Friedrich Kluge

Etymological dictionary of the German language

Friedrich Kluge

Etymological dictionary of the German language

ISBN/EAN: 9783337085605

Printed in Europe, USA, Canada, Australia, Japan

Cover: Foto ©Thomas Meinert / pixelio.de

More available books at **www.hansebooks.com**

AN ETYMOLOGICAL DICTIONARY

OF THE

GERMAN LANGUAGE.

BY

FRIEDRICH KLUGE,
PROFESSOR IN THE UNIVERSITY OF JENA.

TRANSLATED FROM THE FOURTH GERMAN EDITION

BY

JOHN FRANCIS DAVIS, D.Lit., M.A.

LONDON:
GEORGE BELL & SONS.
NEW YORK: MACMILLAN & CO., 112 FOURTH AVENUE.
1891.

TRANSLATOR'S PREFACE.

In preparing an English edition of Professor Kluge's famous work, the Translator has aimed at making the book as easily comprehensible to English students as the original work is to Germans. To this end he has given the chief meanings of all the German words, some of which are rather obscure, and are not to be found in any German-English Dictionaries hitherto published. In assigning the equivalents to the words quoted from foreign languages, great care has been taken to give as closely as possible the corresponding English meaning to the words. In all cases of doubt, the Translator has consulted English, French, and German Dictionaries of foreign languages, such as—

    Sanscrit (Monier Williams).
    Greek (Liddell and Scott; Pape).
    Latin (White and Riddell; Lewis and Short; Smith; Georges).
    Gothic (Skeat).
    Anglo-Saxon (Toller; Bosworth; Leo).
    Middle English (Stratmann).
    Icelandic (Cleasby).
    Old High German (Graff; Schade).
    Middle High German (Müller; Lexer).
    Lithuanian (Schleicher's Handbook).
    Dutch (Calisch).
    Swedish (Holms).
    French (Sachs; Clifton and Grimaud; Littré; Brachet; Fleming and Tibbins).
    Italian (Ferrari; Baretti).
    Spanish (Neumann and Baretti; Lopes and Bensley).
    Welsh (Pugh).

A few misprints and errors in the order of words of the German edition have been corrected, but they are not of sufficient importance to be specially mentioned.

AUTHOR'S PREFACE.

On the completion of the present work, it is to me a pleasant duty to express my thanks to all those who have rendered its execution possible, and have helped to give it its new shape.

I might have mentioned, under the separate words, those scholars who have discovered any etymological data bearing upon the vocabulary of our mother-tongue; the vast extent of etymological literature deterred me, however, from doing so. There is no Teutonic scholar or linguist of any repute who has not by his researches either helped to determine the etymology of some German word or actually settled it. It would have been an extremely toilsome and yet useless task to give the name of the discoverer of the etymology of each word; and how frequently have several scholars at the same time deserved credit for clearing up the history of a word. O. Schade, in his "Old German Dictionary," has with untiring industry collected materials from the copious literature for the older period, and has received the thanks of specialists. I could not expect that those who may use my book would wade through the numerous errors and occasional imperfections of scientific investigation in order to form their own opinion on the evolution of particular words. By foregoing such a plan I obtained space, in spite of the limited compass to which this book was confined, to describe pretty fully the actual development of the word itself.

If my attempt to give a brief, clear, and connected view of the history of each element of our vocabulary has been in any degree successful, a great part of the credit is due to the men who have watched over the germs planted by the great founders of our philology, and have in the course of the last twenty years made them bloom anew. In their foremost ranks I view with pleasure those whose academical instruction I was permitted to enjoy, and others who in friendly intercourse have taught me much and stimulated me in my work. The fact that some of them too have testified their kindly, helpful sympathy with the new edition has been highly grateful to me, in the interest of the subject I have at heart.

I have also received, since the first appearance of my work, encouragement in various ways, even from anonymous and unknown readers of this book, who have made communications to the author respecting dialectic, etymological, and other pertinent facts. Much of it has proved useful for the new edition. Moreover, all reasonable objections of critics have been duly considered. In particular points the book has gained much by the notices of Herren Birlinger, Franck, and Hager; and a detailed, critical letter of my Swedish friends, Prof. A. Noreen and Dr. E. Brate, has placed in the most liberal manner at my disposal numerous valuable improvements and new combinations. For dialectic communications I am indebted to Herren W. Gordack of Königsberg and F. Holthausen of Göttingen, and especially to Prof. Hermann Fischer of Tübingen, who gave me access to his rich stores of Swabian dialectic materials. For the Jewish-German words which the book contains Prof. Euting of Strassburg placed materials at my disposal. Valuable connecting details, for which I had to resort to the liberal help of specialists, I owe to Herren K. von Bahder, O. von Böhtlingk, P. von Bradke, B. ten Brink, K. Brugmann, S. Bugge, C. Cappeller, H. Fischer, W. Franz, F. Holthausen, A. Horning, H. Hübschmann, R. Köhler, Th. Nöldeke, K. Schorbach, O. Schrader, R. Thurneysen, B. Wheeler, and E. Windisch.

I have been especially helped and cheered by the liberal sympathy of Professors A. Leskien of Leipzig, W. Meyer of Jena, H. Osthoff of Heidelberg, and E. Sievers of Halle. They have with praiseworthy liberality made over to me for publication very many new investigations of importance, and have also, by their corrections, objections, and retrenchments, given to many articles a greater fulness and completeness.

For the careful extension and completion of the old Index, the author is much indebted to Herr Vincent Janssen of Kiel, who will very shortly publish independently complete Indexes to this book.

For all the stimulus and sympathy, help and encouragement, I have received in the old as well as in the new edition, I beg to express my most sincere thanks.

F. KLUGE.

STRASSBURG, *July* 1883.
JENA, *October* 1888.

INTRODUCTION.

It cannot be denied that the study of German etymology is held in less esteem among us, and is pursued with less zeal, than that of French. This fact is not surprising; for how easily the results of Romance philology can be made evident to a man of classical training, who has in Latin the chief source, and in his own native German the most important subsidiary source of French entirely under his command! And what gratification there is in viewing through the medium of etymology, well-known words in a new light!

If German etymology could be built up to the same extent as French, from the materials furnished by the better known civilised languages, it would certainly have long ago evoked the same appreciation as is now shown for French. But the perception of historical connections is made more difficult when the earlier stages of the language are not so accessible as Latin is for the history of Romance words. A scientific knowledge of German etymology rests upon facts, whose coherence can only be explained by going beyond the limits of the chief civilised languages. It is impossible, however, for the student to go so far back, unless all the difficulties are smoothed and explained, and all the necessary details for ascertaining the history of a word are placed before him. In investigating a German word, we cannot and must not stop at Middle High German, the only earlier stage of our mother-tongue with which every educated man has some acquaintance; and even Old High German, the oldest literary period of German, is not, except in a very few cases, sufficient for the needs of the etymologist who knows how to appreciate the importance of philology in acquiring a knowledge of the history of the German language.

It is these pre-historic periods of German that furnish the indispensable foundation for etymological inquiry. Not until we have obtained an insight into the difference between the High German and Low German system of consonants can we determine the relations of a German word to its Teutonic cognates; not until we have thoroughly mastered the relations of the Gothic consonants to those of the allied Aryan languages are we able to understand the comparison of a word with its Greek and Latin cognates. To explain the earlier stages of development in German, and to throw light upon them as a chief means of ascertaining the history of a word, is the task of historical grammar. The etymologist must, if he wants to produce conviction, presuppose a general knowledge of the main crises in the history of our mother-tongue.

To the scientific acquisitions of the present century we owe the knowledge of a primary period of the history of the German language, which is authenticated by no other record than the language itself. The literary records of the old Hindus, unlocked to the learned world at the end of the last century, led to the pregnant discovery that the Teutons, several millenniums before our era, spoke one and the same language with the ancestors of the Hindus and Persians, the Greeks and Albanians, the Italics and Kelts, the Slavs and Armenians, a fact which clearly proved that they were descended from the same tribe. The primitive seat of those tribes, which, in conformity with the utmost limits of the settlements of their descendants, have been designated Indo-Teutons, Indo-Kelts, and also Indo-Europeans, was the South of Europe, or more probably Asia.

Scientific investigation, which has been endeavouring for more than half a century to unlock the common source of their language from the later records of the various Aryan tribes, bestows on it the highest praise for its wealth of forms, the development of which has been traced by German grammarians in our mother-tongue down to the present day. The vocabulary of this primitive speech is proved by some of its offshoots to have been exceedingly rich, and at the same time capable of extension; but its fundamental perceptions and ideas were limited. The fact that it expressed the most necessary relations and wants of life has made it the treasury from which the various Aryan languages have drawn their supply of words. Of this old hoard German too has preserved no small a portion, even down to the present time.

Compare our terms for expressing degrees of relationship with those of the allied languages, and these words, with slight divergences in sound, or with unchanged significations, will be found in the whole of the Aryan group. Of course the stock of such terms was far greater than we might suspect from the few which have remained to us. At one time we had, *e.g.*, various designations for 'mother's brother' and 'father's brother' (comp. Oheim and Vetter with Lat. *avunculus* and *patruus*), for 'father's sister' and 'mother's sister' (comp. AS. *faðu* and *módrie* with Lat. *amita* and *matertera*). This implied wealth of pre-historic terms for degrees of kinship can be only understood by us as existing at a time when our ancestors lived together in clans as shepherds and nomads. When with the changing years the more fully developed relations of kinship lost the old inherited terms, how seldom have alien designations attempted to oust the native words, and how seldom with success! Compare Onkel and Tante with Vater and Mutter, Bruder and Schwester, Oheim and Muhme, Neffe and Nichte, Vetter and Base, Schwäher and Schwieger, Schnur and Schwager.

The terms for expressing kinship, whose unimpaired vigour we see in German, are, in combination with the numerals up to a hundred, an infallible indication of the Aryan origin of a language. Thus German testifies also by its old inherited numerals its close relation to the allied languages. Moreover, the designations of parts of the body are specially characteristic of all Aryan tongues. If German in its later development has lost many of them (comp., *e.g.*, OHG. *gëbal*, 'skull,' equiv. to Gr. κεφαλή, under Giebel), yet it preserves in most cases the old inherited words; Hirn, Ohr, Braue, Nase, Zahn, Hals, Bug, Achsel, Arm, Elle, Nagel, Knie, Fuß, Fell recur sometimes in one, sometimes in several of the allied languages. The knowledge too of natural history was displayed in the primitive speech by some essential words. Of the mammals, apart from the domesticated animals (see Vieh, Kuh, Ochse, Hund, Fohlen, Roß, and Schaf), only a few destructive quadrupeds, such as Wolf and Maus, Biber and Hase (see also Bär), have been transmitted to German from that primitive linguistic period. The names for birds and trees are, however, but rarely common to several languages of the Aryan group (see Aar, Kranich, Birke, Föhre, Fichte, and

Buche). Of inanimate nature also the primitive people had only a limited perception; few names for the periods of the day and the year were coined, and, as might have been expected, the circle of their religious ideas was narrow. Only the German words Nacht, Monat, and Sommer have corresponding terms in several allied tongues; the two old Aryan gods of light, *Diêus* and *Ausôs*, have left their final traces in Alemannic Ziestag and in German Ostern.

There is a further rich supply of isolated words in our mother-tongue inherited from the primitive stock. They relate chiefly to the most simple and natural expressions, needs, and activities of life; stehen, gehen, essen, decken, schwitzen, nackt, jung, neu, voll, süß, mitten, dürr, &c., are derived from the primitive speech. In moral conceptions our mother-tongue inherited the stems of Freund and Feind, lieben and hassen, haben and trügen from the old vocabulary.

With the division of the primitive Aryan people into tribes, which may have been caused by religious and political dissensions, or perhaps only by the constant increase in number, and with the migration of these tribes from their primitive home, the Teutonic language may be said to begin. The old materials partly sufficed for the constant growth of perceptions and ideas. Old words received a new shade of meaning; the root (Sans. *mṛ*) for 'to die' acquired the signification of 'murder'; 'the dear, the cherished one' became 'the freeman'; 'to follow' came to mean 'to see' (sehen); 'to split' was extended into 'to bite' (beißen), and 'to persist,' 'to stride,' were developed into 'to live' (leben) and 'to mount' (steigen). Derivatives from existing stems assumed characteristic significations; in this way Gott, König, Kind, schön, and Woge originated. On the other hand, we note the loss of old roots, which in other Aryan groups developed numerous cognates; the roots *pô*, 'to drink,' and *dô*, 'to give,' which we recognise in Lat. *pôtare* and Gr. πέπωκα, and in Lat. *dare* and Gr. δίδωμι, have completely disappeared in Teutonic. Of other primitive roots we find in Teutonic only a few slight relics nearly disappearing, some of which will in course of time vanish altogether. The root *ag*, 'to drive' (in Lat. *ago*, see Acker), the root *an*, 'to breathe' (in Lat. *animus* and Gr. ἄνεμος), the root *glŵ*, 'to live' (in Lat. *vivere*, see queck), have never had in Teutonic, during the period of its independent development, such a wide evolution as in Latin and Greek. In the case of such words, when the idea is a living one, the term that supplants them already exists before they die out; in fact, it is the cause of their disappearance. Occasionally, however, we find in the Teutonic group characteristic word stems, which we look for in vain in the sphere of the allied languages, although they must once have existed there too in a living form. Such primitive stems as Teutonic alone has preserved may be at the base of triefen, geben, fürchten, fechten, fliehen, halten, &c. Other roots peculiar to the Teutonic languages may owe their existence to onomatopoetic creation during the independent development of Teutonic; such are perhaps klingen and niesen.

Only such a pliancy of the primitive speech could keep pace with the higher intellectual development which we must assume for the progress of the Teutonic group after the first division of dialects. The capacity of our race for development is sufficient, even without the assumption of foreign influences, to account for the refinement and development of the conditions of life among the Teutons during the second period of the primitive history of our language. The growing susceptibility to the external world resulted in the extension of the sphere of the gods, the contact with foreign nations led to a refinement of social life, and with both these the conception of propriety grew up. What an abundance of new ideas and words, which were foreign to the primitive speech, had now to be evolved!

In fact, we find among the Aryans but a slight agreement in the designations of ethical ideas; gut and übel, mild and arg, held and treu, are specifically Teutonic; Abel, Ehe, and schwören have no exact correspondences in the remaining Teutonic languages. Gott, Himmel, Hölle, Erde, as well as Wotan (see Wut), Freia (see frei), and Donar (see Donner), owe their existence to the special religious development of the Teutons, while we find the belief in elfish beings (see Elf) even in the Vedas.

It is true that this increase does not altogether suffice to characterise the development of the languages of the Teutonic group. If we assign the year 2000 B.C. as the latest date for the Aryan division of dialects, the second period of the history of the German language would end with the beginning of our era. This interval of two thousand years, at the end of which we assume the development of the consonant and vowel forms peculiar to Teutonic, as well as the settlement of the Teutons in Germany, has no well-defined divisions with prominent characteristics; but the later evidence of the language indicates in this pre-historic period so many points of contact with civilised nations as would in historic times probably be regarded as forming a new epoch.

The Teutonic tribe, with the western group of nations of the Aryan stock, had left its eastern home as a pasturing people. Evidence in the language itself subsequently shows us these people with their flocks on the march. The term *tageweide*, current in Middle High German, could exist as a measure of length only among a race of shepherds in the act of migrating; only nomads could count their stages by periods of rest (Rasten). That the great stream of Aryan tribes poured through the South Russian lowlands (the Italics and Kelts had shown them the way) is antecedently probable, and this theory is finely illustrated by the history of the word Hanf. Here we see the Teutons in contact with a non-Aryan people in the south of Russia; and so, too, the foreign aspect of the Teutonic word Silber (comp. Erbse also) testifies to the pre-historic contact of our ancestors with people of a different race, whose origin can unfortunately no longer be determined. We suspect that its influence on the Teutons and their language was manifested in a greater number of loan-words than can now be discovered.

On the other hand, the emigrant Aryans, whom we find at a later period in our part of the world, and whose languages were differentiated only gradually from one another and from the primitive speech, were led by constant intercourse to exchange a large number of terms expressive of the acquisitions of civilisation, which the individual tribes would perhaps have acquired only after a longer independent development. Numerous words are peculiar to the European Aryans, which we seek for in vain among the Indians and Persians. They relate chiefly to agriculture and technical products, the development of which did certainly not take place at the same time among all the European peoples belonging to the Teutonic stock. Occasionally the language itself bears witness that correspondences in the languages spoken by the Western Aryans are due only to the adoption of words by one people from another (see nähen). Thus the stems of old words such as säen, mahlen, mähen, and melken, whose Aryan character is undoubted, will not necessarily be regarded as genuine Teutonic, since they may have been borrowed from a kindred people.

The evidence of language, which alone gives us a knowledge of the primitive contact of the Teutons with foreign and kindred people, is unfortunately not full enough, and not always transparent enough, to furnish sufficient material for a clear view of these pre-historic events. It is generally acknowledged that the intercourse with the neighbouring Slavonic people took place in the second period of the history of the German language. For the influence of the Kelts upon the Teutons, Amt and Reich afford valuable testimony, which at the same time shows what decisive results can at times be obtained from language itself. We have in the term welſch the last offshoot of the Teutonic word *Walh* (borrowed from the Keltic tribal name *Volcae*), by which the Kelts were formerly designated by the Teutons.

The name by which the Teutons called themselves is unfortunately lost to us. Our learned men have therefore agreed to use the Keltic term which was customary among old historians, and which, according to the testimony of the Venerable Bede, was applied in England to the immigrant Anglo-Saxons by the Britons even in the 8th century. The national character of the Teutons and the type of their language were for a very long period after the division into tribes the same as before. In the last century before our era, when numerous Teutonic tribes became known to the ancient world, we have not the least evidence to show that the language had branched off into dialects. The same may be said of the time of Tacitus; but his account of the genealogy of the Teutonic tribes seems to have some connection with divisions into dialects, recorded at a later period.

The linguistic division of the Teutons into an Eastern group, comprising Goths and Scandinavians, and into a Western, including the English, Frisians, Saxons, Franks, Bavarians, Swabians, and Alemannians, is generally regarded as undoubted. The evidence of language goes, however, to prove that a close connection exists only among the West Teutonic tribes; and unless Tacitus' ethnogony includes all the Teutons, his group of tribes, comprising the Ingaevones, the Erminones, and the Istaevones, are identical in fact with the Western division. The permutation of consonants and the development of the vowel system, which we assume to have been effected before the beginning of our era, were the chief characteristics of all the languages of the second period; but the most important factor in the development of West Teutonic was the uniform attrition of the old final syllables. With the operation of this law in West Teutonic begins the decay of the old inherited forms, most of which were lost in the third period. The German language is now entering upon a stage of development which had been reached by English some centuries ago.

But in spite of this loss of forms, the language retains its old pliancy in undiminished force; after independent words, even in the second period, had been transformed into suffixes and prefixes, the language still possessed new elements which were ready to replace what had been lost. Moreover, the same forces operate in the later history of the vocabulary as in the primitive Teutonic period.

Thus West Teutonic has preserved the stems of old words, which in Gothic and Scandinavian have either died out or have fallen more or less into the background; geben, ſtehen, thun, bin, fechten, ſterben, as well as Buſen, Obſt, Feuer, groß, &c., are the essential characteristics of a West Teutonic language. Other words, such as Nachbar, elend, geſund, Meſſer, Heirat, and Nachtigall, owe their existence to later composition. But, above all, the absence of numerous old words, preserved by Gothic or Scandinavian, is a main feature of the West Teutonic group. But this is not the place to adduce every loss and every compensation which has diminished and re-shaped the old elements in the sphere of languages most closely allied to German.

INTRODUCTION.

The pre-Old High German period—the third period of our mother-tongue, which is not attested by literary records—has, however, acquired its distinctive features by now contact with the languages of civilised nations, which added new elements to the existing material: above all, the contact with the Romans resulted in an exchange of productions and contrivances. However fond we may be of overrating the influence of Latin on the West Teutonic languages, yet it cannot be denied that it materially widened the most various spheres of ideas.

Words which point to active commercial intercourse, such as Münze and Pfund, Straße and Meile, Kiste and Sack, Giel and Pfau, were made known in the pre-High German period, probably even in the first century A.D., to our forefathers both mediately and immediately by the Romans. Contemporaneously with these the Latin nomenclature of the culture of the vine was naturalised in Germany in the words Wein, Most, Lauer, Kelter, and Trichter. Not much later a rich terminology, together with the Roman style of building, was introduced; Mauer, Keller, Söller, Speicher, Kammer, Weiher, Ziegel, Pfeiler, Pfosten, Pfahl, and numerous other cognate ideas, evidently bear the stamp of a Latin origin. The adoption of the Southern method of building in stone, however, brought about a transformation of the entire domestic life. When a migratory life is exchanged for a permanent settlement, the example of a highly civilised people cannot fail to furnish abundant material for imitation. We are not surprised, therefore, to find in the language itself the influence of even Roman cookery and of Roman horticulture before the Old High German period; Koch, Küche, Schüssel, Kessel, Becken, Tisch, Essig, Senf, Pfeffer, Kohl, Pflanze, Rettig, Kürbis, Kümmel, Kirsche, Pfirsich, Pflaume, Quitte, Feige, &c., testify how ready the German of that period was to extend his knowledge and enrich his language when he exchanged the simple customs of his ancestors for a more luxuriant mode of life.

It would, of course, be a too hasty assumption to explain such Southern alien terms (a few Keltic words such as *carrus*, *carruca*, and *paraveredus*, see Karren, Karch, and Pferd, were introduced through a Roman medium) from the importation of products and technical accomplishments which were unknown to our ancestors till about the beginning of our era. We have indubitable reasons, supported by the extent of the Teutonic exports to Rome, and not merely linguistic reasons. We know from Pliny's Natural History that the Teutons furnished effeminate, imperial Rome the material for pillows by the importation of geese; *eoque processere deliciae ut sine hoc instrumento durare jam ne virorum quidem cervices possint*. This suggests to the historian of languages the connection of the Latin origin of Flaum, Kissen, and Pfühl with Pliny's account; our ancestors adopted the Latin designation for the articles which the Romans procured from Germania. Thus our Pfühl with its cognates attests the share Germania had in the decline of Rome.

With Greece the Western Teutons have had in historical times—the word Arzt does not prove much—no immediate contact producing any influence on the German language. It was really the Romans who made known to the new conquerors of the world the name of that nation which at a subsequent period was destined to affect our development so powerfully. But the settlement of the Goths in the Balkan peninsula (their latest descendants were the Crimean Goths, who died out about the beginning of the last century) had such an influence on the Western Teutons that they have left traces even in our mother-tongue; the first knowledge of Christianity spread from them among the other Teutons. Our oldest supply of loan-words bearing on the Christian religion belongs to Greek terminology, which never existed in the

Roman Church; the words Kirche and Pfaffe, Samstag and Pfingtag, we undoubtedly owe to Greek influence, through the medium of the Arian Goths; and probably the same may be said of Engel and Teufel, Bischof and Pfingsten. The connection between the German tribes and the Goths, which we think can be recognised in other words expressive of religious ideas, such as Heide and taufen, lasted till the 7th century; the Alemannians were until the year 635 A.D. under the dominion of the Goths. Orthodox Christianity of the Middle Ages, which supplanted Arianism, was no longer in a position to reject entirely the naturalised terminology, and thus our mother-tongue has preserved down to the present day some expressions of Gothic-Arian Christianity.

All the words that Romish missionaries introduced into German also evidently bear the stamp of a later linguistic period. Not until the development of the peculiar system of sounds in High German—a new permutation of consonants divided from this point High German from Low German—does the influence of Romish Christianity begin to express itself in the language. From the end of the 8th century our mother-tongue remained for more than two hundred years in the service of religious literature. It is the period in our history in which literary records appear, and during that time High German was greatly influenced by Romish Christianity. A large number of Latin words was naturalised among us; for ecclesiastical offices and dignities, for ecclesiastical rites and appurtenances, we adapted the current terms consecrated by the official language of the Church, such as Priester, Probst, Abt, Mönch, Nonne, Sigrist, Küster, Meßner, Messe, Feier, segnen, predigen, fasten, verdammen, Kreuz, Kelch, Orgel, Altar, &c. The unceasing pliancy of our language is attested by the fact that some German words were constructed on the model of the Latin, such as Beichte, from *confessio*, Gevatter, from *compater*, Gewissen, from *conscientia*. The Church brought learning with a new nomenclature in its train; contemporaneously with the ecclesiastical Latin words, Schule, schreiben, Tinte, Brief, received among us the rights of citizenship.

While the Old German vocabulary was enriched by such materials, there existed a store of words which is dying out in the literary language, and is prolonging to some extent its semi-conscious life in the old popular songs. At the same time the terminology of war receives a new impress; old words for 'combat,' such as *gund*, *hilti*, *badu*, *hadu*, disappear as independent words, and leave behind indistinct traces only in proper names, such as Günther and Hedwig. Words such as *marh* (see Mähre), and Ger, Recke, and Weigand have been brought down as archaic terms to the Middle High German period.

With the rise of chivalry the old German terms applied to war must, as may be imagined, have undergone transformation; as it was French in its essential character, it also introduced French loan-words among us. French influence, which first made itself felt in Germany about the year 1000 A.D. (the word fein is, perhaps, the earliest loan-word of genuine French origin), has never ceased to operate on our language. But it reached its zenith with the introduction of chivalry, as it did once again at the time of the Thirty Years' War. It is therefore not to be wondered at that words relating to war and the court, such as Lanze, Soldat, Palast, Kastell, Turnier, Abenteuer, have been borrowed from the French vocabulary in exchange, as it were, for the stock of Teutonic words connected with war which passed some centuries earlier into French (comp. French *auberge*, *gonfalon*, *maréchal*, *héraut* under Herberge, Fahne, Marschall, and Herold). Moreover, courtly and fashionable words, such as kosten, liefern, prüfen, and preisen have also passed into Germany.

INTRODUCTION.

When the linguistic influence of the West had reached its culminating point, Slavonic began to make itself felt on the German Eastern marches. As it was due to neighbourly intercourse among the border tribes, it was at first insignificant and harmless. But several words which came to light in this way, such as Dolmetsch, Grenze, Kummet, Peitsche, Petschaft, and Schöps, gradually won for themselves from the 13th century a place in the language of our literature.

These are in their main features the facts of those periods of the history of the German language whose material has furnished the essential contents of the present work. In those periods lie the beginnings of most of the words whose origin demands a stricter etymological investigation.

LIST OF ABBREVIATIONS.

abstr. = abstract.
acc. = accusative.
adj. = adjective.
adv. = adverb.
adverb. = adverbial.
Alem. = Alemannian.
Americ. = American.
Arab. = Arabic.
Armen. = Armenian.
Armor. = Armorican.
AS. = Anglo-Saxon.

Bav. = Bavarian.
Bohem. = Bohemian.
Bret. = Breton.
Burg. = Burgundian.

causat. = causative.
Chald. = Chaldean.
Chin. = Chinese.
class. = classical.
collect. = collective.
comp. = compare.
conj. = conjunction.
conjug. = conjugation.
contr. = contracted.
Corn. = Cornish.
CrimGoth. = Crimean Gothic.
Cymr. = Cymric.

Dan. = Danish.
dat. = dative.
declen. = declension.
denom. = denominative.
dial. = dialect, dialectic.
dimin. = diminutive.
Dor. = Doric.
Du. = Dutch.

E. = English.
EAryan = East Aryan.
East Teut. = East Teutonic.
Egypt. = Egyptian.
equiv. = equivalent.
Europ. = European.

f. = feminine.
Finn. = Finnish.
Fr. = French.

Franc. = Franconian.
frequent. = frequentative.
Fris. = Frisian.

Gael. = Gaelic.
Gall. = Gallic.
gen. = genitive.
Goth. = Gothic.
Gr. = Greek.

Hebr. = Hebrew.
HG. = High German.
Hung. = Hungarian.

Ic. = Icelandic.
Ind. = Indian.
indeclin. = indeclinable.
infin. = infinitive.
inflect. = inflected.
instrum. = instrumental.
intens. = intensive.
interj. = interjection.
interr. = interrogative.
intrans. = intransitive.
Ion. = Ionian.
Ir. = Irish.
Ital. = Italian.

Jew. = Jewish.

Kelt. = Keltic.

Lapp. = Lappish.
Lat. = Latin.
Lett. = Lettic.
LG. = Low German.
lit. = literal(ly).
Lith. = Lithuanian.
Lombard = Lombardic.
Lower Rhen. = Lower Rhenish.

m. = masculine.
MidDu. = Middle Dutch.
MidE. = Middle English.
MidG. = Middle German.
MidGr. = Middle Greek.
MidHG. = Middle High German.
MidLat. = Middle Latin.
MidLG. = Middle Low German.
ModDu. = Modern Dutch.

ModE. = Modern English.
ModFr. = Modern French.
ModGr. = Modern Greek.
ModHG. = Modern High German.
ModIc. = Modern Icelandic.
ModLG. = Modern Low German.
ModTeut. = Modern Teutonic.
Mongol. = Mongolian.

n. = neuter.
naut. = nautical.
nom. = nominative.
Norw. = Norwegian.
num. = numeral.

OAryan = Old Aryan.
OBulg. = Old Bulgarian.
ODu. = Old Dutch.
OFr. = Old French.
OFris. = Old Frisian.
OHG. = Old High German.
OIc. = Old Icelandic.
OInd. = Old Indian.
OIr. = Old Irish.
OKelt. = Old Keltic.
OLat. = Old Latin.
OLG. = Old Low German.
onomat. = onomatopoetic.
OPers. = Old Persian.
OPruss. = Old Prussian.
ord. = ordinal.
orig. = original(ly).
OSax. = Old Saxon.
OSlav. = Old Slavonic.
OSlov. = Old Slovenian.
OTeut. = Old Teutonic.

partic. = participle.
perf. = perfect.
Pers. = Persian.
Phœn. = Phœnician.
Pied. = Piedmontese.
plur. = plural.
Pol. = Polish.
Port. = Portuguese.
poss. = possessive.
Prak. = Prakrit.
pref. = prefix.

prep. = preposition.
pres. = present.
pret. = preterite.
prim. = primary.
primit. = primitive(ly).
pron. = pronoun.
pronom. = pronominal.
prop. = properly.
Proven. = Provençal.
Pruss. = Prussian.

redup. = reduplicated.
refl. = reflexive.
Rom. = Romance.
Russ. = Russian.

s. = singular.
Sans. = Sanscrit.
Sax. = Saxon.
Scand. = Scandinavian.
Scyth. = Scythian.
Sem. = Semitic.
Serv. = Servian.
Slav. = Slavonic.
Slov. = Slovenian.
Span. = Spanish.
str. = strong.
subst. = substantive.
suff. = suffix.
super. = superlative.
Swab. = Swabian.
Swed. = Swedish.

Teut. = Teutonic.
Thrac. = Thracian.
trans. = transitive.

Umb. = Umbrian.
UpG. = Upper German.

vb. = verb.
voc. = vocative.

W. = Welsh.
West Sax. = West Saxon.
West Teut. = West Teutonic.
wk. = weak.

An asterisk (*) signifies that the form adduced is only theoretical.

KLUGE'S
ETYMOLOGICAL DICTIONARY.

-a, -ach, a frequent suffix in the formation of the names of brooks and rivers (or rather the places named after them); on the whole, -ach (Urach, Steinach, Salzach, Molach, Schwarzach) is more UpG., -a more MidG., and LG. (Fulda, Werra, Schwarza); from OHG. *aha,* 'running water,' Goth. *ahwa,* 'river' (for details see Au), whence also the names of the rivers Aa (Westph.), Ohe (Hesse).

Aal, m., 'eel,' from the equiv. MidHG. OHG. *âl,* m., a term common to the Teutonic dialects; comp. OIc. *áll,* AS. *ǽ',* E. *eel,* Du. *aal* (allied perhaps to Alant i.). No original affinity to the equiv. Lat. *anguilla,* Gr. ἐγχελυς, is possible, for the sounds of the Teut. words differ too much from it; even from *anglu-,* OHG. *âl* or AS. *ǽl* could not be derived. Besides, there is no hereditary stock of names of fishes possessed in common by Teut. and Gr. and Lat. (see Fisch).—**Aalraupe,** f., 'eel-pout' (also called Aalquappe, see Quappe), an eel-like fish, originally called Raupe merely; in MidHG. *rûppe,* OHG. *rûppa;* as the Mid HG. *rutte* (the equivalent and parallel form) indicates, the base of the word is probably supplied by the Lat. *rubéta,* from which, through the Teut. custom of displacing the accent in borrowed words (see Abt), we get *rûbeta,* and then, by the assimilation of the consonants through syncope of the intermediate *e,* the forms mentioned: names of fishes borrowed in OHG. from Lat. rarely occur. See Quappe.

Aar, m., from the equiv. MidHG. *ar,* OHG. *aro,* m., 'eagle'; a prim. Teut. word, which has also cognates outside the Teut. group. Comp. Goth. *ara,* OIc. *are,* m., 'eagle'; further OIc. *ǫrn,* OHG., MidHG. *arn* (to which is allied ModHG. Arnold, OHG. *Aranolt,* orig. sense 'engle-guardian'), AS. *earn,* 'eagle,' Du. *arend,* 'eagle'; primarily cognate with OSlov. *orĭlŭ,* Lith. *erélis,* 'eagle,' Gr. ὄρνις, 'bird,' Corn. and Bret. *er.* W. *eryr,* 'eagle.' See Adler.

Aas, n., from the equiv. MidHG., OHG. and OLG. *âs,* n., 'carcase, carrion'; comp. the equiv. AS. *ǽs;* allied to essen.

ab, adv., also a prep. in older ModHG. (hence the modern abhanden, lit. 'from the hands,' as well as Swiss patronymics like Ab der Flüh, Ab der Halb), 'off, away from,' from MidHG. *abe, ab,* prep., 'down from, away from, off,' adv., 'down,' OHG. *aba,* prep., 'away from, down from here,' adv., 'down.' Corresponding to Goth. *af* (*ab*) prep., 'down from there, from' (also adv.), MidDu. *af, ave,* OLG. *af,* equiv. to AS. *of,* E. *of;* orig. cognate with Gr. ἀπό, Sans. *ápa,* 'away from.' Of course phrases like *ab Hamburg* do not contain the OG. prep., but are due to incorrect Latinity; since the 17th century commercial language has adopted Latin expressions.

Abend, m., 'evening,' from the equiv. MidHG. *âbent* (*âbunt*); OHG. *âband,* m.; corresponding to OSax. *âband,* Du. *avond,* AS. *ǽfen,* 'evening,' whence E. *eve;* also the deriv. AS. *ǽfning,* E. *evening* (comp. *morning*); OIc. *aptann;* similarly Goth. *andanahti,* orig. sense 'forenight,' and *saggs,* lit. 'setting.' The SEurop. term corresponding to Gr. ἕσπερος, Lat. *vesper,* is non-Teut. (comp Weſt and Winter). A verb aben (eben), 'to grow dusk,' adduced from the Swiss dialects to explain Abend, can be none other than a later derivative of Abend. Moreover, Abend (base *ép-*) can scarcely be connected with ab (base *apo*), as if Abend were the waning period of the day. According to old Teut. notions, the evening was regarded rather as the beginning of the following day. See Sonnabend and Fastnacht.

Abenteuer, n., 'adventure,' from Mid

A

HG. *âventiure*, f., 'occurrence, a marvellous, fortunate event, a poem on such a theme, sources of the court poets'; the latter is derived from Fr. *aventure* (MidLat. *adventura*, allied to MidLat. and Rom. *advenire*, 'to happen').

aber, adv. and conj., 'but, however,' from MidHG. *aber* (*aver*), *abe* (*ave*), adv. and conj., 'again, once more, on the contrary, but'; OHG. *abur*, *uvar*, adv. and conj. with both meanings; to this OHG. *avarôn*, 'to repeat,' ModHG. (UpG.) ăfern is allied. Comp. Goth. *afar*, prep., 'after,' adv., 'afterwards,' OIc. *afar*, 'very,' in compounds; the word does not occur in Sax. dialects, but its deriv. OSax. *abaro*, AS. *eafora*, 'descendant' (comp. Goth. *afar*, 'afterwards'), exists. It is probably related to *ab* and its cognates; comp. further Sans. *ápara*, 'the later,' *aparám*, adv., 'latterly, in future,' *apari*, 'future.'

aber, **åber**, adj. (UpG.), ǎfer (Franc.), 'free from snow, laid bare'; from the prim. form *ǎbar, *ǎbiri* (*ǎfiri*); orig. cognate with Lat. *apricus*, 'sunny.'

Aberglaube, m., 'superstition,' first occurs in early ModHG. (15th cent.); since Luther it has made its way into ModHG.; orig. a LG. word (comp. Abebar, Demut), as the vowel-sounds indicate. LG. *aber*, for *over*, *ober*, points to OLG. *obargilôbo (Du. *overgeloof*), 'superstition,' which is formed after the model of Lat. *superstitio;* comp. Dan. *overtro*, Sw. *öfvertro*, but also in MidLG. *biyelôve*, Du. *bijgeloof*.

abermal, adv., first occurs in ModHG., for the equiv. MidHG. *aber*, 'again, once more,' formed with the suffix *mal*.

Aberraute, f., 'southern-wood,' a corruption of Lat.-Gr. *abrotonum* (Fr. *aurone*), due to its supposed connection with Raute; see also Eritz.

Aberwitz, m., 'false wit, craziness,' from MidHG. *aberwitze*, *abewitze*, 'want of understanding,' from MidHG. *abe*, 'away from,' as in MidHG. *abegunst*, 'envy, jealousy.'

abgefeimt, see Feim.

Abgott, m., 'idol,' from MidHG. and OHG. *abgot*, n., 'idol, idolatrous image'; note the retention of the older gender of Gott as late as MidHG.; comp. Goth. *afgups*, 'godless' (antithesis to *gagups*, 'pious'); hence Abgett is properly 'false god'; see Abenwitz.

Abgrund, m., 'abyss, precipice,' from MidHG. *abgrunt*, m., most frequently *ubgründe*, n., OHG. *abgrunti*, n., 'abyss,' properly 'declivity'; comp. Goth. *afgrundipa*, f., 'abyss.'

ablang, adj., 'oblong, oval,' first occurs in ModHG., formed on the model of Lat. *oblongus*.

Ablaß, m., 'sluice, remission,' from MidHG. *ablâz*, m., OHG. *ablâz*, n., 'indulgence, remission, pardon'; comp. Goth. *afléts*, m., 'remission, pardon.' allied to *af-lêtan*, 'to remit, pardon,' OHG. *ob-lâzzan*.

abmurksen, see meucheln.

Abseite, f., 'wing, aisle,' from MidHG. *apsite*, f., 'the domed recess of a church,' a corruption of MidLat. and OHG. *absida* (Gr. ἀψίς), 'vault,' due to its supposed connection with *site*, 'side.'

abspenstig, adj., 'alienated, disaffected,' first occurs in ModHG., from OHG. *spenstig*, 'seductive,' allied to OHG. *spanst*, 'allurement'; see under Gespenst and widerspenstig.

Abt, m., 'abbot,' from the equiv. Mid HG. *apt*, *abbet*, *abbât*, OHG. and MidHG. *abbât*, m.; comp. Du. *abt*, AS. *abbod* (with an abnormal *d*), and less frequently *abbot*, E. *abbot*. Borrowed with a change of accent in OHG. from MidLat. *abbât-* (nom. sing. *abbas*), 'abbot'; comp. Ital. *abáte*, Fr. *abbé*, OIr. *abb*, acc. *abbaith*. It will be seen under Kreuz that in words borrowed from Lat. the stem of the oblique cases as well as the nomin. often forms the base; with regard to the ecclesiastical terms borrowed in OHG. comp. among others Mönch, Nonne, Papst, Priester, Probst.

Abtei, f., 'abbey,' from MidHG. *aptei*, *abbeteie*, OHG. *abbateia*, f., 'abbey' (for *abbeia?), formed from MidLat. *abbatia*, under the influence of OFr. *abbaie*, and based upon *abbât*.

abtrünnig, adj., from the equiv. Mid HG. *abetrünnec* (*abetrünne*), OHG. *abatrunntg*, adj., 'recreant'; orig. sense, 'he who separates himself from,' for trennen contains the same stem. Comp. also OHG. *anttrunno*, 'fugitive,' MidHG. *trünne*, 'a detached troop.'

Abzucht, f., 'drain, sewer,' first occurs in ModHG., germanised from Lat. *aquaeductus* (whence also Swiss Aften, 'conduits'). See Anbauche.

ach, interj., 'ah! alas!' from MidHG. *ach*, OHG. *ah;* to this is allied MidHG. and ModHG. Ach, *ah*, n., 'woe,' and its deriv., which first occurs in ModHG., ächzen,

Achat, m., 'agate,' from MidHG. *achât*, *achâtes*, equiv. to Gr.-Lat. *achates*.

Ache, Rhen. for Nachen.

Achel, see Ähre.

acheln, Jew., 'to eat,' from Heb. *âkhâl*, 'to eat.'

Achse, f., 'axle, axis,' from the equiv. MidHG. *ahse*, OHG. *ahsa*, f.; comp. Du. *as*, AS. *eax*, f., E. *axle* (even in MidE. *eaxel-tree* occurs, E. *axle-tree*), with deriv. *l*, like OIc. *öxull*, m., 'axle'; Goth. *ahsa*, or rather *ahsuls*, is, by chance, not recorded. The stem *ahsô-*, common to the Teut. languages, from pre-Teut. *aksâ*, is widely diffused among the Aryan tongues; it is primitively related to Sans. *âkša*, m., Gr. ἄξων, Lat. *axis*, OSlov. *osĭ*, Lith. *aszìs*, 'axle'; the supposition that the Teut. cognates were borrowed is quite unfounded; comp. Rad. The orig. sense of Aryan *akso-* remains obscure; with the root *ag*, 'to drive,' some have connected Lat. *ago*, Gr. ἄγω. See the following word.

Achsel, f., 'shoulder,' from the equiv. MidHG. *ahsel*, OHG. *ahsala*, f.; comp. AS. *eaxl*, OIc. *ǫxl*, f., 'shoulder'; Goth. *ahsla*, f., is wanting. It is probable that the Teut. word is connected with the O. Aryan Achse; Lat. *axilla* (OIr. *oxal*), 'arm-pit,' and *âla*, 'arm-pit, wing,' are also cognate with it. In OTeut., Goth. *ahsla* (Aryan *aksiâ*) has a still wider family, since forms with Teut. *ô*, Aryan *â* in the stem belong to it; comp. AS. *ôxn*, *ôcusla*, 'arm-pit,' and OHG. *uohsana*, MidHG. *üehse*, *uohse*, f., 'arm-pit,' Du. *oksel*, 'shoulder.'

acht, num., 'eight,' from the equiv. MidHG. *ahte*, OHG. *ahto*, common to the Teut. and also to the Aryan groups. Comp. Goth. *ahtau*, AS. *eahta*, E. *eight*, Du. *acht*, OSax. *ahto*; further, Sans. *aštáu*, Gr. ὀκτώ, Lat. *octo*, OIr. *ocht*, Lith. *asztûnì*, prim. Aryan *oktô*, or rather *oktôu*, 'eight.' Respecting acht Tage see the historical note under Nacht.

Acht, f., 'outlawry, ban,' from MidHG. *âhte*, *æhte*, f., 'pursuit, proscription, outlawry, ban'; OHG. *âhta* (AS. *ôht*), f., 'hostile pursuit.' Goth. *âhtjan*, 'to pursue,' is wanting. Comp. OSax. *âhtian*, AS. *éhtan* (from *anhtjan*), 'to pursue.' Teut. *aňhtian*, 'to pursue,' and *anhtô*, 'pursuit,' seem to be based on a non-dental root, which is perhaps connected with the cognates of *eng* (Aryan root *angh*).

achten, vb., 'to have regard to, esteem, value,' from MidHG. *ahten*, OHG. *ahtôn*, 'to heed, ponder, take care'; allied to MidHG. *ahte*, OHG. *ahta*, f., 'heed, paying attention.' Comp. Du. *achten*, AS. *eahtian*, 'to ponder'; also with deriv. *l*, OIc. *œtla* (Goth. *ahtilôn*), 'to suppose, think.' It is based upon a Teut. root *ah*, 'to suppose, think'; comp. Goth. *aha*, 'understanding,' *ahjan*, 'to believe,' *ahma*, 'spirit.' The Aryan root *ak* is widely diffused, yet no other language coincides with the signification of the Teut. cognates.

achter, LowG. for after.

Achterwasser, 'back-water.' See under After.

ächzen, vb., see ach.

Acker, m., 'field, arable land,' from the equiv. MidHG. *acker*, OHG. *acchar* (*ahhar*), m.; a common Teut. and OAryan word corresponding to Goth. *akrs*, m., AS. *æcer*, E. *acre* (*aker*), Du. *akker*, OSax. *akkar*. Teut. *akra-z*, m., from pre-Teut. *agro-s*; comp. Sans. *ájra-s*, m., 'pasture-ground, plain, common,' Gr. ἀγρός, Lat. *ager* (stem *agro-*), 'field.' It is certainly connected with the Ind. root *aj*, 'to drive' (comp. Trift, allied to treiben), Lat. *ago*, Gr. ἄγω, to which in OIc. *aka*, 'to drive,' was allied. "Thus *ájra-* signifies in the widest sense 'field and common,' orig. as 'pasture-land,' the greatest part of which, when tillage supplanted the rearing of cattle, was used for crops." The transition in meaning was, probably, completed on the migration of the Western Aryans to Europe; moreover, the root *ar*, 'to plough, till,' is West Aryan; comp. Gr. ἀρόω, Lat. *arare*, Goth. *arjan*, OHG. *erian*, OBulg. *orati*, 'to plough.' See Art.

Adebar, m. (Holland. *ooijevaar*), a Low G. name for the stork, MidLG. *odevare*, MidHG. *odebar*, OHG. *odoběro* (in Old Ger. times the term was, moreover, prevalent in Germany). No certain explanation of the word can be given; it is most frequently interpreted as 'bringer of children, of good luck' (comp. Alteb). Respecting the LG. vowel-sounds see Abergaube.

Adel, m., 'nobility,' from MidHG. *adel*, m., n., 'lineage, noble lineage, noble rank, perfection,' OHG. *adal*, n. (and *edili*, n.), 'lineage, esp. noble lineage'; corresponding to OSax. *aðali*, n., 'body of nobles, notables, nobility,' Du. *adel*, AS. *œðelu*, n. plur., 'noble birth,' OIc. *aðal*, 'disposition, talent, lineage.' In Goth. the stem *ap* (by gradation *ôp*) is wanting; to it belong OHG. *uodil*, n., 'patrimony, home' (ModHG. Ulrich, from OHG. *Uodalrîch* or Ubland, from *Uodal-lant*), OSax. ôðil, AS. éðel, m., 'patrimony, home.' Hence the fundamental idea of the Teut. root *ap*, by gradation *ôp* (from Aryan *ât*), seems to be 'by transmission, inheritance.' The aristocratic tinge evinced by the WestTeut. cognates is not remarkable when we consider the early period; only the patrician had a 'family'; genealogies of nobles (in old documents) reach back to the OTeut. period; the names beginning with Abel are primitive, Alfens, influenced by Rom. from OHG. *Adalfuns*, *Adalheid*, *Adalberaht*, Abelf, from *Atha-ulf;* also the deriv. OHG. *Adalung*. See too Alter, edel.

Aber, f., 'vein,' from MidHG. *âder*, OHG. *âdara*, f., 'vein, sinew,' corresponding to MidLG. *ader*, 'vein, sinew,' Du. *ader*, AS. *ǽdre*, f., 'vein' (rarely *ôr*), OSw. *ahra*, ModSw. *âdra;* also without the deriv. r, OIc. *æðr* (the r is simply a nomin. suffix), f., 'vein;' the Goth. cognate *êþ* is not found. The pre-Teut. *êt-* has been connected with Gr. ἦτορ, 'heart,' ἤτρον, 'abdomen,' and here it must be recollected that MidHG. and MidLG. *âder* in the plur. may signify 'bowels.'

Abler, m., 'eagle,' from MidHG. *adel-ar* (also *adel-arn*), m.; prop. a compound, 'noble bird of prey.' It is noteworthy that Aar in ModHG. is the nobler term, while Abler serves as the name for the species without any consciousness of its origin from Abel and Aar. OHG. **adal-aro* appears by chance not to be recorded. Corresponds to Du. *adelaar* (besides *arend*).

äfern, vb., 'to repeat,' an UpG. word; MidHG. *æferen*, OHG. *afarôn*. See under aber.

-aff, suffix used to form names of rivers (Graff, OHG. *Eril-affa*, Aschaff, OHG. *Ascaffa*), and of places (esp. in Franc. and Hess., comp. Honeff), allied to which *-ep, p* (also Westph.), occurs as an unchanged LG. form, *e.g.* in Lennep. The base **apa* is Kelt. (equiv. to Lat. *aqua*, 'water,' Goth. *ahwa*, 'river').

Affe, m., 'ape, monkey,' from the equiv. MidHG. *affe*, OHG. *affo*, m.; also in OHG. the feminine forms *affa*, *affin*, *affinna*, 'female ape.' A word common to the Teut. group, unrecorded by chance in Goth. alone, in which, by inference from OIc. *ape*, AS. *apa*, E. *ape* (whence Ir. and Gael. *apa*), Du. *aap*, the form must have been **apa*. Facts and not linguistic reasons lead to the conclusion that *apan-* is a primitive loanword with which ORuss. *opica*, OBoh. *opice*, is connected, and through commercial intercourse reached the Teutons by some unknown route. On account of the assonance it is very often referred, without sufficient reason, to Sans. *kapi* (Gr. κῆπος), 'ape'; at all events, it is certain that no word for Affe common to the Aryan, or even to the West Aryan, group does exist.

Affolter, m., 'apple-tree.' See Apfel.

After, m., 'buttocks, backside,' from MidHG. *after*, OHG. *aftaro*, m., 'fundament, anus.'; lit. 'the back part,' from MidHG. *after*, OHG. *aftar*, adj., 'behind, following'; akin to Goth. *aftana*, 'from behind,' AS. *æfter*, E. *after* (LG. and Du. *achter*), Goth. *aftra*, 'back, again.' It is certainly allied to Goth. *afar*, 'behind,' and the cognates discussed under aber.—After in compounds is lit. 'after,' whence the idea of 'counterfeit, baseness'; comp. MidHG. *aftersprâche*, 'slander, backbiting,' *afterwort*, 'calumny'; the older meaning, 'after, behind,' is preserved in ModHG. Aftermiete, muse, rede. Note too Sunh. (even in the MidHG. period) *aftermontag* for 'Tuesday.'

Aglei, f., from the equiv. MidHG. *agleie*, OHG. *ageleia*, f., 'columbine,' which is derived from Lat. *aquilegia*, whence too the equiv. Fr. *ancolie*, Du. *akelei*.

Ahle, f., from the equiv. MidHG. *âle*, OHG. *dla*, f., 'cobbler's awl.' To this is allied the equiv. OHG. deriv. *âlunsa*, *âlansa*, f. (with the same suffix as Senfe); prop. *alesna* (Swiss *alesne*, *alsne*), whence the Rom. cognates—Span. *alesna*, Ital. *lesina*, Fr. *alêne*, 'awl,' are borrowed; comp. Du. *els*, 'awl' (from **alisna*), AS. *ǽl* (in the Orkneys *alison*), OIc. *alr*, 'awl.' The consonance with Sans. *ârâ*, f., 'punch, awl,' points to an OAryan word; there existed also a widely ramified Aryan root to designate articles of leather. See Saum and Säule.

ahnen, vb., in nachahmen, which is wanting in MidHG. and OHG.; from the equiv. MidHG. *âmen*, 'to measure a cask, gauge,' figuratively 'to estimate,' from Mid HG. and MidLG. *âme*, 'ohm' (cask = about 40 galls.). See Ohm.

Ahn, m., 'grandfather, ancestor,' from MidHG. *ane* (collateral modified form *ene*), OHG. *ano*, m., 'grandfather'; akin to the

Alem. dimin. **Ähni,** 'grandfather.' Further ModHG. **Ahne,** MidHG. *ane*, OHG. *ana*, f., 'grandmother.' To these are allied Mod HG. **Urahn,** MidHG. *urane, urene*, OHG. **urano*, m., great-grandfather'; in OHG. *alt-ano, altar-ano* (for the force of *ur* in **Urahne** see *ur*). The class is peculiar to G., being foreign to the remaining Teut. dialects; comp. also **Enkel**—really a dimin. form—which belongs to it. There is no doubt that Lat. *ănus*, 'old woman,' is a primit. cognate. Perhaps the Teut. masculine name OHG. *Anelo* (AS. *Onela*, OIc. *Ále*) is allied to it.

ahnden, vb., 'to punish,' from MidHG. *anden*, OHG. *antôn, anadôn*, 'to punish, censure,' allied to OHG. *anto, anado*, m., 'insult, embittered feeling, anger.' It corresponds to OSax. *ando*, 'exasperation, anger,' AS. *anda, onepa*, 'zeal, vexation, hatred,' whence *andian*, 'to be angry'; moreover, Goth. preserves in *us-anan*, 'to die,' the root *an*, 'to breathe, respire, snort,' which appears in these words. Comp. OIc. *ande*, m., 'breath, spirit,' *ǫnd*, f., 'breath, soul'; and also AS. *êðian*, 'to breathe' (implying Goth. **anþjôn*), AS. *oruþ*, 'breath' (Goth. **uzanþ*), or *þian*, 'to breathe,' OIc. *ǫrendi*, 'breathlessness.' The root *an*, preserved in all the cognates, is OAryan, and means 'to breathe'; comp. Lat. *animus, anima*, Gr. ἄνεμος, connected with the Aryan root *an*, 'to breathe, respire.'—**ahnden,** vb., 'to forebode'; see **ahnen.**

Ahne, f., 'boon' (of flax or hemp), from MidHG. *ăne*, older *agene*, f., 'chaff'; OHG. *agana*, f., 'chaff;' also AS. **agon, ægne*, Mid E. *awene*, E. *awns*, Goth. *ahana*, OIc. *ǫgn*, 'chaff.' In these cognates two really different roots seem to have been blended in various ways; the meaning 'chaff' would be applicable to the one, just as the exact Gr. correspondent ἄχνη, 'chaff, foam' (of the sea), likewise points to Aryan *aghná* (comp. besides Gr. ἄχυρον, 'chaff'). The other is perhaps lit. 'prickle, awn,' and belongs to the root *ak* (Aryan *ak*); see **Ähre.**

ahnen, vb., 'to forebode, suspect,' from MidHG. *anen*, 'to foresee, forebode,' foreign to the older period and to the rest of the Teut. dialects; it has been connected with the OAryan root *an*, 'to breathe, respire,' so that it may be a primit. cognate of **ahnten,** under the influence of which it also appears in ModHG. as **ahnten.** It is better, however, to regard it as a derivative of the prep. *an*; *ahnen*, lit. 'to befall, seize, attack' (properly said of ghosts or visions).

ähnlich, adj., from the equiv. MidHG. *ănelich*, OHG. *ánagilth* (**ánalth*), adj., 'similar.' It corresponds to Goth. *ánaleikô*, adv., 'similarly'; from the OTeut. (Goth.) prep. *ana* (see **an**) and the suffix **lich;** see **gleich.**

Ahorn, m.. 'maple,' from the equiv. MidHG. and OHG. *ahorn*, m., the *d* of which is inferred from the Swiss dial.; comp. Du. *ahorn.* It is primit. allied to Lat. *ăcer*, n., 'maple' (Gr. ἄκαστος) and Gr. ἀκαταλίς, 'juniper berry.' The G. word, at all events, cannot be regarded as borrowed from Lat. For another old name see under **Maßholder.**

Ähre, f., 'ear' (of corn), from the plur. of MidHG. *eher*, OHG. *ehir, ahir*, n., 'ear' (of corn); corresponds to Du. *aar*, AS. *éar* (from **eahor*), E. *ear*. As the derivative r stands for an older *s*, Goth. *ahs*, n. (gen. *ahsis*) and OIc. *ax* (also Sw. and Dan.), 'ear' (of corn), are identical with it; so, too, OHG. *ah*, 'ear' (of corn). Comp. besides OHG. *ahil*, ModHG. **Achel,** 'prickle, spike' (of corn), (with regard to the *ch*, comp. Bav. **Ächer,** 'ear of corn,' AS. and Northumb. *æhher*, AS. *egle*, 'spikes' (of corn), E. *ails, eils* 'beard of wheat or barley,' LG. (in Brockes) **Eite,** 'spike' (of corn), Goth. **agiþ*? Comp. also **Ahne.** The Teut. root *ah*, which consequently, specially means 'spike, ear' (of corn), agrees with Lat. *acus* (gen. *aceris*), n., 'corn-prickle.' It may be said generally that a root, *ak*, with the primary meaning 'pointed,' is very widely developed in the Aryan group; comp. Gr. ἄκανος, 'a kind of thistle,' ἄκαινα, 'goad,' ἄκων, 'javelin,' ἄκρος, 'at the point,' Lat. *acus, aculeus, acies* (see **Ecke**).

Ähren, m., 'vestibule' (dial.), from MidHG. *ern*, m., 'floor, threshing-floor,' also 'ground, bottom,' OHG. *erin*, m. (Goth. **arins*), to which OIc. *arenn*, m., 'hearth,' corresponds. Further, OHG. *ëro*, OIc. *jǫrve*, 'earth,' as well as Lat. *area*, 'courtyard, threshing-floor,' Lat. *arvum*, 'plain, cornfield,' and Gr. ἔραζε, 'to the ground,' may be cognate.

aichen, see **eichen.**

Ählei, see **Aglei.**

Alabaster, m., 'alabaster,' from Mid HG. *alabaster* (Goth. *alabastraun*), from Lat-Gr. *alabastrum.*

Alant (1.), m., 'chub' (a fish), from the equiv. MidHG. *alant*, OHG. *alant, alunt*, m., corresponds to OSax. *alund*; allied to

OIc. *blunn*, 'a fish'; of obscure origin, perhaps akin to 𝔄aſ.

𝔄lant (2.), m., 'elecampane' (a plant), from the equiv. MidHG. *alant*, OHG. *alant*, m.; of obscure origin; it has been supposed to be connected with the equiv. Span. and Port. *ala*.

𝔄larm, m., 'alarm,' first occurs in Mod HG., like E. *alarm*, from the equiv. Fr. *alarme*; the latter is derived from Ital. *allarme*, prop., *all' arme*, 'to arms.' See ᛏ𝔄rm.

𝔄laun, m., 'alum,' from MidHG. *alûn*, m., 'alum,' from the equiv. Lat. *alûmen*, whence also Lith. *alunas*, Eng. and Fr. *alun*, E. *alum* (AS. *ælifne*, also *efne*).

𝔄lbe (1.), f., 'alb.' from MidHG. *albe*, OHG. *alba*, f., 'a white vestment used at mass,' formed from the equiv. EcclLat. *alba* (E. *alb*).

𝔄lbe (2.), f., 'bleak, whitebait,' from the equiv. MidHG. *albel*, m., formed from the Lat. *albula*, whence also Fr. *able*.

𝔄lbeere, 𝔄lbeſing, LG. 'black currant,' even in MidLG. *albere*; *al-* is generally connected with 𝔄lant (2). Corresponding to Du. *aalbes*, *aalbezie*.

𝔄lber, f., 'white poplar,' from MidHG. *alber*, OHG. *albâri*, m., 'poplar'; prob. borrowed from Rom.; comp. Ital. *alburo*, which is connected either with Lat. *albus* or with Lat. *arbor*; OHG. *arbar*, 'poplar,' occurs once.

albern, adj., 'silly, foolish,' earlier Mod HG. *alber*, from MidHG. *álwœre*, 'simple, silly,' OHG. *álawâri*, 'kind, friendly, well-disposed' (with an interesting change of meaning from OHG. to MidHG.). The OHG. adj. signifies also 'truly, quite true'; so Goth. *wêrs*, 'true,' also means 'friendly' by inference from *un-wêrjan*, 'to be unwilling, displeased' (comp. too OHG. *mitiwâri*, 'friendly'). See waɦr and all. Moreover, albern has not the present meanings in the UpG. dialects; Luther introduced it from MidG. into the written language.

𝔄lchimie, f., 'alchemy,' from late Mid HG. *alchemie*, f., which is derived from the equiv. Rom. cognates—Ital. *alchimia*, Fr. *alchimie*—the origin of which from Arab. *al-kimtâ* and the earlier Gr. χυμός, 'juice,' is undoubted. *Al-* as the Arab. article is still seen in 𝔄lfali, 𝔄lferan, 𝔄lfabe, 𝔄lhambra, 𝔄lfohol, 𝔄lgebra. See 𝔄lfoven.

𝔄lfanzerei, f., 'foolery,' from MidHG. *ale-vanz*, m., 'trick, roguery, deceit'; connected with OHG. *giana-venzôn*, 'to mock'

(the *al-* of MidHG. as in *albern l*), also Fiſefanz and ʄant.

𝔄lhoven, m., 'bedchamber, alcove,' first occurs in ModHG. from Fr. *alcôve* (comp. also E. *alcove*), which with its Rom. cognates is based upon Arab. *al-qobbah*, 'vault, tent'; comp. 𝔄himie, also 𝔄lhambra, 𝔄lferan.

all, adj., 'all, whole,' from MidHG. and OHG. *al* (infl. gen. *alles*), adj., 'entire, each, every one'; a word common to the Teut. group; it corresponds to Goth. *alls*, OIc. *allr*, AS. *eall*, E. *all*, Du. *al*, OSax. *al*, with the same meanings. There is also an OTeut. form *ala-* in compounds and derivatives; comp. OHG. and OSax. *alung*, MidHG. *alenc*, 'entire, complete,' Goth. *alamans*, plur., 'everybody,' OHG. *ala-wâr*, 'quite true' (see altern), *alaniuwi*, 'quite new.' Probably Goth. *alla-* as a participial form is based upon an older *al-na-* (comp. voll, 𝔚olle), since *ala-* shows that the root was *al* or rather *ol*. Whether Goth. *alan*, 'to grow up' (see alt), is a cognate, remains uncertain; in any case, the Kelt. words, OIr. *uile*, *ule*, 'entire, each, all' (base *olio-*), and W. *oll*, 'entire,' are rightly compared with it, while Gr. ὅλος, on account of Sans. *sárvas* (from Aryan *solvo-s*), 'entire, each,' must be kept apart.—**allein**, adj., 'solitary, sole,' from MidHG. *al-ein*, *al-eine*, like MidE. *al-one*, E. *alone*.—**allmählich**, **allmälig**, adj. 'gradual.' earlier allmädlich and allgemach, from MidHG. *almechlich*, 'slow'; the later form allmälig is based upon 𝔐al, 'time,' but the MidHG. form upon *gemach*.—**𝔄llmende**, f. (Alem.), 'common land,' from MidHG. *almende*, f., 'common'; on account of the MidHG. spelling *almeinde* and *algemeine*, the derivation from *gemeine* is probable (OHG. *alagimeinida). The derivation from an assumed OHG. *alagimannida*, 'community,' must be rejected, as such a form could never have existed.—**𝔄llod**, n., 'allodial estate, freehold.' first occurs in ModHG., adopted from MidLat. *allodium*. which is the latinised form for the OG. and OFranc. *alôdis*, OHG. *al-ôd*, 'entire property or possession, free property'; comp. OSax. *ôd*, AS. *eád*, 'estate, possession,' OHG. *ôtag*, 'wealthy.' To this the Teut. proper name Odoardo, Edward, is allied.

𝔄lm, f., 'mountain pasture,' equiv. to 𝔄lpe.

𝔄lmanach, m., 'almanac,' first appears in early ModHG., from Fr. *almanach*, which with its Rom. cognates is said to have come from Arab. through Span., like other words beginning with 𝔄l: (see 𝔄lchimie, 𝔄lfoven). But as the Arab. word for calendar is certainly not 𝔄lmanach, but *taquim* (Milan. *taccuino*), the derivation from Gr.-Egyp. ἀλμενιχιακά, 'calendar' (found in the Eccl. Hist. of Eusebius), is much more likely to be correct.

𝔄lmoſen, n., 'alms, charity,' from the equiv. MidHG. *almuosan*, OHG. *alamuosan, alamôsan*, n.; corresponds to Du. *aalmoes*, AS. *œlmesse*, E. *alms*, OIc. *ǫlmusa*, f., 'alms.' The derivation from Lat.-Gr. ἐλεημοσύνη, 'sympathy, compassion, alms,' is incontestable; as the OHG. collateral form *elemosyna, elimosina* indicates, the Lat.-Gr. origin was as firmly accepted in the OHG. period as the derivation of OHG. *chirihha*, 'church,' from κυριακόν. Yet the question remains how the ecclesiastical word found its way so early into the Teut. languages, so as to become a common possession of the Mid Europ.and Northern Teutons. The absence of a corresponding Goth. word is explained by the fact that we obtained the word from the Rom. nations, as the congruent phonetic form proves: common Rom. *alimosna*, in accordance with Fr. *aumône*, OFr. *almosne*, Prov. *almosna*, Ital. *limosina;* allied also to OIr. *almsan*, OSlov. *almužino*, Lith. *jalmužnas*.

𝔄lp, m., 'nightmare, incubus,' from MidHG. *alp(b)*, m., 'spectre, incubus, nightmare, oppression caused by nightmare'; prop. a term applied to mythical beings, AS. *œlf*, OIc. *álfr*, 'elf, goblin' (the Scandinavians distinguished between fairies of light and darkness); these appear to be identical with the OInd. *ṛbhú* (lit. 'ingenious, sculptor, artist'), the name of three clever genii (the king of the fairies was *ṛbhukšán*). By the ASaxons, nightmare was called *œlfádl, œlfsogoða*, 'elf-malady, elf-sickness (hiccough),' (lumbago in the Eng. dialects is termed *aweſshots*, AS. *ylfa gesceot*). Comp. further 𝔈lf (proper names like 𝔄lboin, 𝔄lfred, have 𝔄lb as their first component).

𝔄lpe, f., from the equiv. MidHG. *albe*, f., 'mountain pasture,' allied to Lat. *alpes*, so too OHG. *Alpun* and *Alpi*, 'mountain pastures.'

𝔄lraune, f., 'mandrake,' from MidHG. *alrûne*, OHG. *alrûna*, f., 'mandrake, sorceress'; this, as the component *-rûne* indicates, is a primit. term, which has been supposed to be connected with old Teut. mythical beings who do their work secretly (comp. Goth. *rûna*, 'secret'; see raunen).

als, conj., 'as,' from MidHG. *als, alse, alsô*, 'likewise, thus, as, as if, because,' hence prop. identical with *alſo*; OHG. *alsô*, 'likewise, like,' is a compound of *al*, 'entirely,' and *sô*, 'thus,' like the exactly corresponding AS. *ealswâ*, whence E. *as*, from *eal*, 'entirely,' and *swâ*, 'so.'

alſo, adv., related to *als*, like ModE. *also* to *as*, identical in every respect with the preceding.

alt, adj., from the equiv. MidHG. and OHG. *alt*, adj., 'old'; the corresponding OSax. *ald*, AS. *eald*, E. *old*, have the same meaning; Goth. *alþeis* (instead of the expected form **alda-*), 'old.' The West Teut. form *al-da-* is an old *tó-* participle (Lat. *al-tus*, 'high'), like other ModHG. adjs. (see under falt), and belongs to Goth. *alan*, 'to grow up,' OIc. *ala*, 'to bring forth' (primit. related to Lat. *alo*, OIr. *alim*, 'I nourish'), therefore lit. 'grown up.' Hence perhaps it was used orig. and chiefly in reckoning age, &c. (comp. Lat. *X annos natus*), but afterwards it was also used at an early period in an absolute sense, 'vetus.' See 𝔄lter, 𝔈ltern.

𝔄ltar, m., 'altar,' from MidHG. *altêr, altâre, altære*, under the constant influence of Lat. *altâre*, which forms the base. Comp. *altâri, âlteri*, found even in OHG.; the word was introduced by Christianity. Goth. uses *hunsla-staþs*, lit. 'temple-table'; AS. *wîhbed* for *wîhbeód, 'sacred table' (see weihen and 𝔅eute).

𝔄lter, n., 'age, antiquity,' from MidHG. *alter*, OHG. *altar*, n., 'age, old age' (opposed to youth); comp. the corresponding OSax. *aldar*, 'life, time of life,' AS. *ealdor*, 'life,' OIc. *aldr*, 'age, hoary age,' Goth. **aldra-*, in *framaldrs*, 'of advanced age, in years.' An abstract term formed from the root *al*, 'to grow up, bring forth,' mentioned under alt, and the suffix *-tro-* frequent in Gr. and Lat. See further cognates under 𝔚elt.

𝔄ltreife, see 𝔐iefter.

𝔄ltvorbern, plur., from the equiv. MidHG. *altvordern*, OHG. *alt-fordoron*, m. plur., 'forefathers,' lit. 'the old former ones,' from OHG. *fordoro*, 'former.' With regard to the signification of *alt-* in this compound, comp. OHG. and MidHG. *alt-vater*, 'grandfather,' OHG. *alt-hêrro*, 'ancestor,' OHG. *alt-mág*, 'forefather.'

𝔄mboß, m., 'anvil,' from MidHG. *ane-*

bôȝ, OHG. *anabôȝ*, m., 'anvil'; a specifically G. word allied to OHG. *bôȝan*, MidHG. *bôȝen*, 'to beat, strike.' Comp. AS. *beátan*, E. *to beat* (see Weiß, Beutel, Keſſel). Whether OHG. *ana-bôȝ* is formed by the imitation of Lat. *incus* (allied to *cudere*) is uncertain, for the smith's art was early developed among the Teutons without any Southern influence. The corresponding terms AS. *anfilt*, E. *anvil* (also OHG. *anafalz*), Du. *aanbeeld*, MidLG. *anebelte*, Dan. *ambolt*, are similarly formed.

Ameiſe, f., from the equiv. MidHG. *âmeiȝe* (*emeze*, whence ModHG. Emſe), OHG. *âmeiȝȝa*, f., 'ant'; note ModHG. dial. *ametze*, OHG. *âmeitza*. It corresponds to AS. *æmette*, E. *emmet*, *ant*. The derivation can scarcely be ascertained with certainty, as the relations of the vowels of the accented syllable are not clear; the OHG. form *âmeiȝȝa* evidently indicates a connection with emſig; Ameiſe, lit. 'the diligent (insect).' On the other hand, OHG. *â-meizza* and AS. *æ-mette* point to a root *mait*, 'to cut, gnaw' (see under Meißel), so that it would signify 'gnawing insect' (MidHG. and OHG. *â-* means 'off, to pieces'). Du. and LG. *mier*, 'ant,' is more widely diffused than Ameiſe, CrimGoth. *miera* (Goth. *miuzjô), AS. *mŷra*, E. *mire*, Sw. *myra*, 'ant'; orig. 'that which lives in the moss, the moss insect,' allied to Teut. *meuso-* (see Mooß). A word formed from the Lat. *formica* is probably at the base of Swiss *wurmeisle*.

Amelmehl, n., 'starch-flour,' from Mid HG. *amel*, *amer*, OHG. *amar*, 'summer-spelt'; the ModHG. signification seems to be influenced by Gr.-MidLat. *amylon*, 'finest meal' (E. *amel-corn*).

Ammann, m. (Alem.; the Franc. term is Heimbürge), 'chief magistrate, bailiff,' from MidHG. *amman*, a shortened collateral form of *ambetman*, 'magistrate, bailiff'; orig. sense, 'servant, official,' afterwards also 'magistrate.' See also Amt.

Amme, f., '(wet-)nurſe, foster-mother,' from MidHG. *amme*, f., 'mother, in so far as the child is fed by her; (wet-)nurse,' OHG. *amma*, f.; allied to OIc. *amma*, 'grandmother' (Suab. and Bav. even yet 'mother'). Probably an instinctive sound, since, undoubtedly independent of the Teut. group, Rom. also and other languages have similar words for Amme; comp. Span. and Port. *ama*.

Ammeiſter, m., 'chief magistrate,' from MidHG. *ammeister*, from *ambetmeister*, like Ammann, from Ambetmann; MidHG. *ammanmeister* and *ammeister*, 'president of the guilds (of Strasburg).'

Ammer, f., from the equiv. MidHG. *amer*, OHG. *amero* (*amaro), m., 'yellow-hammer,' with the deriv. OHG. and Mid HG. *amerinc*, 'yellow-hammer,' MidLat. *amarellus*, which may have been formed from the G. word; E. *yellow-hammer* (Goldammer) is a corrupt form. Whether OHG. *amaro was derived from OHG. *amar*, 'summer-spelt,' is as doubtful as its relation to Anſel.

Ampel, f., 'lamp,' from MidHG. *ampel* (also *ampulle*), OHG. *ampulla*, f., 'lamp,' also 'vessel.' Borrowed in OHG. from Lat. *ampulla*, 'flask, vessel,' whence also AS. *ampelle*, OIc. *ample*, 'vessel' (LG. *pulle*, 'bottle').

Ampfer, m., 'sorrel,' from the equiv. MidHG. *ampfer*, OHG. *ampfaro*, m.; allied to the equiv. AS. *ompre*; an adj. used as a substantive. Comp. Du. *amper*, 'sharp, bitter, unripe,' OSw. *amper*, 'sour, bitter,' OIc. *apr* (for *ampr), 'sharp' (chiefly of cold); also LG. *ampern*, 'to prove bitter to the taste.' Sauerampfer (also corrupted to Sauerrampf) is a tautological compound like Windhund. In case Teut. *ampra-*, from **ambro-*, represents the prop. Aryan **amrô-*, Sans. *amlá*, 'sour' (also 'wood-sorrel'), and Lat. *amárus*, 'bitter,' are primit. cognate with this word.

Amſel, f., 'blackbird,' from the equiv. MidHG. *amsel*, OHG. *amsala*, f. It corresponds to AS. *ôsle* (*ôs-* from *ams-*), E. *ousel*; the equiv. Lat. *mérula* (Fr. *merle*), whence Du. *meerle* and E. *merl* are borrowed, may represent *mêsula, and have been orig. cognate with Amſel. Its relation to Ammer and to Goth. *ams*, 'shoulder,' is uncertain.

Amt, n., 'office, council, jurisdiction,' from MidHG. *ammet*, older *ambet*, OHG. *ambaht*, *ambahti*, n., 'service, office, occupation, divine service, mass'; a word common to the Teut. group. Comp. Goth. *andbahti*, 'office, service' (from *andbahts*, 'servant,' OHG. *ambaht*, 'servant'), AS. *anbiht*, *ambiht*, n., 'office, service,' *ambiht*, m., 'servant' (obsolete at the beginning of the MidE. period), Du. *ambt*, OSax. *anbaht-skepi*, 'service,' *ambaht-man*, 'servant.' The relation of the common Teut. word to the Gall.-Lat. *ambactus* (mentioned in Cæsar's *Bell. Gall.*), 'vassal,' is much disputed. The WestTeut. words may be best explained from Goth. and OTeut. *ándbahta-*, and the genuinely Teut. aspect of such a word cannot indeed be denied, even if the origin of -*bahts* cannot now be determined (*and-* is a verbal particle, ModHG. ant*s*). The emphatic testimony of Festus, however, is against the Teut. origin of the Gall.-Lat. *ambactus; ambactus apud Ennium lingua gallica servus appellatur*. This coincides with the fact that the word can be fully explained from Kelt.; *ambactus* contains the Kelt. prefix *amb-* (Lat. *amb-*), 'about'; and *ag* is an oft-recurring verbal root (see Acker) in Kelt., meaning 'to go'; hence *ambactus*, 'messenger' (lit. 'one sent hither and thither'), from which comes MidLat. *ambactia, ambactiata*, 'errand' (Ital. *ambasciata*, Fr. *ambassade*, 'embassy'). This explanation of the Lat.-Rom. cognates makes it possible that the OTeut. class was borrowed from Kelt. and transformed (Goth. *andbahts* for *ambahts*); in any case, it was borrowed in prehistoric times (comp. Reich).

an, prep., adv., 'on, by, along,' from MidHG. *ane*, OHG. *ana*, prep., adv., 'on, in, upon'; it corresponds to Goth. *ana*, prep., adv., 'on, upon, in,' AS., E. *on*, prep., adv., Du. *aan*, OSax. *an*. Primit. allied to Gr. *ává*, 'upon, on,' Zend *ana*, 'upon,' Lat. *an-* in *anhēlare*, 'to respire,' OSlov. *vŭ* (for *on).

anberaumen, vb., 'to fix or appoint (a time),' with a dialectic transmutation of *â* into *au* (OBav.), or the word was based by popular etymology on Raum, from MidHG. *râmen* (*ræme*), 'to make proposals, aim, strive' (*berâmen*, 'to fix'), OHG. *râmên*, OSax. *râmôn*, 'to aim, strive,' Du. *beramen*, 'to fix'; allied to MidHG. *râm*, 'goal' (root *rê*, as in Rede?). Further OFr. *aramir*, 'to define legally'?.

Andacht, f., 'devotion,' from MidHG. *andâht*, OHG. *ânadâht*, 'attention, devotion'; MidHG. *dâht*, f., 'thought,' is a verbal abstract from MidHG. and ModHG. *denken*.

Andauche, f., 'drain,' older ModHG. *âdâche*, transformed from Lat. *aquaeductus*. See Abzucht.

ander, adj., 'other, different, second,' from MidHG. *ander*, OHG. *andar*, 'the other'; it corresponds to Goth. *anþar*, 'the other,' OIc. *annarr*, AS. ôðer, E. *other*, Du. *ander*, OSax. ôðar, ôðar. The meanings 'the second, one of two, the other,' are due to a comparative form (Aryan *ánteros*, 'one of two,' Lat. *alter*). Comp. the corresponding Sans. *ántara-*, 'different from,'

Osset. *ändär*, 'otherwise than, with the exception of,' Lith. *ántras*, 'the other.' The root *an-* is proved by Sans. and Zend *an-ya-*, 'another.' With OHG. *andar*, 'other,' is also connected OHG. *antarôn*, 'to imitate.'

Anders, see einst.

Andorn, m., from the equiv. MidHG. and OHG. *andorn*, 'horehound, the plant Marrubium'; the suffix *-orn* as in Ahorn? The root has not yet been explained.

anfachen, see Fächer.

Angel, m. and f., from the equiv. MidHG. *angel*, m., f., 'sting, fish-hook, hinge of a door,' OHG. *angul*, m., 'sting, point, fish-hook'; diminut. of OHG. *ango*, 'sting, door hinge,' MidHG. *ange*, 'fish-hook, door hinge.' Comp. AS. *ongel*, E. *angle*, AS. *onga*, 'sting,' OIc. *ǫngull*, 'fish-hook,' allied to *ange*, 'sting, point' (Alem. *angel*, 'bee sting,' *angelmuck*, 'stinging fly'). The supposition that the primit. and widely diffused cognates are borrowed from Lat. *angulus*, 'angle, corner,' is untenable; OBulg. *ǫglŭ*, E. *angle*, AS. *angul*, 'angle, corner,' are, however, primit. allied to it; so too England, Angelsachsen. The root idea of the Teut. cognates is 'pointed.' An Aryan root *onk*, 'to be pointed,' also lies at the base of Lat. *uncus*, Gr. ὄγκος, ὄγκινος, 'barb,' ἀγκιστροs, 'fish-hook,' Sans. *aṅká*, 'hook,' Osset. *ǻngur*, 'hook, hinge,' OIr. *écad*, 'hook.'

angenehm, adj., 'agreeable, pleasant,' from MidHG. *genæme*, late OHG. *ginâmi*, adj., 'acceptable, agreeable' (without the prefix *an-*), allied to nehmen. Comp. Goth. *andanēms*, 'agreeable,' allied to *and-niman*, 'to accept.'

Anger, m., 'paddock, grass plot,' from MidHG. *anger*, OHG. *angar*, m., 'pasture land, grass plot, arable land'; allied to OIc. *eng*, *enge*, 'meadow, pasture ground.' The cognates can scarcely be derived from *enge*, 'narrow' (Teut. root *ang*). Trustworthy correspondences are wanting.

Angesicht, n., 'face, presence,' from MidHG. *angesiht*, n., 'aspect, view,' MidG. also 'face'; allied to Gesicht, sehen.

Angst, f., from the equiv. MidHG. *angest*, OHG. *angust*, f., 'anxiety, apprehension'; this abstract form is wanting in the other OTeut. dialects, the suffix *st* being also very rarely found; comp. Dienst. But it must not be assumed therefore that the OHG. *angust* is borrowed from Lat. *angustiae*, 'narrowness, meanness.' It is rather to be regarded as a genuine Teut. derivative from the root *ang* appearing in *enge*, especially as the OSlov. in its primit. allied *qzostĭ*, 'contraction,' shows the same derivation. Hence **Ängſt** must be considered as primit. cognate with Lat. *angustiae*. See **bange** and **enge**.

anheiſchig, adj., from the equiv. MidHG. *antheizec*, *antheize*, adj., 'bound, engaged,' influenced by **heiſchen**; the MidHG. adj. is derived from MidHG. and OHG. *antheiʒ*, 'vow, promise,' which, like Goth. *andahait*, 'confession,' AS. *ondettan*, 'to confess,' is composed of the particle *ant*- and the root *hait*, 'to bid.'

Anis, m., from the equiv. MidHG. *anĭs*, also *enĭs*, n., 'anise,' borrowed perhaps even before the MidHG. period from Lat. *anīsum* (Gr. ἄνισον), 'anise,' whence also Fr. *anis*, E. *anise*.

Anke, m., 'butter,' an Alem. word, from MidHG. *anke*, OHG. *ancho*, 'butter'; the genuine G. term for the borrowed word **Butter**, for which, in the OHG. period, *ancsmēro* or *chuo-smēro*, lit. 'cow-fat' (see **Schmeer**), might also be used. Goth. **agqa* for OHG. *ancho* is not recorded. It is certainly allied primitively to the Ind. root *añj*, 'to anoint, besmear,' and to Lat. *unguo*, 'to anoint'; comp. Sans. *ájya*, 'butter-offering,' OIr. *imb* (from *imben*-), 'butter.'

Anker (1.), m., 'anchor,' from the equiv. MidHG. *anker*, late OHG. *anchar*, m.; corresponding to Du. *anker*, AS. (even at a very early period) *oncor*, E. *anchor*, OIc. *akkere*, 'anchor.' A loan-word early naturalised among the English, and before 1000 A.D. even among the MidEurop. Teutons and in the North. From Lat. *ancora* (comp. Ital. *ancora*, Fr. *ancre*, f.; allied also to Lith. *inkaras*, OSlov. *anŭkura*, *ankura*), in connection with which the different gender of the Teut. words is remarkable. In OHG. there exists a genuinely native word for 'anchor'—*senchil*, m., *sinchila*, f.

Anker (2.), m., 'a liquid measure,' ModHG. only, from Du. *anker*, which, like the equiv. E. *anchor*, points to MidLat. *anceria*, *ancheria*, 'cupa minor' (smaller cask); the origin of the cognates is obscure.

Anlehen, n., 'loan,' from MidHG. *anlêhen*, OHG. *analêhan*, n., 'loan of money on interest,' from *an*- and **Lehen**.

anrüchig, adj., also *anrüchtig*, 'disreputable,' ModHG. only, formed from *ruchbar* under the influence of *riechen*. See *ruchbar*.

Anſtalt, f., 'institution,' from MidHG. *anstalt*, 'founding'; *ſtalt* is an abstract from **ſtellen**.

anſtaſſ, see **Staſſ**.

ant-, prefix, preserved in ModHG. only in **Antlitz** and **Antwort** (see also **Amt**, **anheiſchig**, and **Handwerk**). It is found in the early periods in many noun compounds, to which ModHG. *ent*- is the corresponding prefix of verbal compounds. Comp. MidHG. and OHG. *ant*-, Goth. *anda*-, AS. *and*-, *ond*- (comp. E. *answer* under **Antwort**); also the Goth. prep. *and*, 'on, upon, in, along.' The orig. meaning of the prefix is 'counter,' which makes it cognate with Gr. ἀντί, 'against,' Lat. *ante*, 'before,' Sans. *ánti*, 'opposite.'

Antlitz, n., from the equiv. MidHG. *antlitze*, n., late OHG. *antlizzi*, n., 'countenance'; allied to the equiv. collateral forms MidHG. *antlütte*, OHG. *antlutti* (*analŭtti*), n., 'countenance.' Two originally different words have been combined in these forms. It is probable that OHG. and MidHG. *antliʒ* corresponds to AS. *andwlita*, m., OIc. *andlit*, n. (comp. Goth. *andawleizn*, n.); comp. Goth. *wlits*, m., 'face,' *wlaitōn*, OIc. *líta* (for **vlíta*), 'to spy'; the root *wlit* (pre-Teut. *wlĭd*), preserved in these words, has not yet been authenticated beyond the Teut. group. With these cognates were combined those from Goth. *ludja*, 'face,' parallel to which an equiv. **anda-lŭdi*, for OHG. *antlŭtti*, n., 'countenance,' must be assumed.

Antwort, f., from the equiv. MidHG. *antwurt*, f., OHG. *antwurti*, f., 'answer,' beside which there is a neut. form MidHG. *antwürte*, OHG. *antwurti*, Goth. *andawaurdi*; lit. 'counter-words' (collective). Comp. *ant*-; also, AS. *andswaru*, E. *answer*, under **ſchwören**.

Apfel, n., 'apple,' from the equiv. MidHG. *apfel*, OHG. *apful* (also *afful*, plur. *epfili*), m.; a word common to the Teut. group, by chance not recorded in Goth. Comp. Du. and LG. *appel*, m., AS. *æppel*, m. (in the plur. neut.), E. *apple*, OIc. *eple*, n., 'apple' (Goth. **aplus*, m.?). The apple-tree in WestTeut. is **apuldr*, f.; comp. OHG. *affoltra*, AS. *apuldr*, which are preserved in the local names ModHG. **Affeltern**, **Affaltrach**, (**Apolta**?). Du. *Apeldoren*, E. *Appledore*. In spite of this diffusion throughout the entire Teut. group, and of the mention of wild apple-trees in Tacitus, the whole class must be recognised as loan-words (**Obſt** has no connection whatever with them). They must, however, have been borrowed long before the beginning of our era, since the Teut. *p* in *apla-* has, in accordance with the permutation of consonants, originated in a prehistoric *b*; comp. Ir. *aball*, *uball*, Lith. *obůlys*, OSlov. *ablŭko*, 'apple.' As nothing testifies to the Aryan origin of these *oblu-* cognates (in Lat. *mâlum* Gr. μῆλον), found only in the North of Europe, we must assume that the word was borrowed. The derivation from Lat. *malum Abellanum* (the Campanian town Abella was famed in antiquity for its apples), is on phonetic and formal grounds doubtful, although in the abstract (comp. Pfirſich) the combination is interesting. No other explanation of how it was borrowed has yet been found. It is noteworthy that for Augapfel, 'pupil,' *apful* alone (as well as *ougapful*) can be used in OHG.; comp. AS. *æppel*, n. (plur., also masc.), E. *apple of the eye* (also *eyeball*), Du. *oogappel*; but, on the other hand, OIc. *augasteinn*.

April, m., 'April,' from the equiv Mid HG. *aprille*, *aberëlle*, m.; from Lat. *Aprilis* (comp. Fr. *avril*, Ital. *aprile*), borrowed at the beginning of the MidHG. period in place of the genuine OHG. *ôstarmânôd*, 'Easter-month.'

Ar, m., n., a square measure (about 120 sq. yards), ModHG. only, formed from the equiv. Fr. *are* (Lat. *area*).

Arbeit, f., 'work, labour, employment,' from MidHG. *arbeit*, *arebeit*, OHG. *ar(a)beit*, f., 'labour, toil, distress.' Corresponding to OSax. *arbêdi*, n., 'toil, hardship, suffering,' *arbêd*, f., and Du. *arbeid*, m., AS. *earfoð*, *earfeðe*, n., 'toil, hardship,' *earfeðe*, adj., 'difficult,' Goth. *arbaiþs(d)*, f., 'oppression, distress'; OIc. *erfiði*, n., 'toil,' *erfiðr*, adj., 'difficult, toilsome.' Hence 'toil' must be accepted as the fundamental meaning of the cognates, and therefore any connection with the stem of Erbe is improbable. It has been compared with greater reason with OSlov. (Russ.) *rabota*, f., 'servants' work,' and *rabŭ*, *robŭ*, 'servant, thrall,' as prim. cognates, although this comparison is open to doubt. Lat. *labor*, 'work,' is at all events certainly not allied to it.

Arche, f., 'ark,' from MidHG., *arche* (also *arke*), OHG. *arahha* (also *archa*), f., 'Noah's ark.' The ModHG. form with *ch* (instead of *k*) seems to point to Upper Germany (Luther's Bible has Noahs Kaſten); OHG. *buoh-arahha*, 'book-chest,' MidHG. *arche*, 'chest, money-chest.' It corresponds to Du. *ark*, 'Noah's ark,' AS. *earc*, m., *earce*, f., 'chest, covenant, ark, box,' E. *ark*, OIc. *ǫrk*, f., 'chest, coffin, Noah's ark,' Goth. *arka*, f., 'box, money-box, Noah's ark.' This widely diffused word was borrowed at an early period from the equiv. Lat. (also Romance) *arca*, which, as the meanings of the Teut. group coextensive with those of the Lat. indicate, was not perhaps naturalised on the introduction of Christianity, to which the more recent meaning of 'Noah's ark' may refer. Both the word and the thing had probably at the beginning of our era found their way to the Teutons with Lat. *cista*. See Kiſte and Sack.

arg, adj., 'bad, severe, hard,' from Mid HG. *arc(g)*, 'vile, wicked, stingy, avaricious,' OHG. *arg*, *arag*, 'avaricious, cowardly, vile'; also OHG. *ary*, MidHG. *arc(g)*, 'evil, vileness, wickedness,' Comp. AS. *earg*, adj., 'cowardly, slothful' (no longer found in E.), OIc. *argr*, 'cowardly, effeminate' (also *ragr*). Paul the Deacon cites *arga* as an abusive term among the Lombards. Through a Goth. *args the Teut. word may have made its way into Span. and Finn.; comp. Span. *aragan*, 'slothful,' Finn. *arka*, 'cowardly.' As it is not easy to deduce the meaning 'cowardly' from 'avaricious,' which appears chiefly in OHG., we must assume that the root idea of the Teut. *arga-* was 'vile, base,' of which 'avaricious' and 'cowardly' would be specialisations resulting from the liberal hospitality and bravery which characterised the Teutons. This word, like almost all words within the ethical sphere, is peculiar to Teutonic; comp. arm, böſe, gut, übel.—

ärgern, 'to annoy, vex, fret,' from Mid HG. *ergern*, 'to incite to evil, deteriorate, corrupt,' OHG. *ergirôn*, *argirôn*, 'to make worse,' from the comparative of arg. From this ModHG. Ärger, m., is formed (comp. Ausſatz from ausſätzig, Geiz from geizen, Handel from handeln, Opfer from opfern); in MidHG. *erge*, OHG. *argî*, f., 'malice.'—

Argwohn, m., from the equiv. MidHG. *arcwân*, m. (comp. Wahn), 'suspicion, mistrust'; comp. ModHG. Argliſt, f., from Mid HG. *arclist*, f., 'cunning, malice,' from arg; even in OHG. *arcwânen*, 'to suspect,' occurs, MidHG. *arcwænen*.

ärgern, vb., see arg.

Ariesbaum, m., 'service tree,' from MidHG. OHG. *arliz-boum*, m., 'acernus, cornus'; scarcely allied to Erle.

Arm, m., 'arm, branch,' from the equiv.

Arm (12) Arz

MidHG. *arm*, OHG. *aram, arm*, m.; a word common to the Teut. group; comp. OSax. *arm*, Du. *arm*, AS. *earm*, E. *arm*, OIc. *armr*, Goth. *arms*, m., 'arm.' Like many terms for parts of the body (see Arſch, Fuß, Herz, Knie, Nagel, &c.), Arm extends beyond the Teut. dialects. It is primit. related to Lat. *armus*, 'the topmost part of the upper arm, fore-quarter' (Gr. ἁρμός, 'suture, joint, shoulder,' belongs to another division), OBulg. *ramę*, 'shoulder, arm,' Sans. *īrmá-s*, m., 'fore-quarter, arm.' See Ermel.

arm, adj., 'poor, unfortunate, miserable,' from the equiv. MidHG. *arm*, OHG. *aram, arm*, adj.; comp. OSax. *arm*, Du. *arm*, AS. *earm* (obsolete in E.), OIc. *armr*, Goth. *arms*, adj., 'poor.' A term common to Teut., with no correspondence in the allied Aryan group; comp. barmherzig, arg, reich.—**Armut**, f., from the equiv. MidHG. *armuot*, f., *armuote*, n., 'poverty,' OHG. *aramuotî*, f.: a derivative of the Goth. adj. *armôþs; comp. Einöde, Heimat.

Armbrust, f., 'crossbow,' from the equiv. MidHG. *armbrust*, n., which must be a corruption of MidLat. *arbalista, arcubalista*, lit. 'bow for projectiles' (Lat. *arcus*, Gr. βάλλειν). A compound of Arm and Brust is, properly speaking, impossible in G., especially as the MidHG. word is neut. From MidLat. *arbalista* comes the equiv. Fr. *arbalète;* comp. E. *arbalist*, Du. *armborst*, Ital. *balestra*, from the last of which the older ModHG. Balſter, 'crossbow for shooting bullets,' is borrowed.

Ärmel, see Ermel.
Armut, see arm.
Arnold, see Aar.

Arſch, m., 'arse, fundament,' according to the analogous cases cited under birſchen, from an older Ars, MidHG. and OHG. *ars*, m., 'arse.' It corresponds to the equiv. Mid LG. *ars, ers*, Du. *aars, naars* (with prefixed *n*), AS. *ears*, E. *arse*, OIc. *ars* (and *rass*, comp. *argr* and *ragr*, see arg), m., 'arse.' Teut. *arsa-z*, m., from *órso-s*, is rightly held to be primit. allied to Gr. ὄρρος (*pp* for *rs*), 'coccyx, rump'; akin to OIr. *err*, f., 'tail, end, point' ?. Comp. the remark under Arm.

Art, f., 'kind, sort, species, manner,' from MidHG. *art*, m., f., 'innate peculiarity, nature, condition, kind'; OHG. *art*, is not recorded with these meanings, nor is the word found elsewhere. Instead of this there occurs the homonymous OHG. *art*, f., 'tillage, ploughing,' with which *artôn*,

'to inhabit, cultivate,' is connected; further, OSax. *ard*, m., 'dwelling-place,' AS. *eard*, m., 'dwelling, native place,' OIc. *ǫrð*, f., 'harvest, produce.' These cognates, which belong (see Acker) to an OTeut. and Aryan root, *ar*, 'to plough' (Lat. *arare*, Gr. ἀρόω, &c.), are scarcely allied to MidHG. *art*, m., f., 'nature, condition'; comp., however, Wohnung from gewöhnen. It is more probable that Art is connected with Lat. *ars* (gen. plur. *arti-um*), 'method, art,' and Sans. *r̥tá*, 'method.' The compounds Artacker, artbar, arthaft contain MidHG. and OHG. *art*, 'agriculture, tillage,' and belong consequently to the Teut. and Aryan root *ar*, 'to plough.'

Arzenei, f. (in the 17th cent. accented on the A also), 'medicine,' from MidHG. *arzenîe* (*erzenîe*), f., 'art of healing, remedy.' The OHG. word does not occur, but only a derivative OHG. *erzinen*, *giarzinôn*, MidHG. *erzenen*, 'to heal ;' the verb, by its suffix, suggests Goth. *lêkinôn*, AS. *lǽcnian*, OHG. *lâhhinôn*, 'to heal.' From OHG. *gi-arzinôn*, the MidHG. subst. *arzenîe*, which did not appear until a later period, might then have been formed with a Rom. termination. The assumption that MidHG. *arzenîe* referred to Archigenes of Apamea (in Syria), a famous physician, is untenable; if this assumption were correct, we should have expected OHG. *arzin*, or rather *arzino, 'physician,' which, however, is nowhere to be found. Besides, OHG. *arzinôn* formed into *arzât*, 'physician,' under the influence of the genuinely Teut. and Goth. *lêkinôn*, OHG. *lâhhinôn*, 'to heal,' makes any reference to Archigenes quite superfluous. Moreover, MidHG. has also a form *arzatîe* (MidDu. *arsedîe*), 'medicine.' See Arzt.

Arzt, m., 'physician,' from the equiv. MidHG. *arzet, arzât*, OHG. *arzât*, m., a specifically Germ. word, unknown to Eng., Scand. and Goth. Its early appearance in OHG., in which OTeut. *lâhhi* was the more prevalent form, is remarkable (comp. Goth. *lêkeis*, 'physician,' AS. *lǽce*, E. *leech ;* also the ModHG. proper name Lachner, from MidHG. *lâchenære*, 'enchanter,' lit. 'physician'). The MidDu. form *arsatre*, OLG. *ercetere*, 'physician' (MidLG. *arste*), proves the origin from the oft-recurring Franc. and MidLat. *archiater* (ἀρχίατρός), 'physician' (espec. physician-in-ordinary to the king). There are no phonetic difficulties in connecting OHG. *arzât* with *arzâter, arciâter, archiâter*, since the OLG. and MidDu. form itself points to the MidLat. form. Moreover, the technical terms of Greek physic found their way at an early period to the West (comp. Büchſe, Pflaſter), but always through the medium of Lat. and Rom. The unique *arzâte(r)* was entirely unknown to Rom. (Ital. *medico*, OFr. *mire*, Fr. *médecin*, which of course were also unknown to Teut.). Concerning *arz-*, *erz-*, as the representative of Gr. ἀρχι-, see Erz. The theory advanced on account of ModHG. Mühlarzt, 'millwright,' that OHG. *arzât* is from Lat. *artista*, is on phonetic and historical grounds unwarranted. MidLat. *artista* was not used for medical practitioners until late in the Middle Ages (comp. ModFr. *artiste vétérinaire*); the word too is unknown in earlier Rom. On the other hand, we meet with *archiatri* even as far back as the Frank. king Childebert and Charlemagne. See besides Arznei.

As, n., **Aß**, ModHG. only, from the equiv. Fr. *as*, m., 'the ace (of dice or cards),' a small weight' (Lat. *as*). In MidHG. the prevalent term for the 'ace (of dice)' was *esse*, which comes from Lat. *assis* (a later collateral form of *as*). Comp. Daus.

Aſch, see Ariſch.—**Aſch**, m., 'pot, basin, bowl' (to which Aſchfuchen is allied), from MidHG. *asch*, OHG. *asc*, m., 'dish, basin, boat'; lit. 'of ash.' See Eiche.

Aſche (1.), f., 'ashes, cinders,' from MidHG. *asche* (*esche*), OHG. *asca*, f., 'ashes'; corresponds to Du. *asch*, AS. *asce*, *æsce*, f., E. *ashes* (but also sing. in *bone-ash*, *potash*, &c.); OIc. *aska*, f., 'ashes'; akin also to the abnormal Goth. *azgô*, f., 'ashes' (but Span. *ascua* is borrowed). Trustworthy correspondences in other languages are wanting, nor is Eiche allied to it.—**Aſchenbrödel**, see under brodeln.—ModHG. **Aſcher**, 'ash,' in the compound Aſchermittwoch (for which the MidHG. form is *aschtac*), occurs even in MidHG. in compounds.— **Aſchlauch**, m., 'shallot,' MidHG. *aschlouch*, a corruption of the equiv. MidLat. *ascalonium*. See Schalotte.

Aſche (2.), f., 'grayling,' from the equiv. MidHG. *asche*, OHG. *asco*, m.; scarcely allied to Aſche, as if the fish were named from its ash-grey colour; Ital. *lasco*.

Aſſel, m., espec. Kellerassel, 'woodlouse,' ModHG. only; generally derived from Lat. *asellus*, 'little ass,' and might have been named from its grey colour; comp. Gr. ὄνος, ὀνίσκος, 'ass, woodlouse,' Ital. *asello*, 'woodlouse.' Yet the *ff* of the ModHG. word, as well as the dialectic variant *atzel*, might militate against this derivation; hence a pre-Teut. stem *at, att* (allied to eſſen?) seems to be at the base of it. Comp. also Giel.

Aſt, m., 'bough, branch,' from the equiv. MidHG. and OHG. *ast*, m., 'branch,' corresponding to the equiv. Goth. *asts*. The term is unknown to the other dialects, yet its great antiquity is incontestable because of the agreement of Teut. *astaz* (a permutation of the pre-Teut. *ozdos*; comp. Maſt, and the examples cited there of the permutation of the Aryan *zd*, *sd*, to Teut. *st*) with Gr. ὄζος (ὀσθος), 'branch, twig, knot, node (of a tree)'; the latter with Armen. *ost*, 'branch,' is likewise based upon *osdos*. The meanings of the Gr. word admit the supposition of its being allied to MidLG. *ôst* (LG. *aust*), Du. *oest*, AS. *ôst*, 'knot, node' (Aryan stem *ôsdo-*).

Aß, see **Aas** and **As**.

Atem, m., from the equiv. MidHG. *âtem* (*âten*), OHG. *âtum*, m., 'breath, spirit'; comp. MidHG. *der heilege âtem*, OHG. *der wîho âtum*, 'the Holy Spirit;' ModHG. collateral form (prop. dialectic) Odem. The word is not found in EastTeut.; in Goth. *ahma*, 'spirit,' is used instead (see achten). Comp. OSax. *âdom*, Du. *adem*, AS. *œþm* (obsolete in Eng.), 'breath.' The cognates point to Aryan *êtmon-*, Sans. *âtmân*, m., 'puff, breath, spirit'; also OIr. *athach*, 'breath,' Gr. ἀτμός, 'smoke, vapour.' Whether ModHG. Ader and Gr. ἦτορ, 'heart,' are derived from the root *êt*, 'to exhale, breathe,' contained in these cognates, is questionable.

Atte, Atti, m., 'father,' dialectic, from MidHG. *atte*, OHG. *atto*, 'father.' The mutation of the ModHG. is diminutive, as is shown by the final *i* of the Swiss *ätti*. Allied to Goth. *atta*, 'father' (whence *Attila*, MidHG. *Etzel*, lit. 'little, dear father'), perhaps also to OIr. *aite*, 'foster-father' (from *attios*), OSlov. *otĭcĭ*, 'father.'

Attich, m., from the equiv. MidHG. *attech* (*atech*), OHG. *attah* (*attuh*, *atah*), 'danewort,' borrowed and extended at an early period from Lat. *acte* (Gr. ἀκτῆ, ἀκτέα), 'elder-tree.' Comp. Lattich from Lat. *lactuca*, also Dattel from *dactylos*.

Atzel, f., 'magpie'; see under Elſter.

ätzen, vb., 'to corrode, etch, bait,' from MidHG. *etzen*, OHG. *ezzen*, 'to give to eat,' lit. 'to make eat'; factitive of eſſen.

Au, **Aue,** 'river inlet, wet meadow, fertile plain,' from MidHG. *ouwe,* f., 'water, stream, water-land, island, peninsula, meadow-land abounding in water, grassy plain'; OHG. *ouwa,* from old **aujô-* (the presumed Goth. form, comp. OHG.-MidLat. *augia*). It corresponds to OIc. *ey* and AS. *êg, îg,* f., 'island,' to which AS. *êglond, îglond,* E. *island,* Du. *eiland,* 'island,' are allied ; so too Lat. and Teut. *Batavia, Scandinavia;* Goth. **aujô-* (for *aujô-, awiđ-*) has lost a *g* (comp. Niere). The theoretical form *agwjô-,* prop. an adj. used as a subst., ' the watery place,' as it were (hence 'water-land,' *i.e.,* 'island' or 'meadow'), belongs to Goth. *ahwa,* f., 'river,' which with Lat. *aqua* is based upon Aryan *ákwâ.* The names of places ending in *a* (*e.g.* Fulda) and *ach* (*e.g.* Urach) still preserve the OHG. *aha* equiv. to the Goth. *ahwa.* See *a* and *ach*.

auch, adv. and conj., 'also, likewise,' from MidHG. *ouch,* OHG. *ouh,* 'and, also, but.' It corresponds to OSax. *ôk,* Du. *ook,* OFries. *âk,* AS. *eâc,* E. *eke,* OIc. *auk,* 'besides,' Dan. *og,* 'and, also, but,' Sw. *och,* Ic. *ok;* Goth. *auk,* 'then, but'; an adv. common to Teut. Some refer this *auk* to the Teut. root *auk* (Aryan *aug*), 'to increase,' whence OHG. *ouhhôn,* 'to add,' OSax. *ôkian,* AS. *ŷcan,* OIc. *auka,* Goth. *aukan,* 'to increase,' are derived (Lat. *augere, aug-ustus,* Sans. *ugrás,* 'powerful,' *ójas,* 'strength,' are allied to them) ; comp. AS. *tô-eácan,* 'moreover, also.' Others trace Teut. *ank* to a compound of two Aryan particles, *au* and *ge* (Gr. *aũ,* γε).

Aue, f., 'ewe,' dialectic, from MidHG. *ouwe,* OHG. *ou,* f., 'sheep.' Comp. AS. *eowu,* E. *ewe;* primit. allied to Lat. *ovis,* Gr. *ὄïς,* Lith. *avis* (OSlov. *ovĭca*), 'sheep.' See Schaf.

Auer, in Auerochs, m., from the equiv. MidHG. *ûr, ûr-ochse,* OHG. *ûr, ûrohso,* m., 'aurochs'; corresponds to AS. *ûr,* OIc. *ûrr,* (*u-* stem). The fact that even Roman writers knew the Teut. term under the form *ûrus* points to *ûrus (not *ŭrus*) as the Goth. form ; comp. Teut. and Lat. *glêsum,* 'amber,' similar to AS. *glǽre,* 'resin.' Hence the proposed explanation of *ûr* from Sans. *usrá-s,* m., 'bull,' must be put aside. Internal evidence cannot be adduced to show that the OGerm. word is non-Teut. ; the assertion of Macrobius that *ûrus* is Kelt. proves nothing.—**Auerhahn,** m., even in MidHG. the equiv. *ûrhan* (and *orhan*), m., 'blackcock,' with *ûrhuon* (*orhuon*), 'grey hen,' occurs. Auerhahn was evidently compared with Auerochs, the one appeared to be among the birds of the wood what the other was among animals of the chase.

auf, adv., prep., 'up, upwards, on, upon,' from MidHG. and OHG. *ûf,* adv., prep., 'upon'; corresponds to OSax. *ŭp,* AS. *ŭpŭpp,* and its equiv. E. *up;* Goth. *iup,* adv., 'upwards, aloft,' differs remarkably in its vowel. Probably primit. Teut. **ŭppa,* 'up,' is allied to oben and über.

aufmutzen, see mutzen.

Aufruhr, see Ruhr.

aufwiegeln, see wiegeln.

Auge, n., 'eye,' from the equiv. Mid HG. *ouge,* OHG. *ouga,* n. ; a word common to Teut. ; comp. Goth. *augô,* OIc. *auga,* AS. *eáge,* E. *eye,* Du. *oog,* OSax. *ôga,* 'eye.' While numerous terms for parts of the body (comp. Arm, Fuß, Herz, Kinn, Knie, Ohr, &c.) are common to Teut. with the other Aryan dialects, it has not yet been proved that there is any agreement with respect to Auge between Teut. and Lat., Gr., Ind., &c. Of course there is an undeniable similarity of sound between the Aryan base *oq,* 'eye,' and Lat. *oculus,* Gr. ὄσσε for **ὄκje,* ὀφθαλμός, ὦπα, &c., Sans. *akśi,* OSlov. *oko,* Lith. *akì-s,* 'eye.'—**Augenlid,** see Lid.

August, m., formed, after being based anew on Lat. and Rom. *augustus,* from the equiv. MidHG. *ougest, ougeste,* OHG. *augusto, agusto,* m., 'August' (the genuine OGerm. term is Erntemonat, OHG. *aran-mânôt*). Comp. Fr. *août,* Ital. *agosto.* It was borrowed in OHG. at the same time as März and Mai.

aus, adv. and prep., 'out, forth, from, by reason of,' from the equiv. MidHG. and OHG. *ûȝ,* adv., prep. ; corresponds to Goth. *ût,* adv., 'out (thither, hence),' AS. *ût,* 'out (thither, hence), out of doors, outside,' E. *out,* Du. *uit,* prep., adv., 'out,' OSax. *ût.* Comp. außen, äußer. The common Teut. *ût* (from *ût-a ?*) is based upon Aryan *úd* (*ŭd*) ; comp. Sans. *ud,* a verbal particle, 'out, out (thither), aloft, upwards.'

Aussatz, m., from the equiv. late Mid HG. *ûȝ-satz,* m., 'leprosy'; a singular, late and regressive formation from the Mid HG. subst. *ûȝsetze* and *ûȝsetzel,* 'leper,' Mid HG. *ûȝsetzig,* adj., 'leprous,' OHG. *ûȝ-sâzzo, ûȝ-sâzeo,* m., 'leper'; lit. ' one who lives outside, separate' ; those who were afflicted with leprosy were exposed. Considering the very late appearance of the subst. Auſſatʒ, in contrast to the early OHG. ûzsâzeo, 'leper,' there is no doubt that Auſſatʒ is a recent formation, like Ärger from ärgern. The Goth. word for leprosy is þrutsfill.

Auſter, f., 'oyster,' ModHG. only, from earlier ModHG. ûster, from Du. oester, which, with the equiv. AS. ôstre, E. oyster, Fr. huître, Ital. ostrica, is based upon Lat. ostrea, ostreum, Gr. ὄστρεον, 'oyster, mussel.'

ausweiden, see Weide and Eingeweide.

auswendig, see wenden.

außen, adv., 'outside, out of doors, without,' from MidHG. ûzen, OHG. ûzana, ûzdn, adv., prep., 'out of doors, outside, out, without'; corresponding to AS. ûton, adv., 'from without,' Goth. ûtana, adv., prep., 'from without, outside, out'; from OTeut. ût. See aus.

außer, adv. and prep., 'except, unless, apart from, without,' from MidHG. ûzer, OHG. ûzar, prep., 'out—here'; corresponds to OSax. ûtar.

Axt, f. (with a dental added as in Hüfte, Habicht, and Obſt, &c.), from the equiv. Mid HG. ackes (late MidHG. axt), f., OHG. acchus (plur. acchussi), f., 'axe.' It corresponds to OSax. accus, Du. aaks (from akes), AS. œx (from *œcces), E. ax, axe, OIc. öx, Goth. aqizi, f., 'axe.' The Teut. word is based upon Aryan agést, or rather agzi (akst); comp. the prim. cognate Gr. ἀξίνη, 'axe,' with which perhaps the equiv. Lat. ascia, in case it stands for ac-scia, is connected. Lat. acies, 'sharpness,' and Gr. ἀκή, 'point,' as well as Sans. açri, 'edge' (see Ähre, Ecke), are not allied to Axt.

B.

baar, adj., from the equiv. MidHG. and OHG. bar (nom. MidHG. barer, barwer, OHG. barêr), adj., 'naked, bare, denuded, free, empty.' It corresponds to OSax. bar, AS. bær, E. bare, OIc. berr, 'naked, bare'; Goth. *baza- is wanting. The r of the non-Goth. dialects is an old s (not r) as is proved by the affinity to OSlov. bosŭ, Lith. basas, 'bare-footed,' which, as well as the Teut. adjs., point to an Aryan bhosô-s, 'denuded' (with regard to the antiquity of this idea see nackt). Comp. also Armen. bok, 'naked,' which is based upon bhosko-; besides, E. bald (MidE. balled) points to a Goth. participle *bazlôþs (AS. *bællod). Perhaps entbehren is also connected with the root bhes. Comp. further barſch.

Baas, m., 'master,' a LG. word; comp. Du. baas; orig. perhaps it was a term of endearment used in addressing superiors (comp. Amme, Muhme, Bube, Buhle). It is undoubtedly connected with Baſe, 'aunt on the father's side,' because Baſe, Baaſ—Bâſel, are also titles given by domestics to their mistress. Yet it is astonishing that the area of diffusion of Baas, m. (LG.), and Baſe, f. (MidG. and UpG.), is different. Perhaps 'paternal' was the root idea of both words.

babbeln, see pappeln.

Bach, m. (MidLG. and LG., fem.), from the equiv. MidHG. bach (plur. beche), m. (MidG. fem.), OHG. bah, m., 'brook.' Comp. OSax. beki, MidLG. beke, Du. beek; a corresponding Goth. *baki-, m., is wanting; beside which the equiv. AS. bece, and OIc. bekkr (whence E. beck), m., presuppose a Goth. *bakki-. No Aryan root bhag- with a meaning applicable here can be found; both HG. backen and Gr. πηγή, 'source,' are scarcely allied to it, though Sans. bhañga, 'breach, wave' (see Bruch) may be so.

Bachbunge, f., 'speedwell, brooklime' (Veronica beccabunga), from MidHG. bungo, OHG. bunge, 'bulb'; allied to OIc. bingr, 'bolster,' and more remotely with Sans. bahú, 'dense,' Gr. παχύς?.

Bache, f., 'wild sow,' from MidHG. bache, OHG. bahho, m., 'ham, (flitch of) bacon' (Swiss and Bav. bachen); similarly the corresponding MidLat. baco and MidDu. bake mean 'ham, pork,' and 'pig.' Comp. Prov., OFr., and E. bacon, borrowed from Germ. The Teut. root bak contained in these cognates is further allied to the cognates of ModHG. Backe.

Bachſtelze, f., 'water-wagtail,' formed from the equiv. MidHG. wazzerstelze, OHG. wazzerstelza; the second part of the compound is connected with Stelze. This term is only HG.; comp. with it Du. kwikstaart,

Norw. *quickstiert,* E. *wagtail,* LG. *wippstert,* Dan. *vipstiert;* also Gr. σεισοπυγίς Ital. *squassacoda, codatremola, cutretta,* Fr. *hochequeue;* but Span. *andario,* which means lit. 'brook-trotter.'

Bach, n., 'a deep wooden dish, in which food is served for a certain number of the crew'; borrowed, like many technical terms of sea-life, from LG.; LG. *back,* 'dish,' E. *back* ('tub, vat'); comp. ModFr. *bac,* 'brewer's vat or tub,' borrowed from this word or the Du. *bak.* It has been derived from Late Lat. *bacca,* 'water vessel,' whence also Fr. *bac,* 'ferryboat,' Du. *bak,* E. *bac,* 'a flat-bottomed boat.' Probably Becken is allied to it.

Bachbord, n., 'larboard,' from LG. (comp. the preceding word); comp. Du. *bakboord* (AS. *bæcbord),* whence also the equiv. Fr. *bâbord;* lit. 'the left side of the ship to the back of the helmsman, who is steering with his right hand, the left hinder-part of the ship.' Du. and E. *back* is an OTeut. word, which was, however, very early obsolete in HG. (see the following word); OHG. *bah,* OSax. *bak,* AS. *bæc,* E. *back,* OIc. *bak,* n., 'back,' Goth. **bak,* n. From LG. is also derived HG. Borb. See the latter.

Bache (1.), **Bachen,** m., especially used in the compounds with Fisch=, Hinter=, hence the lit. meaning, 'buttock.' The correct HG. form, which has the regular permutation of *k* to *ch,* is seen in MidHG. *bache,* OHG. *bahho,* 'ham, flitch of bacon' (yet MidHG. also *ars-backe,* m.), which as 'bacon' made its way into OFr., and thence into Eng. also. Although it has been connected by the linguistic instinct of ModHG. with the following word, they are not allied; it is more probable that Bache and the stem *bak,* discussed under Backbord, is most closely connected with it.

Bache (2.), m., f., also **Bachen,** m. (the latter espec. in the compounds Backenzahn, =streich), 'cheek'; from MidHG. *backe,* m., 'jaw, jawbone, cheek.' OHG. has the doublets *baccho* (whence the MidHG. and ModHG. *ck*) and *bahho,* which produce MidHG. *bache.* Comp. MidHG. *kinnebache* beside *kinn-backe,* which compound too, even in OHG. (as *chinni-bahho),* is more frequent than the simple word; comp. OSax. *kinni-bako,* Du. *kinnebakken.* It is still uncertain whether Lat. *bucca,* 'cheek,' is allied to it; its initial *b* might have arisen from *bh,* as in *barba* (see Bart); but the two differ in meaning; while the Lat. signifies 'the inflated cheek,' the G. word orig. denoted 'jaw.'

bachen, vb. (dial. UpG. bachen), 'to bake,' from MidHG. *backen, bachen,* str. vb.; doublets are found even in OHG. *bacchan, bakkan,* str. vbs.; OHG. *cch* is based upon the double consonants *kk* (OSax. *bakkeri,* 'baker,' Du. *bakken,* 'to bake'); but *ch* presupposes a simple *k.* Comp. AS. *bacan,* str. vb., E. *to bake,* as well as E. *batch,* from MidE. *bacche,* AS. **bæcce,* where *cc* points to the *ck* of the ModHG. word. Whether a Goth. *bakkan or **baqan,* str. vb., must be presupposed is uncertain; the pre-Teut. form of the verbal root is Aryan *bhôg,* as is shown by its primit. kinship to Gr. φώγω, 'I roast'; the affinity of Lat. *fŏcus,* 'hearth,' is doubtful.

Bad, n., 'bath,' from the equiv. Mid HG. *bat(d),* OHG. *bad,* n.; comp. Du. *bad,* AS. *bæþ,* E. *bath,* OIc. *bað,* 'bath.' An important word in relation to the history of OTeut. civilisation; even the Roman writers testify that bathing (comp. further Laken) was a daily necessity to the Teutons. As a verb, a denominative was already formed in the OTeut. dialects, Mid HG. and ModHG. baten, from OHG. *badôn,* Du. *baden,* AS. *baþian,* E. *to bathe;* Goth. *baþôn is not recorded. The dental of the cognates is derivative, hence *ba* (Aryan *bhâ*) is the root syllable, (comp. Hähen, in that case allied to it), to which OSlov. *banja,* 'bath,' *banjati,* 'to wash, bathe,' belongs.—Baden, the name of a place, is prop. dat. plur. of Bad, 'at the baths' (so too E. *Bath*); probably an imitation of Lat. *aquae* in names of places.

Bader, m., 'barber,' from MidHG *badære,* 'one who looks after the bathers in the bath-house.' "In the later period of the Middle Ages it was a custom to get the beard shaved and the hair cut by the Baber at the end of the bath."

baf! baff! paff! onomatopoetic term for the report of a gun; first occurs in ModHG. Allied to ModHG. bäffen, 'to bark,' from MidHG. *baffen, beffen;* comp. MidE. *baffen,* E. *to beff;* of recent onomat. origin.

bäfzen, 'to yelp,' derivative of bäffen.

bägern, 'to torment, plague,' prob. allied to OHG. *bâgan,* MidHG. *bâgen,* str. vb., 'to contend, quarrel.' Akin to Ir. *bâgim,* 'I contend,' *bâg,* 'combat'; hence the Aryan root is *bhêgh, bhôgh.*

Bagger, m., 'dredging-machine'; like many words with *gg* (comp. Flagge), it is not prop. HG. (since *gg* in HG. must have been changed to *ck*), but from LG. *bagger*, identical with Du. *bagger*, 'mud at the bottom of water.'

bähen, vb., 'to warm by poultices, foment, toast (bread),' from the equiv. MidHG. *bæn*, *bæjen*, OHG. *bâjan*, *bâan*. The Teut. root is *bê*, from pre-Teut. *bhê*, to which *ba-* of the OTeut. words for Bab is related by gradation. The orig. sense of the primit. stem *bhê*, by gradation *bha*, was probably 'to make warm by washing, bathing.'

Bahn, f., 'path, track, career,' from MidHG. *bane*, *ban*, f., m., 'road, way'; allied to MidDu. *bane*, Du. *baan*. No word identical with this is found in any of the older periods of the Teut. group. The cognates of fehnen are probably allied to it.

Bahre, f., 'barrow, bier,' from the equiv. MidHG. *bâre*, OHG. *bâra*, f.; Goth. **bêra* or **bêrô*, f.; AS. *bér*, *bére*, E. *bier*; E. *barrow* (MidE. *barewe*), belongs to a different gradation since it presupposes Goth. **barwa*; comp. OIc. *burar*, plur. 'bier,' Goth. **barôs*. The pre-Teut. phonetic form is *bhérâ-*. From the OHG. word is derived the equiv. Ital. *bara* (*barella*), Fr. *bière*. The root is the primit. Aryan *bher*, 'to carry,' which is widely diffused, and appears in ModHG. Bürde, gebären, Geburt, as well as in Suber; it occurs in Ind. as *bhar*, in Gr. as φερ, in Lat. as *fer*. From this root the OTeut. languages, in agreement with all the other Aryan tongues, formed a str. vb., Goth. *baíran*, OHG. *bëran*, MidHG. *bërn* (the latter means only 'to bear fruit, produce, give birth to'), AS. *bëran*, E. *to bear*. Comp. espec. gebären.

Bai (1.), f., 'bay of a window,' from MidHG. *beie*, 'window,' which with the following word is of Rom. origin; comp. E. *bay*, Fr. *baie*, 'bay (of a window).'

Bai (2.), f., 'bay,' derived through LG. from E. *bay* (MidE. *baie*), which was borrowed from Rom.; Fr. *baie*, Ital. *baja*, Span. and Iber. (in Isidore), *baja*, 'haven'; prop. identical with the preceding word.

Bake, f., 'a mark at the entrance of a harbour as a warning against shallows, buoy'; from Fris. like other technical terms relating to the sea, Fris. *bâken* (comp. Bark), whence LG. *bâke*, Du. *baak*. It is based upon Goth. **baukn*, n., which by a regular change became *beácen*, 'beacon,' in AS.; comp. E. *beacon* and *beckon*. OHG. *bouhhan*, MidHG. *bouchen*, OLG. *bôcan*, 'beacon, model,' are corresponding terms. Thus the OTeut. word meant generally 'sign.' Bake has been restricted to a definite caution signal.

Balbier, m., for Barbier.

Balche, f., see Belch.

Balcon, see Balken.

bald, adv., 'soon, nearly, quickly,' based upon an OTeut. adj. which signified 'quick, bold, brave'; Goth. *balps*, 'bold,' preserved only in derivs., AS. *beald* (with the change of *þ* after *l* to *d*, comp. Wald, falten), E. *bold*, OIc. *ballr*, 'bold, impudent, audacious'; also OIc. *baldr*, AS. *bealdor*, 'prince,' whence the name of the god Balter. In HG. the meaning tended towards 'bold, quick'; OHG. and OLG. *bald*, MidHG. *balt* (gen. *baldes*), 'bold, zealous, quick'; comp. Ital. *baldo*, 'bold.' The development of meaning of the OHG. adv. *baldo*, MidHG. *balde*, is thus 'boldly,—quickly,—immediately.' The abstract Bälde, which is connected with it, meant lit. 'boldness,' like Goth. *balpei* and OHG. *baldî*; MidHG. *belde*, 'audacity'; the meaning of the Mod HG. subst. is based immediately on the adv. To this word are allied proper names like Balduin, as well as Fr. *Baudouin* (applied to the ass).

Baldachin, m., 'canopy,' not from Mid HG. *buldëkîn*, 'raw silk from Bagdad,' but from Ital. *baldacchino*, which is identical with the MidHG. word, but has been specialised in meaning to the canopy made from such stuff.

Baldrian, m., 'valerian,' from MidHG. *baldrian*, from Lat. *valeriana*; comp. the E. term.

Balefter, m., see Armbruft.

Balg, m., 'skin, case, bellows, brat,' from the equiv. MidHG. *balc* (plur. *bëlge*), OHG. *balg*, plur. *balgi*, *bëlgi*, m.; Goth. *balgs*, plur. *balgeis*, 'leather bottle,' lit. 'the flayed skin of an animal for keeping liquids.' On the root *balgi-* is based AS. *belg*, *bylg*, E. *belly* (Balg, with the specialised meaning, 'swollen body'), and E. *bellows*, plur. The primary idea of the root is 'swelling out'; from the same root the OTeut. dialects form a str. vb. *bëlgan* (see Belfter), meaning 'to swell'; OIc. *bólgenn*, 'swollen'; OHG. *bëlgan*, MidHG. *bëlgen*, 'to swell, be angry.' The pre-Teut. form of the stem according to the laws of the permutation of consonants is *bhelgh*, and to this corresponds Ind. *barh* (with the initial aspirate

B

displaced), 'to be great, strong'; also OIr. *bulgaim*, 'I swell,' Ir. *bolg*, Gall.-Lat. *bulga*, 'bag.' It is also possible that HG. Balg is cognate with Lat. *follis* (from *folvis*, *folgvis*). Comp. further Bulge.

balgen, vb., lit. 'to talk angrily, quarrel,' then 'to cudgel'; derived from the verbal root *belg*, 'to swell out,' discussed under Balg; comp. OHG. *bëlgan*, MidHG. *bëlgen*, meaning 'to be angry.'

Balfen, m., 'beam, baulk, loft,' from the equiv. MidHG. *balke*, OHG. *balcho*, m.; comp. AS. *balca*, E. *baulk*, Du. *balk*, 'baulk'; in Scand. beside the corresponding *bálkr*, 'fence, boundary-line,' there occurs with a different gradation *bijálk-*, 'baulk' (Goth. **bilka*), in AS. likewise *bolc-*, 'gangway' (Goth. **bulka*). From Teut. *balkon*, Fr. *balcon* and Ital. *balco* are derived. The Aryan form of the root is *bhalg*, hence Gr. φάλαγξ, φάλαγγ-ος, 'oval piece of wood, trunk of a tree,' has been compared with it, but the nasal of the second syllable renders the comparison dubious.

Ball, (1.) m., 'challenge (of hounds),' belongs to the stem of bellen.

Ball (2.), m., 'ball,' from the equiv. MHG. *bal* (gen. *balles*) or *balle*, *ballen*, m. OHG. *ballo*, m., *balla*, f.; AS. **bealla* is wanting; E. *ball* (MidE. *balle*) is borrowed from the Rom. word Fr. *balle*, which was obtained from German. OIc. *bollr*, 'ball,' presupposes Goth. **ballus*. The root *bal-* appears also with a further gradation in Bolle (in Polster too?); comp. further Bellen.

Ball (3.), m., 'dancing entertainment,' from Fr. *bal*, 'ball'; OFr. *baller*, 'to dance,' and its Rom. cognates have been derived from Gr. βαλλίζω, 'I dance.'

Ballast, m., 'ballast,' like other maritime expressions, from LG.; comp. Du. *ballast*, E. *ballast*. In MidHG. simply *last*, 'ballast,' whence the equiv. Fr. *lest* is derived. The first component of the compound is obscure; it is scarcely of Irish origin (Kelt. *bal*, 'sand'), nor is it likely to be identical with OIc. *bára*, 'sea.' On account of Dan. *baglest*, 'ballast,' the least improbable derivation is from *bak*, 'back,' discussed under Bake (1.). Ballast might perhaps be 'load behind or in the rear.'

Ballei, f., 'jurisdiction,' from MidLat. *ballia*, formed from Fr. *bailli*, *bailif*, 'steward' (MidLat. *ballivus*, E. *bailiff*), which is formed from Lat. *bajulus*, with the suffix *-ivus*.

Ballen, m., 'bale, pack,' identical with Ball, which, as MidHG. *alle* and OHG. *ballo* show, was formerly a weak masc.; in connection with the difference of form arose a difference of meaning; orig. sense 'round bundle of paper,' then 'a certain quantity of rolled or packed paper.' E. *bale* and Du. *baal* are borrowed from Fr. *balle* (also *ballon*), which was again obtained from Germ.

ballen, vb., 'to clench (the fist),' from MidHG. *ballen*, 'to form into a ball.'

ballhornisieren, vb., **verballhornen**, 'to make worse by altering'; derived from Ballhorn, a publisher in Lübeck (1531-1599), who in his 'enlarged and improved' editions of an ABC book was always making fresh mistakes in his 'emendations.'

Balsam, m., 'balm, balsam,' from the equiv. MidHG. *balsame*, *balsem*, m, OHG. *balsamo*, m.; Goth. *balsan*, with a very remarkable deviation; comp. Arab. *balasán*. The Germ. word is derived from Gr.-Lat. *balsamum* (βάλσαμον), whence also Fr. *baume* (E. *balm*), Ital. *balsamo*.

Balz, m., 'pairing time (of birds),' from MidHG. *balze* (besides *ralz*), m.; of obscure origin.

bammeln, also **bambeln**, vb., 'to dangle,' first recorded in ModHG., hence it may be an onomatopoetic word collateral with bimmeln, bemmeln, 'to tinkle.'

Band (1.), m., 'volume,' orig. identical with the following word.

Band (2.), n., 'bund, ribbon,' from binten; MidHG. *bant*, plur. *bender* (and *bant*), n., OHG. *bant*, plur. *bentir* (and *bant*). Comp. OSax. *band*, Du. *band*, m., OIc. *band*; Goth. by another derivation *bandi* (whence AS. *bend*, E. *bend*, as well as a later *band* derived from Fr. *bande*). See the preceding and the following word.

Bande, f., 'cushion,' in Billardbande, from Fr. *bande*; similarly derived in the sense of 'crew.' The Rom. word—Fr. *bande* (Ital. *banda*), 'band, strip, gang, troop,' is derived from OHG. *bant*, Goth. *bandi*.

bändigen, vb., 'to restrain, tame,' from bändig, ordinarily only in the compound unbändig; MidHG. *bendec*, 'tightly bound, fettered,' hence bändigen, 'to put in fetters.'

bange, adj. and adv., 'anxious(ly), uneasy, uneasily,' from MidHG. and MidLG. *bange*, adv., 'anxiously,' and subst. 'anxiety, care.' The root is *ange*, which further appears in Angst; as *enge* is the corresponding adj., bange can only be based on the MidHG. adv. *ange*, OHG. *ango*, the adv. afterwards becoming an adj. The *b* has arisen from the unaccented prefix *be* (*bi*), as *g* in glauben, grabe, from *ge*. See barmherzig, bleiben.

Bangert, m., 'orchard,' for *bān-, bāmgart*, MidHG. *boumgarte;* comp. Baum and Garten.

Bank, f., 'bank, bench, reef,' from the equiv. MidHG. *banc*, plur. *benke*, OHG. *banch*, plur. *benchi*, m., f.; comp. AS. *benc*, f., E. *bench*, OIc. *bekkr*. Besides the stem *banki-* (from pre-Teut. *bhangi-*), Teut. possessed others which are recorded in words borrowed by Romance; comp. Ital. *banco, banca, panca*, Fr. *banc, banque*, &c. See the following words.

Bankert, earlier *Bankart, Baukhart*, m., 'bastard, bantling,' from MidHG. *banchart*, m., 'illegitimate child,' lit. 'a child begotten upon the bench'; a compound of Bank. The second part is *hart*, appearing in proper names as Gebhart, Reinhart, and is formed by assimilation to Bastard (older Bastart, also written Basthart).

Bankett, n., 'banquet,' borrowed before the middle of the 16th cent. from Fr. *banquet*, which (with Fr. *banc*, Ital. *banco*, 'table') was perhaps derived from the German stem of Bank.

Bann, m., 'ban, outlawry, decree,' from MidHG. and OHG. *ban* (*nn*), m., 'order under threat of punishment, prohibition; jurisdiction and its sphere.' It corresponds to AS. *bann*, E. *ban*, and belongs to an obsolete str. vb. *bannan*, of which the primary meaning was 'to order or forbid under threat of punishment.' The root is supposed to be *ba*, pre-Teut. *bha-*; *nn* was perhaps a suffix (comp. rinnen), and properly belonged only to the pres. of the str. vb., but was afterwards joined to the verbal stem. To this pre-Teut. *bha-* belongs, in accordance with the permutation of consonants, Gr. φα in φά-σκω, φη-μί and Lat. *fa* in *fari;* the Teut. meaning must then have been very definitely specialised. From the Teut. word the Rom. cognate Fr. *ban*, 'public proclamation' (OFr. *arban*, 'arrière ban'), is derived.

Banner, m., 'banner, militia,' from MidHG. *baner*, more usual *banier, baniere*, f., from Fr. *bannière*, which has been derived from the stem of Goth. *bandwa, bandwō*, 'sign.' Comp. MidLat. *bandum* in Paul the Deacon, '*vexillum quod bandum appellant*. See Panier.

Banse, f., 'space in a barn near the threshing-floor,' from MidG. and LG.; the word is wanting in MidHG. and OHG. From **bans-* arose AS. *bós*. E. dial. *boose* (*boosy*, 'cattle-trough'), and OIc. *báss*, 'cowhouse.' The Goth. has *bansts*, f., 'barn,' in which the stem has been increased by the deriv. *-ti-*.

*bar, adj. suffix which is derived from a complete adj., properly bāre, MidHG. *bære*, OHG. *bāri;* it means lit. 'bearing,' comp. fruchtbar, lastbar, also tankbar; later on, when it became a suffix, it assumed the present meaning. The older adj. is a verbal form of the str. vb. *bēran* (see under Bahre), Teut. root *ber* (Aryan *bher*), 'to bear, carry.' In AS. too *-bǣre* appears, *e.g.* in *wæstmbǣre*, 'fertile,' *leóhtbǣre*, 'Lucifer.'

Bär (1.), m., '(paving) beetle,' from MidHG. *bern*, 'to strike, beat,' whence also MidHG. *ber*, f., 'blow, stroke.' OHG. *berjan*, Goth. **barjan*, agrees by the permutation of consonants with Lat. *ferio*, 'I strike,' as well as OBulg. *borja*, 'I fight' (OIc. *berjask*, 'to fight'); it is based on the root *bher*, 'to strike.'

Bär (2.), m., 'bear.' The Lat. name of the animal (*ursus*) descends from the pre-Aryan period, just as Gr. ἄρκτος and Ind. *ṛkša-s* (*ursus* for **urcsus*). It is remarkable that the Teutons have abandoned this old Aryan term for 'bear' (*rksós*, Teut. *orhsa-s*), since they have retained other names of animals. In Mid HG. we have *ber*, OHG. *bëro*, AS. *bëra*, E. *bear*, OIc. *björn*, 'bear' (Goth. **baíra*). The Teut. *beron-* is a subst. form based upon an Aryan adj. *bhero-*, equiv. to Lith. *bėras*, 'brown' (Lat. *furvus?*), from the root of which, *bher* and ModHG. Biber, braun, may also be derived; in using the adj. as a subst. the Aryan *rksos* is understood. Note that Braun is the name of the bear in the OG. animal fables.

Bär (3.), m., 'brood-boar,' from the equiv. MidHG. and OHG. *bēr*, m., which, with OSax. *bēr-swīn*, AS. *bār*, E. *boar*, points to Goth. **baira-*.

Barbe, f., 'barbel,' from MidHG. *barbe*, f., OHG. *barbo*, m., which is based upon the equiv. Lat. *barbus*. The fish derived its name from *barba*, 'beard,' on account of its beard-like appendages; from the Lat. word comes Fr. *barbeau* (from Mid Lat. *barbellus*), whence E. *barbel*, as well as *barb;* comp. also Ital. *barbio*, 'barbel.'

Barbier, m., 'barber,' early ModHG. only, borrowed from Fr. *barbier* (MidLat. *barbarius*, 'barber').

Barch), m., 'castrated hog,' from Mid HG. *barc* (*barges*), OHG. *barug* and *barh;* comp. AS. *bearh, bearg,* E. *barrow,* Du. *barg, berg,* OIc. *lǫrgr;* Goth. **bargus* (**borgus*). No evidence of a pre-Teut. stem *bhargh, bhark,* for 'hog,' can be adduced from other languages. Lat. *verres* and Sans. *vardha-s,* 'boar,' cannot be allied to it, any more than Lat. *porcus,* which belongs to Ferkel. It is more probable that Russ. *borov* (primit. Slav. **borovŭ*) is a cognate.

Barchent, m., 'fustian,' from MidHG. *barchant, barchât, barchet,* m., formed from MidLat. *barcânus,* 'cloth from camels' hair'; derived, like Berkan, from Arab. *barrakân,* 'coarse stuff.'

Barett, n., 'skull-cap, hood,' adopted in the 15th cent. from Fr. *barrette,* MidLat. *birrétta,* a deriv. from Lat. *birrus, birrum,* 'cloak, pallium.'

Barke, f., 'barque, boat,' from the equiv. MidHG. *barke,* f.; corresponds to Scand. *barke,* 'barque'; not of Germ. origin. The cognates are based upon an equiv. Rom. class with the primit. forms *barca-barica* (found even in the 7th cent. in Isidore); comp. Fr. *barque* (besides OFr. *barge,* from MidLat. *barica;* whence E. *barge,* LG. Barse), Ital. *barca;* OIr. *barc* is of similar origin. The ultimate source of the cognates (Spain?) is uncertain.

Bärlapp, m., 'club-moss'; orig. sense 'bear's paw'; comp. the Lat.-Gr. term *lycopodium* formed from it; allied to OHG. *lappo,* lit. 'palm of the hand.'

Bärme, f., 'yeast,' borrowed from the equiv. LG. *barme,* m., which corresponds to AS. *beorma* and E. *barm.* Lat. *fermentum* (if it does not belong to *formus,* Gr. θερμός, 'warm') is perhaps akin to it. Teut. *b,* Lat. *f,* are Aryan *bh.*

barmherzig, adj., 'compassionate,' from the equiv. MidHG. *barmherzic;* related to ModHG. and MidHG. *erbarmen,* OHG. *irbarmên.* This stem has been connected with a Teut. word *barm,* 'bosom' (E. *barm,* from AS. *bearm,* Goth. *barms,* OHG. and OLG. *barm,* MidHG. *barm,* m.); hence *erbarmen* means lit. 'to cherish in one's bosom, press to one's heart.' Perhaps the equiv. Goth. *arman,* 'to move to pity,' and *armaiô,* 'compassion,' stand in a similar relation to Arm, the lit. meaning of the verb being 'to take in one's arms, cherish.' Others, however, are of opinion that *erbarmen* contains a *b* derived from *bi* (like *bange,* derived from *biange*), so that it would be more akin

to Goth. *arman.* But in that case either a secondary meaning, 'misericors,' in addition to 'miser,' must be assumed for Teut. *arm,* for which there is no support; or we must regard it as an imitation of a Lat.-Christ. term, Goth. *arman,* from *arms,* like Lat. *misereri,* from *miser;* indeed OHG. *armherzi,* 'misericors,' and *irbarmherzida* (Goth. *armahaírtiþa*), 'misericordia,' render it certain that Christianity coined the words to express a Lat.-Christ. idea; comp. Demut, Gnade, &c.

Barn, m., 'crib, hayrack above the crib,' from the equiv. MidHG. *barn,* m., OHG. *barno,* m.; AS. *bern,* E. *barn,* is equiv. to Germ. Scheuer. The Germ. and Eng. words are not, perhaps, identical, but only of a cognate stem; the stem of the Eng. word is *bar-,* which appears in Goth. **baris,* 'barley,' AS. *bere,* E. *barley,* and is cognate with Lat. *far, farris,* 'spelt,' OBulg. *burŭ,* 'a species of millet'; AS. *bern* is explained from *bere-ern,* 'barley-house.'

Baron, m., 'Baron,' not from the equiv. MidHG. *barân,* but from the Fr. and MidL Rhen. form *baron,* which is found in the 16th cent.; MidLat. *baro, baronis,* is by some based on Kelt. *bar,* 'man,' and by others on AS. *beorn* or on OHG. *baro,* 'man, vassal.'

Barre, f., **Barren**, m., 'bar, ingot,' from MidHG. *barre,* f., 'bolt, railing,' which comes from Fr. *barre.*

Barsch, m., 'perch,' from the equiv. MidHG. *bars,* m.; there is also a deriv. form MidHG. and OHG. *bersich;* comp. the corresponding Du. *baars,* AS. *lærs, bears,* E. dial. *barse* (*bass*); allied to the compounds Sw. *abborre,* Dan. *aborre* (*rr* from *rs*), with the same meaning. The cognates cannot have been borrowed from the equiv. Lat. *perca;* they are more akin to the Teut. root *bars* (*bors*) in Berste, Bürste, signifying 'to be bristly.'

barsch, adj., 'rough, rude,' a modern word, appearing also in Du. (*barsch*) and Sw. (*barsk*), but foreign to the UpG. dialects. It is not found in OTeut. In Swiss dialects the term is *baröösch* (with the accent on the second syllable), in which perhaps the base of barsch is preserved; Ital. *brusco* (Fr. *brusque*) may be connected with it. In Swiss occurs also *barš* in the phrase *barš gâ,* 'to go alone'; it also means 'without a hat, a coat.' Both significations point to its deriv. from *bar.* Yet *barsch* may have originated in the Teut. root *bars,* 'to be bristly, rough,' mentioned under the preceding word, especially as Du. *barsch* means lit. 'rough.'

Bart, m., 'beard, comb, barb,' from the equiv. MidHG. *bart*, OHG. *bart*, m.; comp. Du. *baard*, AS. and E. *beard*. For this Teut. word, the existence of which is proved by the ethnical term Langobarten to be extremely remote, *skegg* was used in Scand. The pre-Teut. form of Goth. **barda*, f., was, in accordance with the permutation of consonants, *bhardhâ*—which is also presumed by OSlov. *brada* (with the usual loss of aspiration and metathesis of the *r*), and Lat. *barba* (with *b* for *dh* when next to *r*, comp. ret, Wort; the initial *b* is from *bh*, as in Backe; in other cases initial *bh* is Lat. *f*). Comp. also Lith. *barzdù*, 'beard' (for **bardà*).

Barte (1.), f., 'broad axe,' from the equiv. MidHG. *barte*, OHG. *barta*, f.; in Bav.-Suab. the word, which is properly North G., does not occur; allied to ODu. and OSax. *barda*, OIc. *barða* (OFr. *barde*, 'hatchet,' is borrowed from Teut.). From this word OSlov. *brady*, f., 'axe,' is borrowed. The words are derivatives of the stem *bhardh-* appearing in Bart; the axe is, as it were, 'the bearded thing,' OIc. *skeggja*, 'broad axe,' being related in a similar way to *skegg*, 'beard'; likewise MidE. *barbe* (from Lat.-Rom. *barba*) signifies, among other things, 'edge of the axe.' Comp. Hellebarte.

Barte (2.), f., 'baleen,' a deriv. of Bart, first occurring in ModHG., and akin to Barte; comp. E. *barbs*, from Lat. *barba*; Du. *baarden*, plur.

Base, f. (dialect. designating any of the remoter degrees of relation on the female side, *e.g.*, in the Basle dial. 'aunt, niece, cousin'), 'cousin, aunt,' from Mid HG. *base*, OHG. *basa*, 'father's sister'; the AS. and Fris. dialects have a word allied to Vater; AS. *fapu*, OFris. *fethe*. The Teut. type *fapôn* is certainly only a term of endearment for *fapar-*, *fadar-swëstar*, 'father's sister.' Probably OHG. *basa* is also a pet or childish name for the proper *badar-*, *fadar-swëssô*. The same might be said of the variant MidG. and LG. Wase, and with the necessary qualifications of the masc. Base.

Bast, m., 'inner bark of trees, husk,' from the equiv. MidHG. *bast*, OHG. *bast* (also *buost* with gradation), OHG. **bast*, m., n. It corresponds to AS. *bæst*, E., Du. and OIc. *bast*, Goth. **bastus*. Hence the deriv. OHG. and MidHG. *besten*, 'to strap,' as well as the Rom. cognate *basto*, 'pack-saddle' (see under Bastart), with which Swiss *bast*, 'saddle,' agrees. There is no justification for deriving the words from *binten*, for the absence of the nasal, the occurrence of *st* (for which we should have expected *ss* from *dh + t*), and the gradation in MidHG. *buost* render such a derivation impossible. The resemblance in sound between this word and *binten* proves nothing as to the etymology; this popular and superficial derivation was suggested by the use of *bast*. The Teut. word, which is more probably connected with the root *bes* appearing in Wesen, found its way into Rom.; comp. Ital. *basta*, 'basting, stitching.'

Bastard, m., 'bastard,' from Fr. *bâtard*, *bastard* (Ital. *bastardo*), borrowed in the Middle Ages (MidHG. *bastart*). MidE. *bast*, 'illegal marriage,' and OFr. *fils de bast*, 'illegitimate son,' indicate the primary meaning of the Rom. word, which came to England with William I., and at a later period made its way to Scandinavia. The OFr. *bastard* (Fr. *bâtard*) has a Teut. termination; see Banfert. The first part of the word, which in MidE. and OFr. signifies 'illegal marriage,' is generally derived from MidLat. and Rom. *bastum*, 'pack-saddle'; comp. Ital. and Span. *basto*, Fr. *bât*, 'pack-saddle.' Bastard would then mean 'the son of a pack saddle' (comp. Bast)—the saddles serving the Spanish muleteers as beds; comp. Bankert. Scand. *bastarðr*, whence some would derive the modern Europ. word, did not reach the North before 1200 A.D. nearly.

Bastei, f., 'bastion,' from earlier Mod HG. *bastie*; comp. OFr. *bastie* (allied to OItal. *bastire*; Fr. *bâtir*); it is akin to Bastion, f., borrowed from Fr. *bastion*, Ital. *bastione*.

Baß (1.), m., 'bass,' derived like many other musical terms from Ital. (*basso*).

baß (2.), compar. adv., 'better,' from the equiv. MidHG. *baʒ*, OHG. *baʒ*; comp. OSax. *bat-bet*, AS. *bet* from *batiz* (Goth. **batis*); it is an old adv. from the adj. discussed under beffer. The almost invariable use at present of the adv. beffer, instead of the older baß, is due to the fact that the formation of the adv. was no longer understood, and that the adj. at the same time has in every case assumed an adv. function.

Bathengel, m., 'germander,' a corruption of Lat. *betonicula*, dimin. of Lat. *betonica*, whence MidHG. *batônje*.

Batzen, m., 'a coin' (about a penny), from MidHG. *batze*, m., 'small coin of the town of Bern with the Bernese coat of arms, a bear' (MidHG. *betz*, ModHG. **Bätz, Petz**); comp. **Kreuzer, Rappen.** Hence Ital. *bezzo*, 'money.'

Bau, m., 'construction, structure,' from the equiv. MidHG. and OHG. *bû*, m. See **bauen, Bube.**

Bauch, m., 'belly, bulge,' from the equiv. MidHG. *bûch*, OHG. *bûh* (*hh*), m.; the corresponding AS. *bûc* (E. dial. *buck*, 'the inner part of a carriage') has the same meaning; OIc. *búkr*, 'body, waist.' It is uncertain whether **Bauch** belongs to the Sans. root *bhuj* (comp. Lat. *fungor*), 'to take food,' or to Sans. *bhuj*, 'to bend' (**Bauch,** lit. 'the flexible part'). Perhaps it is connected with Gr φύσκα (for φυγσκα?), 'stomach, blister'?. It is certainly not akin to AS. *bodig*, E. *body*, OHG. *botah*, 'body,' nor is it allied to Gr. φαγεῖν, 'to eat' (Sans. *bhaj*, 'to enjoy, partake of').

bauchen, vb., 'to steep in hot lye' (LG. *büken*, MidLG. *bûken*), from the equiv. MidHG. *bûchen*, OHG. **bûhhên*; E. *to buck* (dial. *to bouk*), for which even a MidE. term *bouken* occurs a few times, points to AS. **búcian*; to these Swed. *byka*, Ic. *bauka*, and Norw. *boykja*, are allied. The word is, moreover, diffused through most of the Teut. languages, and correctly represents MidHG. *bûchen*; only in the Bav. dialect is the word unrecorded. Hence the existence of a Teut. verbal root *bûk* (to which AS. *bûc*, 'pail,' is allied?) is undoubted, and the Rom. cognate, Fr. *buer* (Ital. *bucare*), 'to wash,' is more probably borrowed from the Teut. than *vice versâ*. The Kelt. origin of **bauchen** (Bret. *boukat*, 'to soften') is impossible.

Baude, see **Bute.**

bauen, vb., 'to build, construct, cultivate,' from MidHG. *bûwen*, OHG. and OLG. *búan* (weak vb. with traces of a strong inflexion), 'to dwell, inhabit, till, plant'; with regard to the meaning 'to dwell,' comp. **Bau, Bauer,** and **Bube.** To the OHG. *búan* corresponds Goth. *bauan*, 'to dwell, inhabit.' The root, in accordance with the law of the permutation of consonants, is pre-Teut. *bhû*, which, on comparison with Sans. *bhû*, Gr. φύω, Lat. *fui* (*futurus*), &c., must mean 'to be, become, arise, beget.' With the same root are connected the following nouns, which are of importance in determining its primary sense : OInd. *bhûmis*, 'earth,' *bhûtis*, 'existence,' φῦμα, 'produce' (comp. also **Baum**), φύσις, 'nature,' φῦλον, φυλή, 'tribe, race.'

Bauer (1.), n. and m., 'birdcage,' a word foreign to the UpG. dialects, from MidHG. *bûr*, used only in the sense of 'sojourn, birdcage;' but OHG. *bûr* has the further meaning of 'house, chamber.' AS. *bûr*, 'dwelling' (to which E. *neighbour* from AS. *neahgebur* is related; similarly the more general meaning of **Bauer** appears in HG. **Nachbar**), E. *bower*, with which E. dial. *bire* ('cowhouse'), AS. *býre*, is connected. The pre-Teut. form would be *bhûró*, with *ro* as a deriv. suffix. See the three following words.

Bauer (2.), m., in **Cräuer, Ackerbauer,** 'tiller,' from MidHG. *bûwære*, OHG. *bûâri* (Goth. **bauareis* is wanting), the term for the agent, from **bauen.**

Bauer (3.), m., 'rustic, peasant,' historically and etymologically different from **Bauer** (2.), for the MidHG. form is *gebûr*, OHG. *gibûro*, m., which belongs to the OTeut. *bûr*, 'dwelling.' discussed under **Bauer** (1.), and means lit. 'co-dweller, joint-occupier,' then 'neighbour, fellow-citizen' (comp. **Geselle,** 'one who shares the same room'), and at a later period 'fellow-villager, peasant, boor.' See also **Nachbar.**

Baum, m., 'tree,' from the equiv. MidHG. and OHG. *boum*, m.; corresponds to OSax. *bôm*, Du. *boom*, AS. *bêam*, m., 'tree,' whence E. *beam* (*beam* in sunbeam is quite another word; G. **Baum** is E. *tree*); E. *boom* is LG. and Du. *bôm*, 'tree.' The corresponding Goth. *bagms* and OIc. *baðmr* have the same phonetic form. The cognates, with Gr. φῦμα, 'produce,'are usually derived from the Teut. root *bû*, Aryan *bhû*, 'to become, arise,' discussed under **bauen.**

baumeln, vb., simply ModHG. 'to hover as on a tree'?. See, however, **bummeln.**

bäumen, vb., 'to rear,' ModHG. only, lit. 'to lift oneself up like a tree.'

Bausch, m., 'pad, bolster,' from MidHG. *bûsch*, m., 'cudgel, blow causing blisters, swelling.' If 'cudgel' is the primary sense, the word may be connected with MidHG. *bôzen*, OHG. *bôzzan*, from *bautan* (see **Amboß, Beutel, Beifuß**); *bût-* would be another stage in gradation, and before the suffix *sch* from *sk* the dental would inevitably disappear; comp. Lat. *fustis*, 'cudgel,' from **bhûd-stis.*

bausen, vb., 'to carouse, swell,' from **Baus,** MidHG. *bûs*, 'inflation, swelling due to repletion'; the like stem also in E. *to bouse*, MidLG. *básen*, 'to carouse' ?.

Bauten, plur., 'buildings,' ModHG. only, from bauen.

baxen, vb., 'to box, cuff,' from LG. *báxen*, which is again allied to OHG. *bágan*, MidHG. *bâgen*. See bägern and Bengel.

Bazar, m., 'bazaar,' ModHG. only; borrowed from Fr. *bazar* (ultimate source Pers. *bázár*, 'market-place').

be-, prefix from MidHG. *be*, properly a verbal prefix from OHG. und Goth. *bi*, which has no definite meaning; identical with the prep. *bei*, from OHG. and MidHG. *bi* (Goth. *bi*), AS. *bî*, E. *by*. For *be* there appears a shorter syncopated form in bange, Grbarmen? barſch? bleiben, Block. See specially bei.

beben, vb., 'to tremble, shake,' from MidHG. *biben*, OHG. *bibên*, 'to shiver, tremble'; Gr. φέβομαι, on account of the non-permutation of β to p and because of the *e* of the root syllable, cannot be originally cognate with beben. The OTeut. word has *i*; comp. OSax. *bibôn*, OIc. *bifa*, AS. *beofian* (from *bibôn*). OHG. *bibêt*, 'he trembles,' corresponds exactly to Sans. *bibhéti*, 'he is afraid,' in which *bi-* (for *bhi*) is the reduplicated syllable, and *bhé* for *bhai* is the augmented root syllable. The OInd. verb *bhî*, 'to be afraid,' forms its pres. by reduplication—*bibhémi*, *bibhési*, *bibhéti*; to these Goth. *bibaim*, *bibais*, *bibaip*, would correspond; this present was then, on account of its apparent deriv. *ai*, classed among the weak verbs in *ai* (Goth. *habaip*, OHG. *habêt*). The root *bhî* (Sans. *bhî*, 'fear,' *bhîmá*, 'fearful') is found in OSlov. *boja ęę*, 'I am afraid,' *běsŭ*, 'demon,' Lith. *byóti-s*, 'to be afraid,' *báimê*, 'fear,' *bajùs*, 'terrible,' *baisà*, 'fright' (and perhaps ModHG. beiſen). *Bi-* is one of the few examples of reduplication in the pres. tense preserved in the Teut. group (comp. zittern), just as the perfect ModHG. thât, from OHG. *têta*, is the sole instance of reduplication preserved in the perf. tense.

Becher, m., 'beaker, goblet,' from the equiv. MidHG. *bëcher*, OHG. *bëhhar*, *bëhhári*, m.; comp. OLG. *bikeri*, Du. *beker*, OIc. *bikarr*, whence MidE. *biker*, E. *beaker*. These cognates are derived from LowLat. *bicarium*, allied to Lat. *bacar* ('vas vinarium,' according to Festus), and still appearing in Ital. *bicchiere*. The Lat. word was naturalised in Germany perhaps as far back as the 7th cent., probably at the same period as Kelch, since its *c* was changed into hh, ch.

Beck, m., 'baker,' only dial. (Alem., Suab., Bav.), from MidHG. *bęcke*, OHG. *bęccho*, akin to backen; the Goth. form may have been *bagja*; ModHG. Becker is a recent form with the termination -*er* denoting the agent (AS. *bœcere*, E. *baker*). In ModHG. Beck, Becth, as well as Bäcker, have been preserved as family names.

Becken, n., 'bowl, basin,' from Mid HG. *bęcken*, *bęcke*, OHG. *bęcchîn*, *bęccht*, n.; the latter comes (comp. Schüſſel) from Low-Lat. and Rom. *baccinum* (comp. Ital. *bacino*, Fr. *bassin*), 'basin'; its *cc* being double, did not undergo permutation, but remained as *cc*, *ck*. *Baccīnum* has been derived from the LateLat. *bacca*, 'vas aquarium,' discussed under Bach; comp. Pickelhaube.

Bede, f., 'gratuity;' borrowed from the LG. *bede*. It corresponds to MidHG. *bëte*, 'command,' which still exists in ModHG. with the meaning 'request, prayer.'

Beere, f., 'berry,' from the plur. of the equiv. MidHG. *bęr*, OHG. *bęri*, n.; comp. Goth. **basi* (only in *weinabasi*, n, 'grape'; OSax. *winbęri*). The OHG. *r* in *bęri* presupposes a Goth. *bazi*; to the *s* of the Goth. word Du. *bes* corresponds; in AS. *bęrie*, E. *berry*, the *s* has been changed into *r*. See, however, Beſing. Foreign cognates are wanting; yet the Sans. root *bhas*, 'to chew,' is perhaps akin (Goth. *basi*, orig. 'the edible substance'?); no connection with OHG. *bëran*, 'to carry' (see gebären), or Lat. *bacca*, 'berry,' is possible.

Beet, n., 'bed (of a garden)'; earlier ModHG. Bett still common to UpG.; really identical with Bett, for the MidHG. has *bęt*, *bętte*, OHG. *bętti*, meaning also '(garden) bed.' According to its form Beet (comp. Biene) has arisen from the neut. sing. *badi*, Bett from the cases in *dj* (gen. *badjis*, dat. *badju*, neut. acc. plur. *badja*, &c.). Comp. Goth. neut. sing. *badi*, neut. plur. *badja*. E. *bed* is also used in the same sense as Beet (so even in AS. *riscbed*), E. *bed of rushes*, *hotbed*.

Beete, f., 'beetroot.' This word, like the names of many other edible vegetables, has come from Lat.; *bêta* was borrowed even before the 8th cent. and naturalised in Germ., for it appears as *bieza* (the *ie* from *ê*, comp. Prieſter, Brief, Ziegel, Rieme, Spiegel, OHG. *Pictar*, from Lat. *Petrum*, &c.), with the permutation of *t* to *z*; whence Mid HG. *bieze*. The ModHG. Beete may have been based anew on Lat. *béta*, or have been taken from the LG. *bete*, thus displacing the older *bieʒe*, which is still found in Bav. From Lat. and Rom. *béta* (Ital. *bieta*, F. *bette*), AS. *béte* (whence E. *beet*) is also derived. In another group of words borrowed from Lat., Lat. *ē* became *î* (comp. Feier, from *ferīae*); hence the dial. *beiſse* (*ei* from Mid HG. *î*) also appears occasionally for *beete*, *bieʒe*.

befehlen, vb., 'to order, command, commend,' MidHG. *berëlhen*, *berëlen*, 'to hand over, entrust, deliver, command'; OHG. *bifëlhan*, *bifëlahan*, 'to hand over' (also 'to hide, bury, entrust, recommend'). The chief meaning of the Goth. str. vb. *fillan* in compounds with the particles *ga-*, *us-*, is also 'to bury'; *anafilhan* approximates the ModHG., 'to command, enjoin'; it means 'to give, hand over, commend, recommend.' AS. *befëōlan* (for *befeolhan*), 'to entrust, make over, devote oneself.' Hence the primary meaning of the primit. Teut. str. vb. *biƶelhan* is 'to entrust, hand over, hide.' The Teut. root *felh-* is based upon pre-Teut. *pelk*; it is a mistake, therefore, to connect the word on account of its earlier meaning, 'to bury,' with Lat. *sepelire*.

Beffchen, n., 'a clergyman's bands,' diminut. of *beffe* (LG.), 'amess, cap worn by officials in Rom. Cath. churches,' the origin of which is obscure. In MidHG. both words are wanting; the latter is found even in MidLG.

begehren, vb., 'to desire, crave, request,' from the equiv. MidHG. *begërn*, chiefly in the simple form *gërn*, OHG. *gërón*; the *r* probably belongs to the stem, because *gern* as a *no*-partic. points in that direction; comp. gern, Gier.

beginnen, vb., 'to begin,' from the equiv. MidHG. *beginnen*, OHG. *beginnan*; it corresponds to Goth *duginnan*, AS. *á-*, *be-*, *on-ginnan*, E. *to begin*, OLG. *biginnan*, with a similar meaning. This verbal stem, which appears at an early period only in a compound form, is based upon a pre-Teut. *to-*, *bhi-kenuô*, with permutation of *k* to Teut. *g*. For the Aryan root *ken* comp. OBulg. *po-činą* (infin. *po-čęti*), 'to begin,' *konī*, 'beginning.'

behagen, vb. (to which behaglich is allied), 'to be comfortable,' from the equiv. MidHG. *behagen*; OSax. *bihagôn*, AS. *onhagian*, 'to suit, please,' OIc. *haga*, 'to arrange.' OG. has only a str. participle, OHG.

bihagan, MidHG. *behagen*, 'fresh, joyous, comfortable' (hence ModHG. das Behagen, Unbehagen); the old str. vb. no longer exists in Teut. Probably the Ind. root *çak* is primitively related to it—*çaknômi*, 'am strong, able, helpful, beneficial,' *çakrá-s*, 'strong'; comp. further Hag, Hede, and hegen, which with the same phonetic form approximate the earlier meaning 'to help, protect.'

behaupten, vb., 'to maintain, assert,' not from MidHG. *behaupten*, which means 'to behead.' This word, which first occurs in ModHG., is rather derived with a change of meaning from MidHG. *behaben*, 'to hold fast, keep, maintain.'

behende, adj., 'nimble, agile, active,' from MidHG. *behende*, adv., 'suitably, conveniently, skilfully, quickly'; in OHG. we should have expected *bi hęnti* (dat.), for which *zi hęnti*, 'at once,' occurs. The prep. is compounded with the dat. of the subst. *hant*, OHG. *hęnti*; comp. the similar origin of abhanden under ab.

Behörde, f., 'the authorities,' first recorded in ModHG. from hören, MidHG. *zuo behœren*, 'to belong to, be one's due.'

Behuf, m., 'behalf, advantage,' from MidHG. *behuof*, m., 'business, purpose, means to an end'; root *haf* (in heben), as also in E. *behoof*, AS. *behóf*.

bei, prep. and adv., 'by, near, about'; the accented form of the unaccented prefix *be*; the Goth used in both cases *bi*; the Englishman makes a distinction like the German; AS. *bí*, E. *by*, but *be* as a prefix. OHG. *bî* and *bi-* (comp. also Beichte, Beiſpiel). In Goth. *bî* means 'around, near'; hence its kinship with Gr. ἀμφί, Lat. *ambi-* is probable; the loss of the first syllable *am-* also occurs in the OTeut. word for beide; the base is probably *ambhi-*; comp. also um.

Beichte, f., 'confession,' from the equiv. MidHG. *bîht*, contracted from MidHG. and OHG. *bijiht*, *bigiht*; a regular verbal noun from MidHG. *bejëhen*, OHG. *bi-jëhan*, 'to confess, acknowledge.' The simple form *jëhan*, usually signifying 'to say, speak out,' also means occasionally 'to avow, confess'; hence OFr. *gehir*. This verb *jëhan* may possibly be connected with ja, which see.

beide, num., 'both,' from the equiv. MidHG. *beide*, *bêde*, m., f., (*beidiu*, n.); OHG. *beide*, *bêde* (*beido*, f., *beidiu*, n.); OHG. and MidHG. have also a remarkable variant with *ê* (OHG. and MidHG. *bêde*), although *ei* in other instances in HG. is not changed into *é* before dentals. In investigating the word **beibe** we must start from the fact that the stem of the num. had really no dental ; AS. *bégen*, *bâ*, Goth. *bai* (OIc. gen. *beggja*), 'both.' Allied in the other Aryan languages to Sans. *ubháu*, Gr. ἄμφω, Lat. *ambo*, OSlov. *oba*, Lith. *abù*, with a syllable prefixed. The G. forms with a dental are undoubtedly secondary ; they obtained their dental by the blending, at a comparatively late period, of the primary *ba-* with the forms of the article, so that OHG. *béde* arose from *bê* and *de*, *beidiu* from *bei* and *diu*, MidE. *bŷthe* (E. *both*) from AS. *bâ* and *þâ* (OIc. *báþer* from *bai* and *þaiz*). In Goth. *ba* is combined with the article *ba þô skipa*, 'both the ships' ; similarly in Gr. ἄμφω. By assuming such a combination in WestTeut. the following ModHG. dial. forms in all genders are explained • Bav. *bed*, *bod*, *beid*, Suab. *béd*, *bued*, *boad*, Wetterau *bed*, *bud*, *bad*.

Beifuß, m., 'a species of wormwood used in seasoning food' ; the MidHG. and OHG. word was written *bibôȝ*, hence the semi-LowG aspect of the ModHG. word. OHG. *bibôȝ* is cognate with *anabôȝ* (see **Amboß**), and connected with an OTeut. verb *bautan*, 'to pound' ; *bibôȝ*, 'spice pounded and mixed with food.' The LG. form of the OHG. word is *bivôt*, and hence arose the ModHG. *Beifuß*, by the awkward attempt of popular etymology to connect *bivôt* with a well-known word.

Beige, Beuge, f., 'a pile arranged in layers' (an UpG. word), from MidHG. *bîge*, OHG. *bîga*, 'shock (of corn)' ; hence Ital. *bica*, 'pile of sheaves' ; comp. E. *bing* (heap of alum), Scand. *bingr*, 'bolster' ; comp. **Bachbunge**. *Benge* has *eu* by being based on *biegen*.

Beil (Bav. **Beichl**), n., 'hatchet,' from the equiv. MidHG. *bîl*, *bîhel*, OHG. *bîhal*, *bîal*, n. (comp. the similar stages in the derivation of **Feile** from *fîhala*) ; comp. Mid LG. *bîl*, 'axe.' On account of OIc. *bîlda*, 'axe,' OHG. *bîhal* must probably be traced to *bîþl*, *bîtl* (for *hl* from *þl* comp. **Gemahl**). Hence there may be a connection with the cognates from *bhid* discussed under **beißen** ; as to the meaning, comp. especially Lat. *findo*, 'I split' (OIr. *biáil*, 'axe,' is primit. akin). On the other hand, it is, of course, not impossible that OHG. *bîhal* may be connected with **Bicke**.

beilen, vb., 'to bring deer to a stand by laying,' formed from MidHG. and OHG. *bîl*, 'the moment when the deer stands at bay ; encircling by the baying hounds' ; MidHG. *bîlen*, 'to bring to a stand by baying,' intr. 'to bark.' No kinship with *beßen* can be proved ; it is more probably connected with the root *bi* in *beben* (for a derivative in *l* from the latter word comp. Lett. *baile*, 'fear,' *bailùs*, 'timid,' Sans. *bhîrú*, 'timid'). In that case MidHG. and OHG. *bî-l* would be lit. 'time of fear.'

Bein, n., 'bone, leg,' from MidHG. *bein*, OHG. *bein*, n. ; comp. OLG. *bén*, AS. *bán*, E. *bone ;* ModHG. preserves the earlier meaning 'bone' still existing in UpG. in the words **Beinhaus, Elfenbein, Fischbein, Salzbein, Gebein** ; the later signification, 'lower part of the thigh,' is recorded even in OHG., MidHG., and OIc. The OIc. *beinn*, adj., 'straight,' favours the supposition that originally at least the straight thigh-bones were termed **Beine** (bones). Goth. ***bain*, n., is by chance not recorded. A primit. Teut. word with the primary meaning 'bone,' which cannot, however, be traced farther back (Lat. *os*, Gr. ὀστέον, Sans. *asthi*, *asthan*, to which an Aryan *osth-*, 'bone,' would correspond, are not represented, on the other hand, in the Teut. group). Comp. further **Eisbein**.

Beispiel, n., 'example,' from late Mid HG. *bîspil*, mostly *bîspel*, n., 'fable, allegory, proverb,' OHG. ***bîspëll* (for *bî* comp. *bei* and **Beichte**). Comp. AS. *bîspell*, 'example, parable' ; formed from OHG. and MidHG. *spël* (*ll*), 'tale, fable, rumour,' Goth. *spill*, 'legend, fable,' AS. *spell*, E. *spell* (*gospel* from *godspell*), 'tale, fable' ; *spell* (to which Fr. *épeler*, 'to spell,' is akin) is the term for literary composition in prose, and hence is as important for the history of primit. Teut. civilisation as **Lied, Sagen,** &c.

beißen, vb., 'to bite,' from the equiv. MidHG. *bîȝen*, OHG. *bîȝȝan* ; cognate with Goth. *beitan*, AS. *bîtan*, E. *to bite*. A primit. Teut. verb with the sense of 'to bite,' which has, however, as is shown by the cognate tongues, been specialised from the more general meaning 'to make smaller, to split with a sharp instrument.' Comp. Lat. *findo*, Sans. root *bhid*, 'to split, break to pieces' ; in OTeut. poetry **beißen** is also used of the sword—a remnant of the earlier meaning. **Beil**, too, if primit. akin to it, must be connected with Lat. *findere*, 'to split.' Comp. **bitter**, which signifies orig. 'piercing.' From the same root **Biß**, Mid HG. and OHG. *bîȝ*, m., is derived, to which

AS. *bite*, E. *bit*, corresponds; Bißchen is a diminutive of it. ModHG. Bissen, from MidHG. *bizze*, OHG. *bizzo*; OLG. *biti*, E. *bit*.

Beißker, m., 'loach,' adopted from Slav. (Bohem. *piskoř*, Russ. *piskárĭ*), and based by popular etymology on beißen (the fish is also called Steinbeißer, 'river-loach,' Schlammbeißer, 'pond-loach').

beizen, vb., 'to cauterise, pickle, etch,' from MidHG. *beizen (beitzen)*, weak vb., 'to macerate, make soft, hawk at birds'; OHG. *beizen (beizzen)*, orig. sense 'to cause to bite,' is the factitive of OHG. *bîzzan*, see beißen. The corresponding E. *to bait* (a hook, a horse on a journey, and hence to put up, halt at a place, also to allure) is derived from the Scand. *beita*, which is identical with OHG. *beizzan*.

beklommen, see Klamm.

Belche (1.), f., 'a kind of salmon'; of obscure origin. See Bolche.

Belche (2.), f., 'coot,' from MidHG. *belche*, OHG. *belihha*; Lat. *fulica* seems allied to it, although OHG. *hh* implies a Lat. *g*; the Germ. guttural suffix is the same as in Goth. *ahaks*, 'pigeon.' See also Habicht, Kranich.

belemmern, vb., 'to cheat,' a LG. word, from MidLG. and Du. *belemmeren*, 'to hinder, molest,' and allied to ModHG. lahm?.

belfern, vb., 'to snarl, nag,' ModHG. only; an intensive form of the following word.

bellen, vb., from the equiv. MidHG. *bëllen*, OHG. *bëllan*, 'to bark, bellow'; AS. *bëllan*, E. *to bell* (of a stag at the rutting period); the E. word indicates accordingly that the primary meaning was more general than simply 'barking, bellowing.' If an *e* root be assumed, OBulg. *blěja*, 'bleat,' and Lat. *fleo*, 'I weep' (*b*, *f* from *bh* and *bhlê* for *bhel*), may be compared. Others have explained the WestTeut. root *bell* from *belz*, *bels*, *bhels*, which would result in its being cognate with Sans. *bhaš*, 'to bark,' *bhâš*, 'to talk.' Comp. Lith. *balsas*, 'voice, tone'; see, too, the following word and Bulle.

Bellhammel, m., 'bell-wether,' ModHG. only; a LG. word (UpG. *herma*, equiv. to Herdmann, 'herdsman'), corresponding exactly to Du. *bel-hamel*, E. *bell-wether*. Fr. *clocheman*, *clocman* (of Germ. origin), also Fr. *mouton à la sonnette*, make the connection of Bellhammel with Du. *bel*, MidDu. and AS. *belle*, E. *bell*, indubitable. In Fr. animal fables the bell-wether has the proper name *Belin* (akin to Fr. *bélier*, 'ram'), from the Du. *bel*, 'little bell,' whence also Fr. *bélière*, 'ring of a bell-clapper.'

Belt, m., 'straits,' akin to OIc. *belte*, AS. and E. *belt*, *baldrick* (OHG. *balz*), 'girdle, shoulder-belt'?. Belt is thus a 'zone of land'?. The cognate Lat. *balteus* is, according to Varro, a Tuscan word.

belzen, vb., 'to graft,' also pelzen; MidHG. *belzen*, OHG. *belzôn* with the same meaning; cognate with Provenç. *empeltar*, 'to graft,' which, with Fr. *pelletier*, 'furrier' (see Pelz), belongs to Lat. *pellis*.

Bemme, f., 'slice of bread,' first occurs in ModHG.; a LG. and MidG. word, a deriv. of the dial. *bammen*, 'to eat,' which may have been *bazmôn* in Goth., and is perhaps primit. allied to the Sans. root *bhas*, 'to chew.'

Bendel, m., from the equiv. MidHG. *bendel*, OHG. *bentil*; comp. MidE. *bendel*, OIc. *bendell*; akin to binden.

Bengel, m., 'cudgel,' then in a figurative sense 'rude person, blackguard,' from MidHG. *bengel*, m., 'cudgel.' Comp. E. *bangle* (club), from the verb to bang, OIc. *banga*, 'to strike, beat,' LG. *bangen*. The Teut. stem *bang*-, 'to strike,' seems to have been nasalised from the root *bâg*, mentioned under baren.

Benne, f., 'wicker cart,' MidHG. only; an old Alem. and perhaps orig. Kelt. word which Festus records as old Gallic *benna*. Comp. Fr. *benne*, 'dosser,' AS. *binn*, E. *bin*.

benschen, Jewish, 'to pronounce the benediction, say grace,' from Lat. *benedicere*.

bequem, adj., 'convenient, comfortable,' from MidHG. *bequáme*, OHG. *biquâmi*, 'suitable, fit.' Akin to AS. *gecwéme*, MidE. *icwéme*, *cwéme*, 'agreeable, suitable'; *qêmi*-, the base, is a verbal adj. from Goth. *qiman*, OHG. *chuman*, 'to come,' for which the meaning 'to be fitting, to suit,' already existing in Goth. *gaqimiþ*, 'it is fitting,' is presupposed; comp. AS. *becuman*, E. *become*. See femmen and Lat. *convenire*, 'to fit in with, be becoming, suit,' which is primit. allied.

berappen, vb., 'to pay,' ModHG. only. The comparison usually made with rupfen must be abandoned; it means 'to give Rappen' (a coin of small value having the impress of a raven). Comp. Rappen and blechen (to give Blech, i.e. money).

beraumen, see anberaumen.

bereit, adj., 'ready, prepared,' from

MidHG. *bereit, bereite*, OHG. *bireiti*, 'ready and willing, obliging; armed, ready'; comp. AS. *gerǽde, rǽde*, E. *ready;* Goth. *garaids*, 'appointed,' does not correspond exactly. The word may belong to the root discussed under reiten (comp. OHG. *reita*, 'carriage'), with the orig. sense of 'to equip with armour'; like fertig, it would thus mean properly 'ready for a journey'; comp. OIr. *riadaim*, 'I am going on a journey,' *riad*, 'practicable (of a route), passable.' On account of the similarity in meaning comp. fertig.

Berg, m., 'mountain,' inherited from the OTeut. vocabulary; OHG. *bĕrg*, MidHG. *bĕrc(g)*, m. Comp. AS. *beorh(g)*, especially 'barrow' (called *byrgels* also), E. only in the deriv. 'to bury' (AS. *byrgan*), from *burgian;* the Goth. form *bairga-* is deduced from the deriv. *bairgahei*, 'mountain range.' The rules for the permutation of consonants demand a pre-Teut. *bhĕrgho-*; with this is connected Sans. *brhant*, 'high' (*b* from *bh*, because the aspiration at the beginning of the root was, on account of the following aspirate, necessarily lost); *h* is *gh*; Zend *barezanh*, 'height,' *berezant*, 'high'; OIr. *brigh*, 'mountain' (*ri*, Sans. *r*, might be compared with the *ur* of Burg), Armen. *berj*, 'height,' *barjr*, 'high,' W. and Armor. *bre*, 'mountain, hill,' W. *bry*, 'high.' Also the Kelt. proper names *Brigiani* and *Brigantes*, like the Teut. *Burgunden, Burgundiones* (lit. 'monticulae'), and the name of the town *Brigantia* (*Bregenz*). Hence to the root *bhergh* belong the primary meanings 'high, rising ground' (OSlov. *brĕgŭ*, 'bank (of a river),' is borrowed from G.); perhaps Burg is derived from this root, if it does not come from bergen. The attempt to connect Berg with Goth. *fairguni* and *Hercynia*, identical with the latter, must be abandoned. With ju Berge, 'up, on end,' comp. MidHG. *ze tal*, 'down.'

bergen, vb., 'to hide, recover (from shipwreck),' from MidHG. *bĕrgen*, 'to hide, secure,' OHG. *bĕrgan;* comp. Goth. *bairgan, gabairgan*, 'to keep, preserve,' AS. *beorgan*, MidE. *bergen*, 'to preserve, protect.' There are other E. words with a different though allied meaning; AS. *byrgan*, E. *to bury;* AS. *byrgels* (OLG. *burgisli*), E. *burials, burial*. For a similar division of a primary meaning see under befehlen. The root *berg, burg*, pre-Teut. *bhergh, bhrgh*, with the primary meaning 'to lay somewhere for safe keeping,' is found outside the Teut. group only in OSlov. *brĕgą*, 'I take care (of), wait upon.'

Bericht, m., 'intelligence, report,' from MidHG. *beriht*, 'report, instruction, reconciliation.' Akin to recht.

Berkan, m., 'a kind of cloth, fustian,' from MidHG. *barragān, barkān*, from Mid Lat. *barracānus* (Fr. *bouracan*, Ital. *baracane*), E. *barracan;* comp. Barchent.

Berline, f., 'coach,' first occurs in ModHG., from the equiv. Fr. *berline*, f. (comp. Lantaner), properly 'a Berlin carriage.'

Bernstein, m., 'amber'; *bern* is a LG. form for brenn, therefore properly Brennstein (combustible stone)?. The Teut.-Lat. word is *glēsum*, preserved in AS. *glǽre*, 'amber, resin.'

Berserker, m., first occurs in ModHG., borrowed from the Scand. *berserkr*, lit. 'bear-skin garment,' then 'a savage warrior who gets furious during the fight'; from OIc. *ber-*, 'bear,' *serkr*, 'garment.'

berſten, vb., 'to burst, crack,' from Mid HG. *brĕsten*, OHG. *brĕstan*, 'to break, tear, burst,' impersonal 'to be wanting, lacking'; *er* for *re* is properly LG. and MidG.; comp. Du. *bersten*, AS. *berstan*, E. *to burst*. Comp. further the Aryan root *bhrest* (cognate with the root of brechen), in OIr. *brissim*, 'I break' (*ss* from *st*).

bert, Bert*, in proper names, from Mid HG. *bĕrht*, OHG. *bĕraht*, 'shining'; comp. Goth. *bairhts*, AS. *beorht*, E. *bright*.

Bertram, n., 'Spanish camomile or pellitory,' based by popular etymology on the proper name Bertram (lit. 'shining raven,' see Rabe), and derived from *bitron*, for Lat.-Gr. *pyrethron* (πύρεθρον).

berüchtigt, adj., 'infamous, notorious,' a partic. adj. from a weak vb. used even by Luther—berüchtigen, 'to defame,' for which berüchten was the common form in the 16th and 17th cents. Comp. Gerücht, as well as anrüchig and ruchbar; all these words are cognate with rufen, and are derived, as is shown by the *ch* for *f* before *t*, from LG.

Beryll, m., 'beryl,' from MidHG. *berille, barille, brille*, m., formed from Lat.-Gr. *beryllus;* also *brille*, 'spectacles'; see Brille, Perle. The Gr.-Lat. term is derived from Prak. *véluriga*, Sans. *vaidūrya*.

Besanmast, m., 'mizzen-mast,' Besanſegel, n., 'mizzen-sail,' from Du. *bezaan*, 'mast nearest the stern of a ship,' which is connected with E. *mizzen*, Fr. *mizaine*, Ital.

mezzana (the Rom. word, a deriv. of Lat. *medius*, is properly 'middle-mast').

beſchälen, vb., 'to cover (a mare),' first occurs in ModHG. ; a denominative from MidHG. *schêl, schêle,* m., 'brood stallion.' See **Schellhengſt**.

beſcheiden, vb., 'to distribute, assign, summon,' from MidHG. *bescheiden,* OHG. *bisceidan,* 'to divide, decide, relate, report.' The ModHG. and MidHG. partic. *bescheiden,* meant orig. 'definite,' then 'clear, distinct, intelligible, prudent.' See **ſcheiben**.

beſchnäufeln, beſchnüffeln, beſchnuppern, vb., 'to sniff at' ; akin to the E. vbs. *to snivel, snuff, snuffle-,* and **ſchnanfen**.

beſchummeln, vb., 'to deceive,' from **ſchummeln**, 'to worry.'

beſchuppen, vb., 'to scale, deceive,' from LG. ; the cognate words of the same group show that *pf,* not *pp,* is the strictly HG. form. It seems to belong to the stem of OIc. *skopa,* 'to deride' ; MidDu. *scop,* 'derision.' To the same stem belongs an OTeut. term for 'poet,' AS. *scop,* OHG. *scopf,* which, on account of its meaning, is important for the right conception of poetic composition among our ancestors.

Beſchwerde, f., 'difficulty, grievance, malady,' from MidHG. *beswærde,* f., 'oppression, grief,' allied to **ſchwer**.

beſchwichtigen, vb., 'to appease, compose.' The Germans connect this word instinctively with **ſchweigen** ; it forced its way, however, in the last half of the preceding cent. from LG. into the written language, and its *cht* is the earlier HG. *ft;* it corresponds to MidHG. *swiften,* 'to pacify,' OHG. *swiftôn,* 'to be quiet.' The stem is the same as in Goth. *sweiban,* 'to cease, leave off' ; with this the cognates of **ſchweigen** accord fairly well both in sound and meaning ; the Teut. root *swîb, swîg,* is based upon the Aryan *sueiq (sueig* in Gr. *σιγάω ;* see under **ſchweigen**).

Beſen, m., 'besom, broom,' from the equiv. MidHG. *bësen, bësem, bësme,* OHG. *bësamo ;* it corresponds to AS. *besma,* E. *besom,* Goth. **bisma,* which have the same meaning ; a pre-Teut. word of obscure origin ; perhaps **Beere** and **Baſt** are allied. Since the Eng. dialects point to an AS. *bisma,* 'besom,' it is possible that the word is connected with **Biesmind**, and the Teut. root *bîs,* 'to move in a restless, excited way.'

Beſing, LG. word, a diminutive form, like the MidLG. equiv. *beseke,* n., 'small berry' ; akin to Du. *bes,* Goth. *basi.* See under **Beere**.

beſſer, compar. adj., 'better' ; see the corresponding adv. **baß** ; superl. **beſt** ; from MidHG. *bezzer, best (bezzist),* OHG. *bezziro, b-zzist,* corresponds to AS. *betera, betst,* E. *better, best ;* Goth. *batiza, batists.* Even in primit. Teut. *gut* formed its degrees of comparison in this way, which might be represented in Ind. by **bhadyas-, *bhadiṣtha-.* The etymology of ModHG. *gut* is difficult to get at ; in the case of **beſſer** we are assisted by the cognate root in **Buße**, the primit. meaning of which is 'utility' ; the ethical notion arose from that of interest. At all events, thus the matter stands from the merely Teut. point of view. It has been connected more remotely with OInd. *bhadrá-s,* to which the primary meaning 'shining' is assigned ; but in this sense the Ind. word cannot be cognate ; it belongs to the root *bhand,* and would consequently become **buntrs* in Goth. The chief significations of *bhadrá-s,* however, are 'capable, salutary, prosperous,' which are in closer approximation to the idea of interest. Of these meanings **beſſer** and **beſt** might form the degrees of comparison.

beſtallt, partic. of **beſteſlen**, for which **beſteſlt** is now used.

beſtatten, vb., 'to convey, bury,' from **ſtatt, Stätte**.

beſulbern, vb., 'to cover with dirt,' from MidHG. *sülwen, sulwen,* 'to soil,' also *süln,* OHG. *süllen,* AS. *sÿlian,* Goth. *sauljan.*

betäuben, vb., 'to deafen, bewilder, confuse,' lit. 'to make deaf.' See **taub**.

beten, vb., 'to entreat, pray,' from the equiv. MidHG. *bëten,* OHG. *bëtôn ;* comp. Goth. *bida,* OHG. *bëta,* 'request, prayer.' Formed from the Teut. root *bid* (Aryan *bhidh*), discussed under **bitten**.

Bett, n., 'bed,' from the equiv. Mid HG. *bet, bette,* OHG. *beti, betti,* n. ; comp. AS. *bedd,* E. *bed,* Goth. *badi.* For ModHG. **Bett** the form **Beth** is found in the 18th cent. (e.g., in Gessner), just as for **Beet** the word **Bett** is used popularly (and in Mid HG.) ; comp. **Beet**. The signification **Beet** ('garden-bed') makes the connection with the Lat. root in *fodio,* 'to bury,' possible (comp. W. *bedd,* 'grave' ; also OSlov. *bo-ṣq,* 'I prick') ; Goth. *badi* (Lat. **fŏdium*), might therefore have arisen from Aryan *bhodhiom.* The primary meaning was probably 'an excavated spot' ; the signification already common to the Teut. group, 'bed, lectus' (akin to OSw. *bædhil*, 'nest'), may be elucidated by reference to the cave-dwellings of the Teutons (see **Ding**). In early times the bed was evidently dug like a niche in the sides of the subterranean dwellings. The meaning 'bolster,' common to OIc. *beðr* and Finn. *patja* (borrowed from Goth.), does not, it is true, harmonise with this explanation.

Bettel, m., 'beggary, trash,' akin to MidHG. *bëtel*, 'begging.'

betteln, vb., 'to beg, live by begging,' from the equiv. MidHG. *bëtelen*, OHG. *bëtalôn*, a frequentative of **bitten**; to this **Bettler**, from *bëtelære*, OHG. *bëtalâri*, is allied.

betuchen, betucht, adj. and adv., 'quiet(ly), reserved(ly)'; of Hebr. origin (*bâtûach*, 'confident, sure').

Betzel, Petzel, m., 'small cap,' from MidHG. (MidG.) *bezel*, f., 'hood.'

beuche, see **bauche**.

beugen, vb., 'to bow, humble,' from the equiv. MidHG. *böugen*, OHG. *bougen, boucken*; it corresponds to AS. *bégan, bígan*, 'to bow,' E. *to bay*, 'to dam (water)'; facitive of **biegen**; hence lit. 'to cause to bend.'

Beule, f., 'boil, swelling,' from the equiv. MidHG. *biule*, OHG. *búlla*, ***búllea***, f., 'blister'; comp. AS. *býle*, E. *bile* (also *boil*), Du. *buil*, 'boil'; Goth. ***baljó***, 'swelling,' is connected with Goth. *ufbauljan*, 'to inflate,' and stands probably for ***búgvliô***, properly **Buckel** (hump); akin to **biegen**.

Beunde, f., from the equiv. MidHG. *biunde*, OHG. *biunt*, 'a vacant and enclosed plot reserved for a special wing or outhouse, enclosure'; no connection with Lat. *fundus* is possible. MidLG. *biwende*, 'an enclosed space,' shows that an OHG. ***bi-want***, 'that which winds round, a hedge,' is implied. Respecting *bi*, 'round about,' see **Bisang**.

Beute (1.), f., 'kneading trough, beehive,' from MidHG. *biute*, f., OHG. *biutta*, f., with the same meaning; it presupposes Goth. ***biudja***. **Bütte** is the most nearly allied, unless the latter is of Rom. origin. The derivation from OHG. *biot*, Goth. *biups*, AS. *beód*, 'table,' seems uncertain; of course AS. *beód* also means 'dish.'

Beute (2.), f., 'booty,' from the equiv. MidHG. *biute*; on account of Du. *buit*, OIc. *býte*, 'booty, exchange,' hence *býta*, 'to exchange, divide,' the *t* indicates that the word was borrowed. E. *booty* is derived from the OIc. *býte*, but it has also been confused with *boot*, 'gain, advantage' (see **Buße**). The *t* would have become *ß, tz* in HG. As *t* would represent the denial in Goth., **bieten**, Goth. *biudan* cannot, according to the laws of the permutation of consonants, be allied to **Beute**; we must assume that the root of the latter is Goth. *bût*, pre-Teut. *bhúd*. Fr. *butin*, 'booty,' is borrowed from these cognates. Comp. OIr. *buaid*, 'victory.'

Beutel (1.), m., 'a ripping chisel, a piece of wood for beating flax,' first occurs in ModHG.; the *t* points to a LG. origin; in HG. we should have expected *ß*, in Mid HG. 3 (MidHG. *bôzel, bæzel*). Comp. LG. *bætel*, AS. *býtel*, E. *beetle* (for beating flax); from a root *baut*, 'to strike, beat' (AS. *beátan*, E. *beat*, OIc. *bauta*, OHG. *bôzzan*), which still appears in **Amboß**.

Beutel (2.), m., 'purse,' from MidHG. *biutel*, m., n., 'purse, pocket,' OHG. *bútil*; comp. Du. *buidel* (*buil*), 'purse'; Goth. ***búdils***. The word cannot, however, be traced farther back than OHG.; its kinship to **bieten**, root *bud*, from *bhudh*, would throw no light on the meaning.

Beutheie, f., 'cooper's mallet for driving on the hoops.' **Beut**, like **Beutel**, 'beetle,' belongs properly to LG.; *heie*, 'rammer, hammer,' from MidHG. *heie*, OHG. *heia*, 'hammer'; hence **Bentheie**, 'driving hammer.'

bevor, conj., 'before,' from MidHG. *bevor*. OHG. *bifora*; comp. the corresponding E. *before*; from AS. *beforan*.

bewegen (1.), vb., 'to move,' from Mid HG. *bewëgen*, OHG. *biwëgan*. See **wegen**.

bewegen (2.), vb., 'to stir, excite,' from the equiv. MidHG. *bewegen*, OHG. *biwecken*, *biwegen*, factitive of the preceding. See **wegen**.

Beweis, m., first occurs in ModHG., from MidHG. *bewîsen*, 'to instruct, show, prove'; comp. **weisen**.

bezichten, bezichtigen, vb.; the former, with a change in meaning due to **züchtigen**, is also written **bezüchten**, 'to accuse of, charge with'; derivatives of a MidHG. subst. *biziht* (*bezîht*), f., 'accusation'; comp. **zeihen**.

Bezirk, m., 'circuit, district, sphere,' from MidHG. *zirc*, 'circle, circumference, district'; from Lat. *circus*, 'circle.' The word, as *z* for Lat. *c* shows, was borrowed very early during the OHG. period.

Bibel, f., 'bible,' from MidHG. *bibel*, of which there is a variant, *biblie* (E. *bible*,

Du. *bijbel*, Fr. *bible*) ; formed from Gr.-Lat. *biblia*. Comp. Fibel.

Biber, m., 'beaver,' from the equiv. MidHG. *biber*, OHG. *bibar*, m. ; it corresponds to AS. *beofor*, E. *beaver*, Du. *bever*, OIc. *björr*, Goth. **bibrus*. A term common to the Aryan family, originally signifying a 'brown' aquatic animal ; Lat. *fiber* (OGall. *Bibracte*), OSlov. *bebrŭ*, Lith. *bébrus* (most frequently *dábras*), 'beaver.' OInd. *babhrús* as an adj. means 'brown,' as a subst. masc. 'great ichneumon' ; *bhe-bhrú-s* is a reduplicated form of the root *bher* in Bär and Braun. The primitive tribe from which the Indo-Teutons are descended had ere its dispersion several fully developed names of animals ; comp. Hund, Kuh, Maus, Wolf, &c. The Teut. word had at an early period supplanted the Lat. *fiber* in Rom., LateLat. *biber*, Ital. *bevero*, Span. *bibaro*, Fr. *bièvre*, from Teut. *bebru-*, *bibru-*.

Bibernelle, **Pimpinelle**, **Pimpernelle**, f., 'pimpernel,' corruptions of the MidLat. botanical term *pipinella*, *pimpinella*. Even in MidHG. various corruptions are produced by popular etymology ; Fr. *pimprenelle*.

Biche, f., **Bichel**, m., 'pickaxe,' from the equiv. MidHG. *bicke*, *bickel*, m. ; comp. MidHG. *bicken*, OHG. *(ana)bicchan*, wk. vb., 'to prick, thrust' ; allied to AS. *becca*, E. *bick-iron*. It is probably connected further with a Kelt.-Rom. class (Ital. *becco*, Fr. *bec*, Du. *bek*, 'beak,' Fr. *bêche*, 'spade,' Ital. *beccare*, 'to hack,' &c.) ; it is possible that AS. *becca*, 'pickaxe,' is allied to Ir. and Gael. *bacc*, 'hook.' Beil seems to come from another stem.

bidmen, wk. vb., an UpG. word equiv. in meaning to beben, 'to tremble, shake,' and allied to it ; MidHG. *bidemen*, 'to tremble,' OHG. **bidimôn*, must represent **bibimôn*, *bibinôn*; respecting the relation of the consonants comp. OHG. *pfêdamo* and its variant *pêbano* under Biber. The OHG. *bibinôn* is an intensive form of OHG. *bibên*. See beben.

Bieber, 'fever' ?. Only in compounds with -illet, -fraut, -wurz. Comp. MidHG. *biever*, n., 'fever.' Its relation to Lat. *febris* is ambiguous ; it is probably a corruption of *vieber*. See Fieber.

bieder, adj., 'staunch, honest,' from MidHG. *biderbi*, OHG. *biderbi*, 'serviceable, useful,' then 'brave, gallant' (comp. besser for a similar change of idea) ; lit. 'suitable to one's need or purpose,' for the adj. is a compound of the stem of dürfen, 'to be in need of,' and the prefix *bi*, which has retained its earlier accent without being replaced, as it usually is, by *bi*. The Goth. form was perhaps **biþarbs*; further, the adj. is identical with derb.

biegen, vb., 'to bend, curve,' from the equiv. MidHG. *biegen*, OHG. *biogan*, Goth. *biugan*, 'to bend.' In Eng. the word belongs to a different class, AS. *búgan*, E. *to bow;* Du. *biugen;* comp. beugen, the factitive of this verb. Root *bŭg*, from pre-Teut. *bhûk*; the *k* of which is changed in the regular manner into *h* in Büchel, OHG. *buhil*. In OInd. we should have expected **bhuc* instead of the recorded *bhuj* (*j* for *g*), which agrees with the Teut. word only in the sense of 'to bend' ; Lat. *fugio*, Gr. φεύγω, have the more remote signification 'to flee,' which AS. *búgan* also shows. Further cognates are Bogen and Biegsam (AS. *búhsom*, *búxom*, whence E. *buxom*).

Biene, f., 'bee,' from the equiv. Mid HG. *bine*, *bin*, f., OHG. *bini*, n.; *bî* is the proper root syllable, as is shown by OHG. *bîa*, Du. *bij*, AS. *beó*, E. *bee*, OSw. *bî* (OIc. *býfluga*); the *n* of the weak declension is retained in the deriv. OHG. *bîni;* the form *binni* (from *binja-*), which we should have expected, is not recorded. Besides these there are OHG. and MidHG. forms with *î*, OHG. *bîna*, f., MidHG. *bîn*, f. (Austr. dial. Bein) ; they are related perhaps to MidHG. *bîn* like Goth. *súnus* to Sans. *súnus*, Goth. *qiwa* to Sans. *jîva-*, &c. ; comp. Sohn, Qued, laut, Schaufel. Lith. *bitis*, Ir. *bech*, 'bee,' seem allied, though they have a different suffix. The word is based on a root *bhî*, 'to be afraid,' discussed under beben ; hence Biene is perhaps 'the trembler' ?. Respecting Bienenbrot comp. Bret. Bienenkorb was an early remodelled form for OHG. *binichar*. Biensaug, n., a botanical term, lit. 'a plant that the bee is fond of sucking.'

Bier, n., 'beer,' from the equiv. MidHG. *bier*, OHG. and OLG. *bior*, n., comp. Du. *bier*, AS. *beór*, E. *beer*, OIc. *björr*; Fr. *bière* is borrowed MidHG. *bier*. There can be no connection with Lat. *bibo*, Sans. *pibâmi;* nor can Gr. πίωρ, OInd. *pivas*, 'a rich drink,' be cognate. It is rightly thought to be akin to an OTeut. term for 'barley,' OLG. and AS. *beó* (OIc. *bygg*), from Teut. **bewwo-*, based on a pre-hist. **bhéwo-*, while the cognates of Bier point to a deriv. **bhewro-*. Thus Bier is equal to 'barley-juice' ?.

Biese, Bise, f., 'north-east wind,' earlier, **Beiswind** (with the regular *ei*), from the equiv. *bise*, OHG. *bisa*, whence Fr. *bise*. A Teut. root *bis, biz*, 'to rush in excitedly,' also appears in MidHG. and ModHG. (dial.), *bisen*, 'to run about like cattle tormented by horse-flies' (with this is connected Mod HG. dial. *beiern*, with a change of *s* into *r*, in Hess. and Henneberg., with the same meaning); comp. further OSw. *bīsa*, 'to run,' Dan. *bisse*, 'to run excitedly.' Perhaps the root *bi*, 'to tremble,' is nearly akin.

Biest, m., in **Biestmilch,** from the equiv. MidHG. *biest*, OHG. *biost*, m.; comp. AS. *beóst*, and its deriv. AS. *bȳsting*, E. *beastings, biestings*. ModHG. dialects have also remarkable parallel forms with *br*, like OIc. *á-brystur*, 'beastings,' *e.g.* Swiss *briescht* (*briest*), which may be connected with **Brust**, OHG. *brust*, AS. *breóst*. Beyond the Teut. group (whence OFr. *bet*, ModFr. *béton* is borrowed) the stem has not yet been traced; it is most frequently compared with the equiv. Gr. πύος, Sans. *pīyūsa*. Yet a Teut. root *bius* seems to underlie *biese, beise*, 'to milk,' in the Wetterau dial.

bieten, vb., 'to offer, make a bid,' from MidHG. *bieten*, OHG. *biotan*, 'to offer, present, command' (similar meanings are united in the MidHG. word for befehlen); AS. *beódan*, 'to announce, offer'; E. *bid* combines the meanings of Germ. bieten and bitten. Goth. *anabiudan*, 'to command, arrange,' *faúrbiudan*, 'to forbid' (OHG. *farbiotan*, MidHG. *verbieten*, AS. *forbeódan*, E. *forbid*). Goth. *biudan*, as well as the whole of this class, points to a pre-Teut. root *bhudh*; Gr. πυθ (according to the well-known rule for φυθ) in πυνθάνομαι, πυθέσθαι, 'to ask, demand, learn by asking, hear,' approaches one of the meanings of the Teut. vb.; the latter has an active signification 'to publish, communicate,' while the Gr. middle vb. means 'to know by report, obtain information.' With the sensuous meaning of HG. bieten is connected the OInd. root *budh* (for *bhudh*), 'to make a present to one'; yet it most frequently means 'to be watchful, astir,' then 'to observe, notice'; and with this is associated OBulg. *bŭdĕti*, Lith. *budėti*, 'to awake'; Lith. *budrùs*, 'watchful'; also Lith. *baústi*, 'to chastise,' and OIr. *buide*, 'thanks.' It is a prim. Aryan verbal stem with a great variety of meanings, the chief of which are 'to present (make a present to one)—to enjoin (to command, communicate)—to be active, awake.' To the same stem belongs an OTeut. word for 'table, dish' (both conceived as the dispensers of food?), which has been mentioned under **Beute** (Goth. *biuþs*, AS. *beód*), also *bote*, from MidHG. *bote*, OHG. *boto* (AS. *boda*, whence E. *to bode*), lit. 'herald.'

Bifang, m., 'enclosure, ridge,' from MidHG *bivanc*. m., 'circuit, ridge between furrows,' OHG. *bifang*, 'circuit,' from *bifāhan*, 'comprise, encircle.' With respect to the accented verbal prefix in the subst. compound, comp. *bei*, where 'around' is also quoted as one of the OTeut. meanings of *bi*. **Bifang** (in opposition to **Beispiel, Bispel**) retains, like **bieder**, the old short verbal prefix; comp. **bieder, Bild, Beunte.**

bigott, adj., 'bigoted,' first occurs in ModHG., borrowed from Fr. *bigot*, but based in spelling on **Gott.**

Bilch, f., 'dormouse,' from the equiv. MidHG. *bilch*, OHG. *bilich* (whence OBulg. *plŭchŭ*, 'dormouse,' is borrowed?); *bil-* is primit. cognate with W. *bele*, 'marten.'

Bild, n., 'image, portrait, representation,' from MidHG. *bilde*, OHG. *bilidi*, n., 'image, figure, parable, prototype'; similarly OSax. *bilithi;* there is no corresponding word in E. or Goth. (*bilipi*). The derivation from a stem *bil-*, with which **Beil** has been absurdly connected, is untenable; *bi-* is probably the prep. *be-* (comp. **bieder, Bifang, Binse**); **liþi* is allied to *lipu-*, 'limb' (see **Glied**); the compound signifies lit. 'a copy of a limb, counterfeit limb'? It is impossible to connect it with E. *build*, which belongs rather to AS. *bold*, 'a building,' and **bauen.**

Bill, f., from the equiv. E. *bill*, which, with Fr. *billet*, belongs to MidLat. *billa, bulla*.

Bille, f., 'hatchet,' from MidHG. *bil* (gen. *billes*), 'pickaxe,' OHG. *bill;* AS. *bill*, 'sword,' E. *bill* ('sword, chopper,' also 'axe'); not cognate with **Beil.**

billig, adj., adv., 'reasonable (-ably), cheap (-ly),' for an earlier **billich**, used even in the last century, from MidHG. *billīch*, OHG. (recorded since Williram) *billich* (adv. MidHG. *billīche*, OHG. *billīhho*). 'conformable, becoming'; cognate with AS. *bilewit*, MidE. *bilewit*, 'simple, innocent.' It has been said, without sufficient reason, that this class was borrowed from Kelt. Comp. other cognates under **Weichbild, Unbill.**

Bilſenkraut, n., 'henbane,' from the equiv. MidHG. *bilse,* OHG. *bilisa,* f.; also a dial. form *bilme,* equal to Dan. *bulme,* AS. *beolene* (Span. *beleño*). The stems *bilisa, beluna,* common to the Teut. group, correspond to Lat. *felix, filix,* 'fern,' but more closely to Russ. *belená,* Pol. *bielun,* 'henbane.' Comp. further MidDu. *beelde,* 'henbane.'

bin, see ſein, vb.

Bims, m., **Bimsſtein,** 'pumice-stone,' from the equiv. MidHG. *bümez,* OHG. *bumiz;* hence we should have expected ModHG. Bümtz. The relation between Kreuz and Lat. *cruc-em* is similar to that between Bimtz and the type, Lat. *pumic-em* (nom. *pumex*). The *i* of the ModHG. form is MidG., as in Ritt, Pilz. From Lat. *pumex* (Ital. *pomice*) are also derived Du. *puimsteen,* and AS. *pūmicstān.* With regard to *s* for *z,* see Binſe.

binden, vb., 'to tie, bind,' from MidHG. *binden,* OHG. *bintan.* corresponds to OSax. and AS. *bindan,* E. *to bind,* Goth. *bindan;* the meaning does not change, hence it was the same in primit. Teut. as in ModHG. and Eng. The pre-Teut. form of the root must have been *bhendh;* comp. the corresponding Sans. root *bandh,* 'to chain, fasten'; Lat. (with *f* for *bh* initially) *offendimentum,* 'bond, cable'; Gr. πεῖσμα for *πένθσμα, 'bond,' also πενθερός, 'father-in-law,' as well as Sans. *bándhu,* 'a relative.' In Teut. numerous forms are derived by gradation from the same root (*e.g.* Band, E. *bond, bend*). Ital. *benda,* 'bandage,' *bendare,* 'to bind up,' are borrowed.

Bingelkraut, n., earlier Büngelkraut, 'mercury'; Büngel, a name of a plant, from MidHG. *bunge,* OHG. *bungo,* 'bulb.' See Bachbunge.

binnen, prep., 'within,' from MidHG. (MidLG. and MidDu.) *binnen;* comp. the corresponding AS. *binnan,* 'within,' from *bi-innan,* with suppression of the *i* of *bi,* as in ſunge, Barmherzig. See innen.

Binſe (Swiss Binz), f., 'rush,' from the plur. of the equiv. MidHG. *binz, binez,* m., OHG. *binuz,* m.; comp. OSax. *binut,* AS. *beonet,* E. *bent, bentgrass,* as well names of places, Bentley, Bentheim, with a LG. vowel. The most probable derivation is that given in the OHG. period, by Notker, from *bi-* and *naz* (see naß); hence lit. 'that which grows in wet places.' LFranc. and LG. have a stem *biusa* corresponding to Du. *bies,* Mid LG. *bese,* which are not cognate with Binſe.

Birke (Swiss Bilche, Birche), f., 'birch,' from the equiv. MidHG. *birke* (UpG. *birche*), OHG. *bircha, birihha;* comp. AS. *birce,* E. *birch;* also Du. *berk,* AS. *beorc,* OIc. *björk,* Goth. **bairka,* f., or **bairkjô,* f. This term, common to the Teut. group, is one of the few names of trees of primit. Aryan origin (comp. Buche); the pre-Teut. form is *bhergâ* (*bhergyâ*), and corresponds to Sans. *bhûrja,* m., 'a kind of birch' (neu. also 'birch bark'), OSlov. *brěza,* f., Lith. *béržas.*

Birne, f., 'pear'; the *n* belongs properly to the inflexion; MidHG. *bir* (and still dialectic), plur. *birn;* OHG. *bira,* 'pear.' Derived from the Lat. *pirum,* or rather plur. *pīra.* On account of the initial *b* of the German word, the date at which it was borrowed can hardly be placed earlier than the 9th cent. The Goth applied to the 'mulberry-tree' the apparently cognate term *batrabagms.* E. *pear,* AS. *peru,* Du. *peer,* are based upon the Rom. word (Ital. and Span. *pera*), derived from Lat. *pirum.* Respecting the change of gender see Pflaume.

birſchen, vb., from the equiv. MidHG. *birsen,* 'to chase with hounds, to shoot deer'; *s* after *r* became *sch,* as in Arſch, Karſch, Dorſche, herrſchen, Hirſch, Kirſche, Kürſchner, wirſch; from OFr. *berser* (MidLat. *bersare*), 'to pierce with an arrow.'

bis, conj., adv., 'until, as far as,' from MidHG. *biz* (for which *unze, unz* most frequently occur); in OHG. it was perhaps *biaz, i.e.* bis is a compound of *bi* (see ki, Goth. *bi*) and *az* (OHG. *az,* 'to,' Goth. *at,* Lat. *ad*); *biaz* became *biz,* 'until.' Earlier ModHG. has a variant *bitze, bitz,* which likewise arose from au older *bi* and *ze,* 'to.' Similarly ModHG. *unz* is composed of *unt* (Goth. *und*) and *ze.—*bislang, from the equiv. MidHG. *bissolange,* 'so long, hitherto,' for *biz sô lange,* 'until so long.'

Biſam, m., 'musk,' from the equiv. MidHG. *bisem,* OHG. *bisam, bisamo,* from MidLat. *bisamum,* which is of oriental origin (Hebr. *besem,* Syr. *besmo*).

Biſchof, m., 'bishop,' from the equiv. MidHG. *bischof* (v), OHG. *biscof* (to which Bistum is related); Du. *bisschop,* AS. *bisceop,* E. *bishop,* with the same meaning. In Goth. with a closer adherence to the primit. form (ἐπίσκοπος), *aípiskaúpus.* This widely diffused word was probably adopted, like the Arianism of the Goths (comp. Kirche), from the Greeks without passing through Romance. The Lat.-Rom. origin is indeed supported by the initial *b* as well as the loss of the original *e* at the beginning; comp. Ital. *vescovo*, OFr. *vesque* (also *evesque*, ModFr. *évêque*, and OIr. *epscop*). Comp. further OSlov. *jepĭskopŭ*.

Bissen, m., 'bit, morsel,' from the equiv. MidHG. *biƺƺe*, OHG. *biƺƺo*; comp. AS. *bita*, E. *bit*, and **beißen**.

Bistum, n., 'bishopric.' Even in MidHG. *bischtuom* and *bistuom*, OHG. *biscetuom*, from *biscoftuom*. By a similar change *Bismarck* was formed from *bischoves marc*; on the borders of such a mark the property of the tribe was situated.

Biß, Bißchen, 'bit, trifle,' from **beißen**.

bitten, vb., 'to beg, entreat, invite,' from the equiv. MidHG. and OHG. *bitten* (from *bitjan*, *bidjan*); it is a str. vb. of the class *e—a—â—e*. Comp. Goth. *bidjan*, *baþ*, *bêdum*, *bidans*; AS. *biddan*; in E. *to bid*, both *bitten* and *bitten* appear; E. *to beg*, from AS. *bedecian* (Goth. *bidagôn ? comp. Teut. and Goth. *bidaga, 'beggar'). The str. vb. belonged originally to the *i* class (Goth. *bidja*, *baiþ, *bidum, *bidans* might therefore be conjectured); a trace of this gradation is shown further by the factitive Goth. *baidjan*, AS. *bœdan*, OHG. *beiten*, with the meaning 'to order, demand, compel.' The root *bheidh*, *bhidh*, accords with Gr. πιθ (for φιθ, according to the well-known rule), πείθω, 'to induce by entreaties, get by asking, persuade, convince'; to this belongs also Lat. *fīdo* (equiv. to the Gr. Mid. Voice πείθομαι), 'to rely on a person.' With this meaning an OTeut. *bîdan*, 'to await, wait with full confidence' (Goth. *b-idan*, OHG. *bîtan*, AS. *bîdan*, E. *to bide*), has been connected. The Germ. noun **Bitte** is OHG. *bita*, most frequently *bëta*, Goth. *bida*. See **beten, Gebet**.

bitter, adj., 'bitter,' from the equiv. MidHG. *bitter*, OHG. *bittar*. This *t*, since it comes before *r*, represents the *t* common to the Teut. cognates ; before *r* the permutation of *t* to *ƺ*, *tz* does not take place (comp. **Eiter, Luter, zittern**); OLG. *bittar*, AS. *bittor*, *biter*, E. and Du. *bitter*; hence we should have expected Goth. *bîtrs, for which a form with a remarkable *ai*, *baitrs*, 'bitter,' occurs. The word is undoubtedly cognate with **beißen** (root *bit*, inf. *bîtan*); the adj. properly signifies ' pricking, sharp,' being now, like **beißen**, restricted to the taste. For other cognates comp. **beißen**.

blach, adj., 'flat,' from MidHG. *blach*;

it is, like Swiss *blacke*, 'a large board,' related to **flach**.

Blackfisch, m., 'cuttlefish,' from LG. *blackfisk*. *Blak* is the LG. term for ink (*blakhorn*, 'inkstand'); comp. AS. *blæc*, 'ink,' E. *black* (a colour and shoemaker's black), OHG. *blach*.

Blahe, f., 'coarse linen,' from MidHG. *balhe*, *blâ*, f.; a dialect. widely diffused word, with the parallel forms *blâhe*, *plane*, *blache*, *plauwe*; the primit. form is Goth. *blahwa ?.

blähen, vb., 'to inflate,' from the equiv. MidHG. *blæjen*, OHG. *blâjan*, wk. vb. (the OHG. word also means 'to blow'); comp. AS. *blâwan*, E. *to blow*. The Teut. root *blâ* (*blê*) agrees partly with Lat. *flare* (Aryan root *bhlâ*); **blasen, Blatt**, and **Blatter** are also closely related to it. **Blasen** especially seems to have arisen from the shorter root, also preserved in **Blatter**, by adding *s* to the stem of the present.

Blaker, m., 'chandelier' (in Voss), from the equiv. LG. and Du. *blaker*; comp. AS. *blæcern*; from the MidLG. and Du. *blaken*, 'to burn, glow.' For further Teut. and Aryan cognates see under **Blitz**.

blank, adj., 'bright, drawn (of a sword),' from the MidHG. *blanc*, OHG. *blanch*, 'gleaming, white, resplendently beautiful.' Comp. E. *blank* ('white'), (AS. *blanca*, *blonca*, OIc. *blakkr*, 'white or grey horse') ; related to OIc. *blakra*, 'to gleam'; formed by gradation from the root *blek* in **Blitz** (comp. also **blecken**). The adj. made its way into Rom. (Ital. *bianco*, Fr. *blanc*), whence **Blankett** with a Rom. suffix; comp. also **blasen**. The less frequent *blink*—a recent formation from the verb—is found as a parallel form to **blank** in ModHG.

Blankscheit, n., 'busk' (whalebone in a corset), corrupted in ModHG. from Fr. *planchette*.

Blase, f., 'blister, bubble, flaw,' from MidHG. *blâse*, OHG. *blâsa*; the last two specially mean 'urinary bladder.' Comp. **Blatter** and **blasen**.

blasen, vb., 'to blow, sound, smelt,' from MidHG. *blâsen*, OHG. *blâsan*, 'to breathe, snort'; comp. the equiv. Goth. *blêsan*; in E. only the deriv. AS. *blæst*, E. *blast*, has been preserved. The *s* of **blasen**, which does not occur in the root *bhlâ* of the cognate languages, is considered by some to be simply a present suffix which was not joined to the stem until a later period ; in that case **blasen** and **Blatter** may be cog-

C

nate. The OTeut. words with initial *bl* separate into two groups; the one, containing blähen, Blatter, blasen, blühen, Blüte, seems to be based on the primary meaning of 'swelling,' the other, comprising blank, blaß, blinken, blecken, blitzen, blau, Blech, Blut, on the notion of 'shining.'

blaß, adj., 'pale, faint (in colour),' from MidHG. *blas*, 'bald,' figuratively 'weak, trifling'; the earlier signification is 'shining' (comp. Glast, from glänzen); allied to OHG. *blas*, 'whitish.' Hence by mutation Blässe, f., 'a white spot on the forehead,' OIc. *bles* (earlier Dan. *blis*), MidLG. *blare* (but *blasenhengst*, 'horse with a blaze'), Du. *blaar*, 'cow with a blaze.' With the meaning 'shining,' AS. *blase*, E. *blaze*, MidHG. *blas*, n., 'a torch,' are connected.

Blatt, n., 'leaf, blade, newspaper,' from the equiv. MidHG. and OHG. *blat*, n.; comp. the corresponding Du. *blad*, AS. *blæd*, 'leaf,' E. *blade*; Goth. *blaþ. The dental of these cognates seems to be a suffix; *bla*- from pre-Teut. *bhlo*-, as well as Lat. *fol-ium*, Gr., φύλλον, 'leaf,' may have been formed from a root *bhol*, *bhlō*. It is uncertain whether Goth. *blada*- is really a partic. with an Aryan suffix *tō*-, with the meaning 'having ceased to bloom' or 'fully grown.' See blühen.

Blatter, f., 'pock, pustule,' from MidHG. *blâttere*, f., 'bladder, pock,' OHG. *blâttara*, f., 'bladder'; comp. Du. *blaar*, AS. *blædre*, E. bladder. The Goth. form would be *blêdrô* (or *bladrô*? see Natter), with *drô*- as a suffix, corresponding to Gr. τρα (see Ater, Natter); for *blê* as a root syllable see blasen, blähen.

blau, adj., from the equiv. MidHG. *blâ* (Gen. *blâwes*), OHG. *blâo*, 'blue'; comp. Du. *blaauw*, AS. *blâw*, and with a suffix *blâwen*; E. blue (from MidE. *blew*) is borrowed from Fr. *bleu*, which, with its Rom. cognates (Ital. *biavo*, from *blawo*), is of Germ. origin. The primit. cognate Lat. *flâvus*, 'flaxen, yellow,' has, like so many names of colours, changed its meaning compared with the Germ. word.

Bläuel, m., 'beetle, rolling-pin,' derived from the following word.

bläuen, vb., 'to beat, drub'; instinctively allied by Germans to blau (blau schlagen, 'to beat black and blue'). It is based, however, on a str. vb., MidHG. *bliuwen*, OHG. *bliuwan*, 'to beat'; comp. the equiv. AS. *blêowan*, whence E. *blow*; Goth. *bliggwan*, 'to beat' (with an excrescent *gg*), for *bliwan*. The root seems to be *blu*, from *bhlu*·; it can hardly be related primitively to blau, nor is it possible to derive *bliwan from a root *bhlīwo* for *b'ligwo* from *bhligh* (comp. Schnee, Niere), and to compare it with Lat. *fligere*.

Blech, n., 'thin metal plate, tin plate,' from the equiv. MidHG. *blëch*, OHG. *blëh*, n.; it corresponds to OIc. *blik*, n., 'gold, thin plate of gold.' In Eng. the word is not to be met with; it is formed by gradation from the root *blik*, which appears in bleichen, and means 'shining.'—**Blechen**, 'to pay money,' comp. berappen.

blechen, vb., 'to show one's teeth, grin,' from MidHG. *blëcken*, 'to become visible, show,' OHG. *b'ecchen* (Goth. *blakjan). Factitive of a Goth. *blikan*, which, according to the law of the permutation of consonants, is cognate with Gr. φλέγω, 'to burn, shine' (comp. φλοξ· in φλόξ, 'flame '), Lat. *flagro*, 'to burn,' and the Sans. root *bhrâj*, 'to shine.' OHG. *blëcchen* also means 'to lighten, gleam, shine forth.' For further details see Blitz.

Blei, n., 'lead,' from the equiv. MidHG. *blī* (Gen. *blīwes*), OHG. *blīo* (for *blīw*), 'lead'; it corresponds to OIc. *blý*; Goth. *bleiwa*- is wanting. The word cannot be traced farther back; it is not found in Eng., the term used being *lead* (Du. *loot*; comp. Lot).

bleiben, vb., 'to remain, continue,' from the equiv. MidHG. *blīben*, OHG. *biliban*; comp. the corresponding AS. *belīfan*, Goth. *bileiban*, 'to remain' (the factitive of which is *bilaibjan*, 'to cause to remain, leave over'; AS. *læfan*, E. *to leave*). It is allied neither to Lat. *linquo* nor to Gr. λείπω, to which leihen is more akin; *biltbo*, 'I remain,' must be based on pre-Teut. *lipô* (Sans. root *lip*, 'to adhere '); Gr. λιπαρός, 'greasy, shining,' λίπος, n., 'fat,' λιπαρόω, 'I persist,' comes nearest to the meaning of the Teut. vb.; comp. OSlov. *lipnati*, Lith. *lipti*, 'to adhere, remain.' With the former meaning, 'to adhere,' ModHG. Leber is connected, and with the latter, 'to persist, abide,' the ModHG. Leib and Leben. See the separate words.

bleich, adj., 'pale, wan,' from the equiv. MidHG. *bleich*, OHG. *bleih*; comp. AS. *blâc*, *blâce*, E. *bleak*, Du. *bleek*, OIc. *bleikr*, 'pale,' from the root *blik* appearing in bleichen. Derivatives: ModHG. Bleiche, f., 'bleaching, bleaching-yard, wan appearance'; bleichen, 'to bleach, turn pale.'

bleichen, vb., 'to lose colour,' erbleichen, 'to grow pale,' from MidHG. blīchen, 'to shine, blush,' OHG. blīhhan; comp. AS. blīcan, MidE. blīken, 'to turn pale'; OIc. blīkja, 'to appear, shine, lighten.' The i root of Slav. bliskati, 'to sparkle' (for *bligskati), blěskŭ, 'splendour,' Lith. blaivýtis, 'to clear up,' is more closely connected with the word than the e root in φλέγω, 'to burn, flame.' The pre-Teut. form of the root was perhaps bhlig, meaning 'lustre' (comp. also **Blech, bleich**; further OHG. blick, see **Blitz**).—**Bleicher(t),** m., 'pale-red wine, claret,' a recent deriv. from bleich.

Bleihe, f., 'whitebait, bleak,' Du. term for a species of white fish; comp. Du. blei, MidLG. and MidDu. bleie, AS. blǽge, E. *blay; from blaijōn for *blaigjōn (comp. OHG. reia, AS. rǽge, from raigjōn; see under Reh). As ModHG. Ricke is a parallel form of OHG. reia, so MidHG. and ModHG. (Swiss) blicke is a variant of LG. bleie. The primary meaning and further cognates are uncertain; OHG. bleihha, MidHG. bleiche, would point to a connection with bleich (comp. OIc. bligja, 'to glance at').

blenden, vb., 'to blind,' from the equiv. MidHG. blenden, OHG. blenten; comp. AS. blendan, whereas E. has to blind based upon blind; factitive of blind. It is remarkable in connection with this word that an old form, *blandjan, as it would be written in Goth., is derived by gradation from an adj. (blinds, Goth.); a str. vb. blindan, 'to be blind,' has never existed. **Blende,** 'blind, screen,' first found in ModHG., is a deriv. of blenden.

Blendling, m., 'mongrel,' from MidHG. blanden, OHG. b'antan, 'to mix'; Goth. blandan. This OTeut. str. vb., meaning 'to mix,' is based, according to the laws of the permutation of consonants, on a pre-Teut. root bhlandh, not found in any other word.

bletzen, 'to patch,' see under Pladen.

Blick, m., 'glance, look, gleam,' from MidHG. blick, 'splendour, lightning, glance'; corresponds to OHG. blic (blicches), m., 'lightning' (also blicfiur, 'electricity'). The orig. sense of the MidHG. word was probably heller Strahl (a bright flash), Strahl being used figuratively of the eye as of lightning; the physical meaning of the stem has been preserved in **Blitz**. The root is shown under bleichen, and especially under **Blitz**, to be the pre-Teut. bhleg.

blind, adj., 'blind,' from MidHG. blint(d), 'blind, dark, murky, hidden, null,' OHG. blint; comp. the corresponding Goth. blinds, AS. blind, E. blind. An ancient but very remarkable factitive form from this adj., with no parallel str. vb., is blendan (Goth. *blandjan). It is still undecided whether d is an old partic. suffix, like Gr. -τος, Lat. -tus, Sans. -tas; considering the meaning of the word, it might easily be connected with the Sans. root bhram, 'to move unsteadily' (partic. bhrāntá-s). Yet its kinship with Lith. blandýti, 'to cast down the eyes,' blindo, blìsti, 'to grow dark,' is more probable (comp. OIc. blunda, 'to close, blink the eyes,' E. to blunder).—Another word for 'blind' in the Aryan group is Lat. caecus, OIr. cáech; Goth. haihs, corresponding to these, means 'one-eyed.' It seems, moreover, that in the Aryan languages there were no terms for 'blind, deaf, lame, dumb,' and other infirmities, common to all of them; there is only an agreement between two or three languages at most.

Blindschleiche, see under schleichen.

blinken, vb., 'to gleam, twinkle, blink,' first occurs in ModHG.; related to blank, blink, adj.; comp. Du. blinken, MidE. blinken, E. to blink. The root may be identical with that of bleichen (blik-en), the i-root becoming nasalised; blinken would then be regarded as a verb of the e class, and blauf a secondary form.

blinzeln, vb., 'to blink, wink.' It may be connected with blind; yet comp. also OIc. blunda, 'to blink,' and Lith. blandýti, 'to cast down the eyes.'

Blitz, m., from the equiv. MidHG. blitze, blicze, blicz, m., 'lightning' (Swiss even now blitzg for blikiz); a derivative of MidHG. bliczen, 'to' lighten,' OHG. blēchazzen (formed like the equiv. Goth. lauhatjan). Allied to the earlier OHG. and MidHG. blic, 'lightning.' The Teut. root blek corresponds to Aryan bhleg, bhlog, in Gr. φλέγω, 'to burn, blaze,' φλόξ, 'flame,' Sans. bhrāj, 'to radiate, sparkle.' (whence Sans. bharga(s), 'splendour,' and bhrgu, 'the special gods of light'), as well as Lat. fulgur, fulmen (for *fulgmen), 'lightning.' To the Aryan root bhleg the following also belong: Du. bliksem, OSax. blikemo, bliksni, 'lightning,' Du. blaken, 'to flame,' AS. blǽcern, blacern, 'candlestick' (see **Blaker**), and perhaps blank (comp. further bleichen and **Blick**).

Block, m., 'block, log, prison,' from MidHG. bloch, 'log, plank, a sort of trap,'

In the latter signification (to which Mid HG. *blocken*, 'to put in prison,' is related) it represents OHG. *bilôh* (with syncopated *i*; see other similar examples under *bei*), 'lock-up,' which belongs to an OTeut. str. vb. *lûkan*, 'to lock' (comp. further E. *lock*; see Loch). The meaning 'log, plank' (Mid HG. *b'och*), is probably based on a different word, which is most likely related to Balken; even in OHG., *bloh* occurs. The cognates passed into Rom. (Fr. *bloc*, *bloquer*), whence again ModHG. blockiren, E. *to block*.

blöde, adj., 'weak, dim-sighted, imbecile,' from MidHG. *blœde*, 'infirm, weak, tender, timid,' OHG. *blôdi*, OSax. *blôði*, 'timid.' Comp. AS. *bleáþ*, 'weak,' OIc. *blauþr*; Goth. **blauþus*, 'weak, powerless,' may be inferred from its deriv. wk. vb. *blauþjan*, 'to render powerless, invalid, to abolish.' According to the permutation of consonants, the pre-Teut. form of the adj. may have been *bhláutu-s*, with the primary meaning 'powerless, weak.' Yet the stem cannot be traced farther back. From this word Fr. *éblouir*, 'to dazzle,' is borrowed.

blöken, vb., 'to bleat,' ModHG. simply, of LG. origin. Comp. LG. *blöken*, *bleken*, MidDu. *bloiken*.

blond, adj., 'blonde, fair,' from MidHG. *blunt(d)*, 'fair,' which first appears when the Fr. influence began (about 1200 A.D.), and is undoubtedly of Fr. origin. Fr. *blond*, Ital. *biondo*, MidLat. *blundus*, give the impression that these words were borrowed from Teut., especially since other Teut. names of colours have been adopted by Rom. (comp. blau, blank, braun). The earlier periods of OTeut. have, however, no adj. *blundu-*. The connection of MidLat. and Rom. *blundo* with blind (OIc. *blunda*) may be possible (comp. Lith. *prý-blinde*, 'twilight'), especially as the meaning of the names of colours is variable.

bloß, adj., 'bare, destitute, mere,' from MidHG. *blôz*, 'exposed, naked'; it corresponds to MidLG. and MidDu. *bloot*, 'bare,' AS. *bleát*, 'poor, wretched' (OIc. *blautr*, 'soft, fresh, tender,' as well as OHG. *blôz*, 'proud,' have a divergent meaning). On account of the UpG. and LG. *blutt* (dial.), Swed. *blott*, 'unfledged, uncovered, unclad,' the origin of Teut. *blauto-*, 'mere,' is dubious. Perhaps blöde is a cognate.

blühen, vb., 'to bloom, flower,' from the equiv. MidHG. *blüen*, *blüejen*, OHG. *bluojan*; a wk. vb., which, however, judging by AS. *blôwan* (E. *to blow*), 'to bloom,' was formerly strong; Goth. **blôjan*. The Teut. stem *blô-* has a wide ramification in particular dialects; the primary sense is 'to bloom.' It is further apparent in many words for Blatt ('leaf') and Blume ('flower'); see the following word, where the non-Teut. cognates are discussed.

Blume, f., 'blossom, flower,' from Mid HG. *b'uome*, m., f., OHG. *bluoma*, f. (*bluomo*, m.); comp. OSax. *blômo*, Goth. *blôma*, AS. *blôma*, E. *bloom*. -*man*- is a deriv. suffix; the root *blô* (see blühen) shows that Blume is lit. 'the blooming plant.' The following are also Teut. cognates of Blume:— Du. *bloesem* (besides *bloem*), AS. *blôstm*, *blôstma*, E. *blossom*; perhaps their *s* belongs, however, to the root; this is indicated by MidDu. *blôsen*, 'to bloom,' which points to the close connection between E. *blossom* and Lat. *florere* for **flôst-re*, *flôs* (*flôr-is* for **flôsis*). A root *bhlô* without this *s* appears in OIr. *bláth*, 'blossom,' E. dial. *blooth*, 'flower.' See further the following word, also Blüte and Blatt.

Blust, m. (Suab. and Swiss, *bluest*, n.), from the equiv. MidHG. *bluost*, f., 'blossom'; Goth. **blôs-ts* is connected perhaps with the Aryan root *bhlôs*, 'to bloom,' preserved in AS. *blôs-tma*, Lat. *flôrere* (for **flôsere*). See Blume and Blüte.

Blut, n., 'blood, race,' from the equiv. MidHG. *bluot*, OHG. *bluot*, n.; it corresponds regularly to Du. *bloed*, AS. *blôd*, E. *blood*. An OTeut. word meaning 'blood,' which is common to all the dialects; comp. Goth. *blôþa-* (for **blôda-*). Pre-Teut. *bhlâto-* does not appear in any cognate language with the same meaning. The Aryan languages have no common word for *blood*. With respect to the Teut. word, it is still undecided whether it belongs to a root *blô*, 'to bloom.' Comp. also E. *to bleed* (for **blodjan*). For Blutegel see Igel. Blut in compounds like blutjung, blutarm, has nothing to do with Blut, but is dial. with the meaning 'bare, naked'; UpG. and LG. *blutt*.

blutsrünstig, see rünstig.

blutt, see blöde.

Blüte, f., 'blossom, bloom, prime,' from the plur. of the equiv. MidHG. *bluot*, plur. *blüete*, OHG. *bluot*, plur. *bluoti*, f.; Goth. **blôþs*, AS. *blêd*. See blühen, Blume, Blust, Blut, and Blatt.

Bocher, Jew., 'youth, student,' from Hebr. *bachûr*, 'youth.'

Bock, m., 'buck, he-goat, ram,' from

the equiv. MidHG. *bock* (gen. *bockes*), OHG. *boc*, m.; corresponds to Du. *bok*, AS. *bucca*, E. *buck*, OIc. *bukkr* and *bokkr* (Goth. *bukks, *bukka, m.). Like so many names of animals (comp. *e.g.* Aue, Geiß), Bock too may have descended from primit. Aryan times; comp. OIr. *bocc*, from primit. Kelt. *bucco-*. Although it is not quite impossible that the whole Teut. class was borrowed from Kelt., yet it seems more probable, on account of Armen. *buc*, 'lamb,' and Zend *būza*, 'he-goat' (Aryan primitive form *bhūga*), that it was only primit. akin to Kelt. Fr. *bouc* may be derived from Teut. or Kelt. Another OTeut. word (related to Lat. *caper*, Gr. κάπρος) is preserved in ModHG. Habergeiß.—Bock, 'mistake,' Mod HG. only, seems to be a pun due to Mod HG. Verstoß, 'blunder.' The origin of the phrase einen Bock schießen ('to commit a blunder') is not clear; note, however, that eine Lerche schießen is 'to fall head over heels.'—Bock (whence Fr. *boc*), for Bockbier, which first occurs in ModHG., is an abbrev. of Einbock (now Eimbecker Bier); comp. the origin of Thaler.

Bocksbeutel, m., 'old prejudice,' first occurs in ModHG., and connected instinctively by Germans with Bock; it is, however, of LG. origin, *bocks-* representing *bōks* ('of the book'). The women of Hamburg used to carry their hymn-books at their side in a satchel, which they were always fond of wearing. When applied to a sort of bottle, Bocksbeutel has a different origin, and means properly 'the scrotum of the buck.'

Boden, m., 'bottom, ground, soil, loft,' from the equiv. MidHG. *boden*, *bodem*, gen. *bodemes* (the dial. ModHG. *bodem* is still used, comp. the proper name Bodmer), OHG. *bodam*, m., which still exists in the cognate dialects and languages. OHG. *bodam* points, however, not to Goth. **buþma-*, but, with a remarkable irregularity, to **budna-*, the corresponding AS. *botm*, E. *bottom*, exhibiting a further irregularity in the dental. Goth. **budna-* seems probable, since the non-Teut. languages of the Aryan stock point to *bhudhmen*, *bhudhnó-* as the stem; Gr. πυθμήν, ὁ (for *φυθμήν, see bieten), 'bottom'; Lat. *fundus* (for *fudnus), Sans. *budhná-* (for **bhudhná-*, by the same rule as in Gr.). It is a primit. Aryan word, with the meaning 'bottom, ground,' but is not connected, however, with a str. vb. in any Aryan language.—Bodensee obtained its name during the Carolovingian period (formerly *Lacus Brigantinus*, 'Lake Constance') from the imperial palace at *Bodema* (now Bodmann), which may be the plur. of the subst. Boten.

Bodmerei, f., 'money advanced on the security of the ship's keel or bottom' (*i.e.* the ship itself), from Du. *bodmerie*, E. *bottomry* (whence Fr. *bomerie*).

Bofist, m., 'puck-ball,' ModHG. only, properly 'knave's fizzling' (see under Fist); comp. AS. *wulfes fist*, the name of the plant (E. *bullfist*), of which Gr.-Lat. *lycoperdon* is a late imitation.

Bogen, m., 'bow, arc, vault, sheet (of paper),' from MidHG. *boge*, OHG. *bogo*, m., 'bow'; comp. AS. *boga*, E. *bow*; Goth. *buga. Properly a deriv. of biegen, hence orig. 'curve, bend,' connected with the equiv. cognates of Bucht; comp. further the primit. Teut. compounds Ellenbogen, Regenbogen.

Bohle, f., 'plank, board,' from the equiv. MidHG. *bole*; comp. OIc. *bolr* (whence E. *bole*), 'trunk (of a tree)'; perhaps connected with MidHG. *boln*, 'to roll,' Gr. φάλαγξ, 'trunk.' See Bollwerk.

Bohne, f., 'bean,' from MidHG. *bōne*, OHG. *bōna*, f.; the corresponding AS. *bēan*, E. *bean*, Du. *boon*, OIc. *baun*, have the same meaning. The early existence of this word is attested by the name of the Fris. islands, *Baunonia*. It has not yet been possible to find a connecting link between the primit. Teut. term and the equiv. Lat. *faba*, OSlov. *bobŭ* (Gr. φακός, 'lentil').

bohnen, vb., 'to wax (a floor), polish,' first occurs in ModHG. from the equiv. LG. *bōnen*; comp. Du. *boenen*, 'to scour,' AS. *bōnian*, 'to polish' (E. dial. *to boon*, 'to mend roads'). Allied to these is the MidHG. *büenen* (orig. HG.), 'to polish' (Goth. *bōnjan). The Teut. root *bōn*, from pre-Teut. *bhān*, 'to shine, glitter,' is probably connected with the Gr. root φαν (φαίνω), Sans. *bhánu*, 'sheen, light, ray,' OIr. *bán*, 'white.'

Bohnenlied, 'bean-song' (in the phrase etwas geht über das Bohnenlied, applied to something incomparably good); the word may be traced as far back as the 15th cent., but the song itself has not been discovered. It may have been an obscene poem, since the bean among various nations is adopted as the symbol of lewdness (comp. the mediæval bean-feast, Gr. πυανέψια).

Böhnhase, m., 'bungler, clumsy workman,' first found in ModHG.; generally asserted to be a popular corruption of Gr. βάναυσος, which means 'artisan;' but it is inexplicable how the Gr. word found its way into popular speech. It is more probably of real German origin, although the primary meaning cannot be got at; we must begin with the fact that the word is native to LG., and is chiefly used in Tailors' Guilds. We must probably regard *hase* as a LG. form for Hofe (see Aberglaube, Abebar). Bühn is generally considered to be a LG. word for Bühne, 'garret'; hence Böhnhase is perhaps 'one who makes breeches in the garret, petty tailor' (opposed to one whose workroom is on the first floor).

bohren, vb., 'to bore, pierce,' from the equiv. MidHG. born, OHG. borōn; comp. the corresponding Du. boren, AS. borian, E. *to bore* (and *bore*, 'hole made by boring'); Goth. *baúrōn*. The prim. Teut. *borōn*, 'to bore,' is primit. cognate with Lat. *forare*, 'to bore,' Gr. φαρόω, 'I plough'; Sans. *bhurij*, 'scissors,' belongs to the same root, and in Ir. there is a verbal root *berr*, from *bherj*, meaning 'to shear.' The primary meaning of this root *bhar*, which differs from that appearing in Geburt and Lat. *fero*, Gr. φέρω, was probably 'to fashion with a sharp instrument.' Comp. ModHG. dial. Behrer, 'woodlouse,' E. *bore*.

Boi, m., 'baize,' ModHG. only, from LG. *baje*, Du. *baai*, which is borrowed from Rom. (Fr. *boie*); perhaps E. *baize* is properly a plur.

Boisalz, m., 'bay-salt,' ModHG. only, of LG. origin, for Baisalz; comp. Bai and E. *bay-salt*.

Boje, f., 'buoy,' from the LG. *boje*, Du. *boei*, E. *buoy*, which are borrowed from Rom.; comp. Fr. *bouée*, 'buoy,' OFr. *buie*, 'chain, fetter,' whence MidHG. *boie*, 'fetter.' The ultimate source of the word is Lat. *boja*, 'fetter'; the buoy was originally a floating piece of wood with a rope fastened to it.

Bolchen, m., 'cod,' like Belche (1.), from the equiv. MidHG. *balche*; of obscure origin.

-bold, in compounds like Raufbold, Witzbold, &c., from MidHG. *bolt*, gen. *boldes*; it is the unaccented form of the MidHG. adj., *balt*, 'bold,' which is discussed under bald.

bölken, vb., 'to roar, bleat,' ModHG. only, and perhaps cognate with bellen, which had formerly a wider signification than in ModHG.; comp. Du. *bulken*, 'to bellow, bleat.'

boll, adj., 'stiff (of leather), brittle, hard'; ModHG. only; origin obscure.

Bolle (1.), f., 'onion,' properly identical with the following word; both are subdivisions of a probable primary meaning, 'bulbaceous.' It is hardly probable that Gr. βολβός, Lat. *bulbus* (whence E. *bulb*), 'bulb, onion,' had any influence on the meaning. See also Zwiebel.

Bolle (2.), f., 'bulb,' from MidHG. *bolle*, OHG. *bolla*, f., 'bud, bowl'; comp. the corresponding AS. *bolla*, 'vessel, bowl,' E. *bowl* (ModHG. Bowle, is borrowed from Eng.). Interesting forms are OHG. *hirnibolla*, 'skull,' and the equiv. AS. *heáfodbolla*. It is evident that there was orig. some such idea as 'boss-shaped' in the O.Teut. word; comp. further MidHG. *boln*, OHG. *bolōn*, 'to roll, throw, hurl.'

Böller, m., 'small mortar (for throwing shells),' ModHG. only, a deriv. of the MidHG. *boln*, 'to throw,' mentioned under the preceding word; comp. late MidHG. *boler*, 'catapult.'

Bollwerk, n., 'bulwark, bastion,' from late MidHG. *bolwerk*, 'catapult, bulwark,' in the former sense cognate with the preceding word; in the latter probably connected with Bohle; Du. *bolwerk*, E. *bulwark*. The Teut. word in the sense of 'bulwark,' which belongs to it since the 15th cent., found its way into Slav. and Rom. (Russ. *bolverk*, Fr. *boulevard*).

Bolz, Bolzen, m., 'short arrow-bolt,' from the equiv. MidHG. *bolz*, OHG. *bolz*, m.; comp. the equiv. OIc. *bolte*, AS. *bolt*, E. *bolt;* allied to Du. *bout*, 'cramp-pin.' The word has the same meaning in all dialects, and in all the various periods of the Teut. languages. We may assume a pre-Teut. *bhļdó-s*, with the meaning 'bolt, dart'; yet no such word outside the Teut. group can be adduced. Belzen cannot be immediately akin to MidHG. *boln*, 'to throw, hurl,' since the Teut. *t* could not be explained as a deriv. from pre-Teut. *d*. But it is at least possible, on account of the great antiquity of the cognates, that they were borrowed from Lat. *catapulta* and remodelled.

Bombasin, m., 'bombasine,' ModHG. only, from Fr. *bombasin*, whence also E. *bombasine;* the original word is Lat.-Gr. *bombyx*, 'silkworm, silk.'

Bombast, m., borrowed in the 18th cent. from E. *bombast*, which is not cognate with τομπή, 'pomp, parade,' Fr. *pompe*; its orig. sense is 'cotton,' then 'padding,' and finally 'inflated language.' Its ultimate source is Lat. *bombyx*; comp. the preceding word.

Boot, n., 'boat,' ModHG. only (not found in Luther), borrowed from LG. *boot*; comp. the equiv. Du. *boot*, AS. *bát*, E. *boat*, OIc. *beitr*. This word, which is still unknown to the UpG. dialects, is at all events native to England, whence it made its way during the AS. period into OIc. (*bátr*), and in MidE. times to the Continent (Du. *boot*). The origin of AS. *bát*, OIc. *beitr*, has not been discovered; like many other nautical terms, this word too is first recorded in Eng. Moreover, the assumption that the word was borrowed in primit. Teut. times must be discarded.

Bord, m., 'board,' borrowed, like many other nautical expressions (see the preceding word), from LG. *Bord*, as a naval term, is found very early in AS., where it is explained by *tabula*; in HG. the word would end in *t*, as MidHG. and OHG. *bort* (gen. *bortes*), 'ship's side,' testify; besides Rand or Ramft is the more frequent term in UpG. for what is called *bord* in LG. E. *board* combines two quite different words; the one, AS. *bord*, signifies lit. 'board, plank' (Goth. *fótubaúrd*, 'footboard,' to which Du. *dambord*, 'draughtboard,' is allied), and is primit. cognate with HG. Brett; the other means only 'edge.' See Bort and Brett.

Börde, f. (the Börde of Soest), 'fertile plain, plain bordering on a river'; from LG. *börde*, MidLG. *gebörde*, 'department,' prop. 'propriety,' corresponding in form to OHG. *giburida*.

Bordell, n., 'brothel,' ModHG. only, from Fr. *bordel* (whence also E. *bordel* and *brothel*), a Rom. deriv. from Ger. Bort, 'board,' and meaning orig. 'a hut.'

bordieren, vb., 'to border (a dress),' from Fr. *border*, which comes from Ger. Borte.

Boretsch, Borretsch, m., 'borage,' from the equiv. Fr. *bourrache* (comp. Ital. *borragine*), whence also the E. term.

borgen, vb., 'to borrow, lend,' from MidHG. *borgen*, OHG. *borgên*, orig. 'to watch over, spare a person,' then 'to remit him his debt, to borrow'; also 'to be surety for something'; similarly AS. *borgian*, 'to protect' and 'to borrow,' E. *to borrow*. Since the meaning 'to watch over' underlies both bergen, 'to borrow,' and bürgen, 'to be responsible,' the word may be compared with OBulg. *brĕgą*, 'I take care of.' The root may have been Teut. *borg-*, pre-Teut. *bhergh-*; perhaps bergen is to be connected with the same root.

Borke, f., 'bark,' a LG. loan-word, which is not found in UpG. The proper HG. is Rinde. Comp. LG. *barke*, Eng. and Dan. *bark*, OIc. *bǫrkr*, 'bark'; Goth. **barkus* is not recorded. Its connection with bergen (in the sense of 'concealing') may be possible as far as its form is concerned; but on account of Sans. *bhûrja*, m. 'birch,' n. 'birch-bark,' its relation to Birke is more probable.

Born, m., 'fountain,' LG. form for HG. Brunnen.

Börse, f., from MidHG. *burse*, 'purse, small bag,' also 'a number of persons living together,' OHG. *burissa*, 'pocket.' Comp. Du. *beurs*; of Rom. origin (Fr. *bourse*, Ital. *borsa*); the Rom. class is derived finally from Gr. βύρσα, 'hide.' This word supplanted an OTeut. term which shows a similar development of meaning—OIc. *pungr*, 'leather bottle, scrotum, purse,' Goth. *puggs*, OHG. *scazpfung*, 'purse.'

Borst, m., 'burst, chink,' from bersten.

Borste, f., 'bristle,' from the equiv. MidHG. *borste*, f., *bürst*, *borst*, m., n., OHG. *burst*, m., n.; comp. AS. *byrst*, and with a suffix *l*, *brystl*, E. *bristle*; Goth. **baúrstus* or **baúrsts*, f., is not recorded. *Bors-* is the Teut. form of the root; comp. further E. *bur*, from AS. **burr* (for **burzu-*, properly 'bristly'). Pre-Teut. *bhers-* shows itself in OInd. *bhrṣ-ṭi-*, 'point, prong, corner'; also in Lat. *fastigium*, 'extreme edge'?. Comp. Bürste.

Bort, n., 'board,' from the equiv. MidHG. *bort*; comp. Goth. *fótubaúrd*, 'footstool,' OSax. and Du. *bord*, AS. *bord*, 'board, shield, table,' E. *board* (see Bord). The OTeut. word *bord* meant the same as Brett, to which it is related by gradation; the apparent metathesis of *re* to *or* is OTeut., as in forschen in relation to fragen; Brett, Bort may be represented in Ind. as *brádhas*, *brdhas*. See Brett.

Borte, f., 'ribbon or trimming of gold thread and silk,' the earlier meaning is simply 'border'; MidHG. *borte*, 'border, frame, ribbon, lace' (comp. further the cognate Bord), OHG. *borto*, 'seam, trimming' (whence Ital. *bordo*, 'border, frame,' Fr. *bord*).

böfe, adj., from the equiv. MidHG. bæse, OHG. bôsi, 'bad, useless, slanderous.' A word peculiar to Germ., not found in the other dialects; the primary meaning, judging from OHG. bôsa, 'buffoonery,' bôsân, 'to vilify,' was probably 'speaking malevolently.' If -si- were regarded as a suffix, Gr. φαῦλος (perhaps for φαῦσ-λος), with the evolution of meaning 'trifling, bad, wicked,' would be connected with böſe.

Böſewicht, m., 'villain, scamp,' from MidHG. bæsewiht, OHG. bôsiwiht. See Wicht.

Bosheit, 'malice,' from MidHG. and OHG. bôsheit, without mutation, because i, the cause of the mutation, was soon syncopated. Empören is not cognate.

boſſeln (1.), vb., 'to play at skittles'; allied to MidHG. bôzen (without the deriv. l), 'to strike' and 'to play at skittles.' See Amboß and Beutel.

boſſeln (2.), vb., 'to work in relief,' from Fr. bosseler, whence also E. to emboss.

Bote, m., 'messenger,' from the equiv. MidHG. bote, OHG. boto; comp. OLG. and ODu. bodo, AS. boda, 'messenger.' To this Botſchaft, from MidHG. boteschaft, botschaft, OHG. botoscaft, botascaf (OSax. bodscepi, AS. bodscipe), is related. See Schaft. Bote (Goth. *buda) is the name of the agent, from the root bud, Aryan bhudh, appearing in bieten.

Böttcher, m., 'cooper,' name of the agent, from the following word.

Bottich, m., 'tub, vat,' from the equiv. MidHG. botech, boteche, m, OHG. botahha, f.; it is probably related to the cognates of Bütte; comp. further AS. bodig, E. body, OHG. budeming, perhaps also ModHG. Beten ?. Considering the deriv. of Mod HG. Biſchof from episcopus, we may assume that Bottich is allied to Lat.-Gr. apotheca; comp. Ital. bottega (Fr. boutique).

Bowle, f., from the equiv. E. bowl. See Bolle (2.).

boxen, vb., ModHG. only, from the equiv. E. to box.

brach, adj. (espec. in compounds such as Brachfeld, &c.), 'uncultivated, fallow,' merely ModHG. In MidHG. there is only the compound brâchmânôt, 'June,' which contains a subst. brâche, f., OHG. brâhha (MidLG. brâke), 'aratio prima,' as its first component; Brache is 'turning up the soil after harvest'; from brechen.

Brach, n., 'refuse, trash,' from Mid LG. brak, 'infirmity, defect,' properly 'breach'; comp. E. brack ('breach, flaw'). See brechen.

Brache, m., 'setter, beagle,' from the equiv. MidHG. and MidLG. bracke, OHG. braccho; scarcely akin to AS. ræcc, E. rach ('setter'), and OIc. rakke; in this case the initial b of the Ger. word would be equal to bi (see be, bri), which is improbable. E. brach ('setter, beagle'), from MidE. brache, is derived from OFr. brache, which, with its Rom. cognates (comp. Ital. bracco, Fr. braque, brachet), is of Ger. origin. If we must assume Goth. *brakka-, the word, on account of the meaning 'hound,' might be connected with Lat. fragrare, 'to smell strongly.'

Brachwaſſer, n., 'brackish water,' first occurs in ModHG., from LG. brakwater, comp. Du. brakwater; to this E. brack ('salt'), Du. brack, 'salty,' are allied; E. brackish water.

Brägen, m., 'brain' (LG.), from Mid LG. bregen, equiv. to Du. brein, E. brain, AS. brægen; no other related words are known.

Bram, see Brembeere, verbrämen.

Bramſegel, n., 'gallant-sail'; Bramſtange, f., 'gallant-mast,' ModHG. only; of Du. origin; comp. Du. bramzeil, with the same meaning.

Brand, m., 'fire, conflagration, mortification, blight,' from the equiv. MidHG. brant(d), OHG. brant, m.; comp. AS. brand, E. brand, OIc. brandr, 'brand, resinous wood'; from brennen. The root is bren (from the Germ., the Rom. cognates Ital. brando, 'sword,' Fr. brandon, 'torch,' are derived). Brandmarken, 'to burn in a mark,' first occurs in ModHG.

branden, vb., 'to surge,' ModHG. only, from LG. and Du. branden, which is connected with Brand, and means lit. 'to blaze, to move like flames'; from this Brandung is formed.

Brander, m., ModHG. only, from the equiv. Du. brander, 'a ship filled with combustibles for setting the vessels of the enemy on fire, fireship.'

Brahne, f., 'outskirts of a wood.' See verbrämen.

Braſſe, f., 'rope at the end of the sailyards, brace,' first occurs in ModHG., from Du. bras, Fr. bras (from brachium), properly 'arm,' then 'a brace (on a yard).' Braſſen, 'to brace, swing the yards of a ship,' is Du. brassen, from Fr. brasser; comp. also E. brace ('a yard rope'), of the same origin.

Braffen, m., 'bream,' from the equiv. MidHG. *brahsen, brasem,* OHG. *brahsa, brahsima, brahsina,* m., f.; the UpG. dialects still preserve the form Brachsme (the forms Brasse, f., Brassen, m., are Mid LG. and MidGer.). Comp. the equiv. Du. *brasem,* E. *brasse.* From OGer. is derived Fr. *brême* (from *brahsme*?), whence E. *bream* is borrowed. The class belongs perhaps to an OTeut. str. vb. *brëhwan,* 'to shine.'

Braten, m., 'roast-meat,' from MidHG. *bráte,* OHG. *bráto,* m.; in the earlier periods of the language the word has the general meaning 'tender parts of the body, flesh,' but in MidHG. the modern meaning is also apparent. To this AS. *bræde,* 'roast-meat,' is allied. Comp. the following word.

braten, vb., 'to roast, broil, fry,' from the equiv. MidHG. *bráten,* OHG. *brátan;* comp. Du. *braden,* AS. *brǽdan,* 'to roast'; a Goth. str. vb. **brédan* is to be assumed. The root may have been a pre-Teut. *bhrédh* or *bhrēt;* in support of the latter we may perhaps adduce OHG. *brádam,* quoted under Brodem. Brüten (Goth. **brôdjan*) might also be assigned to the same root. The pre-Teut. *bhrédh* is also indicated by Gr. πρήθω (if it stands for φρήθω?), 'to consume, set on fire' (chiefly in combination with πυρί). See also Wildpret.

brauchen, vb., 'to use, need, want, require,' from the equiv. MidHG. *brûchen,* OHG. *brûhhan;* comp. the corresponding AS. *brûcan,* 'to enjoy,' also 'to digest, tolerate,' E. *to brook;* Goth. **brûkjan,* 'to use, enjoy.' Not found orig. in Scand. The pre-Teut. form of the root *bhrûg* accords with Lat. *fruor,* which originated in **fruvor* for **frugvor;* the Lat. partic. *fructus,* which phonetically is identical with gebraucht and Goth. *brûhts,* shows the final guttural of the root, and so does Lat. *fruges,* &c. The following are Teut. noun forms from the root *brûk (bhrûg)*: ModHG. Brauch, m. (comp. OHG. *brûh*), Goth. *brûks,* AS. *brýce,* OHG. *brûchi,* 'serviceable, useful.'

Braue, f., 'eyebrow,' from the equiv. MidHG. *brâ, brâwe,* OHG. *brâwa,* f.; a pre-Teut. and more remotely old Aryan word, which was perhaps **brêwa* in Goth. The OGall. and Kelt. *briva,* identical with this word, signifies 'bridge,' and is especially important as proving the connection between these cognates and those of Brücke. OHG. *brâwa* (Aryan *bhrêwâ*) is related by gradation to Aryan *bhrû,* which is proved by AS. *brû,* E. *brow,* OSlov. *brŭvĭ,* Sans. *bhrû,* Gr. ὀ-φρύς. Comp. further OIc. *brú,* OLG. *brâha* (for *brâwa*), AS. *brǽw,* m., and also perhaps Lat. *frons,* 'forehead.' A widely diffused Aryan root. The ModHG. Braune has added to the stem the suffix *n,* which belonged to the declension of the weak form Braue (comp. Biene); similarly OIc. *brûn,* corresponding to AS. *brû,* was formed from *brû* and the *n* of the weak declension (in AS. the gen. plur. is *brûna*). Braue, like the names of many limbs and parts of the body (see Fuß, Niere, Herz, Leber, Nase), originated in the primit. Aryan period. The orig. meaning, however, of the primit. Aryan *bhrû-s* ('(eye)-brow,' is as difficult to discover as that of Herz. See also Brücke.

brauen, vb., 'to brew,' from the equiv. MidHG. *brûwen, briuwen,* OHG. *briuwan;* comp. the corresponding OIc. *brugga,* Du. *brouwen,* AS. *breôwan,* E. *to brew.* To the OTeut. root *bru* (from Aryan *bhru-, bhrēw*), 'to brew,' which may be inferred from these verbs, belongs Phryg.-Thrac. βρῦτος, 'beer, cider,' which perhaps stands for Gr. **φρῦτον,* also Lat. *defrūtum,* 'must boiled down,' OIr. *bruthe,* 'broth,' *bruth,* 'live coals, heat,' *bruith,* 'cooking.' It is shown, moreover, under Brod that the meaning of the root *bhru-* was at one time more general; comp. further Brodeln. On account of the gutturals, Gr. φρύγω, Lat. *frigo,* cannot be cognates. Comp. also Broden, Brod.

braun, adj., 'brown,' from MidHG. *brûn,* 'brown, dark-coloured, shining, sparkling,' OHG. *brûn;* comp. the corresponding Du. *bruin,* AS. *brûn,* E. *brown,* OIc. *brúnn.* This Teut. term passed into Rom. (comp. the cognates of Ital. *bruno,* Fr. *brun;* see Blond); hence also Lith. *brunas,* 'brown.' The proper stem of Aryan *bhr-âna-,* appears in Lith. *beras,* 'brown' (comp. Bär), and reduplicated in OInd. *babhru-s,* 'reddish brown, bay' (this form of the adj. being apparently a common Aryan term for a brownish mammal living in water; comp. Biber); hence it may be right to assign Gr. φρύνη, φρῦνος, 'toad,' to this root. Respecting Braun as a name for the bear, see Bär.—**Braune,** f., from MidHG. *briune,* 'brownness,' related to braun (as a malady, 'brownish inflammation of the windpipe').

Braus, m., from the equiv. MidHG. *brûs,* 'noise, tumult'; perhaps cognate with

AS. *brýsan*, E. *to bruise.*—**braufen,** vb., 'to roar, bluster,' from the equiv. MidHG. *brûsen*; comp. Du. *bruisen*, 'to bluster,' from *bruis*, 'foam, froth'; to this **Braufe,** f., 'watering-pot,' also belongs.

Braufche, f., 'bump, bruise,' from Mid HG. *brûsche*, 'a swelling with blood underneath'; to this E. *brisket* and OIc. *brjósk*, 'gristle,' are allied. The stem common to all these must have meant 'roundish elevation.'

Braut, f., 'bride, betrothed,' from the equiv. MidHG. *brût*, OHG. *brût*, f. Goth. *brûþs* (stem *brû-di-*) means 'daughter-in-law'; from this comes *brûþ-faþs*, 'lord of the bride' (*faþs* corresponds to Gr. πόσις, which stands, as πότνια indicates, for πότις, corresponding to OInd. *patis*, 'lord'), i.e. 'bridegroom.' The MidHG. *brût* signifies 'the young, newly married woman'; the borrowed ModFr. *bru*, earlier *bruy*, is, on account of its meaning, connected most closely with Goth. *brûþs*, 'daughter-in-law'; comp. νύμφη, 'betrothed, bride, daughter-in-law.' In Eng. we may compare AS. *brýd*, 'betrothed,' E. *bride*, which are primit. allied to the Germ.; comp. also E. *bridal*, from AS. *brýd-ealo*, hence orig. 'bride-ale.' E. *bridegroom* is based upon E. *groom*, and represents AS. *brýdguma*, the second component of which is Goth. *guma*, 'man,' corresponding to Lat. *homo* (primary form *ghomon*). The ModHG. **Bräutigam** is identical in etymology with the AS. word; comp. OHG. *brûtigomo*, Mid HG. *briutegome*, in which the first part is properly gen. sing. (comp. **Nachtigall**). The Teut. root form *brûdi-* has not yet been explained etymologically; it is a word peculiar to Teut., like **Weib** and **Frau.** Goth. *qino*, 'woman,' MidHG. *kone*, are based on an ancient form; comp. Gr. γυνή, Sans. *gnâ*, 'woman.'

brav, adj., 'excellent, manly, brave,' ModHG. only, from Fr. *brave*, the origin of which is not established (from Lat. *barbarus*?).

brechen, vb., 'to break,' from the equiv. MidHG. *brëchen*, OHG. *brëhhan*; comp. the corresponding Goth. *brikan*, OLG. and AS. *brecan*, E. *to break*, Du. *breken*, 'to break.' From a root *brek* common to Teut., which is derived from pre-Teut. *bhreg*; comp. Lat. *frangere*, the nasal of which is wanting in *frêg-i*. The ModHG. **Brachfeld, Bruch, Breden,** are formed by gradation from the same root.

Bregen, see **Brägen.**

Brei, m., 'broth, pottage,' from the equiv. MidHG. *brî*, *brîe*. m., OHG. *brîo*, m., allied to Du. *brij*, AS. *brîw*, 'pottage'; Goth. *breiwa- (Goth. *breiws is related to OHG. *brîo* in the same way as Goth. *saiws* to OHG. *séo*). It is hardly possible that the word is connected with the root *brû*, discussed under **brauen.** Did a root *brî*, 'to cook,' exist? comp. OIc. *brîme*, 'fire.' Gr. φρίσσω (root φρίκ) has been suggested.

breit, adj., 'broad, wide,' from the equiv. MidHG. and OHG. *breit*; it corresponds to OSax. *bréd*, Du. *breed*, AS. *brád*, E. *broad*, Goth. *braiþs*, 'broad.' Probably from pre-Teut. *mraitô-*, akin to the root *mrit* preserved in Sans., 'to fall to pieces' (properly 'to extend'?).

Breme, 'edge, border.' See **verbrämen.**

Breme, Bremfe, f., 'gadfly.' Comp. MidHG. *brëme*, *brëm*, OHG. *brëmo*, 'gadfly.' **Bremfe** is LG. for HG. **Breme**; comp. OLG. *brimissa*, AS. *brimse*, MidE. *brimse*. OHG. *brëmo* would be in Goth. *brima, m., **Bremfe,** Goth. *brimisi, f. Yet E. *breeze* (horsefly) cannot be cognate, since *breósa* (and not *brimes*) is its AS. form. The root of **Bremfe,** discussed under **brummen,** is *brem* (pre-Teut. *bhrem*, Lat. *fremere*), 'to buzz, hum,' whence also Sans. *bhramara*, m., 'bee.'

Bremfe, f., 'drag-shoe,' from MidHG. *brëmse*, f., 'barnacle, muzzle.' It cannot be identified with **Bremfe,** 'gadfly' (see **Breme**), because the latter indicates a Goth. *brimisi*, while **Bremfe,** 'drag-shoe,' points to a Goth. *bramisjô*. For **Bremfe,** 'drag,' dialectal forms such as *bram* (with *a* and the loss of the suffix *s*) have been authenticated, but of a root *bram* with some such meaning as 'to press, squeeze,' there is no trace. The suffix *s* recalls Goth. *jukuzi*, 'yoke,' from the equiv. *juk*; comp. also *aqizi*, 'axe.'

brennen, vb., 'to burn, scorch, sting, distill'; it combines the meanings of Mid HG. *brinnen*, str. vb., 'to burn, give light, shine, glow,' and its factitive *brennen*, wk. vb., 'to set fire to, cause to burn'; the former is Goth., OHG. and OLG. *brinnan*, 'to burn' (intrans.), the latter Goth. *brannjan*, 'to set fire to.' Comp. AS. *biernan* (intrans.), *bærnan*, *bernan* (trans.). E. *to burn*, is trans. and intrans., like the ModHG. word. Under **Brand** attention is called to the fact that only one *n* of the Goth. verb. *brinnan* belongs to the root; the second *n* is a suffix of the present tense (comp. also rinnen, rennen); the form with simple n is seen in AS. *bryne*, 'conflagration' (from *bruni*). A root *bren-*, pre-Teut. *bhren*, with the meaning 'to burn,' has not yet been authenticated in the other Aryan languages.

brenzeln, vb., 'to taste burnt,' first occurs in ModHG. a frequentative form of brennen.

Bresche, f., 'breach, gap,' ModHG. only, from Fr. *brèche*, whence also the equiv. Du. *bres*. The Fr. word is usually traced back to the OG. stem of brechen.

Brett, n., 'board, plank, shelf, counter,' from the equiv. MidHG. *brët*, OHG. *brët*, n.; corresponds to AS. *brëd*, n.; Goth. **brid*, n. It has been shown under Bort, 'board,' that the OTeut. word for Brett had two stems, primarily identical and separated only by gradation, viz., *bredo-* and *bordo-*, whose connection might be represented thus: Ind. *bradhas* is related to *bṛdhas*, as Aryan *bhrédhos* is to *bhṛdhós*, n.; MidHG. *brët* combines the meanings 'board, shield,' &c., like AS. *bord*; see also Kerb.

Bretzel, m., f., 'cracknell,' from the equiv. MidHG. *brëzel*, also *breze*, OHG. *brezitella* and *brezita* (*bergita*); allied to Bav. *die bretzen*, Suab. *brützg, brätzet*, Alsat. *brestell*. The Suab. form as well as OHG. *brizilla* presupposes a Teut. *ë*; but the vowel sounds of the remaining forms are uncertain. It is most frequently referred to MidLat. *brácëllum* (whence *brázil*, and by mutation *brëzil*?), or rather *bráchiólum*, 'little arm' (the different kinds of pastry are named from their shape; comp. e.g. Mid HG. *krápfe*, 'hook, hook-shaped pastry'); MidHG. *brazte* would be *bráchitum*. From OHG. *brézitella* the ModHG. Bretstelle (Strassb.) was produced, while *brezitella* was resolved by a wrong division of syllables into Bret-stelle; thus we deduce in Mod HG. Tapfe from Fußtapfe, i.e. Fuß-stapfe. The absence of the word in Rom. (yet comp. Ital. *bracciatello*) seems to militate against the derivation of the whole of this class from Lat. *bracchium*. In that case OHG. *bergita, brezita*, might perhaps be connected with AS. *byrgan*, 'to eat,' OIr. *bargen*, 'cake.'

Brief, m., 'letter, epistle,' from MidHG. *brief*, OHG. *brief*, m.; from Lat. *brëvis* (scil. *libellus*); the lengthened *ë* from *ĭ* in words borrowed from Lat. becomes *ea* and then *ie* (comp. Priester); Lat. *brevis* and *breve*, 'note, document.' The HG. word had originally a more general signification,

'document,' hence the ModHG. verdrießen. MidHG. and OHG. *brief*, 'letter, document,' and generally 'a writing.' When the OTeut. Runic characters were exchanged for the more convenient Roman letters (see schreiben as well as Buch), the Germans adopted some terms connected with writing; OHG. *briaf* appears in the 9th cent. (the Goth. word is *bōka*, 'document').

Brille, f., 'spectacles,' from late Mid HG. *barille, berille, brille*, 'spectacles' (Du. *bril*); properly the gem Lat.-Gr. *beryllus* (the syncope of the unaccented *e* is amply attested by bange, bleiten, glauben, &c.); comp. Beryll.

bringen, vb., 'to bring, accompany,' from the equiv. MidHG. *bringen*, OHG. *bringan*; comp. OSax. *brengian*, Du. *brengen*, AS. *bringan*, E. *to bring*, Goth. *briggan, bringan*, 'to bring.' The Aryan form of this specially Teut. word, which is wanting only in OIc., would be *bhrengh* (*bhrenk*?); no cognates are recorded.

Brink, m., 'grassy hillock, green sward,' from LG. *brink*, comp. OIc. *brekka* (from **brinkô*), f., both meaning 'hill'; akin to E. *brink*, and OIc. *bringa*, 'mead.'

brinnen, see brennen.

Brise, f., from the equiv. E. *breeze* (whence also Fr. *brise*?).

Brocke, Brocken, m., 'crumb,' from the equiv. MidHG. *brocke*, OHG. *broccho*, m.; Goth. **brukka*, m., for which *gabruka*, f., occurs: formed by gradation from brechen (comp. Trette from treten); derivatives bröckeln, bröcklig.

Brockperle, f., 'rough pearl,' ModHG. only, from Fr. *baroque*, Port. *barocco* (Span. *barueco*), 'oval.'

brodeln, brudeln, vb., 'to bubble,' from MidHG. *brodeln*, vb.; hence MidHG. *aschenbrodele*, 'scullion,' from which Aschenbrödel, 'Cinderella,' comes. See Bret.

Brodem, m., 'fume, exhalation,' from MidHG. *brādem*, m., 'vapour,' OHG. *brā-dam*, 'vapour, breath, heat.' AS. *bráþ*, 'vapour, breath, wind,' E. *breath*, are perhaps cognate, so too ModHG. braten?.

Brombeere, f., 'blackberry,' from the equiv. MidHG. *brâmber*, OHG. *brâmberi*; lit. 'bramble-berry,' OHG. *brâmo*, Mid HG. *brâme* (also 'briar' generally), Akin to AS. *brôm*, E. *broom* (ModHG. Bram, 'broom for besoms'; AS. *brêmel*, 'thorny plant,' E. *bramble*, Du. *braam*, 'bramble-bush,' whence Fr. *framboise*.

Brosam, m., **Brosame**, f., 'crumb';

connected instinctively by Germans with **Fret** and **Samen**; comp., however, Mid HG. *brôsem, brôsme*, OHG. *brôsma*, OLG. *brôsmo*, 'crumb, fragment' (Goth. **brausma*, 'crumb,' is not recorded). It is related either to the Teut. root *brut*, which appears in AS. *breótan*, 'to break,' or to AS. *brysan*, OFr. *bruiser* (E. *to bruise*), from a Kelt.-Teut. root *brûs*, which the UpGerm. dialects preserve in *bröfeln*, 'to crumble' (whence, too, OSlov. *brŭsclŭ*, 'sherd,' *brŭsnąti*, 'to wipe off, rub off').

Bröschen, n., 'sweetbread,' first occurs in ModHG., from LG.; comp. Dan. *bryske*, E. *brisket*. See **Braufche**.

Brot, n., 'bread, food, loaf,' from the equiv. MidHG. *brôt*, OHG. *brôt*, n. The form with *t* is strictly UpGer.; comp. LG. *brôd*, Du. *brood*, AS. *breád*, E. *bread*, OIc. *brauð*. The old inherited form for **Bret** was **Laib** (Goth. *hlaifs*); and ancient compounds like AS. *hláford* (for **hláfward*), 'loafward, bread-giver,' E. *lord*, preserve the OTeut. word (see **Laib**), in addition to which a new word peculiar to Teut. was formed from a Teut. root. To this root, which appears in **brauen**, we must assign the earlier and wider meaning of 'to prepare by heat or fire'; comp. AS. and E. *broth* (Ital. *broda*, 'broth,' is of Teut. origin) and **brodeln**. In **Bret** it would have the special signification 'to bake.' There is a strange OTeut. compound of **Bret**-, MidHG. *bî-brôt*, ModHG. **Bienenbrot**, AS. *beóbreád*, E. *beebread*, all of which signify 'honeycomb,' lit. 'bread of bees'; in this compound the word **Bret** appears, singularly enough, for the first time. In earlier AS. the modern meaning, 'bread,' is still wanting, but it is found even in OHG.

Bruch (1.), m., 'breach, rupture, crack,' from MidHG. *bruch*, OHG. *bruh*, m.; formed by gradation from **brechen**.

Bruch (2.), m., n., 'damp meadow, marsh, bog,' a Franc.-Sax. word from Mid HG. *bruoch*, OHG. *bruoh(hh)*, n. m., 'marshy soil, swamp'; comp. LG. *brôk*, Du. *broek*, 'marsh-land,' AS. *brôk*, 'brook, current, river,' E. *brook*. Similarly MidHG. *ouwe* combines the meanings of 'water-stream, watery land, island.' It is possible that WestTeut. **broka-* is allied to **brechen**, a supposition that has been put forward on account of the AS. meaning 'torrent'; in that case the OHG. sense 'swamp' would be based upon 'a place where water gushes out.'

Bruch (3.), f., n., 'breeches,' from Mid HG. *bruoch*, OHG. *bruoh(hh)*, f., 'breeches covering the hip and upper part of the thigh' (akin to AS. *brêc*, E. *breech*); comp. the corresponding AS. *brêc*, plur. *brêc*, E. *breeches*, MidLG. *brôk*, Du. *broek*, OIc. *brôk*, 'breeches.' It has been asserted that the common Teut. *brôk-* has been borrowed from the equiv. Gall.-Lat. *bráca* (likewise Rom., comp. Ital. *brache*, Fr. *braies*); but AS. *brêc*, 'rump,' shows that **Bruch** contains a Teut. stem; hence the Gall.-Lat. word is more likely borrowed from Teut.; comp. **Hemb**.

Brücke, f., 'bridge,' from the equiv. MidHG. *brücke*, OHG. *brucka*, f., which points to Goth. **brugjô*, f.; comp. Du. *brug*, AS. *bryrg*, E. *bridge*. Besides the meaning 'bridge,' common to WestTeut., the OIc. *bryggja* (likewise LG. *brügge*) is used in the sense of 'landing-place, pier,' while *brú* (equal to ModHG. **Braue**) is the proper Scand. word for 'bridge.' **Brücke** (from **brugjô-*) is undoubtedly allied to OIc. *brú*; no common Aryan term for bridge can be found. OSlov. *brŭvĭ* also means both 'eyebrow' and 'bridge,' and OHG. *brâwa* (see under **Braue**) is identical with OGall. *briva*, 'bridge,' both of which point to Aryan *bhrêwâ*. With regard to the transition of **brawi* to **brugî*, see **Jugend**.

Bruder, m., 'brother, friar,' from the equiv. MidHG. *bruoder*, OHG. *bruodar*; comp. Goth. *brôþar*, AS. *brôþor*, E. *brother*, Du. *broeder*, OSax. *brôthar*. Inherited, like most words denoting kinship, from the period when all the Aryans formed only one tribe, without any difference of dialect; the degrees of relationship (comp. **Oheim**, **Better**, **Base**) at that period, which is separated by more than three thousand years from our era, were very fully developed. The primit. form of the word **Bruder** was *bhrâtô(r)*, nom. plur. *bhrâtores*; this is attested, according to the usual laws of sound, both by Goth.-Teut. *brôþar* and Lat. *fráter*, Gr. φράτηρ, OInd. *bhrâtar-*, OSlov. *bratrŭ*; all these words retain the old primary meaning, but in Gr. the word has assumed a political signification.

Brühe, f., from the equiv. MidHG. *brüeje*, 'broth, sauce.' The root of the word must not be sought in **brauen**, which is based upon *bru-*; *brü-je* would be in Goth. *brôja*, Teut. root *brô*, in MidE. *brêie*, MidDu. *broeye*. From the same stem Mid HG. **Brut** has been formed, with a dental suffix. The wk. vb. is **brühen**, MidHG.

brüejen, brüen, 'to scald, singe, burn'; comp. Du. broeijen, 'to warm, brood'; in earlier ModHG., too, brühen signifies 'to brood.' In spite of the meaning, the connection with Bruch is, on phonetic grounds, improbable.

Brühl, m., 'marshy copse,' from MidHG. brüel, m., 'low-land, marshy copse,' OHG. bruil; from Fr. breuil, Prov. bruelh, 'thicket'; of Kelt. origin (brogil).

brüllen, vb., 'to roar, bellow, low,' from the equiv. MidHG. brüelen; in UpG. dialects even now briele, brüele. The remarkable short ü of ModHG. compared with MidHG. üe may be explained by the pret. brüllte, where the shortness of the vowel is produced by the following double consonant; OHG. *bruowilôn is wanting; allied perhaps to E. brawl?. From the root brô ('to scald') in the sense of 'to bubble'?.

brummen, vb., 'to growl, snarl, grumble,' from MidHG. brummen, wk. vb., 'to growl, hum,' a deriv. of the MidHG. str. vb. brimmen, 'to growl, roar' (comp. the equiv. MidE. brimmen). This again is cognate with MidHG. brëmen, OHG. brëman, str. vb., 'to growl, roar,' since mm belongs properly only to the pres. and not to the other tenses. The cognates of the stem brëm-, which these verbs indicate, also includes OIc. brim, 'surge,' MidE. brim, 'glow' (E. brimstone); other related words may be found under Bremse. The Teut. root brem, pre-Teut. bhrēm, appears in Lat. fremere, 'to gnash,' with which some are fond of comparing Gr. βρέμειν, 'to rumble.' The OInd. bhram as a verbal stem signifies 'to move unsteadily'; bhramá, n., 'whirling flame,' bhrmí, m., 'whirlwind.' Hence the meaning 'to rush, gnash, crackle,' seems to have been developed from a vibrating motion, especially that of sound. See the following word.

Brunft, f., 'rutting-time,' from MidHG. brunft, f., 'fire, heat, rutting season of deer, cry.' The MidHG. brunft is of dual origin; in the sense of 'heat' it belongs to brennen, Brand. Brunft, 'the rutting season of deer,' was rightly connected, as early as Lessing, with brummen, since it "indicates the impulse of certain animals to copulation, that is to say, of those that roar or bellow in the act; ignorance and negligence have transformed this word into Brunst" (Lessing).

Brunn, Brunnen, Born, m., 'fountain, spring, well.' The form with the metathesis of the r is LG.; the first two are based upon MidHG. brunne, m., 'spring, spring-water, well'; OHG. brunno (beside which a form pfuzzi, 'well,' from Lat. puteus, appears in OHG.; comp. Pfütze). It is based upon an OTeut. word; Goth. brunna, 'spring,' AS. burna (for brunna), E. bourn ('brook'). Brunnen has been derived from brennen, for which a primary meaning 'to heave, seethe' (comp. MidHG. LG. sôt, 'well, draw-well') is assumed without proof. Gr. φρέαρ, 'well,' scarcely points to a root bhru, 'to heave, bubble' (cognate with brauen?); nn may be a suffix, as perhaps in ModHG. Sonne.

Brünne, f., recently borrowed from the equiv. MidHG. brünne (OHG. brunna), f., 'breastplate'; comp. Goth. brunjô (whence OFr. brunie), OIc. brynja, AS. byrne; not from brennen; the appellations 'glowing, shining,' scarcely suit the earlier leather breastplates. OIr. bruinne, 'breast,' is more probably allied. From Teut. are borrowed OFr. broigne and OSlov. brŭnja, 'coat of mail.'

Brunft, f., from the equiv. MidHG. brunst, f., 'burning, fire, glow, heat, devastation by fire' (Brunstzeit, see Brunst); OHG. brunst, Goth. brunsts. In Eng. this deriv. from the root of brennen is wanting (comp. Kunst from können); the s before the suffix t is due to the double n of the verb.

Bruft, f., 'breast, chest, pap,' from the equiv. MidHG. brust, OHG. brust, f.; it corresponds to Goth. brusts, a plur. noun (conson. stem), f., Du. and LG. borst. In the other OTeut. dialects the words corresponding exactly to Goth. brusts are wanting; they have a peculiar neut. form: AS. breóst, E. breast, OIc. brjóst, OSax. breost, which are related by gradation to HG. Bruft. This term for breast is restricted to the Teut. languages (including OIr. bruinne, 'breast'?), the individual members of the Aryan group differing in this instance from each other, while other parts of the body (see Bug) are designated by names common to all of them. Of the approximate primary meaning of Bruft, or rather of the idea underlying the word, we know nothing; the only probable fact is that the primitive stem was originally declined in the dual, or rather in the plural.

Bruf, f., 'brood, spawn, brats,' from MidHG. and OHG. bruot, f., 'vivified by warmth, brood, animation by warmth, brooding, heat'; comp. Du. broed, AS. brôd,

E. *brood.* The dental is deriv.; *brô*, as the root-syllable, is discussed under Brühe; the primary root signified 'to warm, heat.'— brüfen, 'to brood,' from MidHG. *brüeten*, OHG. *bruoten* (Goth. *brôdjan); comp. AS. *brêdan*, E. *to breed* (with the further signification 'to beget, bring up'). E. *bird*, AS. *bridd*, 'the young of birds, little bird.' are often incorrectly allied to brüten; AS. *bridd* would be in Goth. *bridi (plur. *bridja*), and consequently the connection of the E. word with HG. brüten (Goth. *brôdjan) becomes impossible. It is worth noticing that Du. *broeijen*, LG. *bræjen*, and ModHG. dial. brühen partake of the meaning of brüten. See brühen.

Bube, m., 'boy, lad, rogue, knave (at cards),' from MidHG. *buobe* (MidLG. *bôve*), m., 'boy, servant, disorderly person' (OHG. *buobo and Goth. *bôba are wanting); a primit. Ger. word, undoubtedly of great antiquity, though unrecorded in the various OTeut. periods (yet note the proper names identical with it, OHG. *Buobo*, AS. *Bôfa*). Comp. MidDu. *boeve*, Du. *boef* (E. *boy* is probably based upon a diminutive *bôfig, *bôfing). 'Young man, youth,' is manifestly the orig. sense of the word; comp. Bav. *bua*, 'lover,' Swiss *bua*, 'unmarried man.' To this word MidE. *babe*, E. *baby* are related by gradation; also Swiss, *bâbi, bæbi* (most frequently *tokχebâbi, tittibâbi*), 'childish person' (Zwingli —"Baben are effeminate, foolish youths"); akin to this is OHG. *Bubo*, a proper name. The OTeut. words *baho-bôbo* are probably terms expressing endearment (comp. Atti, Base, Muhme), since the same phonetic forms are also used similarly in other cases; comp. OSlov. *baba*, 'grandmother'; further, Ital. *babbéo*, 'ninny,' Prov. *babau*, 'fop' (late Lat. *baburrus*, 'foolish'), Ital. *babbole*, 'childish tricks.'

Buch, n., 'book, quire,' from the equiv. MidHG. *buoch*, OHG. *buoh*, n. It differs in gender and declension in the various OTeut. dialects: Goth. *bôka*, f., and *bôk*, n., f., signify 'letter (of the alphabet)' in the sing., but 'book, letter (epistle), document' in the plur.; akin to OSax. *bôk*, 'book,' Du. *boek*, AS. *bôc*, f., equiv. to E. *book*. The sing. denoted orig., as in Goth., the single character, the plur. a combination of characters, 'writing, type, book, letter'; comp. Goth. *afstassais bôkôs*, 'writing of divorcement'; *wadjabôkôs*, 'bond, handwriting'; *frabauhta bôka*, 'deed of sale.' The plur. was probably made into a sing. at a later period, so that ModHG. Buch signified lit. 'letters (of the alphabet).' The OTeut. word, which even on the adoption of Roman characters was not supplanted by a borrowed word (see Brief), made its way, like the word Buche, into Slav. at an early period; comp. OSlov. *buky*, 'beech, written character' (plur. *bukŭve*, 'book, epistle'). Buch was used in the earliest times for the runes scratched on the twigs of a fruit-tree (see reißen); hence it results from Tacitus (*Germania*, 10) that Buch (lit. 'letter') is connected with OHG. *buohha*, 'beech.' The same conclusion follows from the Ger. compound Buchstabe, which is based on an OTeut. word—OHG. *buohstab*, OSax. *bôcstaf*, AS. *bôcstæf* (but E. and Du. *letter*), OIc. *bôkstafr*. Undoubtedly the Germans instinctively connect Buchstabe with Buch and not with Buche. As far as the form is concerned, we are not compelled to accept either as the only correct and primit. Teut. word; both are possible. Historical facts, however, lead us to regard Buchstabe as Buchenstab. With the term Buchenstab the early Germans intimately combined the idea of the rune scratched upon it, and constituting its chief value. Comp. the following word and Rune.

Buche, f., 'beech, beech-tree,' from the equiv. MidHG. *buoche*, OHG. *buohha*; AS. *bôc-treów*, with the collateral form *béce* (from *boeciae*), E. *beech*. The form *bôc* has been preserved in E. *buckmast, buckwheat*; comp. OIc. *bôk*, Goth. *bôka, 'beech.' The name of the tree is derived from pre-Teut.; according to Lat. *fâgus*, 'beech,' and Gr. φᾱγός, φηγός, its Europ. form would be *bhâgos*. The Gr. word signifies 'edible oak.' This difference between the Gr. word on the one hand and the Teut.-Lat. on the other has been explained "by the change of vegetation, the succession of an oak and a beech period"; "the Teutons and the Italians witnessed the transition of the oak period to the beech period, and while the Greeks retained φηγός in its orig. signification, the former transferred the name as a general term to the new forests which grew in their native wastes." Comp. Eibe. Buche is properly 'the tree with edible fruit' (comp. Gr. φαγεῖν, 'to eat,' and φηγός), and hence perhaps the difference of meaning in Gr. may be explained from this general signification, so that the above hypothesis was not necessary.

Buchs, m., **Buchsbaum**, 'box, box-tree,' from the equiv. MidHG. and OHG. *buhsboum;* formed from Lat. *buxus*, Gr. πύξος; comp. Ital. *bosso*, Fr. *buis*, E. *box*.

Büchse, f., 'box, pot, jar, rifle,' from MidHG. *bühse*, 'box, magic-box, firelock'; OHG. *buhsa*, from *buhsja*, from Gr. πυξίς, 'a box of boxwood (πύξος), medicine-box.' The Gr. medical art was in vogue in the Middle Ages among all civilised nations, consequently some Gr. medical terms found their way into German. See Arzt, Pflaster. Comp. AS. and E. *box*, Ital. *bossolo*, Fr. *bossette*, 'box.'

Bucht, f., 'bay,' first occurs in ModHG., from LG. *bucht;* comp. Du. *bogt*, E. *bought* (from MidE. *boghti*), 'a twist, bend,' and E. *bight* (from AS. *byht*); properly a verbal abstract from biegen.

Buckel (1.), m., 'boss, stud,' from MidHG. *buckel*, m., f., 'boss of a shield'; from OFr. *bocle* (whence Fr. *boucle*, 'buckle'), which is based on Lat. *buccula*, 'beaver of a helmet, boss.'

Buckel (2.), **Puckel**, m., 'back, hump,' from MidHG. *buckel*. The Swiss *bukel* (not *buxel*) points to a primary form *bugg-* (see biegen, Bühel, Bügel), not directly to bücken, from biegen (root *bug*). Buckel is lit. 'a curve, bend.'

Bücken, vb., 'to stoop, bow,' from MidHG. *bücken*, 'to bend, bow'; frequentative of biegen, like schmücken of schmiegen. The Swiss *bukχe* points to OHG. *bucchen* (Swiss *buckχ*, 'bend'); comp. LG. *bucken*, 'to stoop.' See Buckel.

Bückling, m., 'bloater' (also **Bückling**, based on **Bückling**, 'bow,' from biegen), from the equiv. MidHG. and MidLG. *bückinc;* comp. Du. *bokking*, which is probably a deriv. of Bock, Du. *bok*, 'hircus'; in fact, the fish is also called *boxhorn* (*bockshorn*) in MidDu.

Bude, f., 'booth, stall, shop,' from MidHG. *buode*, f., 'hut, tent'; corresponds to MidE. *bōþe*, 'taberna,' E. *booth*; OIc. *búð*, f., 'dwelling, hut, tent,' has a different vowel, and is based on the widely diffused root *bū-bhū*, 'to dwell, stay.' By a different derivation E. *to bui-ld*, AS. *bold*, *botl*, 'dwelling,' OFris. *bold*, OIc. *ból*, OLG. *bodal*, are produced from the same root. So too OIr. *both* (*bothán*), 'hut,' from *bu-to*, as well as the words discussed under bauen. Lith.-Slav. *buda*, 'booth,' and Bohem. and Silesian Baude, 'shepherd's hut,' are borrowed.

Büffel, m., 'buffalo, boor, buff (leather),' from MidHG. *büffel*, m., 'ox'; borrowed from Fr. *bufle*, Lat. *bubalus*, Gr. βούβαλος; hence also E. *buff*.

Bug, m., 'bend, flexure, hock, bow (of a ship),' from MidHG. *buoc(g)*, OHG. *buog*, m., 'upper joint of the arm, shoulder, upper joint of the leg, hip, hock'; comp. Du. *boeg*, 'ship's bow'; AS. *bóg*, *bóh*, 'armus, ramus,' E. *bough* ('the joint of a tree,' as it were). The Goth. word may have been *bôgus* (from pre-Teut. *bhâghú-s*); comp. Sans. *báhus* (for *bhâghú-s*), 'arm, fore-arm, fore-feet,' also Gr. πᾶχυς, πῆχυς (for φᾶχυς), 'elbow, fore-arm, bend of the arm,' Armen. *bazuk*, 'arm.' On account of the Aryan base *bhâghú-s* the derivation of ModHG. Bug from biegen (root *bug*, pre-Teut. *bhuk*), is impossible. The ancient terms for parts of the body, such as Arm, Bug, Herz, Nase, Niere, &c., are based upon obscure roots, of which we find no further trace anywhere; they belong, in fact, to the most primitive vocabulary of Aryan speech.—**Bugspriet**, n., from the equiv. Du. *boegspriet;* comp. the equiv. MidE. *bousprět*, E. *bowsprit* (Fr. *beaupré*).

Bügel, m., 'curve, arc, guard (of a gun),' ModHG. only, derived from biegen (OTeut. *baug*, 'ring,' corresponding to Hügel from OTeut. *haug*); comp. Du. *beugel*, 'hoop, stirrup.'

Bühel, **Bühl**, m., from the equiv. MidHG. *bühel*, OHG. *buil*, *buhil*, m., 'hill'; it is probably rightly referred to the Aryan root *bhûk*, *bhûg*, 'to bend.' See biegen and Buckel.

Buhle, m., 'lover, paramour,' from MidHG. *buole*, m., 'near relative, lover, sweetheart'; likewise MidHG. *buole*, f., 'lady-love' (OHG. *Buolo*, m., as a masculine name only); the implied correspondences in the cognate Teut. dialects are not recorded. It is scarcely disputable, however, that a primit. Germ. word lies at the base of Buhle. Since Bube in UpGerm. dialects signifies 'lover' also, it is perhaps connected with Buhle, which may be a term of endearment formed from it.

Bühne, f., 'stage, gallery, orchestra,' from MidHG. *büne, bün*, f., 'ceiling of a room (a meaning still preserved in Swiss), board, lath'; the latter is at all events the primary meaning. Perhaps AS. *binn*, 'crib, box,' E. *bin*, are allied by gradation to MidHG. *büne*. The origin of the words has not yet been explained.

Bühre, f., 'bed-tick,' ModHG. only, from LG. büre; probably cognate with Fr. bure, 'coarse stuff.'

Bulge (Swiss, also **Bulgge**), f., 'leather water-pail,' from MidHG. bulge, OHG. bulga, 'leather bag'; MidE. and E. bilje, bulje, from *bylĕje. The cognates are allied to Balg (Goth. balgs, 'leather bottle, bag'), MidLat. bulga.

Bulle (1.), m., 'bull,' MidHG. only, from the equiv. LG. bulle; comp. Du. bul, bol, E. bull (in AS. only the deriv. bulluca, 'bullock,' appears); akin to OIc. bole, 'bull'; Lith. bullus is not a cognate; root bel in tellen ?.

Bulle (2.), f., 'bottle,' first occurs at a late period in ModHG., corrupted from buttel, Fr. bouteille.

Bulle (3.), f., 'bull, papal edict,' from MidHG. bulle, f., 'seal, document, bull' (AS. bulle, E. bull, ModFr. bulle). From Lat. bulla, lit. 'water bubble,' then 'boss, knob (on a door),' finally 'a ball attached as a seal to documents'; whence also Bill.

bumbsen, vb., 'to bounce,' ModHG. only; a recent onomatopoetic word.

bummeln, vb., 'to dangle,' simply Mod HG. from LG. bummeln; an onomatopoetic word of recent origin.

Bund, m., from the equiv. MidHG. bunt(d), 'bond, fetter, confederacy'; related to binden.

Bündel, n., 'bundle, parcel,' ModHG. only, though existing in AS. (byndel, E. bundle); related to binden. See the previous word.

bündig, adj., 'binding, valid, terse,' not from MidHG. bündec, 'firmly bound,' but formed from Du. bondig, 'binding, firm'; the latter word is akin to binden.

bunt, adj., 'gay, mottled, variegated,' a MidG. and LG. word (for which gefleckt, gesprenkelt, &c., are used in UpG.), from the equiv. MidHG. bunt (inflected bunter); nt shows that the word cannot have been handed down from OHG., for nt in OHG. would have become nd in MidHG. Akin to MidLG. bunt, MidDu. bont, also with -nt-. Bunt was borrowed in the MidHG. period; the MidHG. signification, 'with black spots on a white ground' (ModHG. bunt is Mid HG. missevar), supports the view that it was borrowed from MidLat. punctus, 'dotted, spotted' (for the loss of the medial c comp. Ital. punto, 'point,' as well as Tinte). In spite of this explanation the absence of the word in Rom. is remarkable. On account of the earlier reference to fur-skin (Mid HG. and MidLG. bunt, n., also signifies 'fur-skin'), MidLat. mus ponticus, 'ermine,' has been suggested, the meaning of which would suit excellently were there no objection to the form of the expression.

Bunzen, Bunzel, m., 'punch, stamp,' from MidHG. punze, 'burin, chisel'; the latter word is borrowed from Rom. (Ital. punzone, Fr. poinçon, Lat. punctionem), whence also E. punch, puncheon, puncher.

Bürde, f., 'burden, load,' from the equiv. MidHG. bürde, OHG. burdi, f.; it corresponds to Goth. baurþei, 'burden, load'; AS. byrþen, f., E. burthen, burden, have an n suffix; allied to OTeut. beran, 'to carry.' See Bahre.

Burg, f., 'stronghold, citadel, castle, fortified town,' from MidHG. burc(g), OHG. burg, buruc, f., 'enclosed, fortified place, stronghold, castle, town.' Comp. OSax. burg, Du. burg, AS. burh (plur. byrg), E. borough, bury, burrow (especially in compounds), Goth. baúrgs. In the OTeut. dialects Burg corresponded to the modern town. Ulfilas translated πόλις by baurgs. According to the Germania of Tacitus, the Teutons had no urbes, but their oppida were mentioned as early as Cæsar (De Bell. Gall.). With Gr. πύργος, 'tower,' the OTeut. Burg accords neither in form nor meaning. The OTeut. word appears strangely enough in Armen. as burgn, and in Arab. as burg, which probably owed their immediate origin to late Lat. burgus (whence the Rom. words Ital. borgo, Fr. bourg, 'market-town'; so too OIr. borg, 'town'). In this sense the word is solely Teut., and belongs with Berg to an Aryan bhṛgh-, which also appears in OIr. brí (gen. brig), 'mountain, hill,' but scarcely to the verbal stem of bergen. The words for 'town' were not formed until the separate Aryan tribes ceased their wanderings and became permanent settlers; comp. also Garten.

Bürge, m., 'surety, bail,' from the equiv. MidHG. bürge, OHG. burigo, m. We may assume a Goth *baúrgja, which would, however, be distinct from baúrgja, 'citizen.' OIc. á-byrgjast, ':o become bail.' Allied to bergen; the root is pre-Teut. bhergh, with the orig. sense 'to take care of, heed.'

Bursche, m., 'fellow, apprentice, student,' properly identical with ModHG. Börse, from MidHG. burse, f., 'purse, money-bag, society, house belonging to a society, especially to a students' society.' From the last meaning, prevalent in the 15th cent., the ModHG. acceptation of **Burſche** (*s* after *r* became *sch*, as in **Arſch**, **Hirſch**) was developed, just as perhaps **Frauenzimmer** from **Frauengemach**; comp. the existing phrase **altes Hans** among students, AS. *geogoð*, 'a company of young people,' similar to E. *youth*.

Bürſte, f., 'brush,' from MidHG. *bürste*, f., a deriv. of **Berſte**; the equiv. E. term is, however, of Rom. origin (Fr. *brosse*).

Burzel, m., 'purslane,' from MidHG. and OHG. *burzel*, corrupted from the corresponding Lat. *portulaca*.

Bürzel, m., 'hinder part of an animal, buttocks, brush (of a fox), scut,' &c.; Mod HG. only; allied to **burzeln**, *purzeln*?.

burzeln, vb., 'to tumble head over heels,' from the equiv. MidHG. *bürzen*, *burzeln*; the word cannot be traced farther back.

Buſch, m., 'bush, thicket, plume (of a helmet),' from MidHG. *busch, bosch*, OHG. *busc*, m., 'bush, shrubbery, thicket, wood, cluster'; comp. E. *bush*, Du. *bos*, 'cluster,' *bosch*, 'copse,' *bussel*, 'cluster.' There are similar forms in Rom., Ital. *bosco*, Fr. *bois*, which are traced back to a MidLat. *buscus, boscus*.—Allied to **Büſchel**, 'cluster,' from MidHG. *büschel*, m.

Büſe, f., 'herring-boat,' not from Mid HG. *buze*, OHG. *buzo* (*z* for *ts*), but from the equiv. Du. *buis*, to which OIc. *búza*, AS. *bútse* (in *bútsecearlas*), E. *buss*, also correspond. There are similar words in Rom. —MidLat. *buza, bussa*, OFr. *busse, buce*. The origin of the cognates is probably not to be sought for in Teut.; the source whence they were borrowed is uncertain.

Buſen, m., 'bosom,' from the equiv. MidHG. *buosen, buosem*, OHG. *buosam, buosum*, m.; comp. OSax. *bôsm*, Du. *boezem*, AS. *bôsm*, E. *bosom*; in East-Teut. (Goth., Scand.) the corresponding word (Goth. *bôsma-) is wanting. It may perhaps be allied to **Bug**, MidHG. *buoc*, 'arm, shoulder' (pre-Teut. *bhághu*-); but since a pre-Teut. *bhághsmo*, *bháksmo*- does not occur in the cognate languages, nothing can be cited in favour of that explanation; at all events, **Buſen** is not allied to **biegen**.

Büſte, f., 'bust,' ModHG. only, from Fr. *busto*.

Bußaar, Buſſard, m., 'buzzard'; the first form is a popular corruption of the second, which first occurs in Mod HG., from Fr. *busard*, 'mouse-hawk, buzzard.'

Buße, f., 'penance, atonement,' from MidHG. *buoze*, OHG. *buoza*, f., 'spiritual and legal atonement, compensation, relief'; OSax. *bôta*, 'healing, relief'; AS. *bôt*, E. *boot* ('use, gain, advantage'); also E. *bote* ('wergeld'), *firebote*, *fireboot* ('a free supply of fuel'), *housebote* ('prison expenses,' then 'a free supply of wood for repairs and fuel'), Goth. *bôta*, 'use.' Under the cognate adjs. **beſſer, beſt** (comp. **büßen** in **Lücken büßen**, 'to repair,' OHG. *buozzen*; AS. *bêtan*), will be found the necessary remarks on the evolution in meaning of the stem *bat* contained in these words. Comp. **vergüten**, 'to make atonement, give compensation' (**Erſatz**); **Erſatz** denotes a substitute of equal worth. Comp. also **etwas gut machen**, 'to make good a loss,' &c. See **beſſer**.

Butte, f., 'flounder,' first occurs in ModHG., from LG. *butte*; comp. the corresponding Du. *bot*, MidE. *but*. Origin obscure.

Bütte, Butte, f., from the equiv. MidHG. *büte, bütte, büten*, OHG. *butin*, f., 'tub, butt'; the cognate LG. and E. words contain an abnormal medial *t*; AS. *bytt*, 'flagon,' E. *butt*, OIc. *bytta*. These indicate that the HG. word was borrowed in the OHG. period, when the shifting of *t* to *tz* was already accomplished. In the cognates the meaning varies, 'leather pipe, cask,' just as in the Rom. class from which they were borrowed—Span. *bota*, 'leather pipe,' Fr. *botte*, 'butt.' To OHG. *butin* (MidLat. *butina*), MidHG. *büten*, the Mod HG. deriv. **Büttner** (from MidHG. *bütenære*), 'cooper' (likewise a frequent surname), is also related.

Büttel, m., 'beadle, jailer,' from Mid HG. *bütel*, OHG. *butil*, m., 'a messenger of the law'; comp. AS. *bydel*, 'messenger,' E. *beadle* (which is based both on the AS. *bydel* and on a MidE. word of Rom. origin—MidLat. *bedellus*, ModFr. *bedeau*, 'beadle'); allied to **bieten**.

Butter, f., 'butter,' from the equiv. MHG. *buter*, f., m., late OHG. *butera*, f.; the same medial dental appears in Du. *boter*, AS. *butere*, E. *butter*. This necessitates the assumption that the HG. word was first introduced into Germany about the 10th cent. It is derived, though changed in gender (**der Butter**, however, is common to the UpGer. dialects), from the Rom.—

D

MidLat. *butyrum* (whence Fr. *beurre*, Ital. *burro*), late Gr.-Scyth. βούτυρον. Yet the art of making butter was known in Germany ere the introduction of the term from the South of Europe. Butter was called 𝔄nft, as is still the case in Alem.; comp 𝔄nfe and 𝔎erne; perhaps the process in the south was different, and with the new method came the new term. The art of making cheese may have found its way earlier, even before the middle of the 9th cent., from the South of Europe to the North. See 𝔎äſe.

𝔅ul𝔷en, m., 'core, snuff (of candles),' first occurs in ModHG.; cognate with the equiv. Swiss *bǽke*, f. (*bǘlzi, bǘlzgi*). The structure of the word resembles ModHG. (dial.) 𝔊ro𝔷en; see under 𝔊rie𝔟s. Probably, therefore, 𝔅u𝔷en represents **bugze, *búg𝑒𝑧* (Swiss *bǽke*, from *baugnjô)?

C.

See 𝔎.

D.

𝔡𝔞, adv., 'there, then, since,' from the equiv. MidHG. *dâr, dâ*, OHG. *dâr*; the loss of the final *r* (but still remained in ModHG.; see bar) is seen also in other advs.: MidHG. *sâ*, from OHG. *sâ, sâr*, 'soon, at once' (cognate with E. *soon*), comp. we. AS. *þêr*, E. *there*, corresponds to OHG. *dâr*; Goth. *þar* (instead of the expected form *þêr). The adv. is formed from the OTeut. demonstr. pron. *þa-*, Gr. το-, described under ter; the *r* of OHG. *dâr* and Goth. *þar* appears in OInd. *tárhi*, 'at that time' (*hi* is an enclitic particle like Gr. γέ); comp. also Sans. *kárhi*, 'when,' under we. As to the variation of demonst. and relat. meanings in ta, see ter.

𝔇𝔞𝔠𝔥, n., 'roof, cover, shelter,' from MidHG. *dach*, n., 'roof, covering, ceiling, awning,' OHG. *dah*; it corresponds to AS. *þæc*, 'roof,' E. *thatch*, OIc. *þak*; Goth. *þak, 'roof,' is wanting, the term used being *hrôt*, the primit. Teut. term for 'roof,' allied to 𝔇e𝔠𝔨en. The art of constructing houses (see under 𝔊ie𝔟el, 𝔉ir𝔰t, 𝔥au𝔰, 𝔗𝔥ür, 𝔖𝔠𝔥welle, 𝔗enne, 𝔖immer, &c.) was not yet developed when the Teutons were migrating from East to West; hence most of the technical terms are peculiar to Teutonic. The primary meaning of the word 𝔇a𝔠𝔥 is apparent, since it is formed by gradation from a Teut. root *þek*, Aryan *teg*, 'to cover'; Lat. *tego, tegere*; Gr. τέγος, n., 'roof'; the same stage of gradation as in HG. 𝔇a𝔠𝔥 is seen in Lat. *toga* ('the covering garment'), Lat. *tugurium*, 'hut.' The same root appears in Gr. with a prefix *s*, στέγω, 'I cover,' στέγη, 'roof,' as well as in Lith. *stógas*, 'roof,' Ind. *sthágâmi*, 'I cover.' Hence the HG. 𝔇a𝔠𝔥, like the equiv. Gr. τέγος, στέγη, Lith. *stógas* (akin to *stégti*, 'to cover'), signifies properly 'the covering part.'

𝔇𝔞𝔠𝔥𝔰, m., 'badger,' from the equiv. MidHG. *dahs*, OHG. *dahs*, m.; undoubtedly a genuine Teut. word, like 𝔉u𝔠𝔥𝔰, 𝔅a𝔠𝔥𝔰, though it cannot be authenticated in the non-Germ. languages (Du. and LG. *das*). It was adopted by Rom. (MidLat. *taxus*, Ital. *tasso*, Fr. *taisson*). It is probable that the animal, specially characterised by its winter burrow, received its name from the Aryan root *teks*, 'to construct.' In OInd. the root *takš* properly signifies 'to construct skilfully, make, build' (a carriage, pillars of an altar, a settle), while the name of the agent formed from it—*takšan* —denotes 'carpenter, worker in wood.' To the same root belong Gr. τόξον, 'bow,' τέκτων, 'carpenter'; in Teut. also OHG. *dëhsala*, MidHG. *dëhsel*, 'hatchet, axe.'

𝔇𝔞𝔠𝔥𝔱el, f., 'box on the ear'; like 𝔒𝔥r𝔣eige, properly a euphemism used in jest for a blow. 𝔇a𝔠𝔥tel is an older (MidHG.) form for 𝔇attel. Comp. further the term 𝔎op𝔣nu𝔰s, 'blows on the head,' the orig. sense of which expresses, of course, something different from what is usually understood by the word. See 𝔑u𝔰.

𝔡𝔞𝔥𝔩en, vb., 'to talk nonsense,' from the LG.; comp. E. *to dally* (the initial *d* indicates that the word was borrowed), which is traced back to OIc. *þylja*, 'to chatter.'

𝔇𝔞𝔩𝔩e𝔰, m., 'destruction, ruin,' Jew.;

properly the Jewish winding-sheet worn on the great 'day of atonement' (hence orig. 'to wear the Dalles'); from Hebr. *talîth*. According to others, the word is based on Hebr. *dallôt*, 'poverty.'

Damals, adv., 'at that time, then,' Mod HG. only. In MidHG. the expression is *des mâles*, 'at that time.' See Mal.

Damaſt, n., 'damask,' early ModHG., derived, like Du. *damast*, E. *damask*, from Rom. (comp. Fr. *damas*, Ital. *damasto*); based on the name of the city Damaſkus.

Dambock, Damhirſch, m., 'buck'; in ModHG. often written Tamm= in the attempt to find some cognate for this unintelligible word. MidHG. *tâme*, from OHG. *tâmo, dâmo*, m.; the word is of Lat. origin, *dâma* (Fr. *daim*, m., *daine*, f.). It is remarkable that in AS. the labial nasal is lost—AS. *dâ*, E. *doe*; perhaps the latter is of genuine Teut. origin. The initial *d* of the ModHG. word is due to the Lat. original, or to LG. influence.

Dambrett, n., 'draught-board,' for Damenbrett, from Dame, which was first borrowed by ModHG. from Fr. *dame* (Lat. *domina*).

dämiſch, dämlich, adj., 'dull, drowsy, crazy,' ModHG. only; a MidG. and LG. word (Bav. *damiš, taumiš*); from a Teut. root *pêm*, equiv. to Sans. *tam* (*tâmyati*), 'to get tired, out of breath,' whence Lat. *têmulentus*, 'drunk.' Probably allied to the cognates of bämmern.

Damm, m., 'dam, dike, mole,' MidHG. *tam*(*mm*); the *d* of the ModHG. word compared with the *t* of MidHG. points to a recent borrowing from LG.; comp. Du. and E. *dam* (a bank), OIc. *dammr*. Goth. has only the deriv. *faurdammjan*, 'to embank, hinder'; akin to AS. *demman*, E. *to dam*, ModHG. bämmen.

dämmern, vb., 'to grow dusk, dawn,' from MidHG. *dëmere*, f. (also even MidHG. *dëmerunge*, f.), OHG. *dëmar*, n., 'crepusculum,' a deriv. of a Teut. root *pem*, Aryan *tem*, 'to be dusk' (see also bämiſch). OSax. preserves in the *Hêliand* the cognate adj. *thimm*, 'gloomy'; allied to MidDu. and Mid LG. *deemster*, 'dark.' Apart from Teut. the assumed root *tem*, meaning 'to grow dusk,' is widely diffused; Sans. *tamas*, 'darkness' (exactly corresponding to OHG. *dëmar*), *tamrâ-s*, 'obscuring, stilling'; *tâmisrâ*, f., 'dark night'; Ir. *temel*, 'darkness,' *temen*, 'dark grey.' With the latter words Lat. *tenebrœ*, 'darkness,' is connected (*br* in Lat.

from *sr*; *n* for *m* on account of the following labial, a process of differentiation); OSlov. *tĭma*, 'darkness,' Lith. *tamsùs*, 'dark,' *tamsà*, f., 'dusk,' *tèmti*, 'to grow dusk.' In the earlier Germ. periods we have further MidHG. *dinster*, OHG. *dinstar*, which are so related to Sans. *tâmisrâ*, 'night,' and Lat. *tenebrœ*, as to imply a Goth. *þinstra-* as an adj. stem; in that case *t* has intruded between *s* and *r*, as in Schweſter. With regard to MidHG. *dinster* comp. also ModHG. düſter and fluſter.

Dampf, m., 'vapour, steam,' from Mid HG. *dampf, tampf,* m., 'vapour, smoke'; *tampf* seems to have been the strictly HG. form; allied to the equiv. OIc. *dampe*, E. and Du. *damp*, 'moisture'; not recorded in the earlier periods. Formed by gradation from a str. vb.—MidHG. *dimpfen*, 'to fume, smoke,' which has disappeared in ModHG.; its factitive, however, still exists—bämpfen, MidHG. *dempfen*, orig. sense, 'to cause to smoke,' *i.e.* 'to stifle (a fire).' See also bumpf; bunſel may also be allied to it.

Dank, m., 'thanks, acknowledgment, recompense,' from the equiv. MidHG. and OHG. *danc*, m.; corresponds to Goth. *þagks* (*þanks*), AS. *þanc*, E. *thanks*. Etymologically Danf is simply 'thinking,' hence 'the sentiment merely, not expressed in deeds.' See benfen; bünfen.

dann, adv., from the equiv. MidHG. and OHG. *danne*, 'then, at that time, in such a case, thereupon'; properly identical with benn; in MidHG. and OHG. *danne* is used indifferently for benn and bann. AS. *þonne, þænne*, E. *then*. The OTeut. adv. is based on the pronominal stem *þa-* (comp. ber); yet the mode of its formation is not quite clear. Comp. ta, ber, and the following word.

dannen, adv., only preserved in the phrase von tannen, 'thence, from thence'; MidHG. *dannen*, OHG. *dannana, dannân*, and *danân*, 'inde, illinc'; AS. *þanon*, E. *thence*. For Goth. *þanana the word *þaþrô*, formed from the same root, was used.

dar, adv., 'there,' etymologically identical with ba (whence the compounds baran, barin, barum, &c.), and with OHG. *dara*, 'thither.'

darben, vb., 'to suffer want, famish,' from MidHG. *darben*, OHG. *darbên*, 'to dispense with, be deficient'; corresponds to Goth. *gaþarban*, 'to abstain from'; AS. *þearfan*, 'to be in need of.' The verb is derived from the same root (*þerf*) as bürfen which see; its primary meaning is 'to be in need of.'

Darm, m., 'gut, intestine,' from the equiv. MidHG. *darm*, OHG. *daram*, m.; comp. AS. *þearm*, OFris. *therm*, Du. *darm*, OIc. *þarmr*, m., Swed. and Dan. *tarm*. Corresponds in the non-Teut. languages to Lat. *trâmes*, 'way,' Gr. τρῆμα, 'hole, eye,' τράμις, 'perineum,' from root *tar*, 'to traverse.' Hence the orig. sense of **Darm** was probably 'passage.'—Allied to the collective **Gedärm** (ModHG.), n., 'entrails,' from the equiv. MidHG. *gederme*, OHG. *gidermi*, n.

Darre, f., 'kiln for drying fruit, malt, &c.,' from the equiv. MidHG. *darre*, OHG. *darra*, f.; akin to MidLG. *darre*, Swed. (dial.) *tarre*: like *bërren, burr*, from an OTeut. root *þers*, pre-Teut. *ters*, upon which are based ModHG. **Durst, dürsten**, with a specialised meaning. The root *ters* appears in Gr. τέρσομαι, 'to become dry,' τερσαίνω, 'to dry'; in relation to ModHG. **Darre** the equiv. ταρσός and ταρσία, 'hurdle for drying fruit,' deserve special notice. The words connected with the root *ters* are cited under **Durst**, since they, like **Durst**, have been similarly restricted in meaning. Lat. *torreo*, for *torseo*, corresponds in form and idea to ModHG. **bërren**; comp. further Lat. *torris*, 'firebrand,' *torridus*, 'parched.' From Teut. *þarrian*, Fr. *tarir*, 'to dry up,' is derived. See **bërren, burr, Durst**.

daß, conj., 'that,' from MidHG. and OHG. *daz*; corresponds to OLG. and E. *that*, Goth. *þatu*; etymologically identical with **das**, the neut. article. See **ber**.

Dattel, f., 'date' (fruit), from MidHG. *datel, tatel, ta'ele*, f.; from Rom.,—Fr. *datte*, Ital. *dattilo*; the primary source of which is Gr. δάκτυλος, 'date' (comp. **Attich**); hence too Du. *dadel*, E. *date*.

Daube, f., akin to the equiv. MidHG. *dûge*, f., 'stave'; the ModHG. *b* compared with MidHG. *g* shows that the modern word cannot be a continuation of the MidHG. form. UpGer. has preserved the word *dauge*, corresponding to MidHG. *dûge*; comp. Du. *duig*, 'stave.' OIc. *þúfa*, f., 'entrenchment, rampart,' does not appear to be related. In Rom. is found a word phonetically allied and equiv. in meaning— Fr. *douve*, 'stave' (but also 'moat'; hence this is connected with the OIc. word quoted); it was most likely borrowed from Du. or LG. The Scand. *þúfa* and the MidHG. *dûge* look very much like Teut. words whether they are allied or not. We cannot possibly derive MidHG. *dûge* from Gr. δοχή, 'receptacle.' Respecting the permutation of *b* (*f*) and *g*, see **Traube**.

dauern (1.), vb., 'to last, endure,' from the equiv. MidHG. *dûren, tûren*, from Lat. *dûrare* (Fr. *durer*). **Dauer**, f., is simply a ModHG. form from **bauern**. E. *to dure* (*endure*) comes from Fr. *durer*.

dauern (2.), **bedauern**, vb., 'to cause pity, sorrow, regret'; the initial *d* indicates that the vb. was borrowed from MidG. and LG., for the MidHG. form was *tûren; mich tûret ein ding* or *eines dinges*, 'that appears to me to be (too) expensive, dear'; *tûren* is related by gradation to *teuer*, MidHG. *tiure*; for the change from *û* to *iu* comp. *traurig* with AS. *dreórig*, E. *dreary*. It is remarkable that the verb, which, judging by its gradation, must be very old, is utterly wanting in the older dialects.

Daumen, m., 'thumb,' from the equiv. MidHG. and MidLG. *dûme*, OHG. *dûmo*, m.; comp. Du. *duim*, AS. *þûma*, E. *thumb*; OIc. *þumall, þumalfîngr*. The same deriv. with the suffix *l* is seen, but with a change of meaning, however, in AS. *þýmel*, E. *thimble* (Goth. *þúma). This word 'thumb' is consequently common to the Teut. group; even the other fingers had each its special name in the OTeut. period. The AS. terms *middefinger, midlesta finger, se goldfinger, se litla finger*, are in complete accord with ModHG. **Mittelfinger** (middle-finger), **Geldfinger** (ring-finger), and **der kleine Finger** (the little-finger), respectively. These terms are not formed, therefore, like **Daumen** from an old independent stem; in this way **Daumen** is proved to be primit., though etymologically it is not quite clear; the pre-Teut. form may have been *tûmon, perhaps akin to *tûmeo*, 'to swell'?. In that case **Daumen** would be equiv. to 'swollen finger'; comp. also Sans. *tumrá-s*, as 'greasy, fat, vigorous,' and *tûtuma-s*, 'strong,' Zend *tûma*, 'strong,' with Lat. *tum-eo*. Gr. τύλος, τύλη(ϑ), 'callosity, swelling, knob, hump,' are based upon a root *tû*, while the Lat. cognates point to *tûm*. The orig. sense of both may have been 'to swell, be thick.'

Daune, Dune, f., 'down,' ModHG. only, from the equiv. LG. *dûne*, f.; comp. OIc. *dûnn*, m., E. *down*. Hence the initial dental proves that the ModHG. word is of LG. origin, for since the Scand. and Eng. words begin with *d*, a genuine HG. word would necessarily have an initial *t*. The origin of Scand. *dūnn* is obscure. See **Eider, Flaum.**

Daus, n., 'deuce (of dice), ace (of cards),' from MidHG. *dûs, tûs,* with the same meanings; late OHG. *dûs.* From a Rom. word originating in the Lat. *duo;* OFr. *dous* (ModFr. *deux,* Prov. *duas,* from Lat. **duos* for *duo*), whence E. *deuce.* Dice-playing was a favourite amusement even among the Teutons described by Tacitus (*Germ.* 24); unfortunately, however, we can gather nothing from his brief remarks as to the details and technical terms (but see **gefallen, Hund, Sau**) of the OTeut. game; the words died out at an early period, and with the new games from the South new Rom. words have been introduced. See **Aß, Treff, doppeln.**

Dechant, m., 'dean,' from MidHG. *dëchent, tëchant(d),* MidHG. and OHG. *tëchán* from Lat. *decânus,* whence also Ital. *decano,* Fr. *doyen* (E. *dean*).

Decher, m., 'a tale of ten hides,' from the equiv. MidHG. *tëcher, dëcher,* m. n.; borrowed by MidHG. from Lat. *decuria.*

Decke, f., 'cover, ceiling, disguise,' from MidHG. *decke,* f., 'cover, covering, covering up'; OHG. *dechî,* related to the following word.

decken, vb., 'to cover, screen,' from the equiv. ModHG. *decken,* OHG. *dechan;* the latter (with *cch-* from *kj*) from **þakjan,* which was most likely the Goth. form; comp. AS. *þeccan* (obsolete in E.); OIc. *þekja,* 'to cover.' *þakjan* is a deriv. of the Aryan root *teg* (discussed under **Dach**), which appears with the same meaning in Lat. *tegere,* Gr. σ-τέγω, Sans. *sthagâmi.* A str. vb. *þekan* corresponding to *tego,* στέγω, is nowhere recorded within the Teut. group; the wk. vb. has assumed its function.

deftig, adj., ModHG. only, from LG. *deftig;* the latter, with E. *daft,* AS. *gedæft,* 'mild, meek, gentle' (Goth. *gadaban,* 'to be fitting'), and perhaps with HG. *tapfer,* is derived from a Teut. root *dab, dap.* See **tapfer.**

Degen (1.), m., 'valiant warrior'; it is not etymologically a sort of figurative sense of **Degen** (2.), though the tendency of Mod HG. is to regard it thus, in such expressions as *alter Haudegen,* 'a practised swordsman,' &c. While **Degen,** 'sword,' first appears in the 15th cent., **Degen,** 'hero,' is an OTeut. word, which is wanting in Goth. (**þigns*) only. Comp. OHG. *dëgan,* AS. *þëgn,* 'retainer, attendant,' E. *thane* (from *þegn*); MidHG. *dëgen,* 'hero.' There is no phonetic difficulty in connecting these cognates (Goth. *þigna-,* from *teknô-*), as is usually done, with Gr. τέκνον, 'child'; the difference in sense may be paralleled by AS. *magu,* 'boy, son, servant, man.' But since *þëgn* was already an established technical term in the OTeut. system, we must in preference regard 'vassal' as the primary sense of the word. We have too in Goth. *þius* (stem *þiwa-*) for *þigwá-,* 'servant, attendant' (AS. *þëó, þeów,* OHG. *diu;* see **Dirne** and **bienen**), a more suitable connecting link. Moreover, *þëgn,* **Degen,** would, if cognate with τέκνον, be related to τίκτω, 'to give birth to,' τοκεύς, 'begetter,' τόκος, 'birth,' and Sans. *tukman,* 'child.'

Degen (2.), m., 'sword,' first occurs in late MidHG, see **Degen** (1.); from Fr. *dague,* 'dirk.'

dehnen, vb., 'to stretch, extend, lengthen,' from MidHG. and OHG. *denen, dennen,* wk. vb., 'to stretch, draw, strain'; comp. Goth. *ufþanjan,* 'to extend'; AS. *þenian, þennan,* 'to stretch.' The Goth. *þanjan* is a deriv. of a str. vb. **þënan,* like *þakjan,* 'to cover,' from a str. vb. **þëkan* (Lat. *tego*); *þanja* and *þënu* are primit. cognate with Gr. τείνω. The root *ten* is widely diffused in the Aryan group. Sans. root *tan,* 'to strain, widen, extend (of time), endure'; *tántu-s,* m., 'thread,' *tántî-s,* f., 'line, rope'; Gr. τείνω, τάνυμαι, τάσις, τένων, 'sinew,' *ταινία,* 'strip'; OSlov. *teneto, tonoto,* 'cord,' Lat. *tenus,* 'cord,' Lith. *tinklas,* 'net.' The idea of extension is shown also by the root *ten* (Lat. *teneo, tendo*) in an old Aryan adj.; see **dünn** and **Dohne.** A figurative sense of the same root is seen in **bennern**; the evolution of meaning may be 'extension—sound—noise.'

Deich, m., 'dike'; MidHG. *tîch,* m.; since the HG. word would, according to phonetic laws, begin with *t,* we suppose that it has been influenced, like **Dampf** perhaps, by LG.; comp. I.G. *dîk,* Du. *dijk,* AS. *dîc,* E. *dike.* Respecting their identity with HG. **Teich** and E. *dike* ('a ditch'), see **Teich.**

Deichsel (1.), f., 'pole, thill, shaft,' from the equiv. MidHG. *dîhsel,* OHG. *dîhsala,* f.; comp. OIc. *þîsl,* AS. *þîxl, þîsl,* Du. *dissel,* OLG. *thîsla,* f. It has no connection with E. *thill,* which is related rather to ModHG, **Diele.** A word peculiar to the Teut. dialects, and of obscure origin; perhaps Lat. *têmo,* 'pole, shaft,' is primit. allied (if it represents *teixmo;* comp. *ála* from **axla,* under Achſel). The Aryans had learnt the way to build waggons in their Asiatic home ere they separated into different tribes: this is proved by the words Joch, Nabe, Nat, Wagen.

Deichſel (2.), f., 'adze'; comp. MidHG. *dëhsel,* OHG. *dëhsala,* 'axe, hatchet'; from a Teut. root *peh̥s,* equiv. to Aryan *teks.* Comp. OSlov. *tesati,* 'to hew,' Lith. *taszýti,* 'to hew, fashion with an axe,' Sans. *takśan,* 'carpenter' (see under Dachs). The *ei* of the ModHG. word is based upon a variant *pihs,* which is MidG. and LG.; numerous HG. dialects preserve the old *e.*

dein, pronom. adj., 'thy,' from the equiv. MidHG. and OHG. *dîn,* corresponds to Goth. *þeins,* AS. *þîn,* E. *thy, thine;* related to du.

Demant, Diamant, m., 'diamond, adamant,' from the equiv. MidHG. *diamant, diemant,* from Fr. *diamant,* Ital. *diamante* (Lat. *adamantem*).

Demut, f., 'submissiveness, humility,' from the equiv. MidHG. *dêmuot, diemuot, diemüete,* OHG. *deomuoti,* 'condescension, gentleness, modesty.' The correctly developed form from the OHG. *deomuoti* would be ModHG. Diemüte; the present form is due partly to LG. influence, partly to its having been connected with Armut; but while in the latter *ut* is properly a suffix, OHG. *deomuoti,* f., is a compound. The second component is a deriv. of OHG. *muot* (see Mut); OHG. *dio,* however, is Goth. *þius* (stem *þiwa-;* comp. dienen, Dirne, and also Degen), 'hind, servant'; Demut is 'the befitting quality of a servant, the disposition of the attendant.' Neither the word nor the idea is OTeut. (the Goth. said *hauneins,* 'abasement, baseness,' for Demut); both were introduced by Christianity.

dengeln, vb., from the equiv. MidHG. *tengeln,* 'to sharpen by hammering, beat, hammer'; the ModHG. *d* points, as in the case of Deich, to a LG. influence; comp. AS. *dęnęgan,* 'to knock, ding,' E. *to ding.* Akin to OHG. *tangol,* 'hammer'; Goth. **diggwan,* 'to strike,' indicated also by OSwed. *diunga,* ModSwed. *dänga,* is not recorded.

denken, vb., 'to think, call to mind, conceive, believe,' from MidHG. *dęnken,* OHG. *dęnchen,* 'to think, bear in mind, devise, excogitate'; corresponds to Goth. *þagkjan* (*þankjan*), 'to consider, ponder, reflect,' AS. *þęncan.* E. *to think,* is an intermediate form between AS. *þęncan,* 'to think,' and *þyncan,* 'to seem.' Dęnken is in form a factitive of dünfen, which was originally a str. vb., meaning 'to seem'; 'to make a thing seem' is 'to consider, ponder.' See dünfen.

denn, conj., 'for,' from MidHG. *danne, dęnne,* OHG. *danne, danna;* identical with dann.

der, art., 'the,' formed from the OHG. and MidHG. demonstr. and relat. stem *dě-;* comp. Goth. *þa-,* Gr. το-, OInd. *ta-.* The details belong to grammar.

derb, adj., 'compact, stout, blunt, uncouth,' derived in form from MidHG. *derp* (*b*), 'unleavened,' but blended in meaning with a word bėrbe, berb, 'worthy, honest' (see bieder), deduced from OHG. and MidHG. *biderbe.* MidHG. *dërp,* OHG. *dërb,* 'unleavened,' are equiv to OIc. *þjarfr,* AS. *þeorf,* E. *therf.* Bieder is related to bedürfen, but berb, 'unleavened,' on account of its meaning, cannot belong to the same stem; it is connected rather with the root verderben.

desto, adv., 'so much the,' from the equiv. MidHG. *dëste, dëst,* late OHG. *dësde;* in an earlier form two words, *dës diu* (*dës,* gen., *diu,* instr. of the art.); the Goth. word was simply *þê* (instr. of the art.); thus, too, AS. *þŷ* before comparatives, E. *the* (*the more,* desto mehr).

Deube, see Dieb.

Deut, f., 'doit, trifle,' simply ModHG., from Du. *duit,* 'smallest coin' (whence also E. *doit*); the latter is of Scand. origin; OIc. *þveit,* 'a small coin' (from *þvíta,* 'to cut').

deuten, vb., 'to point, beckon, interpret, explain,' from MidHG. *diuken, tiuten,* OHG. *diuten,* vb., 'to show, point, signify, notify, explain, translate'; Goth. **þiudjan;* comp. OIc. *þýða.* In place of *þiudjan,* Goth. has a form *þiuþjan,* 'to praise, laud,' which, however, is scarcely identical with deuten. Probably the latter signifies rather 'to make popular'; *þiuda* is the Goth. word for 'nation' (see deutsch). Comp. MidHG. *ze diute,* 'distinct, evident,' and 'in German' (*diute,* dat. sing. of *diuti, tiute,* f., 'exposition, explanation'); note too AS. *geþeóde,* 'language' (as the main characteristic of the nation).

deutsch, adj., 'German,' from the equiv. MidHG. *diutsch, tiutsch;* the initial *d* of the ModHG. and MidHG. words is MidG., the earlier form, teutſch (MidHG. *tiutsch*), is UpGer., and was, especially by the Up

Ger. writers, constantly used till the end of the last century. OHG. *diutisk* (for MidLat. *theodiscus*, the earliest records of the word are in the years 813, 842, 860), 'German,' properly only 'pertaining to the people' (OSax *thiudisca liudi*, 'Teutons') ; Goth. preserves the corresponding *þiudiskô*, adv., in the sense of 'like a heathen' (in close connection with Gr. ἐθνικῶς. The suffix *isk* denotes 'pertaining to.' The subst. MidHG. *diet*, OHG. *diot*, *diota*, 'people,' upon which this word is based, is preserved in such compound proper names as Dietrich, Detlef, Detmold, Detmar; as an independent word it is also obsolete in Eng.; AS. *þeód*; Goth. *þiuda*, f. The OTeut. subst. is based upon a word—pre-Teut. *teutá*, 'people'—found in many West Aryan languages; comp. Lith. *tautà*, f., 'country,' Lett. *tauta*, 'people, nation'; OIr. *tûath*, 'people'; Oscan *touto*, 'people' (Livy calls the chief magistrate of the Campanian towns '*medix tuticus*'). Thus the word deutsch has a singular and comprehensive history; it was used in the earliest OHG. and MidLat. writings only of the language (since 845 A.D. *Theodisci* occurs also as the name of a people, and first of all in Italy); deutsch, 'popular,' was the term applied to the native language in contrast to the Lat. ecclesiastical speech and the Lat. official phraseology. We may note E. *Dutch*, because it is restricted to the language of Holland; till about 1600 A.D. the people of Holland were convinced that their language was German.

dibbern, vb., Jew., 'to talk' (especially in a low voice), from Hebr. *dibbēr*, 'to talk.'

dicht, adj., 'close, dense,' dial. *d-icht* (Liv. and Esth.), from MidHG. *dîhte*, 'dense.' The absence of the diphthong is probably due to LG., since the word does not occur in UpGer. (Suab. and Bav.). Corresponds to OIc. *þéttr*, 'dense' (related to Goth. *þeihts*, as *léttr*, 'light,' to Goth. *leihts*); allied to the Teut. root *þinh* (see gedeihen), just as Goth. *leihts* to the root ling (see gelingen). E. *tight*, from MidE. *tiht*, has an abnormal *t* for *th* initially, probably due to the influence of Swed. and Dan. *tæt*; in MidE. the normal *thiht* is also found. For another derivation see bid.

dichten, vb., 'to invent, imagine, write, fabricate,' from MidHG. *tihten*, 'to write, draw up (in writing), compose, invent, excogitate'; the ModHG. meaning is very much restricted compared with the fulness of MidHG. Even in the 16th and 17th cents. Dichter (MidHG. *tihtære*) meant generally 'writer, author,' and was applied to the prose writer as well as the poet. The origin of tichten (OHG. *tihtôn*, 'to write, compose'), from Lat. *dictare*, 'to dictate,' late Lat. also 'to compose,' may have favoured the change from tichten to dichten; AS. *dihtan*, which is of the same origin, has the further signification 'to arrange, array.'

dick, adj., 'thick, stout, corpulent,' from MidHG. *dic, dicke*, adj., 'thick, dense, frequent,' OHG. *dicchi*, 'thick, dense'; in Eng. too the double meaning of the adj. obtains; comp. OIc. *þykkr, þjǫkkr*, AS. *þicce*, E. *thick*. Corresponds to OIr. *tiug* (from **tigu*), 'thick,' so that we must presuppose a Goth. **þigus*. Beside which the double sense, 'thick, dense,' makes the kinship with dicht probable. In OHG. the meaning 'dense' has been preserved in Dickicht, lit. 'a place densely overgrown' (orig. used by sportsmen); in MidHG. *dicke* is the equiv. term.

Dieb, m., 'thief,' from the equiv. MidHG. *diep(b)*, OHG. *diob*, m.; common to the Teut. group; comp. Goth. *þiufs(b)*, Du. *dief*, AS. *þeóf*, E. *thief*. The word cannot be traced beyond Teut. In the sense of 'Diebstahl,' E. has a form with a dental suffix—AS. *þýfþ*, f. (OIc. *þýfð*, f., Goth. **þiubiþa*), E. *theft*. The form in HG. is a *j*- stem—OHG. *diuba (diuva)*, MidHG. *diube (diuve)*, earlier ModHG. Deube (as late as Logau, 1604-1655), which is now met with only in Wilddeube, 'petty poaching.' The latter forms the base of ModHG. Diebstahl, in MidHG. *diepstâle* and *diupstâle* (OSwed. *þiufstolet*), lit. 'theft-stealing.' The second part of the compound expresses the same idea as the first; Dieb is simply the concrete which has replaced the abstract; comp. Goth. *þiubi*, n., and its adv. form *þiubjô*, 'secretly.' Besides the masc. Dieb, there existed in OHG. and MidHG. a feminine form, which in Goth. would have been **þiubi*; comp. OHG. *diupa*, MidHG. *diupe*, 'female thief.' We must seek for the primit. word in a pre-Teut. root with a final *p*; this is proved by OHG. *diuva*, MidHG. *diuve*, f., 'theft'; comp. the Aryan root *tup*, 'to duck,' under Duft.

Diele, f., 'plank, board,' from MidHG. *dil, dille*, f., m., 'board, partition of boards, boarded floor' (in LG. 'vestibule'), OHG.

díli, m. (neut. ?), *dílla*, f., with the same meaning. Originally Teut. *þelwz, þiliz*, n., 'board,' was *þiljôn*, 'made of boards'; comp. AS. *þel*, 'board,' OIc. *þilja*, 'rowing seat' (Finn. *teljo* 'ship's beam, oar-bench,' comes from Teut.). Comp. further Du. *deel*, 'board, floor,' MidLG. *dêle*, 'board.' Lith. *tíle*, 'plank of a boat,' OSlov. *tŭlo*, 'ground,' Sans. *tala-m*, 'surface,' seem to be primit. allied ; also Lat. *tellus*, 'earth' ?.

dienen, vb., 'to serve, attend upon, be of use to,' from the equiv. MidHG. *dienen*, OHG. *dionôn* (OSax. *thionôn*) ; comp. Du. *dienen*, Goth. *þiunôn. The latter is formed in the same way as *reikinôn*, 'to rule,' from *reiks*, 'ruler,' *fraujinôn*, 'to be master of,' from *frauja*, 'master' ; that is to say, *dienen* is based upon Goth. *þius* (stem *þiwa-*), 'servant, menial.' Comp. AS. *þeów*, 'servant,' OHG. *deo*, 'menial' (comp. **Demut**) ; also a fem. form, Goth. *þiwi*, OHG. and MidHG. *diu*, 'maid-servant' ; another similar old fem. form is ModHG. **Dirne**. The corresponding abstract—**Dienſt**, MidHG. *dienest*, m., n., OHG. *dionôst*, n. (comp. OSax. *thionost*, n.), is worth noting from the grammatical point of view on account of the suffix *st* (comp. **Angſt**, also AS. *ofost*, 'haste,' with the same suffix). From Goth. *fraujinassus*, 'rule,' *þiudinassus*, 'reign,' we should have expected Goth. *þiunassus*, 'the state of a servant, service,' that is to say, the Germ. suffix *-niss* for *nest*. Moreover, before the *w* of Goth. *þiwa-* a *g* may have disappeared (comp. **Auc, Niere**), so that the Teut. root was possibly *þegw*; in that case the OTeut. *þegnoz*, 'sword' (Goth. *þigns), would belong to the same stem as **dienen** and **Degen**.

Dienstag, m., 'Tuesday,' a West Teut. word, which has quite as important a bearing upon the religious views of the Teutons as **Oſtern**. Originally there were three names for the day. One contains in the first component of the compound the name of the OTeut. god Tiu, to whom the day was sacred ; OIc. *Týsdagr*, AS. *Tíwesdœg*, E. *Tuesday*, preserve this name in the gen. (comp. Goth. *baurgswaddjus*, just as if **Burgsmauer** were used for **Burgmauer** ; see **Nachtigall**). OHG. *Zio* (OIc. *Týr*) is a primit. deity whose worship the Teutons brought with them from their Asiatic home ; it is identical with Gr. Ζεύς (for δjεύς), gen. Διός (for διϝός, hence corresponding to Goth. *Tius-dags); Lat. *Jupiter, Jovis* (for *djovis); Sans. *Djâus*, gen. *Divás*; orig. the word meant simply 'sky,' then the sky personified as a god. Among the Teutons Tiu appears as a god of war ; this change of meaning is explained by the supposition that Tiu, corresponding to the Greek Zeus, was at first regarded simply as the chief god, but was afterwards connected with the main occupation of our ancestors, *i.e.* war (see **fühn**). From *Tiu*, OHG. *Zio*, 'Tuesday' in OAlem. is termed (OHG.) *Ziostac*, (MidHG.) *Ziestac* (*Ziestag* in Hebel). Another appellation is the OBav. *Ertac* (*Erchtag*), instead of which, on the adoption of Christianity in the east of Suabia, the word *aftermœntig*, 'after Monday,' was introduced. In the Franc. and Sax. dialects the term *dingestag* has existed from time immemorial, and was at one time incorrectly thought to mean 'court-day' (see **Ding**). The latter word, however, is based rather on an attribute of the OTeut. *Tiu*, who in a Teut.-Lat. inscription is designated *Mars Thingsus*. *Thinx* is the Lomb. term for **Ding**, 'assembly of the people,' hence *Thinxus*, the god of the assemblies. Among the Sax., Fris., and Francon. tribes Tuesday was sacred to this god ; comp. MidDu. *dinxendach*, MidLG. *dingsedach*, earlier ModHG. *dingsdag*.

dieſer, pron., 'this, the latter,' from the equiv. MidHG. *diser*, OHG. *disêr*, earlier *desêr*; corresponds to AS. *þes*, E. *this*. See the grammars for further details.

Dietrich, m., 'false key' (in UpGer. **Nachſchlüſſel**), occurs late in MidHG. ; the age of the word and of its meaning is attested by the loan-word Swed. *dyrk* (Dan. *dirk*), which has the same signification, and is, like the ModHG. proper name **Dietl**, 'Derry,' a pet name from **Dietrich**, 'Derrick.' Similarly, instead of '**Dietrich**,' **Peterchen** (**Peterſen**), 'Peterkin,' and **Klaus** (**Klöschen**), 'Nick,' are used, probably because **Peter**, 'Peter,' like **Dietrich**, 'Derrick.' and **Niclaus**, 'Nicholas,' are favourite Christian names, which might serve to veil (in thieves' slang ?) the term 'false key' (comp. Ital. *grimaldello*) The word in MidHG. is *müeslüȝȝel*, OHG. *afterslaȝȝil*.

Dill, m., 'dill.' In ModHG. the LG. form is current, just as in the case of **Hafer**. MidHG. *tille*, f., m., is used of the same umbelliferous plant (*anethum*), OHG. *tilli*, n. ; comp. AS. *dile*, E. *dill*; of obscure origin.

Ding, n., 'thing, matter, transaction,' from MidHG. and OHG. *dinc(g)*, n., 'thing, matter,' prop. 'judicial proceeding, court-day' (for a similar change of meaning comp. Sache); the corresponding Scand. þing (thing), meaning 'judicial transaction, court-day, court of justice,' is well known. The OTeut. þing (Lomb. thinx) is therefore connected with the old *mahal*, *maþl*, as 'assembly of the people' (see Gemahl). In Eng. the subst. (AS. þing, n., E. thing) has essentially the ModHG. meaning; but the deriv. þingan, 'to make a treaty,' þingian, 'to settle, adjust,' and þingung, 'mediation,' imply also 'treaty, discussion.' In ModHG. a remnant of the earlier meaning remained in bingen, from MidHG. 'to hold a court, negotiate, make a treaty' (whence ModHG. Bedingung, 'stipulation'), and specially 'to conclude a bargain, buy, hire' (also generally 'to talk,' like AS. þingian, 'to talk'); so, too, in vertheidigen, Dienstag. Hence the primary meaning of the subst. is 'public transaction in the folk-moot,' lit. 'term'; this is supported by Goth. þeihs, 'time,' from preTeut. *tênkos* (equal to Lat. *tempus*). The Aryan base of Lomb. thinx, OHG. ding, is *tenkos*. The OBulg. tęza, f., 'judicial transaction,' is of Teut. origin.

Dinkel, m., from the equiv. MidHG. *dinkel*, OHG. *dinchil*, m., 'bearded wheat, spelt'; of obscure origin.

Dinte, see Tinte.

Diptam, m., 'dittany,' from the equiv. MidHG. *dictam, diptam*; borrowed from Gr. δίκταμνος.

Dirne, f., 'lass, hussy, wench' (not found in UpG.), from MidHG. *dirne*, *dierne*, OHG. *diorna*, 'maid-servant, girl, wench.' Comp. Du. *deern*, OSax. *thiorna*, OIc. *perna*, f.; in Goth. probably *þiwairnô*; comp. *widuwairna*, 'orphan,' orig. sense perhaps 'widow's son.' Thus, too, *þiwairnô*, 'menial's, thrall's daughter, who is therefore herself a slave, *i.e.* a servant.' The deriv. syllable is a diminutive suffix (comp. Eichhorn); the stem is indisputably *þiwa-*, 'menial.' For further cognates, see dienen, Degen.

Distel, f., 'thistle,' from the equiv. Mid HG. *distel*, m. and f., OHG. *distila*, f., *distil*, m.; corresponds to Du. and LG. *distel*, AS. *þistel*, E. *thistle*, OIc. *þistell*. Modern LG. and Eng. dialects have *t* in the accented syllable; hence the root is *þist* ?. Akin to Goth. *wiga-deinô*, 'milk-thistle' ?.

Döbel, m., 'peg, wedge,' from MidHG. *tübel*, m., 'pin, plug, nail'; OHG. *tubili*, n., 'plug.' Comp. E. *dowel*, Du. *deuvik*,

'plug.' The Teut. root *dub*, upon which it is based, appears in Swed. *dubba*; so, too, perhaps in Lith. *dùbti*, 'to get hollow,' *daubà, dùbė*, 'pit.' The *d* of the ModHG. word is due to MidG. influence.

doch, conj., 'yet, however,' from Mid HG. *doch*, OHG. *dôh*, 'yet,' also 'although'; *đ*, on account of the toneless nature of the conj., is shortened from *ô*; Goth. *þáuh*, corresponding to AS. *þéáh*, E. *though*. Scarcely from *þa* (variant of *þata*, HG. *daz*) and *uh*, 'and.' Goth. *þauh* is lit. 'and that' ?.

Docht, m., 'wick.' The strictly ModHG. form should be *ducht*, which is still dialectal, as well as the variant *tacht*, with the *t* from *þ*, as in tausend. MidHG. and OHG. *tâht*, m. n.; comp. OIc. *þáttr*, 'thread, wick.' A Teut. root, *þêh, þêg*, still appears in Swiss *dægel*, 'wick,' Bav. *dähen*, Alsat. *dôche*, 'wick.' In the non-Teut. languages no primit. root *têk* has as yet been found. For another OTeut. term for Docht, see under Wieche.

Dock, n., 'dock,' simply ModHG.; from the equiv. E. *dock*, the origin of which is very obscure. From E. and Du. (*dok*) the word was adopted by Swed., Dan., Mod HG., and ModFr.

Docke, f., 'doll,' from MidHG. *tocke*, f., 'doll,' also 'young girl,' OHG. *toccha*, 'doll.' The word is not found in the oldest periods of the other dialects, nor can the ModHG. meanings, 'skein, yarn,' be authenticated from MidHG., OHG., and the early stages of cognate languages; yet there is no reason to doubt the real Teut. origin of the word.

Dogge, f., 'bulldog, mastiff,' simply ModHG., from the equiv. Du. and E. *dog* (from about 1050 A.D. the word occurs in AS. as *docga*), whence also Fr. *dogue*. With regard to HG. *gg*, as a proof of a word being borrowed from LG., comp. Flagge.

Dohle, f., 'jackdaw,' from the equiv. MidHG. *tâhele, tâle, tâhe*, OHG. *tâha*, f.; primary form **dêhxô, dêwô*, according to AS.*dâwe*, E. *daw*, whence also E. *caddow*, 'daw' (the first part of the compound is AS. *câ*, Du. *ka*, OHG. *châha*, 'daw'; so, too, E. *chough*). From Teut. *þâhwalô* is derived Ital. *taccola*, 'magpie.'

Dohne, f., 'gin, noose, springe,' from MidHG. *don, done*, f., 'stretching,' OHG. *dona*, 'branch, twig.' Dohne is the 'branch bent or stretched for catching birds.' The Aryan root *ten*, 'to stretch, extend,' is discussed under tehnen, dünn. OBulg. *tonoto*, 'cord, noose,' Lat. *tenus*, n., 'cord,' Sans. *tantu-s*, *tantrî*, 'wire, cord,' Gr. τένων, sinew,' are closely allied in meaning to £eßne. So too OHG. *donên* (Goth. *punan), 'to exert oneself.'

Doßes, Douches, m., 'fundament,' a Jewish word, but of doubtful etymology; hardly from Hebr. *tâchath*, 'underneath.'

Dolch, m., 'dagger, dirk,' simply Mod HG. (from the beginning of the 16th cent.), derived like the equiv. Du., Dan., and Swed. *dolk*, from Slav. (Bohem. and Pol. *tulich*?).

Dolde, f., 'umbel,' from MidHG. *tolde*, f., 'top or crown of a plant or tree,' OHG. *toldo*, m.; the ModHG. word has apparently a LG. initial sound. The root is *dul* (pre-Teut. *dhel*), as is indicated by OHG. *tola*, 'grape-stalk.' From Aryan *dhel*, Gr. θόλος, 'dome' (allied in meaning to ModHG. Delve, 'umbel'), is formed by gradation. Yet θάλλω, 'to sprout, bloom,' θάλος, n., 'young shoot, twig,' may also be cognates.

Dole, f., 'canal,' from MidHG. *dol*, OHG. *dola*, f., 'pipe'; akin to LG. and Fris. *dole*, 'pit, ditch.'

Dolmetsch, m., 'interpreter,' from the equiv. MidHG. *tolmetsche*, *tolmetze*, *tulmetsche*; a Turk. word (North Turk. *tilmač*) which found its way into MidHG. through Magyar (*tolmács*) or Slav. (OSlov. *tlŭmačĭ*, Pol. *tłumacz*, Bohem. *tlumač*); also in MidHG. *tolc*, *tolke* (comp. further Du. *tolk*), 'interpreter,' from OSlov. *tlŭkŭ* (whence also Lith. *tulkas*, Lett. *tulks*, 'interpreter').

Dom, m., 'cathedral, dome, cupola,' ModHG. only, borrowed from Lat. *domus* (for *domus dei*; comp. the Goth. word *gudhûs*, 'the house of God, church'). An earlier loan-word is OHG. *tuom* (also *dôm*), MidHG. *tuom*, 'a bishop's collegiate church, cathedral,' which was naturalised in Germany about the 9th cent.; comp. OHG. *scuola* from Lat. *scôla*, as if it were *scôla*; so *tuom* for *tôm* from *dômus*; see Schule. The form Tum, developed from MidHG. *tuom*, kept its ground till the beginning of the last century.

Donner, m., 'thunder,' from the equiv. MidHG. *doner*, OHG. *donar*, m., corresponding to AS. *þunor*, E. *thunder*; Goth. **þunara-*, m. It is the OTeut. name for thunder, under which also the weather-god was worshipped (see Donnerstag). The name comes from the Aryan root *ten*, discussed under behnen, Dehne, and dünn. In its application to sound we meet with this root in Gr. τόνος, 'string, rope, stretching, tone, accent,' Sans. root *tan*, 'to resound, roar,' *tanyitnū-s*, 'roaring, thundering,' Lat. *tonare* (AS. *þunian*, Goth. *þunôn, 'to thunder'), Lat. *tonitrus*; the latter correspondences are, on account of their meaning, the most closely allied to the Teut. words.

Donnerstag, 'Thursday,' from Mid HG. *donerstac*, *dunrestac*, OHG. *donarestag*; comp. Du. *donderdag*, AS. *þunresdæg*, E. *Thursday*, OIc. *þôrsdagr*; the day sacred to the OTeut. god *þunar* (OHG. *Donar*, OLG. *Thunar*, OIc. *þôrr* for *þonraz*); see Dienstag and Woche. A remarkable form occurs in MidHG. (Bav.), *pfinz-tac*, 'Thursday,' from the equiv. Gr. πέμπτη.

Doppeln, vb., 'to play at dice,' from the equiv. MidHG. *deppeln*, from MidHG. *toppel*, 'dice-playing,' which corresponds to Fr. *doublet*, 'doublet' (at dice). See Dame.

Doppelt, adj. (a parallel form, Derrel, occurs in the compounds Doppelader, Derpelgänger), 'double, duplicate, twofold,' Mod HG. only, from Fr. *double*; MidHG. *dublin*, 'double,' is a deriv. from the same source. The final *t* of the ModHG. word is a secondary suffix, as in Art, Obst.

Dorf, n., 'village, hamlet,' from the equiv. MidHG. and OHG. *dorf*, n.; an OTeut. word; comp. OSax. *thorp*, Du. *dorp*, AS. *þorp*, E. *thorp*, *throp* (existing now only in proper names); OIc. *þorp*, 'hamlet'; Goth. *þaúrp* signifies 'fields, land,' while in the other dialects the ModHG. meaning of the word is current (in Goth. *haims*, 'village'; see Heim). The meaning of ModHG. (Swiss) *dorf*, 'visit, meeting,' connected perhaps with OSlov. *trŭgŭ*, 'market,' deserves special notice. If the history of the word is rendered difficult by such variations of meaning, it is made still more so by the Kelt. **trbo*, 'village'; W. *tref*, 'village' (to which the name of the OGall. tribe *Atrebates* is allied), also connected with Lat. *tribus*, 'tribe.' Moreover, OIc. *þyrpa*, 'to crowd,' is closely akin to Gr. τύρβη, Lat. *turba*, 'band.' Note too AS. *þrep*, *þrôp*, 'village,' Lith. *trobà*, f., 'building.'

Dorn, m., 'thorn, prickle,' from the equiv. MidHG. and OHG. *dorn*, m.; corresponds to Goth. *þaúrnus*, OIc. *þorn*, AS. *þorn*, E. *thorn*, Du. *doorn*, OSax. *thorn*, 'thorn'; from pre-Teut. *trnu-*. Comp. OSlav. *trŭnŭ*, 'thorn,' Sans. *tṛna*, 'blade of grass.'

dorren, vb., from the equiv. MidHG. *dorren*, OHG. *dorrên*, 'to get dry, dry up'; comp. OSax. *thorrôn*, Goth. **þaurzan*. A deriv. of *þorz-*, which appears in bürr; comp. Lat. *torrere*, 'to dry' (*torret* is exactly equiv. to OHG. *dorrêt*, Goth. **þaurzaiþ*). Instead of the form **þaurzan*, Goth. has *gaþaursnan* (OIc. *þorna*), 'to get dry, dry up,' which is differently derived (comp. Darre, bürr).

Dorſch, m., 'torsk,' simply ModHG., formed from LG. *dorsch*; corresponds to OIc. *þorskr*, E. *torsk*, *tusk*, from the equiv. Dan. *torsk*.

Dorſche, f., 'cabbage-stump, cole-rape,' with LG. initial *d*, from MidHG. *torse*, 'cabbage-stump,' OHG. *tursô, torso*, 'stalk'; for the change of *s* to *sch* comp. birſchen. There is a parallel Rom. class (Ital. *torso*, OFr. *tros*, 'stump, morsel') which is undoubtedly of Teut. origin. The HG. word is probably primit. allied to the Gr. θύρσος, 'wand.'

dort, adv., 'there, in that place,' from the equiv. MidHG. *dort*, OHG. *dorot*, probably from *darot*; Goth. **þaraþa* (formed like *dalaþa*), would be the corresponding adv. in answer to the question where? The OHG. has *darôt*, 'thither'; derived from þar, þa.

Doſe, f., 'box,' first occurs in ModHG., from LG. *dose*, Du. *doos* (Dan. *daase*).

Doſt, Doſten, m., 'marjoram,' from MidHG. *doste, toste*, OHG. *tosto, dosto*, m., 'wild thyme.' It may be really identical with MidHG. *doste, toste*, m., 'bunch, nosegay,' so that 'thyme' would be a specialised meaning. The Goth. word was probably **þusta*, 'shrub.' Further cognates to help in determining the root are wanting. Comp. Teſt.

Dotter (1.), m. and n., 'yolk,' from the equiv. MidHG. *toter*, OHG. *totoro, tutar-ei*; the ModHG word seems to have a LG. initial sound. Corresponds to OSax. *dôdro*, Du. *dojer*, AS. *dydring*, 'yolk'; a pre-Teut. term for the 'yolk of an egg' (see also Gi). AS. *dott*, m , 'point, spot,' E. *dot* are, on account of LG. *dott, dôtte*, 'yellow part of the egg,' to be derived from the same Aryan stem *dhut*; the orig. sense of Dotter may have been, therefore. 'point in the egg.' The E. term *yolk*, AS. *geolca*, is lit. 'yellow part,' from AS. *geolo*, equiv. to E. *yellow*. In OIc. *blóme*, 'yolk.'

Dotter (2.), m., from the equiv. MidHG. *toter*, m., 'gold-pleasure'; comp. MidE. *doder*, E. *dodder* ('toad-flax'); Dan. *dodder*,

Swed. *dodra*. Perhaps allied to Detter (1.), so that the plant was named from its colour (or from the similarity of its seeds to the yolk of an egg?).

Douches, see Doles.

Douſes, m., 'prison,' Jew., from Hebr. *tafas*, 'to seize, take prisoner.'

Drache, m. (with a MidG. *d*), 'dragon, kite, termagant,' from MidHG. *trache*, (UpG. *tracke*). OHG. *truhho* (UpG. *traccho*), m. ; the ModHG. initial sound is to be regarded in the same way as in tichten (comp. MidLG. and MidDu. *drâke*). The word was naturalised in Germany before the 8th cent. ; as in the case of the bird Greif, 'griffin,' the dragon as a fabulous beast furnished material for the imaginative faculty of the Germans, and supplanted the native mythological creations. The E. loan-word is equally old—AS. *draca*, E. *drake* (in *drake-fly* or *dragon-fly*). The word is based on Lat. (Rom.) *draco* (*dracco*), which again is derived from Gr. δράκων, 'dragon,' lit. 'the sharp-sighted animal' (from δέρκομαι). E. *dragon*, is of recent Rom. origin (Fr. *dragon*).

Draht, m., 'wire, file,' from the equiv. MidHG. and OHG. *drât*, m. ; comp. Du. *draad*, AS. *þrǽd*, equiv. to E. *thread*, OIc. *þrâðr*, Goth. **þrêþs* ; a dental deriv. of the Teut. root *þrê*, 'to turn, twist,' which appears in ModHG. brehen. The pre-Teut *trê* lies at the base of Gr. τρῆσις, 'hole,' which is identical in form with ModHG. Draht ; for the meaning comp. brehen, Darm.

Drake, LG., see Enterich.

drall, adj., 'tight, twisted, stalwart, active,' simply ModHG., akin to MidHG. *drël*, OIc. *þearle*, adv., 'firmly, strongly, very'; from britten?.

Drang, m., 'crowd, throng, pressure,' from MidHG. *dranc(g)*, m., 'throng, oppression.' Comp. Du. *drang*, 'pressure, throng, desire,' AS. *geþrang*, equiv. to E. *throng*; from bringen.

drängen, vb., 'to press, pinch, dun,' from MidHG. *drengen*, factitive of bringen. Drangſal is early ModHG. ; ſal is the frequent ModHG. suffix, the older form of which is as *isal*, Goth. *isl*, AS. and E. *-ls*. Goth. formed from the same stem, but by a different gradation, an abstract *þreihsl*, 'hardship, oppression.'

draus, draußen, 'outside, abroad,' from baraus, baraußen ; comp. MidHG. *drabe*, from *dar abe* ; ModHG. brau, from baran, brin, from barin.

drechſeln, vb., 'to turn (on a lathe),' deriv. of MidHG. *drëhsel, drœhsel*, 'turner,' in Goth. **þrēhs·ls;* trehen (root *þrē, trē*) cannot be closely allied to trechſeln; it must rather be connected with a root containing a guttural, *þrēhs-* or *þrēh*. Gr. τρέπομαι (with *τ* for *k*), and Lat. *torqueo* (Gr. ἄτρακτος, 'spindle,' Lat. *torcular*, 'oil-press'), point to a root *trek*, 'to turn.' The OHG. *drāhsil*, 'turner,' is probably the only remains of this root in Teut.; in Mid HG. and also in UpG. and LG. dialects trehen (MidHG. *drœjen, drœn*) signifies 'to turn (on a lathe).' See trehen.

Dreck, m., 'dirt, mire, filth, dung,' from the equiv. MidHG. *drëc* (gen. *-ckes*), m., 'dirt'; OHG. **drēcch*, Goth. **þrikk*, n., are supported by OIc. *þrekkr*, m., 'dirt' (Dan. *dräck*). Perhaps derived from the meaning 'sediment, lees,' so that Gr. τρύξ, τρυγός, 'lees, sediment, fresh must' (with *υ* for *ο* ?), may perhaps be compared.

drehen, vb., 'to turn, whirl, wind,' from MidHG. *drœjen, drœn*, 'to turn, turn round,' OHG. *drâjan*. The Goth. form may have been *þ aian* (comp. wehen, Goth. *waian;* ſäen, Goth. *saian*); comp. Du. *draaijen*, 'to turn (on a lathe)'; AS. *þrâwan* (comp. *sáwan, wâwan*), and MidE. *þrâwen*, 'to turn,' are str. vbs., while the ModHG. verb is wk. even in OHG. The assumed Goth. form **þraian*, 'to turn,' was undoubtedly conjugated strong (pret. **þaiþrō*). *þrē* is the verbal stem common to Teut., from which a subst., Draht, meaning 'twisted thread,' was formed by adding a dental suffix. This subst. proves most clearly that the root of trehen did not end in a guttural, and that therefore ModHG. Drechſler, from OHG. *drāhsil*, cannot be allied to trehen. In ModE., *to throw* ('to turn'), is obsolete. The root *þrē* is from pre-Teut. *trē, ter;* this appears in Gr., with the meaning 'to bore,' in numerous derivatives. 'To bore' is a specialisation of the meaning 'to turn,' πολύτρητος, 'porous,' τρῆμα, 'hole,' συντρῆσαι, τετραίνω, 'to bore through,' τερέω, 'to bore, turn on a lathe' (comp. MidHG. *drœjen*, 'to turn on a lathe'), τόρνος, 'turner's chisel,' τέρετρον, Lat. *terebra*, 'borer.' Comp. also Darm.

drei, num., 'three,' from MidHG. and OHG. *drî*, which is prop. simply the nom. masc.; the rest of the old cases are obsolete in ModHG.; AS. *þrî*, *þreó*, E. *three*, Goth. *þreis*, from **þrijis*. It corresponds to Aryan *trejes*, equiv. to Sans. *tráyas*, Gr. τρεῖς, from τρέjες, Lat. *trēs*, OSlov. *trĭje*. Drei, like the other units, is a primit. word. See Drilling, Dritte.

dreiſt, adj., 'bold, audacious, self-confident,' simply ModHG., from the equiv. LG. *drīste* (hence treiſt is not found in the UpG. dialects); comp. OSax. *thrīsti*, Du. *driest*, AS. *þrīste*, 'bold, daring.' The similarity in the initial sound with Lat. *tristis*, 'sad,' is perhaps of no etymological value; as, however, a similar change of meaning is met with in the cognates of ModHG. tapfer, Lat. *tristis* and OSax. *thrīsti* may perhaps be derived from a common root. Otherwise it might well be connected with tringen, OSax. *thrīsti*, for *thrīhsti*, from *þrinh-sti*?.

dreißig, see ßig.

dreſchen, vb., 'to thresh,' from the equiv. MidHG. *drëschen*, OHG. *drëskan;* corresponds to Du. *dorschen*, AS. *þerscan* (for *þrescan*), E. *to thrash, thresh* (comp. MidHG. *dreschen*, which also means 'to torment'); Goth. *þriskan*. Threshing was practised in primit. Teut. times, as this common term testifies. The Teutons, even before they became settlers, and hence while they were still migrating, were acquainted with the most elementary methods of agriculture; comp. the various kinds of corn, and also Pflug, Egge, Brot, &c. The Teut. cognates found their way into Rom.,—Ital. *trescare*, 'to trample, move the feet about, dance,' OFr. *tresche*, 'chain-dance.' From these the OTeut. method of threshing may be easily inferred. The flail (Dreſchflegel) came from Italy through the medium of Rom. (see Flegel); for this a simpler term is found in OHG. *driscil*, MidHG. and ModHG. *drischel*. The meaning of the Teut. base *tresk* is probably 'to stamp noisily, tread'; comp. Lith. *trasketi*, 'to rattle, clatter,' OSlov. *trĕskŭ*, 'crack,' *troska*, 'thunderclap.' E. *threshold* is mostly connected with dreſchen, OTeut. *þrëskan*, regarding it as the threshing-staff, or as the place at the entrance to the house where corn was threshed.

drillen, vb., 'to revolve, bore, drill,' from MidHG. *drillen*, 'to turn, make round' (with the partic. *gedrollen*, 'round'). The meaning 'to bore' comes from LG. *drillen* (see drehen, drechſeln, for the connecting link between the meanings), akin to Du. *drillen*, E. *to thrill*, and also LG. *drall* (MidDu. *drel*), 'round, turning,' which is formed by gradation. The cognates point to a Teut. root *þrel*, 'to turn on a lathe).'—**drillen**, 'to plague' or 'to drill (recruits),' may be derived from the first or the second meaning.

Drillich, m., 'ticking,' from MidHG. *drilich, drilch*, m., 'a stuff woven with three threads'; an adj. signifying 'threefold' formed into a subst.; see Zwillich. *Dri-* is the older form for *brei* in compounds (see britte, Zwilz, and Drilling); OHG. *drîfalt*, 'threefold.' OHG. *drilich*, 'threefold, consisting of three threads,' is the convenient Ger. rendering of the Lat. *trīlīx (trīlīcem)*, 'triple-twilled,' from *licium*, 'thread.' Similar formations may be seen in Zwillich and Sammet.

Drilling, m., 'triplet, one of three born at the same time,' simply ModHG., formed like Zwilling.

dringen, vb., 'to press, crowd, pierce,' from MidHG. *dringen*, OHG. *dringan*, 'to compress, throng, press on,' then also 'to plait, weave' (MidHG. *drîhe*, 'embroidering needle'); comp. Goth. *þreihan* (*eih* from *inh*), 'to throng, oppress, cramp, afflict.' The Teut. root is *þrinhw, þrung*; comp. also with OHG. *dringan*, OSax. *thringan*, AS. *þringan*, 'to press,' OIc. *þryngva*. The *h* was retained by MidHG. *drîhe*, f., 'embroidering needle,' whence MidHG. *drîhen*, 'to embroider.' With the general meaning 'to press' are connected ModHG. Drang, drängen, Gedränge (OHG. *gidrengi*), Goth. *þraihns*, 'crowd' (in *faihu- þraihns*, 'wealth'); E. *throng*. With the Teut. cognates Lith. *trénkti*, 'to shake, push,' *tránksmas*, 'din, tumult,' Lett. *trećkt*, 'to shatter,' are primit. allied.

dritte, ord. of brei, 'third,' MidHG. *dritte*, OHG. *dritto*; corresponds to Goth. *þridja;* AS. *þridda*, E. *third*. *þri-* is the stem (see Drillich), *dja* the suffix, which forms the ordinal from the cardinal; it is *-tio-* in Lat. *tertius* Sans. *tṛtīya-s.*—**Drittel**, n., 'third part, third,' from MidHG. *drittteil*.

Droge, f., 'drug,' ModHG. only, from Fr. *drogue*, which with its Rom. cognate *droga* (Ital., Span.) is usually derived from Du. *droog* (see trocken); yet there are essential reasons for ascribing the word to an Eastern origin.

drohen, vb., 'threaten,' from the equiv. MidHG. *dröu*, wk. vb., which is the denominative of an earlier *dro*, f., 'threat.' The more ancient vb. is ModHG. *träuen*, from MidHG. *dröuwen, drouwen*, OHG. *drewen*, *drouwen;* Goth. **þraujan*, AS. *þreán þreáde* (equiv. to E. *to threaten*). OHG. *drô, drôa* (gen. *drawa*), corresponds to AS. *þreá;* Goth. *prawa* is wanting, gen. *þrawôs*, f., 'threat.' In E. the word is obsolete. Beyond Teut. there are no cognates.

Drohne, f., 'drone.' The strict HG. form is Trehne, Trene (so still in Saxony and Austria), according to MidHG. *trēne, trēn*, OHG. *trēno*, m. Drohne is a LG. form derived from Sax. *drân*, plur. *drâni*, to which AS. *drân*, plur. *drēn*, E. *drone*, correspond; both point to Goth. **drainus, *drēnus*, while OHG. *trēno* assumes perhaps Goth. **drina;* the relation between the theoretical Goth. forms has not yet been definitely fixed. The base *drēn* seems to appear in dröhnen (Goth. *drunjus*, 'loud sound'). From the same root probably a Gr. term for 'bee' is formed—τενθρήνη, 'a sort of wasp or humble-bee' (also ἀνθρήνη, 'wild bee'?—comp. too τενθρηδών, ανθρηδών), also Lacon. θρώναξ, 'drone.' Biene, like Drohne, is a primit. Teut. term. See the following word.

dröhnen, vb., 'to roar, rumble, creak, drone,' simply ModHG., borrowed from LG. *drönen;* comp. Du. *dreunen*, OIc. *drynja*, vb., 'to drone, roar,' OIc. *drynr*, m., 'droning,' Goth. *drunjus*, m., 'loud sound.' See derivatives of the same root *drĕn, drhēn*, under Drohne; comp. besides Gr. θρῆνος, 'lamentation.'

drollig, adj., 'droll, ludicrous, queer,' simply ModHG., from LG. *drullig*, Du. *drollig;* E. *droll* (subst. and adj.), also adj. *drollish;* Fr. *drôle*, 'droll, merry.' None of these are recorded in the older periods of the several languages, hence their origin (Rom.? Teut.?) is obscure. The derivation from the Scand. name *trǫll* applied to ghostly monsters is improbable, for in the Scand. dialects the word has an initial *t* while the ModHG. brollig and its cognates have *d*.

Drossel (1.), f., 'thrush,' a LG. form from MidLG. *drosle*, OSax. *throssela, throsla;* the strictly UpG. term for Dressel is Bav. Dröschel, from MidHG. *dröschel*, f.; comp. OHG. *drôscela*, f., also without the deriv. *l, drôsca, drôseca*, f.; the latter form corresponds to AS. *þrýsce* (from **þrauskiô*), E. *thrush*. E. *throstle*, from AS. *þrostle*, 'merula,' corresponds to MidHG. *drostel;* in Goth. the latter would be **þrustla* and the former *þrauska* (or rather **þrauskjô*); akin to Gr. τρυγών, 'turtle-dove,' from **τρυσγων?*.

Comp. on the other hand OIc. þrǫstr, m., 'thrush,' Goth. *þrastus. This abundance of words which are undoubtedly closely allied renders any sure comparison with cognate words beyond Teut. a difficult task. The Lat. turdéla, 'thrush,' may be for *trzdéla; in that case the st of MidHG. drostel, E. throstle, is shifted from sd (see Aſt, Gerſte, Maſt, Reſt); turdéla is a derivative of turdus, 'thrush,' closely connected with OIc. þrǫstr, m. (Goth. *þrastus, m.). Lith. has a longer form for Droſſel, with an initial s—strázdas, which makes the origin of st of MidHG. drostel from zd, sd, a certainty. Russ. drozdŭ, OSlov. drozgŭ, are abnormal. The words of the Teut. group found their way into Rom.: ModFr. trâle (from *þrasla, *þrastla).—Droſſel is one of the few names of birds found in several Aryan languages at the same time, and entirely free from the assumption that they were borrowed.

Droſſel (2.), f., 'throat, throttle, Adam's apple,' preserved only in the deriv. erdroſſeln, 'to throttle, strangle'; not allied to Droſſel (1.), as is shown by MidHG. droʒʒe, f., 'gullet, throat.' Comp. OHG. droʒʒa, AS. þrotu, f., E. throat, and likewise E. throttle (subst. and vb.), an l deriv. There is a parallel group with an initial s added (see Droſſel (1.), Dach); MidHG. stroʒʒe, OLG. strota, 'throat, windpipe,' Du. stroot; see ſtroßen. From HG. the word found its way into Rom.,—Ital. strozza, 'throat,' strozzare, 'to strangle.'

Droſt, m., 'chief magistrate' (a LG. word), from MidLG. droste, drosséte; the latter is identical with MidHG. truhtsæʒe, ModHG. Truchſeß; for Droſtei see also under Truchſeß.

Druck, m., 'pressure, oppression, printing, proof,' from MidHG. druc (-ckes), m., 'pressure, violent impact, rebound, hostile encounter,' OHG. druck; corresponds to AS. þryc (cc supported by ofþryce), 'pressure.'

drücken, **drucken**, 'to press, oppress, hug, print,' from MidHG. drücken, drucken, OHG. drucchen (comp. AS. þryccan, 'to press'), MidHG. drucken, an unmodified UpG. variant, has a specialised meaning in ModHG. In Goth. the subst. would be *þrukks, the vb. þrukkjan. Since the Mid HG. vb. drücken is equiv. to 'to press, throng, oppress, thrust oneself,' the meanings harmonise well with bringen, which is based upon an Aryan root trenk, while trūden would be derived from a root trek

without the nasal; the kk of the theoretical Goth. form originated probably in kn. —**Drückſen**, ModHG. a frequentative form of brücken.

Drude, f., 'sorceress,' LG.; MidHG. trute, f., 'demoness, nightmare'; Drutenſuß, MidHG. trutenvuoʒ. In spite of its wide diffusion (Dan. drude, Gothland. druda), the form of the word is obscure, for it is impossible to see to what the MidHG. initial t and ModHG. d are related. Perhaps MidHG. trute is to be connected with the adj. traut; in that case Drube would be a euphemism similar perhaps to Gr. Eumenides.

Druſe (1.), f., 'ore with a drossy or crystal surface,' simply ModHG.; of obscure origin.

Druſe (2.), 'glanders,' ModHG.; identical with Drüſe.

Drüſe, f., 'gland, kernel, swelling of the glands,' from MidHG. driese, druose (whence the ModHG. variant druse, but only in a special sense); OHG. druos, druosi, f., 'glanders,' Goth. *þros or þróhsi ?, is wanting; so too in E. there is no cognate term.

Druſen, plur., an UpG. word for 'dregs, lees,' from MidHG. druosene, OHG. truosana (UpG. dialects have ue in the accented syllable); corresponds to Du. droesem, Mid Du. droesene, AS. drósn, 'dregs.' The base is perhaps Goth. *dróhsnó, to which E. dregs, ModHG. Treber, Trecher are also allied.

du, 2nd pers. pron., 'thou'; from Mid HG. and OHG. du, and the collateral Mid HG. and OHG. dû; comp. AS. þú, E. thou; Lat. tu, Gr. τό, σύ, and Sans. tvam, are prim. cognates. The details respecting the Aryan pronom. stem belong to grammar.

Ducaten, m. (ducat, m., rarely fem. in earlier ModHG.), 'ducat,' from late Mid HG. ducáte, m. (MidLat. ducátus).

Ducht, f., **Duchtbank**, and **Duft**, 'rowing seat, thwart;' the form with f is HG., that with ch LG.; OHG. dofta, f., OIc. þopta, f., 'thwart'; OHG. gilofto, prop. 'comrade on the thwart,' AS. gebofta, 'comrade.' One of the prim-Teut. naval terms developed during the migrations of the Teutons; see Ruber, Segel, Maſt, Schiff, &c. That the LG. form found its way into HG. is not remarkable after what has been said under Berb, Büſe, and Boot. The OTeut. word for 'thwart' (Goth. *þuftô, f.), belongs probably to a root tup, 'to squat down'; comp. Lith. *tupeti*, 'to squat,' *tupti*, 'to squat down.'

ðucken, vb., 'to bow, duck, stoop, dive,' with LG. initial *d*, from MidHG. *tucken*, *tücken*, 'to incline the body quickly, bend, bow'; prob. a frequentative of MidHG. *tûchen*, 'to dive,' which see.

Duckmäuſer, 'sly, stealthy person,' appears in MidHG. as *tockelmûser*, 'sneak, hypocrite'; the ModHG. form is based anew on bucken, MidHG. *tucken*. A parallel form Tückmäuſer is based on Tücke, 'malice,' the second part of the compound being connected with MidHG. *mûsen*, prop. 'to catch mice,' then (with thievish intent), 'to sneak.'

ðudeln, vb., simply ModHG. formed from the equiv. Pol. *dudlić*, 'to play the bagpipes,' from *dudy*, 'bagpipe.'

Duft (1.), f., see Ducht.

Duft (2.), m., 'exhalation, odour,' with LG. initial *d*, from MidHG. *tuft*, m., 'vapour, fog, dew, rime,' OHG. *tuft*, 'frost'; of obscure origin.

ðulðen, vb. (unknown to the Suab., and perhaps also to the other UpG. dialects), 'to bear, tolerate, suffer,' from the equiv. MidHG. and OHG. *dulten*; a denominative of OHG. *dult*, MidHG. *dult*, f., ModHG. Geduld. The Goth used *þulan* for bulten without the dental deriv. (OHG. *dolên*, MidHG. *doln*, both far more general in meaning than the ModHG. bulten, 'to suffer'; AS. *þolian*, 'to suffer'). The pre-Teut. root is *tel, tol, tlê*, which appears, exactly corresponding to the meaning of the Teut. cognates, in Gr. τλῆ-ναι, 'to suffer,' τλή-μων, 'miserable,' πολύτλας, 'much enduring,'. &c. Lat. *tolerâre* and *ertragen* (Lat. *perferre*), show that Lat. *tollo* (partic. *latus* for *tlâ-tus*; pret. *tuli*, from *affero*), and Gr. τολμᾶν, 'to venture, endure,' may be cognates. Hence the primary sense of the root appearing in the graded forms *tel, tol, tlê, tlâ*, is 'to bear, tolerate.' See Geduld.

Dult, f., Bav. 'fair,' with MidG. initial *d*, from MidHG. *tult*, f., 'fair, church festival, dedication festival,' OHG. *tuld*. The word is the OTeut. term for 'festival'; Goth. *dulþs*, f., 'festival, holiday.'

ðumm, adj., 'stupid, silly,' from Mid HG. *tum* (gen., -*mmes*), *tump* (gen. -*bes*), 'stupid, foolish, weak in understanding, dumb,' OHG. *tumb*. In Goth. *dumbs*, OIc. *dumbr*. the adj. is equiv. to AS. and E. *dumb*; the OHG. word, in addition to the meanings of MidHG., has likewise the signification 'deaf,' which also belongs to bumm in early ModHG. 'Dull in sense and intellect' may be the primary sense of the adj., which has not yet been found in the non-Teut. languages; ſtumm too has a peculiar history; see ſchmecken, hell. Words expressing the perceptions of one sense are often transferred to those of another. Hence Goth. *dumbs*, 'dumb,' OHG. *tumb*, 'deaf, dumb,' may possibly be allied to Gr. τυφλός, 'blind' (root *dhubh*; τυφ by the well-known rule for θυφ). This conjectural etymology is quite as uncertain as that offered under Dieb.

ðumpf, adj., 'damp, dull, heavy,' Mod HG. only; formed by the weakest stage of gradation from MidHG. *dimpfen*, str. vb., 'to fume, smoke'; comp. also MidHG. *dumpfen, dümpfen*, 'to fume, damp.' The orig. sense of the adj. is probably 'smoky,' *i.e.* 'damp,' or 'dimming the sight and dulling the hearing'; bumpf appears in Du. *dompig*, with the meaning 'damp, gloomy.' Perhaps the word is connected with bunſel; comp. E. *dank*.

Düne, f., 'down, dune,' simply Mod HG. from the equiv. LG. *düne* (OSax. *dûna*), Du. *duin* (whence Fr. *dune*); respecting ModHG. *ü* from Du. *ui*, comp. Büſe, Süten. Akin to AS. *dûn*, 'hill,' E. *down* ('plateau'). So too E. *down*, adv.; for AS. *adûne, ofdûne*, 'from the mountain, towards the valley,' corresponds exactly to MidHG. *ze tal* (comp. Fr. *à mont*, 'up the stream'). Likewise Gr. θύραζε, 'before the door,' has the general meaning 'outside'; MidHG. *ze bërge* is 'aloft, upwards'; comp. ModHG. bie, Haare ſtehen einem zu Berge, 'one's hair stands on end.' The *düne* group (E. *down*) seems to have spread from Eng. into Du. and LG. (comp. besides Baſt, Beet, Prahm). Hence the assumption that AS. *dûn* is of Kelt. origin is not to be discarded—OIr. *dûn*, 'hill' (comp. the OKelt. names of towns ending in *dûnum, Augustodûnum, Lugdunum*); though the attempt to show that it is primit. allied to Gr. θίν (nom. θίς), 'sea-beach,' and Sans. *dhânu-s*, 'dry land, continent, inhospitable land,' cannot be recommended; AS. *dûn* would be pre-Teut. *dhûnâ* (the indubitable form of the cognate word in Ind.).

Dung, m., with LG. initial *d*; 'dung, manure,' from MidHG. *tunge*, f., 'dung, manuring'; MidHG. *tunc*, m., f., signifies 'an underground—prop. dung-covered—chamber occupied in winter,' and especially 'the underground weaver's room'; OHG. *tunga*, 'manuring,' E. *dung* (subst. and vb.); OHG. *tunc*, 'weaver's room underground' (Dünger from late MidHG. *tunger*). This double meaning of the cognates is explained by the remarks of Tacitus (*Germania*, § 16) and Pliny (*Hist. Nat.*, 19, 1). 'Dung' is the primary sense of the cognates of Dung and Düngen; in the other Aryan languages, however, no primit. cognates can be adduced.

dunkel, adj., 'dark, gloomy, obscure,' with MidG. initial *d*; from MidHG. *tunkel*, 'dark, dull, damp,' OHG. *tunchal* (with the parallel form *tunchar*, MidLG. *dunker*). By another stage of gradation OIc. *døkkr*, OFris. *djunk* are formed from the same root; they presuppose a Goth. *diggs (pre-Teut. *dhengwos*). The primit. allied E. *dank* points to a connection with Dumpf (Teut. root *ding*, *dump*).

Dünkel, m., 'fancy, imagination, arrogance, prejudice,' simply ModHG. Related to the vb. dünken, from MidHG. *dunken* (pret. *dûhte*), 'to seem, appear to,' OHG. *dunchan* (chiefly impers. with dat.), 'to seem' (pret. *dûhta*); Goth. *þugkjan*, *þûhta*, mostly impers. with dat. 'to seem'; AS. *þyncan*, E. *to think*, which, however, really represents the meanings of AS. *þencan*, OHG. *denchen*, MidHG. and ModHG. denken. Dünken appears to have been originally a str. vb., of which denken was perhaps the factitive form. The Teut. *þunk*, *þank*, is based upon an old Aryan root *tng*, *teng*, and this, again, appears in OLat. *tongêre*, 'to know' (comp. Prænest. *tongitio*, 'notion'). Comp. denken, Dank.

dünn, adj., 'thin, slender, attenuated,' from the equiv. MidHG. *dünne*, OHG. *dunni*; comp. AS. *þynne*, E. *thin*, OIc. *þunnr*, Du. *dun*, Goth. *þunnus. The adj. retained the primit. meaning 'thin' in all the periods and dialects of Teut. The stem *þunnu* is preserved in OHG. *dunwengi*, AS. *þunwenge*, OIc. *þunnvange*, 'temples,' prop. 'thin cheek' (comp. ModHG. dial. Dünninge, Dünege, 'temples'). The adj. is primit. Aryan, in the form *tɩnû-s* (respecting Teut. *nn* comp. Kinn, Mann); comp. OInd. *tanû-s*, 'long, drawn out, narrow, thin'; Lat. *tennis*, 'thin, narrow'; Gr. *ταν-*, existing only in compounds, denotes 'drawn or stretched out, long'; comp. *ταναός*, which has the same

meaning; OSlov. *tǐnǔkǔ*, 'thin,' has a suffix. The idea of attenuation comes from 'extension in one direction, drawn out lengthwise,' still retained by the Ind. and the Gr. adjs. Lat., Teut., and Slav. deprived the orig. meaning of one of its characteristics. In OInd. and Gr. there occurs a verbal stem, *tanu* (*ταν*), with the primary sense 'to stretch out, extend.' Comp. dehnen, Dohne, Donner, and the following word.

Dunst, m., 'vapour, fume, mist,' from MidHG. *dunst*, *tunst*, m., f., 'steam, vapour,' OHG. *tunist*, *dunist*, *dunst*, 'storm, breath'; respecting the MidG. initial *d*. comp. Duft, Tunfel. Corresponds to AS. *dûst* (for *dunst), E. *dust*. Teut. *duns-*, for *dwuns-*, is based upon an Aryan root *dhwens*, which still appears in Sans. *dhvans*, 'to fall to dust' (*dhvasti*, 'falling to dust').

durch, prep., 'through, owing to, by,' from MidHG. *durch*, *dur*, 'through,' also 'for the sake of,' OHG. *duruh*, *durh*; comp. OSax. *thurh*, AS. *þurh*, E. *through* and *thorough*. Goth. *þaírh*, 'through,' with an abnormal vowel, is related to the OHG. *dërh*, 'perforated,' with which are connected OHG. *durhil*, *durihil*, MidHG. *dürhel*, *dürkel*, 'pierced, porous,' AS. *þýrel* (for *þyrhil*), 'hole' (comp. Nüster), as well as Goth. *þaírkó*, f., 'hole' (*k*, from *kk*, for *kn*?). The prepos. might easily be a case of an older adj., perhaps the acc. neut. Besides the passive meaning of OHG. *dërh*, 'pierced,' an active sense, 'piercing,' may also be added. The base *þerh* would be best defined by 'to pierce, penetrate,' which recalls the HG. tringen; the former is based upon a pre-Teut. root *terk*, the latter upon a root *trenk*. The connection with Lat. *trans* is exceedingly problematical.

Durchlaucht, 'Serene Highness,' simply ModHG. with MidG. vowel *au;* MidHG. and MidG. *durchlûht*, partic. for MidHG. *durchliuhtet*, 'illustrious,' from *durhliuhten*, 'to shine, light through, illuminate.' See Gelaucht, leuchten.

dürfen, anom. vb., 'to be allowed, venture, need,' from MidHG. *dürfen*, *durfen*, a preterite pres., 'to have reason, cause, be permitted, need, require'; OHG. *durfan*, preterite pres., 'to lack, be destitute of, require, be in need of'; comp. Goth. *þaúrban*, Du. *durven*, AS. *þurfan*, 'to be in need of.' In addition to the Teut. root *þurf*, *þurb*, Swiss points to an old parallel form *þurp*. In the ModHG. deriv. darben,

Bedürfniß, Notdurft, bieber, &c., the primary sense of the root *þrf*, from *trp*, 'to be destitute of, lack,' still appears.

dürr, adj., 'dry, meagre, barren,' from MidHG. *dürre*, OHG. *durri*, 'withered, dry, lean'; corresponds to Du. *dor*, OLG. *thurri*, AS. *þyrre*, Goth. *þaúrsus*, 'dry' (with regard to HG. *rr*, from Goth. *rs*, comp. irre, Farre). From a pre-Teut. adj. *þurzu-*, 'dry, withered,' which belongs to a root *þurs*, from pre-Teut. *tṛs*. As a result of the restriction of the word—probably in primit. times—to denote the dryness of the throat, we have the OInd. *tṛṣús*, 'greedy, panting,' and ModHG. dürsten; as applied to the voice, or rather speech, *tṛs* appears in Gr. ταυλός, 'lisping,' for *τρασυλός (comp. δαυλός, 'dense,' for *δασυλός, Lat. *densus*), and OInd. *tṛṣṭá-s*, 'hoarse, rough (of the voice).' With the general meaning 'dry,' ModHG. Darre, dörren, and their cognates are connected.

Durſt, m., 'thirst,' from the equiv. MidHG. and OHG. *durst*, m.; comp. MidLG. and Du. *dorst*, AS. *þyrst*, E. *thirst*; Goth. *þaúrstei*, f., 'thirst.' The final *t* of the OHG. and Eng. words is a deriv., as may be inferred from Goth. *þaúrseiþ mik*, 'I am thirsty.' The further comparisons made under Darre, dörren, dürr, amply prove that the short form *þors*, from pre-Teut. *tṛs*, signifies 'to be thirsty'; comp. especially OInd. *tṛ́ṣnaj*, 'thirsty,' *tṛ́ṣnā*, f., 'thirst,' *tṛṣ́*, str. vb. (3rd pers. sing. *tṛ́ṣyati*, Goth *þaúrseiþ*), 'to pant, be thirsty'; *tṛṣú-s*, 'panting.'

Duſel, m., 'dizziness,' simply ModHG., from LG. *dusel*, 'giddiness'; a genuine HG. word would have had an initial *t*, as OHG. *tusig*, 'foolish,' shows; the latter corresponds to AS. *dysig*, 'foolish,' E. *dizzy*. To the root *dus* (*dhus*), contained in this class, belong Thor, thöricht, with the genuine HG. *t* initially. A different gradation of the same root *dus*, from Aryan *dhus*, appears in AS. *dwǽs*, Du. *dwaas*, 'foolish.'

Duſt, m., 'dust, powder,' simply Mod HG., from LG. *dust*; corresponds to E. *dust* (but see further Dunſt). The final *t* is probably a deriv.; *dus*, the root, may be the weakest form of an Aryan *dhwes*; OInd. *dhvas*, *dhvaṅs*, seems to have been always nasalised; it signifies 'fly about like dust, scatter dust when running swiftly,' which is in harmony with the meaning of Duſt, 'dust.'

düſter, adj. (unknown to UpG.?), 'gloomy, dismal, sad,' from the equiv. LG. *düster*, *dûster*; comp OSax. *thiustri*, AS. *þeóstre*, *þýstre*, 'dark.' MidHG. *dinster*, OHG. *dinstar*, OHG. *finstar*, OSax. *finistar* are remarkable parallel forms expressing the same idea; so too AS. *þeóstru*, 'darkness.' The primary form may be seen in the stem of dämmern, Goth. *þimis*, 'twilight,' OInd. *támas*, 'darkness'; Lat. *tenebrae* (for *temebrae*) comes nearest perhaps to MidHG. *dinster*. *f* is interchanged with *þ* in Faſel, AS. *þœcele*; in the same way finſter might be related to *dinstar* (from *þinstar*). These guesses are, however, too uncertain.

Düte, Deute, Tüte, f., 'paper bag, screw'; merely ModHG. from LG. *tüte* (akin to Du. *tuit*, 'pipe'?); respecting the LG. and Du. *ü* sound, see under Büſe. In Swab. and Bav. the terms are *gugge*, *gucken*.

Dutzend, n., 'dozen,' from the equiv. late MidHG. *totzen*, with an excrescent final *d* (see Jemand, Mond); from Fr. *douzaine* (comp. Ital. *dozzina*), whence also E. *dozen*, Du. *dozijn*; ultimately derived from Lat. *duodecim*.

E.

Ebbe, f., 'ebb,' merely ModHG., borrowed, like many terms relating to the sea, from LG.; comp. Du. *ebb*, *ebbe*, f., Dan. *ebbe*, Swed. *ebb*, m. The word is first found in AS., where *ebba*, m., is the form (comp. E. *ebb*, whence also Fr. *ébe*), nautical terms being generally recorded at an earlier period in that language than elsewhere; comp. Boot, Leck, Schote (2.), Steven, and Bord. Had the OTeut. word been preserved in Ger. we should have expected OHG. *eppo*, ModHG. Eppe. It is possible that the word is connected with the cognates of eben (Ebbe, lit. 'leveller,'? 'plain'?). Yet Ebbe, from its meaning, is more appropriately connected with Goth. *ibuks*, 'backwards, back' (OHG. *ippihhôn*, 'to roll back'); hence Ebbe is lit. 'retreat'; the connection with eben (Goth. *ibns*) is not thereby excluded. Scand. has a peculiar word for Ebbe—*fjara*, 'ebb,' *fyrva*, 'to ebb.' No Goth. word is recorded.

eben, adj., 'even, level, plain, smooth,' from MidHG. *ëben*, OHG. *ëban*, adj., 'level, flat, straight'; common to Teut. under these meanings, but it is not found in any other Aryan group; comp. OSax. *ëban*, Du. *even*, AS. *ëfn*, E. *even*, OIc. *jafn*, Goth. *ibns*, 'level.' Akin perhaps to Goth. *ibuks*, adj., 'backward' (see Übel). Apart from Teut. the stem *ib* in the form *ep* or *ebh* has not yet been authenticated; Lat. *œquus* (Sans. *ëka*), cannot, on account of phonetic differences, be regarded as a cognate.— **eben,** adv., 'even, just,' from MidHG. *ëbene*, OHG. *ëbano;* comp. OSax. *ëfno*, AS. *ëfne* (whence E. *even*); the old adv. form of the adj. (Comp. neben.)

Ebenbaum, m., 'ebony-tree,' from the equiv. MidHG. and late OHG. *ebënus*, adopted as a foreign word (still declined after the Lat. method in OHG.) from Lat. *ebenus* (Gr. ἔβενος).

Eber, m., from the equiv. MidHG. *ëber*, OHG. *ëbar*, m., 'wild boar'; corresponds to AS. *eofor*, m., 'wild boar' (E. *York* from AS. *Eoforwic*, lit. 'boar-town'), OIc. *jǫfurr*, 'wild boar,' figuratively 'prince' (also *jǫrbjúga*, 'a kind of sausage'); Goth. **ibrus, *ibarus*. With the pre-Teut. base *eprús* some have connected OBulg. *veprĭ*, m., Lat. *aper*, m., 'wild boar.' Similarly in the terms for Ferkel and Schwein, the West Aryan languages only partially agree.

Ebritz, m., 'southern-wood,' from the equiv. late MidHG. *eberitz (ebereize)*, f., from Lat. *abrotanum* (whence also Aberraute, see after), but corrupted by connection with Eber.

echt, adj., 'genuine, real, legitimate,' simply ModHG. adopted from MidG. and LG., where *echt* is the normal correspondent of MidHG. and OHG. *ëhaft*, 'lawful'; comp. Du. *echt*; akin to OFris. *aft*, 'lawful'; from Ehe, compared with which the adj. has retained the old meaning of Ehe, 'law.' By means of the law-books based on the Saxon Code the LG. adj. found its way into HG., but not until after Luther; yet the word does not occur in the UpG. dialects.

Eck, n., **Ecke,** f., 'edge, corner,' from MidHG. *ëcke*, f. (seldom neut.), 'edge of weapons, point, corner, brim,' OHG. *ëkka*, f., 'point, edge of a sword.' Corresponds to OSax. *eggia*, f., 'edge, sharpness, sword,' AS. *ecg*, 'corner, point, edge (of a sword, &c.), sword,' E. *edg*', OIc. *egg*, f., 'point'; Goth. **agja*, f., is not recorded. The meaning 'point, sharp edge,' which originally was the most prominent in the cognates (see also Gage), recalls the development in ModHG. Ort. The Teut. root *ag(ah)*, pre-Teut. *ak* (Goth. *anjō*-, from Aryan *akyā*-), with the primary meaning 'pointed,' is found in very many non-Teut. languages, since ModHG. Ähre and the non-Teut. words cited under that word are primit. allied to it, as are also Lat. *acies*, Gr. *ἀκίς*, 'point,' both in form and meaning.

Ecker, f., 'acorn,' simply ModHG., from MidG. and LG. *ecker*, 'acorn, beech nut'; there is also in UpG. a word **acheren* primit. allied and equiv. to Swiss *ach-ram* (Bav. *akram*). Comp. the corresponding Goth. *akran*, n., 'produce, fruit (generally),' OIc. *akarn*, n., AS. *œcern*, E. *acorn*, Du. *aker*, 'acorn.' Since the meaning 'acorn, beechnut,' is a recent specialisation in comparison with Goth. *akran*, 'produce, fruit,' the cognates may be connected with Goth. *akrs*, HG. Acker, and perhaps also with Lith. *ůga*, 'berry,' unless the latter is more closely allied to Lat. *uva*. In any case its kinship with Eiche must be denied, since the latter would be **aiks* in Goth. The mutation of the stem in ModHG. and LG. Ecker must be explained by a Goth. **akrin*.

edel, adj., 'of noble birth or qualities, excellent, generous,' from MidHG. *edel, edele*, OHG. *edili (adal-)*, adj., 'of a good family, noble, high-minded'; a deriv. of Adel, OHG. *adal*. Comp. OSax. *ediľi (adal-)*, 'of a good family, noble,' from *aδali*, 'noble family,' AS. *œδele*, 'noble, distinguished.' For details see Adel.

Egel, see Igel.

Egge, f., 'harrow,' simply ModHG., from LG. *egge*; likewise eggen from LG., because a corresponding HG. word would be eden or egen. The MidHG. word is *egede*, OHG. *egida*, f., 'harrow,' OHG. *ecken* (partic. *gi-egit*), 'to harrow,' MidHG. *egen*. Comp. Du. *egge*, AS. *egeδe;* Goth. **agjan*, 'to harrow,' **agiþa*, 'harrow,' are not recorded. The Teut. root *ag (ah)*, 'to harrow,' from pre-Teut. *ak*, *ok*, is most closely connected with Lat. *occa*, 'harrow,' Lith. *akëiti*, 'to harrow,' *akéczos*, 'harrow,' OCorn. *ocet*, W. *oged*, 'harrow.' The West Eur. cognates may also be further connected with Ecke (Lat. *acies*).

ehe, adv., 'before,' from MidHG. *ë*, a parallel form to ModHG. *ehr*, MidHG. *ër*, like ModHG. *bа* from *bar*, *wo* from *war*. See eher.

Ehe, f., 'marriage, wedlock, matrimony,'

from MidHG. *é, ewe*, f., 'customary right, justice, law, marriage,' OHG. *ewa*, f., 'law, marriage'; corresponds to OSax. *éo*, m., 'law,' Du. *echt*, 'marriage' (from *é-haft*, see *echt*), AS. *ǽ, ǽw*, f., 'law, marriage.' These West Teut. cognates *aiwi-* might be derived from *aigwi-, aihwi*, and connected with Lat. *aequum* (base *aiqo-*). To this there is no objection from the linguistic standpoint, for it is probable that the cognates similar in sound and signifying 'time, eternity,' are totally different from those just quoted; comp Goth. *aiws*, OHG. *éwa*, AS. *ǽ, ǽw*, 'time, eternity,' which are allied to Lat. *aevum, aeternus*, Gr. *αἰών, αἰεί*; so too Sans. *āyas*, 'duration of life.' Yet the first group might also perhaps be connected with Sans. *éva*, m., 'progress, course, procedure, custom.'

eher, ehr, adv., 'sooner, earlier, rather,' from MidHG. and OHG. *ér (é)*, 'formerly, previously,' compar. adv.; comp. Goth. *airis*, 'formerly,' from *air*, 'early,' also AS. *ǽr*, E. *ere*. See *ehe, erst*.

ehern, see **Erz**.

Ehni, see **Ahn**.

Ehre, f., 'honour,' from MidHG. *ére*, OHG. *éra*, f., 'honour, fame, sense of honour'; corresponds to OSax. *éra*, f., 'honour, protection, pardon, gift,' AS. *ár*, f., 'honour, help, pardon' (*árian*, 'to spare, pardon'), OIc. *eir*, f., 'pardon, gentleness.' Goth. *aiza* is by chance not recorded; it is probably allied to Goth. *ais-tan*, 'to shun, respect,' which is undoubtedly primit. akin to Lat. *aes-tumare*, 'to acknowledge, value.' It is probably connected with the Sans. root *iš*, 'to desire, seek to obtain.'

Ei, m., 'egg,' from MidHG. and OHG. *ei*, n., 'egg'; common to Teut. with the same meaning, although Goth. *addjis*, n. (comp. OIc. *egg*), is wanting; *ada*, however, is found in Crim. Goth. Comp. OSax. *ei*, Du. *ei*, AS. *ǽ¿*, n. E. *egg* is borrowed from Scand. *egg*. Between the Teut. *aius* (*ajjas*), n., 'egg,' and the corresponding terms in the West Aryan languages there is an unmistakable agreement of sound, although the phonetic justification for the comparison has not yet been found; comp. Lat. *óvum* (LowLat. *ŏvum*, on account of Fr. *œuf*), Gr. *ᾠόν*, OSlov. *jaje, aje* (from the base *ejo-?*), OIr. *og*, 'egg.' Arguing from these cognates, Teut. *ajjas*, n., has been derived from *ewjo-, ŏwjo-*, and connected with Lat. *avis*, Sans. *vi*, 'bird.' In East Aryan no corresponding word is found.

Eibe, f., 'yew,' from the equiv. Mid HG. *iwe*, OHG. *iwa*, f. (MidHG. also 'a yew-tree bow'); comp. the corresponding AS. *iw, éw*, E. *yew*, and OIc. *ýr*, m., 'yew' (and 'bow'). Goth. *eiws* is by chance not recorded. Swiss *tche, ige*, OHG. *iha*, OLG. *ich*, AS. *eoh*, prove that the word had originally a medial guttural; hence the primary form Goth. *eihwa?*. From the Teut. word, MidLat. *ivus*, Fr. *if*, Span. *iva*, 'yew,' are derived. The relation of OHG. *iwa, iha*, AS. *iw, eoh*, to OIr. *eo*, W. *yw*, 'yew' (Lith. *jévà*, 'bird-cherry tree,' OSlov. *iva*, 'willows'), has yet to be determined.

Eibisch, m., 'marsh mallow,' from Mid HG. *ibische*, OHG. *ibisca*, f., 'marsh mallow, dwarf mallow'; borrowed early from the equiv. Lat. *ibiscum* (Gr. *ἰβίσκος*).

Eiche, f., 'oak, oak-tree,' from the equiv. MidHG. *eich*, OHG. *eih (hh)*, f.; a term common to Teut., but by chance not recorded in Goth. (**aiks*, f.); comp. Du. *eek* (*eik*), AS. *ác*, f., E. *oak*. In Iceland, where there are no trees, the old word *eik*, f., received the general meaning 'tree' (for a similar change of meaning see **Esche, Föhre, Tanne**; comp. Gr. *δρῦς*, 'oak, tree (generally).' The term *aik-* is peculiar to Teut.; whether it is connected with OIc. *eikenn*, adj., 'wild,' and with the Sans. root *éj*, 'to shake,' is undecided.

Eichel, f., from the equiv. MidHG. *eichel*, OHG. *eihhila*, 'acorn, fruit of the oak' (corresponding to Du. *eikel*). The form was orig. a diminutive of **Eiche**, 'the offspring of the oak,' as it were; the derivative is wanting in E. and Scand. **Eckern**, ModHG., is not a cognate.—**Eichhorn**, n., 'squirrel,' from the equiv. MidHG. *eichorn*, OHG. *eihhorn* (**eicchorn* according to Swiss *eil·xer*), but corrupted at an early period by connecting it with **Horn**. The primit. Teut. base cannot be discovered with any certainty, since the word has been transformed by popular etymology in all languages. Du. *eekhoren* corresponds to the HG. form. AS. *ác-wern* (earlier *dcweorna*), 'squirrel,' is abnormal, and apparently a compound; still more remote is the equiv. OIc. *íkorne*, from *eik*, 'oak, tree.' The implied Goth (primit. Teut.) word **aikawairna* (**eikawairna*) seems by its formation to resemble Goth. *widuwairna*, OHG. *diorna* (see **Dirne**); in that case AS. *ácweorna* (OIc. *íkorne*) might be a diminutive of *aik* (*ik?*), 'oak,' meaning lit. 'little oak-animal'?. Comp. the diminutive forms MidLat. *squiriolus*, ModHG. Ĝidjĥörndjen, OSlov. *vĕverica*. On the other hand, some maintain that *weorn* in AS. *ácweorna* means 'tail,' while others connect it with Lat. *viverra*, derived from a North Europ. word (Lith. *vover̃*, OSlov. *vererica*). At all events, since the Teut. cognates include OIc., AS., and OHG., we need not suppose the word was borrowed from a Southern Rom. term ; Lat. *sciŭrus* (Gr. σκίουρος), Fr. *écureuil*, Span. *esquilo* (MidLat. *squiriolus*) —whence E. *squirrel*—are too remote in sound from the Teut. words. There is no reason for assuming that the Teut. word was borrowed from another source.

eidjen, aidjen, vb., 'to gauge,' from MidHG. *îchen* (*ühten*), 'to survey, gauge, inspect'; akin to MidHG. *îche*, *ich*, f., 'measure, official standard, office of weights and measures'; corresponds to Du. *ijk*, 'gauge, stamp,' *ijken*, 'to gauge, stamp.' In LG. and MidLG. *ike*, f., means 'gauge mark, instrument for gauging,' generally 'a pointed instrument, lance,' for which reason the cognates have been derived from a Teut. root *îk*, 'to prick.' Yet MidHG. *ühten* points to a connection with *ahten*. In UpG. pfedjten (see Pegel) has a parallel form pjedjen. The solution of the difficulty with regard to eidjen has not yet been found. The spelling of the word with OBav. *ai* is also remarkable, since in Suab. and Bav. *ei* corresponds to the MidHG. *î*.

Eidjhorn, see Eidje.

Eid, m., 'oath, execration,' from the equiv. MidHG. *eit*(*d*), OHG. *eid*, m.; a word common to Teut., but not found in the other groups; Goth. *aiþs*, OIc. *eiðr*, AS. *áþ*, E. *oath*, Du. *eed*, OSax. *éth*, m.; for the common Teut. *aiþa-z*, from pre-Teut. *ói-to-s* (comp. OIr. *oeth*, 'oath'), no suitable cognate has yet been found. Ehe and its cognates are scarcely allied to it, though Eidam may be so.

Eidam, m., 'son-in-law,' from MidHG. *eidem*, m., 'son-in-law,' also 'father-in-law' (comp. Vetter, Schwager, Vase, Neffe, with regard to the fluctuating meaning), OHG. *eidum*, 'son-in-law'; corresponds to AS. *áðum*, OFris. *áthum*, 'son-in-law.' Goth. *aiþmus (?) is wanting, the word *mégs* (see Mage) being used. This merely West Teut. term, the derivation of which appears to be similar to that of Oheim, is connected with MidHG. *eide*, OHG. *eidî*, Goth. *aiþei*, 'mother.' It is not impossible that it may be allied to Eid also ; comp. E. *son-in-law*. In Suab. and Alem. Eidam is unknown, the word used being Tochtermann.

Eide, f., 'awn, beard,' LG. See Ähre.

Eidechſe, f., from the equiv. MidHG. *egedëhse*, OHG. *egidëhsa*, f., 'lizard'; like Eichhorn, the word has been corrupted in various ways in the other languages of the West Teut. group, so that it is impossible to discover its primary meaning. Du. *haagdis*, *hagedis*, 'lizard,' is based on *haag*, 'hedge,' in MidDu. *eggedisse*; AS. *áþexe*, whence E. *ask*, *asker*, 'water-newt,' is altogether obscure. The component OHG. *-dëhsa*, AS. *-þexe* (to use Ochsen, 'lizards,' in natural history as an equiv. term for Saurier, 'Saurians,' is a mistake due to a wrong derivation), may be connected with the Aryan root *teks*, 'to make,' which appears in Dachs ; OHG. *egi-dëhsa*, lit. 'one who inspires fear'?. Comp. OHG. *(gi*, Goth. *agis*, 'fear'; primit. cognate with Gr. ἄχος, 'pain, sadness.'

Eider, Eidergans, f., 'eider-duck,' simply ModHG. from LG. *eider*; the latter, like E. *eider*, *eider-duck*, is from Ic. *æ̂þr* (gen. *æ̂þar*), *æþekolla*, 'eider-duck' (Mod. Ic. *æ* is pronounced like *ei*). Eider-down was brought by the Hanse traders from Iceland to England and Germany, and from the latter imported into Sweden (Swed. *ejder*, *ejderdun*). To the OIc. *æ̂þr*, Sans. *áti-*, 'water-bird,' may correspond ; the latter, it is true, is mostly connected with Ente ; comp. further Norw. *ádder*, Swed. (dial.) *áda*, 'eider-duck' (from OIc. *áþr, without mutation).

Eifer, m., 'zeal, fervour, passion,' from late MidHG. *îfer*, m. (*îfern*, n.), 'zeal, jealousy.' The word appeared at a remarkably late period (15th cent.), and its previous history is quite obscure ; it found its way from UpG., in connection with Luther's translation of the Bible, into LG., Du., Dan. and Swed. Nothing can be adduced in favour of the assumption that the word was borrowed from UpG. eifern. An older Ger. adj., eifer, 'sharp, bitter' (as late as Logau), OHG. *eivar*, *eibar*, 'sharp, bitter,' AS. *áfor*, 'sharp, bitter,' might perhaps be cognate with ModHG. Eifer.

eigen, adj., 'own, pertinent, peculiar, odd,' from the equiv. ModHG. *eigen*, OHG. *eigan*; an adj. common to Teut. ; comp. OSax. *égan*, Du. *eigen*, AS. *ágen*, E. *own*, OIc. *eiginn*; Goth. used *svés* for *aigans. The old adj. eigen is, as the suffix *n* shows, prop. a partic. ending in -ana- of a vb., which only appears, however, as a pret.-pres., meaning 'to possess,' throughout the Teut. group; comp. Goth. *áigan*, (*áihan*), OIc. *eiga*, AS. *ágan*, 'to have' (E. *to owe*), pret. in AS. *áhte*, in E. *ought*, whence also AS. *ágnian*, E. *to own*. The Teut. root *aig* (*aih*), from pre-Teut. *aik*, preserved in these words, has been connected with the Sans. root *íç*, 'to possess, have as one's own,' the partic. of which, *íçâni-s* (*íçána-s*), agrees exactly with HG. *eigan*, Goth. *aigans. In ModHG. Fracht (which see) we have a subst. formed with a dental suffix (Goth. *aihts*, 'property, possession,' OHG. *éht*).

Eiland, n., 'isle,' from MidHG. *eilant*, *einlant*(*d*), n., 'land lying by itself, island' (comp. MidHG. *eilif*, from OHG. *einlif*, see elf). Ein here has the meaning 'solitary, alone,' as in Einsiedler, Einöde. E. *island*, and Du. *eiland*, are not allied; they belong to An; see the latter.

eilen, vb., 'to hasten, hurry,' from the equiv. MidHG. and MidLG. *îlen*, OHG. *îlen* (*îllen* from *îljan*); akin to AS. *île*, OFris. *ile*, OIc. *il* (gen. *iljar*), 'sole of the foot.' If the *l* be accepted as a deriv., as it often is in other words, we obtain the widely diffused root *i*, 'to go,' as the source of the cognates; comp. Gr. ἱέναι, Lat. *ire*, Sans. root *i*, 'to go,' OSlov. *iti*, Lith. *eiti*, 'to go.' See gehen.

eilf, see elf.

Eimer, m., 'pail, bucket,' from the MidHG. *eimber*, *ein-ber*, m., OHG. *eimbar*, *einbar*, m., n., 'pail'; corresponds to OSax. *êmbar* (*ênnar*), Du. *emmer*, AS. *ámbor*, *ombor*, m., 'pail.' Apparently a compound of *ein-* (Goth. *ains*) and a noun formed from the root *ber* (Gr. φερ, Lat. *fer*), 'to carry,' which is discussed under Bahre, Bürde; hence 'a vessel to be carried by one person'; or rather 'a vessel with a handle' ?. In reality, however, the words cited are only popular corruptions, which were suggested by Zuber (OHG. *zwi-bar*) as well as by OHG. *sumbirt*(*n*); for undoubtedly OHG. *ambar*, AS. *ombor*, are the older forms, as is also proved by the borrowed words, OSlov. *aborŭ*, Pruss. *wumbaris*, 'pail'; in that case it would be connected with Gr. ἀμφορά. Note too the diminutives OHG. *amprî* (MidHG. *emmer* ?), AS. *embren*, 'pail,' formed from OHG. *sumbirt*(*n*).

ein, num., from the equiv. MidHG. and OHG. *ein*, 'one,' also the indef. art. even in OHG. and MidHG.; comp. OSax. *ên*, Du. *een*, AS. *ân* (E. *one*, as a num. *a*, *an*, as indef. art.), OIc. *einn*, Goth. *ains*. The num. common to Teut. for 'one,' orig. *ainos*, which is primit. cognate with Lat. *únus* (comp. *commúnis* and gemein, 'common'), and also with OIr. *óen*, OSlov. *inŭ*, Lith. *vénas*, Pruss. *ains*, 'one.' From this old num., which strangely enough is unknown to East Aryan (in which the cognate terms Sans. *éka*, Zend *aéva*, 'one,' occur), Gr. (dial.) has preserved οἰνός, 'one,' and οἴνη, 'the one on dice, ace.' See Einer, Einöde.—**einander**, 'one another,' thus even in MidHG. *einander*, OHG. (in the oblique cases) *einander*, pron., 'one another'—a senseless combination of the nom. *ein* with an oblique case of *ander*; e.g. OHG. *sie sind ein anderen ungelîh*, 'they are unlike one another' (lit. the one to the other), *zeinanderen quédan*, 'to say to one another' (lit. one to the others), for which, however, by a remarkable construction, *zeinen einanderen* may be used in OHG.—

Einbeere, f., 'one-berry, true-love,' simply ModHG.; the assumption that the word is a corruption of *juniperus* is not necessary in order to explain the word. Comp. Ic. *einer*.—**Einfalt**, f., 'simplicity, silliness,' from MidHG. *einvalt*, *einvalte* (-*velte*), f., OHG. *einfaltî*, f., 'simplicity, silliness'; comp. Goth. *ainfalþei*, f., 'silliness, good-nature'—an abstract noun from Goth. *ainfalþs*, 'silly,' OHG. and MidHG. *einfalt*, 'silly,' whence OHG. *einfaltîg*, MidHG. *einveltec*, adj., 'silly.' See falt.—**eingefleischt**, see Fleisch.—**Eingeweide**, n., 'entrails, bowels, intestines,' from MidHG. *ingeweide* (AS. *innoþ* from *invaþ*), n., 'bowels,' for which *geweide*, n., also meaning 'food,' chiefly occurs; ModHG. *ein-* for ModHG. *in*, 'within, inside'; OHG. *weida*, 'food, pasture.' Therefore Eingeweide must have meant lit. 'the food that has been eaten,' and afterwards 'the organs at work in digesting it'; comp. also auswciden, 'to disembowel.' See Weide.—**einig**, adj., 'agreed, sole, only,' from MidHG. *einec*(*g*), OHG. *einag*, adj., 'sole, only'; a deriv. of *ein*.—**Einöde**, f., from the equiv. MidHG. *einœde*, *einœte*, *einôte*, f., 'solitude, desert,' OHG. *einôtî*, n., 'solitude, desert.' By being based on *ôte*, the MidHG. and ModHG. word received its present form; properly, however, -*ôti* in the OHG. word is a suffix (comp. Heimat, Dienat, Armut); Goth. *ainôdus* (comp. *mannisk-ôdus*, 'benevolence') is wanting; comp. AS. *ánad* (from *ánôd*), OSax. *ĕnôdi*, 'desert'; the suffix *-ôdus* corresponds to Lat. *-átus* (*senatus, magistratus*). — **einſam**, adj., 'lonely, solitary,' simply ModHG. derived from *ein* and the suffix of *langſam, wonneſam, ehrſam*. See *ſam*. — **Einſiedel**, m., from the equiv. MidHG. *einsidel, einsidele* (also even *einsidelære*), m., OHG. *einsidilo* (*einsidillo*, Goth. *ainsiþlja), 'hermit;' an imitation of Gr. ἀναχωρητής, Lat. *anachoreta*, basing it on OHG. *sēdal*, 'seat.' See **ſiedeln**.

ein, adv., 'in, into,' from MidHG. and OHG. *în*, adv., 'in, into,' beside which MidHG. and OHG. *in* with the same meaning. The long form was derived from the short, as is proved by the connection with the cognates of *in*, which see.

einſt, adv., from the equiv. MidHG. *einst, einest*, OHG. *einêst*, adv., 'once, at one time'; an obscure deriv. of *ein*; in AS. *ǽnes*, E. *once*, to which OHG. *eines*, MidHG. *eines*, 'once, at one time,' also correspond. Comp. OHG. *anderes, anderêst*, MidHG. *anderes, anderst*, 'otherwise,' as similar formations.

Eintracht, f., 'concord, harmony, agreement,' from the equiv. late MidHG. *eintraht*, f., which, however, belongs, as a MidG. word, to **treffen**; hence MidG. *cht* for *ft*. OHG. preserves the correct form *eintraft*, 'simple.' Comp. Zwietracht.

einzeln, adj. and adv. (in Suab. and Bav. *einzächt*), 'single(ly), sole(ly), individual(ly),' from the equiv. MidHG. *einzel*, a modification of the older and more frequent *einlütze*, OHG. *einluzzi*, 'single, alone'; comp. Thur., and Sax. *eelitzg* (*êlixɣ*), 'unmarried,' from MidHG. *einlützec* (OHG. *einluzzo*), 'unmarried.' The second component belongs to ModHG. **los** (OHG. *hliozzan*); OHG. *ein-luzzi*, 'one whose lot stands alone.' Comp. also OIc. *einhlitr*, 'single'?

einzig, adj., 'only, sole, unique,' from MidHG. *einzec*, 'single,' a developed form of OHG. *einazzi* (adv., *einazzĕm*), the *zz* of which is deriv., as in *emſig* (comp. Gr. κρυπτάδιος with a cognate suffix).

Eis, n., 'ice,' from the equiv. MidHG. and OHG. *îs*, n.; a word common to Teut.; comp. Du. *ijs*, AS. *îs*, E. *ice*, OIc. *iss*, 'ice' (Goth. *eisa is by chance not recorded). Outside the Teut. group no term identical with this can be found. It is still undecided whether it is cognate with **Eiſen** (root *is* 'to shine'?) or with Zend *isi* ('ice'?).

Eisbein, n., a North Ger. word, from the equiv. LG. *îsbên*, MidLG. *îsbên*, 'hip-bone'; comp. Du. *ijsbeen, ischbeen*, 'the socket of the hip-bone,' AS. *îsbân*, n. The first part of the compound seems to contain a subst. *isa-*, 'gait, walking,' which Sans. *ếṣa*, m., 'hastening on,' resembles.

Eiſen, n., 'iron, weapon, sword, fetters,' from MidHG. and MidLG. *îsen* (*îsern*), OHG. *îsan, îsarn*, n., 'iron'; corresponds to Du. *ijzer*, AS. *îsern, îren*, E. *iron*, OIc. *îsarn*, Goth. *eisarn*, 'iron.' Its relation to **Eis** is still undecided; it is most closely connected with OIr. *îarn*, 'iron' (for **isurno-*), whence OIc. *jarn* (Dan. *jern*) is borrowed. It is less certain that OHG. *êr*, Goth. *aiz*, Lat. *aes*, 'bronze,' are allied to it. The deriv. *r* of the earlier forms is retained by ModHG. *eiſern*, which is based on MidHG. *îserin, îsernin*, OHG. *îsarnîn*, adj., 'of iron.'

eitel, adj., 'vain, idle, useless, void,' from MidHG. *îtel*, adj., 'empty, vacant, vain, useless, fruitless, pure, unadulterated,' OHG. *îtal*, 'empty, vacant, vain, boastful'; corresponding to OSax. *îdal*, 'empty, invalid,' Du. *ijdel*, AS. *îdel*, 'empty, useless, worthless,' E. *idle*. The orig. meaning of the adj. was probably 'empty'; but if we accept 'shining' as the primary sense, it follows that the word is connected with Gr. αἴθω, Sans. root *idh*, 'to flame.'

Eiter, n., 'pus, matter, suppuration,' from MidHG. *eiter*, OHG. *eitar* (*eittar*), n., 'poison' (especially animal poison); Goth. **aitra-* is wanting; an old *tr* remains unchanged in HG. (see **treu**, **zittern**). Comp. MidLG. and Du. *etter*, AS. *áttor, attor*, E. *atter* ('pus, poison'), OIc. *eitr*, n. Also a variant without the suffix *r* (Goth. **aita-*); comp. OHG. and MidHG. *eiz* (Alem. *eisse*, Bav. *aiss*), m., 'abscess, ulcer,' with a normal permutation of *t* to 33. The Teut. root *ait*, 'poisonous ulcer,' has been rightly connected with the Gr. οἶδος, n. οἶδμα, n., 'swelling,' οἰδάω, 'to swell'; hence the root is Aryan *oid*.

Ekel, m., 'nausea, disgust, aversion,' a ModHG. word, which has obtained a wide circulation through Luther (he used the form **Gdel**; unknown in the contemporaneous UpG. writings). A MidG. word with obscure cognates; it is perhaps connected with AS. *ácol*, 'burdensome, troublesome' (base *aiklo-*), and probably also to LG. *extern*, 'to vex' (Du. *akelig*, 'terrible,' E. *ache'?). The *h* in UpG. **heikel** (Swiss, *heikxel*) may be excrescent, as in **hitſchen**. These cognates have probably no connection with a Teut. root *erk*, 'to vomit, nauseare,' to which old UpG. *erkelæ*, 'to loathe,' E. *irksome, to irk*, are allied.—**Ekelname**, 'nickname,' simply ModHG., in MidHG. *â-name*, prop. 'false name'; from LG. *œkelname*; comp. Swed. *öknamn*, 'nickname,' OIc. *aukanafn*, 'epithet, surname'; from the Teut. root *auk*, 'to increase.' See *auch*.

Elch, Elen, see **Elentier**.

Elefant, see **Elfenbein**.

elend, adj., 'wretched, pitiful, miserable, despicable,' from MidHG. *ellende*, adj., 'unhappy, woful, living in a foreign country, banished,' OHG. *eli-lenti*, 'banished, living out of one's country, foreign, alien, captive'; corresponding to OSax. *eli-lendi*, 'alien, foreign.' To this is allied the abstract **Elend**, n., from MidHG. *ellende*, OHG. *eli-lenti*, n., 'banishment, foreign country,' MidHG. also, 'want, distress, misery,' OHG. also, 'captivity,' OSax. *eli-lendi*, n., 'foreign country.' The primary meaning of the adj. is 'living in, born in a foreign country' (comp. Elſaß, from early MidLat. *Alisatia*, from OHG. *Elisâȝȝo*, lit. 'incola peregrinus,' or 'inhabitant of the other bank of the Rhine'). Goth. *aljis*, 'another,' is primit. cognate with Lat *alius*, Gr. ἄλλος (for ἄλjος), OIr. *aile*, 'another'; comp. the corresponding gen. OHG. and AS. *elles*, 'otherwise,' E. *else*. The pronominal stem *alja-* was even in the Goth. period supplanted by *anþara-*, 'another.' Comp. Recht.

Elentier, n., also **Elen, Elend**, m. and n., 'elk,' first occurs in ModHG. with an excrescent *d* (as in Mond); borrowed from Lith. *élnis*, 'elk' (OSlov. *jelent*, 'stag'), with which OSlov. *lani*, 'hind' (from *olnia*), is primit. allied. From the Mod HG. word Fr. *élan*, 'elk,' is derived. The genuine OG. term for Elen is Elch (E. *elk*); comp. MidHG. *ëlch, ëlhe*, m., OHG. *ëlaho*, AS. *eolh*, OIc. *elgr*. The last word (originating in *algi-*) is termed *alces* in Cæsar's *Bell. Gall.*, with which Russ. *losī* (from OSlav. *olsī*?) is also remotely connected. Perhaps OG. Elch facilitated the introduction of the Lith. word.

Elf, m., simply ModHG. borrowed from the last century from the equiv. E. *elf* (comp. Halle, Heim); also ModHG. Elfe, f.; for further references see Alp. The MidHG. *elbe, elbinne*, f., shows that a corresponding ModHG. would have *b* in place of *f*.

elf, eilf, num., 'eleven,' from the equiv. MidHG. *eilf, eilif, einlif*, OHG. *einlif;* a term common to Teut. for 'eleven.' Comp. OSax. *elleban* (for *ênliban*), AS. *ándleofan, endleofan* (for *ânleofan*), E. *eleven*, OIc. *ellifu*, Goth. *ainlif*. A compound of Goth. *ains*, HG. *ein*, and the component *-lif* in Zwölf (Goth. *twalif*). In the non-Teut. languages only Lith. has a corresponding formation; comp. Lith. *venólika*, 'eleven,' *twýlika*, 'twelve,' *trý'ika, keturióíika* (and so on up to nineteen); the *f* of the Ger. word is a permutation of *k*, as in Wolf (λύκος). The signification of the second component, which is met with in Teut. only in the numbers *elf* and *zwölf*, is altogether uncertain. Some have derived the compound, upon which the Lith. and Teut. words are based, from the Aryan root *lik*, 'to remain over' (see leihen), or from the Aryan root *lip* (see bleiben), and regarded *elf* as 'one over.'

Elfenbein, n., from the equiv. MidHG. *hëlfenbein*, OHG. *hëlfanbein*, n., 'ivory,' but based anew on Elefant. How the word came b the initial *h* (AS. *ylpenbân*), which is also ound in MidHG. and OHG. *hëlfant* (also less frequently *ëlfant*, equiv. to AS. *ylpend*), 'elephant,' is not known. It is possible that the excrescent *h* at the beginning is due to the word being connected with helfen (in the Middle Ages special healing qualities were ascribed to ivory). Perhaps the word was obtained not from Romance, but from the East, from Byzantium (Gr. ἐλέφαντ-); for the word would probably correspond to Lat. *(ebur; eboreus* had it been introduced into Ger. through a Romance medium. Comp. Ital. *avorio*, Fr. *ivoire*, 'ivory,' Du. *ivoor*, E. *ivory* (yet also Span. *marfil*, Port. *marfim*).—With regard to the meaning of the second part of the compound (Bein, lit. 'bone'), see Bein.

Elle, f., from the equiv. MidHG. *elle, ele, eln, elne*, OHG. *elina* (und *elin*), f. 'ell'; corresponding to Goth. *aleina* (wrongly written for *alina*?), OIc. *eln*, AS. *eln*, f., E. *ell*, Du. *el, elle;* all these words signify 'ell,' which is derived from the lit. meaning 'fore-arm' (comp. Fuß, Spanne, Klafter, as standards of measure). The word in the form *ölënd* is also preserved in other Aryan languages. Comp. Gr. ὠλένη, 'elbow, arm,' Lat. *ulna*, 'elbow, arm, ell,' OIr. *uile*, Sans. *aratnî*, OSlov. *lakŭtĭ* (from *olkŭtĭ*), Lith. *ólektis (ŭlektis)*, 'elbow, ell,' are more remote; they also contain, however, the common Aryan *ŏle-* (whence too Alfe?). From the Teut. *alina the Romance cognates—Ital. *alna* (Fr. *aune*)—are borrowed.

—**Ellenbogen, Ellbogen**, m., from the equiv. MidHG. *ellenboge, elenboge*, OHG. *elinbogo*, m., 'elbow.' Comp. Du. *elleboog*, AS. *elnboga*, m., E. *elbow*, OIc. *ölnboge*, m., 'elbow,' lit. 'bend of the arm.'

Eller, see Erle.—**Elsebeere**, similarly.

Elritze, f., 'minnow,' akin to MidHG. and OHG. *erlinc*. See Erle.

Elster, f. (in Swiss *ægerst*, on the Mid-Rhine *atzel*, Suab. *hätz* and *kägers*), 'magpie,' from the equiv. MidHG. *egelster, agelster, aglaster*, OHG. *aglastra*, f.; corresponding to OLG. *agastria*, LG. *âgster*, Du. *ekster, aakster*, 'magpie.' Its origin is altogether dubious; *-strion* seems here, as sometimes in other cases, to be a fem. suffix. The meaning of the base *ag-ul-* may have already been 'magpie,' as is indicated by OHG. *agazza*, 'magpie' (hence ModHG. *atzel* for *agæ-l*; comp. Blitz, Lenz, Runzel), AS. *agu*, 'magpie.' From the OTeut. (type *agatja), Ital. *gazza*, and Fr. *agace*, are derived.

Eltern, plur., from the equiv. MidHG. (seldom occurs) *eltern, altern*, plur., OHG. *eltiron, (altron)*, plur., 'parents'; corresponds to OSax. *eldiron*, Du. *ouders, ouderen*, AS. *yldran*, OFris. *aldera*, 'parents'; the plur. of the compar. of *alt* used as a subst. in West Teut. only. In AS. the corresponding sing. *yldra* in AS. denotes 'father.' For a similar evolution of meaning comp. Herr, Jünger.

empfangen, empfinden, see ent-.

empor, adv., 'upwards, aloft,' from MidHG. *enbor, enbore*, adv., 'into or in the heights'; OHG. *inbore, in bore*, with the same meaning; a combination of the prep. *in* with the dat. of OHG. and MidHG. *bor*, 'upper space' (OHG. also 'summit'), the origin of which is obscure. It scarcely belongs to the root *ber*, 'to carry' (in Bahre); more probably to empören. The *p* of the ModHG. word is based on an early ModHG. medium form *entbôr*, from which *entper, emper*, must have been produced.

empören, vb., 'to excite, enrage, (refl.) to revolt,' from MidHG. *enbæren*, OHG. (occurs only once) *anabôren*, 'to raise'; akin to MidHG. *bôr*, m., 'defiance, revolt.' The origin of the cognates is uncertain, because it is difficult to determine whether the *r* is primitive or whether it is by a later change based upon *s* (z); with *bor*, 'upper space'—see emper—there seems to be a connection by gradation of *u* to *au*; Mod HG. böse (OHG. *bôsi*) is not allied.

emsig, adj., 'busy, active, assiduous, industrious,' from MidHG. *emzec, emzic*, OHG. *emazzig, emizzig* (also with *tz*), 'constant, persistent, continuous'; Suab. and Alem. have fleißig, instead of the non-existent emsig. A derivative by means of the suffix *-ig* from OHG. *emiz*, whence Mid HG. *emezliche*. Its connection with Muße is questionable, since *ā-* as an accented prefix is not to be found. AS. *æmetig, emtig*, 'free, empty,' E. *empty*, is not allied. With greater probability, the West Teut. term for 'ant' (see Ameise) is related to emsig.

Ende, n., 'end, aim, termination,' from the equiv. MidHG. *ende*, OHG. *enti*, m., n.; corresponds to OSax. *endi*, m., Du. *einde*, AS. *ende*, m., E. *end*, OIc. *ender, ende*, m., Goth. *andeis*, m., 'end.' The common Teut. stem *andja-*, from pre-Teut. *antyá-*, is closely connected with Sans. *ánta-s*, m., 'boundary, end, edge, border,' OIr. *ét* (from *anto-*?), 'end, point.'

Endivie, f., 'endive,' early ModHG. only, formed from the equiv. MidLat. and Rom. *endivia* (Lat. *intibus*).

eng, adj., 'narrow, close, strait, confined,' from the equiv. MidHG. and Mid LG. *enge*, OHG. *engi, angi*; corresponds to Goth. *aggwus*, OIc. *öngr* (seldom *ongr*), 'narrow,' Du. *eng*; from the Teut. root *ang*, Aryan *angh*, preserved also in Angst. Comp. Lat. *angustus, angustiæ, angere* (see also bange), as well as Sans. *aṅhú*, 'narrow,' *áṅhas*, n., 'narrowness, chasm, oppression,' OSlov. *ązŭkŭ*, 'narrow,' Gr. ἄγχω, 'to strangle,' Armen. *anjuk*, Ir. *cum-ung*, 'narrow.'

Engel, m., from the equiv. MidHG. *engel*, OHG. *engil, angil*, m., 'angel'; corresponding to OSax. *engil*, Du. *engel*, AS. *engel* (but E. *angel* is borrowed from the OFr. *angele*), OIc. *engell*, Goth. *aggilus*, m., 'angel.' The cognates which are diffused throughout Teut. are borrowed from the ecclesiastical Lat. *angelus*, or more probably from Gr. ἄγγελος, 'angel.' How they were borrowed cannot, it is true, be discovered with any certainty (comp. Teufel).

Engerling, m., 'grub of the cockchafer,' from MidHG. *engerlinc*, MidHG. OHG. *engerinc(g)*, m., 'corn-weevil,' a derivative of OHG. *angar, angari*, MidHG. *anger, enger*, 'corn-weevil'; scarcely connected directly with *enge.* It is more probable that Lith. *anksztirai*, 'measles (of swine), cockchafer grubs,' Pol. *węgry*, 'measles (of swine),' are primit. cognates.

Enke, m. (unknown to UpG.), from the equiv. MidHG. *enke*, m., 'farm servant, hind,' OHG. *encho*, *ancheo (*ankjo), m., 'servant'; corresponds only to OFris. *inka* and LG. *enke*, 'servant.' It is uncertain whether the word is primit. cognate with Lat. *ancilla*, 'maid-servant,' since Lat. *c* would be normally changed into LG. *h* or *g*; perhaps, however, it is based on the Aryan root *ank* or *ang.*

Enkel (1.), m., 'ankle,' from MidHG. *enkel*, m., OHG. *enchil, anchal*, m.; numerous primit. variants obscure the etymology. OIc. *ǫkkla*, n., AS. *oncleôw*, n. (E. *ankle*), MidDu. *anclau*, OHG. *anchlâo*, 'anklebone,' seem to be modifications of the primary form, but do they suggest any connection with Klaue (comp. AS. *ondcleôw* with *oncleôw*)? There is a difficulty in determining the relation of OHG. *enchil, anchal*, to *anchlâo*, and their further connection with MidHG. *anke*, m., 'joint of the foot, nape' (even now Anke in UpG. and MidG. dialects is the term for 'nape, neck'), OHG. *encha*, f. (from *ankia*), 'thigh, tibia' (Fr. *anche*, 'reed, mouthpiece'). Perhaps allied to Sans *áṅga*, 'limb,' *aṅgûri*, 'finger.'

Enkel (2.), m., from the equiv. MidHG. *enenkel, eninkel*, m., late OHG. *eninchilt(n)*, n., 'grandson.' Since even in MidHG. the forms *enikel* and *enikltn* appear, Mod HG. Enkel is most closely connected with a form *enekel*, in which the medial *e* was syncopated. The termination *inklîn* is frequently found as a diminutive suffix; comp. AS. *scipincel*, 'small ship,' *lipincel*, 'small limb,' OHG. *lęwinchili(n)*, 'small lion,' *huoninchili(n)*, 'chicken.' Hence OHG *eninchilt* is a diminutive of Ahn, OHG. *ano* (Goth. *ana, gen. *amin-s), 'grandfather,' and signifies lit. 'little grandfather, grandfather's child'; comp. the similar evolution of meaning in Lat. *avunculus* (see Oheim). In the non-Teut. languages there is probably another corresponding term besides the word cited under Ahn—OSlov. *vŭnukŭ*, 'grandson.'

ent-, prefix, 'forth, from, out, away,' from MidHG. *ent-*, OHG. *int-*, an unaccented prefix corresponding to the accented *ant-*, which is of the same origin. In words with initial *f*, *ent-* even in MidHG. becomes *emp-*, hence *empfangen* (from fangen), *empfinden* (from finden), *empfehlen* (befehlen), OHG. *int-fâhan, int-findan*, *int-felhan. The meaning of the prefix belongs to grammar.—**entbehren**, vb., from MidHG. *enbërn*, OHG. *(int-?) in-bëran*, 'to do without, want'; a corresponding vb. is wanting in the OTeut. dialects. The meaning of OHG. *in-bëran* can hardly be deduced from *bëran*, 'to carry' (see Bahre, gebaren, Bürde); whether it is connected with bar, OSlov. *bosŭ*, from an Aryan root *bhes*, 'to be empty,' remains uncertain, because the prefix has no very definite meaning, and because no other verb from this root has been found.

Ente, f., 'duck,' from the equiv. MidHG. *ente* (for *enete), *ant* (plur. *ente*), OHG. *anut, enit*, f.; a term common to Teut.; comp. MidLG. *anet(d)*, Du. *eend*, AS. *ǽned*, OIc. *ǫnd*, f., 'duck.' The assumed Goth. form *anups points to a primit. kinship with Lat. *anat-*, 'duck,' with which some have also connected Sans. *âti* (see, however, Eiter), as well as OSlov. *ątĭ*, Lith. *ántis*, 'duck.' For the E. term 'duck' (AS. *dúce*), see tauchen).—**Enterich** (Suab. *antrecht*), m., 'drake,' a modification of MidHG. *antreche*, OHG. *antrahho* (Dan. *andrik*); probably the correct form is *anuttrahho? In LG. simply Drake, equiv. to E. *drake*, which has certainly nothing to do with Drache, 'dragon,' Lat. *draco*. Other terms for *drake* are LG. *erpel* in Pomerania, *weddîk* in Mecklenburg, and *wart* in Holstein, all of obscure origin. Note further Swiss and Bav. Antvogel for Enterich.

entern, vb., 'to board (a ship),' simply ModHG., formed like Du. *enteren*, from Span. *entrar* (Lat. *intrare*).

entgegen, adv., 'against, in opposition, towards,' from MidHG. *engegen*, OHG. *ingegin*, and *ingagan*, adv. and prep., 'towards, against'; comp. OSax. *angegin*, AS. *ongeán*, E. *again*; see gegen.—**entrüstet**, 'exasperated, irritated,' partic. of MidHG. *entrüsten*, 'to take off one's armour, to disconcert' (Du. and LG. *ontrusten*, 'to disturb'); see rüsten.—**entsetzen**, 'to displace, depose'; (refl.) 'to be shocked, terrified,' from MidHG. *entsetzen*, 'to lay aside, disconcert, be afraid,' from MidHG. *entsitzen*, OHG. *intsizzen*, 'to lose one's seat, fear, terrify,' Goth. *andsitan*, 'to shun, fear.'

entweder, particle, 'either,' from Mid HG. *eintwëder*, an uninflected neu., corresponding as a disjunctive particle to an over following; in MidHG. *eintwēder*, is mostly a pron. (sometimes with *oder* following, 'one of two,' corresponding to OHG. *ein-de-wëder* (*ein-dih-wēdar), 'one of two'; see *weber*. The origin of the OHG. *de-* is obscure; see *fein*.

Epheu, m., 'ivy,' from the equiv. Mid HG. *ēphöu, ëbehöu,* OHG. *ëbahęwi,* n.; even at the present day the word is pronounced **Ep-heu** in UpGer. dialects (Franc., Suab., and Alem.), partly corrupted to **Räb-heu,** while the ModHG. pronunciation has been influenced by the written language. Of course it is impossible to say positively whether **heu** is to be regarded as the second component, especially as the other forms are difficult to explain. OHG. has also *ëbawi, ëbah,* AS. *īfig,* E. *ivy,* MidLG. *iflöf, iwlöf,* Du. *eiloof,* 'ivy.' The base of the cognates seems to be a common Teut. *iba-*; yet no definite clue can be found.

Eppich, m., 'celery, parsley,' with LG. consonants, from MidHG. *epfich,* OHG. *epfih,* n., which are preceded by the shorter forms, MidHG. *epfe, effe,* OHG. *epfi,* n. This word, like other names of plants connected with horticulture and cookery, was borrowed previous to the OHG. period (see **Kohl**) from Lat.; the original word in this instance is *apium,* which denotes a species of umbelliferous plants, comprising parsley, celery, &c.; only in ModHG. has **Eppich** been confused in meaning with **Epheu.**

er, pron., 'he, it,' from MidHG. and OHG. *ër,* corresponding to the equiv. Goth. *is,* from a pronom. stem of the third person *i-;* comp. Lat. *i-s* (Lat. *id,* Goth. *ita,* OHG. and MidHG. *ëz,* ModHG. *es*). Akin to the Sans. pronom. stem *i-*.

er-, prefix, signifying 'transition, beginning, attaining,' from MidHG. *er-,* OHG. *ir, ar, ur-,* the unaccented verbal prefix from the accented *ur-.* See the latter.

Erbe, n., 'heritage, inheritance,' from MidHG. *erbe,* OHG. *ërbi, arbi,* n., 'inheritance'; a word common to Teut.; comp. the equiv. Goth. *arbi,* AS. *yrfe* (obsolete in E.), Du. *erf,* OSax. *ërbi.* Akin to **Erbe,** m., 'heir, inheritor,' from the equiv. MidHG. *erbe,* OHG. *erbo, arbeo* (Goth. *arbja*), m. With the Teut. root *arbh,* 'to inherit,' some have connected the OIr. *comarpi,* 'joint heirs,' and Gr. ὀρφανός, Lat. *orbus,* 'orphaned,' Armen. *orb,* 'orphan'; **Erbe,** lit. 'orphan'?.

Erbse, f., 'pea,' from the equiv. MidHG. *arweiz, erweiz, ericiz,* f., OHG. *araweiz, ar-* *wīz,* f.; corresponding to OLG. *ëri,* Du. *erwt, ert,* OIc. *ertr,* plur. The cognates are probably borrowed, as is indicated by the similarity in sound to Gr. ἐρέβινθος and ὄροβος, 'chick-pea' (see **Almofen**); comp. also Lat. *ervum,* 'bitter vetch,' akin to the equiv. AS. *earfe.* Direct adoption from Gr. or Lat. is impossible; the way it was introduced cannot be discovered. Probably **Erbse** is one of the words which Gr. and Teut. have obtained from the same source, as in the case of **Hanf.** In Eng., Lat. *pisum* (Fr. *pois*) was adopted for 'pea' early in the AS. period; comp. AS. *peose, pise,* E. *pease* (and *pea*).

Erchtag, Bav., see **Dienstag.**

Erde, f., 'earth, ground, soil, world,' from the equiv. MidHG. *ërde,* OHG. *ërda,* f.; a word common to Teut.; comp. Goth. *airþa,* OIc. *jǫrð,* AS. *eorðe,* E. *earth,* Du. *aarde,* OSax. *ërtha,* f., 'earth.' To the dental derivative *ër-þō-,* OHG. *ëro,* 'earth,' also belongs; so too Gr. ἔρ-αζε, 'to earth,' and perhaps Lat. *arvum,* 'arable land' (AS. *eard*), as well as the old Aryan root *ar,* 'to plough'; see **Acker, Art.**—**Erdbeere,** f., 'strawberry,' from the equiv. MidHG. *ërtbęr,* OHG. *ërtbęri,* n.; perhaps not really a compound of **Erde,** but of OSax. *erda,* 'honey-flower, common balm'; yet Swed. *jordbär,* tells in favour of a compound of **Erde.**

erdrosseln, see **Drossel** (2).

Ereignis, n., 'event, occurrence,' for an earlier *eröugnis* from MidHG. *eröugen,* OHG. *ir-ougen,* 'to show.' OHG. *ougen,* Goth. *augjan,* 'to show,' are derivatives of **Auge.** Hence *eröugnis* means lit. 'what is shown, what can be seen.' The spelling **Ereignis,** found even in the 16th cent., was due to the corruption of a word no longer understood.

erfahren, vb., 'to experience, come to know, learn, undergo,' from MidHG. *ervarn,* 'to travel, inquire, investigate, proclaim'; akin to **fahren.**—**ergötzen, ergetzen,** vb., 'to delight,' from MidHG. *ergętzen,* 'to cause to forget (espec. grief), compensate for'; factitive of MidHG. *ergeʒʒen,* 'to forget.' See **vergessen.**—**erhaben,** adj., 'sublime, exalted, superior to,' from the equiv. MidHG. *erhaben,* which is properly a partic. of MidHG. *erhęben,* 'to raise aloft.'—**erinnern,** vb., 'to remind, admonish,' (refl.) 'to recollect, remember,' from MidHG. *innern, inren,* 'to remind, inform, instruct,' akin to **inner.**

Erker, m., 'bow, projection (of a building), balcony,' from the equiv. MidHG. *ärker, erker,* m.; the latter is formed from MidLat. *arcora* (a late plur. of Lat. *arcus,* 'bow') ?.

erlauben, earlier erleuben, vb., 'to allow, permit, grant,' from MidHG. *erlouben (erleuben),* OHG. *irlouben (irlouppen),* 'to allow'; comp. Goth. *uslaubjan,* 'to permit, grant,' AS. *âlýfan.* The original meaning of erlauben, like that of glauben, is 'to approve,' which is also inherent in the Teut. root *lub,* upon which the word is based (comp. Lob, lieb, Glaube, which are connected by gradation of the root *lub, liub, laub*). An old abstract of erlauben appears in Mod HG. Urlaub.

erlaucht, adj., 'illustrious, noble,' from MidHG. *erliuht* (with a MidG. vowel *erlâht*), 'illuminated, famous'; a partic. of *erliuhten*. See leuchten and Durchlaut.

Erle, f., 'alder,' from the equiv. Mid HG. *erle,* OHG. *erila, elira* (to this is allied ModHG. Elritze, 'minnow,' OHG. *erlinc,* lit. 'elder fish' ?). Comp. LG. *eller,* Du. *els* (ModHG. Elsbeere, 'wild service-berry '), AS. *alor,* E. *alder,* OIc. *ölr, elrer, elre;* Goth. **alisa(*aluza)* appears in Span. *alisa,* 'alder,' Fr. *alize,* 'wild service-berry.' The change of the orig. OHG. *elira* to *erila* is analogous to Goth. *watrilôs* compared with AS. *wëleras,* 'lips' (see Giffg). Cognates of Erle, like those of Buche, Birke, &c., are found in the non-Teut. languages. Comp. OSlov. *jeltcha,* Lat. *alnus* (for **alsnus*), 'alder.' Comp. Ulme.

Ermel, m., 'sleeve,' from the equiv. MidHG. *ermel.* OHG. *ermilo, armilo,* m.; diminutive of Arm. Comp. the diminutive form of Faust, MidHG. *viustelinc,* 'mitten,' also MidHG. *ringerlîn,* 'ring (worn on the finger),' dimin. of Finger, E. *thimble,* dimin. of *thumb*.

Ernst, m., 'earnestness, seriousness, gravity,' from MidHG. *ërnest,* m., OHG. *ërnust,* n., f., 'contest, earnest, decision of character'; corresponding to Du. *ernst,* AS. *eornost,* 'duel, earnest,' E. *earnest;* the suffix *-n-ust* as in Dienst; see also Angst. Akin also to OIc. *orrostu,* 'battle'; the stem *er* (*erz* ?, *ers* ?) is not found elsewhere with a similar meaning; the evolution in meaning resembles that of Kampf, Krieg. The cognates in other Aryan languages are uncertain.—The adj. ernst, simply ModHG., is represented by *ërnesthaft* in MidHG. and by *ërnusthaft* and *ërnustlîch* in OHG.

Ernte, f., 'harvest,' from the equiv. Mid HG. *ërne,* f., like ModHG. Hüfte, from the equiv. MidHG. *hüffe,* plur. of *huf;* MidHG. *erne* (Franc. and Alem. *ärn*), a plur. used as a sing., is related similarly to OHG. *aran,* 'harvest,' which, like Goth. *asans,* 'harvest, autumn,' is connected with a root *as,* 'to work in the fields,' widely diffused in OTeut. Comp. Goth. *asneis* (OHG. *ësni,* AS. *ësne*), 'day-labourer,' OIc. *önn* (from **aznu*), f., 'work, season for tillage'; akin to OHG. *arnôn,* 'to harvest' (AS. *eornian,* equiv. to E. *to earn,* OIc. *árna* ?), MidHG. *asten,* 'to cultivate.' Probably Lat. *annóna* (for **asnóna*), 'produce of corn,' belongs to the Teut. root *as*.

erobern, vb., 'to conquer, win,' from MidHG. *er-obern,* 'to excel, conquer,' allied to ober, über.—**erörtern,** vb., 'to discuss, determine,' formed from late MidHG. *ortern, ortern,* 'to examine thoroughly,' from MidHG. *ort,* 'beginning, end.'—**erquicken,** vb., 'to revive, refresh,' from the equiv. MidHG. *erquicken,* 'to reanimate, wake from the dead,' OHG. *ir-quicchan;* allied to fect, Quecksilber, verquicken.—**erschüttern,** see Schutt.

erst, adj., 'first,' from MidHG. *ërst,* OHG. *ërist,* 'the first'; corresponding to OSax. *ërist,* AS. *ærest,* 'the first'; superlat. of the compar. form cited under eher. Goth. *airis,* adv., formerly,' *airiza,* 'predecessor, ancestor,' OHG. *ëriro (ëro),* 'predecessor'; the positive is preserved in Goth. *air.* adv., 'early,' AS. *ǽr,* adj., adv., 'early,' OIc. *ár,* adv., 'early' (OHG. *ër-acchar,* 'awake early'). Probably the stem *air-,* on which the word was based, was used orig. like *früh,* only of the hours of the day. It is connected most probably with Gr. ἦρι, 'early in the morning.'

ersticken, vb., 'to stifle, choke,' from MidHG. *ersticken,* intrans., 'to be stifled,' and *erstecken,* trans., 'to stifle.'

erwähnen, vb., 'to mention, call to notice,' formed from the equiv. MidHG. *gewëhenen,* OHG. *giwahinnen, giwahannen* (pret. *gi-wuog,* partic. *giwahtand giwahinit*), allied to OHG. *giwaht,* 'mention, fame.' Goth. **wahnjan* belongs to the root *wok, wôq* (Teut. *woh*), 'to speak,' which is widely diffused in the Aryan languages. Comp. Lat. *vox,* 'voice,' *vocare,* 'to call,' Gr. ὄσσα (for *Fόκγα*) and ὄπ- (for *Fοπ*), 'voice,' ἔπος (for *Fέπος*), 'word,' Sans. root *vac,* 'to say, speak.' In Teut. this old root was not so widely developed.

Erz (76) **Ess**

Erz, n., 'ore, metal, brass, bronze,' from the equiv. MidHG. *erze, arze,* OHG. *grizzi, aruzi, aruz,* n.; an obscure word, which is unknown to the other Teut. dialects; probably borrowed under the form *azuti, aruti?* In Goth. *ais,* AS. *ár,* E. *ore,* OHG. and MidHG. *ér,* 'bronze,' whence the OHG. and MidHG. adj. *érin,* ModHG. **ehern**; these are primitively cognate with Lat. *aes,* 'bronze,' and Sans. *ayas,* 'metal, iron.'

Erz-, prefix, 'arch-, chief,' from MidHG. *erz-*; comp. MidHG. *erz-engel, -bischof, -priester;* OHG. only in *erzi-bischof;* corresponding to Du. *aarts* in *aarts-engel, aartsbisschop,* AS. *arcebiscop,* E. *archbishop,* AS. *arcengel,* E. *archangel;* from the Lat.-Gr. prefix *archi-* (ἀρχι-), much affected in ecclesiastical words. HG. and Du. exhibit the late Lat. pronunciation, *arci* (see **Kreuz**); Goth. *ark-aggilus,* 'archangel,' from *archangelus,* like AS. *arce-,* retain the older sound of the *c.* Comp. also **Arzt**.

es, pron., 'it,' from MidHG. *ëz,* n. sing., and its gen. *ës,* OHG. *ëz* (gen. *ës*); formed from the Aryan pronom. stem of the 3rd pers. (*i-*) mentioned under **er**. See **ihn**.

Esche, f., 'ash, ash-tree,' from the equiv. MidHG. *asch,* OHG. *asc,* m.; corresponding to Du. *esch,* AS. *æsc,* E. *ash,* OIc. *askr,* 'ash.' The remoter cognates, Slav. *jasika,* Lith. *úsis,* with the same meaning; Gr. ὀξύη, 'a kind of beech,' and Lat. *aesculus,* 'winter oak,' are not allied.

Esel, m., 'ass,' from the equiv. MidHG. *esel,* OHG. *esil,* m.; corresponds to OSax. *esil,* Du. *ezel,* AS. *esol, eoso',* Goth. *asilus* (whence OSlov. *osĭlŭ*), 'ass.' It is self-evident that these cognates are related to Lat. *asinus.* Yet it is remarkable that the Romance languages have not an *l,* but an *n* in the suffix; Span. *asno,* OFr. *asne* (whence OIc. *asne*), ModFr. *âne,* Ital. *asino* (the Lat. diminutive *asellus* does not come under consideration, since it is not found in any Romance language; comp. further **Äffel**). For the change of *n* to *l* in the derivatives, see **Himmel, Kümmel, Orgel**. The abnormal AS. *assa* (equiv. to E. *ass*) may be traced back to OIr. *assan,* borrowed, with the usual change of sound, from the Lat. Consequently all the cognates come from Italy; no primit. word for 'ass' can be found in any language of the Aryan group. —The term **Reffercsel** is a late imitation of Ital. *asello;* the equiv. **Äffel** appears, however, to be unconnected with it.

Espe, f., 'aspen-tree,' from the equiv. MidHG. *aspe,* OHG. *aspa* (hence UpG. *aspe*). Comp. the exactly equiv. AS. *æsp,* E. *asp,* OIc. *ǫsp;* scarcely allied to **Eiche**; more probably connected with Lat. *arbor,* 'tree,' if the latter represents an orig. *asbos.*

Esse, f. (the word seems to be unknown to the UpG. dialects), 'forge,' from the equiv. MidHG. *esse,* OHG. *essa,* f., 'chimney, hearth of a worker in metals.' Like OSwed. *æsja,* they indicate a Goth. **asjô,* which is also assumed by the borrowed term, Finn. *ahjo.* Whether **Esse** is allied to OIc. *esja,* 'clay,' and hence means lit. 'what is made of clay,' remains doubtful. Its assumed connection with OHG. *eit,* 'funeral pile,' Gr. αἴθος, 'glow,' Sans. root *idh,* 'to burn,' is untenable.

essen, vb., 'to eat, dine, feed on,' from the equiv. MidHG. *ëzzen,* OHG. *ëzzan;* common to Teut., and orig. an OAryan str. vb.; comp. Goth. *itan,* OIc. *eta,* AS. *ëtan,* E. *to eat,* Du. *eten,* OSax. *ëtan;* see **fressen**. The verbal root *ët,* 'to eat,' common to Teut., to which OHG. and MidHG. *âs,* ModHG. **Aas** (comp. Lat. *ësus* for **ëd-to-,* the partic. of *edere*), also belong, is based upon an Aryan root *ëd;* comp. the Sans. root *ad,* Gr. ἔδομαι, Lat. *ëdo,* Lith. *ëdmi, ëmi,* OSlov. *jamĭ* (from **ëdmĭ*), 'I eat.'—**Essen,** n., 'food, meal, dinner,' even in MidHG. *ëzzen,* OHG. *ëzzan,* n., as an equiv. subst.; it is scarcely an infinitive used as a subst., but rather an independent subst. form like Gr. ἔδανον, 'food,' Sans. *ódana,* n., 'provender.'

Essig, m. (with the normal unaccented *g* for *ch*), 'vinegar,' from the equiv. MidHG. *ezzich* (that the *i* is long is proved by its change into the diphthong *ei* in late MidHG. *ezseich*), OHG. *ezzih (hh),* n. A remarkable loan-word, corresponding to MidLG. *etik,* OSwed. *ætikia,* Swed. *ättika;* also OLG. *ecid,* AS. *eced,* which with Goth. *akeit(s),* 'vinegar,' are based upon Lat. *acétum.* For the HG., LG., and Swed. words we must assume a form **atécum,* produced by metathesis of the consonants— OHG. *ezzih* from *atík* for *atéko,* which, however, is not attested by any Romance form; for such transpositions comp. Romance *alenáre* from Lat. *anhelare,* MidHG. *bierer* from *vieber* (see further citations under **einzeln, Fieber, Erle, Rabeljau, ligesu, Siege**). There is a remarkable form in Swiss dialects, *achiss, echiss,* which is based upon an untransposed form corresponding to Goth. *akeit(s).* The Lat.-Rom. *acétum* (Ital. *accto;* but Fr. *vinaigre* and E. *vinegar* from

Lat. *vinum acre*) has also made its way into other countries—OSlov. *acĭtŭ* (from Goth. *akeits*?), OIr. *acat*.—The UpG. vb. *essĭln*, 'to taste of vinegar,' may perhaps be based upon some such form as OFr. *aisil* (MidE. *aisil*).

Estrich, m., 'floor, plaster-floor, pavement,' from the equiv. MidHG. *estrich*, *esterich*, OHG. *estirih*, *astrih*(*hh*), m. ; comp. MidLG. *astruk*, *esterck*, Du. *estrik* (these two forms are not recorded). In Middle Germany the word, which was unknown to Luther, is not found. Perhaps it is really native to the valleys of the Rhine and Danube, being introduced by Roman colonists. Comp. early MidLat. *astricus, astracus*, 'paving,' Milan. *astregh*, Sicil. *astracu*, Ital. *lastrico* ; OFr. *astre*, Fr. *âtre*, 'hearth,' lit. 'pavement.'

etlich, pron., 'some, sundry,' from MidHG. *ëtelich*, OHG. *ëtalih*, also earlier Mod. HG. *ëtlich*, from MidHG. *ëteslich*, OHG. *ëtteslih*, *ëtteshicëlich*, 'any one' (plur. 'many a one'). The same first component is seen in *etwa*, from the equiv. MidHG. *ëtwâ* (*ëtesuâ*), OHG. *ëttesuâr*, 'anywhere'; *etwas*, from MidHG. and OHG. *ëtewaʒ* (neu. of MidHG. and OHG. *ëtewër*, *ëteswër*, 'any one'). The origin of this pronominal *ëte*, *ëtes*, *ëttes*, *ëddes*, 'any,' is quite obscure. Some have compared it with Goth. *aíþþau*, 'perhaps, nearly' (see oder), and *þishwazuh*, 'every.'

euch, pron., 'you, to you,' from MidHG. *iuch*, *iuwich*, OHG. *iuwih*, accus., the dat. of which, however, is *iu* in MidHG. and OHG.; comp. AS. *eów* (and *eówic*), accus., *eow*, dat. (E. *you*), Goth. *izwis*, accus., dat. Is Lat. *vos, vester*, akin? All other references are dubious.—**euer**, poss. pron. of the preceding, 'your,' from MidHG. *iuwer*, OHG. *iuwar*. Comp. AS. *eówer*, E. *your*, Goth. *izwar*, 'your.'

Eule, f., 'owl,' from the equiv. MidHG. *iule, iuwel*, OHG. *ûwila*, f. Comp. Du. *uil*, AS. *úle* (from *úwle), E. *owl*, OIc. *ugla*, from pre-Teut. *uwicalô, or rather *uwwilô, 'owl.'

Euſt, Swiss, 'sheepfold.' See **Schaf**.

Euter, m. and n., 'udder, dug,' from the equiv. MidHG. *iuter*, *ûter*, OHG. *ûtar*, *ûtiro*, m. ; a word common to Teut. and orig. a primit. Aryan word, which has the same sense everywhere. Comp. Du. *uijer*, AS. *úder*, E. *udder*; also with gradation *cudar* in MidLG. *jeder*, OFris. *iuder*, OIc. *júgr*. The resulting Teut. *údr-, eudr-*, from Aryan *ûdhr-*, corresponds to the equiv. Sans. *ûdhar*, Gr. *οὔθαρ*(with gradation), Lat. *uber*; Slav. *vymę* (from **vyd-men-*), 'udder,' is differently derived.

ewig, adj., 'eternal, perpetual,' from the equiv. MidHG. *êwic*(*g*), OHG. *êwig*; corresponding to OSax. *êwig*, Du. *eeuwig*, 'eternal'; derived from an OTeut. root meaning 'eternity.' Comp. Goth. *aiws*, 'time, eternity,' OHG. *êwa*, 'eternity,' which are primit. cognate with Lat. *aevum*, 'eternity, lifetime,' and Gr. *αἰών*. Comp. *je*.

extern, vb., 'to vex, tease,' a MidG. and LG. word, probably connected with **Eſel** ; allied also to Hess. *ickern* with the same sense.

F.

Fabel, f., 'fable,' even in MidHG. *fabel*, *fabele*, f., from Fr. *fable*, Lat. *fabula*.

Fach, n., 'compartment, shelf, panel, special branch,' from MidHG. *vach*, OHG. *fah*(*hh*), n., 'part, division of space, or a partition, wall, &c.,' also 'contrivance, an enclosed space in water for catching fish, fish-weir, hurdles for fishing'; with the latter meanings some have connected Gr. *πάγη*, 'noose, snare, fishing hurdles,' to which there is no objection phonetically. Yet we must proceed in the case of the HG. word as well as of AS. *fæc*, 'space, time,' from a general and primary sense, such as 'division, a portion of space or time.' Allied to HG. *fügen*.—**-fach**, adj, suffix, '-fold,' from MidHG. (very rare) *vach*, in *manecvach, zwivach*, OHG. not found ; *mannigfach*, lit. 'with many divisions'; moreover, MidHG. *vach*, denotes also 'fold,' and *-fach* as a suffix may be an imitation of the earlier suffix *-falt* in *manecvalt*, 'manifold.'

fächeln, vb., 'to fan,' simply ModHG. from **Fächer**.

Fächer, earlier also **Fächel**, m., 'fan,' ModHG. only ; the derivation is uncertain ; perhaps a diminutive of MidHG. *vach*, 'veil.' Yet the suspicion that the word was borrowed is not unfounded, since MidHG. *foche*, *focher*, 'fan,' point to Lat. *focarius*, *foculare* (from *focus*). The change of *a* to *o* may be due to LG. (comp. Aberglaube, Übeltat), as in anfachen, from Lat. *focare*.

Fackel, f., 'torch,' from the equiv. MidHG. *vackele*, *rackel*, OHG. *facchala*, f.; comp. AS. *fæcele*, f., 'torch,' with the abnormal variant *þæcele*, f. It is usually regarded as a loan-word from Lat. *facula*, (dimin. of *fax*). The sounds, however, point with greater probability to a genuinely Teut. word, which was perhaps connected with Lat. *facula*; Du. *fakkel*, f., has *ck*, like the HG. word, in contrast to AS. *c*; the vowels too of the AS. stem and derivative syllable tell in favour of a genuinely native word; likewise OHG. *rôrea gafacliia*, 'reed shaken to and fro by the wind.'

Faden, m., 'thread, file, shred,' from the equiv. MidHG. *vaden*, *vadem*, OHG. *fadam*, *fadum*, m.; Goth. *faþms is wanting. Comp. OSax. *fathmos*, 'both arms stretched out,' AS. *fæþm*, 'both arms distended, embrace, protection, bosom,' E. *fathom* (a measure), OIc. *faðmr*, 'both arms, bosom.' Consequently the primary sense is 'encompassing with both arms,' which could be adopted as a measure (see Klafter); hence the use of 'fathom' as a measure in Eng., Scand., LG., Du., and also in ModHG. (adopted from LG. and Du.). The ModHG. meaning 'thread' is a recent development; its lit. sense is 'as much yarn as can be measured with the arms stretched out.' The primary sense, 'encompassing,' results from Goth. *faþa*, f., MidHG. *vade*, f., 'hedge, enclosure.' The base of the cognates is a Teut. root, *feþ*, *faþ*, pre-Teut. *pet*, *pot*, which accords with the Gr. πετ in πετάννυμι, 'to spread out,' πέταλος, 'outspread, broad, flat'; Lat. *patere*, 'to stand open,' is even more remote.

fähig, 'capable, competent, able,' from fangen.

fahl, adj., 'dun, fawn-coloured, pale,' from MidHG. *val* (gen. *wes*), adj., 'pallid, discoloured, faded, yellow, fair,' OHG. *falo* (nom. *falawêr*); comp. OSax. *falu*, AS. *fealo* (gen. *fealwes*), E. *fallow*, OIc. *fǫlr*, 'pallid, pale'; comp. falb. Allied primit. to Lat. *palleo*, 'to be pallid,' *pallidus*, 'pallid,' Gr. πολιός (suffix *ιο* as in δεξιός, Goth. *taihswo ι-*) 'grey,' OSlov. *plavŭ*, 'whitish,' Lith. *pálvas*, 'tawny,' Sans. *palita-s*, 'grey.' By this interpretation of the cognates the *ch* of UpG. *falch*, 'cow or horse of fawn colour,' *gefalchet*, 'fallow,' remains unexplained; these suggest a connection with Falte. The cognates, Ital. *falbo*, Fr. *fauve* (comp. also braun, blond, blau), are derived from Teut.

fahnden, vb., 'to inform against,' from MidHG. *vanden*, OHG. *fândôn*, 'to visit'; comp. OSax. *fandian*, AS. *fandian*, 'to test, beseech, demand'; probably from a root *fenþ* in finden (comp. Du. *vanden*, 'to visit a woman in childbed').

Fahne, f. (mas. in UpG.), 'banner, flag, standard, squadron,' from MidHG. *vane*, *van*, m. 'flag, banner'; in this sense OHG. has the compound *gundfano*, m., since *funo* most frequently means 'cloth' (comp. *ougafano*, 'veil,' *halsfano*, 'neckcloth'); allied to Goth. *fana*, 'cloth, stuff, rag,' A.S. *fana* and *gûþfana*, m., 'standard, banner,' E. *fane*, *vane*, Du. *vaan*, 'flag.' The Teut. *fanan*, pre-Teut. *pano-n-*, has in the wider sphere of the Aryan languages many cognates which also point to the general and older meaning, 'stuff, cloth'; Lat. *pannus*, 'small piece of cloth, rag,' OSlov. *o-ponu*, 'curtain,' *ponjava*, f., 'sail.' Akin also perhaps to Gr. πῆνος, n., 'garment,' πηνίον, 'spool, spindle.' An Aryan verbal root, *pen*, appears in OSlov. *pl⌣a (peti)*, 'to span, hang.' The OTeut. *gunþfano*, 'standard,' was adopted with the meaning 'flag' by Romance (comp. Fr. *gonfalon*, Ital. *gonfalone*), while the simple form in Romance retained at different times the earlier and general meaning (comp. OFr. and ModFr. *fanon*, 'rag, towel, fanon (of a priest).'—

Fähnrich, Fähnrich, 'cornet, ensign,' like Gänserich, first formed in ModHG. from the shorter MidHG. word; comp. MidHG. *venre* (the ModHG. *d* is excrescent, as in schaudern, minder), OHG. *faneri*, m., 'standard-bearer.'

Fähre, f., from the equiv. MidHG. *vere*, *ver*, f., n., 'ferry'; comp. Du. *veer* (E. *ferry* is borrowed from OIc. *ferja*, f., 'ferry'). Also akin to OHG. *farm*, MidHG. *varm*, 'skiff, ferry,' and OHG. *ferid*, n., 'navigium'; like Ferge, connected with fahren. See Praam.

fahren, vb., 'to drive, convey, sail,' from MidHG. *varn*, OHG. *faran*, 'to move from one place to another, go, come'; correspond¢ to Goth. (rare) *faran*, 'to wander, march,' OSax. and AS. *faran*, 'to proceed, march,' E. *to fare*, OIc. *fara*, 'to move' (of any kind of motion). The root *jar* in Goth. *farjan* (OHG. *ferian*, MidHG. *vern*) means 'to go by ship,' and is therefore connected with the nouns mentioned under Fähre. The primary meaning of the Teut.

root *far*, 'continued motion of every kind,' is supported also by führen. As derivatives of the Aryan root *per, por*, comp. Gr. πόρος, 'way, passage,' πόρθμος, 'straits' (see Furt), πορθμεύς, 'ferryman,' πορεύω, 'to bring, convey, cross,' πορεύεσθαι, 'to go, travel, march' (hence there is a leaning in Gr. also to the meaning 'to go by ship' in the case of the root πορ); OSlov. *perq. plrati*, 'to fly'; Sans. root *par*, 'to lead across'; Lat. *peritus*, 'experienced.'—Fahrende Habe, 'movables,' from the equiv. MidHG. *varnde habe, varndez guot*, OHG. *faranti scaz*.

Fahrt, f., 'journey, ride, drive, voyage, course,' from MidHG. *vart*, OHG. *fart*; comp. OSax. *fard*, 'journey, voyage,' AS. *fyrd, ferd*, f., 'journey, voyage, expedition, troops on the march,' OIc. *ferð*, f., 'journey'; Goth. *furþs or *fards is wanting, but the term *us-farþō (us skipa,* 'shipwreck') occurs once. From *por-ti-s*, a derivative of the root *por* appearing in fahren; comp. also fertig.

Fährte, f., 'track, trail, scent,' prop. the plur. of MidHG. *vart*, OHG. *fart*, 'track, way, journey, voyage.' See Fahrt.

falb, adj., identical with fahl.

Falbel, f., 'flounce,' simply ModHG., from Fr. and Ital. *falbala*, whence also E. *furbelow*.

Falke, m., 'falcon, hawk,' from the equiv. MidHG. *valke*, OHG. *falcho*, m. (in UpG. still written Falch). In the other Teut. languages the word does not appear till late in the Middle Ages (OIc. *falke*, E. *falcon*, Du. *valk*), yet *Falco* already existed in Lombardic proper names (comp. also AS. *Wester-falcna*). Among the Anglo-Saxons the falcon was called *wealhheafoc*, Welsh hawk'; OIc. *valr*, 'falcon,' is prop. 'the Keltic (bird)'; comp. Walnuß, welsch. Hence it is possible that OHG. *falcho* originated in the tribal name *Volcae*, 'Kelts'; *volcon-* may have become *falkon-*, and the Romance cognates (Ital. *falcone*, Fr. *faucon*) borrowed from it. But it is also possible that the word is connected with the cognates of fahl (UpGer. *falch*, 'a fawn-coloured cow'); hence Falke, 'a fawn-coloured (bird)'?. If, on the other hand, the word originated in the Lat.-Rom. cognates (Lat. *falco* is recorded in the 4th cent.), we must base it on the Lat. *falx*, 'sickle'; *falco*, lit. 'sickle-bearer' (on account of its hooked claws?).

fallen, vb., 'to fall, abate, diminish,' from the equiv. MidHG. *valn*, OHG. *fallan*; the common Teut. word for 'to fall' (singularly, however, it is unknown to Goth.); comp. OIc. *falla*, AS. *feallan*, E. *to fall*, OSax. *fallan*. The Teut. root *fal-l*, pre-Teut. *phal-n*, appears in Gr. and Sans. as *sphal* with an *s* prefixed; comp. Gr. σφάλλω, 'to fell, overthrow,' σφάλλομαι, 'to fall, be deceived.' Lat. *fallo* is based directly upon the root *phal*, 'to deceive'; Sans. root *sphal*, 'to stagger'; also Lith. *pŭlu pŭlti*, 'to fall,' and akin to Sans. *phala*, 'ripe, falling fruit'?. —Fall, m., 'fall, ruin, event, case (in gram., &c.),' OHG. and MidHG *val*. (gen. *valles*), m.; comp. AS. *fyll*, m., 'fall, death, ruin.'— Falle, f., from MidHG. *valle*, OHG. *falla*, f., 'snare, decipula'; AS. *fealle*, f., 'laqueus, decipula' (wanting in E.), Du. *val*, 'snare, noose.'

falsch, adj., 'false, wrong,' from the equiv. MidHG. *valsch*, adj.; OHG. *falsc* is not recorded. On account of late AS. *fals*, E. *false*, Scand. *fals*, which are clearly derived from Lat., the word is doubtlessly connected in some way with Lat. *falsus*. But since the latter retained its *s* unchanged (comp. Ital. *falso*, Fr. *faux*, from OFr. *false*), we cannot imagine that the word was borrowed directly from Lat.-Romance (OIc. *falskr* is a German loanword of the 15th cent.). Probably Mid HG. *valsch*, a comparatively recent formation (comp. fein, wach), from OHG. *gifalscôn, gifelscen*, vb., 'to falsify,' which is derived from a Lat. *falsicâre*, Romance *falscare*, 'to falsify.' The assumption that MidHG. *valsch* (akin to *vâlant*, 'demon'?) is primit. allied to Lat. *fallere*, Gr. σφάλλεσθαι, is scarcely valid.

-falt, -fältig, adj. suffix, '-fold,' from MidHG. *-valt*, OHG. *falt*; comp. Goth. *-falþs*, AS. *-feald*, E. *-fold*, OIc. *-faldr*; a common Teut. suffix in the formation of multiplicatives; it corresponds to Gr. πλάσιος in διπλάσιος, &c. (also δίπαλτος, 'twofold'), for *pltios*, with which *falt seems to be primit. cognate. See falten, and Einfalt under ein.

falten, vb., 'to fold, plait, knit (the brow),' from the equiv. MidHG. *valten*, OHG. *faltan, faldan*; corresponds to Goth, *falþan*, OIc. *falda*, AS. *fealdan*, E. *to fold*; the Teut. root is *falþ*, 'to fold,' pre-Teut. *plt*, with which comp. OSlov. *pleta, plesti*, 'to twist,' Gr. διπλάσιος, 'twofold' (see under -falt), Sans. *puṭa*, 'fold,' for *plta.*— Falte, f., 'fold, plait, crease, hem,' from MidHG. *valte*, OHG. *falt*, m., 'fold,' is primit. cognate with Sans. *puṭa,*, 'fold' (from *pulta*). See falten.—From an OTeut. Faltſtuhl (AS. *fyldstôl*), 'folding stool,' is derived the Fr. cognate *fauteuil*, which has lately been adopted again by ModHG. ; comp. MidLat. *faldistolium, faldistorium*, Ital. *faldistorio.*

Falter, m., simply ModHG., 'butterfly'; the MidHG. term is *vivalter* (corrupted also into *zwivalter*), 'butterfly,' from which the ModHG. word has been corrupted by connecting it with falten. But MidHG. *vivalter* is based upon an OTeut. term for 'butterfly,' which may have been *feifaldrô* in Goth. ; comp. OHG. *fîfaltra*, OSax. *fîfoldara*, AS. *fîfealde*, OIc. *fîfrilde*, 'butterfly'; akin to Du. *vijfwouter*, 'a sort of butterfly.' The origin of this term is not yet established, although it is probably a reduplicated form like beben and zittern.

falzen, vb., 'to fold, groove, rabbet,' from MidHG. *velzen, valzen*, OHG. *falzen*, 'to fold'; Falz, m., from MidHG. *valz*, m., 'fold, joint'; akin to OHG. *anafalz*, 'anvil,' AS. *anfilt*, E. *anvil*, Du. *anbeeld*, 'anvil' (see Amboß). The cognates are undoubtedly connected with falten; MidHG. *valz* may have been *falti* in Goth., which would probably represent *falt-ti, pltni-* (comp. ſchnitzen from ſchneiden).—Falz, see Walz.

fangen, fahen, vb., 'to catch, seize, fish (an anchor), soften (hides),' from MidHG. *vâhen, vân*, OHG. *fâhan*, 'to catch, intercept, seize'; the common Teut. vb.—Goth. *fâhan*, OIc. *fâ*, AS. *fôn* (for *fôhan* from *fôhan*; wanting in E.)—has the same meaning. Root *fanh* (whence *fâh, fâh*), and by a grammatical change *fang* (this form is really found only in the partic. and pret., but it has made its way in ModHG. into the pres. also), pre-Teut. *pank*. With the Teut. cognates some have compared the unnasalised root *pak*, in Lat. *pax, pacem* (lit. 'strengthening'?); akin to the nasalised *pango* (partic. *pactum*), with *g* for *c*?, Sans. *pâçu*, 'cord'; the root *pak* appears without a nasal in Teut. *fôg*; see HG. fügen.—Fang, m., 'catch, capture, fang, clutches, haul,' from MidHG. *vanc*, m., OHG. *fang*; comp. AS. *feng*, 'clutch, embrace,' *fang*, 'capture,' E. *fang* (tooth, claw).

Fant, m., 'coxcomb,' a LG. form (comp. Du. *vent*, 'a would-be wit, fool'), for MidHG. *vanz*, m., 'rogue' (still existing in *alfanz*, lit. 'vagabond'; comp. ModHG. Firle Fanz, the first part of which is obscure, perhaps connected with AS. *fyrlen*, 'foreign'?). See Alfanzerei.

Farbe, f., 'colour, complexion, suit (of cards),' from MidHG. *varwe*, OHG. *farawa*, 'colour'; a fem. subst. from the MidHG. adj. *var*, inflected form *varwer*, 'coloured,' from OHG. *faro* (nom. *farawêr*); comp. Du. *verw*. The word originated probably in Middle Europe, but found its way to the North ; Dan. *farve*, Swed. *fårg*. Is Goth. *farwa-*, adj. (whence Lith. *parvas*, 'colour'), or *fazwa* to be postulated ?

Farn, m., n., 'fern,' from the equiv. MidHG. and OHG. *varn, varm*; corresponds to Du. *varenkruid*, AS. *fearn*, E. *fern*. The interchange of *n* and *m* in OHG. and MidHG. is due to the assimilation of the suffix *na-* to the initial labial; comp. OHG. *feim* with OInd. *phéna*, and OHG. *bodam* with Sans. *budhna*. Farn is wanting in OIc.; yet comp. Swed. dial. *fånne* (Ic. *ferne*). The type is doubtlessly Aryan *parna-*, which is identical with Sans. *parṇa*, n., 'wing, feather, foliage, leaf'; hence Farn is lit. 'feather-like leaf' (Gr. πτερίς, 'fern,' and πτερόν, 'feather'). Probably allied also to Lith. *papartis*, Russ. *paporotĭ* (OSlov. *papratĭ*), 'fern.'

Farre, m., 'bullock, bull,' from the equiv. MidHG. *varre, var*, m., OHG. *farro, far*, m.; corresponding to Du. *varre, var*, 'bull,' AS. *fearr*, m., OIc. *farre*, m., 'bull.' Since there is a corresponding fem. form, Färſe, the *rr* must have originated in *rz(rs)*, (comp. dürr, irre).—Färſe, f. (unknown to UpG.), 'heifer,' from MidHG. (MidG. and LG.) *verse*, f.; comp. Du. *vaars*, 'heifer' (likewise *vaarkoe*, 'heifer'); in Goth. probably *farsi*, gen. *farsjôs*; E. *heifer*, from the equiv. AS. *heáhfore, heáfre*, f., seems to contain Farre, Färſe, in the final syllable. The stem *farz, fars*, does not occur exactly in the cognate languages, yet Gr. πόρις, πόρτις, 'calf, heifer,' agree with it in sound ; likewise Sans. *prṣati*, 'white-spotted cow' (fem. of *prṣati*, 'speckled, spotted') ?.

Färſe, see under Farre.

farzen, vb., 'to fart,' from the equiv. MidHG. *varzen* (also *vurzen, vërzen*), allied to OHG. *fërzan*, 'to fart'; corresponds to AS. *feortan*, E. *to fart ;* OIc. (with transposition of the *r*), *freta*. Teut. root *fert*, from the Aryan *perd*, with the same meaning; comp. Sans. root *pard*, Gr. πέρδειν, Lith. *pêrdžu, pêrsti*, Russ. *perdĕtĭ*.

Faſan, m., 'pheasant,' from the equiv. MidHG. and OHG. *fusân, fasant*, m.; the latter is derived from Lat. Gr. *fasianus* (φασιανός, 'a bird from the Phasis in Colchis'), 'pheasant,' whence also Ital. *fagiuno*, Fr. *faisan*.

Fasching, m., 'carnival,' from MidHG. *vaschanc*, m., 'Shrovetide'; how it is connected with Faſtnacht (Shrove-Tuesday) has not yet been explained.

faſeln, vb., 'to talk irrationally,' only in ModHG., a derivative of OHG. *fasôn*, 'to track, seek here and there'; but the latter word is probably not from the root *fas* in Faſer.

Faſer, f., 'fibre, filament,' from late MidHG. *vaser*, f., 'fringe,' most frequently *vase*, m., f., 'fibre, fringe, border,' OHG. *faso*, m., *fasa*, f.; AS. *fæs*, n., MidE. *fasil*, 'fringe.'

Fasnacht, see Faſtnacht.

faſſen, vb., 'to hold, grasp, comprehend,' (refl.) 'to make up one's mind,' from MidHG. *vazzen*, OHG. *fazzôn*, 'to handle, seize, load, pack, arm oneself, dress, go'; it seems to be a combination of two or more really different roots. Comp. OIc. *fǫt*, neu. plur., 'garments' (Goth. **fata*, 'garments,' may be deduced from Span. *hato*, Port. *fato*, 'stock of clothes, wardrobe'); the West Teut. *fat* (see Faß), has not this meaning, but MidHG. (OHG.) *vazzen*, 'to dress oneself,' points that way. In the sense 'to seize,' the word may be connected with Faß, lit. 'engulphing,' from which the meaning 'to load' would be evolved. In the sense of 'to go' (*sich vazzen*, MidHG.) it must probably be connected with Fuß, or more closely with AS. *fæt*, 'step.' See Fetzen, Fitze.

faſt, adv., 'almost, nearly,' from MidHG. *vaste, vast,* adv. (from *veste*, 'firm'), 'firmly, strongly, powerfully, very, very quickly,' OHG. *vasto*, adv., from *festi*; similar unmutated advs. from mutated adjs. are ſchon from ſchön, ſpat from ſpät. ModHG. has also turned feſt into an adv., the older adv. faſt having been specialised in meaning; even in MidHG. *veste* is an adv.

faſten, vb., 'to fast,' from the equiv. MidHG. *vasten*, OHG. *fastên*; comp. Goth. *fastan*, OIc. *fasta*, AS. *fæstan*, E. *to fast*, Du. *vasten*; a common Teut. verb, invariably used in the sense of 'to fast,' which, therefore, was probably a religious conception even of the heathen Teutons. The corresponding abstract is Goth. *fastubni*, AS. *fæsten*, OSax. *fastunnia*, OHG. *fasta*, *fasto*, m., MidHG. *vaste*, f., *vasten*, n., 'fast'; whence Slav. *postŭ*, 'fast,' was borrowed at an early period. The cognates are probably connected with feſt in the sense of 'to contain oneself, exercise restraint in eating and drinking,' or 'to obey a religious precept'; comp. Goth. *fastan*, 'to adhere to, hold, observe.'—**Faſtnacht,** f., 'Shrove Tuesday,' from MidHG. *vasenaht*, 'eve of the first day of Lent.' According to the OTeut. computation of time (comp. Abend) the evening and night were counted as part of the following day (thus in AS. *frígeǽfen*, 'Thursday evening,' *frígeniht*, 'Thursday night'). The meaning given above did not belong to the word originally. The first part of the compound is an old verb faſeln, 'to play the fool'; the form Faſtnacht may have been introduced by the priests.

Faß, n., 'vessel, cask, vat,' from Mid HG. *vaz*, OHG. *faz*(zz), n., 'cask, vessel, chest'; corresponds to MidLG. and Du. *vat*, AS. *fæt*, 'vessel, receptacle, chest' (E. *vat*), OIc. *fat*, 'cask.' The prim. signification of these cognates (pre-Teut. *podo*-) may have been 'receptacle,' and since Feſſel is an allied word, we have to postulate the meaning 'to hold together' for the Teut. root *fat*. Lith. *púdas*, 'pot, vessel,' would be in Goth. **fôta-* instead of **fata-*. Mod HG. Gefäß is not an immediate derivative of Faß, because it assumes a Goth. **gafêti*, n. See faſſen, Fetzen, Fitze.

faul, adj., 'rotten, worthless, lazy,' from the equiv. MidHG. and MidLG. *vûl*, OHG. *fûl*; comp. Du. *vuil*, AS. *fúl*, E. *foul*, OIc. *fúll*, Goth. *fûls*, 'decayed'; *la-* is derivative; *fû-* as the Teut. root is deduced from OIc. *fúenn*, 'putrefied,' which as a partic. points to an obsolete verb (Goth. **fauan*, formed like *bauan*), of which OIc. *feyja*, 'to allow to putrefy,' is the factitive (Goth. **faujan*). From *fû* several Teut. dialects have formed nouns with the meaning 'cunnus' (OIc. *fuþ*); see Hundsfott. The root *fû*, from Aryan *pû*, is equally represented in the allied languages; Gr. πύον, 'matter,' and the equiv. Lat. *pûs*, n.; Sans. and Zend root *pû* (*pûy*), 'to stink, putrefy,' Lith. *puvú*, *pûti*, 'to putrefy' (akin to Lith. *pùlei*, 'matter,' with a derivative *l* as in faul); also Gr. πύθω, 'to cause to rot,' Lat. *pûteo*, 'to stink,' *pûter*, 'putrid, rotten.' The primary meaning of the root *pû* is 'to emit a smell of putrefaction.'—**faulenzen,** vb. 'to be lazy,' from late MidHG. *vûleízen*, 'to be rotten,' an intensive derivative of faul; comp. blitzen, ſeufzen.

F

Fauſt, f., 'fist,' from the equiv. MidHG. and MidLG. *vûst*. OHG. *fûst*, f.; corresponds to AS. *fýst*, E. *fist*, Du. *vuist*. This term, common to West Teut., is unknown to OIc.; in Goth. it may have been **fûsti-* or **fûhsti-*, f. The possible loss of a *h* before *st* is supported by the connection with Gr. πύξ, 'with the fist,' πύγμαχος, 'boxer,' πυγμή, 'fist, boxing,' Lat. *pugnus*, 'fist,' *pŭgil*, 'boxer,' perhaps also *pugio*, 'dagger' (lit. 'fist weapon'), and further *pugna, pugnare*, &c. The comparison of Fauſt with OSlov. *pęstĭ*, f., 'fist,' is less trustworthy; this is possible only if the assumed Goth. **fûhsti* is further derived from *funhsti-*, pre-Teut. *pnksti-* ; in that case, however, the Gr. and Lat. terms cited would have no connection with the word.

Faxe, plur., 'fooleries, tricks,' ModHG. only ; of obscure origin.

fechten, vb., 'to fight, fence,' from the equiv. MidHG. *vëhten*, OHG. *fëhtan*; a term common to West Teut. for 'to fight, contend,' unknown to Scand. and Goth.; comp. Du. and MidHG. *vechten*, OFris. *fiuchta*, AS. *feohtan*, E. *to fight*. Whether the verb has always belonged to the *e* class is questionable; it may have passed from the pret. plur. and partic. of the *u* class into the *e* class ; in that case, we should have to assume Goth. **fiuhtan, **fauht, **fauhtum, **fauhtans*, instead of **fahtan, **faht, **fauhtam, **fauhtans*. This conceivable assumption facilitates the connection with Lat. *pugna, pugnare*; yet the latter are probably only derivatives of *pugnus*, 'fist'; perhaps the inferred Goth. **fiuhtan*, 'to fight,' is similarly related to Fauſt.

Feder, f., 'feather, pen, plume, spring, flaw (in jewels),' from the equiv. MidHG. *vëder, vëdere*, OHG. *fëdara*, f.; the term common to Teut. for 'feather'; comp. OSax. *fëthara*, AS. *fëþer*, f., 'feather, wing,' E. *feather*, OIc. *fjǫþr*, f., Goth. **fiþra*, f., akin to the collective noun Gefieder (see Fittich). Goth. **fiþra*, from pre-Teut. *petrâ*, f., has in the allied Aryan languages some correspondences which prove the existence of an Aryan root *pet*, 'to fly'; comp. the Sans. root *pat*, 'to fly,' *pátatra*, n., 'wing,' *patarú*, adj., 'flying,' *çatápatra*, 'having a hundred wings or feathers,' Gr. πέτομαι, 'to fly,' πτερόν (for **πετερόν*), 'wing,' πτίλον (for **πετιλον*), 'feather'; it is less certain whether Lat. *penna*, 'feather' (for **petsna ?*), is allied. See Fittich.—**Feder-leſen**, n., lit. 'picking off the feather from a person's dress' as a mark of servile flattery; found even in MidHG.—**Feder-ſpiel**, n., 'lure,' from MidHG. *vëderspil*, n., 'a bird trained for hawking, falcon, sparrow-hawk, hawk.'

Fee, Fei, f., 'fairy,' from the equiv. MidHG. *fei, feie*, f.; borrowed from an OFr. dialect (Burgund.), *feie*, ModFr. *fée* (Ital. and Romance, *fata*, lit. 'goddess of destiny,' from Lat. *fatum*), whence also E. *fay* and *fairy*.

Fegefeuer, n., 'purgatory,' from Mid HG. *vëgeviur*, n., 'purgatory,' from Mid HG. *vëgen*, 'to purify'; formed on the model of MidLat. *purgatorium*.

fegen, vb., 'to sweep, scour, winnow (corn), purge,' from MidHG. *vëgen* (OHG. **fegôn*), 'to purify, adorn, sweep, scour,' Du. *vegen*. Goth. **figôn* is connected with Goth. *fagrs*, 'suitable,' AS. *fǽger*, E. *fair*, OHG. and OSax. *fagar* ; from the root *feh, fah, fag, fôg* in fügen ; OIc. *fægja*, 'to cleanse,' probably belongs to the same root (the Goth. form being *fêgjan*); Aryan root, *pêk, pôk ?*.

Fehde, f., 'feud,' from MidHG. *vëhede, vêde*, OHG. *fêhida*, 'hate, enmity, quarrel, feud'; corresponds to AS. *fǽhþ*, f., 'enmity, revenge, feud'; Goth. **faihiþa*, 'enmity,' is probably an abstract noun from the Goth. adj. **faihs*, 'hostile,' which appears in AS. as *fâh, fâg*, 'exiled, outlawed, proscribed' (AS. *gefâa*, m., 'enemy,' E. *foe* ; comp. OHG. *giféh*, MidHG. *gevêch*, 'hostile, malignant'). A pre-Teut. root, *piq*, 'to injure, cheat' (comp. also Goth. *faih*, 'imposition, deception,' *bifaihôn*, 'to deceive, overreach'), is indicated by the Lith.; comp. Lith. *piktas*, 'angry,' *pýkti*, 'to get angry,' *petkti*, 'to curse,' *paikas*, 'stupid' (akin to Pruss. *po-paikâ*, 'he cheats'). Respecting the interchange of meaning between 'to injure' and 'to deceive,' see trügen. Hence E. *foe* is lit. 'one who injures,' OHG. *fêhida*, lit. 'hurt, injury.'

fehlen, vb., 'to miss, want, err,' from MidHG. *vëlen, vælen*, 'to fail, mistake, cheat, be wanting, miss'; borrowed in the MidHG. period (about 1200 A.D.) from Fr. *faillir*, 'to fail, miss, deceive,' which again, like Ital. *fallire*, is derived from Lat. *fallere*. The word was also adopted by E. in the 13th cent.; comp. E. *fail*, likewise Du. *feilen*, 'to fail, miss, deceive,' Scand. (since the 14th cent.), *feila*.

Fehme, f., 'criminal tribunal' (in Westphalia formerly), from MidHG. *veime*, f., 'condemnation, punishment, secret tribunal.' Goth. **faima*, f., would, on the analogy of τέσσαρες, Goth. *fidvôr*, favour the connection with the root τι in Gr. τίνω, 'to atone for,' derived from *ki*, 'to punish, avenge'; Gr. ποίνη, as a derivative of the same root, may have been formed with a different suffix from that which appears in Fehme. In spite of the late formation of the word, its origin is difficult to discover and uncertain. Its connection with Du. *veem*, 'guild, association,' is also disputed. Others again refer it to OSax. *a-féhian*, 'to condemn' (see *feige*). It is quite impossible to connect it with an older LG. form, Fehme, 'oak-mast,' which, with Bav. *dehme*, *dechel*, 'oak-mast,' belongs to a different stem.

Feier, f., 'holiday, festival, celebration,' from MidHG. *vîre*, f., OHG. *fîra*, *fîrra*, f., 'festival, holiday'; borrowed from Mid Lat. *féria* (formed from Lat. *feriae*), with the lat *ê* strengthened, as Streit, Speise, Seite, Pein; the cause of the *rr* in OHG. *fîrra* is the *i* of *féria*. **Feiertag**, m., 'holiday, festival,' from MidHG. *vîr-*, *vîretac*, OHG. *fîratag*.—**feiern**, 'to celebrate,' from MidHG. *vîren*, OHG. *fîrrôn*, *fîrôn*, 'to celebrate, keep a festival,' formed from Lat. *feriari*. The borrowed word is found in the Teut. languages of Middle Europe (Du. *vierdag*, OFris. *fîra*), but is wanting in E. and Scand. The Romance languages preserve Lat. *feriae* in the sense of 'fair'; comp. Ital. *fiera*, Fr. *foire* (hence E. *fair*). Comp. Messe and Fest.—ModHG. Ferien (since the 16th cent.), 'vacation, holidays,' has been derived anew from Lat. *feriae*.

feige, adj., 'cowardly, dastardly,' from MidHG. *veige*, OHG. *feigi*, adj., 'doomed to death, accursed, unhappy,' then also 'timid, cowardly' (in the ModHG. sense *feige* is wanting in the UpG. dialects); comp. OSax. *fêyi*, 'doomed to death,' Hess. *fêg*, Du. *veeg*, *veege*, 'on the point of death,' AS. *fǽge*, Scotch *fey*, OIc. *feigr*, 'doomed to death, on the point of death.' In the sense of 'fated to die,' the adj. is primit. Teut. (Goth. **faigs*). It has also been compared with Sans. *pakvás*, 'ripe,' so that the Teut. cognates would represent *pêkj*, *pêki* (with an inserted vowel); comp. feil. Far more improbable is the assumption that it is connected with Goth. *faihs*, OHG. *fêh*, AS. *fâh*, 'variegated,' as if it were thought that the person doomed to death by the fates was distinguished by some coloured mark. Some compare it with the cognates discussed under Fehde, some with Lith. *paíkas*, 'stupid, silly,' others again, with an OSax. *féhian*, 'to condemn.' See Fehme.

Feige, f., 'fig,' from the equiv. MidHG. *vîge*, OHG. *figa*, f., 'fig'; comp. OSax. *figa*, Du. *vijg*; derived, like other South Europ. names of trees and fruits, from Rom. Lat. (*ficus*, f.), or more strictly from North Ital. and Provenç. *figa*, whence also Fr. *figue*. The AS. *fîctreów* is connected directly with the Lat., the later E. form *fig-tree* being based upon Fr. *figue*. Comp. Pfirsich, Pflaume, Birne, varieties of fruit, which were borrowed in the OHG. period, or even earlier, from the Lat. Goth. *smakka*, 'fig,' corresponding to OSlov. *smokŭ*, was obtained from a different source. See Ohrfeige.

Feigwarze, f., from the equiv. MidHG. (rare) *vîcwarzen*, n., *vîcwerze*, f., 'venereal ulcer,' for which is found, mostly in the same sense, MidHG. *vîc*, m., from Lat. *ficus*, whence also the equiv. AS. *fîce*; comp. Ital. *fico*, 'fig, venereal ulcer.'

feil, adj., 'for sale, venal,' from Mid HG. *veile*, *veil*, OHG. *feili*, with the curious variant *fâli*, adj., 'purchaseable'; akin to the equiv. OIc. *falr*, with an abnormal vowel. Teut. *faili-* has according to OHG. *fâli*, OIc. *falr*, an inserted vowel in the accented syllable (comp. *feige*); hence it corresponds to Aryan *pêli-*, and is connected with Gr. πωλέομαι, 'to sell,' and more remotely with the OInd. root *paṇ* for *paln-*, 'to purchase, buy, exchange.'— feilschen, with *sch* after *l* for *s*, 'to higgle, bargain,' from MidHG. *veilschen*, OHG. **feilisôn*, 'to bargain for something.'

Feile, f., 'file,' from the equiv. Mid HG. *vîle*, OHG. *fîla*, *fîhala* (not *fîhala*), f.; corresponds to AS. *feól* (dial. variant **fîl*), f., E. *file*, Du. *vijl*, 'file.' The OIc. term is *þél*, f., 'file,' with an abnormal initial sound; Goth **feihala* or **þeihala* must be assumed. The form with initial *f* from Aryan *p* points to the widely diffused root *pik*, 'to scratch,' akin to Lat. *pingo*, *pictor*, OSlov. *pĭsati*, 'to write.' Yet OIc. *þél*, from **pĭthl*, points to Teut. *þinh*, equiv. to pre-Teut. *tek*, *tenk*, in ModHG. Dachs; for the interchange of *f* and *þ* comp. düster (finster), Fackel, Fehme (also OHG. *fîn*, *fîma* compared with LG. *dîme*, 'heap of corn.')

Feim, m., 'foam,' from the equiv. Mid

HG. *veim*, OHG. *feim*, m.; comp. the corresponding AS. *fám*, E. *foam*, which are primit. allied to the equiv. Sans. *phéna*, OSlov. *pĕna*. ModHG. abgefeimt, from an earlier abfeimen, 'to skim' (comp. raffiniert, from Fr. *raffiner*, 'to refine').

fein, adj., 'fine, elegant, cunning,' from MidHG. *vîn*, *fîn*, adj., 'fine, beautiful'; OHG. **fîn* may be inferred from the adv. *finlîhho*, which is first recorded in a gloss of the 10th cent.; comp. Du. *fijn*, E. *fine*. Borrowed from a word common to Romance, Ital. *fino* (Fr. *fin*), with the prim. meaning 'perfect, genuine, pure,' which is a late adj. form from Lat. *finire*.

Feind, m., 'enemy, foe, fiend,' from MidHG. *vînt*, *vîent*, *vîant*, OHG. *fîant*, m., 'enemy'; the common Teut. noun for 'enemy'; comp. OSax. *fîund*, AS. *feónd*, E. *fiend*, Olc. *fjánde*, Goth. *fijands*. In contrast to Lat. *hostis*, discussed under Gast, the Teut. designates his enemy according to the disposition of the latter; Feind (pres. part. of the Sans. root *pî*, *pîy*, 'to scorn, hate') is lit. 'the hater'; comp. OHG. *fîen*, AS. *feógan*, Goth. *fijan*, 'to hate,' akin to Goth. *faian*, 'to blame.' Fehde is perhaps allied to it; for the transformation of the pres. part. into a subst. comp. also Freund, Weigand, and Heiland.

feift, adj., 'fat, in good condition,' from MidHG. *veiʒt*, *veiʒet*, OHG. *feiʒʒit*, adj., 'fat, greasy'; properly a partic. without *gi-*, *ge-* of a Goth. verb **faitjan*, 'to fatten,' OHG. *feiʒʒen*, which is from the nominal stem *faita-*, 'fat,' OIc. *feitr*, MidHG. *veiʒ*. With the assumed Goth. **faitips* are connected AS. *fǽted*, *fǽtt*, and E. *fat* (comp. fett). Goth. **faita-*, from pre-Teut. *paido-*, has no unquestionable cognates in the allied languages; it can scarcely be connected with OSlov. *pitěti*, 'to nourish, feed,' on account of the faulty shifting of the dental (Slav. *t* corresponding to Goth. *t* is impossible); it is more probably related to the root πῖδ, 'to swell, flow forth'; comp. πίδαξ, 'a spring,' πιδύω, 'to gush forth.'

Felber, m., 'white willow,' from MidHG. *vëlwer*, older *vëlwâre*, m., from *vëlwe*, f., 'willow,' OHG. *felawa*, *felwa*, f., 'willow tree.' Probably Osset. *fúrwe*, 'alder,' is primit. allied to it.

Feld, n., 'field, space, square (chessbourd), panel,' from MidHG. *vëlt* (gen. -*des*), OHG. *fëld*, n., 'field, soil, surface, plain'; a word common to West Teut. pointing to Goth. **filþ*, n.; OSax. and AS. *fëld*

(*lþ* in both dialects are regularly changed into *ld*), E. *field*, Du. *veld*. It is still questionable whether OIc. *fjall*, 'mountain,' is identical with it, since the former is more probably connected with ModHG. Fels. On the other hand, the following are certainly allied:—OIc. *fold*, f., 'pasture,' AS. *folde*, f., OSax. *folda*, 'earth, country, ground' (pointing to Goth **fuldô*). Finn. *pelto* is derived from Teut. *fel/þos*, which, with OIc. *folda*, is based upon the Aryan root *plth* (Sans. *pṛth*), 'to be broad, flat'; comp. Sans. *pṛthivî*, 'earth,' as well Flaken.

Felge, f., 'felly (of a wheel),' from MidHG. *vëlge*, OHG. *fëlga*, f., 'rim of a wheel, tyre,' OHG. also 'harrow, roller for breaking clods'; comp. Du. *rudvelge*, 'felloe,' AS. *fëlg*, E. *felly* (rim, fellow). Is OHG. *felga*, 'roller, harrow,' to be connected with AS. **fealge* (MidE. *falge*, 'fallow land'), E. *fallow*, and its *e* to be regarded therefore as formed by mutation? MidHG. *valgen*, 'to plough up, dig,' makes such a supposition very probable. It is possible that the two classes in the sense of 'felloe' and 'harrow' are not allied to each other. Between OHG. *fëlga* and AS. *fëlgu*, 'felloe,' there is no connecting link.

Fell, n., 'hide, skin, fur,' from MidHG. *vël(ll)*, OHG. *fël(ll)*, 'human skin, hide'; comp. Goth. *fill*, n., in *þrúts-fill*, 'leprosy,' *fauru-filli*, 'foreskin'; OIc. *fjall*, 'skin, hide,' in compounds, AS. *fëll*, n., 'skin, hide,' E. *fell*, Du. *vel*. Common to Teut. orig., but universal in the wider sense of 'skin,' both of men and animals. Teut. *fella-* from pre-Teut. *pello-* or *pelno-*; comp. Lat. *pellis*, Gr. πέλλα, 'hide, leather,' ἀπελλος, n., '(skinless) unhealed wound,' ἐρυσίπελας, 'erysipelas, St. Anthony's fire,' ἐπίπλοος, 'caul of the entrails,' the latter for ἐπίπλοFος, akin to Lith. *plévé*, 'caul, skin'; also akin to AS. *filmen*, 'membrane, foreskin,' E. *film*; likewise Gr. πέλμα, 'sole of the foot or shoe,' and perhaps πέπλος, 'garment,' as a reduplicated form (πέ-πλ-ος, root πελ).

Felleiſen, n., from the equiv. MidHG. *rellis*, m., 'valise, knapsack'; the ModHG. form is a corruption of the MidHG. word which is based upon the equiv. Fr. *valise*.

Felſen, m., 'rock,' from the equiv. MidHG. *vëlse*, *vëls*, m., OHG. *felis*, m., *felisa*, f. (from which Fr. *falaise*, 'cliff,' is borrowed); akin to OSax. *felis*, m., probably also to OIc. *fjall*, 'mountain'; the latter would be **filza-* in Goth., the former **falisa-*; in Du. and E. the word is wanting. OIr.

ail (from **palêk*), 'rock,' OSlov. *planina*, 'mountain,' Sans. *parvata*, 'rock, mountain,' may be primit. allied. Connected also with OInd. *pŭr*, 'fastness, citadel,' to which Gr. πόλι-ς has been referred ? or with Sans. *páṣāṇa* (for **palsāna*), 'stone' ?.

Fenchel, m. (Suab. and Alem. Fenkel), from the equiv. MidHG. *venchel, venichel,* OHG. *fenahhal, fenihhal,* m., 'fennel'; comp. AS. *finul,* E. *fennel;* formed from Lat. (*fœniculum, feniculum, feniclum*), *fenuclum;* from the same source the Romance cognates Fr. *fenouil,* Ital. *finocchio,* 'fennel,' are derived.

Fenster, n., 'window,' from the equiv. MidHG. *venster,* OHG. *venstar,* n.; comp. Du. *venster,* n. Based, with a curious change of gender, on Lat. *fenestra,* from which, however, the *fenstar* of the Mid Europ. Teutons could only be produced by shifting the accent back according to the Teut. custom (comp. Abt) and by syncopating the second *e*. This indicates that the word was borrowed very early, in the beginning of the OHG. period. Yet the idea was well known to the older periods, as is testified by the terms naturally applied to the existing object—Goth. *augadaurô,* 'eye-gate,' AS. *ĕgþýrel,* 'eye-hole,' OIc. *vindauga* (whence MidE. *windóge,* E. *window*). By the introduction of the Southern term (comp. also OIr. *senister,* W. *ffenester*) the idea was probably reconstructed. This word was borrowed at the same period as other words—Ziegel, Mauer—relating to the building of houses.

Ferge, m., 'ferryman,' from MidHG. *verge, verje, vere,* OHG. *ferjo, fero* (nom. sing. *ferjo,* gen. and dat. *ferin,* accus. *ferjun*), m., 'mariner, ferryman.' The *j* is changed into *g* after *r* as in Scherge, Lattwerge. Goth. **farja,* m., 'mariner,' is wanting. Most closely allied to Fähre; also akin to Goth. *farjan,* 'to navigate,' see root *far* under fahren.

Ferien, see Feier.

Ferkel, n., 'sucking-pig,' from MidHG. *verker, verchel, verhelin,* OHG. *farhelī(n)*; dimin. of MidHG. *varch,* n., 'pig, sucking-pig,' OHG. *farah, fark,* n.; AS. *fearh,* m., E. *farrow;* Du. *varken,* n., 'pig'; Goth. **farha-* is wanting. In any case it is a pre-Teut. word, since the allied Aryan languages have words corresponding to it both in sound and meaning; **farhaz* from pre-Teut. *porkos,* corresponds to Lat. *porcus* (Gr. πόρκος), Lith. *pàrszas,* OSlov. *prasę,* n.,

OIr. *orc.* Like Eber and Schwein, this word too, unknown to Indian, is essentially West Aryan, while Kuh is a common Aryan word.

fern, adv., 'far, distantly, remotely,' from MidHG. *vërrene, vërren, vërne,* OHG. *vërrana, vërranán,* adv., 'from afar'; the adv. in answer to the question 'where?' is *vërre* in MidHG. and *vërro* in OHG. The adject. form in MidHG. is *vërre,* in OHG. *vër,* which are probably derived from the old adv. The remaining Teut. branches have no old orig. adj.; as an adv., however, we meet with Goth. *faírra,* which is also a prep., 'distant, away from,' OIc. *fjarre,* AS. *feor,* E. *far,* OSax. *ferr.* Besides these words relating to distance in space, O Teut. has also allied terms for distance in time; Goth. *fairneis,* 'old, in the preceding year,' OSax. *firn,* 'preceding, passed away (of years),' OHG. *firni,* MidHG. *virne,* 'old' (see under Firnewein), akin also to OIc. *forn,* 'old,' MidHG. *vorn,* 'earlier, formerly,' with a differently graded vowel. To the Teut. stem *fer-, for-* from pre-Teut. *per, pr,* are allied Gr. πέρᾱ, 'further,' πέραν, 'on the other side,' Armen. *heri,* 'distant,' Sans. *pára-s,* 'more, remote,' *paramás,* 'remotest, highest,' *parás,* adv., 'far off, in the distance.' The cognates of Aryan *per-* have too great and involved a ramification to be fully explained here. See firn.

Ferse, f., 'heel, track, footsteps,' from the equiv. MidHG. *vërsen,* OHG. *fërsana,* f.; corresponds to Goth. *faírzna* (for **fairsna*), f., AS. *fyrsn,* f. (pointing to Goth. **faírsni-*); E. obsolete, the term 'heel' (AS. *hēla*) being used, in Scand. *hǣll;* Du. *verzen,* OSax. *fërsna.* Common, like Fuß, and numerous other terms relating to the body (Herz, Niere, Ohr, Nase, &c.), to Teut. and the allied languages, and hence derived from the OAryan vocabulary; comp. *fersnô, -ni,* from pre-Teut. *pĕrs-nā, -nī-,* with Sans. *pārṣṇi-s,* f. (like AS. *fyrsn* in the formation of its stem), Zend *páṣna,* m., Gr. πτέρνα, f., 'heel, ham,' Lat. *perna,* 'leg (of mutton, &c.), ham,' *pernix,* 'quick, speedy' (for **persna, *persnix*).

fertig, adj., 'ready, complete, dexterous,' from MidHG. *vertec, vertic* (from *vart,* 'journey'), adj., 'able to walk, walking, in motion, ready, fit,' OHG. *fartig;* Du. *vaardig,* 'ready.' The adj., like bereit and rüstig, probably meant orig. 'equipped for a military expedition.'

Feſſel (1.), f., 'fetter, chain, shackle,' from MidHG. *veʒʒel*, OHG. *feʒʒil*, m., 'band for fastening and holding the sword,' then also 'band, fetter'; AS. *fetel*, 'sword-belt,' OIc. *fetell*, m., 'band, bandage, sword-belt'; akin to root *fat* (see **Faß**, **faſſen**), 'to hold'?. The ModHG. has retained its general sense by taking the place of another OTeut. word for 'fetter'; MidHG. *vëʒʒer*, f., 'fetter, shackle for the foot,' OHG. *fëʒʒera*, OSax. *fëter*, AS. *fëter*, E. *fetters* (plur.), OIc. *fjǫturr*. These words, which are usually connected with Lat. *pedica*, Gr. πέδη, 'fetter,' Lat. *compes*, and hence with the cognates of ModHG. **Fuß**, can scarcely be allied to the terms indicating a Goth. *fatils, 'sword-belt.'

Feſſel (2.), f., 'pastern.' See **Fuß**.

Feſt, n., 'festival, fête, feast,' from the equiv. MidHG. *fëst*, n., from Lat. *festum*, whence Ital. *festa*, Fr. *fête* (E. *feast*); **Feier** is the earlier loan-word. Gothic has simply a native *dulþs*, 'feast.' See **Dult**.

feſt, adj., 'firm, solid, strong,' from Mid HG. *vest*, *veste*, OHG. *festi*, adj., 'firm, strong, steadfast'; see the corresponding adv. **faſt**, which is not mutated; neither was the adj. originally formed by mutation, since, according to OSax. *fast*, AS. *fœst*, E. *fast*, OIc. *fastr*, adj., 'firm,' we have to assume a Goth. *fastu-, which is probably an old *to-* partic. like *laut*, *traut*, *ʒart*, *alt*, &c., from the root *fas-*, 'to fasten'; **faſta-*, lit. 'fastened,' then 'firm.' Goth. still retains only the verb *fastan*, 'to keep firm, hold fast.' See **faſten**.

Fetiſch, m., 'fetish,' adopted by Mod HG. at the beginning of the 17th cent. The earlier parallel form **Fetiſſo** is more closely connected with the Port. base *feitiço*, 'enchantment,' but the modern form with Fr. *fétiche*.

fett, adj., 'fat, plump,' only in ModHG., introduced by Luther from MidG. and LG. instead of the genuine UpG. **feiſt**; LG. *fett*, comp. Du. *vet* from an earlier *fêit*, AS. *fǣtt*, 'fat,' which, with OHG. *feiʒʒit*, are derived from Goth. *faitips; see **feiſt**. As to the origin of the ModHG. idiom, **ſein Fett haben**, **jemandem ſein Fett geben**, 'to get one's due, give any one his due,' opinions are divided; although the reference to **einbrocken**, **jemandem etwas einbrocken** (to play one a trick), &c., supports the assumption of a purely Ger. origin, some etymologists regard it as partly translated and partly borrowed from the Fr. *donner à quelqu'un son fait, avoir son fait*, others even as an ironical reference to the Fr. *faire fête à quelqu'un*, 'to make a person heartily welcome.'

Fetzen, m., from the equiv. MidHG. *vëtze*, m., 'rag, tatters'; probably from MidHG. *vazzen*, 'to dress,' OIc. *fǫt*, 'clothes.' From a Teut. (Goth.) *fatu*, 'clothes,' Span. *hato*, and Port. *fato*, 'wardrobe,' are derived. Comp. **faſſen**, **Faß**. In the dialectal compounds **Alltags-**, **Sonntags-fetzen**, **Fetzen** denotes 'clothes.'

feucht, adj., 'moist, damp, humid,' from the equiv. MidHG. *viuhte*, OHG. *fûhti*, *fûht*, (Goth. *fûhtu-* is wanting). The adj. is WestTeut.; comp. LG. *fucht*, AS. *fûht*, E. obsolete, Du. *vochtig*, 'damp.' An allied root (*pûk*), *qûk*, *quak*, is assumed for OSlov. *kysnati*, 'to grow sour,' *kvasiti*, 'to acidify,' which are scarcely connected with this word.

Feuer, n., 'fire, ardour, passion,' from the equiv. MidHG. *viur*, OHG. and OLG. *fiur*, older *fûir*, n.; comp. Du. *vuur*, AS. *fýr* (from *fûir), n., E. *fire*; a word common to West Teut. for 'fire'; in Goth. *fön* (gen. *funins*), OIc. *fune*, 'fire,' but it is doubtful whether they are cognate with HG. **Feuer**; comp. OIc. (only in poetry) *fúrr*, m., and *fýre*, n., 'fire.' The *r* in all the words is a suffix, and *fû* (from pre-Teut. *pû*) the root; comp. Gr. πῦρ and Æol. πύϊρ, n. (πυρσός, 'torch'). In Sans. a verbal root *pû*, 'to flame, beam brightly,' is found, whence *pâvakâ*, 'fire.'

Fibel, f., 'primer,' first occurs in early MidHG. (15th cent.), probably a LG. word orig. formed from **Bibel**; the earlier variant *wibel* (*wirel*?) points to ModGr. pronunciation. Perhaps **Fibel** represents **Bivel** (comp. **Giſig**, **Bieber**).

Fichte, f., 'pine, fir,' from MidHG. *vihte*, f., OHG. *fiohta*, *fiuhta*, f., 'fir.' No cognate term is found in any of the other Teut. dialects, yet **Fichte** is proved from the non-Teut. languages to be primitive; comp. Gr. πεύκη, 'fir,' Lith. *puszis*, 'fir.' The HG. form is fuller by a dental affix than the Gr. and Lith. words.

Fieber, n., 'fever,' from the equiv. Mid HG. *vieber*, OHG. *fiebar*, n.; from Lat.-Romance *febris*, with a change of gender as in AS. *féfor*, n., equiv. to E. *fever*; OHG. and MidHG. *ie* for *e*, as in **Brief**, **Ziegel**, **Spiegel**, **Prieſter**; so too ModHG. **Bieber-**, MidHG. *biever*, from *vieber*, with an interchange of consonants, as in **Eſſig** and **Rabeljau**.

Fiedel, f., from the equiv. MidHG. *videl, videle,* f., OHG. *fidula* (as early as Otfried), f., 'fiddle, violin'; comp. Du. *vedel,* AS. *fiþele,* E. *fiddle,* OIc. *fiþla.* OHG. *fidula* is based, according to AS. *fiþele,* 'fiddle,' *fiþelére,* 'fiddler,' *fiþelestre,* 'fidicina,' upon an older West Teut. **fiþula.* The latter form with *þ* might be deduced from Lat. **fitula* or *fidula* (for *fidicula*?), yet these primary forms are not recorded. There is undeniable connection between the Teut. class and the Romance cognates—Ital. *viola,* Fr. *viole,* 'violin,' the origin of which, it is true, is much disputed. Still Harfe found its way from Teut. into Romance.

fillen, vb., 'to flay,' from the equiv. MidHG. *villen,* OHG. *fillen;* allied to Fell.

Filz, m., 'felt, blanket; miser; reprimand,' from the equiv. MidHG. *vilz,* OHG. *filz,* m.; comp. Du. *vilt,* AS. and E. *felt,* Swed. and Dan. *filt,* 'felt' (Goth. **filtis,* pre-Teut. **peldos,* n.). Lat. *pilus, pileus,* Gr. πῖλος, are scarcely allied; it is more probably connected with OSlov. *plŭstĭ,* 'felt.' From the Teut. word are derived the similarly sounding Romance words, Ital. *feltro,* Fr. *feutre,* MidLat. *filtrum,* 'felt.' Other words also relating to weaving were introduced into Romance from Teut. See Haspe, Rocken.

finden, vb., 'to find, discover; deem, consider,' from the equiv. MidHG. *vinden,* OHG. *findan;* comp. Goth. *finþan,* OIc. *finna,* AS. *findan,* E. *to find,* OSax. *fīthan, findan,* 'to find.' Teut. *fenþ,* as a str. verbal root from pre-Teut. root *pent;* akin to OHG. *fendo,* m., 'pedestrian,' AS. *fēþa,* 'foot-soldier,' OHG. *funden,* 'to hasten'?. Some etymologists adduce Lat. *invenire* and OSlov. *na iti,* 'to find,' to show by analogy that from a verb of 'going' the meaning 'find' can be evolved. With the Teut. root *fenþ* the equiv. OIr. root *et-* (from *pent-*) is most closely connected.

Finger, m., 'finger,' from the equiv. MidHG. *vinger,* OHG. *fingar,* m.; a common Teut. term; comp. Goth. *figgrs,* OIc. *fingr,* AS. and E. *finger.* It is uncertain whether the word is derived from fangen, root *fanh,* and it is questionable whether it comes from the root *finh.* pre-Teut. *pink,* 'to prick, paint,' Lat. *fingo* (see Feile); it is most probably primit. allied to fünf (Aryan *penqe*). The terms Haub, Finger, Zehe are specifically Teut., and cannot be etymologically explained with certainty. Besides there existed even in OTeut. a definite term for each finger. First of all the thumb obtained its name, which is a rudimentary and hence very old form; for the remaining names see under Daumen.

Finth, m., 'finch,' from the equiv. Mid HG. *vinke,* OHG. *fincho,* m.; corresponds to Du. *vink.* AS. *finc,* E. *finch,* Swed. *fink,* Dan. *finke,* 'finch'; Goth. **finki-, *finkjan-,* are wanting. There is a striking similarity of sound in the Rom. words for 'finch'— Ital. *pincione,* Fr. *pinson,* to which the E. dialectal forms *pink, pinch,* 'finch,' belong. Yet there is no suspicion that the Teut. word was borrowed; the Teut. class is probably primit. allied to the Rom. word.

Finne (1.), f., 'fin,' first occurs in Mod HG., from LG. *finne,* Du. *vin,* 'fin'; first recorded in the Teut. group in AS. *(finn,* m., E. *fin),* hence it cannot have been borrowed from Lat. *pinna,* 'fin of the dolphin, feather.' No Teut. word can be proved to have been borrowed from Lat. before the period of the OTeut. substitution of consonants, *i.e.,* before the beginning of our era (see Hanf). Hence AS. *finn* must be assumed as primit. cognate with Lat. *pinna.* Is it, like *penna,* based upon *pesna* (OLat.)? If it were based upon **pis-nā,* 'fin,' it might perhaps be regarded as cognate with *piscis,* Goth. *fiska- (fis-ka),* 'fish.'

Finne (2.), f., 'tumour, scrofula,' from MidHG. *vinne, pfinne,* 'pimple, foul rancid smell'; comp. Du. *vin,* 'pimple.' The relation of the initial sounds is not clear; MidHG. *pfinne* points to Goth. *p,* Du. *vin* to *f* initially; perhaps the double form is due to confusion with Finne (1.); *p* may be the correct initial sound.

finster, adj., 'dark, gloomy, morose, sullen,' from the equiv. MidHG. *vinster,* OHG. *finstar;* OSax. **finistar,* as an adj., is not found, but it may be inferred from a subst. with the same sound, meaning 'darkness'; the stem is essentially Ger., but a series of phonetic difficulties (see düster) hamper the discovery of the type. In OHG. there exists besides finster an OHG. *dinstar,* MidHG. *dinster,* whose initial *d* must have been substituted for an earlier (OSax., Goth.) *þ;* to these OSax. *thimm,* 'dark,' corresponds. The interchange of *þ* and *f,* judging from the parallel forms under Feile and Fadel, cannot be denied. In that case the root would be *þem* (see Dämmerung). But OSax. *thiustri,* AS. *þýstre,* 'gloomy,' have no connection with it.

Finte, f., lit. 'feint,' also 'trick, fib,' first occurs in ModHG., from Ital. *finta,* 'cunning' (Fr. *feinte*).

Firlefanz, m., 'nonsense, drollery,' from MidHG. *virlefanz,* m., 'a sort of dance,' whence the meaning in ModHG. 'foppish, silly manner.' Some have tried to connect it with Norw. *fillefant,* 'scoundrel,' *fantefolk,* 'gipsies,' which would make it akin to Fant. On account of the late appearance of the word it is impossible to decide, however, whether AS. *fyrlen,* 'far, distant,' is the basis of the first part of the compound, or rather MidHG. *ferlei,* 'a dance' (Fr. *virelai,* 'virelay'). See Fant.

firn, adj., 'old, of last year,' from MidHG. *virne,* adj., 'old,' also 'experienced,' OHG. *firni,* 'old'; corresponds to Goth. *fairneis,* 'old,' AS. *fyrn,* 'old,' OSax. *fern,* 'past' (of years). The reference to the year gone by exists in the Goth. and OSax. words, but does not appear to be found in OHG. and MidHG., although the stem is known to modern UpG. dialects; comp. Alem. *fernig,* 'of last year.' 'In the preceding year' is MidHG. *vërt, vërne;* MidG. and UpG. preserve even now an OTeut. adv. *fert, fered,* 'in the preceding year'; comp. OIc. *fjǫrþ,* adv., 'in the preceding year,' from Goth. **fairuþ,* pre-Teut. *peruti* (*perouti*), Gr. πέρυτι, πέρυσι, 'in the preceding year,' OIr. *onn-urid,* 'from the preceding year onwards,' Lith. *pernai,* 'in the preceding year,' Sans. *pa-rut.* Hence the idea of 'the preceding year' is primit. inherent in the stem *per,* Teut. *fer;* the general sense of time gone by appears in the Teut. adj. *frru* and its cognates.

Firn, Firne, m., 'snow of the preceding year or years, glacier,' prop. an adjectival subst. in the sense of 'old snow,' first recorded in the last centnry; see the preceding word.—Firnewein, 'last year's wine'; see firn.

Firnis, m., 'varnish,' from MidHG. *firnis,* 'varnish, rouge'; from Fr. *vernis* (whence also E. *varnish*), Ital. *vernice.* Finally derived from Lat. *vitrum, vitrinus.*

First, m., f., from the equiv. MidHG. *virst,* OHG. *first,* m., 'ridge of a roof, summit'; comp. LG. and Du. (with gradation), *vorst,* 'ridge of a roof,' AS. *first, fyrst,* f.; Goth. **fairsti-* or *fairshti-* is wanting. Allied to Sans. *pr̥ṣṭhá-m,* n., 'back, summit, mountain-peak,' which is nearest in sound to Du. *vorst.* From Teut., OFr. *freste,* Prov. *frest,* 'gable,' are derived.

Fisch, m., 'fish,' from the equiv. MidHG. *visch,* OHG. *fisk,* m.; a common Teut. term; comp. Goth. *fisks,* OIc. *fiskr,* AS. *fisc,* E. *fish,* Du. *visch,* OSax. *fisc.* Teut. *fiska-z,* from pre-Teut. *pisko-s,* corresponds to Lat. *piscis* and OIr. *iasc* (with the normal loss of *p* from prehistoric *peiskos*). The word belongs to the three most western groups of the Aryan division, which have also the word Meer in common; in East Aryan *matsya.* Further, there are no names of fishes common to Teut. and Lat.-Kelt. Perhaps the term was a migratory word of early civilisation, the source of which cannot be discovered.

Fist, m., 'fart,' from the equiv. MidHG. *vist,* m.; akin to the equiv. Du. *veest,* AS. *fist.* A common Aryan root *pezd* appears in Lat. *pēdo* for *pezdo,* as well as in Gr. βδέω, from **βσδέω,* Lith. *bezdù* (*bezdĕti*). Hence Teut. *fisti-* is to be explained by Aryan *pezd-i-.* From the verbal noun *fist* a verbal root *fīs,* 'pedere,' was inferred in very early times. Comp. OIc. *fisa.*

Fistel, f., 'fistula, reed, falsetto,' from MidHG. *fistel,* f., 'a deep abscess in ducts or passages,' even in OHG. *fistul,* formed from the equiv. Lat. *fistula;* the term was first applied to the voice in ModHG.

Fittich, m., from the equiv. MidHG. *vittich, vëttach,* m., n., *vëttache,* f., m., 'wing, pinion,' OHG. *fettah,* older *fëthdhah,* m.; in meaning a collective of Feder; comp. OSax. *fetherac,* OHG. *federah,* MidHG. *fëdrach,* 'wing'; the formation of OHG. *fëthdhah* is not clear; was the Goth. form **fiþþaks?* The dentals are obscure, yet the word is undoubtedly related to Feder.

Fitze, f., 'knot of yarn, skein, wrinkle,' from MidHG. *vitze,* OHG. *fizza,* f., 'a number of reeled threads tied together, skein, yarn'; akin to OIc. *fǫt,* 'clothes,' MidHG. *vaʒʒen,* 'to dress,' root *fat, fet?* 'to spin'? 'to weave'?. Yet it is more closely connected with OSax. *fittea,* AS. *fitt,* 'chapters, divisions in poems.'

fix, adj., 'quick, smart,' first occurs in ModHG.; Lat. *fixus* and its Romance derivatives are not used in this sense; whether borrowed from it or not is doubtful.

flach, adj., 'flat, shallow, superficial,' from MidHG. *vlach,* OHG. *flah*(*hh*), adj., 'flat, smooth'; comp. Du. *vlak,* 'even.' Akin to the graded forms AS. *flóc,* E. *flook, fluke* ('flounder'), North E. *flook-footed,* 'flat-footed.' This suggests Lat. *plaga,* 'district,' or more probably, on account of its meaning, OSlov. *plosku*, 'flat'; Lat. *plānus* scarcely represents *plagnus (see 𝔉lur); related to Gr. πλάξ (stem πλακ), 'surface,' Gr πλακοῦς, Lat. *placenta*, 'cake.' But E. *flat*, OIc. *flatr*, OHG. *flaʒ*, 'flat, level,' have nothing to do with flach. A MidG. and LG. parallel form of flach is mentioned under 𝔅lachfeld.

𝔉lachs, m., 'flax,' from the equiv. Mid HG. *vlahs*, OHG. *flahs*, m.; comp. Du. *vlas*, AS. *fleax*, n., E. *flax*; a common West Teut. term, unknown to Scand. and Goth. Usually referred to the root *fleh* (or *fleht*) in flechten; *s* (Goth. **flahsa-*) is probably a suffix.

flackern, vb., 'to flare, flicker,' from MidHG. *vlackern*, 'to flicker,' OHG. (once) *flagarôn* (for *flaggarôn†*), 'to fly, flutter about'; akin to AS. *flacor*, 'flying, fluttering,' MidE. *flakeren*, 'to fly, flutter about,' MidDu. *flackeren*, Scand. *flökra*, vb., 'to flutter,' as well as the equiv. *flökta*. Comp. the cognate stems AS. *flicorian*, E. to *flicker*, Du. *flikkern*, 'to glimmer, gleam'; this class, on account of the numerous words it comprised at an early period, cannot be derived from Lat. *flagrare*, nor even be connected with fliegen, to which OHG. *flogarôn, flokrôn*, 'to flutter,' and *flogezen*, MidHG. *vlokzen*, 'to flutter, gleam,' may be referred.

𝔉laden, m., 'flat cake, cow dung,' from MidHG. *vlade*, m., 'broad, thin cake,' OHG. *flado*, 'offering-cake'; corresponds to Du. *vlade via*, f., 'pancake,' MidE. *flape* (Goth. *flapa). Pre-Teut. *platan-* or *plathan-* would have to be assumed, perhaps with the primit. sense, 'surface, flat thing'; comp. Gr. πλατύς, 'broad'; Gr. πλάθανον (θ for Aryan *th*), 'cake-mould'; Sans. *prthús*, 'broad' (akin to Sans. *prthivî*, 'earth,' under 𝔉eld), *práthas*, n., 'breadth,' Lith. *platùs*, 'broad.' Allied to the graded forms *plōth*, Lat. *Plōtus, Plautus*, lit. 'flatfooted,' *semiplōtia*, 'slipper,' MidHG. *vluoder*, 'flounder,' lit. 'flat fish.' Remoter cognates of the whole class are OIc. *flatr*, OHG. *flaʒ*, 'level, flat.' From 𝔉laden, which is probably West Teut. only, are derived the early MidLat. *flado*, Ital. *fiadone*, 'honeycomb,' Fr. *flan*, 'flat cake, custard' (whence E. *flawn*, 'a kind of custard'). Comp. for its meaning MidHG. *breitinc*, m., 'a sort of biscuit,' akin to *breit*.

𝔉lagge, f., 'flag, ensign, standard,' borrowed, like most words with *gg* (see 𝔇egge, 𝔅agger), from LG. and Du. in the ModHG. period; comp. Du. *vlag*, E. *flag*, Dan. *flag*, Swed. *flagg*. A modern Teut. word not recorded in the earlier periods. In which of the Teut. maritime tribes this and other nautical terms were first used we know not, for the earlier history eludes us. Since, however, AS. preserves the earliest forms of a number of nautical terms which are afterwards found in all the cognate languages (see 𝔅ord, 𝔅oot, 𝔥elm (2), 𝔖prict, &c.), the silence of the AS. records—no term *flacge is found—may be accepted as a proof that 𝔉lagge is not native to England.

𝔉lamberg, m., 'broad-sword,' simply ModHG. from Fr. *flamberge*, the origin of which is often referred to Ger., though no suitable type can be found.

𝔉lamme, f., 'flame, blaze, flash,' from the equiv. MidHG. *flamme, vlamme*, f.; comp. OLG. *flamma*, Du. *vlam*, formed from Lat. *flamma*.

𝔉lanke, f., 'flank, side,' simply Mod HG., from Fr. *flanc*, which, with its Rom. cognate (Ital. *fianco*), is derived from OHG. *hlanca*, 'side' (see lenfen). For Fr. *fl*, from Teut. *hl*, see flau.

𝔉lasche, f., 'bottle, flask,' from the equiv. MidHG. *vlasche*, OHG. *flasca*, f. (MidHG. also *vlasche* with mutation); comp. Du. *flesch*, AS. *flasce*, f., E. *flask*, OIc. (found early) *flaska*, f., Goth. *flaskô, whence Finn. *lasku*. The word is recorded in Teut. at an early period, but on account of its correspondence with the Rom. words for 'bottle,' it may have been borrowed; comp. MidLat. *flasco* (occurs very early), Ital. *fiasco*, ModFr. *flacon*. Some etymologists derive MidLat. *flasco* from Lat. *vasculum*. An exhaustive history of these cognates has not yet been attempted.

flattern, vb., 'to flutter, dangle,' in Mid HG. *vladern* from MidHG. *vlēdern* (see 𝔉ledermaus); MidDu. *flatteren*, E. *to flatter*, akin to *flutter*, also MidE. *fliteren*, E. to *flitter*; AS. *floterian*, MidE. *floteren*, 'to undulate,' are, however, certainly allied to the root *flut*, 'to flow.'

flau, adj., 'feeble, stagnant, insipid, dull,' simply ModHG.; borrowed in the last century from LG. *flau*, Du. *flauw*, 'languid, faint, indifferent,' which, with E. *flew*, 'soft, tender,' are derived from Rom. Considering the late appearance of the cognates, and the area to which they are confined, it is certain that they originated in Fr. *flou*, OFr. *flau*, *floi*; the latter is of Teut. origin (see lau), so that ModHG. flau is finally derived from a pre-Teut. *hlēwa-*. Comp. Flaufe.

Flaum, m. (UpG. Pflaum also), 'down,' from MidHG. *phlûme*, f., OHG. *pflûma*, 'down,' from Lat. *plûma*, whence also AS. *plûmfëpere*. As the shifting of the initial sound proves, however, the word must have been borrowed in the earlier OHG. period; comp. the OIr. word (also derived from the Lat.) *clûm*, 'feather' (OW. *plumauc*, 'pillow'). Scand. and E. have for Flaum an apparently genuine Teut. word (see Daune. It is certainly recorded by Pliny that Teut. tribes in the olden time sent flocks of geese to Rome; but perhaps it was only 'down' (see also Flode), which was valuable to the Southerners, and so the Lat. *pluma* may have been introduced into Teut. at an early period. The initial *f* of the ModHG. form for *pf* may be due to the connection with Feber.

Flaus, m., orig. 'a tuft of wool,' then 'a woollen coat, pilot cloth,' from MidHG. *vlûs*, 'fleece, sheepskin,' a variant of MidHG. *vlies*. See Flies.

Flaufe, f., 'trick, pretence,' simply ModHG.; MidHG. **vlûse* does not occur; it is probably connected with OHG. *giflôs*, n., 'whispering,' *giflôsida*, f., 'illusion,' *flôsâri*, 'liar.'

Flechfe, f., 'sinew, tendon,' only ModHG., from Lat. *flexus*.

Flechte, f., 'plait, braid (of hair), wattle, lichen,' from late MidHG. *vlëhte*, f., 'plait, lock of hair,' allied to the following word.

flechten, vb., 'to plait, braid, wreathe,' from the equiv. MidHG. *vlëhten*, OHG. *vlëhtan*; a corresponding Goth. **flathtan*, akin to *flahta*, f., 'lock of hair,' is wanting; OIc. *flétta* for *flehta*, Teut. root *fleht*, from pre-Teut. *plekt*; the *t*, as also in Lat. *plecto* compared with *plicare*, was orig. only a formative element of the present tense, for according to Gr. πλέκω, πλοκή, πλόκος, the Aryan root must have been *plek*; comp. Sans. *praçna*, 'braid, basket.' Falten (root *falþ*) and flechten (root *fleh*) are entirely unrelated.

Fleck, Flecken, m., n., with many senses which are historically the same, 'spot, stain, patch,' from MidHG. *vlëc, vlëcke*, m., 'piece of stuff, patch, rag, piece of land, place, spot, differently coloured spot, stain, blemish,' OHG. *flëc, flëccho*; Du. *vlek*, f., 'spot of dirt,' *vlek*, n., 'village'; Goth.

**flikka-* or **flikkan-* (or rather **þl-*) is wanting; comp. OIc. *flekkr* (gen. plur. *flekkja*), m., 'a fleck, spot, stain,' as well as *flik*, f., 'rag, piece of stuff.' Its connection with Scand. *flikke*, AS. *flicce*, E. *flitch*, is dubious. See fliđen.

Fledermaus, f., 'bat,' from the equiv. MidHG. *v/ëdermûs*, OHG. *flëdarmûs*, f.; corresponds to Du. *vledermuis*; E. *flittermouse* does not occur in AS., and may be due to the influence of MidEurop. Teutonic. That the animal was thought to be a mouse is shown by AS. *hreape-*, *hrëremûs*; the E. term *bat*, MidE. *backe*, Dan. *aftenbakke* (*aften*, 'evening'), is unique. Fledermaus, lit. 'fluttering mouse,' from OHG. *flëdarôn*, MidHG. *vlëdern*, 'to flutter.'

Flederwisch, m., first occurs in early ModHG. with a reference to *flëdern*, 'to flutter.' In MidHG. once *vëderwisch*, Du. *vederwisch*; prop. 'a goosewing for dusting,' or rather Federwisch, 'whisk for fanning away.'

Flegel, m. (Suab. Pflegel), 'flail, churl,' from MidHG. *vlegel*, OHG. *flegil*, m., 'flail'; comp. Du. *vlegel*, E. *flail*; probably from MidLat. *flagellum*, 'quo frumeutum teritur' (whence also Fr. *fléau*, 'flail'). On account of its meaning it cannot be connected with the Teut. root *flah*, 'to flay' (OIc. *flá*, 'to flay'). Yet it may be primit. allied to Lith. *plakù*, *plàkti*, 'to strike,' Lat. *plango*, Gr. πλήγνυμι, 'to strike.'

flehen, vb., 'to implore, supplicate,' from MidHG. *vlëhen*, OHG. *flëhan*, *flëhôn*, 'to implore,' OHG. also 'to fondle, flatter '; initial *fl* for earlier *þl*, as in fliehen (Goth. *þliuhan*); comp. Goth. *gapláihan* (*ai* a genuine diphthong), 'to fondle, embrace, console, exhort in a friendly way,' akin to Goth. *gapláihts*, f., 'comfort, warning.' Also allied to OIc. *flár*, 'false, cunning,' AS. *fláh*, 'wily, cunning,' both pointing to Goth. **plaiha-*. The primary meaning of the root *flaih* was perhaps 'importunate, insinuating speech.'

Fleisch, n., 'flesh, meat, pulp (of fruit),' from the equiv. MidHG. *vleisch*, OHG. *fleisk*, n.; it has the same meaning in West Teut. and Scand. Strange to say, a Goth. **flaisk*, **flaiskis*, n. (or *þl-* comp. fliehen), is not recorded, the term used being *leik* or *mims*, n. Comp. Du. *vleesch*, AS. *flǽsc*, n., E. *flesh*; OIc. *flesk* is used only of 'pork,' and more especially of 'ham' and 'bacon,' while *kjöt* was the common Scand. word for 'meat.' It may well be imagined that the Scand. specialised meaning of the word was the oldest, and that the meaning common to West Teut. was established only by generalisation; comp. OIc. *flikke*, AS. *flicce*, E. *flitch* (dial. *flick*), as well as AS. (Kent.) *flǽc* for *flǽsc*, 'meat.' Russ. *poltǐ*, Lith. *páltis*, 'flitch,' cannot, on account of their vowel-sounds, be cognates. The *k* of the OTeut. word is probably a suffix; comp. Du. *vleezig*, 'plump'?.—**eingefleischt**, 'incarnate,' simply ModHG. formed like the Lat. *incarnatus*, 'embodied.'

Fleiß, m., 'industry, application, diligence,' from MidHG. *vlîȝ*, OHG. *flîȝ*, m., 'diligence, zeal, care,' OHG. also 'contest,' from OHG. *flîȝȝan*, MidHG. *vlîȝen*, 'to be zealous, apply oneself,' ModHG. **befleißen**, partic. *be-, geflissen*. Comp. Du. *vlijt*, 'diligence,' AS. *flítan*, 'to emulate, quarrel, contend,' E. *to flite*. On the evolution of meaning see **Krieg**. 'To emulate' seems to have been the lit. meaning of the merely West Teut. root *flīt* (Goth. *fl-* or *þl-*?—see **fliehen**). No further references have been discovered.

flennen, vb., 'to weep ruefully, grin,' from MidHG. *vlennen*; akin to OHG. *flannên*, 'to make a wry face,' from preTeut. *flaznan*?. Root *flas*, from pre-Teut. *plos*, in Lat. *plôrare*, 'to weep'?.

fletschen, vb., 'to beat flat, grin,' from MidHG. *vletsen*, 'to show one's teeth'; remoter history obscure.

flicken, vb., from the equiv. MidHG. *vlicken*, 'to put on a patch, mend'; akin to **Fleck**.

Flieder, m., 'elder,' simply ModHG. from. LG.; comp. Du. *vlier*, 'elder.' Earlier forms are not recorded; the word did not originate in either Scand., E., or HG.

Fliege, f., 'fly, fluke (of an anchor),' from the equiv. MidHG. *fliege*, OHG. *flioga*, f.; comp. Du. *vlieg*, AS. *fleóge*, equiv. to E. *fly*, which is based upon AS. *flýge*, OHG. *fliuga*, MidHG. *fliuge*, 'fly'; hence a mutated form (Goth. *fliugjô*), besides an unmutated Goth. *fliugô*; in OIc. with a different gradation *fluga*, f., 'fly, moth'; akin to **fliegen** (Goth. *fliugan*). For an older term for 'fly' see under **Mücke**.

fliegen, vb., from the equiv. MidHG. *vliegen*, OHG. *fliogan*, 'to fly'; comp. Du. *vliegen*, AS. *fleógan* (3rd sing. *flýhþ*), E. *to fly*, OIc. *fljúga*; the common Teut. term for 'to fly'; Goth. **fliugan* may be inferred from the factitive *flaugjan*, 'to keep on flying.' **Fliegen** is in no wise connected with **fliehen**, as is proved by the initial sound of the root in Goth. *þliuhan*, 'to flee,' compared with *usflaugjan*; see **Fliege**, **Vogel**. Teut. root *flug*, from pre-Teut. *pleugh*, *plugh*; akin to Lat. *plûma* for *plúhma*?. For an older root extending beyond Teut. see under **Feder**.

fliehen, vb., 'to flee,' from the equiv. MidHG. *vliehen*, OHG. *fliohan*; corresponds to OSax. *fliohan*, AS. *fleón* (from *fleóhan*), E. *to flee*, OIc. *flýja*; the *f* before *l* is a common substitution for an older initial *þ*, as in **fliehen** (Goth. *þlaihan*), **flach** (from Goth. *þlaqus*); comp. Goth. *þliuhan*, 'to flee.' This older form was retained only in Goth.; Scand. has *f* (*flýja*), like the West Teut. verbs. Hence the Teut. root is *þluh*, and by a grammatical change *þlug*, preTeut. root *tluk*, *tleuk*. **Fliegen** is primit. allied, since it is based upon the root *plugh*. In the earliest OIc. and in West Teut. the forms of both the verbs must undoubtedly have been confused: thus OIc. *flugu* and AS. *flugon* in the earliest period may mean 'they fled' and 'they flew.' See **Flucht**.

Fließ, **Vließ**, n., 'fleece,' from the equiv. MidHG. *vlies*, n.; comp. Du. *vlies*, AS. *fleós*, n., E. *fleece*; also a mutated form AS. *flýs*, *flýss*, MidHG. *vlius*, earlier Mod HG. *fleusz*, *flüsz*. A second parallel form is represented by ModHG. **Flaus**. In East Teut. the cognates are wanting; whether Goth. **fl-* or **þliusis*, n. (comp. **fliehen**), is to be assumed we cannot say, since satisfactory references to non-Teut. forms have not yet been produced. To explain **Vließ** from Lat. *vellus* is futile, since the latter is more probably primit. allied to **Wolle**, and to regard **Vließ** as borrowed from *vellus* is impossible; **flechten**, **Flache**, &c., are also totally unconnected with the word.

fließen, vb., 'to flow, stream,' from the equiv. MidHG. *vlieȝen*, OHG. *flioȝȝan*, str. vb.; corresponds to OSax. *fliotan*, Du. *vlieten*, AS. *fleótan*, E. *to fleet*, OIc. *fljóta*, Goth. **fliutan*, 'to flow.' The Teut. root *fliut*, *flut*, from pre-Teut. *pleud-plud*, corresponds to Lett. *pludêt*, 'to float,' *plûdi*, 'inundation,' Lith. *plústi*, 'to take to swimming,' *plûdis*, 'floating wood.' Several Teut. terms for 'ships' point to the latter sense, which, of course, is earlier than the ModHG. 'flowing,' though in OHG. Mid HG. and ModHG., **fließen** signifies 'to be driven by flowing water, to swim.' See **Floß**, **Flotte** (**Flut**, Goth. *flôdus*, is not a cognate). Instead of the root *plud*, other

Aryan languages have an allied shorter root *plu;* comp. Gr. πλέω, 'to navigate, swim,' Sans. *plu, pru,* 'to swim,' Lat. *pluere,* 'to rain' (fließen in a restricted sense).

Fliete, f., 'fleam, lancet,' from the equiv. MidHG. *vliete, vlieten,* OHG. *flietuma;* further derived from Gr. and MidLat. *phlebotomum,* 'lancet, an instrument for opening veins,' whence also the equiv. cognates AS. *flýtme,* Fr. *flamme,* E. *fleam,* Du. *vlijm.*

flimmern, vb., 'to glimmer, sparkle, scintillate,' like the older ModHG. flimmen, a ModHG. derivative, by gradation, of Flamme.

flink, adj., 'brisk, nimble, lively,' simply ModHG. from LG. and Du. *flink,* 'brisk, agile, nimble'; akin to earlier ModHG. flinken, 'to glitter, shine'; comp. Gr. ἀργός, 'gleaming, quick.'

Flinte, f., 'flintlock, gun, musket,' first used in the 17th cent.; comp. Dan. *flint,* 'musket'; probably akin to Swed. *flinta,* Dan. *flint,* 'stone,' prop. 'flint-stone.' Du. and E. preserve older terms—Du. *vuurroer,* ModHG. Feuerrohr, E. *firelock. Flint,* 'stone,' AS. and E. *flint,* whence Fr. *flin,* 'thunderstone,' is probably related to Gr. πλίνθος, 'brick.'

Flitter, m., 'spangle, tinsel,' simply ModHG.; orig. 'a small thin tin coin'; akin to MidHG. *gevlitter,* 'secret laughter, tittering,' *vlittern,* vb., 'to whisper, titter,' OHG. *flitarezzen,* 'to coax in a flattering manner'; MidE. *fliteren,* 'to flutter,' E. *flittermouse.* The root idea is 'unsteady motion,' upon which ModHG. Flitter is based. With the meaning of OHG. *flitarezzen,* 'to flatter, fondle,' as well as Mod HG. flittern, 'to whisper, titter,' is connected Flitterwoche, f., which first occurs in early ModHG. The following foreign terms are interesting:—Scand. *hjúnōttsmánapr,* lit. 'a month of the nuptial night'; Dan. *hvedebrodsdage,* lit. 'wheat-brend days'; E. *honeymoon,* derived from the Scand. word ?, or rather formed from the Romance phrases, such as Fr. *lune de miel,* Ital. *luna di miele.*

Flitzbogen, m., 'crossbow,' first occurs in early ModHG. from LG.; comp. Du. *flitsboog,* 'crossbow,' from Du. *flits,* 'javelin'; hence Fr. *flèche,* 'arrow,' and its Romance cognates are probably derived.

Flocke, f., 'flake, flock (of wool), flue,' from MidHG. *vlocke,* m., ' flake, snowflake,' OHG. *floccho;* comp. Du. *vlok,* Dan. *flokke,* Swed. *flokka,* E. (not in AS.) *flock,*

but OIc. *flóke,* 'flock (of hair, wool, &c.).' The supposition that the word was borrowed from Lat. *floccus* is hardly worth considering, since the HG. word is recorded even in the OHG. period, and gives no support to such a derivation (yet comp. Flaum). Besides many possible roots exist within the Teut. group, either in fliegen (Teut. root *flugh,* from pre-Teut. *plugh)* or in AS. *flacor,* 'flying' (see flattern); on account of OIc. *flóke,* the latter is to be preferred. E. *flock,* 'herd,' is beside the mark; like OIc. *flokkr,* 'herd, flock,' and AS. *flocc,* it almost certainly belongs to fliegen, and probably signified orig. 'a swarm of flying creatures' (Stette, 'covey,' on the other hand, meant prop. 'any kind of herd').

Floh, m., 'flea,' from MidHG. *vlóch, vló,* m., f., OHG. *flôh,* m.; a common Teut. term; comp. Du. *floo,* AS. *fleáh,* E. *flea,* OIc. *fló.* It probably means 'fugitive,' and is akin to fliehen; hence a Goth. **pláuhs,* not **fláuhs,* is to be assumed. But even if **fláuhs* is the Goth. form, it cannot be connected with either Gr. ψύλλα or Lat. *pulex,* since neither vowels nor consonants are in accord. Fliegen too is unrelated, since the final sound of its stem is *g* only, and not *h.*

Flor, m., 'gauze, crape, bloom,' ModHG. only; formed from Du. *floers;* akin to Mid HG. *floier,* 'headdress with dangling ribbons' (comp. Schleier)?, *flörsen,* 'adornment, finery'?.

Florin, m., 'florin,' from late MidHG. *flōrīn,* m., 'a gold coin first made in Florence, and stamped with a lily, the armorial bearings of the town' (appeared about the middle of the 14th cent.); MidLat. *florinus,* from *flos,* 'flower'; Ital. *flore.*

Floskel, f., 'flourish, showy phrase,' simply late ModHG., from Lat. *flosculus.*

Flosse, f., from the equiv. MidHG. *vlozze,* OHG. *flozza,* f., 'float'; Floßfeder, 'fin,' even in MidHG. *vlozvēdere,* in OSax. simply *féthara,* 'float,' like Gr. πτέρυξ, 'feather, float,' Lat. *pinna,* 'feather, float.' See Finne. Flosse, akin to fließen, 'to float.'

Floß, n., 'float, raft, buoy, stream, fishing-net,' from MidHG. *vlóʒ,* OHG. *flóʒ,* m., n., 'raft,' also in MidHG. and OHG. in the senses 'current, flood, river'; Du. *vlot,* 'raft'; comp. AS. *fleót,* n., 'ship,' E. *fleet,* AS. *flota,* 'ship' (also 'mariner, sailor'), E. *float,* subst. and verb; note too AS. *flýte,* 'cream, flos lactis,' with which E. *to fleet* ('to skim') is connected, LG. *flot,* 'cream';

comp. Lith. *pluditi*, 'to float,' under fließen (Flosse).

Flöte, f., from the equiv. MidHG. *floite, vloite,* f., 'flute'; corresponds to Du. *fluit,* from OFr. *flaüte,* ModFr. *flûte* (whence also E. *flute,* Du. *fluit*); comp. Ital. *flauto,* 'flute.' In the idiom flötengehen, 'to come to nothing,' a LG. *fleuten,* 'to flow' (OLG. *fliotan*), appears; it meant orig. (in the 18th cent.) 'to go through, run away.'

flott, adj., 'afloat; merry, luxurious,' first occurs in ModHG. from LG.; comp. Du. *vlot,* 'floating, swimming'; it is connected with fließen, Floß, but has, like Flotte, Sax. the dental medially, hence it must be assumed that the word was borrowed from LG.

Flotte, f., 'fleet, navy,' ModHG. only, from Fr. *flotte,* which, with its Rom. cognates, was borrowed from Scand. *flote,* n., 'fleet'; comp. Du. *vloot,* but E. *fleet;* all allied to fließen, Teut. root *flut.*

flößen, flötzen, vb., 'to float (timber), skim (milk),' from MidHG. *vlœzen, vlœtzen,* 'to cause to flow, wash down (soil),' factitive of fließen. The MidHG. forms with ʒ and *tz* correspond to those of heizen, reizen (MidHG. *heizen-heitzen, reizen-reitzen*), and are based upon a Goth. inflexion *flautja, flauteis,* since *tj* leads, through the medium of *tt,* to HG. *tz,* but *t* without *j* to ʒ.

Flöʒ, n., older Fletze, n., 'vein of ore,' from MidHG. *vlęze,* n., 'threshingfloor, vestibule, stratum,' OHG. *flezzi;* comp. AS. *flett,* 'floor of the hall,' OIc. *flet,* 'room, hall'; akin to the OIc. adj. *flatr,* OHG. *flaʒ,* 'flat, wide, level,' mentioned under Flaben and flach.

fluchen, vb., from the equiv. MidHG. *vluochen,* OHG. *fluohhôn,* 'to curse, imprecate,' with an existent str. partic. OHG. *farfluohhan,* 'depraved, wicked'; comp. OSax. *farflôken,* 'accursed'; Goth. *flôkan* (not *flôkan*), str. vb., 'to lament,' Du. *vloeken,* 'to curse, execrate.' In E. and Scand. the Teut. root *flôk* does not occur. Goth. *flôkan,* 'to lament, bewail,' shows the earlier meaning of the cognates; the root *flôk,* from pre-Teut. *plâg,* may be connected with Lat. *plangere,* 'to strike, mourn,' Gr. root, πλαγ in πλήσσω (ἐκπλάγη), 'to strike.' The Lat. verb facilitates the transition of the meaning 'to strike,' 'to lament,' then 'to imprecate, curse.'—

Fluch, from the equiv. MidHG. *vluoch,* m., OHG. *fluoh,* m., 'curse, imprecation'; Du. *vlœk.*

Flucht, f., 'flight, escape, refuge; row, floor,' from the equiv. MidHG. *vluht,* OHG. and OSax. *fluht,* f., a verbal abstract from fliehen; Du. *vlugt,* AS. *flyht,* E. *flight;* Goth. *plauhti-*, 'flight,' is wanting, for which *plauhti-* occurs. In OIc. *flôtte,* m., 'flight,' pointing to Goth. *plauhta.* The verbal abstract of fliegen might in Scand. and West Teut. coincide with this word; in fact, AS. *flyht,* E. *flight,* and Du. *vlugt* signify both 'fleeing' and 'flying.' See fliegen with respect to this confusion.

Fluder, n., 'mill trough,' from MidHG. *vlôder,* n., 'flowing, flooding, mill trough,' OHG. *flôdar,* 'flood of tears.' In Goth. *flaupr,* n., is probably to be assumed, based upon a root *flau, flu;* comp. OHG. *flouwen, flęwen,* MidHG. *vlouwen, vlôun,* 'to wash, rinse.' The prop. sense of the word is exactly that of fließen; comp. OIc. *flau-mr,* 'current, flood'; for pre-Teut. *plu.* see under fließen.

Flug, m., 'act of flying, flight, flock,' from MidHG. *vluc* (pl. *vlüge*), OHG. *flug,* m.; corresponding to AS. *flyge,* OIc. *flugr,* m., 'flight'; verbal abstract of fliegen. For another form see under Flucht. Goth. *flugi-* and *flauhti-* are wanting.—**flugs,** adv., 'hastily, quickly,' a gen. of Flug, MidHG. *fluges,* 'quickly.'

Flügel, m., 'wing, leaf (of a folding door), aisle, grand piano,' from the equiv. MidHG. *vlügel,* m.; comp. Du. *vleugel,* 'wing'; a late derivative of fliegen. Strange to say, a common Teut. word is wanting. For an OAryan root, 'to fly,' see Feder (also Farn).

flügge, adj., 'fledged,' a LG. form for the strictly HG. flücke, MidHG. *vlücke,* OHG. *flucchi,* 'able to fly.' Akin to Mid Du. *vlugghe,* with LG. permutation, E. *fledged;* prop. a verbal adj. from fliegen, with the meaning 'capable of flying.'

flugs, see Flug.

Flunder, m., 'flounder,' a LG. word derived from Scand.; comp. ODan. *flundra,* OSwed. *flundrae,* E. *flounder.* Akin also to OIc. *flyðra,* MidHG. *vluoder,* 'flounder'?.

flunkern, vb., to glimmer,' from the older ModHG. flinfen, 'to shine'; see flinf. In the orig. sense 'to brag,' which is probably LG., it is still the same word; 'to cause to shine' forms the link between the meanings.

Flur, f., m., 'field, meadow, floor, entrance-hall'; the division in meaning in ModHG. Flur, m., 'vestibule,' Flur, f., 'corn-field,' was unknown to the older language; MidHG. *vluor*, m., f., 'corn-field, floor, ground.' The meanings 'entrance to a house, vestibule, paved floor,' belong to MidHG. and LG.; comp. Du. *vloer*, 'vestibule, barn-floor,' AS. *flōr*, m., f., 'vestibule, barn-floor,' also 'storey,' E. *floor* ; Scand. *flór*, 'floor' of a cow-house (Goth. *flōrus* is wanting). The resulting prim. meaning, 'floor,' has been extended only in HG. to 'corn-field.' Teut. *flōru-s*, from pre-Teut. *plōrus*, *plārus*, is most closely related to OIr. *lár* for *plár, ' floor, paved floor.' OPruss. *plonis*, 'barn-floor,' has a different suffix; it is allied to Lith. *plónas*, 'flat' ; hence perhaps it may be connected with Lat. *plānus*.

flüſtern, vb., ' to whisper,' earlier Mod HG. flistern, from OHG. *flūstran*, ' to caress,' to which the old (also Swiss) forms fliſmen, fliſpern, ' to whisper,' are allied ; comp. also Du. *fluisteren*.

Fluß, m., 'river, stream, flow,' from MidHG. *vluz*, OHG. *fluz*, m., 'river, stream, cast, bronze cast, rheumatism'; in these senses simply a ModHG. derivative of fließen, pointing to Goth **fluti-*. E. *flyte* signifies a peculiar kind of 'vessel, pontoon.' For the genuinely Teut. word for ' river, flowing water,' see under **An** ; comp. also **Strom**.

flüſſig, adj., 'fluid, liquid,' from Mid HG. *vlüʒʒec*, 'liquid, flowing,' OHG. *fluʒʒig*; like Fluß, a specifically HG. form.

Flut, f., ' flood, inundation, billow,' from the equiv. MidHG. *vluot*, m, f., OHG. *fluot*, m. ; a word common to Teut. ; comp. Goth. *flōdus*, f., OIc. *flóþ*, AS. *flōd*, m., n., E. *flood*, OSax. *flōd*, Du. *vloed*. Goth. *flōdus*, from pre-Teut. *plōtú-s*, is based upon a Teut. root *flō* (from pre-Teut. *plō*); comp. AS. *flōwan*, equiv. to E. *to flow*, OIc. *flóa*, 'to flow.' Akin to the Gr. root πλω in πλώ-ω, ' to float, sail,' πλωτός, ' floating, sailing, navigable.' Perhaps this Aryan root *plō* is related to the Aryan root *plu* mentioned under fließen and Fluder ; yet there is no direct connection between Flut and fließen and Gr. πλύνω.

Focke, f., 'sail on the foremast,' simply ModHG., borrowed from LG. ; comp. Du. *fok*, ' foremast,' Dan. *fok*, Swed. *fock*, ' foresail.'

Fohlen, n., 'foal,' from MidHG. *vol*, *volе*, OHG. *folo*, m., 'colt, foal'; comp. Goth. *fula*, m., ' foal (of an ass),' OIc. *foli*, ' foal' (of a horse, rarely of an ass), AS. *fola*, m., E. *foal*; a term common to Teut. for the young of a horse or an ass, derived from pre-Teut. *pelón-*. Related by gradation to Gr. πῶλος, ' colt,' as a general term 'young animal,' and Lat. *pullus*, ' the young.' especially of fowls. See **Füllen**.

Föhn, m., a Swiss word, ' humid and tempestuous south wind ' ; the corresponding term in MidHG. is wanting, though OHG. *fōnna*, f. (*fōnno*, m.), 'rainy wind, whirlwind,' is recorded ; from Lat. *favonius* (the intermediate form is *faunio-*), whence also Ital. *favonio*, Rhæto-Rom. *favuogn*.

Föhre, f., ' fir,' from MidHG. *vorhe*. OHG. *forha*, f., ' pine-tree' ; corresponding to AS. *furh*, f., E. *fir* (MidE. *firre*, formed from Dan. *fyr*), OIc. *fura*, f., ' fir'; Goth. *faúrhus, f., is wanting. If the initial *f* is to be regarded as in *vier* related to Lat. *quattuor*, Föhre may be connected with Lat. *quercus*, ' oak ' ; for the change of meaning Eiche and Tanne might be compared. In earlier ModHG. Ferch, ' oak,' is also recorded once, and is akin to OHG. *vereh-eih*, Lomb. *fereha*, ' æsculus.' Thus the connection between Föhre and *quercus* (pre-Teut. *qrku-*) is certain. In any case, Feuer is not a cognate. Fichte, Birke, Buche, Föhre are the few names of trees whose existence can be traced beyond Teut. Comp. also **Kiefer**.

folgen, vb., ' to follow, succeed, result, obey,' from the equiv. MidHG. *volgen*, OHG. *folgēn*; comp. Du. *volgen*, AS. *fylgan*, *folgian*, E. *to follow*, OIc. *fylgja*; the verb common to West Teut. and Scand. for ' follow,' which has supplanted the common Aryan verbal root *seq* (see ſehen), Lat. *sequi*. The origin of the cognates is uncertain. There are indications that the verbal stem is a compound ; the first component may be *vell*; comp. AS. *ful-eōde*. ' he followed,' AS. and OLG. *fulgangan*, OHG. *fola gān*, ' to follow.' Consequently gehen (OHG. *ga gān*) is the second part of the word. The composite nature of the word is supported by the fact that there are no old and widely diffused derivatives of the verb. It is true that the connection between the sense ' to follow ' and the prefix *vell* has not yet been explained.—**Folge**, f., 'sequel, result,' from MidHG. *volge*, f., ' retinue, succession, forced service, pursuit,' &c. OHG. *sēlbfolga*, ' faction.'

foltern, vb., ' to put to the rack, torture,' from late MidHG. *vultern*, ' to put on the rack.' Akin to **Folter**, ' rack,' early ModHG. only, of obscure origin. It is most frequently considered to be partly translated and partly borrowed from Mid Lat. *pulletrus, poledrus*, prop. 'colt,' which signifies 'rack' in Span. and Port. (*potro*), "like Lat. *equuleus* from *equus*, because it bore some resemblance to a horse." Mid Lat. *poledrum* is derived again from Gr. πῶλος, 'foal.' "The wooden horse and the wooden ass—frames with a sharp-edged back, upon which the delinquents were compelled to ride—were favourite instruments of torture."

foppen, vb., 'to quiz, rally, banter,' early ModHG. only, from slang.

fordern, vb., from the equiv. MidHG. *vordern*, OHG. *fordarôn*, 'to demand, request, challenge, summon'; corresponding to Du. *vorderen;* a specifically Ger. form, orig. unknown to the other dialects, yet the word found its way from Ger. into Dan. and Swed. It is a derivative of *verber.*

fördern, vb., from the equiv. MidHG. *vürdern, vurdern*, OHG. *furdiren* (also *fordarôn*), 'to promote, take an active part in, help'; like ferbern, from verber.

Forelle, f., 'trout,' with a foreign accent, for the genuine dialectal (Franc.) *förelle*, still existing; dimin. of an older Forene (whence *Forenle, Forelle*); comp. MidHG. *förelle, förle, forhen, forhe,* f., 'trout,' OHG. *forhana,* f., 'trout'; comp. also OLG. *forna, furnie*, AS. *forne.* Probably not from Föhre, OHG. *foraha,* 'the fish living near firs, in the brooks of fir forests.' It is more probably connected with the Aryan adjs. in the cognate languages, meaning 'spotted, speckled.' Teut. *forhana,* from pre-Teut. *prknâ;* comp. Sans. *pṛ́çni,* 'speckled,' and Gr. περκνός, 'livid, dusky' (πέρκη, 'perch').

Forhe, f., see Fucte.

Form, f., 'form, fashion, pattern, mould,' from ModHG. (post-classical). *forme, form,* f., 'form, shape,' from Lat. and Rom. *forma.*

Formel, f., 'formula, form,' late Mod HG., from Lat. *formula.*

forschen, vb., 'to search, investigate,' from MidHG. *vorsken*, OHG. *forskôn* (rarely Franc. *forspôn*, with assimilation), 'to demand, ask'; a form peculiar to HG. unknown to the remaining dialects, and pointing to Goth. *faúrskôn, *faúrhskôn*. The *sk* is a derivative like Lat. *sc* (comp. treſchen, wünſchen, waſchen). Goth. *faúrskôn would be the normal form for *faúrhskôn, like Goth. *waúrstw,* 'labour,' for *waúrhstw.* The Teut. root *forh* is identical with the root of *fragen*, from the pre-Teut. root *prk* (see *fragen*). An *sc* derivative is also seen in Lat. *poscere* (for *porscere*), 'to demand,' as well as in the Sans. root *pṛch,* 'to ask.'

Forſt, m., 'forest, wood,' from Mid HG. *vorst,* OHG. *forst,* m., 'wood'; also the MidHG. variants *vŏrĕst, fŏrest, fŏrest, fŏreist* (but probably not *fŏrest*), n., 'wood, forest'; these MidHG. forms are certainly of Romance origin,—MidLat. and Romance *foresta,* whence Fr. *forêt.* It is questionable whether the OHG. *forst,* MidHG. *vorst,* m., are also derived from Romance. Opinions are divided on this point; some etymologists connect the Rom. word with Lat. *foris,* 'outside'; others more probably refer OHG. *forst* to OHG. *foraha,* 'fir'; hence *forst* would be lit. 'fir wood.' OHG. *forst* might also be connected with Goth. *faírguni,* 'mountain.' Goth. *faúrst* for *faúrhst,* 'mountain forest,' would have to be construed like the assumed Goth. *faúrskôn for *faúrhskôn, mentioned under ferſchen.

fort, adv., 'forwards, continuously, away,' from MidHG. *vort,* adv., 'forwards, further, continuously.' OHG. *ford* is wanting; it would correspond to OSax. *forth,* AS. *forþ,* E. *forth;* Goth. *faúrþ,* and its compar. *faúrþis,* adv., 'formerly'l. Fort, OTeut. *forþ,* from an earlier *frþo, prto,* is allied to ver. See fürber, fertern, förbern, and verber.

Fracht, f., 'freight, load, cargo,' Mod HG. only, from LG. *fracht;* comp. Du. *vracht,* E. *fraught, freight;* it signified orig. 'reward, charge for conveyance,' and afterwards 'the load itself.' Comp. OHG. *frêht* (probably implying Goth. *frá-aíhts*), 'earnings, reward,' *gifrêhtôn,* 'to merit'; the restricted meaning of the modern dialects is seen first in MidDu. and MidE., and also passed into Romance—Fr. *fret.* Comp. eigen.

Frack, m., 'dress coat,' ModHG. only; comp. Fr. *frac,* 'dress coat'; its etymology and native source obscure, hardly to be sought for in Fr. *froc,* 'monk's habit.' Comp. E. *frock.*

fragen, vb., 'to ask, inquire, interrogate,' from the equiv. MidHG. *vrâgen,* OHG. *frâgên* (with the rare variant *frâhên*); corresponding to OSax. *frâgôn,* Du. *vragen;* confined to the Teuts. of Mid-Europe (Goth. *fréhan, *frégan), with the meaning 'to ask.' from a Teut. root *frêh*, from which the Goth. pret. *frah*

Fra (96) Fra

(*fréhum*) and the partic. *fraihans* are formed. The corresponding pres. has a derivative *n* (comp. ſcheinen), Goth. *fraihnan*, AS. *frígnan*, *frīnan*, beside which appears a form with the present in *io*-, AS. *fricgan* (Goth. *frigjan). For another verbal derivative of the same root see under forſchen, which, like OHG. *jĕrgón*, 'to beg,' has its *r* transposed. The following Teut. words also belong to the root *frĕh*, AS. *frĕht*, 'oracle,' *frihtrian*, 'to predict,' *fricca*, 'herald.' The Teut. root *frĕh* is derived, according to the law of the substitution of consonants, from an Aryan root *prĕk*, *prk*, which may have orig. combined the meanings 'to ask, beg' (*rogare*, *interrogare*). Comp. the prim. allied forms—Sans. root *prch* (for *prç-sk*), 'to ask, long for; to desire, beg for something,' *praçná*, 'inquiry,' Zend root *pares*, *peres*, 'to ask, demand,' Lat. *prĕc*- (nom. plur. *preces*, 'entreaties'), *precári*, 'to beg,' *procax*, 'insolent,' *prŏcus*, 'wooer, suitor,' OSlov. *prositi*, 'to demand, beg.'

frank, adj., 'free, independent,' first occurs in ModHG., from Fr. *franc* (Ital., Span., and Port. *franco*), which was again derived from the Teut. tribal name Franken, OHG. *Franchun*, and may have been applied generally to any freeman. The term Franken is prop. a derivative of a lost OHG. *francho, 'javelin,' preserved in AS. *franca* and OIc. *frakke*; the Saxons (Sachſen) are similarly named after a weapon—OHG. *Sahsun*, from *sahs*, 'sword' (see Meſſer).

Franſe, f., 'fringe,' from MidHG. *franze*, f., 'fringe, ornament, fillet'; hence *franzen*, vb., 'to fringe.' From Romance; comp. Fr. *frange*, Ital. *frangia*. "This orig. Fr. word corresponds exactly to the well-known OHG. *framea*, in the same way as *vendange* to *vindemia*; Franſen are pendant 'darts' or lace, just as the flap of a coat is a broad spear-head (see Schoß, Ochren); the etymology is both grammatically and logically unobjectionable." Though *framea* has certainly not been preserved within the entire Teut. group in the sense of 'javelin,' or in any other sense, yet the Latinised *framea* long remained current in early MidLat. The derivation of the Romance words from Lat. *fimbria*, 'fringe,' is not free from phonetic difficulties.

Fraß, m., 'devouring, gluttony, food, pasture,' from MidHG. *vrāʒ*, m., 'food, feeding'; akin to freſſen; OHG. *frāʒ*, Mid HG. *vrāʒ*, m., also 'gormandiser.'

Fratze, f., 'grimace, distortions, caricature,' f., ModHG. only, whence Du. *fratsen*, f. plur., 'grimaces, distortions,' is borrowed. The absence of the word in OHG. and MidHG. favours the supposition that it was borrowed, and we are compelled to accept that view, since it is impossible to trace the word to a satisfactory Teut. source; the proposed derivation from AS. *fratwe*, f. plur., 'work of art, ornaments (carvings?),' is phonetically impossible. The word might be finally derived from Ital. *frasche*, plur., Fr. *frasques*, 'tricks, hoax.'

Frau, f., 'mistress, lady, wife, woman,' from MidHG. *vrouwe*, OHG. *frouwa*, f., 'mistress, gentlewoman, lady, wife, woman'; orig. perhaps only a HG. fem. form ('wife of the master, mistress of the house'), of OHG. *frô*, 'master,' which became obsolete in Ger., just as in Romance *dominus* disappeared in many dialects while *domina* (in the forms *donna*, *dame*) was retained in the entire group; comp. Schwieger. See Frohndienſt. *Frouwa*, in the form of *frua*, found its way into OLG., and thence as *frû* into Scand.; the word remained unknown to E. The fem. form was OTeut. (Goth. *fraujô, f.), and was used in Scand. —changed according to phonetic laws into *Freyja*—as the name of a goddess. In the MidHG. period *frouwe* was popularly connected by a graceful fancy with freuen, *fröuwen*; comp. Freidank's saw, "Durch vröude vrouwen sind genant, Ir vröude ervröuwet elliu lant, Wie wol er vröude kante, Der sie êrste vrouwen nante"— "Woman is named from the joy she gives, Her favours fill the world with bliss. What a deep sense of joy had he, Who first named it woman." See Jungfer and the following word.

Fräulein, n., 'young lady, damsel, miss,' from MidHG. *vröuwelîn*, n., dimin. of MidHG. *vrouwe*, 'woman,' orig. 'noble maiden, young lady of noble birth, mistress, sweetheart,' also 'girl of mean rank, servant-girl.'—Frauenzimmer, n., 'woman,' from late MidHG. *vrouwenzimmer*, n., 'women's apartment'; the connecting link in meaning is collective, 'the body of women residing in its own apartments, the female inhabitants of the gynæceum,' also 'retinue of a lady of high rank,' just as Hof (court) is used collectively of 'the people at court.' "The application of a collective term to an individual" is analogous to the use of

Burſche and Kamerad; the modern sense dates from the beginning of the 17th cent.

frech, adj., 'bold, insolent, shameless,' from MidHG. *vrëch,* adj., 'courageous, bold, daring,' OHG. *frëh(hh),* 'covetous, greedy'; corresponding to Goth. **friks* only in *faihu-friks,* 'covetous, avaricious' (with respect to *faihu,* 'money,' see Vieh), OIc. *frekr,* 'greedy,' AS. *frec,* 'daring.' 'Greedy' was probably the primary meaning of the adj. stem *freka-* common to Teut.; when specially applied to war it meant 'eager for combat, daring'; AS. *frēca* acquired the meaning 'warlike hero,' earlier E. *freak,* 'hero, man.' For early Teut. words similarly restricted in meaning when applied to a warrior's life, see *bereit, fertig, rüstig.* There are derivatives of the OTeut. *freka-,* Goth. *friks,* in the Romance languages— OFr. *frique,* ModProv. *fricaud,* 'cheerful, lively.' Teut. *freka-,* from pre-Teut. *prēgo-,* scarcely belongs to *fragen.*

frei, adj., 'free, exempt, frank, voluntary,' from the equiv. MidHG. *vrî,* OHG. *frî;* a common Teut. stem *frija-,* 'free' (unknown only to Scand.), which is assumed by Goth. *freis* (acc. sing. mas. *frijana*), AS. *frî, freó* (from *frija-*), E. *free,* OLG. *frî.* From these are formed the abstracts—Goth. *freihals,* 'freedom,' lit. 'having one's neck free,' AS. *freóls,* 'freedom' (also 'peace, quiet'; comp. *freólsdæg,* 'holiday'). Scand. *frjáls* for the non existent **frîr,* 'free,' is identical with these words, being used as an adj. signifying 'with a free neck'; akin to OHG. and MidHG. *frîhals,* 'freeman.' A ring around the neck was an OTeut. mark of a slave. Although *frija-* prevails throughout the Teut. group in its modern sense 'free,' to which W. *ridd,* 'free' (from *prija-*), also corresponds, yet there is some evidence that the meanings 'dear, loved,' once belonged to the adj. in earliest Teut.; comp. the corresponding abstr. Goth. *frijapwa,* 'love,' AS. *freód* (for **frijôdus*), 'love, favour,' AS. *frîgu,* 'love' (also *freódryhten, freóbearn*); allied to Goth. *frijôn,* 'to love,' mentioned under Freund and Friede. All these derivatives point to a Teut. root *frî,* 'to cherish, spare, treat forbearingly' (MidHG. *vrî-ten,* Goth. *freidjan,* 'to spare'); *frei* in an active sense should perhaps be compared with *hold,* which also denoted the relation of the higher to the meaner person. Frei is lit. 'loving, loved, spared.' This sense is placed beyond doubt by the earlier history of the word—Goth. *frija-,* from pre-Teut. *priyó-;* comp. Sans. *priyá-s,* 'dear, favourite,' from the root *prî,* 'to rejoice, make well-disposed.' In OAryan the fem. of the adj. *priyā́* means 'spouse,' also 'daughter'; to this OSax. *frî,* and AS. *freó,* 'wife,' correspond. With the Sans. root *prî,* OSlov. *prijajǫ (prijati),* 'to assist,' *prijatelji,* 'friend,' are also connected. See Freitag, freien, Freund, Friede, Friedhof.

freien, vb., 'to woo,' from MidHG. *vrîen,* 'to woo, marry'; unknown to UpG., prop. a LG. word, made current chiefly by Luther. Comp. Du. *vrijen,* 'to sue for' (MidHG. *vrîen,* 'to set free, rescue,' must in the main be regarded as a different word). In the sense of 'to woo, marry,' the verb must be directly connected with the OTeut. root *frî,* 'to love'; comp. OSax. *frî,* 'wife, beloved.' For the diffusion of the Teut. root *frî* (from Aryan *prî*), see frei, Freitag, and also Freund.

freilich, adv., from the equiv. MidHG. *vrîliche,* adv., 'certainly, by all means,' prop. adv. from *vrîlich,* 'free, boundless.'

Freitag, m., 'Friday,' from the equiv. MidHG. *vrîtac,* OHG. *friatag,* m., 'dies Veneris'; corresponding to Du. *vrijdag,* AS. *frîgdæg, frîgedæg,* E. Friday, 'dies Veneris,' OIc. *Frjádagr* (for which *Föstudagr,* 'fast day,' is used in ModIc.); lit. 'Freia's day' (primit. Teut. *Frijjô*), equiv. to Lat. *dies Veneris. Freia* corresponds to Venus. OIc. *Frigg,* like OHG. *Frîa,* is lit. 'lover, goddess of love'; akin to Sans. *priyā́,* f., 'spouse, beloved' (OSax. *frî,* AS. *freó,* 'wife'). See frei.

Freite, f., 'wooing, courtship,' from MidHG. *vrîât, vrîâte,* f., 'making an offer of marriage'; abstract noun from freien; also in the same sense MidHG. *vrîe;* an essentially MidG. word.

fremd, adj., 'strange, foreign, unfamiliar, peculiar,' from MidHG. *vremede, vremde,* 'foreign, distant, strange, singular, rare,' OHG. *framadi, fremidi,* 'foreign, singular'; a common Teut. adj. for 'foreign,' unknown only to Scand.; comp. Goth. *framaps,* 'foreign, estranged, excluded from,' AS. *frempe, fremte,* 'foreign, alien, estranged' (E. obsolete), OSax. *fremithi,* Du. *vreemd.* A derivative of the stem appearing in the Goth. prep. *fram,* 'far from,' AS. and E. *from,* OHG. *fram,* adv., 'away, forward.'

freſſen, vb., 'to eat greedily, devour, corrode,' from MidHG. *vrëӡӡen,* OHG. *frëӡӡan,* 'to eat up, consume, feed,' of men and animals; derived from an earlier *fraëʒʒan, by syncope of the unaccented a; comp. Goth. fraitan, 'to consume' (E. to fret, 'to cut away'), with the similarly shortened pret. sing. frêt, plur. frêtun, for *fraêt, *fraêtun. The Goth. verbal prefix occurs in other cases in OHG. as fir, far, MidHG. and ModHG. ver, and from êʒʒen combined with this ver a new verb, verêʒʒen, is formed in MidHG. with the same meaning as frêʒʒen, which is etymologically equiv. to it. For the verbal prefix see Frevel, ver.

Frettchen, n., 'little ferret,' diinin. of an earlier ModHG. Frett, n., 'ferret'; first occurs in ModHG. from Romance; comp. Ital. furetto, Fr. furet (E. ferret), MidLat. furetum, furetus, 'ferret,' which is based upon early MidLat. furo, 'polecat,' equiv. to Lat. fur, 'thief.'

Freude, f., 'joy, pleasure, delight,' from the equiv. MidHG. vröude, vreude, OHG. frewida, f.; akin to freuen, MidHG. vröuwen, OHG. frouwen; see froh. For the suffix see Gemeinde, Begierde, Zierde, Beschwerde.

Freund, m., from the equiv. MidHG. vriunt(d), OHG. friunt, m., 'friend, relative'; comp. OSax. friunt, 'friend, relative,' Du. vriend, AS. freónd, E. friend, Goth. frijónds. Goth. frijônds, and hence also the other words, are partic. from an OTeut. and Goth. vb. frijôn, 'to love,' AS. freógan, 'to love' (see frei); therefore the word, signifying lit. 'lover,' is used in many dialects (even yet in LG., Hess., Franc., Alsat., Suab., and Bav.) for 'relative.' As to the formation, see Heiland, Feind.

Frevel, m., 'wanton offence, outrage, sacrilege,' from MidHG. vrevel, f., m., 'boldness, presumption, arrogance, insolence, violence,' OHG. fravilî, f., 'boldness, daring, insolence'; abstr. subst. from the OHG. adj. fravili, frevili, MidHG. vrevele, 'bold, proud, daring, insolent,' ModHG. frevel, adj.; comp. AS. fræfele, 'daring,' Du. wrevel, 'outrage.' Connected with the HG. adj. are two or three difficult forms which furnish a hint for discovering the etymology. OHG. fraballtcho, adv. with b, and frabari, f., 'audacia,' with b and r. Parallel to MidHG. vrevel there exists a form vor-evel, ver-evel, corresponding to MidHG. ver-êʒʒen, compared with vr-êʒʒen. We have probably to assume a Goth. *fra-abls, or rather *fra afls (comp. freffen), and with this OIc. afl, r., 'power, strength,' and OHG. aralôn, 'to torment oneself, work,' are closely connected. In OHG. fru

was preserved as a fully accented prefix in adjs., as in frâ-bald, 'daring,' from bald, 'bold.' See Fracht (a compound containing Goth. fra).—frevenllich, adv., 'sacrilegiously,' first occurs in ModHG., formed like eigentlich, wesentlich, &c., from the Mid HG. adj. vrevele, but with a change of the suffix l into n.

Friede, m., 'peace, tranquillity, quiet,' from MidHG. vride, m., 'peace, armistice, quiet, protection,' OHG. fridu, m., 'peace'; corresponding to OSax. frithu, m., AS. freoðo, friþu, f., OIc. friþr, m., 'peace'; the common Teut. word for 'peace.' Found in Goth. only in Friþareiks, equiv. to Friedrich (lit. 'prince of peace'); akin to Goth. gafriþôn, 'to reconcile.' The Teut. form friþu- contains the suffix þu like Goth. dau-þu-s, 'death'; priþu-s, from an Aryan root pri, Teut. fri, lit. 'to love, spare'; Friede, orig. 'state of love, forbearance' (see frei). It is worth noticing that Teut. first coined a word for 'peace,' for which no common term can be found in the Aryan languages, and the same may be said of 'Krieg.' See Hader.

Friedhof, m., 'churchyard'; the orig. sense is not exactly 'peaceful enclosure,' but rather 'an enclosed place'; akin to MidHG. vride, 'enclosure, a place hedged in'; MidHG. vrîthof, OHG. frîthof, 'enclosed space around a church,' must have given rise to Freithof. In their origin Friede and MidHG. vrît-hof are of course allied; yet vrît-hof must be connected chiefly with Goth. frei-djan, 'to spare,' OHG. fríten, 'to cherish, love, protect'; akin also to einfriedigen.

frieren, vb., 'to freeze, feel cold, be chilled,' from the equiv. MidHG. vriesen (partic., gevrorn), OHG. friosan (partic. gifroran); the change of s into r has obtained in all parts of the verb, yet s has been preserved in Frieseln and Frost. Comp. Du. vriezen, AS. freósan, E. to freeze, OIc. frjósa; Goth. *friusan is wanting, but may be inferred with certainty from frius, n., 'frost, cold.' The change of s into r is also shown by AS. frebrig, adj., 'freezing, frosty, stiff,' OIc. frer, neu. plur., 'frost, cold.' The Teut. root is freus, fruz, from the pre-Teut. root preus, prūs. It appears to lie at the base of Lat. prūrio for *prusio, 'to itch,' if the connecting link in meaning is to be found in the 'piercing, itching, burning nature of frost.' OInd. has a root pruš, 'to inject a substance,' which is more remote in meaning; akin to Lat. *pruĭna*, 'rime' (for **prusvĭna*); Sans. *pruśvá*, 'drop, frozen drop, rime.' Under no circumstances can the word be connected with Lat. *frigere.*

Fries, m., also **Friese**, f., 'frieze (cloth and part of a column),' ModHG. only, formerly also in the sense of 'coarse woollen stuff'; from Fr. *frise*, f., whence E. *frieze ;* the Fr. word, like its Romance cognates, is itself derived from Teut.; comp. AS. *frise,* 'curled,' E. *to friz, frizzle,* OFris. *frisle,* 'hair of the head.'

Frieseln, partic. plur., 'miliary fever,' ModHG. only, from *frieren*, which represents an earlier *friesen*.

frisch, adj., 'fresh, cool, raw (of a wound),' from MidHG. *vrisch,* OHG. *frisc,* adj., 'new, young, cheerful, active, pert'; corresponding to AS. *fersc*, E. *fresh,* OIc. *ferskr,* 'fresh.' The further origin is obscure; on account of its meaning Lat. *priscus* (akin to *prior, prius*) cannot be allied; perhaps OHG. *frisc* is derived from *früh,* OHG. *fruo.* The HG. word found its way at an early period into Romance (comp. Ital. *fresco,* Fr. *frais*), and into E. (*frisk*).

Frischling, m., 'young wild-boar,' from MidHG. *vrischinc, vrischlinc,* m.; a derivative of *frisch* with the suffixes *-ing, -ling.* The OHG. *frisking (fruscing),* 'beast of offering,' was adopted by OFr. as *fresange,* 'young pig.'

frisieren, vb., 'to curl, dress the hair,' ModHG. only, from Fr. *friser,* which is again derived from the cognates mentioned at the end of the article *Fries.*

Frist, f., 'period, appointed time, respite,' from MidHG. *vrist,* f., OHG. *frist,* f. (neu.) 'limited period, postponement, space of time'; OSax. *frist,* AS. *first,* m., OIc. *frest,* n. plur., 'postponement.' Probably not derived from the root *fri* (see *freien*), 'to love.' It might more reasonably be connected with the Goth. verbal particle *fri* in *frisahts,* if the meaning of the latter were clear. See also *Mist.*

froh, adj., 'glad, joyous, happy,' from MidHG. *vrô* (gen. *vrôwes, vrouwes*), OHG. *frô* (inflected form *frawêr*), 'glad'; corresponding to OSax. *frao* (gen. **frawes, frahes*), MidDu. *vro,* 'glad'; a corresponding word in E. is wanting. OIc. *frár,* 'quick, nimble,' closely agrees in sound; with respect to the meaning, comp. the analogous *glatt* and E. *glad.* Thus the sensuous meaning 'nimble' might be taken as the starting-point. If the Scand. word

be disregarded, 'gracious, friendly,' might be assumed as the primary meaning, in order to connect the word with the expressions for 'master, lord,' mentioned under *frohn.*

frohlocken, vb., 'to exult, triumph, shout for joy,' from MidHG. *vrôlocken* (rare), 'jubilate'; according to MidHG. *vrô-sanc,* 'song of joy, hallelujah,' probably a corruption of an earlier form, *frôleichen*; OHG. and MidHG. *vrô-leich would be also lit. 'song of joy.' E. *to frolic* is derived from Du. *vrolijk,* 'joyous.'

frohn, adj., 'lordly, holy,' now only preserved as the first component in archaic compounds; from MidHG. *vrôn,* adj., 'relating to the master or lord, sacred.' In OHG. there appears instead of an adj. *frôn a petrified form *frôno,* 'magnificent, divine, sacred,' which is prop. a gen. plur. of *frô,* 'lord' (used only in the vocative). In MidHG. *vrôn* appears in numerous compounds for the temporal lord, as well as for the κύριος, 'the lord,' κατ' ἐξοχήν, 'Christ'; comp. MidHG. *vrônlîchnam,* m., 'Christ's body, the host,' ModHG. Frohnleichnam; MidHG. *vrônkriuze,* OHG. *daz frôno chrûzi,* 'the cross of Christ'; MidHG. *vrônalter,* 'high altar,' &c.; also *vrônhof,* 'mansion,' *vrônwalt,* 'a wood belonging to the lord,' *vrônrëht,* 'public right.' ModHG. retained Frohndienst, from MidHG. *vrôndienst ;* see *fröhnen.* As to OHG. *frô,* 'O lord,' stress must be laid on its correspondence to AS. *frêa,* 'lord,' as well as OSax. *frao.* Goth. has a form with *j, frauja,* m. (AS. *frêgea*), 'lord,' which is seen in HG. in the fem. forms OHG. *frouwa,* MidHG. *vrouwe,* Goth. **fraujô.* With these some connect in Scand. the names of the deities *Freyr* and *Freyja.* Whether the stem *fraun-,* for *frawun-* and *fraujan-,* in the sense of 'gracious, friendly,' is allied to the adj. *frô,* 'glad,' remains to be proved. Comp. Frau.

Frohne, f., 'compulsory service, villeinage,' from MidHG. *vrône,* f., 'villein socage.' See *frohn.*

fröhnen, frohnen, vb., 'to serve,' from MidHG. *vrônen (vrænen)* 'to serve, perform villein socage.' See *frohn,* Frohne.

fromm, adj., 'worthy, pious, harmless,' from MidHG. *vrum* (inflected form *vrumer*), adj., 'able, excellent, good, gallant, conducive.' The MidHG. adj. is prop. a subst. (comp. Schade); MidHG. *frum, frume,* OHG. *fruma,* f., 'use, advantage' (*frummen,* 'to promote, accomplish'). Akin to the AS. forms with a gradation, *fram*, adj., 'brave, conducive,' *fremman*, 'to promote, accomplish'; comp. OIc. *framr*, 'preferable,' and *fremja*, 'to execute.' Also allied more remotely to the OTeut. terms for 'primus.' See Fürst, fert, fürder, &c.

Frosch, m., 'frog,' from the equiv. MidHG. *vrosch*, OHG. *frosk*, m.; corresponding to Du. *vorsch*, AS. *forsc* (E. dial. *frosk*), OIc. *froskr*, 'frog'; Goth. **frusqa-* is by chance not recorded. Before the deriv. *sk* a guttural has dropped out, as is seen in the cognate terms. AS. *frogga*, E. *frog*, would be in Goth. **frugga (*frugwa?)*; also akin to AS. *frocca*, earlier E. dial. *frock*, as well as OIc. *fraukr*, 'frog' (so too MidE. *frūte*, *froute*, 'toad'). Goth. **frusqa-*, for **fruhsqa-*, would therefore be connected with a *u* root ending in a guttural; perhaps the pre-Teut. root *pruk?*. Hence the attempts to connect the word with frisch or frieren, to which the meaning is also opposed, must be rejected.

Frost, m., 'frost, cold, chill,' from the equiv. MidHG. *vrost*, OHG. *frost*, m.; comp. Du. *vorst*, AS. *forst*, E. *frost*, OIc. *frost*, n., 'frost, cold'; a common Teut. abstract of frieren, Goth. **friusan*. Goth. **frustu-*, m., n., 'frost,' is wanting.

Frucht, f., 'fruit, crop, product,' from MidHG. *vruht*, OHG. *fruht*, f., 'fruit'; corresponding to OSax. *fruht*, Du. *vrucht*, OFris. *frucht*. Based on Lat. *fructus*, which perhaps at the same period as Pflanze and a number of botanical terms, found its way into German.

früh, adj., adv., 'early, premature(ly),' from MidHG. *vrüeje*, adj., 'early,' *vruo*, adv., 'early' (hence sometimes the Mod HG. *fruh* unmodified); OHG. *fruoji*, adj., *fruo*, adv., 'early'; comp. Du. *vroeg*, adj. and adv., 'early.' Goth. **frō* (or rather **fraud* for **frōð?*), adv., is wanting. Pre-Teut. *prō-* appears also in Gr. πρωΐ, 'early, early in the morning,' πρωΐα, f., 'morning,' πρώϊος, 'early'; akin to Sans. *prātar*, adv., 'early in the morning.' Allied more remotely to ver, Fürst, vertere, &c. (also frisch?). It is curious that the OAryan adv., in the sense of 'early in the morning,' is restricted to Ger. In Scand., E., and Goth. it is wanting; the words used being Goth. *air*, OIc. *ár*, AS. *ǣr*, 'early in the morning' (see ehe). Moreover, its special meaning was universally diffused at an early period. See Frühling.

Frühling, m., 'spring,' a deriv. of früh, early ModHG. only—from the 15th cent.; Lenz is the old West Teut. term.

Fuchs, m., 'fox, light bay horse, cunning person, freshman (univ.),' from the equiv. MidHG. *vuhs*, OHG. *fuhs*, m.; corresponding to Du. *vos*, AS. and E. *fox*; Goth. **faúhs-*, m. (weak subst.), is not found. The *s* is a masc. suffix, as in Luchs; it is wanting, therefore, in the older fem. form, OHG. *foha*, MidHG. *vohe*, f., 'vixen' (also 'fox,' equiv. to Goth. *faúhō*, f., 'fox,' OIc. *foa*, 'fox'). OIc. *fox*, n., is used only in the figurative sense of 'deceit.' The ModHG. fem. form Füchsin corresponds to AS. *fyxen*, E. *vixen*. Goth. *faúhō*, f., from pre-Teut. *pŭkā́*, makes it appear possible to connect the word phonetically with Mod HG. Vogel, Goth. *fugls*, pre-Teut. *puklō-s*, in case Sans. *puccha*, 'tail, train,' is of a cognate stem; Fuchs and Vogel, meaning 'tailed creatures,' is quite possible. At all events, there is no connection with Lat. L. *vulpes*.

Fuchtel, f., earlier ModHG. Fochtel, 'broadsword, a blow struck with it,' first occurs in ModHG.; akin to fechten.

Fuder, n., from the equiv. MidHG. *vuoder*, OHG. *fuodar*, n., 'measure (varying from 36 to 72 bushels, of wine about 1200 bottles), waggon-load'; comp. OSax. *fōthar*, Du. *voer*, AS. *fōþer*, 'measure, waggon-load,' E. *fother*, *fodder*, a term in mining. Hence the common West Teut. term *fōþr*, n., 'waggon-load,' from the Teut. root *faþ* in Faden. From HG., Fr. *foudre* is derived.

Fug, m., 'adaptedness, due authority, right,' from MidHG. *vuoc(g)*, m., 'propriety,' as well as the equiv. *vuoge*, f., Mod HG. Fuge, akin to fügen.

Fuge, f., 'fugue,' first occurs in early ModHG., from Ital. *fuga*.

fügen, vb., 'to fit together, connect'; (refl.) 'to accommodate oneself,' from Mid HG. *vüegen*, OHG. *fuogen*, 'to shape or unite suitably'; comp. Du. *voegen*, AS. *gefēgan*, E. *to fay* ('to suit, unite'); Goth. **fōgjan*, 'to make suitable,' is a factitive of the Teut. root *fag*, in Goth. *fagrs*, 'suitable, fitted,' whose nearer cognates are to be found under fegen; E. *to fadge* ('to suit, join'), may also be mentioned here.

fühlen, vb., 'to feel, be sensible of, be sensitive to,' a MidG. and LG. word incorporated in literary Ger. since Luther's time (in Suab. and Alem. spüren and merken, and in Bav. empfinden are used); from the equiv. MidHG. vüelen, OHG. fuolen (OHG. also 'to touch'); comp. OSax. *gifólian*, Du. *voelen*, AS. *félan*, E. *to feel*; a common West Teut. word for 'to feel' (Goth. *földjan*). Akin to OIc. *falma*, 'to grope.' With the Teut. root *fól, fal*, an old term for 'hand' is connected; OSax. *folm*, AS. *folm*, OHG. *folma*, 'hand' (primit. allied to Sans. *páni*, Gr. παλάμη, Lat. *palma*, OIr. *lám* for *plāma*).

Fuhre, f., 'journey, conveyance, waggon, cart-load,' from MidHG. *vuore*, f., journey, way, street, escort, food for a 'journey, fodder,' OHG. *fuora*; comp. AS. *fór*, f., 'journey,' also 'vehicle'; akin to fahren. See also führen.

führen, vb., 'to carry, conduct, deal in, manage,' from MidHG. *vüeren*, OHG. *fuoren*, 'to put in motion, guide, lead'; a factitive of fahren (OHG. *faran*), like ModHG. leiten, a factitive of OHG. *lîdan*, 'to go, drive'; comp. OSax. *fórian*, Du. *voeren*, 'to lead,' OIc. *fœra*, 'to bring.' Goth. *fórjan* is wanting; AS. *féran* means 'to go, march.' Hence the sense 'to lead' is essentially Ger.

füllen, vb., 'to fill,' from MidHG. *vüllen*, OHG. *fullen*, 'to make full'; a derivative of voll. Comp. Goth. *fulljan*, OIc. *fylla*, AS. *fyllan*, E. *to fill*, Du. *vullen*, OSax. *fullian*, 'to fill'; also voll.—**Fülle,** f., 'abundance, plenty,' from MidHG. *vülle*, OHG. *fullî*, 'fulness'; comp. Goth. *ufarfullei*, f., 'superabundance.'

Füllen, n., from the equiv. MidHG. *vüln*, OHG. *fulîn*, n., besides MidHG. *vüle*, OHG. *fulî*, n., 'foal'; for the affix -*in*-, denoting the young of animals, see under Schwein. Based upon Fohlen (Goth *fula*); hence *ful-ein*, n. has to be assumed in Goth.; comp. MidLG. *völen*, Du. *veulen*, OIc. *fyl*. Another derivative of *ful-* is OHG. *fulîhha*, MidHG. *vülhe*, f., 'filly,' pointing to Goth. *fuliki*.

Füllsel, n., 'stuffing,' from the equiv. late MidHG. *vülsel*, n.; a derivative of voll with modification; for the suffix -*sel*, from OHG. *isal*, Goth. *isl*, see Rätsel.

Fund, m., from the equiv. MidHG. *vunt*, m., 'finding, discovery, find'; allied to finden; comp. Du. *vond*, 'discovery, invention,' OIc. *fundr*, *fyndr*.

fünf, card. num., 'five,' from MidHG. *vünf*, OHG. *funf*, also earlier *finf*; corresponding to Goth. *fimf*, OIc. *fimm*, AS. *fîf*, E. *five*, Du. *vijf*, OSax. *fîf*. Goth. *fimf*, from pre-Teut. *pempe, pénqe* (for the permutation of Aryan *q* to Teut. *f* see Fähre, vier, Wolf); comp. Sans. *páñcan*, Gr. πέντε (πέμπε, πέμπτος), Lat. *quinque* (for *pinque*), Lith. *penkì*, OIr. *cóic*, W. *pimp*; a common Teut. term, like all numbers from 2 to 10; the oldest form is *pénqe, pénke*. The attempts to discover the root with some such meaning as 'hand,' and to connect the word with Finger, have produced no result. The Aryan numerals are presented to us as compact forms, the origin of which is obscure. The ord. fünfte is, like all ordinals, a derivative of an old form; Goth. *fimfta*, OHG. *fimfto, funfto*, MidHG. *vünfte*; Du. *vijfde*, AS. *fîfta*, E. *fifth*. Comp. Lat. *quintus* for *pinctus*, Gr. πέμπτος, Sans. *pañcathas*, Lith. *penktas*.

Funke, m., from the equiv. MidHG. (not a classical form) *vunke*, m., OHG. *funcho*, m., 'spark'; comp. Du. *vonk*, 'spark,' MidLG. and MidE. *funke*, 'small fire, spark,' E. *funk*, 'round wood, steam, stink.' Classical MidHG. has *vanke*, m. It is uncertain whether Goth. *fón* (gen. *fúnins*), 'fire,' is allied; it is more probable that Sans. *pájas*, 'splendour, gleam of light,' is primit. cognate.

für, prep., 'for, in behalf of,' from Mid HG. *vür*, OHG. *furi*, 'before, for'; comp. OSax. *furi*, 'before'; a Ger. prep. simply, allied to those discussed under ver.—**fürbaß,** adv., 'forward, further,' from Mid HG. *vürbaz*. adv., from für and baß.

Furche, f., from the equiv. MidHG. *vurch* (plur. *vürche*), OHG. *furuh*, f., 'furrow'; comp. Du. *voor*, AS. *furh*, f., E. *furrow* (akin to AS. and E. *furlong*, 'the length of a furrow'); OIc. *for*, f., 'drain, watercourse.' Goth. **fauŕhus*, f. is wanting. It is based upon pre-Teut *prk-*; comp. Lat. *porca*, 'ridge between two furrows,' and *porculetum*, 'field divided into beds'; akin also to Armen. *herk*, 'freshly ploughed fallow land,' W. *rhych* (OGall. **ricd*, OIr. *rech*), m., f., 'furrow,' from the base *prkd*.

Furcht, f., 'fear, terror, fright,' from MidHG. *vorht, vorht*, f., 'fear, anxiety, apprehension,' OHG. and OSax. *forhta, forahta*; abstr. of fürchten. In AS. a modified abstr. is found; comp. AS. *fyrhto* (Goth. *faurhtei*), hence E. *fright*, whence *to frighten, to fright*; E. *fear* (see Gefahr), is not a cognate.—**fürchten,** 'to fear, dread,' from MidHG. *vürhten* (pret. *vorhte*), OHG. *furihten, forahtan* (pret. *forahta*), 'to be afraid'; comp. OSax. *forahtjan*, AS.

forhtian; Du. and Scand. are wanting; Goth. *faurhtjan*, 'to fear, be afraid,' with the partic. *faúrhts*, 'timid,' used as an adj. The dental of the vb., which was probably strong orig., is a suffix of the present stem, hence Teut. *furh-tjan*; the corresponding abstr. OHG. *forh-ta* is formed like Schande. To the Teut. root *forh* (Aryan *prk̂* ?, *q̂erk̂* ?), Lat. *querquerus*, 'shivering,' and Gr. καρκαίρω, 'to tremble,' have been allied.

fürder, adv., 'further,' from MidHG. *vürder*, OHG. *furdir*, adv., 'further in front, further on, away'; apparently an oblique form of the compar. neut., like Goth. *faurþis*, 'formerly,' from fort, Goth. *faurþ; AS. *furþor*, adv., 'forward, further, more distantly' (Goth. *faúrþōs), E. *further*. See fert.

Furhe, f., 'pitchfork,' from MidHG. *furke*, OHG. *furcha*, f., 'fork'; comp. Du. *vork*, AS. and E. *fork*; from Lat. *furca*, introduced early in the OHG. period along with Southern horticulture.

Fürst, m., 'sovereign, chief, prince,' from MidHG. *vürste*, m., 'the highest, most distinguished, ruler, prince,' OHG. *furisto*, OSax. *furisto*, Du. *vorst*, 'prince'; like Herr, simply a Ger. form. Just as Herr is orig. a compar. of hehr, so is Fürst prop. a superlat. meaning 'first'; comp. OHG. *furist*, AS. *fyrst*, E. *first*, OIc. *fyrstr*; Goth. *faúrists is wanting; the corresponding compar. is OHG. *furiro*, 'the former, preferable,' OIc. *fyrre*, 'former.' The usual OSax. and AS. word for 'first' is *formo*, *forma*, with the suffix *ma* (Goth. *fruma*); from Aryan *pr̥* like Gr. πρόμος, Sans. *pûrva-s*, OSlov. *prŭvŭ*, Lith. *pirmas*, 'first.' It is evident that also ver, für, fert, &c., are derivatives of this Aryan root *pr̥*.

Furt, f. (UpG. masc. also), 'ford,' from the equiv. MidHG. and OHG. *vurt*, m.; comp. OSax. *ford in *Heriford* (lit. 'lord's ford'), Herford; MidDu. *vord*, AS. *ford*, m., E. *ford*; comp. AS. *Oxenaford* (lit. 'oxen's ford'), 'Oxford' (also Schweinfurt, Erfurt). Goth. *faúrdus, 'ford,' is wanting. It belongs to the Teut. root *far*, 'to go, march,' and hence signifies lit. 'a frequented, passable spot'; comp. Gr. πόρος, 'ford,' which has a cognate root, and βόσπορος with *Oxford*; also Zend *peretu*, 'bridge' (*Euphrates*, lit. 'having many bridges'?); so too Lat. *portus*, 'port'; OIc. *fjǫrðr*, m., 'bay.' Lat. *-ritum* (for *pritum) in *Augustoritum*, from Kelt., is also allied to this word.

fuschen, vb., 'to perform hastily, cheat,' ModHG. only, of obscure origin.

Fusel, m., 'bad brandy,' probably from chemical technology (Lat. *fusilis*, 'liquid'?).

Fuß, m., 'foot, base, pedestal, footing,' from the equiv. MidHG. *vuoȝ*, OHG. *fuoȝ*, m., 'foot'; a common Teut. and more remotely a common Aryan term for 'foot'; comp. Goth. *fôtus*, OIc. *fôtr*, AS. *fôt*, E. *foot*, Du. *voet*, OSax. *fôt*. The Teut. *fôt-* (weak subst.), from Aryan *pōd-*, which interchanged with Aryan *pŏd-* and *pĕd* in declension. Comp. Gr. ποδ- in πόδα, nom. sing. πούς (Æol. πώς); Lat. *pĕd-em*, nom. sing. *pes*; πέδιλον, 'sandal,' πεξός (for πεδjός), 'on foot'; *o* gradation in Lat. *tripudium*; OInd. nom. sing. *pád* (locat. *padí*), 'foot,' *padá*, neu., 'tread, footstep.' The *e* gradation is preserved in Teut. by OIc. *fit*, n., 'step,' but as a measure 'foot' (Lith. *pëdì*, 'mark of the foot'); akin to OIc. *feta*, 'to find the way,' OHG. *feȝȝan*, 'to go.' Respecting OIc. *fjǫturr* see Fessel; OIc. *fit*, f., 'the skin of birds between the claws.' MidE. *fetlak*, E. *fetlock*; thus too MidHG. *viȝȝeloch*, 'hough,' earlier ModHG. Fißloch; they are derivatives (not compounds) of **fet-*, 'foot.'—**Fußstapfe**, f., 'footstep, trace,' from stapfen; often divided wrongly into Fußtapfe, which would originate in a verb tarpfen for stapfen.

Futter, n., from the equiv. MidHG. *vuoter*, OHG. *fuotar*, n., 'nourishment, food, fodder, lining, case'; comp. Du. *voeder*, n., 'fodder, lining'; AS. *fôdor*, n., E. *fodder*; OIc. *fôðr*, n., 'fodder'; Goth. *fôdr*, n., 'scabbard.' Two really different words seem to have converged phonetically in this term. Goth. *fôdr, 'nourishment,' seems to be connected with AS. *fôda*, 'nourishment,' E. *food*, Goth. *fôdjan*, AS. *fêdan*, E. *to feed*, and consequently with a Teut. root *fôd*, *fad* (comp. OHG. *fatunga*, 'nourishment, food'), from Aryan *pāt*, which also appears in Gr. πατέομαι, 'to eat'; likewise akin to AS. *fôstor*, 'maintenance,' E. *to foster*, *foster-brother*, &c. The second, Futter, 'case,' Goth. *fôdr*, 'sheath,' has been thought to be allied to Sans. *pâtra-m*, n., 'vessel, receptacle.' The Teut. cognates in both senses found their way into Rom.; comp. Prov. and OFr. *fuerre* (ModFr. *feurre*), 'sheath,' formed from Goth. *fôdr*, OHG. *fuotar*, 'sheath,' ModFr. *feurre*, 'straw for feeding cattle,' ModFr. *fourreau*, 'case, sheath,' &c.

Futteral, n., 'case, lining, sheath,' ModHG. only, from MidLat. *fotrale*, a derivative of OHG. *fôtar*, MidHG. *vuoter*; comp. Futter.

füttern, vb., equiv. to MidHG. *vüetern, vuotern*, 'to feed, nourish,' OHG. *fuotiren* (Goth. *fôdrjan*) ; a derivative of Futter, 'nourishment.'

G.

Gabe, f., 'gift,' from the equiv. MidHG. *gâbe*, f. ; OHG. *gâba* and Goth. *gēba* are wanting ; instead OHG. *gēba* (MidHG. *gēbe* with the dial. variant *gippe*), f., occurs, OSax. *gēba*, AS. *gifu*, OIc. *gjǫf*, Goth. *giba*, f., 'gift.' The forms corresponding to the assumed Goth. *gēba* are seen in Du. *gaaf* and OSwed. *gåfa*.

gäbe, adj., 'acceptable, in vogue, stylish,' from MidHG. *gæbe* (OHG. *gâbi*), adj., 'acceptable, dear, good' ; Goth. *gēbi-* is related to *giban* (see geben) ; just as *nēms* is to *niman* (see gänge, angenehm) ; comp. OIc. *gǣfr*, 'salutary,' Du. *gaaf*, 'suitable.'

Gabel, f., 'fork, shafts (of a vehicle),' from the equiv. MidHG. *gabele*, *gabel*, OHG. *gabala*, *gabal*, f. ; corresponding to Du. *gaffel* (hence ModIc. *gaffall*, 'fork'), AS. rarely, *geaful*, m., 'fork' (for which, even in the AS. period, *forc*, E. *fork* occurs). Gabel seems to be related by gradation to Giebel, and in that case the oldest shape of the fork must have been a sort of acute angle like a gable. Yet the supposition that the word was borrowed is not to be rejected, especially since 'the form of an acute angle' can hardly be the prim. meaning of Giebel. Note the correspondence with Kelt. words ; OIr. *gabul*, 'fork,' *gabhla*, 'shears,' W. *gebe'*, 'tongs,' Lat. *gabalus* '(gable-shaped) gallows' ; to these also OInd. *gâbhasti*, 'fork, shaft,' may be allied, in which case it would follow that the West Teut. Gabel is perhaps primit. allied to the Kelt. class.

gackern, **gackſen**, vb., 'to cackle, chatter,' simply ModHG. ; imitative forms like MidHG. *gâgen*, 'to cackle like a goose.' akin to Du. *gagelen*, 'to gabble,' and even in OHG. *gackizôn*, 'to mutter,' *gagizôn*, *gackazzen*, 'to bawl,' MidHG. *gagzen*, 'to cluck like a hen laying.' Comp. Scand. *gagga*, 'to howl like a fox,' *gagl*, 'wild goose,' E. *to gaggle*.

Gaden, **Gadem**, m. and n., 'room, cottage, storey,' from MidHG. and MidLG. *gaden*, *gadem*, n., 'house containing one room only,' then generally 'apartment, chamber,' OHG. *gadum*, *gadam*, n. ; orig. a merely UpG. word, which found its way, however, even into LG. Akin to Goth. *gatm* (from *ga-* and *tmo-*, the latter related to Gr. δόμος, μεσό-δμη, and HG. Zimmer) ?. Less probably allied to AS. *geat*, E. *gate* (comp. Du. *gat*, 'opening,' under Gaſſe). At all events, the connection with Gr. χιτών, 'garment,' is impossible.

gaffen, vb., 'to gape at,' from the equiv. MidHG. (MidG.) *gaffen*, OHG. *gaffēn* (deduced from OHG. *geffida*, f., 'contemplation') ; Goth. *gapan* is wanting. The ordinary MidHG. and OHG. words for the modern gaffen are *kapfen* and *chapfēn* (Goth. *kappan*, vb., is wanting). Hence, according to the sounds, the two words are radically different ; in the ModHG. period, MidHG. *kapfen* has given way to gaffen. The latter signifies lit. 'to look on with open mouth' ; comp. Du. *gapen* and the equiv. E. *to gape*, OIc. *gapa*, 'to open the mouth wide,' *gap*, 'chaos.' The Teut. root *gap*, 'to gape,' is allied to Sans. root *jabh*, 'to snap' ?.

gähe, see jäh.

gähnen, vb., 'to yawn, gape,' from the equiv. MidHG. *ginen* (*genen*, *geinen*), OHG. *ginēn* (*geinôn*) ; ModHG. *æ* for *ē*. Goth. *gi-nai-* from the root *gi*, 'to gape' ; comp. AS. *ginian*, *gānian*, 'to gape.' OIc. and AS. possess a str. vb. formed from the root *gi*, and *n* orig. a suffix of the present stem— OIc. *gīna*, AS. *tōgīnan*, 'to bark'; comp. also OIc. *gin*, n., 'jaw of animals.' OHG. *gīēn*, 'to gape,' is formed without the suffix *n*; so too with a derivative *w*, OHG. *giwēn*, *gewēn*, MidHG. *giwen*, *gëwen*, 'to open the mouth wide.' The Teut. root *gī*, from pre-Teut. *ghī*, is widely diffused, especially in West Teut. Comp. Lat. *hiare* (for Lat. *h*, representing Teut. *g*, see Gerſte and Gaſt), OSlov. *zijati*, 'to gape, bark,' Lith. *žióti*, 'to open the mouth wide' ; OIr. *gin*, 'mouth' (OIc. *gin*) ; Lat. *hīsco*; Gr. χεω, 'hole,' for χεϝd ?.

Galgant, m., 'galangal,' from the equiv. MidHG. *galgan*, *galgân*, *galgant*, m. ; comp. MidE. *galingale*, E. *galangal* ; a medicinal herb of the Middle Ages, known under the same name to Rom. (comp. Ital. *galanga*, Fr. *galanga*—MidLat. *galanga* ; also Mid

Gr. γαλάγγα). The origin of the term has probably been rightly ascribed to the East; some etymologists compare it with Arab *galang*.

Galgen, m., 'gallows, gibbet, crossbeam,' from MidHG. *galge*, OHG. *galgo*, m., 'gallows (also applied to the cross of Christ, frame over a well from which the bucket is hung to draw water.' It corresponds to OSax. *galgo*, Du. *galg*, AS. *gealga*, E. *gallows* (the plur. used as a sing., yet comp. *gallow-tree*), OIc. *galge*, 'gallows,' Goth. *galga*, m. (applied to the cross of Christ, as also in all the other OTeut. dialects); a common Teut. word, Teut. *galgan-*, pre-Teut. *g'algha-*; comp. Lith. *žalga*, f., 'pole.' Note the double sense of the MidHG. and OHG. word. Probably some such idea as a 'long pliable rod' is the starting-point of the various meanings of the cognates.

Gallapfel, m., 'gall, gall-nut,' first occurs in early ModHG., from Lat. *galla*, whence also, probably, the equiv. AS. *galloc*; comp. E. *oak-gall (galloak)*. See **Galle (2.)**.

Galle (1.), f., 'gall, bile,' from the equiv. MidHG. *galle*, OHG. *galla*, f.; common to Teut. in the same sense (only in Goth. is the weak neu. *gallô* not recorded); comp. OSax. *galla*, Du. *gal*, AS. *gealla*, OIc. *gall*, n. Like a great number of terms relating to the body (see Fuß, Herz, Niere, Nase, Ohr), Galle too has numerous correspondences in the cognate languages, which points to the antiquity of the Aryan term (Goth. *gallin-* or *galzin-*, from pre-Teut. *ghal-*); comp. Gr. χολή, χόλος, Lat. *fel, fellis*, n., 'gall.' Many etymologists connect the word with gelb (OHG. *gëlo*), as if gall was named from its colour; OSlov. *žlŭčĭ*, 'gall' (from *gĭlki*), is certainly allied to Russ. *želknutĭ*, 'to turn yellow.'

Galle (2.), f., 'barbel,' from MidHG. *galle*, f., 'swelling above the knee on the hind-leg of a horse'; comp. E. *gall* (swelling, sore spot, gall-nut); it is questionable whether Gallapfel is allied to the word. Also in Romance, Ital. *galla* and Span. *agalla*, signify 'swelling, tumour, gall-nut.' Hence the Lat.-Rom. *galla*, 'gall-nut,' was perhaps the source of the Teut. terms. Yet it is possible that the foreign word has been confused with a Teut. word similar in sound, especially since Swed. dialects also have a term *gräsgaller*, 'swelling on the hoof of a horse.'

Gallerie, f., 'jelly,' from MidHG. *gal-*
hert, galhart, galreide, f., 'jelly of animal and vegetable matter.' MidLat. *galatina*, 'jelly,' as well as Fr. *gelée* (from Lat. *gelare*), cannot, for phonetic reasons, serve as the source of the MidHG. word; the origin is still obscure.

Galmei, m., 'calamine,' first occurs in early ModHG., with the older variant Kalmei; once in MidHG. *kalemīne*; from MidLat. and Rom.; comp. MidLat. *lapis calaminaris*, Fr. *calamine*; earlier Lat. *cadmia*, Gr. καδμεία, 'calamine.'

Galopp, m., 'gallop,' borrowed from Fr. *galop*, even in the MidHG. period, as is proved by MidHG. *galopieren*, of which the variant *walopieren* occurs (comp. MidHG. *walap*, 'galop,' E. *wallop*). The Rom. words on which they are based are derived by some etymologists from a Teut. source, though it cannot be assigned to any satisfactory root; some assume a Goth-Teut. *walh-hlaup*, which is supposed to denote a Kelt. method of trotting.

Gamander, m., 'germander,' from the equiv. MidHG. *gamandrē*; from MidLat. *chamandreus, gamandraea*, which is based upon Gr. χαμαίδρυς, χαμαίδρυον, 'germander.'

Ganerbe, m., 'joint-heir, co-proprietor,' from MidHG. *ganerbe* (from *ge-an-erbe*), m., 'next co-heir, especially a co-heir with the right of obtaining the property of his fellow-inheritors at their death,' OHG. *ganarbo*, 'co-heir' (Goth. *gaána-arbja*, m.). The prefix *ga*, representing Lat. *con-*, 'together with,' was current in OTeut. See Geneß, Geselle.

Gang, m., 'going, movement, gait, passage,' from the equiv. MidHG. *ganc(g)*, OHG. *gang*, m., 'gait, walking'; corresponding to OSax. *gang*, Du. *gang*, AS. *gong*, m., 'walking, gait' (comp. E. *gang, gangway*, and *gangweek*), OIc. *gangr*, m., 'gait, walking,' Goth. *gagga*, 'lane.' Also in older Teut. a str. vb. *gangan*, 'to go,' of which only the pret. ging and the partic. gegangen are still current in ModHG. In East Teut., in which gehen is wanting, *ganga* (OIc.) and *gaggan* (Goth.) have a wider range; yet comp. OSwed. and ODan. *ga*, 'to go.' In West Teut. part of gehen has been lost; in E., differing in this respect from G., the older *gangan* has become entirely obsolete. Teut. root *gang*, pre-Teut. *ghangh*. The only correspondences in other Aryan languages are Sans. *jáṅghá*, f., 'leg, foot,' Lith. *žengiù* (*žèngti*), 'to step,' akin to Lith. *pražanga*, 'trespass.'

gänge, adj., 'current, in vogue, customary,' from MidHG. *genge*, OHG. *gengi*, 'ordinary, scattered,' orig. 'capable of going, or rather of circulating'; a verbal adj. from the root *ging* (see the preceding word), formed like *gäbe*, *angenehm*, *flügge*.

Gans, f., 'goose,' from the equiv. MidHG. *gans*, OHG. *gans*, f.; a common Teut. term for 'goose,' unrecorded in Goth. only, in which **gans*, f. (plur. **gans*) may have been the form (comp. Span. *gunso*, adopted from it). To this correspond AS. *gós* (*ó* from *an* before *s*), plur. *gés* (owing to the *i* mutation), f., E. *goose*, plur. *geese*; OIc. *gás*, f., from pre-Teut *ghans-*; Du. *gans*; one of the few names of birds to be ascribed to a primit. Aryan origin, since it recurs in most of the languages of the Aryan group; Sans. *hansá-s*, m., *hansí*, f., 'goose,' Mod Pers. *γdz*, Lith. *zasís* (OSlov. *gąsĭ* is borrowed from Teut.), Gr. χήν, Lat. *anser* (for **hanser*), OIr. *géis*, 'swan' (from *ghansi*). The *s* of Aryan *ghans-* seems to be a suffix (comp. Fuchs, Monat); at least Teut. words of cognate stem point to *ghan-* as the more primitive form; comp. OHG. *ganazzo*, MidHG. *ganze*, *genz*, m., 'gander,' Du. *gent*, 'gander,' AS. *ganot*, E. *gannet* ('swan'); AS. *gandra*, E. *ginder*. Pliny informs us that large flocks of geese were kept in Germania, and that the birds or their feathers were sent even to Rome; one species was said to be called *gantae* by the Teutons; a similar term is known in Rom. (Prov. *ganta*, OFr. *gante*, 'wild goose'), which borrowed it from Teut. To the Teut. *ganta*, from pre-Teut. *gandu*, the OIr. *géd*, 'goose' (Lith. *gándras*, 'stork'), is primit. allied.

Gänserich, m., 'gander, wild tansy,' ModHG. simply, formed like Enterich, from an earlier Ganser (still found in many of the UpG. dialects; in Alsat. *gunster*, MidG. *gänsert*), MidHG. *ganzer*, also *ganze*, *ganze*, m., 'gander.' Comp. LG. *gante*, Scand. *gass* for *gåsse*, 'gander'; see Gans. The plant Geuserich is a corruption of an earlier Grensaich; comp. Fr. *bec d'oie*, Ital. *piè d oca*. The MidHG. and OHG. term is *grensinc* (even *gensing* also in OHG.).

Gant, f., 'auction, bankruptcy,' an UpG. word (unknown to the Suab. dial.), from MidHG. *gant*, f., 'sale to the highest bidders, auction.' Not from Fr. *gant*, 'glove.' It is not true that "affixing a glove (in a symbolical way) has given rise to the terms Gant and Vergantung, denoting a distress on real property." The term is more probably derived from Prov. *l'encant*, ModFr. *l'encan*, 'auction' (Ital. *incanto*, from Lat. *in quantum*), whence E. *cant*, 'auction.'

ganz, adj., 'whole, complete, entire,' from MidHG. and OHG. *ganz*, adj., 'uninjured, complete, whole, healthy,' prop. a HG. word simply, which was adopted, however, by the Teut. dialects of MidEurope (Dan. *ganske*, Du. *gansch*, OFris. *gans*; *n* would not have been retained before *s* in a native Dan. or Fris. word. The early history of OHG. *ganz* is obscure; if its primary meaning is 'encircling,' it is perhaps connected with Gr. χανδάνω, 'to comprise'; comp. Gr. χαδός, 'spacious'?.

gar, adj. (and adv.), 'finished, ready, done' (of cooked food), from MidHG. *gar* (inflect. *garwer*), adj., *gare*, adv., OHG. *garo* (infl. *garawér*), adj., *garo*, *garawo*, adv., 'made ready,' armed, prepared, complete, entire'; corresponding to OSax. *garo*, AS. *gearo* (adv., *gearwe* also), E. *yare*, OIc. *gorr* (adv. *gorwa*), 'ready, prepared, made'; Goth. **garwa-* is wanting. The adj. was really used as a partic., the suffix *wo* in Ind., combines with the root *pac*, 'to cook,' forming the partic. *pakvá-s*, 'cooked, done' (of food). Besides AS. *gearo*, 'ready,' a remarkable form, *earo*, is found with the same meaning, and in OSax. *aru* as well as *garu*; these forms point to Goth. **garwa* and **arwa*, 'prepared, made ready.' Hence some have identified the two classes regarding the *g* of **garwa-* as the remnant of the verbal particle Goth. *ga* (HG. *ge*).

Garbe (1.), f., 'sheaf,' from the equiv. MidHG. *garbe*, OHG. *garba*, f.; corresponding to OSax. *garba*, Du. *garf*, 'sheaf'; lit. 'handful, manipulum.' Hence from the Sans. root *grbh*, 'to lay hold of, seize,' *grábhá*, 'handful,' Lett. *grahus*, fem. plur., 'a bundle hastily collected,' Lith. *grėpti*, 'to seize,' and *gróptí*, 'to snatch.' In the HG. dialects grappeln, grapfen, grippen, &c., are also allied to the Aryan root *ghrbh*; so too Du. *grabbelen*, E. *to grabble*. The cognates found their way into Romance (Fr. *gerbe*, f., 'sheaf').

Garbe (2.), f., the same is Schafgarbe, 'milfoil,' f., 'millefolium,' from the equiv. MidHG. *garwe*, OHG. *garwa*, *garawa*, f., 'millefolium'; corresponding to AS. *gearewe*, f., E. *yarrow*, Du. *gerw*, 'millefolium.' Whether it is related to gar (Teut. *garwa-*) is uncertain.

gären, vb., 'to ferment, effervesce, bubble,' a combination as to its form of a str. vb. MidHG. *gëren*; *jësen*; OHG. *jësan*, 'to ferment, foam,' and the corresponding factitive MidHG. *jern (unrecorded, but OHG. jerian occurs), 'to cause to ferment'; OHG. jësan is a str. vb., and jerjan a wk. vb. (comp. ginësan, str. vb., and ginerian, wk. vb.). Noun derivatives of the Teut. root jes retain their s (before t) even as late as ModHG.; see **Gifdjt**, under which the cognate nouns from the other OTeut. dialects are brought together. The root jes, yes, occurs also in Ind. and Gr.; comp. Gr. ζεσ-τός, 'boiled,' ζέσ-μα, hence also ζέω for *ζέσω (perf. έζεσ-μαι), 'to boil, bubble' (ς for earlier j, y as in ζυγόν, see Joch), Sans. root yas, 'to seethe, boil.' Considering this agreement of forms with initial j and y, ModHG. gären with g is remarkable; so too OIc. gerþ, 'yeast' (but E. yeast).

Garn, n., 'yarn, thread, net, snare,' from the equiv. MidHG. and OHG. garn, corresponding to AS. gearn, E. yarn, OIc. garn, n., Du. guren; the common Teut. term for 'yarn' (Goth. *garn, n.); the meaning 'net' was attached to **Garn**, even in the OHG. and MidHG. period, but it never obtained in E. and Scand. We might assume a root gar with some such meaning as 'to turn,' but it is not authenticated. Earlier Teut. has a series of terms corresponding in sound with **Garn** and meaning 'entrails'; comp. OIc. gǫrn (plur. garner), f., 'gut, intestines, entrails,' OHG. mittigarni, mittilagurni, n., 'fat found in the middle of the entrails, arvina,' AS. micgern (cg for dg; comp. AS. orceard, E. orchard, for ortgeard), 'arvina.' These words have been connected with Lith. żarná, f., 'gut,' and Sans. hirá, f., 'gut,' though the latter may be allied to Lat. hīra, f., 'gut,' and hilla for hirla; likewise Lat. haru- in haru-spex, 'one who examines the entrails, soothsayer,' and hariolus, 'soothsayer,' contain the Aryan root ghar. Perhaps—and nothing further can be said—all the words discussed above are based on a Teut. root ghar, 'to turn.'

garſtig, adj., 'filthy, foul, obscene,' an extended form of the late MidHG. garst, adj., 'rancid, tasting "high"'; comp. Du. garstig, 'insipid, rank, rotten'; akin to OIc. gerstr, 'morose' (in appearance). Allied to Lat. fastidium, 'disgust, aversion'?. The latter probably represented *farstidium, like tostus for *torstus, from torreo; Lat. f initially corresponds to Teut. g. See under **Gaſſe** (Lat. fel). But it might perhaps be also connected with Lat. horridus for *ghorsidus.

Garten, m., from the equiv. MidHG. garte, OHG. garto, m., 'garden'; corresponding to OSax. gurdo, OFris. garda, m., 'garden'; Goth. garda, m., 'stable.' Akin to the strong nouns—Goth. gards, m., 'court, house, family'; OIc. garðr, m., 'enclosure, hedge, house, farm,' OHG. gart, m., 'circle, choral dance,' AS. geard (E. yard), 'enclosure, garden' (E. gard-n was borrowed in MidE. from OFr. gardin, jardin, which is of Ger. origin). 'Enclosing,' and 'the enclosed space' are the fundamental ideas of the whole class, which might thus be connected with **gürten**, Teut. root gerd, if the correspondences in the cognate languages did not prove that '**Garten**' is a pre-Teut., perhaps a common West Aryan form, which cannot belong to a specifically Teut. root. But HG. **Garten** is most closely connected with Lat. hortus, 'garden,' Gr. χόρτος, 'enclosure, yard, farmyard, pasture, hay, grass,' OIr. gort, 'cornfield,' also Lat. co-hors, -tis, f., 'courtyard for cattle and fowls'; if the Teut. word is allied to these, the d of the Goth. and Sax. words is derived from Aryan t, i.e. Goth. garda is based on Aryan ghortó- (not ghórto- from χόρτο-). On the other hand, **Garten** may be connected with Slav. and Lith. words, which, however, assume that Goth. and Sax. d originated in Aryan dh; OSlov. gradŭ, m., 'enclosure, citadel, town' (as nu enclosed place; Lith. gàrdas, 'fold'). It is possible that in the Teut. class two words, different in sound but allied in meaning, have been combined; but the Slav. words were more probably borrowed from Teut. Comp. **Zaun**.

Gas, n., 'gas,' a word coined by the Du. chemist, Von Helmont, of Brussels (died 1644 A.D.); comp. Du. gas.

Gaſſe, f., 'lane, road, row,' from MidHG. gazze, OHG. gazza, f., prop. (as even yet in UpG.) 'street'; corresponding to Goth. gatwō, f., 'lane, street,' OIc. gata (accus. gǫtu), 'way, street, path.' From the Scand. word E. gate, 'way,' is derived. Properly speaking, the word is unknown to the LG. languages. Whether **Gaſſe** is allied to AS. geat, E. (Scotch), gate, gait (see **Gatter**), OSax. and Du. gat, n., 'hole, cavern,' OIc. gat, n., 'hole,' and is derived from a prim. meaning, 'inlet, opening'— **Gaſſe**, lit. 'furnished with an entrance, a gate,' on account of the suffix -wôn?—cannot be definitely decided; in any case, it is impossible to connect **Gaſſe** with **gehen**, since the latter is based upon a root *i* (Lat. *ire*, Gr. *lévai*).

Gaſt, m., 'guest, visitor; wight; sailor,' from MidHG. and OHG. *gast* (plur. *geste*, *gesti*), m., 'stranger, guest'; common, in the same sense, to Teut.; comp. Goth. *gasts* (plur. *gasteis*), m. (comp. *gastigôds*, 'hospitable'), OIc. *gestr*, 'guest (uninvited),' AS. *gyst*, *giest*, m., E. *guest*, Du. and OSax. *gast*. Teut. *gastiz*, m., 'stranger, unbidden or chance guest from some foreign part,' from pre-Teut. *ghostis*, which left derivatives in Lat. and Slav.; Lat. *hostis*, 'enemy,' prop. 'foreigner, stranger,' OSlov. *gostĭ*, m., 'guest'; with Lat. *hostis*, 'foreigner,' *hospes* (prop. **hosti-potis*, 'host'?), might also be connected. It is more than questionable whether West Aryan *ghosti-s*, 'stranger,' is prop. 'eater, devourer,' and belongs to the Sans. root *ghas*, 'to eat.' It is worthy of notice in how many ways Teutons and Romans have transformed the idea underlying the old inherited word for 'stranger'; the Roman regards him as an enemy, among the Teutons he enjoys the greatest privileges—a fine confirmation of Tacitus' account in the *Germania*. This evolution of meaning would be still more remarkable if the view were correct that Lat. *hostis*, 'stranger,' is related to Lat. *hostia*, 'victim' (stranger = 'one to be sacrificed'?); this collocation is alluring, but very uncertain.

gäten, jäten, vb., 'to weed,' from the equiv. MidHG. *jëten*, *gëten*, OHG. *jëtan*, *gëtan*; akin to OHG. *jetto*, m., 'weed, darnel.' Perhaps Gr. ζητέω, 'I seek,' is allied, if the Aryan root is *yët*.

gätlich, adj., 'suitable, convenient,' an essentially MidG. and LG. word; derived from a parallel Goth. form **gada-*, to which OHG. *gi-gât*, adj., 'suitable, agreeing with,' also points; comp. **Gatte**, gut; so too OSlov. *godŭ*, 'favourable time,' Lith. *gadas*, 'stipulation,' and Du. *gadelijk*, 'reconcilable.'

Gatte, m., 'spouse, consort, husband,' from MidHG. *gate* (also *gegate*), m., 'equal associate, one's equals, husband'; comp. Du. *gade*, 'husband.' The last meaning is rare in the MidHG. period, and first prevailed over the others in the last century; it is a specialisation of the idea 'belonging to one another'; comp. OSax. *gigado*, 'one's equals,' AS. *gegada*, 'companion'; also Goth. *gadiliggs*, 'relative,' AS. *gædeling*, 'member of the same tribe,' OHG. *gatuling*, 'cousin,' OSax. *gaduling*, 'countryman, member of the same tribe.' ModHG. *gatten* (ſich gatten), vb., is from MidHG. *gaten*, 'to come together, agree'; MidHG. (essentially MidG.) *gater*, 'together,' Du. *te gader*, AS. *geador* and *tôgædere*. E. *together*; AS. *gadrian*. E. *to gather* (Du. *vergaderen*, 'to assemble'); OHG. *geti-lôs*, MidHG. *gete-lôs*, adj., 'wanton, dissolute,' lit. 'free from the restraining bond.' The ideas of 'belonging to one another' and of 'suiti g' are seen in all the cognates of gut.

Gatter, n., 'railing, lattice, rudder,' from MidHG. *gater*, m., n., 'railing, lattice' (as a gate or fence), OHG. *gataro*, m., 'railing.' If the latter represents Teut. *ga-doro*, the word would be a compound of *ga* (see ge) and Thor (Goth. *daúr*). On the other hand, it is possibly allied to AS. *geat*, E. *gate*.

Gau, m., from the equiv. MidHG. *göu*, *gou*, n., OHG. *gewi*, *gouwi*, n., 'district.' According to Goth. *gawi* (*gaujis*), n., 'scenery, country,' we might have expected OHG. *gewi* (*gouwes*), MidHG. *göu* (*gouwes*), since *j* after *au* becomes *w* without producing modification (comp. Frau). Even now Gäu, nen., is found in Bav., Suab., and Swiss, but in the sense of 'country' opposed to town. The word is unknown to Scand., and also to Sax. and E., in which Gau, as the second part of a compound name applied to a district, is met with only in the very earliest period; comp. *e.g.* AS. *ælge*, 'district of eels,' OLG. *Pathergô*, 'Pader district' (around Paderborn). The ModHG. word first obtained currency again in the last century as a result of the study of OGer. (see Hert). No tenable root has yet been found.

Gauch, m., 'simpleton, gawk, crow, owl, cuckoo' (as stupid birds), from MidHG. *gouch*, m., 'dolt, fool, simpleton,' prop. 'cuckoo,' OHG. *gouh*, 'cuckoo'; corresponding to AS. *géac*, OIc. *gaukr* (whence Scotch *gowk*), 'cuckoo.' Is *k* a suffix as in AS. *hafoc*, 'hawk,' and Goth. *ahaks*, 'pigeon'? OHG. *gouh*, Goth. **gauks*, cannot, however, be allied to Lat. *cuculus*, Sans. *kôkila-s*, 'cuckoo,' since Teut. *g* initially cannot represent Lat. and Sans. *k*. Further Gauch is the OTeut. word for the later term Rudud.

Gaudieb, m., formed from the equiv. LG. *gaudeef*, Du. *gauwdief*, prop. 'sharp, cunning thief' (from *gauw*, 'quick, cunning,' see jäh), then generally 'sharper.'

Gauckler, m., 'buffoon, juggler, impostor,' from MidHG. *goukelœre*, OHG. *goukaldri, gouggaldri* (k from *gg*, see *Hafe*), 'magician, conjuror'; from MidHG. *goukeln*, OHG. *goukolôn, gouggolôn*, 'to deal in magic, play the fool.' Apparently allied to OHG. *gougarôn*, MidHG. *gougern*, 'to roam about,' also to MidHG. *gogeln*, 'to act without restraint, flutter about,' *gogel*, adj., 'unrestrained, exuberant,' *giege*, m., 'fool, dupe'; Du. *goochelaar*, 'buffoon.' The cognates point to a Teut. root *gug, geug, gung*, 'to move here and there in a curious fashion like a clown or conjuror'? Considering the numerous correspondences, it cannot be maintained that Gaukler was derived from Lat. *joculari*, or from Gr. καυκίον, 'small dish or bowl'; both these explanations are opposed by the phonetic relations of the words; in the case of the Gr. term there is the further difficulty that we do not know how it was borrowed, and also the fact that no verb 'to juggle' occurs in Gr.

Gaul, m., 'steed, nag,' from MidHG. *gûl*, m., 'boar, male animal (generally)'; only at a late period and rarely 'nag,' which meaning becomes prominent in the 15th cent.; for a 'sorry jade' *runzît* is used in MidHG.; Du. *guil*, f., 'a mare that does not yet bear.' The word is not known to the other dialects; its origin is obscure.

Gaumen, m., 'palate, taste,' from MidHG. *goume, guome*, OHG. *goumo* (*giumo*?), *guomo*, m., 'palate, throat, jaw'; corresponding to AS. *gôma*, m., 'palate,' E. *gums* (probably from AS. *gumma, since, moreover, there are numerous forms in earlier ModHG. which point to an OHG. *gummo, 'palate'); OIc. *gómr*, m., 'palate'; Goth. *gaumô, *gômô, n., are wanting. Allied to Lith. *gomyris*, 'palate.' The relation of the vowels of the stem (OHG. and MidHG. *ou* and *uo*, AS. and Scand. *ô*) is obscure; see Bute. Some etymologists connect the word with a Teut. root *gau* (Gr. χαυ (in χαῦνος, 'gasping, loose,' χάος, 'chasm,' for χάϝος).

Gauner, earlier Jauner, m., 'sharper, knave,' does not occur till the beginning of the last century; in the 15th and 16th cents. the professional swindlers at cards were called Jener, from the slang *jenen*, 'to play,' the ultimate source of which is said to be Hebr. *jáná*, 'to cheat.'

ge-, a proclitic prefix, from MidHG. *ge-*, OHG. *gi*, *ga-* (an accented prefix *ga-* in noun compounds is very rare in OHG. and MidHG.); the prim. idea is 'collectivity, completeness'; comp. Goth. *ga-*, AS. *ge-* (in E. *i* only in *handiwork, handicraft*, AS. *hondgeweorc, hondgecræft*; comp. also E. *enough*, from AS. *genôh*, under *genug*). The prefix is probably allied to Lat. *con-; cum;* comp. geben, glauben, gleich, Glied. &c.

gebären, vb., from the equiv. MidHG. *gëbern*, OHG. *giberan*, vb., 'to give birth to'; corresponding to Goth. *gabaíran* (also *baíran*), 'to give birth to, produce,' AS. *gebëran, bëran*, str. vb., 'to give birth to,' E. *to bear;* in Scand. the compounds with *ga-* are wanting, the simple vb. *bera*, 'to give birth to' being used. See Bahre; where proofs are given of the antiquity of the verbal stem *ber*, pre-Teut. *bher*, within the Aryan group; in Ind. the root *bhr, bhar*, may mean 'to bear offspring' as well as 'to bear' generally; comp. Lat. *fertilis*, from Lat. *fero;* in OIr. the substantives *combairt* and *brith*, corresponding to Geburt, 'birth,' manifest the same specialisation. See Geburt.

Gebärde, Geberde, f., 'bearing, gesture,' from MidHG. *gebærde*, f., 'conduct, appearance, manner,' OHG. *gibârida*, f., from MidHG. *gebâren*, OHG. *gibârên, -ôn;* corresponding to AS. *gebǽran*, 'to conduct oneself,' *gebǽre, gebǽrn*, 'conduct'; from the root *ber* in Bahre, gebären.

geben, vb., 'to give, present, render, yield,' from the equiv. MidHG. *gëben*, OHG. *gëban;* common to Teut. in the same sense; comp. Goth. *giban*, AS. *gifan*, E. *to give*, Du. *geven*, OIc. *gefa*. Comp. Gabe, Gift. Akin to OIr. *gabim*, 'I take,' Lith. *gabénti*, 'to bring, convey to,' *gobinti*, 'to cause to bring'?

Gebet, n., 'prayer,' from the equiv. MidHG. *gebët*, OHG. *gibët*, n. (AS. and OSax. *gebëd*, n., 'prayer'); allied to beten, bitten.

Gebiet, n., 'dominion, jurisdiction, territory, sphere,' from MidHG. *gebiet*, n., 'territory, jurisdiction, order'; allied to gebieten, bieten.

Gebirge, n., from the equiv. MidHG. *gebirge*, OHG. *gibirgi*, n., 'range (of mountains),' a specifically HG. collective form allied to Berg.

Gebresten, n., 'defect, infirmity, grief,' an inf. used as a noun; from MidHG. *ge-brësten*. See bersten.

Gebühr, Gebür, f., 'duty, propriety, dues, fees,' allied to gebühren, MidHG.

gebüren, OHG. *giburien*, wk. vb., 'to occur, happen, fall to one's lot, devolve on by law, be due'; corresponding to OSax. *giburian*, AS. *gebyrian*, OIc. *byrja*, 'to be suitable, becoming, fit'; Goth. **gabaúrjan*, wk. vb., may be inferred from *gabaurjaba*, adv., 'willingly' (lit. 'in a fitting manner'?), and *gabaurjôþus*, m., 'pleasure.' The whole class is probably connected with the root *ber* 'to carry'; comp. LG. büßren, 'to raise aloft,' see empor; hence OHG. *buri dih*, 'go (thou),' lit. 'raise thyself,' *giburita*, 'pervenit'; *burien*, *büren*, also 'to come to pass.' See Bahre, Börde.

Geburt, f., from the equiv. MidHG. *geburt*, OHG. *giburt*, f., 'birth.' Comp. Goth. *gabaurþs*, f., 'birth,' also 'lineage, native town,' OSax. *giburd*, f., AS. *gebyrd*, f., 'birth, rank, dignity,' E. *birth*, OIc. *burþr*, m., 'birth, embryo'; in form it points to Aryan and Sans. *bhṛtí-s*, and both in form and meaning it corresponds to OIr. *brith*, 'birth'; Sans. *bhṛtí-s*, f., 'bearing, nursing, maintenance.' With the simple Teut. *beran*, 'to give birth to,' is connected an O'Teut. neut. subst. *barna-*, 'child' (lit. 'that which is born'), formed from the old *no-*partic. Comp. OIc. *barn*, AS. *bearn*, OSax., OHG., and MHG. *barn*, 'child, son.'

Geck, m., 'fool, fop, buffoon,' orig. MidHG. (and LG.), in which *gëc*, *gëcke*, m., 'silly fellow, fool, droll fellow,' occurs even in the MidHG. period; not allied to MidHG. *giege*, 'fool,' mentioned under gaufeln. Comp. Du. *gek*, m., Dan. *gjæk*, 'fool,' Ic. *gikkr*, 'crafty, coarse person.'

Gedächtnis, n., 'memory, recollection, memorial,' allied to gebenfen, benfen.—**Gedanke**, m., 'thought, idea,' from MidHG. *gedanc(k)*, OHG. *gedank*, m., OSax. *githanko*, m., 'thought,' AS. *geþonc*; allied to benfen.

gedeihen, vb., 'to thrive, prosper,' from the equiv. MidHG. *gedîhen*, OHG. *gidîhan*, str. vb.; Goth. *gaþeihan*, AS. *geþeón* (contracted from *geþíhan*), 'to thrive'; the old AS. form points to the fact that the verbal stem was orig. nasalised; ñ before h is everywhere suppressed in Teut., thus *þhan* for *þiñhan*. The corresponding factitive **þangjan* remained in OSax., where *thengian* means 'to complete'; on the suppression of the nasal the *e* gradation passed into the *i* gradation in Goth. and HG. The simple form *þeihan*, 'to thrive,' is still known in Goth. On account of its meaning, gebeißen (root *þenh*, pre-Teut. *tenk*, *tek*, in Lith. *tenkù*, *tèkti*, 'I have enough,' as

well as in Ir. *tocad*, W. *tynged*, 'fortune,' from the prim. form *tongeto-*) cannot be connected with the root *τεκ* in *τέκνον* (see Degen).—**gediegen**, adj., 'solid, pure, concise, pithy,' from MidHG. *gedigen*, adj., 'adult, firm, hard, clear, pure,' OHG. *gidigan*, adj., 'aged, advanced in years, earnest, pure, chaste'; prop. a partic. of *gidîhan* (g by a grammatical change is the necessary form of h in the partic.); AS. preserves the older participial form of the *e*-gradation, *gepungen*, 'complete,' so too OSax. *thungan*.

Geduld, f., 'patience, forbearance,' from the equiv. MidHG. *gedult*, OHG. *gedult*, f.; allied to bulben.

gedunsen, adj., 'bloated, puffed up,' partic. of a lost str. vb. which is retained in ModHG. dialects (Hess. *dinsen*, 'to draw'); comp. MidHG. *dinsen*, 'to draw, tear, extend,' OHG. *dinsan*; also Goth. **þinsan*, *atþinsan*, 'to draw.' The Teut. root *þens*, pre-Teut. *tens*, corresponds to the Sans. root *tans*, 'to draw,' Lith. *tęstí*, 'to draw, stretch.' The root *tens* seems an extension of the root *ten* appearing in behnen.

Gefahr, f., 'danger, risk, jeopardy,' ModHG. only, for MidHG. *vâre*, OHG. *fâra*, f., 'ambush, deceit, hazard, danger'; AS. *fǽr*, f., 'ambush, unforeseen danger, fright,' E. *fear*, OSax. *fâr*, 'ambush'; Goth. **fêra*, 'ambush,' follows from *fêrja*, m., 'waylayer.' Scand. *fâr*, n., has a somewhat different meaning, 'misfortune, distemper.' Allied to the root *fêr*, Aryan *pêr*, which in Lat. *periculum*, Gr. *πεῖρα*, 'trial, cunning, deception,' furnishes cognate meanings.

Gefährte, m., 'companion, partner, mate,' from MidHG. *geverte*, OHG. *giferto* (**gafartjo*), 'escort,' lit. 'fellow-traveller'; allied to Fahrt.

gefallen, vb., 'to suit, please,' from MidHG. *gevallen*, OHG. *gifallan*, str. vb., 'to happen, fall to one's lot, please,' in Mid HG. always with the complement 'wohl' (well) or 'übel' (ill); probably an expression derived from the OTeut. warlike custom of dividing booty (comp. Hunb) by means of dice; es gefällt mir wohl, 'I am well pleased with it,' lit. das Los fällt gut für mich, 'that was a lucky throw for me' (a similar history is also connected with ModHG. schenfen, which furnishes evidence respecting the Teut. drinking customs). Note too that in ModHG. terms relating to card-playing have been similarly used.

Comp. Eau (lit. 'ace (of cards),' then generally 'good fortune') and $unb.

Gefängnis, n., 'prison,' from MidHG. *gevencnisse*, f., n., 'imprisonment'; allied to fangen.

Gefäß, n., 'vessel, receptacle,' from the equiv. MidHG. *gevæʒe*, n. (OHG. *givāʒʒi*, n., 'transport'). Goth. *gaféti*, n., is wanting; it would probably be connected with Goth. *fêtjan*, 'to adorn' (AS. *fæted*, partic., 'adorned'), and also more remotely with Faß.

Gefieder, n., 'feathers, plumage, fowls,' from the equiv. MidHG. *gevidere*, OHG. *gefidari*, n.; collective of Feder.

Gefilde, n., 'fields, plain,' from the equiv. MidHG. *gevilde*, OHG. *gefildi*, n.; collective of Feld.

geflissen, partic. of a lost vb. fleißen, 'assiduous, busy.' See Fleiß.

gegen, prep., 'against, opposite to, in presence of, in comparison with,' from Mid HG. *gegen*, OHG. *gegin, gagan*, 'against' (in OHG. and MidHG. almost always with a dat.); allied to the MidHG. adv. *gegene*, OHG. *gegini, gagani*, 'towards'; corresponding to AS. *geán, ongeán*, 'against,' E. *again*; OSax. *gegin* and OIc. *gagn*, 'against,' appear only in compounds; in Goth. a corresponding word is wanting. Of obscure origin.—**Gegend**, 'region, neighbourhood,' from the equiv. MidHG. (post-classical) *gegenôte, gegende*, f., which, with the variant *gegene*, f., are imitations of Fr. *contrée* (Ital. *contrada*), 'country,' allied to Lat. *contra*. —**Gegenwart**, 'presence, present time,' from MidHG. *gegenwart*, OHG. *geginwarti*, f., abstract of OHG. *gaganwart*, 'present,' whence MidHG. *gegenwertec*, ModHG. *gegenwärtig*, 'present.' See the adj. suffix -wärts.

gehaben, vb. in sich gehaben, 'to fare, be (in health), behave,' from MidHG. *sich gehaben*, OHG. *sih gihabén*, 'to hold, be (in health)'; allied to haben.

Gehege, n., 'hedge, enclosure, precinct,' from MidHG. *gehege*, n., 'enclosure'; allied to Hag, hegen.

geheim, adj., 'private, secret, hidden, mysterious,' from the equiv. late MidHG. *geheim*, which, with heimlich, means lit. 'belonging to the house.'

gehen, vb., 'to go, walk, go on well, succeed,' from the equiv. MidHG. and OHG. *gên, gân* (some of the inflected forms supplied by the stem *gang*; see Gang); comp. AS. *gân* (stem *ga-*, from *gai*), E. *to go*, OSwed. and ODan. *ga*, 'to go.' The assumed root *ghai-*, meaning 'to go,' cannot be positively authenticated beyond the Teut. group (yet comp. Lett. *gāju*, 'I went'?). The remarkable facts that this Teut. *gaí*, 'to go,' has no primit. noun derivatives in Teut., that it has supplanted the root *i*, which is widely diffused in Aryan, but almost obsolete in Teut. (retained, however, in the Goth. aorist *iddja*, AS. *éode*), and that like the latter it is conjugated like verbs in *mi*—all these lead to the supposition that the assumed Goth. **gaim*, **gais*, **gaiþ* are contracted from the verbal particle *ga* (see ge-) and the old inherited *îmi, îsi, îti* (comp. Gr. εἶμι, Sans. *émi, ési, éti*), 'to go.' From this explanation it follows that gehen is fundamentally identical with Lat. *îre*, Gr. ἰέναι, Sans. root *i*, Lith. *eiti*, OSlov. *iti*, 'to go' (see eilen). For a similar blending of a verbal particle and an old vb. comp. folgen, fressen.

geheuer, adj., 'secure against anything uncanny,' from MidHG. *gehiure*, 'gentle, graceful, free from anything uncanny'; comp. OHG. and OSax. *unhiuri*, 'dreadful, terrible,' AS. *hŷre* (*heóre*), 'friendly, mild,' OIc. *hýrr*, 'mild.' Indubitable cognates in the non-Teut. languages are wanting; perhaps Sans. *çakrá*, 'strong' (of deities) is allied, so that OHG. *-hiuri* would represent *heguro-* (Aryan *keqró-*).

Gehren, m. (dial.), 'lap,' from MidHG. *gêre, yêro*, m., 'wedge-shaped piece of stuff or land, lap'; corresponding to AS. *gára*, 'piece of stuff,' E. *gore*, OIc. *geire*, in the same sense; a deriv. of Ger. For the evolution of meaning comp. Franse, Schoß.—From the OG. word the Rom. cognates, Fr. *giron* and Ital. *gherone*, 'lap, train (of a dress),' are derived.

Geier, m., 'vulture, carrion kite,' from the equiv. MidHG. and OHG. *gîr*, m., akin to LG. *gier*. On account of the early appearance of the G. word we cannot assume that it was borrowed from the Rom. cognates, Ital. *girfalco*, Fr. *gerfaut* (whence MidHG. *gir-valke* is derived), or from Lat.-Gr. *gyrare*, 'to wheel round.' The connection between OHG. *gîr* with OHG. *gîri*, MidHG. *gîre* (geier still occurs in ModHG. dials.), 'greedy, covetous,' and the Teut. root *gîr*, 'to covet,' presents no difficulty. Geier is lit. 'the greedy bird.' See gern, Gier.

Geifer, m., 'slaver, drivel, wrath,' from the equiv. late MidHG. *geifer*, m. (15th cent.), whence also *geifern*, ModHG. geifern. Origin obscure.

Geige, f., 'fiddle, violin,' from the equiv. early MidHG. *gīge,* f.; corresponding to MidDu. *ghighe,* OIc. *gīgja*; in OHG. *fidula,* E. *fiddle*; see Fibel. The Teut. word, like Harfe, found its way into Rom.; comp. Ital. *giga,* Fr. *gigue* (whence further E. *jig*). There is no suspicion that Mid HG. *gīge* was borrowed; it is, however, scarcely allied primit. (pre-Teut. *ghīkā*) to OSlov. *žica,* 'thread' (akin to Lith. *gijà,* 'thread'?).

geil, adj., 'rank, wanton, obscene, lewd,' from MidHG. and OHG. *geil,* 'of savage strength, wanton, exuberant, merry, joyous'; for the change of meaning on the transition from MidHG. to ModHG. comp. Schimpf. The primary meaning, 'unrestrained, joyous,' follows from Goth. *gailjan,* 'to rejoice'; comp. OSax. *gēl,* Du. *geil,* AS. *gâl.* To the Teut. cognates Lith. *gailùs,* 'passionate, furious, sharp, painful, sympathetic,' and *gailéti-s,* 'to injure'; OSlov. *zělŭ* (from *gailo*), 'violent,' adv. *zelo,* 'very.' In the compound Biebergeil appears the MidHG. noun *geil, geile,* 'testicle.'

Geisel (1.), m. and f., 'hostage,' from MidHG. *gīsel,* OHG. *gīsal,* m., n., 'prisoner of war, person held in security'; corresponding to AS. *gīsel,* OIc. *gīsl,* m. To connect it with Geisel (2.), f., as if 'hostage' were lit. 'one who is scourged,' is impossible. It is, probably, most closely allied to the equiv. OIr. *giall* (for **gīsal*).

Geisel (2.), f., 'scourge, whip,' from the equiv. MidHG. *geisel,* OHG. *geisala, geisla,* f.; akin to OIc. *geisl, geisle,* m., 'pole used by persons walking in snow-shoes.' The stem *gais-* is connected with the OTeut. term *gaiza-,* 'spear' (see Ger). Hence 'pole, staff,' must be accepted as the prim. meaning; the second component is Goth. *walus,* 'staff,' so that OHG. *geis-ala* stands for **geis-walu,* just as OHG. *wurzala* for AS. *wyrt-walu* (see under Wurzel).

Geist, m., 'spirit, genius, spectre,' from MidHG. and OHG. *geist,* m., 'spirit (in contrast to body), supernatural being'; corresponding to OSax. *gēst,* Du. *geist,* AS. *gǽst (gést),* E. *ghost*; common to Teut. in the same sense, but in Goth. *ahma* (see achten). The prim. meaning of the word ('agitation'?) is not quite certain; yet OIc. *geisa,* 'to rage' (of fire, passion), and Goth. *us-gaisjan,* 'to enrage,' seem to be allied. Respecting the dental suffix of the Teut. Geist (pre-Teut. *ghaisdos*), note the Sans. root *hīd* (from *hizd*), 'to get angry,' *hḗḍas,* n., 'anger,' to which E. *aghast* also corresponds.

Geiß, f., 'goat, roe,' from the equiv. Mid HG. and OHG. *geiz,* f.; corresponding to Goth. *gaits,* OIc. *geit,* AS. *gát,* E. *goat,* Du. *geit*; also a dimin. Goth. *gaitein,* AS. *gǽten,* OHG. *geizzīn,* n., 'kid' (see Schwein). Primit. allied to Lat. *haedus* from older *ghaido-s* (see Ritze and Ziege). In common with Slav., OTeut. has a different word for Ziege; comp. MidDu. *ho-kijn,* AS. *hécen,* 'kid,' akin to OSlov. *koza,* 'goat.'

Geiz, m., 'avarice,' allied to *grīzen,* Mid HG. *gītsen (gīzen),* beside which MidHG. *gīten,* 'to be greedy, covetous, or avaricious' occurs; comp. AS. *gītsian,* 'to be covetous.' The term for Geiz in MidHG. and OHG. was *gīt,* 'greediness, covetousness, avarice,' for *geizig,* MidHG. *gītec,* OHG. *gītag,* 'greedy, covetous, avaricious'; respecting the derivation of Geiz from *grīzen,* see Ärger, hänseln. Akin to Goth. *gaidw,* n., 'want.' With the Teut. root *gaid, gīd* (Aryan *ghaidh*), are connected Lith. *geidziù (geisti),* 'to desire,' OSlov. *židą, ždati,* 'to expect.'

Gekröse, n., 'giblets; frill, ruffle,' from MidHG. *gekrœse,* n., 'the small intestine,' also the variant *krœse,* OHG. **chrōsi,* akin to Du. *kroes, kroost,* 'giblets of ducks and geese.' All the cognates are probably connected with *kraus*.

Gelage, n., 'feast, banquet, drinking bout,' first occurs in early ModHG., allied to legen. Scarcely derived from the ancient Gelage (banquets); but just as Goth. *gabaur* is lit. 'that which is laid together,' and then 'picnic, feasting' (from *bairan,* 'to carry,' see Bahre), so Gelage is lit. 'that which is laid together,' and then 'feasting'; comp. zechen.

Geländer, n., 'railing, banister, from the equiv. late MidHG. *gelender* (15th cent.), allied to MidHG. *lander,* 'stake, fence,' which may be regarded as a nasalised variant of Latte (Teut. *laþ-*).

Gelaß, m. and n., 'relics, heritage,' from MidHG. *gelâȝe,* n., 'settlement, mode of settlement,' allied to *g-lâzen,* 'to settle.'

gelb, adj., 'yellow,' from the equiv. MidHG. *gēl,* OHG. *gēlo* (gen. *gēlwes*); corresponding to OSax. *gēlo,* Du. *geel,* AS. *geolo,* E. *yellow* (OIc. *gulr*). The common West Teut. *gelwa-,* from pre-Teut. *ghelwo-,* is primit. allied to Lat. *helvus,* 'greyish yellow'; the Aryan root *ghel* appears also in

Gr. χλω-ρόs, χλᾱ-ρόs, 'green, yellow,' χλόη, 'green objects,' OSlov. zelenŭ, 'yellow, green,' Lith. żėlias, 'green' (żėlti, 'to grow green'), Sans. hari, 'yellowish.' Akin also to Galle and Gelb.

Geld, n., 'money, coin, cash,' from MidHG. and OHG. gëlt (t; the d first occurs in ModHG.), n., m., 'recompense, compensation, revenue, income, paying, payment, money,' Du. geld, 'money.' 'Means for paying, coin,' is the latest sense of the words quoted (comp. Goth. gild, 'tax, interest'); it is wanting in the corresponding words of the other dialects; in Goth. the term is faihu (see Vieh), and skatts (see Schatz), AS. feoh, E. money. On the other hand, AS. gild signifies 'recompense, compensation, sacrifice.' See gelten.

gelegen, adj., 'situated, opportune, seasonable,' and adv.; from MidHG. gelëgen, adj. 'neighbouring, at hand, suitable,' OHG. gilëgan, 'nearest, related'; partic. of giligan, MidHG. geligen.—**Gelegenheit**, f., 'opportunity, occasion,' from MidHG. gelëgenheit, 'situation of an affair, condition or nature of things.'—**gelegentlich**, adj., 'occasional, incidental' (and adv.), from MidHG. gelëgenlich, with an inserted t.

Gelenk, n., 'joint, articulation, wrist, link,' from MidHG. gelenke, n., 'waist, bend, bow,' akin to ModHG. gelent, gelentig, adj. formed from MidHG. gelenke, 'pliant, skilful' (see lenken). While the MidHG. gelenke, as a collective of MidHG. lanke, signifies the 'pliable narrow part of the body between the hips and breast,' and hence, as it were, the joint of the entire body, the word in ModHG. is applied to each limb; akin to OHG. lancha, hlancha, 'hip, loins' (whence also the Romance cognates—Ital. fianco, from which ModHG. Flanke is borrowed), likewise OIc. hlekkr, 'link of a chain.'

Gelichter, n., 'likeness, cast, stamp,' lit. 'class of people of like manners'; in this sense glihter and its derivatives occur even in late MidHG. (MidG.); derived from MidHG. gelich, gleich (see the latter). Yet the UpG. form glifter points perhaps to a blending with another word, Goth. *gahliftrja, 'thief's accomplice' (akin to Goth. hlifan, 'to steal,' primit. allied to Gr. κλέπτω). For HG. ft, equiv. to LG. ht, see Sucht, ruchbar, Gerücht.

gelingen, vb., 'to prove successful,' from MidHG. gelingen, OHG. gilingan, str. vb., 'to be successful, prosper'; MidHG. also lingen, 'to prosper, advance, get on.' Allied to AS. lungre, 'quickly,' from pre-Teut. lughró-, to which the equiv. Gr. ἐλαφρόs also points; the Aryan root lengh (lngh) appears also in Sans. laṅgh, raṁh, 'to spring, get on.' See leicht.

gellen, vb., 'to yell,' from MidHG. gëllen, OHG. gëllan, str. vb., 'to sound loud, cry'; corresponding to Du. gillen, AS. gillan, OIc. gjalla, 'to resound'; allied to the Teut. root gel, gal, 'to resound.' Comp. Nachtigall.

geloben, vb., 'to promise, vow,' from the equiv. MidHG. geloben, OHG. gilobōn (akin to loben); lit. 'to assent, applaud.'

gelt (1.), particle. See gelten.

gelt (2.), adj., 'giving no milk, barren,' from the equiv. MidHG. and OHG. galt; corresponding to OIc. geldr, OSwed. galder, which have the same sense. They are connected perhaps with OHG. galza, MidHG. galze, OIc. gpltr, 'gelded pig' (E. dial., gilt, ilt). The stem on which it is based, gald, galt (from pre-Teut. ghal/t, ghaltn-), perhaps meant orig. 'to castrate'; comp. E. to geld, OIc. gelda, 'to geld'; akin to Goth. gilþa, 'sickle'?.

Gelte, f., 'pail, bucket, vessel,' from MidHG. gelt, OHG. gellita, f., 'vessel for liquids'; adopted in the OHG. period from MidLat. galëta, with which are also connected the Romance cognates—Fr. jale, 'pail,' Ital. galea, galeotta, Fr. galiasse, galion, applied to different kinds of ships. The ultimate source of the cognates is obscure.

gelten, vb., 'to be worth, pass current, prove effectual,' from MidHG. gëlten, OHG. gëltan, str. vb., 'to repay, pay, cost, be worth, requite, compensate'; comp. Goth. us-, fra-gildan, 'to requite' (akin to Goth. gild and gilstr, n., 'tax'), OIc. gja/da (OSwed., also gialla, from Teut. gelþan), 'to pay,' AS. gildan, E. to yield, Du. gelden, 'to be worth, cost,' OSax. geldan. The common Teut. stem gelþ, the þ of which is proved by OSwed. from pre-Teut. ghel-t, points to the fact that OSlov. žlédq, 'I pay, atone for,' was borrowed. The prim. meaning of the Teut. cognates is 'to make good, pay oversomething'; it seems to be specially applied to religious sacrifices; comp. AS. gild, OSax. gëld, 'sacrifice' (akin to Gr. τέλθοs, 'duty'?). See Geld, Gilde.—The particle gelt, which first occurs in early ModHG., is properly the subj. pres. of the vb. gelten.

Gelze, f., 'gelded sow,' from the equiv.

MidHG. gelze (galze), OHG. gelza (galza). See gelt.

Gemach, n., 'chamber, apartment; comfort, rest,' from MidHG. *gemach*, m., n., 'rest, comfort, ease, nursing, place where one is nursed, room,' OHG. *gimah(hh)*, 'ease, advantage'; the ModHG. meaning is not found until the classical period of MidHG.; the ModHG. adj. gemach, 'comfortable,' preserves the earlier meaning, MidHG. *gemach*, OHG. *gimah(hh)*, 'comfortable, suitable'; prop., 'suitable to one another' (comp. OIc. *makr*, 'suitable'; see machen). Akin to gemächlich, MidHG. *gemechlîch*, OHG. *gimahlîcho*, adv.

Gemächt, n., 'genitals; handiwork,' from MidHG. *gemaht* (plur., *gemęhte*), OHG. *gimaht*, f., 'testicles'; akin to ModHG. Macht (comp. Du. *gemacht*).

Gemahl, m. and n., 'consort, spouse,' from MidHG. *gemahele*, m., 'betrothed, husband,' and *gemahele*, f. (very rarely n., which is first found in Luther specially), 'betrothed, wife' (the fem. form Gemahlin is wanting in MidHG.); OHG. *gimahalo*, m., 'betrothed, husband,' *gimahala* (*gimála*), 'betrothed, wife.' Simply a G. form from a common Teut. subst. *mapla-* (whence *mahla-*), 'public assembly, negotiation'; comp. Goth. *mapl*, 'assembly, market' (akin to *mapljan*, 'to make a speech'), OIc. *mál*, 'speech' (*méla*, 'to make a speech'), AS. *męðel*, 'assembly' (*maðolian*, *mǽlan*, 'to make a speech'), OHG. *mahal*, 'assembly, contract, marriage contract.' Hence the subst. upon which the word is based has assumed in G. only, the special reference to the act of betrothal in the public assembly before the community.

gemäß, adv., 'conformably, proportionally, suitably,' from MidHG. *gemæze*, OHG. *gimâzzi*, adj., 'adapted'; akin to messen.

gemein, adj., 'common, public; mean, vulgar,' from MidHG. *gemeine*, OHG. *gimeini*, 'belonging to one another, in common, universal, belonging to the great body'; an adj. common to Teut.; comp. Goth. *gamains*, 'in common, joint, general, unholy,' AS. *gemǽne*, E. *mean*, Du. *gemeen*. The common Teut. *ga-maini-s* is primit. allied to the equiv. Lat. *com-mūnis* (for *con-moini-s*); comp. Lat. *ūnus* with Goth. *ains*, Aryan *oino-s*. Since 'in common' is the primary meaning of the class, Meineid (which see) cannot be very closely allied to its OTeut. cognates.

Gemſe, f., 'chamois,' from the equiv. MidHG. *gemeze*, *gamz*, OHG. *gamuz(*gamz*), m.; although a corresponding word is wanting in the other Teut. languages, there is no sufficient reason for regarding OHG. *gamiza, f., as borrowed (formed like OHG. *hiruz*, see Hirſch; AS. *ganot*, 'waterfowl'; MidHG. *krebez*, see Krebs). The Romance cognates (Ital. *camozza*, Fr. *chamois*) which are equiv. in sound tell rather in favour of their own foreign origin than that of the G. word (in Lat. the term was *rupicapra*). Perhaps Span. and Port. *gamo*, 'stag,' is based upon a Goth. *gama, allied to Gemſe (E. *game* has probably no connection with the word?).

Gemüll, see malmen; **Gemüſe**, see Mus; **gemut** and **Gemüt**, see Mut.

gen, prep., 'against, towards,' from the equiv. MidHG. *gen*, a variant of *gein*, *gegen*. See gegen.

genau, adj., 'accurate, precise, strict, parsimonious,' from late MidHG. (MidG.) *nouwe*, 'careful, exact,' akin to *nouwe*, *genouwe*, adv., 'scarcely'; comp. Du. *naauw*, 'narrow, exact, punctual.' Probably these cognates, in their Goth. form *ga-néws, are to be connected with Goth. *néhws*, HG. nahe. Others refer them to a root *nau*, 'to narrow,' in Not and its cognates.

gerehm, see angenehm.

geneſen, vb., 'to get well, recover,' from MidHG. *geneſen*, OHG. *ginësan*, str. vb., 'to be left alive, be healed, escape alive,' also 'to be delivered of a child'; corresponding to Goth. *ganisan*, 'to recover health, be rescued, saved,' AS. *genësan*, OSax. *ginësan*, 'to be rescued, be left alive'; also Du. *geuczen*, 'to heal, cure.' The Teut. root *nes*, with which nähren and its cognates are connected as factitives, corresponds to the Sans. root *nas*, 'to approach' in an affectionate manner, join,' and especially to Gr. νέομαι (root νεσ-), 'to come back,' and νόσ-τος, 'return home.' From Teut. are derived OSlov. *gonĭzęti* (*gonęti*), 'to be redeemed,' and *gonoziti*, 'to redeem,' allied to *gonoziteljĭ*, 'Saviour.' See nähren.

Genick, n., 'back of the neck, nape,' from the equiv. MidHG. *genic*, *genicke*, n.; akin to Nacken, AS. *hnecca*.

genießen, vb., 'to enjoy, partake of,' from the equiv. MidHG. *genießen*, OHG. *giniozan*, str. vb., with the variants Mid HG. *niezen*, OHG. *niozan*; corresponding to Goth. *niutan*, 'to take part in something,' *ganiutan*, 'to catch' (*nuta*, 'captor,

H

fisher'), OIc. *njóta*, 'to enjoy, derive joy from, have the use of,' AS. *neótan*, 'to take, use, enjoy,' Du. *genieten*, OSax. *niotan*, 'to enjoy.' The primary meaning of the Teut. root *nut*, found in str. verbs, was 'to get something for one's own use,' then 'to use or enjoy something, have the use of.' See Nuß, Nießnuß. Akin to the primit. allied Lith. *naudà*, 'use, produce,' *pa-nústu*, *-núdau*, *-nústi*, 'to long, yearn for.' — **Genosse**, m., 'comrade, companion, mate,' from the equiv. MidHG. *genóz*, OHG. *ginóz*, m.; corresponding to OSax. *genót*, AS. *geneát*, Du. *genoot*; lit. 'one who partakes of something with another,' comp. Geselle and Gesinde. — **Genossame**, f., from the equiv. MidHG. *genóz-same*, f., 'fellowship,' OHG. *ginóz-samî*, abstract of OHG. *ginozsam*, MidHG. *genóz-sam*, 'of equal birth or worth.'

genug, adj., 'enough, sufficient,' from the corresponding MidHG. *genuoc(g)*, OHG. *ginuog*; a common Teut. adj. with the Mod HG. meaning; comp. Goth. *ganôhs*, AS. *genôh*, E. *enough*, Du. *genoeg*, OSax. *ginôg*; a deriv. of an OTeut. pret.-pres. Goth. *ganah*, OHG. *ginah*, 'it suffices'; comp. Goth. *ganaúha*, 'sufficiency,' OHG. *ginuht*, MidHG. *genuht*, 'sufficiency.' On MidHG. *genuhtsam*, OHG. *ginuhtsam*, 'abundant, sufficient,' is based ModHG. *genugsam*. To the Teut. root *nŏh* (Aryan *nak*) preserved in these words some refer the Sans. root *naç*, 'to attain,' and Lat. *nancisci*.

Ger, m., 'spear,' formed from the equiv. MidHG. and OHG. *gêr*, m.; corresponding to OSax. *gêr*, AS. *gâr*, OIc. *geirr*. The *r* in the latter word must be based upon an *s*, otherwise the Scand. form would be *gârr*. Goth. *gaizu* may be inferred too from old proper names, such as Hariogaisus. The terms γαῖσος, γαῖσον, are also mentioned by Polybius, Diodorus, &c., as applied to the spear by the North Europ. barbarians. The word is genuinely Teut. (yet comp. also OIr. *gai*, from *gaiso*, 'spear'), and has the approximate meaning, as the allied Geißel shows, of 'shaft, rod (as a missile),' for which reason Gr. χαῖος, 'shepherd's staff,' and Sans. *héśas*, n., 'missile,' are perhaps cognate. The root is Sans. *hi*, 'to urge on,' with which AS. *gâd* and E. *goad* (from Aryan *ghai-tā*) are also connected. The OTeut. term was first used again in ModHG. as a borrowed word, though it continued to exist in the proper names Gerbert (OHG. *Gêr-braht*, lit. 'glittering with spears'), Gerhard (OHG. *Gêrhart*, 'spear-bold'), Gertrud (OHG. *Gêrtrût*). Comp. Gehren and Geisel.

gerad (1.), adv., 'even' (of numbers), from the equiv. MidHG. *gerat*, OHG. *girad*, 'even'; prop. 'equal in reckoning'; akin to Goth. *raþjô*, 'number,' *garaþjan*, 'to count.'

gerade (2.), adj., 'going in one direction, straight, upright,' from MidHG. *gerat*, 'alert, quick, skilful, recently grown up, straight and therefore long'; the primary meaning is 'nimble, rapid'; comp. OHG. *rado* (and *rato, hrato*), 'quick,' AS. *ræðe* (also *hræde*), 'quick,' Goth. *raþs*, 'easy.' Perhaps primit. allied to Rad, Lat. *rota*.

Gerät, n., 'tools, furniture, utensils,' from MidHG. *geræte*, OHG. *girâti*, n., 'equipment'; lit. 'consultation, precaution'; collective of Rat.

geraum, geräumig, see Raum.

Geräusch, n., 'entrails of slaughtered animals,' from the equiv. late MidHG. *ingeriusche*; origin obscure.

gerben, vb., 'to tan, curry, polish,' from MidHG. *gerwen* (*garwen*), wk. vb., 'to make ready, prepare, equip, dress, tan'; a deriv. of *gar* (see gar); OHG. *gariwen* (*garawen*), from *garwjan*, 'to make ready,' *lëdergarawo*, 'tanner.'

gerecht, adj., 'righteous, just, fit,' from MidHG. *gerëht*, 'straight, right, dexterous, skilful, fit, upright, innocent, just,' OHG. *girëht* (*grëht*), 'rectus, directus' (not yet 'justus'); corresponding to *garaihts*, 'upright'; in AS. *rihtwîs* (OHG. *rëhtwîs*), 'justus.' E. *righteous*. See recht.

Gerfalke, Gierfalke, m., 'gerfalcon,' from the equiv. MidHG. *gîr-*, *gërfalke*; from Rom. See Geier.

Gericht, n., 'judgment, tribunal, court, jurisdiction,' in its double sense even in MidHG. *gerihte*, n., 'tribunal, sentence, jurisdiction,' and 'prepared food'; OHG. *girihti*, n., only in the first sense; akin to recht.

gering, adj., 'petty, trifling,' prop. 'insignificant, easy,' from MidHG. *geringe*, 'light and quick, nimble,' *ringe*, 'easy, light, convenient, insignificant, slight, small,' OHG. *ringi, giringi*, 'light'; a specifically G. adj., wanting in the other Teut. dialects; origin obscure. The development of meaning from 'light' to 'slight' through the medium of 'easy' is similar to that of klein.

gern, adv., 'gladly, willingly, fain,' from the equiv. MidHG. *gërne*, OHG. *gërno*, adv., from the MidHG. and OHG. adj. *gërn;* to the latter correspond Goth. *gaírns* in *faíhugaírns,* 'avaricious' (comp. Goth. *gaírnjan,* 'to desire, long for, demand'), OIc. *gjarn,* 'eager,' AS. *georn,* zealous,' Du. *gaarne,* OSax. *gern.* Akin to OHG. and MidHG. *gër* (without the partic. suffix *n*), 'desiring, demanding,' as well as to begehren, Gier. The Teut. root *ger* (from Aryan *gher,* 'to demand violently,' was confused with a derivative form in *r* from a root *gī* (*ghī*), allied in meaning; see Gier, Geier. Whether the Sans. root *har-y,* 'to be fond of,' or Gr. χαίρω, or Oscan *heriest,* 'he will be willing,' is connected with the Aryan root *gher* is uncertain.

Gerfte, f., 'barley,' from the equiv. Mid HG. *gërste,* OHG. *gërsta,* f.; akin to Du. *gerst;* a specifically G. word, unknown to the other dialects; OSax. and AS. *grist,* E. *grist,* are not connected with it, but with OTeut. *grindan,* 'to grind' (equiv. to Lat. *frendere,* 'to gnash'?). In the remaining Teut. dialects the terms for Gerfte are Goth. *baris,* OIc. *bygg* (and *barr*), AS. *bere,* E. *barley.* OHG.*gërstu,*from pre-Teut.*ghŕzdā-,* corresponds only to the equiv. Lat. *hordeum* (from *horsdeum*, prim. form *ghŕzdéyo-*); Gr. κριθή, 'barley,' is scarcely a cognate. From an Aryan root *ghrs,* 'to stiffen' (Lat. *horrere* for *horsere*, Sans. *hŕš,* 'to bristle up'), some have inferred Gerfte to mean orig. 'the prickly plant' (on account of the prickly ears).

Gerte, f., from the equiv. MidHG. *gerte,* OHG. *gartia,* f., 'rod, twig, staff'; a derivative of OHG. and MidHG. *gart,* 'rod, staff, stick.' To the latter correspond Goth. *gazds* (comp. Hort, equiv. to Goth. *huzds*), 'stick,' and OIc. *gaddr* (E. *goad* and its equiv. AS. *gád* are not allied; see Ger). Probably Teut. *gazda-* (OHG. *gerta* would be *gazdjô*) is primit. allied to Lat. *hasta* (from Aryan *ghazdhá*), 'spear.'

Geruch, m., from the equiv. MidHG. *geruch,* m., 'scent, odour, fame'; akin to riechen.

Gerücht, n., 'rumour, report, reputation,' from MidHG. *gerüchte (geruofte),* n., 'calling, cry'; *cht* instead of *ft* (see rufen) is due to LG. influence, as in facht and berüchtigt.

geruhen, vb., 'to deign, condescend, be pleased,' corrupted by connection with Ruhe from the earlier ModHG. geruochen, MidHG. *geruochen,* OHG. *geruochan,* 'to care for, take into consideration' (MidHG. also 'to approve, grant'). Corresponding to ASax. *rôkian,* AS. *récan* (and *réccan,* whence E. *to reck*), OIc. *rœkja,* 'to take care of.' The Teut. root, *rak, rôk,* appears also in OHG. *rahha,* 'account, speech'; so too in rechnen. In the non-Teut. languages no root *rāg* in a cognate sense has yet been found.

Gerüft, n., 'scaffold,' from MidHG. *gerüste,* n., 'contrivance, preparation, erection, frame, scaffold,' OHG. *girusti;* akin to rüften, *rusten, hrustjan.*

gefamt, adj., 'joint, collective,' from the equiv. MidHG. *gesament, gesamnet,* OHG. *gisamanôt;* partic. of OHG. *samanôn.* See fammeln.

Gefchäft, n., 'business, affair, occupation,' from MidHG. *geschefte, gescheffede,* n.; 'creature, work, figure, occupation, business, affair'; abstract of fchaffen.

gefchehen, vb., 'to happen, occur, befall,' from the equiv. MidHG. *geschëhen,* OHG. *giscëhan;* a specifically G. word (MidDu. *geschien,* Du. *geschieden*), as well as the corresponding factitive fchieben. It is uncertain whether the word is connected with Goth. *skêwjan,* 'to go,' and the Teut. root *skeh* (*skêhw, skêw*), from *skek,* or OSlov. *skoků,* 'leap,' and OIr. *scuchim,* 'I go or pass away.' See Gefchichte and fchicken.'

gefcheit, 'sensible, judicious, discreet,' corrupted into gefcheut, from MidHG. *geschîde,* adj., 'sensible, sly'; akin to *schîden,* a variant of *scheiden.* See fcheiben.

Gefchichte, f., 'occurrence, narration, tale, history,' from MidHG. *geschiht,* OHG. *gisciht,* f., 'event, occurrence, cause of an event, dispensation' (MidHG. also 'affair, manner, stratum'; see Schicht); abstract of gefchehen. Similarly ModHG. Gefchick, 'fate, destiny, dexterity,' is based upon MidHG. *geschicke,* n., 'event, order, formation, figure,' as the abstract of ModHG. fchicken.—gefchickt, 'apt, skilful, adroit,' prop. a partic., MidHG. g*schicket,* 'arranged, prepared, ready, suitable,' from MidHG. *schicken,* 'to arrange, set in order.'

Gefchirr, n., 'gear, trappings, implements, ware,' from MidHG. *geschirre,* OHG. *giscirri,* n., 'dishes, vessel, instrument, utensils.' The more general meaning, 'instrument of every kind,' is also seen, especially in anfchirren (ModHG. simply), 'to harness a horse. The origin of the stem, which does not appear elsewhere in Teut., is obscure.

gefchlacht, adj., 'of good quality, soft, tender, shapely,' from MidHG. *geslaht,*

OHG. *gislaht*, 'well brought up, noble, well behaved'; ungeſchlacht, 'uncouth, unwieldy, boorish,' even in MidHG. *ungeslaht*, OHG. *ungislaht*, 'ignoble, base.' Allied to ModHG. Geſchlecht, n., 'species, race, extraction, family,' from MidHG. *geslehte*, n., 'race, tribe, family, quality,' OHG. *gislahti*; comp. OHG. *slahta*, f., 'race, family,' MidHG. *slahte*, 'manner, relation'; akin also to Schlag (*e.g.* Menſchenſchlag, 'race of men'), not found in OHG. and MidHG. It is difficult to determine the relation of these cognates to ſchlagen; even in OHG. *slahan* itself means 'to take after, resemble' (*e.g. náh dén fordŏrŏn slahan*, 'to resemble one's ancestors'), for which in late MidHG. *nâch-slahen* occurs, ModHG. nachſchlagen. Probably the str. vb. in OTeut. once had the meaning 'to beget,' which cannot now be authenticated; of this vb. OHG. *gislaht*, 'of good quality,' would be an old partic. in *to* (see laſt, trant, ſant), with a development of meaning similar to that of König. Comp. Fr. *gentil*, equiv. to Lat. *gentilis*.

Geſchmeide, n., 'ornaments, trinkets, jewels,' from MidHG. *gesmîde*, n., 'metal, metal utensils or weapons, ornaments,' OHG. *gismîdi*, n., 'metal,' and the variant *smîda*, f.; from the root *smî*, widely diffused in Teut.; 'to work in metal,' with which OHG. *smeidar*, 'artificer in metals,' and the cognates discussed under Schmied, are connected. So too geſchmeidig, 'pliant, flexible, tractable, smooth,' from MidHG. *gesmîdec*, 'easy to work, plastic.'

Geſchmeiß, n., 'fly-blows, eggs (of insects), vermin,' from MidHG. *gesmeize*, n., 'excrement'; akin to ſchmeißen.—Geſchoß, n., 'shot, missile, dart,' even MidHG. *geschoz*, OHG. *giscoz*, n., akin to ſchießen. So too Geſchütz, 'artillery, ordnance,' even in MidHG. *geschütze*, n., 'arms, weapons for shooting,' occurs as a collective of Geſchoß.

geſchweige, conj. with a subj. to be supplied, 'much less, to say nothing of, I am silent about it,' &c.—geſchweigen, 'to pass by in silence, omit mentioning,' a factitive of ſchweigen, from MidHG. *gesweigen*, OHG. *gisweigen*, 'to reduce to silence.' See ſchweigen.

geſchwind, adj. and adv., 'swift(ly), rapid(ly), quick(ly),' from *geswinde*, adj. and adv., 'quick(ly), vehement(ly)'; in earlier ModHG. ſchwinde, MidHG. *swinde* (*swint*), 'powerful, strong, quick.' In OHG. the adj. is wanting (yet the proper names Amalswind and Adalswind are recorded). The prim. meaning is 'strong'; the development of meaning to 'quick' is similar to that of balb; Goth. *swinþs*, 'strong, powerful, healthy,' OIc. *svinnr*, 'intelligent,' AS. *swíð*, 'strong, violent,' show various aspects of the primary meaning. The origin of the cognates is obscure; its relation to geſund is dubious.

Geſchwiſter, plur. (prop. neut. sing.), from the equiv. MidHG. *geswister* (*g swister de*), neut. plur., 'brothers and sisters,' OHG. *giswistar*, plur.; akin to Schweſter.

Geſchwulſt, f., 'swelling, tumour,' from the equiv. MidHG. *geswulst*, akin to ſchwellen.—Geſchwür, n., from the equiv. MidHG. *geswêr*, n., 'abscess,' akin to ſchwären.

Geſelle, m., 'comrade, apprentice, journeyman,' from MidHG. *geselle*, OHG. *gisello*, lit. 'fellow-occupant or lodger,' then generally 'companion, friend' (in late MidHG. 'journeyman' also); akin to Saal. Hence the derivatives, MidHG. *gesellec*, 'associate, combined,' ModHG. geſellig; MidHG. *gesellecheit*, 'relation as a comrade'; MidHG. *gesellen*, 'to unite, combine,' ModHG. geſellen, 'to associate.' For the meaning of ge= in Geſelle, comp. Geſinde.

Geſetz, n., 'law, decree, statute,' from the equiv. MidHG. *gesetze*, of which the variant *gesetzede* occurs in the same sense, OHG. *gisetzida*, f.; akin to ſetzen, whence also Satzung.—Geſicht, n., 'sight, countenance,' from MidHG. *gesiht*, OHG. *gisiht*, f., 'seeing, view, dream, sense of sight,' akin to ſehen.—Geſims, see Sims.

Geſinde, n., 'domestics, servants,' from MidHG. *gesinde*, OHG. *gisindi*, n., 'suite, followers in war'; collective of MidHG. *gesint(d)*, OHG. *gisind*, 'follower,' lit. 'one who joins in a *sind*,' from OHG. *sind*, m., 'journey, expedition'; corresponding to AS. *síð*, 'journey,' whence *gesíð*, 'companion, fellow-traveller,' Goth. *sinþs*, 'journey' (*gasinþa*, 'fellow-traveller'). To the OTeut. *sinþa-* (from pre-Teut. *sénto-*) corresponds OIr. *sét*, 'way.' See ſenten and ſinnen.—ModHG. Geſindel, 'rabble, mob, vagabonds,' dimin. of Geſinde, also used in a contemptuous sense, so even in late Mid HG. *gesindelæhe*, *gesindelach* (with a collective suffix).—Geſpan, m., 'companion,' from the equiv. MidHG. *gespan*; lit. perhaps 'one who is yoked along with another.' Comp. Goth. *gajukô*, 'comrade,' lit. 'yoke-fellow.'

Geſpenſt, n., 'spectre, ghost,' from Mid

HG. *gespenste*, n. (*gespenst, gespanst*, f.), 'enticement, allurement, infernal illusion, ghost,' OHG. *gispanst*, f., 'enticement'; the latter meaning is the original one, since Gespenst (see also ab-, widerspenstig), according to its form, is a verbal abstract of an OTeut. *spanan*, 'to entice.' Comp. OSax. and OHG. *spanan*, 'to entice, charm,' Mid HG. *spanen* (comp. Gr. σπάω).

Gest, see Gischt.

Gestade, n., from the equiv. MidHG. *gestat(d)*, n., 'bank, shore.' Comp. Staden.

gestalt, adj., 'having form or shape,' in wohlgestalt, ungestalt; comp. MidHG. *ungestalt*, OHG. *ungistalt*, 'disfigured, ugly,' MidHG. *wolgestalt* (*wol ges'ellet*); a partic. of MidHG. *stellen*, which may also mean 'to shape, make, accomplish, set in order.' To this is allied Gestalt, f., 'external appearance, shape, figure, mien,' MidHG. *gestalt*, f., 'shape, appearance, nature,' OHG. **gistalt*. Considering the comparatively late appearance of the word (not until the end of the 13th cent.), Gestalt may have been derived from the old compound, OHG. *ungistalt*, MidHG. *ungestalt*, adj., 'disfigured.'

gestatten, vb., 'to allow, admit, grant,' from MidHG. *gestaten*, wk. vb., 'to grant, permit,' OHG. *gistatôn*; probably connected most closely with OHG. *stata*, f., 'favourable opportunity' (for details see Statt).—

gestehen, vb., 'to acknowledge, confess,' from MidHG. *gestên, gestân*, OHG. *gistân*, str. vb., 'to stand still, assist, own, confess'; derivatives, ModHG. geständig, Geständnis. See stehen.

gestern, adv., 'yesterday,' from the equiv. MidHG. *gëstern* (*gëster*), OHG. *gëstaron* (*gëstre*), adv.; also, with a divergent meaning, OHG. *ëgëstern*, 'the day after to-morrow' (and 'the day before yesterday'); corresponding to Goth. *gistradagis*, 'to-morrow,' OIc. *tgær*, 'to-morrow, yesterday.' It is evident that the primary word was used in the double sense of 'to-morrow' and 'yesterday' (lit. 'on the second day from this'); comp. also AS. *geostra*, *gistrandœg*, E. *yesterday*, Du. *gisteren*, 'yesterday.' The form and the idea are Aryan; comp. Sans. *hyás*, 'yesterday,' Gr. χθές, Lat. *heri* (for *hjesi*?); *ghyés* is the primit. form, whence with the suffix *tro-, ghistro-, ghyestro-* (Goth. *gistra*). For heute, 'to-day,' and morgen, 'to-morrow' (Lat. *cras*, Sans. *çrás*), an equally diffused form is wanting.

Gestirn, see Stern.—Gestöber, see stöbern.—Gesträuch, see Strauch.—Gestrüpp, see struppig.—Gestüppe, see Stank.—Gestühl, see Stuhl.

gesund, adj., 'sound, healthy, wholesome,' from the equiv. MidHG. *gesunt(d)*, OHG. *gisunt(t)*; also MidHG. *gesunt*, OHG. *gisunt*, m., 'health'; comp. AS. *gesund* and *sund*, E. *sound*, Du. *gezond*, OFris. *sund*. To East Teut. the word is unknown. Its connection with Lat. *sânus*, 'healthy,' is as feasible phonetically as its connection with gesckwind, or with the Teut. root *sinþ*, 'to go,' in Gesinde.

Getreide, n., 'grain, corn,' from Mid HG. *getregede*, n., 'everything that is carried, clothing, luggage; what the soil bears (flowers, grass), corn,' even in late OHG. (11th cent.), *gitreĝidi*, n., 'revenue, possession.' The ModHG. sense is first found in 14th cent.

getreu, see treu.—getrost, see trösten.

Gevatter, m., 'godfather, sponsor, gossip,' from MidHG. *gevatere*, OHG. *gifataro*, 'spiritual co-father, godfather'; an imitation of eccles. Lat. *compater*. From this was also formed OHG. *gifatara*, MidHG. *gevatere*, f., 'godmother.' Comp. also Vetter and Base.

gewahr, adj., 'aware,' from MidHG. *gewar*, OHG. and OSax. *giwar*, 'heedful, attentive, mindful'; hence gewahr werden is lit. 'to grow careful, mindful'; thus even in MidHG. *gewar wërden*, OHG. *giwar wërdan*, OSax. *giwar wërdan*; comp. Du. *gewaar*, E. *aware*. Allied to MidHG. *gewar*, f., 'oversight, headship,' *gewarsame*, 'oversight, certainty,' ModHG. Gewahrsam, m., 'surety, custody.'—gewahren, vb., 'to be aware of, perceive, discover,' from late MidHG. *gewarn*, 'to become aware'; derived from the adj. See wahrnehmen, wahren.

gewähren, vb., 'to be surety for, guarantee, attest,' from MidHG. *gewërn*, OHG. *giwërën*, 'to grant, confess, perform, pay, give security,' also the equiv. MidHG. *wern*, OHG. *wërën*; corresponding to OFris. *wera*, 'to give security.' From the OHG. partic. *wërënto*, 'guarantor,' were adopted the Romance cognates, Ital. *guarento* and Fr. *garant*, 'bondsman' (allied to Fr. *garantir*, Ital. *guarentire*, 'to give security,' whence ModHG. Garantie, E. *warrant*). The connecting link between the OTeut. wk. verbal stem *wërai-*, 'to confess,' and non-Teut. words has not yet been found; perhaps Ir. *ferain*, 'I give,' is allied.

Gewalt, f., 'power, authority, force,' from the equiv. MidHG. *gewalt,* m., f., OHG. *giwalt,* m., f.; allied to *walten.*

Gewand, n., 'garment, dress, garb,' from MidHG. *gewant(d),* n., 'clothing, armour, dress stuff, material' (with the last meaning ModHG. *Gewandhaus* is connected); OHG. only in the late recorded compound, *badagiwant(t),* 'vestis mutatoria.' The older word for '*Gewand*' was MidHG. *gewæte,* OHG. *giwâti,* also OHG. and Mid HG. *wât.* OHG. *giwant,* appears as 'turning, winding,' and upon this sense ('enveloping') the meaning 'clothing' is based; comp. Lat. *toga,* from *tegere,* 'to cover.' See *winten.*—**gewandt,** 'skilled, proficient, adroit,' partic. of *wenten.*

gewärtig, adj., 'expectant, attentive,' from MidHG. *gewertec,* 'careful, obliging'; allied to MidHG. *gewarten,* 'to hold oneself ready, watch with observant eyes in order to be ready, for a service, or to admit visitors,' &c. See *warten.*

Gewehr, n., 'weapon of defence, gun, musket,' from MidHG. *gewer,* f. n., 'guard, defence, bulwark, weapon'; even in OHG. *giwer,* n., 'weapon, goad,' *weri,* 'rampart, means of defence.' Allied to *wehren.*

Geweih, n., 'horns, antlers,' from the equiv. MidHG. *gewîge (hirzgewîge),* n.; in OHG. the corresponding word is wanting; comp. Du. *gewicht,* n., 'stag's antlers,' whence a G. variant *Gewicht.* The cognates have most frequently been connected with the OTeut. root *wîg,* 'to fight' (see *Weigand*); *Geweih* would then be regarded as the weapon of the stag.

Gewerbe, n., 'mode of acquisition, trade, craft,' from MidHG. *gewerbe,* n., 'activity, business'; allied to *werben.*

Geweihl, n., 'antlers,' see *Geweih.*—
Gewicht, n., 'weight,' from the equiv. MidHG. *gewiht, gewihte,* n.; OHG. **giwiht;* verbal abstract of *wiegen;* corresponding to AS. *gewiht,* E. *weight,* Du. *gewigt,* OIc. *vætt.*

gewiegt, adj., ModHG. only, prop. a partic. of *wiegen,* 'to rock,' hence in *etwas gewiegt,* 'rocked into something,' i.e. 'trained up, grown proficient in something.'

gewinnen, vb., 'to win, acquire, prevail on, conquer,' from MidHG. *gewinnen,* OHG. *giwinnan,* 'to attain by work, effort, victory, earn beforehand, conquer, get,' besides which are found MidHG. *winnen,* OHG. *winnan,* 'to toil hard, contend'; corresponding to Goth. *winnan (gawinnan),*
'to suffer, feel pain, torment oneself' (allied to *wunns* and *winnô,* f., 'suffering,' OHG. *winna,* 'strife,' MidHG. *winne,* 'pain'), OIc. *vinna,* 'to work, perform, win,' AS. *winnan,* 'to contend, exert oneself,' E. *to win,* Du. *gewinnen.* The primary meaning of the Teut. root *winn* is 'to toil hard' (especially used of toiling in fight). Whether OHG. *wini,* AS. *wine,* 'friend,' and ModHG. *Wonne* also belong to the same root is doubtful; yet the primit. allied Sans. root *van* signifies 'to procure for oneself, obtain, assist in obtaining, conquer,' and 'to be fond of, favourable to.'

Gewissen, n., 'conscience,' from MidHG. *gewizzen,* f. n., 'knowledge, information, privity, inner consciousness, conscience,' even in OHG. *giwizzant,* f., 'conscience' (Du. *geweten*); probably an imitation of Lat. *conscientia* (G. *ge* equiv. to Lat. *con,* as in *Gevatter*), comp. also *barmherzig*; in Goth. *miθwissei.* OHG. *giwizzant* is most closely connected with *wissen,* OHG. infin. *wizzan.*

gewiß, adj. and adv., 'sure(ly), certain(ly), confident(ly),' from the equiv. MidHG. *gewis(ss),* adj., *gewisse,* adv., OHG. *gewis(ss),* adj., *gewisso,* adv., 'certain, sure, reliable'; corresponding to Du. *wis, gewis;* Goth only in *unwisa-* (misspelt for **unwissa*), 'uncertain.' The OTeut. *wissa- (gawissa-)* is an old partic. of the Goth. pret.-pres. *witan,* OHG. *wizzan* (see *wissen*), from *witta-, widtu-* (allied to the Aryan root *vid*). With regard to the pregnant meaning, 'what is certainly known,' for 'what is known,' comp. *laut,* lit. 'what is heard.'

Gewitter, n., 'thunder-storm,' from MidHG. *gewitere,* OHG. *giwitiri,* 'bad weather'; collective of *Wetter;* corresponding to OSax. *giwidiri,* Goth. **gawidri,* n. The ModHG. meaning is wanting in OHG. and MidHG. OHG. *giwitiri* may also mean 'hail.'

gewogen, adj., 'favourably inclined,' from MidHG. *gewëgen,* 'important, inclined'; prop. a partic. of MidHG. *gewëgen,* 'to be weighty, adequate, help.' See *wägen.*

gewöhnen, vb., 'to accustom, inure, habituate,' from the equiv. MidHG. *gewënen,* OHG. *giwennan* (pret. *giwenita*); corresponding to Du. *gewennen,* AS. *gewęnnan,* OIc. *venja,* Goth. *wanjan,* 'to accustom'; derived from an old adj. or rather partic. *wana-,* 'accustomed' (OIc. *vanr*); for this word a parallel form was chiefly used, the latest derivative of which is **gewohnt,** 'accustomed,' OHG. *giwon,* MidHG. *gewon,* whence, with a dental suffix (see **Mond** and **Habicht**), ModHG. *gewohnt* (yet without *t,* **Gewohnheit** and **gewöhnlich**) ; allied to OHG. *giwona,* MidHG. *gewone (gewan),* ' custom.' For details see *wohnen.*

Gicht, f. and n., 'gout, mouth of a furnace,' from the equiv. MidHG. *giht,* n. f. (chiefly in the collective form *gegihte,* n.), 'gout, convulsions, spasms.' OHG. *gihido may be inferred from AS. *gihða,* m., ' paralysis ' ; this dental suffix is frequent in old names of diseases. The root *gih* is not found elsewhere, and its prim. meaning is obscure. **Gehen** cannot in any case be allied, since it presumes a root *gai* (from *ga* and a root **ĭ**) ; nor could we from this comparison infer the prim. meaning of **Gicht.**

gichsen, vb., from the equiv. MidHG. *çiksen (gëksen),* 'to sigh,' OHG. *gicchazzen;* from an onomatopoetic root *gik,* with a frequentative suffix *sen* (OHG. *azzen, azzen,* Goth. *atjan*).

Giebel, m., 'gable, summit,' from the equiv. MidHG. *gibel,* OHG. *gibil,* m. ; corresponding to Du. *gevel,* OIc. *gafl,* ' gable,' Goth. *gibla,* m., 'spire.' The OHG. word signifies 'front side' (*e.g.,* of the ark of the covenant), as well as ' nap ' (of velvet, &c.), so that 'extreme end' is probably the prim. meaning. It may be assumed, however, that the word was used in a figurative sense, MidHG. *gëbel,* OHG. *gëbal,* m., 'skull, head,' OHG. *gibilla,* f., 'skull' ; primit. allied to Gr. κεφαλή, 'head' (Aryan *ghebhald,* the type of this word and of **Giebel**) ; hence **Giebel** is lit. 'head.'

Giebel, Gieben, m., 'crucian' ; like the equiv. Fr. *gibel,* of obscure origin.

Gienmuschel, f., 'a species of tellina,' allied to MidHG. *ginen (gienen),* 'to gape, open the mouth wide,' OHG. *ginên;* the latter is derived from an OTeut. root *gî* (Aryan *ghî*), 'to bark, gape, open the mouth wide.' See **gähnen.**

Gier, f., 'eagerness, inordinate desire,' from MidHG. *gir (gër),* f., 'longing, craving, greediness,' OHG. *girî,* f. ; abstract of an adj., OHG. *gër* and *giri,* MidHG. *gër, gir,* 'craving, longing,' which is connected with the root *ger* (Aryan *gher*), discussed under *gern.* Another abstract form allied to this is ModHG. **Gierde** (**Begierde**), from MidHG. *girde,* OHG. *girida,* f. (Du. *begeerte*). For the older adj. MidHG. *gir, gër,* only *gierig*

is now used, from MidHG. *girec,* OHG. *girîg,* ' desirous.'

gießen, vb., from the equiv. MidHG. *giezen,* OHG. *giozan,* 'to pour, cast metal, form, pour out, spill, stream' ; corresponding to Goth. *giutan,* 'to pour' (OIc. *giôta,* ' to throw young, blink with the eyes'), AS. *geótan,* Du. *gieten;* a strong verbal root common to Teut., from pre-Teut. *ghud,* whence also the Lat. root *fud* in *fundo,* 'I pour.' This root is probably connected with the equiv. root *ghu* (Gr. χυ-, in χέω, χῦμα, Sans. root *hu,* ' to sacrifice '). See also **Götze.**

Gift in **Mitgift, Brautgift,** f., from the equiv. MidHG. and OHG. *gift,* f., 'gift, present' ; a verbal noun from *gëben* (Goth. *gifts,* E. *gift*).—**Gift,** n., meaning ' poison,' is the same word (for the evolution of meaning comp. Fr. *poison,* from Lat. *potio, potionem,* 'drink'); even in MidHG. and OHG. *gift,* f. (always neut. in this sense in ModHG.), Du. *gift;* in Goth. *lubja,* 'poison' (OHG. *luppi,* MidHG. *lüppe,* ' poison '). The common Aryan term for ' poison ' (Sans. *viša-,* Lat. *virus,* Gr. ἰός) has not been preserved in Teut. See **verwesen.**

Gilbe, f., 'yellow colour or substance,' from the equiv. MidHG. *gilwe,* OHG. *giliwî (gëlawî),* f. ; an abstract of *gelb* (Goth. **gilwei,* akin to **gilwa-*).—To this **gilben,** ' to colour yellow,' is allied.

Gilde, f., 'guild, corporation,' ModHG. only, from the equiv. Du. *gild;* corresponding to OIc. *gilde,* 'guild' (from the middle of the 11th cent.), MidE. *gilde,* E. *guild.* The prim. meaning of the word, which first appears in Scand., is 'sacrifice, sacrificial feast, festive gathering, club' ; allied to *gelten* (in the sense of ' to sacrifice,' in OSax. *geldan,* and in AS. *gildan*).

Gimpel, m., 'bullfinch,' from the equiv. late MidHG. *gümpel;* in ModHG. figuratively 'simpleton.' MidHG. *gümpel* is connected with *gumpel,* 'leaping, jest,' and further with *gumpen,* 'to hop' ; hence MidHG. *gumpelmann* (plur. *gumpelliute*), and *gumpelknëht,* 'tumbler, buffoon, fool.'

Ginst, Ginster, m., ' broom (plant),' first occurs in ModHG., from Lat. *genista,* whence also the Romance cognate, Fr. *genêt ;* the genuine Teut. term is preserved in E. *broom,* Du. *brem.* See **Brombeere.**

Gipfel, m., 'summit, top, climax,' from the equiv. late MidHG. *gipfel,* m., the prim. word cannot be discovered ; **Gipfel** is scarcely an intensive form of **Giebel** ; MidHG. *gupf, gupfe,* 'point, summit,' is still less closely allied, and is rather a variant of *Rappe*.

Gips, m., 'gypsum, plaster of Paris,' from the equiv. MidHG. and late OHG. *gips*, which again is derived from MidLat.-Gr. *gypsum* (γύψος, MidGr. and ModGr. υ being pronounced like *i*, see *Kirche*), whence also Fr. *gypse*, Du. *gips*.

girren, vb., 'to coo,' allied to MidHG. *gërren*, *gurren*, *garren*, which are used for various kinds of sounds.

Gischt, older **Gäschl**, m., 'yeast, foam,' formed from the equiv. MidHG. *jëst*, *gëst*, m., corresponding to E. *yest*, *yeast*, Du. *gest*, 'yeast.' Allied to gischen (MidHG. *gischen*), older gäschen (MidHG. *geschen*, a variant of *jësen*). See gären, a factitive of MidHG. *jësen*.

Gitter, n., 'trellice, lattice, railing,' from the equiv. MidHG. *gëter*, n., a variant of *gater*, **Gatter**; even in late MidHG. *gegitter*.

Glanz, m., 'lustre, splendour,' from the equiv. MidHG. *glanz* (wanting in OHG.), with which is connected the OHG. and MidHG. adj. *glanz*, 'bright, shining'; ModHG. glänzen, from the equiv. OHG. and MidHG. *glenzen*; to the same class belong MidHG. *glander*, 'splendour, shining,' and *glanst*, 'splendour,' further *glinster*, 'splendour,' and the very rare str. vb. *glinzen*. A stem *glint-* is wanting in the rest of the Teut. dialects unless the cognates of glatt (Goth. **glada-*) are allied.

Glas, n., 'glass, tumbler,' from the equiv. OHG. and MidHG. *glas*, n.; a common Teut. word unknown to the other Aryan groups; comp. OSax. *gles*, Du. *glas*, AS. *glæs*, E. *glass*; allied to OIc. *gler*, n., 'glass,' with the change of *s* to *r*, which proves the word to be primit. Teut. (**g'aza-* and **glasa-* in Goth.). Hence it is not very probable that the Teut. word was borrowed, although glass itself was imported by the Phœnicians. The OTeut. term for amber (Lat. *glēsum*) is likewise primit. allied; comp. AS. *glære*, 'resin of trees.' See the following word.

Glast, m., 'splendour,' from the equiv. MidHG. *glast*. It is uncertain whether it belongs, like the cognates discussed under the preceding word, to a Teut. root *glas*, 'to shine.'

glatt, adj., 'smooth, polished, slippery, bald,' from MidHG. and OHG. *glat*, 'smooth, shining'; corresponding to OSax. *gladmôd*, 'gladsome,' Du. *glad*, 'smooth,' AS. *glæd*, 'shining, joyous,' F. *glad*, OIc. *glaðr*, 'joyous, shining.' Goth. **glada-* for pre-Teut. *ghladho-* is primit. allied to OSlov. *gladŭkŭ*, 'smooth,' Lat. *glaber* (for **g'ladhro-*), 'smooth;' hence not 'shining' but 'smooth' is the prim. meaning of the Teut. cognates. The connection with Lith. *glodùs*, 'fitting smoothly' (from the root *glud*, 'to cling to'?), is uncertain. Comp. also the following word, as well as glänzen and gleiten.

Glatze, f., from the equiv. MidHG. *glatz*, 'bald pate, bald spot, surface of the head'; Goth. **glatta-* for pre-Teut. *ghladhno*, allied to glatt (pre-Teut. *ghladho-*); hence Glätte is lit. 'smooth spot.'

Glaube, m., 'belief, credit, creed,' from the equiv. MidHG. *geloube* (by syncope *gloube*), OHG. *giloubo*, m.; an abstract common to West Teut.; corresponding to OSax. *gilôbo*, Du. *geloof*, AS. *geleáfa* (E. *belief*). With this glauben is connected earlier (in Luther) glenben, from the equiv. MidHG. *gelouben* (*glöuben*), OHG. *gilouben*, *gilouppen*; comp. OSax. *g.lôbian*, Du. *gelooven*, AS. *gelýfan*, E. *to believe*, Goth. *galaubjan*, 'to believe.' The prim. meaning is 'to approve.' To the same root *lub* belong erlauben, lieb, leben, and Urlaub.

gleich, adj., 'like, similar, equal, direct,' from the equiv. MidHG. *gelîch*, OHG. *gilîh(hh)*; common to Teut. in the same sense; comp. Goth. *galeiks*, OIc. *glíkr*, AS. *gelic*, E. *like*, Du. *gelijk*, OSax. *gilík*. This specifically Teut. adj. is compounded of the particle ge-, Goth. *ga-*, and a subst. *lîka-*, 'body,' whose cognates are discussed under Leiche; the compound meant lit. 'having a symmetrical body.' The word *lîk*, ModHG. *-lich*, as the second component, is always used in the same sense; *e.g.*, weiblich, lit. 'having a woman's body' (it is preserved also in the prons. welcher, solcher, lit. 'having what kind of body? having a body of that kind'; yet see these words).
—**Gleichen**, in expressions like meines gleichen, is also based upon the adj. gleich, which is here declined in the weak form; comp. MidHG. *mîn gelîche*, OHG. *mîn gilîhho*, 'my equals.'—**Gleichnis**, n., 'similitude, allegory, parable,' from MidHG. *gelîchnisse*, f. n., OHG. *gilîhnissa*, f., 'copy, model, parable.'—gleichsam, adv., 'as it were, as though,' a combination of gleich and sam for gleich wie, 'just as if'; comp. MidHG. *sam*, *same*, adv., 'thus, just as, even as' (OHG. *sama*, from a pronom. stem *sama-*, 'the very same'; comp. E. *same*,

Gr. ὁμός, Sans. *sama-*, 'the same, equal').—See **Gleißner**.

Gleise, n., for **Geleise** (like **glauben**, **gleich**, &c., from **geī**), 'track (of a wheel), rut,' allied to MidHG. *geleis* (rare), f., 'trodden way,' usually MidHG. *leis, leise*, f., 'trace, track,' OHG. **leisa* in *waganleisa*, f., 'track of a waggon'; formed from the OTeut. root *lais*, 'to go,' discussed under **leisten**; Lat. *līra, de-līrare*, OSlov. *lĕcha*, 'ridge' (from **laisā*), Lith. *lýsė*, 'garden bed,' are also allied. Comp. ModHG. **Furche** and Lat. *porca*, 'ridge.'

Gleiß, m., 'fool's parsley,' first occurs in ModHG.; allied to the following word.

gleißen, vb., 'to shine, glitter,' from MidHG. *glizen*, OHG. *glizzan*, str. vb., 'to shine, light, glitter'; corresponding to OSax. *glītan*, to which Goth. *glitmunjan*, OIc. *glita, glitra* (E. *to glitter*), 'to shine.' The OTeut. root *glīt* (pre-Teut. *ghlĭd*) appears also in **glizern**.

Gleißner, m., 'hypocrite,' from the equiv. MidHG. *gelīchesenære*, allied to older ModHG. **gleißen**, 'to dissemble.' The latter is from MidHG. *glīhsen, gelīchesen*, OHG. *gilīhhisôn*, 'to dissemble'; lit. 'to be equal to any one' (from **gleich**), equiv. to the MidHG. parallel form *gelīchsensen*. Comp. further Lat. *simulare*, allied to *similis*.

gleiten, vb., 'to glide, slide, slip,' from the equiv. MidHG. *glīten*, OHG. *glītan*, str. vb.; corresponding to OSax. *glīdan*, Du. *glijden, glijen*, AS. *glīdan*, E. *to glide*. Although the roots of **gleiten** (Aryan *ghlī-dh*, *ghlĭ-t*) and **glatt** (Aryan *ghladh*) are as indubitably allied as those of **Glanz** and **gleißen**, it is impossible to determine the relation between them more definitely.

Gletscher, m., 'glacier,' first occurs in early ModHG., adopted from a Swiss word, which was again obtained from Fr. *glacier*. Comp. **Firne, Fohn, Lawine**.

Glied, n., from the equiv. MidHG. *gelit(d)*, n. and m., OHG. *gilid*, n., 'limb, joint' (in MidHG. 'member' also); likewise in the same sense, mostly without **ge-**, MidHG. *lit(d)*, OHG. *lid*, n. m.; corresponding to OSax. *lith*, Du. *lid* (and *gelid*), AS. *lið*, Goth. *liþus*, 'limb.' The common Teut. stem *liþu* is ordinarily referred to an OTeut. root *līþ*, 'to go' (see **leiben, leiten**), which is scarcely possible, because **Glied** cannot orig. have been confined to the feet. Besides *li-* must be the root and *-þu-* (for Aryan *-tu-*) the suffix, on account of the equiv. words formed with the suffix *m*,

OIc. *li-mr*, 'limb,' *lim*, 'twig,' AS. *lim*, E. *limb*. Also allied perhaps to Lith. *lëmú*, 'stature, growth' (as well as *lëlas*, 'tall, slender'?). Comp. **Bild**.—**Gliedmaßen**, plur., 'limbs,' from MidHG. *lidemâz, gelidemæze*, 'limb'; corresponding to OFris. *lithmâta*, Du. *lidmaat, ledemaat*. The meaning of the second part of the compound is not clear (MidHG. *gelidemâze*, f., signifies 'length of body'). Comp. OSwed. *lipa-, môt*, Ic. *liðamôt*, 'limbs.'

glimmen, vb., 'to shine dimly, glimmer,' from MidHG. *glimmen*, str. vb., 'to glow, glimmer,' allied to MidHG. *glamme*, f., 'glow,' *glim*, 'spark' (OHG. **glimman*); corresponding to Du. *glimmen*; also OHG. *gleimo*, MidHG. *gleime*, 'glowworm' (whence the proper name **Gleim**), MidHG. *glīmen*, 'to light, shine,' OSax. *glīmo*, 'gleam.' To the ModHG. and MidHG. *glimmern* correspond AS. **glimorian*, E. *to glimmer*, to which E. *gleam* (AS. *glǽm*) is allied. The OTeut. root *glimm, glī-m*, contained in these cognates, is perhaps lengthened from a root *glī* (comp. Scand. *glja*, 'to shine'), with which Gr. χλιαρός, 'warm,' χλιαίνω, 'to warm,' as well as Ir. *glé* (from the prim. form *gleivo-*), 'shining, clear,' may be connected.

Glimpf, m., 'moderation, lenity,' from MidHG. *glimpf, gelimpf*, m., 'consistent, courteous demeanour generally,' OHG. *gilimpf*, 'fitness'; to these are allied OHG. *gilimpflih*, MidHG. *gelimpflich*, 'consistent,' whence the ModHG. adv. **glimpflich**; akin to OHG. *gilimpfan*. MidHG. *gelimpfen*, 'to be suitable' (in MidHG. also 'to make suitable'); comp. AS. *gelimpan*, 'to occur.' The West Teut. root *limp* in an appropriate sense has not been found in the non-Teut. languages.

glitzern, vb., 'to glitter, glisten,' from the equiv. MidHG. *glitzern*, frequentative of MidHG. *glitzen*, 'to shine'; comp. OHG. *glizzinôn*; allied to **gleißen**, OHG. *glizzan*. AS. **glitorian*, E. *to glitter*, OIc. *glitra*, 'to shine,' are similarly formed.

Glocke, f., 'bell, (public) clock,' from the equiv. MidHG. *glocke*, OHG. *glocka* (never *chloccha*), f.; corresponding to Du. *klok*, AS. *clugge, clucce*, E. *clock*, OIc. *klukka*, f., 'bell'; not orig. a G. word, since OHG. *chlocchôn*, 'to knock,' cannot well be allied. The MidLat. *clocca* recorded in the 8th cent., from which Fr. *cloche* (in Ital. *campana*) is derived, is probably due, like the Teut. cognates, to Kelt. origin;

comp. W. *cloch*, f., OIr. *cloc*, m., 'bell, clock' (primit. Kelt. *klukko*). It is improbable that the Teut. word is the source of the Rom. and the Kelt. terms, because Teut. itself has usually borrowed the words relating to the Church and its institutions. The OKelt. and Rom. cognates in the form of *klukka* found their way into Teut.; the HG. forms (Swiss *klokke*, not χλωχε) may have been first adopted about 800 A.D., from LG. (AS.).

glosten, vb., 'to glimmer,' from Mid HG. *glosten* (a variant of *glosen*), 'to glow, shine'; allied to E. *gloss*, Scand. *glossi*; derived from the root *glas* appearing in Glas?.

glotzen, vb., 'to stare,' from the equiv. MidHG. *glotzen*; OHG. *glozzōn*, Goth. *gluttōn* are wanting; comp. E. *to gloat*, OIc. *glotta*, 'to sneer'; perhaps primit. allied to OSlov. *gledati*, 'to look, see.'

Glück, n., 'luck, good fortune, success, happiness,' from MidHG. *gelücke* (by syncope *glücke*), n., 'luck, accident'; OHG. *gilucchi* is wanting; a specifically G. word which in the 14th cent. passed in the form *lukka* into Scand. (Swed. *lycka*, Dan. *lykke*), and as *luck* into E. (from Du. *geluk*, 'fortune'). On account of its meaning its connection with leben is dubious.

Glucke, f., 'clucking-hen,' with the variant Kluck (LG. Klusse), from the equiv. MidHG. *klucke*. Comp. MidHG. *glucken*, *klucken*, 'to cluck'; allied to Du. *klokken*, E. *to cluck* (AS. *cloccian*); apparently an onomatopoetic class which is found with corresponding sounds in Rom.; comp. Ital. *chiocciare*, Fr. *glousser* (Lat. *glocire*), 'to cluck,' Ital. *chioccia*, Span. *clueca*, 'clucking-hen.'

Glufe, **Guffe**, f. (UpG. word), 'pin,' from the equiv. late MidHG. *glufe*, *guffe*, f.; origin obscure.

glühen, vb., 'to glow,' from the equiv. MidHG. *glüen*, *glüejen*, OHG. *glōuen*, wk. vb.; corresponding to AS. *glōwan*, E. *to glow*, Du. *gloeijen*, OIc. *glōa*, 'to glow.' From the Teut. root *glō*, *glō*, are also derived ModHG. Glut, MidHG. and OHG. *gluot*, f., to which Du. *gloed*, AS. *glēd* (Goth. *glō-di-*), E. dial. *gleed* correspond, likewise AS. *glōma*, *glōmung*, 'twilight,' E. *gloom*, OIc. *glāmr*, 'moon.' With the Teut. root *glō*, *glī* (from pre-Teut. *ghlā*), Lith. *zlejà*, 'twilight,' is also connected.

Gnade, f., 'grace, favour, mercy, pardon,' from MidHG. *gnāde*, *genāde*, f., 'bliss, rest, condescension, support, favour, mercy,' OHG. *gināda*, f., 'condescension, sympathy, compassion, mercy'; corresponding to OSax. *ginātha*, *nātha*, 'favour, help,' Du. *genade*, OIc. *nāð*, f. (in the plur.), 'rest.' The meanings 'favour, help,' &c., are attested by the Goth. vb. *niþan*, 'to support.' To the Teut. root *nēþ* (from Aryan *nēth*) some assign the prim. meaning 'to incline, decline,' in order to elucidate 'rest' (in Scand.; comp. MidHG. *diu sunne gienc ze gnāden*, 'zur Ruhe,' i.e. 'the sun set'). Comp. the cognates, Sans. root *nāth*, 'to beg,' *nāthā*, 'help, refuge.'

Gnenn, m., 'father' (dial.). See Knan.

Gold, n., 'gold,' from the equiv. Mid HG. *golt(d)*, OHG. *gold*, n.; a common Teut. word; comp. OSax. *gold*, Du. *goud*, AS. and E. *gold*, OIc. *goll*, *gull* (for *golþ-*), Goth. *gulþ*, n., 'gold,' from pre-Teut. *ghlto-*, to which OSlov. *zlato*, Russ. *zoloto* (from *zolto*) are primit. allied; the word Silber is also common to Teut. and Slav. The primary sense of the root *ghel*, of which Gelt is a partic. derivative, is 'to be yellow'; akin to Sans. *hiranya*, 'gold,' from *hāri*, 'gold yellow'; hence probably ModHG. gelb and glühen, with their cognates, are also primit. allied. In any case, Gr. χρυσός has no connection with the Teut. word.

Golf, m., 'gulf,' from the equiv. late MidHG. *golje*; the latter, like E. *gulf*, is derived from Fr. *golfe*, which, with its Rom. cognate (Ital. *golfo*), is based upon Gr. κόλφος (late κόλπος).

gönnen, vb., 'to grant, not to begrudge, wish well to,' from MidHG. *gunnen*, OHG. *giunnan*, 'to grant willingly, bestow, allow'; OHG. and OSax. mostly *unnan*, in the same sense (in OHG. and MidHG. pret.-pres.); comp Du. *gunnen*, AS. *unnan*, OIc. *unna*. The root is *an*; whether this is allied to Lat. *amare*, 'to love,' or to Gr. ὀνίνημι, 'I use,' or to the cognates of ahnden, is uncertain on account of its meaning; most probably Gr. προσ-ηνής, 'inclined,' and ἀπηνής, 'disaffected,' are allied primitively. Comp. Gunst.

Gosse, f., 'sink,' first occurs in Mod HG.; akin to gießen; it corresponds to LG. *gote*, Du. *goot*.

Gote, f., 'godmother,' from MidHG. *gote*, *gotte*, f., 'godmother,' OHG. *gota*; besides these MidHG. *göte*, *götte*, m., 'godfather,' occur. Probably OHG. *goto* and *gota* are pet terms (comp. Base) for the compounds *gotfater*, *gotmuoter*, *gotsunu*, *gottoh-*

tar; comp. the equiv. AS. *godfœder, godsunu, goddohter,* which are equal to E. *godfather, godson,* and *goddaughter*; also Swed. *gubbe,* 'old man,' *gumma,* 'old woman' (dial. 'godmother'), are pet names for *guðfaðer, guðmóðer*. As may be seen under Gevatter and Pate, the godfather is *pater spiritualis,* the child baptized *filius* or *filia spiritualis*; comp. Vetter also.

Gott, m., 'God,' from the equiv. MidHG. and OHG. *got,* m., a term common to Teut., unknown to the rest of the Aryan group; comp. OSax., Du., AS. and E. *god,* OIc. *guð, goð,* Goth. *guþ,* 'God.' The *form* of the Goth. and Scand. words is neuter (comp. Abgott), but the gender is masculine. OIc. *goð,* n., is mostly used in the plur. Goth. *guda-* and *guþa-,* n., 'God,' are based upon Aryan *ghu-to-m,* in which *-to-* is the partic. suffix discussed under *falt, laut,* and *traut.* The Aryan root *ghu-* is Sans. *hū,* 'to invoke the gods' (partic. *hūtá-*). Gott in the orig. neuter form is the 'invoked being'; in the Vedas the epithet *puruhūta,* 'oft-invoked,' is usually applied to Indra. The word Gott being specifically Teut., there is no term common to this group and one of the allied languages (yet comp. OIc. *tívc,* 'deity,' with Sans. *déva,* Lat. *deus ?*). Göttin, the fem. of Gott, is from the equiv. MidHG. *gotinne, götinne, gutinne,* OHG. *gutin* (Goth. **gudini,* AS. *gyden,* Du. *godin*).

Götze, m., 'idol, false god,' from MidHG. *götze,* m., 'statue for ecclesiastical purposes'; lit. 'cast (image),' (allied to gießen, MidHG. *giezen ?*). Perhaps, however, Götz is a short form of Götterbild, just as Götz is pet name for Gottfried; comp. Spatz and Sperling.

Grab, n., from the equiv. MidHG. *grap(b),* OHG. *grab,* n., 'grave'; like **Graben,** m., 'ditch, trench, sewer,' from the equiv. MidHG. *grabe,* OHG. *grabo,* m.; allied to ModHG. **graben,** 'to dig, engrave,' from the equiv. MidHG. *graben,* OHG. *graban,* str. vb.; a common Teut. str. vb., corresponding to the Goth. *graban,* AS. *grafan,* E. *to grave,* Du. *graven (graf,* 'grave'); from a common Teut. root *grab* (pre-Teut. *ghrabh*), which is primit. allied to OSlov. *grcbą,* 'I dig, row,' and *grobŭ,* 'grave'; Gr. γράφω, 'I scratch, write,' has probably no connection with the word. Comp. Griffel, Grube, Gruft, grübeln.

Grad, m., 'degree, step, stage, rank,' from MidHG. *grât (t* and *d),* 'grade, degree,' even in late OHG. *grâd;* from Lat. *gradus,* whence also Fr. *gré* (OIr. *grád*).

Graf, m., 'count, earl,' from the equiv. MidHG. *grâve* (with the variant *grœve,* chiefly in the plur.), OHG. *grâvo, grâvio* (upon the old *j* form is based the ModHG. proper name Gräf, a parallel form of Graf). OHG. *grâvio* assumes a Goth. **gréfja* ('commander'), which is the term for the agent from the verbal noun *gagréfts,* 'command, order,' preserved in Goth. The AS. term *geréfa* (AS. *scîrgeréfa,* E. *sheriff*), which is similar in meaning, is yet radically different, since it points to a Goth. **ga-rófja;* its orig. sense is probably 'head of a troop,' allied to **róf,* OHG. *ruora,* OIc. *róf* (*stafróf*), 'number.' OIc. (MidE.), *greife,* 'count,' is derived from MidLG. *gréve* (from OLG. **grâfio*). All explanations of Graf which do not originate in a Teut. root *gréf,* 'to command,' conflict with the laws relating to the change of sound and meaning. Note the signification of Graf in Du. *pluimgraaf,* 'one who minds the fowls,' Salzgraf, 'manager of a saltwork,' Deichgraf, &c.

gram, adj., 'adverse, hostile, vexed, angry,' from MidHG. and OHG. *gram,* 'angry, peevish, irritated, enraged'; corresponding to the equiv. OSax. *gram,* Du. *gram,* AS. *gram,* OIc. *gramr.* To Goth. **grama-* (from pre-Teut. *ghromo-*), Gr. χρόμαδος, 'gnashing' (and χρεμθω, Lat. *fremo,* 'I gnash'?), seem allied. From the Teut. adj. is derived the Romance cognate, Ital. *gramo,* 'gloomy.'—**Gram,** m., as a subst. even in MidHG. *gram.* From the same root *grimm* is derived. See the latter word.

Gran, m., 'grain,' first occurs in ModHG. from Lat. *granum,* 'grain.' From the same source ModHG. Gran is also derived through the medium of Fr. *grain.*

Granat, m., **Granele,** f., 'shrimp,' from the Du., in which the modern form is *garnaal,* formerly *granaal, graneel,* in the same sense.

Grand, m., 'gravel,' first occurs in ModHG. from LG.; just as Mulm (which see) is allied to mahlen, so Grand is probably connected with an OTeut. root meaning 'to grind'; comp. AS. *grindan,* E. *to grind* (from pre-Teut. root *ghrendh,* whence also Lat. *frendo,* 'to gnash').

Granne, f., 'bristle (of swine), awn,' from MidHG. *gran, grane,* f., 'point of hair, moustache, fish-bone' (in the latter sense Granne is also used dial.), OHG. *grana,* 'moustache'; corresponding to AS.

gronu, OIc. *grọn*, 'moustache.' To the Goth. *grana*, recorded by Isidore, are due Span. *greña*, 'tousled hair,' and OFr. *grenon*, 'moustache and whiskers.' The Teut. cognates are primit. allied to OIr. *grend*, Gael. *greann*, 'moustache' and 'shaggy hair.' See **Grat**.

Grans, m., 'ship's beak,' from MidHG. *grans*, m., 'bird's beak, ship's beak,' OHG. *grans, granso*, 'ship's beak'; a corresponding word is wanting in the other Teut. languages. Origin obscure.

grapfen, vb., 'to grasp, snatch,' simply ModHG.; probably allied primit. to ModHG. **Garbe**, and E. *to grab, to grasp*, Sans. *grbh*, 'to seize,' Lith. *grópti*, 'to snatch, grasp.'

Gras, n., 'grass,' from the equiv. MidHG. and OHG. *gras*, n.; corresponding to OSax. and Du. *gras*, AS. *græs* (*gœrs*), E. *grass*, Goth. *gras*, n., 'herb'; common to Teut. but unknown to the other Aryan languages. Allied to MidHG. *gruose* (Goth. *grōsa*), 'young shoot, green of plants'; probably the *s* in these words is a suffix, so that the Teut. root is *grā-*; comp. Gr. χόρτος, 'grass.' An Aryan root *ghrā*- is also attested by Lat. *grāmen*, as well as by ModHG. **grün** and its cognates.

gräßlich, adj., 'horrible, hideous, ghastly,' formed from early ModHG. *graß*; the latter is derived from MidHG. *graʒ*, 'furious, angry,' of which OHG. preserves only the adv. *graʒʒo*, 'violently, very'; Goth. *grata-*, as well as correspondences in the remaining dialects, is wanting. Goth. *grētan*, 'to weep' (MidHG. *grāʒen*), is scarcely allied.

Grat, m., and **Gräte**, f., 'point, ridge, fish-bone,' from MidHG. *grāt*, m., 'fish-bone, awn, back-bone, mountain ridge'; in ModHG. the word has assumed two forms, according to the meanings. Since **Granne**, 'awn,' has also the dial. sense 'fish-bone,' both words may perhaps be traced back to a common root *gru-*, 'to be pointed, bristly.'

grau, adj., 'grey,' from the equiv. MidHG. *grā* (gen. *grāwes*), OHG. *grāo* (gen. *grāwes*); corresponding to Du. *graauw*, AS. *grǣg*, E. *grey*, *grav*, OIc. *grár*, 'grey.' Its origin and further relations cannot be traced; Aryan *ghrēw*?

Gräuel, m., from the equiv. MidHG. *griul, griuwel*, m., 'terror, horror, abomination' (Du. *gruwel*); allied to ModHG. *grauen*, MidHG. *grūwen*, 'to horrify, terrify,' OHG. *ingrūēn*, 'to shudder.' Akin also to ModHG. *grausam*, from MidHG. *grūwesam*, 'exciting terror'; ModHG. *grăulich*, from MidHG. *griuwelich*. The root *grū*, 'to frighten,' is wanting in the rest of the OTeut. dialects. See **Graus**.

Graupe, f., 'peeled grain or barley,' first occurs in early ModHG.; in the 15th cent. the compound *ts-grāpe*, 'hailstone,' is recorded. Allied to Swed. *grœpe, grjupe*, 'shot,' as well as Russ. *krupa*, OSlov. *krupa*, 'crumb,' Serv. *krupa*, 'hail, sleet.' Probably the cognates are native to Slavonic.

Graus, m., 'horror, dread,' from MidHG. *grūs*, m., 'dread, terror'; allied to ModHG. *grausen*, MidHG. *grūsen, griusen*, OHG. *grūisōn, grūsōn*, 'to be terrified'; formed from the suffix *-isōn* and the root *grū*. See **Gräuel**, where *grausam* is also discussed.

Grauß, m., 'gravel,' from MidHG. *grūʒ*. See **Grieß**.

Greif, m., 'griffin,' from the equiv. MidHG. *grīf, grīfe*, OHG. *grīf, grīfo*, m. Whether the word was adopted from Greek through an Eastern source before the 8th cent. (hence the change of *p* into *f*) is questionable; in any case, Gr. γρύψ, 'griffin' (stem γρῦπ-; υ in the Byzantine and modern pronunciation equal to *i*; comp. **Leier**), must be regarded as the final source of **Greif**; see also **Drache**. Chiefly through the legends concerning Duke Ernst the griffin became popular in Germany, though not among the other Teutons. In Romance too the bird is similarly named—Ital. *griffo, griffone*, Fr. *griffon* (E. *griffin*). Hence OHG. *grīfo* and its Romance correspondences are probably to be traced back to a MidLat. *gryphus*, derived from the Greek word; comp. also OIr. *grīf*. Since, moreover, the belief in fabulous birds that carry off men is genuinely Teut., a Teut. form *grīpo*, 'snatcher' (allied to **greifen**), may have been combined with γρύπ-.

greifen, vb., 'to grasp, seize,' from the equiv. MidHG. *grīfen*, OHG. *grīfan*, str. vb.; corresponding to OSax. *grīpan*, Du. *grijpen*, AS. *grīpan*, E. *to gripe*, Goth. *greipan*, 'to seize, lay hold of'; a common Teut. vb., whence Fr. *gripper*, 'to clutch,' and *griffe*, 'claw.' In the non-Teut. languages there exists an allied Aryan root *ghrīb*, in Lith. *greibiù, greibti*, 'to seize,' and Lett. *grība*, 'will,' *grībēt*, 'to wish.'

greinen, vb., 'to whine, grin,' from the equiv. MidHG. *grīnen*, OHG. *grīnan*, str. vb., 'to distort the mouth with laughing or crying, grumble, snarl,' allied to

MidHG. *grinnen*, 'to gnash,' E. *to grin, to groan*, (AS. *grānian*), also grinfen; from the OG. cognates Ital. *digrignare*, 'to grin,' is derived. The root *grī*, pre-Teut. *ghrī*, is not found elsewhere (Sans. *hrī*, 'to be ashamed'?).

Greis, adj., 'grizzled, hoary, aged,' from the equiv. MidHG. *grîs*, OHG. *grîs* (*grîsil*); comp. OSax. *grîs*, 'hoary'; allied to **Greis** from MidHG. *grise*, 'old man.' From this OG. word, unknown to the other Teut. dialects and obscure in its origin, are derived the Romance cognates, Ital. *griso, grigio*, Fr. *gris*, 'grey' (Ital. *grigio*, from Goth. *greisja*-?. Comp. MidLat *griseus*, 'grey').

Grell, adj., 'shrill, glaring, dazzling,' from MidHG. *grël*(*ll*), 'rough, angry,' allied to MidHG. *grëllen*, 'to cry aloud, angrily'; wanting in OHG.; comp. AS. *griellan*, 'to gnash, sound harshly.' The root and further cognates are unknown; akin to **Grille**?.

Grempelmarkt, m., 'frippery, ragfair,' allied to MidHG. *grempeler*, 'slopseller, retailer, *grempen*, 'to keep a retail shop, deal in second-hand goods'; the latter is akin to Ital. *comprare* (with *r* transposed *crompare*), 'to buy', *compra*, 'purchase.'

Grensing, m., the plant *Potentilla anserina* (silver-weed, goose-grass, or wild tansy), from the equiv. MidHG. and OHG. *grensinc*; akin to MidHG. *grans*, 'beak.' See **Grane**.

Grenze, f., 'boundary, frontier, limit,' from the equiv. late MidHG. *greniz, grenize*, f. (appeared in the 13th cent. in the district belonging to the Teutonic Order), which is again derived from Pol. and Russ. *granica*, Boh. *hranice*. The native word for **Grenze** is **Mark**.

Greuel, see **Gräuel**.

Griebe (Bav. **Grente**), f., from the equiv. MidHG. *griebe* (Bav. *griube*, Swiss *grübe*), OHG. *griobo, griubo*, m., 'greaves' (in OHG. also, 'frying-pan'?); corresponding to AS. *greófa*, E. *greaves*, Swed. *grefwar*; *g* in this word scarcely represents the prefix *ga*-, *ges*, so that the word might be connected with the root of OHG. *girouben*, 'to fry.'

Griebs, r., 'core of fruit,' from the equiv. MidHG. *grobiʒ, grübiʒ* (also 'larynx'), to which the dial. variants MidHG. *grütz* (*gürbsi*), ModHG. **Gretzen**, are akin. OHG. *grobaʒ* and *grubiʒ* are wanting; in form they are connected with OHG. *obaʒ*, 'fruit,' with MidHG. *ebiʒ, ebitz*, 'core of fruit,' and with ModHG. **Butzen**, as well as Swiss *böki*.

Griesgram, m., 'ill-humour, spleen,' from MidHG. *grisgram*, m., 'gnashing of teeth'; allied to MidHG. *grisgramen, -grammen*, 'to gnash with the teeth, snarl,' OHG. *grisgramón, gristgrimmón*, 'to gnash,' AS. *gristbitung*, 'gnashing of teeth.' The first syllable represents *grist*-, but that does not make the early history of the word clearer.

Grieß, m. and n., 'gravel, groats,' from MidHG. *grieʒ* (*grūʒ*), m. and n., 'grain of sand, sand, gravel'; the ModHG. sense has not yet been found in MidHG. (yet late MidHG. *griezmēl*, 'coarse ground flour'), OHG. *grioʒ*, m. and n., 'sand, gravel'; corresponding to OSax. *griot*, AS. *greót*, 'sand,' OIc. *grjót*, 'stones.' On the OG. meaning of these cognates are based Ital. *greto*, 'stony bed of a river,' and Fr. *grès*, 'sandstone,' *grêle*, 'hail.' The ModHG. signification is connected with the closely allied cognates of **Grütze**.

Griffel, m., 'slate pencil, graving tool, stylus,' from the equiv. MidHG. *griffel*, OHG. *griffil*, m.; related to greifen as **Halter** to **halten**?. Yet it is more probably based on a Teut. root *grep*, 'to dig'; comp. Swed. *urgropa*, 'to excavate,' OSwed. and OIc. *grōp*, 'pit,' LG. **Gruppe**, 'gutter').

Grille, f., 'cricket, whim, crotchet,' from the equiv. MidHG. *grille*, OHG. *grillo*, m.; corresponding to Ital. *grillo* (from Gr. γρύλλος, 'grasshopper').

grimm, adj., 'fierce, wrathful, furious,' from MidHG. *grim, grimme*, OHG. *grim, grimmi*, 'unfriendly, frightful, savage' (to which ModHG. *grimmig*, MidHG. *grimmec* and OHG. *grimmig* are allied). Corresponding to OSax. and AS. *grim(mm)*, E. *grim*, Du. *grimmig*, OIc. *grimmr*, Goth. *grimma-*; allied to ModHG. **Gram**, root *grem* (by gradation *gram*).—**Grimm**, m., 'fury, rage, wrath,' from MidHG. *grim (mm)*, m.; comp. Du. *grim*.

Grimmen, n., 'ache, gripe,' in **Bauch**grimmen, from the equiv. MidHG. *grimme*, m.; to this the simply ModHG. **Grimmbarm**, 'colon,' is akin.

Grind, m., 'scab, scurf, itch,' from the equiv. MidHG. *grint*(*d*), OHG. *grint*, m.; allied, like **Grant**, to OTeut. *grindan*? or to **Grund**?.

grinsen, vb., 'to grin, show the teeth,' with a deriv. *s* from MidHG. *grinnen*, 'to gnash.' See greinen.

Grippe, f., 'influenza,' ModHG. only, from the equiv. Fr. *grippe*.

grob, adj., 'coarse, uncouth, rude,' from MidHG. *grop(b)*, *gerop*, OHG. *gerob*, *grob*, 'thick, awkward, indelicate'; comp. Du. and MidLG. *grof*, 'coarse.' The explanation of the word is not certain, since it is wanting in the other Teut. languages; it is undecided whether the term is compounded with *ge-*, Goth. *ga-*; if Goth. **ga-hruba-* were the primit. form, the connection with AS. *hreóf*, OHG. *riob*, 'scabiosus,' would still remain doubtful.

grollen, vb., 'to bear ill-will or a grudge; roll (of thunder,)' allied to Mid HG. *grüllen*, 'to scorn, ridicule'; comp. AS. *gryllan*, 'to gnash,' MidE. *grillen*, 'to vex'?.

Groppe, m. and f., 'miller's thumb,' from the equiv. MidHG. *groppe*; akin to MidLat. *carabus*?.

Gros, Groß, n., simply ModHG., from the equiv. Fr. *grosse*, 'twelve dozen, gross.'

Groschen, m., 'groschen (1½d.),' from the equiv. MidHG. *gros*, *grosse*, m.; like Fr. *gros*, 'groschen,' from MidLat. *grossus*; related to the common Rom. adj., Ital. *grosso*, 'thick' (comp. Fr. *gros*), just as Mid LG. *grote* (whence E. *groat*), 'groschen,' to ModHG. *groß*.

groß, adj., 'great, large, huge, grand,' from the equiv. MidHG. and OHG. *gróȝ*; a specifically West Teut. adj. (in Goth. *mikils*, MidHG. *michel*, Gr. μεγάλη); comp. OSax. *grôt*, Du. *groot*, E. *great*, AS. *greát*. The assumed Goth. **yrauta-* (pre-Teut. *ghraudo-*) has no correspondences in the non-Teut. languages. On account of the Teut. *au* especially, Lat. *grandis* cannot be primit. allied; it is rather connected with Lat. *rûdus*, *raudus*, n., 'lump of bronze, stones broken into small pieces,' and *rudis*, 'raw' (Aryan root *ghrûd*).

Grotte, see **Gruft.**

Grotzen, see **Griebs.**

Grube, f., 'pit, cavity, quarry, mine, ditch,' from the equiv. MidHG. *gruobe*, OHG. *gruoba*, f.; comp. Goth. *grôba*, f., 'pit, cavern' (E. *groove*); allied to graben. Whether **Gruft,** f., 'cave, hollow, sepulchre,' is connected with it is questionable; MidHG. *gruft*, OHG. *gruft*, might well correspond in form to graben, as the vowels of grüfteln prove. But the absence of the word in the other OTeut. dialects probably shows that it was borrowed from the Rom. cognates, Ital. *grotta*, Fr. *grotte*, 'grotto' (whence also **Grotte,** in ModHG. only), which are based on early MidLat. *grupta* (Gr. κρύπτη).—**grübeln,** vb., 'to grub, rack one's brains, brood,' from Mid HG. *grübelen*, OHG. *grubilôn*, 'to excavate by boring, investigate closely'; it is certainly connected with the root *grab*, 'to dig' (comp. E. *to grub*).

Grummet, n., 'aftermath,' from Mid HG. *gruenmât*, *gruonmât*, n., 'grass mown when it is *green*, *i.e.* unripe, aftermath'; the derivation from the root *grô* (see grün), 'to grow,' is less probable (**Grümmet,** lit. 'grass mown during its growth'). Comp. **Mahd.**

grün, adj., 'green, fresh, vigorous, unripe,' from MidHG. *grüene*, OHG. *gruoni*, 'green, fresh'; corresponding to OSax. *grôni*, Du. *groen*, AS. *grêne*, E. *green*, OIc. *grœnn*, Goth. **grô-ni-*, 'green'; allied to a Teut. root *grô*, 'to grow, become green.' Comp. MidHG. *grüejen*, OHG. *gruoan*, 'to grow green'; AS. *grôwan*, E. *to grow*, Du. *groeijen*, 'to grow, thrive.' Akin to **Gras** and its Aryan cognates.

Grund, m., 'ground, earth, basis, rudiment, reason,' from the equiv. MidHG. *grunt(d)*, OHG. *grunt*, m.; corresponding to Du. *grond*, AS. *grund*, E. *ground*, OIc. *grund*, 'meadow land,' *grunnr* (from *grunbus*), 'bottom of the sea;' Goth. *grunduwaddjus*, 'foundation wall.' Goth. *grundu*, from pre-Teut. *ghrentu-* (with *t* on account of OIc. *grunnr*), cannot have originated in the Teut. root *grind* (pre-Teut. *ghrendo-*) mentioned under **Graub.** No cognates are found in the non-Teut. languages.

Grünspan, m., 'verdigris,' from the equiv. late MidHG. *gruënspân*, m., formed like the ordinary MidHG. *spângrüen*, n., 'verdigris,' from MidLat. *viride Hispanum*.

grunzen, vb., 'to grunt,' from the equiv. MidHG. and OHG. *grunzen* (OHG. **grunnazzen*); corresponding to E. *to grunt* (Mid E. *grunten*); intensive form of MidHG. *grinnen*, AS. *grunnian*, 'to gnash.' The stem upon which it is based is probably imitative, as the similarly sounding Lat. *grunnire*, Gr. γρύζειν, lead us to suppose.

gruseln, vb., 'to inspire terror,' Mod HG. simply, intensive of graufen.

Gruß, m., 'greeting, salute,' from the equiv. MidHG. and OHG. *gruoȝ*, m.; corresponding to Du. *groet*. To this is allied grüßen, from MidHG. *grüeȝen* (*grüetzen*), OHG. *gruoȝȝen* (*gruozzen*), wk. vb., 'to address, accost' (also with hostile intent 'to attack'); corresponding to AS. *grétan,* E. *to greet,* Du. *groeten,* OSax. *grôtian,* 'to address,' OIc. *græta.* The latter is probably the primary meaning of the cognates, which are merely West Teut. Origin obscure.

Grütze, f., 'groats, grit, brain,' from MidHG. *grütze,* 'water-gruel'; a variant of the equiv. MidHG. *griuʒe (griutze?);* OHG. *gruzzi* (whence Ital. *gruzzo,* 'pile of collected things'); comp. AS. *grýt* and *grytt,* E. *grit* and *groat* (from AS. **grota?),* OIc. *grautr,* Du. *grut, gort,* 'groats.' From OG. the Romance cognates, Fr. *gruau,* 'groats,' are derived. Besides **Grieß,** MidHG. *grūʒ,* 'grain,' is also allied to **Grütze;** hence 'grain' may be the prim. meaning of the Teut. root *grŭt,* with which the primit. cognates Lith. *grúdas,* 'grain, kernel,' and OSlov. *gruda,* 'clod,' are also connected.

guchen, vb., from the equiv. MidHG. *gucken, gücken,* 'to peep'; the word is wanting in OHG. and in OTeut. generally. Origin obscure.

Gulden, m., 'florin,' from the equiv. MidHG. *guldēn, guldīn,* m., 'the golden coin,' from MidHG. *guldīn,* 'golden.' The absence of mutation from *u* to *ü* is in accordance with the practice of earlier UpG. (Suab. **Gülden**).

Gülte, f., 'payment, interest,' from MidHG. *gülte,* f., 'debt, payment, interest, rent.' Akin to **gelten.**

Gunderrebe, f., 'ground-ivy,' from the equiv. MidHG. *gunderēbe;* the deviation in meaning in OHG. *gundrēba,* 'maple,' is remarkable. Allied to OHG. *gund* (*gunt*), 'pus, poison,' AS. *gund,* Goth. *gunds,* 'pus'?. In that case the word would signify 'poison-vine' (see **Rebe**). Ground-ivy was used as a medicinal herb.

Günsel, m., 'bugle(-plant),' simply ModHG., transformed from Lat. *consolida,* "a name applied by the earlier herb-gatherers to all wound-healing plants."

Gunst, f., 'favour, partiality, permission,' from MidHG. and MidLG. *gunst,* m. and f., 'benevolence, permission,' for **ge-unst,* allied to OHG. *gi-unnan* (see **gönnen**); in OHG. *unst,* f. (MidHG. also *gund;* comp. OIc. *ofund,* 'disfavour'), Goth. *ansts,* 'favour, mercy,' AS. *ést,* OHG. *anst,* 'favour, mercy.'

Gurgel, f., 'gullet, throat,' from MidHG. *gurgel,* OHG. *gurgula,* f.; a remarkably early loan-word (comp. **Körper**) from Lat. *gurgulio,* which supplanted a genuine Teut. word primit. allied to it—OHG. *querchala, quěrcha,* 'gullet,' allied to OIc. *kverk,* 'gullet.'

Gurke, f., 'cucumber,' first occurs in early ModHG.; corresponding to Du. *agurkje,* E. *gherkin,* Dan. *agurke;* borrowed from Pol. *ogurek,* Bohem. *okurka;* the latter has been derived from late Gr. ἀγγούριον, 'water-melon,' and further from Pers. *ankhara.* In UpG. (also in the Wetter and Hess. dials.) **Kukumer** is used instead of **Gurke.**

gurren, vb., 'to coo,' from MidHG. *gurren,* 'to bray'; allied to MidHG. *gërren.* See **girren.**

Gurt, m., 'girth, girdle,' from the equiv. MidHG. *gurt* (in compounds *über-, umbe-, under-gurt*); allied to **gürten** from the equiv. MidHG. *gürten (gurten),* OHG. *gurten (gurtjan);* comp. OSax. *gurdian,* Du. *gorden,* AS. *gyrdan,* E. *to gird;* in Goth. *gairdan,* str. vb. 'to gird.' With the root *gerd* contained in these words are connected OIc. *garðr,* 'fence round the farm,' OSlov. *gradŭ.* 'wall, town' (see **Garten,** and respecting the evolution of meaning see **Zaun**).

Gürtel, m., 'girdle,' from the equiv. MidHG. *gürtel,* m. and f., OHG. *gurtil,* m., *gurtila,* f. Comp. E. *girdle,* from AS. *gyrdel.*

Guß, m., 'shower, torrent, spout, cast,' from MidHG. and OHG. *guʒ(ʒʒ),* 'cast, shower.' Allied to **gießen.**

gut, adj., 'good, virtuous, skilful,' from the equiv. MidHG. and OHG. *guot;* a common Teut. term unknown to the non-Teut. languages; comp. Goth. *gôds,* OIc. *gôðr,* AS. *gôd,* E. *good,* Du. *goed.* Its connection with Gr. ἀγαθός is phonetically uncertain. Only in Teut. are found reliable cognates which may elucidate the primary meaning of *gut* (yet comp. OSlov. *godŭ,* 'suitable time'?). The cognates of **Gatte,** with which E. *together, to gather,* Goth. *gadiliggs,* 'relative,' also seem to be connected, prove that the prim. meaning of *gut* is 'belonging to one another, suitable.' For the comparison of the adj. see **baß, besser.**

H.

Haar (1.), m., 'flax,' from the equiv. MidHG. *har*, OHG. *haro* (gen. MidHG. and OHG. *harwes*), n.; Goth. **harwa-* (gen. **harwis*) is also implied by OIc. *hǫrr* (dat. *hǫrve*), m., 'flax.' As to its connection with **Haar** (2.) see the latter. Perhaps the word is most closely related to E. *hards* ('refuse of flax, tow'). See **Hede**.

Haar (2.), n., 'hair,' from the equiv. MidHG. and OHG. *hâr*, n.; comp. the corresponding OIc. *hár*, n., AS. *hǽr*, n., E. *hair*, Du. *haar*; a common Teut. word (in Goth., however, *tagl* and *skuft*). The following Teut. words are also primit. allied—OIc. *haddr* and AS. *heord*, 'hair' (Goth. **hazda*), as well as Ir. *cass*, 'curled hair.' In the non-Teut. languages comp. OSlov. *kosmŭ*, m., *kosa* (Lith. *kasa*), f., 'hair,' and probably also OSlov. *česati*, 'to comb,' Lat. *carere*, 'to card wool.' The more definite relations in sound existing between these words are difficult to determine (comp. also Gr. κόμη, Lat. *coma*?). On the other hand, there is no phonetic difficulty in connecting the Teut. **hera-*, 'hair,' with *harwa-*, deduced under **Haar** (1.); the mere possibility is, however, all that can be maintained. Comp. also **Lecke** and **Frans**.—An old derivative of **Haar**, AS. *hǽre*, OHG. *hârâ*, *hârrâ*, f., 'hair shirt, coarse garment,' found its way into Romance (Fr. *haire*).

Habe, f., 'possession; handle,' from MidHG. *habe*, OHG. *huba*, f., 'goods, possession'; Du. *have*, 'possession'; allied to the following word.

haben, vb., 'to have, possess,' from the equiv. MidHG. *haben*, OHG. *habên*; corresponding to OSax. *hebbian*, Du. *hebben*, AS. *habban*, E. *to have*, OIc. *hafa*, Goth. *haban*; a common Teut. vb. with the stem *habai-*. Its identity with Lat. *habere* can scarcely be doubted. It is true that Lat. *h* initially requires, according to the laws of substitution, a Teut. *g*, and Teut. *h* a Lat. *c* (comp. **Gast**, **Gerste**, **Geist**, and **Hals**, **Haut**, and **heben**). Probably Lat. *habê-* and Teut. *habai-* are based upon an Aryan prim. form *khabhêj*; the correspondence between Teut. *h* and Lat. *h* is only possible on the assumption of an Aryan *kh*. On this supposition **haben** and **heben** in their etymology are primit. allied, just as Lat. *habere* and *capere*.

Haber (UpG.), m., 'oats,' from the equiv. MidHG. *haber*, *habere*, m., OHG. *habaro*, m. The form **Hafer** first occurs in ModHG.; like **Roggen**, it is derived from LG.; OLG. *haboro*, *havoro* (now *haver*), Du. *haver*. Also allied to OSwed. *hafre*, *hagre*, and further to Finn. *kakra*, borrowed from Teut. In E. the word is wanting, but is found a few times in MidE., which, like Northern E. (*haver*), borrowed it from Scand. The E. term is *oats*, from AS. *âta* (yet Scotch *haver* occurs even in the MidE. period). In investigating the origin of the G. cognates, the *g* in OSwed. *hagre* (Finn. *kakra*) must be taken into account. The usual derivation from OIc. *hafr*, AS. *hæfer*, m., 'he-goat' (Lat. *caper*, Gr. κάπρος, comp. **Habergeiß**), is therefore impossible, especially since this word belongs to the dialects in which **Hafer** is wanting; **Hafer** too must have been the favourite food of the goat ere it could be thus named. Perhaps Gr. κάχρυς, 'parched barley' (Aryan base *khaghru-*), or Lat. *avena*, 'oats' (Aryan base *khaghwes*), are primit. allied.

Habergeiß, f., 'common snipe,' not found in the earlier periods; **Haber** in this compound is the only remnant of the old name for a goat (AS. *hæfer*, OIc. *hafr*; Gr. κάπρος, Lat. *caper*) in G.; the bird is so called because at the pairing season it utters high in the air a sound like the distant bleating of a goat. See **Beck** and **Haber**.

Habicht, m. (with a dental suffix as in **Hüfte** and **Mond**, &c.), 'hawk,' from the equiv. MidHG. *habich*, *habech* (also *hebech*, modified), m., OHG. *habuh*, m.; a common Teut. term by chance not recorded in Goth.; comp. OSax. **haboc* (in the proper names *Hauuchorst*, *Παδοcasbrôc*), Du. *havik*, AS. *heáfoc*, E. *hawk*, OIc. *haukr* (for **hǫbuk-*). The Goth. form would be **habaks*, with a suffix *aks-*, as in *ahaks*, 'pigeon' (comp. also **Kranich**, **Lerche**); comp. the consonantal suffix in Gr. ὄρτυγ-, 'quail.' Against the derivation from the stem *hab*, *haf*, in **heben**, orig., 'to take firm hold of, lay hold of,' there is nothing to object from the Teut. point of view; Italic *capus*, 'hawk,' is certainly derived from the root *kap* (*capio*). The Kelt. cognates, W. *hebauc*, OIr. *sebocc*, 'falcon,' are undoubtedly borrowed from Teut. Comp. also **Falke**.

Hach, m., 'fellow,' from MidHG. *hache*,

m.. 'fellow, churl'; allied to MidHG. *hęchel*, f., 'artful woman, match-maker.' The derivation is not clear, since cognate terms in OTeut. are wanting.

Hächſe, see **Hechſe**.

Hacke, f., 'heel,' prop. a MidG. and LG. word (in UpG. Ferſe); comp. Du. *hak*; not recorded in MidHG., but it occurs once in the transition period from OHG. to MidHG. (*hachun*, 'heels'); usually derived from *hacken*. On account of its meaning, it is more probably related to Du. *hiel*, AS. *hôh*, 'heel,' *héla*, f. (for *$hôhila$), E. *heel*, and the equiv. Scand. *hǽll*, m.

hacken, vb., from the equiv. MidHG. *hacken*, 'to hack, hew'; OHG. *$hacchôn$ is by chance not recorded; comp. AS. *haccian* (*hæccean*), E. *to hack*, OFris. *tohakia*, 'to hack to pieces.' Not found in Goth.; may we assume *$hawôn$, a derivative from the stem *haw* in *hauen*? The medial guttural may have been simply an insertion before *w*, as in *qued* and *ſed*.—**Hacke**, f. (thus even in MidHG.), **Häckerling** (ModHG. only), and **Häckſel** are derivatives.

Hader (1.), m., 'contention, strife, brawl,' from MidHG. *hader*, m., 'quarrel, strife'; unrecorded in OHG. For this word OTeut. has most frequently a deriv. in *u-* (*w-*), signifying 'battle,' which appears in West Teut. only as the first part of compounds; AS. *heapo-*, OHG. *hadu-* (Goth. *$hapu-$). In Scand. *Hǫðr* is the name of a Valkyre, and *Hǫðr* that of a mythological king and the brother of Balder; the names are probably based upon *Hapu-z*, an OTeut. war-god. With these Kότυς, the name of a Thracian goddess, has been compared. The following, however, are certainly allied:—OSlov. *kotora*, f., 'battle,' Ir. *cath*, m., 'battle' (with which Kelt. *Catu-riges*, proper noun, lit. 'warkings,' is connected; Ind. *çátru-s*, 'enemy'; perhaps too Gr. κότος, κοτέω; a deriv. in *r*, like **Hader**, is preserved in OSlov. *kotora*, 'battle'; see also **Haß**. In G. the old form *hapu* became obsolete at an early period, being supplanted by **Kampf** and **Krieg**, but it was retained in OHG. as the first component in some compound proper names, such as *Hadubrant*; Mod HG. **Hedwig** is OHG. *Haduwîg*, 'battle strife.' Similarly appears OHG. *hilta*, f., 'battle,' in MidHG. only in proper names, such as **Hildebrand**, **Brünhild**, &c. It would be very interesting to find out why the OTeut. words gave place to the later forms.

Hader (2.), m., 'rag, tatter, clout,' from MidHG. *hader*, m., 'patch, torn piece of stuff,' OHG. *hadara*, f., 'patch, rag'; also with a suffix *l*, MidHG. *hadel*, from which Fr. *haillon* is borrowed. The word does not seem to have been diffused in the Teut. group. It is not allied to **Hader** (1.); the two words are based on different stems. **Hader**, 'patch' (from Teut. *hapró*, Aryan *kåtrá*), is either connected with the nasalised stem *kant-* in Lat. *cento*, Gr. κέντρων, 'garment made of rags,' Sans. *kanthâ*, f., 'patchwork garment,' or with Sans. *çithirá*, 'loose, unbound.'

Hafen (1.), m., 'pot,' from MidHG. *haven*, m., OHG. *havan*, m., 'pot'; a specifically UpG. word unknown to the other dialects. It belongs to the root *haf* (pre-Teut. *kap*), lit. 'to comprehend, hold,' which appears in HG. **heben**, and not to **haben**, root *hab* (pre-Teut. *khabh*).

Hafen (2.), m., 'port, haven, harbour,' a LG. word, unknown to UpG.; it was first borrowed in ModHG.; in MidHG. *hap*, n., *habe*, *habene*, f., formed from the same root. Du. *haven*, f., late AS. *hœfene*, f., E. *haven*, and OIc. *hǫfn*, f., 'harbour,' correspond in sound to MidHG. *habene*, f. LG. *haven*, Dan. *havn*, Swed. *hamn*, are masc.—Phonetically the derivation from the root *hab* (*khabh*), 'to have,' or from *haf*, *hab* (*kap*), 'to seize, hold, contain,' is quite possible; in both cases the prim. sense would be 'receptacle'; comp. **Hafen** (1.). This is the usual explanation; for another etymology see under **Haff**. Perhaps, however, OIc. *hǫfn* is primit. allied to the equiv. OIr. *cúan* (from *$copno$?).

Hafer, see **Haber**.

Haff, n., 'inland sea, gulf,' a LG. word, orig. 'sea' (generally), which is also the meaning of AS. *hæf* (plur. *heafu*), n., Scand. *haf*, n., MidLG. *haf*; the UpG. words, MidHG. *hap*, *habes*, n., and *habe*, f., which correspond in sound, also signify 'sea,' as well as 'port' (see **Hafen**). As we need not assume an orig. difference between the words for 'harbour' and 'sea,' and since in any case the meaning 'harbour' is derived from the signification 'sea'—the converse would be hardly possible—the usual assumption mentioned under **Hafen** (2.), that **Hafen** is lit. 'receptacle,' is quite problematical. Hence **Hafen** may probably be explained by some such word as 'marina,' in the sense of 'statio marina.' The connection of AS. *hæf*, 'sea,' as 'heaving,' in the sense of Lat. *altum* ('high sea'), with heben (root *haf*, pre-Teut. *kap*), is not impossible, though scarcely probable.

Haft (1.), m., 'hold, clasp, brace, rivet,' from MidHG. and OHG. *haft*, m., 'bond, fetter,' OHG. also n., AS. *hæft*, m., OIc. *haft*, n., 'fetter.' Connected with the root *haf* in heben, lit. 'to seize.'

Haft (2.), f., 'keeping, custody, prison,' from MidHG. and OHG. *haft* (*i* stem) and *hafta*, f., OSax. *hafta*, f., 'imprisonment.' To this are allied OHG. and OSax. *haft*, AS. *hæft*, adj., 'captured,' OIc. *haptr*, m., 'prisoner,' *hapta*, f., 'captured woman.' The root *haf* (comp. heben) has preserved in these forms its old signification; comp. Lat. *captus, captivus*. See the following word.

haft, adj. suffix, as in schmerzhaft, lebhaft, &c.; prop. an independent adj., 'combined with,' which was used as a suffix even in MidHG. and OHG.; in Goth. *audahafts*, 'overwhelmed with happiness, supremely happy.' This suffix is usually identified with the adj. *hafta-*, Lat. *captus*, discussed under Haft (2.). It might also be derived from the root *hab*, 'to have,' Lat. *habere;* the meaning supports the latter supposition.

Hag, m., 'hedge, fence, enclosure,' from MidHG. *hac, hages*, m., n., 'thorn bushes, copse, fence, enclosed wood, park,' OHG. *hag*, in., once as 'urbs' (comp. HG. Hagen, and names of places ending in ⸗hag); Du. *haug*, f., 'enclosure, hedge,' AS. *haga*, m., E. *haw*, 'enclosure, small garden'; OIc. *hage*, m., 'pasture.' Only in Goth. is a cognate word wanting; comp. Hain, Here, Hagen, and Hecke. The derivation is uncertain; it is at all events not connected with hauen, root *haw;* the meaning of ModHG. behagen is unsuitable.

Hagedorn, 'hawthorn,' an OTeut. term, MidHG. *hagedorn*, AS. *hægþorn, hagaþorn*, E. *hawthorn*, OIc. *hagþorn*, m. Comp. Hagestolz.

Hagel, m., from the equiv. MidHG. *hagel*, OHG. *hagal*, m., 'hail'; comp. Du. *hagel*, m., AS. *hagol, hægel*, m., E. *hail;* OIc. *hagl*, n.; the common Teut. word for 'hail,' by chance unrecorded in Goth. only. A single pebble was called a 'stone.' OIc. *haglsteinn*, AS. *hægelstân*, E. *hailstone*, MidHG. and earlier ModHG. Hagelstein. Comp. ModHG. kieseln, 'to hail,' Kieselstein, 'hailstone.' Perhaps Hagel itself signified orig. nothing but a 'pebble'; at least there are no phonetic difficulties against the derivation from pre-Teut. *kaghlo-*, 'flint-stone' (comp. Gr. κάχληξ, 'small stone, pebble').

Hagen, m., 'grave,' from MidHG. *hagen*, OHG. *hagan*, m., 'thorn-bush, fence of thorns'; even in MidHG. a contracted variant *hain*, Hain, occurs. See the latter and Hag.

hagen, behagen, vb., from the equiv. MidHG. *hagen, behagen*, 'to please, gratify,' OHG. *bihagôn;* comp. OSax. *bihagôn*, AS. *onhagian*, 'to please, suit.' The stem *hag*, 'to suit,' is widely diffused in OTeut., and its str. partic. is preserved in OHG. and MidHG. (*gihagan* and *behagen*, 'suitable'). Allied to Scand. *hagr*, adj., 'skilful,' *hagr*, m., 'state, situation, advantage,' *hægr*, 'suitable.' The root *hag*, from pre-Teut. *kak*, corresponds to the Sans. root *çak*, 'to be capable, able, conducive,' whence *çakrá*, 'strong, helpful.'

hager, adj. (in UpG. rahn), 'haggard, lean,' from MidHG. *hager*, adj.; comp. E. *haggard* (MidE. *hagger*), which is usually connected with E. *hag*.

Hagestolz, m., 'old bachelor,' from MidHG. *hagestolz*, m., a strange corruption of the earlier *hagestalt*, OHG. *hagu-stalt*, m., prop. 'possessor of an enclosure' (allied to Goth. *staldan*, 'to possess'); a West Teut. legal term, which originated before the Anglo-Saxons crossed to England (comp. also OIc. *haukstaldr*). It was used in contrast to the owner of the manor-house, which was inherited by the eldest son, in accordance with the OTeut. custom of primogeniture, and signified the owner of a small enclosed plot of ground, such as fell to the other sons, who could not set up a house of their own, and were often entirely dependent on their eldest brother. Even in OHG. glosses, *hagustalt* as an adj. is used for Lat. *caelebs* (*hagustalt lîp*, 'single life'), and even for *mercenarius*, 'hired labourer'; MidHG. *hagestalt*, m., 'single man'; OSax. *hagustald*, m., 'farm-servant, servant, young man'; AS. *hægsteald, hagustealð*, m., 'youth, warrior.' The same phases in the development of meaning may be seen in the Rom.-Lat. *baccalaureus*, Fr. *bachelier*, E. *bachelor*.

Häher, m., 'jay, jackdaw,' from MidHG. *hëher*, m. and f., OHG. *hëhara*, f.; in AS., by a grammatical change, *higora*, m., OIc. *here* and *hegre*, m., 'jay,' MidLG. *heger*. It is rightly compared with Gr. κίσσα (from *κίκjα), 'jay,' or Sans. *çakuná*, 'a large bird' (Lat. *ciconia*, 'stork').

Hahn, m., 'cock,' from MidHG. *han*, OHG. *hano*, m.; comp. AS. *hana* (as well as *cocc*, E. *cock*), OIc. *hane*, Goth. *hana*, m.; a common Teut. word for 'cock,' with the stem *hanan-, hanin-*, which is common to the OTeut. dialects. A corresponding fem. Henne is merely West Teut.; OHG. *henna*, MidHG. and ModHG. *henne*, f., AS. *henn*. On the other hand, Hahn seems to be really of common gender; it may at least be applied in OHG. to 'cock' also; comp. Otfried's *ér thaʒ huan singe*, 'before the cock crows,' lit. 'sings.' In this passage we have a confirmation of the fact that the crowing of the cock was regarded as its song. The term Hahn by general acceptation signifies 'singer.' With this word, according to the laws of substitution, the stem of Lat. *canere*, 'to sing' (comp. Lith. *gaidỹs*, 'cock,' lit. 'singer,' allied to *gédoti*, 'to sing'). A fem., 'songstress,' of Hahn is hardly conceivable; thus it follows that Henne is merely a recent West Teut. form. The common gender Hahn, however, can hardly be connected with the root *kan*, 'to sing,' since it is, at least, a primit. form. The method of its formation, as the name of the agent, has no analogies.

Hahnrei, m., 'cuckold,' ModHG. only; of obscure origin; in earlier G. it signifies 'capon.' Its figurative sense, 'cuckold,' derived from 'capon,' agrees with the expression Hörner tragen, lit. 'to wear horns.' Formerly the spur was frequently cut off and placed as a horn in the comb; the hoodwinked husband is thus compared to a capon. On account of the earlier variant Hahnreh, we may regard Hahnrei as a compound of Reh.

Hai, m., simply ModHG., from the equiv. Du. *haai*, f., 'shark,' Swed. *haj*, Ic. *há-r*.

Hain, m., 'grove,' made current by Klopstock as a poetical term. The form of the word, as is shown under Hagen (1), may be traced back to MidHG., in which, however, Hain is but a rare variant of Hagen; it signified orig. 'thorn-bush, thorn, fence, abatis, enclosed place.' Thus the word does not imply the idea of sacredness which Klopstock blended with it.

Hake, Haken, m., 'hook, clasp,' from MidHG. *hâke, hâken*, m., OHG. *hâko, hácko*, m., 'hook.' The HG. *k* can neither be Goth. *k* nor Goth. *g*; the former would be changed into *ch*, the latter would remain unchanged. The variants OHG. *hâgo, hâggo*, MidHG. *hâgg*, point to Goth. *héyga, n., 'hook' (comp. Raupe, Schuppe). Curiously, however, the corresponding words of the cognate dialects have *k* and are graded: AS. *hôc*, m., 'hook,' E. *hook*, MidDu. *hoek*, 'hook'; comp. also Du. *haak*, AS. *hâca*, OIc. *hâke*, m., 'hook.' The relations of the gutturals (especially of the *gg*) are still obscure; comp. also Kuppe, Schuppe, Raum, Schmauze. A typical form is wanting. It is impossible to connect the word hangen, Goth. *hâhan* (for *hanhan*); it is more probably related to Hechel and Hecht.

halb, adj., 'half,' from MidHG. *halp*, OHG. *halb* (gen. *halbes*), adj.; comp OSax. and LG. *half*, Du. *half*, AS. *healf*, E. *half*, OIc. *hálfr*, Goth. *halbs*, adj.; the common Teut. adj. for HG. halb; there are no undoubted cognates in the non-Teut. languages (Teut. *halba-*, from pre-Teut. *kalbho-*). The fem. of the adj. is used in OTeut. as a subst. in the sense of 'side, direction'; Goth. *halba*, OIc. *hálfa*, OHG. *halba*, MidHG. *halbe*, OSax. *halba*; hence it might seem as if the adj. had orig. some such meaning as 'lateral, that which lies on one side.' But in any case the adj. in the sense of 'half' was purely a numeral in primit. Teut.; the ModHG. method of reckoning anberthalb (1½), britthalb (2½), vierthalb (3½), is common to Teut.; comp. OIc. *halfr annarr* (1½), *halfr þriþe* (2½), *halfr fjorþe* (3½); AS. *óþer healf, þridde healf, feorþe healf*; even in MidE. this enumeration exists (it is wanting in E.); in HG. it has been retained from the earliest period.

halb, halben, prep., 'on account of,' from MidHG. *halp, halbe, halben*, 'on account of, by reason of, from, concerning'; prop. a case of the MidHG. subst. *halbe*, f., 'side,' mentioned under halb (adj.), hence construed with the gen.; MidHG. *minhalp, dinhalp, der herren halbe, sêhens halben*, 'on my, thy account, on the gentlemen's account, for the sake of seeing.' Similarly the ModHG. halber, 'on account of,' recorded in the 15th cent., is a petrified form of the inflected adj.; so too halben, dat. plur., *halbe, halp*, from OHG. *halb*, probably an instr. sing. (since Notker halb has been used as a prep.). This usage is also found in the other Teut. languages; comp. OIc. *af-halfu*, MidE. *on-, bi-halfe*; Goth. *in þizai halbai*, 'in this respect.'

Halde, f., 'precipice, declivity, slope,' from MidHG. *halde*, OHG. *halda*, f., 'mountain declivity.' OIc. *hallr*, 'hill, slope,' corresponds both to the HG. word and to Goth. *hallus*, AS. *heall*, which are translations of 'petra'; see $\mathfrak{Helm}$. These may be further related to HG. $\mathfrak{Halde}$, which, however, is more closely connected with Goth. *halþs, 'inclined'; comp. AS. *heald*, OIc. *hallr*, OHG. *hald*, adj., 'overhanging, inclined'; yet the dental in these words may be a suffix. If Goth. *hallus*, 'rock,' were allied, OIc. *hvǽll*, *hóll* (Goth. *huélus), m., 'hill,' might be compared, as well as AS. *hyll*, E. *hill*. For an Aryan root *kel*, 'to rise,' comp. Lat. *celsus*, *collis*, and Lith. *kalnas*, 'hill.'

$\mathfrak{Hälfte}$, f., 'half.' ModHG. simply, abstract of $\mathfrak{halb}$. Introduced by Luther into the literary language from MidG. and LG. (a strictly HG. word would end in *b* instead of *f*; comp. OSax. *half*, under $\mathfrak{halb}$); the Teut. type is probably *halbiþa?*. In UpG. $\mathfrak{Halbteil}$ (16th cent.) is used.

$\mathfrak{Halfter}$, f., from the equiv. MidHG. *halfter*, OHG. *halftra*, f., 'halter'; comp. Du. *halster*, AS. *hælftre*, E. *halter;* a West Teut. word most closely allied with OHG. *halp*, MidHG. *halp*, plur. *helbe*, 'handle, helve,' AS. *hylf*, m., equiv. to E. *helve;* in earlier ModHG. also $\mathfrak{Helb}$, 'hilt, helve.' From the same root are formed with a suffix *m*, OHG. *halmo* (for *halbmo), in OHG. *jioh-halmo*, MidHG. *giech-halme*, 'rope fastened to the yoke to guide the oxen,' MidHG. *halme*, 'handle, helve, lever of a bell,' *halm-ackes*, 'axe' (comp. also $\mathfrak{Hellebarte}$), likewise MidE. *halme*, 'handle'; so too the modified forms OHG. *joh-helmo*, MidHG. *giech-helme;* AS. *helma*, 'handle' (equiv. also to E. *helm*), and Du. *helmstock*, 'tiller,' are not connected with this word; see $\mathfrak{Helm}$ (2). 'Handle' is the orig. sense of the whole group, and even of $\mathfrak{Halfter}$. Perhaps Lith. *keltuvē*, 'swiple of a flail,' is allied.

$\mathfrak{Hall}$, m., 'sound'; see $\mathfrak{hell}$.

$\mathfrak{Halle}$, f., 'hall, large room. entrance hall, porch,' unknown to MidHG. The word, which was introduced by Luther into the literary language, was originally entirely unknown to the UpG. dials. (in earlier UpG. $\mathfrak{Verschupf}$ was used); it may have originated among the Franc. and Sax. tribes of Germany. It is a thorough OTeut. term ; OIc. *holl*, f., AS. *heall*, f., E. *hall*, OSax. *halla*, MidLG. *halle*, f., 'hall, a large room covered with a roof and open or closed at the side,' sometimes 'temple, house of God.' Not allied to Goth. *hallus*, AS. *heall*, 'rock,' AS. and E. *hill*. From the OG. is derived Fr. *halle*. Against the derivation from the root *hel*, 'to conceal' (comp. $\mathfrak{hehlen}$), there is no weighty objection, $\mathfrak{Halle}$, 'the concealed or covered place.' Yet comp. also Sans. *çálā*, 'house.'— $\mathfrak{Halle}$, f., 'saltern,' is the ordinary G. $\mathfrak{Halle}$, not, as was formerly supposed, a Kelt. term (W. *halen*, 'salt'); $\mathfrak{Halleren}$, a late Lat. derivative of $\mathfrak{Halle}$, 'saltern.' Comp. OHG. *halhūs*, 'salt-house,' MidHG. *halgrāve*, m., 'director and judge in matters connected with salt-mines.'

$\mathfrak{hallen}$, vb., 'to sound, resound'; comp. $\mathfrak{hell}$.

$\mathfrak{Halm}$, m. and n., 'stalk, stem, straw,' from MidHG. *halm*, m., and *halme*, m., OHG. and OSax. *halm*, m.; comp. AS. *healm*, E. *halm;* the meaning in West Teut. is 'grass or corn-stalk'; Scand. *halmr*, 'straw.' In sense and sound corresponding to Lat. *calamus*, Gr. κάλαμος, 'reed, reed-pen, halm' (Ind. *kalamas*, 'reed-pen'), OSlov. *slama*, f., 'halm.' Perhaps the Lat. word is derived from Gr. ; it is also conceivable that $\mathfrak{Halm}$, like $\mathfrak{Hanf}$, was obtained from a South Russ. tribe by the Aryans who had migrated westwards. Yet it is more probable that $\mathfrak{Halm}$ and Gr. κάλαμος, like Lat. *culmus*, 'stalk,' are connected with Lat. *culmen*, 'peak, summit,' and further with *excello*.

$\mathfrak{Hals}$, m., 'neck,' from the equiv. Mid HG. and OHG. *hals*, m. ; corresponding to OSax. and Du. *hals*, AS. *heals* (E. *to halse*, 'embrace,' but now antiquated; the modern word is *neck*), OIc. *hals*, m., 'neck,' Goth. *hals* (gen. *halsis*), m. ; all point to a common Teut. mas. *halsa-*. Primit. allied to Lat. *collum* for *colsum, n., 'neck' (OLat. also *collus*, m.) ; comp. also Gr. κλοιός, 'collar' (from *κλοσιός)?. Whether Lat. *excello*, *excelsus*, are also primit. allied ($\mathfrak{Hals}$, lit. 'prominent part of the body') remains uncertain. From Teut. is derived Fr. *haubert*, OFr. *halberc*, 'hauberk,' from *hals-bērg(a)*.

—$\mathfrak{halsen}$, vb., from the equiv. MidHG. *halsen*, OHG. *halsōn*, ' to embrace, fall on one's neck'; comp. Du. *omhelzen*, AS. *healsian*, 'to implore,' MidE. *halsien*, Scand. *hálsa*, 'to embrace.'

$\mathfrak{halt}$, adv., 'moreover, forsooth, methinks,' prop. a compar. meaning 'rather,' MidHG. and OHG. *halt*, adv., OSax. *hald*, 'rather'; orig. a compar. adv. of the posit. adv. *halto*, 'very.' The compar. ending, according to the law of apocope, has disappeared, as in ħaß for the earlier batiz; orig. halđiz formed, like Goth. haldis, OIc. heldr, 'rather.' In no case is it related to the OHG. adj. hald, 'inclined,' mentioned under Halte; with the exception of the OHG. hallo, adv., no other word in the posit. can be found.

haſſen, vb., 'to hold, support, detain, observe, perform, consider,' from the equiv. MidHG. halten, OHG. haltan; comp. OSax. haldan, 'to preserve, receive, detain as a prisoner, tend (cattle), adhere to, maintain,' Du. houden (see hantern), AS. healdan, str. vb., 'to watch over, lead, possess, rule,' E. to hold; Goth. haldan, redupl. vb., 'to graze cattle'; a redupl. vb. common to Teut. According to the OHG. variant halthan, haltan points to the normal Goth. form *halþan, which is also supported by OSwed. halla. The orig. sense of OTeut. haldan is perhaps 'to keep together by careful watching,' hence 'to tend a herd, govern a tribe, rule.' In the non-Teut. languages an Aryan root kalt of cognate meaning is not found. If the dental belonged orig. to the pres. stem merely, the word might also be derived from the root kol, and hence connected with Gr. βου-κόλος. No relation between haldan and Herde is possible.—ModHG. Halt, m., is wanting both in MidHG. and OHG.

Hamen, m., 'tunnel-net,' from Mid HG. and MidLG. hame; akin probably to the equiv. OSwed. haver, ModSwed. håf, n., OHG. hamo, m., 'tunnel-net.' The latter word is considered identical with OHG. *hamo (in lîhhamo, 'body,' OSax. gûðhamo, feðarhamo; comp. Leichnam, Hemd, and Hämiſch), orig. 'covering, dress.' From the meaning 'Tuch,' in the restricted sense in which it is used by fishermen and huntsmen (i.e. 'toils'), the signification 'net' might of course be developed; but that is not certain. OHG. hamo, MidHG. ham, hame, m., 'fishing-rod, fishing-hook,' and the modern dial. Hamen, are not allied to the words mentioned above; they seem to be cognate with Lat. hāmus, 'fishing-hook, hook'; the h might be explained as in haben.

hämiſch, adj., 'malicious,' from late MidHG. hemisch, adj., 'close, malicious, cunning, perfidious,' orig. perhaps 'veiled, obscure'; allied to OHG. *hamo, 'covering, dress,' mentioned under Hamen, Hemd, and Leichnam.

Hammel, m., from the equiv. MidHG. and MidLG. hamel, OHG. hamal, m., 'wether' (MidHG. also 'steep, rugged height; cliff, pole'); prop. an adj. used as a subst., OHG. hamal, 'mutilated,' which elucidates the MidHG. meanings; OHG. hamalôn, MidHG. hameln (and hamen), 'to mutilate,' AS. hamelian, E. to hamble ('mutilate, lame'); OHG. hamalscorro, m., 'boulder,' OHG. hamal-, hamalung-stat, f., 'place of execution,' MidHG. hamelstat, n. and m., 'indented coast,' hamelstat, f., 'rugged ground.' Allied to OHG. ham (inflected hammēr), adj., 'mutilated, crippled' (comp. hemmen), just as Fr. mouton to Lat. mutilus.

Hammer, m., 'hammer, clapper,' from the equiv. MidHG. hamer (plur. hęmer), OHG. hamar (plur. hamarâ), n.; comp. OSax. hamur, AS. hamor, m., E. hammer, and its equiv. OIc. hamarr, m. (also 'cliff, rock'); the common Teut. word for 'hammer,' by chance unrecorded in Goth. only. For the elucidation of its earlier history the subsidiary meanings in Scand. are important; the cognate term kamy in OSlov. signifies 'stone.' Hence it has been assumed that Hammer is lit. 'stone weapon.' Whether Sans. açman, 'rock, stone weapon, hammer, anvil,' &c., and Gr. ἄκμων, 'anvil' (Lith. akmů, 'stone'), are also allied is uncertain.

Hämmling, Hemmling, m., 'eunuch,' ModHG. simply, a deriv. of Hammel.

Hampfel, f., from the equiv. MidHG. hant-vol, 'a handful.'

Hamſter, m., from the equiv. MidHG. hamster, m., 'German marmot'; OHG. hamastro, m., signifies only 'curculio, weevil,' so too OSax. hamstra, f., for *hamastra. The existing meaning is probably the earlier. In form the word stands quite alone; its occurrence in G. only, perhaps supports the view that it was borrowed. A corresponding word has not yet been found in a neighbouring language.

Hand, f., 'hand,' from the equiv. Mid HG. and OHG. hant, f.; comp. OSax. and Du. hand, AS. hand, f., E. hand, OIc. hǫnd, Goth. handus, f.; a common Teut. word for 'hand,' unknown to the other divisions of the Aryan group, most of the languages having special terms of their own. It is usually derived from Goth. hinþan, 'to catch,' frahunþans, m., 'prisoner' (comp. the cognate E. to hunt, AS. huntian), in the sense of 'the grasping, seizing part,' and to this there is no objection, as far as the sound and meaning are concerned.

Yet the fact remains that the old names of parts of the body have no corresponding str. verbal stems; comp. §erȝ, Ohr, Auge, Finger, Daumen. With regard to the form, it is to be observed that the word, according to Goth. *handus*, was orig. a *u-* stem, but is declined even in OHG. like nouns in *i*, though traces of the *u* declension remain throughout OHG. and MidHG.; comp. abhanden.—Hand, 'kind, sort,' is developed from the medial sense 'side'; comp. MidHG. *ze beiden handen*, 'on both sides,' *aller hande*, 'of every kind,' *vier hande*, 'of four sorts.'

handeln, vb., 'to manage, act, deal, bargain,' from MidHG. *handeln*, OHG. *hantalôn*, 'to grasp with the hands, touch, feel, prepare, perform' (hence O.Lorraine *handeleir*, 'to sweep'); a derivative of Hand; Handel, m., has arisen from the vb. handeln merely, just as Ärger from ärgern (see arg), Geiz from geizen, Opfer from opfern—since it does not appear until late MidHG. (*handel*, m., 'transaction, procedure, event, negotiation, wares'). AS. *handlian*, E. *to handle*, AS. *hendele*, equiv. to E. *handle*; Scand. *hǫndla*, 'to treat.'

Handwerk, n., 'handicraft, trade, guild,' from MidHG. *hantwerc*, n., 'manual labour,' but in the MidHG. period confused with *antwerc*, n., 'tool, machine,' whence the meaning 'any vocation requiring the use of tools' was developed.

Hanf, m., 'hemp,' from MidHG. *hanf, hanef*, m., OHG. *hanaf, hanǫf*, m.; a common Teut. word for 'hemp' (Goth. **hanaps* is by chance not recorded); comp. AS. *hænep*, E. *hemp*, OIc. *hampr*. The usual assumption that the word was borrowed from the South Europ. Gr. κάνναβις (Lat. *cannabis*) is untenable. The Teutons were not influenced by Southern civilisation until the last century or so before our era; no word borrowed from Gr.-Lat. has been fully subject to the OTeut. substitution of consonants (see Fiune (1), Pfad, and the earliest loan-words under Kaiser). But the substitution of consonants in Goth. **hanaps* compared with Gr. κάνναβις proves that the word was naturalised among the Teutons even before 100 B.C. "The Greeks first became acquainted with hemp in the time of Herodotus; it was cultivated by the Scythians, and was probably obtained from Bactria and Sogdiana, the regions of the Caspian and the Aral, where it is said to grow luxuriantly even at the present time."

Thus we can all the more readily reject the assumption of South Europ. influence; comp. Leinen. Why should not the Teutons in their migration from Asia to Europe have become acquainted with the culture of hemp when passing through the south of Russia, where the plant grows wild, and indeed among the very people who directly or indirectly supplied the Greeks with the word κάνναβις? (comp. also Grbse). κάνναβις itself is a borrowed term, and Goth. **hanaps* corresponds in sound quite as well with OSlov. *konoplja*, Lith. *kanápės*, 'hemp.' The word is found even among the Persians (*kanab*). It does not seem to be genuinely Aryan.

Hang, m., 'declivity, propensity, bias,' from MidHG. *hanc (-ges)*, m., 'declivity, hanging.' See hangen.

hangen, vb., 'to hang, be suspended,' from MidHG. *hâhen (hienc, gehangen)*, OHG. *hâhan (hiang, gihangan)*, str. vb.; comp. fangen, from OHG. *fâhan*; before *h* an *n* is suppressed (comp. OHG. *dâhta* from *denchan*, dachte from denken; tracht, OHG. *brâhta*, from bringen). Corresponding to Du. *hangen*, AS. *hón (héng, hangen)*, E. *to hang*, Goth. *hâhan* for **hanhan*, str. vb., 'to hang.' In ModHG., E., and Du., the old str. vb. has been confused with the corresponding wk. vb., so that the trans. and intrans. meanings have been combined; comp. Du. *hangen*, E. *to hang*, 'to suspend and to be suspended'; in MidHG. *hâhen*, is trans. and intrans., while *hang.n* (OHG. *hangên*, AS. *hangian*) is intrans. only, 'to be suspended'; to this is allied OHG. and MidHG. *hengen*, 'to hang down (one's head), give a horse its head, permit, grant,' comp. henfen. The ModHG. vb. is due to a blending in sound of MidHG. *hâhen (hangen)* and *hengen*, yet in meaning it represents only MidHG. *hâhen*, OHG. *hâhan*. Terms undoubtedly allied to the common Teut. root *hanh (hâh)* are wanting in the other Aryan languages; Goth. *hâhan*, 'to leave in doubt,' has been compared with Lat. *cunctari*, 'to delay.'

Hanse, f., 'Hanse,' from MidHG. *hans, hanse*, f., 'mercantile association with certain defined powers as knights, merchant's guild'; orig. an UpG. word (prob. signifying any corporation, association? OHG. and Goth. *hansa*, f., AS. *hôs*, 'troop'), yet it soon became current in all G. dialects, and has been preserved in its application to the towns of the great North G. Hanseatic League, while the orig. sense 'troop' became obsolete even in MidHG. The nominal vb. ḣanſeln is simply ModHG. 'to admit any one into a corporation' (not into the Ḣanſe only).

Ḣanſeln, vb., ModHG. only, different from the earlier homonymous word mentioned under Ḣanſe; lit. 'to make a Ḣanẽ, i.e. a fool, of anybody' (comp. the abusive terms Ḣansвumm, Ḣansnarr, Ḣansмurſt).

ḣantieren, vb., from the equiv. late MidHG. *hantieren*, 'to trade, sell'; not a derivative of Ḣand, meaning 'to handle,' because in that case we should expect *nd* for *nt* in MidHG. and ModHG., but from Fr. *hanter*, 'to haunt, frequent,' which found its way from MidDu. into the Mod Teut. dialects. It is curious to observe in how many ways obscure words have been corrupted in G. Comp. the earlier spelling ḣandtḣieren.

ḣapern, vb., 'to stick, hitch,' formed from Du. (MidDu.) *haperen*, 'to miss, stutter'; yet also Suab. *häperen* (as well as Swiss *hápen*, 'to crawl'?). The corresponding terms, origin, and history of the diffusion of the cognates are obscure.

Ḣarfe, f., 'harp,' from the equiv. Mid HG. *harfe, harpfe*, OHG. *harfa, hurpha*, f.; comp. AS. *hearpe*, f., E. *harp;* a common Teut. word (Venantius Fortunatus calls *harpa* a barbaric, i.e. Teut. instrument), denoting a string instrument peculiar to the Teutons. Its use was confined in earlier times to the OTeut. chiefs, just as the violin or fiddle was to the common folk.

Ḣaring, Ḣering, m., 'herring,' from the equiv. MidHG. *hærinc (-ges)*, m., OHG. *háring*, m.; comp. Du. *haring*, AS. *hǽring*, m., E. *herring*; a specifically West Teut. word (in OIc. *sild*). whose *á* (*ǽ*) is also attested by Fris. dials. and by the Mod HG. pronunciation with *ǽ*. The OHG., MidHG., and MidDu. variant *hering* points to a connection with OHG. *heri*, 'army,' and thus regards the fish as 'one that comes in shoals,' as Ḣerling, 'small army.' Whether the older form *háring* (Anglo-Fris. *hǽring*) is related to these cognates is uncertain. The Teut. word found its way into Rom. (Fr. *hareng*).

Ḣarke, f., 'rake,' a LG. word, in UpG. Redjen; comp. Du. *hark*, AS. *hearge*, E. *harrow*, OIc. *herfe*, n., 'harrow,' Dan. *harv*, Swed. *hærf*. Considering the almost certain identity of the words, their phonetic relations present some difficulties. The root might perhaps be Sans. *kharj*, 'to scratch,' yet AS. *hyrwe (*heurge*)*, E. *harrow*, OIc. *herfe*, 'rake,' are difficult to reconcile with it.

Ḣarlekin, m., 'harlequin,' first naturalised towards the end of the 17th cent. from Ital. *arlecchino* (applied to the masked clown in Ital. comedy), and Fr. *harlequin, arlequin*.

Ḣarm, m., 'harm, distress, sorrow,' very rarely occurs in MidHG. and earlier ModHG., probably formed from E. *harm* and revived in the last cent. through the influence of E. literature (comp. Ḣalle, Ḣeim); MidHG. (entirely disused) *harm*, m., 'injury, pain'; OHG. *haram*, OSax. *harm*, m., 'affront, cutting words, mortification'; AS. *hearm* m., 'insult, harm'; E. *harm;* OIc. *harm*, m., 'grief, care.' From pre-Teut. *karma*, Sans. **çarmá?, çĩrma?*. This is also indicated by OSlov. *sramů* (from **sormŭ*), m., 'shame, disgrace.' An OG. (OHG. and OSax.) compound, OHG. *haramscara*, OSax. *harmscara*, f., 'outrageous, excruciating punishment,' was retained as late as MidHG., in which *harn-, harm-schar*, 'torment, distress, punishment.' remained current, when Ḣarm alone had already disappeared. Comp. ḣerb.

Ḣarn, m., 'urine,' earlier dial. variant Ḣarm (Luther), from MidHG. *harn* (Bav. and East Rhen.), *harm*, m. and n., OHG. *haran*, m., 'urine' (respecting the variant with *m* see Ḣarm); a specifically UpG. word, probably identical orig. with AS. *scearn*, OIc. *skarn*, n., 'mud'; *sk* and *h* (the latter for *k* without *s*) would have interchanged in OTeut. Allied to Gr. σκώρ; comp. ḣeffen, treſſeln, linkṣ, Ṡtier. The derivation of Ḣarn from a root *har*, 'to pour out,' remains dubious.

Ḣarniſch, m., 'harness, armour,' from MidHG. *harnasch*, variants *harnas, harnesch*, m., 'harness'; borrowed at the end of the 12th cent. from OFr. *harnais*, 'armour, gear,' which has come to be a common Rom. term (Ital. *arnese*), but may be traced probably to a Kelt. source (W. *haiarnaez*, 'iron utensils'); the connecting link might be MidE. *harnez*, 'armour' (E. *harness*).

ḣarren, vb., 'to wait, linger in expectation, delay,' from MidHG. *harren*, 'to wait, sojourn'; a MidG. word, entirely unknown to OHG. as well as the other Teut. dialects, but undoubtedly a genuine Teut. term; of obscure origin (allied, like Gr.

καρτερὸν, to ȟart l; comp. Lat. *durare*, akin to *durus*).

ȟarſd), adj., 'hard, rough,' ModHG. simply; E. *harsh* ('bitter, severe'); unknown to AS., OHG., and OIc. Clearly a derivative of ȟart; comp. raſd), allied to grate, Goth. **rusqa-* to *raþa-*, 'quick' (OHG. *rado*), OIc. *horskr*, 'quick,' to AS. *hrade*, OIc. *beiskr*, 'bitter,' to Goth. *bait-ra-*; hence Goth. *hardus*, 'hard,' perhaps presupposes *harsks, *hursqs. Yet it might also be connected with Ic. *hörtl*, 'hardness of the frozen ground'; ModHG. ȟarid), 'snow-crust,' dial. But ȟart ('hard') alone suffices to elucidate this latter sense, as is shown by OHG. *hertemânôt*, MidHG. *hertemânot*, 'hard month,' applied to December and January. See the following word.

ȟart, adj., 'hard, stiff, severe, stern, difficult, hard by,' from MidHG. *herte*, *hart*, adj. (*harte*, adv.; comp. faſt, adv., allied to feſt, ſchen to ſchön, &c.), 'hard, firm, difficult, painful,' OHG. *herti*, *harti*, *hart*, adj. (*harto*, adv.), 'hard'; comp. AS. *heard*, 'hard, strong, brave,' E. *hard* (*hardy* is probably derived directly from Rom.— Fr. *hardi*, which, however, is a derivative of G. ȟart), Goth. *hardus*, adj., 'hardy, severe.' A common Teut. adj. from pre-Teut. *kartús*; comp. Gr. κρατύς, 'strong, powerful, potentate,' καρτερὸς, κρατερύς, 'strong, staunch, mighty, violent,' adv., κάρτα, 'very strongly' (OHG. *harto*, adv., 'very, extremely'); allied perhaps to Sans. *krátu s*, m., 'force, strength' (root *kar*, 'to do, make'), or however to Lith. *kartùs*, 'bitter' (root *krt*, 'to cut, split'). Others compare Sans. *ṣárdha-s*, 'bold, strong,' to the Teut. adj.

ȟart, ȟard, f. and m., 'forest,' from MidHG. *hart*, m., f., and n., OHG. *hart*, 'forest'; comp. also Spessart from *spëhtes hart* (allied to Spedjt); ȟarz for MidHG. *Hart*; ȟaartt in the Palatinate.

ȟarz, n., 'resin,' from MidHG. *harz*, n. and m., 'resin, bitumen,' with the variants *hars*, *harse*; OHG. *harz*, and with a suffix *harzoh*, 'resin'; Du. *hars*, f., with an abnormal *s*, but LG. *hort*, unknown to E. and Scand. as well as Goth.; of obscure origin, scarcely allied to Gr. κάρδαμον, 'cress.' For other OTeut. words with the same meaning see under Bernſtein and Ritt (also Theer).

ȟaſchen, vb., 'to snatch,' a MidG. word made current by Luther, unknown to the modern UpG. dialects as well as to OHG., MidHG., and all other languages. Probably connected with ȟaft, ȟeben, root *haf* (Lat. *capio*); Goth. *hafskôn, 'to seize,' must have become *haskôn in G., just as Goth. *haifsts*, f., 'quarrel, fight,' has become the OHG. adj. *heisti*, 'violent'; comp. OHG. *forscôn*, 'to demand,' for *forhskôn, Goth. *waúrstw*, 'work,' for *waúrhstw. Comp. ȟarſd), ȟaft, ȟannē.

ȟaſe, m., 'hare,' from MidHG. *hase*, OHG. *haso*, m.; a common Teut. term for 'hare'; comp. Du. *haas*, AS. *hara* (with change of *s* into *r*), E. *hare*, OIc. *here*, m.; Goth. *hasa (OHG. *haso*) or *haza (AS. *hara*), is by chance not recorded. To the pre-Teut. *kasa*(*n*), Ind. *çaçá* (instead of *çasá, just as *çváçuras* for *svaçuras, comp. Sdwiȟer), 'hare,' corresponds; the word also occurs in a remarkable manner only once again in OPruss. (as *sasins* for *zasinas*). The primit. word *kasa-*, 'hare,' may be connected with AS. *hasu*, 'grey.' From Teut. is derived Fr. *hase*, f., 'doe-hare.' —The term ȟaſenſdjarte, 'hare-lip,' is not recorded in G. until the 14th cent., but it already exists in AS. as *hǽrsceard* (in E. *hare-lip*); comp. further the OIc. nickname *Skarðe*, also OFris. *has-skerde*, 'hare-lipped.'

ȟaſel, f., 'hazel,' from the equiv. Mid HG. *hasel*, OHG. *hasala*, f., *hasal*, m.; comp. AS. *hæsel*, E. *hazel*, OIc. *hasl* (hence *hoslur*, plur., 'boundary posts'); the common Teut. word for 'hazel,' from pre-Teut. *kósolo-*; hence in Lat., with the normal change of *s* into *r*, *corulus*, 'hazel'; comp. further OIr. *coll*, 'hazel,' for *cosl.

ȟaſpe, ȟäſpe, f., 'hasp, clamp, hinge,' from MidHG. *haspe*, *hespe*, f., 'hinge of a door; windle' (with the variant *hispe*, f., 'clasp'), OHG. *haspa*, 'a reel of yarn'; comp OIc. *hespa*, f., 'hank, skein of wool; bolt of a door'; E. *hasp*, MidE. *haspe*, 'bolt, woollen yarn,' so too AS. *hæsp*, *hæps*, *heps*, f. The double sense 'door bolt, door hook, and hasp,' seems OTeut.; as a technical term in weaving, this word, like Reden, found its way into Rom. (Ital. *aspo*, OFr. *hasple*); see also Runſel. Whether the two meanings have been developed from one, or whether two distinct words have been combined, is uncertain, since we have no etymological data.

ȟaſpel, m., from the equiv. MidHG. *haspel*, m., OHG. *haspil*, m., 'reel, windle'; a derivative of ȟaſpe.

ȟaſt, f., 'haste, hurry,' ModHG. simply;

a MidG. and LG. word; comp. MidDu. *haast*, f., MidE. *haste*, E. *haste*; borrowed from OFr. *haste*, *hâte* (comp. Ital. *astivamente*), which again correspond to the OTeut. cognates of ModHG. heftig; comp. OHG. *heisti*, AS. *hǽste*, 'violent' (Goth. *haifsts*, 'dispute').

Haß, m., from the equiv. MidHG. and OHG. *haʒ*, (gen. *haʒʒes*), m., 'hatred'; in OHG. the older neut. gender occurs once (comp. Goth. *hatis*, n., Scand. *hatr*, n.); AS. *hęte* (E. *hate*) and OSax. *hęti* are also nnsc.; the common Teut. term for 'hate,' pointing to pre-Teut. *kodos*, *kodesos* (Lat. *codus, *coderis), n. ModHG. Hader, and Gr. κότος, may also be allied, since an Aryan root *kôt*, *kôd*, is possible. The orig. sense of Haß is indicated by Haß and hetzen, as well as the wk. vb. haffen, from MidHG. *haʒʒen*, OHG. *haʒʒēn*, *haʒʒôn*, which in OHG. also means 'to pursue' (OSax. *hatôn*, 'to waylay'). Haft too seems allied; hence the prim. meaning of Haß is probably 'hostile, hasty pursuit.' — häßlich, 'ugly, loathsome,' from MidHG. *haʒ-*, *heʒʒelich*, 'malignant, hateful, ugly.'

hätscheln, vb., 'to fondle, pamper,' recently coined in ModHG. ?.

Hatschier, m., 'imperial horseguard,' first occurs in early ModHG., borrowed from Ital. *arciere* (Fr. *archer*, 'archer.'

Hatz, 'baiting, chase'; comp. hetzen.

Haube, f., 'hood, cap (woman's), crest, tuft,' from MidHG. *hûbe*, OHG. *hûba*, f., 'covering for the head worn by men (Mid HG., especially by soldiers, 'peaked helmet, steel-cap') and women'; comp. AS. *hûfe*, in a special sense 'mitre'; Scand. *hûfa*, f., 'cap, hood.' The cognates are connected by gradation with Haupt (Aryan root *kûp*).

Haubitze, f., 'howitzer,' first occurs in early ModHG., introduced during the Hussite Wars from Bohemia (*houfnice*, 'stone slinger'), hence the earliest recorded form, Haunbitze.

hauchen, vb., 'to breathe, respire, exhale,' from MidHG. (rare) *hûchen*, 'to breathe,' an UpG. word; perhaps recently coined in imitation of the sound. Cognate terms are wanting.

Hauderer, m., ModHG. only, from the equiv. Du. *stalhouder*, lit. Stallhalter, 'jobmaster' (in MidG. Geschirrhalter, also Pesthalter); Du. *houden* is ModHG. halten.

hauen, vb., 'to hew, chop, carve,' from MidHG. *houwen*, OHG. *houwan* (MidHG.

houwen, OHG. *houwôn*), 'to hew'; comp. OSax. *hauwan*, AS. *heáwan*, E. *to hew*, Olc. *hǫggva*; Goth. **haggwan*, a redupl. vb., is wanting; Teut. *hauw, haw*, from pre-Teut. *kow*; not allied to κόπτω, but to OSlov. *kovą, kovati*, 'to forge,' Lith. *káuju (káuti)*, 'to strike, forge,' *kovà*, 'combat.' Comp. Hader, Heu, Hick. — Haue, f., 'hoe, mattock, pickaxe,' from MidHG. *houwe*, OHG. *houwa*, f., 'hatchet.'

Haufe, m., 'heap, pile, mass,' from Mid HG. *hûfe, houfe*, m., *hûf, houf*, m., 'heap, troop,' OHG. *hûfo, houf*, m., 'heap, troop'; comp. OSax. *hôp*, Du. *hoop*, AS. *heáp*, m., E. *heap*; Scand. *hôpr*, 'troop,' is borrowed from LG.; Goth. **haups, *hûpa* are wanting; these words, which belong to the same root, are evidently related by gradation (comp. OHG. *hûba*, 'hood,' allied to OHG. *houbit*, 'head'). Probably related to OSlov. *kupŭ* (Goth. **haupa-*), m., 'heap,' Lith. *kaúpas*, 'heap,' *kuprà*, 'hump' (Lett. *kupt*, 'to form into a ball'), although the correspondence of Slav. *p* to LG. and E. *p* is not normal; Slav. *p* is mostly *f* or *b* in LG. and Goth. Since Goth. *p* indicates pre-Teut. *b*, the word may be connected also with Lat. *incubo*, 'the treasure demon who lies on the hoard, nightmare.' Others compare it to Lith. *kugis*, 'heap.'

häufig, adj., copious, abundant,' Mod HG. only, lit. 'by heaps.'

Haupt, n., 'head, chief, leader,' from MidHG. *houbet*, *houpt* (also *höubet*), n., OHG. *houbit*, n.; the OTeut. word for 'head,' supplanted in the 16th cent. by Kopf in all the G. dials. (Kehl-, Kraushaupt, almost the only existing forms, are dialectal), while E. and Scand. have retained the earlier form — AS. *heáfod*, E. *head* (for **heafd*), n., Olc. *haufuþ*, later *hǫfuþ*, n., Swed. *hufvud*, Dan. *hoved*, 'head,' Goth. *haubiþ*, n. Since all the Teut. dialects point to an old diphthong *au* in the stem, of which *û* in OHG. *hûba*, 'hood,' is the graded form (comp. Haute), the Aryan base must be *koupot*, and Lat. *câput*, for which **cauput* might have been expected, was probably transformed by the influence of a word corresponding to AS. *hafola*, 'head,' Sans. *kapâla*, 'skull,' an assumption also supported by Lat. *capillus*, 'hair (of the head).' The MidHG. *höubet* (Luther Heupt), formed by mutation from OHG. *houbit*, is still preserved in zu Häupten, in which primit. phrase the plur. curiously represents the sing.

Haus, n., 'house, household,' from MidHG. and OHG. *hûs,* n., which has the same sound in all OTeut. dials.; ModDu. *huis,* E. *house* (to which *husband, hussy,* and *hustings,* are allied). Goth. **hus* is found only once in *gudhûs,* 'temple,' lit. 'God's house' (for which Goth. *razn* is used; comp. Raft), but may be inferred from the borrowed term, OSlov. *chyzŭ,* 'house.' In the other Teut. dialects it is the prevalent term, corresponding to G. Haus. Probably cognate with Hütte, and like this term allied to a Teut. root *hûd,* 'to hide' (AS. *hŷdan,* E. *to hide*); *hûsa-* for *hûssa-, hûpta-,* lit. 'that which hides'?. See further under Hütte. Others connect Goth. *hûs* with Goth. *huz-ds,* 'refuge,' and Lat. *custos.* In this case too the prim. sense assigned would hold good.

hauß, haußen, adv., 'out of doors, abroad,' from MidHG. *hûʒe* for *hie ûʒe,* 'here outside,' like MidHG. *hinne* for *hie inne.*

Hauste, m., from the equiv. MidHG. *hûste,* m., 'shock of corn, haycock,' cannot be traced further back; evidently for *hûfste,* akin to *hûfe,* 'heap.' Comp. Lith. *kûpstas,* 'tump.'

Haut, f., 'hide, skin, cuticle,' from MidHG., and OHG. *hût,* f., 'hide'; ModDu. *huid,* AS. *hŷd,* f., E. *hide,* Scand. *hûð,* f.; the OTeut. word for 'hide' (Goth. **hûþs,* gen., **hûdais,* is by chance not recorded), from pre-Teut. *kûti-s,* f.; it is Lat. *cûtis* (for the gradation of *û* to *û,* see laut and Sohu); comp. Gr. κύτος, n., 'skin, covering'; the root has a prefix *s* in Gr. σκύτος, n., 'skin, leather,' Lat. *scû-tum.* 'shield,' σκῦ-λον, 'skin, arms, stripped off a slain enemy.' Hence the dental in OHG. *hût,* Lat. *cutis,* would be a suffix merely; for *s-ku* as a root meaning 'to cover, hide,' see under Scheune, Scheuer. The E. vb. *to hide,* from AS. *hŷdan,* may belong to the same root with an abstract dental suffix **hû-ti-,* 'covering,' *hûdjan,* 'to envelop.' Yet traces exist, as may be seen under Hütte, of a root *hud* from *kudh,* 'to veil,' in the non-Teut. languages.

Hebamme, f., 'midwife,' from MidHG. *hebamme;* the latter form, from *heve-amme,* has been modified in sense by connection with heben, its last component representing an earlier *anne* equiv. in meaning, OHG. usually *hevi-anna,* f.; *anna,* f., 'woman' is cognate with Lat. *ănus,* 'old woman' (see Ahn), and hence probably stands for *anua, anva* (comp. Mann, Kinn). Yet OHG. *hevianna* may be really nothing more than the pres. partic. of heben, prim. form *haffan(d)jô,* 'she who lifts,' of which the later forms are modifications. In MidE. *midwif,* E. *midwife,* ModDu. *vroedvrouw,* from *vroed,* 'wise, prudent' (comp. Span. *comadre,* Fr. *sage-femme*); no word common to Teut. can be found. There were probably no regular midwives in the Teut. period.

Hebel, m., 'lever, yeast,' first occurs in early ModHG. in the sense of 'lever'; comp. MidHG. *hebel, hevel,* OHG. *hevilo,* m., 'yeast' (as a means of causing a thing to rise); *v, f,* as the older form, was supplanted by connecting the word with heben.

heben, vb., 'to raise, lift, levy, solve (doubts), settle (disputes), remove,' from MidHG. *heben, heven,* 'to rise, raise, lift,' OHG. *heffan, heman* (prop. *heffu, hevis, hevit, heffames,* inf. *heffun*), from *habjan,* which occurs in Goth. in the sense of 'to raise, lift up'; root, *haf, hab; b* properly belonged in the str. vb. to the pret. plur. and partic., but may have found its way into other stems. AS. *hebban* (sing. *hebbe, hefst, hefþ,* &c.), E. *to heave;* ModDu. *heffen;* OIc. *hefja.* Respecting *j* as a formative element of the pres. stem in str. vbs., see under ſchaffen, lachen, &c.; it corresponds to Lat. *i* in vbs. of the 3rd conjug., such as *facio.* Hence Lat. *capio* corresponds exactly to Goth. *haffan;* Aryan root *kap.* There are numerous examples in Teut. of the sense 'to seize,' which belongs to the Lat. vb.; see under Haft. Since Lat. *capio* is not allied to *habeo,* and Lat. *habeo* is cognate with Teut. haben (*capio,* root *kap, habeo,* 'to have,' root *khabh*), haben is entirely unconnected with heben. Yet in certain cases it cannot be doubted that the words related to haben have influenced the meaning of those connected with heben; some words may be indifferently assigned to the one or the other; comp. e.g. Habe with Handhabe. With the root *kap,* Lat. *capio,* some also connect Gr. κώπη, 'handle.'

Hechel, f., 'flax-comb,' from MidHG. *hechel,* also *hachel,* f.: comp. Du. *hekel;* MidE. *hechele,* E. *hatchel* and *hackle;* wanting in OIc.; Swed. *häckla,* Dan. *hegle* (Goth. **hakila,* **hakula,* is assumed). Probably allied to OHG. and MidHG. *hecchen, hecken (hakjan),* 'to pierce' (espec. of snakes), and further to the cognates of Hafen (E. *hook*). Goth. *hakuls,* 'cloak,' OHG. *hahhul,* MidHG. *hachel,* m., OIc. *hǫkull,* m., AS.

hacele, 'cloak,' are not allied; they belong rather to a conjectural Goth. *hôka, f., 'goat' (AS. *hécen*, 'kid,' from Goth. *hôkein*, n.; see under Geiß), and hence probably mean 'hairy garment.' See also Hecht.

Hechſe, Hächſe, f., from the equiv. MidHG. *hehse*, OHG. *hahsa*, f., 'hock' (especially of horses); the presumable form in Goth. is *hahsi* (gen. *hahsjôs), f. Corresponding in sound to OInd. *kakšâ*, f., 'girth (of a saddle),' a derivative of *kikša-s*, m., 'passage for the girths, armpit'; Lat. *coxa*, 'hip,' whence the adv. *coxim*, 'squatting,' from which a meaning similar to that of the HG. word may be deduced. The signification of the primit. Aryan word fluctuated between 'armpit, hip, and hock.' In the Teut. group the following are also allied to Goth. *hahsi*, f.—OHG. *hahsinôn*, MidHG. *hehsenen*, 'subnervare, to hamstring,' AS. *hôxene*, MidE. *houghsene*, Fris. *hôxene*, 'hock.'

Hecht, m., 'pike,' from the equiv. MidHG. *hechet, hecht*, OHG. *hehhit, hahhit*, m.; comp. OSax. *hacud*, AS. *hacod, hæced*, m., 'pike'; a West Teut. word connected with OHG. and MidHG. *hecken*, 'to pierce,' mentioned under Hechel. On account of its pointed teeth the pike is called the 'piercer.' Comp. E. *pike*, Fr. *brochet*, 'pike,' from *broche*, 'spit,' Scand. *gedda*, 'pike,' allied to *gaddr*, 'prickle.'

Hecke (1.), f., 'hedge,' from MidHG. *hecke*, f., OHG. *hecka, hegga*, f., 'hedge'; the latter from *hagjô-*, whence also AS. *hecg*, f., MidE. *hegge*, E. *hedge*; AS. also *hege*, m., 'hedge' (comp. E. *haybote*, 'an allowance of wood for repairing fences'). Of the same origin as the cognates mentioned under Hag.

Hecke (2.), f., 'the act of breeding,' ModHG. simply, probably neither identical nor even cognate with Hecke (1), 'hedge,' because E. *hedge*, 'Hecke (1),' and *hatch*, 'Hecke (2).' are totally distinct; the former is MidE. *hegge* (AS. *hecg*, f. ?), the latter MidE. *hacche* (AS. *hæcce* ?); E. *hatch*, 'brood, incubation.' MidHG. has a wk. vb., *hecken*, 'to propagate' (of birds), MidE. *hacchen*, E. *to hatch*; OHG. *hegidruosa*, MidHG. *hegedruose*, f., 'testicle,' may be cognate (*g* in AS. *hagan*, 'signalia,' in comparison with the earlier *kk* in MidE. *hacche*, is conceivable), and hence too MidHG. *hagen*, m., 'bull kept for breeding,' earlier ModHG. Hackſch, 'boar kept for breeding.' The cognates seem to indicate a Teut. root *hag, hakk*, 'to propagate.'

Hede, f., 'tow,' ModHG. simply, from LG. *heede*, formed from Herbe by suppressing the *r* (see Miete); comp. MidDu. *herde*, 'flax fibre,' AS. *heorde*, f., 'refuse of flax, tow,' E. *hards* (plur.). Are AS. *heord* and OIc. *haddr*, 'hair,' allied ? For Hede (probably Goth. *hazdô*, *hazdjô*) UjG. has Werg.

Hederich, m., 'hedge-mustard, ground ivy,' from late MidHG. *hederĭch*, m., a corruption of Lat. (*glecoma*) *hederacea*.

Heer, n., from the equiv. MidHG. *here*, OHG. *heri, hari*, n., 'army'; comp. Goth. *harjis*, m., AS. *here*, m., OIc. *herr*, m.; a common Teut. word for 'army,' still current in Swed. and Dan. *här*, Du. *heer-* in compounds. AS. *here* was supplanted in the MidE. period by the Rom. *army*; yet AS. *here-geatwe*, 'military equipment or trappings,' has been retained down to ModE. as *heriot*; similarly the AS. word for *har-bour* (comp. Herberge). The term *chario-*, 'army,' met with in Teut. proper names of the Roman period, corresponds to OIr. *cuire*, 'troop,' OPruss. *karjis*, 'army,' of which Lith. *kâras*, 'war,' is the base (Heer, lit. 'that which belongs to war'); to this OPers. *kâra*, 'army,' is allied ? In MidHG. and earlier ModHG. there is another deriv. of the root *kar*, viz. *harst*, MidHG. also *harsch*, 'body of troops.' The verbal form from the assumed word for 'war' was perhaps Goth. *harjôn*, 'to wage war upon'; comp. OIc. *herja*, 'to go on a predatory expedition,' AS. *herigan*, E. *to harry, to harrow*, OHG. *heriôn*, MidHG. *hern*, 'to ravage, plunder.' Comp. further Herberge and Häring.

Hefe, f., 'yeast, lees, dregs,' from MidHG. *heve, hepfe*, m. and f., OHG. *hevo, hepfo*, m. (from *heppo, huffo*, 'yeast'); as a substance producing fermentation it is derived from the root *haf*, lit. 'raising'; hence also OHG. *hevilo*, MidHG. *hevel*, 'yeast,' as well as AS. *hæf*, Du. *hef, heffe*, f., 'yeast' (see Hebel). Similarly Fr. *levain, levûre*, are related to *lever*. Yet OHG. *hepfo* can scarcely be referred to the Aryan root *kap*, 'to raise.'

Heft, 'handle, hilt, stitched book, number (of a periodical),' from MidHG. *hefte*, OHG. *hefti*, 'haft, handle of a knife, hilt of a sword'; connected with the root *haf* ('to lift') or *hab* ('to have').—**heften,** vb., 'to stitch,' from MidHG. and OHG. *heften*, 'to fasten.'

heftig, adj., 'vehement, violent, impetuous,' from MidHG. *heftec*, adj., 'remaining firm, persistent,' then 'earnest, important, strong.' It seems to be based upon a blending of two words orig. quite distinct, for ModHG. *heftig*, 'vehemens,' is late OHG. *heiftig*, MidHG. *heifte*, adv. *heiftecliche*, with which Goth. *haifsts*, OFr. *haste*, as well as ModHG. $\mathfrak{Haft}$, are connected.

hegen, vb., 'to enclose, cherish, foster,' from MidHG. *hegen*, 'to cherish, keep,' lit. 'to surround with a fence,' OHG. *hegen*, 'to fence in'; allied to $\mathfrak{Hag}$.

$\mathfrak{Hehl}$, m., from the equiv. MidHG. *hæle*, MidG. *hêle*, 'concealment'; also MidHG. *hæle*, adj., 'concealed'; derivatives of MidHG. *hëln*. See **hehlen**.

hehlen, vb., from the equiv. MidHG. *hëln*, OHG. *hëlan*, 'to keep secret, conceal,' AS. *hëlan*, E. *to heal*, 'to cover, conceal,' Du. *helen*, 'to conceal.' Root *hël*, from pre-Teut. *kël* (Sans. *$çal$), in the sense of 'concealing cover'; see further under $\mathfrak{Halle}$, $\mathfrak{Hehl}$, $\mathfrak{Hölle}$, $\mathfrak{Hülle}$, $\mathfrak{Hülse}$, as well as $\mathfrak{hohl}$, $\mathfrak{Höhle}$, and $\mathfrak{Helm}$. The Aryan root is attested by Lat. *célare* (*é* as in Goth. *$hêlei$), which is indicated by MidHG. *hæle*, f., mentioned under $\mathfrak{Hehl}$), *occulo*, Gr. root καλ in καλύπτω, 'I cover,' καλύβη, 'hut,' OIr. *celim*, 'I hide.'

hehr, adj., 'exalted, sublime, sacred,' from MidHG. *hêr*, adj., 'distinguished, exalted, proud, glad,' also 'sacred,' OHG. and OLG. *hêr*, 'distinguished, exalted, splendid.' The corresponding compar. is used in G. in the sense of 'dominus'; comp. $\mathfrak{Herr}$, lit. 'the more distinguished, venerable' (orig. current in the Teut. languages of Mid. Europe only). The orig. sense of the adj. is probably 'venerable,' for the E. and Scand. adj. has the meaning 'grey, hoary, old man'; OIc. *hárr*, AS. *hár*, E. *hoar* (and the lengthened form *hoary*), 'grey.' Goth. *$haira$- (neu. sing. mas. *$haira$) is wanting. The common assumption of a Teut. root *hai*, 'to glitter, shine,' from which an adj. *hai-ra-* can be derived with the double sense given above, is supported by OIc. *heið*, 'clearness of the sky' (see under $\mathfrak{heiter}$), no less by Goth. *hais* (dat. plur. *haizam*), n., 'torch.' With the root *hai* (from pre-Teut. *koi*), Sans. *kê-tú-s*, m., 'light, lustre, torch,' is connected.

$\mathfrak{Heide}$ (1.), f., 'heath, uncultivated land, heather,' from MidHG. *heide*, OHG. *heida*, f., 'heath, untilled, wild, overgrown land, heather'; comp. Goth. *haiþi*, f., 'field,' AS. *hǽþ*, m. and n., 'heath, desert,' also 'heather,' E. *heath*, OIc. *heiðr*, f. The prim. sense of the common Teut. word is 'treeless, untilled plain'; the meaning 'heather' evolved from this is West Teut. (AS. Du. and G.), so too Du. *hei*, *heide*. Goth. *haiþi*, 'field, plain,' from pre-Teut. *káitt*, occurs also in OInd. *kšétra-m*, 'field, cornfield, region, country,' for *skétram*. See the next word.

$\mathfrak{Heide}$ (2.), m., 'heathen, pagan,' from MidHG. *heiden*, m., 'heathen' (espec. 'Saracen'), OHG. *heidan*, m.; comp. Du. *heiden*, AS. *hǽþen*, E. *heathen*, OIc. *heiðenn*, 'heathen.' Ulfilas is acquainted only with the corresponding fem. *haiþnô*, 'heathen woman,' while the masc. plur. equiv. to Lat. *gentes*, Gr. *ἔθνη*, appears as *þiudôs*. The connection of the word with human progress is difficult to decide; on account of the diffusion of the word in all the Teut. dialects, we are evidently not concerned here with a word originating in the OHG. Biblical texts and translations. The usual assumption that Lat. *paganus*, 'heathen,' was the model on which the Teut. word was built needs to be restricted, since it is improbable that all the OTeut. dialects independently of one another should have given an inaccurate rendering of *paganus*, especially since the Slav. languages have borrowed the word directly (OSlov., Russ. *poganŭ*). Lat. *paganus*, 'heathen' (Ital. *pagano*, Fr. *païen*), appears in the second half of the 4th cent. after Christianity was established as the religion of the Empire by Constantine and his sons, and the old worship was forced from the towns into the country districts. The late occurrence of the Lat. word explains the fact that in Goth. first of all a solitary instance of the new term 'heathen' is found in the form *haiþnô*, f., 'a heathen woman.' But the appearance of the word in Goth. is more easily accounted for than in any other dialect from the Goth. forms *haiþi*, f., 'field,' *haiþiwisks*, 'wild' (*miliþ h.*, 'wild honey'). Hence in Goth. a form *$haiþins$ would be connected more closely with Lat. *paganus*, while in the other dialects the corresponding word cannot probably be explained from the Lat. form. Perhaps here, as in the case of $\mathfrak{Kirche}$ and $\mathfrak{Pfaffe}$, the influence of the Goths and of their Christianity upon the other Teutons is discernible. Comp. the history of the word *taufen*.

Heidelbeere, f., 'bilberry, whortleberry,' from MidHG. *heidelber, heitber,* n. and f., OHG. *heidberi,* n., 'bilberry, whortleberry'; corresponds to AS. *hǣð-berie,* with the same meaning. Allied to **Heide,** f.

heikel, adj., 'hooked, captious, nice,' ModHG. only, but widely current in the dials. ; Swiss. *heikχel,* Bav. and Suab. *haikel,* East Fris. *hekel,* 'fastidious with regard to food.' Geographically **heikel** and **Ekel** seem to supplement each other, and hence may be regarded as identical.

Heil, n., 'health, welfare, salvation,' from MidHG. and OHG. *heil,* n., 'health, happiness, salvation'; comp. AS. *hǣl,* n. (for *hâli,* from *hailiz*), 'health, happiness, favourable omen'; OIc. *heill,* n. (f.) (from *hailiz*), 'favourable omen, happiness.' Not the neut. of the following adj., but properly an older *as* stem, pre-Teut. *kâilos* (declined like Gr. γένος, Lat. *genus,* n.). Comp. also the next word.

heil, adj., 'hale, healthy, sound,' from MidHG. and OHG. *heil,* adj., 'healthy, whole, saved'; comp. OSax. *hêl,* AS. *hâl,* E. *whole,* OIc. *heill,* 'healthy, healed,' Goth. *hails,* 'healthy, sound.' In OTeut. the nom. of this adj. was used as a salutation (Goth. *hails!* χαῖρε! AS. *wes hâl!*). Teut. *haila-z,* from pre-Teut. *kailos* (-*lo-* is a suffix), corresponds exactly to OSlov. *cělŭ,* 'complete, whole,' which, like Pruss. *kailûstikun,* 'health' (from **kailûstas,* 'healthy'), is based upon Aryan *kailo-;* the OIr. cognate *cél,* 'augury,' corresponds to AS. *hǣl,* OIc. *heill,* n., 'favourable omen,' as well as to OHG. *heilisôn* and AS. *hǣlsian,* 'to augur.' Sans. *kalya-s,* 'healthy,' *kalyâṇa-s,* 'beautiful,' and Gr. καλός, κάλλος, are probably not related to the root *kai* with the suffix *lo-.*

heilen, vb., 'to heal, cure,' from MidHG. and OHG. *heilen,* 'to heal,' as well as Mid HG. *heilen,* OHG. *heilên,* 'to get well'; comp. AS. *hǣlan,* E. *to heal* (to which *health* is allied, AS. *hǣlþ,* OHG. *heilida,* f., 'health'). — **Heiland,** from the equiv. MidHG. and OHG. *heilant,* m., 'Saviour'; prop. a partic. of **heilen** (a being retained in the partic. derivative as in **Weigand**); the term is HG. and LG.; comp. OSax. *hêliand,* AS. *hǣlend.* In England, where it became obsolete as early as the 13th cent., the word, even in the older period, was never so deeply rooted as in Germany. In Goth. *nasjands,* AS. *nergend.*

heilig, adj., 'holy, sacred, inviolable,' from the equiv. MidHG. *heilec,* OHG. *heilag, heilîg,* adj.; comp. OSax. *hêlag,* AS. *hâleg,* E. *holy,* OIc. *heilagr,* adj.; all have the common meaning, 'sanctus.' In Goth. only is the adj. unknown (yet *hailag* occurs in a Goth. Runic inscription); the earlier old heathen form *weihs* (see **weihen**) was used instead. The development of meaning in **heilig** from the subst. **Heil** is not quite clear. Is the word **Heil** used in a religious sense? Comp. OIc. *heill,* 'favourable omen,' OHG. *heilisôn,* 'to augur,' OIr. *cel,* 'augury'?.

Heim, n., 'home,' from MidHG. and OHG. *heim,* n., 'house, home, dwelling-place,' comp. OSax. *hêm,* 'dwelling-place,' AS. *hâm,* 'home, dwelling-place, house,' E. *home,* OIc. *heimr,* m., 'dwelling world,' Goth. *haims,* f., 'village.' In the 17th cent. and in the first half of the 18th, the ModHG. word vanished from the literary language (the adv. **heim** only being still used), but was restored through the influence of English literature (see **Halle, Elf**). The meaning of the Goth. subst. is found in the remaining dialects only in names of places formed with *heim* as the second component. In Goth. a more general meaning, 'dwelling,' is seen in the adj. *anahaims,* 'present,' *afhaims,* 'absent' (see **Heimat**). The assumption that 'village' is the earlier meaning of **Heim** is also supported by Lith. *kěmas, kaimas,* '(peasant's) farm'; Sans. *kšêma-s,* 'secure residence,' allied to the root *kši,* 'to dwell securely, while away' (*kšitis,* f., 'dwelling, earth'), OSlov. *po-čiti,* 'requiescere,' *po-kojĭ,* 'rest'; perhaps also Gr. κώμη (for κώμη), 'village'?. — **heim,** adv., from MidHG. and OHG. *heim,* acc. sing., 'home(wards),' and MidHG. and OHG. *heime,* dat. sing., 'at home'; in the other dialects, except Goth., the respective substs. in the cases mentioned are likewise used adverbially in the same sense. For further references comp. **Weile.**

Heimat, f., from the equiv. MidHG. *heimôt, heimuot, heimuote,* f. and n., OHG. *heimuoti, heimôti,* n., 'native place'; a derivative of **Heim.** Goth. **haimôdi* is wanting (*haimôþli,* 'native land or fields,' is used instead, OHG. *heimuodili*). Respecting *-ôti* as a suffix, see **Armut, Einöte.**

Heimchen, n., 'cricket,' dimin. of **Heime,** m. and f., from MidHG. *heime,* OHG. *heimo,* m., 'cricket'; AS. *hâma,* 'cricket'; a derivative of **Heim,** hence lit. 'inmate' (a pet term?).

heimlich, adj., 'private, secret, comfortable, snug, from MidHG. *heim(e)lich*, adj., 'secret, confidential, concealed,' also 'home-made, domestic'; allied to $eim.

$eirat, f., from the equiv. MidHG. and OHG. *hîrât*, m. and f., 'marriage,' lit. 'care of a house'; Goth. *heiwa*, 'house,' in *heiwa-frauja*, m., 'master of the house.' The earlier ModHG. form $eirat is due to MidHG. **hia-rât* for *hîw-*. AS. *hîrêd*, *hîrĕd*, 'family,' MidE. *hîred*, and AS. *hîwrǣden*, MidE. *hîreden* in the same sense. The first component, Goth. *heiwa-*, is widely diffused in OTeut. OIc. *hjú*, *hjún*, n. plur., 'man and wife, married couple, domestics,' OIc. *hyske*, n., 'family,' *hîbŷle*, *hŷbyle*, n., 'place of residence.' AS. *hîwan*, plur., 'servants,' E. *hind* (E. *hive*, which is often connected with the cognates in question, is not allied, since it is due to AS. *hŷf*, 'beehive'). Scand. *hyske*, n., corresponds to the West Teut. terms, OHG. *hîwiski*, n., 'family, housekeeping, domestics,' also OHG. *hîun*, plur., 'man and wife, servants,' *hîwo*, 'husband,' *hîwa*, 'wife.' Goth. *heiwa-*, 'house, housekeeping,' has consequently numerous cognates within the Teut. group. Its relation to the non-Teut. words is dubious; Lat. *civis*, 'citizen,' Lith. *szeima*, *szeimȳna*, 'domestics,' OSlov. *sěmija*, *sěmija*, 'domestics,' are usually connected with it. Others refer it to the root appearing in $eim. See Rat.

$eifchen, vb., 'to ask for, demand, require,' from MidHG. *heischen*, prop. *eischen*, OHG. *eiskôn*, 'to ask'; the addition of initial *h* in the MidHG. and ModHG. verbs is correctly ascribed to the influence of $eißen. Comp. OSax. *ēscôn*, Du. *eischen*, AS. *âscian*. E. *to ask*; Goth. **aiskôn* is wanting. It corresponds to Lith. *jëskôti*, OSlov. *iskati*, 'to seek,' also probably to Armen. *aic*, 'investigation,' and Sans. *icch* (*icchati*), 'to seek' (see anheifchig).

$eifer, adj., 'hoarse,' from MidHG. *heiser*, 'rough, hoarse,' with the variant Mid HG. *heis*, *heise*, OHG. *heiri*, *heis*, 'hoarse'; Goth. **haisa-* is also indicated by AS. *hâs*; in MidE. besides *hôse*, an abnormal *hôrse* occurs, whence E. *hoarse*; so too MidDu. *heersch*, a variant of *heesch* (the latter also ModDu.); the *r* of the ModHG. and Mod HG. derivative $eifer is the widely diffused adj. suffix in bitter, lauter, hager, mager, &c. The Scand. *hâss*, for the expected **heiss* (Goth. **hais*), also presents a difficulty. Some have attempted to connect the stem with that in hufften, which is impossible;

hâs, *hœss*, in hufften, cannot, on account of the vowels, correspond to Goth. **haisa*. Others, with greater reason, connect it with E. *to whistle*, AS. *hwistlian*, and with Mod HG. wifpeln, 'to whisper' (the Teut. root *hais*, *hwîs*, appears with a derivative *k* in AS. *hwiskrian*, OIc. *hvîskra*, 'to whisper,' Du. *heesch*, 'hoarse').

$eifter, m., 'beech tree,' a Franc. and Hess. word, which also appears in LG., but is entirely unknown to UpG. and MidG.; even in the MidHG. period *heister* occurs; comp. Du. *heester* (whence Fr. *hêtre*). Note the local term $eifterbach.

$eiß, adj., 'hot, ardent, vehement,' from the equiv. MidHG. and OHG. *heiz*; comp. Du. *he t*, AS. *hât*, E. *hot*, OIc. *heitr*; a common Teut. adj. for 'hot,' pointing to Goth. **haita-*; from the root *hît*, to which $iße is akin. This root may be extended from *ht*, with which OHG. an I ModHG. *hei*, *gelei*, 'heat' is connected. See $eizen.

$eißen, vb., 'to bid, command, be called, signify,' from MidHG. *heizen*, OHG. *heiz-ʒan*, 'to name, be named, be called, command, promise'; the passive sense, 'to be named, nominari,' did not orig. belong to the active, but only to the Goth. and AS. passive form. AS. *hâtan*, 'to name, promise,' *hâtte*, 'I am called' and 'I was called'; OIc. *heita*, 'to name, be named, promise, vow'; Goth. *haitan*, a redupl. vb., 'to name, appoint, call, invite, command,' in the pass. 'to be named.' A common Teut. vb. with the prim. sense 'to call any one by name, to name.' No words undoubtedly allied to the Teut. root *hait*, from pre-Teut. *kaid*, exist in the non-Teut. languages. See anheifchig.

-heit, fem. suffix of abstract terms in the West Teut. dialects; prop. an independent word—MidHG. *heit*, f., 'method, nature,' OHG. *heit*, m. and f., 'person, sex, rank, estate,' AS. *hâd*, 'estate, race, method, quality'; Goth. *haidus*, m., 'method'; see further under $eiter. As an independent word it became obsolete in E. in the MidE. period, and was preserved only as a suffix, as in ModHG.; AS. *-hâd*, E. *-hood* (*boyhood, falsehood, maidenhood*), and also E. *-heal* (*maidnhead*).

$eiter, adj., 'clear, serene, bright, cheerful,' from MidHG. *heiter*, OHG. *heitar*, adj., 'serene, bright, glittering'; comp. OSax. *hêdar*, AS. *hâdor*, 'serene'; a West Teut. adj., but in Scand. *heiþ-r*, 'serene,' without the derivative *r* (all used orig. of the clear, cloudless sky only); comp. OIc. *heiþ*, 'clear sky.' Comp. Teut. *huidra-*, *haida-*, from pre-Teut. *kaitró-*, *kcito-*, with Sans. *kê'ú-s*, m., 'brightness, light, rays, flame, lamp' (identical in form with Goth. *hailus*, m., 'manner, mode,' connected with *ḥeit*), from the root *cit* (*kēt*), 'to shine forth, appear, see'; to this is allied a Sans. adj. *citrá-s*, 'glittering, radiating, bright, glorious,' containing a derivative *r*, but with a differently graded vowel in the stem. A figurative sense is specially attached to OIc. *heiþr* (gen. *heiþar* and *heiþrs*), m., 'honour,' as well as to *ḥeit*.

heizen, vb., 'to heat,' from the equiv. MidHG. and OHG. *heizen*, a variant of *heizen* (comp. *brizen*, *reizen*); a nominal verb from *heiz*, stem *haita-*, Goth. **haitjan*; comp. AS. *hâetan*, 'to make hot, heat' (from *hât*), E. *to heat*. See *ḥeiß*.

Held, m., from the equiv. MidHG. *helt* (gen. *heldes*), m., late OHG. *helid*, 'hero'; corresponding to OSax. *helith*, AS. *hæleþ-* (nom. sing., *hæle*), 'man, hero,' OIc. *holðr*, *holdr* (from **haluþr*), and *halr*, 'man,' Teut. *huléþ-*, from *kalêt-*, *kulêt-*, may most probably be connected with Ir. *calath*, Bret. *calet*, 'hard.'

helfen, vb., 'to help, assist, avail, remedy,' from the equiv. MidHG. *hëlfen*, OHG. *hëlfan*; a common Teut. vb. used in the same sense in all the dialects; comp. Goth. *hilpan*, OIc. *hjalpa*, AS. *hëlpan*, E. *to help*, Du. *helpen*, OSax. *hëlpan*. Teut. root *help* from pre-Teut. *kelb-*; a root of another Aryan dialect apparently allied in meaning curiously ends in *p* (*kelp*); comp. Lith. *szélpti*, 'to help,' *paszalpá*, 'help' (in Sans. the root *çalp* does not occur). Sans. *klp*, 'to accommodate oneself to, suit,' is even less closely connected.

hell, adj., 'clear, bright, evident,' from MidHG. *hël* (gen. *hëlles*), adj., 'loud, sonorous,' OHG. *hël* in *gahël*, *unhël*, *missahëll*; in MidHG. the meaning 'sonorous' was still current, but that of 'glittering' is found neither in OHG. nor MidHG. Comp. OHG. *hëllan*, MidHG. *hëllen*, 'to resound'; MidHG. *hal* (gen. *halles*), m., 'sound, resonance,' whence ModHG. *hallen*; further Scand. *hjal*, n., 'chattering,' *hjala*, 'to chatter'?. Comp. *holen*.

Hellbank, **Höllbank**, f., 'bench near the stove,' allied to earlier ModHG. *Helle*, *Hölle*, f., 'the narrow space between the stove and the wall'; the word is first recorded towards the end of the 15th cent., but was in existence at an earlier period. Comp. AS. *heal*, MidE. *hal*, 'angle, corner' (comp. OIr. *cuil*, 'corner'). The ModHG. form is due to a confusion with **Hölle**, which, like the ModHG. **Hölle** 'winkel', is connected with the root *hel*, 'to veil, conceal.'

Hellebarte, f., from the equiv. MidHG. *helmbarte*, f., 'halberd'; for the second part of the compound see **Barte** (1). The first component has been ascribed to two sources—to the very rare MidHG. *helm*, *halm*, 'helve, handle,' which would probably suit, as far as the sense is concerned, *helmbarte*, 'an axe fitted with a handle'?. But since *helmbarte*, in such a derivation, should have *halm-* as the component, the phonetic relation of the words is in favour of the derivation from *hëlm*, m., hence *hëlmbarte*, 'an axe for cleaving the helmet.' From G. the Rom. words (Fr. *hallebarde*) are derived.

Heller, m., from the equiv. MidHG. *heller*, *haller*, m., 'a copper coin worth about ½d.'; according to the ordinary supposition, "it was so called from the imperial town of Schwäbisch-Hall, where it was first coined." The OHG. term *halling*, 'obolus,' which apparently contradicts this, is perhaps rightly regarded as identical with MidHG. *hëlblinc*, m., 'a fourth of a farthing.'

helligen, **behelligen**, vb., 'to importunate,' from MidHG. *helligen*, 'to weary by pursuit, tease, torment'; a nominal verb from MidHG. *hellic*, adj., 'wearied, exhausted,' ModHG. *hellig*, 'wearied.' The origin of the adj. is obscure.

Helm (1.), m., 'helmet,' from the equiv. MidHG. and OHG. *hëlm*, m.; the same in OSax., OFris., and AS. (AS. *hëlm*, 'helmet, protector,' E. *helm*), OIc. *hjalmr*, Goth. *hilms*, 'helmet'; a common Teut. str. noun, *helma-*, 'helmet,' from pre-Teut. *kelmo-*. Comp. OInd. *çárman-*, n., 'protection' (comp. the AS. meaning), with which the root *kel* in ModHG. *hehlen*, *hüllen*, is connected. Lith. *szálmas*, 'helmet,' and OSlov. *šlěmǔ*, 'helmet,' were borrowed at an early period from Teut.; so too the Rom. class—Ital. *elmo* (Fr. *heaume*), 'helmet.'

Helm (2.), m., 'tiller,' ModHG. simply, from LG., whence a number of nautical terms found their way into HG. (see **Boot**, **Kahn**, **Barke**, **Flagge**, **Spriet**); comp. Du. *he'mstock*, 'tiller.' E. *helm*, AS. *helma*, 'rudder,' Scand. *hjálm*, f., 'tiller.' In this case, as in most of the other nautical expressions, it cannot be decided in which division of the Saxon and Scand. group the technical term originated ; as in other instances—see Beet, Berb—AS. contains the earliest record of the word. The MidHG. *helm* (see Hellebarte), 'helve, handle,' which occurs only once, and its variant *halme*, do not seem to be actually allied to the present term ; they are connected with Halfter.

Hemd, n., 'shirt,' from MidHG. and MidLG. *hemde, hemede*, OHG. *hemidi*, n., 'shirt,' prop. 'long under-garment' ; allied to OFris. *hemethe*, AS. *hemeþe* (Goth. *hameiþi*?) ; a dimin. term, formed like OHG. *jungidi*, 'young of animals.' The sense 'short garment, bodice,' originates in Teut. *hama-*, 'garment,' the same as OIc. *hamr*, m., 'covering, skin, external form.' See further under Leichnam, also Hamen, hämisch. The Goth. form *hameiþja-* previous to its permutation was *kamitjo-*, and with this the late Lat. term *camisia*, 'tunica interior, under-garment, shirt,' recorded at the beginning of the 5th cent., and chiefly in relation to soldiers, must be connected in some way ; it differs little from the assumed form in pre-Teut. ; OIc. *hams*, m. (from *hamisa-*), 'slough of a snake,' has a derivative *s*. Probably Sans. *çamulyá*, 'shirt,' is prim. allied. Since there is no doubt that the HG. word is classical Teut., the vulgar *camisia* must be traced back to a Teut. origin, which is also attested by W. *hefis*, 'chemise,' and OIr. caimmse, ' nomen vestis.' The relation of the initial HG. *h* to Rom. *c* would correspond to that of Fr. *Chivert* to its OHG. original *Hiltibert*, i.e. a Franc. *ch* forms the connecting link. In Lat. *camisia* we obtain for HG. Hemd other related terms in Rom. (Fr. *chemise*, Ital. *camicia*).

hemmen, vb., from the equiv. MidHG. *hemmen* (MidG.), *hamen*, 'to stop, hinder, check' ; OHG. **hamên* and **hemmen* are wanting. The early existence of the word, which is not found in Bav., is proved by OIc. *hemja*, 'to check,' and Sans. *çamay*, 'to annihilate,' which is perhaps cognate with the latter. It is based upon a Teut. root *ham*, meaning 'to mutilate' ; comp. OHG. *ham* (inflected form *hammêr*), 'lame, paralytic' (Goth. **ham-ma-*, from **ham-na-*, orig. a partic.), and further also OHG. *hamal*, 'mutilated' (see Hammel). Scand. suggests the possibility of a different etymology—*hemja*, 'to curb any one, lame, check,' from *hǫm*, f., 'hind-leg of a horse,' *hemill*, 'rope for tethering cattle by the thighs when they are grazing,' *hafa h-mil á*, 'to restrain any one.' In Suab. and Bav. hemmen means only 'to tether horses when grazing.' Comp. also Lith. *kámanos*, plur., 'bridle.'

Hengst, m., 'stallion,' from MidHG. *hengest*, OHG. *hengist*, m., 'gelding, horse (generally),' comp. Du. *hengst*, m., 'stallion,' AS. *hengest*, m., 'male horse (generally),' obsolete at the beginning of the MidE. period ; OIc. *hestr* (from **hinhistr*), m., 'stallion, horse (generally).' The earlier meaning of the HG. word was *equus castratus*, and by the adoption of the general term Pferd, 'horse,' the word obtained in ModHG. (from the 15th cent.) as 'ungelded, male horse.' In Goth. probably **hangists*. The attempt to explain the word etymologically has not yet been successful ; comp. Lith. *szankus*, 'nimble' (of horses)?, or Lith. *kinkyti*, 'to put (horses) to'?.

Henkel, m., 'handle, shank,' ModHG. simply, allied to henken.

henken, vb., 'to hang, suspend,' from MidHG. and OHG. *henken*, prop. a variant of OHG. and MidHG. *hengen* (*k* is Goth. *gj*). To these two words, varying in sound, different meanings were attached ; comp. MidHG. *henken*, 'to hang up,' *hengen*, 'to hang down (one's head),' espec. 'to give a horse the reins.' Yet MidHG. *hengen* is also used in the sense of *henken*, 'to execute by hanging.'

Henker, m., from the equiv. MidHG. (rare) *henker*, *henger*, m., 'hangman,' allied to henken.

Henne, f., 'hen,' from MidHG. and MidLG. *henne*, OHG. *henna*, f.; comp. AS. *henn*, E. *hen* (AS. *hana* was even in the AS. period supplanted by its equiv. *cock*) ; a West Teut. fem. of the common Teut. *hano*, 'cock,' to which are allied the graded forms, OIc. *hœna*, OSwed. and ModSwed. *höna*, 'hen' (OHG. also *henin, heninna*, 'hen'). See Hahn, Huhn.

Heppe, see Hippe.

her, adv., 'hither, this way.' from MidHG. *hêr* (*here*), OHG. *hêra*, adv., 'hither,' formed like OHG. *wara*, 'whither' ; allied to Goth. *hiri*, adv. imperat., 'come here.' Connected with a pronom. stem *hi-*. See heute, hier, hinnen.

herb, adj., from the equiv. MidHG. *here*, inflected *herwer* (also *hare*, inflected *harwer*), 'bitter, harsh' ; Goth. and OHG. **har-wa-* is wanting. Allied to OSax.

har-m, AS. *hear-m*, adj., 'painful, mortifying, bitter'?. See Harm.

Herberge, f. (with *s* as in Herzog, allied to Herr), 'shelter, quarters, inn,' from Mid HG. *herbërge*, f.; lit. 'a sheltering place for the army' (rare in MidHG.), most frequently 'lodging-house for strangers,' also 'dwelling' generally. OHG. *heri-bërga*, 'camp, castra,' then also 'hospitium, tabernaculum.' MidE. *herberge*, 'hospitium,' E. *harbour*; Scand. *herberge*, n., 'inn, lodging, room, chamber.' The compound, in its later form, seems to have been adopted from G. by the other Teut. languages, and also by Rom.; Fr. *auberge*, Ital. *albergo*; OFr. preserves the older meaning 'camp.' Comp. Herr, bergen.

Herbſt, m., 'autumn, harvest,' from the equiv. MidHG. *herbest*, OHG. *herbist*, m.; comp. MidLG. *hervest*, Du. *herfst*, AS. *hærfest*, m., and the equiv. E. *harvest*; a common West Teut. word, archaic in form (whether OIc. *haust*, n., 'autumn,' Swed. and Dan. *höst*, are identical with Herbſt is still very dubious). Hence the statement of Tacitus (*Germ.* 26)—'(Germani) autumni parinde nomen ac bona ignorantur,' can scarcely be accepted. It is true that Herbſt in UpG. is almost entirely restricted to 'the fruit season,' espec. 'the vintage' (the season itself is prop. called Spätjahr, Suab. Spätling). This coincides with the fact that Herbſt is connected with an obsolete Teut. root *harb*, from Aryan *karp* (Lat. *carpere*, καρπός, 'fruit'), 'to gather fruit,' which perhaps appears also in Lith. *kerpù* (*kìrpti*), 'to shear.' In Goth. the term is *asans* ("season for work, for tillage'; comp. Ernte).

Herd, m., 'hearth, fireplace, crater,' from MidHG. *hërt* (-*des*), m., 'ground, earth, fireplace, hearth,' OHG. *hërd*, m., *hërda*, f., 'ground, hearth.' This double sense is wanting in the other West Teut. languages, Du. *heerd*, *haard*, m., 'hearth,' OSax. *herth*, AS. *heorþ*, E. *hearth*. The meaning of *herþa*- (Goth. *hairþs), 'hearth,' is West Teut., while 'ground' is simply HG.; it is not improbable that two orig. different words have been combined (comp. OIc. *hjarl*, 'ground, land'?). Herd, 'hearth,' with Goth. *haúri*, n., 'charcoal' (plur. *haurja*, 'fire'), OIc. *hyrr*, m., 'fire,' may be connected with a Teut. root *hër*, 'to burn' (comp. Lat. *crĕ-mare*).

Herde, f., 'herd, flock, drove,' from the equiv. MidHG. *hërte*, *hërt*, OHG. *hërta*, f.; the common Teut. word for 'herd'; Du. *herde* (obsolete, see Hirte; *kudde*, f., is used instead, see Kette), AS. *heord*, f., E. *herd*, OIc. *hjǫrð*, f., Goth. *hairda*, f., 'herd.' The Teut. type *herdô* (the *d* of the ModHG. form, compared with OHG. *t*, is due to LG. influence), from pre-Teut. *kerdhá*; comp. OInd. *çárdhas*, n., *çárdha-s*, m., 'troop'; also OSlov. *črěda*, f., 'herd'?. See Hirte.

Hering, see Häring.

Herling, Härling, m., 'sour grapes' (ModHG. only), for the earlier, *Herwling, allied to herwe, 'bitter.'

Hermelin, m. and n. (accented like a foreign word), from the equiv. MidHG. *hermelin*, n., 'ermine,' dimin. of MidHG. *harme*, OHG. *harmo*, m., 'ermine'; a G. word merely, wanting in the other OTeut. languages, but in spite of the phonetic correspondence with Lith. *szermú*, 'ermine' (Lith. *sz* for Sans. *ç*, Aryan *k*, whence Teut. *h*), there is no doubt about its being genuinely Teut. From G. are derived the Rom. words similar in sound (ModFr. *hermine*, Ital. *ermellino*) rather than from the Mid Lat. *mus armenius* (for which the earlier *mus ponticus* is found).

Herold, m., 'herald,' late MidHG. only (14th cent.), *hęralt*, *hęrolt* (also *ęrhalt*), m., 'herald'; undoubtedly an OG. military term, which, like a large number of others of the same class (comp. Haber, Kampf), became obsolete at an early period. Herold itself is derived from an OFr. term recorded towards the end of the 13th cent., *héralt*, ModFr. *héraut* (comp. Ital. *araldo*, MidLat. *heraldus*), which is based, however, upon an OG. *hęriwalto, *hariwaldo, 'an army official,' appearing in OSax. as a proper name, Hariold (OIc. *Harald*). OHG. *harēn*, 'to praise,' does not occur in the compound.

Herr, m., 'master, lord, gentleman, sir,' from MidHG. *hërre* (*hēre*), m., OHG. *hēŕro* (*hēro*), m.; comp. OSax. *hērro*, Du. *heer*, OFris. *hēra*, 'lord'; prop. a comparative of hehr (OHG. *hēr*), in Goth. *hairiza. In the OHG. period this origin was still recognised, as is seen by OHG. *hērero*, 'lord' (see Herrschen). Since the orig. meaning of the adj. hehr was 'venerable,' Herr seems to have originated in the relation of the dependants to their master (comp. AS. *hlāford*, 'bread guardian,' under Laib), and was used chiefly as a term of address (see Jünger). Comp. in Rom. the words used in the same sense from Lat. *senior*, viz., Ital. *signore*, Fr. *seigneur*. Herr is orig. native to Germany, but in the form

K

hearra it found its way at a very early period (about the 9th cent.) from the German lowlands to England, and later to Scandinavia (ModSwed. *herre*, 'master'). In ModHG. only a fem. Herrin has been formed from Herr (as in Ital. *signora* from *signore*). The older language used Frau, Herr having supplanted the earlier *frô* (see under frohn).

herrlich, adj. (with shortened *e* before a double consonant, as in the two following words, probably due to its association with Herr), 'lordly, splendid, magnificent,' from MidHG. and OHG. *hêrlich*, adj., 'distinguished, excellent, magnificent.' Allied to hehr.

Herrschaft, f., 'lordship, dominion, master and mistress, employers (as used by servants),' from MidHG. *hêrschaft*, f., OHG. *hêrscaft*, *hêrscaf*, f., lit. 'lordship,' then 'high rank, manor, magistracy.' Allied to Herr, but probably not to hehr.

herrschen, vb., from MidHG. *hersen*, *hêrsen*, OHG. *hêrisôn*, 'to rule, reign,' but also *hêrrisôn* even in OHG., from its association with *hêrro*, 'lord' (for ModHG. *sch* after *r* from an older *s*, comp. Hirsch, Kirsche). The origin of the meaning 'to rule' cannot be explained from the posit. hehr, OHG. *hêr*, 'august, exalted, venerable, glad,' but from the originally compar. *hêrro*, 'lord.' Thus OHG. *hêrisôn*, 'to be lord and master, dominari,' is related to *hêrro*, *hêriro*, 'lord,' as Goth. **hairiza* (compar.) is to **hairisôn*, vb.

Herz, n., 'heart,' from the equiv. Mid HG. *hërze*, OHG. *hërza*, n.; comp. OSax. *hërta*, OIc. *hjarta*, Goth. *haírtô*, AS. *heorte*, and the equiv. E. *heart*; the common Teut. word for 'heart,' which may be traced back even to West Aryan. The Teut. type *hertôn-*, from Aryan *kerd* (*kṛd*), corresponds to Lat. *cor*, *cor-dis*, n., Gr. καρδία and κῆρ for **κηρδ*, n., Lith. *szirdis*, f., OSlov. *srŭdĭce*, n., OIr. *cride*. The corresponding East Aryan word for 'heart' (Sans. *hṛd*, *hṛdaya*, Zend. *zaredaya*), is usually dissociated on account of the initial sound (we should have expected Sans. **ṛrd*) from the West Aryan class.

Herzog, m., 'duke,' from the equiv. MidHG. *hërzoge*, OHG. *hërizogo* (-*zoho*), m. ; comp. OSax. *hëritogo*, AS. *hëretoga*, m., OIc. *hertoge*, m.; a common Teut. term for 'the leader of an army,' in which *zoho*, *zogo*, allied to *ziohan* (as *togo* to *tiuhan*), has the old meaning 'leader.' Comp. ziehen.

hetzen, vb., 'to infuriate, provoke, chase, hunt,' from MidHG. and OHG. *hetzen*, 'to chase, hunt, incite'; by permutation from **hatjan*; comp. Haß. The subst. Hetze, f., is merely a ModHG. formation from the vb.

Heu, n., 'hay,' from MidHG. *höu*, *hou*, *houwe*, n., 'hay, grass,' OHG. *hewi*, *houwi* (prop. nom. *hewi*, gen. *houwes*, dat. *houwe*), n., 'hay.' Comp. Goth. *hawi* (gen. *haujis*), n., 'hay, grass' (with regard to the change of Goth. *j* into OHG. *w* and the consequent absence of mutation, see Frau, Mu, Gau, &c.; in earlier ModHG. the unmutated form Hau is still retained); OSax. *houwi*, AS. *hêg*, *hîg* (with *g* for Goth. *j* as usual), n., MidE. *hei*, E. *hay*, OIc. *hey*, n., 'hay'; common Teut. *hauja-* (in the Goth. stem). Apparently from the root *hau* (see hauen), with the suffix *-ju-*, Heu, meaning 'that which is to be cut.' There is less probability of its being connected with Gr. πόα (Ion. ποίη), 'grass,' from ποFίη, κFοFίη (Teut. *h* equal to Gr. π for κF, both from Aryan *k*, as in ἵππος, equal to Lat. *equus*, Gr. ἕπεσθαι, equal to Lat. *sequi*).

heucheln, vb., 'to feign, dissemble,' ModHG. only, prop. a MidG. word (the corresponding UpG. word is gleißnen), allied to an early ModHG. hauchen, 'to duck, stoop,' from MidHG. *hûchen*, 'to crouch'; comp. the further cognates under hocken. The variation of meaning 'to stoop, dissemble,' is exhibited in an OTeut. root *lut*, AS. *lûtan*, 'to bend, bow,' to which *lot*, 'deceit,' and Goth. *liuta*, 'hypocrite,' are allied.

heuer, adv., from the equiv. MidHG. *hiure*, OHG. *hiuru*, adv., 'in this year'; derived from *hiu jâru* (see Jahr), the chief accent being placed on the pron. Respecting *hiu* see heute, in which the component parts are equally obscure.

heulen, vb., 'to howl, yell, scream,' from MidHG. *hiulen*, *hiuweln*, 'to howl, cry,' OHG. *hiuwilôn*, *hiwilôn*, 'to shout for joy.' Also allied to OHG. *hûwila*, *hiuwila*, MidHG. *hiuwel*, f., 'owl' (as 'the howling bird'), and hence more remotely to OHG. *hûwo*, m., 'owl.'

Heuschrecke, f., from the equiv. Mid HG. *höuschrëcke*, m., OHG. *hewi-skrëkko*, m., 'grasshopper,' lit. 'hay-jumper' (see Schrecken). A distinctly G. term; comp. Du. *sprinkhaan*, AS. *gærs-hoppa*, equiv. to E. *grasshopper*, AS. also *gærs-stapa*, 'grass-stalker.' In Goth. occurs an obscure term *þramstei*, f. (whence OSlov. *chrąstŭ*, 'beetle',

heute, adv., 'to-day,' from the equiv. MidHG. *hiute*, OHG. *hiutu;* comp. OSax. *hiudu, hiudiga* (whence AS. *heódæg*), OFris. *hiudeya*, 'to-day'; a West Teut. adv. for Goth. **hiŏ daga*, 'on this day,' with the accent on the pron., which resulted in the combination of the two words. In the same way **hiutagu* became *hiutgu, hiuttu*, and was finally shortened into *hiutu* (comp. the similar origin of *heuer*). Further, Lat. *ho-die* and Gr. σ-ήμερον are similarly compounded. Likewise for heute Nacht, 'to-night,' OHG. and MidHG. had a parallel adv.; comp. OHG. *hî-naht* (MidHG. *hînet*), 'to-night' (in Bav. and Suab. *heint* is used for 'to-day'). The pronom. stem *hi-* contained in it appears in Goth. in a few cases, and indeed as a temporal pron., 'this'; comp. *himma daga*, 'to-day,' and *hina dag*, 'until to-day,' &c. In the Sax. dials. this pronom. stem, which corresponds to Lat. *ci-* in *ci-s, ci-tra*, appears as a 3rd pers. pron.; comp. E. *he*, AS. *hé*, E. *him*, AS. *him* (Goth. *himma*), &c., OSax. and LG. *hĕ*, 'he.' See further her, hier.

Hexe, f., 'witch, hag, sorceress,' from MidHG. *hecse*, f., OHG. *hagzissa, hagazussa, hagzus* (also *házus, házissa*), f., a gloss for *furia, striga, eumenis, erinnys*; comp. Mid Du. *haghetisse*, ModDu. *heks*, AS. *hægtesse*, f., E. (with the rejection of the apparent termination) *hag*. The word, which is doubtlessly a compound, has not yet been satisfactorily explained; OHG. *hag*, AS. *hag*, 'hedge, wood,' as the first component, seems indubitable. The second part has not been elucidated; some suppose that the prim. meaning of Here is 'forest woman or demon'?. Comp. OHG. *holzmuoja*, Mid HG. *holzmuoje*, f., 'forest woman, witch' (also 'wood-owl').

Hieb, m., 'cut, stroke, blow; sarcasm,' first recorded in the 17th cent., being recently formed from hauen, pret. hieb, hieben; comp. Handel from handeln and Hetze from hetzen.—**Hief**, see Hifthorn.

hier, also **hie**, adv., from the equiv. MidHG. *hier, hie*, OHG. *hiar*, 'here'; comp. Goth., OIc., AS., and OSax. *hér*, equiv. to E. *here*. Allied to *hî-* (see heute)?.

Hifthorn, also **Hüfthorn** (a corruption due to the fact that the horn was carried attached to a belt around the waist—'Hüfte'), 'hunting-horn,' ModHG. simply; the earliest ModHG. form is Hiefhorn; **Hief**, also **Hiff**, 'the blast from a hunter's horn.' Allied to Goth. *hiufan*, AS. *heófan*, OHG. *hiufan*, 'to wail, howl'?.

Hilfe, f., from the equiv. MidHG. *hilfe*, *helfe*, f., OHG. *hilfa, helfa*, f., 'help, aid' (Goth. **hilpi* and **hilpa*, f.). Comp. helfen.

Himbeere, f., 'raspberry,' from the equiv. MidHG. *hintber*, n., OHG. *hint-beri*, n.; lit. 'hind-, doe-berry.' With regard to ModHG. Himbeere, with a distinct second component (in MidHG., however, *hemper*, from *hintbere*, according to strict phonetic laws), see ModHG. Wimper, from *wintbrâ*. In AS. *hindberie*, f., means 'strawberry' and 'raspberry'; comp. E. dial. *hindberries*, 'raspberries' (note too AS. *hindhǽlepe*, 'ambrosia,' MidHG. *hirz-wurz*, AS. *heortclǽfre*, 'camedus,' prop. 'hemp agrimony'). In earlier ModHG. there existed a term Hindsläufte, from MidHG. *hintlouf*, 'a plant growing on the hind's track,' *i.e.*, along forest paths, which was applied to the common chicory.

Himmel, m., 'heaven, sky, canopy, clime,' from the equiv. MidHG. *himel*, OHG. *himil* (OBav. *humil*, m.; comp. OSax. *himil*, Fris. *himul*, Du. *hemel*, Swed. and Dan. *himmel*; the derivative *l* is the result of differentiation from an earlier derivative *n*, formed like Goth. *himins*, OIc. *himenn*, with which the Sax. forms with *f* for *m* are connected; AS. *heofon*, m., E. *heaven*, OSax. *heban*, m., ModLG. *heven*. These forms are based upon a common Teut. *hemono- (humeno-)*; on account of its derivative suffix, note too Gr. οὐρανός. The ModHG. sense, 'sky' is current in all the Teut. dials.; the word is probably connected with the OTeut. stem *ham*, 'to cover, veil,' mentioned under hämisch, Hemd, and Leichnam. OHG. *himil* has also the meaning 'ceiling,' especially in the OHG. derivative *himilizzi*, ModHG. *himelze*, a fact which supports the last assumption; comp. AS. *húsheofon*, Du. *hemel*, MidLG. *hemelte*, 'roof.' The etymology of Himmel (Goth. *himins*), based upon OSlov. *kamy*, Lith. *akmú*, 'stone,' as well as upon Sans. *açmâ*, 'stone, (the stone-roofed) vault of heaven,' and Gr. κάμινος, 'oven,' are not satisfactory, since the word probably denoted the 'covering of the earth' originally.

hin, adv., 'hence, that way,' from Mid HG. *hin, hine*, OHG. *hina*, adv., 'off, away'; AS. *hina (hin-* in compounds, *e.g., hinsîþ*, 'departure, death'), adv. 'away,' allied to the pronom. stem *hi-* discussed under heute.

Hinde, with an affixed fem. termination, also **Hindin**, f., 'hind, doe,' from MidHG. and MidLG. *hinde*, OHG. *hinta*, f., 'hind'; comp. AS. *hind*, f., E. *hind*, OIc. *hind*, 'hind'; the common Teut. fem. of **Hirſch**; Goth. **hindi* (gen. **hindjôs*), f., is wanting. It is generally connected with Goth. *hinþan*, 'to catch' (to which E. *to hunt* is allied). Others relate it to Gr. κεμ-άς, f., 'young deer, pricket'; in that case the dental is a suffix, as in *hun-d* (allied to Gr. κυν-; see **Hund**), and *n* before a dental may originate in *m* (comp. **Sund, Schande,** and **hundert**).

hindern, vb., 'to impede, obstruct, prevent,' from MidHG. *hindern*, OHG. *hintiren* and *hintarôn*, 'to repulse, hinder'; comp. AS. *hinderian*, E. *to hinder*, OIc. *hindra*; an old derivative from the prepos. **hinter**; see the latter and **förbern**.

Hindin, see **Hinte**.

hinken, vb., 'to limp, walk lame, fit badly,' from the equiv. MidHG. *hinken*, OHG. *hinchan*; a word peculiar to HG., if Scand. *hokra*, 'to crawl,' is not connected with it (AS. *hellehinca*, 'devil,' is found). Root *hink*, from Aryan *kheng* (*kh* as in **haben**, from the root *khubh*, in Lat. *habere*; comp. further **Nagel**), based on the Sans. root *khañj*, 'to limp'; allied also to the equiv. Gr. σκάζω for *s-khṇgjô*, with *s* prefixed.

hinnen, von hinnen, adv., from the equiv. MidHG. *hinnen*, OHG. *hinnan, hinnân, hinnana*, adv., 'away from here, from hence'; used in ModHG. only with the explanatory prepos. AS. *heonan, heonon*, adv., 'from here,' E. *hence* (with a suffix *s*, whence *ce*). Formed from the pronom. stem *hi*, like **bannen, von bannen,** from the pron. **þa-**. See **hinten, hinter**.

hinten, adv., from the equiv. MidHG. *hinden*, OHG. *hintana*, adv., 'behind'; Goth. *hinduna*, adv. and prep., 'behind, on the other side'; comp. OSax. *bihindan*, 'behind, along behind,' AS. *hindan*, adv., 'behind,' AS. *bchindan*, E. *behind*; allied to **hinnen** and **hinter**.

hinter, prep., from the equiv. MidHG. *hinter, hinder*, OHG. *hintar*, prep., 'behind'; while OHG. *nt* is changed regularly into *nd* in MidHG., it is frequently retained when *-er* (i.e., vocal *r*) follows as an independent syllable; comp. **Winter**, from OHG. *wintar*, **munter**, from *muntar*. In **hindern** the *d* has been inserted in the normal way, just as in MidHG., and earlier ModHG. **hinter** is found as well as **hinter**. Goth. *hiudar*, prep., AS. *hinder*,

prop. an acc. neu. of an old compar. in -τερο-ν, Sans. *tara-m* (of which AS. and Goth. have preserved a superl. in -*tama-s*, Goth. **hinduma*, whence *hindumists*, 'outermost,' AS. *hindema*, 'the last'). Comp. OInd. *pratarám* (compar. of *pra*), adv., 'further, onwards,' *avatarám* (allied to prep. *ava*), adv., 'further away,' *vitarám* (allied to prep. *vi*), comp. *witer*. The compar. **hinter** is used as an adj. in OHG. *hintaro*, ModHG. *hinter*, 'hinder, posterior.'

Hippe (1.), f., 'sickle,' a MidG. form introduced by Luther into the ModHG. literary language instead of **Heppe**, from MidHG. *heppe, hepe* (*häppe*), f., 'pruninghook'; OHG. *heppa* (*häppa*), f., whence Fr. *happe*, 'axle-tree bed, cramp' (from the type *happia*, Fr. *hache*, 'hatchet,' is derived). Numerous South-Western dials. (Suab. also) use *hâp* (*hôp*), from MidHG. *hâpe*, OHG. *hâppa* (from Goth. **hêb-*). Allied to Gr. κώπη, 'hilt, hand c'?, κωπίς, 'knife, dagger'?.

Hippe (2.), f., **Hipplein**, n., 'goat,' only in ModHG.; the more usual dial. *heppe* (Bav., Thur., and Hess.) makes it probable that the word is a pet or child's term for OG. **haber*, 'he-goat'; on this point see **Habergeiß** and **Hille**.

Hirn, n., from the equiv. MidHG. *hirne*, OHG. *hirni*, n., 'brain.' We should have expected Goth. **hatrni*, n., for which *hwairneins*, 'skull,' occurs once in the gen. sing. OIc. *hjarne*, m., 'brain'; also corresponding in sound to the Goth. word *hrern*, f., 'the two white boat-shaped bones in the brain of fishes, ooliths' (LG. has a peculiar word for **Gehirn**—E. *brain*, AS. *brægen*, Du. *brein*, MidDu. *bregen*; see **Brägen**). The words with initial *h* and those with *hw* must be kept distinct. Du. *hersen*, f., 'brain' (E. dial. *harns*), to which is allied MidHG. *hërsenier*, 'covering for the head worn under the helmet,' proves the origin of OHG. *hirni* from **hirzni, *hirsni* (OIc. *hjarne* from **hjarsne*; comp. **Horniſſe**). This OTeut. *herzn-, hersn-*, is most nearly related to Sans. *çîrṣn-*, 'head' (nom. *çîrṣa*), and the closely corresponding OIc. *hjarse*, 'crown (of the head).' It is also cognate with Gr. κραίνον, 'skull,' whence results the further connection with Gr. κάρα, κάρηνον, 'head,' Lat. *cerebrum* (from **ceresrum*), 'brain,' Sans. *çiras*, 'head'; a common Aryan stem, *ker, kers*, 'head,' to which **Hern** is also allied. Moreover, Gr. κέρνον, 'a large earthen dish,' might, according to the analogies mentioned under 𝔎opf, be closely related to 𝔥irn, 'skull.'

𝔥irſch, m. (in Hess. and Alem. occurs a variant 𝔥irʒ, whence the Alem. proper name 𝔥irʒel), 'stag, hart,' from MidHG. *hirʒ, hirz*, m., OHG. *hiruʒ, hirʒ, hirz*; the *sch* in 𝔥irſch is from an older 𝔥irʒ (comp. 𝔥irſe, 𝔥errſchen, 𝔄rſch, 𝔟irſchen). Corresponding to Du. *hert*, n., AS. *heorot, heort*, m., E. *hart*, Scand. *hjǫrtr*; Teut. **herut-*, from **herwut-, *herwo-t*, with a dental suffix, allied to Lat. *cervu-s* (*t* occurs as a suffix in names of animals in Teut.; comp. 𝔊emſe, 𝔎rebs, and 𝔥erniſſe); the latter is usually connected with Gr. κεραός, 'horned' (allied to κέρας; comp. 𝔥orn). Hence the stag in Lat. and Teut. may have been named from its antlers (the OTeut. languages naturally have a distinct word for the hornless female; see 𝔥inde). A more prevalent term is Aryan *eln-*, in Gr. ἔλαφος, Armen. *eln*, Lith. *élnis*, OSlov. *jelenĭ* (also W. *elain*, 'hind').

𝔥irſe, f. (older ModHG. and even yet MidG., Suab. 𝔥irſche), 'millet,' from the equiv. MidHG. *hirse, hirs*, OHG. *hirsi, hirso*, m.; orig. a HG. word merely, which, however, in modern times has spread to the north (E. and Dan. *kirse*, Swed. *hirs*). Allied to Lat. *cirrus*, 'a tuft (of hair, &c.)'?.

𝔥irte, m. (a strictly HG. form compared with the orig. LG. 𝔥erde), 'herdsman, shepherd, pastor,' from MidHG. *hirte*, OHG. *hirti;* comp. OLG. *hirdi*, AS. *hyrde* (and *heorde*, connected with *heord*, 'herd'), 'herdsman,' still found in E. *shepherd* (*sceáphyrde* in AS.), OIc. *hirðer*, Goth. *hairdeis*, m., 'herdsman'; derived by the addition of *ja-* from Teut. *herdô-*, 'herd.' Hence 𝔥irte is orig. 'he that belongs to the herd.' Another derivative is exhibited by Du. and MidLG. *herder*, m., MidHG. *hertœre*, 'herdsman,' lit. 'herder,' whence 𝔥erber as a proper name. With this word Lith. *kèrdżus, skèrdżus*, 'herdsman,' is also connected ?.

𝔥iſſen, vb., 'to hoist,' ModHG. only, derived as a naut. term from the equiv. I.G. *hissen;* comp. Du. *hijschen*, E. *to hoist*, Swed. *hissa*. Among which of the maritime Teutons this technical term, the etymology of which is still obscure, originated is not known; see 𝔥elm (2); it also found its way into Rom. (Fr. *hisser*).

𝔥itte, f., LG. 'goat' (Bav. 𝔥ette, 𝔥ettel, and without mutation Swiss and Suab. 𝔥attel), a pet term for MidHG. *hatele*, 'goat'; comp. the equiv. OIc. *haðna* as well as 𝔥ippe.

𝔥itze, f., 'heat, ardour, passion,' from the equiv. MidHG. *hitze*, OHG. *hizza*, f. (for **hitja*, the Goth. form); comp. Du. *hitte, hette*, OIc. *hite*, m., 'heat'; all formed by the weakest stage of gradation from the stem of the adj. 𝔥eiß (Teut. root *hit, hait*, 'hot'). OHG. *hizza* was adopted by Rom. (comp. Ital. *izza*, 'anger, indignation').

𝔥obel (dial. 𝔥ofel), m., 'plane,' from the equiv. MidHG. (rare) *hobel, hovel*, m.; comp. MidLG. *hövel*, Swed. *hyfvel*. ModIc. *hefill*, m., 'plane,' proves nothing for the wrongly assumed connection with 𝔥eben. Its relation to OHG. *hovar*, AS. *hofer*, 'hump, boss,' is also dubious.

𝔥och, adj., 'high, lofty, proud, dear,' from the equiv. MidHG. *hôch*, OHG. *hôh*, adj.; a common Teut. adj. with the meaning 'high'; comp. Goth. *hauhs*, OIc. *hár* (for *hauhr*), AS. *heáh*, E. *high*, Du. *hoog*, OSax. *hôh;* Teut. *hauha-*, from the unpermutated pre-Teut. *kâuko-* (the weakest vowel stage of the stem is exhibited by the cognate 𝔥ügel). OTeut. possessed a mas. and neu. subst. formed from the adj. in the sense of 'hill' (type *kauko-s*); comp. OIc. *haugr* (from which E. *how* in proper names was borrowed), MidHG. *houc*(-*ges*), to which such proper names as 𝔇onnerstaugt are akin. Goth. *hiuhma*, m., 'heap, crowd,' seems also allied. In the non-Teut. languages it is rightly compared with Lith. *kaukarà*, 'hill, height,' *kaũkas*, 'boil' (Mid HG. *hübel*, m., 'hill,' is connected with Lith. *kùpstas*, 'tump,' as well as to OHG. *hofar*, AS. *hofer*, 'hump').

𝔥ochzeit, f., 'wedding,' from MidHG. *hôchzît* (also *hôchgezît*), f. and n., 'a great ecclesiastical or lay feast,' then also 'wedding feast.'

𝔥ocke (1.), 'shock (of corn), cock (of hay),' first occurs in ModHG., perhaps from I.G.; yet UpG. (Suab. and Tyrol.) *hock*, m., 'cock.' Perhaps allied to 𝔥och and 𝔥aufe (root *kuk*); Lith. *kúgis*, 'cock,' points, however, to a different root. In West Teut. a cognate term with a prefix *s* appears—MidHG. *schocke, schoche*, 'cock,' E. *shock*, and the equiv. MidE. *schokke*. With regard to the prefix *s* comp. 𝔖tier, 𝔇reſſel, and 𝔩infs.

𝔥ocke (2.), m., 'huckster,' MidHG. *hucke*, m.; MidG. *hoke*, with a long vowel (hence HG. 𝔥öfer, 𝔥öferei, &c.), Du. *hok*, 'booth'?. Comp. MidDu. *heukster*, MidE.

huckstere, E. *huckster*; probably akin to
hocfen, 'to squat.'

hocfen, vb., 'to crouch, squat,' first recorded in ModHG. ; it is, however, an archaic word, as is shown by the prevalence of the root *hăk, hukk*; comp. MidHG. *hŭchen*, 'to duck, crouch,' OIc. *húka* (with a str. partic. *hokenn*), 'to crouch,' Du. *huiken*. OIc. *hokra*, 'to crawl,' is probably not connected with this word, but with hinfen.

höcher, m., 'hump,' from MidHG. *hocker, hogger, hoger*, m., 'hump, humplack'; a subst. peculiar to HG., formed from an adj. *hogga-*, 'hump-backed,' and based on OHG. *hovar*, MidHG. *hover*, 'humpback,' AS. *hofer* (comp. Lith. *kuprà*, f., 'humpback, hump'); *hogga-* represents *hubga*, Sans. *kubja* (for *kubjha*?), 'humpbacked'; comp. Gr. κυφός, 'bent, bowed, stooping,' for κυφφό-s, *kubghás*?.

hode, f., 'testicle,' from the equiv. Mid HG. *hode*, OHG. *hodo*, m.; comp. MidDu. *hode*, and in OFris. *hotha*, 'testicle.' Of obscure origin; perhaps allied to Lat. *côleus*, 'scrotum,' if it stands for *côtleus*?.

hof, m., 'yard, courtyard, manor, court,' from the equiv. MidHG. and OHG. *hof* (*hoves*), m.; comp. OSax. and Du. *hof*, m., AS. *hof*, n. (obsolete at the end of the AS. period); in West Teut. 'courtyard, farm, garden (thus in Du. and OHG.), (prince's) palace,' AS. also 'circle, district, globe.' OIc. *hof*, n. (the same gender as in AS.), 'temple with a roof,' later also (under G. influence) 'palace, courtyard.' Goth. **hufa-*, m. and n., is curiously wanting. Since the cognates are based upon pre-Teut. *kŭpo*, they cannot be allied to Gr. κῆπος, 'garden,' Lat. *campus*.

hoffart, f., 'haughtiness, arrogance,' from MidHG. *hôchvart*, f., 'living in high style, magnanimity, splendour, magnificence, haughtiness'; from *hôch* and *vart*; MidHG. *varn*, 'to live,' as in 𝔚𝔢𝔥𝔩𝔣𝔞𝔥𝔯𝔱.

hoffen, vb., from equiv. MidHG. (espec. MidG.), *hoffen*, 'to hope,' which is not yet used, however, by the classicists of the MidHG. period (they employ the term *gedingen*, wk. vb., with which *gedinge*, 'hope,' is connected ; OHG. *gidingen* and *gidinjo*); it is also unknown to OHG. In OLG., on the other hand, a corresponding *tô-hopa*, 'hope,' is found. The vb. appears earliest in E. ; AS. *tôhopa*, 'hope,' AS. *hopian*, equiv. to E. *to hope*. At a later period Du. *hopen* and MidLG. *hopen* occur.

Not until the latter half of the 13th cent. does MidHG. *hoffen* become more prevalent, after its solitary occurrence since 1150 A.D. It is usually considered as a LG. loan-word. For the early history of the word the corresponding abstract AS. *hyht*, 'hope,' is significant, since it shows that Teut. *hopó-* represents **huqón* (Aryan root *kug*). Its connection with Lat. *cupio* is scarcely possible.

hofieren, vb., 'to court, flatter,' from MidHG. *hovieren*, 'to make a display, serve, pay court to, be courteous, serenade'; from G. 𝔓𝔬𝔣, with a Rom. suffix.

höfisch, adj., 'courtly, flattering, fawning,' from MidHG. *hövesch*, adj., 'courtly, accomplished'; allied to 𝔓𝔬𝔣.

höhe, f., 'height, summit, elevation,' from MidHG. *hœhe*, OHG. *hôhî*, f. ; comp. Goth. *hauhei*, f., 'height.'

hohl, adj., 'hollow, concave,' from the equiv. MidHG. and OHG. *hol*, adj.; comp. Du. *hol*, 'hollow,' AS. *hol*, OIc. *holr*, adj., 'hollow'; E. *hole* is an adj. used as a subst., so too AS., OHG., and MidHG. *hol*, 'cave.' The relation of these cognates, which point to Goth. **hula-*, 'hollow,' to the equiv. AS. *holh*, E. *hollow*, has not been explained. The word is usually connected with the root *hel* (in 𝔥𝔢𝔥𝔩𝔢𝔫), 'to conceal by covering'; Goth. *hulundi*, f., lit. the hiding-place, 'cave.'

höhle, f., 'cavity, cave, burrow,' from MidHG. *hüle*, OHG. *holî*, f., 'excavation, cave'; allied to 𝔥𝔬𝔥𝔩.

hohn, m., 'scorn, scoffing,' from Mid HG. (very rare), *hôn*, m., OHG. (very rare), *hôna*, f., 'scorn, mockery, ignominy'; a fem. subst. formed from an old adj., OHG. **hôn*, represented by *hôni*, 'despised, ignominious, base,' Goth. *hauns*, 'base,' AS. *heán* (obsolete in the beginning of the MidE. period), 'base, miserable, ignominious.' With this is connected the vb. 𝔥𝔬̈𝔥𝔫𝔢𝔫, from MidHG. *hœnen*, OHG. *hônen*, wk. vb., 'to abuse'; comp. Goth. *haunjan*, 'to degrade,' to which *hauneins*, 'humility,' is allied; AS. *hŷnan*, 'to degrade, humble' (from the OHG. vb. Fr. *honnir*, 'to cover with disgrace,' and *honte*, 'disgrace,' are derived). It corresponds in the non-Teut. language to Lett. *kauns*, 'shame, ignominy, disgrace,' Lith. *kuvêti-s*, 'to be ashamed'; hence Goth. *hauns*, 'humble, base,' can hardly have originated in the sensuous meaning 'base.'

höker, see 𝔥𝔢𝔠𝔨𝔢.

Hokuspokus, m., 'hocus-pocus,' ModHG. only. It became current in England, where a book on conjuring, with the title 'Hocus Pocus junior,' appeared in 1634 A.D. The early history of this apparently fantastic and jocose expression is still obscure; its connection with the phrase used in the celebration of mass, 'hoc enim est corpus meum,' cannot be established.

hold, adj., 'favourable, gracious, charming, lovely,' from MidHG. *holt* (gen. *holdes*), OHG. *hold,* adj., 'gracious, condescending, favourable, faithful'; Goth. *hulþs,* 'gracious,' OIc. *hollr,* 'gracious, faithful, healthy,' AS. and OSax. *hold*. The common Teut. adj. originally denoted the relation of the feudal lord and his retainers ('condescending, gracious,' on the one side, 'faithful, devoted,' on the other); comp. MidHG. *holde,* m., 'vassal.' The idea expressed by **hold** was also current in the religious sphere—Goth. *unhulþôns,* f., lit. 'fiends, devils,' OHG. *holdo,* 'genius,' MidHG. *die guoten holden,* 'penates.' **Hold** is usually connected with an OTeut. root *hal,* 'to bow,' to which OHG. *hald,* 'inclined,' is allied; see **Halde**. It has also been referred to **halten** on the supposition that the dental is derivative; **hold,** adj., 'guarded, nursed'?. From the phonetic point of view there is no important objection to either of these derivations.

Holder, UpG., the same as **Holunder**.

holen, vb., 'to fetch,' from MidHG. *holn* (variant *haln*), vb., OHG. *holôn* (*halôn*), 'to call, invite, lead or fetch (hither).' Comp. OSax. *halôn,* OFris. *halia,* Du. *halen,* 'to fetch'; AS. *geholian* and **gehalian,* E. *to hale.* The Teut. root *hal, hol,* corresponds to Lat. *caldre,* 'to convoke,' Gr. καλεῖν. Comp. further **Hall, hell,** which probably belong also to the same root.

Holfter, Hulfter (rarely **Halfter**), f., 'holster,' in which sense it is ModHG. only; MidHG. *hulfter,* 'quiver,' a derivative of *hulft,* 'sheath, covering, case' (OHG. *huluft*). These cognates are often wrongly connected with Goth. *hulistr,* n., 'sheath, covering,' which is said to be supported by the MidHG. variant *huls,* 'sheath, covering,' Du. *holster* and its equiv. E. *holster*. By such an assumption the *f* of the OHG., MidHG., and ModHG. form still remains obscure. It is more probably allied to forms with *f,* such as Goth. *hwilftrjôs,* 'coffin.' It is possible, of course, that there has been a confusion with the words from the stem *hul* (Goth. *hulistr,* 'sheath, covering').

Holt, m., 'large, heavy ship,' from MidHG. *holche,* OHG. *holcho,* 'transport ship'; comp. LG. *holk,* Du. *hulk,* 'transport ship,' E. *hulk.* This word, like other nautical terms (see **Helm**), appears earliest in E., in which *hulc,* 'liburna,' is found in the 9th cent. MidLat. *holcas* is scarcely derived from ὁλκάς?. It is true that some etymologists also ascribe other Teut. naval terms to a Gr. origin. Comp. **Barke**.

Hölle, f., 'hell,' from the equiv. MidHG. *helle,* OHG. *hella,* f., from *hallja*; comp. Goth. *halja,* AS. and E. *hell,* OSax. *hella*; a common Teut. term applied by Christianity to 'hades, infernum'; the Scand. *hel* shows that the earlier word upon which it is based was also used in prehistoric times for a heathen 'infernum.' Comp. also OIc. *Hel,* the goddess of the dead. It was possible for Christianity to adopt the old heathen word in all the Teut. languages; in this case it is quite unnecessary to assume the diffusion of a Goth. or other term (comp. **Heite**). It is usually connected with the root *hel, hal,* 'to cover for concealment,' hence **Hölle,** 'the hiding-place.' See **hehlen, Hülle**.

Holm, m., 'holm,' first occurs in ModHG.; a LG. word; comp. OSax., AS., and E. *holm* (AS. 'sea, lake,' OSax. 'hill'), OIc. *holmr,* 'small island in a bay or river.' Apart from the divergent sense in AS., the words (whence Russ. *cholmŭ,* 'hill,' from Slav. **chŭlmŭ,* is borrowed) are related to the cognates of E. *hill* (allied to Lat. *collis, culmen*). See **Halde**.

holpern, vb., 'to jolt,' ModHG. only (Alem. *hülpen*), for which in late MidHG. *holpeln* once occurs. Of imitative origin.

Holunder, m., from the equiv. MidHG. *holunder, holder,* OHG. *holantar, holuntar,* m., 'elder'; for OHG. *-tar* as a suffix see **Wachholder, Maßholder**. Its relation to the equiv. AS. *ellen,* E. *elder,* is dubious. It is most closely allied to the equiv. Russ. *kalína*.

Holz, n., 'wood, timber,' from MidHG. und OHG. *holz,* n., 'forest, thicket, timber.' In the remaining dialects the meaning 'forest' preponderates. Comp. OIc. *holt,* n., 'forest, thicket,' so too AS. and MidE. *holt,* n. (wanting in E.), but Du. *hout,* 'thicket, wood (as material).' Teut. type *hultos,* from pre-Teut. *kldos;* comp. OSlov. (with a different stage of gradation) *klada,* f., 'beam, wood,' Gr. κλάδο-s, m., 'twig,' OIr. *caill, coill,* 'forest' (with *ll* from *kd*).

Honig, m., 'honey,' from MidHG. *honec* (gen. *-ges*, variant *hünic*), OHG. *honag, honang,* n.; comp. OSax. *honag,* Du. *honig,* AS. *huneg,* n., E. *honey,* OIc. *hunang,* n.; a common Teut. word, wanting only in Goth., in which an older term, *miliþ* (Gr. μέλιτ-, Lat. *mel,* under **Mehltau**), is used. The origin is not certain; it has been referred to Gr. κόνις, 'dust'; **Honig,** 'granular'? .

Hopfen, m., 'hops,' from MidHG. *hopfe,* late OHG. *hopfo,* m.; comp. MidLG. and Du. *hoppe,* MidE. *hoppe,* E. *hop*; MidLat. *hupa* (for *huppa*?). The origin of the cognates is obscure; the term may be borrowed, but there is no proof of this. The assumed relation to OHG. *hiufo,* OSax. *hiopo,* AS. *heópe,* 'brier,' is not satisfactory, since the latter cannot be assigned to a general sense, 'climbing plant.' Nor is it probable that **Hopfen** is connected with **hüpfen.** Scand. has *humall,* m., Sw. and Dan. *humle,* formed from MidLat. *humlo, humulus* (whence Fr. *houblon*?).—**Hopfen**—**herfen,** see **hüpfen.**

horchen, vb., 'to hearken, listen to, obey,' properly MidG. (in UpG. **lofen, hören**), MidHG. *hôrchen,* late OHG. *hôrechen,* from *hôrahhôn;* comp. AS. *heárcian,* E. *to hark,* OFris. *hérkia;* a common West Teut. derivative of **hören.** Goth. *hauzaqôn?* (whence in AS. *hýrcnian,* E. *to hearken*). Comp. E. *to talk,* connected with *to tell, to lurk* with *to lower* (see **lauern**), *to walk,* related to **wallen.**

Horde (1.), f., 'horde,' ModHG. only (from the middle of the 16th cent.); comp. Fr. and E. *horde,* Ital. *orda;* "a word originating in Asia." From Tartar *horda,* 'camp,' Pers. *ordu,* 'army, camp.'

Horde (2.), f., 'frames of wickerwork and the space enclosed by them,' from Mid HG. *horde* (MidG.), 'enclosure, district ;' comp. Du. *horde,* 'wickerwork, hurdle.' Allied to **Hürde.**

hören, vb., 'to hear, give ear to, listen,' from the equiv. MidHG. *hæren,* OHG. *hôren;* common Teut. *hauzjan,* 'to hear'; comp. Goth. *hausjan,* OIc. *heyra,* AS. *hýran, héran,* E. *to hear,* Du. *hooren,* OLG. *hôrian* (comp. also the derivative **horchen**); Teut. root *hauz,* from pre-Teut. *kous,* to which is allied Gr. ἀκούω (for *a-κούσjω?*; Hesychius, κοᾶ ἀκούει). The latter is probably connected with the Aryan stem of **Ohr** (*ous*), just as Lat. *audire* stands for *aus-dire* (comp. *auscultare*); in that case the Teut.

guttural *h,* Gr. ἀκ, would be the remnant of a prefix. A more widely diffused stem for **hören** is OTeut. *hlus* and *klu,* from pre-Teut. *klus* and *klu,* which, however, is nearly obsolete in Teut.; comp. **laut, lauschen, lanftern.** Der. **gehorsam,** from MidHG. and OHG. *gehôrsam* (AS. *gehýrsum*), 'obedient.'

Horn, n., 'horn, peak,' from the equiv. MidHG. and OHG. *horn,* n.; comp. Goth. *haúrn,* OIc. *horn,* AS. and E. *horn,* OFris. *horn,* Du. *horen;* a common Teut. word for 'horn,' cognate with Lat. *cornu,* and Ir., W., and Corn. *corn* (κάρνον την σάλπιγγα Γαλάται, *Hesychius*); allied to Gr. κέρ-ας, 'horn,' with a different suffix (comp. also Teut. **Hirsch,** lit. 'horned animal'), as well as the equiv. Sans. *çṛñ-ga.* See further respecting the Aryan root *ker* under **Hirn.** Comp. **Hahnrei.**

Horniſſe, f., 'hornet,' from the equiv. MidHG. *hôrniȝ, hôrnûȝ* (early ModHG., also **Hermanß**), OHG. *hôrnaȝ, hôrnûȝ,* m.; comp. AS. *hyrnet,* E. *hornet;* probably not a derivative of **Horn.** The Slav. and Lat. words for 'hornet' point rather to a Goth. *hauznuts,* based upon a root *horz,* Aryan *krs* (Ind. *çṛs*); Lat. *crâbro,* 'hornet,' for *crâsro,* OSlov. *sršenĭ,* Lith. *szirszone,* 'hornet.' They point to an old Aryan root *kṛs,* 'hornet'; with this comp. OSlov. *srŭša,* Lith. *szirszŭ,* 'wasp.' A trace of this medial *s* is retained in Du. *horzel,* 'hornet' (Goth. *haursuls*), to which *horzelen,* 'to hum,' is allied.

Hornung, m., 'February,' from the equiv. MidHG. and OHG. *hornunc(g)*; the termination *-ung* is patronymic; February is regarded as the offspring of January, which in earlier ModHG. (dial.) is designated by **großer Horn,** 'great horn,' in contrast with February, **kleiner Horn,** 'little horn.' Comp. AS. and OIc. *hornung,* 'bastard'? .

Horst, m., 'shrubbery, eyrie,' from Mid HG. *hurst,* (MidG.) *horst,* OHG. *hurst, horst,* f., 'shrubbery, copse, thicket'; MidE. *hurst,* 'hill, copse,' E. *hurst;* of obscure origin.

Hort, m. (like **Halle, Heim,** and **Gau,** revived in the last cent., after being long forgotten, by the study of MidHG.), from the equiv. MidHG. *hort,* m., OHG. *hort,* n., 'hoard'; OSax. *hord (hurth),* n., 'treasure,' also 'hidden, innermost room,' AS. *hord,* n. and m., 'treasure, store,' E. *hoard;* Goth. *huzd,* 'treasure,' OIc. *hodd,* n., *hoddr,* m., 'treasure.' Teut. *hozda-,* from pre-

Teut. *kuzdhó-* for *kudhto-*, partic. 'that which is hidden' (comp. Gr. κεύθω, see also Hütte, Haus), Gr. κύσθος, any 'hollow,' espec. 'pudenda muliebria.'

Hose, f., 'hose, stocking, breeches,' from the equiv. MidHG. *hose*, OHG. *hosa*, f.; comp. AS. *hosu*, E. *hose*, and the equiv. OIc. *hosa*; Goth. **hŭsō* is by chance not recorded. 'Hose' was originally (in OHG., MidHG., AS., and OIc.) applied to a covering for the legs reaching from the thigh, or even from the knee only, and often also to stockings and gaiters. Considering the numerous correspondences in Kelt. and Rom. the Teut. term is certainly original; the Teut. words found their way into Kelt. (Corn. *hos*, 'ocrea'), and Rom. (OFr. *hose*). The connection of Hose with OSlov. *košulja*, f., 'shirt,' is dubious.

Hub, m., 'heaving, lift, impetus,' ModHG. only, allied to heben.

Hube, see Hufe.

Hübel, m., 'hillock,' from MidHG. *hübel*, m. (comp. Du. *heuvel*), 'hill'; perhaps cognate with Lith. *kŭpstas*, 'lump,' or the same as MidHG. and UpG. *bühel* (see under biegen).

hübsch, adj., 'pretty, handsome,' from MidHG. *hübesch*, *hübsch*, adj., prop. 'courtly,' then also 'beautiful.' OHG. **hubisc* is connected by a grammatical change with *hof*.

Huf, m., from the equiv. MidHG. and OHG. *huof* (gen. *huoves*), m., 'hoof'; comp. OSax. *hōf*, m., AS. *hōf*, E. *hoof*, Du. *hoef*, OIc. *hófr*. Goth. **hofs*, m., 'hoof,' is by chance not recorded. Teut. *hōfu-*, from pre-Teut. **kōpo-*, to which is allied OSlov. *kopyto*, n., 'hoof' (akin to *kopati*, 'to dig'); others derive *hófa-* from pre-Teut. *kópho-* and compare it with OInd. *çaphá*, Zend *safa*, 'hoof.' Compared with both these explanations, the derivation of Huf from heben must be rejected.

Hufe (LG. form), Hube (UpG. form), f., from the equiv. MidHG. *huobe*, OHG. *huoba*, f., 'hide of land' (about 30 acres), so still in OSax. *hōba*, f. (in E. an independent word is found from the earliest period—AS. *hýd*, E. *hide*). Cognate with Gr. κῆπος, 'garden'; the common type is *kápos*.

Hüfte, f., from the equiv. MidHG. *huf* (plur. *hüffe*), OHG. *huf* (plur. *huffi*), f., 'hip'; comp. Goth. *hups* (nom. plur. *hupeis*), m., AS. *hype* (*hop-*), m. and f., E. *hip*, and the equiv. Du. *heup*, f.; Teut.

hŭpi-, from pre-Teut. *kŭbi*; allied to Gr. κύβος, m., 'hollow near the hips'?. Others comp. Lith. *kumpis*, 'spring or hand of pork' (allied to Lith *kumpas*, 'crooked').

Hüfthorn, see Hifthorn.

Hügel, m., 'hill, knoll,' ModHG. only, introduced by Luther from MidG. into the written language; in MidHG. (UpG.), *bühel*, *kübel*, were used, which, however, must be separated etymologically from Hügel; see Hübel. Hügel (Goth. **hugils*), with dimin. suffix, is related by gradation to OHG. *houg*, MidHG. *houc*(*-ges*), 'hill,' which are explained under hoch.

Huhn, n., 'fowl,' from MidHG. and OHG. *huon* (plur. *-ir*, MidHG. *hüener*), n.; comp. OSax. *hōn*, Du. *hoen*; unknown to E.; OIc. plur. only, *hœns* (AS. *héns-*?), n., 'fowls.' Huhn compared with the related words Hahn and Henne is prop. of common gender, and may in OHG. be used instead of Hahn. The Goth. term may have been **hōn* or **hōnis*. Comp. Hahn.

Huld, f., 'grace, favour, kindness,' from MidHG. *hulde*, f., OHG. *huldi*, OSax. *huldī*, f.; abstract of hold.

Hülfe, see Hilfe.

Hülle, f., 'envelop, covering, sheath,' from MidHG. *hülle*, OHG. *hulla* (Goth. **hulja*), f., 'cloak, kerchief, covering'; allied to the root *hel*, 'to cover for concealment,' in hehlen.—ModHG. in Hülle und Fülle meant orig. 'in food and clothing'; hence Hülle und Fülle was used to denote all the necessaries of life, finally the idea of superfluity was combined with the phrase.

Hülse, f., 'shell, husk,' from the equiv. MidHG. *hülse*, *hülsche*, OHG. *hulsa*, for **hulisa* (Goth. **hulisi* or **huluzi*). f., 'shell'; from the root *hēl*, *hul* (see hehlen, Hülle), like Goth. *jukuzi*, f., 'yoke,' or *aqizi*, f., 'axe' (see Art), in AS. without the suffix *s*, *hulu*, 'pod, husk.'

Hulst, m., 'holly,' from the equiv. MidHG. *huls* (comp. Art, from MidHG. *ackes*), OHG. *huls*, *hulis*, m.; from G., Fr. *houx* is derived. Comp. E. *holly*, AS. *holegn*, E. *kulver*, Kelt. *kelen*, 'holly.'

Hummel, f., 'humble-bee, drone,' from the equiv. MidHG. *hummel*, *humbel*, OHG. *humbal*, m.; comp. Du. *hommel*, 'drone,' MidE. *humbel-bee*, E. *humble-bee* (AS. **humbol-beó*). The origin of the cognates is obscure; the derivation from MidHG. *hummen*, 'to hum,' is not satisfactory, since the soft labial in OHG. *humbal* must be archaic and original.

Hummer, m., 'lobster,' ModHG. only, from the equiv. LG. (Dan. and Swed.) *hummer*; the final source is OIc. *humarr*, m., 'lobster'; comp. Gr. κάμαρος, κάμμαρος, 'a kind of crab,' although the occurrence of the same names of fishes in several Aryan languages is usually very rare. In E. a different word is used—AS. *loppestre*, f., E. *lobster*.

Humpe, f., **Humpen,** m.,'drinking-cup, bumper, bowl,' ModHG. only (from the 17th cent.); it seems, however, to be primitive, since correspondences are found in the Aryan languages, Sans. *kumbha*, m., 'pot, urn,' Zend χumba (the initial *h* of the Mod HG. word probably originated like the *h* in haben, root *khabh*; yet comp. also Gr. κύμβος, m., 'vessel, cup'). However remarkable it may seem that a primit. word like Humpen should have been unrecorded in the entire Teut. group until the 17th cent., yet similar examples of such a phenomenon may be adduced; comp. Schwire, 'stake,' in ModHG. dial. only, which, like AS. *swēr*, 'pillar,' corresponds to Sans. *svāru-s*, 'sacrificial stake.' In this case, however, the supposition that the word has been borrowed is more probable, because Teut. has for the most part adopted foreign terms for drinking vessels (comp. Krug, Kruse, Krust, Kelch); the assumption, on account of Zend χumba, that the word was borrowed at an early period from a Pers. dial. is alluring (as in the case of Pfad).

Humpeln, humpen, vb., ' to hobble'; ModHG. only, from LG. ?. Perhaps allied to hinken.

Hund, m., 'dog, hound,' from the equiv. MidHG. *hunt*(d), OHG. *hunt*(t), m.; a common Teut. word *hunda-*, 'dog'; comp. Goth. *hunds*, OIc. *hundr*, AS. *hund*, E. *hound* (for the chase only, in other cases *dog*, AS. *docga*), Du. *hond*, LG. *hund*. If the second syllable in *hun-da-* is a derivative (comp. Hinte), the Teut. word corresponds to Aryan *kun-*, 'dog'; comp. Gr. κύων (gen. κυν-ός), Sans. *çvā* (gen. *çún-as*), Lat. *canis*, Lith. *szú* (stem *szun-*), OIr. *cú*. Thus the Aryans in their primit. home were already acquainted with the dog as distinct from the wolf. In Teut. it might also appear as if the word were connected with an old str. vb. *hinþan*, ' to catch' (in Goth.); in popular etymology Hund might be regarded as the 'captor, hunter, taker of prey.' The phrase *auf den Hund kommen*, ' to fall into poverty, go to the dogs,' seems to be based upon the OTeut. expression in dice-playing (see gefallen, Sau, and also Daus); probably Hund, like Lat. *canis* and Gr. κύων, denoted an unlucky throw; in Sans. the professional gambler is called ' dog-slayer' (*çvaghnin*). The probable antiquity of dice-playing is attested by Tacitus' account of the Teutons and by the songs of the Vedas.

Hundert, n., 'hundred,' from the equiv. MidHG. and late OHG. *hundert*, n.; comp. OSax. *hunderod*, AS. and E. *hundred*, and the equiv. OIc. *hundraδ*, n.; Goth. **hundarap* (gen. *-dis*) is wanting; the word is evidently a compound, the second part of which is connected with Goth. *rapjan*, 'to count' (comp. Rede). The first component was used alone for ' hundred'; comp. Goth. *twa hunda*, 200, *þrija hunda*, 300, &c.; OHG. *zwei hunt*, *driu hunt*, &c., AS. *tū hund*, *þreo hund*, 200, 300. This simple term is an Aryan form, Teut. *hunda-*, from pre-Teut. *kmtó-*; comp. Lat. *centum*, Gr. ἑκατόν, Sans. *çatám*, Zend *suta*, Lith. *szimtas* (*m* is changed in Teut. into *n* before *d*; see Rand); OSlov. *sŭto* is probably derived from Iran. *sata*. But while the word, judging from the correspondences in these languages, denoted our decimal ' hundred' in primit. Aryan, we find that it is used in OTeut. for 120, the so-called duodecimal hundred. In OIc. *hundraþ* in the pre-Christian period denoted only 120. a distinction being made at a later period between *tólfrætt hundraþ*, 120, and *tírætt hundraþ*, 100; even at the present time *hundraþ* denotes the duodecimal hundred in Iceland. In Goth. we have only indirect evidence of the combination of the decimal and duodecimal numeration, *tuihunté-hund*, ' ten times ten,' but *twa hunda*, 200 (OIc. *tíu-tiger*, 'ten tens, 100'). So too in OHG. and AS.; comp. OHG. *zēhanzo*, '100,' prop. ' ten tens,' and also *einhunt*, AS. *teóntig*, but *tū hund*. In other cases also the co-existence of the duodecimal and decimal system may be seen in OTeut. In G. the word for 120 became obsolete at an early period, but its existence may be inferred from the fact that the old word *hunt* in OHG. and Mid HG. was used only for several hundreds, while hundred was expressed almost entirely by *zēhanzo* and *zēhenzig*.

Hundsfott, m., first occurs in early Mod HG., lit. "' cunnus canis.' Borrowed from the shamelessness of the ' proud' bitch."

Hüne (a LG. form, in earlier ModHG. **Henne**), m., from the equiv. MidHG. *hiune*, m., 'giant,' in which sense it is found in the 13th cent. This word, phonetically identical with MidHG. *Hiune*, OHG. *Hûn*, 'Hun, Hungarian,' existed in Germany in OTeut. names of persons even before the appearance of the Huns. Some etymologists assume, with little probability, that the primit. Teut. *Hûno-* was the name of the aborigines of Germany. Undoubtedly the North G. **Hüne** points rather to a Teut. tribe (Sigfrid in the Eddas is called *enn hunske*). Numerous compound names of places with **Hun** (**Hann**) are found in North Germany (**Hanna**, **Hünfeld**). Note the names of persons such as **Humboldt** (OHG. *Hûnbolt*).

Hunger, m., 'hunger, famine,' from the equiv. MidHG. *hunger*, OHG. *hungar*, m.; comp. OSax. *hungar*, AS. *hungor*, m., E. *hunger*, OIc. *hungr*, m.; Goth. **huggrus* is wanting (it is indicated by *huggrjan*, 'to hunger'), but the term *hûhrus* (for *hunhrus*, *hunhrus*), m., occurs; common Teut. *hunhru-*, *hungru-*, 'hunger,' from pre-Teut. *knkru-*?. The Gr. *gloss*, κέγκει πεινᾷ, points to an Aryan root, *kenk*, *konk*; comp. also Lith. *kankà*, 'torment,' with OIc. *há*, vb., 'to torment, pain' (from Teut. **hanhôn*).

Huntzen, vb., 'to abuse,' ModHG. only, probably 'to call one a dog' (note the formation of *ehen*, *sieten*, *tuhen*); then probably also 'to treat anyone like a dog.'

Hüpfen, vb., from the equiv. MidHG. *hüpfen*, *hupfen*, 'to hop'; OHG. **hupfen* is by chance not recorded; so too AS. **hyppan*, whence MidE. *hyppen*, E. *to hip*. Akin also to ModHG. and MidHG. *hopfen*, AS. *hoppian*, E. *to hop*, OIc. *hoppa*; Goth. **huppôn*, **huppjan*, are wanting. UpG. dialects have besides *hoppen*, from OHG. **hoppôn* (OTeut. **hubbôn*). AS. *hoppettan*, 'to hop,' MidHG. **hopfzen*, ModHG. **hopfen**, are differently formed.

Hürde, f., 'hurdle,' from MidHG. *hurt*, plur. *hürte* and *hürde*, f., 'hurdle, wickerwork,' OHG. *hurt*, plur. *hurdi*, f.; comp. Goth. *haúrds*, f., 'door,' OIc. *hurð*, f., 'door' (this sense is also found in MidHG.), likewise 'wickerwork, hurdle, lid'; AS. **hyrd*, MidE. *hyrde*, AS. *hyrdel*, E. *hurdle*. The meaning 'door' is only a development of the general sense 'wickerwork'; pre-Teut. *krti-*. Comp. Lat. *crâtes*, Gr. κυρτία, 'wickerwork,' κύρτη, κύρτος, 'creel, cage,'

κάρταλος, 'basket'; allied to the Sans. root *kṛt*, 'to spin,' *cṛt*, 'to connect, combine.'

Hure, f., 'whore,' from MidHG. *huore*, OHG. *huora*, *huorra* (from **hôrjô*, Goth.?), f.; comp. AS. and MidE. *hôre*, E. *whore*, with an excrescent *w*, Du. *hoer*, OIc. *hôra*, f., 'whore'; in Goth. *hôrs*, m., is 'whoremonger' (but *kalki*, f., 'whore'). To these are allied OHG. *huor*, n., 'adultery, fornication.' OIc. *hôr*, AS. *hôr*, n.; probably also MidHG. *herge*, f., 'whore' (Goth. **harjô*)?. The Teut. root *hôr-* is related to Lat. *carus*, 'dear,' OIr. *cara*, 'friend,' and *caraim*, 'I love.' Its connection with **Harn** is less probable, although Gr. μοιχός, 'adulterer,' is formed from ὀμιχεῖν, 'mingere.' In Slav.-Lith., too, words with cognate sounds are found in the sense of 'whore.' OSlov. *kurûva*, f. (Lith. *kùrva*, f.), is perhaps derived from the Teut. word.

Hurra, interj., 'hurrah!' from MidHG. *hurrâ*, interj. (allied to MidHG. *hurren*, 'to move quickly').

Hurtig, adj., 'quick, prompt, speedy,' from MidHG. *hurtec*, *hurteclîch*, 'quick.' prop. 'dashing violently against'; Mid HG. *hurt*, m. and f., 'coming into violent collision, impact,' is said to be borrowed from Fr. *heurt* (Ital. *urto*), 'thrust,' which again is derived from Kelt. *hwrdh*, 'thrust.' Yet **hurtig** may be regarded as a genuine Teut. word, allied to OHG. *rado*, AS. *hraed*, 'quick,' with which OIc. *horskr*, 'quick,' is also connected.

Husar, m., 'hussar,' ModHG. only (from the 16th cent.); final source Hungarian *huszár*.

Husch, interj., 'hush! quick!' from MidHG. *husch* (but used only as an interj. to express a feeling of cold); hence Mod HG. **huschen**.

Husten, m., 'cough,' from the equiv. MidHG. *huoste*, OHG. *huosto*, m., from an earlier **hwôsto* with the loss of the *w* (Up. Alsat. and Swiss *wueste* with the *w* retained and the *h* before it suppressed); comp. Du. *hoest*, AS. *hwôsta*, m., E. (dial.) *whoost*, Scand. *hôste* (for **hvôste*), m., 'cough.' The verbal stem *hwôs* was retained in the AS. str. vb. (pret. *hweôs*), beside which a wk. vb. *hwêsan*, E. *wheeze*, occurs. Teut. root *hwôs* (Goth. **hwôs-ta*), from pre-Teut. *kwôs*, *kâs*, corresponds to the Sans. root *kâs*, 'to cough,' Lith. *kôsiu* (*kôséti*), 'to cough,' OSlov. *kašlĭ*, m., 'cough.'

Hut (1.), m., 'hat,' from MidHG. and OHG. *huot* (gen. *huotes*), m., 'hat, cap, helmet'; comp. Du. *hoed*, AS. *hód*, E. hood. It is most closely allied to AS. *hætt*, E. *hat*, and the equiv. OIc. *hǫttr*; in Goth. both **hôps* and **hattus* are wanting. It is probably connected more remotely with Lith. *kúdas*, 'tuft (of hair, &c.), crest of a cock,' and perhaps also with the Teut. root *had*, *hôd*, in the two following words.

Hut (2.), f., 'heed, care, guard,' from MidHG. *huot*, *huote*, f., OHG. *huota*, f., 'oversight and foresight as a preventive against harm, care, guard'; Du. *hoede*, 'foresight, protection.' To this is allied

hüten, vb., 'to heed, take care,' from MidHG. *hüeten*, OHG. *huoten*, 'to watch, take care'; Goth. *hôdjan* is wanting. AS. *hédan*, E. *to heed* (also as a subst.), Du. *hoeden*, OSax. *hôdian*. Teut. root *hôd*, from the Aryan *kâdh* (*kôdh* ?) or *kât*; perhaps allied to Lat. *cassis* (for **cat-i-*), 'helmet,' also to MidHG. *huot*, 'helmet,' E. *hat*. See **Hut** (1).

Hütte, f., 'cottage, hut, foundry, tent,' from MidHG. *hütte*, OHG. *hutta*, f., 'hut, tent'; a specifically HG. word which found its way into Du., E., and Rom.; comp. Du. *hut*, E. *hut*, Fr. *hutte*, 'hut.' In Goth. perhaps **hupja*, and related to AS. *hȳdan*, E. *to hide* (from **húdjan*), Teut. root *hūd*, from Aryan *kûth*, allied to Gr. κεύθω ?. Comp. **Haus**.

Hutzel, f., 'dried pear cuttings,' from MidHG. *hutzel*, *hützel*, f., 'dried pear'; probably an intensive form of **Haut** ?.

I.

ich, pron., 'I,' from the equiv. MidHG. *ich*, OHG. *ih*; corresponding to OSax. *ik*, Du. *ik*, AS. *ic̄*, E. *I*, Goth. *ik*. For the common Teut. *ik*, from pre-Teut. *egom*, comp. Lat. *ego*, Ger. ἐγώ, Sans. *aham*, OSlov. *azŭ*, Lith. *aż*. The oblique cases of this primit. noun were formed in all the Aryan languages from a stem *me-*; comp. mein. The orig. meaning of ich, primit. type *egom* (equal to Sans. *aham*), cannot be fathomed.

Igel, m., 'hedgehog,' from the equiv. MidHG. *igel*, OHG. *igil*, m.; corresponding to Du. *egel*, AS. *igl* (*il*), in E. however, *hedgehog*, to which OIc. *igull* is equiv. Gr. ἐχῖνος, OSlov. *ježĭ*, Lith. *ežỹs*, 'hedgehog,' are undoubtedly cognate. A West-Aryan **eghi-nos*, 'hedgehog,' must be assumed; comp. Goth. *katils*, from Lat. *cattinus*, *asilus*, from Lat. *asinus* (so too Esel, Himmel, Kümmel, Kessel). Very different from this word is the second component of the compound Blutigel, prop. Blutegel; in MidHG. simply *egel*, *egele*, OHG. *egala*, f., 'leech.' That this OHG. *egala* is connected etymologically with OHG. *igil*, 'hedgehog,' is improbable on account of the meaning only.

ihr, poss. pron., 'her, their' (general from the 14th cent.), MidHG. *ir* is rare as a poss. pron.; it is prop. the gen. plur. of er, OHG. *iro* (Goth. *izê*). Further details belong to grammar.

Iltis, m., 'polecat,' from the equiv. Mid HG. *iltis*, *eltes*, OHG. *illitiso*, m. (the long i is assumed by the ModHG. and Bav. form Elledeis); a specifically G. term based upon an old compound which has not as yet been explained.

Imbiß, m., 'lunch,' from MidHG. and OHG. *imbîȝ*, *inbîȝ*, m. and n., 'food, meal,' allied to MidHG. *enbîȝen*, OHG. *inbîȝan*, 'to partake of food or drink, eat,' allied to beißen.

Imme, f., 'bee,' from MidHG. *imbe* (later *imme*), m., OHG. *imbi*, 'swarm of bees' (hence a collective term; the meaning 'bee' first occurs in late MidHG.). In OHG. records *imbi bianô* denotes 'swarm of bees'; comp. AS. *geogoð*, 'a youthful band,' with E. *youth* (see Bursche, Frauenzimmer, Stute). Yet it is questionable whether *imbi* has ever signified 'swarm, herd' (generally). Its direct connection with Biene (root *bî*) is certainly dubious; it is more probably related to Gr. ἐμπίς, 'mosquito, gnat.'

immer, from the equiv. MidHG. *imer*, *immer*, earlier *iemer*, OHG. *iomêr*, 'always' (only of the present and future); OHG. *iomêr* is a compound of *io* (comp. je) and *mêr* (see mehr); comp. AS. *ǽfre* (E. *ever*), from **â-mre* (equiv. to OHG. *io-mêr*).

impfen, vb., 'to ingraft, vaccinate,' from the equiv. MidHG. (rare) *impfen*, OHG. (rare) *impfôn*, for which the usual forms are MidHG. *imp(f)eten*, OHG. *impfitôn*, mostly *impitôn*, 'to inoculate, ingraft'; yet comp. also AS. *impian*, E. *to imp*. Impfen, just like pfropfen and pelzen, seems, on account of OHG. *impfôn* and AS. *impian*, to have been borrowed about the

7th or 8th cent. from Lat.; yet only OHG. *impitôn* can be explained as directly borrowed from a Lat. horticultural term; comp. Lat.-Rom. *putare*, 'to prune' (comp. Ital. *potare*, Span. *podar*), to which Franc. *possen*, Du. and LG. *poten*, 'to ingraft,' are related. The correspondence of OHG. *impitôn*, with Fr. *enter*, 'to ingraft' (from **empter*), is remarkable; comp. Du., Mid Du., and MidLG. *enten*, 'to inoculate' (from *empten*). With the MidLat. base *imputare* (for Lat. *amputare*?), OHG. *impfôn* and AS. *impian* may be connected by the intermediate link *impo(d)are*, unless it is based rather like Fr. (Lorr.) *opé*, 'to inoculate,' upon a Lat. **impuare*. The usual derivation of all the Teut. and Rom. words from Gr. ἐμφυρεύω, ἐμφύω, 'to ingraft,' is perhaps conceivable. Moreover, the medical term impfen has been current only since the 18th cent.

in, prep., 'in, into, at,' from the equiv. MidHG. and OHG. *in*, a common Teut. prep. with the same form; comp. Goth., AS., E., Du., and OSax. *in*, 'in.' Its primit. kinship with Lat. *in*, Gr. ἐν, ἐνί, Lith. *i*, and Lett. *ë* is certain. To this are allied in**t**em, in**t**eß, and in**t**effen.

Infel, Inful, f., from the equiv. Mid HG. *infel*, *infele*, f., 'mitre of a bishop or abbot'; formed from Lat. *infula*.

Ingwer, m., 'ginger,' from the equiv. MidHG. *ingewër*, also *gingebere*, m., derived, like Du. *gember*, E. *ginger*, Fr. *gingembre*, Ital. *zenzovero*, *zenzero*, 'ginger,' from the equiv. late Gr. ζιγγίβερις, which comes from the East; comp. Arab. *zendjebil*, from Prak. *singabëra* (Sans. *çṛṅgavëra*).

inne, adv., 'within,' from MidHG. and OHG. *inne*, OHG. *inna*, 'inwardly'; comp. Goth. *inna*; allied to in.—So too innen, 'within,' MidHG. *innen*, OHG. *innân*, *innana*; Goth. *innana*, 'within.'—inner, 'within,' from MidHG. *innere*, adj. and adv., 'internal,' OHG. *innar*, adj.

innig, adj., 'intimate,' from MidHG. innec(g), adj., 'internal, intimate'; a recent formation from MidHG. *inne;* comp. even in OHG. *inniglih*, 'internal.'

Innung, f., 'association,' from late MidHG. *innunge*, f., 'connection (with a corporate body), association, guild'; allied to OHG. *innôn*, 'to receive (into an alliance), combine'; connected with inne.

Inschlitt, see Unschlitt.

Infel, f., 'island,' from the equiv. Mid HG. *insel*, *insele*, f.; formed from Lat. and Rom. *insula* (Fr. *île*, Ital. *isola*); even in OHG. a divergent form of the word, *isila*, was borrowed. The OTeut. words for 'island' are Aue and Wert.

Infiegel, n., 'seal,' from the equiv. Mid HG. *insigel*, *insigele*, OHG. *insigili*, n.; corresponding to AS. *insegele*, OIc. *innsigle*, with the same sense. See Siegel for the curious history of the cognates.

inständig, adj., 'instant, urgent,' from the equiv. MidHG. **instendec;* OHG. *instendigo* is recorded once. Allied to stehen (gestanden); perhaps an imitation of Lat. *insistere*, 'to pursue zealously'?

inwendig, see wenden.

Inzicht, f., 'accusation,' from the equiv. MidHG. and OHG. *inziht*, f.; an abstract of zeihen; comp. also bezichtigen.

irden, adj., 'earthen,' from MidHG. and OHG. *irdîn*, adj., 'made of clay' (also 'earthly'); an adj. of material allied to OHG. *erda*, 'earth.' Also irdisch, with a different application, from the equiv. Mid HG. *irdesch*, OHG. *irdisc* (prop. 'peculiar or belonging to the earth'; with regard to the suffix comp. deutsch and Mensch). See Erde.

irgend, adv., 'ever, soever, whatever,' with an affix *d* (see Mond, Habicht, and Obst), from the equiv. MidHG. (MidG.) *iergen*, late OHG. *iergen*, for which in earlier OHG. *io wergin* occurs; OHG. *wergin* (for **hwergin*, **hwar-gin*), corresponds to OSax. *hwergin*, AS. *hwergen*, in which *hwar* signifies 'where,' and *-gin*, the indef. particle, 'any,' corresponding to Goth. *-hun* (Lat. *-cunque*, Sans. *-cana*); Goth. **hwar-gin*, **hwar-hun*, 'anywhere.' Respecting OHG. *io*, comp. je. Nirgend, the negative form, occurs even in MidHG. as *niergen* (a compound of *ni*, 'not').

irre, adj., 'in error, astray, insane, confused,' from the equiv. MidHG. *irre*, OHG. *irri*, adj. (OHG. also 'provoked'); corresponding to AS. *yrre*, 'provoked, angry.' Allied to Goth. *airzeis*, 'astray, misled' (HG. *rr* equal to Goth. *rz*). Anger was regarded as an aberration of mind (comp. also Lat. *delirare*, allied to *lira*, 'furrow,' prop. 'rut'). The root *ers* appears also in Lat. *errare*, 'to go astray' (for **ersare*), *error*, 'mistake' (for **ersor*); allied also to Sans. *irasy*, 'to behave violently, be angry'?. —irren, 'to be in error, go astray, mislead, deceive,' from the equiv. MidHG. *irren*, OHG. *irrôn* (Goth. **airzjôn*).—Irre, f., 'mistaken course,' from MidHG. *irre*, f. (comp. Goth. *airzei*, 'mistaken course, leading astray'). **Irrſal**, n., 'erring, erroneous opinion, maze,' from MidHG. *irresal*, n. and m. (Goth. *uirzisl; OHG. -*isal* is a suffix; see **Rätſel**).

Iſop, m., 'hyssop,' from the equiv. early MidHG. *isôpe* (*isôpe*, *ispe*); derived like Ital. *isôpo* from Lat. *hysôpum*, late Gr. ὕσσωπος, which is of Oriental origin.

Itzig, Jew.-G. from Hebr. *Jizcháck*, 'Isaac.'

J.

ja, adv., 'yes,' from the equiv. MidHG. and OHG. *jâ* (for *jă*); corresponding to Goth. *ja*, 'yes,' also *jai*, 'truly, forsooth,' OSax. *ja*, AS. *geá*, also *gese* (for *gê-sweŏ*, 'yes, thus'), whence E. *yea* and *yes*. Allied also to Gr. ἦ, 'forsooth,' and OHG. *jëhan*, 'to acknowledge, confess' (see **Beichte**). Lith. *ja* is derived from G.

jach, **gach**, 'precipitate, hasty,' allied to **jähe**.

Jacht, f., 'yacht, sloop,' ModHG. only, formed from the equiv. Du. *jagt* (comp. E. *yacht*), which is usually connected with **jagen**, and even to **jähe**.

Jacke, f., 'jacket,' first occurs in early ModHG. (15th cent.), formed from the equiv. Fr. *jaque*, whence also E. *jacket*; the derivation of Fr. *jaque* (Ital. *giaco*) from Teut. is quite uncertain.

Jagd, f., 'chase, hunt, hunting-party,' from the equiv. MidHG. *jaget*, n. (and f.), OHG. *jagot, n.; a verbal abstract of **jagen**, 'to hunt, chase' (from the equiv. MidHG. *jagen*, OHG. *jagôn*, wk. vb.), which does not occur in Goth., OIc., AS., or OSax. The connection of this specifically G. word with Gr. διώκω is dubious, and so too its kinship with Gr. ἀἴχνής, 'unceasing,' and Sans. *yahú*, 'restless.'—
Jäger, 'huntsman, sportsman,' is the equiv. MidHG. *jęger*, *jęgere*, OHG. *jageri (*jagâri*).

jäh, **gähe**, adj., 'steep, precipitous, hasty,' from MidHG. *gæhe* (also *gâch*), OHG. *gâhi*, adj., 'quick. suddenly, impetuous'; a specifically G. word (with a dial. initial *j* for *g* as in *jappen*; comp. also **jähnen** with **gähnen**). From this Fr. *gai*, 'gay,' is borrowed. Its connection with **gehen**, **gegangen** (see **Gang**), is impossible. **Gaubieb** is, on the other hand, allied to it.

Jahn, m., 'swath,' first found in early ModHG., yet undoubtedly a genuine G. word, existing throughout South Germany (MidHG. *jân), and also appearing in Swed. dials. as *dn*. In Swiss dials. **Jahn** means 'passage (formed by a swath).' Hence the word is a derivative of the Aryan root *yê*, or rather *ī*, 'to go,' with which Goth. *iddja*, 'went' (Sans. *yâ*, 'to go'), is connected. See **gehen** and **eilen**.

Jahr, n., 'year,' from the equiv. MidHG. and OHG. *jâr*, n.; a common Teut. term; comp. Goth. *jêr*, OIc. *âr*, AS. *geár*, E. *year*, Du. *jaar*, OSax. *jâr* (*gêr*), n., 'year.' The orig. meaning of the word, which also appears in **heuer**, seems to be 'spring,' as is indicated by the Slav. cognate *jarŭ*, 'spring'; comp. also Gr. ὥρα, 'season, spring, year,' and ὥρος, 'year,' so too Zend *yâre*, 'year'; in Ind. a similar term is wanting (comp. **Sommer** and **Winter**). For the change of meaning see the history of the word **Winter**.

Jammer, m., 'sorrow, grief, wailing,' from the equiv. MidHG. *jâmer*, OHG. *jâmar*, m. and n.; prop. a neut. adj. used as a subst., OHG. *jâmar*, 'mournful' (hence **Jammer**, 'that which is mournful'); in OSax. and AS. the adj. only exists, comp. OSax. *jâmar*, AS. *geómor*, 'painful, mournful.' The origin of this word, which is unknown to East Teut. (Goth. *jêmrs), is obscure.

Jänner, m., 'January,' from the equiv. early MidHG. *jęnner*, m.; from the Lat. *januarius*, Rom. *jenuario* (OHG. *jęnneri, m., is wanting, perhaps only by chance).

jappen, vb., 'to gape, pant,' ModHG. only, prop. LG.; comp. Du. *gapen*, 'to gape,' under **gaffen**.

jäten, see **gäten**.

Jauche, f., 'filthy liquid,' first occurs in early ModHG., introduced into HG. from a MidG. and LG. variant, *jûche*. It is based on a Slav. word for 'broth, soup,' which deteriorated in sense when borrowed; e.g. Pol. *jucha*, 'broth' (cognate with Lat. *jús*, Sans. *yûṣan*, 'broth').

Jaucherſ, **Juchert**, m., from the equiv. MidHG. *jûchert*, late OHG. *jukhart* (*ā l*), n., 'acre'; the Bav. and Alem. word for the Franc. and MidG. **Morgen**. The usual derivation from Lat. *jûgerum*, 'acre of land' (prop. ȝ acre), does not offer a satisfactory explanation of the OHG. word, for the equiv. MidHG. *jiuch*, n. and f., 'acre of land,' can only be cognate with Lat. *jūgerum*, and not a mutilated form of the Lat. original. Hence MidHG. *jiuch*, like Lat. *jūgerum*, is doubtlessly connected with ModHG. Joch and Lat. *jugum*; consequently Juchert is lit. 'as much land as can be ploughed by a yoke of oxen in a day'; the suffix of OHG. *juhhurt* suggests that of MidHG. *egerte*, 'fallow land.' See Jod.

jauchzen, vb., 'to shout for joy, exult,' from MidHG. *jûchezen*, 'to cry out, shout for joy,' OHG. **jûhhazzen*; probably a derivative of the MidHG. interj. *jûch*, *jû* (expressions of joy); comp. âchzen, allied to ach.

je, adv., older ie (which in the 17th cent. was supplanted by je, recorded at a still earlier period), 'always, ever,' from Mid HG. *ie*, 'at all times, always (of the past and present), the (with compars., distributives, &c.), at any (one) time,' OHG. *io*, *eo*, 'always, at any (one) time.' The earliest OHG. form *eo* is based on **êo*, *aiw* (comp. See, Schnee, and wie); comp. Goth. *aiw*, 'at any time,' OSax. *êo*, AS. *á*, 'always' (E. *aye*, from OIc. *ei*, 'always'). Goth. *aiw* is an oblique case of the subst. *aiws*, 'time, eternity,' and because in Goth. only the combination of *aiw* with the negative *ni* occurs, it is probable that *ni aiw* (see nie), 'never' ('not for all eternity'), is the oldest, and that the positive meaning, OHG. *eo*, 'always,' was obtained *à posteriori*; yet comp. Gr. *aieí*, 'always,' allied to *aiώv*, and see ewig and the following words.

jeder, pron., 'each, every,' from late Mid HG. *ieder*, earlier *iewĕder*, OHG. *iowĕdar* (*eo-hwĕdar*), 'either,' from weder (OHG. wĕdar, 'which of two') and je; corresponding to OSax. *iahwĕthar*, AS. *ǽhwæðer*; comp. also OHG. *eogiwĕdar*, MidHG. *iegewĕder*, AS. *ǽȝhwæðer*, E. either.—ModHG. jedweder, 'each, every,' is of a different etymological origin, being derived from MidHG. *ietwĕder*, *ie-dewĕder*, 'either' (from *ie* and MidHG. *dewĕder*, 'any one of two'; see entweder). —jeglich, 'each, every,' from MidHG. *iegelich*, OHG. *eo-gilîh*, 'each'; allied to OHG. *gilîh*, 'each' (see gleich). ModHG. jeder, prop. 'either,' has in ModHG. supplanted the MidHG. *iegelich*.—jemand, 'anybody, somebody,' from the equiv. MidHG. *ieman*, OHG. *eoman* (prop. 'any person').

jener, pron., 'you, yonder, that, the former,' from the equiv. MidHG. *jener*, OHG. *jenêr*, allied to the differently vocalised Goth. *jains*, OIc. *enn*, *inn*, AS. *geon*, E. *you* (with which yonder is connected). In late MidHG. *dĕr jener*, 'that,' is also used, whence ModHG. derjenige.—jenseits, 'on the other side, beyond,' from the equiv. MidHG. *jensît*, lit. 'on that side' (MidHG. also *jene sîte*).

jetzt, adv. (older itz, like ie for je), 'now, at the present time,' from the equiv. Mid HG. *ietze*, *iezuo* (hence the archaic ModHG. jetzo), beside which MidHG. *iezunt*, ModHG. jetzund, with a new suffix, occurs. How the adv. *ie-zuo*, recorded in earlier MidHG., can mean 'now' is not clear; comp. MidHG. *iesâ*, 'at once,' from *ie* (see je) and *sâ*, 'at once.'

Joch, n., 'yoke, ridge of mountains,' from the equiv. MidHG. *joch*, OHG. *joh(hh)*, n., 'yoke, ridge of mountains, acre'; corresponding to Goth. *juk*, n., 'yoke of oxen,' OIc. *ok*, AS. *geoc*, E. *yoke*, Du. *juk*; a common Aryan word formed from the Aryan root *yug*, 'to fasten'; comp. Sans. *yugá*, 'yoke, team' (allied to the root *yuj*, 'to put to'), Gr. ζυγόν, from ζεύγνυμι, Lat. *jugum*, from *jungere*, Lith. *jùngus*, OSlov. *igo* (from **jŭgo*); comp. Jauchert. The str. root verb (Teut. root *juk*) has become obsolete in the whole Teut. root.

Joppe, f., 'boddice,' from MidHG. *joppe* (*jope*, *juppe*), f., 'jacket'; borrowed, like Jacke, from Rom.; comp. Fr. *jupe*, *jupon*, 'skirt.' Ital. *giuppa*, *giubba*, 'jacket, jerkin.'

jubeln, vb., 'to rejoice loudly, exult,' allied to MidHG. *jubilieren*. This word (formed like MidLat. *jubilare*, comp. Ital. *giubilare*) is still wanting in MidHG. and OHG. Jubel, 'shout of joy, exultation,' too, first occurs in ModHG.

Juchert, see Jauchert.—juchzen, see jauchzen.

jucken, vb., 'to rub, scratch, itch,' from the equiv. MidHG. *jucken* (*jücken*), OHG. *jucchen*, wk. vb.; corresponding to AS. *gyccan*, E. *to itch* (Goth. **jukkjan*). The stem *juk*, *jukk*, occurs also in OHG. *jucchido*, AS. *gycða*, 'itch' (MidLG. *jöken*, Du. *jeuken*, 'to itch').

Juhs, see Jur.

Jugend, f., 'period of youth, young people,' from the equiv. MidHG. *jugent(d)*, OHG. *jugund*, f.; corresponding to OSax. *juguð*, Du. *jeugd*, AS. *geoguð*, f., 'youth, young troop,' E. *youth* (see Burſche, Frauenzimmer, and Imme); the common Teut.

abstract of jung (in Goth. *junda*, 'youth'); Teut. *jugunþi-* represents pre-Teut. *yuwenti-* (comp. 𝔅𝔯ü𝔠𝔱𝔢). The adj. **jung**, 'young, new, recent,' is the common Teut *junga-* (with a nasal); comp. MidHG. *junc(g)*, OHG. and OSax. *jung*, Du. *jong*, AS. *geong*, E. *young*, Goth. *juggs (jungs)*, 'young.' This common Teut. *junga-* is based, by contraction from *juwunga-*, upon a pre-Teut. *yuwenko-*, 'young,' with which Lat. *juvencus*, 'youth,' and Sans. *yuvaçás*, 'young,' are identical. The earlier Aryan form *yuwén* (*yéwen* ?) appears in Lat. *juvenis*, 'young, youth,' and *juven-ta*, 'youth' (equiv. to Goth. *junda*, f.), as well as in Sans. *júvan*, 'young, youth' (*yóśá*, f., 'maid'), and OSlov. *junŭ*, Lith. *jáunas*, 'young'; they are all based upon an Aryan root *yū*, 'to be young' (comp. Sans. *yáviśtha*, 'the youngest'). **Jüngling**, 'youth, young man,' is a Teut. derivative of *jung*; comp. OHG. *jungalina*, MidHG. *jungelinc*, Du. *jongeling*, AS. *geongling*, E. (antiquated)

youngling, OIc. *ynglingr* (in Goth. *juggalauþs*), 'youth.'—**Jünger**, m., 'disciple,' prop. the compar. of *jung*, used as a subst.; comp. MidHG. *jünger*, OHG. *jungiro*, 'disciple, pupil, apprentice'; the word (as the antithesis to **Herr**, OHG. *hērro*) is probably derived from the OTeut. feudal system.— ModHG. **Jungfer**, f., 'young girl, virgin, maid, maiden,' is developed from MidHG. *juncvrouwe*, 'noble maiden, young lady' (thus, even in MidHG., *ver* appears for the unaccented proclitic 𝔉𝔯𝔞𝔲). To this is allied **Junker**, m., 'young nobleman, squire' (prop. 'son of a duke or count'), from MidHG. *junc-hērre*, 'young lord, noble youth'; corresponding to Du. *jonker*, *jonkheer*, whence E. *younker* is borrowed. **jüngst**, 'recently,' from MidHG. *ze jungest*; comp. 𝔡𝔢𝔯 jüng𝔰𝔱𝔢 𝔗𝔞𝔤, 'doomsday,' for 𝔡𝔢𝔯 𝔩𝔢𝔱𝔷𝔱𝔢 𝔗𝔞𝔤, 'the last day.'

Jux, m., 'jest,' ModHG. only; probably from Lat.-Rom. *jocus* (comp. Ital. *giuoco*), whence also E. *joke*, Du. *jok*.

K.

Kabel, n. and f., from the equiv. Mid HG. *kabel*, f. and n., 'cable'; the latter borrowed, through the medium of Du. and LG., from Fr. *câble*, m., 'rope, cable' (Mid Lat. *capulum*); E. *cable* and Scand. *kabill*, from the same source.

Kabliau, Kabeljau, m., 'cod-fish,' first occurs in early ModHG., recorded in LG. from the 15th cent. and adopted by the literary language; from Du. *kabeljaauw*; Swed. *kabeljo*, Dan. *kabeljau*, E. *cabliau*; also, with a curious transposition of consonants (see 𝔈𝔰𝔰𝔦𝔤, 𝔏𝔦𝔠𝔥𝔢𝔩𝔫, 𝔎𝔦𝔢𝔰𝔢), Du. *bake'jauw*, which is based upon Basque *baccallaba*. The Basques were the first cod-fishers (espec. on the coast of Newfoundland, the chief fishing-place). See 𝔏𝔞𝔟𝔟𝔢𝔯𝔱𝔞𝔲.

Kabuse, f., 'small hut, partition, caboose,' ModHG. only, from MidLG. *kabhūse*; comp. E. *caboose*, which was probably introduced as a naval term into Du., *kabuys*, and into Fr., *cambuse*. The stem of the E. word is probably the same as in E. *cabin*, and hence is Kelt.; E. *cabin* and the cognate Fr. *cabane, cabinet*, are based upon W. *kaban*. The cognates also suggest ModHG. **Kafter**, 'small chamber,' and OHG.

chafteri, 'beehive,' the origin of which is obscure.

Kachel, f., 'earthen vessel, stove-tile,' from MidHG. *kachel, kachele*, f., 'earthen vessel, earthenware, stove-tile, lid of a pot,' OHG. *chahhala*. In E. the word became obsolete at an early period. In Du., *katchel*, borrowed from HG., is still current (in MidDu. *kakele*).

kacken, vb., 'to cack, go to stool,' early ModHG. only. Probably coined by schoolboys and students by affixing a G. termination to Lat.-Gr. *caccare* (κακκᾶν; allied to κακὸς ?. Comp. MidHG. *quât*, 'evil, bad, dirt'); the OTeut. words are 𝔰𝔠𝔥𝔢𝔦𝔰𝔰𝔢𝔫 and dial. 𝔟𝔯𝔦𝔰𝔰𝔢𝔫. In Slav. too there are terms similar in sound, Bohem. *kakati*, Pol. *kakác*. The primit. kinship of the G. word, however, with Gr., Lat., and Slav. is inconceivable, because the initial *k* in the latter would appear as *h* in Teut.

Käfer, m., 'beetle, chafer,' from the equiv. MidHG. *kĕver, kĕfere*, OHG. *chĕvar, chĕvaro*, m.; comp. AS. *ĕafor*, E. *chafer*, Du. *kever*, m. The Goth. term was probably **kifra*, or following AS. *ceafor, *kafrus* also (comp. LG. *kavel*). The name, which has the same import in all the dialects at their different periods, signifies 'gnawing animal' (comp. MidHG. *kifen, kiffen*, 'to gnaw, chew,' MidHG. *kiffel*, under Ṛiefer), or 'husk animal,' from OHG. *chĕva*, 'husk,' MidHG. *kaf*, E. *chaff* (AS. *ĉeaf*).

Ṛaffer, 'uneducated person,' prop. astudent's term, from Arab. *kâfir*, 'unbeliever.'

Ṛäfig, m. and n., 'cage, gaol,' from MidHG. *kęvje*, m., f., and n., 'cage (for wild animals and birds),' also 'prison'; the *j* of the MidHG. word became *g* (comp. Ferge and Scherge). OHG. *chęvia*, f., is derived from Low Lat. *câvia*, Lat. *câvea*, 'birdcage' (respecting HG. *f* for Lat. *v*, comp. Werb, Vers, and Werbift), whence also Mod HG. Ṛaue. Allied to the Rom. words, Ital. *gabbia, gaggia*, Fr. *cage* (hence E. *cage*), and Ital. *gabbiuolo*, Fr. *geôle* (E. *jail, gaol*), 'prison.' Further, Bauer first obtained the meaning 'cage' in MidHG.

Ṛäfter, n., comp. Ṛabufe; the meaning 'little chamber' is ModHG. only; in OHG. *chafteri*, 'beehive,' Suab. *käft*, 'student's room'?. Allied to AS. *ceasforton*, 'hall'?.

kahl, adj., from the equiv. MidHG. *kal* (gen. *kalwer*), 'bald,' OHG. *chalo* (gen. *chalwer, chalawer*); comp. Du. *kaal*, AS. *calu*, E. *callow*. Probably borrowed from Lat. *calvus* (Sans. *khalvâta*, 'bald-headed'), whence Fr. *chauve*, since Lat. *crispus* and *capillare* have also been introduced into Teut.; comp. AS. *cyrsp*, E. *crisp*, OHG. and MidHG. *krisp*, 'curly,' and Goth. *kapillôn*, 'to crop one's hair.' Probably the Teutons and the Romans were equally struck by each other's method of wearing the hair. Other etymologists are inclined to connect Teut. *kalwa-* with OSlov. *golŭ*, 'bare, naked.'

Ṛahm, Ṛahn, m., 'mould on fermented liquids,' from the equiv. MidHG. *kâm (kân)*; comp. Ic. *kám*, n., 'thin coating of dust, dirt,' E. *coom*, 'soot, coal dust' (with *i* mutation, E. *keam*, *keam*); Goth. *kema-*, *kemi-*. The root *ka-* is inferred from MidHG. *ka-del*, m., 'soot, dirt.' Der. fahmig, adj., 'mouldy' (of wine).

Ṛahn, m., 'boat, skiff, wherry,' Mod HG. only (strictly unknown to UpG. and Rhen., as in the case of Boot; in UpG. Nachen); from LG. *kane*, Du. *kaan*; comp. OIc. *kěna*, f., 'a kind of boat.' OIc. *kane* signifies 'wooden vessel,' whence the meaning 'boat' might be evolved according to the analogies adduced under Schiff; comp. Dan. *kane*, with a somewhat different sense 'sleigh.' LG. *kane* looks like a metathesis of AS. *naca* (comp. Fiṇela and Biege).

From the Teut. cognates, OFr. *cane*, 'ship, is derived, but hardly so ModFr. *canot*, which is of American origin.

Ṛaifer, m., 'emperor,' from the equiv. MidHG. *keiser*, OHG. *keisar*; corresponding to AS. *câsĕre*, Goth. *kaisar*. The *ai* of the ModHG. orthography originated in the Bav. and Aust. chancery of Maximilian I., in which the MidHG. *ei* necessarily became *ai* (according to the lexicographer Helvig, A.D. 1620, Meissen-Sax. Ṛeiſer was Bohem.-Bav. Ṛaŋſer). The *ae* of Lat. *Caesar*, upon which the word is based, cannot be made responsible for the ModHG. *ai*. Moreover, the relation of Lat. *ai* to Goth.-Teut. *ai* is not explained. The Romans, it is true, used *ae* for *ai* in Teut. words, comp. Lat. *gaesum*, under Ger; yet the use of Teut. *ḗ* to represent *ae* in Lat. *Graecus* (Goth. *Krêks*, OHG. *Chriah*, 'Greek') is opposed to this. At the same period as the adoption of the names Grieche and Römer (Goth. *Rûmôneis*), i.e., the beginning of our era, the Teutons must have borrowed the Lat. term, connecting it chiefly with Caius Julius Caesar (similarly the Slavs use the name Ṛarl der Große of Charlemagne, in the sense of 'king'; OSlav. *kralji*, Russ. *koroli*, whence Lith. *karálius*, 'king'); yet not until the Roman emperors adopted the title Caesar could this word, which probably existed previously in Teut., assume the meaning 'emperor,' while the Romance nations adhered to the Lat. title *imperator*; comp. Fr. *empereur*. OSlov. *cěsarĭ* (in Russ. contracted *Car*) is derived through a G. medium (which also elucidates MidE. and OIc. *keiser*) from *Caesar*. Thus Ṛaiſer is the earliest Lat. word borrowed by Teut. (see Hanf). For a Kelt loan-word meaning 'king' see under Reich.

Ṛajüte, f., 'cabin,' early ModHG., from LG. *kajüte*, Du. *kajuit*, Fr. *cajute*. The origin of the group is obscure, but is hardly to be assigned to Teut.

Ṛalander, m., 'weevil,' from the equiv. LG. and Du. *kalander* (comp. Fr. *calandre*).

Ṛalb, n., 'calf,' from the equiv. Mid HG. *kalp (b)*, OHG. *chalb* (plur. *chalbir*), n.; comp. AS. *cealf*, E. *calf*, Du. *kalf*, OIc. *kalfr*, m.; Goth. has only a fem. *kalbô* (OHG. *chalba*, MidHG. *kalbe*), 'heifer over a year old that has not calved.' MidHG. *kilbere*, f., OHG. *chilburra*, f., 'ewe lamb,' is in a different stage of gradation; comp. AS. *cilforlamb*, 'ewe lamb,' and ModHG. dial. Ṛilber (Swiss), 'young ram,' (E. dial.

L

chilver). In the non-Teut. languages there is a series of words with the phonetic base *glbh-*, denoting 'the young of animals.' Comp. Sans. *gárbha*, 'covey,' also 'child, offspring'; in the sense of 'mother's lap' the Ind. word suggests Gr. δελφύς, 'womb,' and its derivative ἀδελφός, 'brother'; comp. also δέλφαξ, 'pig, porker.' To the *a* of the Teut. word *o* in Gr. δολφός · ἡ μήτρα, 'the womb,' corresponds.

Kaldaunen, f. plur., 'intestines,' from MidHG. and MidLG. *kaldûne;* a MidHG. and LG. word (in UpG. **Kutteln**). It is based upon a Rom. and MidLat. *caldâmen*, a derivative of Lat. *calidus* (*caldus*) 'warm,' meaning chiefly 'the still reeking entrails of newly slaughtered animals'; comp. South-West Fr. *chaudin*, Bologn. *caldôm*, 'entrails.' From East Rom. (and G. ?) the word found its way also into Slav.; comp. Czech *kaldoun*, 'entrails,' Croat. *kalduni*, 'lung.'

Kalender, m., 'calendar,' from MidHG. *kalender* (with the variant *kalendenære*), m.; the latter comes from Lat. *calendarium*, but is accented like *calendae*.

Kalfatern, vb., 'to caulk a ship,' from Du. *kalefateren;* the latter is derived from Fr. *calfater*.

Kalk, m., 'lime,' from the equiv. MidHG. *kalc*, *kalkes*, OHG. *chalch*, m. The ModHG. variant **Kalch** (occurring in UpG. and MidG.) is based upon OHG. *chalh* for *chalah* (*hh*). Allied to AS. *ċealc;* but E. *chalk* has assumed a divergent sense, just as MidHG. *kalc* means both 'lime' and 'white-wash.' The cognates are derived from the Lat. acc. *calcem* (nom. *calx*), and were borrowed at a very early period, as is indicated by the initial *k*, or rather *c* of the HG. and E. words, for somewhat later loan-words such as **Kreuz** (from *crucem*) have *z* for Lat. *c*; *c* remains as *k* in old loan-words such as **Kaiser**, Goth. *lukarna*, from Lat. *lucerna*, **Keller**, from *cellarium*. The Teutons became acquainted through the Itals. both with the name and thing about the same period as with **Mauer** and **Ziegel** (**Tünche**).

Kalm, m., 'calm,' of LG. origin; LG. *kalm*, E. *calm;* based on the Fr. *calme*.

Kalmank, **Kalmang**, m., from E. *calamanco*, Fr. *calmande*, f., all with the same meaning, 'fine woollen stuff.' MidLat. *calamancus* may be derived from the East.

Kalmäuser, m., 'moping fellow,' simply ModHG., of obscure origin; the second part of the compound is exactly the same as in **Duckmäuser**, which see.

Kalt, adj., 'cold,' from the equiv. MidHG. and OHG. *kalt* (gen. *kaltes*): corresponding to AS. *ceald*, *cald*, E. *cold*, OIc. *kaldr*, Goth. *kalds;* an old partic. formation corresponding to the Lat. vbs. in *-tus*, Sans. *ta-s* (Goth. *d* from Aryan *t*), as in *alt*, *laut*, *tot*, *traut*, *zart*, &c. *kal-* as the root appears in a stronger stage of gradation in ModHG. *kühl*, and in a weaker stage in OIc. *kulde*, 'cold.' In OIc. and AS. the str. vb. of which ModHG. *kalt* and OIc. *keldr* are partics. is retained; Scand. *kola*, 'to freeze,' AS. *calan*, 'to freeze'; allied to Swiss *xale*, 'to cool,' and hence 'curdle.' Note ModE. *chill* from AS. *ċyle* (from *ċeli*, *kali*). The root is identical with that of Lat. *gelu*, 'frost,' *gelâre*, 'to congeal,' *gelidus*, 'cold.'

Kamel, n., 'camel,' from Lat. *camêlus;* in MidHG. *kemmel*, *kêmel*, which point to the Byzantine and ModGr. pronunciation of Gr. κάμηλος, and hence to κάμιλος (the *e* of *kemel* is produced by *i-* mutation from *a*). The ModHG. word is a more recent scholarly term, borrowed anew from Lat. (comp. Fr. *chameau*, Ital. *camello*), while the MidHG. word was brought back from the Crusades, and hence is due to immediate contact with the East. Moreover, at San Rossore, near Pisa, a breed of camels has existed from the Crusades down to modern times, some of which are exhibited in Europe as curiosities. In the OTeut. period there was, curiously enough, a peculiar word for 'camel' current in most of the dialects, which corresponded to Gr. ἐλέφαντ-, Goth. *ulbandus*, AS. *olfend*, OHG. *olbenta*, MidHG. *olbent;* allied to OSlov. *velĭbądŭ*, 'camel.' The history of this word is quite obscure.

Kamerad, m., 'comrade, companion,' ModHG. only, from Fr. *camarade* (Ital. *camerata*, 'society,' lit. 'comrades living together in a room,' then too 'companion'), whence also E. *comrade*. OTeut. had a number of terms for ModHG. **Kamerad**; comp. **Geselle**, **Gesinde**, OHG. *gidofto*, 'companion' (comp. **Decht** and **Deft**), simply forms illustrative of the OTeut. heroic age, which were partly disused in the MidHG. period in favour of the foreign terms **Kumpan** and **Kamerad**.

Kamille, f., 'camomile,' from MidHG. *kamille*, f., which is again derived from MidLat. and Ital. *camamilla* (Gr. χαμαίμηλον).

The term became current in the Middle Ages through medical science, which was learnt from the Greeks (comp. Arzt, Büchse, Pflaster).

Kamin, m., 'chimney, fireplace, fireside,' from MidHG. *kámîn, kęmîn;* the Mod HG. accentuation, which differs from the MidHG., is due to the word being based anew on Lat. *camînus,* while the latter is due to a German version of the foreign word. E. *chimney* is Fr. *cheminée*, 'chimney, fireplace,' which is phonetically cognate with MidLat. *caminata,* prop. 'room with a stove or fireplace,' and hence with MidHG. *kęminâte* (γυναικεῖον); allied also to Czech, Pol., and Russ. *komnata,* 'room.'

Kamisol, n., 'waistcoat, jacket,' simply ModHG. formed like the Fr. *camisole*, 'under-vest' (allied to MidLat. *camisia*, 'shirt'; see Hemd).

Kamm, m., 'comb,' from the equiv. MidHG. *kam (mm), kamp (b)*; it signifies 'comb' in the widest sense; OHG. *chamb*; comp. AS. *comb*, E. *comb* (also AS. *hunig-comb*, E. *honeycomb*?), Goth. **kambs*. The term is undoubtedly OTeut.; our ancestors attached great importance to dressing their hair. The lit. meaning of the word is 'instrument with teeth,' for in the allied Aryan languages the meaning 'tooth' obtains in the cognate words. OHG. *chamb* is based upon pre-Teut. *gombho-*; comp. Gr. γομφίος, 'molar tooth,' γαμφηλαί, γαμφαί, 'jaws, beak'; OInd. *jambha*, m., 'tusk' (plural 'bit'), *jambhya*, m., 'incisor,' O Slov. *ząbŭ*, 'tooth'; Gr. γόμφος, 'plug, bolt,' points to a wider development of meaning. —**kämmen,** vb., 'to comb, card (wool),' is a verbal noun; ModHG. *kęmmen,* OHG. *chemben, chęmpen;* AS. *cęmban*. In UpG. the term sträßlen is current, Strähl too being the word for 'comb.'

Kammer, f., 'chamber, office,' from MidHG. *kamer, kamere,* f., with the general meaning 'sleeping apartment, treasury, storeroom, money-chest, royal dwelling, justice chamber,' &c.; OHG. *chamara,* f., 'apartment, palace.' E. *chamber*, from Fr. *chambre;* but the HG. word is based upon a Rom. word (Span. and Port.) *camara*, 'room' (Ital. *camera*), which again is derived from καμάρα, 'any enclosed space with a vaulted roof,' a term restricted to the more civilised classes in the Middle Ages and current in the Rom. and Teut. groups; comp. further OFr. *camra*, Slav. *komora*. The numerous meanings in MidHG. are also indicated by the ModHG. derivatives and compound terms Kämmerer, Kämmerei, and Kämmerherr.

Kammertuch, n., 'cambric,' manufactured first at Cambray (Du. *Kamerijk*); corresponding to Du. *kamerijksdock*.

Kamp, m., a LG. word, comp. Du. (MidDu.) *kamp;* from Lat. *campus?*. Kamp, however, has a special sense, 'enclosed piece of ground, field.'

Kämpe, m., 'combatant, wrestler,' first introduced into literary ModHG. by the study of the Teut. languages, yet the special history of the word is not known. The form indicates a LG. origin; comp. OLG. *kęmpio,* 'combatant, warrior.' Perhaps it was orig. a legal term of the Saxon Code. See Kamps.

Kampf, m., 'combat,' from MidHG. *kampf*, m. and n., 'combat, duel, tilting'; OHG. *champf,* m., AS. *camp, comp;* OIc. *kapp,* n. The OIc. word is interesting, because it signifies lit. 'zeal, emulation,' which is the orig. meaning of Kampf (Mod HG. Krieg has gone through a similar development of meaning). Hence there is no probability in the assumption that OTeut. **kampa-* is derived from Lat. *campus*, thus connecting it with *Campus Martius*. This older assumption receives no support from phonetic laws, for *kamp* does not look unlike a Teut. word, while the meaning of the Scand. word makes it impossible. We should consider, too, whether the old Teutons, with their numerous terms relating to war, had any need of borrowing such a word. Some connect OTeut. *kampo-* with Sans. *jaṅg*, 'to fight.' HG. Kämpfer, and Kämpfe, Kämpe, prop. 'combatant,' is Mid HG. *kęmpfe,* OHG. *chęmphio, chęmpho,* 'wrestler, duellist'; AS. *cęmpa,* and OIc. *kappe* signify 'warrior, hero'; this term, denoting the agent, passed into Rom. (comp. Fr. *champion*, whence also E. *champion*).

Kampfer, m., 'camphor,' from MidHG. *kampfer, guffer,* m., from MidLat. *camphora, cafura* (Fr. *camphre*; Ital. *canfora* and *cafura,* ModGr. καφουρά); the latter term is derived finally from Ind. *karpûra, kapûr,* or from Hebr. *kôpher,* 'pitch, resin.'

Kanel, m., 'cinnamon bark,' accented on the termination, from MidHG. *kanêl,* 'stick or cane of cinnamon'; the word was borrowed in the MidHG. period from Fr. *canelle, cannelle*, 'cinnamon bark,' which is a diminut. of Fr. *canne* (Lat. *canna*) 'cane,' Ital. *canello*, 'tube.'

Kaninchen, n., 'rabbit,' dimin. of an earlier ModHG. *Kanin*; it is based upon Lat. *cuniculus*, which passed into HG. in various forms; MidHG. *künīclīn* (accented on the first syllable), evidently germanised, also *künolt, künlīn, külle*. The ModHG. form is based upon a MidLat. variant, *caniculus*; the form with *a* is properly restricted to North and Middle Germany, while *ü* (Künchel) is current in the South. Comp. MidE. *coning*, E. *coney*, from Fr. *connin* (Ital. *coniglio*).

Kanker (1.), m., 'spider' (MidG.), from the equiv. MidHG. *kanker* (rare), m. The derivation of the word from Lat. *cancer*, 'crab,' is, for no other reason than the meaning, impossible. It seems to be based upon an OTeut. vb. 'to weave, spin.' This is indicated by the OIc. *kǫngulváfa, kǫngurváfa*, 'spider'; AS. *gongelwǽfre*, 'spider,' must also be based upon a similar word; its apparent meaning, 'the insect that weaves as it goes along,' is probably due to a popular corruption of the obscure first component. We should thus get a prim. Teut. stem *kang*, 'to spin,' which in its graded form appears in ModHG. *Kunkel*. This stem has been preserved in the non-Teut. languages only in a Finn. loan-word; comp. Finn. *kangas*, 'web' (Goth. *kuggs).

Kanker (2.), m., 'canker,' from OHG. *chanchar, cancur*; comp. AS. *cancer*, E. *canker*. Probably OHG. *chanchur* is a real Teut. word from an unpermutated *gongro-*; comp. Gr. γόγγρος, 'an excrescence on trees,' γάγγραινα, 'gangrene.' Perhaps a genuinely Teut. term has been blended with a foreign word (Lat. *cancer*, Fr. *chancre*).

Kanne, f., 'can, tankard, jug,' from the equiv. MidHG. *kanne*, OHG. *channa*, f.; comp. AS. *canne*, E. *can*; OIc. *kanna*, Goth. *kannô. The OTeut. word cannot have been borrowed from Lat. *cantharus* (Gr. κάνθαρος); an assumed corruption of *kantarum*, m. acc. to a fem. *kannô*, is improbable. The derivation of *Kanne*, from Lat. *canna*, 'cane,' is opposed by the meaning of the word. Since ModHG. *Kahn* is based upon a Teut. root *ka-*, the latter can hardly be adduced in explanation of *Kanne*, although the meaning of both might be deduced from a prim. sense 'hollowed wood.' If we assume, as is quite possible, a Goth. *kaznô, 'can,' another etymology presents itself, Goth. *kas*, OIc. *ker*, and OHG. *char*, 'vessel,' would be cognate, and *-nô-*, a suffix of the same root. If we compare, however, with *Kanne* the Suab. and Alem. variant *Kante*, which is based upon OHG. *chanta*, we obtain *kan-* as the root. The G. word passed into Fr. (Mod. Fr. *canette*, 'small can,' equiv. to MidLat. *cannetta*, dimin. of MidLat. *canna*).

Kante, f., 'sharp edge, border, margin, fine lace,' ModHG. only, from LG. *kante*, 'edge, corner'; the latter, like E. *cant*, 'corner, edge,' which is also unknown to the earlier periods of the language, is derived from Fr. *cant*, 'corner,' which, with Ital. *canto*, is said to be based finally on Gr. κάνθος, 'felloe of a wheel.'

Kantschu, m., 'leather whip,' from Bohem. *kančuch*, Pol. *kańczuk*. The word is of Turk. origin (Turk. *kamčí*, 'whip'). Comp. *Karbatsche*.

Kanzel, f., 'pulpit,' from MidHG. *kanzel*, OHG. *cancella, chanzella*, f., lit. 'the place set apart for the priests,' then 'pulpit'; from the equiv. MidLat. *cancellus, cancelli*, 'grating,' *cancelli altaris*, 'the grating enclosing the altar, the part separated from the nave of the church by a grating'; in MidLat. generally 'any part surrounded by a parapet, especially an oriental flat roof.' "Qui vero Epistolas missas recitare volebant populo in regione Palæstinæ antiquitus, ascendebant super tectum et de cancellis recitabant et inde inolevit usus ut qui litteras principibus missas habent exponere Cancellarii usitato nomine dicantur" (du Cange). Hence *Kanzler*. From the same source, MidLat. *cancellus*, is derived E. *chancel*, taken from OFr., the meaning of which forms the starting-point for the development of the signification of the HG. word.

Kapaun, m., 'capon,' from the equiv. MidHG. *kappûn*; borrowed after the era of the substitution of consonants from Rom. *cappônem* (Lat. *capo*, equiv. to Gr. κάπων); comp. Ital. *cappone*, Fr. *chapon* (whence also Serv. *kopun*). Even in the AS. period *capûn*, 'gallinaceus,' is found derived from the same source (E. *capon*); comp. Du. *kapoen*. From the Lat. nom. *cappo* is derived MidHG. *kappe*, and even OHG. *chappo*. For another term see under *Hahnrei*.

Kapelle (1.), f., 'chapel, orchestra,' an early loan-word, which always remained, however, under the influence of MidLat. *capella*, on which it is based, for while numerous other words borrowed from Lat. have their accent changed according to the

Teut. method, the Lat. accent is retained in OHG. *chapélla*, MidHG. *kapélle*, and the ModHG. form. It is true that in MidHG. *káppelle* (ModAlem. *käppelle*), with the G. accent also occurs, and hence the UpG. Kappel, Käppel, frequent names of villages. MidLat. *capella* has a peculiar history; as a dimin. of *capa* (comp. Kappe) it signified 'a cape'; the chapel itself, in which the cloak of St. Martin and other relics were preserved, first obtained the name of *capella;* then from about the 7th cent. the use of the word became general.—
Kaplan, m., 'chaplain,' from MidHG. *kappellän*. It is based on MidLat. *capellānus*, which orig. denoted the priest who had to guard the cloak of St. Martin.— MidLat. *capella* also signifies the body of priests under a bishop, hence the other meanings of ModHG. Kapelle.
Kapelle (2.), f., 'cupel,' ModHG. only; it is based upon a combination of MidLat. *capella*, Fr. *chapelle*, 'lid of an alembic,' and MidLat. *cupella*, Fr. *coupelle*, 'cupel, crucible' (dimin. of Lat. *cupa*).
Kaper, m., 'pirate,' from the equiv. Du. *kaper*.
Kapitel, n., 'chapter,' from MidHG. *kapitel*, 'solemn assembly, convention,' OHG. *capital, capitul*, 'inscription.' Mid Lat. *capitulum* has also both these meanings.
kapores, adj., 'broken, destroyed,' Mod HG. only; according to the general acceptation it is not allied to ModHG. *kaput*, but is rather derived from Hebr. *kappārāh*, 'reconciliation, atonement.'
Kappe, f., 'hood, cowl'; the meaning of MidHG. *kappe*, f., upon which it is based, does not correspond very often with that of ModHG., its usual signification being 'a garment shaped like a cloak and fitted with a cowl as a covering for the head'; hence Tarnkappe, which has first been made current in ModHG. in this century through the revival by scholars of the MidHG. *tornkappe* (prop. 'the cloak that makes the wearer invisible'). OHG. *chappa;* AS. *cæppe*, 'cloak,' E. *cap*. The double sense of the MidHG. word appears in the MidLat. and Rom. *cappa*, 'cloak, cap,' on which it is based (on the prim. form *cāpa* is based E. *cope*, from MidE. *cope*, as well as OIc. *kápa*, 'cloak'). With regard to the meaning comp. ModFr. *chape* (*cape*), 'cope, scabbard, sheath, case,' and the derivatives *chapeau*, 'hat,' and *chaperon*, 'cowl.' The MidLat. word was adopted by the more civilised classes of Europe, passing into Slav. as well as into Rom. and Teut. The word was not borrowed, or rather not naturalised before the 8th cent., for an earlier borrowed term would have been *chapfa in OHG. and *kapfe in MidHG.—Comp. Kapelle.
kappen, vb., 'to chop, lop,' ModHG. simply, from Du. *kappen*, 'to split'; comp. Dan. *kappe* and E. *chap*. In UpAlsat. *kchapfe* is found with the HG. form; allied also to the dial. graded forms *kipfen, kippen;* hence the Teut. root *kep, kapp*.
Kappes, Kappus, m., 'headed cabbage,' from the equiv. MidHG. *kappeʒ, kappūs, kabeʒ*, m. OHG. *chabuʒ, chapuʒ*, directly connected with Lat. *caput*, which strangely enough does not appear in Mid Lat. in the sense of 'cabbage-head'; Ital. *capuccio* (hence Fr. *cabus* and E. *cabbage*) presumes, however, a MidLat. derivative of *caput* in the sense of 'cabbage-head, headed cabbage.' The naturalisation of the Ital. word in HG. may have been completed in the 7th cent. or so; by that time a number of Lat. names of plants, as well as the art of cookery and gardening introduced from the South, was already firmly established in Germany.
Kappʒaum, m., 'cavezon,' ModHG. only, corrupted from Ital. *cavezzone*, whence also Fr. *caveçon*, 'cavezon.'
kaput, adj., lit. 'lost at play,' ModHG. simply, from Fr. *capot; faire capot*, 'to cause to lose,' *être capot*, &c. The Fr. expression was introduced into G. with a number of other terms orig. used at play (comp. Treff).
Kapuʒe, f., 'cowl,' ModHG. only, from Ital. *capuccio*, whence also Fr. *capuce;* Mid Lat. *capúcium;* deriv. Kapuziner (MidLat. *capucinus*).
Karat, n., 'carat,' not derived from MidHG. *gīrât*, f. and n., 'carat,' which in ModHG. must have been Gīrat. The Mod HG. has been more probably borrowed anew from Fr. *carat* or Ital. *caráto;* the Mid HG. word has adopted the G. accent, while the ModHG. term preserves the accent of the Rom. word upon which it is based.
Karausche, f., 'crucian,' ModHG. only; older variants, *karaʒ, karütsch;* from Fr. *carassin*, 'crucian'?. Comp. also E. *crucian*, and its equiv. Ital. *coracino*, Lith. *karósas*, Serv. *karaš*, Czech *karas*, which forms are nearer to HG. than to Fr.; the final source is Gr. κορακῖνοσ (MidLat. *coracīnus*).
Karbatsche, f., 'hunting-whip,' bor-

rowed from Slav. like Rantſchu and Peitſche in ModHG.; Pol. karbacz, Boh. karabáč (from Turk. ḳerbač).

Karbe, Karve, f., 'caraway,' from the equiv. MidHG. karwe and karne, f.; allied to Fr. and Ital. carvi, 'caraway.' The usual assumption that this word as well as E. caraway is based on Lat. careum (Gr. κάρον), 'caraway,' is not quite satisfactory, hence the influence of Arab. al-karavia is assumed.

Karch, m., 'dray,' from the equiv. Mid HG. karrech, karrich, OHG. charrūh (hh), m. Probably current even in the 8th cent. on the Up. and Mid. Rhine, as may be inferred from the initial h, ch (comp. Pferd). It is based upon the late Lat. carruca, 'honoratorum vehiculum opertum, four-wheeled travelling car' (a derivative of carrus; comp. Karren); Fr. charrue,'plough,' is likewise based upon Lat. carrūca, which also signifies 'plough' in MidLat.

Karde, f., 'fuller's thistle,' from Mid HG. karte, f., OHG. charta, f., 'teasel, the instrument made from the thistle and used by cloth-weavers for carding wool.' The final source is MidLat. cardus, carduus, 'thistle' (Fr. chardon, Ital. cardo), the d of the ModHG. word compared with the t of OHG. and MidHG. is due to the word, which was naturalised about the 7th cent., being based anew on the Lat. form.—**Kardelſche, Kardätſche,** f., 'carder's comb'; a derivative of Karte.

Karfreitag, m., 'Good Friday,' from the equiv. MidHG. karvrītac, mostly kartac, m.; Karwoche, 'Passion Week,' is also current even in MidHG. The first part of the compound is OHG. chara, f., 'lamentation, mourning' (charasang, 'elegy'). This OTeut. word for Klage, 'lament,' as distinguished from the other synonyms, signifies properly the silent, inward mourning, not the loud wailing, for in Goth. the cognate kara, f., means 'care,' AS. cearu, f., 'care, suffering, grief,' E. care. A corresponding vb. signifying 'to sigh' is preserved in OHG. quëran (Goth. *qairan). Other derivatives of the Teut. root kar, qer, are wanting. See also karg.

Karfunkel, m., 'carbuncle,' from Mid HG. karbunkel, m., with the variant karfunkel, probably based on MidHG. vunke, ModHG. Funke; b is the original sound, for the word is based upon Lat. carbunculus (comp. E. carbuncle, ModFr. escarboucle).

karg, adj., 'sparing, niggardly,' from MidHG. karc (g), 'prudent, cunning, sly, stingy'; in OHG. charag, 'sad'; a derivative of the OTeut. kara, 'care,' discussed under Karfreitag. From the primary meaning 'anxious,' the three significations 'sad,' 'frugal,' and 'cunning' might be derived; comp. AS. čearig, 'sad,' and E. chary, allied to E. care. The syncope of the vowel in MidHG. karc compared with OHG. charag is normal after r.

Karpfen, m., 'carp,' from the equiv. MidHG. karpfe, OHG. charpho, m.; comp. E. carp; allied to OIc. karfe. It cannot be decided whether Karpfen is a real Teut. word; probably MidLat. carpo, Fr. carpe, and Ital. carpione are derived from Teut. In Kelt. too there are cognate terms for 'carp,' W. carp; comp. also Russ. karpŭ, koropŭ, Serv. krap, Lith. kárpa, 'carp.'

Karre, f., **Karren,** m., from the equiv. MidHG. karre, m. and f., OHG. charra, f., charro, m., 'cart'; the HG. words and also the E. car (OIc. kerra) are based on Mid Lat. carrus, m., carra, f., and their Rum. derivatives (ModFr. char, 'car'). Lat. carrus, 'four-wheeled transport waggon,' is again of Kelt. origin (Gael. carr, Bret. karr); comp. Karch, Pferd.—**Kariole, Karriole,** f., **Kariol,** n., 'jaunting car,' simply Mod HG. from Fr. carriole.—**Kärrner,** m., 'carter.'

Karst, m., 'hoe,' from the equiv. Mid HG. karst, m., OHG. and OSax. carst; the word is not found in other groups. The etymology is dubious; allied to kehren (karjan), 'to sweep'?.

Kartaune, Kartane, f., 'short, heavy cannon,' from Ital. quartana, MidLat. quartāna; this term, as well as its earlier Mod HG. version Viertelbüchſe, signifies a gun "which fired 25 lbs., in comparison with the heaviest piece of artillery firing 100 lbs."

Karte, f., 'card, chart, map,' from late MidHG. karte, f.; formed from Fr. carte.

Karthauſe, Kartauſe, f., 'Carthusian monastery,' from late MidHG. kartūse, f., which is again derived from Cartūsia, Chartreuse (near Grenoble, where the Carthusian order was founded in 1084 A.D.).—**Karthäuſer,** 'Carthusian friar,' from MidHG. kartūser, karthiuser.

Kartoffel, f., 'potato,' derived by a process of differentiation from the earlier ModHG. form Tartuffel. Potatoes were introduced into Germany about the middle of the 18th cent. from Italy, as is proved by the Ital. name (comp. Ital. tartufo, tartufolo; see Trüffel). Another name, Erdapfel, seems to indicate that the plant was brought from the Netherlands and France, Du. *aard-appel*, Fr. *pomme de terre*. The dial. Grumbire is due to a similar conception, its orig. form being Grumbirne. Tuffeln is a shortened form of Kartoffel, resulting from the position of the accent (comp. Kürbis from *cucúrbita*). The rarer dial. Batafen (Franc.), which corresponds to E. *potato*, is based upon Ital. and Span. *patata*, the final source of which is an American word. Potatoes were introduced in the 17th cent. from America into Spain and Italy, and were transplanted from these countries to the north.

Käfe, m., 'cheese,' from the equiv. Mid HG. *kæse*, OHG. *châsi*, m.; Lat. *câseus* (whence also OIr. *caise*), before the 5th cent. at the latest was adopted in the vernacular form *câsius* (variant *câseus*?) by the Teutons; comp. Du. *kaas*, AS. *čýse*, E. *cheese*. It corresponds in Rom. to Ital. *cacio*, Span. *queso*; yet *câseus* was supplanted in the dials. at an early date by Lat. *formaticus*, '(cheese) mould'; comp. Fr. *fromage* (Ital. *formaggio*). OIc. has a peculiar word for 'cheese,' *ostr*, in Goth. perhaps *justs (comp. Finn. *juusto*, 'cheese'); the assumed Goth. *justs is connected etymologically with Lat. *jus*, 'broth,' OSlov. *jucha*, 'soup,' OInd. *yúšan*, 'soup' (comp Jauche), the root of which is *yu*, 'to mix,' in Lith. *jáuju*, *jáuti*, 'to mix (dough).' From this collocation of terms it is probable that *justs is the OTeut. word for 'cheese,' and that the Teutons did not learn how to make cheese from the Southerners, but only an improved method of doing so when they adopted the term Käfe from them. It is true that according to Pliny, *Hist. Nat.* xi. 41, the barbarians generally were not acquainted with the method; yet comp. also Butter.

Kaftanie, f., 'chestnut'; comp. OHG. *chęstinna*, MidHG. *kęstene*, *kęsten*, *kastánie*. The latter is evidently a return to the orig. form, Lat. *castanea*, which had already been transformed to *kęstenne* (comp. UpG. Kęśtę). Moreover, OHG. *chęstinna* and AS. *čísten* (Cistenbeám, MidHG. *kęstenboum*, E. *chestnut*) point to a Lat. *castinia*, *castinja*. Comp. Fr. *châtaigne*, Ital. *castagna*, 'chestnut.' The Lat. word is derived from the equiv. Gr. κασταννία, -νεια, -νειον, -νον; the chestnut was named from the town of Kάσταρα, in Pontus.

Kafteien, vb., 'to chastise,' from Mid HG. *kastîyen* (g for j), *kęstigen*, OHG. *chęstîyôn*, 'to chastise, punish'; the alteration of the accent and the vowels corresponds to that in Kaftanie (which see) compared with the dial. Kęśtę. Lat. *castîgare* (whence also Fr. *châtier*, and further E. *chastise*) was adopted on the introduction of Christianity (comp. Kreuz, Priester, and predigen) from ecclesiastical Lat.; OHG. *chęstîgôn*, like many words borrowed in the OHG. period (see predigen), was accented after the G. method.

Kaften, m., 'chest,' from the equiv. Mid HG. *kaste*, OHG. *chasto*, m.; this word, which is at all events really Teut., is wanting in the rest of the OTeut. dials. Goth. *kasto, 'receptacle,' may be connected with *kasa-*, 'vessel,' so that the dental would be a derivative; yet *kas* signifies specially 'an earthen vessel, pot' (comp. *kasja*, 'potter'). This Goth. *kas*, moreover, became *char* in OHG. by the normal change of *s* into *r*; in the ModHG. literary speech it is now wanting, but it appears in MidHG. *binen-kar*, upon which ModHG. Bienenkorb is based.

Kater, m., 'tom-cat,' from the equiv. MidHG. *kater*, *katere*, m., OHG. *chataro*, m.; the *r* of Kater appears to be a masc. suffix; comp. Marter and Mard, Tauber and Taube; Enterich and Ente?, Ganfer and Gans?, &c. Comp. Kaze.

Kattun, m., 'cotton, calico,' from the equiv. MidHG. *kottûn*, n., which is again derived from Du. *kattoen*, Fr. *coton*, equiv. to E. *cotton*.

Kaze, f., 'cat,' from the equiv. MidHG. *katze*, OHG. *chazza*, f.; a common Europ. word in the Mid. Ages and in modern times; of obscure origin. Comp. also AS. *catt*, m., F. *cat*; OIc. *kęttr*, m. These assume Goth. *katta, *kattus. Early MidLat. *cattus* and its Rom. derivatives (Ital. *gatto*, Fr. *chat*), Ir. and Gael. *cat*, m., and Slav. *kotū*, 'tom-cat,' Lith. *katė*, 'cat,' *kátinas*, 'tom-cat' (allied to Serv. *kotiti*, 'to litter,' &c., *kot*, 'brood, litter'), suggest the possibility that the Teut. term was borrowed from a neighbouring race after the period of the Teut. substitution of consonants, at latest a century before or after the migration of the tribes. It is a remarkable fact, however, that G. retains a prim. and independent masc. form of the word in Kater (Goth. *kaduza?), which also occurs in Du. and LG. *kater* (comp. E. *caterwaul*).

kauderwelſch, adj., 'jargon,' first occurs in early ModHG. allied to an unexplained vb. *laudern*, 'to talk unintelligibly,' hence 'strange, unintelligible foreign tongue.' It seems to have been a Swiss word orig. and allied to Suab. and Swiss *kauder, chúder*, 'tow'; or should it be djunvelfdj?

Šaue, f., 'coop, cage, pen,' from MidHG. *kouwe (kōwe)*, f., 'miner's hut or shed over a shaft' (OHG. **kouwa*, Goth. **kaujô*, are wanting); from Lat. *cavea* (intermediate form *cauja*?), 'cavity.' See also Šáfig.

kauen, vb., 'to chew,' from the equiv. MidHG. *kūwen, kiuwen*, OHG. *chiuwan*; ModHG. *au* and MidHG. *û* in this word compared with *ûu* in wiederfäuen is properly MidG. merely. It corresponds to AS. *cēowan*, E. *to chew*, and the equiv. Du. *kaauwen*. The verb, which is based on a Teut. root *kēw, ku*, pre-Teut. *gew*, is wanting in Goth.; comp. OSlov. *živa, žuja, žīvati*, 'to chew.' The Aryan root is *gjū, gīw*, 'to chew'; see Kierne. Gr. γεύομαι for γεύσομαι is totally unconnected with HG. fauen, being allied to feften.

kauern, vb., 'to crouch'; its relation to MidHG. *hûren* (Du. *hurken*), 'to squat,' is obscure; in E. and in Scand. an initial *k* also appears, MidE. *couren*, E. *to cower*; Dan. *kūre*, Swed. *kūra*, in the ModHG. sense; OIc. *kūra*, 'to be inactive.' Comp. laugen.

kaufen, vb., 'to buy,' from MidHG. *koufen*, OHG. *choufôn*. The meaning in OHG. and MidHG. is somewhat more general, 'to trade, negotiate,' specially also 'to buy, sell, or to barter.' Comp. Goth. *kaupôn*, 'to trade,' AS. *čypan* (Goth. **kaupjan*), 'to buy, sell.' The word has numerous interesting meanings; its primary sense is 'to barter,' and was used by the parties on either side, and hence on the development of the system of paying in specie it signified both 'to buy' and 'to sell'; comp. also AS. *cēap*, 'trade, business, cattle' (cattle was, in fact, the chief medium of payment in exchange; comp. Geld and Vieh). It is most closely allied to Lat. *caupo*, 'retail dealer, innkeeper,' and in connection with this fact it is certainly remarkable that a *nomen agentis* corresponding to Lat. *caupo* is far less widely diffused than the Teut. vb. *kaupôn* (only in OHG. does *choufo* mean 'shopkeeper'). The Teut. vb. in the form of *kupiti*, 'to buy' (allied to *kupŭ*, 'trade,' *kupĭcĭ*, 'merchant,' Lith. *kùpczus*, 'merchant'), passed into prim. Slav. and Finn. (*kauppata*, 'to trade').

The cognates are wanting in Rom. (comp. Kaiſer).—The ModHG. Kauf is OHG. *chouf*, m., 'trade, business'; AS. *čēap*, 'trade'; in E. the cognates *cheap* and *chapman* have been retained.

Kaulbarſch, 'round posterior,' **Kaul-kopf**, 'bull-head,' **Kaulquappe**, 'ruff'; in these compounds Kaul signifies 'a ball of small circumference'; MidHG. *kûle*, a variant of *kugele* (comp. ſtril from ſteigel); older ModHG. Kaule; comp. Keule.

kaum, adv., 'scarcely,' from MidHG. *kûme*, as adj. (?), 'thin, weak, infirm,' as adv. (OHG. *chûmo*), 'with difficulty, hardly, scarcely, not'; to this is allied OHG. *chûmig*, 'powerless, toilsome.' 'Feeble' is the prim. meaning of the adj. and adv., as is shown by Lower Hess. *küme*, MidLG. *küme*, Swiss *chum*, and MidE. *kīme*, 'feeble.' The corresponding AS. *cȳme* signifies 'tender, fine, beautiful' (comp. Klein). Teut. *kûmi-*, 'feeble,' is not found in the other languages.

Kauz, m., 'screech-owl,' from the equiv. MidHG. *kûtze, kûtz*, m. (rarely occurs); in OHG. as well as in the other OTeut. dials. the word is wanting, therefore it is difficult to determine its Goth. form. We might assume Goth. **kutts* or **kûdna*; the first partly suggests Gr. βύξα, 'owl' (for *gûdja*? β as in βαίνα, 'to go,' βύσσος, 'fine flax,' equiv. to ModHG. Raute). Moreover, in ModHG. pet names for birds are formed ending in *tz*, Spatz, Stieglitz, Kiebitz; hence Kauze may have to be divided, and thus Gr. βύας, 'owl,' would be most closely connected with Teut. *kau, kū*.

kauzen, vb., 'to cower'; ModHG. only; like lauern, it is connected with the root *kū*; zen is a suffix from OHG. *zen, azen* (ʒʒen, uʒʒen), Goth. *atjan*; **kûvatjan* would be the Goth. form. Comp. lauern.

Kebſe, f., 'concubine,' from the equiv. MidHG. *kebse, kebese*, OHG. *chebisa, chebis*; in Goth. perhaps **kabisi*. Comp. AS. *čefes, čyfes*. Unfortunately the word is etymologically quite obscure. The meaning is an important one in the history of manners and customs; the AS. word signifies 'concubine' and 'servant,' and the corresponding masc. *kefser* in OIc. 'slave'; it is evident that female captives were made slaves and concubines (comp. AS. *wealh*, 'Kelt, slave,' *wylen*, 'female slave, servant,' under Welsch). The idea of 'concubine,' in spite of Tacitus' highly-coloured picture of the OTeut family life, is not foreign to

OTeut. antiquity; but the important fact is, and this is confirmed by his general statements, that concubines were chosen from the prisoners, or rather the slaves; in antiquity the slaves were regarded as chattels; comp. Lat. *mancipium*, Gr. ἀνδράποδον; OIc. *man*, 'slave,' is neu., and sometimes signifies 'female slave, concubine.'

Ħed̨, adj., 'pert, impudent,' from MidHG. *kĕc*, a variant of *quĕc* (inflected *kĕcker*, *quĕcker*), 'living, fresh'; OHG. *chĕc* (inflected *chĕcchĕr*), *quĕc*, *quĕcchĕr*, 'living.' Corresponding to AS. *cwicu* (*cucu*), 'living,' E. *quick*. The prim. meaning of the adj. is 'living,' and the ModHG. *lebhaft*, 'lively,' illustrates the development of the signification. For further comparison we have to proceed from the corresponding Goth. adj. *qius*, 'living' (the second *c*, *k* of the HG. and E. words, is an insertion before the Goth. *w*). Goth. *qiwa-*, derived from *gwiwo-*, *giwo-*, corresponds exactly to Lat. *vīvus* for *gwivus*, Sans. *jīvás*, 'living,' allied to Lat. *vivere* (*victus*); Sans. *jīvātus*, 'life,' *jīvathas*, 'life'; further, in Gr. with an initial β (comp. βαίνω, 'to go'), βίος, βίοτος, βιόω; allied to OSlov. *živŭ*, Lith. *gývas*, OIr. *beo*, 'living.' All these forms indicate an Aryan root *gīw*, 'to live.' This root seems to be graded in Teut. only, in OIc. *kveykva*, *kveikja* (Goth. *qaiwjan), 'to light a fire,' prop. 'to give life to.' In ModHG. erquicken and Quecksilber are connected with the same root, and in fact with the Aryan adj. *gīwós*, 'living'; the loss of the *u* after *q*, which has differentiated fed from qued, is seen also in tommen, Köter, and Kot.

Kegel (1.), m., 'cone, nine-pin, sight (of a gun),' from MidHG. and MidLG. *kegel*, m., 'nine-pin,' also 'stick, cudgel,' OHG. *chegil*, 'stake, plug,' allied to MidDu. *keughe*, Du. *keg*, 'wedge,' ModHG. and Bav. *kag*, 'stump.' OHG. *chegil*, 'plug,' may have been Goth. *kagils (from pre-Teut. *gagho-*), and might be cognate with Gr. γόμφο-ς (φ for *gh*), 'plug, wooden nail, wedge,' with the root syllable nasalised. It cannot be decided whether Lith. *žaginys*, 'stake, post' (*žágaras*, 'dry branch'), is allied to Regel, or rather to Rufe, 'cheek of a sledge.'

Kegel (2.), m., 'bastard' (retained in ModHG. only in the phrase Kind und Kegel, 'kith and kin'), from MidHG. *kegel*, *kekel*, 'illegitimate child.' Of obscure origin.

Kehle, f., 'throat; channel, fluting,' from the equiv. MidHG. and MidLG. *kĕle*, f., OHG. *chĕla*; corresponding to Du. *keel*, AS. *ċeole* (obsolete in E.) and *ċeolor*. In Goth. perhaps *kilô (gen. *kilôns). Since Teut. *k* is derived from pre-Teut. *g*, we may compare Sans. *gala* and Lat. *gula*, 'throat.' See Herz.

Kehren (1.), vb., 'to turn,' from MidHG. *kêren*, OHG. *chêrren*, 'to turn, direct'; a difficult word to explain both etymologically and phonetically; in AS. *ċĕrran*, *ċyrran* (pret. *ċyrde*), 'to turn.'

Kehren (2.), vb., 'to sweep,' from the equiv. MidHG. *kern*, *keren*, *kerjen*, OHG. *cherian*, *cheren*; the Goth. form is probably *karjan, not *kazjan; also OHG. *ubarchara*, 'offscouring, impurity,' connected with Ic. *kar*, n., 'dirt (on new-born lambs and calves).' Probably primit. allied to Lith. *żeriu*, *żérti*, 'to scrape.'

Keib, **Kaib**, m., 'vulgar person,' prop. 'carrion'; simply ModHG., and only in Suab. and Alem.

Keifen, vb., 'to scold,' with the LG. form for the strictly HG. *keiten*, MidHG. *kiben*, 'to upbraid, quarrel,' with the equiv. frequentative *kibeln*, *kiveln*; MidHG. *kip*, *kibes*, m., 'wrangling manner, defiance, refractoriness.' MidLG. *kiven*, Du. *kijven*, 'to upbraid,' Scand. *kīfa*, 'to quarrel,' *kīf*, 'quarrel.'

Keil, m., 'wedge, keystone,' from Mid HG. *kīl*, 'wedge, plug,' with the curious variant *kīdel* (ModHG. dial. Keidel), OHG. *chil*, 'plug'; both the MidHG. forms assume Goth. **keipls ?*. Scand. *keiler* (Goth. *kaileis), m., 'wedge,' is abnormal; the root is *kī*, *kai*. OIc. *kīll*, 'canal' (comp. the proper name Kiel), is probably not connected on account of the meaning; since OHG. and MidHG. *kīl* signifies 'plug,' the word is more probably allied to AS. *cǣg*, E. *key*.

Keiler, **Keuler**, m., 'wild boar,' Mod HG. only, probably not allied to Keule; borrowed from Lith. *kuilys*, 'boar'?.

Keim, m., 'germ, bud, shoot,' from the equiv. MidHG. *kīm*, *kīme*, m., OHG. *chim*, *chîmo*, m. (Goth. *keima, m.). The Teut. root is *kī*, which is widely diffused in the Teut. group. Goth. has only the partic. of a vb. derived from this root, *us-kijans*, 'sprouted,' for which, however, an earlier variant, *keins*, 'germinated,' is assumed by the vb. *us-keinan* (-*nôda*). With the same root *kī* are connected the dental derivs. AS. *cíþ*, OSax. *kîð*, OHG. *chîdi*. (*frum-*

kidt), MidHG. *kide*, ModHG. dial. Reibe, 'shoot.' OSax. and OHG. *kînan*, 'to germinate,' has a pres. affix *n* of the root *kt*; the identical AS. *cînan*, 'to spring up, burst, burst to pieces, germinate,' and the corresponding AS. subst. *cinu*, MidE. *chine*, 'rift, crack,' prove that the meaning 'to germinate' originated in the actual perception of budding.

fein, num. adj., 'no, none,' from Mid HG. *kein,* shortened from *dechein,* OHG. *dihhein,* also OHG. *dohh-ein, nihhein, noh-hein,* all of which are compounded with *ein.* The meaning of OHG. and MidHG. *dech* is obscure.

Reich, m., 'chalice, cup,' from the equiv. MidHG. *kelch,* OHG. *chelih, kelih (hh),* m.; corresponding to OSax. *kelik;* from Lat. *câlicem (calix),* borrowed at a time when the word was pronounced *kalikem* (comp. Reller); the suggestion that Reich was first adopted from Ecclesiast. Lat. on the introduction of Christianity, is refuted by the changes made in Lat. *crucem,* 'Kreuz' ('cross'), which was certainly not borrowed before this time; the G. *z* for Lat. *c* before *e* points to a far later period than the derivation of Reich from *calicem.* There is greater probability in the assumption that the term was imported with the southern culture of the vine; comp. Reller, Wein, and Becher. In E. and Scand. the Lat. *u* is retained; AS. *calic, cælic,* and Scand. *kalkr;* comp. OIr. *calich.* In almost every language the word is restricted to ecclesiastical uses; comp. Fr. *calice.*—**Rlfilen-held,** 'calyx,' ModHG. is due to a confusion by scientists of Reich (Lat. *calix*), with Gr. κάλυξ, 'calyx.'

Relle, f., 'ladle, scoop, trowel,' from MidHG. and MidLG. *kelle,* f., 'ladle, trowel,' OHG. *chella,* f., 'trowel'; Goth. **kaljô,* f., is wanting. Although there are a few points of contact between HG. Relle and AS. *cylle, cille,* f., 'leather bottle or bag, vessel,' the AS. word is based upon Lat. *culleus,* 'leather bag,' or, as is more probable, a genuine Teut. word has been confused with a borrowed term in AS.

Keller, m., 'cellar,' from the equiv. MidHG. *këller,* m., OHG. *chëllâri,* m.; corresponding to OSax. *kellere,* m.; Scand. *kjallare,* m.; a Teut. loan-word which probably passed from the South through Up. Germany to the North; in England only the word did not obtain in the older period; E. *cellar* originated in the OFr.

celier. The word was borrowed from late Lat. *cellarium* (with a change of gender and accent) in the pre-OHG. period, since the terms borrowed from Lat. in OHG. change Lat. *c* before open vowels into *z* (tz); comp. Kreuz. Keller may have been introduced into Germany from the South at the same time as Reich (which see), perhaps with the culture of the vine; yet the word signifies generally 'subterranean storeroom.'—**Kellner,** m., 'waiter,' from MidHG. *këlnære,* m., 'butler,' from Mid Lat. *cellenarius,* with the equiv. variant *këllære,* m., from Lat. *cellarius,* m., 'steward, butler.'—**Kellnerin,** 'barmaid,' MidHG. *këlnærinne, këllærinne,* f., 'maid, servant, housekeeper.'

Relter, f. and m., 'wine or oil press,' from the equiv. MidHG. *kelter, kalter,* m. and f. OHG. *calcatûra, calctûra* (also *calc-tûrhûs,* MidHG. *kalterhûs*); borrowed, on the introduction of the southern culture of the vine (see Wein, Becher, Reich, and Keller), from Lat. *calcatura,* 'wine-press' *(calcatorium),* derived from *calcare,* 'to tread.' Hence Relter orig. means 'treading press.' For the genuine UpG. for Relter see under Trette and Terfel (in Du. pers, AS. *presse,* from Lat. *pressa*). Relter is MidG., and is found from the Moselle to the Saale. Corresponding to OLorraine *chaucheur,* from Lat. *calcatorium.*

Kemenate, f., from the equiv. MidHG. *kemenâte,* f., 'room with a fireplace,' espec. 'bedroom,' also 'sitting-room, women's apartment.' During the OHG. period Mid Lat. *caminâta,* 'room with a stove or fireplace,' was introduced into G., as is proved by the preservation of the Lat. sharp dental in OHG. *cheminâta,* f. From MidLat. *caminata,* which is recorded as early as the 6th cent., are derived Ital. *camminata,* 'large room,' and Fr. *cheminée,* whence the equiv. E. *chimney,* also Czech, Pol. and Russ. *komnata,* 'room'; comp. Kamin.

kennen, vb., 'to know, be acquainted with,' from the equiv. MidHG. *kennen,* OHG. *chennen.* The simple form was very little used in MidHG. and OHG., the usual words being the compounds OHG. *irchennen,* MidHG. *erkennen,* and OHG. *bichennen,* MidHG. *bekennen,* with the meanings of ModHG. *kennen.* The corresponding Goth. *kannjan (uskannjan),* as well as AS. *cennan, gecennan,* signifies 'to make known.' This double sense, which is combined in OIc. *kenna,* is explained by the fact that OTeut. *kannjan* is a factitive of the OTeut. pret.-pres. *kann*, inf. *kunnan*, 'to know'; erfennen is a derivative 'to inform oneself.' Comp. further references under fönnen.

Kerbe, f., 'notch,' from MidHG. *kërbe*, f., *kërp*, m., 'incision, notch.' Comp. OIc. *kjarf, kerfe*, n., 'bundle,' AS. *cyrf*, 'incision.' **tterben**, vb., 'to notch,' from the equiv. MidHG. *kërben* (with a str. partic. *gekurben* in Lower Rhen.); an orig. str. vb. with the graded forms *kërfan, karf, kurbum, korban* (comp. AS. *ċeorfan*, E. *to carve*, Du. *k-rven*); the final *f* of the stem *kerf* is attested by the MidHG. *kërve*, a variant of *kërbe*; Goth. *kaírfan* is wanting. The root *kerf* is found also in Gr. γράφω, 'to write,' prop. 'to cut in, scratch' (comp. HG. reißen with E. *to write*), which with Teut. *kerf* points to a Sans. root *grph*.

Kerbel, m., 'chervil,' from the equiv. MidHG. *kërvele, kërvel*, f. and m., OHG. *kërvola, kërvela*, f., 'a culinary and medicinal herb'; comp. AS. *ċerfille*, E. *chervil*. It was probably naturalised in Germany before the OHG. period, and is derived from Lat. *cœrifolium* (χαιρέφυλλον), whence also Fr. *cerfeuil*, Ital. *cerfoglio*, which were borrowed at a period when the initial *c* before open vowels was still pronounced *k*; comp. Keller, Kerker, Kaiſer, Kreuz, Pech, &c. In the period before the HG. permutation of consonants, the Ital. art of cookery and horticulture, and with the latter many southern vegetables and herbs, were introduced into Germany; comp. Kappes, Pfeffer, Minze, Kohl, and Keller.

Kerker, m., 'gaol,' from the equiv. Mid HG. *karkœre, kërkœre, kerker*, m., OHG. *karkâri*, m., 'prison'; from Lat. *carcerem*, probably more strictly from *karkerim* (comp. OHG. *krûzi*, from Lat. *crucem* under Kreuz), so that the final *i* of the OHG. word would represent the *-em* of the acc. (comp. Kelch, Pinſe). Even in Goth. *karkara*, f., 'prison,' is found, corresponding to AS. *cearcern*, OIr. *carcar*. In the HG. word the second *k* shows that Kerker was borrowed before the OHG. period, since borrowed terms in OHG. such as *chrâzi*, from *crucem*, pronounce the *c* as *tz* before open vowels; comp. Kaiſer, Kelch, Keller, Kerbel, and Pech.

Kerl, m., 'fellow,' a MidG. and LG. form for MidHG. *karl*, m., 'man, husband, lover,' OHG. *karal*; OIc. *karl*, m., 'man (opposed to woman), old man, one of the common folk, serf, servant,' hence E. *carl*, 'fellow, man.' Besides these terms, which indicate Goth. *karla-*, there appears a form *kerla-* (Goth. *kaírla-*) allied to them by gradation, and assumed by AS. *ċeorl*, 'serf' (hence *ċeorlian*, 'to take a husband, marry'), MidE. *cheorl*, E. *churl*, as well as by Du. *kerel*, Fris. *tzerl*, LG. *kêrl, kerel* (wanting in OSax.). As a proper name the HG. Karl was retained without being supplanted by the MidG. and LG. form; on the adoption of Karl by Slav. see under Kaiſer. Both words denoted a full-grown man (generically, 'husband, lover,' and also 'male of animals' in OHG. and AS.; legally, 'man of the lower orders'); in AS. *ceorl*, 'man,' retained the entire signification, since it is used even of kings, and in the derivative *ceorlian*, 'to marry,' it preserves its generic meaning and its legal aspect in being applied to the common freemen and the serf. References in non-Teut. cannot be adduced with any certainty; the comparison of *kerl, karl*, with Sans. *jâra* (*j* for *g*), 'paramour, lover,' is possible as far as the stem is concerned; the *l* of the Teut. word is at all events a suffix. With regard to the gradation Kerl, Karl, comp. Küſer, Giebel, Rieſer, Laut, &c.

Kern, m., 'kernel, stone (of fruit), pith,' from the equiv. MidHG. *kërn, kërne*, m. OHG. *kërno*, m.; corresponding to OIc. *kjarne*, m., 'kernel.' A corresponding Goth. *kaírnô*, n., is wanting (for which we have *kaúrnô*, n.?). AS. *cyrnel*, and the equiv. E. *kernel* are connected phonetically more nearly with Kern, since a derivative of Kern in E. would have an initial *ch*. OTeut. *kerna-* and *korna-* are allied by gradation to each other just as Brett and Bort, Kerl and Karl.

kernen, vb., 'to churn,' allied to E. *churn*, AS. *ċirne, ċyrne*, Du. *karn*, OIc. *kirna*, f., 'churn,' with which AS. *ċyrnan*, E. *to churn*, and the equiv. Du. *karnen* are also connected. Akin to ModHG. (Up. Palat.) *kern*, 'cream,' MidDu. *kerne*, Scand. (Ic.) *kjarne*, 'cream,' which perhaps are identical with Kern. Probably Teut. *kirnjôn*, 'churn,' and *kirnjan*, 'to churn,' are prim. derivatives of **kerno-*, 'cream.'

Kerze, f., 'taper, wax-light, candle,' from MidHG. *këɼze*, 'candle, taper,' espec. 'wax candle,' OHG. *cherza, charza*, f., *charz*, m., 'taper, wick, tow.' We have to proceed from the latter in tracing the development of meaning in Kerze (comp. OIc. *kerte*, n., 'wax-light'; 'tow, wick made of tow, wick with a covering of wax, taper,' form the series. Hence there is no need to suppose that Kerze has been borrowed from Lat. cerâta, allied to cera, 'wax,' an assumption equally at variance with the phonological relations of the words. It is true that neither *karta-, ' tow,' nor its derivative *kartjô, ' taper,' has any etymological support in the non-Teut. languages. The OHG. doublet karza, kerza, may, however, be explained by the assumption of a Goth. *kartjô, f., the mutation appearing only at a late period before r and consons. in OHG.

Keſſel, m., 'kettle, cauldron, boiler,' from the equiv. MidHG. keʒʒel, OHG. cheʒʒil, m.; corresponding to Goth. katils, OIc. ketell, AS. cytel, m., E. kettle, and the equiv. Du. ketel. This OTeut. word is usually derived from Lat. catînus, 'dish' (Sans. kaṭhina, 'dish'), or its dimin. catillus. Lat. catînus is indicated by OHG. keʒʒîn, cheʒʒî, MidHG. cheʒʒî (Alem.) 'kettle,' AS. cete, 'cooking-pot.' It is shown under Igel that Goth. katils can be derived from Lat. catînus. Schüſſel and Tiſch may have been borrowed at the same period as Keſſel. From Lat. catînus are also derived the Rom. terms, Port. cadinho and Tyrol. cadin, 'wooden dish.' From Teut., OSlov. kotŭlŭ, ' kettle' is derived.

Kette (1.), f., 'covey,' with the earlier variants kitte, kütte, at present dial. ; used in ModHG. only of partridges, &c. Kette is a corruption of the unintelligible kütte, MidHG. kütte, OHG. chutti, n., 'herd, troop'; comp. MidLG. küdde, Du. kudde, f., ' herd.' We might connect the word with Lith. gùtas, m., gaujà, f., 'herd,' and hence further with the Ind. root jû (for gû), ' to drive, urge on,' Lith. gùiti, 'to drive.' Therefore the dental of the OHG. word, as in the equiv. Lith. gûtas, belongs to the suffix. The Aryan root is gu, 'to drive cattle.'

Kette (2.), f., ' chain, fetter,' from the equiv. MidHG. keten, ketene (Ketto is found since the 15th cent.), f., OHG. chetina, chetinna, f., ' chain'; borrowed from Lat. catêna, yet hardly from the latter itself, since the word was probably naturalised in G. before the HG. permutation of consonants (comp. Ketzer), but rather from a vernacular cadéna (thus Prov. and Span., hence Fr. chaine, from which MidE. chaine, F. chain is derived), which by a change of accent and by the HG. permutation and mutation resulted in chetina; Du. keten and MidDu. ketene still point, however, to the t of the Lat. word. For the transition of ê to î, comp. feiern and Pein. The accent is changed, as in OHG. àbbât, from Lat. abbát-em.

Ketzer, m., 'heretic,' from MidHG. ketzer, m., 'heretic,' also 'reprobate, Sodomite' (not recorded in OHG.). The tz presents no difficulties in deriving the word from Gr. καθαρός (καθαροί, a Manichean sect spread throughout the West in the 11th and 12th cents., and persecuted by the Church), if it be assumed that Du. ketter, 'heretic,' is a phonetic version of the HG. word. It is true that HG. tz from Gr. θ (Lat. th) cannot be demonstrated ; the hard fricative th (þ, θ) may, however, be regarded phonetically as tz, since, e.g., King Chilperic's sign for the was none other than z; the þ in OIc. words sounded also to the Germans of the 9th cent. like z; þór seemed to them zor. So too in Italy the καθαροί were called Gazari.

keuchen, vb., 'to gasp,' from MidHG. kûchen, ' to breathe '; MidHG. kîchen, ' to breathe with difficulty, gasp,' has also been absorbed in the ModHG. vb. Corresponding to Du. kugchen, 'to cough,' from Mid Du. kuchen, AS. cohhettan, MidE. coughen, E. to cough.—MidHG. kîchen is based on a Teut. root kik, which appears in LG., Du., and E., in a nasalised form ; LG. (Holstein) kinghosten, Du. kinkhoest, m., E. chincough (for chinkcough), ' whooping-cough '; allied to Swed. kikhosta, Dan. kighoste, AS. cincung.

Keule, f., 'club, pestle ; thigh ; rude fellow,' from MidHG. kiule, f., ' club, stick, pole ' ; cognate with ModHG. Kaule, from MidHG. kûle, a variant of kugele, kugel. See the further references under Kugel.

Keuler, m. See Keiler.

keuſch, adj., 'chaste, pure,' from MidHG. kiusche, kiusch, adj., ' moderate, quiet, modest, bashful '; OHG. chûski, adj., ' continent, moderate.' AS. cûse is borrowed from the OSax. of the Heliand, OSax. *kûsci, of which only the corresponding adv. cûsco is recorded ; Du. kuisch, ' cleanly, chaste.' The prim. meaning of the OTeut. adj., which appears in all these forms, is presumably ' pure '; comp. Du. kuischen, ' to clean, purify '; OHG. unchûski, ' dirt ' (also Hess. unfeuſcher Weg, ' road in bad condition '). — Keuſchlamm, ' chaste tree,' simply ModHG., formed from MidLat. agnus castus, known in Gr. by the term ἁγνός; this being associated with ἁγνός, 'pure,' gave rise to the Lat. *agnus castus*; *agnus*, Gr. ἁγνός, being confused with *agnus*, 'lamb,' led to HG. $\mathfrak{K}$euf$\mathfrak{d}$lamm, one of the strangest products of sciolism (not of popular etymology). The tree is also called $\mathfrak{K}$euf$\mathfrak{d}$baum, Du. *knischboom*.

$\mathfrak{K}$ibi$\mathfrak{z}$, m., 'lapwing,' with numerous dial. forms varying at different periods; they are all due to a corruption of a term the etymology of which was not understood; in MidHG. also there are several forms; *gibitze*, *gȋbitz*, *gȋbiȥ* occur in the written language. The similarity in sound of the equiv. Russ. *čibezŭ* and of MidLG. *kivit*, Du. *kievit*, E. *peewit*, suggests the assumption that $\mathfrak{K}$ibi$\mathfrak{z}$ is of onomatopoetic origin. The suffix resembles that in $\mathfrak{S}$tig$\mathfrak{l}$i$\mathfrak{z}$.

$\mathfrak{K}$i$\mathfrak{d}$er, f., 'chick-pea,' from the equiv. MidHG. *kicher*, OHG. *chihhurra*, *chihhira*, f.; based on Lat. *cicer* (plur. *cicera*), n., 'chick-pea,' *cicera*, f., 'chickling vetch'; MidLat. *cicoria*, *cichorea*, which would be most closely allied phonetically to OHG. *chihhurra*, signifies 'chicory (Gr. κίχώριον). MidE. *chiche*, E. *chiches*, *chickpeas*, plur., with the suffix *r* wanting as in Fr. *chiche*, Ital. *cece*. The term was borrowed before the OHG. period (Du. *sisererwt* is more recent).

$\mathfrak{K}$i$\mathfrak{d}$ern, vb., 'to titter,' ModHG. only; allied to OHG. *chihhazzen*, 'to laugh,' a variant of OHG. *chahhazzen* (MidHG. *kachzen*); comp. also MidHG. *kah*, m., 'loud laughter,' MidHG. *kachen*, 'to laugh loudly'; the *ch* is not based, as in other instances, on Teut. *k*, but following AS. *ceahhet an*, 'to laugh,' on OTeut. *hh*. The cognates are onomatopoetic, the root of which cannot be discovered. In Gr. similar terms were coined, καχάζω, καγχάζω, καγχαλάω, καγχλάζω, 'to laugh loudly,' καχλάζω, 'to splash and bubble.' On account of the non-permutation of the consonants the terms cannot have been orig. allied. The Gr. words may, however, be cognate with Sans. *kakh*, 'to laugh.'

$\mathfrak{K}$iebi$\mathfrak{z}$, see $\mathfrak{K}$ibi$\mathfrak{z}$.

$\mathfrak{K}$iefer (1.), m., from the equiv. MidHG. *kiver* (m., n. ?), *kivel*, *kivele*, 'jaw, jawbone,' besides which there is a form from the stem of *tauen*, MidHG. *kiuwel*, m., and usually *kiuwe*, *këwe*, f., 'jaw, jawbone.' Yet ModHG. *kiver*, *kivel*, have, notwithstanding their rare occurrence, a remoter history in the past; with Goth. **k-fru-* is connected OIc. *kjǫptr*, *kjǫptr* (Goth. *kiftus), 'mouth (of beasts), jawbone,' and also with the *a* stage of gradation, AS. *ceafl*, OSax. *k-fl*, m., 'jaw of animals' (with regard to the gradation comp. $\mathfrak{K}$äfer, $\mathfrak{G}$iebel, and $\mathfrak{K}$erl). The Teut. stem is therefore *kef*, *kaf*, or rather *keb*, *kab* (before *l* and *r* later permutations of *b* to *f* sometimes occur), from pre-Teut. *geph* or *gebh*; comp. Zend. *zafare*, *zafra*, n., 'mouth, jaws' (the corresponding term in Sans. *japhra, *jabhra, is wanting); the nasalised root *jambh*, by gradation *j-bh*, 'to snap at,' leads to Gr. γαμφαί, γαμφηλαί, 'jaws,' yet these are probably connected more closely with the cognates discussed under $\mathfrak{K}$amm. See $\mathfrak{K}$äfer.

$\mathfrak{K}$iefer (2.), f., 'pine,' early ModHG. only; it cannot be traced further back; in UpG. $\mathfrak{F}$öhre simply. Hence $\mathfrak{K}$iefer probably originated in $\mathfrak{K}$ien$\mathfrak{f}$öhre (respecting the obscuration of old compounds comp. $\mathfrak{W}$imper, $\mathfrak{S}$d$\mathfrak{u}$lt$\mathfrak{z}$, and $\mathfrak{S}$d$\mathfrak{u}$ter). The intermediate form *kimfer* is recorded as North Boh. Comp. also MidHG. *kienboum*, m., 'pine,' and *kienforhe, f., 'pine-tree' (attested by the derivative *kienforhin*, adj., 'of pine'). Comp. $\mathfrak{K}$ien and $\mathfrak{F}$öhre.

$\mathfrak{K}$ie$\mathfrak{f}$te, f., 'foot-warmer,' simply Mod HG. from the equiv. LG. *kike*, in Dan. *ildkikkert*, 'foot-warmer.' Of obscure origin.

$\mathfrak{K}$iel (1.), m., from the equiv. MidHG. *kil*, m. and n., 'quill'; not recorded in OHG.; dial. $\mathfrak{K}$eil (MidG.), pointing to Mid HG. *kîl*; LG. *quiele*, *kiel*, is connected with MidE. *quille*, E. *quill*. Goth. *qilus or *qeilus, and further cognate terms are wanting.

$\mathfrak{K}$iel (2.), m., 'keel,' from MidHG. *kiel*, OHG. *chiol*, m., 'a rather large ship'; comp. AS. *ceól*, m., 'ship,' Du. *kiel*, E. *keel*, OIc. *kjóll*, m., 'ship.' Scand. *kjǫlr*, m., 'ship's keel,' is not allied to these; from this the E. word as well as the ModHG. meaning is probably derived (probably through LG. and Dan. influence). The OTeut. *kiuls (the assumed Goth. form), 'ship,' may be connected with Gr. γαυλός (γαῦλος), 'merchant vessel' (orig. 'pail,' also 'articles in the form of a pail, *e.g.* beehive'); *au* would be Goth. *iu*, as in HG. $\mathfrak{S}$tier, Goth. *stiurs*, compared with Gr. ταῦρος. The fact that a naut. term was orig. common to both the Teutons and the Greeks is no more remarkable than the occurrence of the term $\mathfrak{M}$a$\mathfrak{f}$t among the Teutons and the Romans; besides, the terms relating to shipbuilding stretch still further back, as is proved by the correspondence of Lat.

ndvis, Gr. *ναῦς*, Ind. *náus;* comp. 𝔑𝔞𝔠𝔥𝔢𝔫. With the Gr. word, Sans. *gólá, gólam,* 'cone-shaped pitcher' (Sans. *ô* for *au*), has also been compared; hence a similar signification might be assigned to the orig. Teut. word. Comp. 𝔎𝔞𝔥𝔫.

𝔎𝔦𝔢𝔪𝔢, f., 'gill (of a fish),' ModHG. simply, from the equiv. LG. *kîm;* allied to OHG. *chiela, chêla,* as well as AS. *cían, ceón,* with the same meaning. Since the forms corresponding exactly in sound with 𝔎𝔦𝔢𝔪𝔢 are wanting in the earlier periods, its origin is uncertain; some have connected it with 𝔨𝔞𝔲𝔢𝔫, root *kiw* (Aryan *giw*).

𝔎𝔦𝔢𝔫, m., 'resinous wood,' from Mid HG. *kin,* n. and m., OHG. *chien,* 'resinous wood, pine chips, pine torch'; comp. AS. **kén, cén,* m., 'torch pine.' Goth. *kêns or *kizns (comp. 𝔐𝔦𝔢𝔱𝔢 from Goth. *mizdô*) is wanting; further references cannot be found. Comp. also 𝔎𝔦𝔢𝔣𝔢𝔯.

𝔎𝔦𝔢𝔭𝔢, f., 'wicker basket,' ModHG. only, from LG.; comp. Du. *kiepekorf,* m., 'wicker basket, basket for the back,' MidDu. also *cûpe,* AS. *cŷpa,* E. dial. *kipe,* 'basket'; Goth. *kŭpjô or *kiupô is wanting. Whether these terms are borrowed, or rather developed, from MidLat. *cûpa,* 'tun,' and also 'measure of corn' (comp. 𝔎𝔲𝔣𝔢), cannot be decided.

𝔎𝔦𝔢𝔰, m., 'gravel,' from the equiv. Mid HG. *kis,* m.; 𝔎𝔦𝔢𝔰𝔢𝔩, 'pebble,' from MidHG. *kisel,* m., 'flint-stone, hailstone, large hailstone'; OHG. *chisil,* AS. *ćeosel,* MidE. *chisel,* 'pebble.' Goth. **kisuls,* m., is wanting; this would be a derivative of **kisa-,* on which MidHG. *kis* and ModHG. 𝔎𝔦𝔢𝔰 is probably based. Du. *kei* and *kiezel* points to *kî* as the stem.

𝔥𝔦𝔢𝔰𝔢𝔫, vb., 'to select,' from MidHG. *kiesen,* OHG. *chiosan,* 'to test, try, taste for the purpose of testing, test by tasting, select after strict examination.' Goth. *kiusan,* AS. *ceósan,* E. *to choose.* Teut. root *kus* (with the change of *s* into *r, kur* in the partic. 𝔢𝔯𝔨𝔬𝔯𝔢𝔫, see also 𝔎𝔲𝔯, 'choice'), from pre-Teut. *gvs,* in Lat. *gus-tus, gus-tare,* Gr. *γεύω* for *γεύσω,* Ind. root *juś,* 'to select, be fond of.' Teut. *kausjan* passed as *kusiti* into Slav.

𝔎𝔦𝔢𝔷𝔢, f., 'small basket,' ModHG. simply, in MidHG. *kätze,* f., 'basket, basket for the back.' Origin obscure.

𝔎𝔦𝔩𝔩, 𝔎𝔦𝔩𝔩𝔤𝔞𝔫𝔤, in Alem. 'nocturnal meeting'; wanting in MidHG. Comp. OHG. *chwiltiwërch,* n., 'evening work'; OIc. *kveld,* n., 'evening' (in Iceland and Norway the usual word for evening, while *aptann* is used poetically and in stately prose). AS. *cwyldhrepe,* f., 'bat,' lit. 'evening swiftness,' *cwyldseten,* 'evening.' Hence *qeldos,* n., is the oldest word for 'evening.' The loss of the *w* after *k* is normal; comp. 𝔱𝔢𝔡, 𝔎𝔢𝔱, and 𝔎𝔬̈𝔟𝔢𝔯.

𝔎𝔦𝔫𝔡, n., 'child,' from the equiv. Mid HG. *kint* (gen. *kindes*), n., OHG. *chind,* n., 'child'; corresponding to OSax. *kind,* n., 'child'; wanting in Goth., Scand., and E., but a Goth. **kinþa-* may be assumed, whence OSlov. *čędo,* 'child,' is borrowed. In OIc. a form *kundr,* m., 'son,' allied by gradation occurs, and with this an adj. suffix *kunds,* 'descended from,' may be most closely connected, Goth. *himinakunds,* 'heavenly,' *qinakunds,* 'female,' AS. *feorrancund,* 'having a distant origin.' This suffix is an old partic. in *to* (comp. alt, fatt, faut, traut, 𝔊𝔬𝔱𝔱), from a root *kun, ken, kan,* which has numerous derivatives both in the Teut. and non-Teut. languages. The root signifies 'to give birth to, beget'; comp. 𝔎𝔬̈𝔫𝔦𝔤 and also Goth. *kuni,* OHG. *chunni,* MidHG. *künne,* n., 'race' (Goth. *qêns,* 'woman,' E. *queen,* are, however, unconnected). So too AS. *cennan,* 'to give birth to, beget.' Teut. *ken,* Aryan *gen,* has representatives in Gr. *γένος,* n., *γί-γνομαι, γυνή,* in Lat. *genus, gigno, gens,* in OSlov. *žena,* 'wife' (Pruss. *gena,* 'wife'), in Lith. *gentis,* 'relative,' and in the Sans. root *jan,* 'to generate,' *jánas,* n., 'race,' *janús,* n., 'birth, creature, race,' *jant,* f., 'woman,' *jantú,* m., 'child, being, tribe,' *játú,* 'son' (the latter is most nearly connected with Teut. 𝔎𝔦𝔫𝔱).

𝔎𝔦𝔫𝔫, n., 'chin,' from the equiv. Mid HG. *kin, kinne,* OHG. *chinni,* n. (also 'jaw'). The older meaning, 'cheek' (Goth. *kinnus,* f., 'cheek'), has been preserved in 𝔎𝔦𝔫𝔫𝔟𝔢𝔦𝔫, 'cheek-bone,' in OHG. *chinnizën,* MidHG. *kinnezan,* 'molar tooth,' OHG. *kinnibaccho,* 'jawbone'; comp. AS. *ćin,* E. *chin,* AS. *ćinbán,* E. *chin-bone,* ModDu. *kin,* f., 'chin'; OIc. *kinn,* 'cheek.' Comp. Gr. *γένυς,* f., 'chin, jaw, jawbone,' also 'edge of an axe, axe,' *γένειον,* n., 'chin, jaw,' *γενείας,* f., 'chin, beard'; Lat. *gena,* 'cheek,' *dentes genuini,* 'molar teeth'; Ir. *gin,* 'mouth'; Sans. *hánu-s,* f., 'jaw,' *hanavya,* 'jawbone.' Hence the meaning varies considerably between *cheek, jaw, chin;* the prim. sense of the root *gen* in this term cannot be ascertained. On account of the Gr. meaning 'axe' some deduce the word from a root *gen,* 'to cut to pieces.'

Kipfel, dial., also **Gipfel**, m. and n., from the equiv. MidHG. *kipfe*, m., 'roll of fine white bread pointed at both ends' (**Gipfel** is a corrupt form); perhaps allied to OHG. *chipfa*, f., MidHG. *kipfe*, 'drag of a wheel.'

Kippe, f., 'brink, edge,' from MidG. and LG.; the proper HG. form is **Kipfe**, meaning 'point' in Luther; earlier references are wanting. The nominal vb. *kippen* means 'to cut off the point'; in the sense of 'to strike,' allied to OIc. *kippa*, 'to strike,' AS. *cippian*, with which ModHG. *kappen* is also connected.

Kirche, f., 'church,' from the equiv. MidHG. *kirche* (Swiss *chilche*), OHG. *chirihha* (Swiss *chilihha*), f.; corresponding to Du. *kerk*, AS. *ćirice*, *ćyriće*, E. *church*. As is shown by the OHG. *hh* of *chirihha*, the word must have existed before the OHG. period; names of places with **Kirche** are found in Germany even before the beginning of the 8th cent.; yet the word is unknown to Goth. (the terms used were *gwilhûs*, 'the house of God,' *gards* or *razn bidô*, 'house of prayer'; also *aikklêsjô*, 'coetus christianorum'). The other Teut. tribes must, however, have adopted the term from Gr. through the medium of Goth. (comp. **Pfaffe**, also **Heide**, **Taufe**, and **Teufel**). It is true that Gr. κυριακή (with ἡμέρα understood) during the first ten centuries signified 'Sunday' exclusively, and only from the 11th cent. onwards did it obtain the meaning 'house of the Lord.' But since the word is foreign, we may assume that the gender of κυριακόν, 'church' (or its plur. κυριακά), recorded from the 4th cent., was changed (OHG. *chirihha*, f.). Since the Gr. word was never current in the Romish Church (the LatRom. as well as the Kelt. term being *ecclesia*), we have in **Kirche** a term of the Greek Church, though in other cases the words adopted with Christianity are essentially Lat. (from Goth. **kyreika*, Russ. *cerkovĭ*, and OSlov. *crŭky* are also probably derived). The introduction of **Kirche** through a Goth. medium was possible as late as the 9th cent. at least, for, according to Wal. Strabo, divine service was celebrated on the Lower Danube in the Goth. language even at that period.—**Kirchspiel**, n., 'parish,' from MidHG. *kirchspil*, also *kirspel*; the second part of the compound is instinctively connected with **Menschenspiel**, yet its origin has not been definitely ascertained; some have referred it to Goth.

spill, n., 'speech' (comp. **Beispiel**), and have defined **Kirchspiel** as 'the district within which the decision of a church is paramount.' This assumption is not quite satisfactory, because no connecting link between **Kirchenwort**, 'decision of the church,' and **Kirchspiel**, 'parish,' can be discovered. Following the explanation of **Pfarre**, we should rather assume some such meaning as 'district, enclosure, forbearance,' which is supported by AS. *spelian*, 'to spare, protect'; comp. AS. *sp-la*, 'representative' ?.—**Kirchweih**, f., 'dedication of a church,' from MidHG. *kirchwîhe*, f., which thus early signifies also 'annual fair,' and even 'fête' generally, OHG. *chirihwîhî*, f., prop. 'dedication of a church' (comp. Alem. *Kilbe*, *chilbi*).

Kirmes, f., 'village fête,' from MidHG. *kirmësse*, f., 'dedication festival,' for the unrecorded *kirchmësse*, just as MidHG. *kirspil* is a variant of *kirchspel*, n., 'parish,' and *kirwîhe* a variant of *kirchwîhe*, 'dedication of a church.' **Kirmes** (Du. *kerkmis*, *kermis*), lit. 'mass to celebrate the dedication of a church' (in Alem. *chilbe*, from *kilchwîhe*, Bav. *kirta*, from *kirchtac*). Comp. **Messe**.

kirre, adj., 'tractable,' from MidHG. *kürre*, MidG. *kurre*, *kirre*, adj., 'tame, mild'; derived, by suppressing the *w*, from earlier OHG. **churri*, **quirri*; comp. Goth. *qaírrus*, 'meek,' OIc. *kvirr*, *kyrr*, adj., 'still, quiet.' Perhaps based on the Teut. root *gēr* appearing in ModHG. **Kêter**; yet Lith. *gurti*, 'to grow weak, relax,' *gurus*, 'crumbling,' may also be allied.

Kirsche, f., from the equiv. MidHG. *kirse*, *kërse* (Alem. *chriesi*), f., 'cherry' (for the change of *s* into *sch* comp. **Arsch** and **Hirsch**). OHG. *chirsa* (**chirissa*), f., is certainly not derived from Lat. *cerasum*, but, like the cognate Rom. words, from *cerêsia* (prop. n. plur. of the adj. *ceraseus* ?. Comp. Gr. κεράσιον, 'cherry,' κερασία, κερασέα, 'cherry-tree'), only with a Teut. accent; the Alem. form **Kriese** (from the prim. form *krêsia*, which perhaps appears also in Istrian *kriss* and Serv. *krijèša*), like **Kirsche**, is based too on the common primit. form with the Rom. accent; MidLat. **ceresca* (Ital. *ciriegia*, Fr. *cerise*); comp. also OSlov. *črěšnja* (primit. Slav. **čers-*, from **kers-* ?). The adoption of the word by HG. occurred before the 7th cent., as is shown by the preservation of the initial *c* as *k* in HG. For a discussion of the period at which the word was borrowed, and of the gender of the Southern terms for fruit, see Pflaume.

Kissen, Küssen, n., 'cushion,' from MidHG. küssen, küssin, OHG. chussîn, n., 'cushion'; comp. Du. kussen, 'cushion.' The G. word is derived (comp. Pfühl and Flaum) from the equiv. MidLat. cussinus (Fr. coussin), which comes from Lat. *culcitinum, allied to culcita, 'mattress, cushion'; E. cushion and Ital. cuscino are modern Fr. loan-words. The i of ModHG. Kissen comes from MidG. and UpG. dialects (comp. Pilz and Binns).

Kiste, f., 'box,' from MidHG. kiste, OHG. chista, f., 'box, chest'; comp. Du. kist, AS. čest, čiste, E. chest, OIc. kista, 'box.' In Goth. a cognate term is wanting. The assumption that the Teut. languages borrowed Lat. cista (Gr. κίστη) at a very early period, at any rate long before the change of the initial c of cista into tz, presents no greater difficulty than in the case of Arche; comp. Kerb, Keffer, and Sack. Hence between Kasten and Kiste there is no etymological connection; the first has no cognate term in Lat.

Kitt, m., from the equiv. MidHG. küte, küt, m., 'cement, putty,' OHG. chuti, quiti, 'glue, birdlime,' which makes it probable that the Goth. form was *qidus; comp. also AS. cwidu, 'resin of trees.' Prim. allied to Lat. bitumen, Sans. jatu, 'resin of trees'; common type getû. Allied also to OIc. kváða, Swed. káda, 'resin,' MidE. code, 'pitch.'

Kittel, m., 'smock-frock,' from MidHG. kitel, kittel, m., 'smock-frock, shirt, chemise.' AS. cytel, E. kirtle, OIc. kyrtell, on account of the medial r and the abnormal dental correspondence, cannot be compared (they are allied to Furz). Its connection with χιτών is impossible. The origin of the HG. word has not been explained. The strong suspicion that it has been borrowed cannot be proved.

Kitze (1.), f., from the equiv. MidHG. kitze, kiz, n., OHG. chizzî, kizzîn, n., 'kid'; from Teut. *kittîn, n., with the original dimin. suffix -îna, which appears in Küchelein and Schwein. Goth. *kidi (kidjis), n., may be deduced from OIc. kið, n., 'she-goat,' whence E. kid is borrowed (an E. word cognate with Scand. must have had an initial ch). Further, the assumed Goth. *kidi and *kittein, with medial dentals, are related to each other, just as the forms assumed under Ziege, tigô and tikkein, with

medial gutturals. The close correspondence between Kitze and Zicke proves that they are related; both are pet names for Geiß, 'goat' (comp. Swiss gitzi for OHG. chitzi).

Kitze (2.), Kietze, f., 'kitten, kid, fawn,' not found in MidHG. and OHG., but probably existing in the vernacular, as is indicated by the specifically HG. tz compared with LG. tt (kitte); comp. MidE. chitte, 'kitten,' from an unrecorded AS. *citten (E. kitten); MidE. kitlung, E. kitling, are probably borrowed from Scand. ketlingr, 'kitten.' The cognates are related by gradation to Katze.

kitzeln, vb., 'to tickle,' from the equiv. MidHG. kitzeln, kützeln, OHG. chizzilôn, chuzzilôn; comp. MidLG. ketelen, OIc. kitla; AS. cytelian (E. to kittle) is based on the prim. form *kutilôn. E. to tickle, MidE. tikelen, is based on a transposition of consonants in the root kit (so too Alem. zicklen, 'to provoke'); comp. Essig, Fieber, Kabeljau, and Ziege. The Teut. root kit, kut, 'to tickle,' seems to have been coined anew in Teut. on an onomatopoetic basis; hence the OHG. variants chizzilôn, chuzzilôn. In cognate languages similar correspondences are formed anew; comp. Lett. kutêt, 'to tickle.' The subst. Kitzel, m., 'tickling,' first occurs in ModHG, and is formed from the vb.; comp. Handel.

klabastern, vb., 'to run noisily,' Mod HG. only; orig. a LG. term; in consequence of the entire absence of the word in the earlier periods of the languages its origin is dubious; it is most probably akin to OHG. klaphôn, MidHG. klaffen, 'to clatter'; AS. clappian, E. to clap.

Kladde, f., 'rough draft, day-book,' Mod HG. only, from LG. kladde, 'impurity, dirt,' then 'rough draft'; further details for the elucidation of the LG. word (comp. Materia) are wanting.

Klaff, m., 'crash, yelp, bark,' from MidHG. klaf (gen. klaffes) and klapf, m., 'report, crack,' OHG. klaph, m., anaklaph, 'shock'; MidHG. klaffen, klapfen, 'to ring, resound,' ûf kluffen, 'to break asunder, open, gape,' OHG. chlaphôn; Goth. *klappôn is wanting; AS. cluppian, E. to clap. 'Resounding' is the prim. meaning of the stem klapp, while 'cracking, bursting, gaping' is the derivative sense; comp. Klarp and Kleyben.

Klafter, n., m., and f., 'fathom,' from MidHG. klâfter, f., m., and n., OHG.

chláftra, f., 'length of the outstretched arms, fathom'; for a similar development of meaning comp. Ĝlle, Faben, also Spanne and Fuß. Goth. *kléftra or *kléftri, f., is wanting, so too the corresponding forms in the cognate languages. Its connection with AS. *clyppan*, E. *to clip*, 'to embrace,' Swiss χ*lupfel*, 'armful of hay' (Teut. root *klĕp*), makes it probable that the word is related to Lith. *glĕbti*, 'to encircle with the arms,' *glĕbys*, 'armful,' *glóbti*, 'to embrace' (root *glĕb*). The MidHG. variant *láfter* (*láhter*), f. and n., 'fathom,' is obscure.

Ālage, f., from the equiv. MidHG. *klage*, OHG. *chlaga*, f., 'complaint,' prop. 'a wail as an expression of pain'; wanting in all the early periods of the OTeut. languages except OHG.; adopted as a legal term in ModIc. in the form of *klöpun*. ModHG and MidHG. *klagen*, from OHG. *chlagôn*. The pre-Teut. root is probably *glak* or *glagh*; yet cognates are wanting.

Ālamm, m., 'spasm in the throat,' from MidHG. *klam* (gen. *klammes*), m., 'cramp, oppression, fetter'; corresponding to AS. *clom* (*o* before *m*, or rather *mm*, for *a*), m., f., and n., 'firm grip, talon, claw, fetter'; also OHG. *chlamma*, MidHG. *klamme*, f. ModHG. ſlemmen, 'to squeeze,' from MidHG. *klęmmen* (OHG. *bichlęmmen*), 'to seize with the claws, squeeze in, press together'; comp. AS. *beclęmman*, OIc. *klemma*.—ModHG. Ālemme, f., 'defile,' from MidHG. *klemme*, *klemde*, f., 'narrowness, cramping,' OHG. not yet found.

Ālammer, f., 'cramp, clamp, brace,' from the equiv. MidHG. *klammer*, *klamer*, *klamere*, f., OHG. *klamara*, f., is wanting; Scand. *klǫmbr* (gen. *klambrar*), f., 'vice,' and MidHG. *klamere* point to a Goth. *klamra* or *klamara*, f., which is connected with the Teut. root *klam*, 'to press together,' appearing in Ālamm. The equiv. MidHG. *klampfer*, f., and the ModHG. dial. forms Ālamper (Bav.) and Ālampfer (Carinthian) are abnormal; comp. also E. *clamp* and the equiv. Du. *klamp*, m.; the labial following the *m* presents some difficulties. Comp. the next word.

Ālampe, f., 'clamp,' not yet found in MidHG.; from LG.; comp. Du. *klamp*, 'cramp, cleats.' The strictly HG. form is Ālampfe (Bav., Austr.), 'cramp'; comp. Du. *klamp*, E. *clamp*, and the equiv. Scand. *klampi*.

Ālang, m., 'sound, clang,' from the equiv. MidHG. *klanc* (gen. *klanges*), m., with the variant *klanc* (gen. *klankes*), OHG. *chlang*; comp. Du. *klank*, m., 'clang, sound,' as well as E. *clank* and *clang*; AS. **clong*, **clonc*, are wanting, so too Goth. **klaggs* and **klagks*; comp. also MidHG. *klunc* (*klunges*), m., 'sound,' and *klinc* (*klinges*), m., 'tone, clangour.' The form *klank* with a final *k* is to be regarded perhaps like falʒen compared with falten, Bide with Biege, and Bitze with OIc. *kið* (comp. also *franf*), *i.e.*, *k* represents *kk* for Aryan *kn*; *glank* (or rather *glangh*) is perhaps the Aryan root of the Teut. cognates, unless we are tempted to regard Ālang (comp. flingen) as a new onomatopoetic word (comp. Gr. κλαγγή, Lat. *clangor*).

Ālapp, m., 'clap, slap, blow,' ModHG. only, adopted from LG., like its cognates (Ālappe, Flappen, Ālappe). Only flappern, vb., 'to clatter,' is current in MidHG. without any presumption of its being borrowed; perhaps it is onomatopoetic. ModHG. Ālapp, 'blow,' is phonetically MidHG. *klupf*, *klaf*, m., 'report, crack'; comp. Ālaff.

ſlar, adj., 'clear, bright; evident,' from MidHG. *klâr*, 'bright, pure, beautiful'; adopted in MidHG. from Lat. *clârus*; E. *clear*, MidE. *clér*, is borrowed from Fr. *clair*.

ſlaterig, adj., 'slovenly,' a LG. word; prop. 'dirty and wet' (of the weather), then used especially in a figurative sense; comp. LG. *klater*, 'dirt, dung,' allied to Ālabbe.

ſlatſch, 'clap,' onomat. interj., ModHG. simply; allied to onomat. cognates for 'to resound'; comp. Du. *kletsen*, 'to crack a whip,' E. *to clash*.

ſlauben, vb., 'to pick or dig out, cull,' from MidHG. *klûben*, OHG. *chlûbôn*, 'to pluck to pieces, cleave'; Goth **klûbôn* is wanting. The Teut. root *klûb* anciently formed another vb.; see flieben, under which further references are given.

Ālaue, f., 'claw, talon, fang,' from the equiv. MidHG. *kláwe*, *klâ*, OHG. *chláwa*, *chlôa*, f. (comp. Braue, from OHG. *brâwa*). The variants in MidHG. and OHG. render it difficult to determine the Goth. form; AS. *clâ*, *cleô*, *cleô* (plur. *clâwe*), *clawn* (d ?) are also difficult to explain phonetically; Goth. **klêwa*, f., is probable, although OIc. *klô* allows us to infer a graded form, **klôwa*, f. The common Teut. stem means

M

'claw,' but it is not found in the non-Teut. languages. The root is *klu*, pre-Teut. *glu* (comp. Ruäucl); OIc. *klá*, 'to scratch, shave,' based on a Teut *klah*, is scarcely connected with these cognates.

Klause, f., 'cell,' from MidHG. *klûse, klûs*, f., 'hermitage, cell,' also 'monastery,' OHG. *chlûsa*. MidLat. *clausa, clusa, clausum, closum*, with the meanings 'locus seu ager sepibus vel muris septus aut clausus,' also 'monastery'; hence the HG. word is based on *clusa*, which is a later participial form, due to *clâsus*, the partic. of the compounds of *claudere*, in place of the earlier *clausus* (comp. Ital. *chiusa*). On the other hand, MidHG. *klôse, klôs*, f., 'hermitage, monastery,' with the derivative *klôsenære*, 'hermit' (comp. MidLat. *clausarius*, 'monk,' but *clâsinariu*, f., 'virgo deo sacra reclusa'), is based on MidLat. *clausa, *clôsa* (comp. *clôsum*). The MidHG. meanings of *klôse, klâse*, 'rocky cleft, defile, ravine,' are connected with MidLat. *clâsa*, 'angustus montium aditus.' Comp. also Riefter, AS. *clús*, f., 'cell.'

Klausel, f., 'clause,' in use since the 15th cent., from Lat. *clausula*.

kleben, vb., 'to cleave (to),' from Mid HG. *k'ëben*, OHG. *chlëbên*, vb., 'to cleave, adhere, hold on' (for *ê* from Teut. and Aryan *î* comp. Queckſilber, leben, verweſen, &c.); corresponding to OSax. *clibôn*, AS. *cleofian*, E. *to cleave*; Goth. **klibôn* is wanting; Scand. *klifa* has only the figurative sense 'to cling to,' *i.e.*, 'to repeat.' A common Teut. vb. meaning 'to cleave (to),' formed from the weakest vowel stage of the Teut. root *klĭb* (see fleiben).

Klecks, Klechs, m., 'blot,' ModHG. simply; only the vb. flecten (flecken) may be traced further back, MidHG. *klecken*, 'to blot, stain, sputter,' also 'to strike sonorously'; the corresponding *klac (ckes)*, m., signifies 'rent, slit, crack.'

Klee, m., 'clover,' from the equiv. Mid HG. *klê* (gen. *k'ewes*), m., OHG. *chlê, chlêo* (gen. *chlêwes*), m. and n., based on *klaiw-* (see See, Schnee). The remaining LG. dials. have an extended form, in some cases only partially corresponding, AS. *clâfre, clâfre*, f., E. *clover*, Du. *klaver*, LG. *klever* and *klâver*, 'clover.' Perhaps these are based on some obscure compound. Except in the West Teut. languages, too, there are no terms cognate with HG. Klee; in Scand., Ic. *smári (smærur)*, Norw. and Swed. (dial) *smære* are used; Dan. *klöver* is borrowed.

Klei, m., 'clay,' ModHG. only, from LG. *klei*, 'slime, loam, moist earth,' allied to Du. *klei*, f., 'marsh soil, clay, loam'; comp. E. *clay*, from AS. *clǣg*. An assumed Goth. **kladdja*, f., may be connected with the root *klai*, by gradation *kli*, meaning 'to cleave (to),' which has a wider ramification in OTeut.; AS. *clâm* (from *klaim*), 'loam, clay,' E. (dial.) *cloam*, 'pottery,' OHG. *chleimen*, Scand. *kleima, klina*, 'to besmear'; comp. Rleifter and Rlein. It corresponds in the non-Teut. languages to Gr. γλοι, by gradation γλι; comp. γλοιός, 'oil lees, clammy stuff,' as well as γλίνη and γλιά, 'glue'; Lat. *glus, gluten*, with *ŭ* for older *oi*; OSlov. *glina*, 'clay,' *glěnŭ*, 'slime' (Lett. *glīwe*, 'slime'?). Further MidHG. *klěnen*, 'to cleave (to), spread over,' is connected with the Gr. and Slav. noun with the suffix *na*.

kleiben, vb., 'to stick, glue,' from Mid HG. and OHG. *kleiben*, 'to fix firmly, fasten,' prop. 'to cause to adhere or hold on'; a causative of the vb. *klīben*, obsolete in ModHG. and rarely found even in MidHG., OHG. *chlīban*, OSax. *biklīban*, 'to cleave, adhere.' OIc. *klifa*, 'to climb,' proves the connection of ModHG. flimmen (which see) with the root *klīb, klīf*, 'to cleave (to),' from pre-Teut. *glīp* (Teut. *f* in Swiss *xlefe*, 'box on the ear.'

Kleid, n., 'dress,' from the equiv. Mid HG. *kleit* (gen. *kleides*), n.; wanting in OHG. till the middle of the 12th cent.; hence the word is supposed to be borrowed from Du. *kleed*. Unknown orig. to OSax. also, as well as to Goth. and several AS. records (AS. *clâþ*, n., 'cloth, dress,' E. *cloth*; OIc. *klæþi*, n., 'stuff, cloth, dress'). The history of the word, which is more widely diffused in the modern Teut. languages, is obscure on account of the want of early references and the divergence of the earliest recorded forms, AS *clâþ*, n., and OIc. *klæði*, n. (the latter too has an abnormal *d* instead of *ei* for the Teut. *ai*). If the dental of AS. *clâþ* be regarded as derivative (Goth. **klai-þa*), we may infer from the AS. and OIc. meaning 'stuff, cloth' (AS. *cildclâþ*, prop. 'child's clothes,' with the special sense 'swaddling cloth'), a root *klai* signifying perhaps 'to weave.'

Kleie, f., 'bran,' from the equiv. Mid HG. *klîe*, usually plur. *klîen*, with the earlier variant *klîwen*, OHG. *chlīa, chlīwa*, plur. *chliwân*, f.; wanting in Goth., E., and Scand.; comp. further MidLG. *clîge*, Mod. Du. wanting; Swed. *kli*, 'bran.'

klein, adj., 'little,' from MidHG. *klein, kleine*, adj., 'clean, pretty, fine, prudent, slender, lean, little, insignificant'; OHG. *chleini*, 'pretty, shining, neat, careful, slight' (Alem. dials. point to an OHG. variant *chlîni). AS. *cléne*, adj., 'clean, neat,' E. *clean*, proves that 'pretty, clean,' is the prim. idea of the various senses of the Mid HG. word (comp. Schmach). Scand. *klénn* was borrowed at a late period from E., LG., or Fris. Goth. **klai-ni-* is wanting; the nasal belongs, as in several other adjs. (see rein and schön), to the suffix. It is uncertain whether the root is to be connected with Gr. γλοι-όs, 'greasy, sticky oil,' and its cognates, discussed under Klei (the meanings 'to shine, cleave (to)' interchange, e.g., in the root λιπ, Gr. λίπα, λιπαρέω, λίπος, λιπαρός). Gr. γλῆνος, n., 'wonders, ornaments,' and γλήνη, 'pupil (of the eye),' are, however, both on account of their forms and meanings, still less allied.—

Kleinod, n., 'jewel,' from MidHG. *kleinôt*, n., with the variants *kleinœte, kleinœde*, n., lit. 'fine, pretty thing,' then 'costliness, ornament,' not recorded in OHG.; *ôt* is a suffix (see Heimat, Armut, and Einöde). Hence the derivative has retained another feature of the earlier varied senses.

Kleister, m. and f., 'paste,' from the equiv. MidHG. *klîster*, m., with the equiv. variant *klênster* based on the vb. *klênen*; OHG. *chlîstar* and Goth. **kleistra-* are wanting; *stra* is a suffix, as in Laster; the stem *kli* is the root *klî*, by gradation *klai*, 'to cleave (to)' (discussed under Klei and Klein), which forms a vb. only in OHG., but it passes at the same time into the *e*-class, *chlênan*, 'to cleave (to), smear,' for *kli-na-n*, with *na* as a suffix of the pres., as in Lat. and Gr. (sper-ne-re, li-ne-re, δάκνειν, &c.); comp. MidHG. *klênen*, vb., Ic. *klîna*, 'to smear,' *klîningr*, 'bread and butter,' *klîstra*, 'to paste.'

klempern, vb., 'to tinkle,' ModHG. simply, allied to MidHG. *klamben, klampfern*, 'to clamp'; Klempner, 'tinker,' also ModHG. simply, allied to the equiv. MidHG. *klampfer*.

klengen, vb., 'to force the seeds from cones by heat,' from MidHG. *klengen, klenken*, 'to cause to ring'; factit. of klingen, which see; comp. henken, allied to hangen.

Klepper, m., 'nag,' early ModHG., orig. not in a contemptuous sense; a LG. form; it is connected with LG. *kleppen*, 'to strike rapidly' (espec. also 'to ring with a sharp sound'), MidHG. *klepfen*. Perhaps the term Klepper is derived from the bells on the harness of the horse.

Klette, f., 'bur,' from the equiv. Mid HG. *klêtte*, f., with the variant *klête*; OHG. *chlêtto*, m., *chlêtta*, f. (also OHG. *chlêta*). AS. *clipe, clâte*, f., E. *clotbur*, 'large bur'; further from the root *klîb*, 'to cleave (to), adhere' (comp. bleiben), the equiv. OHG. *chlîba*, AS. *clife*, MidE. *clive*, as well as MidDu. *klijve*, MidLG. *klive*; finally also ModDu. *klis*, f., 'bur.' OHG. *chlêtta* is the most closely connected with AS. *clipe*. It has been compared with Lat. *glis* (*ss*) as a cognate. From the G. word, OFr. *gleton, gletteron*, and ModFr. *glouteron* are derived. Comp. also the next word.

klettern, vb., 'to climb,' early ModHG only, probably allied to Klette, and derived like the latter from a root meaning 'to cleave (to)'; comp. kleben and klimmen. Akin to Du. *klauteren*, LG. *klâtern, klattern*, South Franc. *klôteren*, 'to mount, climb' (with an abnormal vowel and dental); root *klêt*?.

klieben, vb., 'to split,' from MidHG. *klieben*, OHG. *chlioban*, vb., 'to split, cleave'; corresponding to OSax. *clioban*, AS. *cleófan*, E. *to cleave*. From the correspondence of the other Teut. dials. we may assume Goth. *klûban, *kliuban, 'to split.' Under klauben a vb. from the same root *klûb*, by gradation *kleub*, 'to work with a sharp instrument,' has been discussed, to which is allied Gr. γλυφ (γλύφω, 'to hollow out, carve,' γλύφανος, 'chisel,' γλύπτης, 'carver'), perhaps also Lat. *glûbo*, 'to peel.' With the Aryan root *glûbh*, by gradation *gleubh*, Kleben, Kluft, and Kluppe are also connected.

klimmen, vb., 'to climb,' from a Mid HG. *klimmen, klimben*, OHG. *chlimban*, str. vb., 'to climb, mount'; corresponding to AS. *climban*, E. *to climb*. The nasal was orig. a part of the pres. stem; it did not belong to the root, as is proved by OIc. *klîfa*, vb., 'to climb.' As to the identity of *klimban* with OTeut. *klîban*, 'to cleave (to), hold firm,' comp. bleiben; hence klimmen is prop. 'to adhere.'

klimpern, vb., 'to clink,' ModHG. only, a new onomatopoetic term.

Klinge (1.), f., from the equiv. Mid HG. *klinge*, f., 'sword-blade'; the word, which is not recorded in OHG., is probably a derivative of Klingen (from the ringing sound made by the sword on the helmet).

Klinge (2.), f., 'ravine,' from MidHG. *klinge*, f., 'mountain stream,' OHG. *chlinga, chlingo*, m., 'torrent'; like **Klinge** (1), a derivative of Klingen.

klingeln, vb., 'to ring,' from MidHG. *klingelen*, OHG. *chlingilôn*, vb., 'to sound, roar, splash,' dimin. and frequent. of Klingen.

klingen, vb., 'to sound,' from MidHG. *klingen*, OHG. *chlingan*, str. vb., 'to sound, resound'; corresponding to Ic. *klingja*, 'to ring.' E. *to clink* has adopted the same final stem sound (*k* for *g*), which the subst. *clank*, connected with it by gradation (comp. **Klang** and **Klenken**), has always had. The stem, like the derivative **Klang** (comp. also **Klinge, Klinke**, and **Klenken**), is common to Teut., but on account of the non-permutation it cannot be cognate with Gr. κλαγγή, Lat. *clangor*. Both roots are independent onomatopoetic forms in each separate language.

Klinke, f., 'latch,' from MidHG. *klinke*, f., 'bolt of a door'; allied to Klingen.

Klinse, Klinze, f., 'cleft,' from Mid HG. *klinse, klimse*, and with a different stage of gradation *klunse, klumse, klumze*, f., 'slit'; OHG. *chlumuʒa, chlimuʒa*, is wanting. Origin obscure.

Klippe, f., 'cliff,' from the equiv. Mid HG. (Lower Rhen.) *klippe*, f., borrowed from MidDu. *klippe*; comp. Du. *klip*; allied to a Teut. root *klib*, as is shown by OIc. *k'eif*, n., 'cliffs'; comp. also AS. *clif*, n., E. *cliff*, OIc. *klif*, n., OSax. *klif*, OHG. *klëb*, n., all pointing to a Goth. **klif, klibis*, n., 'rock, hill.' They have been connected with Ic. *klífa*, vb., 'to climb' (see under **kleiben**), but on account of the prim. meaning 'to cleave (to),' this is scarcely satisfactory.

klippern, vb., 'to click,' ModHG. only, a recent onomatopoetic term.

klirren, vb., 'to clash,' ModHG. only, a recent onomatopoetic term.

Kloben, m., 'log of wood, block, pulley,' from MidHG. *klobe*, m., 'log of wood with a slit to act as a vice, fetter, stick with a slit for catching birds, bolt, slit,' &c.; OHG. *chlobo*, m., 'stick for catching birds'; allied to Klieben, MidHG. *klieben*, vb., 'to split, cleave' (comp. Begen, allied to biegen). OLG. *klobo*, m., 'fetter'; OIc. *klofe*, m., 'crevice in a rock, door joint'; Du. *kloof*, f., 'slit, rift, cleft.' Comp. **Knoblauch**.

klopfen, vb., 'to knock,' from MidHG. *klopfen*, OHG. *chlopfôn*, wk. vb., 'to knock, rap'; Goth. *kluppôn is not warranted by corresponding forms in the other OTeut. dials.; comp. also Du. *kloppen*. Further, OHG. *chloechôn*, MidHG. *klocken*, 'to knock,' which are not indubitably allied to klopfen. With the latter the cognates discussed under **Klaff** are connected by gradation, and these point to a Goth. *kluppôn, 'to strike.'

Kloster, m., 'monastery,' from the equiv. MidHG. and OHG. *klôster*, n., borrowed on the introduction of Christianity from MidLat. and Rom. *claustrum* (Ital. *chiostro*, Fr. *cloître*), 'monastery'; comp. **Klause**.

Kloß, m., 'clod, dumpling,' from Mid HG. *klôʒ*, m. and n., 'lump, bulb, clew, bullet, pommel of a sword, wedge,' OHG. *chlôʒ*, m., 'ball, round mass, bowl (at play)'; corresponding to MidLG. *klûte*, Du. *kloot*, m., 'bullet, ball.' AS. *cleát, E. *cleat*, 'wedge' (Ic. *klót*, 'pommel of a sword,' has an abnormal *ó* for *au*, which indicates that the word has been borrowed, unless it is cognate with Lat. *glâdius*). Goth. **klauta-* is wanting; the Teut. root *klut* appears also in the following word.

Kloß, m. and n., 'block, log, stump,' from MidHG. *kloz* (gen. *klotzes*), m. and n., 'lump, bullet,' hence equiv. to MidHG. *klôʒ*; AS. *clot, E. *clot*; we may therefore assume Goth. **klutta-*, the relation of which to *klauta-*, mentioned under **Kloß**, is evident. In the non-Teut. languages the Teut. root *klut* ('bale'?), adduced under **Kloß**, has not been definitely authenticated; a root *glud* appears in Lith. *gludus*, 'clinging to,' *glausti*, 'to cling to.'

Klucke, Glucke, f., 'clucking hen,' from MidHG. *klucke*, f., 'brood hen,' allied to MidHG. and ModHG. *klucken* (*glucken*). Comp. AS. *cloccian*, E. *to cluck*, Du. *klokken*. The Teut. cognate, *klukk*, is of onomatopoetic origin; comp. the phonetic cognates, Lat. *glôcîre*, Gr. γλώζειν, 'to cluck.'

Kluft, f., 'chasm,' from MidHG. *kluft*, f., 'cleft, chasm, cave, vault, tongs,' OHG. *chluft*, f., 'tongs, shears,' prop. 'splitting' (as a verbal abstract of the OTeut. *kliuban*, 'to split,' discussed under Klieben). The tongs, as an instrument with a slit, is called dial. **Knift**; comp. **Kluppe**. The Mid HG. meaning 'vault' (*crypta*) seems to be due to a confusion of **Kluft** with the foreign word *crypta* (see **Gruft**). Goth. **klufti-*, f.;

AS. *clyft, E. cleft, clift; Du. kluft, f., 'cleft, notch, chasm.'

klug, adj., 'knowing, prudent, shrewd,' from MidHG. *kluoc (g)*, 'fine, pretty, tender, superb, brave, polite, prudent, sly'; in OHG. not recorded, whether by chance or no is not known. It is thought to have been borrowed from LG., although the word in the non-HG. languages has a final *k*, LG. *klôk*, Du. *klock*, 'prudent, brave, great, corpulent' (not found in E.; Scand. *klôkr*, 'prudent, cunning,' is supposed to be a G. loan-word). No clue to an etymological explanation of the adj. can be discovered.

Klumpe, Klumpen, m., 'clump, lump,' ModHG. only; from the equiv. LG. *klamp*, Du. *klomp*, m.; comp. E. *clump*. Scand. *klumba*, f., 'club,' with a different labial, also a variant *klubba; klubbu-fótr*, whence the equiv. E. 'club-foot.' Further references have not been discovered. Comp. Kolben.

Klüngel, n., 'clew,' from MidHG. *klüngel*, *klüngelin*, OHG. *chlungilîn*, n., 'clew,' dimin. of OHG. *chlunga*, f., 'clew'; if *ng* be a suffix, as in jung, the word may be allied to Knäuel, OHG. *chliuwa* (root *klu*, Aryan *glu*), in which case it would be brought into connection with other terms; it is, however, more probably allied to E. *to cling*, from AS. *clingan*, 'to cling to, hold fast, adhere.'

Klunker, f., 'clot, tassel,' ModHG. only; allied to MidHG. *klungeler*, 'tassel,' *glunke*, f., 'dangling curl,' *glunkern*, 'to swing, dangle.'

Kluppe, f., 'pincers,' from MidHG. *kluppe*, f., 'tongs, barnacles, splinter,' OHG. *kluppa*, f., 'tongs.' Kluppe, like Mod HG. Kluft (dial.) 'tongs,' is also derived from OTeut. *kliuban*, 'to split, cleave'; unfortunately correspondences in other dialects are wanting (Goth. *klubjô ?). Comp. klieben, klauben, and Kluft.

Knabe, m., 'boy, lad, youth,' from MidHG., late OHG. *chnabo*, m., 'boy'; also 'youth, fellow, servant,' with the originally equiv. variants, ModHG. Knappe, MidHG. *knappe*, OHG. *chnappo* (OHG. *chnabo* and *chnappo* are related like Rabe and Rappe). AS. *cnapa*, OSax. *knapo*, and OIc. *knapc*, 'attendant, squire,' present some difficulties compared with AS. *cnafa*, E. *knave*. Equally obscure is the relation of the entire class to the root *ken*, Aryan *gen* (Lat. *genus*, *gi-gn-o*, Gr. γένος, γι-γν-ομαι, &c.), with which some etymologists would like to connect it; if it were allied, OHG. *chnëht* (kn-ëht) also might perhaps be compared.

knacken, vb., 'to crack,' from MidHG. *knacken*, *gnacken*, 'to split, crack,' wanting in OHG.; E. *knack*, MidE. *cnak*, 'crack,' Ic. *knakkr*; ModHG. Knack, 'crack,' Mid HG. not yet found. To the same root OIc. *knoka*, AS. *cnocian*, E. *to knock*, formed by gradation, seem to belong. The words are based on an imitative root which is peculiar to Teut.

Knall, m., 'sharp report, explosion,' ModHG. only; allied to MidHG. *er-knëllen*, 'to resound.' Comp. AS. *cnyll*, *cnell*, m., 'signal given by a bell,' E. *knell*.

Knan, Knän, m., 'father,' from Mid HG. *genanne*, *gnanne*, from *genamne*, prop., 'of the same name' (for MidHG. *ge-* comp. gleich and Geselle), 'namesake.' Used even in MidHG. by sons addressing their father or grandfather.

knapp, adj., 'scanty,' ModHG. only; wanting in MidHG. and OHG.; probably from LG., for *gehnapp*. Comp. OIc. *hneppr*, 'narrow.'

Knappe, m., 'squire, attendant,' from MidHG. *knappe*, m., 'youth, bachelor, servant, squire,' OHG. *chnappo*, m.; in the rest of the OTeut. languages there are no cognates pointing to Goth. *knabba*; two variants of the assumed *knabba* are mentioned under Knabe, where the further etymological question is discussed. Comp. also Rabe with Rappe, Goth. *laigân*, 'to lick,' with AS. *liccian*.

knappen, vb., 'to make scarce, hobble, nibble,' ModHG. only, from Du. *knappen*, 'to eat, lay hold of quickly.'—**Knappsack**, 'knapsack,' from Du. *knap-zack*, 'saddle-bag,' whence probably also E. *knapsack*.

knarren, vb., 'to creak,' from MidHG. *knarren*, *gnarren*, 'to creak, snarl'; a recent onomatopoetic term like knirren and knurren.

Knaster, m., 'best tobacco,' borrowed at the beginning of the 18th cent. from Du. *knaster*, *kanaster*, m., 'canister tobacco,' which comes from Span. *canastro*, 'basket' (comp. Lat. and Gr. *canistrum*, κάναστρον).

Knäuel, m. and n., 'clew,' from Mid HG. *kniuwel*, *kniulîn*, *kniul*, n., 'small clew or ball'; the *n* by differentiation represents *l* on account of the final *l* (see Kuckuck); MidHG. *kliuwel*, *kliuwelîn*, dimins. of MidHG. *kliuwe*, n., 'clew, ball';

OHG. *chliuwelin*, dimin. of *chliuwa*, *chliwa*, f., 'ball, clew'; AS. *cleówe*, *clýwe*, n., MidE. *cleewe*, E. *clew*; also AS. *cleówen*, *clíwen*, n., like MidG. *kláwen*, Du. *kluwen*, 'skein.' OHG. also *kliwi*, *kliuwi*, n., MidHG. *kliuwe*, n., 'clew.' A richly developed nominal stem peculiar to West Teut.; the Goth. form is probably *kliwi (kliujis), n. or *kliujô, n.; the root *klû*, by gradation *klêu*, appears also perhaps in Klaue (Goth. *klêwa), which in that case was so called from its contracting; comp. Lat. *gluere*, 'to contract,' *glûma*, 'husk,' also Sans. *glâus*, 'bale,' hence Aryan root *glu*. Lat. *glôbus* and *glômus* are not connected with this word.

Knauf, m., 'button, pommel,' from MidHG. *knouf*, m, 'pommel (of a sword), pinnacle,' also a dimin. *knoufel*, *knöufel*, m., OHG. *chnouf* not recorded; Goth. *knaups is also indicated by Du. *knoop*, m., 'button, knob.' A Goth. graded form *knupps may likewise be inferred from the cognates discussed under Knopf, which see.

Knauser, m., 'niggard,' ModHG. only, probably from MidHG. *knûz*, 'impudent, daring, haughty (towards the poor).'

Knebel, m., 'branch, peg, moustache, knuckle,' from MidHG. *knebel*, m., OHG. *knebil*, 'crossbeam, girder, crossbar, cord, fetter, knuckle'; Du. *knevel*, m., 'packing-stick'; Scand. *knefill*, m., 'stake, stick'; Goth. *knabils is wanting. Considering the relation of Goth. *nabala, m., 'navel,' to Gr. ὀμφαλός, we may assume for Goth. *knabils, a root *gombh (goubh) in the non-Teut. languages (comp. γόμφος, 'plug, nail, wedge'; this word, however, is usually connected with the cognates of ModHG. Ramm).—It is still doubtful whether Knebel in Knebelbart '(twisted) moustache,' first recorded in ModHG. and borrowed from LG. and Du., is of a different origin, i.e. connected with AS. *cenep*, OFris. *kenep*, OIc. *kanpr* (Goth. *kanipa-), 'moustache,' MidDu. *cane/been*, 'cheek-bone.'

Knecht, m., 'servant,' from MidHG. *knëht*, OHG. *chnëht*, m., 'boy, youth, fellow, man, squire,' often also 'hero'; comp. AS. *cniht*, m., 'boy, youth, man capable of bearing arms, hero,' E. *knight*; probably a West Teut. word, unknown to Goth. and Scand. (Dan. *knegt* and Swed. *knekt* are borrowed). The same variety of meanings in West Teut. words is found in Knabe and Knappe (comp. also AS. *mago*, 'son, boy, man, champion,' see too Kerl). However probable its close connection with Knabe and Knappe may be, yet it is not possible to define it strictly. Knecht is more probably allied to the root *ken*, from Aryan *gen* (Lat. *genus*, γένος, Lat. *gi-gn-o*, γίγνομαι), than Knabe, because a suffix -*ëht* exists in Teut.

kneifen, vb., 'to nip,' ModHG. only, a phonetic rendering of LG. *knipen*, adopted by the written language. Comp. kneipen.

Kneipe, f., 'pincers, gripes,' ModHG. only, of obscure origin; its cognate relation to kneipen can only be assumed, since an older connecting link between it and Kneipe, 'tavern,' is wanting; orig. Kneipe was a low tavern. Is it related to Du. *knijp*, f., 'narrowness, embarrassment'? or rather Du. *knip*, m., 'bird-snare, brothel'?

kneipen, vb., 'to pinch,' early ModHG., orig. LG. *knipen* (see also kneifen); Du. *knijpen*, 'to nip, twitch'; probably not allied to AS. *hnípan*, *hnipian*, 'to bow,' but to a root *hnîp*, 'to nip,' not recorded in OTeut., from which also MidE. *nipen*, E. *to nip*, are derived; *kn* initially may be explained from *gahnípan. The pre-Teut. root *knîb* appears in Lith. *knibti*, 'to pick, pluck,' *knebti*, 'to nip.' If the E. word is unconnected with Du. *knijpen* on account of the initial sound, we might assume a root *knib, gnib* (Lith. *gnýbti*, 'to nip,' *gnýbis*, 'nip'), though this too is not recorded in OTeut.

kneten, vb., 'to knead,' from the equiv. MidHG. *knëten*, OHG. *chnëtan*; comp. Mid LG. and Du. *kneden*, 'to knead,' AS. *cnëdan*, MidE. *cneden*, E. *to knead*; a Goth. *knidan, or rather *knudan (comp. treten), 'to knead,' may be assumed; Scand. has only a wk. *knoða*, pointing to Goth. *knudan. Since HG. *t*, LG., E., and Goth. *d* may have originated in *t* owing to earlier positions of the accents (comp. Vater, AS. *fæder*, with Lat. *pater*, Gr. πατήρ), *gnet* may be regarded as the pre-Teut. root. Comp. OSlov. *gnetą*, *gnesti*, 'to crush, knead.'

knicken, vb., 'to crack,' ModHG. only; from LG. *knikken*, 'to burst, split, crack'; E. (dial.) *to knick*, 'to crack.'

Knie, n., 'knee,' from MidHG. *knie*, *kniu* (gen. *knies*, *kniewes*), OHG. *chniu*, *chneo* (gen. *chnëwes*, *chniwes*), n., 'knee'; comp. Du. *knie*, f., AS. *cnëó* (gen. *cneowes*), n., MidE. *cnee*, E. *knee*; Goth. *kniu* (gen. *kniwis*), n., 'knee'; a common O. and Mod Teut. word with the prim. meaning 'knee,' which also belongs to the allied Aryan words; *genu-*, *gonu-*, *gnu-* are the Aryan stems of the word; comp. Lat. *genu*, Gr. γόνυ (comp. γνυ-πετεῖν, γνύξ, *gnóa*), Sans. *jánu*, n., 'knee' (*abhijñu*, 'down to the knee,' *jñu-bādh*, 'kneeling'). This Aryan stem *gnu* had when declined the variant *gnew-*, which appears extended in Teut. by the *a* of the *a*-declension, Goth. *kniwa*-. The shorter Teut. form *knu-*, Aryan *gnu-*, has been retained in Goth. *knu-ssus (inferred from *knussjan*, 'to kneel'), 'kneeling' (the suffix *-ssus* is current in Goth.), and probably also in OIc. *knūe*, m., 'knuckle' (presupposing Goth. *knuwa, m.); there are also some abnormal *l*-derivatives, MidE. *cnélien*, E. *to kneel*, Du. *knielen*, and Swiss *chnü'e*, 'to kneel.'

Sniff, m., 'pinch,' ModHG. only, allied to ſneifen; Du. *kneep*, f., 'pinch, pinching.'

Snirps, m., 'pigmy,' ModHG. only, a MidG. word, by syncope from *knürbes, *knirbes* (comp. LG. *knirfix*, Lower Rhen. *knirwes*). MidE. *nûrvel*, *nirvel* (AS. *cnyrfel?), 'pigmy,' are formed with a different dimin. termination. Allied to Suab. *knorp*, 'pigmy'; and to Du. *knorf*, 'knot'?.

knirren, vb., 'to creak,' from MidHG. *knirren*, 'to jar.' A recent imitative word.

knirſchen, vb., 'to gnash,' MidHG. *knirsen, may be inferred from *knirsunge*, f., 'gnashing,' and *zerknürsen*, 'to crush, squash'; for *sch* from *s* after r comp. Hirſch and Arſch; comp. ModDu. *knarsen*, *knersen*, 'to gnash, crash,' *knarsetanden*, 'to gnash with the teeth.'

kniſtern, vb., 'to crackle,' from Mid HG. *knisten, on which the noun *knistunge*, f., 'gnashing,' is based; an onomatopoetic formation.

Sniffelvers, m., 'doggerel,' ModHG. only; Knittel for Knüttel, 'cudgel.' E. *staff*, in the sense of 'stick,' and also 'verse, strophe, stanza,' may be adduced as an approximate parallel. The Dutchman Junius says of the refrain in Du. popular songs, 'In vulgaribus rhythmis versum identidem repetitum scipionem aut baculum appellant'; the Romans had *versus rhopalici*, the Scandinavians the *stef*.

kniffern, vb., 'to rumple,' ModHG. only; an imitative word.

knobeln, vb., 'to fillip,' ModHG. only, allied to a widely diffused dial. form *knöbel* (UpG.), *knöwel* (MidG. and LG.), 'joint,' espec. of the fingers.

Knoblauch, m., 'garlic,' from MidHG. *knobelouch*, m., with the orig. variant *klobelouch*, m., OHG. *chlobolouh*, *chlofolouh*, *chlo-*

volouh, m.; with regard to *b* for *f*, comp. Schwefel; the *kn* of the MidHG. and Mod HG. words may be explained as in Knäuel by a process of differentiation, *i.e.* the *l* of the next syllable produced the change of the first *l* into *n*; comp. ModDu. *knoflook* and MidLG. *kloflôk*. In the ordinary explanation of 'cleft leek' no regard is paid to the fact that the first part of the compound, which is identical with ModHG. Rleben, appears elsewhere in the Teut. group, AS. *clufe*, E. *clove* (of garlic), AS. *clufþung*, 'crowfoot,' *clufwyrt*, 'buttercup.'

Knöchel, m., from the equiv. MidHG. *knöchel*, *knüchel*. m., 'knuckle'; dimin. of Knochen, MidHG. *knoche*; AS. *cnucel*, Mid E. *knokil*, E. *knuckle*, and the equiv. Du. *knokkel*.

Knochen, m., 'bone,' from MidHG. *knoche*, m., 'bone, knot of a branch, fruit capsule.' The ModHG. word, almost unknown to Luther, rarely occurs in MidHG., and is entirely wanting in OHG. (Bein is the genuine UpG. and HG. word for Knochen, which again is orig. native to the MidG. and LG. dialects.) Knochen is, however, proved by the corresponding dimin. Knöchel to be a good OTeut. word; Goth. *knuqa, m., may be assumed. It is still uncertain whether it is connected with E. *to knock*, AS. *cnucian*, OIc. *knoka*, MidHG. *knochen*, 'to cuff,' or is related to OIc. *knūe*, 'knuckle,' which would favour its further kinship with Knie. From *knuqa, UpG. Knocke, 'snag, knot,' MidHG. *knock*, 'nape,' may be derived; their *ck* correctly represents the old *q*. Allied words with final *g* in the stem are, however, obscure, MidHG. *knögerlin*, 'little knot,' and MidHG. *knügel*, 'knuckle.'

Snocke, f., 'bundle, bunch,' ModHG. only, from LG. *knocke*; proved to be a genuine OTeut. word by AS. *cnycće, Mid E. *knuecche*, 'bundle' (*e.g.* 'bundle of hay'), E. *knitch*, 'faggot'; Goth. *knuka, or rather *knukja, m., are wanting.

Knödel, m., 'dumpling,' from MidHG. *knödel*, m., 'seed-bud, dumpling'; dimin. of MidHG. *knod-*, 'knot,' discussed under Knoten.

Knollen, m., 'clod, bulb,' from Mid HG. *knolle*, m., 'clod, lump'; OHG. *chnollo, m., is wanting. With the Mid HG meaning are connected AS. *cnoll*, m., E. *knoll*; Du. *knol*, 'turnip.'

Knopf, m., 'button, knob, pommel,' from MidHG. and OHG. *knopf*, m., 'protuberance on plants, bud, pommel of a sword, knot, loop'; comp. AS. *cnopp, m., E. knop, 'button, bud'; Du. knop, 'bud, button, knot on plants.' Goth. *knuppa- is wanting; under Knauf its graded form Goth. *knaupa- was assumed, which would represent *knauppa-, for the stem loses its final b, as is shown in MidHG. knübel, m., 'knuckle,' as well as AS. *cnobba, MidE. knobbe, E. knob; comp. also ModDu. knobbel, m., 'knot, bulb, weal,' and HG. Knubbe. Besides the words hitherto adduced, from which we may infer an old u root (comp. especially Knauf), there are some abnormal forms, OIc. knappr, 'button, pommel,' AS. cnæp, MidE. knap. Comp. Knospe, Knubbe, Knüpfen, and Knüppel.

Knorpel, m., 'gristle,' from MidHG. knorpel-, knorbel-, bein knospel, 'cartilage.' It cannot be certainly decided whether the word is based on a Goth. knuzba- or *knaûrba-; the former is the more probable for grammatical reasons; ModDu. knobbel, ModLG. knusperknaken, 'cartilaginous bone.'

Knorre, m., 'knotty excrescence,' from MidHG. knorre, m., with the equiv. variant knûre, m., 'knot, protuberance' (on trees, the body, &c.); knûre also signifies 'rock, cliff, summit'; in the sense of 'cuff, push,' it is connected with MidHG. knûsen (from *knusjan), 'to push, strike.' For the other meanings too we must probably proceed from a Goth. word with s (z), as the dial. forms indicate, Suab. Knaus, 'knob on a loaf,' Swiss knus, 'knot, excrescence.' E. knar, 'knot in wood,' MidE. knarre, with the variant knorre, 'knot, excrescence.'— OHG. has only the adj. chniurig, 'knotty, stout, firm,' derived from *knûr.—Comp. Knospe and Knust.

Knorz, m., 'snag,' from MidHG. and OHG. knorz, 'excrescence, knot'; Dan. knort, Swed. knört. Allied to the preceding word?.

Knospe, f., 'bud,' from MidHG. knospe, m., 'protuberance'; the modern meaning is one of the varied senses in earlier Mod HG.; 'protuberance' is the prim. signification, hence it is natural to connect Knospe etymologically with Knopf; the latter is to be represented in Goth. by *knuppa-, the former by *knuspan- for *knufspan-; in that case -span would be a suffix; *knuspan- may, however, stand for *knusspan-, and be connected with the root knus appearing in Knorre.

Knoten, m., 'knot,' from MidHG. knote, knode, m., 'natural knot (on the body and plants). artificial knot in a thread, noose'; OHG. chnodo, chnoto, m. (the OHG. and MidHG. doublets with t and d appear in Knote and Knödel even as late as ModHG.). Allied to AS. cnotta, m., E. knot, with differently related dentals; comp. OIc. ú-knytter, 'dirty tricks,' and Mid HG. knotze, f., 'protuberance'; E. to knit, AS. cnyttan, LG. (Voss) kniitte, f., 'knitting-needles,' &c. OIc. knûtr, m., 'knot,' knûta, f., 'dice'; they are related to AS. knotta, like Goth. *knaupa- to *knuppa- (comp. Knauf and Knopf), and just as a form with a in the stem (AS. cnæpp) is connected with these words, so is OIc. knttr (Goth. *knattus), m., 'ball,' related to the cognates of Knoten. No indubitably allied term can be adduced from the other Aryan languages. Comp. also Knüttel.

Knöterich, m., 'knot-grass'; found only in ModHG.

Knubbe, Knuppe, m., 'knot in wood,' ModHG. only; from LG. knubbe, the cognates of which see under Knopf. We may also mention MidHG. knübel, to which Stumpf is related, as Hauben to Klumpe.

Knuffen, vb., 'to cuff,' wanting in the earlier periods; of obscure origin.

Knüpfen, vb., from the equiv. MidHG. knüpfen, OHG. knupfen, 'to unite, tie, fasten together' (Goth. *knuppjan is wanting); a nominal vb. from Knopf, which see; MidHG. knopf, 'knot.'

Knüppel, m., 'wooden bar, stick, cudgel,' from LG.; in MidHG. knüpfel, m., 'cudgel,' was used. It is connected with MidHG. knopf, 'knot on plants.' See Knopf.

Knust, Knaust, m., 'crusty piece of bread,' prop. 'protuberance,' especially 'corner of a loaf,' from LG.; t is a suffix; for knûs- in the sense of 'knot,' see under Knorre.

Knute, f., 'knout,' ModHG. only; borrowed from Russ. knut; comp. Peitsche.

Knüttel, m., from the equiv. MidHG. knüttel, knüttel, OHG. chnutil, m., 'cudgel,' prop. 'stick or string with knots'; allied to Knoten.

Kobalt, m., 'cobalt,' ModHG. only; of uncertain origin, probably equiv. to Kobold.

Koben, m., 'hovel,' from MidHG. kobe, m., 'stable, pigsty, cage'; the ModHG. variant Kofen is derived, as the f indicates, from LG. The word had orig. a more general sense, and was not restricted merely to a shed for animals and pigs. Even in Mod HG. the earlier meaning 'hut' is found; comp. MidHG. *kobel*, 'narrow house'; Ic. *kofi*, m., 'hut, penthouse, partition.' In AS. the corresponding *cofa* is specially used as a choice poetic term for 'apartment, bed-chamber'; hence E. *cove* and *pigeon-cove*. Goth. *kuba, on which these words are based, is wanting. The word is genuinely Teut., as is proved by OHG. *chubisi* (Goth. *kubisi), 'hut', which, from its form, is a derivative of a far earlier period; comp. also MidHG. *kober*, 'basket, pocket,' AS. *cofl*, 'basket.' See Kobelb and Kübel.

Kobold, m., 'goblin,' from MidHG. *kóbolt*, with the variant *kobólt*, m., 'fantastic familiar spirit, goblin.' As the genuinely Teut. household deities, the Kebelbe may be regarded as equiv. to the AS. *cofgodu*, *cofgodas*, 'penates, lares' (unfortunately AS. *cofold or *cofweald, 'household deity,' lit. 'protector of the bed-chamber,' is not recorded); in Goth. probably **kubawalda-*. The first component is OIc. *kofe*, AS. *cofa*, 'apartment, chamber' (see Kieben). The MidHG. and ModHG. variants Oppelt and Opelt may have been *ôtwalt, Goth. *audawald, 'Lord of wealth'; the old *ôt*, 'wealth,' has been retained only in proper names like Ottekar, Otfried (Eduard, E. *Edward*). For the ending felb see under Herelb and walten.

Koch, m., 'cook,' from the equiv. Mid HG. *koch*, OHG. *choh(hh)*; comp. Du. and OSax. *kok*, 'cook'; adopted before the HG. permutation of consonants, at latest in the 6th cent. (contemporaneously with Küche), when the art of cookery and horticulture were introduced from Italy; the word is based on Lat. *coquus*, or more accurately on the form *koko-* (comp. Ital. *cuoco*). The word passed into E. in a different form—AS. *côc*, E. *cook*, where the *ô*, compared with HG. and Lat. *ŏ*, is due to a change of quantity in an open syllable (comp. Schule and Kuchen); on the other hand, the *ô* of the HG. word is probably derived from the vb. fochen. The earlier Teut. word for fochen is fieben; an OTeut. word for 'cook' is wanting.—fochen, 'to cook,' from the equiv. Mid HG. *kochen*, OHG. *chohhôn*, from Lat. *coquere* (more accurately *coquĕre ?). The HG. word could not remain a str. vb., because the vowel of the stem differed from the analogy of verbs of that class. In Rom. note Fr. *cuire*, Ital. *cuocere*. Comp. also Kuchen.

Köcher, m., 'quiver,' from MidHG. *kocher*, OHG. *chohhar*, m., 'quiver,' yet also generally 'receptacle' with the variants, MidHG. *kochære*, OHG. *chohhári*, MidHG. *koger*, *keger*, with an abnormal *g* apparently in harmony with the obscure OIc. *kǫgurr* ('quiver' ?), preserved only in *kǫgursweinn*, *kǫgurbarn*; OIc. *kǫgurr*, 'quilted counterpane, coverlet,' is an entirely different word, and is connected with a remarkable G. form Köcher, 'cover.' AS. *cocur*, MidE. *coker*, 'quiver'; also in MidE. and E. *quiver*, from OFr. *cuivre*, which is again derived from the Teut. word (Teut. *kokro-*, whence MidLat. *cucurum*, 'quiver').

Köder, m., 'bait.' The word, on account of its very varied forms and senses, is difficult to explain etymologically, perhaps several words, originally different, have been combined with it; MidHG. *kŏder*, *koder*, *kĕder*, *korder*, *kŏrder*, *kĕrder*, *quĕrder*, m., 'lure, bait, patch of cloth or leather,' OHG. *quĕrdar* also means 'wick of a lamp'; in ModHG. it signifies, in the various dialects and at different periods, 'double chin, slime, rag, leather strap, bait.' With Köter, 'double chin,' we may perhaps compare E. *cud*, AS. *cudu*, *cweodu* (Goth. *qipus*, 'belly' ?). With the meaning 'bait,' Goth. *qairrus* and HG. firre may be most closely connected, because *quĕrdar*, as the oldest HG. form, points to a Goth. **qairþra-*; with this the Gr. compound δέλεαρ (δελ- for δερ- may be due to a process of differentiation, since a G. form *kerdel* occurs; and δ, according to Æol. βλῆρ, is perhaps an old guttural, root *ger*) may be certainly associated, and its variant δέλετρον, which more nearly corresponds with the G. word; the latter form is usually approved, since it combines the meanings of 'bait' and 'torch' (corresponding to OHG. *quĕrdar*, 'wick'); in either case E. *cud* is abnormal. For the other meanings of the G. word no satisfactory etymologies can be found.

Koffer, m., 'trunk,' MedHG. only, from Fr. *coffre*.

Kohl, m., 'cabbage,' from the equiv. MidHG. and OHG. *kôl*, m., with the variants OHG. *chôli*, MidHG. *kœle*, *kœl*, m. (comp. Alem. *chœl*, *kœl*), as well as OHG. *chôlo*, *chôlo*, m., MidHG. *kôle*, *kœle*, *kôl*, and

OHG. *chóla*, f. Adopted with the South Europ. culinary art and horticulture from Lat. *caulis*, m., 'cabbage'; E. *cole;* MidE. *caul, coul,* AS. *cáwl,* as well as OIc. *kál,* n., point to Lat. *caulis,* whence also Ital. *cavolo,* Fr. *chou,* 'cabbage,' and W. *cawl.* The 'apparently vernacular' Lat. *cólis* would have left no trace in the history of language if the MidHG. forms *kŏle, kŏl,* with a short accented syllable, were not derived from it. Most of the G. varieties of fruits and vegetables may have been introduced into Germany with the art of cookery in the 6th or 7th cent.; comp. Eppich, Fenchel, Pfeffer, Minze, Pflaume, and Kirsche.

Kohle, f., 'coal, charcoal,' from the equiv. MidHG. *kole,* f., mostly *kole, kol,* m., and *kol,* n., OHG. *cholo,* m., *chol,* n.; comp. AS. *col,* n., E. *coal* (E. *colemouse,* see under **Kohlmeise**), OIc. *kol,* n. plur., 'coals.' Akin to the deriva. OIc. *kylna,* f., 'kiln,' AS. *cylne,* E. *kiln,* as well as Swed. *kylla,* 'to heat.'

Kohlmeise, f., 'coalmouse,' from Mid HG. *kŏlemeise,* f., allied to **Kohle,** not to **Kohl;** lit. 'titmouse with a black head'; AS. *cólmáse,* E. *colemouse* (a corruption of *coalmouse,* just as the Germans instinctively connect **Kohlmeise** with **Kohl**).

Kohlrabi, m., 'turnip-cabbage,' from Ital. *cavoli rape* (plur.); comp. Fr. *chourave,* Germanised **Kohlrübe.** For further references see **Rübe.**

Kolben, m., 'club,' from MidHG. *kolbe,* 'mace, club, cudgel,' OHG. *cholbo,* m.; Ic. *kólfr,* m., 'javelin, arrow, bulb,' with the derivative *kylfi,* n., *kylfa,* f., 'club, cudgel.' Goth. **kulba-n-,* 'stick with a thick knob at the end.' From its meaning the word seems to be related to the cognates with the nasal form *klumb,* discussed under **Klumpen;** in that case the Aryan root may be *gl-bh,* and the word compared with Lat. *globus,* 'round mass' (also 'clique,' comp. E. *club*).

Kolk, m., 'deep pool,' LG.; Du. *k·lk,* m., 'eddy, abyss, hole.' Comp. Sans. *gárgara,* m.; yet according to Lat. *gurges,* 'eddy, whirlpool, abyss,' Teut. *r* and not *l* ought to correspond to Ind. *r.*

Koller (1.), n. and m., 'lady's ruff,' from MidHG. *koller, kollier, gollier, goller,* n., 'neckcloth,' derived from Fr. *collier* (Lat. *collarium*).

Koller (2.), m., 'staggers,' from Mid HG. *kolre,* m., 'staggers, frenzy, silent rage,' OHG. *cholero,* m.; derived, like a number of medical terms, mediately from Gr. χολέρα, Lat. *cholera;* the *ch* has also in Rom. the value of a *k;* comp. Ital. *collera,* Fr. *colère.*

Koller, m., 'coverlet,' from MidHG. *kolter, kulter,* m., f., and n., 'quilted counterpane,' from OFr. *coultre* (comp. Ital. *colíra*); for further references see **Kissen.**

kommen, vb., from the equiv. MidHG. *komen,* OHG. *chuĕman,* 'to come,' a common Teut. vb. The proper form of the initial *k* is *qu,* as is proved by ModHG. *bequem,* and hence OHG. *quĕman·* is the base; the *w* of an initial *kw* is frequently suppressed in HG. (comp. *feď* and *furr*) before *e* and *o* (not before *a*). Goth. *qiman,* AS. *cuman,* E. *to come,* OSax. *cuman,* OIc. *koma.* The prim. Teut. vb. *qeman,* 'to come,' thus deduced has a remoter history; it is identical with the Ind. and Zend root *gam,* 'to come,' and allied to Lat. *vĕnio* for **gvĕmio,* Gr. βαίνω for **βanjw* (for **gvĕmiō*); comp. **bequem** and **Kunft.** The assumed Aryan root is *gem,* The evolution of a *v* after the *g* is normal; comp. Goth. *qinō* with Gr. γυνή and Ind. *gnā* (**gánā*), 'woman'; Goth. *qiws-,* Lat. *vivus* (Gr. βίος, subst.), Ind. *jivá* (see **feď,** comp. the similar evolution of a *kv* akin to Teut. *hw* from Aryan *k* under **wer** and **welcher**).

Komtur, m., 'commander of an order of knighthood,' from MidHG. *kommentiur, komedûr,* m., from OFr. *commendeor* (Lat. *commendator*), 'commander, holder of an estate belonging to a priestly order.'

König, m., 'king,' from the equiv. Mid HG. *künic, künc (g),* OHG. *chunig, chuning;* corresponding to OSax. *cuning,* AS. *cyning (cyng),* E. *king,* Du. *koning,* OIC. *konungr;* a common Teut. term, wanting only in Goth. The high antiquity of the term is attested by its being borrowed at an early period by Finn. and Esth. as *kuningas,* 'king,' by OSlov. as *kŭnęgŭ, kŭnęzĭ,* 'prince,' Lith. as *kùningas,* 'lord, pastor ' (Lett. *kungs,* 'lord '). The word may be most probably explained by connecting it with Goth. *kuni* (gen. *kunjis*), OHG. *chunni,* MidHG. *künne,* AS. *cynn,* 'family.' Regarding *-ing* as a patronymic (AS. *Wódening,* 'son of Woden'), the meaning would be 'a man of family,' *i.e.* of a distinguished family, 'ex nobilitate ortus'(Tacitus, *Germ.* vii.). This simple and satisfactory explanation is opposed by the fact that in OTeut. *kuni-* alone means 'king,' which has been preserved especially in compounds such as AS. *cyne-helm,* 'king's helmet,' *i.e.* 'crown,' *cynestól*, 'king's seat,' *i.e.* 'throne,' *cynerice*, equiv. to OHG *chunirthhi*, 'kingdom,' &c.; the simple form is perhaps found only in OIc. poetry as *konr* (*i*-stem), 'man of noble birth, relative of the king.' In tracing the evolution in meaning, this fact can no more be rejected than the former; in this case too König would contain the essential idea of distinguished birth, but perhaps more accurately 'the son of a man of distinguished birth'; comp. Fr. and E. *prince*, signifying both Prinz (male member of the royal family) and Fürst (a sovereign ruler, and also a title next above Count). The etymological connection between E. *king* and *queen* must be discarded, since the latter signified 'woman' generally; yet it is of some value in illustrating the development of meaning in the word König; AS. *cwén* is espec. 'the noble lady.'

können, pret. pres., 'to be able,' from MidHG. *kunnen*, OHG. *chunnan*, pret. pres. (sing. *kan*, plur. *kunnum*, pret. *konsta*), prop. 'to be capable intellectually, know, be acquainted with, understand,' then also 'to be able, be in a position (to).' AS. *cunnan* (sing. *can*), pret. pres., 'to be acquainted with, know, be able,' E. *can*; Goth. *kunnan* (sing. *kann*, plur. *kunnum*), pret. pres., 'to be acquainted with, know.' In the earlier periods the verbal stem fönnen had exclusively an intellectual sense in contrast to that of mögen, vermögen. Besides the stem *kann*- preserved in the vb. *kunnan* (comp. also Goth. *kunnan*, 'to recognise,' AS. *cunnian*, 'to explore, attempt,' see also Kunst, fund, fennen), there exists in the OTeut. languages a verbal stem which may be represented in Goth. as *knê*, *knô*; AS. *cnáwan*, 'to recognise, know,' E. *to know*; OHG. *irchnáan*, *bichnáan*, 'to recognise'; OHG. *úrchnát*, f., 'perception' (Goth. *knêps*, f., is wanting); the OHG. nominal vb. *irchnuodilen*, 'to become perceptible,' points to a Goth. *knôpla*-, 'knowledge.' The three Teut. stems *kann*, *knê*, *knô* occur in the non-Teut. languages, Gr. and Lat. *gnô* in γιγνώσκω (ἔ-γνω-ν), 'to recognise,' γνῶσις, 'knowledge,' Lat. *gno-sco*, *nô-tus*, *nô-tio*; OSlov. *znajq*, *znati*, 'to recognise'; OIr. *gnáth*, 'acquainted.' Ind. forms a pres. from a root *jan*, the pret. from a root *jnâ*, *jánâmi*, *jajnáu* (comp. part. *jnátá*), 'to know'; the Teut. root *kann* from *gen-n* appears in Lith. *žinaú*, 'to know, recognise, perceive,' *pa-žintis*, 'knowledge,' Zend *á-zaiñti*, f., 'information,' OIr. *ad-géin*, perf.,

'cognovit.' This wide ramification of the closely allied Aryan root *gen*, *gnô*, 'to recognise, know,' is generally recognised, but its connection with the root *gen*, 'to beget, bring forth,' and the variants *gnâ*-, *gnî*-, discussed under Kind, König, and fennen, is problematical. Both seem to be united in AS. *cennan*, 'to bring forth,' and 'to generate,' Gr. γνωτός, 'related by blood,' and 'discernible, known.' The distinction, however, between the physical and intellectual senses of the word must have been made previous to the division of languages, since it exists in all the Aryan groups. Comp. fühn.

Kopf, m., 'head,' from MidHG. *kopf*, m., 'drinking vessel, cup, pint measure, skull, head'; OHG. *choph*, *chuph*, m., 'goblet'; AS. *cuppa*, E. *cup*; Scand. *koppr*, m., 'crockery in the form of cups.' This class is one of the most difficult to explain. Haupt, E. *head*, is certainly the real Teut. and earlier term for Kopf, and only in ModHG. has the latter finally supplanted the former. The numerous senses of the cognates further involves us in doubt, although analogies may be adduced in favour of the evolution of the notion 'head' from an earlier meaning 'cup'; comp. OIc. *kolla*, f., 'pot,' *kollr*, m., 'head'; ModHG. Hirnschale; Ital. *coppa*, 'cup,' and Prov. *cobs*, 'skull'; Fr. *tête*, from Lat. *testa*; Goth. *hwaírni*, 'skull,' allied to AS. *hwér*, 'kettle,' Du. *hersen-pan*, 'skull,' MidE. *herne*-, *brainpanne*, 'skull,' allied to Pfanne, 'pan'; Du. *hersen-becken*, 'skull,' allied to Becken, 'basin.' Thus in fact the ordinary assumption might be allowed to stand, according to which the entire class is based on MidLat. *cuppa* (Ital. *coppa*), 'cup,' Lat. *cûpa*, 'cask.' There are, however, cognate terms in Teut. which induce us to proceed, not from Lat. *cûpa*, 'cask,' but from a prim. Teut. word meaning 'point, summit,' AS. and MidE. *copp*, 'summit, point,' MidE. also 'head,' E. *cop* (for the evolution in meaning comp. Giebel, allied to Gr. κεφαλή, dial. Dach, 'roof,' for Kopf); OSax. *coppod*, 'cristatus' of serpents, is also worthy of note. The Teut. origin of the word Kopf in its ModHG. sense is also supported by the fact that OHG. *chuppha*, MidHG. *kupfe*, f., 'head-dress,' evidently connected with Kopf, is necessary to explain some Rom. cognates—Ital. *cuffia*, Fr. *coiffe*, and MidLat. *cofea*, are derived from OHG. *chuppha*. Besides, Lat. *cûpa*, *cuppa*, as a fem. is not well adapted in form to explain the Teut. masc., especially since *koppa-* (Goth. **kuppa-* is certainly wanting) had already too wide a ramification in the OTeut. languages. But in any case, it is conceivable that the assumed genuine Teut. word was confused at an early period with a MidLat. and Rom. term, and thus incorporated a number of foreign meanings. Comp. Kuppe.

Koppe, see Kuppe.

Koppel, f. and n., 'leash,' from MidHG. *koppel, kopel, kuppel,* f. (m. and n.), 'tie, connection,' especially 'leash,' then collect. 'pack of hounds,' also 'band' generally; from Lat. *copula,* MidLat. also *cupla* (the latter also 'couple of hounds in a leash'), whence also Fr. *couple,* E. *couple,* Du. *koppel,* 'couple, multitude, troop.'

Koralle, f., 'coral,' from MidHG. *koralle,* m., formed from MidLat. *corallus,* Lat. *corallium.*

Korb, m., 'basket,' from the equiv. Mid HG. *korp* (*b*), OHG. *chorp, korb* (gen. *korbes*), m.; comp. Du. *korf,* m., 'dosser.' The usual derivation from Lat. *corbis* is opposed by phonetic considerations, and also by the fact that nouns equiv. in meaning but with differently graded forms also occur; according to ModHG. Brett and its gradation Bord (which see), MidHG. *krêbe,* m., 'basket,' and hence further ModHG. Krippe may also be connected with Korb (comp. too ModIc. *karfa,* f., and *körf,* f., 'basket' ?). It is not impossible that, in addition to an inherited OTeut. word, the Lat. term was borrowed at a later period; OHG. *churib,* plur. *churbī,* points perhaps to Lat. *corbis* (E. *corb*); further ModHG. Ren (1) seems to be an old cognate of Lat. *corbis.*

Korde, Kordel, f., 'cord, tow-line,' ModHG. only, from Fr. *corde, cordelle;* comp. Du. *koord,* f., and the equiv. E. *cord,* from the same Rom. source, ultimately derived from Lat. and Gr. *chorda.*

Koriander, m., 'coriander,' ModHG. only, from Lat. *coriandrum;* in MidHG. *koliander, kullander, kollinder,* from Mid Lat. *coliandrum.* Comp. Du. *koriander* and E. *coriander.*

Korinthe, f., 'currant,' early ModHG. only, from Fr. *corinthe.*

Kork, m., 'cork,' early ModHG. only, through the medium of Du. (*kork, kurk,* n., 'corkwood, cork, stopper') and LG. commerce, from Span. *corcho,* 'corkwood, stopper,' whence also E. *cork* at an early period. The ultimate source is Lat. *cortex,* 'bark.'

Korn, n., 'grain, corn,' from MidHG. *korn,* OHG. *chorn* (gen. *chornes*), n., 'corn' (in MidHG. also 'grape-stone, corn-field, corn-stalk'). Goth. *kaúrn,* n., with the variant *kaúrnō,* n.; OIc. *korn,* AS. and E. *corn,* Du. *koren;* common Teut. stem *korna-* meaning 'single grain,' then also 'stone' and 'fruit.' For the meaning 'stone' comp. OHG. *berikorn,* MidHG. *wīn-, trūben-korn,* 'stone of a berry'; OHG. *korn-* and *kërnapful* (AS. *cornæppel*), 'malum punicum, calville,' are interchangeable; for the derivative AS. *cyrnel,* E. *kernel,* see under Kern. Thus it is probable that there exists a close connection between Kern and Korn, their phonetic relation being similar to that between Brett and Bord; for further examples of gradation in nouns, see under Korb. Another graded form of Korn, from pre-Teut. *grnó-m,* is furnished by Lat. *grānum,* 'grain, core'; see Hirse, equiv. to Lat. *crates;* vell, equiv. to Lat. *plēnus,* OIr. *lán. Grnō* is exactly the same as OSlov. *zrŭno,* n., 'grain.'

Kornelle, f., 'cornel-cherry,' even in OHG. *cornul, cornul-baum,* from MidLat. *cornolium* (Fr. *cornouille,* Ital. *corniolo*); a derivative of Lat. *cornus,* f., 'cornel-cherry'; comp. AS. *corntreó,* E. *cornelian-tree.*

Körper, m., 'body, substance, carcass,' in the MidHG. period (13th cent.) *korper, körpel, körper,* m.; borrowed from Lat. *corpus,* or more accurately from the stem *corpor-,* a prim. cognate of which exists in OTeut. from the same source (Aryan *krp*), OHG. *hrêf,* AS. *hrif,* 'womb.' Leich (see Leichnam) is the OTeut. word for ModHG. Leib and Körper. "The sacrament of the Church and the elevation of the Host, and perhaps medical art, led to the naturalisation of the Lat. word."

koscher, kauscher, adj., 'pure,' Med HG. only, from Jew. Chald. *kāschēr,* 'pure, according to prescription.'

kosen, vb., 'to chat, caress,' from Mid HG. *kôsen,* OHG. *chôsôn,* 'to converse, talk.' The meaning of the vb. is opposed to any connection with OHG. *chôsa,* 'lawsuit,' and Lat. *causa, causari,* for it nowhere shows an indication of a legal origin; Mod Fr. *causer,* 'to chat,' is also derived from G., since in Lat. *causa,* Fr. *chose* originated. As a native word kosen (Goth. **kausôn*) is of uncertain origin; it is certainly connected, however, with AS. *cedst,* MidE. *cheeste,* 'argument, dispute,' Du. *keuzelen,* 'to caress.'

Kossat, see Kot (1).

Koſt (1.), f., 'cost,' from MidHG. *koste kost*, f. and m., 'value, price, expense,' even in OHG. *kosta*, f.; borrowed in the OHG. period from MidLat. *costus*, m., *costa*, f. (comp. Ital. *costo*, m., Fr. *coût*, m., Span. *costa*, f.; ultimate source Lat. *constare*, 'to come to, cost'). From Rom. are derived MidE. *costen*, E. *to cost*, whence Scand. *kosta*, 'to cost.'

Koſt (2.), f. (in the 16th cent. also m.), 'board,' from MidHG. *koste, kost*, f., 'living, food, victuals'; comp. Scand. *kostr*, m., 'victuals, provisions.' In Scand. as in the G. word, the meanings of (1) and (2) overlap; at all events (2) is a later development of (1). We must certainly assume that the Scand. loan-word *kostr*, 'expense, victuals,' was confused with an OTeut. word which would be most closely connected with Goth. *kustus*, m., 'trial, proof,' and *gakusts*, 'test'; OIc. *kostr*, m., 'choice, condition, circumstances.' With regard to these nouns see **fieſen**.

koſten (1.), vb., 'to cost,' from MidHG. *kosten*, 'to come to, cost'; from MidLat. and Rom. *costare* (Lat. *constare*); Fr. *coûter;* see **Koſt** (1) and (2); E. *to cost.*

koſten (2.), vb., 'to taste,' from MidHG. 'to scrutinise, test by tasting'; OHG. and OSax. *costôn*, AS. *costian* (wanting in E.); a common Teut. vb. meaning 'to put to the test, scrutinise, try.' **Koſten**, like the Teut. words mentioned under **Koſt** (2), is connected with **fieſen**, and is identical in form with Lat. *gustâre*, 'to taste.' Teut. *kus*, pre-Teut. *gus*, is the root. Comp. **fieſen**.

koſtſpielig, adj., 'expensive,' first used towards the end of the 18th cent.; it contains, however, an old word which has elsewhere disappeared, and even in this compound has been corrupted; MidHG. *spildec*, 'extravagant'; OHG. *spilden*, 'to squander, dissipate' (from OHG. *gaspilden*, Fr. *gaspiller* is derived). Hence *kostspildig is probably 'squandering money'; *spildig*, which was etymologically obscure, was corrupted into *ſpielig*.

Kot (1.), **Kote**, f., 'cot'; prop. a LG. word; LG. *kote, kot*, Du. *kot*, 'hut'; corresponding to AS. *cot*, n., and *cote*, f., 'hut'; from the former E. *cot* is derived (E. *cottage* is the same word with a Rom. suffix; comp. MidLat. *cotagium*, OFr. *cotage*), from the latter came *cote* in *dove-cote* and *sheep-cote;* comp. Scand. *kot*, n., 'small farm.' Goth. *kut, n., or *kutô, f., is wanting. The widely ramified class is genuinely Teut., and passed into Slov. (OSlov. *kotĭcĭ*, 'cella') and Kelt. (Gael. *cot*). Rom. words have also been derived from it—ModFr. *cotte, cotillon*, Ital. *cotta*, all of which denote some article of dress, though this sense does not belong to the Teut. word (E. *coat*, at all events, is probably derived from Rom.). The Teut. word means only 'apartment, hut, room of a house'; *gudo-* is perhaps the pre-historic form.—**Kotſaſſe**, also by assimilation **Koſſaſſe, Koſſat, Koſſe**, 'person settled in a small farm'; also spelt **Kötter**.

Kot (2.), m., 'dirt, mire, dung,' from the equiv. MidHG. *kôt, quât, kât*, n., OHG. *quât;* Goth. **qêda-*, 'dirt,' is wanting. Prop. neut. adj.; MidG. *quât*, ModDu. *kwaad*, 'wicked, ugly, rotten' (MidE. *cwêd*, 'bad'). **Unflat** and **Harst** are in the same way veiled terms for *stercus*. In its pre-Teut. form *guêtho*, **Kot** might be related by gradation to Ind. *gûtha*, Zend *gûtha*, 'dirt, excrementa,' so that the Teut. subst. may have been formed from the adj. even in pre-historic times; the Sans. and Zend word seems, however, to be connected with the Ind. root *gu*, 'cacare' (OSlov. *govĭno*, n., 'dirt').

Kote, Köte, f., 'pastern joint,' Mod HG. only, from LG. *kote;* comp. ModDu. *koot*, Fris. *kate*, f., 'knuckle-bone.' No other cognates are found.

Köter, m., 'cur,' prop. 'farmer's dog,' allied to LG. *kote*, 'small farm.' See **Kot** (1).

Kotze, f., 'coarse cloth,' from MidHG. *kotze*, m., 'coarse, shaggy woollen stuff, cover or garment made of it,' OHG. *chozzo*, m., *chozza*, f.; comp. OSax. *cot (tt)*, 'woollen cloak, coat'; a specifically G. word, wanting in Goth., Scand., and E. The Rom. words mentioned under **Kot** (1)— Fr. *cotte*, 'petticoat,' Ital. *cotta*—seem to have been borrowed from G., since in OHG. other words belong to the same class, OHG. *umbichuzzi*, 'upper garment,' *umbichuzzen*, vb., 'amicire.' On the assumption that **Kotze** is a genuine Teut. word, some have connected it with Gr. βεῦδος (from the root *gud*), 'woman's dress.' MidE. *cote*, E. *coat* are certainly of Rom. origin, OFr. *cote*, MidLat. *cotta*. Comp. **Kutte**.

Kötze, f., 'basket,' from the equiv. MidHG. *koetze;* of obscure origin; comp. **Kieſe**.

fol𝔷en, vb., 'to vomit,' first occurs in early ModHG.; of uncertain derivation.

Krabbe, f., 'crab,' borrowed, like most words with medial *bb*, from LG.; comp. MidLG. *krabbe*, Du. *krab*, AS. *crabba*, E. *crab*, Scand. *krabbi*; the strictly HG., i.e. permutated, form Krappe, appears in the 16th cent., yet the word was native only to the maritime Teutons. Krebs is from a cognate stem, but Gr. κάραβος, Lat. *carabus*, 'sea-crab,' are neither prim. allied, nor are they the forms from which the Teut. words were borrowed. Fr. *crabe*, 'crabfish,' is most closely connected with the Teut. and with the Lat. word.

krabbeln, vb., 'to crawl,' with LG. permutation, in contrast to MidHG. *krappeln*, of which the variant *krabelen* occurs, whence also earlier ModHG. *frabeln*. The form with a double labial may be due to its being popularly connected with Krabbe (Krappe), for in Scand. also a simple form is found without this double labial, Scand. *krafla*, 'to scratch with the nails,' and *krafsa*, 'to shuffle with the feet.' E. *grabble*, *grapple*, *grab* are connected with LG. and Du. *grabbeln*.

krachen, vb., 'to crack, crash, break,' from the equiv. MidHG. *krachen*, OHG. *chrahhôn*; comp. Du. *kraken*, 'to crack (nuts, &c.), burst, crack, crackle,' AS. *cracian*, E. *to crack*; Goth. *krakôn is wanting. AS. *cearcian*, 'to crack' (Goth. *karkôn), is worthy of note; comp. respecting the apparent transposition of the *r*, Brett and Bord, fragen and forschen. Teut. root *krk* from *qrg*; comp. Sans. *grg, garj*, 'to rustle, crackle.'—**Krach**, m., from the equiv. Mid HG. *krach*, OHG. *chrah*, 'crack, crash.'

krächzen, vb., 'to croak,' ModHG. only, a deriv. of frachen; in MidHG. *kroehzen*, OHG. *chrocchezan*, 'to croak,' which is related by gradation to the stem of frachen. From AS. *cracian, cracettan* was formed, like ModHG. frächzen, from frachen.

Kracke, f., 'sorry nag,' ModHG. only, of obscure origin. Perhaps akin to Du. *kraak*, Fr. *caraque*, 'clumsily built merchant ship'?.

Kraft, f., 'strength,' from MidHG. *kraft*, OHG. *chraft*, f., 'strength, power, force of an army, multitude, abundance'; comp. OSax. *craft*, m. and f., Du. *kracht*; AS. *cræft*, m., with the HG. meanings, also 'mental capacity, art, science,' hence E. *craft* (the corresponding *crafty* shows prominently the last specialisation of meaning within the mental sphere); OIc. *kraptr*, m., 'strength.' ModIc. *kræfr*, 'strong,' exhibits the stem without the dental suffix; yet OIc. *krefja*, 'to beg, demand, challenge,' as well as AS. *crafian*, E. *to crave*, seems, on account of its meaning, not to be connected with the subst. No certain cognates are found in the non-Teut. languages.

kraft, prep., 'in virtue of,' prop. dat. sing. of the preceding word, originally combined with the preps. *aus* or *in*. Mid HG. *kraft*, with the gen. of a noun, is often simply a pleonasm for the noun itself— *hôher wunne kraft* for *hôhiu wunne*, 'great bliss'; *az zornes kraft*, 'in anger.'

Kragen, m., 'collar,' from MidHG. *krage*, m., 'neck' (of men and animals), also 'nape,' then further, 'article worn round the neck, collar'; wanting in OHG., OSax., AS., and OIc. MidE. *crawe*, E. *craw*, 'crop' (of birds), point to AS. *craga; E. variant *cray*, 'neck, nape,' dial. also 'crop'; ModIc. *kragi*, m., 'collar,' is of G. origin. Goth. *kraga*, m., 'neck, throat,' is wanting. Further references are uncertain; Gr. βρόγχος, 'windpipe,' may be allied, since its initial β may represent *g* (grogho-, gronyho-); comp. also βρόχθος, 'gullet, throat.' MidHG. *krage* is also used personally as an abusive term, 'fool'; hence ModHG. Geizkragen, 'niggard.'

Krähe, f., 'crow,' from the equiv. Mid HG. *krêe* (rare), f. (usually *krâ* and *krâwe*, f.), OHG. *chrâia, chrâwa*, and *chrâ*, f.; comp. Du. *kraai*, OSax. *krâia*, f., AS. *crâwe*, f., E. *crow*; a West Teut. word allied to frähen, which was orig. a str. vb. The Scand. term *kráka*, f., 'crow,' cannot be immediately connected with the cognates adduced; it is only very remotely allied.

krähen, vb., 'to crow,' from the equiv. MidHG. *kræn, kræjen* (pret. *kráte*), OHG. *chrâen*, vb.; corresponding to AS. *crâwan* (pret. *creôw*), E. *to crow*, and the equiv. Du. *kraaijen*; a specifically West Teut. vb., in Goth. *hrûkjan*. That it was not orig. used of the cock alone is attested by the etymology of Krähe, and also by the compounds, OHG. *hanachrât*, OSax. *hanocrâd*, AS. *hancrêd*, 'cock-crow, crowing.' The Teut. stem. *krê-, krêw* may be connected with OSlov. *graju, grajati*, 'to croak,' and Lith. *gróju, gróti*, 'to croak.'

Krahn, m., 'crane' (machine), Mod HG. only, formed from LG. and Du.; prop. identical with Kranich, of which it is a shorter form; see Kranich. Gr. γέρανος also means 'crane'; comp. too Lat. *aries*, HG. **Bod**, as well as Lat. *grus*, as terms for machines.

Krakeel, m., 'uproar,' ModHG. only; comp. Du. *krakeel*; of obscure origin.

Kralle, f., 'claw, talon, clutch,' Mod HG. only; wanting in the earlier periods. Allied to Gr. γράω, 'to gnaw,' Sans. root *gras*, 'to devour'?. MidHG. *krellen*, 'to scratch' (Goth. **krazljan*?), is more closely connected.

Kram, m., 'retail trade,' from MidHG. *krâm*, m., prop. 'stretched cloth, marquee,' espec. 'covering of a stall,' then the 'stall' itself (also called *krâme*, f.), 'trade wares'; corresponding to Du. *kraam*, f., 'retail shop, wares,' then, strangely enough, 'child-bed,' which must have originated in the meaning 'stretched cloth,' as the covering for the bed. A specifically G. word introduced into the North by commerce (Ic. *kram*, n., 'wares,' Lith. *krômas*). 'Tent-cloth' may have been the prim. meaning of Goth. **krêma-*.

Krammetsvogel, m., 'fieldfare,' from MidHG. *kramat(s)vogel, krambitvogel, kranewitvogel*, m., 'fieldfare,' prop. 'juniper bird.' The juniper in MidHG. is *kranewite, kranwit (kramwit, kramat)*, OHG. *chranawitu* (prop. 'crane-wood'), from *krana*, 'crane,' mentioned under **Krahn** and **Kranich**, and OHG. *witu*, 'wood' (note the similarity in the E. word); comp. E. *craneberry, cranberry*, from *crane*.

Krampe, f., 'staple, cramp,' from LG., since we should have expected *pf* in HG.: comp. Du. *kram* for *kramp*, 'hook, clamp,' E. *cramp*, also *cramp-irons*; OHG. *chrampf*, 'hook.' From the Teut. cognates, which are based on the adj. **krampa-*, discussed under **Krampf**, Fr. *crampon*, 'cramp,' is derived; see the next word.

Krämpe, f., 'brim of a hat,' ModHG. only; from LG. *krempe*, allied to the OHG. adj. *chrampf*, 'curved' (OIc. *krappr*, 'close, narrow'); OHG. *chrampf*, quoted under **Krampe**, combines the meanings 'hook' and 'border, brim.'

Krämpel, f., 'carding-comb,' borrowed from LG., but it occurs even in the Mid HG. period; dimin. of **Krampe**, 'hook.'

Krampf, m., 'cramp, spasm, convulsion,' from the equiv. MidHG. and OHG. *krampf* (OHG. also *chrampfo*); comp. OSax. *cramp*, Du. *kramp*, f., E. *crump*; the common West Teut. term for 'cramp'; orig. an adjectival subst. from OHG. *chrampf*, 'curved,' OIc. *krappr* (normal for **krampr*), 'narrow, pressed close.' The Teut. stem *krampa-* has numerous cognates in G.; besides the LG. loan-words *krampe, krämpe, krämpel*, we may mention OHG. *chrampf*, 'hook, border,' *chrimpfan*, MidHG. *krimpfen*, 'to contract in a crooked or spasmodic fashion,' MidHG. *krimpf*, adj., 'crooked' masc. subst. 'cramp'; ModHG. *frumm* is also allied, as is indicated by its OHG. and MidHG. variant *krumpf*, 'bent, twisted.' Comp. *frumm*, and OHG. *chrimpfan*, Mid HG. *krimpfen*, 'to be convulsed,' ModDu. *krimpen*, 'to draw in, shrivel,' MidE. *crimpil*, 'wrinkle,' *crumbe*, 'hook,' *crumpe*, 'crump,' E. *to crimple*, 'to contract,' &c.; OIc. *krappr*, 'narrow,' and its nominal vb. *kreppa*, 'to compress.' Comp. **Krüppel** and **Krapfen**.

Kranich, m., from the equiv. MidHG. *krenech (krenich)*, n., OHG. *chranuh, chranih (hh)*, m., 'crane' (bird); also without the guttural suffix, MidHG. *krane*, which agrees with the MidG., LG., and E. forms (Du. *kraan*, f., 'crane'—bird, and then machine; AS. *cran* and *cornuc*, E. *crane* in both senses). In the Scand. languages, OIc. *trane*, m., 'crane,' seems to be connected with these. The suffix *ch* in ModHG. is Goth. *k* in *ahaks*, 'pigeon,' AS. *hafoc*, '*habicht*' (hawk). The corresponding words for 'crane' in the other West Aryan languages (prim. form *ger-w*) are the most closely allied—Gr. γέρανος, Kelt. and W. *garan*; also OSlov. *žeravl*, Lith. *gérwė*, f., Lat. *grus* (gen. *gru-is*), corresponds to OHG. *chreia*, 'crane.' The derivation of Gr. γέρανος, from γεράσκω, root *ger*, 'to grow old,' as if the crane were remarkable for its great age, is open to objection. Further, the crane is one of the few names of birds (see **Drossel**) in which several Aryan stems coincide. Comp. also **Krahn** and **Krammetsvogel**.

kraŋf, adj., 'sick, ill,' from MidHG. *kranc (k)*, adj., 'narrow, slender, slight, powerless, weak, null' (in OHG. not yet found). The earliest references are in the first half of the 12th cent., therefore *franf* is most frequently regarded as a LG. loanword; but the late appearance of the word cannot be accepted as a proof of its having been borrowed, since this is not supported by its form, which may be derived from an OTeut. source; comp. OHG. *chrancholôn*, 'to grow weak, stumble'; AS. *cranc*, 'feeble, infirm,' also occurs rarely. For the further history of the word we must at all events proceed from the latter meaning (ſich is the OTeut. adj. for 'sick'); Scand. *krankr*, 'sick,' is borrowed from G. (**krakkr* must have been the native form); a genuine Scand. *krangr*, 'feeble,' also occurs. The common West Teut. adj. *kranka-* is connected with AS. *cringan*, lit. 'to writhe like one mortally wounded, fall in fight, fall with a crash' (thus closely allied in meaning to AS. *cranc*, 'infirm, tottering'). With the same root *kring*, *krink*, are connected ModHG. Kring, 'circular pad for the head,' E. *crank, to crankle, crinkle*.— **kränken**, 'to make ill,' from MidHG. *krenken*, 'to torment, grieve,' prop. 'to lessen, humiliate.'

Kranz, m., 'wreath,' from the equiv. MidHG. and late OHG. *kranz*, m.; a specifically HG. word, which in this form has passed within historic times into other Teut. languages (Ic. *krans*, Du. *krans*). Perhaps allied to Sans. *grunth*, 'to tie (a knot), bind,' *granthi-s*, m., 'knot,' or even with Lith. *grandis*, m., 'bracelet, tyre of a wheel' (Lett. *grùdi*, 'wood for framing,' from the base **grandai*).

Kräppel, Kräpfel, dimin. of Krapfen.

Krapfen (1.), **Krappe**, m., from the equiv. MidHG. *krâpfe* (MidG. *krâpe*), m., 'a kind of pastry, fritter'; OHG. *chrâpfo*, m., orig. identical with the following word; so called from the hooked form of the pastry.

Krapfen (2.), m., 'cramp, hook, dungfork,' from MidHG. *krâpfe, krâpe*, m., 'hook, cramp,' OHG. *chrâpfo*, 'hook,' also 'claw, talon'; the Goth. form **kræppa* is wanting, nor is the word found in the other Teut. languages; before the HG. permutation of consonants it passed in the form *grappo, grapo* into Rom. (Ital. *grappa*, 'cramp, talon,' Fr. *grappin*, 'grapnel'). Comp. further E. *craple*, 'claw, talon.' It is doubtful whether OHG. *chrâcho* (Goth. *krékka*), m., 'hooked instrument,' and Scand. *kraki*, m., 'stake,' are allied. The stem of Krapfen appears in a nasal form in OHG. *champf*, 'curved,' and OHG. *champfa, chrampho*, m., 'iron hook' (comp. Fr. *crampon*, 'cramp,' borrowed from OHG.). Consequently Krapfen is connected with Krampf.

Krätze (1.), f., 'dosser,' from MidHG. *krezze*, also *kratte*, m., 'basket'; OHG. *chrezzo* and *chratto*, m., 'basket.' Perhaps the word is allied, on account of the Mid-HG. variant *krenze*, with Kranz. On the other hand, OHG. *chratto* and MidHG. *kratte* suggest AS. *cradol*, E. *cradle*, and also Du. *krul*, AS. *cræt*, E. *cart* (orig. 'cartbasket'?), E. *crate*. With Gr. κάρταλλοι, 'basket,' these cognates cannot be connected.

Krätze (2.), f., 'itch,' from MidHG. *kretz, kratz*, allied to Fratzen.

kratzen, vb., from the equiv. MidHG. *kratzen, kretzen*, OHG. *chnazzôn*, 'to scratch' (allied to Scand. *krota*, 'to dig in,' Goth. *gakrutón*, 'to grind'); previous to the HG. permutation of consonants **kratton*, whence Ital. *grattare*, Fr. *gratter*, 'to scratch.' Comp. kritzeln.

krauen, vb., 'to tickle,' from the equiv. MidHG. *krouwen*, OHG. *chrouwôn, krouwen*; Goth. **kraujón*, or rather **kragguón*, and other correspondences are wanting. With this vb. is connected OHG. *chrouwil*, MidHG. *kröuwel*, m., 'three-pronged fork, talon, claw,' to which Swiss and ModHG. Kräuel, 'fork with hooked prongs'; comp. Du. *kraauwel*, m., 'pitchfork, fork, claw, finger-nail,' allied to *kraauwen*, 'to scratch.' Connected with Krume.

kraus, adj., 'frizzled,' from MidHG. *krûs*, 'curled, frizzled'; unknown to all the OTeut. languages; retained in Mid Du. *kruis*, ModDu. *kroes*, 'dishevelled, entangled, frizzled, stubborn'; MidE. *crûs*, 'frizzled, angry.' The genuine Teut. origin and great antiquity of kraus are certified by the equiv. parallel cognates, Mid HG. *krol* (*ll*), 'curly, lock of hair,' Du. *krul*, 'lock,' *krullig*, 'frizzled, curly,' MidE. *crul*, 'curly.' Comp. Krolle.

Krause, f., 'pitcher with a lid,' from MidHG. *krûse*, f., 'pitcher, earthenware drinking vessel'; OHG. **chrûsa*, f.; Mid Du. *kruise*, AS. **crûse*, MidE. *crûse*, E. *cruse*; Scand. *krús*, 'pitcher with a lid.' It is not immediately connected with HG. Krug. That the word is of foreign origin seems certain, yet the ultimate source cannot be Gr. κρωσσός, 'pitcher.' See the following word.

Kräusel, m., 'top,' with the more frequent variant Kreisel, a corrupt form which arose from connecting Kräusel with the circular (kreisförmig) movement of a top; MidHG. **kriusel*, MidG. *krûsel*, m., 'top,' a dimin. of Krause, hence lit. 'small pitcher.' Comp. the UpG. term Topf for 'top.'

Kraut, n., 'herb, vegetable, weed,' from

MidHG. *krŭt*, n., 'small foliated plant, herb, vegetable,' espec. 'cabbage,' OHG. *krŭt*, OSax. *crūd*; Du. *kruid*, n., 'herb, spice, gunpowder' (the last meaning is also found in MidHG. from the 14th cent.); MidE. *crūdewain* (Du. *kruidwagen*), 'ammunition waggon,' seems to have been borrowed. Goth. *krūþ (gen. *krūdis), n., might be taken for *krū-da-*, with the suffix *da-* from *tó* (Aryan *grū-tó-*). Gr. γρύτη, 'lumber, trash,' does not agree in meaning. Perhaps the word should be connected rather with the Gr. root βρυ- for *gru-*; comp. βρύω, 'to swell,' ἔμβρυον, 'embryo,' βρύον, 'moss.' From G. is derived Fr. *choucroute*, m., 'pickled cabbage.'

Krebs, m., 'crayfish,' from the equiv. MidHG. *krëbeʒ*, *krëbeʒ*, OHG. *chrëbiʒ*, *chrëbuʒo*, m.; comp. Du. *kreeft*, m., 'crayfish'; allied to LG. *Krabbe*. The G. word passed at an early period into Rom. (comp. Fr. *écrevisse*, 'crayfish,' and *crevette*, 'shrimp'). It is not connected with Gr. κάραβος, but rather with OHG. *chrāpfo*, 'hook'; **Krebs**, lit. 'hooked or claw fish'?. See **Krapfen** (2).

Kreide, f., 'chalk,' from the equiv. MidHG. *krīde*, late OHG. *krīda*, f.; ultimate source Lat. *créta*, f., 'Cretan earth.' The change from Lat. *ē* to HG. *ī* cannot be explained by the ModGr. pronunciation of Crete (comp. MidHG. *Krīde*, Scand. *Krīt*, 'Crete'), since there are other instances in which Lat. *ē* appears in HG. loan-words, as *ī*; comp. **Feier**, and espec. **Seide**. Besides, the word *créta*, 'Cretan earth,' is unknown to Gr. The more precise history of the adoption of HG. *krīda* is obscure (the corresponding words in Rom. are Ital. *creta* and Fr. *craie*).

Kreis, m., 'circle, orbit, sphere,' from MidHG. *kreiʒ*, m., 'circumference, circuit, division of a country district'; OHG. *chreiʒ*, pointing to Goth. *kraits, and D. *krijt* to Goth. *kreits. Comp. MidHG. *krīʒen* (MidG.), 'to make a circle.' The word cannot be traced beyond G.; it is not allied to **Kranz** and **Kring**. Comp. **kritzeln**.

kreischen, vb., 'to shriek,' from Mid HG. *krīschen*, 'to screech, shriek'; OHG. *chrīskan and Goth. *kreiskan are wanting. MidHG. *krīʒen*, 'to shriek' (Goth. *kreitan), points to the fact that a dental (Goth. *t*) has been lost before the suffix *sk* of **freifchen**, just as a guttural has been dropped in **forschen**, OHG. *forskôn*. Comp. Du. *krijschen*, 'to shriek, yell.' Comp. **kreifen**.

Kreisel, see **Kräusel**.

kreisen, kreißen, vb., 'to be in labour,' from MidHG. *krīʒen*, 'to screech, shriek, groan'; comp. Du. *krijten*, 'to shriek, shout.' For further cognates see **kreischen**; akin also to MidHG. *krīsten*, earlier Mod HG. **kreisten**, 'to groan.'

Kreppel, see **Kräppel**.

Kresse (1.), f., 'cress,' from the equiv. MidHG. *kresse*, OHG. *chresso*, m., *chressa*, f.; corresponding to Du. *kers*, *kors*, f., AS. *cærse*, f., E. *cress*. This word, which is probably peculiar to West Teut., found its way to the North—Dan. *karse*, Swed. *krasse*, Lett. *kresse*; it was also adopted by the Rom. languages—Fr. *cresson*, Ital. *crescione*. The assumption that the Rom. words contain the orig. form is opposed by the early appearance of the term in the old West Teut. languages. It is true that no plausible explanation of OHG. *chresso* (Goth. *krasja?) has been put forward; OHG. *chrēsan*, MidHG. *krēsen*, *krisen*, 'to crawl,' seems unrelated.

Kresse (2.), f., 'gudgeon,' from the equiv. MidHG. *kresse*, OHG. *chresso*, m. Different from **Kresse** (1). The fish is thus named only in G., and hence the term is not diffused in West Teut. like the preceding word.

Kretschem, Kretscham, m., from the equiv. MidHG. *kretschem*, *kretscheme*, m., 'village tavern,' a Slav. loan-word; Bohem. *krčma*, Wend. *korčma*, Pol. *karczma*, 'tavern.'

Kreuz, n., 'cross,' from the equiv. Mid HG. *kriuz*, *kriuze*, n., OHG. *chrūzi*, n.; from Lat. *crūci-* (dat. *cruci*, acc. *crucem*), with change of vowel quantity in the stem as in **Leier, Lilie**, and **Pilz**, and also of gender (comp. **Abt, Orden**, and **Pech**). The change of medial *c* in the Lat. word to HG. *tz*, though in another group of (older) loan-words Lat. *c*, even before open vowels, appears as *k* in HG. and Teut., is due to the fact that words like **Keller** and **Kaiser** were introduced into Germany at a far earlier period than **Kreuz**, which was adopted with Christianity in the 8th and 9th cents. The Goths used Teut. **Galgen** (Goth. *galga*), the English of the earliest period, *rood* (comp. **Rute**). The loan-word is now found in all the Mod. Teut. languages—Ic. *kross*, Swed. and Dan. *kors*, Du. *kruis*, E. *cross*.

Kreuzer, m., 'kreutzer' (about ⅓d.), from MidHG. *kriuzer*, *kriuzære*, m., a small coin, orig. marked with a cross (Mid HG. *kriuze*), 'kreutzer.'

N

fribbeln, vb., 'to crawl, tickle,' ModHG. only, MidHG. *kribeln* (MidG.), 'to tickle'; a recent formation; comp. Mod Du. *kribeln*, 'to itch, prick,' *kribbelen*, 'to grumble, wrangle.'

Sribsfrabs, Sribbelfrabbel, m., ModHG., an onomatopoetic term for 'utter confusion'; comp. ModDu. *kribbelen*, 'to scrawl'?.

Sriecbe, f., 'early sloe,' from the equiv. MidHG., f., 'early sloe-tree,' OHG. *chriehboum*; comp. Du. *kriek*, f., 'wild cherry.' Phonetically it might be derived from OHG. *Chriah*, MidHG. *Kriech*, 'a Greek,' if *græca* could be found in MidLat. denoting the tree and the fruit. The word must have been introduced from Italy, on account of the Lat. term (comp. Ririche), for it is inconceivable that the Germans, of their own accord, and without foreign precedent, should have termed the fruit 'Greek' because it was imported, as we assume for the moment, from Greece. At all events, the name has not yet been explained (comp. further the Fr. loan-word *crèque*).

fricdjen, vb., 'to crawl,' from the equiv. MidHG. *kriechen*, OHG. *chriohhan*, str. vb.; corresponding to OSax. *kriupan*, Du. *kruipen*, AS. *creópan*, E. *to creep*, OIc. *krjúpa*. The relation of the HG. form with *ch* from *k* to the remaining Teut. languages with *p* has well-authenticated analogies; see Rufe (1), werfen, and Strumf. The guttural appears again in MidE. *crúchen*, E. *to crouch*. Rraufen, 'to crawl,' is the MidHG. (MidG.) *krúfen*.

Sriedjente, see Rriefente.

Srieg, m., 'war,' from MidHG. *krieg(g)*, m., 'exertion, endeavour to obtain something,' then also 'opposition, resistance, argument, discord, combat.' The predominant meaning in ModHG. is the latest and 'counter-effort' the earliest; comp. MidHG. *einkriege*, adj., 'self-willed.' For a similar evolution of meaning comp. OHG. *flîz*, 'exertion, zeal, quarrel'; see Fleiß. The word is almost entirely unknown to OHG.; it occurs once as *chrêg*, 'pertinacia,' with which *to'darkrêgi*, 'controversia,'*widarkriegelín*, 'obstinatus' (with obscure *l*, *ia*, *ie*), are connected. This word, obscure in origin, is shared only by Du. (*krijg*) with G.; in all the other Teut. languages it is wanting, Dan. and Swed. *krig* being borrowed from G. Comp. the following word.

friegen, vb., 'to get,' from MidHG. *kriegyen* (in MidG. *krigen* is str., so too the corresponding vb. in LG. and Du.), 'to exert oneself, strive, aim at, oppose, struggle,' then also 'to defend, maintain an opinion,' MidG. also 'to obtain, receive'; the latter meaning is LG. and Du. (*krijgen*, 'to obtain, receive'). With regard to the numerous meanings comp. OHG. *winnan*, 'to exert oneself, struggle,' *giwinnan*, 'to win.' Hence the various senses of the vb. are the outcome of a prim. meaning 'to make an effort against,' just as in the case of the noun Srieg, on which it is based.

Sriekente, f., 'teal,' a LG. form for HG. Rriech-Ente; wanting in MidHG. and OHG.; it is based on Lat. *anas crecca*, hence also Swed. *krücka*. Fr. *sarcelle*, 'teal,' like Ital. *cerceta*, is traced to Lat. *anas querquedula*; thus it has no etymological connection with Rriechente; the same may be said of E. *crake*, *corncrake*.

Sring, m., 'circular pad for the head,' from MidHG. *krinc(g)*, m., 'circle, ring, district,' with the MidG. variant *kranc(g)*; LG. has a variant *krink* with final *k*, since in the whole of the corresponding class *k* and *g* at the end of the stem interchange (comp. fraufy). Scand. *kring*, *kringum*, adv., 'round about,' *kringja*, 'to encircle,' *kringlóttr*, adj., 'round.'—E. *crank*, MidE. *cranke*; E. *to crankle*, 'to run in a winding course,' *crinkle*, 'wrinkle, bend.' ModHG. Ring and its cognates differ etymologically from Rring. In the allied Aryan languages some connect Lith. *grężiù*, *gręžti*, 'to twist, turn,' with the Aryan root *grengh*, authenticated by Rring. Gr. βρόχος, 'noose, cord,' is scarcely akin.

Sringel, Srengel, m., 'cracknel,' dimin. of Rring, or rather Rrang; used even in MidHG. as a term in pastry.

Srippe, f., 'crib,' from the equiv. Mid HG. *krippe*, OHG. *chrippa*, f., for *chrippju* (Goth. **kribjô*; for HG. *pp* from Goth. *bj*, comp. further Rippe, Suppe, and úppiq); corresponding to OSax. *kribbia*, *kibbu*, AS. *cribb*, E. *crib*. In HG. occurs a variant with *pf*, which is phonetically obscure, OHG. *chripfa*, MidHG. and ModHG. *kripfe*; there are also dial. forms with *u* in the stem, Swiss *krüpfti*, LG. *krübbe*, AS. *crybb*, Scand. *krubba*, 'crib.' This word, in Goth. *uzéta*, 'the thing from which one feeds,' is connected with MidHG. *krêbe*, 'basket'; hence 'resembling a basket, woven,' was perhaps the prim. meaning of Rrippe. The West Teut. word passed into

Rom.—Ital. *greppia*, Prov. *crupia* (the latter connected with the Teut. forms in *u* mentioned above), ModFr. *crèche* (whence E. *cratch*, 'a grated crib,' MidE. *crache*).

Krittelu, vb., 'to find fault, carp,' Mod HG. simply from a popular term, *gritteln*, 'to wrangle' (wanting in MidHG. and OHG.), with an allusion to Kritif, &c.

Kritzeln, vb., 'to scribble,' dimin. of MidHG. *kritzen*, 'to scrawl,' OHG. *chrizzōn*, 'to scratch or cut into.' It is probably connected with fraķen, OHG. *chrazzōn*, as well as with OIc. *krota*, 'to engrave, stamp.' If this is not approved, it may be allied to Kreis (root *krĭt*); *kritjōn* (whence *chrizzōn*) would then mean 'to draw lines.'

Krolle, f., 'curl' (Rhen.), from the equiv. MidHG. *krolle*, *krol(-les)*, m.; comp. Du. *krul*, f., 'curl.' MidHG. *krol*, adj., Du. *krullig*, MidE. *crul*, adj., 'curly'; Du. *krullen*, MidE. *crullen*, 'to frizzle.' For the connection between MidHG. *krolle*, f. (Goth. *krŭzlô), and ModHG. *kraus*, Mid HG. *krūs*, see under Kraus.

Krone, f., 'crown,' from the equiv. Mid HG. *krōne*, *krōn*; in OHG. *corōna* (with the foreign accent preserved), from Lat. *corōna* (the unaccented *ŏ* disappeared in MidHG.); comp. MidE. *corūne*, *croune*, E. *crown*; in MidDu. the double form *crône*, *krûne*, existed, Du. *kroon*, *kruin*. Scand. *krūna*, f. In AS. the term *cyne-helm*, lit. 'king's helmet,' was substituted for Lat. *corona* of the Biblical texts (just as *sceptrum* was rendered by *cynegerd*, lit. 'king's staff'); in OSax. and OHG. *hôbidband*, *houbitbant*, 'crown.' These words show that the Teutons had their own distinctive terms for the royal insignia. With the Lat. name they also borrowed a new idea —**krönen**, 'to crown,' from MidHG. *krœnen* and a denominative from Krone; thus it is not Lat. *coronare*, to which OHG. *chrōnōn* more accurately corresponds.

Kropf, m., from the equiv. MidHG. and OHG. *kropf*, m., 'goitre, crop, craw'; corresponding to Du. *krop*, m., 'crop, bosom, bow of a ship,' E. *crop* (of birds, top, harvest), AS. *cropp*, which has the special meanings 'crop, summit, top (of trees), ear (of corn), cluster of grapes'; OIc. *kroppr*, 'trunk, body' (also 'hump'), is still more remarkable. To these numerous senses, a primary meaning, 'a round mass in the shape of a ball, a projecting spherical body,' has been assigned; with this the Rom. loan-words such as Fr. *groupe*, 'group, cluster, knot,' coincide. Goth. **kruppa-* might be related to Gr. γρυπός, 'curved,' if 'crop, excrescence,' represented the prim. meaning of the group.

Kropzeug, n., 'rogues,' a LG. word, formed from LG. *krŏp* (comp. friechen), 'crawling creature, small cattle,' but this is not quite certain. Others connect it with the preceding word Kropf, which also signifies in Suab. and Bav. 'small, crippled creature, little man.'

Kröte, f., from the equiv. MidHG. *krote*, *kröte*, *krēte*, f. (even now dial. Krete, Krette), OHG. *chrota*, *chrēta*, f., 'toad.' The forms with *ē* and *o* are related by gradation; comp. Brett and Berb. The word is peculiar to G.; in OIc. *padda*, Du. *padde*, AS. *tâdie*, E. *toad*. Etymologically all three are equally obscure.

Krücke, f., 'crutch,' from the equiv. MidHG. *krücke*, *krucke*, OHG. *chruccha* (for *krukjō), f.; comp. Du. *kruk*, AS. *cryćć*, f., E. *crutch*. Certainly a genuine Teut. word ('staff with a curved handle'); it is most closely connected with Scand. *krōkr*, 'hook, curve'; it may also be related to friechen. In the MidHG. period it was confused with a Rom. term based upon Lat. *crucea*, and meaning 'crosier.' On the other hand, the Teut. word was submerged in many of the Rom. languages in the old inherited term; Ital. *croccia*, 'crutch,' *crocco*, 'hook,' Fr. *crosse*, 'crook,' *croc*, 'hook'; MidLat. *croca*, 'baculus episcopalis,' *crocea*, 'baculus pastoralis,' and 'baculus incurvus,' *croceus*, *croccia*, *crucia*, *crucca*, 'crutch.' Krücke can scarcely be explained from MidLat. *crucea*, 'cross-bar' (of a window), because this must have become *chruzza* (*ce* changed to *tz*); comp. Kreuz.

Krug (1.), m., 'jug, pitcher,' from the equiv. MidHG. *kruoc* (*g*), OHG. *chruog*, m.; corresponding to AS. *crōg*, *crōh*, 'pitcher,' also 'bottle.' Besides these terms, based upon a common form *krōga-*, there are several words allied in sound and meaning; comp. OSax. *krāka*, Du. *kruik*, f., AS. *crūce*, MidE. *crouke*; MidHG. *krūche*, f., ModHG. (dial.) Krauche. AS. *crocca* (and *crohh*), MidE. *crokke*, 'pitcher,' Ic. *krukka*, 'pot.' Since it is not improbable that all these terms were borrowed, we may perhaps connect them further with Kranse. Their source, however, cannot be assigned, since the corresponding words in the allied languages may also have been borrowed, and are insufficient phonetically to account for the numerous Teut. terms. Some etymologists derive them from Kelt. words such as W. *crwc*, 'pail,' from which Fr. *cruche*, 'pitcher,' may be derived, if it is not of G. origin. The Goth. term for 'pitcher' is *aúrkeis* (borrowed from Lat. *urceus*). Comp. Krug (2).

Krug (2.), m., 'alehouse,' comp. Du. *kroeg*; it passed into HG. and Du. from LG., where it is recorded since the 13th cent. The quondam assumption that the word is identical with Krug (1), "because formerly an actual or a carved pitcher was hung in front of a tavern," is demolished by the fact that Krug, 'urceus,' is entirely unknown to LG. (and Du.); the OSax. term *krōka* was used. On the other hand, Krug, 'alehouse,' was orig. wanting in HG., in which Krug, 'pitcher,' was current at the earliest period.

Kruke, see Krug (1).

Krume, f., 'crumb,' a LG. loan-word, wanting in MidHG.; comp. LG. *krûme*, Du. *kruim*, AS. *crûme*, E. *crumb*, *crum*. The root *krū* appears also in frauen, OHG. *chrouwôn*, 'to scratch, operate with the nails.' Allied to Gr. γρυμέα, 'rubbish' (Aryan root *grū*)?.

krumm, adj., 'crooked,' from MidHG. *krump(b)*, OHG. *chrumb*, 'crooked, curved, twisted, perverted' (comp. fraus); rare variants OHG. and MidHG. *krumpf*, OHG. *chrampf*, as well as MidHG. *krimpf*, in the same sense. Comp. OSax. *crumb*, AS. *crumb*; E. *crump*, 'crooked,' is abnormal (with this E. *to crumple*, MidE. *crumpeln*, and also E. *crimple*, 'wrinkle, fold,' are connected). Under Krampf it is shown how the graded and permutated forms are widely ramified; the Teut. root signified 'spasmodically contracted, curved.' Besides the cognates of West Teut. *krumba*-, from preTeut. *grumpó*-, quoted under Krampf, comp. the unnasalised Gr. γρυπός, 'curved, bent'?. OIr. *cromm*, W. *crwm*, seem to have been borrowed from AS.

Kruppe, f., 'crupper,' ModHG. only, borrowed from Fr. *croupe*, whence E. *croup*. The Fr. word has been derived from Scand. *kryppa*, f., 'hump, excrescence' (allied to *kroppr*, 'hump'). See the following word.

Krüppel, m., 'cripple,' from the equiv. MidHG. *krüppel*, *krüpel*, m.; it passed in the MidHG. period from LG. into HG.; Du. *krenpel*, E. *cripple*, MidE. and AS. *cryppel*, Scand. *kryppell*, *kryplingr*. The *p* of these forms is HG. *pf* (Alsat. Krüpfel), hence we must assume that HG. Krüppel was borrowed from LG. and MidG. Allied in the UpG. dials. to Swiss *chrüfi*, *chrüpfe*, Suab. *kropf*, *kruft*, *krüftle*, Bav. *krapf*, comp. 'deformed person,' and the cognate Bav. *krüpfen*, 'to become crooked,' akin to OIc. *kroppr*, *kryppa*, 'hump,' and the cognates discussed under Kropf. Besides Gr. γρυπός, 'curved,' we may also refer to OSlov. *grŭbŭ*, 'back,' ModSlov. *grbanec*, 'wrinkle,' Serv. *grba*, 'hump' (*grbati se*, 'to stoop').

Kruste, f., 'crust,' from the rare Mid HG. *kruste*, OHG. *crusta*, f., 'crust'; a learned term which has been first naturalised in ModHG. Derived from Lat. *crusta*, whence also Du. *korst*, E. *crust*, as well as Rom. words like Fr. *croûte*.

Krystall, m., from the equiv. MidHG. *kristâl*, *kristálle*, m. OHG. *krystálla*, f., 'crystal.' The retention of the Lat. accent (*crystállus*, m. and f.) preserved the foreign aspect of this merely learned term, which was borrowed at a very early period.

Kübel, m., 'tub, bucket,' from the equiv. MidHG. *kübel*, OHG. *chubil, m.; comp. OHG. *miluh-chubili*, -*chubilîn*, n., 'milkpail'; allied to AS. *cŷf* (from *kûbi*-), Mid E. *kīve*, 'cask.' The stem is genuinely Teut.; it is doubtful whether it is connected with the cognates ('narrow space') discussed under Koben. Its Rom. origin at all events must be rejected.—ModLat. *cupella*, *cupellus*, 'mensura frumentaria' and 'vas potorium,' do not coincide in meaning; Du. *kuip*, 'vat, cask,' is alone connected with Lat. *cûpa*, 'cask.' Some Rom. words, such as Prov. *cubel*, 'tub,' are derived from the Teut. cognates, from which Slav. and Lett. words are borrowed; Lith. *kúbilas*, 'tub,' OSlov. *kŭbŭlŭ*, 'vessel,' as a corn measure. Comp. Koben, Kopf, and Kufe.

Küche, f., 'kitchen,' from the equiv. MidHG. *küche*, *küchen*, *kuchîn* (UpG. without mutation *kuche*, *kuchi*), OHG. *chúhhîna*, f.; corresponding to AS. *cycene*, f., E. *kitchen*, Du. *keuken*. An old West Teut. word, probably not derived immediately from late Lat. *coquina*, 'kitchen,' but rather from a common Rom. and MidLat. *cūcina* (*kukîna*; comp. Ital. *cucina*, Fr. *cuisine*). The HG. *ch* (OHG. *hh*) for *c*, *k*, in consequence of the HG. permutation points to the adoption of the term about the 6th cent., at which period the South Europ. arts of cookery and horticulture were introduced into Germany; comp. Koch, Kuchen, Kohl, Kümmel, and Pfeffer.

Kuchen, m., 'cake,' from the equiv. MidHG. *kuoche*, OHG. *chuohho*, m. ; comp. MidLG. *kôke*, Du. *koek*. Besides these forms with old ô in the stem (comp. AS. *côcil*, MidE. *kéchel*, 'little cake,' E. dial. *keech*) there occurs in the Scand. and E. languages an apparently graded form with *a*—E. *cake*, and the equiv. Scand. *kaka*, f. This gradation seems to point to a Teut. origin of the cognates, yet their relation to the Rom. class (Catal. *coca*, Rheto-Rom. *cocca*, Picard. *couque*, 'cake'), connected with Lat. *coquus*, *coquere* (AS. *côc*, OHG. *chohhôn*), is not clear. Moreover, on the assumption that the word was borrowed, ô in OHG. *chuohho* would correspond exactly to the ô in AS. *côc*, 'cook.'

Küchenschelle, f., 'pasque flower,' ModHG. only, interpreted from one of the variants *Kuh-*, *Kühschelle* as *Küchenschelle* ; its relation to the equiv. Fr. *coquelourde* is obscure ; the ModHG. form is certainly a corruption.

Küchlein, n., 'chicken,' ModHG. only ; a MidG. and LG. word introduced by Luther into HG. (in UpG. dial. *hüenli*, West MidG. *hünkel*, Suab. *luggele*). To the MidG. and LG. *küchen*, *küken*, correspond AS. *čýčen* (plur. *čýcnu*), MidE. *chiken*, E. *chick*, *chicken*, Scand. *kjúklingr*, Du. *kieken*, *keuken*. The Goth. dimin. termination -*ina*- (**kiukein*) frequently occurs in the names of animals, Goth. *gait-ein*, AS. *tiččen* (Goth. **tikkein*), AS. *héčen* (Goth. **hôkein*), n. 'kid' ; see Füllen, Geiß, Schwein, Zicklein, and Mädchen. The substan. on which the word is based is AS. *cocc*, E. *cock*, Scand. *kokkr* (to which Goth. **kiukein*, n., is related by gradation). There is no reason for thinking that the Teut. word was borrowed from Rom.— Fr. *coq*, like AS. *cocc* (UpG. *gockel*, *gückel*), is a recent onomatopoetic term also, for W. and Corn. *cog*, 'cuckoo,' points also to the base *cucû* (so too OIr. *cúach*, 'cuckoo,' from *coucú*). Comp. Kuckuck.

kuchen, see gucken.

Kuckuck, m., 'cuckoo,' from the equiv. late MidHG. *kuckuk* (rare), m. ; the usual term in MidHG. is *gouch*, which was introduced in the 15th cent. from Du. (*koekoek*, early MidDu. *cuccûc*). An onomatopoetic term widely diffused, but it is not necessary to assume that it was borrowed in most of the languages, E. *cuckoo*, Fr. *coucou*, Lat. *cuculus*, W. and Corn. *cog*, OIr. *cúach*. See also Küchlein.

Kufe (1.), f., 'runner of a sledge' ; Mid HG. **kuofe* and **küoche* are wanting with this meaning, so too OHG. **chuofa* ; OHG. *chuohha* is found, however, in *dito-chôha*, 'runner of a sledge' (see examples of the interchange of *k-ch* and *p-f* under kriechen) ; comp. MidLG. *kôke*, 'runner of a sledge.' Perhaps Lith. *žagrè*, f., 'forked piece of wood on a plough,' is allied, and also its cognates *žaginjs*, m., 'stake, post,' *žagarus*, m., 'dry twig.' From these the evolution of meaning in Kufe may be inferred.

Kufe (2.), f., 'coop, vat,' from the equiv. MidHG. *kuofe*, OHG. *chuofa*, f. The prim. form of the word previous to the HG. permutation of consonants is represented by OSax. *côpa*, f., and the equiv. E. *coop*. From MidLat. *côpa*, a variant of *cûpa*, 'cask,' whence Du. *kuip*, 'coop' ; comp. also Kübel. The word must have been borrowed before the 7th cent., since it has undergone permutation in HG. ; perhaps it was introduced with the culture of the vine.

Küfer, m., from the equiv. MidHG. *küefer*, m., 'cooper' ; comp. Du. *kuiper*, E. *cooper*.

Kugel, f., 'ball, bullet, globe,' from the equiv. MidHG. *kugel*, *kugele*, f. ; comp. MidLG. and Du. *kogel*. The word is not recorded in the other languages. It is allied to ModHG. *Kaule*, from *kûl*, *kugl*, and also to ModHG. *Keule*, with which E. *cudgel* and AS. *cyčgel* is closely connected ; *Keule* is a 'pole with a ball-shaped end.' *Kugel* and *Kegel* cannot possibly be related by gradation.

Kuh, f., 'cow,' from the equiv. MidHG. and OHG. *kuo*, f. ; comp. MidLG. *kô*, Du. *koe*, E. *cow*, AS. *cû*, OIc. *kýr*, f. (Goth. **kôs*) ; Teut. type *kô-*, f., 'cow.' This word, like the names of other domestic animals, is found in the non-Teut. languages, and in the form of *gôw* (*gô*) it is common to the Aryan group ; comp. Ind. *gâus* (acc. *gâm*), f., Gr. βοῦς (stem βοF), Lat. *bos* (stem *bov-*). These terms are both mas. and fem., hence Sans. *gâus*, m., 'bull, cattle,' f., 'cow' ; Gr. βοῦς, 'cattle, ox, cow' ; Lat. *bos*, 'ox, cow' ; Lett. *gûws*, 'cow.' This term, like other primit. Aryan words (comp. Pferd, Schaf, Hund, Ochse, &c.), proves that the Aryans, before the division into the later tribes, were already acquainted with domestic animals.

kühl, adj., 'cool,' from the equiv. Mid HG. *küel*, *kücle*, adj., also a regularly non-mutated form *kuol-* in compounds such as *kuolhûs*, n., 'cooling-house,' and in the adv. *kuole* (comp. ſchen, ſpät, faſt); OHG. *chuoli*, adj., 'cool' (**chuolo*, adv.). It corresponds to MidLG. *kôl*, Du. *koel*, AS. *côl*, E. *cool*. In the form of *kôli-* (orig. *kôlu-*) the adj. is common to West Teut.; the adj. laſt is the old partic. form from the stem of fühl, from which in Scand. (*kala*) and AS. (*calan*) str. vbs. are formed; the further cognates E. *chill*, AS. *ĕĕle*, *ĕyle*, 'cold,' are based on a Goth. **kali-* (n. sing. **kals*). Comp. faſt.

kühn, adj., 'bold, daring,' from Mid HG. *kiien*, *küene*, OHG. *chuoni*, 'bold, eager for combat, strong'; comp. the non-mutated variant in the MidHG. and OHG. derivative *kuonheit*, 'boldness,' and in the OHG. adv. *chuono*. It corresponds to MidLG. *koene*, Du. *koen*, AS. *céne*, 'bold,' E. *keen* (the adj. is obsolete in Suab. and Bav.); Scand. *kœnn*, 'wise, experienced.' The latter must at one time have been the prevalent sense in West Teut. also, as is proved by the ModHG. proper name Ronrad; OHG. and MidHG. *Kuonrât* (without mutation, like OHG. and MidHG. *kuonheit*), AS. *Cénréd* (Goth. **Kôniréps*), may have meant 'giving wise advice.' Teut. *kôn-i-* (lit. 'one that can understand, sensible') is orig. a verbal adj. from the vb. ſennen, ſönnen, hence the West Teut. sense 'bold,' compared with the OIc. meaning, must be regarded as derivative. All intellectual and moral conceptions of the OTeut. period are related more or less to war and conflict (comp. bald, ſchnell, and Krieg).

Küchen, LG., see **Küchlein**.

Kümmel, m., 'cummin, caraway seeds,' from the equiv. MidHG. *kümel*, OHG. *chumil*, m., with the variants MidHG. *kümin*, OHG. *chumîn*; comp. AS. *cymen*, Du. *komijn*, MidLG. *kömen*; from Lat. and Rom. *cŭmînum*. The change of *n* into *l* is the same as in Jgel (in UpG. still *kümi*, *kümich*). With regard to the period of the adoption of Lat. words relating to horticulture and the art of cookery, comp. Käſe, Küche, Minze, Pfeffer, &c.

Kummer, m., 'grief, sorrow, distress,' from MidHG. *kumber*, m., 'rubbish, refuse (thus still dial.), encumbering, oppression, distress, grief'; ModHG. *mm*, from Mid HG. *mb*, as in Zimmer, Lamm, and Ramm. The word is wanting in all the OTeut. dials.; comp. ModDu. *kommer*, m., 'grief, affliction; hare's dung'; MidE. *combren*, 'to encumber, molest,' E. *to cumber*. The cognates are very similar in sound to a Rom. class—Fr. *décombres*, 'rubbish,' Port. *comoro*, *combro*, 'mound of earth, hillock,' Ital. *ingombro*, 'hindrance,' Fr. *encombrer*, 'to obstruct (with rubbish), block up'; MidLat. *combrus*, 'mound of earth, barrier of felled trees, obstructing pile.' The Teut. cognates seem to have passed into Rom.; for, besides the more recent form with *r*, we find in AS. and Scand. a variant with *l*, OIc. *kumbl*, 'tumulus, barrow.'

Kummet, n., 'horse-collar,' from the equiv. MidHG. *komat*, n.; borrowed in the MidHG. period from Slav. (comp. OSlov. *chomątŭ*, Pol. *chomąt*); hence not diffused beyond the HG. group. The Slav. cognates of OSlov. *chomątu* are derived from OTeut.; comp. MidE. and ModE. *hame*, Du. *haam*, Westphal. *ham*, Rhine Prov. *hamen*, *hammen*, 'horse-collar.'

Kumpan, m., 'companion, mate,' from MidHG. *kumpân*, *kompân*, m., 'comrade, associate'; the latter is derived from OFr. Prov. *compaing*, 'companion, partner.' MidLat. *companio*, lit. 'one who shares the same food,' is based on OTeut. expressions such as Goth. *gahlaiba*, OHG. *gileibo*, m., 'associate, comrade,' and the equiv. OHG. *gimazzo*, from *maz*, n., 'food'; see Laib.

Kumpeſt, **Kompôſt**, m., 'preserves, heap of rubbish or dung,' from MidHG. *kumpost*, also *kumpôst*, m., 'preserves,' espec. 'pickled cabbage,' from Rom. (Ital. *compôsto*).

Kumpf, m., 'basin, bowl,' from Mid HG. *kumpf*, m., 'vessel'; comp. LG. *kump*. A MidLat. *cumpus* as the source of the G. word does not exist; MidLat. *cumba*, *cumbus*, have too no such meaning as Kumpf, hence they cannot be adduced to explain the dial. ModHG. Kumme, 'deep bowl.' Kumme and Kumpf are more probably genuine Teut. words, and allied to AS. *cumb* and the equiv. E. *coomb*.

Künchel, see Kaninchen.

kund, adj., 'known, manifest,' from MidHG. *kunt(d)*, OHG. *chund*, adj., 'become acquainted, noted, known.' It corresponds to Goth. *kunþs*, 'noted,' OSax. *cûth*, AS. *cûþ*, 'noted,' E. *couth* (now only in the compound *uncouth*). A common Teut. adj. in the form *kunþa-*, from the non-permutated *gn̂-to-*, which is prop. a partic. in *to-* from the verbal stem of the root *gŏn*, *gnō*, discussed under ſennen, ſennen, and fühu. For other particles. formed into adjs. see under laut.

Kunft, f., 'arrival,' from MidHG. and OHG. *kunft, kumft,* f., 'coming, arrival'; comp. Goth. *gaqumþs,* f., 'meeting, assembly,' the corresponding verbal abstract to Goth. *qiman,* HG. fommen, with the suffix *þi-,* from *-ti-* (comp. Schult, Durst, and Gift). The insertion of an *f* in the combination *mþ* (*mfþ* becoming *mft*; comp. further Vernunft, Zunft, Ramst) corresponds to the addition of an *s* to *nþ* (*nsþ* becoming *nst*), mentioned under Kunst.—**künftig,** adj., 'to come, future,' from the equiv. Mid HG. *künftec,* OHG. *kumftig.*

Kunkel, f., 'distaff,' from the equiv. MidHG. *kunkel,* f., OHG. *chunchala,* f.; a Suab., Alem., and Rhen. word, for which Rocken occurs in other dials. (Bav. and also MidG.). It is wanting in the remaining OTeut. dials., and its diffusion supports the assumption that it has been borrowed from Rom., especially since the earlier OHG. form *chonachla* closely resembles the equiv. Rom. words in sound; MidLat. *conucla* (for *colucula* ?, dimin. of *colus,* 'distaff' ?), equiv. to Ital. *conocchia,* Fr. *quenouille,* 'distaff,' whence also the equiv. OIr. *cuicel.* Others refer the word to the cognates discussed under Kaufer, with the prim. meaning 'to spin.'

Kunst, f., 'skill, art, address,' from MidHG. and OHG. *kunst,* f., 'knowledge, wisdom, skill, art'; comp. OSax. *cunsti,* plur., 'knowledge, wisdom,' Du. *kunst;* wanting in E. and Goth. A verbal abstract from können, like Kunst from fommen; *s* is a euphonic insertion before the dental; comp. Brunst from brennen, Gunst from gönnen.

kunterbunt, adj., 'higgledy-piggledy,' ModHG. only; in MidHG., however, *kunterbéch,* adj., which means 'variegated, strange as a Kunter,' *i.e.* 'monster'?. But while MidHG. *kunter,* 'monster,' and OHG. *chuntar,* 'herd, drove of cattle' (cognate with OSlov. *ženą,* Lith. *genù,* 'I drive cattle'?), are UpG., funterbunt is prop. LG. Both MidHG. *kunterbéch* and Mod HG. funterbunt are imitations of MidHG. *kunterfeit,* lit. 'contralactus, not genuine'; from this in MidHG. (MidG.) a word *kunter,* 'what is false, deceptive,' was deduced.

Kupfer, n., 'copper,' from the equiv. MidHG. *kupfer,* OHG. *chupfar,* n.; an old loan-word from which *kuppor must have been the earliest form; the word was bor-rowed before the 7th cent.; comp. Du. and MidLG. *koper,* AS. *copor,* E. *copper,* Scand. *kopar.* These are probably based on MidLat. *cuper* (gen. *-eris*). Late Lat. *cvprum,* or rather *æs cyprium,* or simply *cyprium* (whence Fr. *cuivre*), is an Italian (not a Greek) term; the Teuts. probably owe to the Italians their earliest knowledge of copper. The island of Cyprus was called Kipper by the Germans of the Middle Ages, following the Byzant. and ModGr. pronunciation of Κύπρος; hence MidHG. *kippor* or *kipperwin,* 'Cyprian wine.'

Kuppe, f., 'peak, summit,' adopted by the written language in the last century from MidHG.; in HG. the form would have *pf.* Koppe and Kuppe, as well as Kaupe ('crest of birds,' also termed Koppe, comp. OSax. *coppod,* 'cristatus' of snakes, under Kopf), are allied words, with the prim. meaning 'point, extreme end,' which belonged orig. to the strictly HG. permutated form Kopf. The further history of all these terms is obscure; under Kopf it is assumed that they are of genuine Teut. origin, though the possibility of their being blended with MidLat. and Rom. *cupa,* 'beaker,' is granted. In MidHG. *kuppe,* f., OHG. *chuppa,* f., means 'covering for the head' (espec. under the helmet); see Kopf.

Kuppel, f., 'cupola, dome,' ModHG. only, from Ital. *cupola* (Fr. *coupole*).

kuppeln, vb., 'to couple, fence (a field),' from MidHG. *kuppeln, koppeln,* 'to leash, bind, fetter, unite'; MidHG. *kuppelspil,* 'coupling,' *kuppelære,* 'match-maker, procurer,' and *kuppelærinne,* the fem. form; a deriv. of Koppel, Lat. *copulare.*

Kur, Chur, f., 'election,' in Kurfürst connected with erkoren, erkiesen; MidHG. *kür, küre,* f. (MidG. *kur, kure,* without modification), 'consideration, selection,' espec. 'election of a king' (MidHG. *kür-, kurvürste,* MidG. *korvürste,* 'Elector'); OHG. *churi,* f., is preserved in HG. Willfur in the regularly mutated form. AS. *cyre,* m., 'choice'; Scand. *kør, keyr,* n., 'choice.' See kiesen.

Kurbe, Kurbel, f., 'crank, winch,' from MidHG. *kurbe,* OHG. *churba,* f., 'windlass over a well'; generally traced to Fr. *courbe,* and further to Lat. **curva,* 'bent piece of wood,' from *curvus.*

Kürbis, m., 'gourd, pumpkin,' from the equiv. MidHG. *kürbeʒ, kürbiʒ,* OHG. *churbiʒ,* m. (rarely f.); borrowed previous to the HG. permutation (of *t* to *z*) from Lat. *cucŭrbita*, whence also AS. *cyrfet*. Whether the reduplicated form of the Lat. word was influenced by Teut. itself cannot be determined. From Lat. *cucurbita* are also derived Ital. *cucuzza*, Fr. *gourde*, whence E. *gourd*, Du. *kauwoerde*.

Küren, vb., 'to choose, select,' ModHG. only, derived from an older *kür*, f., 'choice,' equiv. to Kur.

Kürſchner, m., 'furrier,' from the equiv. MidHG. *kursenǣre*, m. (*sch* from *s*, as in Arſch, birſchen, and Hirſch), a derivative of MidHG. *kürsen*, f., 'fur coat,' OHG. *chursinna*, *chrusina*, AS. *crūsne*, 'fur coat'; MidLat. *crusna*, *crusina*, *crusinna*. Cognate terms also occur in Slav. (OSlov. *krŭzno*, Russ. *korzno*), in which, however, the word did not originate any more than it did in G., yet it may have been introduced into G. through a Slav. medium, perhaps from some Northern language. The prim. kinship of OHG. *chursina* with Gr. βύρσα, 'hide, skin,' is scarcely conceivable.

kurz, adj., 'short,' from the equiv. Mid HG. and OHG. *kurz*; a very curious loan-word from Lat. *curtus*. What may have led to its adoption is even more obscure than in the case of ſicher (from Lat. *securus*). The assumption of its being borrowed is supported only by the form *kurt* (without the change of *t* to *z*), which appears also in strictly UpG. records; comp. OHG. *porta*, *pforta*, and *pforza*, from Lat. *porta*. The form *curt* is OSax. and OFris.; comp. also Du. *kort* and Ic. *kortr*. The Lat. loan-word passed by degrees into all the Teut. dialects except E., which preserved an OTeut. word for 'short' with which the Lat. word, from its close resemblance in sound, has been confused—AS. *sceort*, E. *short* (comp. OHG. *skurz*, 'short'); these cannot, on account of their want of permutation, be primit. allied to Lat. *curtus*. For the cognates of E. *short* see Schürze.

Kuß, m., 'kiss,' from the equiv. Mid HG. and OHG. *kus* (gen. *kusses*); corresponding to Du. *kus*, OSax. *cus*, *cos* (gen. *-sses*), AS. *coss*, OIc. *koss*, m.; a common Teut. word for 'kiss,' wanting only in Goth. (*kussus, comp. Goth. *kukjan*, East Fris. *kükken*, 'to kiss'). A pre-Teut. root *gut*, *gud*, 'to kiss,' does not occur. Indubitable cognates are not found in the non-Teut. languages unless Ir. *bus*, 'lip,' and Gael. *bus*, 'mouth with thick lips,' are allied.— küſſen, vb., 'to kiss,' from MidHG. and MidLG. *küssen*, OHG. *chussen*; AS. *cyssan*, E. *to kiss*, OIc. *kyssa*.

Küſſen, see Kiſſen.

Küſte, f., ModHG. only, from the equiv. Du. *kuste*, *kust*, 'coast,' which, like E. *coast*, MidE. *coste*, is of Rom. origin, OFr. *coste*, *côte*, MidLat. *costa*, 'coast.'

Küſter, m., 'sacristan,' from the equiv. MidHG. and OHG. *kustor*, *kuster*, m. Adopted on the introduction of Christianity. While Kreuz, from OHG. *chrūzi*, is based upon the Lat. stem *cruci-*, acc. sing. *crucem* (and not the nomin. *crux*), Küſter, on the other hand, is not derived from Lat. *custodem* (stem *custodi-*), or even from the nom. sing. *custos*, since in the OHG. period the change of *s* into *r* no longer occurs. We have rather to proceed from an actually recorded MidLat. *custor*, *custorem*, a rare variant of the more prevalent form *custod-*, which appears also in Fr. *coutre*, OFr. *costre*, 'sacristan.' Mid Lat. *custos* (scil. *ecclesiae*), 'warden, guardian of the church jewels, holy vessels, &c., presbyter s. clericus cui ecclesiae et templi cura incumbit.' With the same sense Mid Lat. *costurarius*, whence OSax. *costurdri*, as well as ModHG. dial Guſterer.

Kutſche, f., 'coach,' first occurs in early ModHG. from Hungar. *koszi*, 'a carriage from Koszi' (near Raab); a characteristic modern term common to the Europ. languages; comp. Fr. and Span. *coche* (E. *coach*), Ital. *coccio*, Du. *koets*.

Kutte, f., 'cowl,' from MidHG. *kutte*, f., 'monk's habit'; comp. MidLat. *cotta*, *cottus*, 'tunica clericis propria,' which, however, with the corresponding Rom. words (Fr. *cotte*, 'petticoat,' Ital. *cotta*), may be traced back to Teut. *kotta-*, appearing in OHG. *chozzo*, MidHG. *kotze*, 'coarse woollen stuff, cover.' Comp. Ketze.

Kutteln, f., 'chitterlings, tripe,' from MidHG. *kutel*, f., 'gut, tripe'; as a genuine UpG. word it is probably not cognate with LG. *küt*, 'entrails,' but connected rather with Goth. *qiþus*, 'belly.'

Kux, m., 'share in a mine,' earlier Mod HG. and dial. Kuckus; first occurs in early ModHG., perhaps introduced from the Slav. frontier mountains.

Lab (201) **Lad**

L.

Lab, n., 'rennet,' from MidHG. *lap(b)*, n., 'rennet,' also 'acid fluid,' OHG. *lab*, 'broth'; it is not improbable, since the latter is the prim. meaning, that the word is further cognate with OTeut. terms for 'medicine.' Goth. *lubja*, f., 'poison,' AS. *lyb*, 'poison,' OIc. *lyf*, 'medicine,' OHG. *luppi*, n., 'deadly juice.' Note specially MidHG. *kœseluppe*, f., OHG. *châsiluppa*, AS. *cýs-lyb*, equiv. to MidHG. *kêse-lap*. The way in which **Lab** is related by gradation to *lubja* corresponds perhaps to that of HG. Nase to AS. *nosu*, E. *nose*. The prim. meaning of the stem seems to be 'strong, sharp perfume; plant juice'; OIc. *lyf*, 'medicine,' and Goth. *lubja*, 'poison,' are differentiations of the same orig. sense.

Labberdan, m., 'codfish,' ModHG. only, from LG.; to this are allied, with remarkable divergences, Du. *labberdaan*, earlier *abberdaan* and *slabberdaan*, and E. *haberdine*, with the same sense. The word is based not on the name of the Scotch town Aberdeen, but on *tractus Laburdanus*, a part of the Basque country (Bayonne used to be called *Laburdum*, Fr. *Labourd*). It must have been introduced into the Netherlands through a Fr. medium; the form *abherdaen* is due to the error of regarding the initial *l* as the article. Comp. also Kabliau.

laben, vb., 'to refresh,' from MidHG. *laben*, OHG. *labôn* (comp. AS. *gelafian*), 'to wash, quicken, refresh.' If we take into consideration Tacitus' account of the fondness of the Teutons for bathing, we can readily conceive how the meaning 'to refresh' was evolved from 'to wash'; the reverse course is also possible, as is shown perhaps by ModHG. sich erfrischen, sich stärken, in the sense of 'to drink.' The former is the more probable, on account of MidHG. *lap* (*b*), 'bilge water'; there is, however, no connection with Lat. *lavare*, Gr. λούειν. —**Labe,** f., 'refreshment,' from the equiv. MidHG. *labe*, OHG. *laba*, f.

Lache, f., from the equiv. MidHG. *lache*, OHG. *lahha*, f., 'puddle, pool, water in an excavation.' The OHG. word cannot be derived from Lat. *lâcus*, 'lake,' which may, however, be the origin of Mid E. and E. *lake*, while AS. *lagu*, 'lake,' shows what form the Teut. word cognate with the Lat. term would assume. The attempt to connect **Lache** (Bav. *lacke*) and *lacus* is also opposed by the difference in meaning; Ital. *lacca*, 'low ground,' and OSlov. *loky* are G. loan-words. The origin of **Lache** remains obscure; it is scarcely allied to leck and its cognates.

lachen, vb., 'to laugh,' from the equiv. MidHG. *lachen*, OHG. *lahhên*, *lahhan*, earlier *hlahhan*; the *hh* of the HG. is due, according to Goth. *hlahjan* (pret. *hlôh*), 'to laugh,' to an older *hj*, AS. *hlyhhan*, E. *to laugh*, and the equiv. Du. *lachen*. In the non-Teut. languages the stem *hlah*, pre-Teut. *klak* (probably onomatopoetic, like the cognates of klingen or Lith. *klegėti*, 'to be noisy, laugh loudly'), is not positively authenticated.—Derivative **Lache,** f., 'laugh,' from MidHG. *lache*, f., 'laughing,' comp. E. *laughter*, AS. *hleahtor*, MidHG. *lahter*, 'laughter.' **Lächeln,** vb. 'to smile,' from MidHG. *lęcheln*, is a frequentative of lachen.

Lachs, m., 'salmon,' from the equiv. MidHG. *lahs* (plur. *lęhse*), OHG. *lahs*; corresponding to AS. *leax*, OIc. *lax*, Scotch *lax*; a common and prim. Teut. term for 'salmon'; in Goth. perhaps **lahs*. The Slav. and Lith. words are cognate; Lith. *laszisza*, Lett. *lasis*, Russ. *lososŭ*, 'salmon trout,' Pol. *lasóś*, 'salmon.' Hence the *s* in OHG. *lahs* is a suffix (comp. Fuchs), and not a part of the root.

Lachter, n. and f., 'fathom,' from the equiv. MidHG. *lâhter*, *lâfter* (MidG.); its early history is obscure; the stem is not the same as in Klafter.

Lade, f., 'chest, box, press,' from Mid HG. *lade* (OHG. **lada*, **hlada*?), f., 'receptacle, chest'; Lade is prop. an 'arrangement for loading'; the corresponding OIc. *hlaþa* means 'barn, storehouse,' so too MidE. *laþe*, whence E. *lathe*. For further references comp. the vb. laden. It is also probable that Lade is connected with the following subst. Laden; in that case the prim. meaning would be 'trunk made of boards.'

Laden, m., 'shop, shutter,' from Mid HG. *laden*, *lade*, m., 'board, plank, shutter, shop.' The meaning of MidHG. *lade*, 'board,' is the orig. one, hence the derivation of the word from the vb. laden must be rejected in favour of its connection with ModHG. Latte; since the latter in Goth.

would be represented by *lappô, and later by *lapa, we might assume a root lap, pre-Teut. lat, meaning 'board'; comp. Latte.

Laden (1.), vb., 'to load, charge, burden,' from the equiv. MidHG. laden, OHG. ladan (earlier hladan); corresponding to Goth. hlapan, AS. hladan, E. to lade. The d of the AS. word compared with the þ of the Goth. and d of the HG. is abnormal; the irregularity is probably on the side of the Goth. and OHG., which produced a grammatical change as though the Aryan dental were t. In fact, however, it is dh (hladan, hlôd, hlôdum, hladans, not hlapan, hlôp, hlôdum, hladans); comp. OSlov. kladą (klasti), 'to lay,' which, with E. to lade, proves the existence of an Aryan root kladh. Comp. Last and Lade.

Laden (2.), vb., 'to summon, invite,' from the equiv. MidHG. laden, OHG. ladôn; distinguished from laten (1) by the initial sound; laten, 'onerare,' had orig. initial hl, while laten, 'invitare,' has always had a simple l only; Goth. lapôn, 'to summon,' AS. lapian (obsolete in E.). The Teut. root is lap, the meaning of which is indicated by Goth. lapôns, f., 'calling, consolation, redemption,' the adv. lapaleikô, 'very willingly,' and ModHG. Luter. Some such idea as 'to treat affectionately, beg,' must be regarded as the orig. sense; a root lat with this meaning has not yet been found in the other Aryan languages. Further, the word cannot possibly be connected with Gr. καλεῖν, κλη-τός, &c., to which Mod HG. holen more probably belongs.

Laffe, m., 'puppy, dandy,' from Mid HG. lape, lappe, m., 'simpleton, dandy.' The relation of ModHG. Lump to Lumpen makes the existence of MidHG. lappe, 'dandy,' as well as *lappe, 'rags,' conceivable; yet the ModHG. form has ff compared with the MidHG. pp; comp. läppisch. Others refer Laffe to Du. and LG. laf, 'stale, insipid.'

Lage, ., 'situation,' from MidHG. lâge, OHG. lâga, f., 'putting, arranging, situation'; from liegen. So too ModHG. Lager, n. (prop. Leger), from MidHG. lēger, OHG. lēgar, m., 'camp'; comp. E. lair.

Lägel, see Legel.

Lahm, adj., 'lame,' from MidHG. and OHG. lam (gen. lames), 'weak in the limbs, lame.' The more general meaning, 'weak in the limbs,' is the orig. one, since an adj. with a different gradation belonging to the same stem—OHG. luomi, Mid

HG. lüeme—signifies 'wearied, relaxed,' and even 'gentle.' Yet OIc. lame, AS. lama, E. lame, OSax. lamo, and Du. lam, 'lame,' show that the prevalent ModHG. meaning is primitive (in Goth. halts, AS. halt, equiv. to Lat. claudus, Sans. khoḍa). An old lama-, 'weak, infirm' (from which Prov. lam is borrowed), suggests OSlov. lomlją (lomiti), 'to break' (root lam); Russ. lomôta, 'rheumatic pains.' Comp. also Scand. lemja, 'to lame, disable.'

Lahn, m., 'tinsel,' ModHG. only, from F. lame, f., 'thin metal plate, wire.'

Laib, m., 'loaf,' from MidHG. and OHG. leip(b), m. (early OHG. hleib), 'bread.' It is the earlier Teut. term for the modern Brot, which is unknown to Goth., and almost so to AS. Comp. Goth. hlaifs (gen. hlaibis), AS. hlāf, E. loaf; to these Goth. gahlaiba and OHG. gileibo, m., 'companion,' are allied; comp. Rumpan. E. lord, from AS. hlâford (Goth. *hlaibwards), 'lord,' lit. 'bread guardian,' as well as E. lady, from AS. hlâfdige, 'domina' (lit. 'bread distributor'), contains HG. Laib in the compound; comp. E. Lammas (Aug. 1), from AS. hlâfmœsse, 'bread-feast as a sort of harvest thanksgiving festival.' These primit. compounds prove the great antiquity of Laib and the more recent origin of Brot. Slav. borrowed its chlěbŭ, 'bread' (whence Lith. klépas, Lett. klaipas, 'bread'), from an OTeut. dialect (the OTeut. word being also found in Finn and Esthon.—Finn. leipä, Esthon. leip, 'bread'). See Lebkuchen.

Laich, m. and n., 'spawn,' doubtlessly a prim. word, though first recorded in late MidHG.; corresponding to MidLG. lêk, Swed. lek, Dan. leeg. The Goth. form is perhaps *laik, and thus the connection of Laich with Teut.-Goth. laikan, 'to leap,' is conceivable. Dialectically Laich signifies 'lusus venereus' (comp. Leich).

Laie, m., 'layman, novice,' from the equiv. MidHG. leie, leige, OHG. leigo, leijo, m., 'laïcus.' (It is based on a Romanised Lat. laïcus, whence also AS. lœwed, 'layman,' E. lewed). The word was probably borrowed at a later period than the other ecclesiastical terms Priester and Probst.

Laken, m. and n., 'sheet, shroud,' Mod HG. only, from LG. (OLG. lakan); in HG. prop. Lachen, MidHG. lachen, OHG. lahhan. Westphalia sent a great deal of linen (comp. Linnen) to South Germany, hence the LG. may have supplanted the HG. form. Allied to MidE. lake and ModHG. Leilach.

Lakritze, f., 'licorice,' from the equiv. late MidHG. *lakeritze*; from MidLat. *liquiritia* (the *a* in the first syllable of the G. word is due to the unaccented *i*), equiv. to Gr. γλυκύρριζα (with the modern pronunciation of the vowels). Words originally Gr. and used by medical science in the Middle Ages are preserved in Arzt, Büchſe, Pflaſter, Lawerge, &c.

lallen, vb., 'to stammer,' from MidHG. 'to speak indistinctly, stammer'; the corresponding OIc. *lalla*, 'to totter like a child walking' shows a curious figurative application of the word. Gr. λαλεῖν, Lat. *lallāre*, and HG. lallen are scarcely cognate; they are rather independent imitative words separately coined in each language.

Lambertsnuß, f., 'filbert,' instinctively connected by Germans with St. Lambert, but the historic term is lombardiſche Nuß, 'Lombard nut'; MidHG. *Lambardie*, *Lombardie*, and *Lámpart*, 'Lombardy, Italy.' Comp. Walnuß.

Lamm, n., 'lamb,' from the equiv. Mid HG. *lamp* (plur. *lember*), OHG. *lamb* (plnr. *lembir*), n. It corresponds to Goth. *lamb*, AS. *lomb*, E. *lamb*, Du. *lam*, 'lamb'; a prim. Teut. term which passed also into Finn. (*lammas*, gen. *lampaan*). Cognates in the non-Teut. languages have not yet been found.

Lampe, f., 'lamp,' from the equiv. Mid HG. *lampe*, f., which is formed from Fr. *lampe* (Gr. λαμπάς), whence also E. *lamp*. Comp. Ampel.—**Lampe,** m., 'hare,' is probably a pet term for Lamprecht, Lantbrecht, Lambert; its relation to Fr. *lapin*, Du. *lamprei*, 'rabbit,' is obscure.

Lamprete, f., 'lamprey,' from MidHG. *lampréte*, also corrupted into *lemfride*, *lantfride*, &c. OHG. *lampréta*, formed from Lat. *lampréda* (whence Fr. *lamproie*, E. *lamprey*), with the variant *lumpetra*, lit. 'stone-licker.'

Land, n., 'land, country,' from the equiv. MidHG. *lant* (d), OHG. *lant* (t), n.; a common Teut. word; comp. Goth. *land*, 'district, estate, native country,' OIc., AS., E., Du., and OSax. *land*, 'country, land.' To these are prim. allied Ir. *land*, *lann*, W. *llan*, Corn. *lan* (from the primit. form **landhā*), 'open space, area, small enclosure, yard,' Bret. *lan*, 'heath,' as well as OSlov. *lędina*, 'heath, uncultivated land' (Russ. *ljada*, *ljadina*), with which Swed. dial. *linda*, 'fallow field,' agrees in the vowel sounds. Hence Land is native to the North of Europe, while Acker has a far wider diffusion. The Rom. cognates, Ital. *landa* and Fr. *lande*, 'heath, plain,' are derived from Kelt. rather than from Teut.

lang, adj., 'long,' from the equiv. Mid HG. *lanc* (g), OHG. (and OSax.) *lang*; it corresponds to AS. and E. *long*, Goth. *laggs*, OIc. *langr*, Du. and LG. *lang*. A common Teut. adj. primit. allied to Lat. *longus*; it also cognates, perhaps, with OPers. *dranga*, so that in Lat. and Teut. a dental (*d* or *dh*) may have been lost; Gr. δολιχός, OSlov. *dlŭgŭ*, Sans. *dīrghás*, 'long,' are certainly not allied.—ModHG. **langſam,** adj., 'slow,' is one of the earliest forms ending in *sam* (in Goth. only *lustusams*, 'delightful, longed for'); AS. *longsum*, 'tedious, continuous,' OSax. *langsam*. In OHG., besides *langsam*, 'lasting a long time,' there exists a form *langseimi*, 'lingering,' and in MidHG. *lancsam*, adj. and adv., 'slow'; as well as *lancseime*, 'lingering, slow'; in ModHG. langſeim became obsolete, and its meaning has been transferred to langſam.

Lanze, f., 'lance,' from the equiv. Mid HG. *lanze*, f., which was formed from OFr. *lance* (Lat. *lancea*, comp. Ital. *lancia*).

Lappalie, f., 'trifle, bauble, nonsense,' ModHG. only, from ModHG. Lappe, with a Lat. termination and accent; comp. Schmieralien.

Lappen, Lappe, m., 'rag, patch,' from MidHG. *lappe*, f. and m.; OHG. *lappa*, f., 'piece of stuff hanging loose, rag'; comp. AS. *læppa*, 'hem, lappet,' E. *lap*, and Du. *lap*. The irregular correspondence of AS. *pp* to HG. *pp* is obscure (AS. *pp* ought to be *pf* in HG.). We may compare Gr. λοβός, 'lobe,' or preferably Lith. *lópas*, 'patch, rag,' *lópyti*, 'to patch.'

läppiſch, adj., 'silly, foolish,' ModHG. only, allied to MidHG. *lappe*, 'dandy, simpleton,' which is preserved in earlier HG., and still in the dial. Lappe; comp. Laffe.

Lärche, f., 'larch,' from the equiv. MidHG. *lerche*, *larche*; OHG. **larihha* is by chance not recorded, but Lat. *larix* (acc. *larĭcem*, comp. Reich from Lat. *calicem*) necessarily leads to OHG. **larik*, and then by permutation and mutation to **lĕrihha*. The permutation of *k* to *ch*, and the fact that the word is based on a Lat. term pronounced *larikem* (E. *larch*), point to a very early adoption; comp. Reich.

Lärm, m., 'alarm, noise,' ModHG. only; like E. *larum*, it originated in Fr.

alarme (from Ital. *allarme*) by dropping the unaccented initial vowel; prop. a military term identical with **Alarm**.

Larve, f., 'spectre mask, larva, grub,' ModHG. only, from Lat. *larva*, with the *v* pronounced as *f*, as in HG. Brief, Käfig, and Vers.

lasch, adj., 'slack,' from MidHG. und OHG. *lasc*; comp. OIc. *lǫskr* (Goth. *lasqs*), adj., 'slack, weary'; formed with a suffix *sk* from the root laß, laſſen (Goth. *lasqu-* would represent *latsqa-*). Yet it is not improbable, since laſch is first recorded in ModHG., that the root was borrowed from a Rom. class similar in sound (comp. Fr. *lâche*, Ital. *lusco*, 'idle').

Lasche, f., 'flap, lappet,' from MidHG. *lasche*, f., 'shred, rag'; it is conceivable that the word is related to Lappe, whose labial may have been lost before *sch*; hence OHG. *laska* for *lafska*?.

Lase, f., 'pitcher, can,' a MidHG. word, not recorded in OHG. and MidHG.; probably connected with laſſen.

laſſen, vb., 'to let, leave,' from the equiv. MidHG. *lâzen*, OHG. *lâzzan*, str. vb.; comp. AS. *lǽtan*, E. *to let*, Du. *laten*, OIc. *láta*, Goth. *lêtan*; the pre-Teut. form of the common Teut. root *lêt*, 'to leave,' is *lêd* (with *lad* as a weaker gradation, comp. laß). The only certain cognate in the other Aryan languages is the Lat. word *lassus*, 'faint, languid,' quoted under laß; hence 'to relax, release,' is probably the prim. meaning of the verbal stem. From this, MidHG. *lâzen*, both simply and in compounds, evolved the meanings 'to set free, omit, leave behind,' &c., as in ModHG.

Laſt, f. (UpG. masc.), from the equiv. MidHG. and MidLG. *last*, f. and m., 'burden,' OHG. (earlier *hlast*); allied to laten Goth. *hlaþan*); the *st* is a suffix before which the final dental of the verbal stem *hlaþ* necessarily disappeared, AS. *hlæst*, n., E. *last*. In Scand. an old *to-* partic. assumed the meaning 'waggon-load,' *hlass*, n. (for *hlapto-*). The G. word passed into Rom. (Fr. *lest*, m., 'ballast,' *laste*, m., Ital. *lasto*, 'load of shipping'). For further references comp. laten.

Laſter, n., 'vice, crime,' from MidHG. and MidLG. *laster*, n., 'abuse, disgrace, mistake,' OHG. *lastar*, n. It is connected with a str. vb. *lahan* (for the loss of *h* before *s* comp. Miſt) preserved in OHG., equiv. to AS. *leán*, 'to blame.' Pre-Teut. *lahstra-* is formed from the verbal stem

lah with the suffix *stra-*, which represents the earlier form *tra* seen in AS. *leahtor*, n., 'reproach, sin' (obsolete in E.). Another derivative from the same stem is seen in Scand. *lǫstr* (Goth. *lahstus*), MidE. *last*, 'mistake, defect.' In the non-Teut. languages the word may be compared with OIr. *locht* (from *lokto-*), 'mistake.'

laß, adj., 'inactive, idle,' from MidHG. *laz* (zz), 'faint, idle, tardy' (see leßen); it corresponds to Goth. *lats*, OIc. *latr*, AS. *læt*, MidLG. *lat*, adj., 'sluggish, idle, lazy.' A pre-Teut. adj. formed by gradation from the stem of laſſen, *lêt*, of which *lǎt-* is the weak form (see ſchlaff, OHG. *slâf*, from the root *slêp*). The close correspondence with Lat. *lassus* may be accounted for historically; *lassus* is an old partic. for *ladtus*; *lad* is the pre-Teut. root on which Mod HG. laß is based; comp. laſch, laſſen, and leßt. The assumption, however, that HG. laß was borrowed from the Rom. cognates (Ital. *lasso*, Fr. *las*, Lat. *lassus*) is inconceivable.

lateiniſch, adj., 'Latin,' with the foreign accent, in contrast to the E. term. The diphthong of the second syllable proves that the adj. was naturalised previous to ModHG. MidHG. *latînisch*, OHG. *latînisc*, which was adopted in the OHG. period, as is proved by the non-permutation of *t* (*latînus*) to HG. zz, was used chiefly in the monastic schools, in which Latin was cultivated as the language of the Church.

Laterne, f., 'lantern,' from the equiv. MidHG. *latërne* (*lantërne*), f.; borrowed with the retention of the foreign accent from Lat. *laterna* (Fr. *lanterne*, E. *lantern*).

Latte, f., 'lath,' from the equiv. Mid HG. *late*, *latte*, OHG. *latta*, f.; it corresponds to Du. *lat*, AS. *lætta* (*læþþa*?), Mid E. *laþþe*, E. *lath*; a difficult word both grammatically and etymologically. The correspondence of *tt* in AS. *lætta* and OHG. *latta* is abnormal (AS. *tt* ought to be HG. *tz*, only AS. *þþ* corresponds to a HG. *tt*). Unfortunately a corresponding word is wanting both in Scand. and Goth. Yet there is no need to regard the cognates as foreign; since ModHG. Laten is cognate, the Teut. origin of the word is established. Hence from HG. Latte an allied Rom. class has been rightly derived—Fr. *latte*, Ital. *latta*, 'flat wooden pole.' To the Teut. cognates Ir. *slath* (Bret. *laz*), 'rod, pole,' from the base *slattâ*, is primit. akin.

Lattich, m., 'lettuce,' from the equiv.

MidHG. *lattech, latech, lateche,* OHG. *lattuh* (*lato!hha*), borrowed in the OHG. period from Lat. *lactūca* through the intermediate forms *lattūca, lattuca;* comp. AS. *leahtric,* 'lactuca' (comp. Alltch from Lat. *acte*).— In Huflattich, 'colt's foot,' Lattich represents Lat. *lapatium* (MidHG. *huofḷeteche,* OHG. *huofḷetihha*), or more correctly Mid Lat. *lapatica* (intermediate forms *lápatica, láptica, lattica*).

Latwerge, f., 'electuary, confection,' from the equiv. MidHG. *latwērge, latwērje, latwārje,* f. ; the *t* as in Lattich represents *ct* (assimilated *tt*) ; *lactuárium* has *a* in the unaccented first syllable for *e*, as in Lafritze. This foreign term is based on the equiv. MidLat. *electuarium,* which sometimes in MidHG. preserves its prim. form, *electuárje, lectquerje*. The MidLat. word, which originated in Gr. ἐκλεικτόν, ἔκλειγμα, 'medicine that dissolves in the mouth,' belongs to the medical art of the Middle Ages, which was learned from the Greeks (comp. also Lafritze, Büchse, Arzt, &c.), and was introduced into G. through a Rom. medium—Ital. *lattovaro,* Fr. *electuaire* (whence E. *electuary*).

Latz, m., 'stomacher, bodice,' first occurs in early ModHG. from Rom. (Fr. *lacet,* m., 'lace, stay-lace,' whence E. *lace*; Ital. *laccio,* 'cord'; the prim. word is Lat. *laqueus,* 'noose, snare').

Lau, adj., 'lukewarm, tepid,' from the equiv. MidHG. *lā* (inflected *lāwer*), OHG. *lāo* (inflected *lāwēr*); probably for an earlier *hlāo* (Goth. *hlēws*); comp. OIc. *hlýr, hlúr,* 'warm, mild,' Du. *lauw*. In the non-Teut. languages indubitable cognates are wanting, yet the Rom. cognates of flau (Fr. *flou*) are derived from OG.

Laub, n., 'foliage,' from the equiv. MidHG. *loup* (*b*), OHG. *loub,* m. and n.; a primitive and common Teut. term; comp. Goth. *laufs* (plur. *laubōs*), m., AS. *leáf,* n., E. *leaf,* Du. *loof*. Some connect the word with Lith. *lápas,* 'leaf,' which, however, compared with the diphthong of the Teut. word has an abnormal *a* (comp. Haupt with Lat. *caput*); Gr. λέπος, 'scale, rind,' is even less akin.

Laube, f., 'arbour, bower,' from Mid HG. *loube* (*löube*), f., 'porch, market, court of justice, gallery round the upper storey of a house,' OHG. *louba* (*louppea*), f., 'penthouse, hall, front building' (the mutated *läube* is met with in MidG. dials.; comp. LG. *löve*). The OIc. *lopt,* 'upper storey, balcony' (whence E. *loft*), is probably connected with this word. The ModHG. meaning, 'arbour,' wanting in MidHG. and OHG., is due to the term being popularly connected with Laub. The OHG. word passed in the form of MidLat. *laubia* into Rom. (Ital. *loggia,* Fr. *loge,* 'hut, tent, tier of boxes').

Lauch, m., 'leek, garlic,' from. the equiv. MidHG. *louch,* OHG. *louh* (*hh*), m.; comp. the corresponding OIc. *laukr,* Du. *look,* AS. *leác,* E. *leek,* with which *lic* in garlic is connected ; a primitive and common Teut. word, which was adopted in Finn. as *laukku* and in OSlov. as *lukŭ*. Like most of the old names of plants and animals, it is of obscure origin. Gr. λύγος, 'a pliant rod or twig for wicker-work, willow-like tree,' cannot be allied on account of its meaning. Perhaps OIr. *luss,* 'herb, plant' (from *luksu-*), is a cognate.

Lauer, m., 'tart wine.' "It is derived from Lat. *lōra,* which denotes the tart wine that is made from the skins and stones of grapes by pouring water on them" (Lessing). Even in OHG. *lūra,* MidHG. *lūre,* f. (OHG. *lūrra,* MidHG. *liure,* from the prim. form *lōrea,* appears in the equiv. Suab. *leier;* to this Swiss *glöri* from OHG. *glūrra* is allied ?). As to the period of the introduction of Italian vine-culture into Germany, comp. Wein, Winzer, Keller, Kelch, and Most. Lat. *lōrea* is also indicated by Ital. *loja,* 'dirt.'

lauern, vb., 'to lie in wait,' from the equiv. late MidHG. *lūren,* wk. vb. ; it corresponds to Scand. *lūra,* 'to slumber,' Mid E. *lūren,* E. *to lower, lour*. Comp. further MidE. *lurken* (for *lūr ken*), E. *to lurk,* which seems the prim. meaning of the G. and Scand. word. "To the G. term is traced Fr. *lorgner,* 'to leer, ogle,' from which the foreign words Fr. *lorgnon, lorgnette,* were introduced into G."

Läufel, Laufft, 'shell' (espec. nutshell), a Hess. and Franc. word, corresponding to OHG. *louft,* 'nutshell, bark of trees.' Prim. cognate with Lith. *lupinai,* 'peel, skins of fruit' (*lùpti,* 'to skin, peel'), Pol. *lupina,* 'husk.'

laufen, vb., 'to run,' from the equiv. MidHG. *loufen,* OHG. *louffan,* str. vb. ; from an earlier *hlauffan,* equiv. to Goth. *hlaupan,* 'to run.' It corresponds to AS. *hleápan,* str. vb., 'to run, leap, dance,' E. *to leap,* Du. *loopen,* OIc. *hlaupa;* a specifically Teut. word common to all the dialects. For the prim. meaning we have absolutely no clue (Gr. κραιπνός, 'swift,' is not allied to Goth. *hlaupan*, which may be preferably compared with Lith. *klupti*, 'to stumble'). The Teut. root *hlaup* has a collateral form *hlūp*, by gradation *hlōp* (MidHG. and Mod HG. dial. *geloffen*, partic.), of which a variant *hlaubt* appears in Swiss *lōpen*, 'to run' (comp. ḫūrfen, Bav. *hoppen*). ModHG. Lauft, plur. Läufte, m., from the equiv. Mid HG. and OHG. *louft*, m., 'course (of time),' (MidHG. plur. *löufte*, 'conjunctures').

Lauge, f., 'lye,' from the equiv. MidHG. *louge*, OHG. *louga*, f.; corresponding to MidLG. *lôye*, Du. *loog*, AS. *leáh*, and the equiv. E. *lye*. In OIc. *laug*, f., means 'warm bath' (preserved in ModIc. in numerous proper names, and signifying 'hot spring'). Perhaps this Teut. word for 'warm bath' is connected with the Aryan root, *lowe*, *lu*, 'to bathe' (comp. Lat. *lavâre*), like the equiv. Swed. *lut*, of which an extended Aryan *luk*, equiv. to Teut. *luh*, 'to wash,' may appear in OHG. *luhhen*, 'to wash,' Suab. *lichen*, North Franc. and Henneberg *lüen*, 'to rinse washed linen.' The HG. word occurs in the Slav. languages as *lug*, 'lye.'

läugnen, vb., 'to contradict, deny,' from the equiv. MidHG. *lougenen*, *lougenen*, *lougen*, OHG. *louginen*, *lougnen*, wk. vb.; corresponding to OSax. *lôgnian*, AS. *léhnan*, *lŷgnan*, Goth. *laugnjan*, wk. vb., 'to deny'; OIc. *leyna*, 'to conceal' (Goth. *galaugnjan*, 'to be concealed'), with the loss of a *g* before the *n*. A common Teut. wk. vb. with the meaning 'to deny'; it is a derivative of an OHG. noun *lougna*, f., 'denial' (OIc. *laun*), which is formed by gradation from the stem of lügen (root *lug*). Comp. lügen.

Laune, f., 'humour, freak,' from Mid HG. *lûne*, f., 'humour, mood'; the Mod HG. word also signifies 'phase of the moon, quarter of the moon, change of fortune.' This series of meanings shows that the word is based on Lat. *lûna*, and that the astrology of the Middle Ages in its attempt to read the fortunes of men by the stars determined the different significations. Ital. *luna*, Fr. *les lunes*, E. *lunatic*, *lunacy*, *lune*, all referring to mental states, give evidence of the belief that the moon influenced the moods of men.

Laus, f., 'louse,' from the equiv. Mid HG., MidLG., and OHG. *lûs*, f.; corresponding to AS. *lûs*, E. *louse*, Scand. *lûs* (plur. *lýss*), Du. *luis*, 'louse.' The word is common to Teut., occurring everywhere in the same sense. The usual derivation of Laus from the stem of verlieren, Berlust, lose, löse (root *lus*), although supported by the analogy of Gr. φθείρ, 'louse,' from φθείρω, is dubious, since MidHG. *verliesen* (prop. 'to lose') does not occur at an early period in the sense of 'to spoil.' Neither is the derivation from the Teut. root *lût*, 'to hide oneself' (OHG. *lâʒʒên*, see lauschen), certain.

lauschen, vb., from the equiv. MidHG. (rare) and MidLG. *lûschen*, wk. vb., 'to listen, lurk'; the meaning points to the oft-recurring OTeut. stem *hlûs*, 'to hear,' so that *hlûskan* for *hlûs-skai-, with a derivative *sk*-, may be assumed. Comp. OHG. *hlosên*, MidHG. *losen*, 'to listen to, hearken,' OIc. *hlus-t*, 'ear.' Eng. has preserved the cognates in AS. *hlyst*, f., 'hearing,' *hlystan*, 'to listen or hearken to,' E. *to list*, *listen*; OHG. *lûs-trên*, MidHG. *lûstren*, Suab. and Bav. lauftern, 'to hearken,' MidHG. *lusmen*, *lüsenen*, 'to hearken.' The OTeut. verbal stem *hlus*, authenticated by this group, from pre-Teut. *klus*, has cognate terms in Ind. and Slav.; Ind. *cruṣṭis*, f., 'hearing, obedience'; OSlov. *slyšati*, 'to hear,' *sluchŭ*, m., 'hearing,' Lith. *klausà*, f., 'obedience,' *paklùsti*, 'to obey,' *klausýti*, 'to hear.' To this root *klus*, 'to hear,' a shortened form *klu* is allied; comp. laut and Leumund. ModHG. lauschen also seems to be connected in a subsidiary manner with MidHG. *löschen*, OHG. *lôscên*, 'to be hidden, concealed.' Comp. MidDu. *luuschen*, 'to be concealed,' allied to the equiv. OHG. *lâʒʒên* (Bav. laußen, 'to lie in ambush,' still exists).

laut, adj., 'loud,' from the equiv. Mid HG. and OHG. *lût* (for an earlier *hlût*, Goth. **hlûda*-); a common Teut. adj. (comp. Du. *luid*, AS. *hlûd*, E. *loud*), which, like laft, alt, tot, gewiß, traut, zart, schaft, sund, satt, wund, was orig. an old partic. in *to* (Lat. *tus*, Gr. τος, Ind. *tas*). The meaning of **klû-dâ-s*, pre-Teut. *klû-tó-s*, from the root *klû*, 'to hear,' is lit. 'audible, heard.' Another shade of meaning was assumed by the Aryan partic. in the cognate languages —Sans. *crutás*, Gr. κλυτός, Lat. *inclūtus*, 'famous.' In Teut. also there are traces of the short vowel (*hlŭda*-), especially in proper names, Ludwig, Lothar, Ludolf, Chlothilde, &c. Moreover, the root *klû* (Gr. κλύω, 'I hear,' κλέος, 'fame'); Ind. *çrâvas*, 'fame'; OSlov. *sluti*, 'to be called,' *slovo* for **slevo*, 'word'; Lat. *cluo*, *clueo*, 'to hear oneself called') is also widely diffused in OTeut. ; Goth. *hliuma*, 'hearing, ear,' OIc. *hljómr*, AS. *hleóþor*, 'tone, voice, melody.' Comp. laufdjen and Leumunb.

Laut, m., 'sound,' from MidHG. *lût*, m., 'sound, tone, voice, cry.'—**lauf**, prep. with gen., is a form of the subst. ; lit. 'according to the sound of,' &c.; MidHG. *nâch lût*, e.g. *der briefe*, 'according to the letters,' *nâch lût des artikels*, 'according to the article,' then also simply *lût des artikels*. Orig. used only of the contents of documents read out.

Laute, f., 'lute,' from the equiv. late MidHG. *lûte*, f., which is derived from Fr. *luth* ; comp. OFr. *leüt*, Ital. *liûto*, the origin of which from Arab. *al'ûd*, 'musical instrument,' is accepted ; hence the connection between Laute and Laut or Lieb must be rejected.

läuten, vb., 'to ring, chime,' MidHG. *liuten*, wk. vb., 'to utter a sound, cause to resound, ring,' OHG. *lûten*, 'to make audible.' Comp. AS. *hlýdan*, 'to be audible, make a loud noise, shout, sound.'

lauter, adj., 'pure, mere,' from MidHG. *lûter*, adj., 'bright, pure, clear,' OHG. *hlûttar*, *hlûttar*. Since Goth. and LG. *tr* is not permutated in HG. (comp. zittern, Winter, Eiter, Otter, and bitter), Goth. *hlûtrs*, 'pure,' AS. *hlûttor*, 'pure, clear' (wanting in E.), and Du. *louter* are corresponding forms. A prim. Teut. adj. perhaps orig. signifying 'washed' (like Lat. *lautus*, lit. 'washed,' then 'splendid, magnificent'). This prim. meaning may be assumed since the Teut. root *hlût*, preserved only in the adj. lauter, is cognate with Gr. κλυδ and κλύζω, 'to rinse out, wash, cleanse,' and κλύδων, 'beating of the waves.'

Lavendel, m. and f., 'lavender,' from the equiv. MidHG. *lavendel*, f. and m.; MidLat. *lavendula* (Ital. *lavendola*).

lavieren, vb., 'to veer, tack,' ModHG. only, from Du. *laveeren*, whence also Fr. *louvoyer*.

Lawine, f., 'avalanche,' ModHG. simply ; from Swiss, in which Lauwin, pronounced with a G. accent, was current at an earlier period. The word passed in the 18th cent. into the written language, orig. with the variants Lauwine, Lauine, Läue, Loewin. Although we might regard the word as a derivative of Lat. *labina* on account of Föhn, which is undoubtedly of Lat. origin, yet it probably comes from a genuine Teut. source ; for the medial Lat. *b* would be represented only by *b* or *f* (*v*) in G. (MidHG. **levene*). Moreover, the numerous dial. variants point to a G. root, and, indeed, to kinship with lau ; thus with Bav. *läuen*, *läunen*, 'to be softened by a mild temperature, thaw,' is connected Bav. *läuen*, *läun*, 'thaw, mass of half-melted snow, avalanche,' and Swiss *läue*, *läui* (plur. *läuine*), 'avalanche,' with *läu*, 'warm enough to thaw.' Even in OHG. an allied word *lewina*, 'cascade,' occurs.

leben, vb., 'to live,' from the equiv. MidHG. *lëben*, OHG. *lëbén*; corresponding to Goth. *liban* (pret. *libaida*), AS. *libban*, E. *to live*, Du. *leven*; Scand. *lifa*, 'to live,' and also 'to be remaining.' This proves the identity of the stem *lib*, 'to live,' with that of bleiben (Goth. *bileiban*) ; hence the connection with Gr. λιπαρεῖν, 'to persist,' to which λιπαρής, 'persistent, industrious,' is allied, probably also Lith. *lipti*, 'to adhere.' Comp. bleiben and Leib.

Leber, f., 'liver,' from the equiv. Mid HG. *lëber*, *lëbere*, OHG. *lëbara*, f.; the *ë* of the stem is an old *i* (comp. leben and leben) ; corresponds to Du. and MidLG. *lever*, AS. *lifer*, E. *liver*, OIc. *lifr*, f. Some have attempted to connect with this common Teut. word equiv. terms in the non-Teut. languages—Gr. ἧπαρ, Lat. *jecur*, Sans. *yakṛt*, and have assumed two stems, *lik* and *ljëk* (*jëk*) ; in that case the medial *labial* in Leber would represent an orig. guttural as in vier, fünf, eilf, Wolf, &c. Equally uncertain is the explanation from the Gr. λίπα, 'fat,' λιπαρός, 'sticky, greasy' ; nor does it seem probable that Gr. λαπάρα, f., 'loins, flanks,' is allied, because the OTeut. word has an old *i*.

Lebkuchen, m., 'gingerbread,' from the equiv. MidHG. *lëbekuoche*, m., allied to the equiv. MidHG. *lëbezelte*. The derivation of *lëb-*, from Slav. *lipa*, 'lime-time,' Pol. *lipiec*, 'finest honey (lime-tree honey),' is improbable ; Lat. *libum*, too, hardly suffices to explain the HG. word. MidHG. *lëbe-* is more probably a graded form of MidHG. *leip* (see Laib), 'bread.' Or is it connected with ModSlov. *lepenj*, 'a sort of cake' ?

lechzen, vb., 'to be parched with thirst,' from MidHG. *lëchzen*, *lëchezen*, prop. 'to dry,' then 'to be parched with thirst' (comp. Durst). It is connected with the earlier ModHG. adj. *lëch*, 'leaky,' for which the LG. form is used (comp. led), MidHG. *lëchen*, 'to dry up, crack and leak through dryness' ; in Goth. probably a str. vb.

*_likan;_ comp. OIc. _leka_, 'to drip, leak'; E. _to leak_, AS. _leccan_, 'to water.' The Goth. stem is probably _lik_, by gradation _lak_ (or rather _hlak_). OIr. _legaim_, 'to melt away, dissolve,' is closely related in sound and meaning. Comp. also the following word.

Ledʃ, adj., 'leaky,' ModHG. only, a LG. form for an earlier and strictly HG. ledʃ, for, according to the words quoted under _ledʒen_, the Goth. root is _lik_ (_hlik_?), and this adj. corresponds to the OIc. adj._lekr_, 'leaky,' whose _k_ would be represented in HG. by _ch_. The borrowing of the ModHG. word from LG. is explained by the fact that a great number of nautical expressions in ModHG. are of LG. origin; the HG. form ledʃ is also found in the dials. MidHG. _lęcken_, vb., 'to moisten' (_lęcke_, f., 'moistening'), has _ck_ for earlier _kj_, as is shown by AS. _lęččean_, 'to moisten' (from _lakjan_). Both vbs. prove that 'to be watery' is the prim. meaning of the Teut. stem _lek_ (by gradation _lak_). ModHG. lecken, 'to leak,' is no more connected with MidHG. _lęcken_, 'to moisten,' than it is with ModHG. lecken, 'to lick'; it is a derivative of the adj. ledʃ, and hence has the variant ledʒen.

Ledʃen (1.), vb., 'to lick,' from the equiv. MidHG. _lęcken_, OHG. _lęcchôn_ (for Goth. *_likkôn_). It corresponds to Du. _likken_, AS. _liccian_, E. _to lick_. The vb. _likkôn_, 'to lick,' common to E. and G., is related to Goth. _laigôn_, apart from the gradation, as HG. Ziege (Goth. *_tigô_) is to Zicklein (Goth. *_tikkein_), or as Hut (Goth. *_hôda_-) is to AS. _hætt_ (Goth. *_hattu_-). Goth. *_likkôn_, 'to lick,' is also authenticated by the equiv. Rom. cognates borrowed from it, Ital. _leccare_, Fr. _lécher_. A Teut. root _slikk_ seems to be preserved in ModHG. ſchlecken, OIc. _sleikja_, 'to lick.' Goth. *_laigôn_ is based on an Aryan root _līgh_, _leigh_, _loigh;_ Gr. λείχω, 'to lick,' λιχνεύω, 'to lick, taste by stealth,' λίχνος, 'glutton, dainty'; Sans. _rih_, _lih_, 'to lick'; OSlov. _lizą_ (_lizati_), and Lith. _lēžiù_ (_lēžti_), 'to lick'; Lat. _lingo_, 'to lick,' and allied to this perhaps Lat. _lingua_ (Lith. _lēžùvis_), 'tongue'; OIr. _ligim_, 'to lick.'

Ledʃen (2.), lödʃen, vb., 'to kick, hop,' from the equiv. MidHG. _lęcken_, wk. vb., in Goth. perhaps *_lakjan_, which may be connected with Gr. λάξ, adv. λάγ-δην, 'with the foot.' Its kinship with Goth. _laikan_, 'to spring, hop,' is improbable.

Leder, n., 'leather,' from the equiv. MidHG. _lëder_, OHG. _lëdar_, n.; a common Teut. word pointing to Goth. *_liþra_-, n.; comp. AS. _lęþer_, E. _leather_, Du. _leder_, OIc. _leþr_, n., 'leather.' The pre-Teut. form is _lëtro-m_, to which Ir. _lethar_, W. _lledr_, 'leather,' are traced.

Ledig, adj., from the equiv. MidHG. _lëdic_, _lëdec_ (_g_), 'unoccupied, free, untrammelled'; the modern UpG. dials. point to MidHG. _lędic_. OHG. *_lëdag_, _lędlig_, as well as Goth. *_liþags_ are wanting; the following, however, are recorded: OIc. _liþugr_, 'free, untrammelled,' MidE. _lęþi_, adj., 'unoccupied, empty,' MidDu. _lëdech_, Mid LG. _leddich_, _ledich_, 'at leisure, unemployed.' The prim. word is MidE. _lịthe_, 'leisure, spare time' (AS. _leoþu_?), to which is allied _lëthen_ (_lęþin_), 'to set free' (AS. _āt_-, _a-leoþian_?), as well as MidDu. _onlëde_, 'want of leisure, grief.' On account of the absence of the word in the OTeut. dials. it is difficult to determine the evolution in meaning. Must we connect it with Goth. _unlēds_, AS. _unlǽde_, 'poor, unhappy,' or with Lat. _liber_ (for _líthero_?), 'free'?

Lee, n., 'lee,' ModHG. only, from LG. _lee_, 'place where a calm prevails'; comp. Ic. _hlé_, E. _lee_ (from AS. _hleó_, 'protection').

Leer, adj., from the equiv. MidHG. _lǽre_, OHG. and OSax. _lâri_, 'empty, void'; comp. AS. _lǽre_, _gelǽre_, MidE. _ilẹre_, E. dial. _leer_, 'empty, with an empty stomach, hungry.' It can hardly be determined whether the _r_ represents by rhotacism an earlier _s_. Perhaps Goth. _lasius_, 'powerless, weak,' AS. _lęsve_, 'weak' (MidHG. _erlęsmen_, 'to grow weak'), as well as OIc. _lasenn_, 'demolished,' are the nearest cognates of _leer_.

Lefze, f., 'lip,' from the equiv. MidHG. _lęfs_, _lęfse_, f. and m., OHG. _lęfs_, m., an UpG. term (in Suab. lengthened to _lif͡sg_) for the properly LG. Lippe. Both terms are primit. allied; Lippe may come from Teut. *_lipjô_, f., and Lefze (with the OHG. variant _lëffur_, OSax. _lëpur_), from primit. Teut. _lepas_, gen. _lepaziz_, or _lęfs_, gen. _lęfsis_ (with _fs_ for _ps_); comp. Goth. _ahs_, gen. _ahsis_, 'ear (of corn),' with OHG. _ahir_, AS. _eár_ (from *_eahor_), E. _ear_. For the further cognates comp. under Lippe. Goth. and Scand. have a totally different term for 'lip'; Goth. _wairilô_ (AS. _weler_), OIc. _vǫrr_, f.

Legel, m., 'keg, cruse,' from MidHG. _lägel_, _lâgel_, _lägele_, f., 'small cask,' OHG. _lâgila_, _lâgella_, f., which is derived from MidLat. _lagëna_, 'a measure for liquids and for dry goods' (Lat. _lagōna_, _lagoena_, 'flask.'

from Gr. λάγηνος, λάγυνος ἡ, 'flagon'); with respect to *l* for Lat. *n* in words borrowed from Lat. comp. Kümmel (also Himmel, Schlenig). Moreover, the primit. kinship of the HG. cognates with OSlov. *lakŭtĭ*, Lith. *lakas*, 'earthen pitcher,' is perhaps conceivable.

legen, vb., 'to lay, put,' from the equiv. MidHG. and OHG. *legen*, *lecken*, wk. vb.; prop. 'to cause to lie,' hence a factitive of liegen. It corresponds to OSax. *leggian*, Du. *leggen*, AS. *lećǵan*, E. *to lay*, OIc. *leǵja*, Goth. *lagjan*, wk. vb., 'to lay.' Comp. liegen.

Legenbe, f., 'legend,' from MidHG. *legende*, f., 'story of a saint'; from MidLat. *legenda*, neu. plur. (sic dicta, quia certis diebus legenda in ecclesia et in sacris synaxibus designabatur a moderatore chori).

Lehbe, **Lebe**, f., 'waste land,' simply ModHG., from earlier Du. *leeghde*, ModDu. *laagte*, 'low ground, valley,' through a LG. medium. Allied to the ModDu. adj. *laag*, 'low,' to which E. *low* and the equiv. OIc. *lágr* correspond; in miners' language the adj. appears also in G.; *lâg*, 'sloping, awry,' from MidHG. *lǣge*, 'flat, low.' The whole class belongs to the stem of liegen.

Lehen, n., 'fief,' from MidHG. *lêhen*, n., 'feudal estate, fief,' OHG. *lêhan*, n.; corresponding to OIc. *lán*, n., 'loan, fief' (whence E. *loan*), AS. *lǽn*; in Goth. probably *laihwnis*, n., to which Sans. *rekṇas*, n., 'estate, wealth,' prop. 'inheritance,' corresponds in construction and derivation. For further cognates comp. leihen.

Lehm, m., 'loam, clay,' with a LG. and MidG. form (*è* for HG. *ei*); the strictly HG. form Leimen has a restricted sphere. Comp. MidHG. *leim*, *leime*, m., 'loam,' from OHG. *leimo*, m. It corresponds to AS. *lám*, E. *loam* (Goth. *laima*). The root *lai* appears with a derivative *s* in OIc. *leir*, n., from *laiz*, which may have been contracted from *laj-is*, like Goth. *ais*, 'brass,' from *ajis*, Sans. *ayas*. Allied to Lat. *límus*, m., 'slime, dirt.' The form of the gradation between Teut. *laima* and Lat. *límus* is *ai* to *i*. Comp. Leim.

Lehne (1.), f., 'back or arm (of a chair), balustrade, railing,' from the equiv. Mid HG. *lëne*, *line*, f., OHG. *lina*, f., 'reclinatorium' for *hlina*, which was probably the form in Goth. also. Comp. Gr. κλίνη, 'couch, mattress' (these meanings also belong to Lehne in earlier ModHG.), and for further cognates see lehnen and Leiter.

Lehne (2.), f., from the equiv. MidHG. *liene*, with the remarkable variant *liehe*, f., 'wild sow'; its further connections are difficult to determine; the similarity in sound with the equiv. Fr. *laie* and MidLat. *léfa* (for *léha*?) must not be overlooked. It is doubtful whether Lehne is of Teut. origin.

Lehne (3.), f., 'linch-pin'; comp. Lünse.

Lehne (4.), **Lenne**, f., 'Norwegian maple'; MidHG. and OHG. *lin-*, *limboum*, hence also earlier ModHG. Leinbaum; the ModHG. form is borrowed from a Northern dial.; Dan. *lön*, Swed. *lönn*. Moreover the term was orig. common to Teut.; it was applied to the 'maple' in all the older dials. except Goth.; OIc. *hlynr*, AS. *hlyn* (*hlynn* or *hlîn*?), and with these in the non-Teut. languages Slav. *klenŭ*, and Lith. *klévas*, 'maple,' are primit. allied.

lehnen (1.), vb., 'to lean, recline'; it combines MidHG. *lënen*, *linen*, intr., 'to rest (on),' and (through the medium of MidG.) MidHG. *leinen*, trans., 'to lean,' OHG. *linên*, earlier *hlinên*, intr., and *leinen*, *hleinen*, trans.; corresponds to AS. *hlinian*, *hleonian*, intr., and *hlǽnan*, trans., 'to lean.' The real stem is *hli*, the *n* is a verbal suffix (in Lehne, however, corresponding to Gr. κλί-νη, a nominal suffix). The graded form of *hlĭ*, *hlai*, has been preserved in Leiter; it also existed in an O'Teut. *hlaiwaz*, *hlaiwiz*, n., 'hill' (Goth. *hlaiw*, AS. *hlǽw*, OHG. *lêo* for *hlêo*), as well as in Goth. *hlains*, m., 'hill,' OIc. *hlein*, f., 'projecting rock.' The root *hlĭ*, unpermutated *klĭ*, appears in the non-Teut. languages with numerous cognates; Gr. κλί-νω, 'to lean,' κλῑ-μαξ, f., 'ladder, stairs' (comp. Leiter), κλί-νη, 'couch,' κλι-σία, 'couch, easy-chair, tent' (comp. Goth. *hlei-þra*, f., 'tent'), κλι-τύς, 'hill,' κλῑ-τος, κλίτος, n., 'hill' (comp. ModHG. Leite, f., OIc. *hlíþ*, f., AS. *hlíþ*, n., 'hill'); Lat. *clinare*, 'to incline,' *clivus*, m., 'hill,' with which are allied Lith. *szlýti*, 'to incline to one side,' *szlėti*, 'to lean against,' *szlaitas*, 'slope.' Hence, according to these allied meanings, the idea is 'to rise gradually, assume a wry form or a slanting position.'

lehnen (2.), vb., 'to lend,' from MidHG. *lêhenen*, OHG. *lêhanôn*, 'to bestow as a fief, lend'; comp. Lehen, and further also leihen; allied to AS. *lǽnan* (pret. *lǽnde*), E. *to lend*.

lehren, vb., 'to teach,' from MidHG. and OHG. *lêren*, 'to instruct, teach, make one acquainted with,' sometimes also 'to learn'; corresponding to Du. *leeren*, AS. *lǽran* (whence OIc. *lǽra* is borrowed), Goth. *laisjan*, 'to teach.' A common Teut. vb. with the primit. meaning 'to cause to know'; *laisjan* is the factitive of a pret. pres. *lais*, 'I know,' preserved in Goth. only. In G. and E. only a partic. derivative was retained, which was probably represented in Goth. by *lisnan* or *liznan*; comp. lernen. Allied also to Goth. *leis*, 'knowing,' *leisei*, 'knowledge,' in *lubja-leis*, -*leisei*, 'skilled in poisons, witchcraft.' We have data for assuming that Goth. *lais*, 'I know,' is based on a prim. meaning 'I have experienced,' for the stem *lis* of lehren and lernen appears also in Gleise and leisten in the old sense of ' to go,' with which Lat. *lira*, ' furrow,' and its derivative *delīrare* (lit. ' to slip away from') are connected, as well as OSlov. *lěcha*, 'ridge (of a furrow),' mentioned under Gleise; comp. leisten.—**Lehre**, f., 'teaching, doctrine,' from MidHG. *lēre*, OHG. *lēra*, f.; comp. AS. *lár*, f., whence E. *lore*.—**gelehrt, gelahrt**, part., 'learned,' even in MidHG. *gelĕrt* and *gelărt*, with the ModHG. sense, prop. however, ' one who is instructed'; comp. MidE. *ilǽred*, Scand. *lǽrþr* (comp. *doctus* from *docere*). -**lei**, suffix, ModHG. simply; from Mid HG. *leie*, f., ' manner, method.' In MidHG. there was no compound corresponding to ModHG. mancherlei, the expression *maneger leie* being used as a gen., e.g. *maneger leie liute*, ' various sorts of people,' equiv. to ModHG. mancherlei Leute. MidHG. *leie, lei*, is generally considered to be a Rom. word borrowed from OFr. and Prov. *ley*, 'method' (Span. and Port. *laya*, ' manner,' is said to be of Basque origin).

Lei, Leie, m. and f., 'rock, stone' (in proper names like Lorelei), from MidHG. *lei, leie*, f., ' rock, stone,' also ' paved way, schist,' corresponding to OSax. *leia*, f., 'rock.' Further cognates, whether in the Teut. or non-Teut. languages, are uncertain (allied perhaps to Gr. λᾶας, 'stone'?). It has been assumed that Ital. *lavagna*, 'slate,' was borrowed from the G. cognates.

Leib, m., 'body, waist,' from MidHG. *lîp* (b), m., ' life, body, substance '; the meaning 'life' has been preserved in Mod HG. only in compounds such as Leibzucht, 'sustenance,' Leibrente, 'life-annuity.' OHG. *lîb*, m. and n., ' life,' AS. *lîf*, E. *life*; Goth. **leif* (b) is wanting (' life ' is rendered by *faírhwus*); Scand. *líf*, n., ' body, life.' The phonetic kinship with Leben may be represented in Gr. by λιπ, λιπ; just as leben, following Gr. λιπαρεῖν, means lit. ' to persist,' so too OTeut. *liba*- is lit. ' persistence, continuance '; the meaning ' body, substance,' is simply G. Gr. λείπω cannot on account of Lat. *linquo* be connected with λιπαρέω; it is allied to Teut. leiben, while λιπαρέω with Leib and Leben are based on an Aryan root *lîp* in bleiben.

Leich, m., ' lay,' a term borrowed anew from MidHG. *leich*, m., ' song consisting of unequal strophes,' orig. in a general sense ' instrumental melody' (whence OFr. *lai* was borrowed). It corresponds to Goth. *laiks*, 'dance,' from *laikan*, ' to dance,' AS. *lác*, n., ' play, tilting,' from *lácan*, ' to leap, dance.' Since ModHG. Leich is only a loanword, no further remarks are necessary concerning the specifically OTeut. root *laik* and its wide ramifications.

Leiche, f., 'corpse,' from MidHG. *lich*, *lîche*, f., ' body, substance,' also ' dead body, corpse '; in ModHG. the specialised meaning, which in the earlier Teut. dials. was subordinate to the more general sense ' body ' as substance, has now become the prevalent one. OHG. *lîh (hh)*, f. and n., ' body, flesh,' AS. *líc*, n., ' body, substance, corpse' (for E. *like* comp. gleich); Goth. *leik*, n., ' flesh, body, corpse.' In a possessive compound *lîk* assumed even in the OTeut. period the definite meaning ' body,' but was modified afterwards in numerous dials. to a suffix equiv. to HG. -lich (which see). The signification ' body ' has been retained in ModHG. Leichbern, ' corn,' lit. ' thorn in the body' (Ic. *líkþorn*).—**Leichnam**, m., ' dead body, corpse,' from Mid HG. *lîchname*, OHG. *lîhhinamo*, m., ' body, substance, corpse '; OHG. *lîhhinamo* for **lîhhin-hamo* is based on a wk. form **lîkan-*, **lîkin-* (comp. Goth. *manleika*, 'image '); at all events, OHG. *lîhhin-amo* is not a corruption of OTeut. *lîkhamo*, m., ' body'; OHG. *lîhhamo* (by syncope *lîhmo*), MidHG. *lîchame*, m., AS. *líc-ȝoma*, OIc. *líkamr* (*líkame*), m., ' body.' The second component is an obsolete noun (*ham, hamo*), meaning ' form, covering '; comp. OIc. *hamr*, ' skin, shape,' AS. *homa*, ' covering '; Goth. *anahamón, gahamón*, 'to put on (clothes), dress ' (comp. Hemd, hämisch, and Hemd). Therefore Leichnam probably signified orig. ' body; ' lit. ' covering or form of flesh,' *i.e.* ' body of flesh, in so far as it is endowed with life.' The compound has a rather poetical air about it, and in fact

Scand. and AS. poetry coined many similar circumlocutions for 'body.' In AS. poetry comp. *flǽsc-homa*, 'flesh-covering,' also *bán-fœt*, lit. 'bone-vessel,' *bánhús*, lit. 'bone-house,' *bánloca*, lit. 'bone-cage,' *báncofa*, lit. 'bone-dwelling,' as synonyms of AS. *líc-homa*, 'body.' Hence it is quite possible that OTeut. *lík-hamo* was adopted from poetry in ordinary prose.

leicht, adj., 'light,' from the equiv. Mid HG. *lîht*, *lîhte*, OHG. *lîhti*; corresponding to Du. *ligt*, AS. *lîht*, *leôht*, E. *light*, OIc. *léttr*, Goth. *leihts*, 'light.' The further cognates of the word are uncertain, since there are too many adjs. in the allied languages closely resembling leicht both in sense and sound. Some etymologists derive Lat. *lēvis*, 'light,' from *lévis*, *lenhvis*, in order to connect it with the common Teut. adj. as well as with Gr. ἐλαχύς, 'petty, small,' Lith. *lengvùs*, *lĕngvas*, 'light'; in that case *lîht* would represent *linht*, *lenht*. If leicht be connected with ModHG. gelingen, it might be compared with Gr. ἐλαφρός, 'light, nimble' (see lungern). No explanation has been hitherto quite satisfactory, since in the non-Teut. languages there is no adj. corresponding in form to G. leicht.—In E. *lights* (see Lunge) is also connected with the adj. *light*.

Leid, n., 'harm, hurt, sorrow,' from MidHG. *leit (d)*, n., 'affliction, pain, evil' (as adj. 'afflicting'), OHG. *leid*, n., 'that which causes affliction; harm, pain' (*leid*, adj., 'afflicting, repugnant, hateful'). Comp. AS. *lāþ*, 'offence, wrong, hostile, hateful, inimical'; E. *loath*, adj., *to loathe*, OIc. *leiþr*, 'hostile, hateful.' Probably the abstr. subst. is orig. nothing more than the neut. of the adj., which passed into Rom. at a very early period (comp. Ital. *laido*, 'ugly,' Fr. *laid*). See further under leiben and leider.

leiden, vb., 'to suffer, endure, bear,' from the equiv. MidHG. *líden*, OHG. *lídan*, str. vb. It is ordinarily identified with an OTeut. str. vb. *líþan*, 'to go' (comp. leiten); comp. OHG. *lídan*, 'to go, proceed,' AS. *líþan*, Goth. *leiþan*, 'to go.' It is assumed that *líþan*, from the meaning 'travelling to a foreign land (*alilandi*, whence Mod HG. elend) and across the sea' (*líþan* is frequently used of a voyage), has acquired the sense of 'indisposition, enduring, and suffering.' This explanation is too artificial, and when it is urged in its favour that the latter meaning does not occur in Goth.,

OSax., and AS., the fact is overlooked that it is assumed as primit. by the common Teut. adj. *laipa-*, 'painful, repugnant, hostile,' which is wanting only in Goth. (comp. Leid). It might be conceivable if a compound of *liþan*, 'to go,' formed by prefixing a verbal particle, had assumed within the historic period the meaning 'to suffer,' but that the simple verb evolved such a sense immediately from 'to go' in primit. Teut. times is scarcely credible. The proof of this lies in the fact that the derivative *laiþa-*, from the stem of *liþan*, is more widely diffused, and is recorded at an earlier period. Thus we are led to the orig. meaning 'to put up with what is repugnant,' and therefore the early existence of the adj. and subst. discussed under Leid causes no surprise. For the further history of the word the OHG. interject. *léwes*, *lés*, 'oh! alas!' appears to be valuable; in form it is the gen. of a noun, and presumes Goth. *laiwis*, from a stem *lai-wa-*. Since it is used in a way similar to HG. leider, they are probably cognate. Thus the root would be *lai*, by gradation *lî*; the dental of *lídan*, leiden, was probably therefore a part of the present stem originally. See the following word.

leider, interj., 'alas!' from the equiv. MidHG. *leider*, OHG. *leidôr*; prop. a comparat. of the OTeut. adj. mentioned under Leid. With regard to the possibility of its being allied to OHG. *léwes*, *lés*, 'alas!' comp. leiden.

Leier, f., 'lyre,' from the equiv. Mid HG. *líre*, OHG. *líra*, f.; from Lat. and Gr. *lyra*, with the Byzantine pronunciation of the *y* current in the Middle Ages, but with an abnormal change of quantity (as in Kreuz, Schule, and Lilie). The lyre of the Middle Ages, except when imported, was essentially different from the antique lyre; it was an instrument of the same sort as a guitar, and was played by a wheel turned by a winch; hence it was something very like a barrel-organ (hurdy-gurdy). Through the influence of classical studies, the term Leier is now applied again to the antique instrument without entirely supplanting the earlier meaning (comp. Leierkaften). Comp. also Ital. *lira*, Fr. *lyre*, E. *lyre*, and Du. *lier*.

leihen, vb., 'to lend, borrow,' from Mid HG. *líhen*, OHG. *líhan*, str. vb., 'to take on credit,' rarely 'to give on credit'; so too Goth. *leihwan*, AS. *león* (contracted from *lîhan*), of which only the allied forms *loan* and *to lend* have been preserved in E. (comp. Leben and Leben). These derivatives, which appear in several dialects, are based on the common Teut. meaning 'to lend.' The correspondences in the cognate languages prove that this is only a specialisation of a general sense, 'to leave.' The Aryan root *lik* occurs with the meanings 'to leave behind, forsake, set free, relinquish'; Sans. *ric* (for *lik*), pres. *riṇḍcmi*, 'to abandon a thing, give up, set free, empty, clear, give way for a certain sum'; to this are allied *rikthám*, n., 'bequest, inheritance,' *reknas*, n., 'property left behind, wealth' (see Lehen), *riktás*, adj., and *rékn-s*, adj., 'empty'; also Lat. *linquo, relinquo, reliquus;* Gr. λείπω, with very numerous meanings, 'to forsake, leave over or behind, omit'; λοιπός, adj., 'remaining'; OIc. *léicim* (prim. form *leiqô*), 'I leave, relinquish'; Lith. *lēku, likti*, 'to leave behind,' *pálaikas*, 'remnant,' OSlov. *otŭ-lěkŭ*, 'remnant, relic.'

Leilachen, Leilach, n., 'sheet,' from MidHG. *lilachen, lilach*, n., 'bed-linen, sheet.' The ModHG. and MidHG. word originated in *lin-lachen*, which form is often recorded in MidHG. (Leinlachen in earlier ModHG.), and appears in OHG. as *lîn-lahhan*; *lînl-* was assimilated in MidHG. to *lill-* and *ll* simplified after a long vowel. A similar course was followed by the OIc. cognate *lé-rept* for **línrept, *línript*, 'linen.' The derivation of Leilachen from MidHG. *lihlachen*, OHG. *lih-lahhan*, 'body-linen' (comp. Leicht, for OHG. *lîh*), is less probable, because an assimilation of *chl* to *ll*, *l*, is scarcely credible.

Leim, m., 'glue, birdlime,' from the equiv. MidHG., MidLG., and OHG. *lîm*, m.; corresponding to Du. *lijm*, AS. *lîm*, E. *lime;* Scand. *lím*, n., 'glue, lime'; Goth. **leima* is wanting. The common Teut. *lîma-* is related by gradation to the common Teut. *laima-*, mentioned under Lehm; the prim. meaning, 'earthy, adhesive substance,' is deduced from the E. and Scand. signification 'glue, lime.' Lat. *limus*, 'slime,' is more closely connected with HG. Lehm in meaning, but with HG. Leim in its graded form *î*. The root *lai*, by gradation *lî*, is authenticated by OIc. *leir*, n. (see Lehm), and Lat. *li-no*, 'to rub over.' Its relation to Gr. λειμών, 'marsh,' and γλοιός, 'sticky, clammy stuff,' is less certain.

Lein, m., 'flax,' from the equiv. Mid HG. and OHG. *lîn*, m. and n.; comp. Leinen.

Leine, f., 'line,' from MidHG. and Mid LG. *lîne*, f., late OHG. *lîna*, f., 'rope, cable, line,' espec. 'towline.' The derivation from Lat. *línea* is doubtful, because the latter does not signify 'cable' even in Mid Lat., but specially 'plumb-line,' and in Mid Lat. 'measure of length.' As far as the sense is concerned, the word is more closely connected with Lat. *línum*, 'thread, cable, rope'; hence OHG. *lîna* is the plur. of the Lat. word. In Rom. and MidLat., however, *línum* does not occur in this sense. Perhaps Leine, as an independent Teut. derivative of *lin*, 'linen,' corresponds to Gr. λινέα, λινέα, 'rope, cord'? In that case AS. *line*, E. *line*, and OIc. *lína* (Goth. **leinjô*, lit. 'what is prepared from flax'), are also formed according to the genuinely Teut. principle (suffix, *jôn*).

Leinen, n., 'linen,' prop. a neut. adj. used as a subst., MidHG. *lînen, lînîn*, '(of) linen.' It is based on MidHG. *lîn*, m., 'flax, linen, linen garment,' OHG. and OSax. *lîn*, n., Goth. *lein*, n., 'linen.' In this case, as in that of Hanf, it is doubtful whether the term (common Teut. *lîna-*) is cognate with or borrowed from the similarly sounding words in Lat. and Gr. If the Teut. word is really borrowed, the relation of the consonants proves that Hanf was known to the Teutons previous to the permutation of consonants, *i.e.*, long before our era; the same may be said of *lîna-*, 'flax,' since Pliny and Tacitus testify that linen was used among the Teutons when they wrote. Perhaps we may regard Scythian as the source of the cognates, as is indicated by the absence of the word among the Eastern Aryans. Comp. Lat. *lînum*, Gr. λίνο-ν, OSlov. *lĭnŭ*, Lith. *línaî*, 'flax'; λι- was retained in the dat. λι-rí, plur. λί-τα, hence the root of *línum*, λίνον, is *lî-* and *no*, the suffix. Comp. Leilachen and Leine.—

Leinwand, f., is a ModHG. corruption of MidHG. *lînwât*, f., 'linen,' connecting it with HG. Gewand. The old *wât* (OHG. and MidHG.) has become obsolete in Mod HG.; like AS. *wǽd*, 'garment,' it is allied to a lost Aryan root, *wê*, 'to weave.'

Leis, m., 'canticle,' borrowed from Mid HG. and early ModHG. *leis, leise*, m., 'spiritual song,' shortened from *kírléise*. *Kyrie eleison* was the refrain of hymns.

leise, adj., 'low, soft, gentle,' from Mid

HG. *lîse*, OHG. *lîsi* (adv. *lîso*), 'low,' also 'slow.' Under lehren, Lift, and lernen, a Teut. root, orig. meaning 'to go,' is discussed, with which Goth. *leis*, 'familiar,' seems to be connected. The HG. word can, however, scarcely be directly allied to this adj., since the difference in meaning is too great. It is also questionable whether leife belongs at all to the root *lis*. Perhaps it is connected with Gr. λεῖος, λιαρός, 'soft, gentle, mild'; both, however, are better referred to Lat. *lēvis*, 'smooth.' The nasal in Suab. *lins (læñs)*, 'low,' presents a difficulty.

Leiſte (1.), f., 'list, border, selvage,' from MidHG. *lîste*, OHG. *lîsta*, f., 'long strip, edge, lace, list'; comp. AS. *list*, f., E. *list*; Ic. *lista (lísta ?)*, f., 'border, strip'; in the non-Teut. languages there are no cognates. Note, however, the words borrowed in Rom., Ital. *lista*, Fr. *liste*, 'strip, lace.'

Leiſte (2.), f., 'groin,' ModHG. only, probably not connected with the preceding word, but with Goth. **laistô*, f. The latter is indicated also by E. *last* (dial.), 'groin.' The equiv. AS. *leósca*, MidE. *léske*, ModDu. *liesche*, OSwed. *liuske*, Dan. *lýske*, diverge too widely in sound from the HG. form; the attempt to connect it with MidLat. *laisius*, 'lap' (Lex Salica), is also dubious.

Leiſten, Leiſte, m., from the equiv. MidHG. *leist*, m., 'last'; OHG. *leist* (n. ?), 'forma.' Corresponding to AS. *lást, lǽst*, m., 'footprint, track, forma,' E. *last*. Goth. *laists*, m., 'track, goal,' with the facts mentioned under leiſten, indicate that 'footprint' is the orig. meaning of the HG. and E. words; this is probably an important fact in the history of the word. It is true that OIc. *leistr*, m., signifies 'foot,' and 'short stocking, sock.'

Leiſten, vb., 'to perform, accomplish,' from MidHG. and OHG. *leisten*, 'to adhere to and execute an order, fulfil one's promise or duty'; corresponds to Goth. *laistjan*, 'to pursue, yield.' On account of its kinship with Gleiſe and Leiſten, m., the meaning of the HG. word (as well as the equiv. OSax. *léstan*) must be based on the Goth. vb. AS. *lǽstan*, 'to perform, accomplish, hold, sustain, endure,' whence E. *to last*. The common Teut. wk. vb. *laistjan*, 'to pursue' (whence Span. and Port. *lastar*, 'to pay on behalf of another,' was borrowed), is derived from Goth. *laists*, m., AS. *lást*, m., 'footprint' (see under Leiſten), which are again derived from a root *lis*, 'to go.'

This root has a constant tendency to pass from the sensuous meaning 'to go, follow,' into an intellectual notion (see Lehre, lernen, and Liſt); comp. also Leiſe.

Leite, f., from the equiv. MidHG. *lîte*, f., 'mountain, slope, declivity,' OHG. *lîta*, from an earlier **hlíta*, f. (Goth. **hleida*, f.). The Teut. root *hlî* is discussed more fully under lehnen, where also the allied terms signifying 'hill' may be compared.

Leiten, vb., from the equiv. MidHG. and OHG. 'to lead, guide'; corresponding to OSax. *lédan*, Du. *leiden*, AS. *lǽdan*, E. *to lead*, OIc. *leiða*. All point to a non-recorded Goth. **laidjan*, which (as factitive of the OTeut. *lîþan*, 'to go,' discussed under leiten) signifies lit. 'to cause to go'; comp. ſenden, which also had orig. this same meaning. With the factitive **laidjan* is connected a Teut. *laidô-*, f., 'leading,' whence AS. *lád*, 'road, journey,' in E. current only in *loadstar*, *loadstone*, and *loadsman* (AS. *ládmann*), equiv. to ModHG. Leiſt. ModHG. Leitſtern, MidHG. *leitstërne*, m., 'the polar star that guides the mariners, loadstar.'

Leiter, f., from the equiv. MidHG. *leiter, leitere*, OHG. *leitara* (earlier **hleitir*), f., 'ladder.' It corresponds to Du. *ladder*, *leer*, AS. *hlǽlder, hlǽder*, f., E. *ladder*; the Goth. term **hlai-dri* (gen. *-drjôs*), f., 'ladder,' with a fem. suffix identical with Gr. *-τρια*, is wanting : **hlat-dri* is based on the *hlî* (pre-Teut. *klî*) discussed under lehnen, and in Gr. κλῖ-μαξ this root has a meaning corresponding to that of the West Teut. word; Leiter is as it were 'that which slants or leans.' Scand. *hleiðr*, 'tent,' may be connected with the equiv. Goth. *hleiþra*, f., and Gr. κλισία. Comp. Lehne, lehnen, and Leite.

Lende, f., 'loins,' from the equiv. Mid HG. *lende*, OHG. *lentin*, f.; corresponding to Du. *lende*, AS. *lÿnden*, f. (in the plur. *lẏndenu*, m.) ; OIc. *lend*, Dan. *lynd*, 'loins' (allied to Ic. *lundir*, 'sirloin, saddle of mutton'?); in Goth. perhaps **landini*, f. In case the *b* of Lat. *lumbus*, 'loins,' represented Aryan *dh*, or rather *dhw* (for Lat. *barba*, representing *bhardhâ*, see Bart, and Lat. *ruber*, representing Aryan *rudhros*, ἐρυθρός, see ret), HG. Lende might be compared with it. The prim. form *lndhwi-* is also indicated by OSlov. *lẹdvija*, f., 'loins, kidney.'

Lenken, vb., 'to guide, direct,' from MidHG. *lenken*, 'to bend, turn, direct'; a denominative of MidHG. *lanke*, OHG.

lanca, hlanca, 'hip, loins.' For further details see under Flanke and Gelenk; it is also perhaps allied to *link,* lit. 'oblique'; hence lenken orig. means 'to direct obliquely or sideways' (comp. linf). It is also thought to be connected with Lith. *lĕnkti,* 'to bend.'

Lenz, m. (Bav. *längess, längsing,* Swiss *langsi),* from the equiv. MidHG. *lęnze,* m. and f., 'spring' (from the variants *langeʒ, langeʒe);* OHG. *lęnzo, lęnzĭn, langiʒ,* m.; the loss of the *g* is normal, as in Blitz and Munzel. Comp. Du. *lente,* AS. *lęncten,* m., 'spring,' E. *Lent.* This West Teut. word was probably the term for spring, and Tacitus in the *Germania* seems to have a dim idea that it was used by the Teutons (OIc. *vár,* MidE. and Scotch *wĕr,* North Fris. *ûrs, woos,* represent the North Teut. term primit. allied to Lat. *vĕr,* Gr. ἔαρ, Sans. *vasar)* ; for the other observations of Tacitus on the OTeut. divisions of time, comp. Herbst (also Frühling, which has supplanted the old word Lenz in most of the modern dials. of Upper Germany; see an old Aryan term for Lenz under Jahr). The word is peculiar to Teut.; it has not been authenticated in the non-Teut. languages; its prim. meaning is therefore dubious. Some etymologists, misled simply by the similarity of sound, have connected Lenz with lang (Goth. *laggs),* and opined that it was so named from the lengthening of the days; such a derivation is at all events uncertain.

Lerche, f., 'lark,' from the equiv. Mid HG. *lĕrche,* from *lĕreche, lĕwreche,* OHG. *lĕrahha,* f.; it is shown by the equiv. Du. *leeuwerik,* AS. *lǽwrice, lǽwerce, lǽwerce,* E. *lark,* Scotch *lavrock,* OSwed. *lǽrikia,* as well as the MidHG. variants *lĕwerich, lĕwerech, lĕwerch,* that a fuller form would have been *lĕwarahha in OHG. The Goth. form cannot be determined with any certainty, nor can we say definitely whether the OHG. and AS. words are compounds or simply unusual derivatives.

lernen, vb., from the equiv. MidHG. *lĕrnen,* 'to learn' (more rarely 'to teach'), OHG. *lirnên, lërnên,* 'to learn'; comp. AS. *leornian,* E. *to learn,* OSax. *lînon* for Goth. **liznan* (pret. **liznóda);* an OTeut. derivative of the partic. of the Goth. str. vb. *lais,* 'I know,' discussed under Lehre and lehren; hence lernen means 'to become experienced, informed.' The cognates of the stem *lis* fall into two classes; to one belongs the sensuous notion 'to go' (comp. Leisten, Leiste, Gleise, and leise), the other comprises the words Lehre, lehren, and Goth. *leis,* 'knowing.'

lesen, vb., 'to gather, glean, read,' from MidHG. *lësen,* OHG. *lësan,* 'to pick out, pick up, read,' also 'to narrate, relate.' Goth. *lisan, galisan,* and AS. *lesan,* simply mean 'to gather, collect'; from the latter E. *to lease* is derived. So too in earlier OIc. *lesa* merely signifies 'to collect, glean.' There can be no doubt that this was the prim. meaning of HG. lesen; hence it is probable that the common Teut. *lesan,* 'to gather up,' is connected with Lith. *lesù (lèsti),* 'to peck, pick up grains of corn.' There is no relation between Goth. *lisan,* 'to gather,' and *lais,* 'I know,' *laisjan,* 'to teach' (see lehren, and lernen). The development of the meaning 'to read' from 'to gather' is indeed analogous to that of Lat. *lego* and Gr. λέγω, which the HG. significations combine. Yet the state of OTeut. culture affords a finer and wider explanation of lesen, 'legero'; since the modern term Buchstabe, 'letter,' is inherited from OTeut. times, when runic signs were scratched on separate twigs, the gathering of these twigs, which were strewn for purposes of divination, was equiv. to 'reading (lesen) the runes.' Hence OTeut. *lesan* expressed the action described by Tacitus (*Germ.* 10) as "surculos ter singulos tollit;" in pre-hist. G. it also signified "sublatos secundum impressam ante notam interpretatur." It is worthy of remark too that the OTeut. dials. have no common term for 'to read,' and this proves that the art was not learnt until the Teutons had separated into the different tribes. It is also certain that runic writing was of foreign, probably of Italian origin. The Goth used the expressions *siggwan, ussiggwan,* 'to read,' the Englishman AS. *rǽdan,* E. *to read;* the former probably signified orig. 'loud delivery,' the latter 'to guess the runic characters.'

Letten, m. '(potter's) clay,' from Mid HG. *lëtte,* OHG. *lëtto,* m., 'loam' (*ë* is due to the Bav. and Alem. dials.); to this is probably allied the Ic. graded form *lepja,* f., 'loam, dirt.' It is connected by some etymologists with Lat. *lŭtum,* n., 'mud, dirt,' and by others, less probably, with OPruss. *laydis,* 'loam,' whose diphthong, compared with the *a* of the Teut. word, presents a difficulty.

letzen, vb., 'to injure,' from *letzen*, OHG. *lezzen*, 'to check, stop, hinder, damage, hurt'; corresponding to Goth. *latjan, galatjan*, 'to stop, check,' AS. *lettan*, E. *to let*; a common Teut. denominative from the adj. *lata-*; comp. laß and laſſen.—ſich letzen, 'to indulge oneself,' from Mid HG. *letzen*, 'to liberate, do one a kindness, take one's leave, regale oneself.' See also the following word.

letzt, super. adj., 'last,' from the equiv. MidHG. *lest, lezzist*, super. of laʒ, adj., 'faint'; the ModHG. form seems to be due to LG., which must have produced *letist* and *lezt* (for *letst*). These forms actually occur in the *Heliand*. In OHG. *lezzist, lazzóst*, AS. *lætma* and *lætmest* (pointing to a Goth. *latuma*, 'latest'); also AS. *latost*, E. *last*. The posit. of these OTeut. superlats. is the OTeut. adject. stem *lata-* (see laß), lit. 'lazy, inactive, dilatory'; letzter orig. means 'most dilatory, latest' (comp. AS. and E. *late*). In the phrase ʒu guter Letzt, 'for the last time, finally,' the noun is a corruption of Letʒ, which is connected with MidHG. *letzen*, 'to end, take one's leave, take refreshment,' mentioned under letʒen, hence the expression meant orig. 'as a choice farewell-banquet.'

Leuchſe, f., 'rail-tie,' a Bav. and Suab. word, from the equiv. MidHG. *liuhse*; probably cognate with the equiv. Czech *lušně*, Pol. *lusnia*, Russ. *ljusnja*, if these are not connected rather with Lünſe.

Leuchte, f., 'light, lamp,' from MidHG. *liuhte*, f., 'light, apparatus for giving light,' also 'brightness, lustre'; a derivative of Licht.—leuchten, vb., from the equiv. Mid HG. and OHG. *liuhten*, 'to shine, give light,' corresponding to Goth. *liuhtjan*, 'to shine, give light'; an OTeut. denominative from the adj. *liuhta-*, 'light'; leuchten meant lit. 'to be light, bright.' Comp. licht.

Leumund, m., 'reputation, character,' from MidHG. and OHG. *liumunt*, m., 'reputation, fame, report.' In ModHG. it is perhaps instinctively interpreted as Leute Mund, 'mouth of the people'; but the word is not a compound. In Goth. probably *hliumunds*, m., which must be referred to *hliuma*, 'hearing, ear'; *-munda-* is perhaps an affix corresponding to Gr. *-μαρ-* and Lat. *-mento-* (in *co-gnō-mentum*). The root *hliu-* has numerous derivatives, both in the Teut. and non-Teut. languages (comp. lauf, lauten, Gr. κλέος, Sans. *çrávas*, 'fame'); Sans. *çrómata-m.*, n., 'hearing,'

corresponds most nearly in form to HG. Leumund. Lat. *crīmen* has absolutely nothing to do with these last two terms.—Verleumden, 'to calumniate,' is not based directly on Leumund, but on a MidHG. *liumde*, normally abbreviated from it.

Leute, plur only, 'people,' from Mid HG. *liute*, m. and n. plur., 'people, persons,' with the sing. *liut*, m. and n., 'nation'; OHG. *liuti*, m. and n. plur., 'people,' also *liut*, m. and n., 'nation'; corresponding to AS. *leóde*, plur., 'people.' It is uncertain whether we have to assume *liudus*, 'nation,' in Goth. The word is common to Teut. and Slav.; OSlov. *ljudŭ*, m., 'nation,' plur., *ljudije*, 'people,' Lett. *laudis*, m. plur., 'people, nation.' They are connected with an Aryan root *ludh*, 'to grow,' which retained its meaning in Goth. *liudan*, OSax. *liodan*, AS. *leódan*, OHG. *liotan*; comp. the Sans. root *ruh*, 'to grow.' The following Teut. words are also connected with the same stem, Goth. *laups* (gen. *laudis*) in *svalaups*, 'so great,' *samalaups*, 'equally great, equal,' *juggalaups*, 'youth,' MidHG. *lóte*, 'constituted'; Goth. *ludjó-*, f., 'face'; AS. *leód*, m., 'king.'

-lich, adj. suffix, from MidHG. *-lich*, *-lich* (the short vowel on account of its position in an unaccented syllable), OHG. *-lich*; corresponding to Goth. *-leiks*, AS. *-lic*, E. *-ly*. Orig. identical with the OTeut. *lîka-*, 'body,' discussed under Leichnam and gleich; Goth. *wairaleiks*, 'male,' lit. 'having a male body.' In this manner *-lika* is used in all the dials. as an adj. suffix. In some pronominal forms (ſolcher and welcher) the old *-lik* represents a suffix corresponding to Gr. -λίκος in τηλίκος, πηλίκος. See gleich and männiglich.

licht, adj., 'light, luminous,' from Mid HG. *lieht*, OHG. *lioht*, adj., 'bright, radiant, shining'; corresponding to AS. *leóht*, E. *light*, adj.; Goth. *liuhts*, 'bright,' may be inferred from its derivative *liuhtan*, 'to give light' (see leuchten). It is questionable whether the dental licht is of particip. origin, as in alt, ſaſt, ſant, &c.

Licht, n., 'light, luminary, candle,' from MidHG. *licht*, OHG. *lioht*, n., 'light, lustre, brightness'; corresponding to OSax. *lioht*, Du. *licht*, AS. *leóht*, n., E. *light*. The dental of the word is a suffix, as is shown by Goth. *liuh-aþ* (gen. *-adis*), n., 'light, sheen.' OIc. *ljós*, n., 'light,' formed with a different suffix would be in Goth. *liuhs* (gen. *-sis*); they are based on Aryan *leukot-, leukt-*, and *leukos-*, *leuks-*, as a double stem; comp. Sans. *rocis*, n., Zend *raocanh* (for **rócas*), 'lustre, light.' The Aryan root *luk*, by gradation *leuk*, has numerous derivatives, Sans. *ruc* (*rócámi*), 'to give light,' *rukmá-s*, adj., 'glittering,' subst. 'jewels,' *róká-s*, m., *róc iní*, n., 'light'; Gr. λευκός, adj., 'white,' ἀμφιλύκη, 'morning twilight'; Lat. *lucerna*, *lúceo*, *lux*, *lucidus*, *lúna*, *lúmen*, *diluculum*; OIr. *lóche* (*t*), 'lightning,' *lón*, 'lustre'; OSlov. *luča*, 'ray,' *luna*, f., 'moon.' In Teut. there are also other derivatives of the Aryan root *luk*; comp. Leuchte, licht, adj., Lohe and Luchs, as well as Goth. *lauhmuni*, f., 'lightning,' *lauhatjan*, 'to give light'; OIc. *ljóme*, AS. *leóma*, OSax. *liomo*, m., 'lustre'; AS. *légetu*, MidE. *leit*, 'lightning,' and OHG. *lôhazzen*, 'to lighten'; comp. also Luchs. With Sans. *rukšá*, Zend *raokšna*, adj., 'bright,' Pruss. *lauksnos*, f., plur., 'stars,' and OIc. *ljós*, 'light,' are also connected OHG. *liehsen*, adj., 'bright,' and AS. *líxan*, 'to give light.'

lichten, vb., 'to lighten, weigh (anchor),' ModHG. only; MidHG. *lüften*, 'to raise aloft, lift up, air,' as well as E. *to lift*, are unconnected with this word. Lichten, as a nautical term, is borrowed from LG. lichten, lit. 'to make light,' then 'to lift up.'

Lid, in Augenlid, n., from MidHG., *lit*(*t*), n., 'lid' (espec. of a vessel), OHG. *lit*, earlier *hlit*, n.; corresponding to AS. *hlid*, n., 'lid, door,' E. *lid*; OIc. *hlíþ*, n., 'gate.' 'Evelid' in Ic. is *augnalok*, n., lit. 'eyelock'; in MidE. also *eielid*, E. *eyelid* (MidHG. *ougelit*), and hence the term, like Augapfel, is common both to G. and E. *hlid*, 'lock-up, lid,' is connected with an old verbal stem, OSax. and AS. *hlí lan*, 'to cover, lock up.'

lieb, adj., 'dear, esteemed,' from the equiv. MidHG. *liep* (inflected *lieber*), OHG. *liob* (inflected *liobér*). It corresponds to Goth. *liufs* (*b*), AS. *leóf*, E. *lief*, adj., Du. *lief*, OIc. *ljúfr*; a common Teut. adj. with the general meaning 'dear'; it is regularly derived from pre-Teut. **leubho-*, which is accurately represented by OSlov. *ljubŭ* (Aryan root *leubh*, by gradation *lubh*). An OAryan adj. for 'dear' (Sans. *priyá-s*) was changed in meaning at an early period in Teut. (see frei) and supplanted by lieb; ModHG. and MidHG. *lieben*, OHG. *liubôn*, 'to love'; to this is allied AS. *lufian*, E. *to love*, with a weaker vowel stage of the root (AS. *lufu*, equiv. to E. *love*). Since HG. Leb, geleben, erlauben, glauben belong to the same Teut. root *lub*, by gradation *leub* (pre-Teut. *lubh*, *leubh*), we must assign to the latter a wider meaning, something like 'pleasure' and 'approbation'; Sans. *lubh*, 'to demand violently,' Lat. *lŭbens*, *libens*, 'with pleasure, willingly,' *lŭbet*, 'it pleases, is agreeable,' *lŭbĭdo*, *libído*, 'pleasure, longing, desire.' With these perhaps the common Teut. word *lustus*, equiv. to Lust, is also connected.

Liebstöckel, n. and m., 'lovage,' even in MidHG. *liebstuckel*, usually, however, *lübestecke*, m., which is based on Lat. *ligusticum* (whence the equiv. Ital. *levistico*, Fr. *lirèche*). The unintelligible Lat. form was corrupted in the Middle Ages in the most varied ways; AS. *lufestice* is also based on AS. *lufu*, 'love.' OHG. *lubistêchal*, MidHG. *lübestecke* seem to be formed in allusion to OHG. *luppi*, MidHG. *lüppe*, 'juice of a plant producing strong effects' (see Lab).

Lied, n., from the equiv. MidHG. *liet*(*d*), OHG. *liod*, n., 'song' (Goth. **liup*, n., may be inferred from *liupareis*, m., 'singer,' and *liupôn*, 'to sing praises'); comp. Du. *lied*, AS. *leóþ*, n., 'song.' The Teut. term for poetical productions, such as existed far earlier than the time of Tacitus (comp. "carmina antiqua," *Germania*, 2). Poetry flourished long before the adoption of the letters of the runic alphabet, which was derived from the Lat.

liederlich, adj., 'dissolute,' from MidHG. *liederlich*, adj., 'light, pretty, trifling, frivolous' (not recorded in OHG.). AS. *lȳþre*, adj., 'miserable, bad,' points to **liuþrs*. To this is doubtlessly allied letter in compounds pointing to a Goth. **ludrs*. Probably Gr. ἐλεύθερος, 'free,' like the Teut. words, may be traced to a root *leuth*. Lüderlich for liederlich is a recent form of the adj., connecting it with Luder (MidHG. *luoder*).

liefern, vb., 'to deliver, furnish, supply,' first occurs in early ModHG., formed from MidLat. *liberare*, 'dare, praebere' (Fr. *livrer*).

liegen, vb., 'to lie, be situated,' from the equiv. MidHG. *ligen*, *licken*, OHG. *licken*, *ligen*, str. vb.; corresponding to Du. *liggen*, AS. *licǵan*, E. *to lie* (*ligjan*, *lag*, *legans*, was the orig. gradation, but Goth. *ligan* in the pres.); the common Teut. vb. for liegen, which has numerous cognates in Aryan (root *legh*). Comp. Gr. λέκτρον, λέχος, n., 'bed,' ἄλοχος, 'bed-fellow, wife,' also λεχώ, 'woman in childbed,' λοχέω, 'to give birth to'; λόχος, 'lying in wait, ambush,' also 'lying-in, childbirth.' In Gr. epic poets aorist forms of a verb formed from a root *legh*, λεχ, have been preserved, λέκτο, λέξατο, &c., with the meaning 'to lie down, encamp.' The vb. is also wanting in Lat., where, however, *lectus*, 'bed,' a derivative of the root *legh*, is retained. OSlov. *lęgą* (*ležti*), 'to lie down,' *leža* (*ležati*), 'to lie.' In East Aryan the root is unknown. Comp. legen, Lager, and fechen.

Lilie, f., 'lily,' from the equiv. MidHG. *lilje*, OHG. *lilja*, f.; borrowed in OHG. from Lat. *lilia*, plur.; the brevity of the *i* of the accented syllable in the G. word and also in E. (AS. *lilie*, E. *lily*) is the same as in Linie and Lite, from Lat. *linea* and *licium*. Comp. Reſe.

lind, gelinde, adj., 'gentle,' from MidHG. *linde*, OHG. *lindi*, adj., 'soft, gentle, tender, mild' (Goth. **linþs* is wanting); corresponding to OSax. *līthi*, AS. *līþe*, 'mild, friendly, soft,' E. *lithe*. In Scand. an exact correspondence is not found; the term used is *linr*, 'friendly, mild, soft' (whence Lapp. *lines* is borrowed), which with Bav. *len*, 'soft,' Du. *lenig*, 'pliant,' points to the fact that the dental of the G. and E. words is a suffix. Hence *lin-* is the root from which are formed in OTeut. Goth. *af-linnan*, 'to go away, yield,' OIc. *linna*, 'to cease,' AS. *linnan*, 'to cease, part from, lose,' OHG. *bilinnan*, 'to relax, leave off.' Therefore the Teut. root meant orig. 'yielding disposition.' Comp. OSlov. *lěnŭ*, 'lazy,' Lat. *lēn-i-s*, 'gentle, mild,' and *lentus*, 'flexible, pliant.'

Linde, f., 'linden, lime-tree,' from the equiv. MidHG. *linde*, OHG. *linda*, f.; corresponding to Du. *linde*, AS. *lind*, f. E. *lind*, *linden*, *linden-tree* (E. *lime-tree*='linden' is obscure); OIc. *lind*, f., 'lime-tree'; a common Teut. term for 'linden,' also, as an OTeut. warlike term, 'shield,' lit. 'linden shield.' Its earlier history is obscure; ModHG. dial. Lint, 'bast,' and Scand. *linde*, 'girdle,' derivatives of Linde, give no clue to the prim. meaning of the word. If we consider the change in meaning to which names of trees have been subject (see under Buche, Eiche, and Tanne), we might assume that Linde is related to Gr. ἐλάτη (from *lentā*), 'pine tree, white pine'; it can scarcely be connected with Lat. *lentus*, 'flexible' (comp. lind), as if the inner bark of the linden were used at an early period for cords.

Lindwurm, m., 'winged serpent or dragon,' borrowed, with the revival of MidHG. literature in the last century, from MidHG. *lintwurm*, OHG. *lindwurm*, m., 'dragon' (comp. also Wurm). The first component is identical in meaning with the second, which is only an explanation of the obscure term Lind, which was no longer understood; comp. OHG. *lind, lint*, 'serpent'; OIc. *linnr*, 'serpent' (for **linþr*). Windhund is a similar compound.

Linie, f., 'line, lineage,' from the equiv. MidHG. *linie*, f., from Lat. *līnea*, f., with a change of quantity. It occurs even in OHG.

link, adj., 'left,' from the equiv. MidHG. *linc*, adj., with the variant *lęnc* (gen. *-kes*); the form with *sl* is probably quite as old as that with initial *l* (comp. drefſeln, Stier, Heden, and ſeden). In OHG. only *lęncha*, f., 'left hand,' is recorded; the adj. is rendered by *winistar*, MidHG. *winster*, in Bav. *lërz, lërc*, and *tenk*, Lower Rhen. *slinc* (this is doubtless a primitive variant of *link*, as is shown by the analogies under dreffeln, Stier, Heden, and ſeden); in E. *left* (AS. **lyfte*? Du. *lucht*). In the OTeut. dials. there are no other correspondences of link; perhaps ModHG. lenken is allied to this word with the prim. meaning 'oblique, awry'; lenken signifies lit. 'to direct obliquely.' Schlimm may also be a cognate.

Linnen, n., a LG. form for Leinen, 'linen,' which was introduced in the last century into Upper Germany through the Westphalian linen trade. OSax. *līnīn* is still used as an adj., 'flaxen, linen.'

Linſe, f., 'lentil, lens,' from the equiv. MidHG. *linse*, OHG. *linsi*, f., with the MidHG. and OHG. variant *linsīn*. It is not certain whether the word comes from Lat. *lens*, f., because other borrowed terms are based not on the nomin. of the Lat. word (comp. Kreuz, Reich, yet also Pabst), but on the stem appearing in the oblique cases; hence Lat. *lent-* (as is shown by AS. *lens*) ought to have appeared as **linz-* in HG. An analogous case of an apparent permutation of *nt* to *ns* is furnished by E. *flint*, equiv. to OHG. *flins*, MidHG. *vlins* (see Flinte); these difficulties are not yet solved. Grbſe, however, testifies that we are not compelled to assume that Linſe was borrowed from Lat. Comp. also OSlov. *lęšta* (from **lentja*), Lith. *lénszis*, 'lentil.'

Lippe, f., 'lip,' unknown to MidHG. and OHG.; it has appeared in the written language since Luther. It is the LG. and

MidG. word for UpG. Lefje; comp. OSax. *lippa, Du. lip, AS. lippa, E. lip; in Goth. we have perhaps to assume *lipjô, f. According to OSax. lėpur the Teut. root is lep, and this, following the permutation of consonants, is based on leb. The correspondence with Lat. labium is generally accepted; but when this is connected with lambere, 'to lick,' difficulties are presented, especially by the meaning. To represent the lip as 'that which licks' is not satisfactory. In Teut. a vb. (OHG. laffan, pret. luof) corresponding to Lat. lambere has been retained, and the rules of gradation show that HG. Lippe cannot be allied to this; Lippe is connected rather with a Goth. vb. *lipan, not *lapan (OHG. laffan). Lat. labium was derived perhaps from *lebium (Goth. *lipjô) and connected with lambere; to this ModPers. lab, 'lip,' is allied. The LG. word passed through Du. into Fr. lippe, f., 'blobber lip.'

Lifpeln, vb., 'to lisp,' with a diminutive or frequentative suffix from MidHG. and OHG. lispen, vb., 'to stammer'; never 'to speak through the lips' as a derivative of Lefje (see Lippe); it rather represents wlispen (thus in Lower Rhen. in the 15th cent., also by transposition, wilspen?). Comp. AS. wlisp, wlips, OHG. lisp, 'stammering'; E. to lisp, Du. lispen.

Lift, f., 'craft, cunning, deceit,' from MidHG. and OHG. list, m. (f. in MidG. and OHG.), 'wisdom, prudence, slyness, sly purpose, cunning, art.' Goth. lists is by chance recorded with the ModHG. sense only. The meaning 'prudence' is the orig. one; AS. list, f., 'art, propriety, cunning,' E. list; OIc. list, f., 'prudence, skill in an art, propriety.' Thus the signification of the word fluctuates in several dials. between the prim. meaning 'prudence' and 'cunning.' The subst., as an old abstract in ti (Goth. listi-ns, acc. plur.), belongs by its structure to the Goth. pret. pres. lais, 'I know'; the verbal stem lis, with the orig. sense 'to know,' is still widely diffused in HG., comp. lehren and lernen. Moreover, on the common Teut. listi- are based the Slav. cognates of OSlov. ltstĭ and the Rom. class comprising Fr. leste and Ital. lesto, 'skilful, nimble.'

Lifte, f., 'list, roll,' ModHG. only, from Fr. liste, Ital. lista, which are again derived from HG. Leifte (MidHG. lîste).

Lilge, f., 'twisted lace, bobbin,' from MidHG. lize, f., 'twisted lace, cord as a barrier'; from Lat. lĭcium, n., 'thread.' The change made in the quantity when the word was borrowed in MidHG. as litze is analogous to that in Pilie and Linie. From the Lat. lĭcium (whence Fr. lice, 'lists, arena') are also derived Zwilliĉ and Drilliĉ, which see.

Lob, n., 'praise,' from MidHG. lop (b), OHG. lob, n. and m., 'praise, reward, glorification'; corresponding to Du. lof, AS. lof, m., 'praise, fame'; OIc. lof, n., 'fame, reward, praise, laudatory poem,' also 'permission,' points to the similarity of the roots of loben and erlauben (comp. MidHG. urloup and urlop, 'permission'). The old gradation lub-liub-laub comprises ModHG. Lob, lieb, glauben, and erlauben; in AS., lufu (equiv. to E. love) is the weakest form of the root with the meaning corresponding to HG. lieb (Goth. liufs). Under lieb the prim. sense of the Aryan root leubh (Sans. lubh, Lat. lubet, lubido) is assumed to be 'inclination'; in meaning, Lith. liaupsė, 'hymn,' lảupsinti, 'to extol,' are the most closely allied. With regard to the gradation, it is also noteworthy that MidHG. and ModHG. loben, OHG. lobôn, lobên, vb., AS. lofian, vb., 'to praise,' are represented in OIc. by lofa, vb., 'to praise, commend, permit,' and that OIc. leyfa (from *laubjan) has also the same double sense.—ModHG. and MidHG. lobesam, adj., 'laudable,' OHG. lobosam, AS. lofsum; Goth. galufs, galaufs, 'precious,' lit. 'having praise,' so too OHG. gilob, 'precious.'

Loĉ, n., 'hole, dungeon, haunt,' from MidHG. loch, n., OHG. loh, gen. lohhes, n., 'enclosed place, prison, lurking-place, cave, hole, opening.' Comp. AS. loc, n., 'enclosed place, lock'; loca, m., 'enclosed place, prison'; from the former E.l ock is derived. The various meanings all originate in 'enclosed place'; comp. Goth. usluka-, 'opening.' The subst. is formed by gradation from an old Teut. vb. (obsolete in ModHG.), MidHG. lûchen, OHG. lûhhan, Goth. lûkan, AS. lûcan, 'to lock,' which may be compared (since the pre-Teut. root is lûg) with Lith.l ùżtu (lùżti), 'to be broken,' as well as with Sans. ruj, 'to break.'

Loĉe, f., 'lock, curl, tress,' from the equiv. MidHG. loc (plur. locke), OHG. loc (plur. locchâ), m.; comp. AS. locc, E. lock, OIc. lokkr, Du. lok, 'lock.' A common Teut. word for 'lock' (Goth. *lukks is by chance not recorded), and peculiar to the

Teutons, who from the earliest times laid special stress on the mode of wearing the hair; the freeman was distinguished by his long streaming locks, while the bondman wore his hair short. The Southerners (see Fahl) were specially struck with the golden curly hair of the Teutons when they first came into contact with them. It is true that curls were considered effeminate by the earlier Northmen, though in Germany they were fondly cherished. Comp. also Haar, Schopf, Zette, and other words for 'hair' peculiar to Teut. The primit. history of the word is obscure; Locke (as 'that which is bent') is most probably connected with an Aryan root, *lug*, 'to draw, bend, curve'; comp. Gr. λυγ- in λυγόω, λυγίζω, 'I bend, tie,' also λύγος, 'young, pliant twig' (Lith. *palugnas*, adj., 'pleasing'?). In Teut. the following are also probably allied to these—Goth. *lûkan*, 'to draw' (*uslúkan*, 'to unsheathe a sword'), North. Eng. *to look*, 'to weed,' Bav. *liechen*, 'to pluck' (e.g. the flax out of the ground).

Lochen, vb., 'to curl, entice,' from MidHG. *locken*, OHG. *locchôn*, 'to entice, allure, decoy,' with the equiv. variant MidHG. *lücken*, OHG. *lucchen*. OIc. only has a corresponding *lokka*, 'to entice.' To these Lith. *lugsti*, 'to beg,' is primit. allied. Comp. Luder, allied to laden.

Locker, adj., 'loose, spongy, dissolute,' first occurs in early ModHG. with the MidHG. variant *loger*; in UpG. *lucke*, *lücke* (now Luck); from the same root as Lücke (Teut. root *lug*).

Lodern, vb., 'to blaze, flare,' first occurs in early ModHG.; lit. perhaps 'to spring up (of plants)'; a LG. word. Comp. Westphal. *lodern*, 'to grow luxuriantly,' to which OHG. *lota*, 'young shoot,' is allied; for the root *lud* see under Leute.

· Löffel, m., 'spoon, ladle,' from the equiv. MidHG. *leffel*, OHG. *leffil* (*lepfil*), m.; corresponding to LG. and Du. *lepel* (whence Ic. *lepill*, 'spoon'). Derived from a Teut. root *lap*, 'to drink, lick,' which is assumed by OHG. *laffan*, 'to lick,' AS. *lapian*, 'to drink, lap'; further by Lat. *lambere*, 'to lick'; hence Löffel means lit. 'a utensil for sipping liquids' (see Lefze and Lippe). The Scand. term is *spánn*, which was adopted in E. as *spoon* (in AS. *cucelére*, equiv. to Lat. *cochlear*); see under Span.

Loh, adj. (espec. in lichterloh, 'in full blaze'), 'blazing, flaring,' ModHG. only; allied to the following word.

Lohe (1.), f., 'blaze,' from MidHG. *lohe*, m. (MidG. also f.), 'flame, lurid ray,' OHG. *loho* (Goth. *laúha*); the term used in OHG. was *louc*, MidHG. *louc* (AS. *lég*, *ltg*). These, like OIc. *loge*, m., 'flame,' are derived from the Teut. root *luh*, 'to give light,' which still exists in HG. Licht, and which as Aryan *luk* appears in Lat. *lucere*, *lux*, OSlov. *luču*, 'ray,' and the Sans. *ruc*, 'to shine,' *rocis*, 'light.'

Lohe (2.), f., 'tanning bark,' from the equiv. MidHG., MidLG., and OHG. *lô* (gen. *lôwes*), n.; comp. Du. *looi*. Distinct from Lohe (1), since it presumes a Goth. *lawa-*; origin obscure.

Lohen, vb., 'to flare, blaze,' from the equiv. MidHG. *lohen*, OHG. *lohén*; allied to Lohe (1).

Lohn, m., 'reward, wages,' from the equiv. MidHG. and OHG. *lôn*, m. and n.; a word common to OTeut.; comp. the equiv. Goth. *laun*, OIc. *laun*, AS. *leán*, Du. *loon*, OSax. *lón*. Since *na-* is the suffix, we may connect the root *lau-* with OSlov. *lovŭ*, 'booty, chase,' Lat. *lu-crum*, 'gain,' Gr. ἀπολαύω, 'to partake of'; others make it cognate with OIr. *lúag*, 'reward.'

Lolch, m., 'darnel,' from the equiv. MidHG. *lulch*, *lullich*, *lulche*, m.; the OHG. word is wanting, therefore it is difficult to determine when the term was borrowed from the equiv. Lat. *lollum*. It is also conceivable that the G. word is independent of the Lat., especially as the former is lengthened by a guttural.

Loos, see Los.

Lorbeer, m., 'laurel,' from MidHG. *lôrber*, OHG. *lôrberi*, n. and f.; lit. 'the berry of the lôrboum' (OHG. and MidHG.); *lôr-* in *lôr-boum*, *lôr-beri*, is Lat. *laurus*, 'laurel tree,' which was probably known in Germany even before the 7th cent. (comp. Ital. *lauro*, Fr. *laurier*).

Los, Loos, n., 'lot, fate, chance,' from MidHG. and OHG. *lôz*, m. and n., 'lot, casting lots, drawing a lot, disposal by lottery, division of an inheritance'; comp. Goth. *hlauts*, 'lot, inheritance,' OIc. *hlaut* (*hlutr*), 'lot, portion, sacrifice,' AS. *hlýt* and *hlot*, E. *lot*. To these are allied the str. vbs.—OIc. *hljóta*, AS. *hleótan*, OSax. *hliotan*, OHG. *liozan*, MidHG. *liezen*, 'to obtain by lot, acquire.' This verbal stem in heathen times was probably a sacrificial term (comp. MidHG. *liezen*, 'to predict,' OIc. *hlaut*, 'sacrifice'; also Tacitus, *Germania*, 10). Old derivatives of this root *hlut*, which is peculiar to Teut., passed also into Rom. ; comp. Ital. *lotto*, 'lottery urn,' Fr. *lot*, 'share,' OFr. *lotir*, 'to cast lots, predict,' Fr. *loterie*, 'lottery.'

los, adj., 'loose, released,' from MidHG. *lôs*, 'free, unimpeded, bare, plundered, released, wanton, not solid, frivolous'; corresponding to Goth. *laus*, 'empty, invalid, vain,' OIc. 'loose, free, unimpeded,' AS. *leás*, 'loose, false, deceitful' (to this is allied E. *leas*, 'lie,' and E. *-less*, only as the second part of a compound; E. *loose* is borrowed from Scand.), Du. *los*, OSax. *lôs* ; the adj. form *lausa-*, common to Teut., is from the root *lus*, 'to be loose,' discussed under verlieren. From the Teut. adj. is derived Span. *lozano*, 'merry, cheerful.' See löfen.

löſchen (1.), vb., 'to extinguish, go out'; in the ModHG. vb. two MidHG. vbs. are comprised, MidHG. *leschen* (most frequently *erleschen*), str. vb., 'to cease to burn, go out,' and the corresponding factitive *leschen*, 'to extinguish' ; comp. OHG. *leskan*, *irleskan*, intrans., and *lesken*, trans.; this verbal stem is unknown to the other Teut. languages. The *sk* of OHG. *leskan* is really a suffix of the pres. stem (see dreſchen and waſchen), as may be inferred from the connection with the Teut. root *leg* (see liegen); erlöſchen is lit. 'to lie down.'

löſchen (2.), vb., 'to discharge a ship,' borrowed from the equiv. LG., Du. *lossen* ; comp. Dan. *losse*, Swed. *lossa;* the origin and early history of the cognates are unknown (comp. Boot, Verb, and Rahe).

löſen, vb., 'to loosen, free,' from the equiv. MidHG. *lœsen*, OHG. *lôsen* (*lôsjan*) ; a derivative of the MidHG. and OHG. adj. *lôs* (see los) ; comp. Goth. *lausjan*, 'to loosen,' from *laus*, 'loose.'

Loſung, f., 'war-cry, watchword,' from the equiv. late MidHG. *losunge*, *lôzunge*, the first appearance of which in the 15th cent. makes it impossible to determine the correct MidHG. form and its derivation (from Los ? or from loſen, 'to hear'? see lauſchen).

Lot, n., 'lead (or soft metal), half an ounce,' from MidHG. *lôt* (in OHG. by chance not recorded), n., 'lead, weight cast from lead'; corresponding to Du. *lood*, 'lead, kind of weight,' AS. *leád*, E. *lead*. The old West Teut. *lauda-*, n., 'lead,' is connected with the equiv. OIr. *luáide*.—**löten**, vb., from the equiv. MidHG. *lœten*, 'to solder,' is a derivative of Lot.—**lötig**,

'of due alloy,' corresponds in compounds to MidHG. *lœtec*, 'of full weight, containing the due proportion of a noble metal.'

Lotſe, m., 'pilot,' like löſchen (2) Mo l HG. only ; borrowed from LG. and Du. *loots*, *loods*, 'pilot.' Perhaps the word originated in E., in which *loadsman*, 'steersman,' occurs as an old compound of *load*, AS. *lád*, 'street, way' (see leiten). With regard to the *o* in Lotje, see Boot.

Lotter-, in compounds like Lotterbube, 'vagrant, knave,' from MidHG. *loter*, 'slack, light-minded, frivolous, knave, ne'er-do-well, buffoon,' OHG. *lotar*, 'empty, vain'; comp. AS. *loddêre*, 'villain.' Allied to liederlich.

Löwe, m., 'lion,' from the equiv. Mid HG. *lewe*, *lêwe* (*louwe*, *löuwe*), OHG. *lêwo*, *lewo* (*louwo*), m. ; comp. OSax. and AS. *leo*, Du. *leeuw;* undoubtedly a loan-word, since there is no common Teut. and no old Aryan term for 'lion.' Lat. *leo*, however, does not suffice to explain all the G. forms of Middle Europe. OHG. *louwo* and MidHG. *löuwe*, 'lion,' are specially abnormal; *E. lim* is derived from Fr. *lion*). These late occurring OHG. forms with *ou* are preserved in ModHG. names of places and streets, such as Lauenburg, Lauengaſſe. The MidHG. fem. *lunze* (also *lewinne*), 'lioness,' still remains obscure.

Luchs, m., 'lynx,' from the equiv. Mid HG. and OHG. *luhs*, m. ; corresponding to OSax. *lox*, Du. *losch*, AS. *lox*, m. The *s* of this OTeut. stem is a suffix, as in Fuchs ; hence Swed. *lo* (Goth. **laûhô*), and in the non-Teut. languages Lith. *lússis*, Gr. λυγκ-, 'lynx.' It is probably related to the root *luh* in Licht (OIc. *ljós*, 'light,' AS. *líxan*, 'to give light'), since the sharp, gleaming eyes of the lynx may have given rise to the name.

Lüche, f., 'gap, chasm,' from MidHG. *lücke*, *lucke*, OHG. *lucka*, from **luggja*, f., 'hole, gap,' closely allied to locker (MidHG. *loger*, UpG. *luck*). The UpG. dials. contain a prim. form **luggia* (Swiss *lugg*, not *lukχ*), hence OHG. *luccha*, 'gap,' is abnormal. For this reason too the phonetic relation of the word to Loch is obscure.

Luder, n., 'lure, decoy, bait,' from Mid HG. *luoder*, n., 'bait, gluttony, dissolute life, loose woman' (from an OTeut. *lôþra-* is derived Fr. *leurre*, 'lure, bait'). Its connection with ModHG. laben is probable, since 'bait' is the orig. sense.—**Lüderlich**, see liederlich.

Luft, f. (UpG. masc.), 'air, breeze,' from the equiv. MidHG. and OHG. *luft*, m. and f.; a common Teut. term; comp. Goth. *luftus*, OIc. *lopt*, AS. *lyft* (E. *lift*, dial. only), OSax. *luft*, Du. *lucht*, 'air.' Whether OIc. *lopt*, 'loft' (comp. Laube), is a derivative of the same word remains dubious; nor is it of any help in determining the primit. sense of the specifically Teut. *luftu*-, especially as indubitable cognates in the non-Teut. languages are wanting.

Lug, m., **Lüge**, f., 'lie, falsehood,' from the equiv. MidHG. *luc* (*g*), *lüge* (*lügene*), OHG. *lugin*, f.; an abstract of *lügen* (dial. *liegen*), MidHG. *liegen*, OHG. *liogan*, str. vb. 'to lie.' Comp. OSax. *lugina*, 'lie,' from *liogan*, Du. *leugen*, *logen*, from *liegen*, AS. *lyge* (E. *lie*), from *leógan*, Goth. *liugn*, 'lie,' from *liugan*, str. vb. 'to lie.'—**Lügner**, m., 'liar,' from MidHG. *lügenære*, OHG. *luginâri*. To this common Teut. root *lug* (Aryan *lugh*), 'to lie,' Goth. *liugan* (pret. *liuⳉaidu*), 'to marry,' has no relation; the latter, like OFris. *logia*, 'to marry,' is connected rather with OIr. *luige*, 'oath' (primit. form *lughio*-). ModHG. *lügen* is more probably allied to OSlov. *lŭžą* (*lŭgati*), 'to lie,' *lŭža*, 'lie.' From Teut., Ital. (dial.) *luchina*, 'false story,' is derived.

lugen, vb., 'to look out, spy,' from the equiv. MidHG. *luogen*, OHG. *luogên*; corresponding to OSax. *lôcôn*, AS. *lôcian*, E. *to look*, with an abnormal *k* for *g*. From these Norman *luquer* is borrowed. The early history of this West Teut. stem *lôkai*, *lôgai*-, is obscure.

Luke, f., 'dormer window, hole, hatchway,' prop. a LG. word meaning 'opening'; allied to Loch.

lullen, vb., 'to lull,' ModHG. only; a recent onomatopoetic term.

Lümmel, m., 'lubber, scoundrel,' first occurs in ModHG.; probably derived from the antiquated adj. *lumm*, 'relaxed, loose,' which is based on MidHG. *lüeme*, OHG. *luomi*, 'mild, languid' (MidHG. *lüemen*, 'to slacken, relax, be wearied'), and connected with lahm.

Lump, m., 'scamp, ragamuffin,' Mod HG. only; prop. identical with Lumpen, m., 'rag, tatter,' which in late MidHG. appears as *lumpe* with the same sense. It was probably introduced from LG.; comp. Du. *lomp*, 'rag, tatter, patch,' *lomperd*, 'lout' (to this OIc. *leppr*, 'shield,' is allied?); comp. Lappen and Laffe.—**lumpen**, vb., lit. 'to treat or regard as a ragamuffin.'

Lunge, f., 'lung,' from the equiv. Mid HG. *lunge*, OHG. *lungun* (plur. *lungunnâ*), f.; corresponding to the equiv. Goth. *luggô, OIc. *lunga*, AS. *lungen*, E. *lungs* (prop. plur. on account of the two lobes), Du. *long*. Some etymologists connect these cognates with the OTeut. root *ling*, 'to be light,' which appears in leicht and gelingen. Comp. Port. *leve*, 'lung,' from Lat. *levis*, 'light,' E. *lights* from *light*, Russ. *legkoe* from *legkij*.

lungern, vb., 'to seek prey, yearn,' Mod HG. only; a derivative of the West Teut. adj., MidHG. *lunger*, OHG. *lungar*, 'speedy, quick,' AS. *lungor*, 'quick,' which, with Gr. *ἐλαφρός*, 'quick,' is connected with the Aryan root *lengh*, discussed under the preceding word (see leicht).

Lüning, m., 'sparrow' (LG.), from the equiv. OSax. *hliuning*. Origin obscure.

Lünse, f., 'linch-pin,' from the equiv. late MidHG. *luns*, *lunse*; comp. OSax. *lunisa*, Du. *luns*, *lens*. In OHG. *lun*, *luna*, MidHG. *lun*, *lune*, f., also OHG. *luning*, MidHG. *lüninc*, *lüner*, 'lungs'; comp. AS. *lynes*, m., E. *linch-pin* (Goth. *lunisi is wanting); it may have been formed like Goth. *aqizi*, *jukuzi*. Some etymologists connect these cognates with the Aryan root *lu*, 'to loosen,' discussed under verlieren, so that Lünse is lit. "peg for loosening the wheel." Comp. further AS. *ălynnan*, 'to release.'

Lunte, f., 'lunt, match,' ModHG. only; corresponding to Du. *lonte*, E. *lunt*, Dan. *lunte*. In earlier ModHG. and in modern dials. it signifies 'wick of a lamp' (prop. 'tow'?), allied to MidHG. *lünden*, 'to burn' (OHG. *lunda*, 'tallow'?). Further cognates are uncertain.—**Lunte**, f., 'brush of a fox,' is a figurative sense of Lunte, 'lunt' (*i.e.*, from its fiery colour).

lüpfen, 'to set free and then raise aloft,' an UpG. vb., from the equiv. MidHG. *lüpfen*, *lupfen*. Since the word is not found in other languages (Goth. *luppjan?), its origin cannot be discovered; perhaps it is connected with the cognates of Läufel. In ModHG. a modern vb., lüften (allied to Luft), 'to lift,' has supplanted the cognate phonetic form lüpfen.

Lust, f., 'pleasure, delight, fancy, lust,' from the equiv. MidHG. *lust*, m. and f., OHG. *lust*, f.; corresponding to Goth. *lustus*, OIc. *lyst*, AS. *lyst*, *lust*, E. *list*, *lust*, Du. and OSax. *lust*; a common Teut. abstract, the origin of which is still dubious. Its relation to lieben (Teut. root *lub*, 'to desire'), as well as to the root *lus* (see **verlieren**) is improbable; it is rather connected with a root *las*, 'to desire,' to which is allied Gr. λιλαίομαι, Sans. root *laš* (for *lals*), 'to desire,' and also with the Sans. root *lod, lud,* 'to move.'

Iutſchen, vb., 'to suck,' ModHG. only, a recent onomatopoetic term.

M.

machen, vb., 'to make, produce, cause, perform,' from the equiv. MidHG. *machen,* OHG. *mahhôn;* corresponding to the equiv. OSax. *makôn,* Du. *maken,* AS. *macian,* E. *to make;* a common Teut. vb. for 'to make,' but existing also as a borrowed term in the Northern dials. The OHG. vb. further signifies 'to combine, join.' As allied to Goth. **makôn,* comp. the adjs.—OIc. **makr,* only in the compar. *makara,* 'more suitable or convenient,' AS. *gemœr,* 'suitable, fit,' OHG. *gimah,* 'combined with, belonging to, corresponding, convenient,' MidHG. *gemach,* ModHG. gemach; OHG. *gimah,* neut. of the adj., 'combination, convenience, agreeableness,' MidHG. *gemach,* m. and n., 'comfort, agreeableness, place where one rests, dwelling, room,' ModHG. Gemach; further, AS. *gemœčča,* 'husband, wife,' E. *make,* 'companion, spouse,' E. *match,* OHG. *gimahho,* 'companion,' *gimahha,* 'wife,' OHG. *gimahhidi,* MidHG. *gemęchede,* n., 'spouse.' Hence results a Teut. root *mak,* 'to join or belong to in a suitable manner' (equiv. in meaning to the root *gad* in Gatte). A non-Teut. root *mag,* with this sense, has not yet been found.

Macht, f., 'might, force,' from the equiv. MidHG. and OHG. *maht,* f., 'might, power, ability'; comp. OSax. *maht,* Du. *magt,* AS. *meaht, miht,* E. *might,* OIc. *máttr,* m., Goth. *mahts,* f., 'might, power, capacity.' The common Teut. **mahti-,* f., which may be deduced from these words, is an old verbal abstract of Goth. *magan.* See mögen and Gemächt.

Mädchen, n., 'maiden, girl, servant,' ModHG. only, a derivative of Magd, with the dimin. suffix chen (in UpG. Maitle, Mädel, &c., with dimin. *l.*

Made, f., 'maggot,' from MidHG. *made,* m., 'worm, maggot,' OHG. *mado;* corresponding to Du. *made,* AS. *maþa,* Goth. *maþa,* 'maggot, worm.' Hence the equiv. OIc. *maþkr,* m. (with a suffix), from which is derived MidE. *maþek,* E. *mawk,* 'maggot'; Goth. *maþaks (E. *maggot* is probably not allied). The orig. sense of the OTeut. **maþan-,* 'maggot,' is perhaps 'gnawer'; it has been connected with the root *mê,* 'to mow'; Mette (MidHG. and ModHG. variant *matte*) may also be akin.

Magd, f., 'maid, servant,' from Mid HG. *maget* (plur. *megde*), *meit,* 'maiden, virgin,' also 'bond girl, servant,' OHG. *magad* (plur. *magidi, męgidi*), f., 'maiden'; corresponding to Goth. *magaþs* (wanting in OIc.), AS. *mœgþ,* OSax. *magath,* f.; the common OTeut. word (unknown only in Scand.) for 'maiden,' in OSax. and Mid HG. also with the ModHG. sense 'maid, servant.' From these are derived the diminutives (see Küchlein and Schwein), Goth. **magadein,* n., OHG. *magatîn,* Mid HG. *magetîn,* n., 'girl,' AS. *mœgden,* E. *maid, maiden* (AS. *mœgþ,* f., 'maiden,' became obsolete at the beginning of the Mid E. period), Goth. *magaþs,* 'maiden,' and its cognates in the other languages are old femin. derivatives from an archaic term, *magus,* 'boy, youth'; comp. Goth. *magus,* 'boy, servant,' OIc. *mǫgr,* 'son,' AS. *mago,* 'son, youth, man, servant.' To this is allied another femin. derivative, Goth. *mawi,* OIc. *már* (for **maguî,* with the loss of a *g,* see Niere); comp. further AS. *meôwle,* 'girl.' Teut. *magus,* 'son, boy, servant,' is equiv. to OIr. *macc,* 'boy, youth, son' (comp. the Ir. proper names MacCarthy, &c.).

Mage, m., formed from the equiv. Mid HG. *mâc (g),* m., OHG. *mâg,* m., 'kinsman'; corresponding to OSax. *mâg,* AS. *nuêg,* m., 'kinsman.' The allied terms in the East Teut. languages denote special degrees of relationship; comp. Goth. *mêgs,* 'daughter's husband,' OIc. *mágr,* 'brother-in-law, son-in-law, father-in-law.' Probably *mâg* signified orig. 'one who is related by marriage.' HG. distinguishes between Schwert and Spillmagen, just as MidHG. does between *swertmâge,* 'relatives on the male side,' and *spinnelmâge,* 'relatives on the female side'; similarly in AS. *spermagas* and *spinelmâgas.*

Magen, m., from the equiv. MidHG. and MidLG. *mage,* OHG. *mago,* m., 'stomach';

comp. Du. *maag*, AS. *maga*, MidE. *mawe*, E. *maw*, OIc. *mage*, Dan. *mave*, 'stomach'; Goth. **maja* (gen. **magins*) is wanting. From Teut. is derived Ital. (dial.) *magone*, 'crop (of birds),' or rather *magon*, also *magon*, 'vexation,' to which Rhaeto-Rom. *magún*, 'stomach,' is allied.' For the early history of the word we have no definite clue; to derive Wagen from mögen, root *mag*, 'to be able, have strength' (as if the stomach were the 'nourishing, strength giving part'), is not to be commended. The names of parts of the body need not, however, be traced back to a verbal root; comp. Herz, Niere, and Leber.

mager, adj., 'lean, lank, meagre,' from the equiv. MidHG. *mager*, OHG. *magar*, adj.; corresponding to MidLG. and Du. *mager*, AS. *mæger*, OIc. *magr*, adj., 'lean'; a common Teut. word, wanting only in Goth. Considering the wide and early diffusion of the term, its similarity to Lat. *macer* (Ital. *magro*, Fr. *maigre*) is remarkable. While MidE. *mēgre*, E. *meagre*, are certainly of Rom. origin (comp. Fr. *maigre*), Teut. *mager*, like Lat. *macer*, 'lean,' and Gr. μακεδνός, 'tall,' μακρός, 'long,' may be derived from an Aryan root *māk*, 'long, thin'; Lith. *mážus*, 'little,' may, like OHG. *magar*, point to a common root, *magh*. Yet the supposition that the Teut. cognates are derived from Low Lat. and Ital. *magro* is more probable; note furz, from Lat. *curtus*.

Mahd, f., 'mowing, swath,' from MidHG. *māt* (gen. *mādes*), n. (also f.), 'mowing, what has been mown, hay, meadow,' OHG. *mād*, n.; hence OHG. *mādāri*, MidHG. *mādære*, *mæder*, ModHG. Mäher, 'mower'; AS. *mǽþ*, n., 'mowing, what has been mown, hay,' E. *math* in *aftermath* and *lattermath*. HG. Mahd, and E. *math*, Goth. **mēþ* (gen. **mēþis*), are properly verbal abstracts of the root *mē*, 'to mow,' just as the cognate Gr. ἄμητος, 'harvest,' is derived from ἀμάω, 'I mow'; comp. also ἀμητός, 'crop, the field when reaped.' See Grummet, Matte, and Ómet.—mähen, vb., 'to mow,' from the equiv. MidHG. *mæjen*, OHG. *māen*; corresponding to Du. *maaijen*, AS. *māwan* (pret. *meōw*), E. *to mow*. A common West Teut. root *mē*, 'to mow,' has already been deduced from the previous word; it appears in Gr. with a vowel prefixed in ἀ-μη-τος, 'harvest,' and ἀ-μάω, 'to mow'; the *t* in the Lat. root *mĕt*, 'to mow, harvest,' which orig. belonged to the pres. stem only, may have been regarded as a part of the root; to this is allied OIr. *meithel*, 'a party of reapers.'

Mahl (1.), n., obsolete except in compounds; Mahlschatz, m., 'dowry,' from MidHG. *mahelschaz*, m., 'dowry,' and espec. 'engagement ring'; Mahlstatt, 'place of public assembly or of execution,' Mid HG. *mahelstat*, f., 'court of justice, place of execution,' OHG. *mahalstat*, f., 'court of justice.' See Gemahl.

Mahl (2.), n., 'meal, repast,' from Mid HG. *māl*, n., 'banquet, meal-time'; OHG. **māl*, n., not recorded in this sense; allied to MidE. *mǽl*, E. *meal* (wanting in AS.). Probably identical in orig. with the cognates discussed under mal(2), so that 'mealtime,' as 'time' par excellence, may have led to the meanings 'banquet, repast.' OIc. *māl*, n., also signifies, among other things, 'meal-time.'

mahlen, vb., 'to grind,' from the equiv. MidHG. *maln*, OHG. *malan*; in the latter form the common Teut. word for 'to grind' (but wanting in E. even in AS.); comp. OSax. *malan*, Du. *malen*, OIc. *mala*, Goth. *malan*, 'to grind.' The root *mal* (*mol*, *ml*), 'to grind,' is common to the West Aryan languages, and this fact indicates the very early existence of grinding; comp. Lat. *molo*, Gr. μύλλω (to which μύλη, μύλος, μυλίται are allied), OSlov. *melja* (*mlěti*), Lith. *máļù* (*málti*), OIr. *melim*, 'I grind.' This community of terms in the West Aryan languages does not necessarily point to a primit. period when the tribes speaking the languages mentioned formed one body. It is more probable that the use of mills was learnt by one tribe from another. The influence of a foreign civilisation (comp. Hanf) is also quite conceivable. Comp. malmen, Malter, Maulwurf, Mehl, Mühle, and Müller.

mählich, adv., see allmählich.

Mähne, f., 'mane,' earlier ModHG. also Mane (the mutation, which also occurs in Suab. and Bav., seems to be due to the plur.), from the equiv. MidHG. *mane*, *man*, f. and m., OHG. *mana*, f.; comp. Du. *maan*, AS. *manu*, E. *mane*, OIc. *mǫn*, f., 'mane' (to this is allied the derivative OIc. *makke*, Swed. and Dan. *manke*, 'upper part of the neck of a horse'). The common Teut. *manō*, f., 'mane' (Goth. **mana*, f., is by chance not recorded), shows a later development of meaning, for the earlier sense of the word was certainly 'neck' merely; in OTeut. occurs a derivative signifying 'necklace'; comp. OIc. *men*, AS. *mene*, OSax. *meni*, OHG. *menni*, n., 'necklace.' To these are allied, in the non-Teut. languages, Lat. *monile*, 'necklace, collar,' Dor. μάννος, μάδρος, μόννος, 'necklace,' Kelt. μανάκης, equiv. to OIr. *muince*, 'necklace,' Sans. *maṇi*, m., 'string of pearls.' An OInd. *mand, f., 'neck,' is wanting, though *manyá*, f., 'nape,' occurs. Further, OIr. *muin*, *muinél*, 'nape,' *mong*, 'hair, mane,' with which Swed. and Dan. *manke*, mentioned above, is closely connected.

mahnen, vb., 'to warn, admonish,' from MidHG. *manen*, OHG. *manôn*, *manên*, 'to remind, warn, challenge'; corresponding to OSax. *manôn*, AS. *manian*, 'to warn'; a derivative of the Aryan root *mon*, *men*, widely diffused in OTeut., to which are allied the Goth. pret. pres. *munan*, 'to be of opinion,' Lat. *memini*, *reminiscor*, *men-s* (*men-te-m*), Gr. μένος, μιμνήσκω, and the Sans. root *man*, 'to think' (see Mann, meinen, and Minne). To OHG. *manên* (with the variant *monên*), Lat. *monêre*, 'to warn,' with *ô* equiv. to Teut. *a* (as in Lat. *molere*, Goth. and OHG. *malan*), which is likewise formed from the root *men*, is most closely allied in sound and meaning.

Mahr, m., from the equiv. MidHG. *mar*, *mare*, m. and f., 'incubus, nightmare,' OHG. *mara*, f.; comp. AS. *mara*, m., E. *mare* in *nightmare*, OIc. *mara*, f., 'incubus.' The derivation from Goth. *marzjan*, 'to vex,' OHG. *marren*, *merren*, 'to hinder, disturb,' is scarcely possible. Some etymologists connect the word with Slav.-Russ. *kikimora*, 'ghost,' Pol. *mora*, Bohem. *můro*, 'nightmare.' From Mahr, Fr. *cauchemar*, 'nightmare,' has also been derived (*caucher*, from Ital. *calcare*, 'to tread, press').

Mähre, f., from the equiv. MidHG. *merhe*, OHG. *meriha*, *marha*, f., 'mare'; fem. of the OHG. *marah*, *mark*, 'horse,' discussed under Marschall; comp. AS. *myre*, E. *mare*, Du. *merrie*, OIc. *merr*, pointing to a Goth. *marhi (gen. *marhjôs). In G. the fem. form has been preserved longer than the masc., on which it is based (comp. Frau, Magd, and Schwieger).

Mai, m., from the equiv. MidHG. *meie*, OHG. *meio*, m., 'May.' Borrowed from Lat. *Május* (comp. Ital. *maggio*, Fr. *mai*), 'May,' at the same period as August, März, and Jänner (old form for Januar).

Maid, f., 'maid, servant,' from MidHG. *meit*. See Magd.

Maie, m., 'green boughs for adornment,' from late MidHG. *meie*, m., 'birch tree,' whence Ital. *majo*, Fr. *mai*, 'green boughs, maypole'; identical with Mai.

Mais, n., 'maize,' ModHG. only, a recent word in the ModEurop. languages, of American origin (*mahis* in Hayti); comp. Fr. *maïs*, E. *maize*, and Span. *maíz*. Columbus is said to have imported the corn and its name.

Maische, see Meische.

Majoran, m., 'marjoram,' in MidHG. *meigramme*, m., and also *meiron*, *meieron*, 'marjoram.' From MidLat. *majorana*; the MidHG. words seem to be based in sound on *meie*, 'May.' Comp. Ital. *majorana*, Fr. *marjolaine*, E. *marjoram*; the last two have also been corrupted ?. The ultimate source of the word is Gr. ἀμάρακον, whence Lat. *amaracus* and *majoracus* (based on *major*).

Makel, m., 'stain, blot,' from late Mid HG. *mâkel*, m., which was borrowed from Lat. *macula*, 'spot.'

mäkeln, makeln, vb., 'to transact business as a broker,' ModHG. only; from the equiv. LG. *mäkeln*, Du. *makelen*, which are allied to *maken*, 'to make' (handeln also combines the meanings 'to make' and 'to traffic'). Fr. *maquereau* (whence E. *mackerel*), 'pimp,' is said to be derived from these cognates on account of OHG. *huormahhári*, 'pimp.'

Makrele, f., 'mackerel,' from late Mid HG. *makrële*, f.; borrowed from the equiv. Du. *makreel* (comp. E. *mackerel*), which is of Rom. origin; MidLat. *macarellus*, *maquerellus*, OFr. *maquerel*, ModFr. *maquereau*.

Mal (1.), n., 'mark, spot,' from MidHG. *mâl*, n., 'spot,' OHG. *mâl in the compound *anamâli*, 'spot, scar'; identical with MidHG. and OHG. *mâl*, 'period, point'; see mal (2). Its primit. kinship with Goth. *mail*, n., 'spot,' is uncertain, yet Mal has at all events assumed the meaning of Goth. *mail*, which is normally represented by OHG. and MidHG. *meil*, n.; to this corresponds AS. *mâl*, whence E. *mole*. Goth. *mél*, 'time,' points to the Aryan root *mê*, 'to measure' (Gr. μέτρον, Lat. *métiri*).

-mal (2.), suffix of the multiplicatives and temporal advs. (also a noun); it is based on MidHG. and OHG. *mâl*, 'period'

(Goth. *mél*, see the preceding word). Even in OHG. the expressions *z' einemo mâle*, 'once,' *ze drin mâlen*, 'thrice,' *manigen mâlen*, 'many a time,' were formed ; hence lit. 'at one period, at two, at many periods' ; so too *z' andermo mâle*, 'at another time' ; hence MidHG. *eines mâles*, 'once,' lit. 'at one period.' For the OHG. and MidHG. dat. plurs. *mâlum, mâlen (ze drin mâlen*, 'thrice'), the apocopated form maſ first appears in early ModHG.

maledeien, vermaledeien, vb., from the equiv. MidHG. *vermaledien*, later also *maledien*, 'to curse' ; from Lat. *maledicere*, whence also Fr. *maudire*, Ital. *maledire*.

malen, vb., 'to paint,' from MidHG. *mâlen*, lit. 'to furnish with a mark or sign,' then 'to colour, paint, write,' OHG. *mâlôn, mâlên*, 'to paint, draw' ; allied to OHG. *mâl*, 'point,' signifying also 'period' according to maſ (2), mentioned under Maſ (1). Akin also to Goth. *méla*, neu. plur., 'writing, documents,' *méljan*, 'to write, record.'

malmen, zermalmen, vb., 'to crush to pieces, grind,' ModHG. only, but apparently, on account of the infrequency of the *m*-suffix, far older. The non-occurrence of OHG. *mâlmôn and MidHG. *malmen is probably only an accident ; in Mid HG. *zermaln* and *zermüln*, 'to grind,' are used. The suffix *m* is seen in the nouns, Goth. *malma*, m., 'sand,' and OSax., OHG., and MidHG. *mëlm*, m., 'dust' ; to these are allied Müll and Gemüll, MidHG. *gemülle*, OHG. *gimulli*, 'dust, mould.' For the root *mal* see under mahlen.

Malter, m. and n., 'measure' (in Pruss. formerly about 18 bush.), from MidHG. *malter, malder*, n., 'corn measure' ; comp. OHG. *maltar*, OSax. *maldar*, n., 'measure.' Formed by means of the Teut. suffix -*þra-*, -*dra-* (Gr. τρο-, Lat. *tro-*, comp. Alter), from the root *mal* ; see mahlen. Malter means lit. 'grinding,' then 'the quantity given to be ground at one time.'

Malve, f., 'mallow,' ModHG. only, from Lat. (Ital.) *malva* ; if it were borrowed at an early period, *lv* in Lat. ought to have changed into *lb* in ModHG. In England the Lat. term was adopted in very early times ; hence AS. *mealwe*, E. *mallow* (Du. *maluwe*). Comp. also Fr. *mauve*.

Malz, n., 'malt,' from the equiv. Mid HG. and OHG. *malz*, n. ; comp. OSax. and OIc. *malt*, n., AS. *mealt*, E. *malt* (Goth. *malt, n.) ; a common Teut. word for 'malt,' which passed into Slav. and Finn. (comp. OSlov. *mlato*, Finn. *mallas*), and also into Fr. as *malt*. Teut. *maltas belongs to a Teut. root *melt*, in AS. *mëltan*, 'to dissolve, liquefy, melt,' to which is allied an OIc. adj. *maltr*, 'rotten,' similar to OHG. and MidHG. *malz*, 'melting away, soft, relaxed.' Perhaps the subst. Malz (Goth. *malt, n.) is only the neu. of this adj., meaning 'that which is soft.' See further ſchmelzen.

mampfen, vb., 'to stutter,' ModHG. only, of obscure origin.

man, pron., 'one, they, people,' from MidHG. and OHG. *man*; corresponding to OSax. and AS. *man*, Du. *men*; prop. nom. sing. of the ModHG. subst. Mann, 'homo'; so too Lat. *homo* appears as a pron. in Fr. *on* (as well as *homme*). In the early periods (MidHG., OHG., and AS.) *man* was again represented by the 3rd pers. pron. sing. (MidHG. and OHG. *ër*, AS. *hé*); hence man is lit. 'any man'; in Goth. *manna* is found only with a negation (*ni manna*, 'nobody') ; see jemand. The sing. may have here a collective meaning, just as Sans. *mánus* (comp. Mann), and *pūrús* in the sing. signify 'person, people, mankind.'

manch, adj., 'many a,' from MidHG. *manec (g)*, OHG. *manag*, adj., 'much, many a.' The *g* has been preserved in ModHG. mannigfalt ; the change of *g* to *ch* in this word, which is first found in ModHG., is due to LG. influence. ModHG. *manec*, OHG. *manag*, 'much' ; akin to Goth. *manags*, 'much,' so too AS. *monig*, E. *many*, OSax. *maneg*, Du. *menig*. From the Teut. standpoint, the adj. may be derived from Goth. and OHG. *mana-*, 'man, person,' which orig. always occurred in compounds ; comp. Goth. *ga-man*, n., 'fellow-man,' *mana-sëþs*, 'mankind,' OHG. *manaheit*, 'valour,' *manalihho*, 'likeness,' &c. In that case, since the suffix *ga-*, equiv. to Gr. κο-, Lat. *c*, denotes 'providing with something,' the prim. meaning of Goth. *managa* may have been 'to provide with people.' Yet OIr. *menice*, 'frequent,' and OSlov. *mănogŭ*, 'much,' point to a prim. word probably unconnected with Goth. and OHG. *mana-*, 'person.'

Mandel (1.), 'fifteen,' ModHG. only ; the other meaning, which appears in earlier ModHG., 'shock of corn (of 15 sheaves),' may be the older. The G. word cannot be etymologically explained. (MidLat. *man-*

P

dala, '15 articles,' is met with even in the 13th cent.); its relation to Du. *mand*, E. *maund*, 'basket,' is obscure.

Mandel (2.), f., 'almond,' from the equiv. MidHG. *mandel*, OHG. *mandala*, f.; from Ital. *mandola*; corresponding to MidLat. *amandola*, Fr. *amande* (hence Du. *amandel*, E. *almond*). Gr. ἀμυγδάλη is usually regarded as the ultimate source of these cognates.

Mange, Mangel, f., 'mangle,' from MidHG. *mange*, f., 'machine for rolling woven stuffs, catapult'; comp. Du. *mangel*, equiv. to E. *mangle*. The origin of the word is sometimes ascribed, on account of the dial. forms Mande, Mandel, to the Sans. root *manth*, 'to turn,' which appears in OIc. *mǫndull*, 'handle' (espec. of a handmill). Allied terms in Rom. show, however, that *g* in the word Mangel must be very old; Ital. *mangano*, 'sling,' OFr. *mangoneau*, 'sling,' whence MidE. *mangonel*. There is no Teut. type of the whole class; its source is said to be Gr. μάγγανον, 'warlike machine'; perhaps an instrument of this kind furnished the model for the mangle.

mangeln, vb., 'to want, lack, be lacking,' from MidHG. *mangeln*, OHG. *mangolôn*, 'to dispense with, miss, be in want of'; **Mangel**, from MidHG. *mangel*, m., 'want, defect.' To this is allied MidHG. *manc*, 'want, defect,' also OHG. *mangôn*, *mengen*, 'to be deficient'; Du. *mangelen*, 'to dispense with.' A Teut. root *mang*, *mangu*, does not occur elsewhere; it may be primit. allied to Lat. *mancus*, 'mutilated, powerless, deficient,' from which early derivatives were formed in E., AS. *gemancian*, 'to mutilate'; to this Du. *mank*, 'limping, deficient,' and E. *to mangle* are also akin.

Mangold, m., 'beet,' from MidHG. *mangolt*, m.; its connection with Gelb does not seem to be orig. If it is to be connected, as is usually done, with the proper name *Managolt*, the prim. meaning is 'powerful ruler' (*manag* and *waltan*; comp. Πολυκράτης), but scarcely 'very gracious' (Bielbold). See Markolf. By what means the plant acquired this name can no longer be discovered. Others regard Mangold as Halsgold, 'gold-neck' (comp. Mähne); but *mane*-, 'neck,' is not found elsewhere in Teut.

Manier, f., 'manner, fashion, mannerism,' from MidHG. *maniere*, f., 'manner,' from Fr. *manière*.

manig, see manch.

Mann, m., 'man, husband,' from MidHG. *man* (*nn*), OHG. *man* (*nn*), m., 'person, man.' The general meaning 'person' still appears in MidHG. jemand, niemand, as well as in the pron. discussed under man. In AS., *man*, *mǫn* (*n* equiv. to *nn*), might be used equally of a male or female, although the former sense preponderated; AS. *man*, 'person, man, woman,' E. *man*, OIc. maðr, Goth. *manna*, 'person, man.' The word followed the declension of the two stems *mann*- and *mannan*- (thus in Goth., AS., OHG., und MidHG.); from the latter the modern plur. Männer has been obtained. Goth. and Teut. *mann*- for *manw*- is based on an older *manu*- (like Finn on *kenie*-, *genu*-; see also bünn). This Aryan *mănu*-, 'person,' appears also in Ind., but it was used also as *Manu*, 'the father of mankind.' To this corresponds the Teut. *Mannus* in Tacitus, 'the progenitor of the West Teutons'; comp. further Sans. *manus*, m., and *manuša*, 'person,' perhaps also OSlov. mąžĭ, 'man.' The Ind. *manu*- is usually connected with the root *man*, 'to think' (comp. mahnen); in that case the orig. sense is 'thinking being.' This cannot, however, be definitely regarded as the primit. source of the word. It is scarcely probable that the primit. Aryans considered 'thinking' to be the essential characteristic of a man. We should rather assume from the earliest Aryan literature, the OInd. Vedas, that the primit. Aryan felt he was closely allied to the brutes, since the Vedic Indian actually calls himself *paçu*, 'beast.' The literal meaning of Aryan *manu*-, 'person,' can hardly be ascertained now. See Mensch.

mannig, see manch.

männiglich, pron. 'everybody,' from MidHG. *manne-gelich*, *menneclich*, 'every'; lit. *manne gelich*, OHG. *manno gilih*, 'each of men,' whence OHG. *manniclich* and *mannolich*, 'every, each.' Similarly täglich is based on OHG. *tagogilih*, 'every day.' OHG. *gilih*, 'every,' is identical with gleich.

manschen, vb., for earlier mantschen, 'to splash, dabble,' from MidHG. *mangezen, OHG. *mangazzen; allied to mengen.

Mantel, m., 'cloak, mantle,' from the equiv. MidHG. *mantel*, *mandel*, OHG. *mantal*, *mandal*, m.; on account of the non-permutation of *t* to *z* the word cannot be cognate with MidE. *mantel*, E. *mantle*, OIc. *mǫttull*, m., 'cloak,' and hence it is not derived from the same root as Gr. μανδύας, 'upper garment.' The Teut. cognates are more probably based on Lat. *mantellum*, from which Ital. *mantello* and Fr. *manteau* are derived.

Märchen, n., 'fairy story, tale,' dimin. of **Mär**, f., from MidHG. *mære*, n. and f., 'tale, fiction, report, information,' whence in MidHG. the dimin. *mærelîn*, n., 'short story, fairy story.' Comp. OHG. *mâri*, f., *mâri*, n., 'rumour, information'; an abstract from OHG. *mâri* (MidHG. *mære*), Goth. *mêrs*, 'known, famed,' which is recorded by old historians in many OTeut. proper names in the form *mêrus*, *mêris*; akin to Slav. *měrŭ* in *Vladiměrŭ*, 'Vladimir, Waldemar,' Gr. -μωρος in ἐγχεσίμωρος, 'famed for wielding the spear,' OIr. *mâr*, *môr*, 'great, of repute'; for the compar. of this primitive adject. stem *mê-ro-*, see under *mehr*.

Marder, m., 'marten,' from the equiv. MidHG. *marder* (and *mader*), m., OHG. *mardar*, m.; allied to OIc. *mǫrðr*, 'marten,' and AS. *mearþ* (also *meard*), 'marten, wensel' (without the suffix r, like MidHG. *mart*, 'marten'). Whether we are to assume Goth. *marþus* or *marþuza* remains uncertain. Yet the cognates are probably of genuine Teut. origin (from pre-Teut. *martu-*), to which MidLat. *martus* (Ital. *martes*), with the corresponding Rom. class also point—Ital. *martora*, Fr. *martre*, f. (whence E. *marten*).

Mark (1.), f., 'marches, frontier,' from MidHG. *marc*, 'mark, token,' OHG. *marcha*, f., 'frontier, marches'; comp. OSax. *marca*, 'territory,' AS. *mearc*, f., 'frontier, territory' (E. *march* is not based on the AS. form, the *c* of which would not have changed to *ch*, but on OFr. *marche*, 'frontier,' which is of Teut. origin). To Goth. *marka*, f., 'frontier,' corresponds OIc. *mǫrk*, 'wood,' with a remarkable change of meaning; woods in Teut. times were often the natural boundaries between nations. The orig. meaning of the cognates of 'frontier' is supported by their primit. kinship with Lat. *margo*, 'border,' as well as by OIr. *brû* (from the prim. form *mrog*), 'border,' Ir. *bruig*, W. and Corn. *bro*, 'district, country, region,' ModPers. *marz*, 'frontier, marches.' From Teut. are derived Ital. *marca*, Fr. *marche*, 'frontier.' See **Mark** (2) and **Marke**.

Mark (2.), f., 'mark' (coin), from Mid HG. *marc*, *marke*, f., 'mark, half a pound of silver or gold'; OHG. *marka* (whence MidLat. *marca*, which first appears in documents in the latter half of the 9th cent.), AS. and MidE. *marc*, OIc. *mǫrk*, f., 'mark, half a pound of silver.' Its origin is obscure; the assumption that **Marke**, 'designation, sign' (with reference to the stamp), is a cognate, is not proved, since **Mark** orig. denoted a definite weight, and not a particular coin.

Mark (3.), n., from the equiv. MidHG. *marc* (gen. *marges*), n., 'marrow, pith'; the MidHG. *g* has been preserved in *mergelîn*; OHG. *marg*, *mara-y*, n., OSax. *marg*, n., Du. *merg*, n., AS. *mearg*, n., E. *marrow*, OIc. *mergr*, m., 'marrow'; in this word *r* is due to Goth. *z*, according to the law of rhotacism; Goth. *mazga-* is wanting. The latter points to pre-Teut. *mazgho-*, to which OSlov. *mozgŭ*, m., Zend *mazga*, Sans. *majjan*, 'marrow,' all with a normal loss of the aspirate, correspond. The root is Sans. *majj*, 'to immerse,' to which Lat. *mergere* is allied.

Marke, f., 'mark, token'; from Mid HG. *marc* (gen. *markes*), n., 'sign'; comp. Du. *marke*, 'mark, characteristic'; AS. *mearc*, n., E. *mark*, OIc. *mark*, n., 'sign'; Goth. *mark* is wanting. Whether these cognates are connected with those of **Mark** (1), 'frontier, marches,' lit. 'border,' is uncertain; the meaning 'frontier,' which was proved by the allied languages to be primitive, can scarcely be the starting-point for 'sign'; the contrary is the more probable. It has with greater reason been compared with Lith. *márgas*, 'variegated.' Comp. *merfen*. From Teut. a Rom. class is derived; comp. Fr. *marque*, *remarquer*, &c.

Markolf, m., 'jay,' first occurs in early ModHG.; it has passed from the fables of animals into general use; liter. *Markwolf*, 'boundary wolf,' used in the OHG. period as a proper name (*Marcolf*). Similarly in Reineke Vos, *Marquart* is the name of the jay, formed from the OHG. proper name *Marcwart*, lit. 'frontier guardian.'

Markt, m., 'market, market-place,' from MidHG. *markt*, *mark t*, m., 'fair, market, market-place,' OHG. *markât*, *mërkât*, *mërchât*, m.; borrowed in OHG. from the equiv. Lat. *mercâtus* with a G. accent; from the same source come Du. *markt* and E. *market*. ModHG. **markten**, vb., 'to buy, bargain,' from MidHG. *marketen*, 'to be at the market, to bargain.' The *e* of the Lat. original has been preserved in

Suab. and Alem. 𝔐ärft; the variant with a points to the Fr. *a*. Comp. in Rom., Ital. *mercato*, Fr. *marché* (whence MidE. and E. *market*).

𝔐armel, m., from the equiv. MidHG. *marmel*, OHG. *marmul*, m., 'marble'; from the Lat. word by differentiating *r-r* to *r-l*.

𝔐arſch, f., 'marsh, moor,' ModHG. only, a LG. word. LG. *marsch*, MidDu. *maersche*, 'pasture ground,' AS. m*e*rsc, m., and the equiv. E. *marsh*, Dan. *marsk*, 'bog.' Goth. *marisks may be assumed as a derivative of Goth. *marei*, 'ocean' (see 𝔐eer); similarly ModHG. 𝔄u is a derivative of Goth. *ahwa*, 'water.' Comp. MidLat. *mariscus*, 'marsh,' and some of the Rom. words connected with it, such as OFr. *maresc*, ModFr. *marais*, Ital. *marese*, which may, however, be partly derivatives of Lat. *mare*.

𝔐arſchall, m., 'marshal,' derived, partly under the influence of Fr. *maréchal*, from MidHG. *marschale*, m., which lit. and orig. signified 'horse-servant,' then 'overseer of the train of servants on journeys and expeditions, as a municipal or court official; marshal.' OHG. *maruhscalc* is a compound of 𝔖chalf, 'servant,' and *marah*, 'horse'; even the Lex Salica and the Leg. Alem. record the term *mariscalus*, besides which, in MidLat. *marscallus* occurs. From Teut. are derived the Rom. cognates —Ital. *mariscalco*, Fr. *maréchal*, 'farrier, marshal,' as well as the MidLat. version, *comes stabuli*, Fr. *connétable*. OHG. *marah*, n., MidHG. *marc*, n., 'steed, horse,' AS. *mearh*, Scand. *marr*, n.; Goth. *marh is wanting. It originated, in exact accordance with the permutation of consonants, from pre-Teut. *marka-*, in which form it is recorded as OKelt. by Pausanias; comp. with this OIr. *marc* and W. *march*, 'horse.' There is, however, no linguistic necessity for deriving Teut. *marha-* from Kelt. The word *marh*, the fem. of which, 𝔐ähre, has been preserved, was supplanted at a later period by 𝔑eß and then 𝔓ferd. To this word 𝔐arſtall is akin.

𝔐arſtall, m., 'royal or public stable,' from MidHG. *marstal* (gen. *-stalles*), m., 'stable for horses.' For the orig. *marhstal*, like MidHG. *marschalc*, for *marh-schalc*, see 𝔖tall; and with regard to *marh-*, comp. the preceding word.

𝔐arter, f., 'torture, rack,' from Mid HG. *marter*, *martere*, f., orig. 'martyrdom,' espec. 'the Passion,' then 'torture, torment, persecution, rack,' OHG. *martira*, *martara*, f. (also with *l*, OHG. *martela*, MidHG. *martel*); formed from Gr. and Lat. *martyrium*. The derivative 𝔐ärtyrer is from MidHG. m*e*rterer, *marterer*, OHG. *martirâri*, 'martyr,' for which the forms *martir*, *martyr*, equiv. to Lat.-Gr. *martyr*, 'martyr for the truth of Christianity,' rarely occur. The Eccles. Lat. meaning 'torture,' which is foreign to Gr., is found also in the Rom. cognates of *martyrium*. Comp. Ital. *martirio*, Fr. *martyre*.

𝔐ärz, m., from the equiv. MidHG. m*e*rze, m., OHG. m*e*rzo, *marzeo*, m., 'March,' from Lat. (*mensem*) *Martium*. The corresponding Westphal. *märte*, MidLG. m*e*rte, as well as Du. *maart*, make it probable that 𝔐ärz was borrowed previous to the OHG. permutation of consonants about the era of the Merovings, and in fact contemporaneously with 𝔄uguſt, 𝔍änner, and 𝔐ai. E. *March*, MidE. *marche*, was borrowed at a somewhat later period from OIr. *march* (ModFr. *mars*).

𝔐aſche, f., 'mesh, stitch,' from MidHG. *mâsche*, OHG. and OLG. *mâsca*, f., 'mesh, snare'; comp. AS. *mâsce*, E. *mesh*, OIc. *mǫskve*, m.; Goth. *mêsqa, *masqa, are by chance not recorded. According to the permutation of consonants, the latter is based on pre-Teut. *mêzga-* (*mosga-*); comp. Lith. *mázgas*, 'threads interlaced, knot,' which is connected with a vb. *mezgù* (*mégsti*), 'to tie knots, knit (nets).' Thus 𝔐aſche may be traced to a Teut. root *mêsq* (pre-Teut. and Aryan *mêzg*', 'to plait.'

𝔐aſer, f., 'vein (in wood), speck, spot,' from MidHG. *maser*, m., OHG. *masar*, n., 'vein, knotty excrescence on the maple and other trees' (MidHG. also 'goblet of speckled wood'); comp. AS. *maser*, 'knot in wood,' E. *measles*; OIc. m*ǫ*surr, m., 'maple' (*mǫsur-bolle*, 'maple bowl'). Allied to OHG. *masa*, f., 'wound, scar.' The Teut. class is the source of Rom. derivatives. Comp. Fr. *madré*, 'speckled,' Mid Lat. *scyphi maserini*, 'drinking vessels.'

𝔐aske, f., 'mask, disguise, masquerader,' from Fr. *masque*; the equiv. Suab. and Bav. *maskere* is more closely connected with Ital. *maschera* as well as Span. *mascara*, 'division'; comp. also Du. and E. *masker*. Perhaps the origin of the entire class is to be sought for in Rom.

𝔐aſſe, f., 'mass, bulk, heap,' from Mid HG. *masse*, f., 'misshapen stuff, mass,' espec. 'lumps of metal.' Borrowed in the late OHG. period (by Notker), as *massa*, f., from Lat. *massa*.

Maſt (1.), m. (probably quite unknown to Suab. and Bav.), 'mast,' from MidHG. and OHG. *mast*, m., 'pole, flagstaff, spearshaft,' espec. 'ship's mast, tree fit for a mast'; comp. LG. and Du. *mast*, AS. *mæst*, m. E. *mast*, OIc. *mastr*, 'mast.' Goth. **masta-*, m., 'mast, pole,' is wanting. According to the permutation of consonants, the latter is based on pre-Teut. *mazdo-* (comp. Aſt, Gerſte, and Neſt); did Lat. *mâlus* for **mâdus* originate in this? (also Ir. *matan*, 'club,' *maite*, 'stick'?). Similarly Fiſch (*piscis*) and Meer (*mare*) are primit. allied.

Maſt (2.), 'mast (for fattening),' from MidHG. and MidLG. *mast*, m., f., and n., 'food, acorns, fattening,' OHG. *mast*; comp. AS. *mæst*, f., E. *mast*. Goth. **masta* is derived, according to the permutation of consonants, from a primit. form *mazdo-*, to which Sans. *mêdas*, n., 'fat,' *mêdây*, 'to fatten,' also points. The ModHG. verbal noun mäſten comes from MidHG. and OHG. *mesten*; Du. *mesten*, AS. *mæstan*, 'to fatten'; to this is allied the ModHG. adj. partic. maſt, OHG. *mast*, AS. *gemæst*, 'fat, fattened.' In MidHG. *gemast, gemęstet*.

Maſs, n., 'measure, standard, proportion,' from MidHG. *mâʒ*, n., 'measure, manner'; usually in MidHG. *mâʒe*, f., 'measure, definite extent of time, space, weight, strength; moderation, temperance,' OHG. *mâʒa*, f.; comp. Du. *maat*, OIc. *mát*, m., 'method.' With the Teut. root *mĕt* (in meſſen), from pre-Teut. *mĕd*, Lat. *mŏdus*, 'manner,' is also connected.

Maſse, f., 'measure,' allied to MidHG. *mâʒe*; see under Maſs, n.

maſsen, conj., 'whereas,' from the dat. plur. *mâʒen* (of MidHG. *mâʒe*), 'in the method'; orig. used only as an adv., but in ModHG. as a conj. also; allied to Maſs.

Maſsholder, m., 'maple,' from MidHG. *mazalter, mazolter*, m., OHG. *mazzaltra, mazzoltra*, f., 'maple'; the ModHG. form is due to its connection with Holunder (older variant Holder). The OHG. *mazzoltra* is like *affoltra*, 'apple tree,' from *apfol*, a derivative of a primary Goth. **matls*. AS. *mapuldr*, E. *maple tree*, with the recorded base *mapol*, E. *maple*, has, instead of the HG. dental, an abnormal labial, presupposing Goth. **maple;* so too OIc. *mǫpurr*, m., 'maple.' On account of OHG. *mazzaltra* (ʒʒ for Goth. t), Maſsholder cannot be connected with Maſer (s equiv. to Goth. s); nor does it belong to OHG. *maʒ*, n., 'food,' Ahorn as 'food tree' being improbable, although maple-juice is used as a medicinal draught. Goth. **matla-*, or rather **mapla-*, is of obscure origin. Comp. also Ahorn, where an earlier term is given. The ModHG. form Maſseller is, like Maſsholder, a corruption of the MidHG. word. With regard to the OHG. suffix *-tra*, comp. Apfel, Wacholder, and Holunder.

mäſsig, adj., 'moderate,' from MidHG. *mæʒec*, OHG. *mâʒîg*, adj., 'moderate, temperate; of moderate size'; a derivative of Maſs, Maſse. Comp. Du. *matig*, 'moderate.'

Maſslieb, n., 'daisy, Easter daisy,' ModHG. only, formed from MidDu. *matelief*, ModDu. *madelief*, f., 'daisy'; of obscure origin; perhaps allied to Matte?.

Matratze, f., 'mattress,' from MidHG. *matraʒ, materaʒ*, m. and n., 'couch stuffed with wool, divan'; comp. Du. *matras*, E. *mattress*. The HG. form with *tz* is formed from MidLat. *matratium*, which, with its corresponding Rom. cognate, Fr. *matelas*, is usually derived from an Arab source; Arab. *mutrah*, 'pillow,' lit. 'place where something is thrown.'

Matroſe, m., 'sailor,' ModHG. only, from the equiv. Du. *matroos*; Dan. and Swed. *matros*. They are based on Fr. *matelot* (OFr. *matenot*), 'sailor,' which again is derived through a Norman medium from Scand. *mǫtunautr*, 'messmate' (the crew was divided into companies, who took their meals together).

matt, adj., 'checkmated; faint, languid, insipid,' from MidHG. *mat* (gen. *mattes*), adj., 'checkmated' (also figuratively), which was adopted from Rom. in the latter half of the 12th cent.; comp. Fr. *mat*, Ital. *matto*, MidLat. *mattus*, whence also Du. *mat*, E. *mate*. This characteristic term, which was introduced with chess, is formed from Arab. and Pers. *schâh mât*, 'the king is dead.' See Schach.

Matte (1.), f. (an Alem. word unknown to Suab. and Bav.), from the equiv. Mid HG. *mate, matte*, f., 'mead, meadow'; OHG. **matta*, f., is wanting (but OHG. *mato-scrëch*, 'grasshopper,' is preserved). Goth. **mapra, *mëdwa*, is not recorded; comp. E. *meadow*, *mead*, from AS. *mǣd* (gen. *mǣdwe*), 'meadow,' MidLG. *mâde*, OLG. *mâtha, mada*, OFris. *mêth*. They seem to be based on a Teut. root *mâp, mad*, which is connected with Lat. *mêto*, 'to mow, reap,' and which has a shorter form, *mê*, in ModHG. mähen.

Matte (2.), f., 'mat,' from MidHG. *matte* (late MidHG. also *matze*), OHG. *matta*, f., 'covering woven of straw, rushes, &c., mat'; Du. *mat*, AS. *meatte*, f., E. *mat*. The correspondence of the HG. and LG.-Eng. dental indicates that the word was borrowed, and as a fact it was introduced during the OHG. period. It is based on Lat. *matta*, 'mat made of rushes.'

Matz, m., 'Mat; simpleton; pet name for tame birds'; ModHG. only; probably a pet name for 𝔐𝔞𝔱𝔥𝔦𝔞𝔰, 'Matthias,' and 𝔐𝔞𝔱𝔱𝔥ä𝔲𝔰, 'Matthew'; the intermediate form is 𝔐𝔞𝔱𝔱𝔢𝔰.

Matzen, m., 'passover bread,' early ModHG.; from Jewish *mazzo*, Hebr. *mazzóth*, 'unleavened bread,' whence also late MidHG., or rather early ModHG. 𝔐𝔞𝔰𝔞𝔲𝔷𝔢, 'passover bread.'

mauen, vb., from the equiv. MidHG. *mâwen*, 'to mew like a cat'; an imitative word; comp. 𝔐𝔦𝔢𝔷𝔢.

Mauer, f., from the equiv. MidHG. *mûre*, *mûr*, f., 'wall,' OHG. *mûra*, f. (*mûrî*, f.), 'wall,' from Lat. *mûrus*, with an abnormal change of gender, which is probably caused by an OTeut. word for 'wall'; comp. Goth. *waddjus*, f. At the same period, before the HG. permutation, OSax. *mûr*, AS. *mûr*, m. (OIr. *mûr*), were also borrowed from the Lat., like other words relating to stone buildings; comp. 𝔖𝔦𝔢𝔤𝔢𝔩, 𝔉𝔢𝔫𝔰𝔱𝔢𝔯, 𝔓𝔣𝔢𝔯𝔱𝔢, 𝔖𝔭𝔢𝔦𝔠𝔥𝔢𝔯, &c.

Mauke, f., with a LG. guttural, from the equiv. MidHG. *mûche*, f., 'malanders,' hence the strictly HG. form 𝔐𝔞𝔲𝔠𝔥𝔢 (Bav.). Of obscure origin; perhaps allied to Goth. *mûks*, 'soft, tender'?.

Maul (1.), n., 'mouth (of beasts), muzzle' (in UpG. 𝔐𝔞𝔲𝔩 is also used for 𝔐𝔲𝔫𝔡, 'mouth of men'). from MidHG. *mûl*, *mûle*, n., *mûle*, f. (MidG.), 'mouth,' OHG. *mûla*, f., 'mouth,' also 'beak'; Du. *muil*, OIc. *mûle*, m., 'mouth, snout'; Goth. **mûlô*, n., 'mouth,' is wanting, but is authenticated by the derivative *faurmûljan*, 'to muzzle.' This word is an *l* derivative from the root *mû*, from which HG. 𝔐𝔲𝔫𝔡, with a particip. suffix. *nþ*, is also formed; see 𝔐𝔲𝔫𝔡.

Maul (2.), n., 'mule,' in 𝔐𝔞𝔲𝔩𝔱𝔦𝔢𝔯, n., 𝔐𝔞𝔲𝔩𝔢𝔰𝔢𝔩, m., from MidHG. *mûltier*, n., *mûlesel*, m., yet ordinarily simply *mûl*, m. and n., *mûle*, m., 'mule,' OHG. *mûl*, m.; borrowed from Lat. *mûlus*. From the same source Du. *muil*, *muilezel*, AS. *mûl*, E. *mule*, as well as OIr. *mûl*, are derived.

Maulbeere, f., from the equiv. MidHG. *mûlber*, n. and f., 'mulberry,' which originated, by differentiating *r* to *l*, from OHG. *mûr-beri*, *môr-beri*, n. The fluctuation from *ô* to *û* in OHG. indicates that the word was borrowed from Lat. *môrum*, 'mulberry,' *môrus*, 'mulberry tree,' whence also Du. *moerbes*, AS. and MidE. *môrberie* and *mûrberie*, MidE. also *mulberie*, E. *mulberry*.

Maulwurf, m., from the equiv. Mid HG. *môltwërf*, *moltwërfe*, m., 'mole,' lit. 'the animal that throws up the soil' (Mid HG. *molte*, f.). The ModHG. form is a corruption of the MidHG. word, which is recorded even in the MidHG. and OHG. periods in various forms (MidHG. *mûwërf*, *mûlwërf*, *mûlwëlf*, *mûrwërf*). Other Mod HG. corrupt forms are the dial. 𝔐𝔢𝔩𝔱𝔴𝔲𝔯𝔪, 𝔐𝔞𝔲𝔩𝔴𝔲𝔯𝔪, and 𝔐𝔞𝔲𝔩𝔴𝔢𝔩𝔣. OHG. *moltwerf*, *multiwurf*, m., 'mole,' are connected with MidHG. *molte*, f., *molt*, m., 'dust, mould, soil,' OHG. *molta*, f., *molt*, m.; comp. Goth. *mulda*, f., 'dust, mould,' AS. *molde*, E. *mould*; prop. a fem. subst. from the partic. formed with *da-* from the root *mal*, 'to crush, pulverise,' hence *mul-da*; comp. 𝔪𝔞𝔩𝔱, 𝔞𝔩𝔱, 𝔟𝔲𝔫𝔱, and 𝔷𝔞𝔯𝔱. In MidE. also *moldwerp*, 'mole' occurs; of this MidE. *mole*, Du., Westph., and Fris. *mol* are shortened forms?. These, however, are probably independent forms from the root *mal*. Another name for *mole* appears in OHG. *scêro*, MidHG. *schêr*, Suab. and Alem. 𝔖𝔠𝔥ä𝔯𝔪𝔞𝔲𝔰.

Maus (1.), 'mouse,' from the equiv. MidHG. and OHG. *mûs*, f.; comp. Du. *muis*, AS. *mûs*, f., E. *mouse*, OIc. *mûs* (Goth. **mûs*), f., 'mouse.' In the consonantal form of the stem, *mûs-*, it is the common Teut. as well as the common Aryan term for 'mouse.' The name occurs in almost all the Aryan languages, a proof that the Aryans in their primit. Asiatic home were already acquainted with the tiny animal, chiefly through its thefts, *mûs-* being derived from an OAryan root, *mûs*, 'to steal,' which exists in the Franc. *chreomosido*, 'plundering dead bodies,' of the Lex Salica, and signifying 'thief' (it is possible, however, that the *mûs*, 'to steal,' is deduced from *mûs*, 'mouse'). Comp. Sans. *mûś*, 'mouse,' with the root *muś*, *muśdy*, 'to take away, rob'; also Gr. μῦς, OSlov. *myšĭ*, f. Comp. further the following word.

Maus (2.), prop. 'muscles on the arm and foot,' now espec. 'ball of the thumb,' from MidHG. *mûs*, f., 'muscles especially of the upper part of the arm'; OHG. *mûs*, AS. *mûs*, Du. *muis*, have the same sense; prop. identical with 𝔐𝔞𝔲𝔰 (1). In other cases too names of animals are applied to parts of the body. Comp. Gr. μῦς, 'muscle,' μυών, 'cluster of muscles,' Lat. *mus-culus*, 'muscle,' lit. 'little mouse,' OSlov. *myšca*, 'arm,' Sans. *muš-ka*, 'testicle, pudenda muliebria,' lit. 'little mouse.'

𝔪𝔞𝔲𝔰𝔠𝔥𝔢𝔩𝔫, vb., 'to act like a cheat,' lit. 'mosaizare'; allied to 𝔐𝔞𝔲𝔰𝔠𝔥𝔢, equiv. to Hebr. *Móschäh*, 'Moses.'

𝔐𝔞𝔲𝔰𝔢, 𝔐𝔞𝔲𝔰𝔢𝔯, f., 'moulting, casting the skin, moulting season,' from MidHG. *mûze*, f. (in compounds *mûzer*). 'mewing, moulting'; OHG. *mûzza*, f., 'moulting,' is not recorded; allied to OHG. *mûzzôn*, MidHG. *mûzen*, 'to exchange for,' MidHG. also espec. 'to moult, cast the skin.' Borrowed before the OHG. period (contemporaneously with 𝔎𝔞𝔣𝔦𝔤, 𝔓𝔣𝔞𝔲, and 𝔓𝔦𝔭𝔢) from Lat. *mutâre*, hence the permutation of *t* to *z* (MidLat. *mûta*, 'moulting'); *sz* has been preserved in Bav. maußen. From the same source are derived AS. *bimútian*, 'to change, exchange,' MidE. *moutin*, E. *to moult*, as well as Fr. *muer*, 'to moult,' *mue*, 'moulting.'

𝔪𝔞𝔲𝔰𝔢𝔫, vb., 'to catch mice, pilfer,' from MidHG. *mûsen*, 'to creep, deceive'; a derivative of MidHG. *mûs*, equiv. to 𝔐𝔞𝔲𝔰.

𝔪𝔞𝔲𝔰𝔦𝔤, adj., 'pert, saucy,' ModHG. only (𝔰𝔦𝔠𝔥, mauſig 𝔪𝔞𝔠𝔥𝔢𝔫, 'to bray, bluster'), allied to 𝔐𝔞𝔲𝔰𝔢𝔯, 'moulting,' lit. 'one that moults, mews, dresses smartly in order to make himself conspicuous.'

𝔐𝔞𝔲𝔱, f., 'toll, duty,' a Bav. word, from MidHG. *mûte*, f., OHG. *mûta*, f., 'toll.' The current derivation from Mid Lat. *mûta* is not satisfactory, since the latter word is not recorded until late (first half of the 9th cent.), and that as a G. word, *nullum telonenm neque quod lingua theodisca Muta vocatur*; ann. 837. Goth. *môta*, f., 'toll,' is the earliest recorded term. Yet OHG. *mûta* and Goth. *môta* (also OIc. and OSwed. *múta*, 'fee, gratuity, bribe') are not equiv., since Goth. *môla* (AS. *môt*) leads to OHG. **muoza*, and OHG. *mûta* to Goth. **mûda*. Probably the OBav. word was borrowed about the 8th cent., after the HG. permutation of consonants, from a dial. closely allied to the Goth. (Goth. *ô* tended towards *û*); to this is also allied OSlov. *myto*, 'toll.' An earlier loan-word is also recorded in Mid HG. *muoze*, 'toll, tax,' which points to OHG. **muoza*, and which has been preserved in Bav. 𝔐𝔲𝔢𝔰, 'miller's fee.' Yet the word may have been primit. allied to the Goth. The term 𝔓𝔬𝔩𝔩, which is cognate in meaning, is also of obscure origin.

𝔪𝔢𝔠𝔥𝔢𝔯𝔫, vb., 'to bleat,' ModHG. only; MidHG. has an equiv. word by a different derivation from the same stem, *mêchzen*, 'to bleat,' allied to MidHG. *mëcke*, m., 'he-goat,' as a nickname (Goth. **migga*, 'he-goat,' is wanting). Comp. the pre-Teut. root *mak* in Gr. μηκάομαι, 'to bleat.'

𝔐𝔢𝔢𝔯, n., 'ocean, sea,' from MidHG. *mer*, n., OHG. *meri*, earlier *mari*, m. and n., 'ocean'; comp. OSax. *meri*, f., Du. *meer*, n., AS. *mere*, m., E. *mere* (to which *merman*, *mermaid*, are allied), OIc. *marr*, m., Goth. *marei*, f. (and **mar*, n., preserved in the compound *mari-saivs*, 'ocean'). The common Teut. word for 'ocean,' prim. Teut. *mari*, n. (or *mori*, recorded by Pliny as a Cimbrian form), which is partly common to the West Aryan tribes (so too Lat. *lacus*, OIr. *loch*, equiv. to OLG. *lagu*, 'ocean'); Lat. *mare*, n., OSlov. *morje*, n., 'ocean,' Lith. *mares*, 'Kurisches Haff,' OIr. *muir* (from *mori*), 'ocean'; to these are allied Gr. 'Αμφίμαρος, 'son of Poseidon,' as well as ἀμάρα, f., 'trench, conduit' (comp. OFris. *mar*, 'trench, pond') ?. These cognates are usually connected with the Aryan root *mar*, 'to die' (comp. 𝔐𝔬𝔯𝔡, Lat. *morior*), so that the ocean was named in "contrast to the living vegetation" of the mainland, just as in Ind. also *marus*, 'desert,' is referred to the root *mar*, 'to die'; this, however, is no more probable than the derivation of 𝔐𝔞𝔫𝔫 from the root *men*, 'to think.' Comp. 𝔐𝔞𝔯𝔰𝔠𝔥 and 𝔐𝔢𝔢𝔯.

𝔐𝔢𝔢𝔯𝔯𝔢𝔱𝔱𝔦𝔤, m., 'horse-radish,' allied to 𝔐𝔢𝔢𝔯, like 𝔥𝔢𝔯𝔷𝔬𝔤 to 𝔥𝔢𝔢𝔯, 𝔳𝔦𝔢𝔯𝔱𝔢 (?) to *vier* (?), &c.; corresponding to MidHG. *merrettich*, OHG. *meri-ratich*, m., 'radish that has come from over the sea, transpontine radish.' The E. term *horse-radish*, 𝔐𝔢𝔢𝔯𝔯𝔢𝔱𝔱𝔦𝔤, is curious, and suggests the idea that 𝔐𝔢𝔢𝔯 in this case is equiv. to 𝔐𝔞𝔥𝔯𝔢. Du. *mierikwortel*, Westph. *mirrek*, Hess. 𝔐𝔢𝔯𝔠𝔥𝔥𝔢𝔯𝔫, seem to be of the same origin.

𝔐𝔢𝔥𝔩, n., 'meal, flour, dust,' from Mid HG. *mël* (gen. *mëlwes*), n., OHG. *mëlo* (gen. *mëlawes*), n.; corresponding to OSax. *mël*, Du. *meel*, AS. *mëlu* (gen. *mëlwes*), n., E. *meal*, OIc. *mjǫl* (gen. plur. *mjǫlva*), 'meal'; the common Teut. word for 'meal'; Goth. **milwa* (gen. **milwis*) is by chance not recorded. It is a specifically Teut. derivative of the root *mal*, 'to grind,' of which the form *mel* is authenticated by Slav. and Ir.; see mahlen. While the vb. mahlen is common to West Aryan, the form of the word Mehl, from the root *mel*, is peculiar to Teut.; it may also be remarked that the subst. is found in E., though not the corresponding vb. There is also a derivative from the same root in Kelt.; comp. W. *blawd*, Bret. *bleud* (from *mlât*).

Mehltau, m., 'mildew, blight,' corrupted from the equiv. MidHG. *miltou*, n., OHG. *mili-tou*, n.; comp. AS. *meledeáw* (*miledeáw*), E. *mildew*. The opinions as to the origin of the first component are various. The most probable derivation is that from Goth. *milip*, n., 'honey' (comp. OIc. *milska*, f., 'sweet drink'), to which in West Teut. a subst. *mili* (Gr. μέλι, stem μέλιτ-, Lat. *mel*) is possibly akin; hence Mehltau, 'honeydew'?. It is less probable that the word was borrowed from or was primit. allied to the equiv. Gr. μίλτος, so that Tau may have been an explanatory addition (comp. Lindwurm and Windhund). It is also possible that OHG. *mili-*, AS. *mele-*, *mile-*, is connected with Mehl, and a special formation from the root *mel*, 'to grind.' In that case the ModHG. change of Miltau into Mehltau is warranted by etymology; Mehltau is defined as 'a greyish-white, meal-like coating on plants in summer.'

mehr, adj. and adv., 'more,' from MidHG. *mêr*; compar. of viel; also, doubly compared, *mêrer*, *mêrre*, 'greater or larger' (of space, number, and value); further indeclin. *mêre*, *mêr*, *mê*, 'plus'; OHG. *mêr*, undeclin. neu. and compar. adv., 'more, plus, magis, amplius,' adj. *mêro*, 'major, greater' (also with the addition of the compar. suffix *mêrôro*, *mêriro*, 'major'). OHG. *mêro* originated in *maizo*, Goth. *maiza*, the *-iza-* of which is the OTeut. compar. suffix (comp. besser, Goth. *batiza*; höher, Goth. *hauhiza*); comp. AS. *mâ*, adv. and neu. subst., 'more,' adj. *mára*, E. *more*. The corresponding superl. is meist. Goth. *maiza*, for *majiza, belongs, with the Goth. superl. *maists* (see meist), to the Teut. adj. *mê-rs*, 'projecting,' discussed under Märchen.

mehrer, adj., 'greater, several,' from MidHG. *mêrer*, compar. adj. See mehr.

meiden, vb., 'to avoid, shun, refrain,' from MidHG. *míden*, 'to dispense with, suffer want, eschew, forsake, refrain from'; OHG. *mídan*, 'to hide oneself from, keep secret, eschew, refrain from'; comp. OSax. *míthan*, AS. *mîðan*, 'to hide, conceal, refrain from.' The orig. sense of the cognates seems to be 'to hide, remain far from,' but definitely related terms are wanting; Lat. *amitto*, Lith. *pa-metù*, 'to throw away,' are not connected. For other words similar in sound see under miß and missen.

Meier, n., 'head-servant on an estate, land-steward, farmer,' from MidHG. *meier*, *meiger*, m., OHG. *meior*, *meier*, m.; it corresponds to the early MidLat. *major domus*, which lit. denoted 'the steward of the household servants'; hence OHG. and MidHG. *meier*, 'steward of an estate, manager or lessee of an estate.' From Lat. *major*, Fr. *maire* is also derived.

Meile, f. (rare in Suab. and Bav.), 'mile' (about five E. miles), from the equiv. MidHG. *mîle*, OHG. *mîla*, *mîlla* (for *milja*), f.; corresponding to Du. *mijl*, AS. *mîl*, E. *mile*, Scand. *míla*, £, 'mile'; from Lat. *mîlia* (*passuum*), 'thousand paces,' whence also Ital. *miglia*, Fr. *mille*. It prop. denotes 'a measure of a thousand paces (sing. *mille passuum*).' The more frequent plur. *milia* was adopted in Rom. and G., chiefly as a fem. sing., without the addition of *passuum* (Ital. formed the sing. *miglio*, 'mile,' from the plur. *miglia*). The word was borrowed in the first cent. contemporaneously with Straße (Ital. *lega*, Fr. *lieue*, 'league,' a later word of Kelt. origin, was never adopted in G.).

Meiler, m., 'charcoal-kiln,' from late MidHG. *meiler*, *miler*, m., 'stack of wood for making charcoal'; the *č* of the Mid HG. prim. form is attested by ModHG. and LG. dials. The word cannot be derived from Slav. (Czech *milíř*, Pol. *mielerz*, 'charcoal kiln,' are themselves of G. origin). Since it may have denoted orig. a definite number of objects (comp. Carinth. *meiler*, 'a definite number of bars in a stack of pig-iron'), we might connect it with Lat. *mîliarium*, 'thousand' (see the similar case of Decher).

mein, poss. pron., 'my,' from MidHG. and OHG. *mîn*; in the same form it is the common Teut. poss. pron. from the stem *me-* of the pers. pron. (mir, mich, thus even in MidHG. and OHG.). This stem *me-* (in Goth. *mi-s*, 'to me,' *mi-k*, 'me,' acc.) is according to Lat. *meus, mihi*, Gr. μέ, Sans. *ma*, common to the Aryan division. Further details belong to grammar.

Meineid, m., 'false oath, perjury,' from the equiv. MidHG. *meincit*, OHG. *meincid*, m.; corresponding to OSax. *mênêth*, Du. *meineed*, AS. *mánáþ*, OIc. *meineiðr*, m., 'perjury.' It is the common Teut. word for 'false oath'; only Goth. **main-aiþs* is wanting. The first component is an adj. (or rather an adj. used as a subst.), MidHG. and OHG. *mein*, 'false, deceitful,' as masc. and neut. 'falsity, injustice, outrage.' In MidHG. *ein meiner* was also used for *ein meineit*; comp. OSax. *mên*, AS. *mán*, m., 'falsity, crime, outrage,' OIc. *mein*, n., 'damage, injury, misfortune' (allied to *meinn*, adj., 'hurtful'). ModHG. gemein (Goth. *gamains*) does not seem to be directly akin, although MidHG. *mein*, 'outrage,' may have been the source of the bad sense attached to the modern word. They are, however, finally connected with Slav. words for Tausch, 'exchange' (comp. Tausch and. täuschen), Lith. *mainas*, 'exchange,' OSlov. *mêna*, 'change, alteration' (Lett. *nút*, 'to exchange'). In that case Lat. *commūnis* and Goth. *gamains* (see gemein) would mean lit. 'being on a footing of barter.' It is probably not related to Lat. *mentīri*.

meinen, vb., 'to think, opine, mean,' from MidHG. *meinen*, 'to direct one's thoughts to, have in view, aim at, be affected towards a person, love,' OHG. *meinen, meinan*, 'to mean, think, say, declare'; comp. OSax. *mênian*, Du. *meenen*, AS. *mǽnan*, E. *to mean* (to this AS. *mǽnan*, E. *to moan*, are supposed to be allied); Goth. **mainjan* is wanting. The most closely allied term is OSlov. *mênja, mêniti*, 'to mean.' The latter, as well as West Teut. *meinen* (assuming *mainjan* from *mênjan*) is usually rightly connected with the man, 'to think' (comp. mahnen, Manu, and Minne). The meaning 'to love' appears only in MidHG. literature it has been introduced into ModHG. poetry.—**Meinung**, f., 'opinion, meaning,' from MidHG. *meinung*, OHG. *meinunga*, f., 'thought, disposition, view.'

Meisch, m., **Meische**, f., 'mash,' from MidHG. *meisch*, m., 'grape mash,' also 'mead, drink mixed with honey'; allied to E. *mash*, which by chance is not recorded in AS. and MidE. It is very likely related by gradation to mischen, if the latter, as is probable, is a genuine Teut. word; comp. MidE. *máschien* and the equiv. E. *to mash*. With this agrees the further assumption that MidHG. *meisch*, 'mead,' is primit. allied to OSlov. *mêzga*, 'tree-juice' (for OSlov. *zg*, equiv. to Teut. *sk*, see mischen and Masche).

Meise, f., 'titmouse,' from the equiv. MidHG. *meise*, OHG. *meisa*, f.; comp. Du. *mees*, AS. *máse* (E. only in *titmouse*, a corruption of *tit-moase*; AS. *á* is equiv. to E. *oa*); OIc. *meisingr*, m., with a suffix 'titmouse.' A term peculiar to Teut., which passed also into Fr. (Fr. *mésange*, 'titmouse,' formed from Scand. *meisingr*?); origin obscure. Only a few names of birds can be traced beyond the Teut. group (comp. Aar, Drossel, Specht, and Kranich).

meist, adj. and adv., 'most, mostly,' from MidHG. *meist*, adj., 'greatest, most,' adv., 'mostly, at best, very specially' (a superl. of the compar. mehr, MidHG. *mêr*); comp. OHG. *meist*, Goth. *maists*, from the OHG. posit. *mihhil*, Goth. *mikils*, 'great.' Goth. *ma-ists* has the old superl. suffix *ist* like Goth. *but-ists*, OHG. *bezzist*; from the stem *ma-* the Goth. compar. *ma-iza* is also formed. The forms of comparison seemed to be based on the Goth. adject. stem *mêrs*, OHG. *má-ri*, 'projecting.' Comp. also OSax. *mêst*, Du. *meest*, AS. *mǽst* (*mást*), E. *most*.

Meister, m., 'master, chief, leader,' from MidHG. *meister*, m., 'learned poet, meister-sänger (poets who were members of guilds), mayor, burgomaster,' OHG. *meistar*; OSax. *mêstar*, Du. *meester*, AS. *mǽgster*. Borrowed from Lat. *magister*, which in MidLat. was applied to numerous offices. Comp. further Ital. *maestro*, Fr. *maître*, E. *master, mister*.

Meißel, m., 'chisel,' from MidHG. *meizel*, OHG. *meizil*, m., 'chisel, tool for dressing and chipping'; allied to OHG. *meizan*, MidHG. *meizen*, 'to hew, cut,' Goth. *maitan*, 'to hew, hew off'; thus too OIc. *meitell*, m., 'chisel,' allied to *meita*, 'to cut.' All these belong to a Teut. root *mait*, 'to hew,' which has been connected with the Teut. root *mat*, 'to hew,' in Metze (Steinmetze). Comp. also E. *mattock*.

Melde (Bav. *molten*), f., 'orache' (a plant), from the equiv. MidHG. and Mid LG. *mëlde*, and with a different gradation *mulde, molte*, f., OHG. *mola, mulda* (*muolhta* is incorrectly written for *molta*), f.; of obscure origin. The derivation from the root *mal*, 'to grind,' to which 𝔐𝔢𝔥𝔩 is allied, does not give a suitable sense. Gr. βλίτον (for *μλίτον), 'orache,' should rather be compared with the G. word.

melden, vb., 'to mention, notify, announce,' from MidHG. *mĕlden*, 'to inform against, betray. announce, show, name'; comp. OHG. *mĕldôn*, OSax. *mĕldôn*, AS. *mĕldian*, 'to inform against, betray'; a West Teut. vb. simply, meaning 'to betray,' to which other senses have been given in MidHG. Goth. *milþôn points to a Teut. root *melþ, 'to betray'; an equiv. pre-Teut. *melt has not yet been authenticated.

melk, adj., 'giving milk, milch,' from the equiv. MidHG. *mĕle*, *mĕlch*, OHG. *mĕlch* (equiv. to AS. *mĕlc*), adj.; comp. OIc. *mjolkr*, *milkr*, MidE. *milche*, E. *milch*, adj. (AS. *mylce is wanting); a verbal adj. from melfen.

melken, vb., from the equiv. MidHG. *mĕlken*, *mĕlchen*, OHG. *mĕlchan*, 'to milk'; comp. Du. *melken*, AS. *mĕlcan* (wanting in E., in which *to milk* is used); Ic. *mjalta*, and also *mjalter*, 'milking,' *mjaltr*, 'milch,' but also from *mjolk*, 'milk,' *mjolka*, 'to milk,' and *mjolkr*, 'milch'; Goth. *milkan is by chance not recorded. The Teut. root *melk* is derived from the Aryan *melg*, which occurs with the same meaning in the West Aryan languages; comp. Lat. *mulgere*, Gr. ἀμέλγειν, OSlov. *mlĕsti* (pres. *mlŭzǫ*), Lith. *milšti* (pres. *mélžu*). In the East Aryan languages the corresponding root appears with an older signification, 'to wipe or rub off' (comp. Sans. *mṛj*, *mṛj*, Zend *marez*). 𝔐𝔢𝔩𝔣𝔢𝔫 is one of the characteristic words which point to a closer connection between the West Aryans compared with the East Aryans; comp. 𝔥𝔞𝔫𝔣 and 𝔪𝔞𝔥𝔩𝔢𝔫. See also 𝔐𝔦𝔩𝔠𝔥, 𝔐𝔬𝔩𝔣𝔢, and 𝔪𝔢𝔩𝔣.

Memme, f., 'poltroon,' ModHG. only. A derivative of late MidHG. *mammie*, *memme*, f., 'woman's breast'; lit. 'effeminate being, effeminate man.'

Menge, f., 'crowd, multitude, mass,' from MidHG. *menege*, OHG. *menigi*, *managi*, f., 'multiplicity, great number, crowd'; an abstract from OHG. *manag*, 'much'; Goth. *managei*, f., AS. *menigo*, 'multiplicity.' Originally it was not connected with the following word, but in modern times it may be dimly thought to be akin to it.

mengen, vb., 'to mingle, mix, blend,' from MidHG. *mengen*, 'to mix, mingle,' f., introduced from MidG. and LG.; in OHG., *mengan* occurs once as a Franc. word (in Isidore); OSax. *mengian*, Du. *mengen*, AS. *mengan*, MidE. *mengen*, 'to mix' (whence E. *to mingle*); Goth. *managjan is wanting. Allied to OSax. *gimang*, AS. *gemong*, 'mingling, commixtio, company, troop'; AS. *on gemong*, E. *among*, so too OSax. *an gimange*. From these may be deduced a West Teut. root *mang*, 'to mix,' which, however, is unknown to Suab. and Bav. It has been connected, with hardly sufficient reason, with the root *mik*, 'to mix' (see 𝔪𝔦𝔣𝔠𝔥𝔢𝔫), which appears in most of the Aryan languages; it is more probably allied to Lith. *mìnkau*, *mìnkyti*, 'to knead,' *mìnklas*, 'dough' (OSlov. *mękŭkŭ*, 'soft,' *maka*, 'meal'). In that case mengen would be traced to a pre-Teut. root *meng*, 'to knead.'

Mennig, n., 'vermilion,' from the equiv. MidHG. *mĕnig*, *minig*, late OHG. *minig*, n.; based on Lat. *minium*, 'vermilion.'

Mensch, m. and n., from the equiv. MidHG. *mensch*, *mensche*, m. and n., 'man, person, fellow,' OHG. *mennisco*, *mannisco*, m.; comp. OSax. *mennisco*, Du. *mensch*, 'person.' Simply a West Teut. form, prop. an adj. used as a subst., hence 'humanus' for 'homo.' The adj. on which it is based is derived with the suffix *iska* (HG. iſch) from *mann-*, 'homo'; Goth. *mannisks*, OIc. *mennskr*, AS., OSax., and OHG. *mennisc*, 'humanus, human' (comp. further AS. *mennesc*, 'humanity'); comp. *manuśja* as an adj., 'human,' and as masc. subst. 'man,' with Sans. *mánu*, *mánus-*, 'man' (see further under 𝔐𝔞𝔫𝔫).—𝔐𝔢𝔫𝔣𝔠𝔥 in the neut. gender appears even in MidHG., and was used till the 17th cent. without any contemptuous meaning; the neut. was generally applied to female servants, but that signification became obsolete in the last cent., and a moral sense was attached to the word.

Mergel, m., 'marl,' from the equiv. MidHG. *mergel*, OHG. *mergil*, m.; from MidLat. *margila*, with the primary form *marga*, which is recorded by Pliny as a Kelt. word; comp. Bret. *marg*, W. *marl*. From the same source the equiv. Rom. words are derived—Fr. *marne* (from OFr. *marle*), Ital. and Span. *marga*.

mergeln, vb., 'to emaciate, enervate,' ModHG. only; derived with the compounds abs and aus-mergeln from Mark (3), MidHG. marc, marges.

merken, vb., 'to mark, note, observe,' from MidHG. and OHG. merken, 'to give heed to, perceive, understand, note'; a derivative of Marke (Goth. *markjan); hence OFr. merchier, 'to designate.'

meschugge, adj., 'crazy,' from the equiv. Hebr. meschuggá.

Messe, f., 'mass, fair,' from MidHG. mësse, misse, f., 'mass, church festival, fair'; OHG. mëssa, missa, f. So too the word on which it is based, MidLat. missa, signifies not only 'incruentum christianorum sacrificium,' but also 'feast of a saint' ("quod in eo Missa sollemnis peragitur"). The latter sense led to MidLat. missa, MidHG. mësse, 'fair,' because this "was wont to be held on account of the great concourse of people" on saints' days (comp. Fr. foire, 'fair,' lit. 'holiday,' under Feier). MidLat. missa, "as is well known, originated in missa est, scil. concio, the words spoken by the deacon when dismissing the congregation which did not partake of the sacrament"; from this the corresponding Rom. cognates, Ital. messa and Fr. messe, are derived. The vowel in AS. mœsse, f. (Northumbr. messe), E. mass, is abnormal; the latter also signifies feast in Christmas and Lammas (see Laib). Comp. Feier, Mette, Nonne, Opfer, and Vesper.

messen, vb., 'to measure, survey,' from MidHG. mëzzen, OHG. mëzzan, 'to measure, mete out, distribute, consider, test'; comp. OSax. mëtan, Du. meten, 'to measure,' AS. mëtan, 'to measure, value, deem,' Goth. mitan, 'to mensure'; also allied to Goth. mitôn, 'to ponder, reflect on'; OHG. mëzzôn, 'to moderate.' The Teut. stem mët, 'to measure, estimate, ponder' (comp. Maß), is based on pre-Teut. mêd, and cannot, because of the non-permutation, be connected with Lat. metiri; comp. Lat. modus, Gr. μέδομαι, μήδομαι, 'to consider, estimate,' μέδων, 'adviser,' μέδιμνος, 'medimnus' (about 12 galls.), Lat. modius, Goth. mitaþs, 'corn measure.' See Metze (2).

Messer, n., from the equiv. MidHG. mëzzer, 'knife.' The word has undergone strange transformations; it is an abbreviation of mëzzeres, OHG. mëzziras, mëzzirahs, n., the etymology of which had grown obscure; the variants maz-sahs, mëzzi-sahs, show, however, that mëzzirahs is a compound meaning 'food-sword.' With regard to Goth. mats, n., OHG. maz, n., AS. mëte, n., E. meat, comp. Mus and Mettwurst. OHG. sahs, AS. seax, n., 'sword, knife,' whence the name Saxons, is usually connected with Lat. saxum, because knives were orig. made of stone. The OHG. compound mëzzi-rahs shows the change of medial s (z) to r. Goth. *matisahs is also indicated by OSax. mëzas for *mëtsahs, Du. and LG. mes, AS. mëte-seax, 'food-knife, dagger.'

Messing, n., from the equiv. MidHG. messinc (gen. -ges), m., 'brass, latten'; a derivative of Masse, OHG. massa (from Lat. massa?), 'sow-metal'; AS. mœstling (with a suffix), 'brass' (whence E. maslin?), is also derived from the same source; see too OIc. messing, f., 'brass.' Contrary to this prevalent opinion, we have to observe that the derivative is more widely diffused than the primit. word, and it is inconceivable that the word was derived independently in the various languages; hence these cognates cannot be associated with Lat. massa unless a derived word can be adduced as the base of the Teut. words.

messingisch, adj., 'hybrid, composed of HG. and LG. elements in the same word'; the term was first recorded in the last cent., but it originated probably in the 16th or 17th cent., when HG. and LG. were struggling for the mastery.

Mesner, m., from the equiv. MidHG. mesnære, messenære, m., 'sexton, sacristan' (the latter connected with Messe), from late OHG. mesindri (not messindri), m., based on MidLat. *masinarius for mansionarius, 'custos et conservator aedis sacrae, aedituus, ostarius'; MidLat. mansionarius was also an official in the court of the Frankish kings (MidLat. mansio, 'house,' equiv. to Fr. maison). Comp. Küster and Sigrist.

Met, m., 'mead,' from MidHG. mët, mëte, OHG. mëtu, mitu, m., 'mead'; comp. AS. meodo, E. mead, OIc. mjǫðr; Goth. *midus, m., 'mead,' is by chance not recorded. A common Teut. and also common Aryan word; Aryan *medhu, Sans. mádhu, n., 'sweetness, honey, sweet drink,' Gr. μέθυ, 'wine' (to which μεθύω, 'to be drunk,' and μέθη, 'drunkenness'), OSlov. medǔ, 'honey, wine,' Lith. midùs, 'mead,' medùs, 'honey,' Ir. mid. To these is allied OInd. mádhu, 'sweet, lovely,' hence the various meanings of medhu, 'mead, honey, wine,' lit. 'that which is sweet,' perhaps (according to Gr. μεθύω,) 'intoxicating liquid.' Comp. süß.

Mette, f., 'matins,' from MidHG. *metten, mettene, mettī, mettīn*, f., 'early mass,' late OHG. *mettīna, mattīna*, f.; from MidLat. *mattīna* for *matutīna hora* (hence also OIr. *maten*). From Lat. *matutīnum* are derived Fr. *matin* (*mutines*), and Ital. *mattino*. Comp. Meſſe, Mette, and Veſper.

Mettwurſt, f., 'pork sausage,' ModHG. only, from the equiv. LG. *metwurst*, lit. 'food sausage,' allied to LG. *met*, 'minced meat,' OSax. *meti*, Goth. *mats*, 'food.' See Meſſer.

Metze (1.), m., from the equiv. MidHG. *steinmetze*, OHG. *steinmezzo*, m., 'stone cutter'; also once in OHG. *steinmeizzo*, which is clearly connected with OHG. *meizzan*, 'to hew,' mentioned under Meißel. But whether OHG. *steinmezzo* originated in *steinmeizzo*, or whether Metze, Goth. *matja (comp. Fr. *maçon*, 'mason, bricklayer') is connected with the root *mat*, 'to hew' (AS. and E. *mattock*), remains obscure.

Metze (2.), f., 'corn measure, peck,' from MidHG. *mëzze*, OHG. *mëzzo*, m., 'small dry measure.' Tent. *ë* results from the Bav. and Alem. pronunciation. This word, like Goth. *mitaps*, 'measure' (about 18 bush.), is connected with the Teut. root *met*, 'to measure'; AS. *mitta*, 'corn measure,' is also equiv. to OHG. *mëzzo*. The masc. is still the gender in UpG., the fem. seems to be of MidG. and LG. origin. To the pre-Teut. root *mod* (*med*) belongs Lat. *modius*, 'peck,' which (see Pfund and Münze) before the OHG. period passed into West Teut.; comp. OSax. *muddi*, OHG. *mutti*, MidHG. *mütte*, 'bushel.'

Metze (3.), f., 'prostitute,' from MidHG. *metze*, f., which is "literally a pet name for Mathilda, then 'a girl of the lower class,' often with the accessory notion of a loose life." For other abbreviated forms with the suffix *tz* or *z* used as pet names, comp. Friz and Kunz.

Metzger, m., from the equiv. MidHG. *metzjære, metzjer*, m., 'butcher.' Adopted in the MidHG. period from MidLat.; at least no better explanation can be found than the derivation from MidLat. *macellarius*, from which, through the medium of *mazil-*, OHG. *mezijári, with a G. accent and mutation, would be evolved. Allied to MidLat. *macellum*, 'shambles,' *macellarius*, 'qui carnem in macello vendit'; yet the change of *ll* into *j* is not clear, therefore a MidLat. *macearius (OHG. *mezziyári) has been assumed. From Mid Lat. *macellarius* were derived MidHG. *metzler*, OHG. *mezzilári*, 'pork-butcher.'

meuchel-, derived, as the first part of a compound, from MidHG. *miuchel-*, 'secret.' Earlier ModHG. Meuchler, from the equiv. MidHG. *miuchelære, miucheler*, late OHG. *mûhhildri*, m., 'plotter, assassin.' Allied to MidHG. *miuchelingen*, 'insidiously, like an assassin'; OHG. *mûhhilswërt*, 'assassin's sword, sword for assassination'; OHG. *mûhhari, mûhho, mûhheo*, 'brigand, footpad'; also *mûhhen, mûhhôn*, 'to attack from an ambush'; MidHG. *vermûchen*, 'to get out of the way secretly, conceal,' and MidHG. *mocken*, 'to lie hidden'; further E. dial. *to mitch* (AS. *myčan), 'to be hidden,' MidE. *micher*, 'thief.' The entire class points to a Teut. root *mûk*, 'to lurk in ambush with weapons'; a pre-Teut. root *mûg* appears in Kelt.; comp. OIr. *formûigthe, formûichthai*, 'absconditus,' *formûichdetu*, 'occultatio.' Since these words well accord in meaning with the HG. cognates, Goth. *muks, OIc. *mjûkr*, E. *meek* (to which Du. *meuk*, 'mellow, ripe' is allied), cannot be associated with them, since their meaning does not correspond to that of the class under discussion. See muden and munfeln.

Meute (1.), f., first occurs in early Mod HG. from the equiv. Fr. *meute*, f., 'pack of hounds.'

Meute (2.), Meuterei, f., first occurs in early ModHG. from the equiv. Fr. *meute*, 'mutiny, riot.'

mich, see mein.

Mieder, n., 'bodice, corset' (with Mid HG. and UpG. *i* instead of *ü*, MidHG. *üe*); from MidHG. *müeder, muoder*, n., lit. 'body, bodily form, skin, article of dress enveloping the upper part of the body, stays, bodice, vest,' OHG. *muodar*, 'alvus, belly of a snake'; comp. OLG. *môder*, OFris. *môther*, 'breast bandage' (worn by women); Goth., AS., and OIc. *môþr are wanting. The various meanings are specially ascribed to the relation of Leib, 'body,' to Leibchen, 'stays.' The word has also been connected further with Gr. μήτρα, 'womb,' as well as with Lat. *mâtrix*; this leads to its kinship with the cognates of Mutter.

Miene, f., 'mien, look, bearing,' Mod HG. only, from Fr. *mine*.

Mies, see Moos.

Miete, f., 'pay, hire, rent,' from Mid HG. *miete*, OHG. *mieta, miata*, earlier *mêta*, f., 'payment, wages'; the orig. form is preserved by Goth. *mizdô*, 'reward,' the *z* of which, however, by the lengthening of the *ĭ* to *ê* has been lost in Teut.; OHG. *mêta*, OSax. *mêda*, AS. *mêd* (once with the normal change of *s* into *r*, *meord*), E. *meed*. Goth. *mizdô*, from pre-Teut. *mizdhá-*, is primit. allied to Gr. μισθός, 'wages, hire,' OSlov. *mĭzda*, f., 'wages,' Zend *mĭzda*, n., 'wages,' OInd. *mídhá* (for *miždhá*), 'contest, match, booty' (orig. sense probably 'prize,' by inference from the Sans. adj. *mĭdhvás*, 'distributing lavishly'). Hence the primit. Aryan form of the cognates is *mizdho-*, *mizdhá-*, orig. meaning 'wages, prize.'

Miezc, f., 'pussy,' ModHG. only; it is either the modern Bav. pet name for **Maria**, 'Mary,' just as **Hinz**, the pet name for the tom-cat, is connected with **Heinrich**, 'Henry,' or it is a recent onomatopoetic form like the phonetically cognate Ital. *micio*, and the corresponding Rom. class. The ModHG. *miauen*, *mauen*, are also onomatopoetic forms.

Milbe, f., from the equiv. MidHG. *milwe*, OHG. *milwa*, *miliwa*, f., 'mite, moth'; Goth. **milwjô*, or rather **milwi*, f., are wanting. To this Goth. *malô*, f., 'moth,' and OIc. *mǫlr*, 'moth,' are allied. These terms are derived from the root *mel*, *mal*, 'to grind'; **Milbe**, Goth. *malô*, 'the grinding (i.e., producing dust or meal) insect'; to the same root OSlov. *molĭ*, 'moth,' also belongs.

Milch, f., from the equiv. MidHG. *milch*, OHG. *miluh*, f., 'milk'; the common Teut. term for 'milk'; comp. Goth. *miluks*. f., OIc. *mjólkr*, f., AS. *meoluc*, *milc*, f., E. *milk*, Du. *melk*, OSax. *miluk*. The direct connection of the Teut. cognates with the root *melk* in **melfen** is indubitable. It is remarkable, however, that a common Aryan, or at least a West Aryan term for 'milk' is wanting, although the root *melg*, Teut. *melk*, 'to milk,' occurs in all the West Aryan languages. Gr. γάλα (stem γάλακτ-), Lat. *lac* (stem *lact-*), cannot be connected with the root *melg*, and OSlov. *mlěko* (from **melko*) with its Slav. cognates must have been borrowed from the OTeut. word, since in a primit. allied word we should have expected a *g* instead of the *k*.

mild, adj., 'mild, meek, gentle,' from MidHG. *milte*, 'friendly, kind, liberal, gracious,' OHG. *milti*; comp. OSax. *mildi*, AS. *milde*, E. *mild*, Goth. *mildeis* (hardly **milds*), adj., 'loving, mild'; a common Teut. adj. of disputed origin. A word corresponding exactly in sound does not occur in the cognate languages. Lat. *mollis*, if it represents **molvis*, **moldvis* (like *suāvis* for **suādvis*; comp. füß), might with Teut. **mildu-*, 'mild,' belong to the root *mol*, 'to grind,' with which also OIr. *mláith* (prim. form *mláti-*), 'soft, gentle,' or OIr. *meldach*, 'pleasant,' is connected.

Milz, f., 'milt, spleen,' from the equiv. MidHG. *milze*, OHG. *milzi*, n.; from the HG. form are derived the Rom. cognates, Ital. *milza*, Span. *melsa*, 'spleen.' Corresponding forms are found in OIc. *milte*, n., AS. *milte*, n. and f.; E. *milt* and Du. *milt* signify both 'spleen' and 'soft roe.' The cognates are probably connected with the Teut. root *melt* (see **Malz**), 'to soften, melt,' "with respect to the properties ascribed to the spleen of manufacturing, decomposing, and liquefying the various humours of the body." The term **Milz** is found in Teut. only; so too **Haub**, **Finger**, **Daumen**, **Zehe**, **Leber**, &c. The names of other parts of the body, such as **Herz**, **Niere**, **Fuß**, **Arm**, **Rippe**, have, however, a history that can be traced farther back.

minder, compar. of *gering* and *wenig*, 'less, inferior, lower'; from MidHG. *minre*, *minner*, OHG. *minniro*, compar. of *luzzil*, 'little, small.' To this is allied the OHG. and MidHG. adv. *min* (like *baz* allied to *bezziro*). A common Teut. compar. formed like Goth. *minniza*, *mins*, AS. *mins*; the corresponding superl. is Goth. *minnists*, OHG. *minnist*, MidHG. *minnest*, ModHG. *mindest*, with the *d* of the compar. which has been evolved in ModHG. between the *n* and *r*; the positive is wanting, as in the case of *ehr*, *besser*, *seit*, &c. Since *en* in these cognates, as in **Mann**, has originated in *nw* for *nv*, the word is based on the Lat.-Gr. verbal stem *minu-*, whence also Lat. *minor*, *minimus*; comp. Lat. *minuere*, Gr. μινύω; OSlov. *mĭnij*, 'minor,' Gr. μινύ-ϝθα, 'a little while.' The oldest form of the root is Aryan *mĭ* (*mī́*), with the pres. stems *mĭnā-* and *mĭnu-*, 'to lessen, shorten,' of which the OInd. would be **meymas* (equiv. to Gr. μείων); comp. also Gr. μειόω, 'to diminish.'

Minne, f., reintroduced in the latter half of the 18th cent. on the revival of OG. studies, from the equiv. MidHG. *minne*, f., 'love,' which became obsolete in the transition from MidHG. to ModHG.; OHG. *minna*, f., OSax. *minna*, *minnia*, f., 'love,' lit. and orig. 'recollection, memory';

comp. OIc. *minne*, n., 'remembrance, recollection, toast.' E. *mind*, from AS. *mynd*, is also connected with the same root *man*, *men*; comp. Goth. *muns*, 'meaning.' These belong to the common Aryan and also Teut. root *men*, *man*, 'to think'; comp. Gr. μένος, 'temper, disposition,' μιμνήσκω, 'I remember,' Lat. *memini*, *reminiscor*, *mens*, *moneo*, Sans. root *man*, 'to opine, believe, think of, purpose'; comp. mahnen and Mann.

Minze, f., from the equiv. MidHG. *minze*, OHG. *minza*, f., 'mint'; comp. AS. *minte*, f., E. *mint*; borrowed previous to the HG. permutation of consonants from the equiv. Lat. *mentha*, *menta* (Gr. μίνθα), at the same period as the other terms relating to horticulture and the art of cookery; see Pfeffer. The variants, OHG. *munza*, MidHG. *münze*, ModHG. Münze, have a remarkable form, and cannot be explained by the Lat. word; comp. Pfefferminz.

mis, miß, 'mis-, dis-, amiss, wrong,' in compounds; from MidHG. *misse*-, OHG. *missa*-, *missi*-, which express the perversity or failure of an action; comp. Goth. *missadêps* (OHG. *missitât*, MidHG. and ModHG. *missetât*), 'sin,' *missataujands*, 'sinner,' Goth. *missa*-, for *miþtó*- (lit. 'lost'), is an old to-partic. from the root *miþ* (see meiden); comp. OIr. *mí*, 'amiss.' Hence the derivative missen.

mischen, vb., from the equiv. MidHG. and MidLG. *mischen*, OHG. *misken*, 'to mix'; comp. AS. *miscian*, E. *to mix*. In the other OTeut. languages a corresponding vb. is wanting. The agreement with Lat. *misceo* (*miscere*), 'to mix,' is evident. The only question is whether the word was primit. allied or was borrowed; that is difficult to determine, since, judging by sound and sense, both are possible. The assumption that the word was borrowed is supported by the loan-words relating to the Ital. culture of the vine, which are quoted under Most. On the other hand, the Rom. languages have instead of *miscere* a derivative *misculare* (Fr. *méler*, equiv. to OHG. *misculôn*, Suab. *misle*); yet comp. Ital. *mescere*. On the supposition that the word was primitively allied, which is supported by Meisch, we should have to compare, in addition to the Lat. term, Gr. μίσγω (σγ equiv. to Teut. *sk*?), μίγνυμι, the Sans. root *miç* in *miçrá-s*, 'mixed,' OSlov. *měsiti*, 'to mix,' Lith. *misti*, 'to mingle' (*maisz-tas*,

'riot'). Hence Lat. *misceo*, and, if mischen is primit. allied to it, OTeut. *miskja* represent a pre-historic *mik-skejo* (with *sk* as a suffix of the pres. stem, like forschen for pre-historic **forhskôn*; comp. waschen and wünschen). Comp. Meisch.

Mispel, f., from the equiv. MidHG. *mispel*, with the variants *mespel*, *nespel*, f., OHG. *mespila*, f., 'medlar,' with the variant *nespila*. From MidLat. *mespila*, whence also, with the change of the initial *m* into *n*, the corresponding Rom. cognates (Ital. *nespola*, Fr. *nèfle*). The ultimate source is Gr. μέσπιλον, 'medlar.'

missen, vb., 'to be without, do without,' from MidHG. and OHG. *missen*, 'to miss'; comp. AS. *missan*, E. *to miss*, and the equiv. OIc. *missa*; Goth. **missjan* is wanting. It is clearly connected with West Teut. *míþan*, 'to avoid,' which is related to an old partic. *missa*- (for **miþta*- with -*tó*-), meaning 'avoided, frustrated'; comp. meiden and miß.

Mist, m., 'excrement, dung,' from Mid HG. and OHG. *mist*, m., 'mud, manure, dunghill'; it represents **mihst*, like OHG. *forskôn*, 'to demand,' for **forhskôn*; see mischen. Goth. *maíhstus*, m., 'excrement,' AS. *m·ox* (for **meoxt*?), 'excrement,' MidE. *mix*, obsolete in E.; the derivative AS., MidE., and E. *mixen*, 'dunghill,' has been preserved, and appears in OHG. as *mistunnea*, *mistina*, f., and also in Franc. as *misten*, 'dunghill.' Since *stu* in Goth. *maíhstus* is a suffix, HG. Mist is connected with Lith. *mẽz-ti*, 'to dung,' *mėžlai*, 'excrement,' or with the Aryan root *mīgh*, 'to make water,' which has been retained in LG. as *migen*; comp. AS. *mígan*, OIc. *míga*, 'to make water.' This latter verbal stem is found in the non-Teut. languages; comp. the Sans. root *mih*, Lat. *mingere*, Gr. ὀμιχεῖν, with the same sense; Lat. *méjo* and Lith. *mẽžu*, 'mingo,' also belong to the same Aryan root *mīgh*. Since ὀμίχλη, ὀμίχλη, OSlov. *mїgla*, Lith. *miglà*, 'mist,' are also allied to Gr. ὀμιχεῖν, 'to make water,' the following have also been connected with Mist, AS. and E. *mist*, LG. and Du. *mist*, 'mist,' Ic. *mistr*, 'misty air'; Sans. *meghá*, 'cloud,' *míh*, 'rain, mist,' belong also to the root *mih*, which in OInd. means both 'to make water' and 'raining, gushing forth.'

Mistel, f., from the equiv. MidHG. *mistel*, OHG. *mistil*, m., 'mistletoe': comp. AS. *mistel*, E. *mistle*, OIc. *mistelteinn*, 'mistletoe.' An OTeut. word not derived from the equiv. Lat. *viscus*, and scarcely allied to E. *mist* (see 𝔐𝔦𝔰𝔱). Origin obscure.

mit, prep. and adv., from the equiv. MidHG. and OHG. *mit*, prep., 'with,' and the MidHG. adv. *mite*, OHG. *miti*; corresponding to Goth. *miþ*, *mid*, adv. and prep., 'with,' AS. *mid*, obsolete in E. (except in *midwife*). Teut. *mid*, earlier *midi*, represents, according to the permutation of consonants, pre-Teut. *miti* or *meti*, and hence is allied to Gr. μετά, Zend *mat*, 'with.' It might also be connected with the cognates discussed under *miß*, meaning 'reciprocal.'

Mittag, m., 'midday, noon, south,' from *mitt* and *Tag*. Comp. MidHG. *mettetac*, OHG. *mittitag*.

mitte, adj., obsolete as an independent word, but preserved in derivatives; MidHG. *mitte*, OHG. *mitti*, adj., 'medius'; comp. AS. *midd*, preserved in E. only in *midriff*, AS. *mid-hrif* (*hrif*, 'body,' Lat. *corpus*), E. *midnight*, *mid-Lent*, *midland*, *midwinter*, &c., and in the derivatives *midst*, *middle*, &c.; Goth. *midjis*, 'medius.' It is a common Teut. and Aryan adj., prehistoric *médhyo-s*; comp. Sans. *mâdhyas*, Gr. μέσος for *μέθjος, Lat. *medius*, OSlov. *mežda*, f. (from *medja*), 'middle.'—**Mittag**, 'mid-day,' 𝔐𝔦𝔱𝔣𝔞𝔰𝔱𝔢𝔫, 'mid-Lent,' 𝔐𝔦𝔱𝔱𝔴𝔬𝔠𝔥, 'Wednesday'; 𝔐𝔦𝔱𝔱𝔢𝔯𝔫𝔞𝔠𝔥𝔱, 'midnight,' is prop. a dat. sing., originating in MidHG. *ze mitter naht*, OHG. *zi mitteru naht*, its frequent locative use (in this case to denote time when) becoming predominant as it did in names of places (*e.g.* 𝔅𝔞𝔡𝔢𝔫, prop. dat. plur., originated in MidHG. *ze Baden*, 'at the baths,' 𝔖𝔞𝔠𝔥𝔰𝔢𝔫, dat. plur., MidHG. *ze Sahsen*, 'in Saxony,' lit. 'among the Saxons'). In MidHG., however, *mitnaht* was also used for OHG. *mittinaht*.—

Mitte, f., 'middle,' from MidHG. *mitte*, OHG. *mitti*, f., an abstract form of the adj. Comp. the following article.

mittel, adj., 'middle, interior,' from MidHG. *mittel*, OHG. *mittil*, adj., 'medius, situated in the middle'; AS. *middel*, E. *middle*, adj., a derivative of OTeut. *midja*-, 'middle,' discussed under *mitte*; the orig. form of this derivative was Goth. *midala-, authenticated by OHG. *metal*, adj., 'middle.'—**Mittel**, n., 'middle, means, resource,' from MidHG. *mittel*, n., 'middle, centre, something intermediate, means,' an adj. used as a subst.; comp. AS. *middel*, E. *middle*. Prepost. derivatives *mittels*, *mittelst*. Comp. *mitte*.

Moder, m., 'mud, mould, decay,' from late MidHG. (MidG.) *moder*, m., 'body that has been decomposed, decay, bog, moor'; comp. Du. *modder*, 'slime,' E. *mother*, 'slimy substance' (espec. in vinegar), Du. *moer*, 'yeast, lees.' The entire class has become current only in the modern languages; comp. the corresponding MidG. *mot*, 'moor, morass, marsh,' MidE. *mudde*, E. *mud*. The early history of the cognates is obscure; Gr. μυδών, 'fungous flesh,' on account of its permutation does not belong to the cognates.

mögen, vb., 'to like, choose; may,' from MidHG. *mugen*, *mügen*, OHG. *mugan*, earlier *magan*, pret. pres., 'to be able, have power,' Goth. *magan*; a common Teut. pret. pres. with the OHG. and MidHG. meaning, 'to be able, have power,' as it appears in the ModHG. abstract form 𝔐𝔞𝔠𝔥𝔱, and in the compound *vermögen*; AS. *mæg* (plur. *magon*, pret. *mihte*), whence E. *may* (pret. *might*). The Teut. stem. *mag* (*mug*), from pre-Teut. *magh*, is most closely allied to OSlov. *mogą*, *mošti*, 'to be able, have power.'

Mohn, m., from the equiv. late MidHG. *mân*, earlier *mâhen*, m., 'poppy'; OHG. *mâhan is wanting, for which OHG. *mágo*, MidHG. *máge*, m., 'poppy,' with a change of *h* to *g* (see 𝔣𝔯𝔞𝔤𝔢𝔫 and 𝔍ä𝔥𝔯𝔢), is used (comp. Goth. *þahan* with OHG. *dagén*, Lat. *tacere*); to this UpG. *mâgsame* (Alsat. *màss*), 'poppy,' is allied. It corresponds to OSwed. *valmoghe*, Swed. *vallmo*, 'poppy.' The word points to pre-Teut. *mékon-*, besides which the form *mâkon-* is presupposed by Gr. μήκων (Dor. μάκων), OSlov. *makŭ*, 'poppy.' These correspondences, however, do not necessarily imply that the cognates are of genuine Aryan origin (comp. 𝔥𝔞𝔫𝔣). For OHG. *mágo* a form *popig* (E. *poppy*) was used in AS., based on Lat. *papaver*.

Mohr, m., 'Moor,' from MidHG. and OHG. *môr*, m.; derived from MidLat. *Maurus*, whence also Fr. *More*, Ital. and Span. *Moro*.

Möhre, f. (not current in Suab. and Bav.), from the equiv. MidHG. *mörhe*, also *more*, *morhe*, f., OHG. *moraha*, *morha*, 'carrot'; a non-mutated form occurs in Mod HG. 𝔐𝔢𝔥𝔯𝔯ü𝔟𝔢; Goth. *maúrhô may be also assumed from AS. *moru* (for *morhu), f., and *more*, f., E. (dial.) *more*, 'turnip.' For a derivative of these cognates see under 𝔐𝔬𝔯𝔠𝔥𝔢𝔩. From OTeut. *morhô-n-*, 'carrot,' Slov. *mrkva* and Russ. *morkovĭ* (prim. Slav. *mrŭky) seem to be derived.

Molch, m., 'salamander'; the suffix *ch* first appears in early ModHG. (comp. *Habicht*); from MidHG. *mol*, m., *molle*, m., 'lizard, salamander,' OHG. *mol*, with the variants *molm* and *molt*. Du. *mol* and MidE. *molle* signify 'mole.' It is not certain whether the word in both senses is orig. the same. OHG. *mol*, 'lizard,' has also been connected with the root *mal*, 'to grind, pulverise.'

Molke, f., 'whey,' from MidHG. *molken*, *molchen* (also with *u-ü* instead of *o*), n., 'whey,' also 'milk and that which is prepared from milk'; OHG. *molchan* is wanting. AS. *molcen*, n., testifies, however, to the antiquity of MidHG. *molken*, which is a derivative of *melken*, Teut. root *melk*; comp. melken and Milch.

Monat, m. (with ModHG. *ô* from Mid HG. *â* before a nasal, as in Mohn, Mond, Brombeere, ohne, &c.), from the equiv. Mid HG. *mânôt* (*d*), OHG. *mânôd*, m., 'month'; comp. Goth. *ménôþs*, AS. *mônaþ*, E. *month*. The common Teut. term *ménôþ-*, 'month' (pre-Teut. *ménôt-*), seems identical with Mont, OTeut. *ménin-*. The computation of time according to the periods of the moon is perhaps OAryan, since the terms for month in the Aryan languages agree approximately. See under Ment.

Mönch, m., 'monk, friar,' from the equiv. MidHG. *münch*, *münech*, OHG. *munih* (*hh*), n. From the prim. form *muniko-*, *monico-*, the equiv. Fr. *moine* is also derived. In the original Lat. word *monachus* (μοναχόs), 'monk,' the *ch* was probably pronounced as *c;* comp. Ital. *monaco*, OIr. *manach*, AS. *munuc*, E. *monk;* so that OHG. *ch* is the HG. permutation of *k*. In that case Mönch was borrowed at an earlier period than Abt and Papst (see Münster). OSlov. *münichŭ* is a G. loanword.

Mond, m., 'moon,' from MidHG. *mâne*, m., 'moon, month' (MidHG. rarely fem.), OHG. *mâno*, m., 'moon'; even in MidHG. occurs a form with a final dental, *mânt*, *mânde*, which is due to confusion with *mânet* (yet comp. Glentier and niemand), Goth. *ména*, AS. *môna*, m., E. *moon*, Du. *maan*. In the form *mêno* m., a common Teut. term for 'moon' (a later fem. form appears in MidHG. *mænin*, OHG. *mânin*); it is based, like most of the terms for 'moon' and 'month' in the cognate Aryan languages, on Aryan *mên*, *ménôt*, or *mênes*. Comp. Sans. *mâs*, m. (for *mâns*, *mêns*), 'moon, month,' *mása*, m., 'month,' Gr. μήν (for *μήνs*), 'month,' Lat. *mensis*, 'month,' OSlov. *mesęcĭ*, m., 'moon, month,' Lith. *mėnů*, 'moon,' *mėnesis*, 'month,' OIr. *mí*. The exact relation of Teut. *ménôþ-*, *ménan-*, to Lat.-Gr. *mêns-* (*mênes-*) is disputed. The derivation of the stems *mên*, *mêns*, from the Aryan root *mê*, 'to measure' (Sans. *mâ*, 'to measure, mete out,' *mâtram*, Gr. μέτρον, 'measure,' see Mahl, messen), may accord with the facts of the case (the moon was regarded as the measurer of time), yet from the historical and linguistic standpoint it cannot be considered a certainty. Comp. Menat and Mentag.

Montag, m., 'Monday'; with the *môn* of Mond without the later *d;* MidHG. *mântac* (Suab. and Bav. *mæntac*, with mutation), OHG. *mânatag* (*mânintag?*), m., 'Monday'; comp. Du. *maandag*, AS. *mônandæg*, E. *Monday* (*môn* equiv. to 'moon'), OIc. *mânadagr*. The common Teut. term for Lat. *dies Lunae* (Fr. *lundi*, Ital. *lunedi*).

Moor, m. and n., 'moor,' ModHG. only, from Lg. *môr;* comp. Du. *moer*, OSax. *môr*, n., AS. *môr*, n., 'moor, swamp,' E. *moor;* corresponding to OHG. and MidHG. *muor*, n., 'swamp,' seldom 'sea'; scarcely akin to OIc. *mô-r* (gen. *mô-s*), m., 'moor, dry heath.' OHG. *muor*, as well as AS. *môr* (Goth. **môra-* is wanting), is rather related by gradation to Meer, OHG. *meri*, AS. *mere*, Goth. *marei*, or, if *r* is derived by rhotacism from *s*, the cognates are connected with OHG. and MidHG. *mos*, 'swamp'; this, however, after the remarks made under Mees, is hardly probable.

Moos, n., 'moss,' from MidHG. and OHG. *mos*, n., 'moss, moor, swamp' (whence Fr. *mousse*, 'moss'); corresponding to Du. *mos*, 'moss,' E. *moss*, OIc. *mose*, m., 'moss, swamp,' to which OIc. *myrr* (E. *mire*), 'slime,' is allied. To these are related by gradation AS. *meôs*, OHG. *mios*, MidHG. *mies*, m. and n., 'moss,' whence also ModHG. Mirs. The senses 'moss, swamp,' may be associated by the connecting link 'mossy ground,' hence the assumption of two orig. different words is not required, **mosa-*, 'moss' (by gradation **miusa*, 'moss,' OHG. *mios*, AS. *meôs*, 'moss'), and *mosa-*, 'swamp' (by gradation **môsa*, 'moor,' OHG. *muor*, comp. Mees). Goth. **musa*, by gradation **miusa-*, 'moss,' is connected with OSlov. *múchŭ* 'moss,' Lith. *mŭsaĭ*, 'mould' (on liquids), and Lat. *muscus*, 'moss,' which has a derivative *c* for *sc*; and also with Gr. μυῖα, 'horse-fly,' for μύσια, and μύαξ (for μύσαξ), 'sea-mussel.' The meaning 'swamp' is still current in Suab. and Bav.; comp. Dachauer Moos.

Mops, m., ModHG. only, from the equiv. LG. *mops*, Du. *mops* and *mop*, 'pug-dog.' Akin to a Teut. root *mup*, 'to distort the face, make grimaces'; comp. late MidHG. *muff, mupf*, m., 'wry mouth,' Du. *mopper*, 'to wear a peevish look,' E. *to mop*, 'to gibber,' MidE. *moppe*, 'fool.' ModHG. Mops, in the sense of 'stupid fellow,' may be explained as indicated by the MidE. word without reference to the name of the Lat. author Mopsus.

Moraſt, m., 'morass,' ModHG. only from LG. *moras*; comp. Du. *moras*, *moeras*, E. *morass*, MidE. *mareis*. The cognates, as is indicated by the non-Teut. accent, are borrowed from Rom.; comp. Ital. *marese*, Fr. *marais*, MidLat. *maragium*, 'morass, swamp.' The *o* of the Teut. words is due to their being connected with Meer. Unknown to Suab. and Bav.

Morchel, f., from the equiv. MidHG. *morchel, morhel*, late OHG. *morhila*, f., 'moril' (Du. *morille*, 'moril'); the apparent derivation from OG. *morha-*, 'carrot' (see Möhre), is explained under Wurzel. The Suab. and Bav. variants *maurache*, *môraûχ, môroχ*, present a difficulty.

Mord, m., 'murder,' from MidHG. *mort* (-*des*), m. and n., OHG. *mord*, n.; comp. OSax. *morth*, Du. *moord*, AS. and OIc. *morð*, 'murder,' with the common meaning 'intentional, secret death-blow.' Goth. *maurþ*, n., is wanting; it is based on pre-Teut. *mpto-m*, n., and orig. meant 'death' simply, as the root *mor*, 'to die,' widely diffused through all the Aryan languages, indicates. Comp. the Sans. root *mṛ*, 'to die,' *mṛtá-m*, n., 'death,' *amṛta-m*, 'immortality,' *mṛtus*, 'dead,' *márta-s*, 'mortal,' *amṛta-s*, 'immortal,' *mṛtyús*, 'death'; Lat. *mori*, 'to die,' *mortuus*, 'dead,' *mors* (Sans. *mṛti-s*), 'death'; OSlov. *mrěti*, 'to die,' *morŭ-sŭ-mrŭtl*, 'death,' *mrŭtvŭ* (Lat. *mortuus*), 'dead'; Lith. *mirti*, 'to die,' *mirtis*, 'death.' In Gr. as well as in OTeut. the strong root *mṛ* is wanting, but its derivatives βροτός, 'mortal' (for *μρο-τό-s), ἄμβροτός, 'immortal,' have been preserved; OIr. *marb*, 'dead.' In Teut. the root has assumed the sense of 'intentional, secret killing,' the older meaning 'to die, death,' supplanted by ſterben and Tod, having become obsolete; MidHG. *mort*, 'dead,' was borrowed from Fr. *mort*. Comp. further Goth. *maúrþr*, n. (in Sans. *mṛtra-m), AS. *morþor*, n., equiv. to E. *murder*; also OHG. *murdiren*, Goth. *maurþrjan*, 'to murder'; hence Fr. *meurtre*, MidLat. *mordrum*, 'murderous deed.'

Morgen (1.), m., 'morning,' from the equiv. MidHG. *morgen*, OHG. *morgen*, m.; comp. OSax. *morgan*, Du. *morgen*, AS. *morgen, mergen*, m., E. *morning* (with the suffix -*ing* as in *evening*), OIc. *morgunn* and *myrgenn*, Goth. *maurgins*, m.; the common Teut. term for the first half of the day, commencing with the dawn. It does not obtain, however, in the non-Teut. languages, being, like Tag and Abend (Goth. *undaurns*, 'midday'), specifically Teut. The pre-Teut. *mṛkeno-* or *mṛgheno-* is still obscure; some etymologists connect it with Goth. *maúrgjan*, 'to shorten,' but this gives no definite sense for Morgen. With greater probability may OSlov. *mrŭknqti*, 'to grow dark,' *mrakŭ*, 'darkness,' be allied to the Teut. cognates, so that Morgen might be regarded as 'dawn'; comp. the development of meaning in Dämmerung.— morgen, in the sense of 'to-morrow,' is from MidHG. *morgen*, OHG. *morgane*, prop. a dat. sing., 'in the morning, especially of the following day, (on) the next day'; similarly Fr. *demain, lendemain*, from Lat. *mane*. This use of morgen is unknown to Goth. (comp. gestern); Scand. has *á morgun*, E. *to-morrow*; MidE. *tô morwe*, dat., from *morge*(n), Du. *morgen*, 'to-morrow.' Abend is similarly used of the preceding day (see also Sonnabend).—Morgen, 'east,' is similar to the meaning of Lat. *mane* in the Rom. languages. Comp. the origin of Often.

Morgen (2.), m., from the equiv. Mid HG. *morgen*, OHG. *morgan*, m., 'acre' (or nearly so); usually identified with Morgen (1), 'morning's work for a team, the space ploughed by a team in a morning'; similarly MidLat. *dies*, 'tantum terrae quantum quis per diem uno aratro arare potest.' So too MidLat. *diurnalis*, 'a square measure.'

morſch, adj., 'decaying, rotten,' a MidG. and LG. word with the variant *mers*; a recent derivative of the root *murs*. See Mörſer.

Mörſer, m., 'mortar (bowl),' from the equiv. MidHG. *morsære*, OHG. *morsåri*, m.; allied to Suab., Alem., and Hess.

Mörſchel, 'mortar,' and merſch. The combination rs instead of rsch (see under herrſchen, Hirſch, birſchen, &c.) occurs also in Hirſe, compared with the dial. Hirſche. The HG. form, OHG. mors-âri, is based on a verbal root murs; comp. MidHG. zermürsen (MidG. zermorschen), 'to crush to pieces,' Swiss morsen, mürsen, 'to grind, pound small,' Du. morzelen, 'to pulverise, mangle.' On the other hand, the equiv. Lat. mortarium (Fr. mortier) is indicated by Du. mortier, AS. mortére, MidE. mortér, E. mortar.

Mörtel, m., from the equiv. MidHG. mortel, morter, m., 'mortar (cement),' from MidLat. mortarium. Comp. Fr. mortier, 'mortar' (bowl and cement), whence also E. mortar.

Moſt, m., 'must, new wine,' from Mid HG. and OHG. most, m., 'fermenting new wine, wine must;' borrowed, like other words relating to vine-growing (see Wein, Winzer, Lauer, Preſſe, Torfel, and Relch); the Lat. origin is mustum, 'must,' whence also AS., MidE., and E. must, the equiv. Du. mo t, and in the Rom. group, Ital. mosto, Fr. mout. Comp. further OSlov. mŭstŭ.

Moſtert, Moſtrich, m. (the second word is a corruption of the first), 'mustard,' MidHG. mostert, musthart, m., 'mustard mixed with must'; corresponding to the Rom. terms, Ital. mostarda, Fr. moutarde, whence MidE. and E. mustard, Du. mosterd. A derivative of Lat. mustum, 'must,' mustard being mixed with must. Comp. Senf.

Motte, f., from the equiv. late MidHG. motte, f., 'moth' (tt originated in Goth. and OTeut. þþ, as in Fittich, Latte, and fretten). Goth. *muþþô is wanting; comp. AS. moþþe, f., MidE. moþþe, E. moth, Du. mot (t for tt from þþ), 'moth'; also the curious variants, MidHG. matte, f. (Goth. *maþþa), AS. mohþe, f., MidE. moughþe, 'moth' (OIc. motte, m.. 'moth,' with the same permutation of þþ to tt as in Du.). Perhaps the cognates discussed under Mate are akin.

Möwe, f., ModHG. only, from the equiv. LG. mew-, Du. meeuw, f., 'mew, seagull.' The word existed in OHG. as mêh; Goth. *maihws is wanting; comp. OIc. mâ-r, m., 'seagull.' A variant *maiwi is indicated by AS. mǽw, E. mew (for the interchange of hw and w see Niere), as well as by the Du. form meeuw. A pre-Teut *maiko-, *maiki, has not yet been found with a meaning similar to that of the Teut. cognates.

Mucke, f., 'whim, freak,' a LG. form for the rare MidHG. muoche, 'vexatious thought'; yet the word may be regarded as the normal UpG. form for Mücke, so that its derivation should be similar to that of Grille.

Mücke, f., 'gnat, midge,' from MidHG. mücke, mucke, f., 'gnat, fly' (hence still ModHG. dial. 'fly'), OHG. mucca, f. Goth. *muggjô is by chance not recorded; it is indicated by AS. myčge, f., E. midge, OSax. muggia, Du. mug. OIc. mý, n., 'gnat,' suggests the idea that the West Teut. guttural is a suffix, as in Brücke (see also Jugend). The common Teut. form of the noun is muwi, to which also Gr. μυῖα corresponds.

mucken, vb., 'to grumble,' first occurs in early ModHG., probably akin to late MidHG. mûgen, 'to roar,' which may be allied to μυκάομαι, 'to roar' (see Mücke). Perhaps it is also connected with Mucker; it is based on MidHG. muckzen, muchzen, OHG. muccazzen, 'to whisper, grumble'; apparently, however, it is better connected with the Teut. root mûk, 'to pretend to know secrets,' discussed under meuheln. To this also belongs the simply ModHG. Mucker, 'sulky person, grumbler,' prop. 'religious hypocrite,' in which sense the word first appeared in Jena in the early part of the 18th cent. to denote the adherents of the pietist theologian Buddens.

Mucker, see mucken.
muckſen, see mucken.

müde, adj., from the equiv. MidHG. müede, OHG. muodi, adj., 'tired, weary'; comp. OSax. môði, Du. moede, AS. mêðe, 'tired' (Goth. *mô-þeis, 'tired,' is wanting); comp. also OIc. môðr, 'tired.' The dental is a partic. derivative of the root *mô- (comp. mühen), of which mûte is a verbal adj. meaning 'having wearied oneself.'

Muff (1.), m., 'muff,' ModHG. only; from LG. muff, Du. mof, 'muff,' E. muff; a modern Teut word connected with Fr. moufle, 'mitten,' MidLat. (even in the 9th cent.) muffula. The origin of the cognates has not yet been determined; they are generally connected with MidHG. mouwe, 'sleeve.'

Muff (2.), 'mould,' MidHG. only, allied to Du. muf, 'musty, moist, mouldy'; late MidHG. müffeln, 'to smell bad or rotten.' With these are connected the widely-diffused Rom. cognates, which are said to have originated in the G. words: Fr. *moufette*, 'firedamp (in mines),' Ital. *muffo*, 'mouldy.'

muhen, vb., 'to low,' from late MidHG. *miihen, müwen, mügen*, 'to roar'; perhaps allied to Gr. μυκάομαι, but more probably a recent onomatopoetic form.

mühen, vb., 'to trouble, vex,' from MidHG. *müen, müejen*, OHG. *muven*, wk. vb., 'to burden, torment, vex'; Du. *moeijen*, 'to molest, take pains.' The verbal adj. müde (Goth. *mōþeis*) points, like the vb., to an OTeut. and Aryan root *mō*, of which there are derivatives in the cognate languages, Gr. μῶ-λος, 'toil, labour, espec. in war,' μῶ-λυς, 'exhausted by toil, languid, weak,' Lat. *mō-les*, f., 'exertion, toil, distress,' &c., *mōlior*, 'to exert oneself.'—

Mühe, f., from the equiv. MidHG. *müeje*, OHG. *muot*, f., 'toil,' is a verbal abstract of the vb. mühen.

Mühle, f., from the equiv. MidHG. *mül (müle)*, OHG. *muli, mulin*, f., 'mill'; comp. AS. *myln*, E. *mill*, OIc. *mylna* (derived from E.), f., 'mill.' Hardly a Teut. derivative of the root *mal*, discussed under mahlen; it is rather borrowed from common Rom. *mŏlina*, 'mill' (for classical Lat. *mola*); comp. Ital. *mulino*, Fr. *moulin*, 'mill' (Du. *molen*, OIr. *mulen*, and Slav. *mŭlinŭ*'. The formation of an OTeut. *mulinō* with a suffix *-inō* has no parallels in Teut. The genuine Teut. word for 'mill' is preserved in Goth. *qaírnus*, AS. *cweorn*, OHG. *quirn*.

Muhme, f. (in UpG. almost obsolete), 'aunt, female relative, nurse,' from MidHG. *muome*, OHG. *muoma*, f., 'mother's sister,' also 'sister-in-law, female relative.' That the earlier meaning, 'mother's sister' (comp. Base), is the orig. one is shown by the connection of the word with Mutter. OHG. *muoma* points to Goth. *mōna, as is indicated by LG. and MidE. *mōne*, 'aunt' (for the change of n to m, see Pilgrim). The word is a pet form of or child's term for AS. *mōdrie*, LG. *mödder* (equiv. to W. *modryb*, 'aunt'), which have the same form as Gr. μητρυιά (comp. Vetter with Vater); likewise Du. *moei* from MidDu. *moeie*, 'aunt.' An old synonym occurs in AS. *faþu*, 'aunt on the father's side, father's sister,' allied to Vater. OIc. *mōna*, 'mother,' and the equiv. LG. *mœme*, Lith. *momà*, OSlov. *mama*, seem to be pet terms for 'mother'; so too Du. *moei*, 'aunt' (OHG. *muoia*, Gr. μαῖα).

Mühsal, n., from the equiv. MidHG. (rare) *müesal*, n., 'trouble, affliction'; formed by means of the oft-recurring suffix *-sal*, from the MidHG. vb. *müejen, Mod HG. mühen.

Mulde, f., 'trough, tray, pail,' from MidHG. *mulde*, f., 'semicircular hollow vessel, espec. used for cleaning corn, flour-bin, kneading-trough,' with the equiv. variants MidHG. *muolte, muolter, multer*, OHG. *muoltera*. The *w* before an *l* and a consonant points to the fact that the cognates were borrowed; they are usually referred to Lat. *mulctra*, 'milk-pail.'

Müller, m., 'miller,' from MidHG. *müllner, mülnære*, n. (ln is preserved in the surname Müllner, in other cases it is represented by *ll*), OHG. *mulinári*, m., 'miller.' A derivative of Mühle (OHG. *mulina*), or borrowed directly from MidLat. *molinarius* (Ital. *mulinaro*, Fr. *meunier*), 'miller.' See Mühle.

Mulm, m., 'loose, dry mould, dust,' first recorded in ModHG., but probably of an earlier origin; allied to the root *mal*, 'to grind,' lit. 'to pulverise,' with which Goth. *mulda*, 'dust, earth,' and E. *mould* are connected; see under Maulwurf. Comp. also Staub.

Mumme (1.), f., 'mum (kind of beer),' ModHG. only, whence Du. *nom*, E. *mum*. The word is usually derived from Christian Mumme of Brunswick, who first brewed this beer in the year 1492.

Mumme (2.), f., 'mask, masked person, disguise,' first occurs in early ModHG.; comp. Du. *mom*, 'mask, mummery,' E. *to mumm*, to which is allied OFr. *momer*, 'to masquerade,' ModFr. *momerie*, 'mummery'; they are probably connected with an old verbal stem, *mum*, 'to buzz, growl.' Comp. Du. *mommelen*, 'to mumble, grumble,' MidE. *mummen*, 'to roar,' E. *to mumble*, ModHG. mummeln.

mummeln, vb., 'to mumble.' See the preceding word.

Mund (1.), m., 'mouth,' from MidHG. *munt*, OHG. *mund*, m., 'mouth, outlet,' OSax. *mŭđ*, m., Du. *mond*, 'mouth,' AS. *mūđ*, m., E. *mouth*, OIc. *munnr, muđr*, Goth. *munþs*, m., 'mouth.' The common Teut. word *munþa-z*, m., may be based on pre-Teut. *mṇto-s* and connected with Lat. *mentum*, 'chin' (of men and beasts). In the non-Teut. languages also evidence of the kinship of 𝔐und and 𝔐aul may be found, since the latter is an old *mŭ-lo-, while the former may represent *mu-npo (with a partic. suffix, see 𝔅ahn). Comp. Sans. mū-kha, 'mouth.'

𝔐und (2.), f., 'protection,' from MidHG. and OHG. munt, f., 'protection, hand'; comp. AS. mund, 'hand, protection,' OIc. mund, f., 'hand'; the Du. term still exists in mond-baar with the variant momber, 'guardian,' OSax. mundboro, AS. mundbora, OHG. muntboro, MidHG. muntbor, m., 'protector, tutor'; comp. also 𝔅ermund and 𝔐ündel. 𝔐und is certainly not connected with Lat. munire (with regard to ū from Aryan ai, comp. moenia), but is probably derived from a root cognate with that of Lat. manus, 'hand.'

𝔐ündel, m. and f., 'ward, minor,' ModHG. only; in MidHG. mundelinc, 'ward' and 'guardian.' A derivative of 𝔐und (2).

mündig, adj., from the equiv. MidHG. mündec, adj., 'of age,' from 𝔐und (2).

munkeln, vb., 'to whisper secretly,' ModHG. only; from the Teut. root munk, mūk. See meucheln.

𝔐ünster, n. and m., 'minster, cathedral,' from MidHG. münster, OHG. munustiri, munistri, n., prop. 'monastery, convent' (OHG.), then (MidHG.) 'monastery or convent church, collegiate church, cathedral'; comp. AS. mynster, E. minster. Formed from Lat. and Gr. monastérium, 'monastery,' whence also ModFr. moutier, 'monastery, convent' (comp. also OIr. munter, manister, as well as OSlov. monastyrĭ, 'monastery'). MidLat. monasteria were orig. cellae in quibus unicus degit monachus, then generally 'monastery,' finally 'cathedral,' quod plerisque in ecclesiis cathedralibus monachi, non ut hodie canonici, olim sacra munera obirent (this signification is found even towards the end of the 11th cent.). 𝔐önch was borrowed at the same period as 𝔐ünster; comp. 𝔄bt and 𝔓robst.

munter, adj., 'cheerful, lively, brisk,' from MidHG. munter, munder, OHG. muntar, adj., 'fresh, lively, zealous, wakeful'; probably allied to Goth. mundrei, f., 'aim,' and mundôn, vb., 'to fix one's eyes upon,' so that 'striving' is the orig. meaning of the adj. It is also primit. allied to OSlov. mądrŭ, 'wise,' Lith. mundrùs, mandrùs, 'cheerful.' Moreover, OHG. muntar may also be connected with OHG. menden,

OSax. mendian, 'to rejoice' (Teut. root manp).

𝔐ünze (1.), f., from the equiv. MidHG. münze, OHG. muniʒʒa, f., 'coin.' The word was adopted in West Teut. previous to the HG. permutation, probably even before the time of Tacitus, from Lat. monéta, 'coin, money'; comp. AS. mynet, E. mint, Du. munt. Lat. monéta, on its adoption, was probably pronounced, with a Teut. accent, móněta; ě passed into ĭ and ŏ into ŭ, later ü; mänĭta is the initial stage of OHG. munĭʒʒa. That Lat. words were introduced with Lat. money (Tacit. Germ. 5) is antecedently probable. Comp. 𝔓funt.

𝔐ünze (2.), f., equiv. to 𝔐inze.

mürbe, adj., 'tender,' from MidHG. mürwe, mür, OHG. muruwi, murwi, adj., 'tender, mellow'; also, with the same sense, OHG. marawi, maro, MidHG. mar (inflect. marwer), AS. mearu. The root mar appears further in Gr. μαραίνω, 'to cause to wither,' Sans. mlâ, 'to fade'; also in OIr. meirb, 'soft.'

murmeln, vb., 'to murmur,' from MidHG. murmeln, OHG. murmulôn, with the parallel form murmurôn, 'to murmur, grumble'; either from Lat. murmurare, or rather a native onomatopoetic form. See murren.

𝔐urmeltier, n., 'marmot,' corrupted in late MidHG. from MidHG. mürmendîn, n., OHG. murmunti, n., 'marmot' (OHG. variant muremunto, m.). The ultimate source of the word is Lat. murem montis (mus montis, mus montanus), whence also the corresponding Ital. marmotta, Fr. marmotte. The OHG. form murmunti is extended by a diminut. suffix.

murren, vb., 'to grumble, mutter,' first occurs in early ModHG. Allied to the equiv. Du. morren, AS. murcnian.

𝔐us, n., 'pap, porridge, confection of fruit,' from MidHG. and OHG. muos, n., 'cooked food, espec. pap-like food; food, meal'; OSax. and AS. môs, n., 'food.' The assumed Goth. *môsa-, 'food,' may be connected with mati-, 'food,' while *môsa- may represent *môtta- with a dental suffix; in that case the root would be Teut. mat, pre-Teut. mâd, 'to cook, prepare food' (for Goth. mats, 'food,' see 𝔐esser and mästen). To this is allied 𝔊emüse, 'vegetables,' from MidHG. gemüese (OHG. *gimuosi), n., which as a derivative presumes the more general sense of OHG. muos. See 𝔐usteil.

Muſchel, f., from the equiv. MidHG. *muschel,* OHG. *muscula,* f., 'mussel, shellfish.' Borrowed from the equiv. Lat. *musculus,* m.

Muskel, m., 'muscle' (of the body), ModHG. only, borrowed from the equiv. Lat. *musculus.*

müſſen, anom. vb., 'to be obliged; must,' from MidHG. *müezen,* OHG. *muozan,* pret. pres., 'to like, be able, be allowed, be obliged' (see **Muſe**); comp. OSax. *motân,* Du. *moeten,* 'to be obliged; ought,' AS. **motan,* 'to be allowed, be able, like, be obliged,' in E. only the pret. *must* (AS. *môste,* 'was obliged') has been preserved with the meaning of the pres.; Goth. *gamôtan,* 'to take place, have room.' The origin of these cognates is doubtful; they can scarcely be connected with meſſen.

Musteil, m. and n., allied to **Mus** (**Gemüſe**), "half the stock of provisions left on the death of a husband, and what remains thirty days later when an inventory is made; one half belongs to the widow and the other to the heirs" (Lessing); the share of the widow is called **Musteil.** Even in MidHG. (in the MidG. of the Saxon Code) *musteile* for *muosteile occurs.

Muſter, n., 'sample, model, paragon,' first occurs in early ModHG., from the equiv. Ital. *mostra;* comp. Fr. *montre* (E. *muster,* Du. *monster*), 'sample.' Allied to Lat. *monstrare.*

Muſe, f., 'leisure, ease,' from MidHG. *muoze,* OHG. *muoza,* f., 'leisure, ease, inactivity,' OHG. also 'possibility, suitable occasion'; allied to the OTeut. pret. pres. *môtan* (see müſſen).—**mūſſig,** adj., 'at leisure,' from MidHG. *müezec,* OHG. *muozzîg,* 'at leisure, unemployed.'

Mut, m., 'courage, mood,' from MidHG. and OHG. *muot,* m., 'sense, mind, spirits, courage,' OSax. *môd,* 'spirits, inner self, heart, courage,' Du. *moed,* m., 'courage,' AS. *môd,* n., 'mind, spirits, heart, courage, zeal,' E. *mood,* Goth. *môds,* m., 'anger.' 'Strong emotion, violent excitement,' is the primary idea of the common Teut. stem *môda-,* the origin of which cannot be traced with certainty in the non-Teut. languages. The usual derivation from the root *mā,* Gr. μαίομαι, 'to desire,' is possible. Comp. the Slav. root *mě* in *sǔměją* (*sǔměti*), 'to venture.'—ModHG. *gemut* in *wohlgemut,* from MidHG. *wol gemuot,* 'courageous,' and the simple *gemuot,* 'minded, disposed.' — ModHG. **Gemüt,** 'spirits, disposition,' from MidHG. *gemüete,* OHG. *gimuoti,* n., prop. a collective of **Mut,** 'totality of thoughts and feelings,' MidHG. also 'mood, longing,' OHG. 'joy.'

Mutter, f., 'mother,' from MidHG. *muoter,* OHG. *muotar,* f.; comp. OSax. *môdar,* Du. *moeder,* AS. *môddôr, môdor;* E. *mother* (with *th* when followed by *er,* as in *father, weather*); OIc. *môðer.* The common Teut. word for 'mother,' wanting only in Goth., in which *aipei* (comp. **Eibam**) was the current term, just as *atta* was used for 'father' instead of *fadar.* Teut. *môdar,* 'mother,' from pre-Teut. *mâtér,* is, like many other terms denoting degrees of relationship, common also to the Aryan languages; comp. Ind. *mātṛ,* Gr. μήτηρ, μάτηρ, Lat. *māter,* OSlov. *mati,* OIr. *máthir* (Lith. *môtė,* 'married woman'). It is allied to **Muhme** and its cognates, as well as to Gr. μαῖα, 'good mother' (as a kindly address). Whether these words are based on an Aryan root *mā,* meaning 'to mete out' (**Mutter,** 'apportioner, distributor'?), or in its OInd. sense, 'to form' (of the embryo in the womb), is uncertain.—**Mutterkrebs,** 'female crayfish,' prop. 'a crayfish at the period when it casts its shell,' had orig. nothing to do with **Mutter;** it contains rather OHG. *muter,* HG. **Mauſer** (Lat. *mūtare*). Comp. mauſern.

Müke, f., from the equiv. late MidHG. *mütze, mutze,* f., 'cap, bonnet,' which is a shortened form of the equiv. *armuz, almuz.* It is derived from MidLat. *almutia, armutia, almutium,* prop. 'amictus quo Canonici caput humerosque tegebant,' worn also at a later period by laymen; the development of meaning is similar to that of ModHG. **Kappe.** MidLat. *almutia,* the origin of which is entirely obscure (*al* is thought to be the Arab. article), appears in Rom. Comp. Fr. *aumusse* or *aumuce,* 'amess' (fur cap worn by officials in Roman Catholic churches).

mutzen, vb., 'to dress up, adorn'; in the sense of 'to be out of humour,' from muckſen, like **Blitz** from **Blitz,** ſchmatzen from ſchmackzen; but ModHG. aufmutzen, 'to throw in one's teeth, blame,' from MidHG. *uſmützen,* 'to dress up, adorn,' MidHG. *mutzen, mützen,* 'to dress, adorn.' **Aufmutzen** thus means 'to puff.'

N.

na, particle, 'well then! now!' ModHG. only, unknown to MidHG.; scarcely identical with the interrog. particle *na*, which Notker (OHG.) uses at the end and in the middle of interrog. sentences expressed negatively.

Nabe, f., from the equiv. MidHG. *nabe*, OHG. *naba*, f., 'nave (of a wheel)'; corresponding to Du. *naaf*, *aaf*, *nave* (see Näber, Matter), AS. *nafu*, f., E. *nave*, OIc. *nof*, f., all of which have the same meaning; Goth. *naba, f., is by chance not recorded. Both the word and the idea are OAryan (primit. form *nobhá*); comp. OInd. *nábhi*, f., and *nábhya*, n., 'nave (of a wheel).' Undoubtedly the cognates discussed under Nabel with the meaning 'navel' are primit. allied, the Ind. word *nábhi* just quoted also signifying 'navel,' as well as Lett. *naba*, f., which is exactly equiv. in sound to OHG. *naba*. Hence Lat. *umbo* (for *onbo, *nobo), 'boss (of a shield),' may also be connected with *umbilicus*, 'navel'; comp. Gr. ὀμφαλός, 'navel, boss (of a shield).' With regard to the antiquity of the terms denoting parts of a waggon see Rad, Achse, Künse, and Deichsel.

Nabel, m., 'navel,' from the equiv. MidHG. *nabel*, OHG. *nabolo*, m.; corresponding to Du. *navel*, AS. *nafela*, E. *navel*, OIc. *nafle*, m., 'navel'; Goth. *nabala is by chance not recorded. A common Aryan word in the primit. forms *nobhelo-*, *onbhelo-*; comp. Gr. ὀμφαλός, Lat. *umbilicus* (for *unbilicus, *nobilicus), Sans. *nábhîla*, OIr. *imbliu*, 'navel.' These words are primit. *l*- derivatives of OAryan *nóbhá*, *onbhá*, 'nave, navel,' appearing in Nabe. In other cases the OAryan terms for parts of the body are mostly underived forms (see Herz and Ohr).

Naber, **Näber**, m., 'auger, gimlet,' from MidHG. *negber*, *nageber*, m., a strange corruption (probably by connection with Nagel) of *nebe-gêr*, *nabe-gêr*, m., 'auger' (comp. Essig). Corresponding to OHG. *naba-gêr*, m., 'auger,' lit. 'spear, pointed iron tool to bore naves,' also AS. *nafogâr*, 'auger,' MidE. *nevagêr*, *nauger*, E. *auger* (with regard to the apparent loss of an initial n comp. E. *adder*, equiv. to ModHG. Otter; similarly Du. *avegaar*, 'auger,' as well as *aaf*, *are*, 'nave '), equiv. to OLG. *nabugêr*, Scand. *nafarr*, 'auger.' An OTeut. compound, whence Finn. *napakaira*, 'auger.'

nach, prep., 'after, behind, in accordance with,' from MidHG. *nâch*, OHG. *nâh*, prep., 'after, near to, beside'; comp. Goth. *nêhw*, *nêhwa*, prep., 'near to'; allied to the adj. nah, OHG. *nâh*, Goth. *nêhws*.

nachahmen, see ahmen.

Nachbar, m., 'neighbour,' from the equiv. MidHG. *nâchgebûr*, OHG. *nâhgibûr*, *nâhgibûro*, m.; corresponding to Du. *nabuur*, AS. *nêhhebûr*, m., E. *neighbour*; a common West Teut. compound, pointing to Goth. *nêhwagabûr, m.; it signifies 'he who lives near to another.' Comp. Bauer.

Nachen, m., 'boat, skiff,' from the equiv. MidHG. *nache*, OHG. *nahho*, m.; corresponding to OSax. *naco*, Du. *naak*, *aak* (respecting the form without n see Näber), AS. *naca*, m. (obsolete in later E.); OIc. *nǫkkve*, m., 'boat'; Goth. *naqa, m., is by chance not recorded (see also Kahn). Its origin is obscure; perhaps Lat. *nâv-is*, Gr. ναῦ-ς, Sans. *nâus*, are allied, Lat. *nav-* being changed to *nag*. Comp. queb.

nachschlagen, see Geschlecht.

Nächste, m., the superl. of nahe used as a subst., 'neighbour, fellow-man'; comp. OHG. *nâhisto*, m., 'neighbour'; in Goth. *nêhwundja*, m., 'neighbour.'

Nacht, f., 'night,' from the equiv. OHG. and MidHG. *naht*, f.; corresponding to Goth. *nahts*, OIc. *nótt*, AS. *neaht*, *niht*, E. *night*, Du. *nacht*, OSax. *naht*, f.; a common OTeut. *naht-*, f., from common Aryan *nokt-*, 'night.' Comp. Lat. *nox* (stem *nocti-*), Gr. νύξ (νυκτ-), Sans. *nuikta-*, *naktan-*, n, *nákti-*, f., Lith. *nuktìs*, OSlov. *noštĭ*. While the word 'night' is common to all the Aryan languages, they differ considerably in the terms for 'day'; this is due to the fact that time in the primit. Aryan period was counted by nights and not by days; relics of this method are seen in Fastnacht, 'Shrove Tuesday,' Weihnachten, 'Christmas,' and E. *fortnight, sennight* (comp. Ostern and Osten). Only a few main divisions of time, such as Monat and Jahr, are widely diffused.

Nachtigall, f., 'nightingale,' from the equiv. MidHG. *nahtegal*, OHG. *nahte-gala*, f.; a term common to the West Teut. languages for 'luscinia,' prop. 'singer in the night' (allied to OTeut. *galan*, 'to sing'); OSax. *nahtigala*, Du. *nachtegaal*, AS. *nihtegale*, E. *nightingale*.

Nacken, m., 'nape,' from MidHG. *nacke, nac* (gen. *-ckes*), m., 'hind part of the head, nape,' OHG. *nac hnac* (*cch*), m.; comp. Du. *nek*, AS. *hnĕcca*, m., 'neck, nape,' E. *neck*, OIc. *hnakke*, m., 'hind part of the head' (Goth. *hnakka, *hnikka, is wanting). In Suab. and Franc. Anſe or Geniď is mostly used, and in Bav. Genáď (the Bav. meaning of *nacken*, 'bone,' is remarkable). The graded form with *ē* (AS. *hnĕcca*) parallel to *a-o* is preserved by ModHG. in Geniď; E. *nape* (AS. *hnapa* ?) seems to be a corresponding form with a medial labial. In the non-Teut. languages the word may be cognate with OIr. *cnocc*, OBret. *cnoch*, 'hill, elevation' (stem *cnocco-*).

nachť, nachenď, adj., 'naked, bare, nude,' from the equiv. MidHG. *nacket*, *nackent*, OHG. *nacchut, nahhut*, adj.; corresponding to Du. *naakt*, AS. *nacod*, E. *naked*, OIc. *nøkkveðr*, Goth. *naqaþs*, with the same meaning; a partic. derivative (see falt) *naqe-dó* from pre-Teut. *nogetó-* (OIr. *nocht*, 'naked,' from the prim. form *nokto-*). In Ind. the form *nagná* occurs with a particp. *na* for *ta*; OSlov. *nagŭ*, Lith. *nŭgas*, 'naked,' are formed without a suffix. Nothing further is known concerning the Aryan root *nŏg* (allied to Lat. *nūdus* for *novdus, *nogvidus?), which has a bearing on the history of civilisation, since it implies the correlative 'non-naked,' i.e. 'clad,' and thus assumes that a sort of dress was worn in the primit. Aryan period. See also bar.

Nadel, f., 'needle,' from the equiv. MidHG. *nâdel*, OHG. *nâdal, nâdala*, f.; corresponding to Goth. *nêþla*, OIc. *nâl*, AS. *nêdl*, f., E. *needle*, Du. *naald*, OSax. *nâdla*. A common Teut. form for 'needle,' with the suffix *þlô-* (*tlâ-*), from the root *nê* (Natel, lit. 'an instrument for sewing'), appearing in ModHG. näḫen.

Nagel, m., from the equiv. MidHG. *nagel*, OHG. *nagal*, f., 'nail'; corresponding to OSax. *nagal*, Du. *nagel*, AS. *nœgel*, E. *nail*, OIc. *nagl*, 'nail'; Goth. *nagls may be deduced from the recorded vb. *nagljan*, 'to nail.' The West Teut. words have mostly the double sense 'nail of the finger or toe' and 'wooden, iron nail.' The former meaning, in accordance with the corresponding words in the other Aryan languages, is the original one (in OIc. there

is a distinction between *nagl*, 'finger-nail,' and *nagle*, 'wooden, iron nail'). Teut. *naglo-* originated in Aryan *noghlo-*, or rather *nokhló-;* comp. OInd. *nakhá*, m. and n., 'finger or toe nail, claw of birds,' Gr. ὄνυχ- (nom. ὄνυξ), 'claw, talon, hoof,' then also 'hook,' Lat. *unguis*, 'claw, talon,' OSlov. *nogŭtĭ*, 'nail, claw' (from OSlov. *nogò*, f., 'foot'); Lith. *nágas*, 'finger-nail,' *nagù*, 'horse's hoof.' The root *nokh, nogh*, is unknown; it must not be sought for in *nagen*, the root of which was rather pre-Teut. *ghnagh*. See Nelfe.

nagen, vb., 'to gnaw, nibble,' from the equiv. MidHG. *nagen*, OHG. *nagan*, with the earlier variant *gnagan;* comp. OSax. and AS. *gnagan*, E. *to gnaw*, OIc. *gnaga*, 'to gnaw.' There are also forms with initial *k* instead of *g*, Du. *knagen*, OLG. *cnagan*, likewise HG. *chnagan*, 'to gnaw'; the form *nagen* originated in *gnagen*. To the Teut. root *gnag, knag*, no correspondences have been found as yet in the non-Teut. languages.

naḫ, adj., 'near, impending,' from Mid HG. *nâch* (inflect. *nâher*), OHG. *nâh* (inflect. *nâhêr*), adj., 'near'; corresponding to OSax. *nâh*, LG. and Du. *na*, AS. *neáh*, E. *nigh*, adj. (whence the comp. AS. *near*, adv., E. *near;* superl. *next*, E. *next*); OIc. *nâr*, Goth. *nêhws*, 'near.' To the Goth. stem *nêhwa-* (for further derivatives see under Nachbar and nach) we should have expected *néko-, néqe-*, in the non-Teut. languages, but they do not occur. Gr. ἐγγύς, 'near,' is no more equiv. in sound to naḫe than Sans. *nâhuša*, 'neighbouring.'—**naḫe,** adv., from the equiv. MidHG. *nâhe*, OHG. *nâho*, adv., 'near, nearly.'—**Näḫe,** f., 'nearness, proximity,' from the equiv. Mid HG. *nœhe*, OHG. *nâhî*, f.; an abstract of the adj. *nâh*.

näḫen, vb., 'to sew, stitch,' from the equiv. MidHG. *nœjen*, OHG. *nâjan;* corresponding only to Du. *naaijen;* Goth. *naian is wanting, neither is the word found in the other Teut. languages. The verbal stem *nê* contained in näḫen was at one time more widely diffused in the Teut. group, as may be inferred from the common Teut. Natel (*nêþlô-*); comp. further Naḫt. In the non-Teut. languages a root *nê*, 'to spin,' is found, which is usually connected with the root of näḫen; comp. Lat. *neo*, Gr. νέω, 'I spin,' νῆμα, 'thread,' νῆτρον, 'spindle'; to this is allied a root *snd* in OIr. *snáthe*, 'thread,' *snáthat*, 'needle' (comp. Schnur). The cognates were probably borrowed in pre-historic times by one tribe from another (comp. nähen), so that nähen may not be a genuine Teut. word.

nahr- in nahrhaft, from MidHG. *nar*, OHG. *nara*, f., 'rescue, maintaining, sustenance.' To this is allied the derivative Nahrung, f., 'nourishment, food,' from MidHG. *narunge*, f., maintenance, nourishment'; allied to nähren.

nähren, vb., 'to nourish, support, foster,' from MidHG. *nern*, *nerigen*, OHG. *neren*, *nerian;* prop. causative of genesen, hence 'to cause to recover, make healthy, heal, rescue, keep alive.' The modern sense is found as early as MidHG. The word corresponds to OSax. *nerian*, AS. *nerigan*, Goth. *nasjan*, 'to rescue.' The change of *s* (for *z*) to West Teut. and Scand. *r* at the end of the stem in causative vbs. is normal (comp. lehren); allied to OIc. *nœra*. See nahrhaft and genesen.

Naht, f., 'seam,' from the equiv. Mid HG. and OHG. *nât*, f.; corresponding to Du. *naad*. Allied to nähen, root *nê* (Goth. *nêþs), and to OHG. *nâtâri*, *nâteri*, Mid HG. *nâtœre*, m., 'sewer, tailor,' of which the fem. form is MidHG. *nâtœrin*, Mod HG. Näherin. See Natel and nähen.

naiv, adj., 'naïve, artless,' borrowed in the last cent. from Fr. *naïf*.

Name, m., 'name,' from the equiv. Mid HG. *name*, OHG. *namo*, m. This word, to which there are corresponding terms in all the Teut. and Aryan languages, is of the greatest antiquity, and is most widely diffused. Comp. OSax. *namo*, Du. *naam*, AS. *nǫma*, *nama*, m., E. *name;* Goth. *namô*, n. OIc. *nafn*, n. (for *namn*), 'name'; equiv. to the corresponding Sans. *nâman*-, Gr. ὄ-νομα, Lat. *nômen*, OSlov. *imę*, n. (from *ĭn-men, *n-men), Pruss. *emmens*, OIr. *ainm*. The Aryan primit. form may have been *nômen*-. Aryan *nômen* is indicated by MidHG. *benuomen* and Du. *noemen*, 'to name,' yet the OSlov. and OIr. words present some phonetic difficulties. Formerly Gr. ὄνομα and Lat. *nômen* were derived from the root γνω-, gnô-, 'to recognise' comp. E. *to know*, see kennen), so that Aryan *nômen* would represent *gnômen*, and have orig. signified 'means of recognition'; this view wants phonetic confirmation. Others derive Name from the root *nem* in nehmen, so that the word would mean 'that which is accepted,' which is likewise improbable; see further nennen and nämlich.

Napf, m., 'bowl, basin,' from MidHG. *napf*, OHG. *napf*, for an earlier *hnapf*, m., 'goblet, dish'; corresponding to MidLG. and Du. *nap*, 'bowl,' AS. *hnæp* (gen. *hnæppes*), 'goblet.' Of obscure origin. The Teut. cognates passed into Rom.; comp. Ital. *nappo*, Fr. *hanap*, 'goblet.'

Narbe, f. (apparently hardly known in UpG.), 'scar,' from the equiv. MidHG. *narwe*, late OHG. *narwa*, f., lit. 'narrowness, contraction'; a fem. subst. from the adj. *narwa*- (OSax. *nuru*, AS. *nearu*, E. *narrow*), 'narrow' (comp. Nehrung). Comp. in the non-Teut. languages, Lith. *nër-ti*, 'to thread (a needle),' *nurvà*, 'cell of the queen-bee.'

Narde, f. 'nard, spikenard,' from the equiv. MidHG. *narde*, OHG. *narda*, f.; formed from Gr. and Lat. νάρδος, *nardus*, introduced also through the translation of the Bible into other languages.

Narr, m., 'fool,' from MidHG. and MidLG. *narre*, m., 'simpleton, fool,' OHG. *narro*, m., 'madman'; a word peculiar to G., the origin of which is totally obscure. The derivation from MidLat. *nârio*, 'sneerer, scoffer, subsannans,' is not satisfactory, since the Lat. word would be represented by a different form in G.; moreover, there is no reason, as far as the meaning is concerned, to suppose that the word was borrowed (see Gauller). Allied to OHG. *murring*, MidHG. *snürring*, 'buffoon, fool'?.

Narwal, m., 'sea-unicorn,' ModHG. only, borrowed from Dan. and Swed. *narhval* (equiv. to OIc. *nâ-hvalr*), whence also E. *narwal*. The origin of these cognates, introduced from the North, is obscure. See Walfisch.

naschen, vb., 'to pilfer dainties,' from MidHG. *naschen*, OHG. *nascôn*, 'to partake of dainties, pilfer dainties'; for *hnaskôn, allied to Goth. *hnasqus*, 'soft, tender,' AS. *hnesče*, 'soft, tender,' E. *nesh*?.

Nase, f., 'nose,' from the equiv. Mid HG. *nase*, OHG. *nasa*, f.; corresponding terms occur in the other Teut. languages, but Goth. *nasa is by chance not recorded. OIc. *nǫs*, f. (for *nasu*, *nasô*); AS. (with gradation *o*, *a*) *nosu*, *nasu*, E. *nose* (the form with *a* in the stem appears in numerous AS. compounds as *næs*-), Du. *neus*. Like other terms for parts of the body, this too is common Aryan (see Fuß, Herz, Ohr, Niere, Zahn, &c.); comp. OInd. *nâsâ*, *nas*, f.,

OSlov. *nosŭ*, m., Lith. *nósis*, Lat. *násus*, *náres*. See further 𝔑üſtern.

naß, adj., 'wet, moist,' from the equiv. MidHG. and OHG. *naȝ*, adj.; corresponding to Goth. **nata*-, nom. **nats*, 'wet' (deduced from *natjan*; see neÿen); OSax. and Du. *nat*. Teut. *nata*- can scarcely be connected with Sans. *nadī̆*, ſ., 'river,' because the latter is derived from a root *nad*, 'to rush, roar.' Perhaps Gr. νοτερός, 'wet' (νοτέω, 'I am wet'), points, like the Teut. cognates, to a root *not, nod* (comp. Haß with Gr. κότος). Neÿ likewise may be primit. allied; see Neÿ and neÿen.—**Naß**, n., 'humidity,' from MidHG. *naȝ*, n., 'fluid, moistness'; the adj. naß used as a neut. subst.—**Näſſe**, f., 'humidity, moisture,' from MidHG. *neȝȝe*, OHG. *neȝȝī*, f., an abstract form from naß.

Natter, f., 'adder, viper, asp,' from the equiv. MidHG. *náter, nátere*, OHG. *nátara*, f.; corresponding to OSax. *nādra*, Du. *adder* (for *nadder*; see under Nabt, Näber), AS. *nǣddre*, E. *adder* (likewise, with the loss of the initial *n*, see Otter). Goth. **nēdro* is wanting, the graded form *nadrs*, m., 'adder,' being used; Olc. *naðr, naðra*, 'adder.' A specifically Teut. word, the early history of which is not quite clear; it can scarcely be connected with Lat. *natrix*, 'water-snake,' which belongs to *nare, natare*, 'to swim.'

Naue, f., 'barque,' from MidHG. *nāwe, nǣwe*, f. and m., 'small ship,' espec. 'ferryboat'; not primit. allied to Lat. *nāvis*, but rather borrowed from it in the MidHG. period. The Teut. cognate of Lat. *nāvis*, Gr. νηῦς, Sans. *nāus*, is Olc. *nór*, 'ship,' of which we should have expected the corresponding MidHG. form **nuowe*. It is certainly remarkable that the Teut. primit. word corresponding to the Aryan terms adduced has been preserved only in Scand.

Nebel, m., 'mist, fog, haze,' from the equiv. MidHG. *nëbel*, OHG. *nëbul*; corresponding to OSax. *nëbal*, m., Du. *nevel* (in E. *mist*; see Mist). Goth. **nibls* is wanting; allied to the Olc. compounds with *nifl*-, 'darkness,' to which *njól*, 'night,' is akin (comp. AS. *nifol*, 'dark'). OHG. *nëbul*, from pre-Teut. *nebhelo*-, corresponds to Gr. νεφέλη, 'cloud, mist,' Gr. νέφος, n., 'cloud, mist,' Lat. *nebula*, 'mist,' Sans. *nábhas*, n., 'mist, cloud, dampness,' OSlov. *nebo* (stem *nebes*-), n., 'sky,' OIr. *nel*, 'cloud.'

neben, adv. and prepos., 'beside, along with, in addition to,' from MidHG. *nëben*, shortened form of *enëben*, OHG. *nëben, inëben*, 'beside'; as a compound of in and ëben it signifies lit. 'in the same line with,' similarly AS. *on efn, on emn*, 'alongside.' Comp. the following word.

nebſt, prep., 'along with, together with,' first occurs in early ModHG., with the variant nebenſt. Borrowed from Du., in which *nevens*, 'near to,' occurs, which is etymologically equiv. to neben.

necken, vb., 'to tease, banter,' from MidHG. (MidG.) *necken*, 'to excite the appetite,' to which is allied MidHG. (MidG.) *nachaft*, 'malicious, crafty,' *nac-heit*, 'malice, cunning'; not found in OHG. Of obscure origin. See Schabernack.

Neffe, m. (with abnormal *ff*), 'nephew,' from MidHG. *nëve*, OHG. *nëvo*, m.; orig. existing in all the OTeut. dials. (now obsolete in Suab. and Bav.). The meaning in the older languages was not so definite as at present; MidHG. *nëve*, most frequently means 'sister's son,' also more rarely 'brother's son,' likewise 'uncle,' then generally 'relative'; Du. *neef*, 'grandson, nephew, cousin,' AS. *nëfa*, 'grandson, nephew' (E. *nephew* is based on Fr. *neveu*), Olc. *nefe*, m., 'relative.' Goth. **nifa*, m., is by chance not recorded. The cognates are primitive and common to the Aryan group; Teut. **nefód*, nom. sing. (of which there is a fem. form *niftī*; see Nichte), from pre-Teut. *nepót*, appears in Ind. *nápāt* (stem *náptṛ*), 'descendant, son, grandson,' Lat. *nepos*, 'grandson,' Gr. ἀνεψιός, 'first cousin,' νέποδες, 'brood,' OIr. *nia*, 'sister's son.' With regard to the fluctuation of meaning see Braut, Oheim, Vetter, and Schwager.

nehmen, vb., 'to take, accept,' from the equiv. MidHG. *nëmen*, OHG. *nëman*; a common Teut. str. vb. with the same signification throughout the group; comp. Goth., OSax., and AS. *niman*, Olc. *nema*. The most nearly allied in sense to these are Lat. *emere* and OIr. *em* (OSlov. *imą* ?), 'to take,' with which nehmen is connected in sound if its initial *n* is the relic of a particle. OTeut. *nëman* may, however, be compared more probably with Gr. νέμω, 'to distribute, pasture' (trans.), νέμος (νόμος), 'pasturage,' equiv. to Lat. *nemus*, 'grove,' Gr. νόμος, 'law,' in which case it is especially connected with the mid. vb. νέμεσθαι, 'to distribute among themselves, possess, consider as, hold.'

Nehrung, f., 'a long narrow strip of

land separating a Haff from the sea,' first occurs in ModHG., allied to MidHG. (14th cent.) *Nerge*, 'Kurische Nehrung': "since Nehrung is a narrow strip of land, it may be derived from OSax. *naru*, 'narrow.'" See Marк.

Neid, m., 'envy, grudge,' from MidHG. *nît* (gen. *nîdes*), m., 'hostile disposition, warlike fury, grudge, jealousy, envy,' OHG. *nîd*, m., 'hatred, anger, envy.' It corresponds to OSax. *nîð*, m., 'zeal, hostile conflict, hatred,' Du. *nijd*, m., 'envy,' AS. *nîþ*, m., 'endeavour, effort, hostility' (obsolete in E.). In East Teut. the corresponding word is neut., Goth. *neiþ*, n., 'envy,' OIc. *nîð*, n., 'disgrace, opprobrious term.' Teut. *nîþa-*, connected with Lat. *nîtor*, 'to exert oneself' ?.—**Neidnagel**, see Niet.

neigen, vb., 'to tilt, bend, incline,' from MidHG. *nîgen*, str. vb., 'to bow,' and *neigen*, wk. vb., 'to cause to bow, humiliate, lower'; OHG. *nîgan*, from *hnîgan*, str. vb., 'to bow,' and *neigen*, wk. vb., 'to incline, bend.' It corresponds to OSax. *hnîgan*, *hnêgian*, AS. *hnîgan*, *hnǽgan*, Goth. *hneiwan*, vb., 'to bow, sink,' *hnaiwjan*, vb., 'to humiliate, bend' (for *hneigwan*, *hnaigwjan*); the wk. vb. is the causative of the str. vb. The Teut. root *hnîgw*, from pre-Teut. *kn̂igh* (or rather *kn̂iq̂*?), is uncertain in the other Aryan languages. Perhaps Lat. *co-nîveo*, *nîco*, *nicto*, 'to wink, nod,' are connected with the Teut. cognates.

nein, adv., 'no,' from the equiv. MidHG. and OHG. *nein* (negative adv.); so too OSax. *nên* (in the *Heliand*), 'no'; derived from the Goth. adv. of negation *ni*, OHG. *ni*, MidHG. *en-ne* (which also appears in the *n* of nicht, nit, and nirgend), and the neut. of the indefinite article OHG., MidHG., and ModHG. *ein*, equiv. to Goth. *ains*; *nein* is therefore 'not one' (comp. nichts, meaning 'not something'). The approximate source of E. *no* is the equiv. AS. *nâ* (OIc. *nei*), in Goth. *nê*, 'no.' The Goth. negative *ni*, etymologically cognate with un- and ohne, belongs to the same class as Gr. νη (e.g. νη-κερδής, 'unprofitable'), Lat. *nê* (in *nêfas*) and *nê*. 'not, lest, in order that not,' Sans. *na*, OSlov. *ne*, 'not,' Lith. *ne*, 'not.'

Nelke, f., 'pink carnation,' a LG. form for Nägelchen (LG. *negelkin*), n.; in Mid HG. *negellîn*, n., 'clove.' Comp. Ic. *negull*, m., 'clove,' Du. *nagelbloem*, 'carnation.'

nennen, vb., 'to name,' from the equiv. MidHG. and OHG. *nennen* (also *nemmen*); originated in *namnjan* by the assimilation of *mn*; a verbal noun from Name (OHG. *namo*). Comp. Goth. *namnjan* from *namô*, AS. *nam an*, wk. vb., equiv. to E. *to name* (AS. also *nemnan*, equiv. to OSax. *nemnian*). See Name and the remarks there on Du. *noemen*, 'to name.'

nergeln, **nörgeln**, vb., 'to grumble, growl,' ModHG. only, of obscure origin; in Bav. the vb. signifies 'to speak indistinctly' (espec. in a guttural fashion or through the nose). Allied perhaps to Du. *nurken*, 'to grumble, growl'?.

Nerv, m., 'nerve, sinew,' ModHG. only, from Lat. *nervus*.

Neſſel, f., 'nettle,' from the equiv. Mid HG. *nezzel*, OHG. *nezzila*, f.; corresponding to MidLG. and Du. *netel*, AS. *netele*, f., E. *nettle*; allied to earlier OHG. equiv. *nazza* (the same as Ic. *notr*?), 'nettle.' Goth. *natus*, f., and *natilô*, f., 'nettle,' are by chance not recorded. Since the HG. word can never have had an initial *h* before the *n*, Gr. κνίδη, 'stinging nettle,' cannot be regarded as a cognate. The word has more correctly been connected with the common Teut. Netz (Goth. *nati*), on the assumption that nets in early times were made of nettle-threads. Further cognates are wanting. The term has also been compared with Pruss. *noatis*, Lith. *noterė́*, and OIr. *nenaid*.

Neſt, n., 'nest, haunt,' from MidHG. and OHG. *nest*, n., 'nest, resting-place for birds and also for sucking animals'; corresponding to MidLG., Du., AS., and E. *nest*; Goth. *nista-* is wanting. The cognates are primit.; the OTeut. form previous to the permutation of consonants was *nizdo-*, which is indicated likewise by Sans. *nîḍa-s*, 'lair of animals,' also 'dwelling,' as well as by OIr. *net*, 'nest,' Lat. *nîdus*, 'nest,' for *nizdus* (Lith. *lizdas* and Slav. *gnězdo*, 'nest,' are abnormal). The form *nizdo-* is prop. a compound of the root *sed*, 'to sit, seat oneself,' and the verbal particle *ni* preserved in Sans. (see nieder; *nizdo-*, from *ni-sedô-*, therefore means lit. 'place of settling'; comp. Sans. *ni-sad*, 'to sit down, settle.' In Lat. and Teut. *nîdus* and *nest* assumed the special meaning 'bird's nest'; similarly in Scand. a general word for 'couch' (Gr. κοίτη) was restricted to a bear's haunt (OIc. *hlý*; it belongs, like Gr. κοίτη, κεῖμαι, to the Aryan root *ḱî*, 'to lie'). The Goth. term for 'nest' is *sitl*, lit. 'seat,' which therefore is of a cognate root with Neſt.

Neſtel, f. and m., 'lace,' from MidHG. *nestel*, f., OHG. *nestilo*, m., *nestila*, f., 'knot of ribbons, bow, lace (for stays, &c.), bandage'; allied to MidLG. and Du. *nestel*, 'girdle, lace,' OIc. *nist, niste*, n., 'stitching needle,' and with further gradation OHG. *nusta*, f., 'tying together,' as well as *nuska*, MidHG. *nüsche*, 'clasp of a cloak.' If *st* and *sk* in these words be regarded as a part of the derivative, they may be compared with Lat. *necto*, 'to join' (and the Sans. root *nah*, 'to connect'?). OHG. *nestilo* (Goth. *nastila*) has also been connected with Lat. *nôdus* (for *nozdus*, like *nidus* from *nizdus*; see Neſt). The form *nastila* passed into Rom.; comp. Ital. *nastro*, 'silk ribbon.'

nett, adj., 'neat, nice, pretty,' first occurs in early ModHG.; from Du. and Fr. *net* (Lat. *nitidus*).

Netz, n., 'net,' from the equiv. MidHG. *netze*, OHG. *nezzi*, n.; corresponding to OSax. *net* (and *netti*), n., Du., AS., and E. *net*, Goth. *nati*, OIc. *net*, n., 'net'; a common Teut. term, to which the graded Scand. *nót*, 'large net,' is allied. The etymology is obscure; it is scarcely allied to naß, Teut. *naṭa-*; it is rather connected with Neſſel, with which it may be based on a pre-Teut. root *nădd*, 'to sew, knit.' Comp. also Lat. *nassa*, 'creel, net.'

netzen, vb., 'to wet, moisten,' from MidHG. *netzen*, OHG. *nezzen* (Goth. *natjan*), 'to wet'; a verbal noun from naß.

neu, adj., 'new, fresh, modern, novel,' from the equiv. MidHG. *niuwe*, *niu*, OHG. *niuwi*. Corresponding forms exist in the Teut. and Aryan group; Goth. *niujis*, OIc. *nýr*, AS. *níwe*, E. *new*, Du. *nieuw*, OSax. *niuwi*. Teut. *ninja*, from pre-Teut. *neuyo-*, appears also in Sans. *nâvyas* (and *nâvas*), Lith. *naújas* (OSlov. *novŭ*, Lat. *novus*, Gr. *véos*). The prim. meaning of this primit. Aryan *nenjo-, newo*, cannot be determined with certainty; it is probably connected with the OAryan particle *nû*, 'now,' so what was new was regarded as 'that which has just come into being' (comp. nun). Its relation to the following word is very doubtful.

neun, num., 'nine,' from the equiv. MidHG. and OHG. *niun*; corresponding to Goth. *niun*, 'nine,' OSax. *nigun*, Du. *negen*, AS. *nigun*, E. *nine*, OIc. *nīu* (all these represent *nījun*?); a common Aryan numeral, like all the units. Comp. Sans. *návan*, Lat. *novem*, Gr. ἐννέα, OIr. *nói*. It has been supposed that the common Aryan word for *neun* (*newn*) is derived from *neu* (*newos*), 'nine' being regarded as the 'new number' of the third tetrad; the system of reckoning by fours must be assumed as the oldest in the Aryan languages, since the numeral acht, 'eight,' is a dual form.

nicht, particle, 'not,' from MidHG. *niht*, pronom. subst., 'nothing,' OHG. *niwiht*, *neowiht*, 'not'; it is used even in OHG. and MidHG. to strengthen the negative *ni*, *en*. In the 12th cent. this negative begins to be omitted, and towards the end of the 15th cent. it entirely disappears, its place being taken by nicht. In zu nichte machen, 'to bring to nought, ruin,' and mit nichten, 'by no means,' nicht is still used as a subst. (see Nicte). OHG. *neowiht* is a compound from *ni eo wiht*, 'never a whit' (comp. Wicht); so OSax. *neowiht*, Du. *niet*, AS. *náwiht, náuht*, E. *not* and *naught*; Goth. *ni waihts*, 'nothing,' *ni waihtai*, 'by no means.' See nein, nie, uech, and nur.

Nichte, f., 'niece,' ModHG. only (unknown to UpG. dialects in which Baſe is used), from LG. *nicht*, in MidHG. *niftel*, OHG. *niftila*, f. (dimin. of OHG. *nift*); comp. AS. *nift*, OIc. *nipt*. These are fem. forms of Neſſe, pointing to Goth. *nifti*, pre-Teut. *nepti*, f., from *nepôt*, m. The meaning of Nichte fluctuates as in the case of Neſſe; MidHG. *niftel*, 'niece, mother's sister, first cousin,' OIc. *nipt*, 'sister's daughter, niece,' OHG. *nift*, 'neptis privigna.' Comp. also Lat. *neptis*, 'granddaughter,' with *nepos*; Sans. *naptî*, f., 'daughter, granddaughter,' with *nápât*.

nichts, pronom. subst., 'nothing,' ModHG. only, in MidHG. *niht*. It originated from MidHG. *nihtes niht*, an emphatic form of the simple *niht*, which was ultimately omitted; the ModHG. dial. form *nichtst* is probably based directly on the MidHG. phrase, which in late MidHG. appears as *nihtzit*.

Nickel, m. and n., 'nickel,' ModHG. only, from the equiv. Swed. *nickel*.

nicken, vb., 'to nod, doze,' from Mid HG. *nicken*, OHG. *nicchen*; the iterative of neigen (like ſchmücken of ſchmiegen, bücken of biegen). Nacken is not allied.

nie, adv., from the equiv. MidHG. *nie*, OHG. *nio, neo*, 'never'; a compound of *ni* and *eo*, 'not ever,' like OSax. *nio* from *ni io*, AS. *ná* from *ne â*; in Goth. the two words were kept separate, *ni aiw,* 'never.' With regard to the negative *ni* see **nidjt**; and for OHG. *io,* Goth. *aiw,* comp. **je.**

nieð, prep., 'below,' from MidHG. *nide,* 'under, below,' OHG. *nida,* prep., 'under, beneath'; allied to **nieðer.**

nieðen (in **hienieden**), adv., 'below, beneath,' from MidHG. *niden, nidene,* OHG. *nidana,* adv., 'below'; comp. OSax. *nithana,* AS. *neoþan* (from AS. *beneoþan* is derived E. *beneath*); allied to **nieðer.**

nieðer, adv., from the equiv. MidHG. *nider,* OHG. *nidar,* adv., 'down, downward'; corresponding to OSax. *nithar,* Du. *neder,* AS. *niþer,* E. *nether,* OIc. *niðr;* Goth. **niþar,* is by chance not recorded. A derivative of the Aryan verbal particle *ni,* 'down' (see **Neft**), which is preserved in other Teut. forms (see **nieð** and **nieten**); comp. OSlov. *nizŭ,* 'below,' as well as Sans. *ni,* 'down,' and Sans. *nitarām,* which is closely allied to the Teut. adv.— **nieðer,** as an adj., 'nether, lower, base,' has been recently formed from the adv.; OHG. *nidari,* MidHG. *nider, nidere,* adj., 'nether, low'; akin to OSax. *nithiri.*

nieðlich, adj., 'pleasant, pretty, nice,' from MidHG. **nietlich,* of which only the adv. *nietliche,* 'zealously, diligently,' is recorded; late OHG. *nietsam,* 'desiderabilis, desirable, pleasant'; comp. OSax. *niudsam,* 'pleasant.' The cognates are connected with OHG. *niot,* m., 'lively longing, zealous endeavour,' OSax. *niud,* AS. *neód,* 'zeal, longing.'

Niednagel, Neidnagel, m., see **Niet.**

niemals, see **nie** and **mal.**

niemand, pron. with an excrescent final *d* (as in **Mond**), from *nie* and *man,* 'nobody'; comp. MidHG. *nieman, niemen,* OHG. *nioman,* 'nobody'; see **nie** and **jemand.**

Niere, f., 'kidney,' from the equiv. MidHG. *nier, niere,* OHG. *nioro,* m. (OHG. also 'testicle'); corresponding to Du. *nier,* f., MidE. and MidLG. *nére* (to which are allied E. *kidney,* MidE. *kidenére,* from AS. **cýdneóre, *cýdneóra*?), 'kidney'; in Scand. *nýra,* 'kidney,' with *i-* mutation. If the latter indicates Goth. **niuzô,* n., the Teut. class has no further cognates; but if we are to assume Goth. **niurô, niurjô,* corresponding forms may be found in the other Aryan languages, which have numerous terms for parts of the body in common with Teut.; Goth. **niuró* for **niuró, *neguró,* from preTeut. **neghrón,* which is represented in Gr. by an equiv. *νεφρός,* 'kidney, testicle' (φ for *gh*); akin further to Lat. *nefrones.* With regard to Goth. **niu-* for **niu-,* **nique-,* see **Nu.**

niefen, vb., 'to sneeze,' from the equiv. MidHG. *niesen,* OHG. *niosan,* str. vb.; corresponding to Du. *niezen,* OIc. *hnjósa* (to which *hnore,* m., 'sneezing,' is allied), MidE. *nésin;* also AS. *fneósan,* MidE. *fnésen,* equiv. to Du. *fniczen,* 'to sneeze.' The two Teut. roots *hnus* and *fnus* seem to have been orig. identical; with these are connected MidE. *mésen,* E. *to sneeze.* The pre-Teut. root *qnus, ksnus,* may be onomatopoetic.

Niesiwurz, m., 'hellebore,' from the equiv. MidHG. *nieswurz,* f.; akin to the preceding word. "The name is due to the fact that the pulverised root has been used from the earliest times to produce sneezing."

Nießbrauch, m., 'usufruct,' allied to **nießen;** see **genießen.**

Niet, n., from the equiv. MidHG. *niet,* m. and f., 'bolt'; OHG. **hniot* is not recorded with this sense. The word is connected with OHG. *hniotan,* 'to fasten,' OIc. *hnjóða,* vb., 'to strike, hammer, fix firmly'; the Teut. root *hnud,* pre-Teut. *knut,* has not yet been found in other languages.

Niete, f., 'blank (in a lottery)'; "adopted in the first half of the 18th cent. after the introduction of lotteries in the Du. fashion, from the equiv. Du. *niet,* m. and n., 'nothing, nought,' the gender of which was changed to fem.; the Du. word exactly corresponded orig. to Mod HG. *nichts, nicht.*" See the latter words.

Niflel, f., see **Nichte.**

nimmer, adv., 'never, never again,' from MidHG. *niemer, nimmer, nimer* (from *nie mér*), 'never (of present and future actions)'; comp. ModHG. *nimmer* in the sense of 'no more, never again,' for which *nimmermehr* is used in preference. From MidHG. *niemér, nimmér,* 'never more.' Both forms are derivatives of OHG. *nio* and *mér* (like AS. *néfre,* E. *never,* from **námire*); *nimmermehr* contains the second component twice. See **nicht** and **nie.**

nippen, vb., ModHG. only, from LG. and Du. *nippen,* 'to sip'; in Henneb. and Bav. *nepfen, nöpfen,* with the HG. *pf.* Comp. further AS. *nipele,* E. *nipple* l.

Nippsache, f., 'toy, trinket,' ModHG. only, formed from Fr. *nippe.*

nirgend, nirgends, adv., 'nowhere,' from MidHG. *niergen, niergent;* see irgend.

nisteln, nisten, vb., 'to build a nest, nestle,' from the equiv. MidHG. *nisteln, nisten,* OHG. *nisten;* a verbal noun from Nest. Comp. AS. *nistlian,* E. *to nestle,* Du. *nestelen.*

Niß, f., 'nit,' from the equiv. MidHG. *niz* (33), f., for *hniz;* corresponding to Du. *neet,* AS. *hnitu,* f., and the equiv. E. *nit;* Goth. *hnits is not recorded. According to the permutation of consonants Gr. *κονίς,* plur. *κονίδες,* 'eggs of lice, bugs, fleas,' &c., may be akin, if the words in both languages be based on *knid.* It has also been connected with Slav. *gnida.* Nuß is not allied.

nit, the same as nicht.

Nix, m., 'nixey, water-fairy,' from MidHG. (very rare) *nickes,* OHG. *nihhus,* n. and m., 'crocodile'; comp. AS. *nicor,* 'hippopotamus,' E. *nick,* 'water-sprite' (Old Nick, applied to the devil), MidDu. *nicker,* 'water-sprite,' by OIc. *nykr* (from *niqiza), 'water-sprite in the form of a hippopotamus,' also 'hippopotamus.' The OHG. and MidHG. sense 'crocodile' is easily associated with the other meanings of the cognates; the prim. signification may be 'fabulous sea-monster.' The word is probably based on a Teut. root *niq* from pre-Teut. *nig* (Sans. *nij,* Gr. *νίπτω*), 'to wash oneself'; thus Nir would mean orig. 'a sea-animal that delights in bathing, sea-spirit,' while the masc. Nir, like AS. *nicor,* points to Goth. **niqiza,* **nikuza-,* the corresponding fem. Nirt, preserved only in HG., indicates Goth. **niqisi;* OHG. *nicchessa,* MidHG. **nickese,* **nixe,* in *wazzernixe,* f., 'female water-sprite,' for which in MidHG. *merwip* and *mermeit* are used.

Nobistrug, m., 'underwold, hell,' borrowed, like Krug, 'tavern,' the second part of the compound, in early ModHG. from LG. The first component is MidHG. *abis, abyss,* m., 'abyss,' whence with *n* prefixed (comp. Ital. *nabisso,* from the usual combination *in abysso*), the LG. form Nebistrug, hence lit. 'tavern in hell.'

noch (1.), adv., from the equiv. MidHG. *noch,* OHG. *noh,* 'still'; corresponding to OSax. *noh,* Du. *nog,* Goth. *nauh,* 'still'; a compound of *nu,* 'now,' and *h,* equiv. to Lat. *que,* Gr. *τε,* Sans. *ca,* 'and also'; therefore the orig. meaning is probably 'also now,' or 'even, just now'; comp. nun, and with regard to Goth. *h-,* equiv. to Lat. *que,* see noch (2).

noch (2.), conj., 'nor,' from MidHG. *noch,* OHG. *noh,* 'nor, not even, and not even'; OHG. *noh—noh,* MidHG. *noch-, noch,* 'neither—nor,' also even in MidHG. *wëder—noch.* Corresponding to OSax. *noh,* Du. *noch;* in Goth. *nih,* 'nor, not even,' Goth. *nih—nih,* 'neither—nor.' Goth. *nih* is exactly equiv. to Lat. *ne-que* (with regard to Goth. *ni,* Lat. *ne,* see nicht). The particle *-h, -uh,* corresponding to Lat. *que,* Gr. *τε,* Sans. *ca,* 'and,' had a definite meaning in Goth.

Nock, n., 'yard-arm,' ModHG. only, borrowed, like other nautical terms, from LG.; comp. Du. *nock,* 'summit, point.'

None, f., 'afternoon prayers,' from MidHG. *nône,* OHG. *nôna,* f., 'hora nôna, the ninth hour of the day' (reckoned from six A.M.), also 'the prayers said at that hour.' The term was borrowed during the OHG. period from Lat. *nôna* (scil. *hora;* comp. Fr. *none,* Ital. *nona*); comp. also OSax. *nôna, nôn,* AS. *nôn,* E. *noon* (the difference in time is said to be due to the shifting of the canonical 'nona' to midday).

Nonne, f., 'nun,' from the equiv. MidHG. *nunne,* OHG. *nunna,* f.; corresponding to Du. *non,* MidLG. and AS. *nunne,* f., E. *nun,* adopted, like the previous word, in connection with monastic life, both in G. and E. about the beginning of the 9th cent., from Lat. *nonna* (Gr. *νόννα*), which passed also into Rom.; comp. Fr. *nonne, nonnain,* 'nun,' Ital. *nonna,* 'grandmother,' like Ital. *nonno,* 'grandfather.' The early history of the cognates is obscure; late Lat. *nonna* was an 'expression of reverence' (hence its meaning in Ital.).—

Nonne, f., 'gelded sow,' is, like the corresponding words in MidHG. and Du., identical with Nonne, 'nun,' and was thus termed for sexual reasons.

Nord, m. (almost obsolete in the UpG. vernacular), 'north,' from MidHG. *nort* (gen. *nordes*), m. and n., OHG. *nord,* m.; corresponding terms are found in all the OTeut. languages (whence Ital. *norte* and Fr. *nord*), the names of the cardinal points being formed independently in Teut.; in this case the Aryan languages possess no common term. Comp. OSax. *north (recorded only as an adv. 'northwards'), AS. *norþ,* m., E. *north.* Goth. **naúrþs,* or rather *naúrþr (equiv. to OIc. *norðr*), is by chance not recorded. It has been connected with Gr. νέρτερος, 'that which exists below, lower down,' which would involve the assumption that the word was coined at a period when the Teutons were descending the northern slope of a mountain range. Yet it must also be remembered that Umbr. *nertro* signifies 'on the left.'—To this **Norden**, m., 'northern region,' is allied; from MidHG. (MidG.) *norden*, OHG. *nordan*. n.; comp. also **Süden**.

Norne, f., ModHG. only, naturalised, espec. by Klopstock, from the equiv. OIc. *norn* (plur. *norner*), 'goddess of fate'; the origin of the term is disputed.

Nößel, n., 'pint' (nearly), allied to MidHG. *næzelîn* (ö?), n., 'a small liquid measure,' dimin. of an obsolete primit. word, the origin of which is obscure.

Not, f., 'need, compulsion, distress,' from MidHG. and OHG. *nôt*, f. (seldom masc.), 'toil, oppression, danger, struggle, compulsion'; a common Teut. form; comp. Goth. *naubs*, f., 'necessity, compulsion, force,' OIc. *naudr*, f., 'necessity,' AS. *nêd*, *neád*, f., E. *need*, Du. *nood*, OSax. *nôd*. The common Teut. stems *naudi*, *naubi*, from pre-Teut. *nauti*-, have been connected with Pruss. *nauti*-, 'distress'; *nau*- (see genau) is probably the root.—**Notdurft**, f., 'necessaries' (of life), from MidHG. *nôt-durft*, f., 'necessity, need, needs of nature, want of necessaries, livelihood,' OHG. *nôtduruft*, f. (OSax. *nôdthurft*); allied to Goth. *naudibaurfts*, adj., 'necessary.'—**Noterbe**, m., early ModHG., equiv. to 'necessary, legitimate heir, who may not be passed over.'—**Notwehr**, f., 'self-defence,' from MidHG. *nôtwer*, f., 'warding off force.'—**Notzucht**, f., 'rape,' formed from MidHG. (Lower Rhen.) *nôtzühten*, 'to ravish, violate,' and also the equiv. MidHG. *nôtzogen*, lit. 'to treat in a violent manner,' even in OHG. *nôtzogôn* (MidHG. and OHG. *nôtnumft*, 'rape').

Note, f., 'note, annotation,' from Lat. *nota* (Fr. *note*); in the sense of 'musical note, melody,' *note* appears even in MidHG.

nu, adv., 'well now, well,' equiv. to nun.

nüchtern, adj., from the equiv. MidHG. *nüchtern*, *nüchter*, OHG. *nuohturn*, *nuohtarnîn*, adj., 'without food or drink, fasting, temperate,' comp. Du. *nuchter*, AS. *nixtnig*. The assumption that the word is based on Lat. *nocturnus* does not suffice to explain the meaning of nüchtern, since the Lat. term signifies only 'nocturnal, at night'; nor is it possible to regard OHG. *nuohturn* as a genuine Teut. derivative of Aryan *nôkt*, 'night' (OIc. *nôtt*), since it must have been equiv. in meaning to Lat. *nocturnus*. It may more probably be compared with Gr. νήφω, 'I am sober,' νηφάλιος, νήπτης, 'sober, without wine,' the φ-τ of which may represent an old guttural. In spite of this probable connection of the root, the suffix of nüchtern is still obscure.

Nücke, **Nucke**, f., 'freak, artfulness,' ModHG. only, from LG. *nücke*; comp. Du. *nuk*, 'freak.'

Nudel, f., 'vermicelli, dumpling,' first occurs in ModHG., whence Fr. *nouilles*; of obscure origin.

nun, adv., 'now, at present,' from MidHG. and OHG. *nu* (with the variant *nû*), 'at the present time, now,' rarely in MidHG. with the adverbial suffix *n* (*nun*, *nuon*). Further in ModHG. nu (from MidHG. *nû*); corresponding to OSax. *nû*, Du. *nu*, AS. *nû*, E. *now*, Goth. *nû*, 'now.' A common Teut. temporal adv.; comp. Sans. *nu*, *nû*, 'now,' *nûnam*, 'now,' Gr. νύ, νῦν, Lat. *nunc* (with the *c* of *hi-c*), OSlov. *nynĕ*, 'now,' Lith. *nu*. Comp. neu and noch (1).

nur, adv., 'only, simply,' from MidHG. *newære*, OHG. *niwâri* (OSax. *ne wâri*); lit. 'it would not be, if it were not.' MidHG. and the ModHG. dials. have numerous intermediate forms between *n·wære* and ModHG. nur, espec. *nûer*, *neur*, *niur*, *nuor*. For the negative *ne* see nicht.

Nüster, f., 'nostril,' ModHG. only, from LG. *nuster*, E. *nostril*, is demonstrably a compound, signifying lit. ' nose-hole' (comp. AS. *næs-þýrel*, *nos-þyrl*). We cannot so positively assume that the G. word is also a compound, for the *l* of the E. word is wanting. Hence some etymologists regard it as an *r*-derivative from *nos*- (a graded form of Nase, comp. earlier Mod HG. nuselu, in Logau, 'to snivel'), with a *t* inserted, and connect it with Lith. *nasrai*, 'mouth, jaw,' and OSlov. *nozdri*, 'nostrils.' Niesen is not allied; comp. Nase.

Nuß (1.), f., 'nut,' from the equiv. Mid HG. and OHG. *nuz*, f., neither cognate with nor borrowed from Lat. *nux* (*nucem*). It is rather a genuine Teut. word, orig. with initial *h*; comp. OIc. *hnot*, f., AS. *hnutu*, f., E. *nut*, Du. *noot* (Goth. **hnuts*, f., is wanting). The genuine Teut. cognates point to a pre-Teut. *knud*-, which appears with the same sense in OIr. *cnú*.

Nuß (2.), f., 'blow, push,' ModHG.

simply; only apparently identical with the preceding word (comp. Dachtel); historically, however, it is probably allied to Goth. *hnutó*, 'prick.'

Nute, f., from the equiv. MidHG. *nuot*, f., 'joint, groove'; allied to OHG. *hnuo, nuoa*, 'groove,' as well as OHG. *nuoil*, Mid HG. *nuowel, nüejel*, 'groove, plane,' *nuotîsen*, 'iron of a groove plane.' MidHG. *nüejen*,

vb. (OHG. *nuoen*, from **hnôjan*), 'to smooth, fit exactly,' also belongs to a Teut. root *hnô*.

nütze, adj., 'useful,' from MidHG. *nütze*, OHG. *nuzzi*, adj., 'profitable'; Goth. *un-nuts*, 'useless'; comp. AS. *nytt*, 'useful.' Allied to genießen, where other derivatives and cognates of the str. vb. are adduced.

O.

ob (1.), prep. and adv., 'over, above,' from MidHG. *obe, ob*, prep. and adv., 'aloft, above, across,' so too OHG. *oba;* comp. AS. *ufe-weard*, 'upper.' ModHG. *ob* has been retained chiefly in compounds such as Obdach and Obdach. Allied to oben.

ob (2.), conj., 'whether, if,' from MidHG. *obe, ob*, op. conj., 'if, as if, although, whether,' so too OHG. *oba*, with the earlier variant *ibu*, 'if, whether'; corresponding to OSax. *ef, of* (AS. *gif*, E. *if*). Goth. *ibai, iba*, 'whether then, perhaps, probably, lest perhaps,' with the corresponding negative *nibai, niba*, 'unless.' The OHG. form is the dat. and instrum. of *iba*, f., 'doubt, condition,' OIc. *ife, efe*, m., and *if, ef*, n., 'doubt.' Hence the lit. meaning of the conj. is 'in doubt, on condition.'

oben, adv., 'above, aloft,' from MidHG. *obene*, OHG. *obana*, adv., 'above, from above'; so too OSax. *oban, obana*, 'down from above,' AS. *ufan*, 'from above,' E. preserved only in *ab-ove*. Allied to ober.

ober (1.), compar., 'upper, higher,' from MidHG. *obere*, OHG. *obaro*, 'the superior'; prop. the compar. of *ob*. From this was formed, even in OHG., a new superl. *obarôst* (MidHG. *oberest*).

ober (2.), prep., 'over, above, beyond,' of MidG. and LG. origin, as is indicated by the stem vowel, for the *o* which prevails in MidG. and LG. *obar, obar*, AS. *ofer*, E. *over*, and the equiv. Du. *over*, is always represented in HG. by *u*. See über and auf.

Oblate, f., from the equiv. MidHG. *oblât, oblâte*, f. and n., 'the Host, wafer'; from Lat. *oblâta* (from *afferre*, which was adopted as opfern), whence also the equiv. AS. *oflête*; MidE. *oblé* is formed, however, from OFr. *oublee*, whence ModFr. *oublie*. See Opfer.

Obst, n., with an excrescent dental as in Art, Mond, niemand, Palast, Papst; from the equiv. MidHG. *obez*, OHG. *obaz*, n., 'fruit.' It is a West Teut. word; comp. Du. *ooft*, AS. *ofet* (Goth. **ubat* is wanting, in OIc. *alden*). It is uncertain whether Goth. **ubat* is akin to ober, über, root *up-*, thus signifying 'what is above.'

Ochse, m., from the equiv. MidHG. *ohse*, OHG. *ohso*, m., 'ox'; corresponding terms occur in all the OTeut. dials.; Goth. *auhsa*, OIc. *oxe*, AS. *oxa*, E. *ox*, Du. *os*, OSax. *ohso*, 'ox.' The common Teut. *ohsan-* (from pre-Teut. *uksén-*) is primit. cognate with Sans. *uksán*, 'bull,' the words Kuh and Stier being also common to the Aryan group. The Sans. root is *ukš*, 'to spurt out,' or *ukš*, 'to grow strong, grow up.' If the latter is correct, Ochse is connected with wachsen, yet it may be a masc. form of Lat. *vacca*, 'cow.'

Ocher, m., from the equiv. MidHG. *ocker, ogger*, n. and m., 'ochre.' Borrowed from Lat. *ochra* (ὤχρα), 'ochre,' whence also Ital. *ocra*, Fr. *ocre*.

öde, adj., 'deserted, waste,' from MidHG. *œde*, adj., 'uncultivated, uninhabited, empty, foolish, poor, infirm,' OHG. *ôdi*, 'desolate, empty'; corresponding to Goth. *auþs*, 'desolate, solitary, unfertile,' OIc. *auðr*. In some of the languages of the Teut. group there occurs an adj. similar in sound, but apparently of a different etymology, with the meaning 'easy.' Comp. OSax. *ôði*, OHG. *ôdi*, AS. *ýþe, eáþe*, OIc. *auð-* (in compounds), 'easy.' The prim. meanings of both classes are uncertain.—

Öde, f., 'waste, solitude, wilderness,' from MidHG. *œde*, OHG. *ôdî*, f., 'desert.' Comp. the Goth. derivative *auþida*, 'desert.'

Odem, equiv. to Atem.

oder, conj., from the equiv. MidHG. *oder*, OHG. *odar*, 'or, else'; the OHG. and MidHG. ordinary form are without *r*;

OHG. *odo*, earlier *ëddo*, MidHG. *ode*, *od*. This abnormal *r* is, according to some, a compar. suffix; according to others it is simply an affix due to the influence of OHG. *wëdar*, MidHG. *wëder*, 'neither.' OHG. *ëddo*, *ëdo*, correspond further to Goth. *aíþþau*, 'or,' which is a compound of Goth. *iþ*, 'and' (Lat. *et*), and *þau*, 'or.' E. *or* has no connection with this word, since it originated in AS. *áhwæþer*; Goth. *aíþþau* is AS. *oþþe* and *ëþþa*, 'or,' which became obsolete at an early period.

Odermennig, m., 'agrimony,' a corruption of the equiv. Lat. *agrimonia*, which appears under various forms in MidHG. *odermenie, adermonie.*

Ofen, m., 'from the equiv. MidHG. *oven*, OHG. *ovan*, n., 'oven'; so too with the same meaning MidLG. and Du. *oven*. AS. *ofen*, E. *oven*, OIc. *ofn*, *ogn* (Swed. *ugn*), Goth. *aúhns*; the word is common to Teut., hence the thing signified must also be primit. The variation of guttural and labial is seen also in the forms primit. cognate with these, Sans. *ukhá*, 'pot,' and Gr. *ἰπνός*, 'oven' (for *uknos*, which is indicated by Goth. *aúhns*). The orig. sense, 'pot,' seems also to follow from AS. *ofnet*, 'little vessel.'

offen, adj., from the equiv. MidHG. *offen*, OHG. *offan*, adj., 'open'; it has the same meaning in all the Teut. languages except Goth., where *upans is wanting. Comp. OIc. *openn*, AS. and E. *open*, Du. *open*, OSax. *opan*; the adj. seems similar in form to a partic., but the primit. verb cannot be adduced. It is also doubtful whether *auf*, OSax. *upp*, Goth. *iup*, is allied, so that *offen* would mean lit. 'drawn up.'

oft, adv., from the equiv. MidHG. *oft*, *ofte*, OHG. *ofto*, adv., 'often, frequently'; corresponding to Goth. *ufta*, OIc. *opt*, AS. *oft*, E. *oft* (extended form *often*), OSax. *oft*, *ofto*, 'often.' These adv. forms seem to be petrified cases of an obsolete subst. or adj. partic; they have also been connected with the partic. of the Sans. root *uc*, 'to be fond of doing.'

Oheim, Ohm, m., from the equiv. Mid HG. *ôheim*, *œheim* (also with final *n* instead of *m*), OHG. *ôheim*, m., 'uncle'; corresponding to Du. *oom*, AS. *eám*, 'uncle' (contracted from *eáhám), MidE. *ûm*, 'uncle,' also early ModE. *eme* (whence, *Eames* as a prop. name). By inference from OFris. *ém*, 'mother's brother,' and Lat. *avunculus*, the lit. meaning of Oheim is 'uncle on the mother's side' (in contrast to Vetter, Lat. *patruus*). Goth. *áuháims, corresponding to the simply West Teut. cognates, is wanting. The etymology of the word is difficult to determine. The first syllable is generally regarded as cognate with Lat. *avun-culus*, 'uncle,' which is the dimin. of *avus*, 'grandfather' (so too Lith. *avynas* and OSlov. *ujĭ*, from *aujos, 'uncle'); to Lat. *avus* (to which OIr. *aue*, 'grandson,' is allied), Goth. *awô*, f., 'grandmother,' OIc. *áe*, 'great-grandfather,' corresponds. With reference to the second syllable a Teut. *haima-*, 'honour,' is assumed; therefore Oheim means lit. 'enjoying the honours of a grandfather.' A more probable assumption is 'possessing the grandfather's house,' 'grandfather's heir' (hence Lat. *avunculus*, lit. 'little grandfather'). Others join the *h* to the first syllable and regard it as the representative of the Lat. *c* in *avuncu-lus*, and divide the Goth. word thus, *auh-aims, so that *aima* is a dimin. suffix for *aina*. It is to be observed that after the remarks under Neffe and Vetter, MidHG. *ôheim* may also mean 'nephew, sister's son.'

Ohm, n. and m., 'awm' (liquid measure, about 40 galls.), from MidHG. *âme*, *ôme* (*â* before nasals is changed into *ô*; comp. Mohn, Mont, Ohmet, and ohne), f., m., and n., 'awm, measure'; corresponding to Du. *aam*, E. *awm*, Scand. *áma*. They are based on MidLat. *ama*, 'vessel,' wine measure' (Gr. *ἄμη*, 'water-pail,' Lat. *ama*, 'water-bucket'). See ahmen.

Ohmet, n., 'aftermath,' from the equiv. MidHG. *âmât*, OHG. *âmâd*, n.; also in the same sense with a different prefix Mid HG. *uëmet*, OHG. *uomât*, n., 'second mowing of the grass'; for OHG. *mâd* see under Mahd. The OHG. syllables *â* and *uo* are nominal prefixes; OHG. *uo* also signifies 'after' in the compounds *uo-quëmo*, 'descendant,' *uo-chumft*, 'succession'; *â-*, which is usually a negative prefix (see Ohnmacht), means 'remaining,' in OHG. *â-leiba*, MidHG. *âleibe*, 'relics.'

ohne, prep., from the equiv. MidHG. *ân*, *âne*, OHG. *âno*, prep., 'without'; corresponding to OSax. *âno*, MidDu. *aen*, OIc. *án*, earlier *ón* (from *ánu), 'without'; in Goth., with a different gradation, *inu*. Undoubtedly the negative *un-* and Goth. *ni*, 'not' (see nie), are also allied to ohne, as well as Gr. *ἄνευ*, 'without.'—ohne in ohngeachtet, 'notwithstanding,' ohnlängst, 'not long since,' represents un= under the influence of Du. *on*, 'un-.'—**Ohn=** in **Ohnmacht** is due to the attempt to assign a more intelligible meaning to **Omacht**, which originated in OHG. and MidHG. *â-maht*; the prefix *ô* from the old *â* had become obscure in the compound. With regard to OHG. *â*, 'un-,' comp. *â-teili*, 'having no share in,' MidHG. *â-seize*, 'unoccupied,' AS. *œ-men*, 'devoid of men.'—**ohngefähr**, adj., 'casual, accidental,' adv., 'about, not far from,' from MidHG. *ân gevære*, mostly *ân gevœrde*, 'without evil intention, without deceit.'

Ohr, n., from the equiv. MidHG. *ôre*, *ôr*, n., OHG. *ôra*, n., 'ear'; corresponding terms are found in all the Teut. languages; OSax. *ôra*, Du. *oor*, AS. *eâre*, n., E. *ear*, OIc. *eyra* (with mutation on account of *r*, equiv. to Goth. and Teut. *z*), Goth. *ausô*, n., 'ear.' Like many other terms for parts of the body (comp. **Fuß, Herz, Nagel, Niere**, &c.), this word occurs also in other Aryan languages, Lat. *auris* for **ausis* (to which *aus-cultare* is akin, see **hören**), Gr. οὖς (from **οὖσος*), gen. ὠτός from (οὐσατός, allied to an *n*- stem like the Teut. cognates), OSlov. *ucho* (gen. *ušese*), n., 'ear,' from *ausos* (with the dual *uši*), Lith. *ausis*. Comp. the following word.

Öhr, n., 'eye' (of a needle), from Mid HG. *œre, œr*, n., 'ear-like opening, eye (of a needle), hole in a handle, handle,' so too late OHG. *ôri*, n.; a derivative of OHG. *ôra*, 'ear'; comp. further **Öse**. Moreover, Gr. οὖς, E. *ear*, and Du. *oor* also signify 'handle.'

Ohrfeige, f., 'box on the ear,' first occurs in early ModHG., similar to Du. *oorvijg*; usually regarded as a facetious corruption of Du. *oorveeg*, 'box on the ear,' in which *veeg* (cognate with ModHG. **fegen**) signifies 'stroke, cut.' It may, like **Dachtel, Kopfnüsse, Maulschelle** (prop. a kind of pastry), be a euphemistic expression.

Öl, n., from the equiv. MidHG. *öle, öl*, n. (with the variants *ole, ol*, and *olei*), OHG. *olei, oli*, n., 'oil'; corresponding to OSax. *olig*, Du. *olie*, AS. *ele*, n., 'oil.' Lat. *oleum*, 'oil,' passed into HG. before the 8th. cent. Goth. adopted the term probably even half a century earlier from the Lat., the only assumption that can explain the remarkable Goth. form *alêw*. The approximate source of E. *oil*, MidE. *oile*, is OFr. *oil*, which with its Rom. cognates (ModFr. *huile*) are also based on Lat. *oleum*.

Oleander, m., 'oleander, rose-bay,' first occurs in early ModHG., from the equiv. Fr. *oléandre*, or rather Ital. *oleandro*.

Olive, f., 'olive,' from MidHG. *olîve*, f. and m., from Lat. *oliva*.

Onkel, m., 'uncle,' ModHG. only, from Fr. *oncle*.

opfern, vb., from the equiv. MidHG. *opfern*, OHG. *opfarôn*, 'to sacrifice'; so too OSax. *offrôn*, Du. *offeren*, AS. *offrian*, 'to sacrifice,' whence E. *to offer*, under the influence of Fr. *offrir*. Introduced by the Church from Lat. *offerre*. With regard to the change of accent in Teut., comp. **predigen**, from *praedicare*, in which the verbal particle likewise assumed the accent.—**Opfer**, n., 'offering, sacrifice,' from MidHG. *opfer*, OHG. *opfar*, n., is not based on a Lat. word, but coined from the G. vb. (comp. **Handel**); see also **Oblate**. Moreover, the Teutons had their own special word for 'to sacrifice'; Goth. and AS. *blôtan*, OIc. *blôta*, OHG. *bluozan*.

Orden, m., 'order, class, badge,' from MidHG. *orden*, m., 'rule, regulation, uses, management, decree, rank, spiritual order'; borrowed from Lat. *ordin-em* (acc. of *ordo*), even in the OHG. period; comp. OHG. *ordina*, f., whence *ordinhaft*. The oblique case of the Lat. word determined the form of the OHG. term; so too in **Kreuz, Abt**, &c.—**ordnen**, 'to order, regulate,' even in MidHG. *ordenen*, OHG. *ordinôn*, formed from Lat. *ordinare*.

Orgel, f., 'organ' (mus. instrument), from MidHG. *organâ, organe*, OHG. *organâ*, f., of which a rare variant in *l* occurs, OHG. *orgela*, MidHG. *orgel*, f., 'organ.' OHG. *organa* is derived from MidLat. *organum* (Ital. *organo*, Fr. *orgue*, E. *organ*), or rather its plur. *organa*, 'organ.' Properly, however, "*organa dicuntur omnia instrumenta musicorum*; *non solum illud organum dicitur quod grande est et inflatur follibus*, &c." (Augustine). Organs were known to the MidEurop. Teutons as early as the latter half of the 8th cent., espec. in the reign of Charlemagne, for Charlemagne himself received a magnificent organ, which was described by a monk of St. Gall, as a present from the Byzantine emperor Michael.

Orkan, m., ModHG. only, from the equiv. Du. *orkaan*, E. *hurricane*; comp. Fr. *ouragan*, Ital. *uracano*, 'hurricane'; "it is a modern word introduced from America, said to be of Caribbean origin."

R

Orlogſchiff, n., ModHG. only, formed from the equiv. Du. *oorlogsschip*, n., 'man-of-war,' which is derived from *orlog*, 'war,' corresponding to OSax. *orlag*, 'war,' AS. *orlege*, MidHG. *urliuge*, OHG. *urliugi*, 'war.'

Ort (1.), m., 'awl,' in this sense Mod HG. only, and identical with Ort (2).

Ort (2.), m., 'place, spot, region,' from MidHG. *ort*, n. and m., 'sharp point, end, beginning, corner, angle, border, place,' OHG. *ort*, m. and n., does not occur in the ModHG. sense of 'place.' The meaning 'point, corner,' is the orig one; comp. OSax. *ord*, m., 'point,' AS. and MidE. *ord*, 'point of a weapon' (for a similar evolution of meaning comp. Ede). The *r* of the word originated in *s*, *z*; Goth. **uzda-* is by chance not recorded; it is assumed by OIc. *oddr*, 'point,' the *dd* of which points to Goth. *zd*. In Ort (1) the earlier meaning is still dimly seen. See also Ort (3).

Ort (3.), n. and m., 'quarter, quart,' from MidHG. *ort*, m. and n., 'fourth part of a measure, weight, or coin'; corresponding to Du. *oord*, 'a fourth part of a coin, measure, &c.' Identical with Ort (2). "This meaning is approximately derived from the square coins divided by a cross into pieces with four Orte, *i.e.*, 'corners,' and afterwards transferred to measure and weight. Thus in Germany and Austria, when, in the year 1849, the florin notes were divided into four parts to serve as change, a single part was called Edele or Örtel, 'a little corner,' and this expression was then generally used for a quarter of a florin." The earlier assumption that this word was based on MidLat. *quarto*, 'fourth part,' must be rejected.

Öſe, f., 'ear, hook,' from late MidHG. and early ModHG. (MidG. and MidLG.) *ose*, f., 'ear, hook, handle'; the usual assumption that the word is borrowed from Lat. *ansa*, 'handle,' is not to be preferred to the opinion that Öſe and Öhr are identical, and that the *s* from which the *r* of Öhr and Öhr is derived is preserved in Öſe; see Öhr.

Oſten, m., from the equiv. MidHG. *ôsten*, m. and n., OHG. *ôstan*, m. and n., 'east'; the form Oſt is wanting in MidHG. and OHG.; it has probably been recently coined; comp. Nord and Norden, Süd and Süden, Weſt and Weſten. Yet even in AS. *eást*, E. *east*, occurs, whence Fr. *est.—oſten,* adv., from MidHG. *ôsten, ôstene,* 'in, to, or from the east,' OHG. *ôstana,* 'from the east,' so too AS. *eástene,* 'in the east,' *eástan,* 'from the east,' OSax. *ôstan, ôstana,* 'from the east'; OHG. and OSax. *ôstar,* 'to the east.' The stem *austa-* (in OIc. *austr,* gen. *austrs,* m.), on which these words are based, is undoubtedly connected with the OAryan term for 'dawn'; primit. Aryan **ausôs,* Sans. *uśás,* Lat. *aurôra* (for **ausôs-a*), Gr. ἠώς, Lith. *auszrà*, 'dawn.' Since, in other instances, the names for the periods of the day have been applied to the cardinal points, *e.g.,* Mittag, Morgen, &c., the dawn might be used for the east, especially as Morgen in UpG. signifies 'east' (in UpG. the old terms for the cardinal points are almost obsolete). Comp. also Oſten.

Oſterluzei, f., 'birth-wort,' first occurs in early ModHG.; corrupted from the Lat. term *aristolochia,* "in order to give at least a G. air and some apparent meaning to the word."

Oſtern, fem. plur, from the equiv. Mid HG. *ôster,* f., more usual *ôsteren,* plur., OHG. *ôstarûn,* f. plur., *ostara,* f., 'Easter'; corresponding to AS. *eáster,* n., *eástro,* f. plur., whence the equiv. E. *Easter*. Probably applied at an earlier period to an old heathen festival of the West Teutons. It is based upon the name of an OTeut. goddess of spring, *Austrô,* which must be identical with Ind. *usrá,* 'dawn' (between *s* and *r*, *t* is inserted in Teut., see Schweſter). The OAryan *Aurôra* had among the Teutons, to some extent at least, exchanged the character of a goddess of dawn for that of the light-bearing goddess of spring. This is indicated by the time of the Easter festival; the Christian season must have coincided with the heathen, since the name of the latter was appropriated. Bede testifies to the existence of the OTeut. goddess by the mention of the E. dial. form *Eostra* (for West Sax. *Eástre*). *Ausôs,* the OTeut. name of *Aurôra,* was the origin of the Teut. derivatives for 'east,' as well as AS. *eárendel,* 'morning star, daybreak,' whence the OHG. proper name *Ôrentil* in the later Orendel legends. See Oſten.

Otter, f., from the equiv. MidHG. *otter,* OHG. *ottar,* m., 'otter'; corresponding to Du. *otter,* AS. *otor,* E. *otter,* OIc. *otr,* 'otter'; Goth. **utra* is by chance not recorded. Goth. *tr* remains unaffected by the HG. permutation; see bitter, lauter, treu, zittern. The term *udrá-* is applied in several Aryan languages to aquatic animals; *udra- belongs to the same root as Gr. ὕδωρ, 'water,' ἄνυδρος, 'waterless, dry,' Sans. udan, 'water,' ánudra-s, 'waterless, dry,' hence ModHG. Otter is etymologically connected with Waſſer. Comp. Gr. ὕδρα, ὕδρος, 'water-snake,' Lith. údra, 'otter,' OSlov. vydra, 'otter,' Sans. udra, m., 'otter.'—Otter, f. (thus in Luther), for 'adder,' is East MidG.; comp. Du. and LG. adder, E. adder (also Suab. ádr).

Oxhoft, n., 'hogshead,' MidHG. only, from the equiv. LG. and Du. okshoofd, n., to which Swed. oxhufoud and Dan. oxehoved are allied; the origin of the word cannot be ascertained. The sounds point rather to a Scand. dial. than to LG. and Du., because in the latter os signifies 'ox.' It is not certain whether the prim. meaning is 'head of an ox,' though it was thus popularly understood in LG., as is seen by the corrupt form hogshead, which it assumed on being adopted by Eng.

P.

Paar, n., from the equiv. MidHG. and OHG. pâr, 'pair, two of the same sort'; formed from Lat. par, 'pair,' whence also ModFr. paire, and from this comes E. pair.

Pacht, f., 'compact, lease, tenure,' from MidHG. (MidG.) paht, with the strictly HG. permutated and more usual forms phaht, phahte (MidHG.), f. and m., 'rent, lease, justice, law'; so too Du. pacht. The ModHG. form is due to LG. influence, as is indicated by the initial sound compared with MidHG. phahte. It is based on Mid Lat. pactum, pactus, 'compact, a sum stipulated by the compact.' OHG. *pfahta is not recorded, probably only by chance, though OHG. (also MidHG.) pfât occurs a few times.

Pack, m. and n., 'pack, bundle,' to which late MidHG. backen, packen, 'to pack up, load,' is allied; it is connected with a ModTeut. and Rom. class, the source of which has not yet been discovered; comp. Du. pak, Scand. pakke, MidE. packe, E. pack; Ital. pacco, Fr. paquet, &c.; also Ir. and Gael. pac, Bret. pak, which some regarded as the origin of the cognates, though others refer them, with greater probability, to OIc. baage, 'burden.'—**Pack**, n., 'rabble,' is LG., and is historically identical with Pack, 'bundle.'

paff, interj., 'puff! bang!' ModHG. only, agreeing with LG. and Du. paf, 'puff!'; scarcely allied to late MidHG. baffen, 'to bark'; it is rather a recent onomatopoetic form.

pah! interj., 'pooh!' ModHG. only, of a similar origin to paff.

Palaſt, m., 'palace,' from MidHG. palast (comp. Art, Obſt, Papſt), more usual palas, n. and m. (with a varying accent), 'large building with one main room, used for the reception of guests, for festivities, and espec. for meals,' and then 'palace.' It was adopted in late OHG. (the end of the 11th cent.) from Fr. palais, MidLat. palatium. See Pfalz.

Pallaſch, m., 'sword, falchion,' Mod HG. only, from Russ. palásch, Pol. palasz.

Palliſade, f., 'palisade,' ModHG. only, from Fr. pallisade, which comes from Ital. palizzata.

Palme, f., from the equiv. MidHG. palme, balme, f. and m., OHG. palma, f., 'palm-tree, palm.' Borrowed in OHG. from Lat. palma through an ecclesiastical medium. Very many names of plants and trees had been previously introduced from the South of Europe.

Pamphlet, n., ModHG. only, from Fr. pamphlet, which was again derived from the equiv. E. pamphlet. The E. word is not a native term, though its origin is not yet determined.

Panier, n., from the equiv. MidHG. panier, usually banier, f. and n., 'banner, standard.' From Fr. bannière, hence of the same origin as ModHG. Banner.

Panther, m., from the equiv. MidHG. panter, pantel, n., 'panther,' late OHG. panthera, f., formed from Lat. panther, panthera.

Pantoffel, m., 'slipper,' first occurs in early ModHG., from Ital. pantofola (Fr. pantoufle), the origin of which has not yet been explained.

Panzer, m., from the equiv. MidHG. panzer, panzier, m., 'coat of mail,' from Ital. panciera, MidLat. pancerea, 'coat of mail,' which is connected with Ital. pancia, 'belly, body' (Fr. panse, whence also Mid HG. and ModHG. dial. Panſe, 'belly'), and signifies lit. 'the part of the armour covering the abdomen.'

Papagei, m., from the equiv. MidHG. *papagey*, most frequently *papegân*, m., 'parrot'; corresponding to Du. *papagaai*, E. *popinjay* (MidE. *pŏpejai*); borrowed from the equiv. Rom. cognates, espec. from OFr. *papegai* (Ital. *pappagallo*). The origin of these words is not yet determined; they are most probably derived from Arab. *babaghâ*.

Papier, n., 'paper,' from late MidHG. *papier*, n., which is derived from Lat. and Gr. *papyrum*, whence also the Rom. cognate, Fr. *papier* (E. *paper*).

Pappe, f., 'pap, paste,' from MidG. and LG.; comp. Du. and E. *pap*; MidHG. (MidG.) *pap, peppe*, 'pap.' It is usually derived from Ital. and MidLat. *pappa*, 'pap,' allied to Lat. *pappare*, 'to eat.'

Pappel (1.), f., from the equiv. MidHG. *papel, papele*, f., OHG. (MidLat.) *papula*, f., 'mallow.' Of obscure origin; probably cognate orig. with Pappel (2).

Pappel (2.), f., from the equiv. MidHG. *papel, popel*, f., 'poplar,' Lat. *pŏpulus* (Fr. *peuplier*), with the MidLat. variant *papulus*; from the Fr. form (OFr. *poplier*) are derived the equiv. Du. *populier* and E. *poplar* (MidE. *popler*). In the Rom. class, Lat. *populus* was changed in many curious ways in most of the dials.; comp. Ital. *pioppo* (from *ploppus* for *populus*). Since the HG. form is closely connected with the Lat., it must have been introduced by scholars, probably in the MidHG. period.

pappeln, vb., 'to babble, prate,' Mod HG. only, an onomatopoetic term (comp. Fr. *babiller*), but linked perhaps to the equiv. LG. *babbeln*, Du. *babbelen* (MidE. *babelen*, E. *to babble*), whence the ModHG. form may be derived by permutation.

Papst, Pabst, m., 'pope,' from Mid HG. *bâbes*, and with an excrescent *t* (see Obst and Palast), *bâbest*; OHG. *bâbes* first occurs about 1000 A.D. (in Notker); from the equiv. Lat. *pâpa*. The initial and medial *b* in OHG. and MidHG, in contrast to Lat. *p* may be compared with *bĕch, balme, bapel*, and their variants *pĕch, palme, papel*, in MidHG. The *s* of the OHG. form *bâbes* (earlier *bâbas*?) is both strange and difficult to explain; comp. OSlov. *papeẑi*, borrowed from it. This Latin Church word, which passed into G. at a late period, cannot be connected with ModGr. πάππας (comp. Pfaffe); most of the corresponding Rom. words have, however, no *s* (Ital. *papa*, Fr. *pape*). Yet OFr. has sometimes *pape-s* instead of *pape*, with an inorganic *s* in the nom. (comp. Bjau), for in OFr. numerous mascs. in *a* could take an *s* in the nom. (*poetes* from *poeta*, *prophetes* from *propheta, hermites* from *eremita, homicides* from *homicida*, &c.). In MidEuropean Ger. this form in *s* afterwards constituted the stem; besides OHG. *bâbes* comp. also Du. *paus* (from OLG. and ODu. *pâvos*, recorded even in the 9th cent.). The LG. form seems to have passed in the 10th cent. to the south of Germany. OIc. *pâfe* was probably formed under the influence of AS. *pâpa* (Lat. *pâpa*), E. *pope*. Moreover, MidLat. *pâpa* was a respectful term used in addressing bishops, and since Leo the Great a title of the Roman pope, and also since Hierocles the title of the patriarch of Alexandria. Gregory VII. decreed in 1075 the exclusive right of the Roman pontifex to the title *papa*. The fact that AS. has preserved the Lat. word in a purer form is explained by its having been borrowed at an earlier period.

Paradies, n., 'paradise,' from MidHG. *paradise, paradis, pardis* (its accent fluctuates), n., OHG. *paradisi, paradis*, n. (Mid HG. *t* explains the earlier ModHG. Paradeis). It corresponds to OSax. *paradis*, Du. *paradijs*, MidE. *paradise*; the cognates are derived from the biblical and ecclesiastical *paradisus*, παράδεισος (prop. 'pleasure-ground, park'), which again is of Pers. origin. Comp. Zend *pairidaeza*, 'rampart, enclosure.'

Pardel, Parder, m., from the equiv. MidHG. *parde*, OHG. *pardo*, m., 'panther, leopard'; borrowed from Lat. *pardus*; MidHG. variant *part* (*pardes*), m.; the *l* or rather *r* of the ModHG. form is due to Gr. and Lat. *pardalis*.

Park, m., 'park,' early ModHG., borrowed from Fr. *parc*. See Pferch.

Partei, f., 'party, faction, league,' from MidHG. *partîe*, f., 'party, division,' borrowed from Fr. *partie* (Lat. and Ital. *partita*, E. *party*), whence also ModHG. Partir.

Pasch, m., 'doublet, pair royal (at dice),' first occurs in early ModHG.; from Fr. *passe-dix*, 'above ten (at dice).'

paschen, vb., 'to smuggle,' ModHG. only, probably from Fr. *passer*, Ital. *passare*, 'to go beyond,' with 'frontier' understood.

Paspel, m., ModHG. only, from the equiv. Fr. *passe-poil*, 'piping' (for clothes).

passen (1.), vb., 'to forego one's turn in playing,' ModHG. only, formed from Fr.

passer, 'to omit, pass.' Numerous words relating to play are derived from the Fr.; comp. 𝔓𝔞𝔣𝔠𝔥 and 𝔇𝔞𝔲𝔰.—The meaning 'to lie in wait, watch,' comes, however, from Du. *passen.*

paſſen (2.), vb., 'to pass muster, suit, be convenient,' ModHG. only, corresponding to Du. *passen,* which is found even in the 13th cent.; from Fr. *passer.* Deriv. päßlich, 'tolerable.'

paſſieren, vb., 'to befall, happen, occur to,' from Fr. *se passer.*

𝔓𝔞𝔣𝔱𝔢𝔱𝔢, f., 'pie, pastry,' from MidHG. *pastête, pastêde,* f., from MidLat. *pastâta,* whence Fr. *pâtée,* 'paste' (for poultry), *pâté,* 'pie' (allied to *pâte,* Ital. *pasta,* 'dough'). Akin also to Du. *pastie,* E. *pasty* (comp. *paste*).

𝔓𝔞𝔥, m., 'pass, mountain road, passport,' ModHG. only, from Du. *pas,* 'step, passage, pass.'

𝔓𝔞𝔱𝔢, m., from the equiv. MidHG. *pate (bate),* m., 'godfather, godmother,' from Lat. *pater,* the declension being changed to the wk. masc.; Lat. *pater spiritualis,* 'sponsor,' mostly MidLat. *patrinus,* whence Ital. *patrino,* Fr. *parrain* (Du. *peet, petekind*). MidHG. also *pfetter,* 'sponsor' and 'child to be baptized,' from *patrínus,* whence ModHG. dial. 𝔓fetter, 𝔙etter. The initial *pf* may be due to its having been borrowed at an early period (similarly Du. *meter,* 'godmother,' is borrowed from Lat. *matrina*). In Suab. *dête,* m., and *dôte,* f., are chiefly used for 𝔓ate (*dêtle,* 'godchild'), in Bav. Tett, m. and f. With regard to UpG. 𝔊ette, 𝔊etti, see under 𝔊ett.

𝔓𝔞𝔲𝔨𝔢, f., from the equiv. MidHG. *pûke (bûke),* f., 'kettledrum'; a difficult word to explain. The Suab. variant *baoke* seems to be formed by gradation from MidHG. *pûke.* Perhaps the primit. word is *bûggn, bauggn,* an old onomatopoetic form.

𝔓𝔞𝔲𝔰𝔟𝔞𝔠𝔨, m., 'person with puffed cheeks,' allied to MidHG. *pfûsen (pfnûsen),* 'to snort,' with MidG. and LG. initial *p.*

pauſchen, bauſen, vb., 'to puff up, blow up,' ModHG. only, formed from Fr. *poncer,* 'to pounce,' and *ébaucher,* 'to sketch' (hence the dial. form 𝔱𝔲𝔯𝔠𝔥𝔭𝔬𝔲𝔰𝔢𝔫).

𝔓𝔞𝔲𝔰𝔢, f., from the equiv. MidHG. *pûse,* f., 'pause, rest'; borrowed in MidHG. from Fr. *pause* (Lat. and Ital. *pausa*), whence also Du. *poos* and E. *pause.* The Lat.-Rom. word passed through a G. medium to the North. Comp. Dan. *pause,* Swed. *paus.*

𝔓𝔞𝔳𝔦𝔞𝔫, m., 'baboon,' ModHG. only, formed from Du. *baviaan* (HG. *p* for Du. *b,* as in 𝔭𝔲𝔭𝔭𝔢𝔩𝔫); the latter, like E. *baboon,* is derived from Fr. *babouin,* 'baboon' (Ital. *babbuino,* MidLat. *babuinus*). The derivation of these cognates from MidLat. *papio,* 'wild dog,' is not satisfactory; their origin must be sought for somewhere in the South. Late in the 13th cent. the term passed into Rom. and then into E.; in Germany the animal seems to have been shown for the first time at the Imperial Diet at Augsburg in the year 1552 A.D.

𝔓𝔢𝔠𝔥, n., from the equiv. MidHG. *pěch, běch* (comp. 𝔓apſt), OHG. *pěh, běh,* n., 'pitch'; MidHG. *pfich* (very rare), from OHG. **pfih,* unless it is a phonetic transcription of the Lat. or LG. word. It corresponds to OSax. *pik,* n., Du. *pik, pek,* AS. *piċ,* n., E. *pitch;* OIc. *bik.* The Teut. cognates are based on a Lat.-Rom. word; Lat. *picem,* acc. of *pix* (with regard to the oblique case as the base comp. 𝔎𝔯𝔢𝔲𝔷). Compared with 𝔎𝔯𝔢𝔲𝔷 from *crûcem,* the preservation of the guttural as *k* and of the vowel quantity in the stem is an important element in the history of the word. Lat. *picem* was naturalised at a much earlier period in G. than *crûcem,* probably in the 7th cent. Comp. further Ital. *pece,* Fr. *poix,* 'pitch,' from Lat. *picem* (nom. *pix*).

𝔓𝔢𝔡𝔞𝔫𝔱, m., 'pedant,' ModHG. only, from Fr. *pédant,* Ital. *pedante,* of which the orig. meaning was 'instructor' (the ultimate source is Gr. παιδεύειν). "How the word obtained its modern sense is easily seen."

𝔓𝔢𝔡𝔢𝔩𝔩, m., 'beadle, messenger of a court or council,' first occurs in early ModHG.; from MidLat. *bidellus, pedellus; bedelli universitatum* is recorded in 1350. As the usher of a court of justice the word *bedellus* appears as early as the 13th cent., and, like its Rom. cognates (Ital. *bidello,* Fr. *bedeau,* 'beadle'), is derived from OHG. *bital, pital* (MidHG. *bitel*), a derivative of OHG. *bitten,* 'to invite, cite.' See 𝔅üttel.

𝔓𝔢𝔤𝔢𝔩, m., 'water-mark,' ModHG. only, from the similar LG. form; comp. Du. *pegel,* 'gauge-mark, standard,' and *peil,* 'gauge-mark, scale on which the height of the water is marked.' These words are derived, like AS. *pægel,* E. *pail,* from a Teut. root *pag,* which also appears in Alem. pſexle, pſexe, 'to gauge.'

Pein, f., from the equiv. MidHG. *pîne*, *pîn*, OHG. *pîna*, f., 'pain, punishment, torture'; adopted during the OHG. period on the introduction of Christianity from Lat. *poena*, which was pronounced *pēna* in MidLat. (comp. Ital. *pena*); MidLat. *ê* appears in HG. as *î* in other cases also (see **Streit** and **Feier**). Comp. OSax. *pîna*, Du. *pijn*, AS. *pîn*, E. *pine* (a later variant of *pain*); also OIr. *pían* (gen. *péne*).

Peitsche, f., 'whip, lash,' early Mod HG., from Bohem. *bič* (Pol. *bicz*).

Pekesche, f., 'laced coat, hussar's jacket,' from Pol. *bekiesza*.

Pelikan, m., 'pelican,' from MidHG. *pellicân*, m., formed from Lat. *pelicanus*.

Pelle, f. (LG.), equiv. to Du. *pel*, E. *peel*.

Pelz, m., from the equiv. MidHG. *bellîz*, *belz*, *pelz*, m., 'fur,' borrowed in the 10th cent. (OHG. *pellîz*) from the equiv. Mid Lat.-Rom. *pellicia*, 'fur'; comp. Ital. *pelliccia*, Fr. *pelisse*. It corresponds to AS. *pylce*, E. *pelt*.

Pennal, n., 'pen-case,' ModHG. only, formed from MidLat. *pennale*; with this comp. **Pennal** meaning, 'grammar-school, high-school, pupil.' To the students at the university the school might seem as a huge array of pen-cases, and "in jest the freshman too was called a 'pen-case,' probably because he attended lectures regularly, and so carried his pen-case with him."

Perle, f., 'pearl,' from the equiv. Mid HG. *përle*, *bërle*, OHG. *bërla*, *përala*, f.; a foreign word, as the fluctuating initial sound indicates. It corresponds to the Rom. cognates, Ital. *perla*, Fr. *perle*, whence also E. *pearl*; derived probably from Lat. **pirula*, 'little pear.' In Goth., *marikreitus*, a corrupt form of Lat. *margarita*, was used, corresponding to AS. *mere-greót*, OHG. *meri-grioz*, MidHG. *meregriez*. — **Perlmutter**, f., 'mother of pearl,' late Mid HG., formed like Fr. *mère-perle* (Ital. *madre-perla*); so too E. *mother of pearl*. **Perlmutter** is lit. 'producer of pearls inside the mussel.'

Pest, f., 'pest, plague,' ModHG. only, from Lat. *pestis*. — **Pestilenz**, f., 'pestilence,' even in MidHG. *pestilenzie*, *pestilenz*, f., from Lat. *pestilentia*.

Petersilie, f., 'parsley,' from MidHG. *pêtersil*, m., *pêtersilje*, m., OHG. *pêtarsile*; borrowed from MidLat. *petrosilium* (Gr. πετροσέλινον), 'parsley.' In the UpG. dials. a shortened form is found, **Peterli**, **Peterle** (**Peterling**).

Petschaft, n., 'signet, seal,' from Mid HG. *petschat*, *petschaft*, n.; borrowed from the equiv. Bohem. *peĕet* (OSlov. *peĕati*); the *f* of the MidHG. and ModHG. words was introduced by associating them with **Schaft**.

Petze, f., 'bitch, she-bear'; early Mod HG.; its relation to the equiv. E. *bitch* (from AS. *bičče*) and Fr. *biche* is uncertain.

Pfad, m., from the equiv. MidHG. *pfat* (gen. *pfades*), OHG. *pfad*, m., 'path, track'; OSax. **path* is wanting; Du. *pad*, AS. *pæþ*, m., E. *path*. The word is unknown to East Teut., and thus the difficulty of determining its origin is greatly enhanced. The prevalent opinion, which is based on the supposition, probably correct in the main, that the words beginning with HG. *pf* and LG. *p* are borrowed, is satisfied with the phonetic similarity to Gr. πάτος, 'path, road,' to prove the fact that **Pfad** is borrowed from the latter. With regard to this point we have to take into account the *p* of the E. word, which is assumed by HG., and which proves the existence of **Pfad** in G. before the beginning of our era. But Teut. has no such early loan-words of Gr. origin (see **Hanf**). As we have no data, we cannot decide whether the word was introduced through a foreign medium; it is possible the word was borrowed indirectly from Gr., but the assumption that it was adopted directly from Scyth. is equally valid; comp. Zend *paþ* (also *paþan*, *panþan*), 'way.' In the latter case it must have passed into G. after the primit. Teut. permutation; **Hanf** was borrowed before this period. Its primit. kinship with Gr. πάτος, 'way' (Sans. *panthan*, *path*, Zend *paþan*), must be decidedly rejected, because Teut. *f* would correspond to *p* in the non-Teut. languages. Comp. **Humpen**.

Pfaffe, m., 'priest, parson,' from Mid HG. *pfaffe*, OHG. *pfaffo*, m., 'priest'; corresponding to LG. and Du. *pape*, 'priest'; the common prim. form is *pâpo*. The MidLat. term is *clericus*. The usual assumption that the word is derived from Lat. *pâpa*, which was in the Western Church a respectful term applied to bishops and a title of the Pope, does not account for the fact that the term means 'priest' in all the Teut. dialects of MidEur., and therefore must be decidedly rejected. In the Greek Church a distinction was made between πάπας, 'pope,' and παπᾶς, 'clericus minor'; with the latter sense the G. cognates are connected. It would also be remarkable if the *p* of a Latin word introduced into G. at the period of the Roman conversion had undergone permutation (comp. Priester, predigen, and Propst). The Gr. word (possibly in the vocat. form παπᾶ?) may have been widely diffused throughout Germany even in the 6th cent.; it was introduced perhaps at a somewhat later period than Kirche, as might be inferred from the absence of the word *pāpa*, 'priest,' in AS. and E. Here too we have a trace of the influence of the Greek Church on the Teutons; yet we cannot determine which tribe adopted Gr. παπᾶς as *pāpa* in its vocabulary and passed on the term (the meaning of Goth. *papa* in the Milan Calendar is obscure). It found its way even into OIc., in which *pape*, however, was strangely enough used by the Irish anchorites found in Iceland by the Northmen when they colonised the island. With regard to Lat. *pāpa* see Papst.

Pfahl, m., from the equiv. MidHG. *pfâl*, OHG. *pfâl*, m., 'pale, stake'; allied to the equiv. Du. *paal*, AS. *pál*, E. *pole, pale*. The cognates were undoubtedly borrowed from Lat. *pālus* (whence also Fr. *pal*) contemporaneously with the cognates of Pfosten, and probably also with the technical terms relating to building in stone (Ziegel, Schindel, Wall, Mauer, and Pforte); all these words have undergone permutation in HG.; see also the following word.

Pfalz, f., 'palace, high official residence, palatinate,' from MidHG. *pfalz, pfalze, phalenze*, f., 'residence of a spiritual or temporal prince, palatinate, town-hall,' OHG. *pfalanza, pfalinza*, f.; corresponding to OSax. *palinza, palencea* (used in the *Heliand* of the palace of Pilate). The current view is content with the assumption that the word is based on Lat. *pālātium*, yet the relation of the one to the other is more difficult to determine than is generally imagined. As the permutation of LG. *p* to HG. *pf* indicates, the word must have been naturalised in G. as early as the beginning of the 8th cent.; in the age of Charlemagne it already existed in G. Besides, the nasal of the OSax. and OHG. derivative, which was retained down to MidHG. even, cannot be explained by the form of Lat. *palatium*, nor can we discover why it was inserted. OHG. *pfalanza* and OSax. *palinza* clearly point to MidLat. *palantium*, 'murus, fastigium,' *palenca, palencum, palitium*, 'contextus ac series palorum'; we are thus led to 'the fortress.' or, more accurately, 'the district enclosed by pales,' as the orig. sense of the word Pfalz. When, at a later period, under the Carlovingians, *palatia* were built in Germany, the word, which had been adopted long previously from the Lat., acquired the meaning of the similarly sounding *palatium*. In later MidLat. appears also *palantia* for *palatinatus*, 'the district of a count palatine.'

Pfand, n., from the equiv. MidHG. *pfant* (gen. *-des*), OHG. *pfant* (gen. *-tes*), n., 'pawn, pledge, security'; it corresponds to MidLG. and Du. *pand*, and OFris. *pand*, which have the same meaning. It is usually derived from OFr. *pan*, 'cloth, rag' (from Lat. *pannus*); the West Teut. word is more closely connected, however, with OFr. *paner*, Prov. *panar*, Span. *apandar*, 'to fleece a person,' *apañar*, 'to take away'; hence Pfand, 'taking way,' or 'that which is seized' (OFr. *pan*, 'the thing seized,' whence E *pawn*) f.

Pfanne, f., from the equiv. MidHG. *pfanne*, OHG. *pfanna*, f., 'pan'; widely diffused in Teut. with the same sense, Du. *pan*, AS. *ponne*, f., E. *pan*. The permutation of *p* to HG. *pf* indicates the early existence of the word in the form *panna* in G., perhaps about the 7th cent., or, on account of the coincidence of the E. with the MidEur. Ger. word, far earlier. The Lat. form of *patina*, 'dish, pan,' is scarcely adequate to serve as the immediate source of the Teut. words; comp. further Pfennig. From Teut. is derived the equiv. Slav. *pany*.

Pfarre, f., 'parish, parsonage, living,' from MidHG. *pfarre*, OHG. *pfarra*, 'parish'; corresponding to LG. *parre*. The current assumption that Pfarre is derived from the MidLat. and Rom. *parochia* (Ital. *parrochia*), *paroecia* (Gr. παροικία, Fr. *paroisse*), and E. *parish* (borrowed from Fr.), is not quite satisfactory as far as the sound is concerned, since it assumes too great a modification of the word; note OIr. *pairche* from *parochia*. The later *parra* recorded in MidLat. is clearly an imitation of the G. word, and therefore the latter cannot be based on it. Perhaps the ecclesiastical division was connected with an OTeut. **parra*, 'district,' which is similar in sound and is assumed by the derivative **Pferch**; the idea associated with **Pfarre** in historic times originated, of course, in *parochia*, παροικία.—**Pfarrer**, m., 'clergyman, minister,' MidHG. *pfarrære*, OHG. *pfarrâri*, a G. derivative of *pfarra*. Note that the word is not based on MidLat. *parochus* (Ital. *parroco*), 'priest.' There also exists a later variant, **Pfarr**, MidHG. *pfarre*, m.; hence the derivative **Pfarrei** (Suab. and Bav.).

Pfau, m., from the equiv. MidHG. *pfâwe*, OHG. *pfâwo*, m., 'peacock'; the OHG. form, with its permutated initial sound and its preservation of the *v* as *w* (see **Räfig**, **Pferd**), points to a very early loan-word from Lat. *pâvo* (whence also Fr. *paon*, Ital. *pavone*). With regard to the form of the word, it may be remarked that while other loan-words from Lat. are based on the oblique case (see **Kreuz**), in this instance the G. word is classified under the n- declension, to which Lat. *pâvo* (acc. *pâvôn-em*) also belongs. The peacock (comp. **maufern** and **Räfig**) may have been known in Germany about the 7th or 6th cent., or even earlier. Comp. Du. *paauw*, AS. *pâwa* and *peâ*, E. *peacock*, which were borrowed contemporaneously from the same source; OSlov. *pavŭ* is also allied.

Pfebe, f., from the equiv. MidHG. *pfëben*, OHG. *pfëban, *pfëbano, m., 'pumpkin,' formed from Lat. *pepon* (Gr. πέπων), 'pumpkin.' MidHG. *pfëdem*, 'pumpkin,' and OHG. *pfëdemo*, are peculiar; besides these, OHG. *pëpano*, *bëbano*, and MidHG. *bëben* also occur without permutation. Comp. **Kitmen**.

Pfeffer, m., from the equiv. MidHG. *pfëffer*, OHG. *pfëffar*, m., 'pepper'; borrowed, as the unvarying permutation indicates, prior to the OHG. period from Lat. *piper* (whence Fr. *poivre*, Ital. *pepe*), which assumption is supported by Du. *peper*, AS. *pipor*, E. *pepper*, Ic. *piparr* (note in the non-Teut. languages OSlov. *pĭprŭ*). The early adoption of the Lat. word in Teut. is confirmed by history. In 410 A.D. Alaric, before Rome, granted a truce, for which the city was obliged to supply, among other things, 3000 lbs. of pepper.—**Pfeffermünze**, n., 'peppermint,' is connected with **Münze**, or rather its OHG. variant *munza*. See **Münze**.

Pfeife, f., from the equiv. MidHG. *pfîfe*, OHG. *pfîfa*, f., 'pipe'; borrowed prior to the OHG. period from MidLat. *pîpa* (allied to Lat. *pîpare*, 'to pip, chirp'); hence also Du. *pijp*, AS. *pîpe*, f., E. *pipe*, OIc. *pípa*; so too the Rom. cognates, Ital. *piva*, Fr. *pipe*.—**pfeifen**, 'to pipe,' from MidHG. *pfîfen*, from Lat. *pipare*, from which we should have expected an OHG. wk. vb. *pfîfôn.

Pfeil, m., from the equiv. MidHG. and OHG. *pfîl*, m., 'arrow, dart'; corresponding to MidLG. *pîl*, Du. *pijl*, AS. *pîl*, E. *pile*, Scand. *píla*, 'arrow.' Borrowed at an early period from Lat. *pîlum*, n., 'heavy javelin,' with a change of gender and meaning. The OTeut. word for arrow, Goth. *arhwazna*, OIc. *ǫr*, AS. *earh* (etymologically the same as Lat. *arcus*, 'bow'), disappeared on the introduction of the word.

Pfeiler, m., from the equiv. MidHG. *pfîlære*, OHG. *pfîlâri*, m., 'pillar'; borrowed prior to the OHG. period from MidLat. *pîlâre*, *pîlarius* (Lat. *pîla*), 'pillar,' whence also Du. *pijlaar*. Comp. Ital. *piliere*, Fr. *pilier*, E. *pillar* (to which E. and Fr. *pile*, formed from Lat. *pîla*, is allied).

Pfennig, m., 'a coin, one-tenth of a penny,' from MidHG. *pfennic*, *pfenninc* (gen. -ges), OHG. *pfenning*, m., 'denarius, a silver coin, a twelfth of a shilling.' Its form and origin are difficult to determine. It may be derived from **Pfanne**, and thus its name may be due to its shape (perhaps 'pan-shaped' or 'made in the pan'). A variant with *nd*, from the connection of the word with **Pfand**, is seen in OHG. *pfenting* and AS. *pending* (variants of the more usual *penning*, *pennig*, whence E. *penny*). With regard to the diffusion of the word, comp. further OSax. *pending*, Du. *penning*, OIc. *penningr*; in Goth. a presumptive form *panniggs or *pundiggs is wanting. The suffix *-ing* frequently occurs in names of coins in the earlier periods; comp. **Schilling**, **Silberling**, OHG. *cheisuring*, 'imperial gold coin,' E. *farthing*, from AS. *fëorþing*, 'quadrans.' From the Teut. cognates are derived OSlov. *pěnęgŭ*, *pěnędzĭ*, 'coin, money.'

Pferch, m., 'fold, pen,' from MidHG. *pfërrich*, OHG. *pfërrih*, *pfarrih* (hh), m., 'fence, enclosure, espec. for sheep'; corresponding to AS. *pearroc*, m., 'enclosure, park,' Du. *perk*, 'enclosed space.' If the words with initial *p* in LG. and initial *pf* in HG. are of foreign origin, the term on which they are based must have been introduced, on account of the correspondence between the Continental Ger. and E. words, at a very early date (about the 4th cent.). "It appears even in the earliest MidLat.; *parcus, parricus* (Leg. Rip. and Leg. Angl.), *parc* (Leg. Bajuv.), in the latter instance as 'granary,'" and also in early Rom.; comp. Fr. *parc*, 'pen, park' (see Parf), Ital. *parco*. E. *park* is based partly on Rom. and partly on the AS. word. The source of all the cognates is incorrectly ascribed to Kelt.; comp. Gael. *páirc*, W. *parc, parwg*.

Pferd, n., 'horse,' from MidHG. *pfert* (*-des*), n., 'horse,' espec. 'riding-horse, lady's horse' (in contrast to Roß, 'war-horse'), with the earlier variants *pferit* for **pferirit*, OHG. (from the 10th cent.) *pferfrit, pfarifrid;* corresponding to LG. *perid*, Du. *paard*. The word seems to be Franc. and Sax. (in the UpG. dials. the old terms Roß and Gaul are still the prevalent terms; it was probably borrowed (about the 8th cent.?) from the early MidLat. *paraverēdus, parifredus* (*f* for *v* as in Räftg; the change of *v* into *f* in this case, however, is common to Teut.). *Parverēdus,* 'horse,' lit. 'near horse,' is derived from Gr. παρά and MidLat. *verēdus,* 'horse' (allied to Kelt. *rēda*, 'waggon'). In the Kelt. group, W. *gorwydd,* 'steed,' was retained. The Rom. languages retain the MidLat. word (in the MidLat. collateral form *palafrēdus, palafrēnus* in the sense of 'palfrey'; comp. Fr. *palefroi* (E. *palfrey*), Lat. *palafreno*.

Pfelter, see Pate.

Pfifferling, m., 'toadstool,' from MidHG. *pfifferling, pfefferling,* m., 'curry mushroom.'

Pfingsten, plur. 'Whitsuntide,' from MidHG. *pfingsten,* which in form is really a dat. plur. (comp. Mitternacht), and was used at an early period for all cases; OHG. zi **pfingustin,* 'Whitsuntide,' is by chance not recorded (Notker uses a pedantic semiversion, zi *finfchustin*). Formed from Lat. and Gr. πεντεκοστή (Ital. *pentecoste,* Fr. *pentecôte*), lit. 'fiftieth day after Easter'; OSax. *te pincoston,* 'at Whitsuntide,' Du. *pinksteren,* as well as OSlov. *petikostij,* 'Whitsuntide.' While the term Oftern, applied to the Christian passover, was orig. a heathen word, which has been retained in E. and G., in this instance the ecclesiastical name obtained on the Continent, and that probably prior to the OHG. period, as the initial *pf* in MidHG. indicates; it was perhaps introduced through a Goth. medium contemporaneously with

Kirche and Pfaffe. In E., *Whitsunday* (Scand. *hottadagr*) was retained from a very early period, since it was the chief day for baptism, and the newly baptized were wont to wear white garments during that week; hence the G. term 'der weiße Sonntag' (Dominica in Albis). From *quinquagesima,* the frequent rendering in MidLat. of *pentecoste,* are derived MidDu. *sinxen,* OIr. *cincgigais,* 'Whitsuntide.'

Pfinztag, m., 'Thursday,' from Mid HG. *pfinztac;* a word peculiar to Bav.-Austr., based on Goth. **pinta,* equiv. to Gr. πέμπτη (Mod. Gr. πέφτη), 'Thursday.' It seems to have been introduced by Arians with Pfingsten and Samstag (see also Kirche and Pfaffe); comp. OSlov. *petŭkŭ,* 'Friday.'

Pfirsich, m. and f. (*s* after *r* as in Mörser and Hirse; yet Suab. *pfersix*), from the equiv. MidHG. *pfersich,* m., 'peach' (comp. Ital. *pesca,* Fr. *pêche,* whence E. *peach*). Although the word is not recorded until the 12th cent., Lat. *persicum* was naturalised in Germany even prior to the OHG. period (so too in England; comp. AS. *persoc,* as the permutation of the initial *p* to *pf* indicates (comp. Lärche and Pflaume), while Birne was adopted within the latter era. With regard to the gender see Pflaume. With the introduction of horticulture and fruit-growing from the South, numerous names of fruit passed into G.; see Kirsche, Pflaume, and Pfropfen.

Pflanze, f., 'plant, vegetable,' from MidHG. *pflanze,* OHG. *pflanza,* f.; from the equiv. Lat. and Rom *planta* (Fr. *plante,* Ital. *pianta*), whence AS., E., and Du. *plant* (so too Ir. *cland,* W. *plant*). This term was borrowed at the same period as the words mentioned under Pfirsich.

Pflaster, n., 'plaster, pavement,' from MidHG. *pflaster,* OHG. *pflastar,* n., 'plaster, court-plaster, cement, mortar, floor of cement or stones'; borrowed, perhaps contemporaneously with Büchse, in the 8th cent., from Gr.-Lat. ἔμπλαστρον (comp. Ital. *empiastro,* Fr. *emplâtre*), 'plaster,' which in MidLat. also assumed the meaning 'gypsum' (comp. ModFr. *plâtre*), and was shortened to *plastrum;* comp. Ital. *piastrello,* 'small plaster.' In the sense of 'pavement' MidHG. *pflaster* was first used at the end of the MidHG. period. Comp. E. *plaster* and *to emplaster*.

Pflaume, f., from the equiv. MidHG. *pflûme,* f., 'plum'; borrowed, as the permutated initial *pf* from *p* indicates, previous to the OHG. period (see Pfirfich) from Lat. *prūnum*, 'plum,' or rather its plur. *prūna*. The change of gender in names of fruit was made even in the Rom. group, as is shown by the words corresponding to Lat. *cerasum*, *pomum*, *morum*, and *pirum*; see Birne and Kirsche. Hence the late OHG. *pfrūma*, f., 'plum,' in closer connection with the Lat. form, and also *pflūmo*, 'plum-tree.' The *r* of the Lat. word is changed into *l*, as in Lat. *morus*, equiv. to Maulbeerbaum (comp. also Pilgrim, from Lat. *peregrinus*, which has, besides, *m* for Lat. *n*). Numerous MidHG. and Mod HG. dial. forms, as well as the corresponding Du. *pruim*, likewise contain *r*; comp., on the other hand, AS. *plúme*, E. *plum*. The Rom. derivatives of Lat. *prūnum* are Fr. *prune*, Ital. *prugna*, Span. *pruna* (in MidLat. too forms with *l* and *m* occur instead of *r* and *n*; *m*, moreover, appears in South-East Fr. dials.). As to the time when the word was borrowed, see Pfirfich.

pflegen, vb., 'to nurse, cherish, indulge in, be accustomed to,' from MidHG. *pflēgen*, OHG. *pflēgan*, 'to take care of, take a friendly interest in, provide for, protect, carry on, be wont or accustomed to,' OHG. and early MidHG. also 'to promise, stand security for.' It corresponds to OSax. *plēgan*, 'to promise, stand security, be answerable for,' Du. *plegen*, 'to nurse, execute, do, be accustomed'; also to AS. *plëgian*, 'to move on rapidly, play,' E. *to play*. The Prov. and OFr. *plevir*, 'to assure, stand security,' to which no definite Lat. and Rom. original can be assigned, is derived rather from MidEurop. Teut. (OSax. and OHG.) than the reverse. E. *pledge* originated in OFr. *pleige*, MidLat. *plegium*. Although the West Teut. cognates must have existed perhaps as early as the 4th cent., nothing definite can be asserted concerning their origin and their numerous meanings, the base of which seems to be 'to act affectionately for, or in conjunction with, some one'; to this Gr. βλέφαρον, 'eye,' as well as βλέπειν, 'to see' (Aryan root *glegh*?), is perhaps primit. allied. If the cognates have been borrowed, their source cannot be determined; Rom. is out of the question, since it contains no suitable root from which they can be derived. See Pflicht.

Pflicht, f., 'obligation, duty, allegiance,' from MidHG. and OHG. *pflihi*, f., 'friendly care, nursing, intercourse, sympathy, service, obligation'; a verbal abstract from *pflegen*; allied to AS. *pliht*, 'danger,' E. *plight*, as well as AS. *pleón*, 'to risk,' and *pleóh*, 'danger.'

Pfloch, m., from the equiv. late MidHG. *pfloc* (gen. *-ckes*), m., and *pflocke*, m., 'plug, peg'; corresponding to Du. *plug*, vb. and subst., equiv. to the E. vb. and subst. *plug*. The word seems to be unknown to UpG.

pflücken, vb., 'to pluck, gather,' from the equiv. MidHG. *pflücken* (MidG. *pflocken*); OHG. **pfluccben* is by chance not recorded; comp. Du. *plukken*, AS. *pluccian* (AS. **plyccban* may be inferred from MidE. *plicchen*), E. *to pluck*, OIc. *plokka*, 'to pluck' (birds). Since the word is so widely diffused in OTeut. (it is wanting only in UpG.; yet note Swiss *blucke*, 'to pluck,' from the prim. form **bluggōn*) there is absolutely no foundation for supposing that it has been borrowed. If it be assumed that the cognates found their way to the North with the South Europ. culture of the vine in the 2nd or 3rd cent., from Ital. *piluccare*, 'to gather grapes' (Prov. *pelucar*, 'to pluck out,' Fr. *éplucher*), then the early existence of the Rom. word must be more definitely established.

Pflug, m., from the equiv. MidHG. *pfluoc* (gen. *-ges*), m., OHG. *pfluog*, *pfluoh*, m., 'plough'; corresponding to the equiv. Du. *ploeg*, AS. *plóh*, E. *plough*, OIc. *plógr*. These cognates, which were diffused in Teut. at an early period, as may be inferred from the agreement of the dialects, curiously correspond to the Slav. class, Serv. and Russ. *plugŭ* (Lith. *pliugas*), though the normal permutation does not take place in Teut. The Slav. word is probably borrowed from the Teut. original, which was perhaps acquired during the migratory period; comp. Pfad. Teut. *plōgo* also appears in Rhæto-Rom. and in Upper Ital. ; Tyrol. *plof*, Lombard. *piò*. OTeut. likewise contained many terms for 'plough' which afterwards became obsolete; AS. *sulh* (primit. allied to Lat. *sulcus*), Goth. *hóha*, OIc. *arl*, OSax. *erida*.—**Pflugschar**, f., 'ploughshare,' late MidHG. *pfluocschar*, MidE. *plowschare*, E. *ploughshare*; allied like MidHG. *schar*, m. and n., OHG. *scaro*, 'ploughshare,' to scheren.

Pforte, f., 'door, gate, portal,' from the equiv. MidHG. *pforte*, OHG. (Franc.) *pforta*, f.; borrowed in the OHG. period, in the 8th cent., from Lat. *porta*; hence the absence of the permutation of *t* to *z*, which had been accomplished even in the 7th cent. (it is seen in OHG. *pforzih*, MidHG. *pforzich*, from Lat. *porticus*, which was introduced in the 5th or 6th cent. with the Southern art of building in stone; comp. AS. *portič*, E. *porch*). In MidG. and Lower Rhen., in which the permutation of *t* to *z* did not take place until later, we find in the MidHG. period the permutated form *porze*. ModHG. Porte, MidHG. *porte*, OHG. (UpG.) *porta*, is due to a more recent introduction into UpG.

Pfosten, m., 'post, stake,' from Mid HG. *pfoste*, OHG. *pfosto*, m., 'post, beam'; comp. Du. *post*, 'door-post,' AS. and E. *post*; from Lat. *postis*, the dimin. of which, *postellus* (Fr. *poteau*), is preserved in the Rom. languages. The word was borrowed in pre-HG. times contemporaneously with Pfuhl.

Pfote, f., 'paw, claw'; MidHG. **pfôte* is wanting, though Lower Rhen. *pôte*, f., 'paw,' is recorded in the 14th cent.; corresponding to Du. *poot*, 'paw, foot, leg.' The prim. form *pauta* is also indicated by OFr. *poe* and Prov. *paute*, 'paw' (comp. also Fr. *patte*, 'paw, claw'?). Whether the Rom. word is the source of the G. is uncertain; allied also to E. *paw*?. It has not yet been ascertained how the prevalent UpG. terms *dáp*, *dôpe*, 'paw' (MidHG.*tápe*), are related to these cognates.

Pfriem (1.), m., from the equiv. Mid HG. *pfrieme*. m., 'awl'; corresponding to Du. *priem*, 'awl, dagger'; allied to AS. *preón*, 'awl, needle,' E. *preen*, 'tool for carding wool,' OIc. *prjónn*, 'nail, plug.' With regard to the interchange of *n* and *m* comp. Boten, Feim, Pflaume, and Pilgrim.

Pfriem (2.), m., 'broom' (plant), based on Pfriem (1); from MidHG. *pfrimme*, OHG. *pfrimma*, f., 'broom,' with the variant *brimma*, which indicates that the word was borrowed; corresponding to Du. *brem*, 'broom.' The source of the cognates has not yet been discovered.

Pfropfen, m., 'stopper, cork' (first recorded in the last cent.); its form is based on the equiv. LG. *propp*, Du. *prop*, 'plug, cork, stopper'; allied to E. *prop*. The cognates cannot be derived from Lat. *proponere*; they are more probably connected with the following group of words.

pfropfen, vb., 'to plug up, cork,' from MidHG. *pfropfen*, allied to OHG. *pfroffo*, **pfropfo*, 'layer of a vine, slip,' MidHG. *pfropfœre*, 'graft.' OHG. *pfroffo*, *pfropfo*, m., is derived from Lat. *propágo*, m. (for the retention of the nom. form instead of the oblique case see Pfau), 'layer, slip,' whence also Ital. *propaggine*, Fr. *provin*. With regard to the period when the word was borrowed see Pfirfich.

Pfründe, f., 'benefice, living,' from MidHG. *pfrüende*, *pfruonde*, OHG. *pfruonta*, f., 'food, maintenance; espec. the provisions supplied according to agreement; spiritual office and its revenue'; corresponding to the equiv. OSax. *prevenda*, f., Du. *prove*. Borrowed in the 8th cent. from MidLat. *provendu*, a variant of the earlier and more frequent *praebenda* (see Propst), which signified 'cibi ac potus portiones diurnae, quae monachis, canonicis &c. praebentur'; hence Ital. *provenda*, Fr. *provende*, 'store of provisions,' Ital. *prebenda*, Fr. *prébende*, 'prebend.'

Pfuhl, m., 'pool, puddle,' from the equiv. MidHG. and OHG. *pfuol*, m.; corresponding to Du. *poel*, AS. *pól*, E. *pool*. On account of the numerous West Teut. cognates, as well as the difficulties presented by its sound and form, the word cannot have been borrowed at an early period from Lat. *pălus* (acc. *pălŭd-em*). The early history of the Teut. *pôlo-* is obscure.

Pfühl, m. and n., 'bolster, pillow,' from MidHG. *pfülwe*, n., OHG. *pfuliwī*, n., 'feather cushion'; also OHG. *pfulwo*, Mid HG. *pfulwe*, m.; borrowed at the beginning of our era, as is indicated by the invariable permutation of *p* to *pf*, and the retention of the Lat. *v* as *w*, from Lat. *pulvīnus* (*pulvīnar*), 'pillow, cushion, bolster,' probably contemporaneously with Flaum, Kissen, and Pips. Comp. AS. *pyle*, *pylwe*, E. *pillow*, Du. *peuluw*, 'pillow.' The early period at which the West Teut. form *pulwīn* was borrowed is attested by the fact that Lat. *pulvīnus* is not preserved in the Rom. languages.

Pfund, n., from the equiv. MidHG. *pfunt* (gen. *-des*), OHG. *pfunt* (gen. *-tes*), n., 'pound'; corresponding to Goth., OIc., and AS. *pund*, E. *pound*, Du. *pond*, OSax. *pund*. Since the Goth. word coincides with the terms in the other dials., Pfund must be one of the earliest loan-words from Lat.; it passed into Teut. probably at the same period as Münze, about the 2nd cent., from Lat. *pondo* (indecl.), 'pound' (not from *pondus*, 'weight').

pfuſchen, vb., 'to bungle, botch,' Mod HG. only, of obscure origin. Allied to the equiv. Fr. *bousiller*?.

Pfütze, f., 'puddle, slough,' from Mid HG. *pfütze*, f., 'pool, puddle, well,' OHG. (MidG.) *pfuzzi, pfuzza* (UpG.), *buzza*, f.; corresponding to OLG. *putti*, 'well,' Du. *put*, 'well, puddle,' AS. *pytt*, 'well, pit,' E. *pit*. The permutation of LG. *t* to *zz*, and the diffusion of the word throughout West Teut., proves the existence of the cognates in Germany in the 6th or 7th cent.; yet UpG. *buzza* seems to be a recently borrowed term. The word is based on Lat. *puteus*, 'well, cistern,' whence also Ital. *pozzo*, 'draw-well,' *pozza*, 'puddle, pool,' Fr. *puits*, 'well'; likewise OIr. *cuithe*, W. *peten*, 'well.'

Pich, Pick, m., 'grudge, pique,' Mod HG. only; formed from LG. and Du. *pik*, 'grudge, anger, hate,' which is derived from Fr. *pique*, 'pike; grudge, pique' (comp. Ital. *picca*, 'pike, pique'). The HG. word may, however, be borrowed directly from Fr. See Pike.

pichen, vb., prop. LG. equiv. to E. *to pick*, AS. *pican*, 'to pick' (E. *pike* comes from AS. *pīc*).

Pichelhaube, f., 'peaked helmet'; MidHG. (13th cent.) *beckenhūbe* (also *beckelhūbe*), f., 'peaked helmet,' allied to Becken; MidLat. *bacinetum, bacilletum*, 'helmet,' whence also Ital. *bacinetto*, 'flat helmet, morion,' is named from the orig. basin shape of the helmet.

Pichelhering, m., 'merry-andrew, buffoon,' borrowed in the beginning of the 17th cent. from E. *pickle-herring*, a term introduced by the English comedians into Germany.

Picknick, m., 'picnic,' ModHG. only, formed from Fr. *pique-nique*, whence also E. *picnic*. The origin of the word has not yet, however, been definitely established.

piepen, vb., 'to pipe, pip, chirp,' from LG. *piepen*, which, like Lat. *pipare*, is an onomatopoetic form; comp. the equiv. E. *to peep*, Gr. πιππίζω, Fr. *pépier*, Ital. *pipillare*, Lith. *pypti*, Czech *pípati*.

Pilger, m., and in an elevated antiquated style Pilgrim, 'pilgrim,' from Mid HG. *pilgrīn, bilegrīm* (Pilger, from MidHG. *pilgrī*), m., OHG. *piligrim*, m., 'pilgrim,' formed from MidLat. *peregrinus*. From OHG. is derived E. *pilgrim*. The change of Lat. *r* and *n* into HG. *l* and *m* is similar to that in Pflaume; the *l* in this word is found also in Rom.; comp. Fr. *pelerin*, Ital. *pellegrino*, 'pilgrim'; in Italy, and espec. in Rome, the change of meaning from 'foreigner' to 'pilgrim' was easily suggested. The word was borrowed by HG. in the 9th, and by E. in the 12th cent.

Pille, f., from the equiv. MidHG. *pillele*, f., 'pill'; formed from Fr. *pilule*, Lat. *pilula* (Ital. *pillola*).

Pilot, m., 'pilot,' from Fr. *pilote*, probably through the medium of Du. *piloot*; the ultimate source is said to be Gr. πηδόν, 'rudder.'

Pilz, m., 'mushroom, fungus,' from the equiv. MidHG. *bülez* (*bülz*), OHG. *bulīz* (ModHG. *i* for *ü* is UpG. and MidG., as in Stitt); a specifically G. loan-word (comp. LG. *bülte*) from Lat. *bōlētus* (Gr. βωλίτης), 'mushroom'; probably naturalised in G. before the 7th cent., as may be inferred from the permutation of *t* to *z* (for Lat. *t*, represented by OHG. *t* and *z*, comp. Kette and Münze). Its rare occurrence in Rom. (Grisons *bulieu*, Fr. *bolet*, Vosges *bulo*) supports the very early adoption of the word in HG. (comp. Pfühl).

Pimpernelle, f., 'pimpernel,' ModHG. only, formed from Fr. *pimprenelle* (Lat. *pimpinella*); MidHG. has the corrupt forms *bibenelle, bibernelle*.

Pinn, m., 'peg, pin,' from LG. and Du. *pin* (comp. MidE. *pinne*, E. *pin*); from MidLat. and Lat. *pinna*.

Pinsel, m., from the equiv. MidHG. *pensel, bensel* (MidG.), *pinsel*, m., 'painter's brush'; formed from MidLat. *pinsellus* from *penicillus*, 'little tail,' whence also the equiv. Fr. *pinceau*.

Pips, m., 'pip,' a LG. and MidG. form for the earlier ModHG. Pfipf, from Mid HG. and OHG. *pfifflz, pfifflz, pfipflz*, m., 'pip' (horny pellicle on the tip of a fowl's tongue). Borrowed at the beginning of the OHG. period or earlier (perhaps contemporaneously with Flaum and Kiſſen?) from MidLat. *pipita*, whence also Ital. *pipita*, Fr. *pépie*; likewise Du. and E. *pip*. The ultimate source of all the cognates is Lat. *pītuīta*, 'slime, phlegm, pip.' In Henneberg the equiv. Zipf originated in the same prim. word through the intermediate form *tipuita*.

piſſen, vb., first occurs in early Mod HG. from the similarly sounding LG. and

Du. vb.; allied to the equiv. E. *to piss*, Fr. *pisser* (Ital. *pisciare*). The origin of this now widely diffused term cannot be easily determined.

pfachen, vb., 'to plague,' ModHG. only, intensive form of plagen.

Pfachen, m., 'patch, piece,' from MidHG. *placke,* m., 'spot, place, district'; comp. Du. *pluk,* 'spot, blot,' E. dial. *platch* (variant of *patch*). From these G. words, the origin of which is obscure (they can scarcely have originated in Lat. *plaga*), are derived Fr. *plaque, placard,* &c. Perhaps UpG. bletzen, 'to patch,' which has probably lost a guttural before the *tz*, is also connected with these cognates.

Pfage, f., 'plague, calamity,' from MidHG. *pláge,* OHG. *plâga,* f., 'divine punishment'; adopted on the introduction of Christianity during the OHG. period (comp. Pein) from Lat. *plâga*, 'blow, thrust.' From the same source the Rom. cognates, Ital. *piaga,* Fr. *plaie,* 'wound' (E. *plague*), are derived.

Pfan, m., 'plain, plan, project,' from MidHG. *plân,* m. and f., 'open space, plain'; from the equiv. Fr. *plan.*

Pfanke, f., 'plank, board,' from MidHG. *planke, blanke,* f., 'thick board, plank, fortification'; corresponding to Du. and E. *plank;* borrowed in the MidHG. period from the equiv. Rom. and MidLat. *planca;* comp. Fr. *planche,* Ital. (Pied.) *pianca.*

pfappern, vb., ModHG. only, an onomatopoetic form of a lost stem, *blab*, which is also indicated by the equiv. MidHG. *blepzen,* OHG. *blabbizôn,* 'to blab, babble'; allied to ModHG. (dial.) and Du. *blaffen,* 'to bark, yelp,' Alem. *plapen,* E. *to blab.*

plärren, vb., from the equiv. MidHG. *blerren, bléren,* 'to cry, bleat'; an imitation of sound like Du. *blaren,* 'to bleat,' and E. *to blare.*

pfatt, adj., 'flat, level, dull, downright'; in MidHG., only MidG. *blatefuoʒ* and *platehuof,* 'flat foot, sole of the foot,' are recorded. It is most closely connected with Du. (LG.) *plat,* 'plat,' which, like E. dial. *plat-footed* (i.e. *flat-footed*), is derived from Rom., Fr. *plat,* Ital. *piatto.* Their origin is ascribed to Gr. πλατύς. To this **plätten** (Du. *pletten*), 'to flatten, iron (clothes),' is allied, as well as **Pfatte,** f., 'flat, dish' (MidHG. *blate, plate,* signify only 'covering for the breast, baldness'), formed from Du. *plat,* 'flat,' Fr. *plat,* E. *plate.*

Pfalleise, f., 'plaice,' formed from the equiv. Du. *pladijs* (*platdijs*), which is based on MidLat. *platessa;* comp. E. *plaice.*

Pfatz (1.), m., 'place, row, seat, situation,' from MidHG. *plutz,* m., 'open space, place'; formed, like Du. *plaats,* from the Rom. cognates, Ital. *piazza,* Fr. and E. *place,* which are derived from Lat. *platēa* (Gr. πλατεῖα), 'street.' The word seems to have been borrowed towards the end of the 13th cent.

Pfatz (2.), m., 'pancake, fritter'; MidHG. only in MidG. *platzbecke,* 'pastrycook'; allied to platt, or from Pol. *placek,* 'flat cake'?. The word is also current in UpG.

platzen, vb., 'to crash, burst,' from MidHG. *platzen, blatzen,* 'to fall with a noise, strike.' This word and *blesten,* 'to splash,' are derived from an onomat. stem, *blad.* Blatschen and Plätschern, Du. *plassen,* 'to plash' (*plasregen,* equiv. to Platzregen), are intensive forms of plagen.

plaudern, vb., 'to chatter, chat,' from late MidHG. *plûdern,* a variant of *blâderen, blôdern,* 'to rustle, roar'; a recent form in imitation of sound, like Lat. *blaterare,* 'to babble.'

Pfinze, f., 'coiled fritter or pancake'; ModHG. only, an East MidG. word of Slav. origin; comp. Russ. *blin, blince,* 'flat, round cake.'

plötzlich, adv., 'suddenly,' from the equiv. late MidHG. *plozlich* (also earlier ModHG. *plotz* merely); allied to **plotz,* 'sudden blow.' In UpG. the adv. is quite unknown.

Pluderhose, f., 'wide breeches,' first occurs in early ModHG.; origin uncertain.

plump, adj., 'plump, unwieldy, coarse,' ModHG. only, from LG. and Du. *plomp,* 'thick, coarse, blunt' (whence in Swiss *pflumpfig,* with the HG. permutation); from Du. the word seems to have passed into E. and Scand. as *plump.* The term *plump* was orig. an imitation of sound.

Pfunder, m., 'trash, lumber, plunder,' from late MidHG. *plunder, blunder,* m., 'household furniture, clothes, linen,' which is probably a LG. loan-word (MidLG. *plunde,* 'clothing'). Hence **plündern,** 'to plunder,' lit. 'to take away the household furniture' (also Du. *plunderen,* 'to plunder').

Pflüsch, m., 'plush,' ModHG. only, formed from the equiv. Fr. *peluche* (Ital. *peluzzo*).

Pöbel, m., 'populace, rabble,' formed

from Fr. *peuple; povel, pövel, bovel* are found in MidHG. from the 13th cent. (comp. E. *people* in its orig. sense).

pochen, vb., 'to knock, beat,' from Mid HG. *puchen, bochen;* comp. MidLG. *boken,* Du. *pogchen,* 'to boast,' E. *to poke.* The ModHG. vb. is not borrowed from the LG.; comp. Alem. *bochen.* It is derived from a Teut. root *puk, buk.*

Pocke, f., 'pock,' properly a LG. word, unknown in this form to MidHG. and OHG.; comp. the equiv. Du. *pok,* for which we should have expected Pjeche in HG., and in fact the dials. preserve this form. Allied to AS. *pocc,* E. *pock.* The cognates seem to be based on a Teut. root *puh,* 'to swell,' which appears also in AS. *pohha, poca,* E. *poke* and *pocket.*

Pokal, m., 'drinking cup,' first occurs in ModHG. from Ital. *boccale* (Fr. *bocal*), 'beaker, mug,' which with its Rom. cognates is usually traced back to Gr. βαυκάλιον, 'vessel'; comp. Becher.

Pökel, m., 'pickle, brine,' ModHG. only, prop. a LG. word; comp. the equiv. Du. *pekel,* E. *pickle* (see also Pickelhering). Origin obscure; perhaps the cognates are connected with E. *to pick.*

Polei, m., 'penny-royal,' from the equiv. MidHG. and OHG. *polei, pulei,* n.; based on Lat. *pulējum,* 'penny-royal' (whence Ital. *poleggio,* Fr. *pouliot*).

Polster, m. and n., 'cushion, bolster,' from the equiv. MidHG. *polster, bolster,* OHG. *bolstar.* m.; corresp. to Du. *bolster,* AS. and E. *bolster,* and its equiv. OIc. *bólstr.* The cognates are connected with the OTeut. root *belg,* 'to swell,' to which Balg also belongs, hence the orig. sense is 'swelling' (Teut. *bolstra-,* from *bolhstro-*). With the corresponding Sans. root *bṛh,* 'to be great,' Sans. *upabarhaṇa,* 'bolster,' is connected; comp. also Pruss. *pobalso, balsinis,* 'pillow,' Serv. *blazina* (from *bolzina*), 'pillow.'

poltern, vb., 'to make a row, rattle,' from late MidHG. *buldern* (a variant of *bollern*?); allied to the equiv. Ic. *baldrast;* probably an imitation of sound akin to Russ. *boltatĭ,* 'to vibrate,' Lith. *bildeti,* 'to rattle.'

pomadig, adj., 'slowly,' ModHG. only, borrowed from the equiv. Pol. *pomalu.*

Pomeranze, f., 'orange,' adopted in the 15th cent. from the equiv. MidLat. *pomarancia,* a compound of Ital. *pomŏ,* 'apple,' and *arancia,* 'orange'; the latter word and Fr. *orange* are usually derived from Arab. *nârang,* Pers. *nâreng,* and further from Sans. *nâranga,* 'orange.'

Pomp, m., 'pomp, splendour,' first occurs in early ModHG., from Fr. *pompe,* f. (Lat.-Gr. *pompa*).

Popanz, m., 'bugbear,' ModHG. only, from Bohem. *bobak,* 'frightful object.'

Port, m., 'port, harbour,' from the equiv. MidHG. *porte,* f., *port,* m. and n.; borrowed at a late period from Lat. and Rom. *portus* (Ital. *porto,* Fr. *port*), 'port.'

Porzellan, n., 'porcelain,' ModHG. only. "This ware, at first obtained from China and Japan, was introduced into Europe by the Italians; *porcellana* in Ital. orig. denoted a sea-mussel, *concha veneris;* since this bore a great resemblance to porcelain, the name was easily transferred from the one to the other."

Posaune, f., 'trumpet, trombone'; a loan-word, as is indicated by the accent; it is met even during the MidHG. period as *busûne, basûne, bosûne.* On account of the remarkable variant *bustne* the word has been derived from OFr. *buisine,* which, like Ital. *búccina,* 'trumpet,' is based on Lat. *búcĭna.* Comp. further Du. *bazuin,* 'trumpet.'

Posse, f., 'drollery, fun, farce,' first occurs in early ModHG.; corresponding to Du. *poets, pots.* OHG. *gibôsi,* 'tricks, nugae' (comp. böse), cannot be allied to it. In earlier ModHG. Posse also signified the decoration, the accessories in works of art; hence the word has been connected with Fr. *ouvrage à bosse,* 'work in relief' (comp. Ital. *bozzo,* 'rough stone, stone blocks,' *bozzetto,* 'slight sketch'; also E. *bosh*?).

Post, f., 'post, post-office,' first occurs in early ModHG., formed from Ital. *posta* (Fr. *poste*), which is based on MidLat. *posita,* 'standing-place' (for horses?). Similarly ModHG. Posten, 'post, station, item, entry,' is derived from Ital. *posto,* 'place, post,' which again comes from MidLat. *positus,* 'standing-place.'

Pott, m., 'pot,' a LG. word; comp Du. *pot,* E. *pot,* and the equiv. Scand. *pottr.* From the Teut. cognates are derived those of Fr. *pot* and Span. *pote.* The Teut. word is said to be of Kelt. origin; comp. W. *pot,* Gael. *poit.* Topf is not akin.—**Pottasche**, f., equiv. to E. *potash;* hence Fr. *potasse,* Ital. *potassa.*

Pracht, f., 'state, pomp, magnificence,' from MidHG. and OHG. *praht, braht,* m. and f., 'noise, shouting.' The evolution in meaning is similar to that of *hell*; Mid HG. *brëhen*, 'to light, shine,' may also have exercised some influence, as well as ModHG. prangen, the abstract of which could only be a form identical with Pracht. OHG. and OSax. *braht*, 'noise,' like the equiv. AS. *breahtm*, may be traced to a Teut. root *brah*, 'to make a noise.'

prägen, vb., 'to stamp, impress,' from the equiv. MidHG. *præchen, bræchen*, which come from *bráhhjan, a derivative of brechen ?. Akin to MidHG. *bræch*, 'stamp, impression.'

prahlen, vb., 'to parade, vaunt, boast,' from MidHG. *prâlen*, 'to make a noisy parade, shout'; comp. the equiv. Du. *brallen* and *pralen*, as well as E. *to brawl*. Its connection with Fr. *brailler*, 'to bawl,' and W. *bragal*, 'to brag, bawl,' is uncertain.

Prahm, m., 'ferryboat, punt,' ModHG. only, borrowed from LG.; comp. Du. *praam*, 'transport,' Dan. *pram*, OIc. *prâmr*, E. *prame*. The whole of the cognates are derived from Slav.; comp. Slav. *pramŭ*, which is connected with the Aryan root *par*, 'to carry across,' preserved in HG. fahren (OHG. *faran*).

prallen, vb., 'to strike, rebound,' from MidHG. *prellen* (pret. *pralte*), 'to strike violently against, recoil.' Further references are wanting.

prangen, vb., 'to make a parade, display,' from MidHG. *prangen, brangen*, 'to adorn oneself, boast' (comp. Pracht); origin obscure. Its relation to the following word is uncertain.

Pranger, m., from the equiv. MidHG. *pranger, branger*, m., 'stocks, pillory.' It is impossible to regard this word as a euphemistic term connected with prangen, on account of Du. *prang*, 'pressure, oppression,' *prangen*, 'to press, squeeze,' *pranger*, 'iron collar, barnacles, cooper's hook,' E. dial. *prong*, 'fork.' These words show that LG. Pranger (the HG. dials. have Pfranger) is connected with Goth. *praggan*, MidHG. *pfrengen*, 'to crowd, oppress.' The further history of the word is obscure.

prasseln, vb., 'to crackle, rustle,' from the equiv. MidHG. *prasteln, brasteln*, OHG. *brastalôn; comp. the equiv. AS. *brastlian*. These words are connected, like MidHG. *brasten*, OHG. *brastôn*, 'to crack,' with the OHG. str. vb. *brëstan*, MidHG. *brësten*, 'to break.'

prassen, vb., 'to riot, carouse,' Mod HG. only, from Du. *brassen*, 'to gormand-

ise' (akin to *bras*, 'feast'). OIc. *brass*, 'cook,' and *brasa*, 'glowing coal' (comp. OFr. *brese*, Prov. *brasa*), may be connected with it.

predigen, vb., 'to preach,' from the equiv. MidHG. *predigen, bredigen*, OHG. *predigôn, bredigôn (brédión)*; corresponding to OSax. *predigôn*, Du. *prediken*. Borrowed in the OHG. period from the ecclesiastical Lat. and Rom. *prædicâre* (Fr. *prêcher*, whence E. *preach*, Ital. *predicare*), from which OIr. *pridchim*, 'I preach,' is also derived. — Predigt, f., 'sermon'; UpG. Predig; MidHG. *bredige, bredigát*, OHG. *brediga (brédia)* and *bredigunga*.

Preis, m., 'price, cost, prize, reward,' from MidHG. *prîs (brîs)*, m., 'praise, splendour, noble deed'; borrowed in the 12th cent. from OFr. *pris* (ModFr. *prix*), whence also E. *price, prize*, Du. *prijs*. The ultimate source is Lat. *prëtium* (whence also Ital. *prezzo*). The expression preisgeben has nothing to do with this word, but is due rather to the equiv. Ital. *dar presa*; Ital. *presa* (equiv. to Fr. *prise*), 'seizure, booty, catch,' may be traced back to Lat. *præhendere*. Comp. further preisen.

Preiselbeere, f., 'cranberry,' ModHG. only; the dial. variants Preusel:, Praus:, Brausbeere seem to indicate a MidHG. *briuzelbere; their relation to the equiv. Bohem. *brusina, bruslina*, Lith. *brúkné*, Lett. *bruklene* is not quite clear.

preisen, vb., 'to praise, commend,' from MidHG. *prîsen*, wk. vb., 'to assign the prize, praise, extol' (in the 15th cent. it passed over to the str. vbs.); formed from Fr. *priser*, 'to value, estimate' (comp. Ital. *prezzare*, MidLat. *prëtiare*), whence Du. *prijzen*, E. *to praise*. With regard to the period at which the word was borrowed comp. Preis.

prellen, vb., 'to swindle, cheat,' lit. 'to squeeze, push'; prop. identical with Mod HG. prallen, which see.

Presse, f., 'press, pressure, strait, printing-press'; from Fr. *presse*; MidHG. *prësse*, OHG. *prëssa (pfrëssa)*, 'winepress,' is like the equiv. AS. *presse (persa)*, Du. *presse*, an earlier loan-word from MidLat. *pressa*. MidHG. *prësse*, 'crowd, throng,' is connected with the equiv. Fr. *presse*.

Priamel, f., from the equiv. late Mid HG. *preambel, priamel*, 'a short gnomic poem,' which is derived from MidLat. *præambulam*, 'proverb.'

prickeln, vb., 'to prick, goad,' ModHG.

only, prop. a LG. word, of which the strictly HG. variant *pfrecken* is once recorded in late MidHG. Comp. Du. *prikkelen* (*prikken*), 'to prick, stitch,' AS. *prician*, E. *to prick*, and *prickle*, equiv. to Du. *prikkel*; these words are based on an OTeut. root *prik*, which, in spite of the initial *p*, cannot have been borrowed.

Priester, m., 'priest,' from the equiv. MidHG. *priester*, OHG. *priestar* (*préstar*), m.; corresponding to OSax. *prēstar*, Du. *priester* (AS. *preóst*, E. *priest*, OIc. *prest-r*). The cognates were borrowed, at a comparatively late period, from Lat. and Rom. *presbyter* (Gr. πρεσβύτερος), or rather from its shortened variant **préster*, whence also Fr. *prêtre* (OFr. *prestre*), as well as Ital. *prete*, Span. *preste* (likewise OIr. *cruimther*). The orig. sense, 'elder,' was a respectful term applied to the spiritual head of the community (orig. used perhaps only in addressing him); comp. Abt, Papst, and also Herr. The Lat. word was not adopted in OHG. before the 9th cent. (contemporaneously with prebigen).

Prinz, m., 'prince (of the blood),' from MidHG. *prinze*, m., 'prince (sovereign ruler)'; borrowed in the 13th cent. from the equiv. Fr. *prince* (whence also E. *prince*, Ital. *prence*), which is derived from Lat. *princeps*.

Prise, f., 'capture, prize ; pinch (of snuff)'; ModHG. only, from Fr. *prise*.

Pritsche, f., 'bat, racket, wooden sword of a harlequin,' from late MidHG. **britze*, f., which is only implied, however, by the two compounds — *britzelmeister*, ModHG. Pritschelmeister, 'a harlequin carrying a wooden sword with which he directs the order of the game,' and *britzelslahen*, 'blow with the wooden sword.' The meaning 'wooden couch' points to a connection between Pritsche and Brett.

Probe, f., 'proof, trial, test, sample,' from the equiv. late MidHG. *próbe*, f., which is derived from Ital. *proba*, 'proof' (comp. Fr. *épreuve*).

Probst and **Provess**, see Propst.

prophezeien, vb., 'to prophesy,' Mod HG. only, a derivative of MidHG. *prophezîe* (*prophetîe*), f., 'prophecy.' Allied to Mid HG. *prophezieren*, 'to prophesy.'

Propst, m., 'provost,' from MidHG. *probest, brobest*, OHG. *probost, probist* (*provost*), 'superintendent, overseer, provost,' a loan-word from Lat. and Rom. *propositus* (syncopated *propostus*), *præpositus*, whence Ital. *prevosto*, 'provost,' Fr. *prevôt*, 'assistant, provost.' The word was borrowed by OHG. in the 9th cent. Profess is a later loan-word, which, like Du. *provoost*, 'marshal (navy), provost-marshal,' E. *provost*, has assumed different meanings by connection with OFr. *prevost*. AS. *profast* agrees with the G. words in substituting the prefix *pro* for *præ*. Comp. Pfründe.

prüfen, vb., 'to try, examine, prove, test,' from MidHG. *prüeven, brüeven* (pret. *pruofte*), wk. vb., 'to demonstrate, consider, count, test, put right'; this vb., which is of frequent occurrence from the 12th cent., is based on OFr. *prover* (ModFr *prouver*), which is again derived, like Ital. *provare*, from Lat. *probáre*. The abnormal *üe* of the MidHG. vb. comes from East Fr. *üe* (East Fr. *prüeve*, from Lat. *probat*). Comp. Fr. *prouver, éprouve*, E. *proof* (even in AS. *prófian*, 'to demonstrate'). With regard to the treatment of Lat. *ô* in recent loan-words see further Schule.

Prügel, m., 'cudgel,' from late MidHG. *brügel*, m., 'club'; allied to MidHG. *brüge*, 'wooden platform.' The history of the word is obscure.

Prunk, m., 'parade, ostentation,' Mod HG. only, prop. a LG. word. Comp. the equiv. Du. *pronk*, which is perhaps allied to prangen.

Psittich, see Sittich.

Pudel, m., 'poodle, slattern; blunder,' ModHG. only ; of obscure origin.

Puder, m., 'powder, hair-powder,' Mod HG. only, from Fr. *poudre*.

puffen, vb., 'to puff, buffet, cuff,' Mod HG. only, prop. a LG. word; comp. Du. *pof*, 'thrust, blow, credit' (whence ModHG. Puff in the sense of 'credit'), probably allied also to *bobbien, buffen*, 'to strike,' E. *buffet*, subst. and vb. ; *puff* (hence the meaning of Puff, 'puffing of a sleeve'), and *to puff* (AS. *puffan*). "The close proximity of the meanings 'to blow' (inflate) and 'to strike' is not unusual ; Fr. *souffler* and *soufflet* furnish a ready example ; the Rom. languages have the same stem," though it is not necessary to assume that one was borrowed from the other ; the stem *buf* may have originated independently as an imitative form in both groups. Comp. Ital. *buffo*, 'blast of wind,' *buffettare*, 'to snort,' Span. *bofetada*, 'box on the ear.'

Puls, m., 'pulse,' from the equiv. late MidHG. *puls*, m. and f. ; Lat. *pulsus* (akin to *pulsare*, 'to beat'), 'beat' (of the pulse), is shown by Du. *pols*, E. *pulse*, Fr. *pouls*, Ital. *polso*, &c., to be a common term in medicine in the Middle Ages.

Pult, m. and n., 'desk, writing-desk,' from the equiv. late MidHG. *pult*, n., with the older variants *pulpt*, *pulpet*, *pulpit*. A later loan-word from Lat. *pulpitum*, 'wooden platform,' whence also Ital. *pulpito*, 'pulpit,' Fr. *pupitre*, 'desk' (E. *pulpit*).

Pulver, n., 'powder, gunpowder,' from MidHG. *pulver*, m. and n., 'dust, ashes' (also in the 15th cent. 'gunpowder'). From Lat. *pulver* (Fr. *poudre*, Ital. *polvere*).

Pumpe (East MidG. variant *Plumpe*), f., 'pump,' ModHG. only, prop. a LG. word; comp. the equiv. Du. *pomp*, E. *pump*. The further history of the word is obscure.

Puppe, f., 'puppet, doll,' even in late MidHG. *puppe*, *boppe*, from the equiv. Lat. *pupa*, whence also Fr. *poupée*, 'puppet,' *poupon*, 'chubby child' (from which Du. *pop* and E. *puppet* are formed).

pur, adj., 'pure, downright, mere,' ModHG. only, from Lat. *purus*.

purzeln, vb., 'to tumble head over heels.' Alem. *bürzle* seems to suggest that this word is connected with Bürzel.

pusten, vb., 'to blow, puff,' ModHG. only, prop. a LG. word; the strictly HG. forms are seen in MidHG. *pfûsen*, 'to sneeze, snort,' and *pfûsel*, 'catarrh.' Akin to E. *pose*, 'catarrh'?.

Pute, f., 'turkey-hen,' ModHG. only, perhaps a subst. form of the cry of the bird. Its connection with E. *pout* (Turkey-pout) is not clear.

putzen, vb., 'to deck, dress, polish,' from late MidHG. *butzen*, 'to adorn.'

Q.

quabbeln, vb., 'to shake or tremble' (of fat and jelly), ModHG. only, orig. a LG. word, which is usually derived from LG. *quabbel* (Du. *kwabbe*), 'dewlap.'

Quacksalber, m., 'quack'; ModHG. only; orig. a LG. word; corresponding to E. *quack*, Du. *kwakzalver*, a compound of *zalf*, 'salve' (comp. OHG. *salbâri*, 'seller of ointment, physician'). The first part of the compound seems to come from the vb. *quafen* (which see), 'to boast'; hence Quacksalber, 'boasting physician'?.

Quader, m., 'squared stone,' from the equiv. MidHG. *quâder*, m. and n., which is based on Lat. *quâdrum*, 'square,' or rather *quâdrus* (scil. *lapis*), 'square stone.' Comp. Ital. *quadro*, 'square,' Prov. *caire*, 'square stone' (Ital. *quadrello*, Fr. *carreau*).

quaken, vb., 'to quack, croak,' ModHG. only, orig. a LG. word; comp. Du. *kwaken*, 'to croak,' to which *kwakken*, 'to make a noise,' is allied, E. *to quack*. A late onomatopoetic term.

Qual, f., 'torment, pain,' from MidHG. *quâl*, *quâle* (*kâle*), OHG. and OSax. *quâla*, f., 'anguish, torture'; comp. Du. *kwaal*, 'pain,' AS. *cwalu*, 'violent death.' To this word is allied a str. root vb. OHG. *quëlan* (MidHG. *quëln*), 'to be in violent pain' (AS. *cwëlan*, 'to die'), of which the factitive is ModHG. *quälen*, MidHG. *quëln*, OHG. *quellen* (from *qualljan*), 'to torture, torment to death.' The Teut. root *gel* (*qal*) is primit. connected with Lith. *gelti*, 'to prick' (*gélia*, 'it pains'), *gélà*, 'pain,' OSlov. *žalĭ*, 'hurt' (Aryan root *gēl*).

Qualm, m., 'vapour,' ModHG. only, formed from the equiv. LG. and Du. *kwalm*, the early history of which is obscure. It is identical probably with MidHG. *twalm*, 'stupor, faint.'

Quappe, f., 'eel-pout, tadpole,' ModHG. only, from LG. in which the OLG. word *quappa* occurs (comp. Du. *kwab*); the latter is primit. allied to OPruss. *gabawo*, 'toad,' OSlov. *žaba* (from the prim. form *gēba*), 'frog.' The assumption that the word is borrowed from Lat. *capito* is less probable.

Quark, m., 'curds, filth,' from late MidHG. *twarc* (*g*), *quarc* (*zwarc*), 'whey cheese,' which is usually connected with MidHG. *twërn*, 'to turn, stir, mix.' It is more probably related to the equiv. Slav. cognates; comp. Russ. *tvarogŭ*, Pol. *tvarog*. Since Quark first appears in late MidHG., and is unknown to the other Teut. languages, it may be assumed that it was borrowed from Slav. Comp. Quirl.

Quart, n., 'quart, quarto,' from MidHG. *quart*, f. and n., 'fourth part of anything'; formed like Du. *kwart* and E. *quart* from the Rom. cognates, Ital. *quarto*, Fr. *quart*.

Quarz, m., 'quartz,' from the equiv. MidHG. *quarz*; its relation to Du. *kwarts*,

S

E. *quartz*, Ital. *quarzo*, and Fr. *quartz* has not yet been explained.

Quaſt, m., 'tuft, tassel,' from MidHG. *quast* (*queste, koste*), m. and f., 'cluster of leaves, bath-brush' (OHG. *questa*, 'apron of leaves'); comp. Du. *kwast*, 'brush for sprinkling holy water, brush' (Dan. *kost*, 'besom.' akin to OIc. *kvistr*, 'branch').

quecch, adj., 'lively, quick,' from Mid HG. *quëc* (*ck*), OHG. *quëc* (*cch*), 'living, fresh, gay'; for its early history see under the variant *fecḟ*.—**Quechſilber,** n., 'quicksilver,' from the equiv. MidHG. *quëcsilber*, OHG. *quëcsilbar*; an imitation, like Du. *kwikzilver*, E. *quicksilver* (AS. *cwicseolfor*), of the common Rom. *argentum vivum*; comp. Ital. *argento vivo*, Fr. *vif-argent*.

Queche, f., 'quick-grass,' ModHG. only, from LG.; comp. Du. *kweek*, AS. *cwiče*, E. *quitch-, couch-grass*; these words seem to be connected with *quecḟ*, 'living,' as a term for a luxuriant weed. "No plant has more vitality than this species of grass, which is propagated by its root, and therefore is very difficult to extirpate."

Quelle, f., 'spring, source,' first occurs in early ModHG. (naturalised by Luther); a late derivative of the ModHG. str. vb. *quellen*, MidHG. *quëllen*, OHG. *quëllan*. From the variant *kal* (by gradation *qel*), derived from OIc. *kelda*, 'spring' (whence Finn. *kaltio*), and Goth. *kaldiggs, which is implied by OSlov. *kladęzĭ*, 'spring'; likewise AS. *collen*, 'swollen.' The prehistoric root *gel* (*gol*) is related to Sans. *jala*, 'water,' *gal*, 'to curl.'—**quellen,** 'to soak, cause to swell,' is a factitive of OHG. *quël'an*, 'to swell.'

Quendel, m., 'wild thyme,' from the equiv. MidHG. *quëndel*, most frequently *quënel 'konel*), OHG. *quënala* (*chonala*), f.; comp. Du. *kwendel*, AS. *cunele*. It is hardly probable that this is an early loan-word from Lat. *conīla* (Gr. κονίλη), 'thyme,' since the Rom. languages have not preserved the word.

quengeln, vb., 'to be peevish, grumble,'

ModHG. only, an intensive form of ModHG. *twęngen*, 'to press' (with East MidG. *qu* for *tw*); see *zwängen*.

Quentchen, n., 'drachm, dram,' from MidHG. *quëntin* (*quinttn*), 'fourth (orig. perhaps fifth?) part of a Lot(half-an-ounce)'; from MidLat. *quintīnus*, which is wanting in Rom.

quer, adv., 'athwart, crosswise,' from the equiv. MidHG. (MidG.) *twër* (hence *twër*, f., 'diagonal'); for further references see Zwerchs.

Querche, f., see Zwerche.

quelſchen, vb., 'to crush, squeeze,' from the equiv. MidHG. *quętzen* (even yet dial. *quętẓen*), *quętschen*; akin to MidLG. *quattern*, *quettern* (Du. *kwetsen*, borrowed from HG.?).

quiehen, vb., 'to squeak, squeal,' Mod HG. only, a recent onomatopoetic word.

Quirl, m., 'whisk, twirling stick,' from the equiv. MidHG. *twirel*, *twirl*, OHG. *dwiril*, 'stirring stick'; akin to MidHG. *twërn*, OHG. *dwëran*, 'to turn, stir'; allied to the equiv. OIc. subst. *þvara*. With the Teut. root *þwer* (Aryan *twer*), are connected Gr. *τορύνη*, and Lat. *trua*, 'stirring spoon.' It is doubtful whether Quarl is allied.

quitt, adj., 'quit, rid,' from MidHG. *quit*, 'released, unencumbered, free'; borrowed about 1200 A.D. from the equiv. Fr. *quitte*, whence also Du. *kwijt*, E. *quit* (also E. *quite*); Fr. *quitte* and *quitter*, 'to let go, forsake,' are derived from Lat. *quietare*.

Quitte, f., 'quince,' from the equiv. MidHG. *quiten*, f. (OHG. *quitina is wanting), with the remarkable variant *kiiten*, from OHG. *chutina* (Swiss *χütene*), 'quince.' This latter form alone renders it possible that Quitte was borrowed from the equiv. Rom. *cotōneu*, which is probably represented by Ital. *cotogna* and Fr. *coing* (whence E. *quince* and Du. *kwee*). The connection between Lat. *cotōnea* (parallel form *cottanum*) and Gr. *κυδώνεα* is obscure, and so is the relation of OHG. *quitina to *chutina*. If the word was borrowed, it was introduced contemporaneously with Pflaume.

R.

Rabe, m., 'raven,' from the equiv. Mid HG. *rabe* (*rappe*), OHG. *rabo* (*rappo), m., also MidHG. *raben*, OHG. *raban, hraban,* and MidHG. *ram* (*mm*), OHG. *ram, hram* (with *mm* for *mn*), m., 'raven'; all these

forms point to Goth. *hrabns. Comp. OIc. *hrafn*, AS. *hræfn*, m., E. *raven*, Du. *raaf*, *rave* (comp. Rappe). The proper names *Wolf-ram*, OHG. *Hraban*, and ModHG. *Rapp* preserve the old variants. Perhaps these cognates with Lat. *corvus*, Gr. κόραξ, 'raven,' Lat. *cornix*, and Gr. κορώνη, 'crow,' belong to the same root; yet the Teut. form has a peculiar structure of its own, which, contrary to the usual assumption, presents some difficulties.

Rache, f., 'revenge, vengeance,' from MidHG. *râche*, OHG. *râhha*, f.; allied to râchen.

Rachen, m., 'throat, jaws, abyss,' from the equiv. MidHG. *rache*, OHG. *rahho*, m., for the earlier *hrahho; comp. AS. *hracu*, m., 'throat,' perhaps also AS. *hracca*, 'back of the head, nape,' E. *rack*, 'neck of mutton'; also Du. *raak*, 'back part of the palate, inner parts of the mouth.' Further references for determining the origin of the word are wanting; no relation to Rragen is possible.

rächen, vb., 'to revenge, avenge,' from MidHG. *rëchen*, OHG. *rëhhan*, older *wrëhhan, 'to revenge, obtain satisfaction for some one'; corresponding to Goth. *wrikan*, 'to persecute,' *gawrikan*, 'to avenge,' AS. *wrëcan*, 'to drive out, revenge, chastise,' E. *to wreak*, to which *wreak* is akin, Du. *wreken*, 'to revenge,' and *wraak*, *wrake*, f., 'revenge,' OSax. *wrekan*, 'to chastise.' The Teut. root *wrek* (comp. also Rache, Recke, Wraf) with the prim. meaning 'to pursue, or rather expel, especially with the idea of punishment,' is derived from a pre-Teut. *wreg*, *wery*. It is usually compared with Lat. *urgeo*, 'I oppress,' Sans. root *vrj*, 'to turn away,' Gr. εἴργω, 'to enclose,' OSlov. *vragŭ*, 'enemy,' Lith. *vàrgus*, 'distress' (*várgti*, 'to be in want'), which imply an Aryan root *werg*, *wreg*.

Racher, m., 'slayer, hangman's servant,' ModHG. only; comp. Du. *rakker*, 'beadle, hangman.' Lessing suggested that it was allied to recten, 'to put to the rack.' It is now usually connected with LG. *racken*, 'to sweep together,' and MidLG. *racker*, 'flayer, knacker, nightman.'

Rad, n., 'wheel,' from the equiv. MidHG. *rat* (gen. *rades*), OHG. *rad*, n.; corresponding to LG. and Du. *rad* (comp. also OFris. *reth*). The word is confined to Mid Europ. Teut.; it is wanting in E., Scand., and Goth.; this, however, is no reason for assuming that the word is borrowed from Lat. *rota*. Since OHG. *rad* is based on pre-Teut. *rotho-m*, *rothos*, n. (Goth. **raþa-*), 'wheel,' it is primit. cognate with the equiv. OIr. *roth*, m., and Lat. *rota*, and likewise with Lith. *rátas*, 'wheel.' The corresponding Sans. *ratha-s* (*rathas*, n. in *ráthas-páti*) signifies 'car,' espec. 'war chariot' (for the root *roth* see under rasch), while Sans. *cakra*, Gr. κύκλος, corresponding to AS. *hweol*, E. *wheel*, also means 'wheel' in Aryan.—**radebrechen**, vb., from the equiv. Mid HG. *radebrechen*, 'to break on the wheel, mangle,' akin to Du. *radbraken*, 'to mutilate, mangle, murder a language.' See Achse, Künie, Wagen.

Rädelsführer, m., 'ringleader,' ModHG. only, allied to Bav. Rädel (dimin. of Rad), 'small circle of persons, ranks, dancing-song'; as to the evolution of meaning comp. E. *ringleader*, allied to *ring*.

Raden, m., 'cockle-weed,' from Mid HG. *râde*, usually *râte*, *ratte*, *râten*, *ratten*, m., 'a weed among corn,' OHG. *râto*, *ratto*, m.; so too OLG. *râda*, f., 'weed.' In Franc. and Henneberg *râdne* occurs, in Swiss and Suab. *ratte*. Perhaps the numerous forms of this simply MidEurop. Teut. word point to a primit. G. *râpwo-* (prim. form *rétwo-*). Cognate terms in the non-Teut. languages have not yet been discovered.

Räder, m., also **Rädel**, 'sieve,' allied to MidHG. *rëden*, OHG. *rëdan*, 'to sift, winnow.' The Teut. stem is probably *hreþ-*, hence the word may be related to Lith. *krétalas*, 'sieve,' *kreczù*, 'to shake'; allied also perhaps to Lat. *cer-nere*, 'to sift' (*creteus*, 'sifted').

raffen, vb., 'to snatch, carry off suddenly,' from MidHG. *raffen*, OHG. *raffôn (by chance not recorded), 'to pluck, pull out, snatch away'; corresponding to LG. and Du. *rapen*, 'to gather hastily.' E. *to raff* is derived from Fr. *raffer*, which, like Ital. *arraffare*, is borrowed from HG.; on the other hand, E. *to rap* is primit. allied to HG. raffen. MidHG. *raspôn* (for *rafspôn*), MidHG. *raspen*, 'to collect hastily,' and Ital. *arrappare*, 'to carry off,' are also connected with the Teut. root *hrap*.

ragen, vb., 'to project, stand forth,' from MidHG. *ragen* (OHG. *hragen*?), 'to project, become rigid, be prominent'; allied to MidHG. *rac*, adj., 'tense, stiff, astir'; also to AS. *oferhragian*, 'to tower above'; see Rahe and regen.

Rahe, f., also **Raa** (under LG. and Du. influence), 'yard' (of a ship), from MidHG. *rahe*, f., 'pole'; corresponding to Du. *ra*, 'sail-yard,' OIc. *rá*, f., 'sail-yard' (Goth. *rāha, f., 'pole'). Rahe is native, both to UpG. and LG.; comp. Bav. *raχe*, 'pole.'

Rahm, m., 'cream, crust of mould or mildew,' from the equiv. MidHG. *roum*, m.; comp. Du. *room*, AS. *reám* (earlier ModE. *ream*), OIc. *rjóme*, 'cream.' The *d* of the ModHG. form compared with OHG. *roum (Thuring. *roum*) is dialectal (comp. MidHG. *strâm* and *stroum* under Strom). The origin of these cognates has not yet been discovered.

Rahmen, m., 'frame, border,' from MidHG. *ram, rame*, m. and f., 'prop, framework, frame for embroidery or weaving,' OHG. *rama*, 'pillar, prop'; comp. Du. *roum*, 'frame.' Allied probably to Goth. *hramjan*, 'to crucify,' lit. 'to fasten to a pillar or prop'(?), which may, however, be cognate with Gr. κρεμάννυμι. Rahmen, prop. 'setting,' is usually connected with OSlov. *kroma*, f., 'border.'

Raigras, n., ModHG. only, from the equiv. E. *ray-grass*, or rather from its phonetic variant *rye-grass*.

Rain, m., 'strip or belt of grass as a dividing line between fields, ridge,' from MidHG. and OHG. *rein*, m., 'ridge' (as a line of division between fields); corresponding to LG. *reen*, 'field boundary,' OIc. *rein*, f., 'strip of land.' Perhaps cognate with Sans. *rékhâ*, f., 'row, line, strip.'

Ralle, f., 'corncrake,' ModHG. only, from Fr. *râle*, whence also E. *rail*.

Ramme, f., from the equiv. MidHG. (MidG.) *ramme*, f., 'rammer, pile-driver,' prop. identical with MidHG. *ram* (gen. *rammes*), m., 'ram,' OHG. *ram, rammo*, m., 'ram' (comp. Bock, Rahn); corresponding to Du. *ram*, 'ram, battering-ram,' AS. *ramm*, E. *ram*. No connection with Gr. ἀρήν is possible; it is more probably allied to OIc. *ramr, rammr*, 'strong, sharp, powerful.' See the following word.

rammeln, vb., 'to buck, rut, ram, force in,' from MidHG. *rammeln*, OHG. *rammalón*, 'to rut'; akin to Rammler, 'buck rabbit,' from MidHG. *rammeler*, 'ram during the rutting season.' A derivative of the cognates discussed under Ramme.

Rampe, f., 'sloping terrace,' ModHG. only from, Fr. *rampe*.

Rand, m., 'rim, border, brink,' from MidHG. *rant* (gen. *randes*), m., OHG. *rant* (gen. *rantes*), m., 'boss of a shield,' then 'rim of a shield,' and finally 'rim' (generally); so too Du. *rand*, 'edge, rim,' AS. *rond*, n., 'rim of a shield, shield, rim,' E. *rand*, OIc. *rǫnd* (for *randô-*), 'shield, rim of a shield.' Goth. *randa, 'rim,' is also implied by Span. *randa*, 'lace on clothes.' Pre-Teut. *ram-tâ points to a root *rem* (AS. *ríma, reoma*, 'rim'), the *m* of which before *d* would be necessarily changed to *n* (see hundert, Sand, Sund, and Schande). From the same prim. form is derived the modern dial. term Ranft for Rand; comp. OHG. *ramft* (with an excrescent *f* as in Kunft? yet comp. the equiv. OSlov. *rabŭ* and Lith. *rŭmbas*), m., 'rim, rind, border,' MidHG. *ranft*, m., 'frame, rim, rind.' Rinde also belongs probably to the same stem.

Rang, m., 'rank, order, row,' ModHG. only, from Fr. *rang* (whence also Du. *rang*, E. *rank*), which again is derived from G. Ring, OHG. *ring, hring*.

Range, m., 'dissolute youth,' first occurs in early ModHG. Allied to ringen.

Ranft, plur. Ränfte, m., 'winding, intrigue, wile,' from MidHG. *ranc* (*k*), m., 'rapid winding or movement'; corresponding to AS. *wrenc*, 'bend, cunning, plot,' E. *wrench*. See renfen.—**Ranke**, f., 'tendril, creeper,' ModHG. only, from MidHG. *ranken*, 'to move to and fro, extend, stretch.' See renfen.—**Rankhorn**, n., from the equiv. MidHG. *rankorn, rankhorn*, n., 'quinsy (in pigs)'; allied to Du. *wrong*, which is used of the diseases of cows. Whether it belongs, by inference from the Du. word, to the pre-Teut. root *wrank* (see renfen), is uncertain.

Ranzen, m., 'belly, knapsack, satchel,' from MidHG. *rans*, m., 'belly, paunch.' Comp. Du. *ranzel*, 'knapsack.'

ranzen, vb., 'to speak rudely or harshly to,' ModHG. only, probably for *ranfzen, allied to MidHG. *ranken*, 'to bray.' Scarcely cognate with E. *to rant*.

ranzig, adj., 'rancid, fetid,' ModHG. only, from the equiv. Fr. *rance* (Lat. *rancidus*), like, or through the medium of, Du. *rans*, 'rotten, rancid.'

Rapp, m., 'grape-stalk,' from the equiv. MidHG. *rappe, rape*, m., borrowed from the equiv. Fr. *râpe* (comp. Ital. *raspo*), whence also the equiv. E. *rape*.

Rappe (1.), m., 'black horse,' ModHG. only in this sense, which is a figurative use of MidHG. *rappe*, 'raven,' the variant of MidHG. *rabe* (Alem. *rap*, 'raven'). OHG. *rappo is wanting; it would be related to *rabo* like *knappo, 'squire,' to *knabo*, 'boy.' See Rappen.

Rappe (2.), f., 'malanders,' from MidHG. *rappe, rapfe*, f., 'itch, scab'; allied to Du. *rappig*, 'scabby.' The root is seen in

OHG. *rapfen*, 'to harden (of wounds), form a scab,' and in *räffi*. From HG. the equiv. Fr. *râpes*, pl., is formed.

Rappe (3.), f., 'rasp,' ModHG. only, from the equiv. Fr. *râpe*, which again corresponds to OHG. *raspôn*, 'to sweep off,' MidHG. *raspeln*. See raffen, Rupp, and Raspe.

rappeln, vb., 'to rattle,' ModHG. only, from LG.; the correct MidHG. form is *raffeln*, 'to bluster, clatter'; allied to E. *to rap*, MidE. *rappien*.—In the sense of 'to be crack-brained, rave,' rappeln may be derived from the meaning 'to bustle'; it is usually connected, however, with MidHG. (MidG.) *rëben*, 'to dream, be confused,' which is derived from Fr. *rêver*, whence also E. *to rave*.

Rappen, m., 'centime,' from MidHG. *rappe*, m., 'the name of a coin first made in Freiburg in Baden, and stamped with the head of a raven, the Freiburg coat of arms.' See krappen and Rappe (1).

Rapier, m. and n., first occurs in early ModHG., from Fr. *rapier*, whence also the equiv. E. *rapier* and Du. *rapier*. The Fr. word is generally regarded as Teut. and derived from *râpe*. See Rappe (3).

Rappufe, f., 'common prey, scramble,' from late MidHG. *rabusch*, m., 'tally,' which is again derived from the equiv. Bohem. *rabuše*.

Raps, m., 'rape-seed,' ModHG. only, from Lat. *rapicium*. See Rübe.

rapfen, vb., 'to sweep off,' intensive of raffen. LG. *rapen*.

Rapunzel, m., 'rampion, corn-salad,' ModHG. only, not from Lat. *rapunculus*, but rather an extended form from MidLat. *rapunciun* (Fr. *raiponce*, comp. Du. *rapunsje*), whence also Ital. *ramponzolo*; comp. further E. *rampion*. Allied to Lat. *rapa* (see Rübe).

rar, adj., ModHG. only, from Fr. *rare* (Lat. *rarus*), whence also Du. *raar*, E. *rare*.

Rafch, m., 'arras, serge,' ModHG. only, from the equiv. Du. *ras* (E. *arras*). In late MidHG. *arraz*, *arras*, 'light woollen fabric, serge,' which was named from Arras, a town in the north of France.

rafch, adj., 'impetuous, speedy, swift, rash,' from MidHG. *rasch*, OHG. *rasc*, adj., 'quick, prompt, skilful, powerful,' of which the equiv. variants MidHG. and OHG. *rosch*, and MidHG. *resch*, *risch*, occur. Corresponding to E. *rash*, Du. *rasch*; OIc. *rǫskr* (Goth. *rasqs*), 'brave.' The final dental of the root has disappeared before the suffix *sqa*, *ska* (*rasqa- for *rat-sqa*); comp. OHG. *rado*, AS. *ræde*, 'quick.' Comp. also OIc. *horskr*, AS. *horsc*, 'quick, clever,' with AS. *hrædlîc*, 'quick.' The Teut. root *rap*, Aryan *rot* (*roth*), in OHG. *rado*, 'quick,' may have meant 'to hasten'; it appears also in ModHG. Rab.

rafcheln, vb., 'to rustle, rattle,' ModHG. only, probably a derivative of rafch, like OHG. *rascezzen*, 'to sob, emit sparks,' because of the successive short and lively movements. Comp. AS. *ræscetung*, 'sparkling.'

Rafen, m., from the equiv. late Mid HG. *rase*, m., 'turf, sward'; comp. MidLG. *wrase*, LG. *frasen*. The word is wanting in the other dials. (Goth. **wrasa* may perhaps be assumed); in UpG. Wafen, which is primit. cognate with the primary form *wrasa*.

rafen, vb., 'to rave, rage,' from Mid HG. *rasen* (rare), 'to storm, rave'; corresponding to LG. *rasen*, Du. *razen*. It is usually thought that the word was borrowed from LG., since it is not found in HG. till the end of the 13th cent. Allied to AS. *ràsettan*, 'to rave,' *rǽsan*, 'to make a violent attack,' *ræs*, 'attack, charge' (comp. E. *race*), OIc. *rás*, 'race, running,' and *rasa*, 'to rush headlong.'

Rafpe, f., 'rasp,' ModHG. only, from Fr. *raspe* (now *râpe*), hence prop. identical with Rappe (3).

Rafpel, f., 'large rough file, rasp,' Mod HG. only, a derivative of the preceding; comp. E. *rasp*, *rasper*. As to the ultimate connection of the cognates with OHG. *raspôn*, 'to scrape together,' comp. Rappe (3).

Raffe, f., 'race, breed,' borrowed in the 18th cent. from Fr. *race*, which is recorded as early as the 16th cent., at which period the E. word *race* was also borrowed; the Fr. term and its Rom. cognates (Ital. *razza* is met with even in the 14th cent.) are derived from OHG. *reitza*, *reizza*, f., 'line.'

raffeln, vb., 'to rattle, clatter,' from MidHG. *razzeln* (from *razzen*), 'to bluster, rave,' but based in meaning on LG. *rateln*, 'to clatter'; comp. MidHG. *ratzen*, 'to rattle,' Du. *rateln*, 'to clatter, chatter,' *ratel*, 'rattle, clapper,' AS. *hrætele*, E. *rattle*. The Teut. root *hrat* appearing in these words is connected with Gr. κραδαίνω, 'I swing.'

Raft, f., 'rest, repose,' from MidHG. *rast*, *raste*, f., OHG. *rasta*, f., 'repose, rest, permanence,' also in OHG. and MidHG.

'stage of a journey,' which is the only sense borne by Goth. *rasta* and OIc. *rǫst*. Comp. AS. *ræst*, E. *rest*, OSax. *rasta*, *resta*, 'couch, deathbed,' Du. *rust* (see Rüste), 'rest, repose.' The common Teut. word is based on a root *ras*, 'to remain, dwell,' which may also be inferred from Goth. *razn* and OIc. *rann*, 'house.' Rast, in the sense of 'stage,' comes from the period when the Western Aryans were migrating to Europe; only a wandering tribe could adopt the intervals of reposing and encamping as a measure of distances. Moreover, the older language preserves a few other words as relics of the migratory period; comp. MidHG. *tageweide*, f., 'day's journey, the distance traversed in a day' (prop. said of nomadic marches, 'the length of pasture grazed by cattle in one day'); see Hanf. Whether the assumed root *ras*, 'to remain, dwell,' is connected with the root *rô* in Ruhe is doubtful.

Rat, m., 'counsel, advice, deliberation, council,' from MidHG. and OHG. *rât* (gen. *râtes*), m., 'counsel, means at hand, store of provisions'; these meanings are still partly preserved by ModHG. Gerät, Vorrat, Hausrat, Unrat. A verbal abstract of ModHG. raten, MidHG. *râten*, OHG. *râtan*, 'to advise'; comp. the equiv. Goth. *rêdan*, OIc. *râða*, AS. *rǽdan* (to which E. *to read* is akin?), OSax. *râdan*. Some etymologists have connected the common Teut. *rêdan*, 'to advise,' with Lat. *reor*, 'to suppose'; in that case the dental of the Teut. verb is prop. only part of the pres. stem, which was afterwards joined to the root. Others with equal reason have referred to the Sans. root *râdh*, 'to carry out a project, put to rights, obtain; to appease,' and to Sans. *râdíti*, 'to feel solicitous, trouble oneself about.'—**ratschlagen**, vb., 'to deliberate,' from the equiv. late MidHG. *râtslagen*, the origin of which is obscure. See Rätsel.

Ratsche, f., 'rattle, clapper,' ModHG. only, allied to MidHG. *rutzen*, 'to clatter'; see rasseln.

Rätsel, n., 'riddle, perplexity,' from the equiv. MidHG. *râtsal*, *rætsel*, n., OHG. *râtisal, n.; comp. OLG. *râdisli*, MidLG. *rêdelse*, Du. *raadsel*, AS. *rǽdels* (for *rǽdesl), m., whence the equiv. E. *riddle*, the *s* of the AS. word being regarded as a sign of the plur. The formation of the subst. from raten corresponds to that of Mühsal from müßen, of Labsal from laben, and of Trübsal from trüben. The notion 'riddle' was current among the Teutons from early times; the Goth. term was *frisahts*; in OHG. we find *tuncal*, n., and *râtussa*, *râtissa*, f., 'riddle.'

Ratle, f., from the equiv. MidHG. *ratte*, *rate*, f., *rat*, *rate*, m., OHG. *rato*, m., *ratta*, f., 'rat' (in MidHG. there also appears another variant *ratz*, *ratze*, m., whence Bav. and Swiss Ratze). It corresponds to OLG. *ratta*, f., Du. *rat*, *rot*, m., AS. *rǽtt* (?), E. *rat*, Dan. *rotte*. Besides these are found the Rom. words Fr. *rat*, Ital. *ratto*, and also Gael. *radan*. The origin of all these cognates is unknown. The Rom. class has been derived from Lat. *raptus*, *rapidus*; in that case Ital. *ratto*, 'quick, nimble,' would be the primary meaning. The phonetic relations of the Teut. words are not sufficiently clear to pronounce a decided opinion (comp. Ratze).

Raub, m., 'robbery, spoil,' from the equiv. MidHG. *roup* (gen. *roubes*), m., OHG. *roub*, m.; comp. OSax. *rêf* in *nôdrôf*, 'violent wresting,' Du. *roof*, m., 'robbery,' AS. *reáf*, n., 'robbery, booty,' allied to AS. *reófan*, 'to break, rend,' OIc. *rjúfa*, str. vb., 'to break, rend' (espec. used of a breach of contract); these are further connected with Lat. *rumpo* (Aryan root *rup*); comp. the Sans. root *lup*, 'to shatter.' Hence Raub seems to mean lit. 'breach of contract.'?—**rauben**, vb., 'to rob, plunder,' from Mid HG. *rouben*, OHG. *roubôn*; OSax. *rôbôn*, AS. *reáfian*, whence E. *to reave* (the AS. subst. *reáf* has become obsolete in E.), Goth. *biraubôn*, 'to plunder, despoil.' The Teut. cognates passed with two distinct meanings into Rom.; comp. on the one hand Ital. *ruba*, 'robbery,' *rubare*, 'to rob,' Fr. *dérober*, 'to steal,' and on the other Ital. *roba*, 'coat, dress,' Fr. *robe*. The latter are connected with Raub, since by inference from OHG. *roub* and AS. *reáf*, 'robbery, booty, armour, dress,' the OTeut. word had probably acquired the meanings of 'garments got by plundering, dress (generally).' See also raufen.

Rauch, m., from the equiv. MidHG. *rouch*, OHG. *rauh* (*hh`*, m., 'smoke, steam'; corresponding to OSax. *rôk*, m., Du. *rook*, AS. *réc* (from Goth. **rauki-*), m., E. *reek*, OIc. *reykr*, m., 'smoke'; Goth. *rauks (*rauki-*) is by chance not recorded. The common Teut. is connected by gradation with the Teut. root *rûk*, 'to smoke.' See riechen.

rauch, adj., 'rough, hairy'; equiv. to

rauh; Rauchwerf, 'furs, skins' (MidHG. rûchwêrc) contains ModHG. rauh, 'hairy, covered with hair'; Rauchhandel (ModHG. only), 'trade in furs, furred skins.'

Räude, f., from the equiv. MidHG. riude, rûde, f., OHG. rûda, f., 'scab, mange, scabies,' for an earlier *hrûda, since it is allied to OIc. hrûðr, m., 'scab of a wound'; comp. Du. ruit, 'scab, itch.'—räudig, 'scabby, mangy,' from MidHG. riudec, OHG. riudig, older rûdig, 'scabiosus.' Perhaps OHG. rû-da (from the Teut. root hrû) is connected with Lat. cruor, 'gore,' crû-dus, 'bloody, raw,' to which AS. hrûm, 'soot,' is probably akin.

raufen, vb., 'to pluck, pull out,' from the equiv. MidHG. and OHG. roufen (Mid HG. also rôufen); corresponding to Goth. raupjan, 'to tear out, pluck off.' A Teut. root raup (see rupfen) has not yet been found elsewhere; it is, however, probably connected with the Aryan root rup, 'to break' (see Raub).—Raufe, f., 'rack' (for fodder), from late MidHG. roufe, f.; derived from raufen, just as MidLG. roepe from roepen; but in what way is it connected with Du. ruif, 'rack,' ruiffel, 'wrinkle'?

Raugraf, m., 'Raugrave,' from Mid HG. rû-grâve, m., a title like MidHG. wilt-grâve; prop. perhaps 'Count in a rough or uncultivated country'; from rauh.

rauh, adj., 'rough, harsh, coarse,' from MidHG. rûch (infl. rûher), OHG. rûh (infl. rûhêr), adj., 'rough, shaggy, bristly'; comp. MidDu. ruch, ModDu. ruig, ruw, 'rough,' AS. rûh, E. rough. Goth. *rûhs, rûhws, are wanting. Perhaps primit. allied to Lith. raũkas, 'wrinkle,' rùkti, 'to become wrinkled.' The compound Rauchwerf, 'furs, skins,' preserves normally the uninflected form of MidHG. rûch. See rauch.

Rauke, f., 'rocket,' ModHG. only, from Lat. erûca, 'a sort of colewort,' whence also Ital. ruca, ruchetta, Fr. roquette (E. rocket).

Raum, m., from the equiv. MidHG. and OHG. rûm (MidHG. rân), m., 'room, space'; corresponding to OSax., m., rûm, m., Du. ruim, AS. rûm, m., E. room, Goth. rûm, n., OIc. rûm, n., 'room, open space, bed, seat.' The common Teut. subst. originated in the adj. rûma-, 'spacious'; comp. Goth. rûms, MidHG. rûm and gerûm, Mod HG. geraum, Du. ruim, AS. rûm, 'spacious.' The root is usually considered to be rû, and the class connected with Lat. rû-s (gen. rû-ris), 'country,' and Zend ravanh, 'space, distance.'

raumen, see anberaumen.

raunen, vb., from the equiv. MidHG. rûnen, OHG. rûnên, 'to whisper, to utter in a low, soft tone,' allied to MidHG. rûne, f., 'whisper, secret conference.' Corresponding to OLG. rûnôn, AS. rûnian, E. to roun (round), also AS. rûn, f., 'secret deliberation, secret,' Goth. rûna, f. (see Alraune), 'secret, secret resolution'; OIc. rûn, f., 'secret, rune.' It has also been compared further with the cognates, Gr. ἐρευνάω, 'to search, track,' as well as with OIr. rûn, 'secret.' ModHG. Rune, f. (AS. rûnstafas, 'secret characters, runes'), was introduced from the Scand. dials. by the literary movement for the promotion of Teut. studies in the last cent.

Raupe (1.), f., 'caterpillar,' from Mid HG. rûpe, rûppe, OHG. rûpa, rûppa, f., 'larvæ of insects, caterpillar.' In Suab. and Bav. (partly also in Swiss) the word is wanting, the term used being Graswurm, in OHG. grasawurm (yet in Suab. ruopen, 'to clear the trees of caterpillars,' with an abnormal û for û); in Swiss roup, which probably originated in the written language (in Henneberg abnormally roppe).

Raupe (2.) in Rasraupe is an entirely different word; see the latter.

Rausch (1.), m., 'cranberry,' from Mid HG. rûsch, rusch, f., 'rush,' from Lat. ruscum, whence also Du. rusch, m., 'rush,' AS. rysce, f., E. rush; see Risch and Rush.

Rausch (2.), m., 'carouse, rush, roar,' ModHG. only (corresponding in MidHG. to rûsch, m., 'onset, attack'; see rauschen); its relation to LG. roes, 'intoxication,' E. rouse, OIc. rûss, 'drunkenness,' is still obscure. The ModHG. word has certainly been borrowed.

rauschen, vb., 'to rustle, roar, be excited,' from MidHG. rûschen (riuschen), 'rustle, roar, swell, hurry along'; corresponding to Du. ruischen, 'to rustle,' E. to rush (MidE. ruschen).

Rauschgelb, n., 'red sulphuret of arsenic,' first occurs in early ModHG., corresponding to Du. rusgeel; earlier ModHG. also Ruß, Roßgelb; allied to Rom. and Lat. russus (Ital. rosso), 'red.'

räuspern, vb., 'to hawk, clear the throat,' from the equiv. MidHG. riuspern (riustern). This verb, which is not recorded prior to MidHG., belongs to a root frequently occurring in Teut., rûk (Aryan *räg*), 'to belch, eructate,' the *k* disappearing before the suffix *sp, st;* comp. AS. *roccettan*, 'to belch,' OHG. *itarucchen*, MidHG. *itrücken*, AS. *edorcan (eodorcan)*, 'to chew the cud.' Comp. Lat. *ē-rūgere*, 'to spit out,' *rūminare* (for *rūgminare*), 'to chew the cud,' and *ructare*, 'to belch,' Gr. ἐρεύγεω, 'to spit out,' ἐρυγή, f., 'vomiting,' OSlov. *rygati sę*, 'to belch,' Lith. *atrūgas*, f. pl., 'rising of the stomach.'

Raute (1.), f., 'rue,' from the equiv. MidHG. *rūte*, OHG. *rūta*, f. This, like the equiv. Du. *ruit*, is usually considered to be borrowed from Lat. *rūta* (comp. Ital. *ruta*); yet AS. *rūde*, 'rue,' might prove that the G. word is cognate with Lat. *rūta*. E. *rue*, from Fr. *rue*.

Raute (2.), f., 'quadrangle, square,' from MidHG. *rūte*, f., 'lozenge in heraldry, pane' (hence Du. *ruit*, 'square'). As to OHG. *rūta* for *hrūta*, equiv. to Aryan *krūtā, klrātā*, see vier.

Rebe, f., 'vine, vine-branch,' from MidHG. *rëbe*, OHG. *rëba*, f., MidHG. *rëbe*, OHG. *rëbo*, m., 'vine, tendril, creeper' (comp. Weinrebe); corresponding words are wanting in the other dials. OHG. has a remarkable form, *hirnirëba*, 'skull,' lit. perhaps 'entwining the brain'; hence with this word is connected the common Teut. Rippe, as well as OSlov. *rebro*, 'rib' (see Rippe). The primary idea of all these terms, and of the Aryan root *rebh*, deduced from them, is 'winding, entwining.'—

Rebhuhn, n., 'partridge,' from the equiv. MidHG. *rëphuon*, OHG. *rëba-huon*, *rëbhuon*, n.; it is not probable that Rebenhuhn signifies 'the fowl that is fond of frequenting vines (Reben).' Perhaps *reba-* has here another sense. To assume also, on account of LG. *raphon*, Swed. *rapphöna*, 'partridge' (OIc. *rjúpa*, 'ptarmigan'), that the word is derived from LG. *rapp*, 'quick,' is inadmissible, since the HG. term occurs at a very early period. It is most probably connected with the equiv. Russ. *rjabka* (allied to OSlov. *rębŭ*, Russ. *rjaboj*, 'variegated').

Rebus, m. and n., a modern term like the equiv. E. *rebus* and Fr. *rébus;* the source and history of the cognates are unknown. The word is based on Lat. *rebus*, 'by things,' since the meaning of a rebus is illustrated by pictorial objects.

Rechen, m., 'rake, rack,' from the equiv. MidHG. *rëche*, OHG. *rëhho*, m.; corresponding to Du. *reek*, f., 'rake,' and OIc. *reka*, f., 'rake'; allied to MidHG. *rëchen*, OHG. *rëhhan*, 'to scrape together,' Goth. *rikan*, 'to heap up, collect,' also to MidLG. and MidDu. *rake*, AS. *racu*, f., E. *rake*, with a different gradation. The Teut. root *rak, rēk*, from Aryan *reg, rog*, is compared by some with Gr. ὀ-ρέγειν, 'to stretch out,' by others, without reason, to Lat. *legere*, 'to collect.' See rechnen and reden.

rechnen, vb., 'to reckon, estimate, deem,' from MidHG. *rëchennen*, OHG. *rëhhanôn*, 'to count, reckon, render an account' (*ë* is proved by modern dials.). The assumed Goth. *rikanôn*, which is also implied by AS. *rëconian*, E. *to reckon*, and likewise the equiv. LG. and Du. *rekenen*, is abnormally represented by the strange word *rahnjan*. The West Teut. *rēkanôn* is connected, probably in the sense of 'to compute, collect' (comp. the meanings of lesen), with the root *rak*, 'to collect' (see Rechen), to which AS. *rëččan* (from *rakjan*), 'to count up, compute, arrange,' and AS. *racu*, OSax. *raka*, OIc. *rahha*, f., 'speech, account, affair,' also belong; so too gerußen.

recht, adj., 'right, just,' from MidHG. and OHG. *rëht*, adj., 'straight, right, just, correct'; common Teut. *rehta-*, with equiv. meaning in all the dials., Goth. *raihts*, OIc. *rēttr*, AS. *riht*, E. *right*, Du. *regt*, OSax. *reht*. Lat. *rectus*, Zend. *rāšta*, 'straight, right, correct,' are also primit. allied. This adj., which has a particip. ending *to-*, is usually considered to be orig. a partic. of the root *rēg*, 'to direct,' in Lat. *regere;* with this is also connected Sans. *rjú*, 'straight, correct, just,' superlat. *rájištha*, whereby the Aryan root *rēġ* is authenticated.—In the sense of 'to or on the right' (the antithesis of links, 'to or on the left'), the adj. rarely occurs in MidHG., since in the earlier period an adj. primit. allied to Lat. *dexter* was used (comp. Goth. *tathswa-*, OHG. *zëso*, MidHG. *zëse*, 'to or on the right').—

rechtfertigen, vb., 'to justify, vindicate,' from MidHG. *rëht-vertigen*, 'to put into a right state, mend, justify.' Allied to MidHG. *rëhtvertic*, 'just, upright.'

Reck, n., 'wooden frame, rack,' ModHG. only, prop. a LG. word. Comp. LG. and Du. *rek*, 'pole, clothes-horse.' Allied to recken.

Recke, m., 'hero, champion, paladin,' from MidHG. *rëcke*, m., 'warrior, hero,' orig. however, 'knight-errant, adventurer, stranger'; comp. OHG. *reccho*, earlier *wreccho*, m., OSax. *wrekkio*, m., 'vagrant, outlaw, stranger,' AS. *wrëčča*, 'fugitive, exile, unfortunate wretch,' whence E. *wretch*. These interesting West Teut. cognates implying Goth. *wrakja* are connected with ModHG. räd̄en, Goth. *wrikan*, 'to persecute.' ModHG. *ťfenb* has a somewhat similar development.

reden, vb., 'to stretch, rack, reach forth,' from MidHG. *recken*, OHG. *recchen*, 'to stretch out, extend,' corresponding to Du. *rekken*, 'to stretch out,' whence E. *to rack* is borrowed, Goth. *uf-rakjan*, 'to stretch out,' to which Goth. *rahtōn*, 'to proffer.' From Teut. is derived Ital. *recare*, 'to bring.' The assumed direct connection between the common Teut. vb. and Goth. *rikan*, 'to collect,' lit. 'to scrape together,' must on account of the meaning be abandoned in favour of its relation to Lith. *ręžau, ręžyti*, 'to stretch,' Lat. *por-rigo*, 'I stretch,' and Gr. ὀρέγειν, 'to stretch.'

Rede, f., 'speech, discourse, oration,' from MidHG. *rede*, OHG. *redia, reda*, f., 'account, speech and reply, speech, narrative, information'; corresponding to OSax. *redia*, f., 'account,' Goth. *rapjō*, f., 'account, bill, number'; to this is allied Goth. *garapjan*, 'to count,' and further the phonetic equivalent Lat. *ratio*, 'computation, account, number,' &c. From the same Teut. root *rap* (pre-Teut. *rat*), signifying 'number,' *ȟunbert* (which see) is derived.—**reden**, vb., 'to speak, talk, converse,' from the equiv. MidHG. *reden*, OHG. *redion, redōn*, also OHG. *redinōn*, just as in the case of OHG. *redia* the equiv. variant *redina* occurs (comp. OSax. *reδion*, 'to speak'); from this OHG. *redinōn*, is derived OHG. *redinâri*, MidHG. *redenære*, ModHG. *Redner*, 'orator.'

rediid̄, adj., 'honest, candid,' from Mid HG. *redelich*, 'eloquent, intelligent, upright, sturdy,' OHG. *redilih*, 'intelligent'; allied to OHG. *redia*, MidHG. *rede*, 'understanding, account.' See *Rede*.

Reff (1.), n., 'dosser, framework of staves for carrying on the back,' from the equiv. MidHG. *ref*, n., OHG. *ref*, n., for earlier Goth. *hrip*; comp. OIc. *hrip*, n., 'wooden frame for carrying coals or peat,' MidE. and E. *rip*, 'fish-basket.' To the assumption that the word is primit. akin to Lat. *corbis*, 'basket,' there is no phonetic objection (see *Rerb* and *Rrebe*), yet the Alem. variants seem to imply a Teut. primary form *hrēfo-.

Reff (2.), n., also **Reef**, n., 'reef,' ModHG. only, a nautical term borrowed from LG.; comp. Du. and E. *reef*, also Du. *reven*, 'to reef a sail.' It is noteworthy that in OIc. *rif*, 'rib,' is used in the same sense. OIc. *rifa*, 'to tack together,' is probably most closely connected with the cognates.

reffen, vb., 'to hatchel hemp or flax,' from MidHG. *reffen* (a variant of *raffen*), 'to tug, pluck.' The ModHG. sense is probably based on a LG. word. Comp. Du. *repel*, 'breaking flax,' *repelen*, 'to break flax,' E. *ripple*, 'hatchel.'

rege, adj., 'astir, lively, active,' ModHG. only; see *regen*.

Regel, f., 'rule, regulation, principle,' from MidHG. *rëgel, rëgele*, OHG. *rëgula*, f., 'rule, especially of an order'; borrowed in this latter sense during the OHG. period when the monastic system was adopted (see Kloſter, Münſter, Abt, and Mönd̄), from Lat. *rēgula*, pronounced *rĕgula* in MidLat. (Lat. *ē* would be changed into OHG. *î*, see Feier, Kreide, and Pein). This pronunciation is also implied by AS. *regul*, m., and OFr. *riule*, 'rule' (E. *rule*, from MidE. *reule*, is derived from OFr. *reule*, Lat. *regula*).

Regen, m., from the equiv. MidHG. *rëgen*, OHG. *rëgan*, m., 'rain'; common to Teut. in the same sense; comp. the corresponding Goth. *rign*, n., OIc. *regn*, n., AS. *regn*, m., E. *rain*, Du. *regen*, OSax. *rëgan*. Primit. Teut. *regna-*, from pre-Teut. *reghno-*, probably represents *mreghno-*, if the word be connected with Gr. βρέχειν (for μρεχ-, μβρεχ-), 'to wet'; Lat. *rigare*, 'to water, wet,' may belong to the same Aryan root *mregh*. The compound Regenbogen is found in all the Teut. languages; MidHG. *rëgenboge*, OHG. *rëganbogo* (Du., however, *waterboog*), E. *rainbow*, from AS. *rëgnboga*, OIc. *regnboge*, Goth. *rignbuga*.

regen, vb., 'to stir up, move, excite,' from MidHG. *regen*, 'to cause to project, set up, excite, move, awaken,' a factitive of MidHG. *rigen*, 'to rise, tower,' hence primit. allied to ragen. Akin also to MidHG. *rahe*, 'rigid, stiff.' The Teut. root *rag, rēh*, of these cognates has not yet been found in the allied languages. See *rege*.

Reh, n., 'roe, deer,' from the equiv. MidHG. *rēch* (gen. *rēhes*), OHG. *rēh* (gen. *rēhes*), n.; the stem *raiha-* is common to Teut.; comp. Du. *ree*, AS. *rāhdeór*, E. *roe*, OIc. *rā*; Goth. *raih* is by chance not recorded. Allied also to OHG. and OLG. *rēho*, m. (like AS. *rā*, m., from *rāha*), 'roe,' and *reia* (AS. *rāge*), f., 'caprea'; for another fem. form see *Ride*. Teut. *raiha-* from *raiko-* can scarcely be related to Sans. *ṛçya*, 'buck of a species of antelopes.' See further §ajntet.

reiben, vb., 'to rub, scratch, scour,' from the equiv. MidHG. *riben*, OHG. *rîban*, for an older **wrîban*, whence Fr. *riper*, 'to scrape'; comp. LG. *wrîven*, Du. *wrijven*, 'to rub.' The Teut. root *wrîb* has not yet been found in the other Aryan languages.

Reich, n., 'empire, realm, kingdom,' from MidHG. *rîche*, n., OHG. *rîhhi*, n., 'country under sovereign sway, kingdom, Roman-German emperor, authority, dominion'; corresponding to Goth. *reiki*, n., 'realm, dominion, power, authority,' AS. *ríce*, n., 'realm, dominion, reign,' OSax. *riki*, n., 'realm, dominion, authority.' A derivative with the suffix *ja* from Teut. **rîk-*, which has been preserved only in Goth. as *reiks*, 'ruler, chief' (yet also in proper names like Friedrich and Heinrich). The rare OHG. str. vb. *rîhhan*, 'to reign over, take possession of, be mighty,' is prop. a derivative of **rîk-*, 'ruler,' which again is a pre-Teut. loan-word from the equiv. Kelt. *rîg* (for another word, probably borrowed from Kelt. at the same period, see under Amt). The latter is primit. allied to Lat. *rêg-em*, Sans. *râjan*, 'king' (Aryan *rêg-* would be orig. akin to Teut. *rêk*, *râk*), which are connected with the Aryan root *rêg*, 'to direct' (see recht). See the following word.

reich, adj., 'rich, copious, abounding,' from MidHG. *rîche*, OHG. *rîhhi*, adj., 'mighty, rich, splendid'; corresponding to OSax. *rîki*, 'mighty, powerful,' AS. *ríce*, 'mighty, powerful,' E. *rich*, Goth. *reiks*, 'mighty, distinguished.' From the G. adj. the equiv. Rom. cognates are derived; comp. Ital. *ricco*, Fr. *riche*, 'rich.' The common Teut. adj. is a derivative of the root **rîk*, 'king,' discussed under the preceding word, hence 'mighty' is the earlier meaning of the cognates; 'royal' (Lat. *régius*) is the orig. sense.

reichen, vb., 'to reach, extend, suffice,' from MidHG. 'to arrive at, attain, proffer, suffice, extend,' OHG. *reihhen*, 'to proffer, extend'; corresponding to AS. *ræ̂can* (from **raikjan*), and the equiv. E. *to reach*. Its connection with Goth. *rakjan*, 'to reach,' *rahtôn*, 'to proffer,' is not probable, for phonetic reasons; and on account of its meaning, the word can scarcely be related to the cognates of **rîk*, 'ruler,' mentioned under Reich.

Reif (1.), m., 'encircling band, hoop, ring,' from MidHG. and OHG. *reif*, m., 'rope, cord, coiled rope, hoop, band, fetter, circle'; corresponding to Du. *reep*, 'hoop, rope,' AS. *ráp*, m., 'strap, cord, rope,' E. *rope*, OIc. *reip*, n., 'rope,' Goth. *skaudaraip*, 'shoe-thong,' Gr. ῥαιβός, 'crooked,' is probably not allied, and is best compared with Goth. *wraiqs*, 'crooked.'

Reif (2.), m., 'rime, hoar-frost,' from the equiv. MidHG. *rîfe*, OHG. *rîfo*, *hrîfo*, m.; corresponding to OLG. *hrîpo*, Du. *rijp*, 'rime, hoar-frost' (Goth. **hreipa*). The other dials. have a similarly sounding form, which is not, however, closely allied phonetically; OIc. *hrím*, AS. *hrím*, n., E. *rime*, Du. *rijm*, with the same meaning; comp. MidHG. *rimeln*, 'to cover with hoar-frost.' Does *hrîm* represent Teut. **hrîpma-*, and thus belong to Reif? The comparison of AS. *hrím* with Gr. κρῡμός, 'frost,' is untenable.

reif, adj., 'ripe, mature,' from the equiv. MidHG. *rîfe*, OHG. *rîfi*, adj.; corresponding to the equiv. OSax. *rípi*, Du. *rijp*, AS. *rípe*, E. *ripe;* a verbal adj. allied to AS. *rípan*, 'to reap' (whence E. *to reap*), signifying 'that which can be reaped.' The Teut. root *ríp*, with the orig. sense 'to cut, reap' (comp. AS. *rífter*, 'sickle'), has not yet been found in the other Aryan languages.

Reigen, see Reihen (1).

Reihe, f., from the equiv. MidHG. *rîhe*, f., 'row, line,' allied to MidHG. *rîhen*, OHG. *rîhan*, 'to range, put on a thread, fix,' to which MidHG. *rige*, f., 'row, line,' OHG. *rîga*, 'line, circular line,' and Du. *rij*, 'row,' are akin. AS. *ráw*, 'row, line' (Goth. **raiwa*, for **raigwa*, allied to **reihwan*), whence E. *row* is also probably connected with these. The Teut. root *rîhw*, *raihw*, is related to Sans. *rêkhâ*, 'streak, line' (Aryan root *rikh*).

Reihen (1.), **Reigen**, m., 'chain-dance, roundel, dance and song, frolic,' from MidHG. *reie*, *reige*, m., 'a sort of dance in a long row across the field'; origin obscure. Comp. also E. *ray*, 'a sort of dance,' the etymology of which is equally obscure.

Reihen (2.), m., 'instep,' from the equiv. MidHG. *rîhe*, m.; OHG. *rîho*, m., 'calf of the leg, hock.' An older **wrîho* may be assumed, since ModHG. Rist seems to be allied.

reihen, vb., see Reihe.

Reiher, m., 'heron,' from the equiv.

MidHG. *reiger*, m. ; OHG. **reiar, *reijar*, are by chance not recorded ; comp. OSax. *hreiera*, Du. *reiger*, AS. *hrágra*, m., 'heron.' OHG. *heigir* and MidHG. *heiger*, 'heron,' are abnormal forms.

Reim, m., 'rhyme,' from MidHG. *rîm*, m., 'verse, line.' To the assonant OHG. *rîm*, m., this sense is unknown ; it signifies 'row, succession, number,' and these meanings are attached to the corresponding words in the other OTeut. dials. ; comp. OSax. *unrim*, 'innumerable quantity,' AS. *rîm*, 'number.' From these OTeut. words Mid HG. *rîm*, 'verse,' must be dissociated, and connected rather with Lat. *rhythmus* (versus *rhythmicus*). The ModHG. word acquired the sense of Fr. *rîme*, 'rhyme,' in the time of Opitz. In the MidHG. period *rîme binden* was used for *reimen*, 'to rhyme,' and Gebäude by the Meistersingers for Reim. E. *rhyne* (MidE. *rîme*, 'rhymed poem, poem, rhyme') is also borrowed from OFr. *rime*.

rein, adj., 'pure, clean, downright,' from the equiv. MidHG. *reine*, OHG. *reini*, older *hreini*, adj. ; corresponding to Goth. *hrains*, OIc. *hreinn*, OSax. *hrêni*, North Fris. *rian*, 'pure'; in Du. and E., correspondences are wanting. The ModHG. sense (for which in Bav. and Swiss sauber is mostly used) is not found in the dials. ; *e.g.*, in Rhen.-Franc. and Swiss it signifies only 'fine ground, sifted' (of flour, sand, &c.), and belongs therefore to the Teut. root *hrî*, pre-Teut. *krî, krei*, 'to winnow, sift,' whence OHG. *rîtara* (see Reiter), Lat. *cri-brum*, Gr. κρί-νειν (for the adj. suffix *-ni-* see stein and schön). Hence 'sifted' may be assumed as the orig. sense of *rein*; comp. OLG. *hréncurni*, 'wheat.'

Reis (1.), m., 'rice,' from the equiv. MidHG. *rîs*, m. and n., which was borrowed from the equiv. MidLat. and Rom. *riso-*, n. and n. ; comp. Ital. *riso*, Fr. *riz* (whence also E. *rice*, Du. *rijst*) ; the latter is usually traced to Lat. and Gr. ὄρυζον (also ὄρυζα), 'rice,' which is derived from Sans. *vrîhi* through an Iran. medium.

Reis (2.), 'twig, sprout,' from MidHG. *rîs*, OHG. *rîs*, earlier *hris*, n., 'branch'; corresponding to Du. *rijs*, AS. *hrîs*, OIc. *hrîs*, n., 'twig, branch'; Goth. **hreis*, n., is wanting. The Teut. cognates (Zweig, 'that which shakes, lives') accord well with Goth. *hrisjan*, 'to shake,' OSax. *hrissian*, AS. *hrissan*, 'to tremble, quake.' —**Reisig, Reisich**, n., 'small twigs, brushwood,' from MidHG. *rîsech*, OHG. *rîsach*, n. ; the collective of Reis (OTeut. *hrîsa-*).

Reise, f., 'journey, travel, voyage,' from MidHG. *reise*, f., 'departure, march, journey, military expedition,' OHG. *reisa*, f., 'departure'; allied to OHG. *rîsan*, Mid HG. *rîsen*, 'to mount, fall,' OSax. *rîsan*, 'to rise,' AS. *rîsan*, E. *to rise*, and the equiv. Goth. *ur-reisan*. The idea of vertical, and espec. of upward motion, thus belongs everywhere to the root *rîs*; therefore Reise is lit. 'departure.' Further, MidHG. and ModHG. *reisen* is a derivative of the subst. ; comp. also with the root *rîs*, E. *to raise* and (by the change of *s* into *r*) *to rear*.

Reisige, m., 'trooper, horseman,' from MidHG. *reisec*, adj., 'mounted.'—**Reisigen**, pl., 'horsemen,' usually connected with MidHG. *reise*, 'military expedition,' yet it may be also a derivative of *rîten*, 'to ride,' since OHG. *rîso*, 'horseman,' occurs (*rîplan-* gives *rîssan-, risan-*).

reißen, vb., 'to tear, drag ; sketch,' from MidHG. *rîzen*, OHG. *rîzan*, earlier **wrîzan*, 'to tear, tear in pieces, scratch, write'; corresponding to OSax. *wrîtan*, 'to tear in pieces, wound, write,' AS. *wrîtan*, E. *to write*, OIc. *rîta*, 'to write'; Goth. **wreitan*, 'to rend, write,' is wanting, but is implied by Goth. *writs*, 'streak, point.' The various meanings of the cognates are explained by the manner in which runes were written or scratched on beech twigs. The Teut. root *writ*, which has been preserved also in ModHG. Riß, Ritz, ritzen, and reizen, has not yet been found in the non-Teut. languages.

reiten, vb., 'to ride,' from MidHG. *rîten*, OHG. *rîtan*, 'to move on, set out, drive, ride'; corresponding to Du. *rijden*, 'to ride, drive, skate,' AS. *rîdan*, E. *to ride*, OIc. *rîða*, 'to ride, travel ; swing, hover.' These words are based on the common Teut. *rîdan*, with the general sense of continued motion. This, as well as the fact that in Teut. there is no vb. used exclusively for 'to ride,' makes it probable that the art of riding is comparatively recent. Besides, in the allied languages no single term expresses this idea. It is also known that the art among the Greeks appears after the time of Homer, and that it was still unknown to the Indians of the Rig-Veda. It is true that the Teutons are known to us as horsemen from their earliest appearance in history, but the evolution of the word reiten (comp. Lat. *equo vehi*) proves that the art is of recent origin. The Teut. verbal stem ri̥d, for pre-Teut. ri̥dh, reidh, corresponds to OIr. *riad*, 'driving, riding' (*riadaim*, 'I drive'), OGall. *rēda*, 'waggon' (comp. Gr. ἔ-ριθος, 'messenger, servant'?). The general meaning is seen also in AS. *rád*, f., 'journey, expedition,' E. *road*, as well as in the cognates under bereit.

Reiter, f., 'coarse sieve, riddle,' from MidHG. *rīter*, OHG. *rītara*, f., 'sieve,' for earlier **hrītara;* corresponding to AS. *hridder*, f., 'sieve,' whence E. *riddle*. For the Teut. root *hrī* in the sense of 'to sift, winnow,' see rein. The OHG. suffix *tara*, from pre-Teut. *thrā* (Goth. **hrei-dra*, f.), corresponds to *-brum* for *-thrum* in Lat. *cribrum* (br from *thr*, as in *ruber*, ἐρυθρός), equiv. to OIr. *criathar*, 'sieve'; Aryan *kreithro-* may be assumed. ModHG. Räber, 'sieve,' is not connected with this word.

reizen, vb., 'to stimulate, excite, charm,' from MidHG. *reitzen*, *reizen*, OHG. *reizzen*, *reizen*, 'to charm, entice, lead astray'; the form with *tz* is due to Goth. *tj*. Apparently a factitive of *reißen*, hence lit. 'to cause to drag, make one come out of oneself'; comp. OIc. *reita*, 'to stir up, irritate.' Comp. reißen, heißen.

renken, vb., 'to twist, wrench,' from MidHG. *renken*, OHG. *renchen*, 'to turn this way and that,' for an earlier **wrankjan* (from the stem *rank*, 'to dislocate,' are derived the Rom. cognates, Ital. *ranco*, 'lame,' *rancare*, 'to halt'). AS. *wrenć*, 'bend, artifice,' AS. *wrenćan*, 'to turn,' E. *wrench*, subst. and vb. The corresponding vb. is ringen, Teut. *wringan;* the *k* of renfen (probably for *kk*) compared with the *g* of ringen resembles the variation in büden and biegen, ſeđen and Goth. *bilaigōn*, &c. With the pre-Teut. root *wrenk* (*wreng*) comp. Gr. ῥέμβω, 'to turn,' ῥόμβος, 'top.' Comp. Rauf.

rennen, vb., 'to run,' from MidHG. and OHG. *rennen*, prop. 'to cause to flow, chase, drive,' espec. 'to make a horse leap, burst,' hence the reflexive meaning of the ModHG. word; corresponding to OSax. *rennian*, Goth. *rannjan*, which are factitives of rinnen.

Renntier, n., 'reindeer,' ModHG. only, from the equiv. Swed. *ren*, which is derived from OIc. *hreinn* (AS. *hrán*), whence also Du. *rendier*, E. *reindeer;* from the same source probably are Ital. *rangifero*, Fr. *rangier* (and *renne*), 'reindeer.' OIc. *hreinn* is usually considered to be a Finn. and Lapp. loan-word (*raingo*).

Rente, f., 'rent, rental,' from MidHG. *rēnte*, 'income, produce, advantage; contrivance.' Borrowed from Fr. *rente*, MidLat. *renta*, Ital. *rendita*, whence even in OHG. *rentōn*, 'to count up.'

Reſt, m., 'rest, remnant, remains,' ModHG. only, from Fr. *reste*, m.

retten, vb., 'to rescue, save,' from MidHG. and OHG. *retten*, 'to snatch from, rescue'; comp. Du. *redden*, OFris. *hredda*, AS. *hreddan*, 'to snatch from, set free,' E. *to rid;* Goth. **hradjan* may be assumed. The Teut. root *hrad*, from pre-Teut. *krath*, corresponds to the Sans. root *çrath*, 'to let go' (pres. *çrathāyāmi*).

Rettich, **Rettig**, m., 'radish,' from the equiv. MidHG. *retich*, *rætich*, OHG. *retih*, *ratih*, m.; corresponding to AS. *rœdić*, borrowed from Lat. *rādīc-em* (nom. *rādix*), which, as the HG. guttural indicates, is found with the Teut. accent prior to the OHG. period. E. *radish* is a later loan-word from Fr. *radis*.

Reue, f., 'repentance,' from MidHG. *riuwe*, f., 'sadness, pain, mourning, repentance,' OHG. *riuwa*, earlier *hriuwa*, f.; corresponding to Du. *rouw*, AS. *hreōw*, 'grief, mourning, repentance.' Allied to an obsolete OHG. vb. *hriuwan*, MidHG. *riuwen*, 'to feel pain, be sorry'; corresponding to AS. *hreōwan*, 'to vex, grieve,' E. *to rue*, to which *ruth* is akin; OIc. *hryggva*, 'to sadden.' Goth. **hrigguan* is wanting. The Teut. *hrū*, 'to be sad, sadden,' has no correspondences in the other Aryan languages.

Reuſe, f., 'weir-basket, weel,' from MidHG. *riuse*, OHG. *rūsa*, *rūssa*, f., 'weel, fish-basket' (from Goth. **rūsjō*); a graded and lengthened form of Goth. *raus* (see Rohr). Hence Reuſe means lit. 'that which is made of reeds.'

reuten, vb., 'to root out, grub up,' from MidHG. *riuten*, 'to root out, make fertile'; to this is allied OHG. *riuti*, MidHG. *riute*, n., 'land made fertile by uprooting,' OIc. *ryðja*, 'to make fertile.' Whether OHG. *riostar*, *riostra*, MidHG. *riester*, 'plough, plough-handle,' dial. Riester, is connected with this word is uncertain. See reben.

Reuter, m., 'trooper,' first occurs in early ModHG., formed from Du. *ruiter*, 'trooper,' which has nothing to do with reiten, 'to ride.' The word is based rather on MidLat. *ruptarii* (for *ruptuarii*), *rutarii* (ex Gallica pronuntiatione); thus were "dicti quidam praedones sub XI. saeculum ex rusticis collecti ac conflati qui provincias populabantur et interdum militiae principum sese addicebant": "these people were often on horseback." Thus Du. *ruiter* could easily acquire the meaning 'horseman'; comp. Du. *ruiten*, 'to plunder.' See Rette.

Rhabarber, m., 'rhubarb,' ModHG. only, from Ital. *rabarbaro*, Fr. *rhubarbe;* also earlier ModHG. Rhapontif, from Fr. *rapontique*. The word is based on the Mid Lat. *ra-, reu-ponticum, -barbarum*, also *radix pontica, -barbara*, 'a plant growing on the banks of the Volga.'

Rhede, f., 'roadstead, road,' ModHG. only, from LG.; comp. Du. *ree, reede*, MidE. *rāde*, E. *road;* from the E. class are derived the equiv. Ital. *rada* and Fr. *rade*. Orig. sense probably 'place where ships are equipped'; allied to the Teut. root *raid*, 'to prepare'; comp. OIc. *reiðe*, 'ship's equipment.' See *bereit*.

ribbeln, vb., 'to rub briskly, scour,' ModHG. only, intensive of *reiben*.

richten, vb., 'to regulate, direct, judge, condemn,' from MidHG. and OHG. *rihten*, 'to set right,' denomin. from *recht*.

Riche, f., 'doe,' by chance recorded only in ModHG.; MidHG. *riche* and OHG. *riccha* are wanting, but may be assumed from the archaic form of ModHG. Ricke (Swiss *rikye*). In Goth. *rikki*, 'doe,' would be a derivative fem. form of Reh (*raiha-*).

riechen, vb., 'to smell,' from MidHG. *riechen*, OHG. *riohhan*, str. vb., 'to smoke, steam, emit vapour, smell'; comp. Du. *ruiken, rieken*, 'to smell,' AS. *reócan*, 'to smoke, emit vapour,' OIc. *rjúka*, 'to smoke, exhale.' The Teut. root *rūk* signified 'to smoke'; see further under Rauch and Geruch. In the non-Teut. languages the stem is not found.

Riefe, f., 'furrow in wood, stone, &c.,' ModHG. only, from LG.; comp. AS. *gerifian*, 'to wrinkle,' with which E. *rifle*, lit. 'the fluted weapon,' and *rivel*, 'wrinkle, fold,' are connected. OIc. *rífa*, f., 'slit, rift,' allied to OIc. *rífa*, 'to tear to pieces, slit.'

Riege, f., 'row,' from MidHG. *rige*, OHG. *rīga*, f., 'line, row' (Goth. *rīga, f., is wanting); allied to Reihe, OHG. *rîhan*, 'to form in a row.' From G. are derived Ital. *riga*, 'line, strip,' and *rigoletto*, 'chain-dance.'

Riegel, m., 'rail, bar, bolt,' from Mid HG. *rigel*, OHG. *rigil*, m., 'crossbar for fastening'; corresponding to MidE. and E. *rail*, Du. and Swed. *regel*, 'bolt.' It is scarcely allied to OHG. *rîhan*, 'to form in a row.'

Riemen, m., 'strap, thong, string,' from MidHG. *rieme*, OHG. *riomo*, m., 'band, girdle, strap'; corresponding to OSax. *riomo*, m., Du. *riem*, AS. *reóma*, 'strap'; Goth. *riuma, m., is wanting. Gr. ῥῦμα, 'towing-line, rope,' is primit. allied, and hence the Aryan root was probably *rū́* (Gr. ἐρύω), 'to draw.'

Ries, n., 'ream,' from the equiv. late MidHG. *ris (riʒ, rist)*, m., f. and n.; in Du. *riem*, E. *ream*. These late Teut. cognates are borrowed from Rom.; comp. the equiv. MidLat. and Ital. *risma*, Fr. *rame*. It is true that the MidHG. form still requires further explanation. The ultimate source of MidLat. and Ital. *risma* is Arab. *rizma*, 'bale, bundle,' espec. 'packing-paper.'

Riese, m., 'giant,' from the equiv. Mid HG. *rise*, OHG. *risi, riso*, m.; comp. OSax. *wrisi-lic*, 'gigantic,' OLG. *wrisil*, Du. *reus*, 'giant.' Goth. **wrisi-*, or rather **wrisjan-*, is wanting. It seems primit. allied to Sans. *vṛṣan*, 'mighty, manly, strong,' to which OIr. *fairsing*, 'great, powerful,' is also probably akin.

Riester, m., 'wrist, instep, patch (on a shoe),' ModHG. only; probably a primit. word, but of obscure origin. This word, which is unknown to Bav., has, according to Swiss *riester, riestere*, m. and f., a genuine diphthong equiv. to Goth. *iu;* hence Mid HG. *altriuze, riuze*, 'cobbler,' preserved in ModHG. dials. as Altreise, 'second-hand dealer,' is perhaps allied.

Rieschling, m., 'small white field-grape,' ModHG. only; perhaps a derivative of Riess, 'Rhætia' (Tyrol), so that Rieschling is lit. 'Rhætian' (wine).

Riet (in the LG. form Ried), n., 'reed,' from the equiv. MidHG. *riet*, OHG. *riot*, earlier *hriot*, n.; common to West Teut. in the same sense; comp. OSax. *hreod*, Du. *riet*, AS. *hreód*, E. *reed*. Goth. *hriuda is wanting. Pre-Teut. **kreudho-* is not found in the other groups.

Riff, n., 'reef,' ModHG. only, from LG. *riff, reff;* comp. the equiv. Du. *rif*, n., E. *reef*, and OIc. *rif*. The latter is equiv. in sound to Goth. *rif*, 'rib,' but this is probably only an accident. It has been thought to be allied to OIc. *rífa*, 'to slit, split,' *rifa*, 'rift, split'; hence probably Riff means lit. 'the dissevered, cleft, mass of rock,' then 'reef.'

Riffel, Rüffel, n., 'flax-comb, ripple; censure,' probably allied to MidHG. *riffeln, rifeln,* 'to comb or hatchel flax,' *riffel,* 'mattock,' OHG. *riffila,* 'saw.' G. has similar figurative terms for ' to find fault with, inveigh against' (similar to *thwas turchhecheln,* ' to censure'). Comp. reffen.

Rind, n., 'horned cattle,' from the equiv. MidHG. *rint* (gen. *rindes*), OHG. *rind,* earlier *hrind,* n.; Goth. **hrinþis,* n., is wanting; AS. *hryþer* (*hriðer, hrið-*), MidE. *rother,* Du. *rund,* 'horned cattle,' imply Goth. **hrunþis,* a graded variant allied to Rind, Goth. **hrinþis.* OHG. *hrind* is usually connected, like Hirsch, with the stem *ker,* 'horn, horned' (see Horn), appearing in Gr. κέρας, and also with Gr. κριός, 'ram.' The G. word is, however, probably not allied to these words.

Rinde, f., 'rind, crust, bark,' from Mid HG. *rinde,* OHG. *rinta,* f., 'rind of trees, crust,' also (rarely) 'bread-crust'; corresponding to AS. *rind,* E. *rind.* Its kinship with Rand and Ramft is undoubted; their common root seems to be *rem, ram,* 'to cease, end'; comp. espec. AS. *reoma, rima,* E. *rim.* Some etymologists connect it with Goth. *rimis,* 'repose'; comp. Sans. *ram,* 'to cease, rest.'

Ring, m., 'ring, circle, link,' from MidHG. *rinc* (gen. *ringes*), OHG. *ring,* earlier *hring,* m., 'ring, hoop, circular object'; comp. OSax. *hring,* Du. *ring,* AS. *hring,* E. *ring,* OIc. *hringr,* m. The common Teut. word, which implies a casually non-existent Goth. **hriggs,* denoted a circle, and everything of a circular form. Pre-Teut. *krengho-* appears also in the corresponding OSlov. *krągŭ,* m., 'circle,' *krąglŭ,* 'round.' From the Teut. word, which also signifies 'assembly' (grouped in a circle), are derived the Rom. cognates, Ital. *aringo,* 'rostrum,' Fr. *harangue,* 'public speech,' and Fr. *rang.*

Ringel, m., 'ringlet, curl,' dimin. of the preceding word; MidHG. *ringele,* 'marigold,' OHG. *ringila,* f., 'marigold, heliotrope.'

ringen, vb., 'to encircle; wring, wrestle, strive,' from MidHG. *ringen,* 'to move to and fro, exert oneself, wind,' OHG. *ringan,* from an earlier **wringan;* comp. Du. *wringen,* 'to wring, squeeze,' AS. *wringan,* E. *to wring,* Goth. **wriggan* is implied by *wruggô,* 'snare.' The root *wring,* identical with the root *wrank* (see renfen), meant orig. 'to turn in a winding manner, move with effort.' With this are connected Mod HG. Rank, E. *wrong,* MidE. *wrang,* 'bent, perverted, wrong' (OIc. *rangr,* 'bent, wrong,' ModDu. *wrang,* 'sour, bitter'), and E. *to wrangle.* Perhaps würgen (root *worg*) is allied; E. *to ring* is, however, not connected, since it comes from AS. *hringan.*

Rinken, 'large ring, buckle,' an Up G. word, from MidHG. *rinke,* m. and f., 'buckle, clasp,' whence MidHG. *rinkel,* 'small buckle'; an old derivative of Ring (OHG. *rinka,* from the primit. form **hringjôn*).

Rinne, f., 'channel, gutter, groove,' from MidHG. *rinne,* f., OHG. *rinna,* f., 'watercourse,' MidHG. also 'gutter, eavestrough.' Comp. Goth. *rinnô,* f., 'brook,' and AS. *rynele,* E. *rindle.* Connected with the following word.

rinnen, vb., 'to run, flow, leak, drop,' from MidHG. *rinnen,* OHG. *rinnan,* 'to flow, swim, run.' This vb. is common to Teut. in the same sense; Goth. *rinnan,* AS. *irnan,* E. *to run,* Du. *rennen,* OSax. *rinnan;* the orig. sense of all these is 'to move on rapidly.' The *nn* of Goth. *rinnan* is usually regarded as a part of the pres. stem for *no* (comp. Gr. δάκνω, Lat. *sper-no*), and a root *ren, run,* is assumed, which is preserved in AS. *ryne* (from **runi-*).

Rippe (Luther, Riebe), f., 'rib,' from MidHG. *rippe* (*ribe*), n. and f., OHG. *rippa,* f., *rippi* (*ribi*), n., 'rib'; corresponding to the equiv. Du. *rib, ribbe,* AS. *ribb,* E. *rib,* OIc. *rif;* Goth. **ribi,* n. (plur. **ribja*), is by chance not recorded. Teut. *ribja-,* from pre-Teut. *rebhyo-,* is cognate with ModHG. Rebe and OSlov. *rebro,* n., 'rib,' from *rebhro-.* See Rebe, where 'entwining' is deduced as the prim. meaning of Rippe.

Rispe, f., 'panicle,' from MidHG. *rispe,* f., 'branches, bushes,' akin to OHG. *hrispahi,* n., 'bushes'; of obscure origin. The derivation from OHG. *hrespan,* MidHG. *respen,* 'to pluck, gather,' is not quite satisfactory.

Rist, m., 'wrist, instep; withers,' from MidHG. *rist, riste,* m., f., and n., 'wrist, instep'; OHG. **rist,* as well as the implied earlier **wrist,* are by chance not recorded; comp. Du. *wrist* (dial. Frist), AS. *wyrst, wrist,* E. *wrist,* OFris. *riust, wirst,* 'wrist, ankle,' OIc. *rist,* f., 'instep'; Goth. **wrists* is not recorded. The primit. meaning of the cognates is usually assumed to be 'turning-point,' Rift being referred to a

Teut. root *wrīp*, 'to turn,' which has been preserved in E. *to writhe*, as well as in ModHG. Reitel, 'packing-stick' (MidHG. *reitel* for an earlier *wreitel*). Other etymologists connect the word with Gr. ῥίζα (from *Fριϝδαἰ), 'root.' Yet OHG. *rîho* (for earlier *wrîho*), ModHG. Reihen, is probably most closely connected with the cognates of Riß, so that Goth. *wristi-* would represent *wrihsti-*, and thus imply an Aryan root *wrîk*.

Riß, m., 'cleft, gap, schism,' from MidHG. *riz*, n., 'cleft'; the corresponding OHG. *riz*, m., in contrast to the MidHG. and ModHG. which are connected with the vb. reißen, preserves the earlier meaning 'letter' (Goth. *writs*, 'stroke, point'), which connects it with Goth. *writan*, 'to write, draw' (see reißen). Comp., moreover, Riß, in the earlier sense of 'sketch.'

Ritt, m., 'ride,' first occurs in early ModHG.; a derivative of reiten.

Ritten, m., 'fever,' from the equiv. MidHG. *rite, ritte*, OHG. *rito, ritto*, m., for an earlier *hripjo*, 'fever'; so too AS. *hripa*, m., 'fever'; allied to OHG. *ridon*, MidHG. *riden*, 'to shiver,' AS. *hrîpian*, 'to shiver in a fever,' OHG. *rido*, 'shivering,' AS. *hrip*, 'storm.' The root *hrīp*, pre-Teut. *krīt*, 'to move wildly,' appears also in OIr. *crith*, 'shivering.'

Ritter, m., 'chevalier, knight,' from MidHG. *ritter, riter*, m., 'horseman, knight' (also *rîtære*): the form with *tt* is due to a confusion with OHG. *ritto*, 'horseman' (from *ridjo*). See reiten and Reuter.

Ritze, f., 'rift, rent,' from MidHG. *riz* (gen. *ritzes*), m., 'rift, wound,' like ritzen, from MidHG. *ritzen*, 'to scratch, wound,' OHG. *rizzen, rizzôn*; allied to reißen.

Robbe, f., 'sea-dog, seal,' borrowed from LG., like most ModHG. words with a medial *bb* (Ebbe, Krabbe, &c.); comp. Du. *rob*, m., 'sea-dog, seal'; the equiv. Scand. *kobbi*, similar in sound (akin to *kôpr*, 'young sea-dog'), is not allied. The Teut. word, Goth. *silha-* (comp. AS. *seolh*, E. *seal*, OHG. *sëlah*, OIc. *selr*) became obsolete in G. at an early period. The source and history of the LG. term is obscure.

Roche (1.), m., 'ray, thornback,' from LG. *ruche*; comp. the equiv. Du. *roch*, *rog*, AS. *reohha, *rohha*, whence MidE. *reihe*, *rouhe*; also E. *roach, roche*? (E. *ray* is derived from Lat. *raja*, whence also Ital. *raja*, Fr. *raie*).

Roche (2.), m., 'castle' (at chess), from the equiv. MidHG. *roch*, n.; borrowed with chess-playing from the Fr. (*roc*, whence also MidE. and E. *rook*). The ultimate source is Pers. *rukh, rokh*, 'archer mounted on an elephant' (at chess). Deriv. rochieren.

röcheln, vb., 'to rattle,' from MidHG. *rücheln, rüheln*, 'to neigh, roar, rattle'; allied to OHG. *rohôn*, MidHG. *rohen*, 'to grunt, roar'; comp. Du. *rogchelen*, 'to spit out.' The Teut. root *ruh, ruhh*, preserved in these words, has been connected with the Slav. root *ryk* (from *rūk*); comp. OSlov. *rykati, ryknqti*, 'to roar' (Lett. *rûkt*), to which has to be added perhaps the Gr.-Lat. root *rug* in *rugire*, 'to roar,' ὀρυγμός, 'roaring.'

Rock, m., 'coat, robe, petticoat,' from MidHG. *roc* (gen. *rockes*), OHG. *rocch*, m, 'outer garment, coat'; corresponding to the equiv. Du. *rok*, OFris. *rok*, AS. *rocc*, OIc. *rokkr*; the implied Goth. *rukku-* is wanting. From the Teut. cognates is derived the Rom. class, Fr. *rochet*, 'surplice' (MidLat *roccus*, 'coat'), which again passed into E. (*rochet*). The early history of the Teut. cognates is obscure; allied to Rocken?

Rocken, m., 'distaff,' from the equiv. MidHG. *rocke*, OHG. *roccho*, m.; common to Teut. in the same sense; comp. Du. *rok*, *rocken*, AS. *rocca*, MidE. *rocke*, E. *rock*, OIc. *rokkr*; Goth. *rukka* is by chance not recorded. The Teut. word passed into Rom.; comp. Ital. *rocca*, 'distaff.' It may be doubted whether Rocken and Rock are derived from an old root *ruk*, 'to spin,' which does not occur elsewhere. At any rate, Rocken is not connected with the equiv. LG. *wocken*, since the cognates of Rocken, according to the LG. and E. terms, have not lost an initial *w*.

roden, vb., 'to root out,' from MidHG. *roden*, the MidG. and LG. variant of *riuten*, 'to root out.'

Rodomontade, f., 'boasting, bluster, swaggering,' from the equiv. Fr. *rodomontade*, Ital. *rodomondata*, f. Rodomonte is derived from Ariosto's *Orlando Furioso*, and is the name of a boastful Moorish hero; it first appears in Boiardo's *Orlando Innamorata*, and means lit. 'roller of mountains, one who boasts that he can roll away mountains.'

Rogen, m., 'roe, spawn,' from the equiv. MidHG. *rogen*, OHG. *rogan*, m., for an earlier *hrogan*, m.; also MidHG. *roge*, OHG. *rogo*, m.; corresponding to the equiv. OIc. *hrogn*, n. plur., AS. *hrogn*, E. *roan*, roe. Goth. *hrugna- is by chance not recorded. The true source of the word cannot be found; some connect it with AS. hrog, 'nasal mucus,' others with Gr. πρόκη, 'pebble,' Sans. parkara, 'gravel.'

Roggen, m., for the genuine HG. Rocke, Recken (in Bav. and Hess., Kern is almost invariably used), 'rye.' The gg of the ModHG. written form is either LG. or Swiss (see Gyge in list of corrections); in MidHG. rocke, OHG. rocko, m., 'rye, secale'; corresponding to OSax. roggo, Du. rogge. UpG., as well as LG. and Fris., imply the prim. form *ruggn-. On the other hand, E. and Scand. assume a Goth. *rugi-; comp. AS. ryge, E. rye, and the equiv. OIc. rūgr. Pre-Teut. rughi- is proved by Lith. rugýs, 'rye-corn' (rugei, pl., 'rye'), OSlov. růžĭ, 'rye' (Gr. ὄρυζα, 'rice,' from Sans. vrīhi, is not allied). Among the East Aryans this term is wanting.

roh, adj., 'rude, raw, crude, rough,' from MidHG. rô (infl. râwer), OHG. rô (infl. râwêr), 'raw, uncooked, rude' (for earlier hrâwa-); comp the equiv. OSax. hrâ, Du. raauw, AS. hreá, E. raw, OIc. hrár (for *hrávr), 'raw, uncooked.' This adj., which is wanting in Goth. (*hrawa-, *hrêwa-), points to a Teut. root hrū, from pre-Teut. krū, which appears in numerous forms, such as Lat. cruor, cruentus, crūdus (for *cruvidus?), Gr. κρέας, 'flesh,' Sans. kravis, 'raw meat,' Sans. krūras, 'bloody,' OSlov. krŭvi, Lith. kraūjas, 'blood.'

Rohr, n., 'reed, cane, rush,' from the equiv. MidHG. and OHG. rôr (gen. rôres), n.; an earlier *rauza is to be assumed; comp. Goth. raus, n., OIc. reyr, m., Du. roer, 'reed' (wanting in OSax., AS., and E.). The Teut. form in s, closely allied to the Goth., passed into Rom.; comp. Fr. roseau, 'reed,' and the equiv. Prov. raus. The form rausa-, with which Reuse and Röhre (Rest, (1)?) are also connected, is related to Lat. ruscum, 'butcher's broom'; comp. Meer with Lat. muscus.

Rohrdommel, f., 'bittern,' from the equiv. MidHG. rôrtumel, m.; the word has been variously corrupted in OHG. and MidHG., finally resulting in the ModHG. form. In OHG. occur horo-tukel, horotumil, lit. 'mud, slime tumbler' (*rôrtumil is not found in OHG.). MidDu. roesdomel; AS. has a remarkable form, râradumbla, with the same meaning. The wide diffusion of these cognates, transformed in various ways by popular etymology, but closely resembling one another in sound, leaves no doubt as to their genuine Teut. origin. The usual assumption that they are all corruptions of Lat. crecopulus, cretobolus, onocrotalus won't bear investigation.

Röhre, f., 'tube, pipe, flue,' from Mid HG. rœre, OHG. rôru, rôrra, from an earlier rôrea, f., 'reed stalk, hollow stalk, reed'; a derivative of Rohr, OHG. rôr (Goth. *rauzjô, f., is wanting); hence Röhre is lit. 'the reed-shaped.'

röhren, vb., 'to bellow,' from MidHG. rêren, OHG. rêrên, 'to bleat, roar'; corresponding to AS. rârian, E. to roar.

Rolle, f., 'roll, roller, pulley, scroll, actor's part,' from MidHG. rolle, rulle, f., 'rotulus,' also rodel, rottel, m. and f., 'scroll, list, document'; formed from MidLat. rotulus, rotula, or rather the corresponding Rom. cognates. Comp. Ital. rotolo, rullo, Fr. rôle; whence also E. to roll, MidHG. and ModHG. rollen, Fr. rouler, Ital. rullare.

Römer, m., 'green, bulging wine-glass; rummer' ('Roman glass'?).

rösche, adj., 'prompt, lively, alert, fresh,' an UpG. word (Bav. and Swiss rêš, 'lively, precipitous, harsh'), from MidHG. rôsch, rœsche, OHG. rôsc, rôsci, 'nimble, hasty, fresh'; cognate terms from which we may infer the prim. form (Goth. rausqa-?) are entirely wanting. The connection of the word with rasch is uncertain.

Rose, f., 'rose,' from the equiv. Mid HG. rôse, OHG. rôsa, f.; comp. the equiv. Du. roos, AS. rôse, E. rose; adopted in the OHG. period from Lat. rôsa. Had the word been borrowed earlier, the Lat. quantity would have been retained in G. (in Lilie, from Lat. lilia, the vowel was shortened, because lilja was the pronunciation in Mid Lat.). Lat. *rôsa is, however, implied also by the Rom. cognates, Ital. rosa and Fr. rose. A Lat. ŏ must have led in OHG. to the form *ruosa; comp. OHG. scuola, school,' from Lat. scôla.

Rosine, f., 'raisin,' from the equiv. late MidHG. rôsîne (rasin), f.; the latter, like MidLat. rosina, is a corruption of Fr. raisin (sec, 'raisin'), which, with Ital. racimolo, 'bunch of grapes,' is due to Lat. racémus, 'berry'; comp. further Du. rozijn, razijn, E. raisin.

Rosmarin, m., 'rosemary,' first occurs in early ModHG., formed from the equiv. Lat. rosmarinus, whence also Du. rozemarijn and MidE. rosmarine, E. rosemary (implying a connection with Mary); the word in

G. and E. is instinctively connected with Ṙoſe, 'rose.'

Roſt (1.), m., 'grate, gridiron,' from MidHG. rôst, m., 'grate, funeral pile, glow, fire,' OHG. rôst, m., rôsta, f., 'small gridiron, frying-pan.' The current derivation from Roḣr, in which case we should have to assume 'iron grating' as the primit. sense of Roſt, does not satisfy the meaning (OHG. rôstpfanna, MidHG. rôstpfanne). Derivative röſten, 'to roast, broil,' Mid HG. ræsten, OHG. rôsten, 'to lay on the gridiron, roast'; hence the Rom. cognates, Ital. arrostir, 'to roast,' Fr. rôtir, and from this again comes E. to roast.

Roſt (2.), m., 'rust, mildew, blight,' from MidHG. and OHG. rost, m., 'rust, aerugo, rubigo'; corresponding to the equiv. OSax. rost, Du. roest, AS. rûst, E. rust (Scotch roost). For Goth. *rûsta-, 'rust,' nidwa, f., was used. Reſt belongs to the Teut. root rŭd (pre-Teut. rudh), 'to be red,' appearing in ModHG. rct. From the same root was formed the equiv. OHG. rosamo, which assumed early in MidHG. the meaning 'freckle,' as well as OIc. ryð, n., MidHG. rot, m. and n., OSlov. rŭzda (for rudja), f., Lith. rûdis (rudĕti, 'to rust'), Lat. robigo, 'rust'; also Lett. rûsa, 'rust,' rusta, 'brown colour.'

röſten (1.), see under Roſt (1).

roſten (2.), vb., 'to steep, water-rot flax or hemp,' from MidHG. ræʒen, rætzen, 'to rot, cause to rot,' implying a connection with röſten (1); allied to rôʒ, adj., 'mellow, soft,' rôʒʒen, 'to rot,' and OHG. rôʒʒên, 'to rot.' From a Teut. root raut, 'to rot'; comp. Du. rot, 'rotten, decayed,' OSax. rôtôn, 'to rot,' AS. rotian, E. to rot, to ret (from AS. *reátian?), 'to steep, water-rot,' OIc. rotenn, 'putrefied'; see rotten (2).

Roſs (1.), n., 'horse, steed,' from MidHG. and OHG. ros (gen. rosses), n., 'horse,' espec. 'charger,' for earlier *hrossa-; comp. OSax. hross, Du. ros, AS. hors, E. horse, OIc. hross, n., 'horse.' Goth. *hrussa- is wanting, the term used being OAryan aḣhwa- (OSax. ĕhu, AS. eoh, OIc. jôr), equiv. to Lat. equus, Gr. ἵππος, Sans. áçva-s (Lith. aszvà, 'mare'). In MidHG. the term Pferd appears; Roſs is still used almost exclusively in UpG. with the general sense of 'horse.' From the Teut. cognates is derived the Rom. term, Fr. rosse, 'sorry horse, jade.' The origin of Teut. hrussa- is uncertain; as far as the meaning is concerned, it may be compared, as is usually done, with Lat. currere for *curs-ere, *crs-ere, root krs, 'to run,' or with the Sans. root kûrd, 'to leap,' with which OIc. hress, 'quick,' may also be connected. For another derivation see rüſten.—Roſsläuſcher, m., 'horse-dealer,' from the equiv. MidHG. rostûscher, rostiuscher, m. (see tauſchen), retains the orig. sense of the old word Rcſs.

Roſs (2.), n., 'honeycomb,' from the equiv. MidHG. râʒ, râʒe, f.; OHG. *râʒa is by chance not recorded; corresponding to OLG. râta, 'favus,' Du. raat, f., 'virgin honey'; undoubtedly a genuine Teut. term. The derivation from Lat. radius is unfounded; OFr. raie de miel (from raie, 'ray,' radius) is due to the influence of the Teut. word, in Goth. *rêta, f., which cannot, however, be traced farther back.

rot, adj., 'red,' from the equiv. MidHG. and OHG. rôt, adj.; corresponding to the equiv. Goth. raups, OIc. rauðr, AS. reád, E. red (AS. also reód, OIc. rjóðr, 'red'), Du. rood, OSax. rôd. Goth. and common Teut. rauda-, from pre-Teut. roudho-, is a graded form of the widely-diffused Aryan root rŭdh, 'to be red,' which appears also in ModHG. Roſt (2), as well as in OHG. rutichôn, 'to be reddish,' MidHG. rôten, 'to redden,' and MidHG. rôt, 'red'; also in Goth. gariudjô, 'shamefacedness,' and perhaps Goth. *bi-rusnjan, 'to honour,' AS. rudu, 'redness,' and rúd, 'red,' E. rud (AS. rudduc, E. ruddock). In the non-Teut. languages, besides the words adduced under Roſt (2), the following are the principal cognates: Sans. rudhirá-s, 'red,' rôhita, 'red' (for *rôdhita); Gr. ἐρυθρός, 'red,' ἔρευθος, 'redness, flush,' ἐρυσίπελας, 'erysipelas,' ἐρεύθω, 'to redden' (OIc. rjóða; AS. reódan, 'to redden, kill'); Lat. ruber (rubro- for *rudhro-, Gr. ἐρυθρός, like barba for *bardhâ, see Bart), rufus, 'red,' rubidus, 'dark red,' rubeo, 'to blush with shame'; OSlov. rŭdrĭ, 'red,' rŭdĕti sę, 'to blush'; Lith. rùdas, rùavas, 'reddish brown,' raũdas, raudônas, 'red,' raudâ, 'red colour.' It is noteworthy that red in several of these languages is a sign of shame. Moreover, the Teut. cognates may be explained from an Aryan root rut, which appears also in Lat. rût-ilus, 'reddish.'—Derivatives Rötel, m., 'red chalk,' from MidHG. rœtel, rœtelstein, m., E. ruddle; comp. the equiv. Lat. rubrica, from ruber.—Röteln, plur. 'measles.'—Rotwelſch, 'jargon, cant,' from MidHG. rôticalsch, 'sharpers' language, gibberish,' allied to rôt, 'red-haired, deceptive'? rôt,

T

'false, cunning,' frequently occurs in MidHG.

Rotte, f., from the equiv. MidHG. *rotte, rote*, f., 'troop, detachment'; borrowed in the MidHG. period from OFr. *rote*, 'division of an army, troop,' whence also E. *rout* (MidE. *route*), Du. *rot*. The OFr. term is derived from MidLat. *rutta, rupta*; comp. Meuter.

rotten (1.), vb., 'to root out,' formed from the earlier MidG. *roten*, a variant of MidHG. *riuten*, 'to root out'; comp. Bav. *rieden*, Swiss *ussrüde*, 'to root out.'

rotten (2.), vb., 'to cause to rot or decay,' ModHG. only, from the equiv. LG. and Du. *rotten;* see röſten (2).

Rotz, m., 'mucus, snot,' from the equiv. MidHG. *roz, rotz*, OHG. *roz*, earlier *hroz*, m. and n., formed from a Teut. root *hrût* (Aryan *krud*); comp. OHG. *râzan*, AS. *hrûtan*, 'to snore, snort,' OIc. *hrjóta*. It can scarcely be compared with Gr. κόρυζα, 'cold, catarrh.'

Rübe (UpG. Rube), f., 'rape, turnip,' from the equiv. MidHG. *rüebe, ruobe*, OHG. *ruoba, ruoppa*, f. The OHG. word cannot have been borrowed from Lat. *râpa*, 'rape,' although names of vegetables (comp. Kohl, Rappes, and Rettich) have passed directly from Lat. into OHG.; for if the word were borrowed thus, the sounds of Lat. *râpa* must have been preserved, or rather the *p* must have been changed into *ff*. The assumption that the prim. Teut. form *rôbî* appearing in Rübe was borrowed is opposed by the OHG. graded form *râba*, MidHG. *râbe*, 'rape' (Swiss *räbi*). The pre-Teut. word is therefore related to Lat. *râpum, râpa*, with which Gr. ῥάπυς, ῥάφυς, 'turnip,' ῥάφανος, ῥαφάνη, 'radish,' OSlov. *rêpa*, Lith. *rôpė*, 'turnip,' are also connected. These cognates are wanting in East Aryan, hence the supposition that they were borrowed, as in the case of Hanf, is not to be discarded.—**Rübezahl,** 'Numbernips, a fabulous spirit of the Riesengebirge,' is a contraction of MidHG. *Ruobezagel*, 'turnip-tail' (MidHG. *zagel* is equiv. to E. *tail*, AS. *tægel*).

Rubrik, f., 'rubric,' from late MidHG. *rubrike*, f., 'red ink,' from Fr. *rubrique*, whence also E. *rubric;* for Lat. *rubrica* see Röthel.

ruchlos, adj., 'infamous, flagitious,' from MidHG. *ruoche-lôs*, 'unconcerned, reckless,' allied to MidHG. *ruoche*, f., 'care, carefulness'; comp. E. *reckless;* see ruhen and geruhen.

ruchtbar, ruchbar, adj., 'notorious,' ModHG. only, from LG., as is indicated by the LG. and Du. *cht* for the HG. *ft;* allied to MidHG. *ruoft*, 'fame, reputation'; see anrüchig, berüchtigt, and Gerücht.

Ruck, m., 'jerk, tug,' from MidHG. *ruc* (gen. *ruckes*), OHG. *ruc* (gen. *rucches*), m., 'sudden motion, jerk.'—**rücken,** vb., 'to jerk,' from MidHG. *rücken*, OHG. *rucchen*, 'to push along'; Goth. **rukki*, m., 'jolt,' and **rukkjan*, 'to jerk,' are wanting; comp. OIc. *rykkja*, 'to jerk,' and *rykkr*, m., 'jolt,' AS. *roccian*, 'to jerk,' E. *to rock*.

rucken, vb., 'to coo' (of pigeons), allied to MidHG. *ruckezen*, 'to coo,' and *rucku*, interj., 'coo!' (of pigeons); onomat. forms.

Rücken, m., 'back, rear, ridge,' from the equiv. MidHG. *rücke*, OHG. *rucki*, earlier *hrukki*, m. (Goth. **hrugja-* is to be assumed); comp. the equiv. OSax. *hruggi*, Du. *rug*, AS. *hrycg*, E. *ridge*, OIc. *hryggr*. Gr. ῥάχις, 'back,' is not allied, because *krukjô-* is the OAryan form for Rücken. It is more probably related to OIr. *crocen*, 'skin, back,' and the Sans. root *kruñc*, 'to bend,' so Rücken may have been named from its flexibility. See zurück.—**Rückgrat,** 'spine'; see Grat.—**rücken,** vb.; see Ruck.

Rüde, m., 'hound,' from MidHG. *rüde*, m., 'big hound,' OHG. *rudo, hrudeo;* OHG. **rutto* (comp. ModHG. dial. Rütte) is by chance not recorded, but it may be assumed from the equiv. AS. *ryþþa*, 'hound,' m. Their origin is not certain, espec. as it cannot be determined whether the initial *h* of the AS. word is permanent; we have probably to assume Goth. **ruþja*, m. Akin to AS. *roðhund* l.

Rudel, n., 'flock, herd, troop,' ModHG. only, of uncertain etymology, perhaps a dimin. of Rotte, 'host' (comp. MidHG. *rode* with *rotte*). OIc. *riðull*, 'small detachment of soldiers,' can scarcely prove the genuine G. origin of Rudel, since it probably belongs to *riða*, 'to ride.' The kinship of Rudel with Goth. *wriþus*, 'herd,' is also uncertain.

Ruder, n., 'oar, rudder,' from the equiv. MidHG. *ruoder*, OHG. *ruodar*, n.; corresponding to the equiv. Du. *roer*, AS. *rôþor*, E. *rudder* (Goth. **rôþr*, n., 'oar,' is by chance not recorded); in OIc. with a different suffix *ræði*, n., 'oar,' while *rôðr*, m., signifies 'rowing.' Goth. **rô-þra-*, 'oar,' belongs to AS. *rôwan*, str. vb., E. *to row*, OIc. *róa*, Du. *roeijen*, MidHG. *rüejen, ruon*, all of which signify 'to row.' The Teut.

root *ró* appears with the same meaning in the other Aryan languages, as *ró, rē, er, ar*; comp. OIr. *rám*, Lat. *ré-mus*, 'oar' (*ratis*, 'raft'), Gr. ἐ-ρέ-της, 'rower,' τρι-ήρης, 'trireme'; ἐρετμός, 'oar,' Sans. *arítra-s*, 'oar'; also the Aryan root *rē*, 'to push,' in OSlov. *rinąti, rējati*, 'to push,' Sans. *ar*, 'to drive.' Moreover, E. *oar*, from AS. *ár* (OIc. *ár*) is the relic of another OTeut. term (whence Finn. *airo*, 'oar').

Ruf, m., 'call, cry; report, fame, reputation,' from the equiv. MidHG. *ruof*, OHG. *ruof*, m., for an earlier **hruof;* corresponding to Goth. *hróps*, m., 'cry, clamour.' — **rufen**, vb., 'to call out, cry,' from the equiv. MidHG. *ruofen*, OHG. *ruofan;* corresponding to OSax. *hrópan*, Du. *roepen*, AS. *hrópan* (wanting in E.), 'to call out'; in Goth. *hrópjan*, OHG. *ruofen*, ModHG. *rüefen*, wk. vb., with the same meaning. In the non-Teut. languages there are no terms corresponding to the Teut. root *hróp*. See *ruchbar*.

rügen, vb., 'to denounce, censure, reprove,' from MidHG. *rüegen*, OHG. *ruogen*, 'to accuse, charge with, blame,' for an earlier *wrogjan;* comp. Goth. *wróhjan*, OSax. *wrógjan*, AS. *wrégan*, 'to accuse, charge with.' Allied to ModHG. **Rüge,** 'censure, blame, crime,' MidHG. *rüege*, Goth. *wróhs*, 'accusation,' OSax. *wróht*, 'strife,' AS. *wróht*, 'accusation, strife, crime.' The Goth. forms with *h* compared with the *g* in the other terms point to Aryan *k*, which was the cause of the grammatical change of *h* to *g*. An Aryan root *wrók, wrák*, has not yet been discovered.

Ruhe, f., 'rest, repose, calm, peace,' from the equiv. MidHG. *ruowe*, OHG. *ruowa*, f. (also MidHG. *ráwe*, OHG. *ráwa*, in the same sense); comp. OIc. *ró*, AS. *rów*, f., 'rest.' Goth. *rówa (with the graded form *réwa) corresponds exactly to Gr. ἐ-ρωή, 'desisting, ceasing, rest,' from Aryan *rówā;* the root *ró* contained in these words is probably allied to *ra-* in ModHG. **Rast;** yet the East MidG. **Ruge** used by Luther presents a difficulty. — **ruhen,** vb., 'to rest, repose, be calm,' from the equiv. MidHG. *ruowen* (*ráwen*), OHG. *ruowen* (*ráwen*); a denom. of **Ruhe.**

Ruhm, m., 'fame, celebrity; rumour,' from MidHG. *ruom* (*ruon*), m., 'fame, honour, praise,' OHG. *ruom*, earlier *hruom*, m.; comp. OSax. *hróm*, m., 'fame,' Du. *roem*. From the root *hró* are derived, with a different suffix, the equiv. OIc. *hróðr*, m.,

AS. *hréþ*, m., OHG. *hruod-, ruod-*, in compounds like Rudolf, Robert, &c.; also Goth. *hróþeigs*, 'victorious.' The Teut. root *hró* is based on Aryan *kar, krā*, to which Sans. *kīr*, 'to commend,' and *kīrtí*, 'fame,' are allied.

Ruhr, f., 'stir, disorder, diarrhœa, dysentery,' from the equiv. MidHG. *ruor*, *ruore*, f., lit. 'violent, hasty motion'; allied to *rühren;* comp. MidHG. *ruortranc*, 'purgative.' The general meaning 'violent motion' is still preserved in the compound Aufruhr, 'riot.' — **rühren,** vb., 'to stir, move (the feelings); touch,' from MidHG. *ruēren*, OHG. *ruorern*, 'to put in motion, incite, stir up, bestir oneself, mix, touch'; comp. OSax. *hrórian*, 'to move, stir,' Du. *roeren*, AS. *hréran* (to which AS. *hréremús*, E. *reremous*, is allied), OIc. *hréra*. We have probably to assume Goth. *hrózjan, to which *hrisjan*, 'to shake,' and OIc. *hress*, 'quick,' are perhaps allied. See **Ruhr.** The Teut. root *hrós* (Aryan *krás*) has no cognate terms in the other groups.

rülpsen, vb., 'to belch, eructate,' ModHG. only, early ModHG. *rültzen;* of obscure origin. Yet late MidHG. *rülz*, 'coarse fellow, peasant,' seems to be allied.

Rum, m., late ModHG. from the equiv. E. *rum*, whence also Fr. *rhum, rum*. The source of the word is said to be some American language; formerly it was wrongly derived from Sans. *róma*, 'water.'

Rummel, m., 'rumble, din, lumber, lump,' ModHG. only, from LG. *rummel*, 'heap' Du. *rommelen*, 'to tumble,' *rommelzo*, 'medley'; see **rumpeln.** In the sense of 'noise' **Rummel** is connected with Du. *rommelen*, 'to rattle, roar, drink (of beasts),' to which OIc. *rymja*, 'to roar, make a noise,' must be related.

rumpeln, vb., 'to rumble, rummage, throw into confusion,' from MidHG. *rumpeln*, 'to make a noise or din, fall with a clatter'; probably an intensive form on account of the *p*. Comp. the equiv. MidE. *romblen*, E. *to rumble;* allied to Du. *rommelen*, 'to make a noise,' the *mb* being assimilated to *mm;* hence **Rummel** means 'lumber.'

Rumpf, m., 'trunk, body,' from the equiv. MidHG. (MidG.) *rumph*, m.; in UpG. and MidG. *botech*, OHG. *botah* (AS. *bodig*, E. *body*). Comp. LG. *rump*, Du. *romp*, 'trunk,' MidE. *rumpe*, E. *rump*, Scand. *rumpr*, 'rump.' Allied to **rümpfen** ?.

rümpfen, vb., 'to turn up (the nose),' from MidHG. *rümphen,* 'to turn up (the nose), wrinkle'; OHG. **rumpfen* is wanting, *rimpfan* (MidHG. *rimphen*), 'to contract, wrinkle,' being used; comp. Du. *rimpelen,* 'to wrinkle,' and *rompelig,* 'rugged.' The cognates have scarcely lost an initial *h* in spite of the existence of AS. *hrympele,* 'wrinkle,' and *gehrumpen,* 'wrinkled,' since *gerumpen,* 'bent,' is also recorded in AS. without an initial *h.* The Teut. root *rimp* (comp. further E. *rimple, rumple,* and Du. *rimpel,* 'wrinkle') has been connected with Gr. ῥάμφος, 'curved beak, espec. of birds of prey,' as well as ῥέμβομαι, 'to roam,' ῥαμφή, 'curved dagger.'

rund, adj., 'round,' from the equiv. Mid HG. *runt* (gen. *rundes*), adj.; borrowed from Fr. *rond* (from Lat. *rotundus*), whence also E. *round,* Du. *rond,* Dan. and Swed. *rund.*

Rune, f., see **rannen.**

Runge, f., 'rung; bolt, pin; trigger,' from MidHG. and MidLG. *runge,* f., 'dragshoe'; OHG. **runga,* older **hrunga,* f., are by chance not recorded; comp. Goth. *hrugga,* f., 'staff,' AS. *hrung,* E. *rung.* The prim. sense is probably 'spar,' therefore the connection with ModHG. Ring is doubtful.

Runkelrübe, f., 'beetroot,' ModHG. only, of obscure origin.

runflig, adj., 'flowing, running,' in blutrünftig, 'bleeding, bloody,' from Mid HG. *bluot-runsec, -runs,* adj., 'bloody, wounded,' allied to MidHG. and OHG. *bluot-runs,* 'hæmorrhage, bleeding wound.' *Runs* is an abstract from rinnen; comp. Goth. *runs* (gen. *runsis*), 'course,' *runs blôþis,* 'issue of blood.' Hence also Mod HG. (dial.) Runß, 'course of a torrent.'

Runzel, f., 'wrinkle, fold, rumple,' from the equiv. MidHG. *runzel,* OHG. *runzila,* f.; dimin. of OHG. *runza,* MidHG. *runze,* f., 'wrinkle.' By inference from OIc. *krukka,* MidHG. *runke,* and E. *wrinkle* (AS. *wrincle*), the OHG. from *runza* represents **wrunkza, *wrunkiza,* with a dimin. suffix; the loss of the guttural is normal as in Bliß from **blikz,* Lenz from **lenkz.* In the non-Teut. languages comp. Lat. *rūga,* Lith. *rùkti,* 'to become wrinkled,' *raũkas,* 'wrinkle' (see further rauh).

Rüpel, m., 'coarse fellow, lubber,' prop. a Bav. abbreviation of Ruprecht (hence Rüpel and Rüppel as surnames); for a similar use of proper names comp. Meße. Probably the meaning of Rüpel was occasioned by Knecht Ruprecht, 'Knight Robert' (bugbear in nursery tales), in whose character maskers disported themselves in a rude and coarse manner.

rupfen, vb., 'to pluck (feathers), pick,' from MidHG. *rupfen, ropfen,* an intensive form of raufen. To this is allied *ruppig,* 'battered,' from LG. *ruppen* for UpG. rupfen.

Rüffel, m., 'trunk (of an elephant), snout,' from the equiv. MidHG. *rüezel,* m.; ModHG. has shortened the real stem vowel as in laffen, from MidHG. *lâzen.* OHG. **ruozil,* earlier **wruozil,* are unrecorded. Comp. the equiv. AS. *wrôt,* East Fris. *wrôte,* formed without the *l* suffix; also OHG. *ruozzen,* 'to root or tear up the earth,' Du. *wroeten* and North Fris. *wretten,* 'to root,' AS. *wrôtan, wrôtian,* E. *to root.* The Teut. root *wrôt,* 'to root up' (Rüffel is lit. 'the uprooting snout of a pig'), from pre-Teut. *wrôd* (yet see Wurzel), has not yet been discovered in the non-Teut. languages; perhaps Lat. *rôdere,* 'to gnaw,' is primit. allied.

Rüfte, f., from the equiv. late MidHG. *rust,* f., 'repose, rest,' a variant of Raft, derived from LG. Comp. Du. *rust,* 'rest.'

rüften, vb., 'to prepare, equip, arm,' from MidHG. *rüsten,* OHG. *rusten,* earlier **hrustjan,* 'to arm, prepare, adorn'; comp. Du. *rusten,* AS. *hyrstan* (for *hrystan*), 'to deck, adorn.' A denom. of OHG. *rust,* 'armour,' AS. *hyrst,* 'decoration, adornment, armour,' which again are verbal abstracts from a Teut. root *hruþ,* 'to adorn.' Comp. AS. *hreôdan,* 'to adorn,' OIc. *hrjôða,* 'to cleanse, discharge (a ship).' May we also connect with this root *hruþ,* Teut. **hrossa-,* 'charger,' as a partic. in *ta-* in the sense of 'that which is adorned,' in so far as it is an object of adornment? The Teut. root *hruþ* (from Aryan *kruth, krut*?) has been said, probably without any proof, to exist in Gr. κεκορυθμένος, 'armed,' κορύσσω, 'to arm,' κορυθ-, 'helmet'; yet the dissyllable root κορυθ- cannot be made to tally with the Teut. *hruþ* of one syllable. See also Gerüfte.

rüftig, adj., 'prepared for action, vigorous, robust,' from MidHG. *rüstec,* 'vigorous, armed,' OHG. *rustîg,* 'prepared, adorned.' With regard to the evolution of meaning comp. fertig, also entrüftet. OIc. *hraustr,* 'brave, competent,' is more remote.

Ruß, m., 'soot,' from the equiv. Mid HG. and OHG. *ruoz,* m.; comp. Du. *roet,* 'soot.' LG. *sot*, E. *soot*, and its equiv. AS. *sót* are scarcely allied. OHG. *ruoʒ* probably represents *hruoʒ,* *hrôta-*, but whether it is to be connected with Goth. *hrót*, 'roof,' is more than questionable; it is more probably allied to AS. *hrót*, 'dirt.' No cognate terms are found in the non-Teut. languages.

Rute, f., 'rod, switch, wand, rod (about 15 feet),' from MidHG. *ruote*, OHG. *ruota*, f., 'switch, rod, pole, rod (a measure)'; corresponding to OSax. *rôda*, f., 'cross,' Du. *roede*, 'rod (also a measure),' AS. *ród*, f., 'cross,' E. *rod*, *rood*. Goth. *ráda, f., 'pole, stake,' is wanting. A pre-Teut. *rádhá-* is not found elsewhere; but is Lat. *rādius*, 'staff,' primit. allied ?

rutſchen, vb., 'to slide, glide, slip,' from late MidHG. *rütschen*, 'to glide,' with the variant *rützen*. Perhaps it belongs to the same root as *rütteln*, *rütten* (*zerrütten*), which are based on MidHG. *rütteln*, *rütten*, 'to shake.'

S.

Saal, m., 'hall, large room, drawing-room,' from MidHG. and OHG. *sal*, m. and n., 'house, large room, hall, building generally containing only one room, especially used for assemblies'; OSax. *seli*, m., 'building consisting of only one large room.' In OHG. and OSax. the term *selihûs*, 'house with a large room,' is also used; AS. *sęle*, *salor*, *sæl*, 'hall, palace,' OIc. *salr*, m. (OTeut. *saloz*, *saliz*, n., may be assumed). Goth. preserves only the allied *saljan*, 'to find shelter, remain,' and *salipwôs*, f. plur., 'lodging, guest-chamber'; comp. with the latter OHG. *sęlida*, f., 'dwelling,' MidHG. *selde.* To these OSlov. *selitva*, f., 'dwelling,' and *selo*, n., 'courtyard, village,' and also Lat. *sŏlum*, 'soil, ground.' From the Teut. cognates are derived the Rom. class, Ital. *sala*, Fr. *salle*, 'hall, room.'

Saat, f., 'sowing, seed, crop,' from the equiv. MidHG. and OHG. *sât*, f.; corresponding to OSax. *sâd*, n., Du. *zaad*, AS. *sǽd*, m. and n., E. *seed*, OIc. *sǽðe*, and *sáð*, n., 'seed,' Goth. only in *mana-sêþs* (þ equiv. to *d*), f., 'mankind, world.' OTeut. *sê-di-* and *sê-da-* are abstract forms from the primit. root *sê*, 'to sow,' contained in ſäen and Same.

Säbel, m., 'sabre,' from the equiv. late MidHG. and early ModHG. Sabel and Sebel, m., which, like the equiv. Fr. and E. *sabre* and Ital. *sciabla*, seems to be derived from the East; the ultimate source is still uncertain. The Slav. words, such as Russ. *sablja*, Pol. *szabla*, Serv. *sablja*, as well as Hun. *száblya*, appear to have been borrowed.

Säbenbaum, see Sebenbaum.

Sache, f., 'thing, matter, affair, business, case,' from MidHG. *sache*, OHG. *sahha*, f., 'quarrel, cause of dispute, lawsuit, opportunity, affair, cause, reason'; corresponding to the equiv. OIc. *sǫk*, f., and OSax. *saka*, f.; comp. Du. *zaak*, 'thing,' AS. *sacu*, 'strife, feud,' E. *sake*, Goth. *sakjô*, f., 'strife, dispute.' The cognates are connected with Goth. *sakan*, 'to strive, dispute,' AS. *sacan*, OSax. *sakan*, OHG. *sahhan*, 'to blame, scold; sue (at law).' The root *sak*, 'to contend, sue (at law),' is peculiar to Teut. The evolution in meaning is worthy of special notice. The general sense 'case' is a later development of 'lawsuit, dispute,' which has been preserved in ModHG. Sachwalter, 'attorney, advocate' (see further Widerſacher). Old legal parlance developed the former from the latter.

ſacht, adj., 'soft, gentle, slow, gradual,' ModHG. only (unknown to UpG.), from LG. *sacht*, comp. Du. *zacht;* LG. and Du. *cht* for HG. *ft*. It corresponds to HG. ſanft, the nasal of which has disappeared even in OSax. *sâfto*, adv., 'softly, gently.'

Sack, m., 'sack, bag, pocket,' from the equiv. MidHG. *sac* (gen. *sackes*), OHG. *sac* (gen. *sacches*), m.; corresponding to the equiv. Goth. *sakkus*, m., OIc. *sekkr*, m., AS. *sæcc*, m., E. *sack*, and Du. *zak*. A loan-word from Lat. *saccus* (Ital. *sacco*, Fr. and OIr. *sac*), which came through the medium of Gr. σάκκος, from the Hebr. and Phœnic. *sak*. The Lat. word seems to have been introduced into G., through commercial intercourse with Roman merchants, at a very early period (in Cæsar's time ?), probably contemporaneously with Arche, Kiſte, and Schrein.

ſackerlot, interj., 'zounds !' late Mod HG., remodelled from Fr. *sacré nom de Dieu;* also corrupted into ſapperlot. Sackerment (Sacrament), from *sacramentum*, signifies 'body of Christ.'

Säen, vb., 'to sow (seed),' from the equiv. MidHG. *sæjen, sæn*, OHG. *sáen* (from an orig. *sèjan*); comp. the equiv. Goth. *saian*, OIc. *sá*, AS. *sáwan*, E. *to sow*, Du. *zaaijen*, OSax. *sájan*. The Teut. root *sê*, 'to sow,' of which Saat and Same are derivatives, is common to the Aryan group; comp. the Lat. root *sê* in *sê-vi, sa-tum, sê-men* (Lat. *sero* is a reduplicated pres. for *si-so); OSlov. *sěja (sěti)*, 'to sow,' Lith. *sèja (sěti)*, 'to sow.'

Safran, m., 'saffron,' from MidHG. *safrán*, m., which is derived from Fr. *safran* (comp. E. *saffron*); comp. Ital. *zafferano*, the ultimate source of which is the equiv. Arab. *záfarán*.

Saft, m., 'sap, juice,' from the equiv. MidHG. *saft*, usually *saf*, OHG. *saf* (gen. *saffes*), n.; corresponding to AS. *sæp*, n., E. *sap*, Du. and LG. *sap*. Its connection with Lat. *sapio* (OHG. *seven, seppen*, MidHG. *seben*, 'to observe') and *supor* is conceivable on account of OIc. *safe*, 'sap,' provided that an Aryan root *sap, sab* (comp. Sans. *sabar*, 'nectar') seems possible (on the other hand, Gr. ὀπός, 'sap,' and OSlov. *sokŭ* are not allied). The prevalent view that AS. *sæp* and OHG. *saf* were borrowed from Lat. *sápa*, 'thick must,' is unsatisfactory.

Sage, f., 'legend, report,' from MidHG. *sage*, OHG. *saga*, f., 'speech, declaration, tale, rumour'; an abstract from *sagen*, like AS. *saga*, f., from *secgan*; E. *saw*.—**sagen**, vb., 'to say, tell, utter,' from the equiv. MidHG. *sagen*, OHG. *sagên*; corresponding to OSax. *seggian*, LG. *seggen*, Du. *zeggen*, AS. *secgan* (from *sagjan). E. *to say*, and its equiv. OIc. *segja*. In Goth. both *sagan and every other derivative from the same root are wanting. Teut. *sagai-*, which comes by the rule of grammatical change from Aryan *sokêy-*, is closely allied to Lith. *sakýti*, 'to say,' OSlov. *sočiti*, 'to notify'; with this OLat. *insece*, 'I narrate' (*in-sectiones*, 'tales'), is usually connected, as well as the Gr. root σεπ, σεκ in ἔννεπε for ἐν-σεπε, ἴ-σπ-ετε, 'tell (thou or ye).' OIr. *sagim, saigim*, 'I speak, say,' also point to a similar class. In Rom. only one loan-word of this class is found; comp. Span. *sayon*, 'usher' (of a law-court), lit. 'speaker.'

Säge, f., 'saw,' from the equiv. MidHG. *sëge, sage*, OHG. *sëga, saga*, f.; comp. Du. *zaag*, AS. *sage*, f., and *sagu*, f., E. *saw*; OIc. *sǫg*, f. (Goth. *saga, f., is wanting). A derivative of an Aryan root *sek, sok*, whence also Lat. *secáre*, 'to cut,' *securis*, 'hatchet'; see further under Eichel. The *ä* of ModHG. Säge is based, as is indicated by the modern Alem. dials., on *ē*; hence there is the same gradation in OHG. *sëga* and *saga* as in OHG. *rëhho* and AS. *racu* (see Rechen), or in HG. Nachen and E. *neck*. With the Aryan root *sek, sok*, are also connected in Teut., OHG. *sahs*, 'sword' (see Messer), E. *scythe*, and AS. *sīðe*, from Sichel; comp. OIc. *sigðr*, m., 'sickle,' OHG. *sëh*, MidHG. *sëch*, 'ploughshare,' and the cognates of Sense.

Sahne, f., 'cream,' from the equiv. late MidHG. (MidG. and LG.) *sane*, f.; comp. Du. *zaan*. The word orig. also belonged probably to UpG., as is indicated by the derivative Senne (for Sahne the UpG. and MidG. word Rahm is now used, in Swiss also *nidel*, and in other dials. Schmant). The origin of the cognates is obscure.

Saite, f., 'string' (of a musical instrument), from MidHG. *seite*, m. and f., OHG. *seita*, f., *seito*, m., 'string, cord, fetter'; comp. OHG. *seid*, n., 'cord, noose,' AS. *sáda*, m., 'cord, noose,' derived by means of the Aryan suffix *t* from the Teut. and Aryan root *sai*, by gradation *sī*, 'to bind,' which appears in Seil; comp. further OIc. *seimr*, m., 'string' (Goth. **sai-ma-*), and *sīma*, n., 'string,' AS. *sīma*, OSax. *sīmo*, m., 'cord'; also Gr. ἱ-μάς, 'strap,' and the Sans. root *si*, 'to bind, fetter.' The derivatives most closely allied to the Teut. word are OSlov. *sě-tl*, f., 'cord,' and Lith. *saitas*, m., 'cord.' With regard to the pre-Teut. root *sī, sai*, see further under Seil.

-sal, in Mühsal, see selig.

Salamander, m., 'salamander,' from the equiv. MidHG. *salamander*, m. and f.; the origin of the meaning 'toast' (drunk in special honour of a guest at students' clubs), which first became current between 1830 and 1840, is very much disputed.

Salat, m., 'salad,' late MidHG. *salát*, m., from the equiv. Ital. *salata, insalata*.

Salbader, m., 'idle talker, quack,' ModHG. only (the earliest reference is in the Epistolæ Obscurorum Virorum); its origin is wrongly attributed to the owner of a bathing establishment (ein Bader) at Jena, who bored his guests with his stale stories. Others prefer to connect it with *salvator*, 'saviour,' so that Salbadern would mean 'to have the *name* salvator on one's lips, and nothing more,' an equally improbable explanation.

Salbe, f., 'salve,' from the equiv. MidHG. *salbe,* OHG. *salba,* f.; a common Teut. term; comp. OSax. *salba,* Du. *zalf,* AS. *scalf,* E. *salve* (Goth. *salba,* f., may be inferred from *salbôn,* 'to anoint'). The Teut. *salbô-,* from pre-Teut. *solpā-,* is entirely unrelated to Gr. ἀλείφω; Gr. ἔλπος, 'oil,' ἔλφος, 'butter,' ὄλπη, 'oil-flask,' Sans. *sarpis,* n., 'grease,' are more probably allied to Salbe.

Salbei, m., 'sage,' from MidHG. *salbeie, salveie,* OHG. *salbeia, salveia,* f., from Mid Lat. *salvegia,* a variant of Lat. and Rom. *salvia* (Fr. *sauge,* whence E. *sage*).

Salbuch, n., 'register of the survey of lands,' from MidHG. *sal-buoch,* n., 'register of lands belonging to the community, a record of receipts and donations,' from Mid HG. *sal,* f., 'legal assignment of an estate,' which, with MidHG. *sal,* m., 'legacy,' is connected with OHG. *sellen,* AS. *sellan,* 'to surrender.' The corresponding E. verb *to sell* has acquired a different shade of meaning.

Salm, Salmen, m., 'salmon,' from MidHG. *salme,* OHG. *salmo,* m., from the equiv. Lat. *salmo.*

Salweide, f., 'sallow, round-leaved willow'; allied to MidHG. *salhe,* f., OHG. *salaha* (Goth. *salhô*), f., 'willow'; the second part of the ModHG. compound serves as an explanation of the old term, which is undoubtedly of genuine Teut. origin; comp. OIc. *selja,* f. (Goth. *salhjô*), and AS. *sealh,* E. *sallow.* Primit. allied to Gr. ἑλίκη (Arcad.), Lat. *sălix* (acc. *salicem*), 'willow'; Fr. *saule* is based not on the Lat., but on the HG. word.

Salz, n., 'salt,' from the equiv. MidHG. and OHG. *salz,* n.; corresponding to the equiv. Goth. *salt,* AS. *sealt,* n., E. *salt,* Du. *zout,* OSax. *salt* (also an adj. OIc. *saltr,* AS. *salt,* 'salty, saline'). The specifically Teut. form *sal-ta-* (whence Lapp. *salte*) is of course related to Lat. *sal,* Gr. ἅλς; comp. further OSlov. *solĭ,* Lett. *sāls,* OIr. *salann,* 'salt.' The lengthened pre-Teut. root *sald* appears also in Lat. *sallere,* 'to salt,' with the assimilation of *ld* to *ll;* in Lith. the corresponding adj. *saldùs* has the remarkable signification 'sweet' (Lith. *druskà,* 'salt,' is connected with Lett. *druska,* 'crumb.' Among the Eastern Aryans a cognate term is wanting, the word salt, curiously enough, not being mentioned in the Rig-Veda. Perhaps the Western Aryans, in their migration, got their knowledge of the mineral from a civilised tribe that has also exercised an influence on European languages in other instances (comp. Silber). That a graded form could be constructed from even a foreign term admits of no doubt (see Sülze). Perhaps the divergence between Teut. *salta-* and Gr.-Lat. *sal-* is due to differences anterior to the period in which the word was borrowed.

sam, see langsam.

Same, m., 'seed, semen, spawn,' from MidHG. *sâme,* OHG. and OSax. *sâmo,* m., 'grain of seed, seed, descendants, field, soil'; a derivative of the root *sê,* 'to sow,' contained in Saat and säen. Corresponding to Lat. *sēmen,* OSlov. *sĕmę,* 'seed,' Lith. *sėmi,* 'seed'; an Aryan neut. *sê-mn-,* with a suffix *men,* is implied; the same suffix appears in Keim and Blume. A different derivation is indicated by OIr. *sil* and Lith. *sėklà,* 'seed' (prim. form *sétla*).

Sämischleder, n., ModHG. only, corresponding to the equiv. E. *chamois leather* (also *shammy*), Fr. *peaux chamoisees;* of obscure origin, perhaps from Russ. *zamša,* 'wash-leather.'

sammeln, vb., 'to collect, gather,' from the equiv. MidHG. *samelen,* prop. with a n- suffix, *samenen,* OHG. *samanôn;* corresponding to OSax. *samnôn,* Du. *zamelen,* AS. *samnian,* OIc. *samna,* 'to collect'; a derivative of the OG. adv. *saman.* Primit. allied to Sans. *samand,* 'together.' See zusammen and gesamt.

Samstag, m., 'Saturday,' prop. a UpG. and Rhen. word (in MidG. and LG. Sonnabend), from MidHG. *samztac, sampstac,* OHG. *sambaztac.* In Du. *zaterday,* LG. *sáterdach,* AS. *sæternesdæg,* E. *Saturday,* which, like the equiv. OIr. *dia sathairnn* and Alban. *šëtúne,* are based on Lat. Saturni dies, unknown to Rom.; in OIc. *laugardagr, þváttdagr* (lit. 'bathing day'). From the ecclesias. Lat. *sabbati dies* (whence Fr. *samedi,* Ital. *sabbato,* Prov. *dissapte,* and Ir. *sapait*), OHG. *sambaz-tac,* ModHG. Samstag cannot be derived, for such a derivation does not explain the HG. nasal; nor can the *t* of an ecclesias. Lat. word be changed to z. Since OSlov. *sgbota,* Magy. *szombat,* and Rouman. *sâmbâtâ* are the most closely allied to OHG. *sambaz-,* we may perhaps assume that it is of Eastern origin, which supposition is supported by the fact that Bav. *pfinz-tac*, 'Thursday,' is borrowed from Gr. πέμπτη (see Pfingſtag). Although Gr. *σαμβατον, a parallel form of σάββατον, has not yet been discovered, we may infer its existence from Pers. *šamba* almost with certainty ; the corresponding Arab., Ethiop., and Abyss. words have also a medial *mb*. It is manifest that an Oriental term, *sambata*, of the 5th cent. was introduced into UpG. and Slav. through Gr. (along with Arianism, see Kirche and Pfaffe) ; yet it is strange that Ulfilas uses *sabbatō dags* without any nasal (comp. Goth. *aíkklēsjō* with West-Teut. *kirika*, from κυριακόν).

Samt, m., 'velvet,' from the equiv. Mid HG. *samît, samât*, m. ; borrowed in the MidHG. period from Rom. ; comp. Mid Lat. *samitum*, Ital. *sciamito*, OFr. *samit*. The ultimate source is MidLat. *examitum*, ModGr. ἑξάμιτον, 'a stuff made of six twisted threads' (Gr. μίτος, 'thread '), whence also OSlov. *aksamitŭ*, 'velvet.' Span. and Port. *terciopelo*, 'velvet,' lit. 'consisting of triple threads,' is similarly formed.

ſamt, prep. adv., 'together with,' from MidHG. *samt*, earlier *sament*, OHG. *samant*, adv. 'together,' also a prep. with dat. 'together with.' See zuſammen and ſammeln.

Sand, m., 'sand,' from the equiv. Mid HG. *sant* (gen. *sandes*), OHG. *sant* (gen. *-tes*), m. ; corresponding to the equiv. OSax. *sand*, m. and n., Du. *zand*, AS. *sǫnd*, n., E. *sand*, Olc. *sandr*, m. (Goth. **sanda-*, m. and n., is by chance not recorded). They represent pre-Teut. *samdho-, samadho-* (in Teut. *m* before *d* is changed into *n*; see Mand, Hundert, and Schande) ; comp. Gr. ἄμαθος, 'sand.' The equiv. Bav. and Tyrol. *samp* (MidHG. *sampt*), from OHG. **samat*, corresponds exactly to the Gr. word ; comp. further E. dial. *samel*, 'sandy soil,' with Lat. *sabulum*, from **samulum* ?.

Sandel, m., 'sandal - wood,' ModHG. only, from Ital. *sandalo* (Fr. *sandal*), 'an Indian dyeing wood ' ; "from Gr. σάνταλον, which comes from Arab. *zandal*, but orig. derived from Sans. *candana*. The tree grows in the East Indies, whence the wood was brought to the West as an article of commerce."

ſanft, adj., 'soft, gentle,' from MidHG. *senfte*, adj., *sanfte*, adv., OHG. *semfti*, adj., *samfto*, adv., 'softly ' ; corresponding to the equiv. OSax. *sāfti*, adj., *safto*, adv. (comp. ſacht), AS. *sēfte*, adj., *sōfte*, adv.,

'softly' (E. *soft*) ; wanting in East Tent. Do the cognates belong to Goth. *samjan*, 'to please'? (comp. Ranft, from the root *ram*). Deriv. Sänfte.

Sang, m., 'song,' from MidHG. *sanc* (gen. *-ges*), OHG. *sang*, m., 'singing, song ' ; see ſingen.

ſapperlot, see ſackerlot.

Sardelle, f., 'sardine,' first occurs in ModHG., from Ital. *sardella* (MidLat. *sarda*, prop. ' the Sardinian '), a variant of *sardina*.

Sarder, m., 'sardel, sardine,' from late MidHG. *sarde*, MidHG. usually *sardîn*, m., 'a precious stone'; from MidLat. *sarda* (Gr. σάρδιον).

Sarg, m., 'coffin,' from MidHG. *sarc* (gen. *sarkes*) and *sarch* (gen. *sarches*), m., 'coffin, vault, grave,' also generally 'shrine, receptacle,' OHG. *saruh, sarch*, m., 'sarcophagus, coffin ' ; comp. Du. *zerk*, 'gravestone.' Rom. has a corresponding class in ModFr. *cercueil*, 'coffin,' and its earlier cognates. The ordinary derivation from σαρκοφάγος, 'sarcophagus,' was repudiated as early as Lessing, because Sarg in MidHG. ' signified in countless passages a receptacle generally, a water vessel, a trough, a shrine for idols or saints ' ; perhaps the Gr. term has helped to determine the Mod HG. meaning and the spelling of the word with *g*. As yet nothing definite has been discovered concerning this probably Teut. word. It may be connected with Olc. *serkr*, 'shirt,' since the Aryan root *serg* in Lith. *sérgėti* (OSlov. *strěga, strěšti*), ' to watch over, guard,' has a general signification (Sarg, 'receptacle ').

ſatt, adj., 'sated, satiated,' from the equiv. MidHG. and OHG. *sat* (gen. *sates*), adj. ; corresponding to the equiv. OSax. *sad*, AS. *sæd*, 'sated' (E. *sad*), Olc. *saðr* (*saddr*), Goth. *saps*, 'sated.' A Teut. partic. in *-da-* (see ſaut and ſalt) connected with an Aryan root *sā*, 'to satiate,' from whose long vowel form Goth. *sō-þjan*, ' to satisfy,' and *sō-þs*, ' repletion,' are constructed. Comp. Lat. *sat, satis, satur* ; Lith. *sōtas*, m., 'repletion,' *sōtus*, 'satiating, easily satiated ' ; Gr. ἄμεναι (ἅ), 'to satiate,' ἇ-ατος, 'insatiable,' and ἅ-δην, 'sufficiently' ; OIr. *sathach*, 'sated,' *sásaim*, 'to sate, satiate,' *sáith*, 'repletion' (OSlov. *sytŭ*, 'sated,' is, on account of its vowel, not allied). The meaning of E. *sad* is curiously developed from the idea expressed by ſatt.

Satte, Sette, f., 'bowl, porringer,

milk-pan,' ModHG. only, from LG. *satte, sette*, a derivative of ſiṭen, 'to sit'; the milk is kept in Satten, so that the cream may set. OHG. *satta*, 'basket, provision basket,' which became obsolete as early as the beginning of the MidHG. period, does not appear to be allied.

Sattel, m., 'saddle,' from the equiv. MidHG. *satel*, OHG. *satal, satul*, m.; corresponding to Du. *zadel*, AS. *sadol*, E. *saddle*, OIc. *spðull*, m.; Goth. *saduls is by chance not recorded. The assumption that the word is borrowed from Lat. *sedīle* is not supported either by the sound or the meaning. The common OTeut. **sadula-* cannot, however, be primit. allied to ſiṭen (Teut. root *set*). Perhaps the word was anciently borrowed from another Aryan tongue, which could probably form *sadula-* from the root *sed*, 'to sit' (comp. Reich); comp. Slav. *sedlo* (*sedīlo*), 'saddle.'

Saturei, f., 'savory' (bot.), from the equiv. MidHG. *satereie*; comp. Ital. *satureja*, Fr. *sarriette*, MidLat. *saturēja*.

Satz, m., 'sediment; sentence; set; wager,' from MidHG. *saz* (gen. *satzes*), m.; a graded form of ſiṭen, signifying in Mid HG. 'place where something lies or is put, position, situation, mandate, law, purpose,' &c.

Sau, f., 'sow, hog,' from the equiv. Mid HG. and OHG. *sû*, f.; corresponding to AS. *sû*, E. *sow*, OIc. *sýr*, 'sow.' Du. *zog, zeug*, 'sow,' belong further, like AS. *sŭgu* (Goth. *sugus), and Suab., MidLG., and MidE. *suge*, to OTeut. *sû*, whence also Schwein (Goth. *swein*, n.) is derived. The term *sû*, 'pig,' is essentially West Aryan; comp. Lat. *sû-s*, Gr. *ὗ-s, σῦ-s*, to which Zend *hu*, 'boar,' is allied; for further references see under Schwein. The root is Sans. *sû*, 'to bring forth' (comp. Sohn), so that the 'sow' was probably named from its fecundity; others regard *sû* as an imitation of the grunting of the pig, because in Sans. the animal is termed *sûkara*, lit. '*sû* maker.' Sau, in its prov. sense, 'ace' (of cards), seems, like Hund, to have been an old technical term in dice-playing, yet early references are wanting.

ſauber, adj., 'neat, clean, nice, pretty,' from MidHG. *sûber, sûver*, 'neat, clean, pretty,' OHG. *sûbar, sûbiri*; OSax. *sûbri, Du. *zuiver*, AS. *sŷfre*, 'clean, purified, spotless'; Goth. **sûbri-* is wanting. Since the agreement of the OWest Teut. dials. proves the early existence of the Teut.

word, the assumption that it was borrowed from Lat. *sobrius* or Gr. σύφαρ cannot be maintained.

ſauer, adj., 'sour, acid, bitter,' from the equiv. MidHG. and OHG. *sûr*, adj.; corresponding to Du. *zuur*, MidLG. and AS. *sûr*, E. *sour*, OIc. *sûrr*; Goth. *sûra-* is by chance not recorded. Pre-Teut. *sû-rô-s is further attested by OSlov. *syrŭ*, 'raw,' and Lith. *sûras*, 'salty.' Perhaps Gr. ξυρός, 'sour' (in Hesych.), and the root ξυ, 'to scrape, scratch,' are also allied; in that case ſauer would mean 'scratching.' From Teut. is derived Fr. *sur*, 'sour.'

ſaufen, vb., 'to drink' (of beasts), from MidHG. *sûfen*, OHG. *sûfan*, 'to sip, lap, drink'; MidLG. *sûpen*, AS. *sûpan*, and OIc. *sûpa* have the same sense; comp. further Du. *zuipen*, 'to drink,' E. *to sup* (the verb *to sip* seems to be connected with Goth. *sûpjan). For the Teut. root *sûp*, which has not yet been found in other groups, see Seff and Suppe; comp. further ſeufzen.

ſaugen, vb., 'to suck, absorb,' from the equiv. MidHG. *sûgen*, OHG. *sûgan*; Du. *zuigen*, MidLG. *sûgen*, AS. *sûgan* (also *sûcan*, E. *to suck*), OIc. *sûga* have the same meaning; Goth. *sûgan, *sûkan are by chance not recorded. Teut. root *sûg* (*sûk*), from pre-Teut. *sûk* (*sûg*); comp. Lat. *sûgere*, Lett. *sûzu* (*sûkt*), 'to suck,' OIr. *sûgim* (also OSlov. *sŭsa. sŭsati*, 'I suck')?

ſäugen, vb., 'to suckle,' from the equiv. MidHG. *söugen*, OHG. *sougen*, prop. 'to cause to suck'; a factitive of *sûgan*; see ſaugen. Goth. *saugjan is wanting.

Säule (1.) (Bav. Saul), f., 'pillar,' from the equiv. MidHG. *sûl* (plur. *siule*), OHG. *sûl* (plur. *sûli*), f.; comp. Du. *zuil*, AS. *sŷl*, OIc. *sûla*, 'pillar'; also, with gradation, Goth. *sauls*, f., 'pillar.' Perhaps Schwelle is primit. allied.

Säule (2.), f., 'awl,' from MidHG. *siule*, OHG. *siula*, f., 'awl, punch' (Goth. *siwila, f.); connected with the Aryan root *sīw*, "the primit. word for leather-work" (see Ahle). Comp. Goth. *sinjan*, OHG. *siuwan*, AS. *seówian*, E. *to sew*; also Lat. *suo*, 'I sew,' *sutor*, 'cobbler,' Gr. κασ-σύω, 'to patch, stitch,' Sans. root *sīv*, 'to sew,' OSlov. *ši-ti*, 'to sew.' In a sense corresponding to that of MidHG. *siule* we find Lat. *subula* and OSlov. *šilo*, which are formed from the same root. Comp. the following word.

Saum (1.), m., 'border,' from MidHG. and OHG. *soum*, m., 'sewn edge of a garment, border'; corresponding to Du. *zoom*, AS. *seám*, m., E. *seam*, OFris. *sâm*, OIc. *saumr*, m., 'border, seam' (Goth. **sauma-* is by chance not recorded). A graded form of the Aryan root *sū-*, a variant of the root *sīw*, 'to sew,' discussed under Säule (2). Comp. Sans. *sûtra*, 'thread.'

Saum (2.), 'load,' from MidHG. and OHG. *soum*, m., 'load of a beast of burden' (also as a measure of weight), 'beast of burden'; corresponding to AS. *seám*, 'horse-load,' E. *seam*. Borrowed prior to the OHG. period, probably even before the AS. migration, from Low Lat. *sauma* (σάγμα), 'pack-saddle,' whence also Ital. *salma*, Fr. *somme*.—Säumer, 'beast of burden, driver of sumpter-beasts,' from MidHG. *soumære*, OHG. *soumâri*, 'beast of burden,' AS. *seámere*; formed from MidLat. *sagmarius*.—Saumsattel, 'pack-saddle,' MidHG. *soumsatel*, AS. *seámsadol*.

säumen, vb., 'to linger,' from MidHG. *sûmen*, 'to stay, defer, loiter, linger'; OHG. only *virsûmen* (MidHG. *versûmen*), 'to let slip,' and *ar-sûmen*, 'to omit.' The history of the word is very obscure, because it is peculiar to G., and appears only in a compound form in OHG. The great antiquity of the compound is attested by MidHG. *frá-sûme*, m., 'delay,' which points to Goth. **frá-sûma*, m.; we should have expected MidHG. *versûme*. Probably the meaning, which properly belongs only to the compound, has been transferred to the simple form.—Saumsal, 'procrastinating disposition,' from the equiv. MidHG. *sûmesal*, *sûmesele*, with the suffix *-sal*: hence Mod HG. saumselig, MidHG. (MidG.) *sûmeselic*.

Saurach, m., 'barberry, pepperidge bush,' from the equiv. MidHG. *sûrach*, m. A derivative of sauer, MidHG. *sûr*.

Saus, m., 'buzz, bluster,' from MidHG. *sûs*, m., 'drinking, blustering, revelling and rioting'; even in MidHG. occurs *in dem sûse lében*, 'to revel and riot,' lit. 'noisy doings'; comp. OIc. *sús*, 'roar of the surf.' —sausen, 'to rage, bluster, buzz,' from MidHG. *sûsen* (*siusen*), OHG. *sûsôn*, 'to bluster, hum, hiss, creak, gnash'; derived from an OAryan root *sûs* (OSlov. *sysati*, 'to whistle, bluster,' Sans. root. *çuś*, 'to snort').—säuseln, vb., 'to rustle, murmur,' dimin. of MidHG. *siusen*, 'to bluster.'

Schabe (1.), 'mill-moth, cockroach,' from the equiv. MidHG. *schabe*, f.; OHG. **scaba*, f., is by chance not recorded in this sense; comp. AS. *mælsceafa*, 'caterpillar.'

Derived, like the following word, from schaben.

Schabe (2.), f., 'scraper, spokeshave,' from MidHG. *schabe*, OHG. *scuba*, f., 'spokeshave, plane.' Comp. Du. *schaaf*, 'plane,' AS. *sceafa*, E. *shave* (knife for shaving, hoop-axe), OIc. *skafa*, f., 'spokeshave.'

schaben, vb., 'to shave, scrape, scratch,' from MidHG. *schaben*, OHG. *scuban*, 'to scratch, erase, scrape,' corresponding to Goth. *skaban*, 'to shear'; OIc. *skafa*, 'to scratch, shave,' AS. *sceafan*, E. *to shave*, Du. *schaven*, 'to shave, smooth.' Teut. root *skab*, from the pre-Teut. root *skâp*; comp. Gr. σκάπ-τω, 'to dig,' σκαπάνη, 'spade,' Lith. *skópti*, 'to hollow out,' *skiptas*, 'woodcarver's knife'; allied also probably to Lat. *scabo*, 'to scratch, shave,' OSlov. *skoblĭ*, 'spokeshave,' Lith. *skabùs*, 'sharp' (Aryan root *skâb*). See the preceding words as well as Schuppe and Schaft.

Schabernack, m., 'hoax, practical joke,' from MidHG. *schabernac*, *schavernac*, m., 'hoax, mockery, scorn,' also chiefly 'shaggy (lit. neck-rubbing?) fur cap,' and 'a kind of strong wine.' Allied to OHG. *ir-scabarôn*, 'to scratch out, scrape together.' It is uncertain whether the second part of the compound is connected with ModHG. Nacken or with the verb neden. The Mid HG. word with its numerous senses may have also meant orig. 'prankish hobgoblin.' Comp. den Schelm im Nacken haben, 'to be a sly dog'?.

schäbig, adj., 'shabby, sordid, scabby,' from an earlier ModHG. Schabe, 'scab, itch'; comp. MidHG. *schębic*, 'scabby.' Allied, like AS. *sceabb*, E. *shab* (*shabby* perhaps influenced the ModHG. meaning of schäbig), to schaben.

Schach, n., 'chess,' from MidHG. *schâch*, m. and n., 'king (at chess), chessboard, checkmating move'; the chessboard was usually termed *schâch-zabel* in MidHG, *zabel* (even in OHG. *zabal*, 'chess or draught board'), being changed by permutation from Lat. *tabula*. MidHG. *schâch* was obtained through a Rom. medium from Pers. *schâh*, 'king'; it is strange, therefore, that the HG. word ends in *ch* in contrast to the Rom. *cc*; comp. Ital. *scacco*, Fr. *échec*. This must be ascribed to a fresh influence of the orig. word.

Schächer, m., 'robber,' from the equiv. MidHG. *schâchære*, OHG. *scâhhâri*, m., connected with MidHG. *schâch*, OHG. *scâh*, m., 'robbery, rapine'; comp. Du. *schaak*, 'rape, seduction,' OFris. *skák*, 'booty, robbery,' AS. *sceácere*, 'robber'; Goth. *skéka*, 'robbery,' is wanting. The Teut. cognates passed into Rom.; comp. OFr. *échec*, 'robbery.' Other terms related to the Teut. cognates are not found in the Aryan languages.

Schachern, vb., 'to chaffer, haggle,' Mod HG. only, allied to Hebr. *suchar*, 'gain.'

Schacht (1.), m., 'shaft' (of a pit), from the equiv. MidHG. *schaht*, m.; prop. the LG. form of Schaft. See the following word.

Schacht (2.), m., 'square rood,' Mod HG. only, from the equiv. LG. *schacht*, which is identical with HG. Schaft.—

Schachtelhalm, m., 'shave-grass,' likewise from LG., for the MidHG. equiv. term is *schaftel*, n., a dimin. of the MidHG. word for Schaft.

Schachtel, f., 'box, bandbox,' from the equiv. late MidHG. *schahtel*, f., which, with its equally late variant *schatel*, is borrowed from Ital. *scatola*, 'bandbox, box.' The change of the simple *t* into *cht* in Mid HG. and ModHG. has not yet been explained; comp., however, MidHG. *schahtelân* and *schatelan* for *kastelân*.—Schatulle is a recent loan-word with the same signification. Schachtel, 'old woman,' occurs even in late MidHG., in which *schahtel* also means 'female.' The latter looks a LG. loan-word for HG. *schaftel*, from Schaft.

Schade, n., 'damage, harm, injury,' from MidHG. *schade*, OHG. *scado*, m., 'damage, destruction, disadvantage'; corresponding to the equiv. Du. *schade*, OIc. *skaðe*, m. Further OIc. *skaðe*, OHG. *scado*, OSax. *scaðo*, AS. *sceaþa*, m., 'robber, foe,' allied to Goth. *skaþjan*, 'to injure, act unjustly,' AS. *scéþþan*, 'to injure,' OHG. *scadôn*, MidHG. and ModHG. *schaden*. An Aryan root *skâth*, corresponding to the Teut. root *skaþ*, appears in Gr. ἀσκηθής, 'unscathed.'

Schädel, m., 'skull,' from MidHG. *schëdel*, m., 'skull,' and also 'a dry measure'; unknown to Du. *schedel*, m.; unknown to the other OTeut. dials. (in OHG. *gëbal*, 'skull,' like Gr. κεφαλή; see Giebel) Its connection with Scheitel is conceivable.

Schaf, n., 'sheep,' from the equiv. Mid HG. *schâf*, OHG. *scâf*, n.; common to West Teut. in the same sense; comp. OSax. *scâp*, n., Du. *schaap*, n., AS. *sceáp*, n., E. *sheep*; in Goth. *lamb* (see Lamm), OIc. *fœr*, f., 'sheep,' whence *Fœr-eyjar*, 'the Faroe Isles' (lit. 'sheep isles'). Teut.

skêpo- (for *skéqo*-) corresponds perhaps to Sans. *chága*, 'he-goat.' Yet Aryan *owis*, by inference from Lat. *ovis*, Gr. ὄϝις, Sans. *ávis*, and Lith. *avìs* (OSlov. *ovĭca*), was the oldest term which is preserved in OTeut. and a few ModTeut. dials.; comp. Goth. *awistr*, 'sheepfold,' *awethi*, 'flock of sheep,' OHG. *ou*, OLG. *ewi*, AS. *eowu*, and E. *ewe* (to which *to yean* from *ge-eánian* is allied?).—**Schäfchen**, in the phrase sein Schäfchen ins Trockene bringen, 'to feather one's nest,' is usually explained as a corruption of LG. *schepken*, 'barque.' Perhaps it is, however, an ironical application of a passage in the parable of the Good Shepherd.

Schaff, n., 'vessel,' UpG.; see Scheffel.

schaffen, vb., 'to create, procure, obtain, bring,' from MidHG. *schaffen*, OHG. *scaffan*, 'to create, effect, arrange, do, make.' Also in a similar sense OHG. *scepfen*, *skeffen*, Goth. *gaskapjan*, AS. *scÿppan*, OSax. *sceppian* and Goth. **skapôn*, OHG. *scaffôn*, Mid HG. *schaffen*. These imply a root *skap* peculiar to Teut., the connection of which with schaben is not quite certain; see also schöpfen. OTeut. had a number of substant. derivatives from the same root, such as ModHG. Schöpfung, Geschöpf, and E. *shape*; see the following word and Schöffe.

Schaffner, m., 'purveyor, steward, manager,' from the equiv. MidHG. *schaffenære*, m., of which the equiv. variant *schaffaere* occurs; allied to schaffen; see al-o Schöffe.

Schafott, n., 'scaffold,' ModHG. only, from Fr. *echafaut*, earlier *chafaut*, through the medium of Du. *schavot*?.

Schaft (1.), m., 'shaft, handle, trunk, stalk,' from MidHG. *schaft*, OHG. *scaft*, m., 'shaft, spear, lance'; comp. OSax. *skaft*, m., 'spear,' Du. *schacht*, m., 'quill, shaft of a lance,' AS. *scëaft*, E. *shaft*, OIc. *skapt*, n., 'pole, spear'; Goth. **skafta*- is by chance not recorded. These substant. cognates can scarcely be related to schaffen, they are connected rather with schaben (lit. 'that which has been scraped or made smooth'?). It is most closely allied to Gr. σκῆπτρον, 'staff,' akin to Dor. (Pindar) σκᾶπτον, σκήπων, 'staff'; further Lat. *scâpus*, 'shaft'; hence OAryan *skâp*-, 'shaft.'

Schaft (2.), m., 'shelves, bookcase,' ModHG. only; from MidHG. *schaf*, 'vessel for containing liquids'?. For the latter see Scheffel.

Schakal, m., 'jackal,' ModHG. only,

from Pers. and Turk. *schakal;* through the medium of Fr. *chacal?*.

Schäkern, vb., 'to jest, joke, play,' late ModHG. (last cent.), from Jew.-Hebr. *scheker,* 'lie.'

Schal, adj., 'hollow, stale, flat,' from MidHG. (rare) *schal,* adj., 'turbid,' to which MidHG. *verschaln* and *schaln,* 'to become dim'; comp. Du. *verschalen,* 'to get flat or stale,' E. *shallow.* The term, the origin of which is obscure, is wanting in the UpG. dials.

Schale, f., 'shell, peel, scale, dish,' from MidHG. *schâl, schâle,* OHG. *scâla,* f., 'husk of fruit, egg-shell, &c., drinking cup' (hence Fr. *écale,* 'egg-shell, nut-shell'). It is questionable whether the two different senses are evolved from the same word. It is at all events probable that one of the meanings was connected with a form containing *â* (in the sense of 'husk'), the other with a form containing *â,* just as North Fris. distinguishes *skal* (orig. *â*), 'scale of animals,' &c., from *skeel* (orig. *â, ê*), 'bowl.' Comp. OSax. *scâla,* f., 'drinking cup,' AS. *scâlu,* 'husk,' E. *shale* and (under OIc. influence?) *scale,* OIc. *skâl,* f., 'drinking cup, scale (of a balance).' Akin to Goth. *skalja,* f., 'tile' (lit. perhaps 'shingle, similar to a scale'), OIc. *skel,* f., AS. *scyll,* f., E. *shell,* Du. *schel,* f., 'shell, husk.' The Goth. and Teut. form *skalja* passed into Rom.; comp. Ital. *scalgia,* Fr. *écaille,* 'scale, shell, crust.' The Teut. cognates are usually connected with an Aryan root *skel,* 'to split'; comp. Schelle, as well as Lith. *skélti,* 'to split,' OSlov. *skoltka,* 'mussel, shell-fish,' Russ. *skala,* 'crust.'—**schälen,** vb., 'to shell, scale, peel,' MidHG. *scheln,* OHG. *schellen,* 'to strip off, peel off'; allied to Schale.

Schalk, m., 'rogue, knave,' from Mid HG. *schalc,* m., 'servant, serf; person of servile character, espec. cunning person,' OHG. *scalch,* m., 'servant'; corresponding to Goth. *skalks,* OIc. *skálkr,* AS. *scealc,* m., 'retainer, man' (so too the corresponding fem. *scylcen,* 'maid-servant'). The evolution in meaning is similar to that of AS. *ĉyfes* and *wealh;* see Kebse and welsch. Schalf passed at an early period into Ital., in which *scalco* signifies 'head-cook.' It is worthy of note that the meaning of the word is lifted into a higher plane in its transition from MidHG. to ModHG.; it is thus defined by Goethe, 'one who plays a good-humoured practical joke.'

Schall, m., 'loud sound, noise,' from the equiv. MidHG. *schal* (gen. *schalles*), OHG. *scal* (*ll*), m.; from this is derived MidHG. and ModHG. **schallen,** akin to OHG. *scëllan,* MidHG. *schëllen,* 'to sound loudly, resound,' OIc. *skjalla,* 'to rattle.' From the Teut. verb is derived the Rom. term Ital. *squillare,* 'to ring, resound.' See Schelle and Schilling.

Schalmei, f., 'reed pipe, shepherd's pipe,' from the equiv. MidHG. *schalemîe,* f., which is again derived from the equiv. Fr. *chalumeau,* or rather Burg. and Wall. *chalemie,* MidLat. *scalmeia* (akin to Lat. *calamus*).

Schalotte, f., 'shallot,' formed from the equiv. Fr. *échalotte,* from MidLat. *ascalonium,* 'onion from Ascalon (in Palestine),' whence also ModHG. Aschlauch.

schalten, vb., 'to go or push against the stream, direct, regulate,' from MidHG. *schalten,* 'to push, impel (espec. a ship), set a-going, drive.' Just as Lat. *gubernare* came to mean 'to direct, rule,' so schalten acquired in ModHG. the sense of 'to direct,' OHG. *scaltan,* 'to push,' OSax. *skaldan,* 'to impel a ship'; a corresponding term is wanting in the other Teut. dials. Origin obscure. For derivatives see schelten. In ModHG. **Schalter,** 'sash window,' MidHG. *schalter, schelter,* 'bolt,' the prim. meaning of schalten gleams through; so too in **Schaltjahr,** MidHG. and OHG. *schalt-jâr,* n., 'intercalary year,' so named because a day is inserted.

Schaluppe, f., 'sloop,' ModHG. only, from the equiv. Fr. *chaloupe,* which is derived from Du. *sloep,* whence also the equiv. E. *sloop;* the E. variant *shallop* comes from Fr.

Scham, f., 'shame, disgrace, bashfulness, pudenda,' f., from MidHG. *scham,* OHG. *scama,* f., 'sense of shame, confusion, infamy, disgrace (MidHG.), pudibunda.' Comp. OSax. *skama,* f., 'confusion,' Du. *schaam-* (in compounds), AS. *scëamu,* f., 'shame, infamy, disgrace,' E. *shame;* Goth. **skama,* f., may be inferred from *skaman,* 'to be ashamed' (OHG. *scamên*). The Aryan root *skam,* which also appears in ModHG. Schande, is connected with the Aryan root *kam,* 'to cover oneself,' preserved in Hemd (which see, as well as Leichnam) and in Goth. *hamón,* so that Goth. *sik skaman,* 'to be ashamed,' would signify lit. 'to cover oneself.'

Schande, f., 'disgrace, infamy,' from the equiv. MidHG. *schande,* OHG. *scanta,* f.; corresponding to the equiv. Goth. *skanda*, AS. *sćeond*, Du. *schande*, f.; an abstract form from the root *skam* (see Sd&ant), with the change of *m* into *n* before *d*, as in Manb. Comp. further the partic. in *da-* formed from the same root, OHG. *scant* (see lant, fatt, and zart); from this is derived ModHG. ſchänben, MidHG. *schenden*, OHG. *scenten*, 'to dishonour, ravish.'

Schanf, m., 'retail,' from late Mid HG. **schanc*, m., in *win-schanc*, m., 'wine tavern'; the simple MidHG. word *schanc* signifies 'vessel to pour from; present.' Allied to ſd)enfen.

Schanker, m., 'cancer, chancre,' Mod HG. only, formed from Fr. *chancre*.

Schanze (1.), f., 'chance, fortune'; comp. etwas in die Schanze schlagen, 'to hazard something.' From MidHG. *schanze*, f., 'throw at dice, lucky throw, game'; borrowed from the equiv. Fr. and E. *chance* (MidLat. *cadentia*, 'throwing of the dice,' Ital. *cadenza*, 'fall').

Schanze (2.), f., 'redoubt, earthwork,' from late MidHG. *schanze*, f., 'bundle of faggots, redoubt'; akin to Du. *schans*. Of obscure origin.

Schar (1.), see Pflugschar.

Schar (2.), f., 'host, troop, crowd,' from MidHG. *schar*, f., 'division of an army, drawn up detachment of soldiers, knot of four or more men, crowd, heap,' OHG. *skara*, f., 'host.' The meaning is not connected with ſd)eren. AS. *sćealu*, *sćeolu* (E. *shoal*), 'host,' is abnormal. From Teut. is derived the Rom. word *schiera*, 'host, troop, swarm.' See Sd)erge.

Scharbe, f., 'cormorant,' from MidHG. *scharbe*, OHG. *scarba*, *scarva*, f., 'diver, cormorant'; comp. OIc. *skarfr*, 'pellicanus graculus'; AS. *scræfl*.

Scharbock, m., 'scurf, scurvy,' early ModHG., a corruption of MidLat. *scorbûtus*. From the same source are derived the equiv. Du. *scheurbuik*, E. *scurvy*, Ital. *scorbuto*, and Fr. *scorbut*. The ultimate source of the cognates is Du. *scheurbuik*, or rather its older forms with a dental in the suffix, as in *scorbutus* (Du. *scheur*, 'rift, cleft,' *buk*, 'bone'); ModDu. *scheurbuik* is also very probably a corruption, the word being connected with *buik*, 'belly.'

ſcharf, adj., 'sharp, acrid, acute,' from the equiv. MidHG. and OHG. *scharf*, *scharpf;* in the same sense occur the corresponding forms OSax. *scarp*, Du. *scherp*, AS. *sćearp*, E. *sharp*, OIc. *skarpr;* Goth. **skarpa-* is

by chance not recorded. In the sense of 'sharp, cutting,' the following are also allied:—OHG. *scrēvōn*, 'to cut in,' OHG. *scarbôn*, MidHG. and ModHG. *scharben*, 'to cut in pieces,' as well as AS. *sćeorfan*, 'to tear off' (see ſd)ürfen), MidHG. *schrapfe* (Goth. **skrappō*), 'tool for scratching,' E. *to scrape;* yet the final labials present a difficulty. OHG. and MidHG. *sarpf*, as an equiv. variant of ſd)arf, is abnormal, so too OIc. *snarpr*, 'sharp.' From Teut. are derived Fr. *escarper*, 'to cut steep down, escarp,' *escarpe*, 'slope,' Ital. *scarpa*, 'slope; locksmith's chisel.' In the non-Teut. languages Gr. ἅρπη, 'sickle,' OSlov. *srŭpŭ*, 'sickle,' are allied to OHG. *sarf*, though, of course, this does not explain the form ſd)arf, Goth. **skarpa-*, which is perhaps connected with the Teut. root *skrap* (*skrub*, *skrb*), 'to slit, cut in' (see ſd)rèpfen).

Scharlach, m., 'scarlet,' from the equiv. MidHG. *scharlach*, *scharlachen*, n., which is, as is shown by Du. *scharlaken*, a corruption of MidHG. *scharlât*, the word being thus connected with Lafen (MidHG. *lachen*, 'cloth'); *scharlât* (comp. E. *scarlet*, MidE. *scarlat*) is formed from OFr. *escarlate* (Mod Fr. *écarlate*), 'scarlet stuff.' Comp. Mid Lat. *scarlatum*, Ital. *scarlatto*. The ultimate source of the word is Oriental; comp. Pers. *sakirlât* (Turk. *iskerlet*).

Scharlei, m., 'sage' (bot.), from Mid HG. *scharleie*, f., 'borrago, clary'; of uncertain origin, which the equiv. Ital. *schiarea*, MidLat. *sclareia*, *scarleia*, are not able to elucidate.

Scharmützel, n., 'skirmish,' from the equiv. MidHG. *scharmützel*, *schurmutzel*, m., which, like Du. *schermuscling*, are derived from Ital. *scarmuccia* (Fr. *escarmouche*), 'skirmish,' which again comes from Ital. *schermire*, 'to fight.' The ultimate origin of the word is OHG. and Mid HG. *schirmen*, 'to fight.' Comp. further E. *skirmish*.

Schärpe, f., 'scarf, sash,' ModHG. only, formed from the equiv. Fr. *écharpe*, of which the OFr. form *escharpe*, 'wallet hung round the neck of a pilgrim,' is derived, like Ital. *sciarpa*, 'scarf, girdle,' from late OHG. *scharpe*, 'pocket.' Note Bav. Sd)ärpfen.

Scharreifen, n., 'scraper,' from the equiv. MidHG. *scherre*, OHG. *scërra*, f., under the influence of ſd)arren.—**ſd)arren,** vb., 'to scrape, scratch,' from the equiv. MidHG. *scharren*, a graded form of the

MidHG. vb. *schërren*, OHG. *scërran*, whence ModFr. *déchirer*, OFr. *eschirer*, 'to tear to pieces,' is borrowed.

Scharte, f., 'notch,' from MidHG. *scharte*, f., 'an opening or indentation made by cutting, hewing, or fracture; notch, wound'; comp. Du. *schaard*, 'notch, potsherd.' Allied to MidHG. *schart*, adj., 'hewn to pieces, full of notches, wounded,' OHG. *scart*, AS. *sceard*, E. *sherd*, OIc. *skarðr*, which were orig. *da-* (*to-*), partics. of ſcheren. MidHG. *scharte*, OHG. *scartisan*, 'skillet, pan,' must, like their ModHG. corresponding forms, be kept apart from these cognates on account of their meaning, especially since they are derived from *skarithâ* (not from *skartâ*), as is proved by OSlov. *skvrada*, *skrado*, 'skillet, pan, hearth.'

Scharteke, f., 'worthless book, trash,' ModHG. only: prop. 'waste book'; formed from Ital. *scartata*, 'refuse.'

ſcharwenzeln, vb., 'to bow and scrape, be obsequious, fawn'; it is uncertain whether the word is derived from Fr. *servant*, 'servant.'

Schatten, m., 'shade, shadow,' from the equiv. MidHG. *schate*, m. (rarely f.), OHG. *scato* (gen. *-awes*), m.; corresponding to Goth. *skadus*, AS. *sceadu*, E. *shade, shadow*, Du. *schaduw*, OSax. *skado*, 'shadow.' Perhaps Gr. σκότος, 'darkness,' is allied; OIr. *scáth*, *scáil*, 'shadow,' are, however, more closely akin. For another OTeut. word for 'shadow,' see under ſchauen.

Schatz, m., 'treasure, store; sweetheart,' from MidHG. *schaz* (gen. *-tzes*), OHG. *scaz*, m.; its chief senses down to the 13th cent. are 'money, property, wealth,' and only later 'valuables stored up'; OHG. *scaz*, m., is only 'money, a definite coin.' Comp. Goth. *skatts*, 'coin, money,' OIc. *skattr*, 'tax, tribute,' AS. *sceatt*, 'a certain small coin, money, property,' OFris. *sket*, 'money, cattle,' OSax. *scat*, 'piece of money, property.' The early history of the cognates is unfortunately too obscure; opinions are divided whether the Teut. word *skatta-* is derived from OSlov. *skotŭ*, 'cattle,' or whether the latter comes from Teut. The variation in meaning, 'cattle' and 'money,' is analogous to Lat. *pecunia* from *pecus*, E. *fee* from AS. *feoh*, 'cattle' (see Vieh); in bartering, cattle played the part of money. Yet we cannot prove that the prim. meaning of OTeut. **skatta-*, 'money, coin,' is 'cattle.' On the other hand, the assumption that the word is primit. allied to Gr. σχέδη, 'board, tablet,' is certainly not satisfactory on account of the meanings of the Teut. words.

Schaub, m., 'bundle or truss of straw, sheaf,' from MidHG. *schoup* (gen. *-bes*), m., 'bundle, truss of straw, wisp of straw,' OHG. *scoub*, m., 'sheaf, truss of straw'; comp. Du. *schoof*, AS. *sceáf*, E. *sheaf*, OIc. *skauf*, 'sheaf'; allied to ſchieben. Hence Schaub is lit. 'what is gathered together'; akin further to Schober.

ſchaudern, vb., 'to shudder, shiver,' ModHG. only, from LG. *schuddern*; comp. Du. *schudden*, 'to quake, tremble'; MidE. *schudderen*, E. *to shudder*. Schütten is of a cognate stem, and, like the words of this class, is based on a Teut. root *skul-*, 'to be shaken'; allied to OHG. *scutisón*, 'to shudder,' *scutisôd*, 'quaking, trembling.' The assumption that Schauder is connected, like Schauer, with MidHG. *schûr* is not warranted, because the MidHG. word does not mean 'shudder.' See Schutt.

ſchauen, vb., 'to look at, gaze,' from MidHG. *schouwen*, OHG. *scouwôn*, 'to see, look at, contemplate'; comp. OSax. *scauwôn*, Du. *schouwen*, AS. *sceáwian*, 'to look at' (whence E. *to show*); Goth. **skaggwôn* is wanting to this *usskaujan*, 'to restore to consciousness.' From the root *skau-*, *skû-*, 'to see' (see ſchön), are also derived Goth. *skuggwa*, m., 'mirror,' OHG. *scû-char*, 'mirror,' further OHG. *scûwo*, AS. *scûa*, OIc. *skugge*, m., 'shadow' (see Spiegel); also OIc. *skygna* (Goth. **skuggwinôn*), 'to spy,' *skyn*, n. and f., 'perceiving,' *skoða*, 'to spy.' In the non-Teut. languages, Sans. *kavis*, 'sage, poet,' Lat. *cavere*, 'to beware,' Gr. κοέω, 'I mark,' OSlov. *čuja*, *čuti*, 'to be sensible of, feel, perceive,' are also connected with the root *skû*, *skau*, or rather *kû*, *kau*.

Schauer (1.), m., 'penthouse, shed'; see Scheuer.

Schauer (2.), m., 'shower,' from MidHG. *schûr*, OHG. *scûr*, m., 'storm, hail'; comp. OSax. *skûr*, m., 'weather, shower,' Du. *schoer*, 'pouring rain,' AS. *scûr*, E. *shower*, and the equiv. OIc. *skúr*; Goth. only *skûra windis*, 'gale.' Origin obscure.

Schaufel, f., 'shovel,' from the equiv. MidHG. *schûvel*, OHG. *scûvala*, f., pointing to Goth. **skûfla* (*skûbla*). The forms of the other Teut. languages point to Goth. **skûbla*, f.; comp. Du. *schoffel*, f., 'shovel,' AS. *scĕofl*, f., E. *shovel*. Allied to the root *skûb* (*skûf*?) in ſchieben; hence Schaufel is lit. 'a tool on which something is put to be thrown away.' For the change of *ŭ* to *û* comp. Sehn and laut.

Schaufel, f., 'swing,' ModHG. only, derived, however, under LG. influence, from MidHG. *schoc* (gen. *-ckes*), m., and *schoke,* f.; comp. LG. *schuckel,* f., 'swing'; MidHG. *schoc,* OHG. *scoc,* 'rocking motion' (whence Fr. *choc,* 'shock'). In East Thuringian 'swing' is Schaukel, in Suabian Gautsche, in Swiss Gireiz:, Gigerreize.

Schaum, m., 'foam, froth, scum,' from the equiv. MidHG. *schûm,* OHG. *scûm,* m.; corresponding to Du. *schuim,* OIc. *skûm,* 'foam' (whence E. *scum*). The other dials. have a different word; comp. AS. *fám,* E. *foam,* under Feim. It is questionable whether Lat. *spuma,* 'foam' (with *p* for *k*, comp. *lupus* with λύκος?), is connected with the Teut. cognates. Schaum is usually connected with the root *skû,* 'to cover,' appearing in Scheuer; hence it means lit. 'covering, that which covers.' From Teut. are derived Ital. *schiuma,* Fr. *écume,* 'foam.'

Schaute, see Schote.

ſchechig, adj., 'dappled, spotted, pied,' from MidHG. (rare) *schëcke,* 'striped, spotted,' to which are also allied MidHG. *schëcken,* 'to make of various colours,' *schëckëht,* 'spotted,' also MidHG. *schëcke,* 'a closely-fitting striped coat,' AS. *sciccels,* 'coat.' It is, on the other hand, assumed that the word is borrowed from Fr. *échec,* 'check' (Ital. *a scacchi*); comp. E. *checky*.

Scheebe, see Schieber.

ſcheel, adj., 'oblique, awry,' from Mid HG. *schël, schëlch* (gen. *schëlhes, schëlwes*), OHG. *scëlah* (gen. *scëlhes, scëlawes*), adj., 'awry, squinting, athwart, oblique, crooked'; comp. Du. *scheel,* AS. *scëolh,* OIc. *skjalgr,* 'awry, squinting' (Goth. **skilhwa-,* or rather **skilwa-,* **skilga-,* is by chance not recorded). Pre-Teut. **skelko-, skëlgo-,* must be assumed; hence Gr. σκολιώς, 'aslant, awry,' is not quite adequate to explain phonetically the Teut. forms; perhaps both the Teut. and Gr. terms are based on a root *skel*.

Scheffel, m., 'bushel,' from MidHG. *scheffel,* OHG. *scëffil,* m., 'bushel, corn measure'; comp. the equiv. OSax. *scëpil,* Du. *schepel* (see also Wiſpel). Allied to OSax. *skap,* n., 'vessel, cask,' OHG. *scaf,* MidHG. *schaf* (see Schaff). 'vessel for holding liquids'; in Bav., *ſaſſl,* n., is a dimin. of the equiv.

ſaff. The assumption that the word was borrowed from Lat. *scaphium* (Gr. σκάφιον), 'drinking vessel,' is not satisfactory; Mid Lat. *scaphum, scapellus* (Ital. *scaffale,* 'bookshelves'), are only imitations of the G. words. Perhaps the terms are primit. G.; comp. also OIc. *skeppa,* 'bushel'; also the root *skap,* 'to contain,' under ſchöpfen.

Scheibe, f., 'slice, pane, wafer,' from MidHG. *schibe,* OHG. *sciba,* f., 'pane, ball, wheel'; corresponding to OLG. *sciva,* 'sphaera,' Du. *schijf,* 'slice,' MidE. *schive,* 'circle, slice' (E. *shive, sheave*), Ic. *skifa,* f., 'shaving, slice.' Teut. *skîbô-,* from pre-Teut. *skipā-,* is most closely related to Gr. σκοίπος, 'potter's wheel,' with which Gr. σκίπων, 'staff,' is usually connected. ModHG. Schiefer is scarcely allied.

Scheide, f., 'sheath,' from MidHG. *scheide,* OHG. *sceida,* f., 'scabbard'; comp. OSax. *scêðia,* f., Du. *scheede,* f., AS. *scêð,* f., E. *sheath,* OIc. *skeiðer* (plur.), 'sheath'; Goth. *skaipi (from *skaiti*), f., 'sheath,' is wanting (the term used being *fôdr,* n., 'sheath,' see Futteral). Allied to ſchieben, hence lit. 'separation, the separating covering'?. ModHG. Scheibe, 'separation, parting,' is the same word; comp. MidHG. *scheide,* f., 'separation, severing, departure, distinction, boundary'; OHG. *sceida.*

ſcheiden, vb., 'to separate, divide; depart,' from MidHG. *scheiden,* OHG. *sceidan,* str. vb., 'to separate, sever; decide, adjust, appoint' For the expected Goth. *skaipan (comp. OSax. *skêðan,* 'to separate,' OFris. *skêtha*) occurs *skuidan* with grammatical change; comp. AS. *scêádan,* 'to separate,' whence E. *shed*. The Teut. root *skaiþ,* the dental form of which may be inferred from ModHG. Scheide, f., is based on Aryan *skhait,* of which *skhaid* and *skhid* are parallel forms; comp. Gr. σχίζω, 'I split,' σχίζα (see Scheit); Sans. *chid,* 'to split,' Lat. *scindo* (also *cuedo*?), Lith. *skědzu,* 'I separate.' See further geſcheit and ſcheißen.

Schein, m., 'shining, sheen, semblance, appearance,' from MidHG. *schîn,* OHG. *scîn,* m., 'lustre, shining, brightness, clearness,' late MidHG., also 'evidence, testimony, appearance'; comp. OSax. *skîn,* m., 'lustre,' Du. *schijn,* AS. *scîn,* 'ghost.' An abstract of ſcheinen, vb., from MidHG. *schînen,* OHG. *scînan,* 'to glitter, appear; show oneself'; comp. the equiv. OSax. *scînan,* Du. *schijnen,* AS. *scînan,* E. *to shine,* OIc. *skína,* Goth. *skeinan.* The Teut.

root *skī*, whence *skinan*, str. vb., is formed with a present suffix *na-*, appears with a suffix *m* in ſdjimmern. Akin probably to Gr. σκιά, 'shadow,' see Sdjemen; also Gr. σκίρον, 'parasol'?. See ſdjier.

ſdjeiſjen, vb., 'to go to stool, excrete,' from MidHG. *schīzen*, OHG. *scīzan*; corresponding to the equiv. Du. *schijten*, AS. *scītan*, E. *to shit*, OIc. *skīta*. The common Teut. root *skīt*, 'to excrete,' is probably connected with the Aryan *skhīd*, discussed under ſdjeiben; its lit. meaning is perhaps 'to dissever'?. From the Teut. cognates are derived Ital. (dial.) *scito*, 'excrement,' and OFr. *eschiter*.

Sdjeit, n., 'log, billet, fragment,' from MidHG. *schīt*, OHG. *scīt*, n., 'log of wood'; corresponding to the equiv. OFris. *skīd*, AS. *scīde*, E. *shide*, OIc. *skīð*. The root is the Aryan form *skhait*, *skhīt*, discussed under ſdjeiben, the prim. meaning of which, 'to split,' appears still in ModHG. Sdjeit; comp. Gr. σχίζα (from *σχίδja), 'splinter,' Lith. *skëdrà*, Lett. *skaida*, 'chip,' from the root *skhit* (see ſdjeiben).—Sdjciterhaufcn, 'funeral pile,' ModHG. only, formed from MidHG. *schīter*, plur. of *schīt*.—ſdjeifern, 'to go to pieces, be wrecked,' ModHG. only, from MidHG. *schīt*, plur. *schīter*.

Sdjcttel, m., 'crown (of the head), vertex,' from MidHG. *scheitel*, OHG. *sceitila*, f., 'vertex, crown, parting of the hair from the crown to the forehead'; corresponding to Du. (*haer*) *scheel*, MidLG. *schēdel*. Allied to ſdjeiben; lit. 'part of the head where the hairs separate, i.e., where they are parted to either side.' Akin to AS. *scēada*, 'crown,' E. *to shed*.

Sdjellad, m., 'shellac,' ModHG. only, from the equiv. LG. and Du. *schellak;* comp. E. *shellac;* lit. 'scale lac, lac thin like scales.'

Sdjelle, f., 'small bell,' from the equiv. MidHG. *schëlle*, OHG. *schëlla*, f.; allied to MidHG. *schëllen*, OHG. *scëllan*, 'to sound loudly, resound,' to which Ital. *squilla*, 'little bell,' is also akin.—ModHG. and Mid HG. ſdjellen, lit. 'to cause to resound,' is the factitive form. Comp. verſdjollen, 'vanished,' as a relic of the MidHG. str. verb.

Sdjellfiſd), m., 'codfish, haddock,' ModHG. only, formed from LG. and Du. *schellvisch;* allied to Du. *schel*, 'shell,' E. *shell;* so called "because the cod lives chiefly on shellfish"?. See Sdjale.

Sdjcllhengſt, m., 'stallion,' an explanatory compound for the equiv. MidHG. *schële*, OHG. *scëlo*, m.; see beſdjälen.

Sdjellkraut, n., 'swallow-wort, celandine,' from MidHG. *shëlkrut*, *-wurz;* probably an abbreviation and corruption of the equiv. MidLat. *chelidonia* (*ch* pronounced as in the corresponding Fr. *chélidoine*); comp. Gr. χελιδόνιον, 'celandine.'

Sdjelm, m., 'rogue, knave, villain,' from MidHG. *schelme*, m., 'pest, plague; those who have fallen in battle,' then, as an abusive term, 'wretch, seducer,' OHG. *scalmo*, *scëlmo*, 'plague.' In MidDu. and MidLG. *schelm* has the old sense of 'carrion, cadaver,' so too in Bav. For the development of the meaning 'rogue' from 'wretch,' comp. Sdjalf, which has also acquired a milder signification. From the ModHG. word are derived Du. *schelm* and Ic. *skelmir*, 'rogue.'

ſdjellen, vb., 'to reprove, revile,' from MidHG. *schëlten*, OHG. *scëltan*, str. vb., 'to reprove, abuse, insult'; comp. MidLG. and Du. *schelden*, OFris. *skelda*, 'to reprove.' Akin to the cognates discussed under ſdjalten; 'to push' is the prim. meaning of ſdjellen.

Sdjcmel, m., 'stool, footstool,' from the equiv. MidHG. *schëmel*, *schamel* (*schāmel*?), m.; OHG. *scamal* (*scāmal*?), m., which, like OSax. *fōtscamel*, 'footstool,' and AS. *scēamul* (espec. *fōt-scēamul*), m., is derived from Lat. *scamellum*. Du. *schabel*, 'stool,' as well as the equiv. Rom. terms, Fr. *escabelle*, *escabeau*, and Ital. *sgabello*, is based on Lat. *scabellum;* hence in MidRhen. Sdjawell, Sdjabell.

Sdjcmen, m., 'phantom,' from MidHG. *schëme*, m., 'shadow,'(MidG.) *schime;* comp. AS. *scīma*, OSax. *scīmo*. Allied to the root *skī*, 'to glitter,' discussed under ſdjeinen, with which Gr. σκιά, 'shadow,' with the same evolution in meaning, is also connected; see Sdjimmer and Sdjönbartſpiel.

Sdjcnk, m., 'publican, cupbearer,' from the equiv. MidHG. *schenke*, OHG. *scencho* (OSAX. *scenkio*), m., 'cupbearer.' From Teut. is derived Fr. *échanson* (OFr. *eschançon*, MidLat. *scancionem*).—ſdjenken, vb., 'to pour out for drinking, bestow, give,' from MidHG. *schenken*, 'to pour in, give to drink, water, make a present of, give'; OHG. *scenchen*, 'to pour in, give to drink.' The meaning 'to give' first appears in the post-classical times of MidHG. 'To pour in, give to drink,' is the prim. meaning; it is characteristic of G. that the sense 'to give,' could be developed from this (similarly ModHG. **gefallen** attests the importance of dice-playing in Teut. life; comp. also **zechen**). The prim. meaning appears in AS. *scëncan*, OFris. *skenka*, OIc. *skenkja*; from Teut. is also formed OFr. *escancer*, 'to pour in.' Goth. *skagkjan* is wanting. Some etymologists regard the common Teut. vb. as a derivative of AS. *scëonc*, *scëonca*, 'shank,' assuming that shanks were used as taps in the earliest times; hence **schenken** would mean lit. 'to put the tap in a cask.' See the next word.

Schenkel, m., 'thigh, shank,' from the equiv. MidHG. *schenkel*, m.; comp. Du. *schenkel*; unknown to OHG. as well as to the other OTeut. dials. A dimin. of AS. *scëonca* (see **schenken**), E. *shank*, which is further connected with ModHG. **Schinken**; comp. also Du. *schonk*, 'bones in meat,' Swed. *skänk*, Dan. *skank*.

schenken, see **Schenk**.

Scherbe, f., 'fragment, sherd, flowerpot,' from MidHG. *schërbe*, *schirbe*, OHG. *scirbi*, f. and m., 'sherd, fragment, earthenware pot'; comp. Du. *scherf*, f., 'sherd'; a derivative of pre-Teut. *skerpo-*; comp. OSlov. *črěpŭ*, 'sherd,' Lett. *schkirpta*, 'notch,' *schkërpele*, 'splinter of wood.' Akin to **Scherflein**?

Schere (1.), f., 'scissors, shears,' from the equiv. MidHG. *schære*, f., which is probably plur., OHG. *scârî*, plur. of *skar* and *skâra*, 'shears'; with regard to the plur. comp. Ital. *cesoje* and *forbici*, plur., Fr. *ciseaux*, equiv. to E. *scissors*. In Sans. the word was of course dual; comp. *bhurijâ* (Rig-Veda), dual 'shears.' Comp. Du. *schaar*, MidE. *schêre*, E. *shears* (plur.), and the equiv. OIc. *skâre*, neut. plur. See **scheren**.

Schere (2.), f., 'rock, reef,' ModHG. only, formed from the equiv. Swed. *skär* (Dan. *skjær*), n.; comp. OIc. *sker*, 'cliff.'

scheren, vb., 'to shear, fleece, molest,' from MidHG. *schërn*, OHG. *scëran*, 'to shear, cut off'; comp. Du. *scheren*, AS. *scëran*, 'to shear, cut or hew to pieces,' E. *to shear*, OIc. *skera*, 'to cut, shear, slaughter.' The prim. meaning of the root *sker* contained in these vbs. is 'to cut or hew to pieces' (comp. Lith. *skirti*, 'to sever,' *skard*, 'rag'), as is shown by the OTeut. *skarda-* 'hewn or cut to pieces,' which originated in *skr-tô-* (see **Scharte**). Yet the meaning 'to shear' is very old; comp. the derivative **Schere**. The root *sker* (whence Sans.

kšurás, 'razor'?) appears in Gr. as *ker* in κείρω, 'I shear.'

Scherflein, n., 'mite' (coin), from the MidHG. *schërf*, OHG. *scërf*, n., 'mite, very small coin'; comp. MidLG. *scharf*, *schërf*, 'one-seventeenth of a penny'; allied to AS. *scëorfan*, 'to tear off'?. Comp. for a similar development of meaning ModHG. **Deut**, as well as Gr. κέρμα, lit. 'part cut off,' then 'small coin.' **Scherbe** is scarcely allied.

Scherge, m., 'beadle, sergeant,' from MidHG. *schërge*, *schërje*, m. (for the change of *rg* to *rj*, ModHG. *rg*, see **Ferge**), 'usher (of a court), bailiff, beadle,' OHG. *scerjo*, *scario*, *scaro*, 'captain, leader of a troop'; a derivative of **Schar**.

Scherz, m., 'joke, jest,' from MidHG. *schërz*, m., 'pleasure, play'; allied to ModHG. **scherzen**, vb., from MidHG. *schërzen*, 'to cut capers, hop, amuse oneself'; comp. MidHG. *scharz*, 'leap.' These cognates, which are found neither in the MidHG. classical writers, in OHG., nor in OTeut. generally, are met with, however, in Ital. *scherzare*, 'to jest,' borrowed from G.

Scheu, f., 'shyness, reserve, timidity,' from MidHG. *schiuhe*, f., 'shyness, horror,' also 'bugbear, scarecrow,' whence ModHG. **Scheuche**. Allied to **scheuen**, **scheuchen**, vb., from MidHG. *schiuhen*, 'to be shy of, avoid, scare or chase away,' OHG. *sciuhen*. Both the noun and vb. are derivatives of MidHG. *schiech*, OHG. *scioh*, 'shy, bashful.' ModHG. **schen**, adj., is based anew on the vb.; comp. AS. *scêoh*, 'timid,' to which E. *shy* is allied; Du. *schuw*, 'timid, shy.' From the G. cognates Ital. *schivare*, 'to avoid,' is derived. See **Scheusal**.

Scheuer, f. (in Bav. and East Suab. **Stadel**), 'barn, shed,' from the equiv. MidHG. *schiure*, OHG. *sciura*, f.; a derivative of OHG. *scûr*, MidHG. *schûr*, 'penthouse, protection,' ModHG.(dial.)**Schauer**. Comp. OIc. *skjól*, n., 'place of refuge, shelter,' *skaunn*, m., 'shield.' The Aryan root, *skû*, 'to cover, protect' (comp. **Scheune**), contained in these words, is widely diffused; comp. Lat. *scûtum*, 'shield,' Gr. σκῦ-λον, 'armour,' Lat. *ob-scû-rus*, 'dark' (covered), and the Sans. root *sku* 'to cover.' See **Scheune** and **Schote**.

scheuern, vb., 'to scour, rub,' early ModHG. (unknown to UpG., the term used being **fegen**), formed from MidG. and LG. *schüren*; comp. Du. *schuren* (MidE. *scouren*, E. *to scour*, borrowed from Du.?), Dan. *skure*, Swed. *skura*. Although the

U

word is wanting in the OTeut. dials., it need not be regarded as borrowed from Mid Lat. *scurare* (Lat. *ex-curare*), Ital. *scurare*, Fr. *écurer*, 'to scour.'

Scheune, f. (unknown to UpG.), 'barn, shed,' from the equiv. MidHG. *schiune*, f., which is derived by the loss of the *g* (equal to *j*?) from OHG. *scugin*, *scugina*, 'barn.' If the *g* is equal to *j*, **Scheuer** (MidHG. *schiure*) is closely allied. If this is not the case, no certain connecting link has been discovered.

Scheusal, n., 'object of horror, monster,' a derivative of *scheu*, like late MidHG. *schûsel*, 'monster, scarecrow.' To this is allied ModHG. **scheußlich**, corrupted from MidHG. *schiuzlich*, 'shy, despairing,' which is connected with *schiuzen*, 'to feel horror,' from *schiuhezen (allied to **scheuen**, MidHG. *schiuhen*).

Schicht, f., 'layer, stratum, day's work,' from MidHG. *schiht*, f., 'history, affair, accident, arrangement, division, row of things laid on one another, layer, beds of soil, day's work (in mines)'; allied to (ge)**schehen**; see **Geschichte**.

schichen, vb., 'to bring about, send, despatch,' from MidHG. *schicken*, 'to bring about, do, create, prepare, set going, depute, send.' This vb., undoubtedly a primit. form, which is wanting in OHG. and the OTeut. dials. generally, seems, like Goth. *skêwjan* and OIc. *skáva*, 'to go,' to be connected with a primit. Teut. root *skêhw* (*skêw*) from pre-Teut. *skêq* (to which OIr. *scuchim*, 'I go away,' from *skok*? is allied). Akin to late MidHG. *schic*, m., 'method,' and **schicklich**, which first occurs in ModHG.; see **geschickt**. These specifically G. cognates, which passed into Du., Fris., and Scand., are wanting in OHG. until the 12th cent.; on account of their formation, however, they must be very old; OHG. *sciechen*, Goth. *skikkjan*. Allied to (ge)**schehen**. Deriv. **Schicksal**.

Schicksel, n., 'young girl,' ModHG. only, formed from Hebr. and Jew. *schickzah*, 'Christian girl,' Hebr. *schikkâz*, lit. 'abomination.'

schieben, vb., 'to shove, push,' from the equiv. MidHG. *schieben*, OHG. *scioban*; comp. Goth. *af-skiuban*, 'to thrust away,' OIc. *skúfa*, *skýfa*, 'to push,' AS. *scúfan*, 'to shove, push,' E. *to shove*. The root *skûb*, 'to shove' (from pre-Teut. *skûp*), which appears also in **Schaufel**, **Scheber**, and **Schuppe**, corresponds to the Sans. root *chup*, 'to touch,' with which Lith. *skubrùs*, *skubùs*, 'quick,' and *skùbti*, 'to make haste' (Aryan root *skub*), and OSlov. *skubati*, 'to pluck,' are also probably allied. See **Schurf**.

Schiedsrichter, m., 'arbiter,' ModHG. only, in MidHG. *schideman*; allied to Mid HG. *schit* (gen. *schides*), 'judicial decision,' akin to OHG. *scidôn*, 'to separate, distinguish, decide.' The Teut. root *skip* is connected with **scheiden**.

schief, adj., 'oblique, awry, sloping,' a MidG. and LG. word; MidHG. and MidG. *schief*, 'awry, distorted'; cognate with AS. *scâf*, *scâb*, OIc. *skeifr*, 'awry,' North Fris. *skiaf*, Du. *scheef*, 'awry' (whence E. *skew* is borrowed), Schmalkald. *seip*. HG. dials. also imply a MidHG. *schêp* (pp), 'awry'; Hess. and Franc. *sêp*, Suab. *seps*. Besides these primit. Teut. cognates *skibb*, *skaib* (whence Lett. *schkîbs*, 'awry,' is borrowed), UpG. has *skieg*, which is represented by MidHG. *schiec*, 'awry,' Bav. and Alem. **biegen**, *kieggen*, 'to waddle' (respecting the *ie* see **Stiege** and **Wiege**). They are all connected, like Gr. σκίμπτω, 'to bend,' with an Aryan root *sklêq*, *skaiq*.

Schiefer, m., 'slate, shist,' from Mid HG. *schiver*, *schivere*, m., 'splinter of stone, and espec. of wood,' OHG. *scivaro*, 'splinter of stone'; the modern meaning is Mod HG. only (in UpG. the prim. meaning 'stone splinter' has been preserved). Goth. **skifra*, m., is wanting. Allied to ModHG. **Schebe**, f., 'chaff, boon' (of flax or hemp), which is derived from LG.; comp. E. *shive* (AS. **scîfa*); MidE. *schivere* (AS. **scîfera*), E. *shiver*. These are derivatives of a Teut. root *skîf*, 'to divide, distribute'; comp. AS. *scîftan*, 'to divide,' E. *to shift*, OIc. *skipta*, 'to divide' (OIc. *scîfa*, 'to cut in pieces'; allied to **Scheibe**? or to this word?), Du. *schiften*, 'to separate, sever.' **Schiefer** and **Schebe** are lit. 'fragment, part.'

schielen, vb., 'to squint, leer,' from the equiv. MidHG. *schilen*, *schilhen*, allied to **schel**.

Schienbein, n., 'shin-bone,' from Mid HG. *schinebein*, n., allied to MidHG. *schine*, OHG. *scina*, f., 'shin-bone'; comp. AS. *scinu*, f., E. *shin* (also AS. *scinebân*, MidE. *schinebône*); Du. *scheen* and *scheenbeen*, 'shin-bone.' **Bein** in this compound has preserved its older meaning of 'bone'; see **Bein**. Scarcely allied to **Schiene** and **Schinken**, for the secondary meaning of ModHG. **Schiene** (MidHG. *schine*), 'narrow wood or metal plate, strip,' as well as OHG.

scina, 'needle,' points to a Goth. **skinô*, f., 'narrow piece of bone or metal.' Of the primit. history of the cognates it can only be said, however, that by inference from AS. *scíæ*, *sceó*, 'shin,' the root must be *skí*. From Teut. are derived Ital. *schiniera*, 'greaves for a horse,' and probably also Ital. *schiena*, Fr. *échine*, 'spine,' with their Rom. cognates.

Schiene, f., see **Schienbein**.

schier, adj., 'clear, pure, simple, sheer,' from MidHG. (MidG.) *schîr*, 'mere, pure, glittering'; comp. OSax. *skîr*, *skîri*, AS. *scîr*, 'pure, glittering,' E. *shere*, *sheer*, OIc. *skîrr*, Goth. *skeirs*, 'clear, manifest'; a derivative of the root *skî*, 'to shine, glitter.' In ModHG. this adj. has been confused in sound with the following adv., yet the ModHG. form may be also of LG. origin. See **scheinen**.

schier, adv., 'almost,' from MidHG. *schiere*, adv., 'quickly, soon,' OHG. *sciaro*, older *skêro*, adv., 'quickly'; allied to OHG. *sciari*, *scêri*, adj., 'sagacious, zealous in tracing out'; comp. Du. *schier*, 'almost' (OIc. *skŷrr*, *skǽrr*, 'bright, clear').

Schier, n., 'lawn, veil,' ModHG. only, borrowed from LG.; prop. the neut. of the adj. *schier*.

Schierling, m., 'hemlock,' from the equiv. MidHG. *schirlinc*, *scherlinc* (gen. -*ges*), OHG. *sceriling*; comp. Du. *scheerling*. Derived, like the variants MidHG. *schernine*, OHG. and OLG. *scerning*, 'hemlock,' from the equiv. OHG. *scarno*, m.; the *l* of the OHG., MidHG., and ModHG. forms is due to the current G. suffix -*ling*. The term is unknown to the other OTeut. dials. (in AS. *hymlic*, *hemleác* occur, E. *hemlock*).

schießen, vb., 'to shoot,' from the equiv. MidHG. *schiezen*, OHG. *sciozan*; the corresponding vb. occurs in the same sense in all the OTeut. dials.; comp. OSax. *skeotan* (Du. *schieten*), AS. *sćéotan* (E. *to shoot*), OIc. *skjóta*, Goth. (by chance not recorded) **skiutan*. The root *skut*, 'to shoot,' from pre-Teut. *skud*, is widely diffused in Teut., and corresponds to the Sans. root *kṣud*, 'to shatter, excite,' or better with Sans. *skund*, 'to leap forth.' For derivatives see **Schoß**, **Schuß**, **Schutz**, and **Schütze**.

Schiff, n., 'ship,' from the equiv. MidHG. *schif*, OHG. *scif*, *scëf* (gen. -*ffes*), n.; a common Teut. term; comp. Goth. and OIc. *skip*, n., AS. *sćip*, n., E. *ship*, Du. *schip*, OSax. *scip*. The OHG. word also signifies 'vessel,' being rendered in a gloss as equiv.

to its derivative OHG. *scipht*, 'phiala' (comp. **Kahn**; E. *vessel* in its double sense, borrowed from Fr. *vaisseau*, 'vessel (a utensil), ship,' Gr. σκάφις, 'bowl, skiff'). The Gr. term with σκάφος, 'boat, ship,' cannot be allied to the Teut. word, since the latter implies an Aryan *i* in the stem syllable. No certain etymological explanation can be given of Teut. *skipa*-; the suspicion that the word was borrowed at a primit. period may not be unfounded, for there are only a very few nautical words possessed in common by several Aryan languages (comp. **Mast**). From OHG. the word passed into Rom.; comp. Ital. *schifo*, Fr. *esquif*, 'boat,' to which is allied OFr. *esquiper*, 'to equip a ship,' with a LG. *p*, ModFr. *équiper*, 'to equip, endow,' which passed again into Teut.

Schild (1.), m., 'shield, coat of arms,' from the equiv. MidHG. *schilt*, OHG. *scilt*, m.; a common Teut. term; comp. Goth. *skildus*, m., OIc. *skjǫldr*, AS. *scyld*, E. *shield*, Du. *schild*, OSax. *scild*. The word first signified 'signboard' in early ModHG. The specifically Teut. term *skildu-s* (from *skeldhus*, *skeltús*?) cannot be traced farther back; it can scarcely be related to **schallen** (**Schild**, lit. 'that which gives a loud sound or resounds'?).

Schild (2.), n., 'signboard,' ModHG. only, a variant of the foregoing; hence **Schilder** (neut. stem) in compounds such as **Schilderhaus**, 'sentry-box.'

schildern, vb., 'to paint, depict, describe,' allied to MidHG. *schilt*, 'coat of arms'; comp. MidHG. *schiltære*, m., 'artist'; the shields were orig. painted in the MidHG. age of chivalry with coats of arms, and even, according to Tacitus, *Germ.* vi. ("scuta lectissimis coloribus distinguunt"), in the OTeut. heroic period. Comp. Du. *schilderen*, 'to paint, depict, describe.'

Schildpatt, n., 'tortoise-shell,' ModHG. only, from LG. and Du. *schildpad*, 'tortoise' and 'tortoise-shell.' The early history of Du. *padde*, 'toad,' E. *puddock* and OIc. *padda*, 'toad,' is obscure.

Schilf, n., 'rush, bulrush, reed,' from the equiv. MidHG. *schilf*, OHG. *sciluf* (m. and n.?); unknown to the other Teut. dials.; perhaps it is an early loan-word from Lat. *scirpus*, 'rush,' to which it cannot be primit. allied. Others, regarding **Schilf** as a genuine Teut. word, connect it with OHG. *sceliva*, MidHG. *schelfe*, 'bowl of fruit and pulse.'

ſchillern, vb., 'to change or vary in colour,' ModHG. only, a derivative of MidHG. *schillen*, a variant of *schilen*, 'to squint, blink.'

Schilling, m., 'shilling, money,' from the equiv. MidHG. *schillinc*, OHG. *scilling*, m., a common Teut. term for a coin ; comp. Goth. *skilliggs*, OIc. *skillingr*, AS. *scilling*, E. *shilling*, Du. *schelling*, OSax. *scilling*. Formed from OTeut. *skellan*, 'to sound,' with the suffix *-inga-*, a favourite termination in OG. names of coins (see **Pfenning**, OHG. *cheisuring*, E. *farthing*) ; hence Schilling is lit. 'ringing coin.' From Teut. are derived Ital. *scellino* and Fr. *escalin*, a coin worth about sixpence, as well as the equiv. OSlov. *sklęzĭ*.

Schimmel, m., 'mould,' from the equiv. MidHG. *schimel*, m., for an older *schimbel*, OHG. *scimbal*, which may be inferred from the OHG. derivatives *scimbalên*, 'to get mouldy,' *scimbalag*, 'mouldy.' The MidHG. form is due to a confusion with *schîme*, m., 'glimmer'; comp. Du. *schimmelen*. OHG. *scimbal* has no corresponding form in the other Teut. dials.—Schimmel, m., 'white horse,' late MidHG., identical with Schimmel, 'mucus.'

Schimmer, m., 'glimmer,' early ModHG., formed from LG. and Du. *schemeren*, 'to glimmer, gleam.' This is connected, like MidHG. *schîme*, 'glimmer, lustre,' OHG. *scîmo*, Goth. *skeima*, 'light, lamp,' with the root *skî*, 'to shine, glitter'; comp. MidE. *schimeren*, 'to shimmer,' E. *shimmer*, E. *shim*, 'white spot,' Swed. *skimra* (see Schemen).

Schimpf, m., 'insult, abuse, affront,' from MidHG. *schimpf* (parallel form *schampf*), m., 'jest, pastime, play, tournament.' The current meaning first appeared in early ModHG. ; yet the older sense 'jest,' which belongs to OHG. *scimpf*, MidHG. *schimpf*, was retained till the 17th cent. (Logau) ; comp. Du. *schimp*, 'scorn, mockery,' MidHG. *schumpfe*, f., 'paramour' (lit. 'she who jests'). The root *skimp*, 'to jest,' which appears in OHG. *scimpf*, is wanting in the other Teut. dials. It has been connected with Gr. σκώπτω, 'to jest, deride,' which, with its double meaning, certainly furnishes an analogy for MidHG. Schimpf.

Schindel, f., 'shingle, splint,' from the equiv. MidHG. *schindel*, OHG. *scintila*, f., formed from MidLat. *scindula, scandula*, 'shingle,' the sound of which was perhaps influenced by Gr. σχινδαλμός. The word was borrowed from MidLat. about the 6th cent., contemporaneously with Ziegel, Mauer, &c. The MidE. form *schingel*, E. *shingle*, is peculiar. The Rom. languages preserve the *a-* form, Lat. *scandula*; comp. Ital. (dial.) *scandola* and Fr. *échandole*.

ſchinden, vb., 'to skin, flay,' from MidHG. *schinden*, 'to skin, peel, ill-treat severely,' OHG. *scintan*; a denominative from a lost OHG. *scind*, n., 'hide, skin,' which may be assumed in OHG. from OIc. *skinn* (see Schinne), n., 'skin, hide, fur, leather.' E. *skin*, from MidE. *skinne* (AS. *scinn*), is borrowed from Scand., since AS. *sci, sci*, must have become *shi* in ModE. Goth. *skinþa-*, from pre-Teut. *skénto-*, has not yet been found in the non-Teut. languages.

Schinken, m., 'ham,' from MidHG. *schinke*, m., 'thigh, ham,' OHG. *scincho*, m., *scincha*, f., 'tibia, thigh.' They are related by gradation to the cognates adduced under Schenkel, to which Suab. and Alem. (and Bav.) Schunke, OFris. *skunka*, meaning 'bone, thigh, ham,' are also to be added as further graded forms. Its connection with Schiene is probable on account of the meaning. From the Teut. cognates Ital. (dial.) *stinco (schinco)*, 'shin-bone,' is borrowed.

Schinnen, plur., 'dandruff, scurf,' ModHG. only, from MidG. and LG. ; connected with the cognates discussed under ſchinten ; lit. 'that which comes off in scales from the skin of the head ' ; hence allied to OIc. *skinn* (from *skinþ*), 'skin ' ?.

Schirling, see Scherling.

ſchirmen, vb., 'to protect, defend,' from MidHG. *schirmen, schërmen*, 'to protect, defend, fight,' OHG. *scirmen*, 'to serve as a bulwark, protect,' allied to OHG. *scirm, scërm*, m., 'bulwark, shield, protection,' MidHG. *schirm, schërm*, m., 'shield, penthouse, shelter, defence'; to these Schirm and beſchirmen are allied. From Teut. are derived the Rom. cognates of Ital. *schermo*, 'screen,' *schermire*, 'to fight.' The early history of these words, which are wanting in the rest of the Teut. dials., is obscure ; Gr. σκίρον, 'parasol,' is perhaps primit. allied.

ſchirren, see Geſchirr.

Schiß, m., 'ordure,' a ModHG. form from ſcheißen.

ſchlabbern, vb., 'to slobber, slaver,' ModHG. only, formed from LG. and Du. *slabben*, 'to flap,' *slabberen*, 'to spill.'

Schlacht, f., 'battle, engagement,' from MidHG. *slahte, slaht,* f., 'killing, slaughter, battle,' OHG. *slahta,* f., OSax. *man-slahta,* f., 'death-blow, killing'; an abstract formed by the fem. suffix *-ta-* (as in **Schande**), from the Teut. root *slah,* 'to slay.' For **Schlacht** in the sense of 'sort' see **Geschlecht**. **Schlacht,** 'dyke, embankment,' is also a derivative of **schlagen**, 'to make firm by beating,' which sense MidHG. *sluhen* may have even in the classical poets.—**schlachten,** vb., 'to slaughter, slay,' MidHG. *slahten,* OHG. *slahtôn,* 'to kill, slaughter,' is a derivative of **Schlacht** (OHG. *slahta*), with the preservation of its more general meaning; so too **Schlächter,** m., 'butcher,' MidHG. *slahtære,* OHG. *slahtâri,* 'butcher'; allied to E. *slaughter.*

Schlacke, f., 'slag, dross,' ModHG. only, from LG. *slacke,* 'scales that fly off when metal is struck' (E. *slag*); allied to **schlagen**.

Schlaf (1.), m., **Schläfe,** f., 'temple,' from the equiv. MidHG. and OHG. *slâf,* m.; **Schläfe** is prop. the plur. of **Schlaf,** referring to both the temples (comp. Lat. *tempora*); Du. *slaap,* 'temple.' In AS. *þunwenge,* allied to OHG. *tinna,* MidHG. *tinne* and OHG. *thinna-bahho,* m., 'temple,' MidHG. *tünewenge,* 'temple' (comp. **Wange**), OHG. *dunwengi,* OIc. *þunnvange,* 'temple.' Beneath these similarly sounding terms lies the older Teut. term for 'temple.'

Schlaf (2.), m., 'sleep, slumber,' from the equiv. MidHG. and OHG. *slâf,* m.; a verbal abstr. from **schlafen,** MidHG. *slâfen,* OHG. *slâfan,* str. vb., 'to sleep.' This form is peculiar to Teut. in this sense, and is wanting only in OIc., which has preserved *sofa* (Teut. root *swef,* Aryan *swep*), primit. allied to Lat. *somnus,* Gr. ὕπνος; Goth. *slêps,* 'sleep,' *slêpan,* 'to sleep,' AS. *slǽp,* E. *sleep,* AS. *slǽpan,* E. *to sleep,* Du. *slaap, slapen,* OSax. *slâp, slâpan.* Comp. also the derivatives with *r,* OHG. *slâfarag,* MidHG. *slâfrec, slæfric,* 'sleepy,' OHG. *slâfarôn* (and *slâfôn*), MidHG. *slâfern,* 'to be asleep, get sleepy.' With the Teut. root *slêp,* 'to sleep,' appearing in these cognates, are also connected ModHG. **schlaff** and its Teut. correspondences; hence the prim. meaning of **schlafen** is probably 'to be relaxed.' For further references see under **schlaff**.

schlaff, adj., 'relaxed, loose, indolent,' from MidHG. and OHG. *slaf* (gen. *slaffes*), 'relaxed, idle, impotent'; comp. LG. and Du. *slap,* 'relaxed, impotent,' whence ModHG. **schlapp**, retaining the LG. *p,* is borrowed. Goth. **slapa-* is perhaps a graded form of the root *slêp,* as *lata-*, 'idle, lazy,' is of the root *lêt,* 'to omit' (see **laß**). OSlov. *slabŭ,* 'relaxed, weak,' and Lat. *lăbi,* 'to glide,' *lābare,* 'to totter,' have been rightly compared with the prim. Teut. *slupa-,* 'relaxed.' See **schlafen**.

Schlag (1.), m., 'sort, race, family, class'; see **Geschlecht**.

Schlag (2.), m., 'stroke, blow,' from the equiv. MidHG. *slac* (gen. *slages*), OHG. *slag,* m.; a verbal abstr. of the root *slah,* 'to strike.' ModHG. **schlagen,** 'to strike, beat, pulsate,' MidHG. *slahen,* OHG. *slahan,* 'to strike'; the *g* of the ModHG. vb. is due to the grammatical change of *h* to *g.* Comp. Goth *slahan,* OIc. *slâ* (also 'to mow down'), AS. *sleán* (from *sleahan*), E. *to slay,* Du. *slaan,* OSax. *slahan,* 'to strike.' Teut. root *slah* (*slaȝ*), from pre-Teut. *slâk*; akin to Gr. λακίζω, Lat. *lacerare,* 'to tear to pieces or rags,' for *slak-?*. A root similar in sound appears in OIr. *slechtaim, sligim,* 'I strike' (root *sleg*). See **Geschlecht** and **schlau**.

Schlamm, m., 'slime, mud,' from the equiv. MidHG. *slam* (gen. *slammes*), m.

Schlamp, m., 'carouse'; see **schlemmen**.

Schlange, f., 'serpent,' from the equiv. MidHG. *slange,* m. and f., OHG. *slango,* m.; comp. OIc. *slange,* m., 'serpent,' Du. *slang;* a graded form of **schlingen,** hence **Schlinge** is lit. 'that which coils.'—**schlängeln,** vb., 'to wind, twist,' ModHG. only, seems a diminut. derivative of **Schlange**.

schlank, adj., 'slender, slim,' from Mid LG. (MidG.) *slanc,* 'slim, lean'; comp. Du. *slank,* 'thin, nimble'; to this OIc. *slakke* (for *slankæ*), 'mountain slope,' is also probably allied. Goth. **slanka-* would be connected with the root *sling* in **schlingen,** like **kranz** with the root *kring* in AS. *cringan;* see **schlingen**.

Schlappe (1.), f., 'slipper,' ModHG. only, from LG. *slappe,* which is derived from LG. *slapp,* 'loose.'

Schlappe (2.), f., 'slap; discomfiture, defeat,' ModHG. only, from LG. *slappe;* comp. MidE. *slappe,* E. *slap;* hence also in earlier ModHG. 'slap in the face.' From a HG. *slapfe is derived Ital. *schiaffo,* 'slap in the face.'

schlappen, vb., 'to slap, hang down, go slipshod,' ModHG. only, from LG. and Du. *slabben;* see **schlabbern**.

Schlaraffe, m., 'sluggard, lubber,' for earlier ModHG. **Schlauraffe,** which is met with as late as the first half of the last cent. ; from MidHG. *slûr-affe* (*sluder-affe*), 'luxurious, thoughtless idler, sluggard,' recorded in the 14th cent., and certainly of not much earlier date ; the latter term is from MidHG. *slûr*, 'sluggishness, lazy person,' see ſchlentern, ſchlummern. The first detailed description of Schlaraffenland, of which the earliest mention is made in the 15th cent., was given in a farce by Hans Sachs in 1530 A.D.

ſchlau, adj., 'sly, crafty, cunning,' early ModHG. only, formed from LG. *slū* ; comp. Du. *sluw*, 'sly' ; akin also probably to OIc. *slœgr*, MidE. *sleigh*, E. *sly*, which, as Mod HG. verſchlagen, 'cunning,' indicates, is perhaps connected with the root *slah*, 'to strike.' It is uncertain how far these terms are due to earlier loan-words, and whether OIc. *slœgr* is the ultimate source of them all.

Schlauch, m., 'leather bag, bottle, or pipe, funnel,' from MidHG. *slûch*, m., 'skin, slough (of a snake), leather bag, pipe' ; corresponding to E. *slough*, Swed. dial. *slug*. MidHG. *slûch*, 'gullet, throat ; gulf, abyss,' is a different word ; late OHG. *slûch*, m., 'yawning chasm' (allied to ſchluden). ModHG. Schlund, as well as Lat. *vorāgo*, 'abyss,' allied to *vorare*, 'to swallow up,' shows a similar evolution in meaning ; comp. Lat. *faux*, 'gullet, throat, abyss.'

Schlauchmaul, n., 'glutton,' Mod HG. only, connected with the cognates of ſchluden.

ſchlecht, adj., 'bad, base, mean,' from MidHG. *slëht*, adj., 'honest, straight, smooth, simple, clear, correct,' OHG. *slëht*, 'straight, even, honest, simple, gentle, friendly' ; corresponding to Goth. *slaihts*, 'even, straight,' OIc. *slēttr*, 'straight, even, smooth, gentle,' OFris. *sliacht*, 'honest, simple' ; Du. *slecht*, 'honest, bad.' MidE. and E. *slight*, since the AS. word is not recorded, is probably a Du. loan-word. The meanings are evolved from 'straight, even, simple' (see ſchlicht and ſchlichten), and has led in ModHG. to a peculiar development *in malam partem*. The origin of the common Teut. adj. (or *to*-partic. ?) *slehta*- is obscure ; it cannot, on account of its form and meaning, be connected with ſchlagen ; Gr. ὀλίγος, 'trifling,' does not suit the earlier meaning, 'straight, even, simple.'

ſchlecken, vb., 'to lick, lap, be dainty,' from late MidHG. *slëcken*, 'to eat dainties by stealth' ; allied to MidHG. *slëc*, m., 'daintiness, dainty mouth,' and *havenslëcke*, 'glutton' ; OHG. **slëcchōn*, 'to be fond of dainties,' is wanting, as well as a corresponding term in any of the other OTeut. dials. Not allied to ſchluden, but an intensive form of OIc. *sleikja*, 'to lick,' which implies a Teut. root *slīk*, *sloiq*.

Schlegel, m., 'mallet, sledge-hammer, drumstick,' from MidHG. *slegel*, OHG. *slegil*, m., 'implement for beating, club, flail, hammer' ; from the root *slah*, 'to strike.' Comp. E. *sledge*, AS. *sleçge*, f., 'hammer,' from the same root.

Schlehe, f., 'sloe,' from the equiv. Mid HG. *slēhe*, OHG. *slëha*, f. ; a common Teut. term ; comp. Du. *slee*, AS. *slā*, *slāhœ*, f., E. *sloe*, Swed. *slån*, Dan. *sluaen*, 'sloe' ; Goth. **slaihō*, or rather **slaihwō*, are by chance not recorded. The cognates are usually connected with LG. *slee*, 'blunt' ; comp. OHG. *slēo*, OSax. *slēo* (Du. *sleeuw*, 'bitter, harsh'), AS. *slāw* (E. *slow*), OIc. *sljór*, *slœr*, 'blunt,' hence the lit. meaning of Schlehe is perhaps 'the fruit that makes the teeth blunt.' Yet since the latter terms imply Goth. **slaiwa*-, and the former Goth. **slaihō* (**slaihwō*), the explanation is dubious. So too, for the same reason, is the comparison with OSlov. *sliva* (Lith. *slywas*), 'plum,' for which we should expect a Goth **slāiwō* (though AS. *slā* points to **slāihō*).

ſchleichen, vb., 'to creep, crawl, slink,' from MidHG. *slîchen*, OHG. *slîhhan*, 'to walk with a light sliding motion, creep' ; akin to MidHG. *slîch*, m., 'slime, mud,' Du. *slik*, *slijk*, 'slime, mud,' MidE. *sliken*, 'to creep,' with which E. *sleek* and *slick* are connected ; in the other languages the Teut. root *slīk* (pre-Teut. *slīg*) rarely occurs. —To this is allied Schleiche in Blindſchleiche, f., 'blind-worm,' MidHG. *blintsliche*, OHG. *blintsliicho*. m. See Schlich.

Schleie, f., 'tench,' from the equiv. Mid HG. *slîe*, OHG. *slîo*, m. ; corresponding to AS. *slīc*, m., 'tench' ; Goth. **sleivs*, m., or rather **sleiwa*, m., is wanting. Perhaps the fish was so named from its slimy scales, so that Schleim may be allied.

Schleier, m., 'veil, pretence,' from Mid HG. *sleier*, earlier variants *sloier*, *slogier*, m., 'kerchief, veil' (the MidHG. term *floier* is curious) ; comp. Du. *sluijer*, MidE. *sleir*. MidHG. *sloier*, first recorded in the 13th cent., is certainly a borrowed term ; the assumption that it was introduced by the Crusaders from the East leads to no definite result. Perhaps it is connected with OIr. *sról*, 'silk.'

Schleife, f., 'slide ; slip-knot, bow of

ribbons, favour,' for earlier ModHG. (still dial.) Schläufe, f., allied to MidHG. *sloufen, slôufen*, 'to push, slip, dress'; also Goth. *slaupjan*, 'to strip off'; AS. *slúpan*, 'to glide, slip' (E. *slop*), Goth. *sliupan*, 'to slip,' OHG. *sliofan*, MidHG. *slie-fen*, 'to slide, slip.' The Teut. root *slûp*, from pre-Teut. *slûb*, contained in these words, has been connected, perhaps rightly, with Lat. *lûbricus* (for *slûbricus*), 'slippery,' and Lith. *slúbnas*, 'weak.'

Schleifen, vb., 'to slide, sharpen, whet,' from MidHG. *slîfen*, 'to glide, sink, grind a weapon,' &c. (prop. 'to sharpen by letting it slide '), OHG. *slîfan*, 'to glide, sink, smooth'; comp. Du. *slijpen*, 'to sharpen,' AS. *tô-slípan*, 'to dissolve,' to which are allied E. *to slip*, and *slippers* (Ital. *schippire*, 'to escape'). How the Teut. root *slîp*, 'to glide, slip,' is connected with the equiv. root *slûp*, discussed under the preceding word, and further also with schleichen (root *slîk*), has not yet been ascertained. The corresponding factitive schleichen, vb., 'to trail,' from MidHG. and OHG. *sleifen*, lit. 'to cause to slide along,' hence 'to drag along, trail,' even late MidHG. *eine burc sleifen*, 'to raze a city'; comp. LG. and Du. *slepen*, 'to drag along the ground, trail,' whence ModHG. schleppen is borrowed. See Schiff.

Schleim, m., 'slime, mucus, phlegm, filth,' from MidHG. *slîm*, m., 'slime, mire, sticky fluid'; OHG. *slîm* is wanting. Comp. Du. *slijm*, 'slime,' AS. *slím*, and the equiv. E, *slime*, OIc. *slím*, n.; Goth. **sleims* is wanting. The root *slî*, 'to be smooth, slippery,' contained in these words, which is especially apparent in OHG. *slîmen*, 'to make smooth, brighten by grinding,' is closely related to Lat. *limare*, 'to file, polish, smooth,' *lima*, 'file,' with which probably Lat. *lévis* and Gr. λεῖος, 'smooth,' are also connected. In Lat. and Gr. initial *s* disappears before *l*. Perhaps Lat. *límus*, 'slime' (see under Lehm), may be adduced here; comp. further Schleie.

schleißen, vb., 'to slit, split, gash,' from MidHG. *slîzen*, OHG. *slîzan*, 'to split, tear to pieces, wear out'; corresponding to OSax. *slîtan*, 'to tear to pieces,' Du. *slijten*, 'to wear out,' AS. *slítan*, 'to tear to pieces,' to which E. *to slit* is allied, OIc. *slíta*, 'to tear to pieces.' The Teut. root *slît*, 'to tear to pieces' (Goth. **sleitan*), from pre-Teut. *slîd*, has not yet been found in the non-Teut. languages. See schlitzen, the intensive form. Schleißen, wk. vb., as the factitive of the str. vb., is MidHG. and OHG. *sleizen, sleitzen*, 'to tear to pieces, split.'

Schlemmen, 'to carouse,' from late MidHG. *slemmen*, 'to squander,' allied to late MidHG. *slamp*, 'carouse'; comp. Du. *slemp*, 'dainty meal,' *slempen*, 'to carouse,' with which Schlempe, f., 'rinsings,' is connected. The term is wanting in the other Teut. languages.

Schlempe, f., see schlemmen.

schlendern, vb., 'to lounge, saunter,' ModHG. only, formed from the equiv. LG. *slendern*, Du. *slenderen*.—Schlendrian, m., 'old practice or custom, loafer,' Mod HG. only, formed from LG.; in Du. *slender*, 'sauntering gait.' The *d* after *n* represents an older *t*, which is correctly permutated in HG. schlenzen, 'to saunter'; comp. MidE. *slenten*, 'to saunter.'

schlenkern, vb., 'to sling, fling; loiter, lounge'; from late MidHG. *slenkern*, 'to sling,' allied to MidHG. *slenge, slenger, slenker*, 'sling,' OHG. *slengira*, f., 'sling'; derivatives from a root *sling* (see schlingen). From this was formed OHG. *slinga*, f., MidHG. *slinge*, f., 'sling,' whence the Rom. term Fr. *elingue* was borrowed; comp. E. *sling*, and see Schlinge.

Schleppe, f., 'train (of a dress), trail,' ModHG. only, from LG. *slepe*, Du. *sleep*, 'train.'—schleppen, 'to drag along, trail'; it occurs even in MidHG.; from MidG. and LG.; comp. LG. and Du. *slepen*. See schleifen.

Schleuder, f., 'sling, swing,' from the equiv. late MidHG. *slûder*, f.; probably borrowed (whence ?). The equiv. G. word is quoted under schleufern.

schleudern, vb., 'to perform in a slovenly manner, bungle'; it is not really related to the preceding word, though it is instinctively connected with it by Germans, in Schleuderpreis, 'undervalue,' for example. The vb. is allied to MidHG. *slûderer*, 'he who works hastily and negligently,' which again, with an excrescent dental (as in hautern), is akin to MidHG. *slûr*, m., 'bungling, idling, idler'; comp. Schlaraffe and schlummern.

schleunig, adj., 'hasty, speedy,' from MidHG. *sliunec*, OHG. *sliunig*, 'quick, speedy,' in OHG. also 'thriving.' A lengthened form of Goth. **slû-na-*, for which we have, however, *snú-na-*; the *l* seems to have been produced by assimilation on account of the suffix *n*. Allied to the OTeut. root *snĕll*, 'to hasten, move quickly, turn'; comp. OHG. *sniumo*, AS. *sneóme*, adv., 'speedily, quickly,' Goth. *sniumundô*, 'hastily,' AS. *snúde*, adv., 'quickly'; as a vb. Goth. *sniumjan*, 'to hasten,' Goth. *sniwan*, 'to hasten,' AS. *sneówian*, 'to hasten,' OIc. *snúa*, 'to turn.'

Schleuse, f., 'sluice,' ModHG. only, formed from LG. *slüse*, Du. *sluis*, 'aqueduct,' which is derived from OFr. *escluse*, ModFr. *écluse*, 'sluice' (from early Mid Lat. *sclusa*, *exclusa*). From the same source E. *sluice* is derived.

Schlich, m., 'byway, trick,' from MidHG. *slich*, m., 'light, gliding gait,' allied to *schleichen*.

schlicht, adj., 'plain, homely, honest,' ModHG. only, formed to represent the meanings of MidHG. *slëht* (see *schlecht*), which became obsolete in ModHG. *schlecht*, from the MidHG. and OHG. vb. *slihten*, 'to make plain, smooth over,' and the MidHG. abstract form *slihte*, f., 'straightforwardness'; comp. OHG. *slihten*, 'to make plain,' *slihtt*, allied to *slëht*, 'straight, even.'

schliefen, vb., see **Schleife**.

schließen, vb., 'to close, shut, include, infer,' from MidHG. *sliezen*, OHG. *sliozan*, 'to shut,' OSax. *slûtan* (equiv. to MidLG. and LG. *slûten*), is attested by *slutil*, 'key'; Du. *sluiten*, 'to lock up,' OFris. *slûta*; further Northern E. *sloat*, *slot*, 'bolt of a door.' In OIc. and Goth. the corresponding vbs. and derivs. are wanting. The Teut. root *slût* certainly originated in pre-Teut. *sklâd*—the combination *skl* is not tolerated in Teut.,—and hence it may be compared with Lat. *claudo* for *sclaudo* (Aryan root *klaud*, as well as *sklaud*), as a cognate term. See **Schloß** and **Schlüffel**.

Schliff, m., 'sharpening, grinding, edge,' from MidHG. *slif* (gen. *sliffes*), m., 'polish, slipping'; allied to *schleifen*.

schlimm, adj., 'bad, wicked,' from MidHG. *slimp*, adj., 'awry, aslant,' whence the adv. *slimbes*, 'obliquely'; OHG. **slimb*, 'aslant,' may be assumed from the derivative abstr. form *slimbî*, 'slope.' The moral signification of the adj. first occurs in ModHG.; a similar development is seen in Du. *slim*, 'bad' (beside which occurs *slimbeen*, 'person with bandy-legs'). E. *slim* and OIc. *slœmr*, 'vile,' were borrowed from the Continent. The remoter history of OTeut. *slimba-*, 'aslant, awry,' from which Ital. *sghembo*, 'awry, bent,' was borrowed at an early period, is quite obscure.

Schlinge, f., 'knot, loop, noose, snare.' ModHG. only; corresponding in form to MidHG. *slinge*, 'sling,' f. (see *schleudern*), which meaning was retained in ModHG. till the 17th cent. (so too Span. *eslingua*, Fr. *élingue*). On account of its sense, however, **Schlinge** is not to be derived from this MidHG. word, but from the ModHG. vb. —**schlingen**, vb., 'to wind, twine, twist, sling,' from MidHG. *slingen*, OHG. *slingan*, 'to wind, entwine, swing to and fro,' MidHG. also 'to creep,' OHG. 'to move'; comp. Du. *slingeren*, 'to hurl, swing.' AS. *slingan*, E. *to sling*, OIc. *slyngva*, 'to throw'; Goth. **slingwan* (or rather **sleihwan*) is wanting. The prim. idea of the root *slingw*, to which both *schleudern* and **Schlange** are allied, was 'a revolving, swinging motion.' The Teut. root *slingw* (**slinhw*) originated in pre-Teut. *slenk*, as is indicated by Lith. *slinkti*, 'to creep' (OSlov. *sląkŭ*, 'crooked'?).—**Schlingel**, m., 'sluggard, rascal, blackguard,' earlier ModHG. *Schlüngel*, prop. perhaps 'sneak'; wanting in MidHG. and in the other languages.

schlingen (1.), vb., 'to twine, wind.' See the preceding article.

schlingen (2.), vb., 'to swallow, engulf,' a MidG. term introduced by Luther, for (UpG.) MidHG. *slinden*, OHG. *slintan*, 'to devour'; in MidG. *nd* changes to *ng*, as, e.g., Thuring. *linge*, 'Linde' (linden), *gebungen*, *gebunden* (bound), *schlung*, **Schlund** (gullet). Comp. Goth. *fra-slindan*, 'to devour,' Du. *slinden*, 'to devour'; further corresponding vbs. are wanting in OTeut. The Teut. root *slind*, 'to devour,' seems to be cognate with the root *slŭl*, 'to slide.' See **Schlitten** and also **Schlund**. The change from *schlinden* to *schlingen* is due to connecting the word with *schlingen* (1); comp. *hinunter würgen*, 'to swallow.'

Schlitten, m., 'sleigh, sledge,' from the equiv. MidHG. *slitte*, usually *slite*, m., OHG. *slita*, f., *slito*, m.; comp. Du. *slede*, MidE. *slede*, E. *sled*, *sledge*, OIc. *sleðe*, m., 'sleigh.' From HG. is derived Ital. *slitta*, 'sleigh.' The Teut. cognates are based on a Teut. root *slĭd*, 'to slide,' which is preserved in the E. vb. and subst. *slide*; comp. the equiv. MidHG. (MidG.) *slîten*, whence ModHG. (dial.) *schlittern*, 'to slide (on ice),' AS. *slîdan*. Pre-Teut. *slidh*, 'to slide,' is also attested by Lith. *slidus*, 'smooth' (of ice), *slýsti* (root *slyd*), 'to slide,' Lett. *slîdas*, 'skates,' and Sans. *srîdh*, 'to stumble'; the root seems to have been often used in primit. Teut.

times, and perhaps still earlier, for 'to slide (on ice).'—Schlittschuh, m., 'skate,' ModHG. only in its present sense, for earlier ModHG. Schrittschuh. Comp. MidHG. *schriteschuoch*, n., 'league-boot, shoe for flying.'

Schlitz, m., 'slit, gash,' from MidHG. *sliz* (gen. *slitzes*), OHG. *sliz, slíz*, m., 'cleaving, breach' (comp. E. *slit*); allied to schleißen.—schlitzen, vb., 'to slit, gash, cleave,' from the equiv. MidHG. *slitzen*, intensive of schleißen.

schlohweiß, adj., see Schleße.

Schloß, n., 'lock, clasp; castle, palace,' from MidHG. *slôȝ*, n., 'bolt, band, lock, fetter, castle, citadel,' OHG. *slôȝ*, n., 'lock, bolt'; corresponding to Northern E. *slot, sloat*, 'bolt, crossbar'; allied to schließen.

Schloße, f., 'hail, hailstone, sleet,' from the equiv. MidHG. *slôȝe*, f., *slôȝ* (m. and n.?); OHG. **slôȝa* is wanting; comp. Du. *slote* (OSax. **slôta*), AS. **slýt, *sléte*, E. *sleet* (Goth. **slauti-* is wanting). The origin of the cognates is obscure; it is scarcely derived from the root *slût*, 'to lock,' as if hail were regarded as 'that which is bound together compared with the soft snowflakes and the streaming rain.'—schloßweiß, or, by a curious corruption, schlohweiß, lit. 'white as hail' (MidHG. *wiȝer dan ein slôȝ*, 'whiter than a hailstone,' occurs once).

Schlot, m., 'chimney, flue, channel,' from MidHG. and OHG. *slât*, m., 'chimney, fireside, mouth of an oven.' A word peculiar to MidG.; of obscure origin.

schlottern, vb., 'to shake, hang loose, dangle,' from the equiv. MidHG. *slottern*, intensive of MidHG. *sloten*, 'to quiver.' Comp. Du. *slodderen*, 'to shake'; of obscure origin.

Schlucht, f., 'ravine, gorge,' ModHG. only, formed from LG., for earlier ModHG. and HG. Schluft; for LG. *cht*, representing HG. *ft*, see Sacht, beichwichtigen, and Nichte. MidHG. (rare) *sluft*, 'ravine,' belongs to the Teut. root *slûp*, 'to slip,' discussed under Schleife.

schluchzen, vb., 'to sob,' from the equiv. late MidHG. *sluckzen*; prop. a frequentative of schlucken, which in MidHG. also means 'to sob.' See seufzen (OHG. **sluhhazzen, *slucchazzen*, are wanting).—schlucken, vb., 'to gulp down, swallow,' from MidHG. *slucken*, 'to swallow, gulp down, sob'; OHG. **slucchôn* may be inferred from *sluccho, slûkho (hh* as in schluchzen?), m., 'gormandiser, glutton.' Allied to MidHG. *slûchen*, 'to swallow, gulp down,' and *slûch*, 'gullet, throat; sot, glutton' (comp. ModHG. Schlauchmaul). The Teut. root *slûk*, not allied to schlecken, originated in Aryan *slûg*, which has been identified in Gr. as λυγ (for σλυγ); comp. λυγγάνομαι, λύζω, 'to have the hiccup, sob,' λύγδην, 'sobbingly,' λύγξ (λυγγός), 'violent sobbing, hiccup.' In OIr. the root appears with initial *s* as *slug*, 'to devour.' Akin also to Schlauch.

Schluft, see Schlucht.

schlummern, vb., 'to slumber,' from the equiv. late MidHG. (MidG.) *slummeren, slumen*; comp. Du. *sluimeren*; AS. *slûmerian*, E. *to slumber*, AS. *slûma*, Northern E. *sloom*, 'to slumber.' The root (Alem. *slûne, slâre*, 'to slumber') contained in these words appears in Goth. *slawan (slawaida)*, 'to be silent,' in a curious divergent meaning, to which MidHG. *slûr*, m., 'idling, idler' (comp. Schlaraffe), is also allied. The prim. idea of the whole group is 'to be quiet, inactive.'

Schlund, m., 'gullet, throat, chasm,' from MidHG. and OHG. *slunt*, m., 'gullet, throat, neck, abyss'; allied to MidHG. *slinden*, ModHG. schlingen (2), but with the preservation of the old dental, which schlingen has changed into a guttural.

Schlupf, m., 'slip, refuge, pass, defile,' from MidHG. *slupf*, 'noose, cord,' allied to MidHG. *slüpfen*, MidHG. and OHG. *slupfen*, ModHG. schlüpfen, 'to slip,' which is an intensive of MidHG. *sliefen*, 'to slide, slip,' corresponding to Goth. *sliupan*, 'to slip'; Lat. *lûbricus* seems to be primit. allied to it.—schlüpfrig, adj. 'slippery, unstable,' from late MidHG. *slupferic*, 'slippery,' of which the variant *slupfer* occurs.

schlürfen, vb., 'to sip, lap, drink,' ModHG. only; probably, however, its nonoccurrence in earlier HG. is only an accident (MidHG. **slürfen*, OHG. **slurfen*); according to the HG. permutation Du. *slurpen*, 'to sip,' is allied. The stem is not found elsewhere; its origin is obscure.

Schlüssel, m., 'key,' from the equiv. MidHG. *slüzzel*, OHG. *sluȝȝil*, m.; corresponding to OSax. *slutil*, Du. *sleutel*. This derivative of schließen (Goth. **slutila-*) is wanting in E., OIc., and Goth.

Schluß, m., 'end, conclusion,' from the equiv. late MidHG. *sluȝ*, m., of which the variant *sloȝ* occurs in *sloȝrede*, 'syllogism,' *sloȝstein*, 'keystone.' Allied to schließen.

Schmach, f., 'outrage, ignominy,' from MidHG. (rare) *smâch, smâhe*, usually *smæhe*, f., 'insult, abuse, ignominy' (to which Ital. *smacco*, 'affront,' is allied?). An abstract from MidHG. *smæhe*, adj., 'little, trifling, contemptible'; comp. OHG. *smâhi*, adj., 'little, trifling, base,' *smâhi*, f., 'trifle, baseness'; also OIc. *smár*, 'little,' and, with a different development of meaning, AS. *smeálic*, 'fine, careful.' A similar variety of meanings is seen in the history of ModHG. *klein*, for which we must assume (as for OHG. *smâhi*) the prim. meaning of 'little, pretty.' If Gr. μικρός, σμικρός, represents *σμεκρός, OHG. *smâhi* (as if corresponding to *σμήκιος) may be connected with it. The earlier sense still appears faintly in ſchmachten and verſchmachten; comp. MidHG. *versmahten* (ā or ä?), 'to pine away,' OHG. *gismahtēn*, 'to disappear.' Allied to ſchmächtig, adj., 'pining, languishing,' from MidHG. (MidG.) *smahtec*, from MidHG. (MidG.) *smaht*, 'pining away'; if these latter cognates contain ā, they may be connected with ModHG. *smēcker*, 'slender, narrow, pining.' See ſchmähen.

Schmach, see ſchmecken.

Schmache, f., 'smack' (vessel), ModHG. only, formed from the equiv. LG. and Du. *smak*, E. *smack*, Dan. *smakke* (comp. Fr. *semaque*); its history and origin are obscure.

ſchmähen, vb., 'to abuse, revile, rail,' from MidHG. *smæhen*, 'to treat contemptuously,' OHG. *smâhen*, vb., 'to make small, lessen,' see Schmach. Allied to ModHG. ſchmählich, adj., 'abusive,' MidHG. *smæhelich*, OHG. *smâlich*, adj., which are identical with the OHG. adj. *smâhi*, MidHG. *smæhe*, adduced under Schmach.

ſchmal, adj., 'narrow, slender, scanty,' from MidHG. and OHG. *smal*, adj., 'small, trifling, slender, scanty, narrow'; corresponding to Goth. *smals*, 'small, trifling,' AS. *smæl*, 'small, trifling,' E. *small*, Du. *smal*, OSax. *smal*, 'small, trifling.' The ModHG. sense is to be regarded as a specialisation of the older and wider meaning. The word is usually compared with OSlov. *malŭ*, 'small,' as well as Gr. μῆλα, 'small cattle' (for σμ-?), OIr. *mīl*, 'animal,' espec. since OIc. *smale*, 'small cattle,' has the same meaning. The older and wider meaning of the adj. is still faintly seen in ſchmälen, 'to put down with reproof'; comp. MidHG. *smeln*, 'to make narrower, lessen.'

Schmalte, f., 'smalt,' ModHG. only, formed from Ital. *smalto*, or Fr. *smalt*, 'glass of a deep blue.'

Schmalz, n., 'fat, grease, suet,' from MidHG. and OHG. *smalz*, n., 'melted fat for cooking, grease, butter' (comp. Ital. dial. *smalzo*, 'butter'); allied to ſchmelzen, 'to melt,' which, in the sense 'to cook with fat,' is derived from Schmalz.

Schmant, m. (Livon., LG., and Hess.), 'cream,' from the equiv. late MidHG. *smant*, borrowed in the 15th cent. from Slav.; comp. Bohem. *smant*. With Bohem. *smetana* (Russ. *smetana*, 'cream') is connected the dial. (Siles., Bohem., and Austr.) Schmetten, 'cream,' to which Schmetterling is probably related.

ſchmarotzen, vb., 'to spunge on,' from late MidHG. *smorotzen*, 'to beg, be sordid, spunge on.' On account of the narrow area and the late appearance of the word, its history and origin are obscure.

Schmarre, f., 'slash, scar,' ModHG. only; corresponding to LG. *smarre*; unknown to the OTeut. languages; only in MidHG. does a cognate *smurre*, f., 'cut, stroke,' occur. Of obscure origin.

ſchmatzen, vb., 'to smack the lips in eating,' from the equiv. MidHG. *smatzen*, which also means 'to kiss with a smack.' The MidHG. word comes from an older equiv. variant *smackezen*, a derivative of MidHG. *smacken*, 'to taste, savour.'

Schmauch, m., 'thick smoke,' from MidHG. *smouch*, 'smoke, vapour' (AS. *smēč*). Allied to a Teut. root *smūk*- (pre-Teut. *smūg*), 'to smoke'; comp. AS. *smēocan*, *smōcian*, and the equiv. E. *to smoke*, Du. *smoken*, 'to smoke,' *smook*, 'smoke'; also LG. *smōken*. Perhaps Gr. σμύχω (Aor. ε-σμύγ-ην), 'to consume in a smouldering fire,' is allied.

Schmaus, m., 'feast, banquet'; its history and origin are obscure. Yet Du. *smullen*, 'to eat or drink immoderately, carouse,' *smuisteren*, 'to feast,' Du. and LG. *smudderen*, *smodderen*, 'to feast,' are probably cognate. The word is unknown to the OTeut. period.

ſchmecken, vb., 'to taste, savour, relish,' from MidHG. *smęcken*, *smacken*, 'to try by tasting; savour, smell, scent; perceive'; the meaning 'to smell' is still partly retained by Alem. and Bav. OHG. *smęcchen*, only 'to taste' (trans. and intrans.), *smacchēn*, 'to smack of.' Comp. OHG. and MidHG. *smac*, m., 'taste,' Du. *smaak*, AS. *smæc* (*cc*), 'taste,' *smeččan*, 'to taste,' E. *smack*, vb. and subst. In OIc. and Goth. there are no corresponding vbs. from the Teut. root *smak* (pre-Teut. *smág*), with which Lith. *smagùs*, 'agreeable,' lit. 'pliant,' has wrongly been connected as cognate terms.

Schmeer, m., 'fat, grease, smear,' from the equiv. MidHG. *smër* (gen. *smërwes*), OHG. *smëro* (gen. *smërwes*), n.; comp. **schmieren**. From the root *smër*, contained in these words, are derived Goth. **smair-þr*, n., 'fat, fatness,' Du. *smeer*, 'fat, grease, tallow,' AS. *smeoro*, E. *smear*, OIc. *smjǫr*, 'butter'; also, with a different meaning, Goth. *smarna*, 'dirt, excrement' (comp. its relation to **Schmeer** and **schmieren**), and, in a figurative sense, OHG. and AS. *bismer*, 'contumely.' In the non-Teut. languages the word has been compared, probably without any justification, with Gr. μύρω, 'to trickle,' μύρον, 'salve.'

schmeicheln, vb., 'to caress, coax, flatter,' from MidHG. *smeicheln*, *smeichen*, 'to flatter, praise, extol'; OHG. **smeihhen* is wanting; comp. MidLG. *smeken*, Du. *smeeken*, 'to implore' (conversely, Du. *vleijen* signifies 'to flatter'). These cognates, which have no corresponding terms in other languages, probably belong, like the words adduced under **Schminke**, to a Teut. and Aryan root *smî-w*, 'to be insinuating, friendly,' to which MidHG. *smieren*, *smielen*, 'to smile' (comp. **Speichel** from the root *spîw*, 'to spit'), is allied. In that case E. *to smile*, Sans. *smêra-s*, 'smiling,' Sans. root *smi*, 'to laugh,' Lett. *smêt*, 'to laugh,' and OSlov. *smĭjǫ*, *smijati sę*, 'to laugh,' are probably allied. If from its relation to HG. **glatt** and E. *glad* it is assumed that the prim. meaning of the root *smî-w* is 'to be smooth,' the root *smî* (see **Schmied**), 'to work artistically' (lit. 'to do polished work'), may be regarded as cognate with the former; similarly OHG. *gi-slihten* signifies 'to smooth over, polish,' and 'to flatter.'

schmeißen, vb., 'to smite, fling, kick (of horses),' from MidHG. *smîzen*, 'to rub, strike'; the latter meanings are the earlier, as is shown by Goth. *smeitan* (only in *ga-smeitan* and *bi-smeitan*), 'to spread over, besmear'; comp. AS. *smîtan*, E. *to smite*. The meaning of ModHG. **schmeißen**, compared with that of OHG. and MidHG., is due to LG. and Du. influence; comp. Du. *smijten*, 'to fling, throw.' Yet it is to be observed that the OHG. and MidHG. vbs. are compounded usually with *bi*, or rather *be* (as in Goth. and AS.), hence the OTeut. root *smît* probably signifies 'to throw at.'

The corresponding ModHG. vb. **schmeißen**, 'cacare' (MidHG. *smeizen*, 'cacare'), is a factitive of **smîzen**. See **schmitzen**.

schmelzen, vb., 'to melt, dissolve,' from the equiv. MidHG. *smëlzen*, OHG. *smëlzan*; also as factitive ModHG. **schmelzen**, MidHG. and OHG. *smęlzen*, 'to smelt, liquefy'; comp. E. *to smelt*. The pre-Teut. root *smeld*, contained in these words and in the allied term **Schmalz**, is cognate with the root *meld* (see **Malz**), and Gr. μέλδω, 'to melt.' From the Teut. cognates the Rom. terms, Ital. *smalto* and Fr. *émail*, 'enamel,' are usually derived.

Schmergel, m., 'emery,' early ModHG. only, from the equiv. Ital. *smeriglio*.

Schmerl, m., **Schmerlin**, 'merlin,' from MidHG. *smirl*, m., *smirlîn*, 'mountain falcon,' OHG. *smirl*, m., OIc. *smyrell*; loan-words from Rom.; comp. Ital. *smerlo*, *smeriglione*, Fr. *émerillon*, 'stone-falcon'; E. *merlin* comes from Fr. The Rom. name of the bird is usually derived from Lat. *merula*, 'blackbird'; "it is said that the Lat. word is applied to a bird similar to the blackbird."

Schmerle, f., 'loach,' from MidHG. *smërl*, *smërle*, f., 'loach, groundling'; Mid HG. also *smërlinc*, m., and *smërlîn*, n.; of obscure origin.

Schmerz, m., 'pain,' from the equiv. MidHG. *smërz*, m., OHG. *smërzo*, m., *smërza*, f.; allied to OHG. *smërzan*, vb., MidHG. *smërzen*, 'to smart, pain,' AS. *smeortan*, 'to pain, smart,' E. *smart*, vb. and subst. MidE. *smerte*, E. *smart*, adj., make it probable that the cognates are related to Lat. *mordēre*, 'to bite,' Gr. σμερδνός, σμερδαλέος, 'horrible'; the Aryan root *smerd*, Teut. *smert*, signifies perhaps 'to stick, bite.' Comp. **bitter**.

Schmetten, see **Schmant**.

Schmetterling, m., 'butterfly,' Mod HG. only; in the earlier periods a term closely connected with ModHG. **Falter** (Zweifalter) is used. In most of the ModHG. dials. this literary term is also wanting; in Bav. *müllermaler* (so too in the Fulda dial.) or *sommervogel*, Suab. *baufalter* or *weifalter*. In other dials. occur **Milchdieb**, **Molkendieb** (Westph. also *molkentövener*, *smantlecker*), LG. **Buttervogel** or **Butterfliege** (AS. *butorfleóge*, E. *butterfly*), which may perhaps explain ModHG. **Schmetterling**. The latter term is probably derived from ModHG. **Schmetten**, 'cream,' which, like **Schmetterling**, is native to the eastern part of Middle

Germany (see **Schmant**). Comp. further Du. *vlinder*.

Schmettern, vb., 'to hurl, smash, bray (of trumpets), peal (of thunder),' MidHG. *smetern*, 'to clatter,' an onomatopoetic word.

Schmied, m., 'smith,' from MidHG. *smit*, OHG. *smid*, m., 'worker in metal.' Goth. *aiza-smiþa*, 'smith,' lit. 'worker in brass,' and *ga-smiþôn*, 'to work (do smith's work),' show that the HG. meaning is specialisation of the signification 'faber, worker in art'; OIc. *smiðr*, m., 'worker in metal or wood'; comp. AS. *smiþ*, E. *smith*, Du. *smid*. ModHG. **Schmiede**, f., based on **Schmied**, is derived from the equiv. Mid HG. *smitte*, OHG. *smitta*, f., 'smithy.' which again comes from Goth. *smiþjo (*þj* became *þþj* in West Teut., and the *þþ* was permutated to *tt* in HG.; comp. **Sittich**); comp. OIc. *smiðja*, AS. *smiþþe*, f., E. *smithy*, and the equiv. Du. *smisse*. With the root *smi*, 'to work artistically in hard material—wood, brass,' preserved in Goth. *smi-þa, m., are connected OHG. *smeidar*, 'artist, artifex daedalus,' and the words discussed under **Geschmeide**. Comp. also Gr. σμίλη, 'graving tool,' σμι-νύη, 'hoe.' For its supposed connection with other terms see under **schmeicheln**.

schmiegen, vb., 'to wind, incline; (refl.) twine, nestle,' from MidHG. *smiegen* (OHG. *smiogan is by chance not recorded), 'to cling close to, contract, stoop'; comp. AS. *smúgan*, 'to creep,' OIc. *smjúga*, 'to creep through something'; the prim. idea of these cognates, which do not occur elsewhere in Teut., is 'to press closely to anything and to be swayed by its movements.' Teut. root *smûg*, from pre-Teut. *smûk*; comp. OSlov. *smykati sę*, 'to creep,' Lith. *smùkti*, 'to slide.' See **schmücken** and **schmygeln**.

Schmiele, f., 'hair-grass, bulrush,' from the equiv. MidHG. *smilehe*, *smēlehe*, f.; OHG. *smēlaha, *smilaha*, or rather *smēlawa*, *smilawa*, and Goth. *smilhwi, f., are wanting; allied to MidHG. *smëlhe*, adj., 'narrow.'

Schmieralien, plur., 'bribes,' ModHG. only, formed like **Lappalien** (trifles), with a foreign suffix from a G. stem; comp. also **Schwulität**. Allied to **schmieren**, MidHG. *smirn*, *smirwen*, 'to smear, salve, bribe,' OHG. *smirwen*, a denominative of **Schmeer**.

Schminke, f., 'paint (for the face), rouge,' from the equiv. MidHG. *sminke*,

smicke, f., allied to OHG. *smëcchar*, *smëhhar*, adj., 'fine, pretty,' AS. *smicere*, 'fine, pretty.' These are connected with **schmeicheln** (root *smaikw*?). Comp. Dan. *smigre*, Swed. *smickra*, 'to flatter,' E. *to smicker*, 'to ogle.'

Schmiß, m., 'blow, stroke, trick,' Mod HG. only, allied to MidHG. *smiz*, 'spot' (*smîzen*, 'to strike').

schmitzen, vb., 'to lash, whip,' from Mid HG. *smitzen*, 'to beat with rods, scourge, besmear.' To this is allied ModHG. **verschmitzt**, 'wily, cunning,' lit. 'beaten away.'

Schmöker, m., ModHG. only, prop. 'smoker,' then 'book strongly scenting of tobacco'; allied to LG. *smöken*; see **Schmauch**.

schmollen, vb., 'to pout, be sulky,' from MidHG. *smollen*, 'to be silent from vexation, pout.' also 'to smile'; a late form of MidHG. *smielen*, 'to smile'; see **schmeicheln**.

Schmollis, m., 'good-fellowship, fraternisation,' ModHG. only; its history is obscure, yet it seems to be connected with Du. *smullen*, 'to feast, gormandise' (see **Schmaus**), *smul*, 'feast, good cheer.'

schmoren, vb., 'to swelter, stew, fry,' ModHG. only, formed from LG. and Du. *smoren*, 'to roast, stew,' also 'to stifle, fume'; comp. AS. *smorian*, 'to stifle.' Those who regard 'to roast, stew,' as the prim. meaning of the cognates may trace AS. *smorian* to Goth. *smuzôn*, and explain ModHG. **Schmaus** from some such orig. sense as 'cook-shop.' Yet AS. and MidE. *smorþer*, 'steam,' E. *smother*, probably points to a root with a final *r*.

Schmuck, m., 'adornment, finery,' Mod HG. only, in MidHG. *gesmuc*, 'adornment, embellishment,' allied to **schmücken**, MidHG. *smücken*, 'to wind, press close, dress, adorn.' The Teut. root *smug* (pre-Teut. *smuk*) in **schmiegen**, of which **schmücken** is an intensive form, was frequently used orig. to form words signifying 'to dress,' and is also found in the name of a sort of under-garment or shirt, OHG. *smoccho*, AS. *smoc* (comp. E. *smock*). The adj. **schmuck**, 'tidy, smart,' ModHG. only, is derived from LG. (comp. North Fris. *smok*), whence also E. *smug* (or from Dan. *smuk*).

schmuggeln, vb., 'to smuggle,' Mod HG. only, formed from the equiv. LG. *smuggeln*; comp. Du. *smokkeln*, E. *to smuggle* (borrowed from the same source?). The orig. word is connected with the root *smug*, 'to wind,' to which the secondary sense of 'secrecy' may belong; comp. Du. *smuigen,* 'to enjoy oneself secretly.'

Schmunzeln, vb., 'to smile good-naturedly, simper,' frequentative of MidHG. *smutzen, smotzen,* 'to smirk, smile good-naturedly,' to which MidHG. *smutz,* ModHG. (dial.) **Schmuß,** 'kiss,' is also probably allied. It is perhaps connected with **Schmatz, schmatzen** (from MidHG. *smackezen*).

Schmus, m., 'talk, chaffering,' ModHG. only; from Hebr. *schĕmûôth,* 'news, tales'; hence Du. *smousen,* 'to chaffer'?.

Schmutz, m., 'dirt, filth,' from the equiv. MidHG. *smuz (-tzes),* m., allied to MidHG. *smotzen,* 'to be dirty'; also to Du. *smet,* 'spot, dirt,' *smetten,* 'to get stained,' *smodderen,* 'to soil,' E. *smut,* vb. and subst., MidE. *bismitten, bismoteren, bismudden,* 'to stain, soil.' It is uncertain whether these words are late graded forms of MidHG. *smitzen,* 'to rub over.'

Schnabel, m., 'beak, bill,' from the equiv. MidHG. *snabel,* m., OHG. *snabul,* m.; corresponding to Du. *snavel,* 'beak, trunk' (of an elephant), *sneb,* 'beak,' OFris. *snavel,* 'mouth.' To these, from the relation of **Malz** to **schmelzen** (Aryan root *meld, smeld*), the following are also allied—Du. *neb,* f., 'beak,' E. *nib,* AS. *nębb,* 'beak, face,' OIc. *nef,* n., 'nose' (as well as *snafōr,* 'sharp-scented'). From Teut. are derived the cognates of Ital. *niffo,* 'snout, trunk.' Teut. *snabja-, snabula-* (from an Aryan root *snap, nap*), agrees with Lith. *snápas,* 'beak.' Comp. **schnappen, Schnepfe,** and **Schnepfe.**

Schnack, m., 'chit-chat, talk,' ModHG. only, formed from MidG., LG., and Du. *snakken,* 'to chatter, babble'; to this is allied ModHG. **Schnake,** 'merry tale,' from LG., also 'merry fellow.' Comp. Du. *snaak,* 'buffoon.'

Schnake, f., 'gnat, midge,' from the equiv. MidHG. *snāke,* m. and f.; the sounds point to OHG. **snāko* (from the base **snāggo;* comp. **Hafen,** from the base **hăggo*). The prop. LG. *schnake,* f., 'water-snake,' is different from this word, and corresponds to E. *snake,* AS. *snăcu,* 'snake,' OIc. *snákr, snókr,* 'snake' (Swed. *snok,* 'water-snake').

Schnalle, f., 'buckle, clasp,' from MidHG. *snalle,* f., 'buckle,' shoe-buckle,' allied to MidHG. *snal,* m., 'quick movement' (for the proper term for buckle see **Rinken**). Hence the word is probably named from the rapid movement of the spring. See the following word and **schnell.**

Schnalzen, vb., 'to smack, snap, crack,' from MidHG. *snalzen,* intensive of MidHG. *snallen,* 'to move with a noise peculiar to the rapid movement of the fingers or the tongue'; allied to **Schnalle.**

Schnappen, vb., 'to snap, snatch,' from MidHG. (MidG.) *snappen,* 'to snap, chatter.' The latter, like Du. *snappen* (E. *to snap*), is an intensive of MidHG. *snaben,* 'to snap, snort'; allied to the root *snab* contained in **Schnabel.**—ModHG. **schnappen** (dial.), 'to limp,' MidHG. *snappen,* 'to stumble,' is etymologically distinct from this verb.

Schnapphahn, m., 'highwayman,' from the equiv. late MidHG. *maphan;* yet it seems that the word signified orig. a sort of musket, although this meaning is first recorded at the end of the 17th cent., and hence is later than 'mounted highwayman,' which occurs even in the 15th cent.; the signification 'musket' was afterwards transferred to the man armed with such a weapon. Comp. Du. *snaphaan,* 'gun, musket, bandit.'

Schnaps, m., 'dram, glass of gin or brandy, liquor,' from the equiv. LG. *snapps,* which means lit. 'draught, mouthful,' and is connected with **schnappen.**

Schnarchen, vb., 'to snore, snort,' from the equiv. MidHG. *snarchen, snarcheln;* allied to MidHG. *snarren,* 'to rattle, crash,' like **herschen** to **hören.** Comp. Du. *snorken,* 'to snore, chatter, boast'; also MidE. *snur-ten,* 'to snore,' with a different intensive suffix, E. *to snort* (comp. MidHG. *snar-z,* 'twittering of the swallow,' also an abusive epithet), and without a suffix MidE. *snorin* (AS. **snorian*), E. *to snore.* From the root *snar* numerous terms have been formed in imitation of sound (see also **schnarren** and **schnurren**); comp. Du. *snorren,* 'to hum, whiz, chirp,' E. *to snarl,* and *snurls,* 'nostrils,' and in the non-Teut. languages perhaps Lith. *snarglýs,* 'snot.'

schnarren, vb., 'to rattle, drone,' from MidHG. *snarren,* 'to rattle, crash, chatter': see the preceding word.—To this is allied **Schnarre,** 'landrail,' ModHG. only, in MidHG. *snarz,* 'landrail.'

schnattern, vb., 'cackle, gabble, chatter,' from MidHG. *snateren,* 'to cackle, croak (of frogs), clatter (of storks), chatter'; comp. Du. *snater,* 'beak,' *snateren,* 'to chatter, boast.' The stem is not found elsewhere.

schnauben, vb., 'to snort,' from MidHG. (MidG.) *snûben,* 'to snore'; comp. Du. *snuiven,* 'to snort.' From the corresponding Du. *snúven* is usually derived ModHG. **ſchnaufen**, which, however, may come from MidHG. *snûfen*, 'to snuff.' The Teut. root is *snupp*, *snûf*, *snûb*. Comp. **Schnupfen**.

Schnauc, f., 'snow' (vessel), from the equiv. LG. *snau*, Du. *snaauw*, whence also E. *snow*, Fr. *senau*; "orig. a ship with a beak, from LG. *snau*, 'beak.'" Yet comp. also OHG. *snacga*, 'navis rostrata' ?.

Schnauze, f., 'snout, muzzle, nozzle,' MidHG. only; an imitation of LG. *snûte*, Du. *snuit*, 'snout,' though wrongly influenced in its dental sound perhaps by Mid HG. *sniutzen*, ModHG. **ſchnenzen**; comp. E. *snout* and the equiv. MidE. *snoute*. The form with a correctly permutated MidHG. *z*, equiv. to ModHG. *sz*, is preserved in ModHG. (dial.) **ſchnaußen**, 'to snarl, junket, suck.' For further remarks see **ſchnenzen**.

Schnede, f., 'snail, slug, spiral staircase,' from MidHG. *snĕcke*, m., 'snail, tortoise, spiral staircase,' OHG. *snĕcko*, m., 'snail'; corresponding to LG. *snigge* (Goth. **snigga*, m., is wanting). Goth. **snagils* is implied by MidHG. *snegel*. ModHG. (Hess.) **Schnegel**, 'snail,' LG. *snagel*, AS. *snagel*, E. *snail*. Comp. further OIc. *snigell*, 'snail.'

Schnee, m., 'snow,' from the equiv. MidHG. *snê*, OHG. *snêo*, m.; a common Teut. term which may be traced back to OAryan; this is all the more remarkable, since no words common to the Aryan group can be adduced for 'hail' and 'rain.' Goth. *snaiws*, OIc. *snêr*, AS. *snâw*, E. *snow*, Du. *sneeuw*. The common Teut. *snaiwa-z*, m., 'snow,' from an earlier *snoiguô-s* (prior to the OHG. permutation *snoighwôs*) corresponds to OSlov. *snĕgŭ*, Lith. *snĕgas*, 'snow'; allied to the Teut. root *snîw*, from pre-Teut. *snîgh*, preserved in ModHG. **ſchneien** MidHG. *sníen*, OHG. *snîwan*. To this corresponds Lat. *ninguere*, 'to snow,' and *nix (nivis)*, 'snow,' Gr. νίφει, 'it snows' (φ equiv. to *ghw*), acc. νίφα, 'snow' (all these have lost an initial *s* before *n*); Lith. *snigti*, 'to snow,' OIr. *snechta*, 'snow,' Zend *snîž*, 'to snow.' The Sans. root *snih*, 'to become damp, melt away,' is divergent in meaning; it must also be noted that the term for 'snow' differs in most of the Aryan dials. (Zend *vafra*, 'snow'). Thus we have a West Aryan and Pers. (but not an Ind. and Armen.) verbal root *snîgh*, 'to snow'; the term 'snow' is of more recent origin. See **Winter**.

Schneide, f., '(cutting) edge, snare, gin,' from MidHG. *snide*, f., 'edge of a sword or a knife'; allied to **ſchneiten**, from MidHG. *snîden*, OHG. *snîdan*, 'to cut, carve, make (clothes)'; comp. Goth. *sneiþan*, 'to cut, reap,' OIc. *sníða*, AS. *sníþan* (obsolete at the beginning of the MidE. period), Du. *snijden*, OSax. *snîthan*. A common Teut. vb. from the root *snîþ (snîd)*, 'to cut,' which has no correspondences in the other Aryan languages. See **ſchnitzen**.—**Schneider**, m., 'cutter, tailor,' from the equiv. MidHG. *snîdære*, m., is connected with the meaning of MidHG. *snîden*.

ſchneien, see **Schnee**.

Schneiſe, f., 'path hewn through a wood,' in this sense a MidG. and LG. word, in MidHG. *sneite*; both are derived from **ſchneiten**. The word also signifies 'noose, snare.'

ſchneiteln, **ſchneideln**, vb., 'to lop, prune,' from late MidHG. *sneiteln* (also *sneiten*), 'to strip off the branches.' Allied to **ſchneiten**.

ſchnell, adj., 'quick, speedy, hasty,' from MidHG. *snël (ll)*, adj., 'quick, nimble, brave,' OHG. *snël (ll)*; comp. OSax. and AS. *snël (ll)*, 'fresh, energetic, courageous,' Scotch *snell*, 'bitter' (comp. E. *keen* in the same sense, ModHG. **fühn**), Du. *snel*, OIc. *snjallr*, 'eloquent, capable, brave.' The earlier meaning (comp. the ModHG.), was much more general, equiv. perhaps to 'capable'; comp. **Taft**. This common Teut. adj., unknown only to Goth., passed into Rom.; comp. the cognates of Ital. *snello*, 'quick, lively.' The origin of the Teut. adj. is obscure.—Comp. **Schnalle**. ModHG. **ſchnellen**, vb., 'to jerk, toss,' from Mid HG. *snellen* (pret. *snalte*), 'to send off with a jerk; move on rapidly.'

Schnepfe, f., 'snipe,' from the equiv. MidHG. *snëpfe*, m., OHG. *snëpfo*, m., *snëpfa*, f.; comp. Du. *snep*, MidE. *snipe*, E. *snipe*, from the root *snĭpp*. Also AS. *snîte*, E. *snite?*. The HG. word passed as *sgneppa* into the Ital. dials. The origin of the cognates is obscure.

Schneppe, f., 'nozzle, spout,' ModHG. only, a phonetic rendering of the earlier LG. *snebbe*. Comp. Du. *sneb*, 'beak'; hence connected with **Schnabel**.

ſchneuzen, vb., 'to blow one's nose, snuff (a candle),' from the equiv. MidHG. *sniuzen*, OHG. *snûzen*; comp. the equiv. Du. *snuiten*; OIc. *snýta*. To this **Schnauze** is allied. The Teut. root *snût* appears as *snutt* in MidHG. *snuz*, 'clogging of the nose,' Du. *snot*, 'snut' (*snottolf*, 'snotty nose'), AS. *snot* (*tt*), E. *snot*. Allied to a Teut. root *snûp*, in MidHG. *snudel*, *snuder*, 'stoppage of the nose,' MidHG. and OHG. *snûden*, 'to snort, snore.'

Schniegeln, vb., 'to trim up, dress smartly,' ModHG. only, allied to a dial. **Schniegel**, 'adornment, finery'; unknown to the older dials. Of obscure origin.

Schnippchen, n., 'snap' (of the fingers), ModHG. only, allied to ſchnippen, MidHG. *snipfen*, (MidG.) *snippen*, 'to snap.' Akin to ſchnippeln, 'to snip, chip,' formed from LG.; comp. Dn. *snippelen*, 'to cut in pieces, mutilate,' E. *snip*.—ſchnippig, adj., 'snappish,' ModHG. only, formed from Du. *snebbig*, 'flippant,' which is connected with *sneb*, 'beak'; allied also to MidE. *snibbin*, 'to blame'?.

Schnitt, m., 'cut, incision, slice, fashion,' from MidHG. and OHG. *snit*, 'cut, wound, circumcision, harvest'; allied to ſchneiten. So too **Schnitte**, f., 'cut, slice, chop,' from MidHG. *snite*, OHG. *snita*, f., 'slice of bread, morsel,'—**Schnittlauch**, m., 'chive,' from MidHG. *snitilouch*, OHG. *snitilouh*, lit. 'leek for cutting.'—ſchnitzen, vb., 'to cut, carve, chip,' MidHG. *snitzen*, intensive of ſchneiten, 'to cut in pieces, carve.'—**Schnitzer**, m., 'blunder,' allied to ſichſchneiten, 'to deceive oneself'? or to **Schnitzel**, 'trifle'?.

ſchnoben, vb., 'to snuff, pant,' Mod HG. only, formed from ſchnauben; so too ſchnoobern, 'to sniff.'

ſchnöde, adj, 'worthless, base, vile, insolent,' from MidHG. *snœde*, adj., 'contemptible, poor, pitiable, trifling, bad, arrogant, ruthless'; in MidHG. the passive sense preponderates, so too in Luther. From the 17th cent. the modern active signification 'contemptuous' appears. OHG. *snôdi* is not recorded; comp. Du. *snood*, 'base, malicious'; OIc. *snauðr*, 'poor, needy,' *sneyða*, 'to rob,' AS. *besnyþian*, 'to rob.' Akin to OIc. *snoðenn*, 'thin-haired'; this meaning also belongs to MidHG. *snœde*, which is therefore identical in form with MidHG. *besnoten*, ModHG. (dial.) beſchnolten, 'close, sparing.' The pre-Teut. root *snaut*, *snût*, appearing in these cognates, probably meant orig. 'needy'; it is scarcely connected perhaps with MidHG. and OHG. *snûden* (see ſchneuzen), 'to mock, scorn.'

Schnörkel, m., 'spiral, scroll,' Mod HG. only, probably akin to OHG. *snarha*, *snaraha*, f., 'noose'?.

Schnucke, f., 'sheep with a short tail,' ModHG. only, formed from the equiv. LG. *snucke*.

Schnüffeln, vb., 'to sniff, smell,' Mod HG. only, formed from LG. and Du. *snuffelen*, 'to smell,' allied to Du. *snuf*, 'scenting'; comp. E. *to snuff, sniff, to snivel* (also the subst. *snivel*, AS. *snofl*); see the following word.

Schnupfen, m., 'cold (in the head), rheum,' from the equiv. MidHG. *snûpfe*, m. and f. The Teut. root *snûpp* contained in these words, with which **Schnuppe** and OIc. *snoppa*, f., 'snout,' are connected, is identical with the Teut. root *snuf* (*snûb*) in ſchnauben and ſchnüffeln. It may be also allied to the Aryan roots *snûp* and *snût* (in ſchneuzen).

Schnuppe, f., 'candle-snuff,' ModHG. only, formed from LG. *snuppe*, lit. bas ſchneuzen, 'blowing one's nose,' ſchneuzen being also used of 'snuffing a candle'; comp. Du. *snuiten*, 'to blow one's nose, snuff a candle,' E. *snuff*.

Schnur (1.), f., 'string, cord, line,' from MidHG. and OHG. *snuor*, f., 'string, bond, rope'; comp. Goth. *snôrjô*, f., 'basket, basket-work,' OIc. *snœre*, 'twisted cord,' Du. *snoer*, 'string'; allied to the Aryan root *snô, snē*, 'to plait' (comp. näſjen), with which AS. *snô-d*, 'fillet,' as well as OIr. *snáth*, 'thread,' is connected.

Schnur (2.), f. (mostly obsolete in the dials., *e.g.*, Swiss and Bav.), 'daughter-in-law,' from the equiv. MidHG. *snur* (*snuor*), OHG. *snura* (*snora*), f.; with this is connected the equiv. derivative MidHG. *snürche* (OHG. *snurihha). Corresponding to MidLG. *snore*, AS. *snoru*, MidE. *snore* (obsolete in E.), OFris. *snore*, OIc. *snor, snør*, 'daughter-in-law' (Goth. *snuzô, f., is by chance not recorded). A common Aryan term for 'daughter-in-law' (comp. also other terms common to Aryan for degrees of relationship, such as Sohn, Tochter, &c.), in the Aryan form *snusā́* (Sans. *snuśā́*, OSlov. *snŭcha*, and Aryan *snusŭs*, in Lat. *nurus* (for *snusus*), Gr. *νυός* (for *σνυσός). Aryan *snusā́*, 'son's wife,' has been regarded as a derivative of Aryan *sūnŭ-*, 'son,' on account of Söhnerin, the Suab. term for Schnur.

ſchnurren, vb., 'to hum, whiz, buzz, purr,' from MidHG. *snurren*, 'to rustle, drink (of beasts).' Allied to ModHG. **Schnurre**, f., 'humming-top, farce,' and the derivative ſchnurrig, 'droll'; comp. OHG. *snurring*, MidHG. *snürrinc* (also *snurrære*), 'buffoon, fool'; perhaps Narr, 'fool,' OHG. *narro*, is a cognate term. — **Schnurre,** **Schnorre,** f., 'snout, mouth,' genuine UpG., though not recorded in MidHG. and OHG.; lit. perhaps 'that which drinks or purrs.'

Schnule, f., 'muzzle, snout,' ModHG. only, formed from LG. *snûte;* see **Schnauze.**

Schober, m., 'stack, rick,' from the equiv. MidHG. *schober,* OHG. *scobar,* m.; allied, like **Schaub,** to **schieben.**

Schoch, n., 'shock, heap, threescore,' from the equiv. MidHG. *schoc,* m.; comp. OSax. *scok,* 'threescore,' Du. *schok,* 'threescore.' Orig. used perhaps only of sixty sheaves; comp. MidHG. *schocken,* 'to put corn in a heap,' *schoche,* 'rick,' *schoc,* 'heap.' See **Stiege.**

schofel, adj., 'paltry,' ModHG. only, formed from Hebr. *schâfêl,* 'low.'

Schöffe, m., 'assessor, sheriff, juryman,' from MidHG. *scheffe, scheppfe, scheffen,* m., 'presiding judge, assessor,' OHG. *sceffin, scaffin,* and *sceffino,* with the same sense; comp. OLG. *sceppino,* 'assessor,' Du. *schepen,* 'sheriff.' The term is not found before the time of Charlemagne, who first created the office of assessor; yet the origin and form of the word points to an earlier period, although Goth. **skapja* or **skapeins* and the corresponding words in OIc. and AS. are wanting. Teut. *skapjan* (see **schaffen**) also signified 'to arrange, decree, decide,' hence **Schöffe,** lit. 'ordainer'?. From Teut. the office and the term applied to it passed into Rom. as MidLat. *scabīnus;* comp. Ital. *scabino,* Fr. *échevin.*

Scholle (1.), f., 'clod, floe,' from the equiv. MidHG. *scholle,* m., OHG. *scolla,* f., *scollo,* m.; comp. Du. *schol,* 'clod, floe'; prop. a partic. of the root *skel,* 'that which is split,' and is therefore allied to **Schale,** and with Goth. *skilja,* 'butcher,' OIc. *skilja,* 'to divide, separate'; also with OSax. *scola,* AS. *scęōlu* (equiv. to E. *shoal*).

Scholle (2.), f., 'plaice, sole,' ModHG. only, formed from LG.; comp. the equiv. Du. *schol.*

Schöllkraut, see **Schellkraut.**

schon, adv., 'already, even,' from Mid HG. *schôn, schône,* adv., from *schœne,* adj., 'beautiful'; the ModHG. sense occurs very seldom in MidHG., and is entirely unknown to the courtly poets; MidHG. *schône,* OHG. *scôno,* 'in a handsome manner,' are formed without the mutation of **schön**; comp. **fast** from **fest.**

schön, adj., 'beautiful, handsome, fine,' from MidHG. *schœne,* OHG. *scôni,* 'shining, bright, splendid, beautiful'; comp. OSax. *skôni,* 'shining, light, beautiful,' AS. *scếne,* 'beautiful,' E. *sheen.* Orig. 'perceptible, worth seeing, noteworthy' (comp. **laut,** lit. 'that which is heard'); a verbal adj. from the Teut. root *skau,* 'to look,' in OHG. *scouwôn* (for the formation of the word see **rein**). Goth. has preserved only the cognate compounds, *guþaskaunei,* 'form of God,' and *ibnaskauns,* 'of like appearance with,' which imply a Goth. **skauns,* 'form'?. At all events, they show that the modern sense 'beautiful' did not orig. belong to the word. With the same root are connected the words adduced under **schauen** and OIc. *skjóne,* 'dapple-grey horse,' *skjóme,* 'ray.' See **schon, schauen,** and espec. **schauen.**

Schönbartspiel, n., 'mummery, carnival play,' a corruption of MidHG. *schëmebart,* m. (also *schëme-houbet*), 'mask,' connecting the word with the adj. **schön;** *schëmebart* is prop. 'bearded mask,' from MidHG. *schëme,* m., 'shadow, mask.'

schonen, vb., 'to take care (of), spare, economise,' from early MidHG. *schônen,* 'to treat indulgently, spare'; comp. Du. *schoonen;* a derivative of the adj. **schön.** OIc. *skaunn,* m., 'shield,' is not allied.

Schoner, m., ModHG. only, formed from the equiv. E. *schooner.*

Schooß, see **Schoß.**

Schopf (1.), m., 'top, crest, tuft,' from MidHG. *schopf,* m., 'hair on the top of the head,' OHG. **scopf,* and Goth. **skuppa-* are wanting; in OHG. and Goth. *skuft* is used, OIc. *skopt,* 'hair of the head,' allied also to OIc. *skupla,* 'old woman's hat.' In the non-Teut. languages corresponding terms are wanting.

Schopf (2.), UpG. 'shed, stable'; see **Schuppen.**

schöpfen, vb., 'to draw (water, &c.),' from the equiv. MidHG. and OHG. *scheppfen;* comp. OSax. *skeppian,* Du. *scheppen,* 'to draw (water).' The verbal root *skap* does not occur elsewhere in this sense; the same dials. have also corresponding noun derivatives. Under **Scheffel** a root *skap,* 'to contain,' is deduced; with this the cognates of **schaffen** are also primit. allied. See **Scheppen.**

Schöpfer, m., 'creator,' from the equiv. MidHG. *schepfære,* OHG. *scepfâri,* allied to MidHG. *scepfen* (*scaffan*), 'to create.'

Schöppe, m., LG. form of **Schöffe.**

Schoppen (1.), m., 'pint,' ModHG. only, formed from the equiv. LG. schopen; connected with MidHG. schuofe, f., 'scoop'?.

Schoppen (2.), see Schuppen.

Schöps, m., 'wether, mutton, simpleton,' an East MidG. and Bav. word (unknown to Hess., Rhen., and Francon.), from MidHG. schöpez, schopez, m., 'wether, mutton'; borrowed in the MidHG. period from Slav. Comp. Czech skopec, 'wether,' OSlov. skopĭcĭ, 'eunuch,' allied to skopiti, 'to castrate.'

Schorf, m., 'scurf, scab,' from the equiv. MidHG. schorf, OHG. seorf, m.; corresponding to MidDu. scorf, ModDu. schurft, AS. sčeorf, scurf, E. scurf, Ic. skurfur, 'scurf, scab.' Comp. schürfen.

Schornstein, m., 'chimney,' from the equiv. MidHG. schornstein, schorstein, m.; comp. Du. schoorsteen; prob. allied to AS. sčeorian, 'to project,' E. to shore, Du. schoor, 'support, brace'?.

Schoß (1.), m., 'shoot, sprout, sprig,' from the equiv. MidHG. schoz (zz), n., and with the same meaning even OHG. scoz, n., and scozza, f.; allied to the root skŭt, 'to shoot.' From the OHG. word with the LG. dental is derived Fr. écot, 'stump of a tree.' To this ModHG. Schößling, from MidHG. schüzzelinc, is allied.

Schoß (2.), 'tax, scot,' from MidHG. (MidG.) schoz, m., 'tax, rent'; comp. Du. schot, AS. sčeot (E. scot), 'tax, score.' The great antiquity of the West Teut. cognates is attested by the Rom. loan-words, Ital. scotto, 'score,' Fr. écot, 'score.' The Teut. words are formed from the root skŭt, 'to shoot,' which in AS. sceótan, 'to shoot,' has also the secondary meaning, 'to contribute money.'

Schoß (3.), Schooß, m., 'lap,' from Mid HG. schoz, m., f., and n., OHG. scôz, scôzo, scôza, m. and f., 'skirt of a garment, petticoat, lap' (to this Lombard. scoss, 'lap,' is allied). Comp. Goth. skauts, m., 'border, hem of a garment,' OIc. skaut, n., 'tuft, corner, end, skirt,' AS. sčeát, 'corner, wedge, bosom' (whence AS. sčýte, 'cloth,' E. sheet), Du. schoot; allied to the root skŭt, 'to shoot.' It is uncertain whether the orig. sense was a descending or hanging part of the dress or a projecting corner of the land, or whether (as in the similar cases of Franse and Gehren) the skirt was so named from its resemblance to a missile?. See Schote (2).

Schote, Schaude, m., 'simpleton,' Mod HG. only, formed from Hebr. schôtêh, 'foolish.'

Schote (1.), f., 'pod, cod, shell,' from MidHG. schôte, schotte, f., 'pod, seed-case, pericarp'; allied to OIc. skauðer, pl., 'sheath.' Connected with the root skŭt, 'to cover,' which is discussed under Scheune.

Schote (2.), f., 'sheet' (of a sail), Mod HG. only, formed from LG.; comp. Du. schooten, AS. sčeáta, 'pes veli' (sceát-líne, 'propes'), E. sheet. These are identical with HG. Schoß (3). The AS. word is recorded the earliest; comp. Boot, Ebbe. From LG. is also derived Ital. scotta, 'cable.'

schraffieren, vb., 'to hatch (drawings),' ModHG. only, formed from the equiv. Du. schrafferen (Ital. sgraffiare).

schräg, adj., 'aslant, oblique,' from the equiv. late MidHG. (rare) schrege; allied to UpG. Schragen, from MidHG. schrage, m., 'wooden cross-legs of a table'; comp. Du. schraag, 'aslant, trestle.' Probably from an Aryan root skrak, 'to be aslant,' which, with the final consonant modified and nasalised, appears as skrang in schränken.

Schramme, f., 'slight wound or scratch,' from MidHG. schram (mm), f., 'sword wound'; comp. Du. schram, 'scratch,' OIc. skráma, 'wound'; allied to MidHG. schramen, 'to open, tear open,' schram, 'hole.'

Schrank, m., 'cupboard, chest, press,' from MidHG. schranc (k), m., 'that which shuts off, railing, enclosure, barrier, enclosing, space shut off, cupboard.' From the meaning 'enclosure, space shut off,' which still appears in the fem. form Schranke, the early ModHG. signification 'cupboard' was developed. The corresponding OHG. scranch, m., 'deception, deceit,' points to the vb. schränken, root skrank, 'oblique.' The subst. does not occur elsewhere; in Francon., Hess., and LG. Schank is used; in Swiss chaste or säfräti, Alsat. špint. See the following words.

Schranke, f., 'railing, barrier, limit,' from MidHG. schranke, f., with the same meanings as MidHG. schranc, m.; see the preceding word.

schränken, vb., 'to cross, entwine, enclose with a railing, limit,' from MidHG. schrenken, 'to lay aslant, fence in, plait,' OHG. skrenchen, 'to lay aslant, deceive,' MidE. schrenchen, 'to cheat.' The root implied is Teut. skrank, Aryan skrang (see

X

Sch (322) Sch

Schraut), which is identical with the Aryan root *skrak* appearing in ſchräg.

Schranz, m., 'flatterer, parasite ; slit, cleft,' from MidHG. *schranz*, m., 'breach, rift, cleft, hole, wound, slashed garment, an overdressed young man (with slashed sleeves, &c.), fop'; with the last of these varied meanings ModHG. Hofſchranze, 'flattering courtier,' is connected. On the other hand, the prim. meaning 'rift' points to a connection with Schraube, so that two roots *skrant* and *skrand*, have to be assumed in Teut.

ſchrappen, vb., 'to scrape,' ModHG. only, from LG. *schrappen*, an intensive form of Du. *schrapen*, *schrabben*, 'to scratch,' MidE. *scrapien* (*schrapien*), E. *to scrape*, OIc. *skrapa*. From the LG. cognates OFr. *escraper*, 'to scratch off,' is derived. See urther under ſchröpfen and ſchrubben.

Schraube, f., 'screw,' from the equiv. late MidHG. *schrûbe*, f.; allied to Du. *schroef* (E. *screw*), Ic. *skrûfa*; these terms, some of which may have been borrowed, and hence do not correspond exactly in sound, are essentially ModTeut. Note Suab. *schrauf*, Bav. *schraufen* (compared with Swiss *strûbe*). Origin obscure.

Schreck, m., 'fright, terror, scare,' from MidHG. *schrëcke*, m., allied to ſchreďen, vb., from MidHG. *schrëcken*, OHG. *scrëcchôn*, 'to start up, spring up, spring, leap'; the early sense (comp. the evolution in meaning of ſich entſeßen) is preserved in the compound Heuſchrecke. From this vb. comes the causative *schrëcken*, 'to cause to spring up, terrify.' In connection with the intensive form OHG. *scricch*, MidHG. *schric*(*ck*), m., 'starting up suddenly, fright'; Du. *schrikken*, 'to frighten,' Scand. *skrika*, 'to glide.' The root is essentially HG.

Schrei, m., 'cry, scream,' from MidHG. *schri*, *schrei*, OHG. *screi*, m., 'cry, call, shout,' allied to ſchreien, MidHG. *schrien*, OHG. *scrîan*, str. vb., 'to cry out.' The str. verbal root *skrî*, which is without doubt genuinely Teut., is wanting in the other OTeut. dials.

ſchreiben, vb., 'to write,' from the equiv. MidHG. *schrîben*, OHG. *scrîban*; corresponding to the equiv. Du. *schrijven*, OSax. *scrîƀan*, OFris. *skrîva*. Also with a remarkably divergent meaning, AS. *scrîfan*, 'to inflict a punishment, impose penance, receive confession,' E. *to shrive*, AS. *scrift*, E. *shrift*, so too OFris. *scrîva*, 'to inflict a punishment,' OIc. *skript*, 'confession, punishment,' *skripta*, 'to confess, cause to confess, punish.' In the latter cognates there appears at all events a genuine Teut. verbal root, *skrîƀ*, 'to inflict a punishment,' which was transferred by Christianity to ecclesiastical affairs; with this root OSax. *biscrîƀan*, 'to concern oneself about,' is also probably connected. On the adoption of Roman characters, and the introduction of the art of writing (in contrast to the earlier Runic system; see reißen, Buch, and Rune), Lat. *scribere* was now combined with this genuine Teut. vb., and in the South of Germany entirely supplanted the meaning of the old *scrîƀan*; comp. Brief and Tinte. In UpG. especially, *scrîƀan*, 'to write,' took firm root, as might have been expected; in E. the AS. vb. *wrîtan* (E. *to write*), orig. used of scratching runes, was retained.

ſchreien, see Schrei.

Schrein, m., 'box, chest, shrine, coffin,' from MidHG. *schrîn*, m. and n., 'chest for clothes, money, or valuables, coffin,' OHG. *scrîni*, n.; comp. the corresponding Du. *schrijn*, AS. *scrîn*, E. *shrine*, Scand. *skrín*. From Rom. and Lat. *scrinium*, 'box, case for papers, &c., escritoire,' whence also Ital. *scrigno*, 'clothes-press,' Fr. *écrin*, 'casket.' The diffusion of the term through the old West Teut. languages makes it probable that the Lat. word was borrowed at an early period,—contemporaneously with Arche, Kiſte und Sact l.

ſchreiten, vb., 'to step, stride, stalk,' from the equiv. MidHG. *schrîten*, OHG. *scrîtan*, MidHG. also 'to leap into the saddle.' Comp. OSax. *skrîdan*, *skrîdan*, 'to stride, go' (*ti-scrîdan*, 'to dissolve'), Du. *schrijden*, 'to stride,' AS. *scrîðan*, 'to stride, go, wander' (whence E. *to stride* is allied ?), OIc. *skríða*, 'to crawl, glide.' The signification of the OTeut. verbal root *skrîþ* (*skrîd*), Aryan *skrît*, was at first general (perhaps 'to move slowly'), in contrast to the special sense in ModHG.

Schrift, f., 'writing, letters, inscription,' from MidHG. *schrift*, OHG. *skrift*, f., a verbal abstract from ſchreiben, connected with Lat. *scriptum*.

ſchrill, adj., 'shrill.' ModHG. only, formed from the equiv. LG. *schrell*; comp. MidE. *schrillen*, E. *to shrill*, AS. *scralletan*, 'to sound loudly,' Scand. *skrölta*, 'to sound loudly.' Teut. and Aryan root *skrel*, *skral*.

Schritt, m., 'step, stride, gait,' from the equiv. MidHG. *schrit*, OHG. *scrit*, m.; a verbal abstract from ſchreiten; in OHG. also *scriti-mâl, -mēz*, 'step.'

Schroff, adj., 'rugged, rough, steep,' ModHG. only, allied to MidHG. *schrof* (*v*), *schroffe, schrove*, m., 'rocky cliff, stone wall'; allied to early MidHG. *schruffen*, 'to split,' OHG. *screvōn*, 'to cut into' (*scrēvanga*, 'incision '), MidHG. *schraf*, 'rocky cliff,' AS. *scræf*, 'cave.'

ſchröpfen, vb., 'to crop young wheat, tap (trees), cup,' from the equiv. Mid HG. *schrepfen, schreffen;* comp. AS. *scrēpan*, 'to scratch'; also LG. *schrappen*, prop. an intensive form. The prim. meaning of the Teut. root *skrēp* is 'to scratch, cut into' (to this ſcharf is allied?). Ital. *scaraffare*, 'to snatch away,' is borrowed from HG.

Schrot, n., 'block, log of wood, shot, groats,' from MidHG. *schrôt*, m., 'cut, incision, piece cut or sawed off,' OHG. *scrôt*, 'cut'; allied to ſchroten, MidHG. *schrôten*, OHG. *scrôtan*, 'to hew, cut, cut off, hack to pieces,' MidHG. also 'to cut out clothes' (whence *schrôtære*, 'tailor,' and the proper name Schröter), 'to roll, revolve.' Comp. Scand. *skrjōðr*, 'torn book,' AS. *screádian*, 'to cut,' E. *to shred*, to which also AS. *scrúd*, 'dress,' E. *shroud*, are allied. Root *skrúd* from *skrût*? With this is connected Lat. *scrūtari*, 'to examine,' to which AS. *scrudnian* and OHG. *scrotōn*, 'to examine,' are allied?. ModHG. Hornſchröter, 'horn-beetle,' from MidHG. *schrœtel*, lit. 'gnawer.'—**ſchrötig,** in ein verſchrötiger Baum, 'a tree from which four posts can be made,' early ModHG. only, is probably connected with OHG. *riorscōzzi*, 'four-cornered'; comp. MidDu. *vierscoot*, 'square-built, thick-set,' earlier LG. *vierschötig*, 'four-cornered'; comp. Scheß (3).

ſchrubben, vb., 'to scrub, rough-plane,' ModHG. only, from LG.; comp. Du. *schrobben*, 'to scour,' E. (borrowed) *to scrub*. Probably connected with ſchrappen.

Schrulle, f., 'freak, whim,' early Mod HG. only, allied to Du. *schrollen*, 'to revile, be discontented.'

ſchrumpfen, vb., 'to shrink, shrivel, crumble,' from MidHG. *schrimpfen*, 'to wrinkle'; allied probably to E. *shrimp*, Du. *schrompelen*, Swed. *skrumpa*, Dan. *skrumpe* (E. *scrimp*). Besides the Teut. root *skrimp* contained in these cognates there is also an equiv. Teut. root *rimp* (see rümpfen), *krimp* (comp. Du. *krimpen*, AS. *crimpan*, 'to shrivel'), as well as *skrink*, in AS. *scrincan*, E. *to shrink*.

Schrunde, f., 'cleft, gap, crevice,' from MidHG. *schrunde*, f., 'rift, notch, rocky cave'; comp. the equiv. OHG. *scrunta, scruntunna, scruntussa*. Allied to OHG. *scrintan*, MidHG. *schrinden*, 'to burst, fly open, crack.' Teut. root *skrend*, from pre-Teut. *skrent;* comp. Lith. *skrentu* (*skręsti*), 'to form into a crust.'

Schub, m., 'shove, push, thrust,' from MidHG. *schup*, m.; allied to ſchieben.

ſchüchtern, adj., 'shy, timid, bashful,' early ModHG. only, allied to ſchen, root *skuh* (*skeuh*)?. It may be connected even with the abnormal OHG. *skihtig*, 'shy,' but we must assume the influence of MidHG. *schiuhen* on the stem vowel; see ſcheu.

Schuft, m., 'wretch, rascal, scamp,' ModHG. only, formed from LG. *schuft*, Du. *schoft*, which is usually derived from LG. *schuf ût*, 'thrust out'; comp. Du. *schavuit*, 'rascal,' lit. 'scrape out'; hence Schuft, lit. 'offscouring'?.

Schuh, m., 'shoe,' from the equiv. Mid HG. *schuoch* (*h*), OHG. *scuoh*, m.; a common Teut. word; comp. the equiv. OSax. *skôh*, Du. *schoen*, AS. *scéôh*, E. *shoe*, OIc. *skôr*, Goth. *skôhs*, m., which point to primit. Teut. *skôha-, skôhwa-*, from pre-Teut. *skôqos. A pre-Teut. verbal root *skēq* (*skôq*) appears in Goth. *skēwjan*, OIc. *skévu*, 'to go,' and in ſchicken; hence Schuh, 'walking gear'?. See further Schuſter.

Schuhu, m., 'horned owl,' ModHG. only, borrowed from Fr. *chouette* (Ital. *ciovetta*), 'screech-owl,' and influenced by Uhu, 'horned owl.'

Schuld, f., 'debt, crime, guilt,' from MidHG. *schult* (*d*) and *schulde*, OHG. *sculd, sculda*, f., 'obligation, debt, culpability, sin'; comp. OSax. *sculd*, f., 'debt, culpability, sin'; AS. *scyld*, 'guilt, sin.' An old verbal abstract from the root *skal*, which appears also in Lith. *skold*, 'guilt,' *skilti*, 'to get into debt,' and *skelēti*, 'to be indebted,' as well as in Pruss. *skallisnan*, 'duty'; Lat. *scelus* does not appear to be connected with it.

Schule, f., 'school,' from MidHG. *schuole*, f., 'school, university,' OHG. *scuola*, f., 'school'; comp. Du. *school*, AS. *scôl* (*scôlu*), E. *school* (OIc. *skôle*, 'school,' is of E. origin). Borrowed at the same period as the ecclesiastical words from Lat. *scôla*, as pronounced in Rom. *scôla* (with regard to Lat. *ō* see prüfen); comp. Brief, Dom, and Prieſter.—**Schüler,** m., 'scholar, pupil,' MidHG. *schuolære*, OHG. *scuolâri*.

Schuller, f., 'shoulder,' from the equiv. MidHG. *schulter*, OHG. *scultarra*, f., corresponding to Du. *schouder*, AS. *sculdor*, E. *shoulder*, Dan. *skulder*, Swed. *skuldra*. This undoubtedly genuine Teut. word is wanting in Goth.; its origin is obscure.

Schultheiß, m., 'chief magistrate,' from MidHG. *schultheiȝe* (*schultheitze*), m., 'he who assigns duties, judge,' OHG. *scultheiȝo*, *scultheitzo*, m., 'tribunus, praefectus, centurio.' It is remarkable that "this term, purely judicial in its etymological origin, should have been transferred to captains of an army" in OHG., and "that this judicial term does not appear in the older laws, except in the Lombardic, although it has been diffused from the Middle Ages till the present day throughout the greatest part of Germany." Comp. LG. *schulte*, from *schuldhete*, Du. *schout* (from *scholthete*), 'village magistrate,' Fris *skeldata*, *skelta*; AS. *scyldhǣta*; the compound is wanting in Goth. The ModHG. form **Schulze** (also as a proper name; comp. LG. *Schulte*) is based on MidHG. *schuldheize* (as well as *-heiȝe*), OHG. *schuldheizo* (as well as *-heiȝo*), and ultimately on Goth. **haitja* (*tj* produces *tz*, but *ti* changes into *zi*, see **Grüße, Weizen**).

Schulz, see the preceding word.

Schund, m., 'offal, refuse, excrement,' ModHG. only, recently derived from **schinden**. Orig. perhaps 'filth of the sewer.'

Schupf, m., 'push, jerk,' from MidHG. *schupf*, m., 'swing, rocking movement,' allied to MidHG. *schupfen*, 'to waver,' OHG. *scupfa*, 'see-saw'; intensive forms of **schieben**.

Schuppe, f., 'scale (of fish, &c.),' from the equiv. MidHG. *schuoppe* (*schuope, schuppe*), m., OHG. *scuoppa*, f. Comp. Du. *schob*, 'scale'; a derivative of the Teut. root *skab* (*skôb*), 'to shave, scrape.'

Schüppe, f., 'spade, shovel,' ModHG. only, from East MidG. and LG. *schüppe*; comp. Du. *schup, schop*, 'shovel, spade,' allied to **schupfen.—Schüppen,** 'spade (at cards),' is identical with **Schippe**, and is formed on the model of Fr. *pique*. Comp. Du. *schoppen*, 'spade (at cards).'

Schuppen, Schoppen, m., 'shed, coach-house,' ModHG. only, formed from MidG. and LG.; corresponding to AS. *scypen*, E. dial. *shippen*, 'stable'; in OHG. and Mid HG. *schopf, schof* (Bav. and Alem. **Schopf**), 'structure without walls, penthouse, vestibule.' Comp. AS. *sc̔oppa*, 'hall, hut,' E. *shop* (from AS. is also probably derived Fr. *échoppe*, 'booth').

Schur, f., 'shearing, vexation, fleecing,' from MidHG. *schuor*, m. and f., 'shearing,' a graded form of the root *skĕr*, *skŏr*, 'to shear.'

schüren, vb., 'to stir, poke,' from Mid HG. *schürn*, 'to urge on, irritate, stir (the fire)'; allied to MidHG. *schorn*, 'to sweep together,' MidHG. *schor*, OHG. *scora* (Goth. *skaúrô*), 'shovel.'

schürfen, vb., 'to scratch, scrape, dig,' from MidHG. *schürfen, schürpfen*, 'to cut up,' to which *schürfære*, 'flayer, executioner,' OHG. *scurfen*, 'to cut up,' and AS. *screpan, sceorpan*, are allied. Probably connected with the root *skrĕp, skĕrp*, 'to be sharp.' See **scharf, schrappen,** and **schröpfen**.

Schurke, m., 'rascal, knave, villain,' ModHG. only, allied to OHG. *fir-scurgo*, 'rascal,' which is connected with *fir-scurigen*, 'to thrust away.'

Schurz, m., **Schürze,** f., 'apron,' from MidHG. *schurz*, m., 'shortened garment, apron'; allied to OHG. *scurz*, 'short,' AS. *sc̔eort*, E. *short*, whence also MidHG. *schürzen*, 'to shorten, tuck up the dress under the girdle to make it shorter below, gird up.' A Teut. derivative *skurtjôn* is also indicated by AS. **scyrte*, E. *shirt*, OIc. *skyrta*, 'shirt' (OIc. *skorta*, 'to be in want of'). These genuinely Teut. cognates imply a Teut. root *skrt* (MidHG. *schërze*, m., 'piece cut off'), which has not yet been found elsewhere. With regard to the union of this word with Lat. *curtus* in some languages, see under **furz**.

Schüssel, f., 'dish, platter,' from the equiv. MidHG. *schüȝȝel*, OHG. *scuȝȝila*, f.; comp. Du. *schotel*, 'dish,' AS. *scutel*, OIc. *skutell*, m., 'dish, small table.' With regard to the meaning see **Tisch**, with which it was borrowed, probably contemporaneously (about the 6th cent.) with the adoption of Roman cookery, from Lat. *scutula, scutella*, 'small dish.' Comp. further from the same source AS. *scutel*, E. *scuttle*; also Fr. *écuelle* (*scutella*), Ital. *scodella*, 'bowl.'

Schuster, m., 'shoemaker, cobbler,' from the equiv. MidHG. *schuoch-sútære*, m.; OHG. and MidHG. also merely *sútári, sútære*, m., 'cobbler'; corresponding to AS. *sútére*, Northern E. and Scotch *souter*. Borrowed from Lat. *sutor*, with a G. suffix denoting the agent; *sútári*, as a genuine Teut. derivative from the Teut. root *siw*, 'to sew,' discussed under **Saum** and **Säule**, is not probable. The genuine G. word for the UpG. Schuster is MidHG. *schuoch-würhte* (allied to wirken), which has been preserved only in the proper names Schuchart or Schubert.

Schuß, m., 'shot, report, charge,' from MidHG. *schuʒ* (ʒʒ), OHG. *scuʒ* (ʒʒ), m., 'shot'; allied to the root *skut*, 'to shoot.' See schießen.

Schüte, f., 'barge, ferryboat,' ModHG. only, derived, like Du. *schuit* and E. *skute*, from OIc. *skúta*, f., 'small swift boat.' Allied to the root *skut*, 'to shoot' (see schießen). With regard to ModHG. *ü* comp. Büse.

Schutt, m., 'rubbish, refuse, debris,' ModHG. only; in MidHG., *schüt*, f., 'alluvium, deposition (of soil), rubbish'; allied to ModHG. schütten, 'to shed, pour, discharge, heap up,' MidHG. *schütten*, 'to shake, swing, shed'; OHG. *scutten, scuten* (Ital. *scotolare*, 'to beat flax'); comp. OSax. *skuddian*, 'to shake, convulse,' Du. *schudden*, 'to shake, convulse.' Teut. root *skud*, 'to convulse, shake,' with which MidHG. and ModHG. *schütteln*, OHG. *scutilôn*, and ModHG. schüttern are connected as frequentatives. See schaudern.

Schutz, m., 'protection, defence, dike, fence,' from MidHG. *schuz* (tz), m., 'surrounding with a dike, protection,' allied to ModHG. schützen.

Schütze, m., 'marksman, archer,' from MidHG. *schütze*, m., 'cross-bowman,' also late MidHG., 'beginner, young pupil' (to which ModHG. ABC-schütze, 'pupil beginning to read, tyro,' is allied); OHG. *scuzzo*, m., 'sagitarius' (equiv. to AS. *scytta*, Goth. **skutja*). Allied to the root *skut*; see schießen.

schützen, vb., 'to protect, guard, defend, shelter,' from MidHG. *schützen*, 'to embank, dam up, protect,' which, according to ModHG. *beschütten*, 'to protect,' implies OHG. **skutisôn*. The prim. meaning is evident from MidHG. *schüte*, *schüt*, f., 'earth-wall,' which is identical with Schutt.

schwach, adj., 'weak, infirm, feeble,' from MidHG. *swach*, adj., 'low, poor, despised, weak, infirm'; wanting in OHG. as well as in the other Teut. dials. The usual derivation from a Teut. root *swek*, 'to swell' (schwach, orig. 'that which has lost its savour'), must be abandoned; schwach is rather allied to siech, so that the Teut. roots *suk, swak*, are to be assumed (comp. the following word).

Schwaden, Schwadem, m., 'vapour, damp, exhalation,' from MidHG. *swadem, swaden*, m., 'vapour'; allied to North Fris. *swesh*, AS. *swaðul*, m., 'smoky vapour,' OHG. *swëdan*, 'to burn slowly with a smoky flame.' The Teut. root *sweþ* contained in these words seems to correspond to the root *sûp* contained in sieben (comp. *suk, swak*, under the preceding word; see toll).

Schwadron, f., 'squadron,' ModHG. only, formed from the equiv. Ital. *squadrone* (Fr. *escadron*).—**Schwadronieren**, see schwätzen.

Schwager, m., 'brother-in-law,' from MidHG. and MidLG. *swâger*, m., 'brother-in-law, father-in-law, son-in-law' (with regard to the variation in meaning see Neffe); OHG. **swâgar* is not recorded; a specifically G. word, unknown to the OTeut. diala. Since the word is cognate with Schwäher and Schwieger, and has also an archaic gradation, an Aryan form *swêkrô-s* may be assumed for Schwager (note OIc. *svára*, from **swâhrjon*, 'mother-in-law'). See the following word.

Schwäher, m., 'father-in-law,' from MidHG. *swêher*, OHG. *swëhur*, m., 'father-in-law,' late OHG. also 'brother-in-law'; comp. AS. *sweór* (from *sweohor*), 'father-in-law' (obsolete even at the end of the AS. period), Goth. *swaihra*, 'father-in-law.' A primit. Teut. and old Aryan word, with the primary form *swekros*, *swekuros*; comp. Gr. ἑκυρός, Lat. *socer* (for **swecuro-*), Sans. *çvaçuras* (for **svaçuras*), OSlov. *swokrŭ*, Lith. *szészuras*, 'father-in-law.' The orig. sense of the common Aryan word cannot be ascertained; it is, however, cognate with Schwager (Aryan *swêkrôs*) and Schwester (Aryan *swesô*). Corresponding to the now almost obsolete Schwäher, there has existed from primit. Teut. times a fem. *swekrû*, 'mother-in-law,' just as from Sans. *çvaçrû* (for **svaçrû*) are derived Lat. *socrûs* (for **swecrus*), Gr. ἑκυρά (the Goth. form must have been **swigrus*, f., for which *swaíhrô* is used). The word was current in AS. as *swëger*, which also became obsolete at an early period. Only in G. was it retained, OHG. *swigar*, MidHG. *swiger*, f., 'mother-in-law,' from which ModHG. constructed the tautological compound Schwiegermutter, while the corresponding ModHG. masc. Schwiegervater, formed from the latter, supplanted the old term Schwäher; similarly we have the compounds Schwiegereltern, -sohn, -tochter, &c. It is evident that the mother-in-law plays a more important rôle in marriage than the father-in-law.

Schwalbe, f., 'swallow,' from the equiv. MidHG. *swalwe*, OHG. *swalawa*, f.; a common Teut. term; corresponding to the equiv. Du. *zwaluw*, AS. *swealwe*, E. *swallow*, OIc. *svala* (gen. *svǫlu*), f., 'swallow.' No certain explanation can be given of the prim. form *swalwôn*, f.; perhaps it represents *swalgwôn-*, pre-Teut. *swalkuán*, to which Gr. ἀλκύων is also traced.

Schwalch, m., 'gullet, opening in a furnace,' from MidHG. *swalch*, m., 'gullet,' allied to ſchwelgen.

Schwall, m., 'swell, billow, flood,' from MidHG. *swal* (*ll*), m., 'swollen mass'; allied to ſchwellen.

Schwamm, m., 'sponge, fungus,' from the equiv. MidHG. *swam* (*mm*), swamp (*b*), m., OHG. *swam* (*mm*), *swamb*, m.; comp. Goth. *swamms*, 'sponge,' OIc. *svǫppr*, 'sponge.' Within these groups, which are very possibly connected together, we must distinguish three words, probably of different origin, of which the Goth. stems were *swammu-*, **swamba-*, and **swampu-*. In ModHG. Schwamm the first two forms have been united; to the second form Gr. σομφός (for σFo-), 'spongy, loose, porous,' is primit. allied; the first is formed from ſchwimmen.

Schwan, m., 'swan,' from the equiv. MidHG. *swane*, *swan*, m., OHG. *swan*, m. (*swana*, f.); corresponding to Du. *zwaan*, AS. *swǫn*, E. *swan*, OIc. *svanr*, m., 'swan'; Goth. *swans is by chance not recorded. Probably allied to the Sans. root *svan*, 'to rustle, resound' (comp. Hahn, allied to Lat. *canere*), Lat. *sonare* (for *svonare); prop. only of the singing swan ?.—ſchwanen, vb., 'to presage, forebode,' ModHG. only, lit. 'to have a presentiment,' like the swan that sings before its death.

Schwang, m., only in the phrase im Schwange ſein, 'to be in vogue,' from Mid HG. *swanc* (*g* or *k*), m., 'swinging motion, swinging, stroke, cut'; allied to ſchwingen.

ſchwanger, adj., 'pregnant, teeming,' from the equiv. MidHG. *swanger*, OHG. *swangar*; comp. Du. *zwanger*, 'pregnant,' but AS. *swǫngor*, 'awkward, idle'; the latter meaning makes the derivation from ſchwingen improbable. AS. has also the curious form *swǫncor*; see ſchwanf.

Schwank, m., 'prank, drollery, farce,' from late MidHG. *swanc* (*g* or *k*), m., 'prank, trick, an anecdote about it,' identical with MidHG. *swanc*, 'swing, stroke, cut' (see Schwang), OHG. *swanch*, m., allied to *swingan* (just as OHG. *chlanch* to *chlingan*; see Klang).

ſchwank, adj., 'staggering, unsteady,' from MidHG. *swanc* (*k*), adj., 'pliant, thin, slender'; so too the equiv. MidHG. *swankel*, AS. *swǫncor*, OIc. *svang-r*; allied to the root *swink*, *swing*, in ſchwingen; hence ſchwanf is lit. 'easily swung, pliant.' With the Teut. cognates Ital. *sguancio*, 'wryness,' has been connected.

Schwanz, m., 'tail, trail, train,' from the equiv. MidHG. *swanz*, m. (for OHG. *swanz a form *zagal*, MidHG. *zagel*, equiv. to E. *tail*, is used). Through the medium of the intensive forms *swangezen*, *swankzen*, MidHG. *swanz* is connected with ſchwingen: MidHG. *swansen*, 'to shake to and fro,' Du. *zwanselen*, 'to reel.'

Schwäre, f., 'ulcer, boil, sore,' from MidHG. *swër*, OHG. *swëro*, m., 'physical pain, disease, swelling, ulcer'; allied to MidHG. *swërn*, OHG. *swëran*, 'to hurt, pain, fester, ulcerate.' The root *swer* orig. perhaps 'to press, torment'; comp. the Sans. root *sṽr*, 'to torment, injure.' See ſchwer and Geſchwür.

Schwarm, m., 'swarm, cluster, throng,' from MidHG. *swarm*, OHG. *swaram*, m., 'swarm (of bees)'; allied to the Sans. root *svar*, 'to rustle, resound.' Comp. AS. *swearm*, 'swarm (of bees),' E. *swarm*, OIc. *svarmr*. See ſchwirren.

Schwarte, f., 'thick, hard skin; rind, bark,' from MidHG. *swarte*, *swart*, f., 'hairy scalp, hairy or feathered skin' (OHG. *swarta, f., is by chance not recorded). A common Teut. word; comp. Du. *zwoord*, 'bacon rind,' OFris. *swarde*, 'scalp,' AS. *sweard*, MidE. *sward*, 'skin,' OIc. *svǫrðr*, 'scalp, skin, whale-hide'; Goth. *swardus, f., 'scalp.' Origin obscure. Note the evolution in meaning of E. *sward*, Scand. *jarðan-srǫrðr*, *gras-srǫrðr*, Dan. *jord-*, *grön-sweard*.

ſchwarz, adj., 'black, swarthy, gloomy,' from MidHG. and OHG. *swarz*, 'dark-coloured, black'; a common Teut. term, most of the words denoting colour, except the recent loan-words, being part of the primit. Teut. vocabulary (comp. gelb, rot, braun, &c.); Goth. *swarts*, OIc. *svartr*, AS. *sweart*, E. *swart*, Du. *zwart*, OSax. *swart*. OIc. *sorta*, 'black colour,' *sorte*, 'black cloud,' and *Surtr* are in a different stage of gradation. The common Teut. *swarta-*

is usually connected with Lat. *sordes* (for **svordes?*), 'dirt,' and *sudsum* (for **suarsum*), 'black colour, dirty spot'; Lat. *surdus*, 'deaf,' has also been referred, but with less probability, to the root *sword*, *surd*, 'dark.'

Schwälzen, vb., 'to chatter, prate, gossip,' from the equiv. MidHG. *swetzen*, allied to MidHG. *swaz(tz)*, 'talking, chattering'; an intensive form of a Teut. root *swap*. Comp. MidHG. *swadern*, *swatern*, 'to chatter, rustle, clatter,' of which the simply ModHG. Schwabronieren is a Rom. derivative. There is no relation to Lat. *suadere*. Origin obscure.

Schweben, vb., 'to soar, hover,' from MidHG. *swëben*, OHG. *swëbên*, 'to soar, move to and fro in or on water or in the air': allied to OIc. *svifa*, 'to rove, ramble,' OHG. *sweibôn*, MidHG. *sweiben*, 'to soar. roam.' The Aryan root *swip*, 'to move.' on which these words are based, had also a variant *swib* preserved in ModHG. schweifen.

Schwefel, m., 'brimstone, sulphur,' from the equiv. MidHG. *swëvel*, *swëbel*, OHG. *swëval*, *swëbal*, m.; the *f* of the Mod HG. form can only be explained by the influence of LG., as is shown by the double forms in MidHG. and OHG. A common Teut. word; comp. Du. *zwavel*, AS. *swefl*, Swed. *swafvel*, Goth. *swibls*, 'sulphur.' Lat. *sulpur* (for **suplur?*) is probably not allied. If the OTeut. *swebloz*, 'sulphur,' is a primit. loan-word, it may perhaps be connected with the old Aryan root *sweep*, 'to sleep' (Sans. *svápnas*, Lat. *somnus*, Gr. ὕπνος, AS. *swefn*); comp. AS. *swebban*, 'to kill,' OIc. *svæfa*, 'to kill, lull to sleep'; Schwefel may then be lit. 'stifling, killing, soporific stuff.'

Schweif, m., 'tail, train, suite,' from MidHG. *sweif*, m., 'rotation, encircling band, trimming of a garment, tail,' OHG. *sweif*, OIc. *sveipr*, 'encircling band'; allied to OHG. *sweifan*, 'to cause to rotate, turn.' With the Teut. root *swaip*, Gr. σόβη, 'horsetail,' cannot be connected. See the following word.

Schweifen, vb., 'to roam, rove, wander,' from MidHG. *sweifen*, OHG. *sweifan*, 'to cause to rotate, swing, wind '; comp. AS. *swápan*, 'to swing, sweep, tear,' E. *to swoop*, *to sweep*, to which AS. and E. *swift*, Du. *zweep*, and LG. *swipe*, 'whip,' are allied.

Schweigen, vb., 'to keep silence, be silent,' from the equiv. MidHG. *swîgen*, OHG. *swîgên*; comp. OSax. *swîgôn*, Du. *swijgen*, OFris. *swîgia*, AS. *swîgian*, 'to be silent.' The connection with Gr. σιγάω, σῑγή, 'silence,' is undoubted, in spite of the abnormal correspondence of Gr. γ to Teut. *g* (for *k*); we must assume a double Aryan root *swig*, *swiq* (the latter for the West Teut. words). ModHG. schweigen, vb., 'to silence,' from MidHG. and OHG. *sweigen*, 'to reduce to silence,' is a factitive of the foregoing schweigen.

Schwein, n., 'pig, hog,' from the equiv. MidHG. and OHG. *swîn*, n.; corresponding to the equiv. OSax. *swîn*, Du. *zwijn*, AS. *swîn*, E. *swine*, OIc. *svîn*, Goth. *swein*. These imply a primit. Teut. *sweino-m*, n., 'pig,' which must have been orig. a dimin. of Sau, 'sucking pig, young pig' (the OTeut. suffix *-ina-* was a favourite one in designating the young of animals; see Küchlein and Füllen), in the form of *su-îna-m*, 'the young of the sow' (primit. Teut. *sû*, 'sow'). On account of the great prolificness of pigs, and hence the immense number of young pigs, the dimin. was used for the species ?.

Schweiß, m., 'sweat, perspiration,' from the equiv. MidHG. and OHG. *sweiz*, m.; MidHG. also 'blood,' a meaning still current among sportsmen (so too schwitzen, 'to bleed'); OSax. *swêt*, 'sweat,' AS. *swát*, 'sweat, blood,' E. *sweat*, Du. *zweet*. For the Teut. root *swît*, *swait*, Aryan *swoid*, *suêd*, see under schwitzen; comp. Sans. svêda-s, m., Lat. *sudor* (from **svoidos*), 'sweat.' To this is allied schweißen, vb., 'to begin to melt, weld,' from Mid HG. *sweizen*, *sweitzen*. 'to weld,' OHG. *sweizen*, 'to roast, broil.'

Schwelen, vb., 'to burn slowly, smoulder,' ModHG. only, from LG. For the Teut. root *swel* in OHG. *swîlizôn*, 'to burn slowly,' and AS. *swëlan*, 'to glow,' see under schwül.

Schwelgen, vb, 'to guzzle, carouse, revel,' from MidHG. *swëlgen*, *swëlhen*, 'to swallow, gulp down, drink,' OHG. *swëlgan*, *swëlahan*, 'to swallow, gulp down'; comp. OSax. *far-swëlgan*, 'to gulp down,' Du. *zwelgen*, 'to swallow, *zwelg*, 'draught,' AS. *swëlgan*, E. *to swallow*, OIc. *svelgja*, 'to swallow'; Goth. **swilhan* is wanting. A Teut. root *swëlh* (*swëly* by grammatical change), from pre-Teut. *swelk*, is not found elsewhere. See Schwalch.

Schwelle, f., 'threshold, sill,' from Mid HG. *swelle*, f. and n., 'beam, threshold.' OHG. *swelli*, m., 'threshold'; Goth. **swalli*, 'threshold,' is wanting. Comp. AS. *syll*, f., E. *sill*, and the equiv. OIc. *syll*, *svill*, f.; allied to Goth. *ga-suljan*, 'to establish,' root *srol*, *sŭl*, 'to establish'; comp. Lat. *solea* (for *sro'ea*) ?. Akin also to OHG. *sŭl*, 'pillar' ?.

Schwellen, vb., 'to swell, rise,' from the equiv. MidHG. *swëllen*, OHG. *swëllan*; corresponding to the equiv. OSax. *swëllan*, Du. *zwellen*, AS. *swëllan*, E. *to swell*, OIc. *svella*; Goth. **swillan* is wanting; for the Teut. root *swell*, *swel*, see **Schwiele**. To this is allied the vb. *schwellen*, 'to swell, expand' (trans.), from MidHG. and OHG. *swęllen*, 'to cause to swell,' a factitive of *schwellen*. See **Geschwulst**.

Schwemmen, vb., 'to wash, soak, water,' from MidHG. *swęmmen*, 'to cause to swim, dip in water, wash in it'; a factitive of *schwimmen*.

Schwengel, m., 'pendulum, clapper, beam,' from MidHG. *swęngel*, *swęnkel*, m., 'that which swings, pendulum.' See the following word and *schwingen*.

Schwenken, vb., 'to swing, wave to and fro, brandish,' from MidHG. *swęnken*, 'to swing, hurl, roam, soar,' OHG. *swęnchen*, 'to strike'; comp. Du. *zwenken*, 'to swing,' AS. *swęncęan*, 'to strike, worry,' and allied to the root *swink*, *swing*, in *schwingen*; comp. *Hingen* with regard to the change of *k* to *g* at the end of the root.

Schwer, adj., 'grievous, heavy, difficult,' from MidHG. *swære*, adj., OHG. *swári*, *swár*, adj., 'heavy,' with the adv. form OHG. *swáro*, MidHG. *swáre*; OSax. *swár*, Du. *zwaar*, AS. *swér*, *swár*, OIc. *svárr*, 'heavy.' Akin also to Goth. *swêrs*, 'honoured, respected, weighty, as it were, for heart and sense'?. See **wichtig**, **Gewicht**. Comp. Lith. *swerìù* (*svérti*), 'to lift, weigh,' *swarùs*, 'heavy,' *svóras*, *sváras*, 'weight.'

Schwert, n., 'sword,' from the equiv. MidHG. and OHG. *swërt*, n.; a common Teut. term; comp. the equiv. OSax. *swerd*, Du. *zwaard*, AS. *sweord*, E. *sword*, OIc. *sverð*. Goth. **swairda-*, n., is wanting, *hairus* being used. This latter term is the earliest recorded in Teut.; it is preserved in old West Teut., almost exclusively in old compounds, and is connected with Sans. *çáru*, m., 'missile, spear.' The later OTeut. term **swerda-* has no correspondences in the non-Teut. languages.

Schwertel, n., 'sword-lily, fleur-de-luce, iris,' from MidHG. *swërtele*, OHG. *swërtala*, f., a derivative of **Schwert**, in imitation of Lat. *gladiolus*.

Schwester, f., 'sister,' from MidHG. *swëster*, OHG. *swëster*, f.; a common Teut. and also primit. Aryan word. Comp. Goth. *swistar*, OIc. *syster*, AS. *sweostor*, E. *sister*, Du. *zuster*, OSax. *swëstar*. The common Teut. stem *sw-str-*, originated in Aryan *swesr-* (comp. **Strom** for the insertion of *t* in *sr*), nom. sing. *swésô*; comp. Sans. *svasr-*, nom. sing. *svasâ*, Lat. *soror* for **swesô-r*, OSlov. *sestra*, Lith. *sesù* (for **swesô*). The orig. meaning of the cognates, as in the case of **Bruder**, Aryan *bhrâtô* (*brâthr*), cannot be discovered; yet **Schwäher**, **Schwieger**, and **Schwager** (Aryan *swekuros*, *swekrû*, *swekrôs*) are similar in sound, so too OIc. *sviljar*, 'husbands of two sisters,' OSax. *swiri*, 'nephew, sister's child' (Aryan *swesrjo-*?), &c., whose common component *swe-* signified 'own, his,' according to Sans. *sva*, Lat. *suus*; comp. **sein**. For the Aryan terms of consanguinity comp. **Vater**, **Mutter**, &c.

Schwibbogen, m., 'stone arch, arcade, flying buttress,' from MidHG. *swiboge*, OHG. *swibogo*, m.; the ModHG. form is an early corruption, connecting *sweiboge*, which had become obscure even in Mid HG., with *schweben* and **Bogen**. OHG. *swibogo*, 'arched vault,' if this too is not a corruption, appears to be either an old derivative from the root *swib* (see *schweben*), hence Goth. **swib-uga*, or a compound of OHG. *bogo*, 'bow, arch,' with a prefix *swi-*, the meaning of which is certainly not clear; comp. Goth. *swi-kunþs*, 'manifest,' OIc. *sve-víss* (?), *svi-dauðr* (?), AS. *sweo-tol*.

Schwichtigen, see **beschwichtigen**.

Schwieger, f., 'mother-in-law,' from the equiv. MidHG. *swiger*, OHG. *swigur* (AS. *swégyer*), f.; Aryan *swekrû*; see under **Schwäher**.

Schwiele, f., 'hard skin, weal,' from the equiv. MidHG. *swil*, m. and n., OHG. *swilo*, m., *swil*, n.; Teut. **swiliz*, pre-Teut. **swelos*, n., is to be assumed; allied to the root *swel* in *schwellen*, **Schwulst**. **Schwiele**, lit. 'swelling.'

Schwierig, adj., 'difficult, hard,' from MidHG. *swiric* (*g*), m., 'full of sores or ulcers,' a derivative of **Schwäre**; instinctively connected by Germans, however, with *schwer*, and hence transformed in meaning.

Schwimmen, vb., 'to swim,' from the equiv. MidHG. *swimmen*, OHG. *swimman*; corresponding to the equiv. OSax. *swimman*, Du. *zwemmen*, AS. *swimman*, E. *to swim*; OIc. *symja* points to Goth. **sumjan*, (pret. *swam*). Akin also to Goth. *swamms*, 'sponge,' *swumfsl*, m., 'pond.' The Teut. root *swēm*, *sŭm*, appears also in Snub; comp. also OIc. *svamla*, MidHG. *swamen*, 'to swim.' In the non-Teut. languages the root *swem*, *sŭm*, 'to swim,' has not yet been found.

Schwind, see geschwind.

schwindeln, vb., 'to be dizzy or giddy,' from the equiv. MidHG. *swindeln*, OHG. *swintilōn*, allied to MidHG. *swindel*, 'giddiness, vertigo,' equiv. to OHG. *swintilōd* and *swintilunga*. Further akin to schwinden, 'to dwindle away,' hence MidHG. also 'to faint, become unconscious.'

schwinden, vb., 'to vanish, dwindle away, decay, perish,' from MidHG. *swinden*, OHG. *swintan*, 'to vanish, pass away, grow lean, become unconscious, faint'; corresponding to AS. *swindan* (wanting in E.), 'to vanish'; probably allied to a root *swī* (like Goth. *standan* to the root *stā*?). The root *swī* appears in OHG. *swinan*, MidHG. *swīnen*, 'to decrease, disappear, grow lean, become unconscious,' OIc. *svīna*, 'to subside,' *svīa*, 'to abate,' OIc. *svīme*, AS. *svīma*, Du. *zwijm*, 'giddiness, vertigo.' In the non-Teut. languages the root *swī*, 'to decrease,' has not yet been authenticated; the comparison with Gr. σίνομαι, 'I plunder, damage,' is dubious.—Schwindsucht, f., 'consumption,' MidHG. *swintsuht*, *swinsuht* (allied to *swīnen*), also *swindelunge*.

schwingen, vb., 'to swing, brandish, wave,' from MidHG. *swingen*, *swinken*, OHG. *swingan* (*swinchan*?), 'to swing, throw, hurl, strike, scourge, vault, fly, soar'; corresponding to OSax. *swingan*, 'to vault,' AS. *swingan*, 'to scourge, fly, flutter,' E. *to swing*; from Goth. *swiggwan* was formed *swaggwjan*, 'to swing about.' Under schwank and schweifen, an Aryan root *swenk*, *sweng*, was adduced; AS. *swincan*, E. *to swink*, is a variant of AS. *swingen*, E. *to swing*; comp. Du. *zwenken*, 'to swing.'

Schwire, f., 'stake'; see Humpen.

schwirren, vb., 'to whiz, whir, chirp,' ModHG. only, allied, like Schwarm, to a root *swer*, 'to rustle, drink (like beasts).'

schwitzen, vb., 'to sweat, perspire,' from the equiv. MidHG. *switzen*, OHG. *swizzen*; Goth. *switjan* is wanting. The Teut. root *swit*, Aryan *swīd*, is primit. Aryan, as was observed under Schweiß (a common Aryan root for 'to freeze' is wanting; comp. Winter, Schnee, frieren, and

Sommer); comp. Sans. *svidyá-mi*, from the root *svid*, 'to perspire,' Gr. ἰδίω, 'I perspire,' ἰδρώς, 'perspiration,' for σFιδ-, and further Lat. *sūdare*, 'to perspire' (for *swoidare*), Lett. *swīdrs*, 'perspiration.'

schwören, vb., 'to swear,' from the equiv. MidHG. *swęrn*, *swęrjen*, OHG. *swęren*; a specifically Teut. word (like Sib); comp. Goth. *swaran*, OIc. *sverja*, AS. *swęrian*, E. *to swear*, Du. *zweren*, OSax. *swęrian*, 'to swear.' The Teut. root *swar* contained in these words had, however, a wider sense orig. than the one given, for traces in particular dials. lead us to infer that 'to answer' was the meaning of the root; comp. OIc. *svęr*, n. plur., 'answer,' *svara*, vb., 'to answer,' in the legal sense also 'to give security,' *andsvar*, n., 'legal decision,' AS. *andswaru*, f., 'answer,' E. *to answer* (see Antwort), OSax. *andswor*, 'vindication.' The prim. idea of the Teut. root *swar* is therefore, perhaps, 'to be responsible'; it has been compared to Lat. *respondeo* from *spondeo*.

schwül, adj., 'sultry,' ModHG. only, from LG. *swûl*; comp. Du. *zwoel*, 'sultry,' AS. *swōl* (Goth. **swōls* is wanting); allied, like schwelen, to OHG. *swilizzōn*, 'to burn slowly,' AS. *for-swēlan*, 'to burn,' OIc. *svæla*, 'thick, choking smoke.' The root *swel*, *swōl*, appears also in Lith. *svilti*, 'to smoulder,' *svīlus*, 'glimmering,' *svilmis*, 'burnt smell,' and in Lett. *swelt*, 'to singe.' Deriv. Schwülität, 'sultriness,' with a Lat. ending like Lappalien and Schmieralien.

Schwulst, f., 'swelling, bombast,' from MidHG. *swulst*, *geswulst*, OHG. *giswulst*, f., 'swelling'; allied to schwellen.

Schwung, m., 'swing, vibration, soaring, flight,' from the equiv. late MidHG. *swunc* (*g*), m.; allied to schwingen.

Schwur, m., 'swearing, oath, curse,' ModHG. only, in MidHG. found only in the compound *meinswuor*, 'perjury,' in OHG. only in *eidswuor*, 'oath'; allied to schwören.

Sebenbaum, m., 'savin (species of juniper),' from the equiv. MidHG. *sęvenboum*, OHG. *sęvina*, *sęvinboum*, formed from Lat. *sabina* (*arbor Sabina*, lit. 'Sabine tree'); corresponding to AS. *safine*, E. *savin*.

Sech, n., 'coulter,' from MidHG. *sēch*, OHG. *sēh* (*hh*), n., 'mattock, ploughshare' (Goth. **sika-* is wanting); allied, like Sichel and Sense, to a Teut. root *sch*, *seg*, *sek*, from Aryan *sek*, *seg*.

ſechs, num., 'six,' from MidHG. and OHG. *sëhs;* a common Teut. and primit. Aryan num.; comp. OSax. *sehs*, Du. *zes*, AS. and E. *six*, OIc. *sehs*, Goth. *saíhs;* primit. Aryan *seks* (and *sweks*). Comp. Sans. *ṣaṣ*, Zend χšvaš, Gr. ἕξ, Lat. *sex*, W. *chwech*, OSlov. *šestĭ*.

Sechter, m., 'two pecks,' from MidHG. *sëhter, sëster, sëhster*, m., 'a dry measure,' OHG. *sëhtâri, sëhstâri*, 'two pecks (about)'; derived, like OSax. *sëster*, from Lat. *sextarius*, whence also AS. *sëster*, Ital. *sestiere*, Fr. *setier*.

Seckel, m., 'purse, bag, pocket,' from MidHG. *seckel*, OHG. *secchil*, m., 'purse'; dimin. of Sack, Lat. *sacellum;* comp. OFr. *suchel*, E. *satchel*.

See, m. and f., 'lake, sea,' from MidHG. *sê*, m. and f., 'sea, lake, ocean' (the masc. predominates, and is used without distinction in all the senses); OHG. *sêo*, m., 'sea, ocean,' and in these significations occur OSax. *sêo*, Du. *zee*, f., AS. *sǽ*, m. and f., E. *sea;* OIc. *sær*, m., 'ocean'; Goth. *saiws*, m., 'lake, marsh.' The common Teut. **saiwi-*, 'ocean, lake,' does not belong to any Teut. verbal stem; Lat. *saevus*, 'savage' (Gr. διόλος, 'mobile'), seems to be allied (See, lit. 'the savage element'). While See is peculiar to Teut., Meer is common to some of the West Aryan languages.

Seele, f., 'soul,' from the equiv. Mid HG. *sêle*, OHG. *sêla* (*sêula*), f.; a word peculiar to Teut. Comp. Goth. *saiwala*, f., OIc. *sala*, f., AS. *sáwl, sáwul*, f., E. *soul*, Du. *ziel*, OSax. *sêola*, f. The origin of the primit. Teut. *saiwolô*, f., 'soul,' is obscure; it may be allied to See (Seele, lit. 'that which moves'); comp. Gr. αἰόλος. Its connection with Lat. *saeculum*, 'age, generation' (lit. 'vital power'?), is equally possible; comp. Sans. *âyu*, 'vital power,' similar to Lat. *aevum*, 'age, time.'

Segel, n., 'sail,' from the equiv. Mid HG. *sëgel*, OHG. *sëgal*, m.; comp. OSax. *sëgel*, n., Du. *zeil*, n., AS. *sëgel*, m. and n., E. *sail*, OIc. *segl*, n., 'sail' (Goth. **sigla-* is not recorded). The word cannot have been borrowed from Lat. *sagulum*, 'military cloak,' on account of the sounds, and because no other OTeut. nautical expressions have been derived from Lat.; besides, *sagulum* is not a naut. term. Segel (Teut. **segla-*) looks very much like a Teut. term (comp. Maſt), yet the root cannot be ascertained. From the Teut. cognates Fr. *cingler* and Span. *singlar*, 'to sail,' are derived.

Segen, m., 'blessing, bliss, enchantment,' from MidHG. *sëgen*, OHG. *sëgan*, n., 'sign of the cross, blessing resulting from it, magic spell'; borrowed on the introduction of Christianity (see Kreuz, Altar, and Prieſter) from Lat. *signum;* so too OHG. *sëganôn*, 'to bless,' OSax. *sëgnôn*, 'to bless,' lit. 'to make the sign of the cross,' from Lat. *signáre*. AS. *sëgen*, 'banner, military emblem,' must have been borrowed at an earlier period from Lat. *signum;* with the *ë* of the Teut. words comp. the OIr. loan-word *sén*, as well as Ital. *segno* (Fr. *enseigne*).

ſehen, vb., 'to see, look,' from the equiv. MidHG. *sëhen*, OHG. *sëhan;* a common Teut. vb., and in this sense peculiar to this group. Comp. Goth. *saíhwan*, OIc. *sjá*, AS. *seón* (from **seohan*), E. *to see*, Du. *zien*, OSlov. *sëhan*, 'to see.' The common Teut. root *sehw* (with grammatical change *segw*, *sew*), from the pre-Teut. *seq*, closely agrees in sound with the Aryan root *seq*, 'to follow, pursue, accompany'; comp. Sans. *sac*, 'to escort, promote,' Gr. ἕπεσθαι, 'to follow,' Lat. *sequi*, Lith. *sekti*, 'to follow'; the assumption that these words are primitively allied presents no difficulty (hence ſehen is perhaps lit. 'to follow with the eyes'). The supposition that the term is connected with Lat. *secare*, 'to cut' (Aryan root *sek*, 'to penetrate'?), is untenable.

Sehne, f., 'sinew, tendon, nerve, string (of a bow),' from MidHG. *sëne, sënewe*, f., 'sinew, string (of a bow), nerve,' OHG. *sënawa*, f., 'sinew'; comp. Du. *zenuw*, AS. *sinu*, f., and the equiv. E. *sinew*, OIc. *sin*, f.; Goth. **sinawa*, f., is wanting. The word is usually connected with Sans. *snâva-s*, m., 'sinew' (the Teut. words would also imply a Sans. **sanâva-*); its kinship with Gr. ἵ-ες. 'sinew,' is improbable.

ſehnen, vb., 'to long, yearn,' from Mid HG. *senen*, 'to long, inspire with longing'; allied to MidHG. *sene*, f., 'yearning, longing.' Unrecorded in OHG. and the other OTeut. dials. perhaps only by chance; of obscure origin, but probably genuine Teut.

ſehr, adv., 'very greatly, very much' (unknown to Suab. and Bav., arg, recht, gar being used), from MidHG. *sêre, sêr*, adv., 'with pain, painfully, powerfully, very'; OHG. and OSax. *sêro*, 'painfully, with difficulty, violently'; adv. form of OHG. and OSax. *ser*, 'painfully,' AS. *sár*, adj., 'painful, wounding.' Allied to the substs. Goth. *sair*, AS. *sár*, 'pain' (E. *sore*), OSax. *sêr*,

OHG. and MidHG. *sêr*, n., 'pain'; from the OTeut. adj. is derived Finn. *sairas*, 'sick.' The common Teut. *saira-* seems, like OIr. *sáeth*, *sóeth*, 'hurt, disease,' to point to a root *sai*, 'to pain.' The earlier meaning is preserved by Suab. and Bav. *sêr*, 'wounded, painful,' and verſehren, 'to wound'; comp. Du. *zeer*, 'injured, injury, sickness, scab.'

ſeichen, vb., 'to make water,' from the equiv. MidHG. *seichen*, OHG. *seihhen;* allied to ModHG. Seiche, 'urine,' and the equiv. MidHG. *seiche*, f., *seich*, m., OHG. *seih*, m.; Goth. **saiqjan*, 'to make water,' is wanting; with these ſidern, 'to ooze,' and LG. *seken*, 'to make water' (Teut. root *saik*, *saiq*), are connected. The Aryan root *sīq*, mentioned under ſeihen, appears in OSlov. as *sicati*, with the same meaning, 'to make water'; comp. OSlov. *sĭcĭ*, m., 'urine.'

ſeicht, adj., 'low, shallow, flat,' from MidHG. *sîhte*, adj., 'low, shallow'; OHG. **sîhti* not recorded; probably allied to ſinken, hence lit. 'where the water has sunk into the ground,' or 'that which has sunk, or is low'; scarcely akin to ſeihen, lit. 'where it gently flows'?.

Seide, f., 'silk,' from the equiv. Mid HG. *sîde*, OHG. *sîda*, f.; derived from MidLat. *sêta*, 'silk,' like OHG. *chrîda*, from Lat. *crêta*. The *d* of the HG. words must be explained by the soft mute of the Rom. languages, appearing in Span., Prov. and North Ital. *seda* and Ital. *seta*, 'silk' (Fr. *soie*), just as in Span. *greda*, 'chalk,' compared with Ital. *creta* (comp. Seidel). MidLat. *sêta*, *crêta* (*ê* closed; see Preiſ, Bein, Sweiſe, and ſeiern), may have been borrowed about the 10th cent. From Lat. *sêta* (lit. 'bristle') OIr. *sita* is also derived. For the assumption that the Phoenician town of Sidon furnished both the material and the name Seide, or rather Lat. *sêta*, there is no historic proof. In E. another term is used, AS. *seole*, *seoloc*, E. *silk*, to which the equiv. OIc. *silke*, n., is allied. It is usually assumed that these latter terms come from the Lat., in which *sericus* (Ir. *stric*) means 'of silk'; they must, however, especially since their forms can scarcely be deduced from the Lat., be more fittingly connected, like OSlov. *šelkŭ*, m., 'silk,' with an Eastern term; comp. Mongol. *sirgek*, 'silk.' The Seres, from whom the Greeks obtained their term σηρικός (Lat. *sêricus*), adj., cannot, as an East Asiatic people, be regarded as the immediate source of the North Europ. loanwords.

Seidel, n. and m., 'pint,' from the equiv. late MidHG. *sîdel*, *sîdelîn*, n.; from Lat. *situla* (Ital. *secchia*, 'pail'), 'bucket,' whence also OIr. *sithal;* with regard to the lengthening of Lat. *ĭ* to MidHG. *î* in an open syllable, see Schule, and for *d* representing *t*, see Seite.

Seidelbaſt, m., 'spurge-laurel, mezereon,' derived under the influence of Seite (on account of the fine bast?) from the equiv. MidHG. *zîdelbast* (also *zîtzelbast*), m., called also *ztlant;* origin obscure. Perhaps *zîdel-weide*, 'rearing of bees,' is allied.

Seife, f., 'soap,' from the equiv. Mid HG. *seife*, OHG. *seifa*, f. (OHG. also 'resin'); comp. Du. *zeep*, AS. *sápe* (hence OIc. *sápa*), E. *soap;* Goth. **saipjô* is implied by OHG. *seipfa* (Suab. and Swiss Seipfe), and by the Finn. loan-word *saippio*. OHG. *seifa*, AS. *sáp*, 'resin,' might suggest the assumption that Seife belongs, like AS. *sípan*, MidHG. *sîfen*, and Du. *zijpelen*, 'to trickle,' to the Teut. root *sîp*, to which Lat. *sêbum*, 'tallow,' is usually referred. But Pliny says that 'soap' (*sâpo*) was an invention of the Gauls, "Gallorum hoc inventum rutilandis capillis; fit ex sebo et cinere . . . apud Germanos majore in usu viris quam feminis." The Lat. *sâpo* of Pliny, however, is, like its derivatives Fr. *savon*, Ital. *sapona*, none other than the Teut. **saipô;* perhaps soap (the Romans were not acquainted with it) may be regarded as a Teut. invention. Yet it is remarkable that Pliny speaks of soap only as a "pomade for colouring the hair." The term *sâpo*, 'soap,' was not frequently used in Lat. until the 4th cent. Another Teut. word for soap is represented by E. *lather*, AS. *leáðor*, OIc. *lauðr*.

Seihe, f., 'straining, strainer, colander,' from the equiv. MidHG. *sîhe*, OHG. *sîha*, f. Allied to ſeihen, 'to strain, filter,' from MidHG. *sîhen*, OHG. *sîhan*, 'to strain, filter, trickle'; comp. Du. *zijgen*, 'to filter through, decay, faint,' AS. *seón* (from **sîhan*), 'to strain,' and the equiv. OIc. *sia*. Identical with these are MidHG. *sîgen*, OHG. and AS. *sîgan*, 'to fall down, trickle.' Teut. root *sîh*, *sîhw* (with grammatical change *sîg*, *sîw*), from pre-Teut. *sîq*, 'to trickle down'; comp. OSlov. *sicati*, 'to make water,' Sans. *sic*, 'to pour out' (Gr. ἰκμάς, 'moisture'?). An equiv. Teut. root *sik* is also indicated by ModHG. ſeichen, ſinken, and ſickern.

Seil, n., 'rope,' from MidHG. and OHG. *seil*, n., 'rope, cord'; corresponding to OSax. *sêl*, AS. *sâl*, OIc. *seil*, Goth. **sail*, n., 'rope' (from *insailjan*, 'to lower or let down with cords'). A common Teut. word *sailo-m*, which, like the equiv. OSlov. *silo*, is derived from the widely diffused Aryan root *sî*, 'to bind.' Comp. the Sans. root *si*, 'to bind,' *sêtu*, 'bond, fetter,' Gr. *ἱ-μάς*, 'strap,' and *ἱ-μονιά*, 'well-rope,' Lett. *sinu*, 'to bind'; also OHG. *si-lo*, MidHG. *sil*, m., 'traces of draught cattle'; OSax. *sîmo*, 'strap,' OIc. *sîme*. See Seile and Siele.

Seim, m., 'strained honey, sweetness,' from MidHG. *seim* (*honecseim*), OHG. *seim* (*honangseim*), m., 'virgin honey'; comp. Du. *zeem*; OIc. *seimr, hunangsseimr*, 'honeycomb.' On account of this divergence of meaning in Teut. the connection of the word with Gr. *αἷμα*, 'blood' (lit. 'juice'?), is improbable. It may be allied to the cognates discussed under Seihe.

sein, poss. pron., 'his, its,' from MidHG. and OHG. (also OSax.) *sîn*; comp. Goth. *seins*, 'his'; allied to Goth. *si-k*, 'himself,' formed with the poss. suffix -*tna*- like *mein* and *dein*. Comp. sich; the further discussion of the word belongs to grammar.

sein, anomal. vb.; its tenses are formed from various stems. The Teut. prim. stems are *es, -s*, with the same meaning (OHG., MidHG., and ModHG. *ist*, OHG. and MidHG. *sint*, ModHG. sind; subj. mood, OHG. and MidHG. *sî*, ModHG. sei; inf. MidHG. *sîn*, ModHG. sein; comp. Goth. 3rd pers. sing. *ist*, plu. *sind*; optat. *sijau*; AS. and E. 3rd pers. sing. *is*, 3rd pers. plur. AS. *sind*); corresponding to the Aryan root *es* in Lat. *es-t*, Gr. *ἐστί*, Sans. *ás-ti*, Lat. *sunt, sim*, Sans. *sánti*, &c. The second stem begins with *b*, ModHG., Mid HG., and OHG. *bin*, OSax. *bium*, AS. *beó*, 'I am' (AS. also 'I shall'), connected with the stem of Lat. *fio*, Gr. *φύω*, Sans. *bhû*, 'to become.' For the third stem (of gewesen and war) see under Wesen. Further details belong to grammar.

seit, prep. and conj., 'since,' from Mid HG. *sît*, prep. and conj., 'since,' adv., 'since then,' OHG. *sîd*, adv., 'since then, later,' conj. 'since, as, because,' prep. 'since.' Comp. OSax. *sîð* (also *sîðor*), 'later, afterwards, since then, if'; orig. a compar. adv.; comp. Goth. *þanaseiþs*, 'further,' allied to *seiþus*, 'late.' As new equiv. compars. comp. also OSax. *sîð-or*, OHG. *sîdôr*, Mid HG. *sîder*. MidHG. *sint*, a variant of *sît*, is implied by *sintemal*; E. *since* is based on MidE. *sithens, sithen*, AS. *sîððan*.

Seite, f., 'side, flank, page,' from Mid HG. *site, sît*, OHG. *sîta* (*sîtia*), f., 'side'; comp. Du. *zijde*, f., 'side,' and the equiv. AS. *síde*, E. *side*, OIc. *sîða*, f.; Goth. **seidô* (**seidjô*), f., is wanting. Allied to OIc. *sîðr*, 'hanging down,' AS. *sîd*, adj., 'wide, large, extended'?—feits, in einerseits, anders, jenseits, &c., with adv. *s* from MidHG. -*sît* in einsit, ander-sit, jensît, which are accus. advs.

Sekt, m., 'Canary wine, sack,' ModHG. only, from the equiv. Du. *sek*, which, like E. *sack*, is said to have been formed from Ital. *vino secco*.

selb, selber, selbst, pron., 'self-same, self, himself,' &c., from MidHG. *sëlp* (*b*), OHG. *sëlb*, pron., 'self, himself,' &c.; comp. OSax. *self*, Du. *zelf*, AS. *sylf*, OIc. *sjalfr*, Goth. *silba*, 'self, himself,' &c. A pron. peculiar to Teut., which signified lit. perhaps 'master, possessor' (thus Sans. *p-tiḥ*, 'master,' is similar to Lith. *pats*, 'self'). Comp. OIr. *selb*, f., 'possession'?.

selig, adj., 'happy, blessed, deceased, late,' from MidHG. *sælec*, OHG. *sâlig*, adj., 'happy, blessed, blissful, salutary'; lengthened by the suffix -*ig* from an older **sâl*, which was preserved in MidHG. *sælliche*, 'in a lucky manner'; comp. Goth. *sêls*, 'good, suitable,' AS. *sælig*, 'good, happy,' OHG. *sâlida*, MidHG. *sælde*, f., 'happiness, welfare.' Goth. *sêls* is usually compared with Gr. *ὅλος* (Ion. *οὖλος*), 'whole,' from *solvos, οὖλε*, as a greeting, Sans. *sarva s*, 'whole, all,' Lat. *sollus*, 'whole.'—felig, in the adjs., just as trübselig, faumselig, and mühselig, has nothing to do with OHG. *sâlig*, since it is a suffix of the neuts. Trübsal, Saumsal, Mühsal. In substs. of this kind -*sal* itself is a suffix formed from OHG. *isal* (gen. -*sles*), which appears in Goth. as -*isl*, n.

Sellerie, m., 'celery,' ModHG. only, from Fr. *céleri*.

selten, adj. and adv., 'rare, rarely,' from MidHG. *sëlten*, OHG. *sëltan*, adv., 'rarely'; corresponding to the equiv. AS. *sëldan*, adv., E. *seldom*, OIc. *sjaldan*, OFris. *sielden*, adv. The corresponding adj. is OHG. *sëltsâni*, MidHG. *sëltsæne* (AS. *sëld-sêne*), 'rare, strange,' the suffix of which has been supplanted in ModHG. by the more familiar -*sam*. In Goth. *sildaleiks*, 'wonderful,' to which is allied Goth. *sildaleikjan*, 'to be astonished' (akin to AS. *syllic*, E.

silly). Cognate terms in the non-Teut. languages are wanting.

Semmel, m., 'roll,' from MidHG. *sëmel,* sëmele (also *simel*), OHG. *sëmala, simila,* f., 'fine wheat flour or bread, roll'; a word peculiar to HG., allied to OHG. *sëmon,* 'to eat.' Lat. *simila,* 'wheat flour,' whence also Ital. *semola,* Fr. *semoule,* 'bran from fine wheat flour,' has been influenced by the HG. word.

Semperfrei, adj., 'free-born, entitled to act as assessor of the synod,' from Mid HG. *sëmpervrî,* 'subject only to the emperor and empire, authorised to hold a synod or to take part in it.' Allied to MidHG. *sënt,* m., 'senatus, diet, imperial diet,' also 'ecclesiastical assembly,' like OHG. *sënot* (Lat. *synodus*); MidHG. *sëmpœre, sëntbœre,* prop., 'authorised to take part in a synod.'

senden, vb., 'to send, dispatch,' from the equiv. MidHG. *sęnden,* OHG. *sęnten*; a common Teut. vb.; comp. Goth. *sandjan,* AS. *sęndan,* E. *to send,* Du. *zenden,* OSax. *sęndian,* OIc. *senda,* 'to send.' Factitive of a lost OTeut. **sinþan,* 'to go, travel'; thus *senben* is lit. 'to cause to go.' Comp. Gesinde and sinnen.

Senesbaum, m., 'senna (tree),' ModHG. only, formed from the equiv. Fr. *séné* (E. *senna*), Ital. *sena.* The ultimate source is Arab. *sana.*

Seneschall, m., 'seneschal, high steward,' from the equiv. MidHG. *seneschalt, sineschalt,* m., which is derived from Rom.; comp. the cognates Fr. *sénéchal,* Ital. *siniscalco* (MidLat. *siniscalcus*), 'high steward.' The Rom. words are based on an OTeut. word (Goth. **sinaskalks,* 'head servant'); comp. Goth. *sinista,* 'eldest,' which is primit. allied to OIr. *sen,* Lat. *senex, senior,* Lith. *sénas,* Sans. *sánas,* 'old.' With regard to the second part of the compound comp. Schalf (and Marschall). The invariable *t* at the end of the MidHG. word is remarkable.

Senf, m., 'mustard,' from the equiv. MidHG. *sënf, sënef,* m., OHG. *sënaf,* m.; corresponding to Goth. *sinap,* AS. *sënep,* 'mustard.' The other dials. have, like Rom., the term Mostert. It cannot be determined through what medium Gr. and Lat. σίναπι, *sinápi,* 'mustard,' were introduced at so early a period that the Goth. and HG. terms correspond; but since they are not genuine Aryan words, it is possible the South Teutons and Græco-Itals. obtained them independently from the same source.

sengen, vb., 'to singe, scorch,' from MidHG. *sęngen,* 'to singe, burn,' lit. 'to cause to singe or crackle'; a factitive of MidHG. and ModHG. *singen,* with a peculiar development of meaning, which is shared by the E. *to singe,* from AS. **sęnğean.*

Senkel, m., 'plumb-line,' from MidHG. *sęnkel,* m., 'plumb-line, lace,' also 'anchor, drag-net,' OHG. *sęnchil,* 'anchor, drag-net.' Allied to senken, MidHG. *sęnken,* OHG. *sęnchen,* 'to lower' (factitive of sinken; comp. OSax. *sęnkian,* Goth. *sagqjan,* 'to lower, let down').

Senne, m., 'cowherd,' ModHG. only, MidHG. **sęnne* is not recorded, but in late MidHG. (rarely), *sęnnœre,* 'herdsman, cowherd.' The antiquity of the ModHG. term is attested, however, by OHG. *sęnno,* m., 'herdsman,' as well as by late MidHG. *sęnne,* 'pasture on the Alps.' On account of the restriction of the cognates to UpG. the origin of the word is not quite certain; it is usually connected with Sahne (Goth. **sana,* 'cream,' **sanja,* 'cowherd').

Sense, f., 'scythe,' from MidHG. *sënse, sëgense,* OHG. *sëgansa,* f., 'sickle, scythe' (for the suffix see Axt); corresponding to OSax. **sëgasna (sëgisna),* Du. *zeissen,* 'scythe.' From a Teut. root *seg,* 'to cut' (see Säge), whence OIc. *sigðr,* AS. *sigðe, sîþe,* f., E. *scythe,* LG. *sicht*; primit. allied to Lat. *secare* and *securis,* Aryan root *sek,* 'to cut.'

Sente, f., 'herd,' ModHG. only; allied to Senne.

Sessel, m., 'settle,' from the equiv. MidHG. *sëʒʒel,* OHG. *sëʒʒal,* m.; corresponding to AS. *setl,* E. *settle,* Goth. *sitls,* m., 'seat, stool.' A derivative of the Teut. root *set,* 'to sit,' like Lat. *sella,* for **sedla* from **sédeo*; comp. also Gr. ἕδρα, from ἕζομαι, OSlov. *sedlo,* 'saddle,' from *sésti,* 'to sit down'; comp. sieben.

Sester, m., 'bushel,' of the same origin as Sechter.

seßhaft, adj., 'settled, stationary, residing,' from MidHG. *sëʒhaft,* 'settled, residing,' allied to MidHG. and OHG. *sëʒ,* 'seat, residence'; akin to sitzen.

setzen, vb., 'to set, put, place,' from MidHG. *sętzen,* OHG. *sęzzen,* 'to set, cause to sit'; an OTeut. factitive of sitzen. Comp. Goth. *satjan* (whence Ital. *sagire,* Fr. *saisir*), AS. *sęttan,* E. *to set,* Du. *zetten,* OSax. *sęttian,* OIc. *setja,* 'to set.'

Seuche, f., 'epidemic, plague,' from

MidHG. *siuche*, OHG. *siuhht*, f., 'disease'; abstract of ſiech.

ſeufʒen, vb., 'to sigh, lament,' from the equiv. MidHG. *siufzen*, *siuften*; the *z* of the MidHG. form is due to the influence of the intensives in *-zen*; in OHG. *sûftôn*, *sûfteôn*, 'to sigh,' allied to MidHG. *sûft*, 'sigh.' The latter is an abstract from OHG. *sûfan*, 'to drink'; hence ſeufʒen, lit. 'drawing in the breath'; it is related to ſaufen, as ſchluchʒen is to ſchluden. Note, however, E. *to sob*, MidE. *sobbin*, AS. *sobbian*, 'to sob, sigh,' which may be allied to OHG. *sûfteôn*.

ſich, pron., 'himself, herself,' &c., from the equiv. MidHG. *sich*, acc. and dat., OHG. *sih*, acc.; corresponding to the equiv. OLG. and Goth. *sik*, acc. Comp. Lat. *se*, Gr. *é*, OSlov. *sę*, acc., 'himself,' &c. (*sebě*, dat., like Lat. *sibi*); Sans. *sva*, 'own,' Lat. *suus*, Gr. *ŏs*, *ős*. Hence even in Aryan there existed a reflex. pron. *swe-*, *se-*. Further details belong to grammar.

Sichel, f., 'sickle,' from the equiv. Mid HG. *sichel*, OHG. *sihhila*, f.; corresponding to Du. *zikkel*, AS. *sicol*, E. *sickle*. It is perhaps borrowed from Lat. *secula* (Ital. *segolo*, 'bill, hedging bill'). On account of the agreement of the E. with the G. term, it must have been introduced in the 5th cent., which date also explains the permutation of Lat. *k* to HG. *ch*. On the other hand, Sichel and its cognates may be regarded as genuine Teut. words (Teut. *sikilô-*); the G. word looks like a diminutive of ModHG. Sech, which points to Teut. *sěko-*, and more remotely to the Aryan root *seg*, *sok* (see Senſe).

ſicher, adj., 'sure, certain, trusty,' from MidHG. *sicher*, OHG. *sihhûr*, 'careless, unconcerned; sure, protected, confident'; to these are allied OSax. and AS. *sicor*, 'free from guilt and punishment,' MidE. *siker*, Du. *zeker* (OHG. *sihhorôn*, 'to justify, protect, promise, vow,' OSax. *sicorôn*, 'to set free'). It is based on the common West Teut. loan-word Lat. *sěcûrus* (phonetic intermediate form *sěcûrus*, the accent of which was Germanised when the word was borrowed); comp. Ital. *sicuro*, Fr. *sûr*. The term was naturalised in G. before the 7th cent., as is shown by the permutation of *k* to *ch*. Was it first introduced through the medium of legal phraseology? Comp. OHG. *sihhorôn*, 'to justify, purgare.'

Sicht, f., 'sight,' from MidHG. *siht*, f., 'appearance, view'; verbal abstract from ſehen; comp. E. *sight*, from *to see*.

ſichten, vb., 'to sift, winnow,' ModHG. only, formed from LG. *sichten*, earlier Du. *zichten*, 'to sift'; these are derived from an older *siften*, with a LG. change of *ft* to *ht*; ModDu. *ziften*, with an abnormal *ft* (for *gt*), is based on *zeef*, 'sieve.' Comp. AS. *siftan*, E. *to sift*. A derivative of the root *sib*, 'to sift'; see Sieb.

ſickern, vb., 'to trickle, drop,' ModHG. only, from LG. ?. Comp. AS. *sicerian*, 'to trickle, ooze'; allied to ſeichen and ſiufen (Teut. root *sîk*, *sîh*, from Aryan *sig*, *sik*).

ſie, pron., 'she, her, it, they, them'; from MidHG. *sie*, *si* (*si*), nom. and acc. sing. f., nom. and acc. plur., m., f., and n. OHG. *siu*, *sî*, nom. sing. f., *sié*, nom. and acc. plur. For further details see grammars.

Sieb, n., 'sieve,' from the equiv. Mid HG. *sip* (*b*), OHG. *sib*, n.; comp. the equiv. Du. *zeef* (and *zift*); AS. *sife*, n., E. *sieve*; derived, like *siftan*, 'to sift' (see ſichten), from a root *sib* (*seb*), which is not found elsewhere.

ſieben, num., 'seven,' from the equiv. MidHG. *siben*, OHG. *sibun*; corresponding to Goth. *sibun*, AS. *seofon*, E. *seven*, Du. *zeven*, OSax. *sibun*, 'seven'; orig. *septn*. Like all units, a common Aryan word; comp. Sans. *saptan*, Gr. *ἑπτά*, Lat. *septem*, OSlov. *sedmĭ*, OIr. *secht*, 'seven.' The *t* of the Aryan prim. form *septn-* disappears in primit. Teut. between *p* and *n*.

ſiech, adj., 'sickly, infirm,' from MidHG. *siech*, OHG. *sioh* (*hh*), adj., 'sick'; corresponding to OSax. *siok*, Du. *ziek*, AS. *seóc*, E. *sick*, OIc. *sjúkr*, Goth. *siuks*, 'sick.' The OTeut. term for 'sick, ill,' compared with the ModG. word *frant*; comp. the difference in meaning between ModHG. ſiech and Seuche. To this Sucht is allied (and ſchmach?), as well as Goth. *siukan*, str. vb., 'to be weak.' A pre-Teut. root *sug* is wanting.

ſiedeln, vb., 'to settle, establish,' from the equiv. MidHG. *sidelen*; allied to Mid HG. *sědel*, OHG. *sědal*, m. and n., 'seat, settle, residence,' a variant of Seſſel, Goth. *sitls* (**sipls*). There are several examples of the change of *tl* to *pl* (parallel to that of *tn* to *pn* in Boten). Comp. also Einſiedel.

ſieden, vb., 'to seethe, boil, stew,' from MidHG. *sieden*, OHG. *siodan*, 'to seethe, cook'; comp. Du. *zieden*, AS. *seóðan*, E. *to seethe*, OIc. *sjóða*, 'to seethe, cook.' In

Goth. the only allied term is *saups*, m.,
'offering' (OIc. *sauðr*, 'sheep,' prop. 'sacrificial animal'). An Aryan root *sut* seems
to be wanting in the cognate languages.

Siedler, m., 'settler'; comp. Einſiedel.

Sieg, m., 'victory, triumph, conquest,'
from the equiv. MidHG. *sige*, also *sic (g)*,
OHG. *sigi*, *sigu*, m.; a common Teut.
word; comp. Goth. *sigis*, OIc. *sigr*, AS.
segor and *sige*, Du. *zege*. The great antiquity of the Teut. stem *segoz*, *sigiz*, is
attested both by the proper names *Segimérus*, *Segi-mundus*, and *Segestes*, mentioned by Tacitus, and by the terms in
the cognate languages; Aryan *séghos*, n.,
'prevailing might,' is implied also by Ind.
sáhas and Zend *hazañh*, 'power, might,
victory.' Comp. Sans. *sah*, 'to overpower,
vanquish, conquer,' to which Gr. ἔχω (aor.
ἔ-σχ-ον) and OIr. *segaim*, 'I attain,' are
closely allied.

Siegel, n., 'seal, signet,' from the equiv.
late MidHG. *sigel*, m. (wanting in OHG.);
in the classical period MidHG. *insigel*, *insigele*, OHG. *insigili*, n. It cannot be determined whether MidHG. *sigel*, which
was substituted for the latter term, was
borrowed at a later period from Lat. *sigillum*, or whether it was formed again from
MidHG. *besigelen* (OHG. *bisiyelen*), 'to seal,'
and *entsigelen* (OHG. *intsigilen*), 'to unseal'; nor is it known how OHG. *insigili*
is related to Lat. *sigillum*. In Goth. a term
sigljô, n., occurs.

Siele, f., 'brace, strap,' from the equiv.
MidHG. *sile*, OHG. *silo*; the latter is allied
to the root *sî*, 'to bind,' in Seil: on the
MidHG. variant *sil* are based ModHG. Sill,
n., and Sille, f.

Sigrist, m., 'sexton, sacristan,' from the
equiv. MidHG. *sigriste*, OHG. (also OLG.)
sigristo; borrowed during the OHG. period
contemporaneously with Priester, predigen,
and especially with Küſter and Meßner, from
Lat. *sacrista*, whose MidLat. variant *segrista(nus)* leads to OFr. *segretain* (in ModFr.
sacristain, Ital. *sagrestano*, E. *sexton*).

Silbe, f., 'syllable,' from the equiv. Mid
HG. *silbe*, earlier *sillabe*, OHG. *sillaba*, f.;
borrowed from Lat. and Gr. *syllaba*, probably at the same period as Schule, and the
words relating to writing, such as Brief and
ſchreiben.

Silber, n., 'silver,' from the equiv. Mid
HG. *silber*, OHG. *silbar*, earlier *silubar*, n.;
a common Teut. word with corresponding
forms; comp. Goth. *silubr*, AS. *seolofer*,

seolfor, E. *silver*, Du. *zilver*, OSax. *silubar*.
This primit. Teut. term is pre-historically
connected (comp. Gelt) with the equiv. Slav.
cognates, OSlov. *strebro*, Lith. *sidabras*.
The implied *silobro*- is certainly not an
Aryan word; perhaps the Teutons adopted
it in their migration from a non-Aryan
tribe and transmitted it to the Slavs. The
Lat.-Gr. term *argentum*, ἄργυρος, seems,
like the equiv. Sans. *rajatá* (in the Vedas
silver is unknown), to point to a primit.
Aryan term of which Teut. has retained no
trace. Another non-Aryan word of prehistoric Teut. is Hanf.

Sill, n., 'tether, string'; see Siele, so
too Sille.

Simmer, n. 'half a bushel,' for earlier
ModHG. and MidHG. *sümmer*, whose variants *sümber*, *sumber* (*sümbrin*), lead to OHG.
sumbir (*sumbrîn*). 'basket.' The suffix *in*
occurs in several terms denoting vessels
(see Keſſel); the syllable *ber* in MidHG.
sümber recalls Eimer and Zuber.

Simpel, m., 'simpleton,' ModHG. only,
from the adj. ſimpel, which comes from Fr.
simple.

Sims, m. and n., 'cornice, shelf, mantelpiece,' from the equiv. MidHG. *simȝ*, *simeȝ*,
OHG. *simiȝ* (OHG. *simiȝstein*, 'capitellum'); a corresponding *simito*- is wanting
in the other Teut. languages; its prehistoric existence is proved by its kinship
with Lat. *sima*, 'ogee, moulding.' To Mid
HG. *simeȝ* belongs the prop. collective
gesimeȝe, ModHG. Geſimſe. The derivation
from Fr. *cymaise* (Gr. κυμάτιον) is inconceivable.

Sinau, m., 'lady's mantle'; the earlier ModHG. variants Sinbau and Sinbawe
point to MidHG. and OHG. *sinton*, whose
lit. sense, 'ever-dew' (see Singrün), characterises the plant more simply than the terms
Taubehalt, lit. 'dew-holder,' and Tauſchlüſſel,
lit. 'dew-key,' which are applied to it.

Sindflut, see Sündflut.

ſingen, vb., 'to sing, chant,' from the
equiv. MidHG. *singen*, OHG. and OSax.
singan; a common Teut. vb. occurring in
the same sense in all the dials.; comp.
Goth. *seggwan*, OIc. *syngra*, AS. *singan*, E.
to sing, Du. *zingen* (yet Goth. also 'to read,'
OHG. also 'to crow'). The Teut. root
singw, which appears also in Sang, &c., is
only doubtfully related to some terms in the
non-Teut. languages; it is said to be primit. allied to ſagen (Teut. root *sag*, from
Aryan *seq*), and to this there is no phonetic

objection. It is more probably connected with Gr. ὀμφή, 'voice, speech, oracle,' if a pre-historic root *sengh* be assumed. Comp. *jengen*, and, for other Teut. artistic expressions, 𝔏ieb and 𝔐arfe.

Singrün, n., 'periwinkle,' ModHG. only, prop. a LG. word ; comp. AS. and MidE. *singréne*, OIc. *sí-grœnn*, 'semperviva'; *sin*, 'always,' is an OTeut. prefix connected with Lat. *sem-per*. Comp. 𝔖ünbflut.

finken, vb., 'to sink, fall, abate,' from the equiv. MidHG. *sinken*, OHG. *sinchan*; a common Teut. str. vb. (for its causative see *fenfen*). Comp. Goth. *siggan*, OIc. *sokkva*, AS. *sincan*, E. *to sink*, Du. *zinken*, OSax. *sincan*. The α-root *senq*, contained in these words, seems to have originated in an *i*-root *sig*, which appears in the parallel form *síhw* in ModHG. *feiḥen*, as well as OHG. *sígan*, MidHG. *sígen*, 'to drip.' The pre-Teut. root *síg, síq*, appears in OSlov. *sĭkati*, 'to make water,' *sĭkĭ*, 'urine,' as well as in Sans. *sic*, 'to wet, pour out,' whose pres. appears in a nasalised form *siñcati*. Mod HG. *feiḥen* is based upon Teut. *saik*, pre-Teut. *sig*.

Sinn, m., 'sense, meaning, import,' from the equiv. MidHG. and OHG. *sin* (nn), m.; comp. OFris. *sin*. It cannot be borrowed from Lat. *sensus*, since a MidHG. and ModHG. str. vb. *sinnen* co-exists with the subst. The corresponding OHG. vb. *sinnan* signifies only 'to travel, strive, go'; which certainly suggests that MidHG. and ModHG. *sinnen* derived its meaning from OHG. *sin*, 'sensus.' The relation of OHG. *sin*, 'sensus,' to *sinnan*, 'to set out, go in any direction,' may be inferred from its early history. The root of OHG. *sinnan* is the same as that of Teut. *sinþo-*, 'way, journey' (comp. 𝔊efinbe), *sinnan* being based on a pre-historic *sentno-*. In Lat. *sentire*, 'to feel,' the Aryan root *sent* (comp. Ir. *sét*, 'way') has an abstract meaning (see *feḥen*), which is also shared by OHG. *sinno-*. From the OHG. word the equiv. Rom. cognate Ital. *senno* is derived.

fintemal, conj., 'since, whereas,' from MidHG. *sintemál*, for *sint dem mále*, 'since then.' Comp. *feit*.

Sinter, m., 'dross of iron, scale,' from MidHG. *sinter* (*sinder*), OHG. *sintur*, m., 'slag, slack'; comp. OIc. *sindr*, AS. *sinder*, 'slag, dross' (E. *sinter* is a HG. loan-word). References in the non-Teut. languages are uncertain.

Sippe, f., 'kin, kindred, family,' from MidHG. *sippe*, OHG. *sippa*, f., 'consanguinity'; corresponding to the equiv. OSax. *sibbea*, AS. *sibb*, Goth. *sibja*. The pre-historic form *sebhyá* indicates a kinship with Sans. *sabhá*, 'tribe, tribal union, kin.' In OIc. mythology *Sif* is worshipped as the goddess of the family, and espec. of marriage.—**Sippfchaft,** from MidHG. *sipschaft*, f., equiv. to MidHG. *sippe*.

Sitte, f., 'custom, manner, good-breeding,' from the equiv. MidHG. *site*, m. (rarely f.), OHG. *situ*, m. ; a common Teut. word ; comp. the equiv. Goth. *sidus*, OIc. *siðr*, AS. *sidu* (wanting in E.), Du. *zede*, OSax. *sidu*. It is very probably allied primit. to Gr. ἔθω, gen. ἔθεος (Aryan prim. form *sédhos*), 'custom,' but its connection with Gr. ἦ-μος, 'true,' is less likely.

Sittich, m., 'parrot,' from the equiv. MidHG. *sittich*, m., beside which MidHG. and ModHG. *psittich* also occurs. Borrowed in the OHG. period from Lat. and Gr. *psittacus*, contemporaneously with ℜfau.

fitzen, vb., 'to sit, fit, suit,' from the equiv. MidHG. *sitzen*, OHG. *sizzen* (from **sizzean*, earlier **sittian*) ; a primit. Teut. and also common Aryan str. vb. from the Aryan root *sěd*, Teut. *sět*. Comp. Goth. *sitan*, AS. *sittan*, E. *to sit*, Du. *zitten*, OSax. *sittian*, 'to sit, be seated.' It corresponds to Sans. *sad*, Gr. ἔζομαι (for **σεδjo-*), Lat. *sêdeo*, OSlov. *sęda* (*sěsti*). For the corresponding causative see *feßen*. It is unnecessary to adduce further derivatives from this very large Aryan class (such as Lat. *sido*, Gr. *ἱδρύω*, Lat. *sella*, &c.).

Six, f. (in the asseveration bei meiner 𝔖ir, 'in faith, forsooth'), ModHG. only ; early history obscure.

Skizze, f., 'sketch,' ModHG. only, formed from Ital. *schizzo*, which comes from Lat. *schedium?*. Comp. also 𝔷ettel.

Sklave, m., 'slave,' from late MidHG. *slave, sklave*, m., 'slave,' prop. 'a captive of war.' Derived from the national designation 𝔖lave (MidLat. *Sclavus, Slavus*) during the G. war of annihilation against the Slavs. AS. *wealh*, 'Celt' and 'slave,' is similarly derived. The G. word 𝔖flave passed into other Teut. and Rom. languages; comp. Du. *slaaf*, E. *slave*, Fr. *esclave*, Ital. *schiavo*.

Skrupel, m., 'scruple,' early ModHG. only, formed from Lat. *scrupulus*.

Smaragb, m., 'emerald,' from the equiv. MidHG. and OHG. *smaragd* (*smarát*), m.

A learned term formed from Lat. *smaragdus*.

So, adv., 'thus, so,' from MidHG. and OHG. *sô*; corresponding to OSax. *sô*, which seems to represent *swô, although its relation to AS. *swâ* (E. *so*) and Goth. *swa*, 'thus,' cannot be accurately ascertained. Comp. alſo, alſie, and ſolch. The early history of this pronom. adv. ('in this way') is obscure; the fact that it assumed the function of a relative (*i.e.*, was used as a conjunction) corresponds to a similar change in the use of baƶ; *sô* appears as a relative particle in MidHG., but rarely in OHG.

Socke, f., 'sock,' from MidHG. *soc* (*ck*), *socke*, OHG. *soccho*, m., 'stocking'; borrowed like Du. *zok*, E. *sock*, OIc. *sokkr*, from the Lat.-Rom. term *soccus* (Ital. *socco*, 'light shoe worn by comedians,' Fr. *soc*). It was introduced contemporaneously with the term derived from Lat. *sûtor* (see Schuſter) and with Sohle (2).—Sockel, m., 'plinth,' ModHG. only, formed from Fr. *socle* (Lat. *socculus*).

Sod, m., usually Sodbrennen, 'heartburn,' from the equiv. MidHG. *sôt* (*d*), m. and n., which lit. means 'bubbling, boiling,' a derivative of MidHG. *sieden*. Hence ModHG. Sod, signifying 'broth, well,' as well as the local name Soden.

Sofern, conj. (inſofern), 'so far, in case,' even in MidHG. *sô verre*.

Sohle (1.), f., ModHG. only, formed like the equiv. E. *sole*, Swed. *sola*, from the Lat.-Rom. term *solea*, 'flat fish'; comp. Fr. *sole*, Ital. *soglia*. Is the term Schelle (Du. *schol*) derived from the same source?

Sohle (2.), f., 'sole (of the foot),' from the equiv. MidHG. *sol*, *sole*, OHG. *sola*, f.; borrowed contemporaneously with Socke prior to the OHG. period from Lat. *sôla* (a variant of *sôlea*), which is implied by Ital. *suolo*, Fr. *sole*, 'sole.' Lat. *sôlea*, whence Ital. *soglia*, Fr. *seuil*, 'threshold,' is probably the source of Goth. *sulja*, 'sole.' The prim. kinship of OHG. *sola* with Lat. *sôlea* (Gr. ὑλαί) is conceivable if Schwelle is allied.

Sohn, m., 'son,' from the equiv. MidHG. and OHG. *sun*, earlier OHG. *sunu*, m.; a common Teut., and further a common Aryan word (comp. Tochter, Vater, and Mutter); corresponding to Goth. *sunus*, AS. *sunu*, E. *son*, Du. *zoon*, OSax. *sunu*. To these Sans. *sûnû*, Zend *hunu*, OSlov. *synŭ*, and Lith. *sūnùs*, 'son,' are primit. allied. The root *sû* (comp. Sans. *sû*, 'to give birth to'; see Sau), contained in this stem *sû-nû-*, also forms the base of Gr. υἱός (dial. υἱύς), 'son,' which points to Aryan *sû-yu-* (*suivo-*). Comp. Schnur.

Solch, pron., 'such,' from the equiv. MidHG. *solich*, *solh* (*sülich*), OHG. *sulih*, *solih* (*hh* and single *h*); corresponding to OSax. *sulic*, and Du. *zulk*. Just as AS. *swâ* and Goth. *swa* represent HG. and LG. *sô*, so AS. *swylc* (E. *such*), and Goth. *swaleiks*, 'such,' represent *sulîk*. For the form and meaning of the Teut. suffix *lîko* (*liho-*) comp. lich and welcher.

Sold, m., 'pay, salary,' from MidHG. *solt* (*d*), m., 'reward for service done,' also 'that which is to be performed, duty, service.' It first appears in MidHG. about 1200 A.D., and is derived from Fr. *solde*, 'soldier's pay,' which is prop. the coin, Lat. *solidus*, Ital. *soldo* (ModFr. *sou*); yet the double sense in MidHG. can only be explained by the influence of the vb. ſollen.—Soldat, m., 'soldier,' an early ModHG. loan-word, based on Ital. *soldato*, whence also Fr. *soldat* (E. *soldier* comes from OFr. *soldoier*); in MidHG. the term *soldenœrs* with a Teut. suffix was used, and signified 'paid warrior, mercenary.'

ſollen, vb., 'to owe, be in duty bound, be said to,' from MidHG. *soln* (*scholn*), OHG. *solan* (*scolan*), pret. pres., 'to owe, be obliged, be allowed, become, be indebted, be fitting.' The corresponding abstract Schuld, f., 'debt, guilt,' proves, like Goth. *skulan*, 'to be indebted, be bound to pay,' that *skal*, 'to owe,' is the root (the loss of the guttural, by which the 1st per. *skal* became *sol* in OHG. and MidHG., is surprising). From this root a pret. pres. common to Teut. was formed, which assumed the function of an auxiliary vb.; comp. E. *shall* and Du. *zal*. For further details see grammars.

Söller, m., 'upper room, garret, balcony,' from MidHG. *sölre* (*solre*), m., 'flat roof, floor in the first storey,' OHG. *soleri* for *soldri*, orig. *sôldri*, from Lat. *sôldrium*, 'flat house-top, terrace, balcony,' whence also OSax. *soleri*, Du. *zolder*, E. *sollar*, 'open gallery or balcony, loft, garret' (AS. *solor*). Corresponding to OFr. *solier*, 'granary,' Ital. *solujo*, *solare*, 'ceiling.' The word was borrowed prior to the OHG. period, contemporaneously with Speicher, Keller, Mauer, and Ziegel.

Solper, m., 'brine, pickle,' prop. a Lower Rhen. word, whose first component is Du. *solt*, 'salt'; probably Du. *soltbrijn*, 'brine,

Y

pickle,' appears in the compound, which has also been regarded as identical with Salpeter.

Sommer, m., 'summer,' from the equiv. MidHG. sumer, OHG. sumar, m.; common to Teut. in a similar form; comp. Du. zomer, AS. sumor, E. summer, OIc. sumar. Sans. samá, 'year,' Zend ham, 'summer,' Armen. amarn, 'summer' (but am, 'year'), OIr. sam, samrad, Cymr. ham, haf, 'summer,' are cognate terms with different suffixes. Comp. Lenz, Winter, and Herbst.

sonder, prep., 'without,' from the equiv. MidHG. sunder, which is prop. an adv., 'aside, separately,' but in OHG. and Mid HG. it is frequently a conj., 'but, rather.' Comp. OHG. suntar, adv., 'separately, especially, but,' Goth. sundrô, 'separated, alone,' AS. sundor, E. asunder, Du. zonder, 'without.' Allied to Gr. ἄτερ, 'without,' from the prim. form sntér?. With this word is connected besonders, from MidHG. besunder, 'separately, singly.'—sonderbar, adj., 'peculiar, strange, odd,' from MidHG. sunderbære, 'distinguished,' sonderlich, adj., 'special, peculiar,' from MidHG. and OHG. sunderlîch, 'singly, especially, distinguished'; sondern, vb., 'to separate, sever,' from the equiv. MidHG. sundern. OHG. sun'arôn; sondern, conj., 'but,' from MidHG. suntern, a variant of sunder, 'but, meanwhile.'

Sonne, f., 'sun,' from the equiv. Mid HG. sunne, OHG. sunna, f.; a common Teut. term; comp. Goth. sunnô, f. and n., AS. sunne, f., E. sun, Du. zon, OSax. sunna, f. In OSax. and OHG. (MidHG.) sunno (sunne) also occurs as masc., which is similar to OHG. stër-no, mâ-no (see Stern). OIc. sól (corresponding to Goth. souil, AS. sól), the only term used in Mod. Scand., is primit. allied to Lat. sôl, Gr. ἥλιος, 'sun,' which, like Sans. svar, 'sun,' are based on an Aryan root sâw, sû, 'to give light'; on this root the common Teut. term sunnôn- may also be based.—Sonnabend, m., 'Saturday,' even in MidHG. sun-âbent, sunnen-âbent, OHG. sunnân-âband (also Samstag, OHG. sambaʒ-tac). MidHG. âbent is frequently used of the eve of a festival. In AS. the corresponding sunnan-æfen is used only of the 'eve of Sunday.' It follows from what has been said under Fastnacht that the name of a part of the day was in G. applied to the whole day. According to the article Samstag, a native term for Saturday seems to have been wanting among the Teutons (perhaps they had orig. a week of only six days). Moreover, Sonnabend is really MidG. and LG.—Sonntag, m., 'Sunday,' from MidHG. sun-tac, sunnen-tac, OHG. sunnûntag, seems to have been even the pre-Christian term, as may be inferred from the agreement with OSax. sunnun-dag, Du. zondag, E. Sunday (but OIc. dróttensdagr, 'Lord's day'). Comp. Montag.

sonst, adv., 'else, otherwise, formerly,' from MidHG. sunst, sust, earlier MidHG. and OHG. sus, 'thus' (the change in meaning from 'thus' to 'else' is generally explained by the ellipse of a negative particle). OHG. and OSax. sus, Du. zus, 'thus,' seem to be of the same stem as OHG. and MidHG. sô.

Sorge, f., 'care, anxiety, sorrow,' from the equiv. MidHG. sorge, OHG. soraga, f., whose Franc. variant sworga makes it probable that the word was derived from an Aryan root swerk (to which OIr. serc, 'love,' is allied?) or Aryan swergh (comp. Lith. sergëti, 'to guard'). Yet the forms in the other Teut. dials. have not the w; comp. Goth. saúrga, AS. sorh, E. sorrow, Du. zorg, OSax. sorga. Nothing certain can be asserted concerning the early history of the word.

Sorte, f., 'sort, kind, species,' ModHG. only, formed from Ital. sorta.

spähen, vb., 'to spy,' from the equiv. MidHG. spëhen, OHG. spëhôn. This word and the OHG. and OSax. adj. spâhi, Mid HG. spæhe, 'prudent, skilful' (and Du. bespieden, 'to spy'?), are the sole relics of the OTeut. root speh, 'to see,' which, through Lat. spec in speculum, conspicio, adspectus, as well as through Sans. spaç, 'to see' (Gr. σκέπ-τω for *σπέκτω?), is proved to be primit. Aryan (Aryan root spek). From the Teut. cognates those of Ital. spiare, Fr. épier, 'to spy out' (Ital. spione, Fr. espion, 'spy,' whence E. spy), were borrowed at an early period.

spalten, vb., 'to split, cleave,' from the equiv. MidHG. spalten, OHG. spaltan; comp. MidLG. spolden, MidDu. spalden, 'to split.' A str. vb. peculiar to the Teutons of Middle Europe, and based on an Aryan root, sphalt; comp. Sans. sphuṭ, sphaṭ (for sphlṭ), 'to crack' (causat. 'to split'). Probably connected with MidHG. spëlte, 'lance splinter,' Goth. spilda, 'tablet,' OIc. spjald, 'tablet.'

Span, m., 'shaving, chip, splinter,' from MidHG. and OHG. spân, m., 'chip,' Du. spaan, 'chip, blade of an oar,' AS. spón,

E. *spoon*, as well as OIc. *spónn*, *spánn*, 'splinter of wood, spoon,' attest the double sense of primit.' Teut. *spénu-*, of whose early history, on account of the want of cognate terms in the non-Teut. languages, nothing can be definitely ascertained. The connection with Gr. σπά-θη, 'spoon for stirring' (see Spaten), is uncertain.

Spanferkel, n., 'sucking pig,' a diminutive of MidHG. *spenvarch*, n., 'sucking pig' (also in MidHG. *spen-sū-*, *-swīn*). The first component is MidHG. *spen*, f., 'breast, milk,' on whose equiv. variant *spüne*, *spünn-*, MidHG. *spünneverchelīn*, 'sucking pig,' is based. Comp. Du. *speen*, 'udder,' and OHG. *spunni*, f., 'breast,' whose root is perhaps the same as that of spannen; akin also to Lith. *spenys*, 'teat.'

Spange, f., 'clasp, buckle, bracelet,' from the equiv. MidHG. *spange*, OHG. *spanga*, f.; a common Teut. term; comp. OIc. *spǫng*, AS. *spange*, 'clasp' (to which E. *spangle*, prop. a diminutive, is allied), Du. *spang*. Its early history is obscure.

Spanne, f., 'span,' from MidHG. *spanne*, OHG. *spanna*, f., 'width of the outstretched hand' (from this Ital. *spanna* and Fr. *empan*, 'a measure of length,' are borrowed); allied to spannen, 'to stretch, expand, span,' MidHG. *spannen*, OHG. *spannan*, str. vb., which corresponds to Du. *spannen*, AS. *spannan*, E. *to span*. The root *span*, 'to draw,' seems to be connected with the cognates discussed under Spanferkel and Gespenst, perhaps united with those of spinnen.

sparen, vb., 'to save, economise, lay up,' from MidHG. *sparn*, OHG. *sparôn*, 'to save, spare, preserve, lay up.' Denomin. of OHG. *spar*, 'thrifty' (AS. *spær*, for which sparsam, 'thrifty,' first occurs in ModHG.; MidHG. *sperlîche*, 'in a frugal manner,' is the corresponding adv., but it was changed in ModHG. into an adj., spärlich, 'frugal'); in OHG. *sparhenti*, AS. *spærhende*, 'thrifty.' Comp. Du. *sparen*, AS. *sparian*, E. *to spare*, OIc. *spara*. No connection with Gr. σπαρνός, 'scarce, few, seldom' (allied to σπείρω, 'to sow, scatter '), is conceivable.

Spargel, m., 'asparagus,' from the equiv. MidHG. *spargel*; the latter was formed from Lat. *asparagus*, which was also the source of the equiv. Du. *aspersie*, Fr. *asperge*, Ital. *sparagio*. Note Swiss sparse.

spärlich, see sparen.

Sparren, m., 'spar, rafter,' from Mid HG. *sparre*, OHG. *sparro*, m., 'pole, beam'; corresponding to Du. and E. *spar*, OIc. *sparre*, 'beam.' There are no cognate terms in the non-Teut. languages. See sperren.

Spaß, m., 'jest, joke, fun,' ModHG. only, formed from Ital. *spasso*, 'pleasure, pastime.'

spät, adj. and adv., 'late(ly), backward,' from the equiv. MidHG. *spæte*, OHG. *spâti*, adj. (but MidHG. *spâte*, OHG. *spâto*, adv.); comp. Du. *spade*, 'late.' Goth. preserves only *spêdiza*, 'later,' and *spêdists*, 'latest, last, least.' The Teut. *spêd-* cannot be traced farther.

Spat, m., 'spar' (mineral), from Mid HG. *spât*, m., 'foliated stone, splinter,' whence Du. *spaath*, Fr. *spath*, and Ital. *spato*, 'felspar,' seem to be derived. Its origin is obscure, as in the case of Quarz.

Spaten, m., 'spade,' ModHG. only; MidHG. *spate* may be inferred from the MidHG. and ModHG. dimin. *spatel*, 'little shovel'; the implied OHG. **spato* agrees with OSax. *spado*, Du. *spade* (*spa*), AS. *spada*, E. *spade*. These OTeut. cognates are primit. allied to Gr. σπάθη, '(blade of a) sword.' Ital. *spada*, 'sword' (to which Fr. *épée* is allied), is usually derived from Gr. rather than from Teut.

Spatz, m., 'sparrow,' from the equiv. late MidHG. *spatz*, m.; a pet term peculiar to HG., and allied to MidHG. *spar* (see Sperling). The assumed orig. connection with the equiv. Lat. *passer* (for **spat-ter*?) is less probable.

spazieren, vb., 'to walk,' from the equiv. MidHG. *spatzieren*. Borrowed in the 13th cent. from Ital. *spaziare*, 'to roam.'

Specht, m., 'woodpecker,' from the equiv. MidHG. and OHG. *spëht*, m.; Du. *specht* and E. *speight*, 'woodpecker,' are G. loan-words; also OHG. and MidHG. *spëch* (from a Teut. *spëcca* are derived OFr. *espeche*, ModFr. *epeiche*, 'woodpecker'). Probably cognate with Lat. *picus*, 'woodpecker'; the name is said to mean 'speckled,' and is usually connected with Lat. *pingo*, 'I paint,' *pictus* (Gr. ποικίλος), 'ornate,' or with E. *speck*, AS. *specca*, 'spot.' If OHG. *spëht* (Du. *specht*) be not allied to Lat. *picus*, it may be referred as 'spy, watcher,' to the root of spähen, 'to spy.' Deriv. Speßart, equiv. to *Spëhtes hart*, lit. 'woodpecker's forest.'

Speck, m., 'bacon, lard, fat,' from the equiv. MidHG. *spëc (ck)*, OHG. *spëch*, m.; corresponding to Du. *spek*, AS. *spic*, OIc. *spik*, n., 'blubber.' A primit. Teut. term, which is usually connected with Sans. *pîvan*, 'fat,' Gr. πίων, 'fat,' Zend *pivaṅh*, 'bacon,' the *w* being assumed to be changed into *q* (see **fett** and **Speichel**).

Speer, m., 'spear,' from the equiv. Mid HG. and OHG. *spër*, n.; common to Teut., with the corresponding terms, OIc. *spjǫr*, plur., 'spear,' AS. *spëre*, E. *spear*, Du. *speer*, OSax. *spër* (from Teut. *spër* is derived OFr. *espier*). It is uncertain how the word is connected with Lat. *sparus*, 'hunting-spear'; it may be cognate, or the two languages may have borrowed it from a third. Its relation to **Sparren** and **Sporn** is doubtful.

Speiche, f., 'spoke,' from the equiv. Mid HG. *speiche*, OHG. *speihha*, f.; a West Teut. word; comp. AS. *spáce*, E. *spoke*, Du. *speek*, OLG. *spéca*, 'spoke.' Its connection with OHG. *spahha*, 'chip, stick,' Du. *spaak*, 'rafter,' is not certain. **Speiche** is derived from a primit. Teut. *spīk;* so too the cognates of ModHG. **Speichernagel**, whose first component is ModHG. (simply MidG.) *spīcher*, m.; 'nail.' This corresponds to Du. *spijker*, 'nail,' OIc. *spīk*, 'spike, sprig,' and E. *spike*.

Speichel, m., 'spittle, saliva,' from the equiv. MidHG. *speichel*, OHG. *speihhilla*, *speihhila*, f.; allied to Du. *speeksel* (Goth. **spaikuldr ?*), 'spittle.' It is uncertain in what way these cognates are connected with the root *spīw*, 'to spit' (see **fpeien** and **fpuden**).

Speicher, m., 'granary, corn-loft,' from the equiv. MidHG. *spīcher*, OHG. *spīhheri* (*spīhhāri*), n.; corresponding to OSax. *spikâri* and Du. *spijker*. The permutation of the medial *k* to *hh* in HG. indicates that the word was borrowed before the 8th cent. (see **Spelt**). Lat. *spīcārīum*, 'granary,' was probably introduced in the 4th cent. from the South of Europe with the art of building in stone (see **Reller**, also **Söller** and **Ziegel**); it is remarkable, however, that the word rarely occurs in the Rom. languages; **Speicher** is also wanting in Bav. Comp. also **Speiche**.

fpcien, vb., 'to spit, vomit,' from the equiv. MidHG. *spīen*, OHG. *spīwan*, str. vb.; a root vb. common to Teut. and found also in other Aryan languages. Comp. Goth. *speiwan*, OIc. *spýja*, AS. and OSax. *spīwan*, E. *spew* and Du. *spuwen*, 'to spit'; corresponding to the equiv. Lat. *spuo*, Gr. πτύω, Lith. *spiáuju*, OSlov. *pljuje*, Sans. *ṣṭhīv*. **Speichel** and **fpeußen** are also connected probably with this common Aryan root *spīw*, 'to spit.'

Speife, f., 'food,' from the equiv. Mid HG. *spīse*, OHG. *spīsa*, f.; borrowed in the beginning of the 9th cent. from Ital. and MidLat. *spësa* for *spensa* (with regard to OHG. *î* for Lat. *ê*, see **Feier** and **Seite**). Comp. Ital. *spesa*, 'expenditure, expenses' (whence **Spesen**), from Ital. *spéndere*, 'to spend' (see **fpenden**), equiv. to Lat. *expendere*. **Speife** may have been borrowed contemporaneously with **Schüssel**; comp. further Goth. *mésa* and OHG. *miasa*, from Lat. *mensa*.

Spelt, Spelz, m., 'spelt,' from the equiv. MidHG. *spëlte*, *spëlze*, OHG. *spëlta*, *spëlza*, f.; corresponding to AS., E., and Du. *spelt*. The OHG. form *spëlza* (equiv. to AS. *spelt*) was borrowed, as the *z* indicates, prior to the OHG. period (perhaps contemporaneously with **Speicher**, **Pflanze**, and **Kochen**) from Lat. and Ital. *spelta*, while the OHG. variant *spëlta* points to Ital. *spelda*. Comp. also with these Fr. *épeautre*, 'spelt.'

Spende, f., 'spending, alms,' from Mid HG. *spënde*, OHG. *spënta*, f., 'present, gift, alms.' ModHG. **fpenden**, vb., 'bestow as a gift, spend, distribute,' from MidHG. *spënden*, OHG. *spëntôn*, 'to distribute gratuitously,' which was borrowed about the 7th cent. from MidLat. and Ital. *spéndere* (equiv. to Lat. *expendere*), 'to spend' (to which ModHG. **Speife** belongs); allied to E. *to spend*.

Spengler, m., 'tinker,' from the equiv. MidHG. *spengeler;* a derivative of MidHG. *spengel* and *spange*, 'metal ornament, clasp.'

Sperber, m., 'sparrow-hawk,' from the equiv. MidHG. *spërwære*, *sparwære*, OHG. *sparwâri*, m. (comp. Du. *sperwer*). A derivative of the Teut. *sparwa-*, 'sparrow' (see **Sperling**); hence *sparwâri* is lit. 'bird of prey that lives on sparrows' (in MidHG. also *sprinze*, f., 'female sparrow-hawk'). OHG. *sparwâri* is a compound of *aro*, 'eagle'; comp. OHG. *mûs-ari*, *chranuh-ari*, and AS. *gós-heafoc*, *mûs-heafoc*, *spear-heafoc* ('sparrow-hawk,' like OHG. *sparw-ari*). OHG. *aro*, 'eagle,' may appear as *ari* in the second part of a compound. From Teut. are derived the Rom. terms, Ital. *sparaviere*, Fr. *épervier.—***Sperberbaum**, m., 'service-tree,' is a corruption of MidHG. *spërboum*, the origin of which is obscure.

Sperling, m., 'sparrow,' from the equiv. MidHG. *spërlinc* (*g*), a dimin. of MidHG. *spar*, OHG. *sparo*, m., 'sparrow' (comp. E. *starling*, allied to ModHG. **Staar**), which represents the common Teut. name of the bird. Comp. Goth. *sparwa*, OIc. *spǫrr*,

AS. *spearwa*, E. *sparrow* (in Du. *mosch, musch*; for the LG. term see **Lüning**). Of this stem *sparw-*, which is based on the root *spor*, 'to sprawl' (see **Sporn**), **Spatz** seems to be a pet form; note also Franc. **Sperf**, 'sparrow' (in Suab. and Bav. the usual term is **Spatz**). Comp. **Sperber**.

sperren, vb., 'to bar, obstruct, fasten,' from MidHG. and OHG. *sperren* (pret. *sparte*, OHG. *sparta*), wk. vb., lit. 'to provide with spars.' Deriv. of **Sparren**.

speutzen, vb., 'to spit,' from late Mid HG. *spiutze-n*, an intensive of *spîwen*, to which ModHG. **spützen**, equiv. to E. *to spit*, and AS. *spyttan*, is also allied.

Spezerei, f., 'spice, groceries,' from late MidHG. *specerîe*, f., which is formed from Ital. *spezieria*.

spichen, vb., 'to lard; provide richly,' a ModHG. derivative of **Speck**.

Spiegel, m., 'mirror, looking-glass, reflector,' from the equiv. MidHG. *spiegel*, OHG. *spiagal*, m. (comp. Du. *spiegel*). The OHG. term is derived, with a change of gender, from MidLat. *spēgulum* (equiv. to Lat. *spĕculum*), to which Ital. *speglio* (also *specchio*), 'mirror,' points. The word must have been borrowed, on account of the change of vowels, prior to the OHG. period. OTeut. has a peculiar word for 'mirror'; comp. OHG. *scûchar*, lit. 'shadow container,' from OHG. *scûwo*, AS. *sĉúa*, 'shadow,' in Goth. *skuggwa*, 'mirror.'

Spiel, n., 'play, game, sport,' from the equiv. MidHG. and OHG. *spil* (gen. *spiles*), n., 'jest, pastime, pleasure'; allied to **spielen**, 'to play, sport, gamble,' MidHG. *spiln*, OHG. *spilôn*, wk. vb., 'to amuse oneself'; comp. Du. *spelen*, AS. *spilian*, OIc. *spila*, 'to play.' There are no undoubted cognates in the non-Teut. languages.

Spieß (1.), m., 'spear, lance, pike,' from MidHG. *spiez*, OHG. *spioz*, m., 'warrior's or hunter's spear'; corresponding to the equiv. Goth. **spiuta-* (whence OFr. *espiet*, 'spear'), OIc. *spjót*, n. (in AS. *spreôt*, see **Spriet**). Cognate terms in the non-Teut. languages are wanting.—ModHG. **Spießgeselle**, 'accomplice,' lit. 'comrade in arms.'

Spieß (2.), m., 'spit' (cooking), from the equiv. MidHG. and OHG. *spiz* (gen. *spizzes*), m.; corresponding to Du. *spit*, AS. *spitu*, E. *spit*. These cognates, whence the equiv. Rom. term, Ital. *spito*, are connected with the adj. **spitz**, of which AS. *spitu* is a subst. form. **Spieß** (Fr. *épois*) is also used in the sense of 'dags or croches

of a stag,' a meaning not found in the earlier periods; yet ModHG. **Spießer** (OHG. *spizzo, spizzo*, 'hinnulus'), 'young stag,' and the borrowed Fr. term *épois*, 'trochings of a stag,' implies the existence of such a meaning. See **Spitz**.

Spille, f., see **Spindel**.

Spilling, m., 'large yellow plum,' from the equiv. MidHG. *spillinc, spinlinc* (g), m. Probably connected, like OHG. *spĕnala*, MidHG. *spĕnel*, 'pin,' with a primit. Teut. *spĭna-*, 'thorn,' which is cognate with Lat. *spīna*, 'thorn' (comp. Ital. *spillo*, 'pin').

Spindel, f., 'spindle, distaff, pivot, peg,' from the equiv. MidHG. *spinnel*, OHG. *spinnala*, f.; the ModHG. variant **Spille**, MidHG. *spille*, is based upon MidHG. *spinle*.—ModHG. **Spinne**, f., 'spider,' from the equiv. MidHG. *spinne*, OHG. *spinna*, f., lit. 'spinner.'—**spinnen**, vb., 'to spin,' from the equiv. MidHG. *spinnen*, OHG. *spinnan*, str. vb.; common to Teut. in the same sense. Comp. Goth. *spinnan*, OIc. *spinna*, AS. *spinnan*, E. *to spin*, Du. *spinnen*. While the cognates of ModHG. *weben* are common to Teut., those of *spinnen* have only Lith. *pinti*, 'to plait' (*pintis*, 'cord'), and OSlov. *peti*, 'to stretch,' connected with them; comp. the pre-Teut. roots *pen* and *spen*, which occur also in **Fahne**. It is also frequently assumed that *spinnen* and *spannen* are allied.—ModHG. **Spinnewebe**, f., 'cobweb,' from the equiv. MidHG. *spinnewĕp, -weppe*, OHG. *spinnûn weppt*, m.

Spion, m., 'spy,' from Fr. *espion*; see **spähen**.

Spital, Spittel, n., 'hospital,' from the equiv. MidHG. *spitâl* and *spittel*, n.; which is derived from Lat. *hospitâle*.

spitz, adj., 'pointed, acute, sharp,' from the equiv. MidHG. *spitz, spitze*, OHG. *spizzi*; Goth. **spitj-* (nom. **spitus*) is wanting; comp. **Spieß** (2). No corresponding term is found in the non-Teut. languages.—**Spitz**, m., 'Pomeranian dog,' ModHG. only; an adj. used as a subst.

splitzen, vb., 'to split, cleave,' from the equiv. MidHG. *splitzen*; corresponding to E. *to split* and the equiv. Du. *splijten*; an OTeut. root vb. which does not occur elsewhere. To this is allied ModHG. **Splitter**, m., 'splinter,' from MidHG. *splitter*, m. and f. (Goth. **splitra-*); an old *tr* in HG. is not permutated; comp. **bitter, treu,** and **zittern**, but in MidHG. a term *spelter*, 'splinter,' connected with **spalten**, is mostly used. Comp. Du. *splinter*, and the equiv. E. *splint, splinter*, derived from the nasalised root.

Spor, m., 'mould,' allied to MidHG. *spar*, 'dry, rough,' OHG. *spôri*, 'mellow, rotten'; cognate terms are wanting.

Sporn, m., **Sporen**, plur., 'spur,' from the equiv. MidHG. *spor, spore*, OHG. *sporo*, m.; corresponding to Du. *spoor*, AS. *spora, spura*, E. *spur*, and the equiv. OIc. *spore*. From the Teut. cognates are derived the Rom. terms, Ital. *sprone* and Fr. *éperon*, 'spur.' Teut. *sporo*, m., 'spur,' is based on a str. verbal root *sper*, 'to kick,' which is preserved in ModHG. **Spur**, fpüren, and E. *to spurn*. Comp. OHG., OSax., and AS. *spurnan*, 'to tread,' with which Sans. *sphur*, 'to kick away,' Gr. σπαίρω, 'to struggle' (Lat. *sperno*, 'I despise,' has a figurative sense), and Lith. *splrti*, 'to tread,' are primit. allied. Comp. also Sperling (lit. 'sprawler'?). Since the orig. sense of the Aryan root *sper* is 'to kick,' Speer cannot be connected with it.

Sporteln, plur., 'fees, perquisites,' ModHG. only, formed from the equiv. Ital. *sportula*.

Spott, m., 'mockery, banter, scorn, laughing-stock,' from MidHG. and OHG. *spot* (gen. *spottes*), m., 'mockery, scorn, disgrace'; its early occurrence in OHG. shows that it is a genuine HG. word. It is remarkable that the LG. dials. have a medial *tt* in the corresponding words; comp. Du. *spot*, OIc. *spott*, n., 'mockery.' ModHG. and MidHG. *spotten*, 'to mock, scoff at,' OHG. *spottôn*, equiv. to Du. *spotten* and OIc. *spotta*. The cognates seem to imply a Goth. *spuþþôn (for Goth. *þþ*, equiv. to HG. *tt*, see Schmiede), whose origin cannot be discovered. Lat. *spūtum* is scarcely allied.

Sprache, f., 'speech, language, utterance,' from the equiv. MidHG. *sprâche*, OHG. *sprâhha*. An abstract of fprechen (comp. AS. *spréć*), 'to speak, say, utter,' which comes from the equiv. MidHG. *sprëchen*, OHG. *sprëhhan*, a str. vb. peculiar to the West Teut. languages; comp. OSax. *sprêkan*, Du. *spreken*, AS. *sprëcan*. The corresponding E. *to speak* (and *speech*), from AS. *spécan* (and *spéć*), points to a Teut. root. *spek*, which appears also in MidHG. *spëhten*, 'to chatter.' The Teut. root *sprek* has no cognates in the non-Teut. languages; it is perhaps related to Sans. *sphûrj*, 'to rustle.' For an obsolete term, also meaning 'to speak,' see under Beichte; the current term in the UpG. dials. is reden.

Sprehe, f., 'starling,' ModHG. only, prop. a LG. word; comp. OSax. *sprâ*, Du. *spreeuw*, North Fris. *sprian*, 'starling.' Origin obscure. From an OTeut. dial. the equiv. OFr. *esprohon* was borrowed.

fpreiten, vb., 'to spread, strew,' from MidHG. and OHG. *spreiten*, wk. vb., 'to unfold'; a primary form also occurs, MidHG. *sprîten, sprîden*, 'to spread.' Comp. Du. *spreiden, spreijen*, AS. *sprédan*, E. *to spread*. The Teut. root *sprĭþ* has not yet been found in the non-Teut. languages; no connection with breit is possible.

fpreizen, vb., 'to spread open, stride,' earlier ModHG. fprengen, lit. 'to stretch upwards like a prop or buttress,' from MidHG. and OHG. *spriuzen* (*spriuzen*), 'to prop, support.' Allied to MidHG. *spriuz*, f., 'buttress,' which is derived from the stem of fprießen.

Sprengel, m., 'sprinkling brush; diocese, jurisdiction,' from MidHG. *sprengel*, m., 'brush for sprinkling holy water, sprinkle,' with a remarkable change of meaning.—fprengen, vb., 'to burst, break open, blow up,' from MidHG. and OHG. *sprengen*, 'to cause to spring,' is a causative of fpringen.

Sprenkel (1.), m., 'springe, noose, snare,' ModHG. only, from LG.; comp. Du. *sprenkel*, 'loop in a cable.' The latter, like MidHG. *sprinka*, MidHG. *sprinke*, f., 'bird-trap,' is based on a prim. form *springô*, from which E. *springe* is also derived. This prim. form is probably cognate with Lith. *springti*, 'to choke,' *sprangùs*, 'choking,' Lett. *sprangât*, 'to cord, confine.'

Sprenkel (2.), m., 'speck, spot,' from MidHG. (MidG.) *sprenkel, sprinkel*, m., 'spot,' for which in MidHG. a form *sprëckel* without a nasal is used (also *sprünkel in *sprünkelëht*, 'spotted'), allied to Ic. *sprekla*, Swed. *sprükla*, 'little spot,' Swiss *sprigel, sprägel*. These cognates may be connected with E. *to freak, freckle*, and further with Gr. περκνός, Sans. *pṛçni*, 'spotted, variegated,' if *sprek* (*spreg*) and *prek* (*preg*) be regarded as the Aryan roots (with regard to the interchange of *sp* and *p*, comp. that of *st* and *t* under troffeln and Stier). In that case there would probably be no historic connection between fprenfeln and fpringen.

Spreu, f., 'chaff,' from the equiv. MidHG. and OHG. *spriu* (gen. *spriuwes*), n.

A specifically HG. word, which, like MidHG. *spræxen*, MidDu. *spraeien* (Goth. **sprēvjan*), 'to emit sparks, fly as dust, scatter,' is based on a Teut. and an Aryan root *sprēw*, 'to emit sparks,' of which, however, no further traces can be found (see further **fprüfjen**). The corresponding LG. word is represented by the cognates, E. *chaff* and Du. *kaf*.

Sprichwort, n., 'proverb,' from the equiv. MidHG. *sprichwort*, n. (the form **Sprüchwort** first occurs in early ModHG. only), lit. 'uttered word.'

Spriegel, with the variant **Sprügel**, m., 'support of an awning, tilt,' a ModHG. word of the MidG. group; not recorded, probably only by chance, in the earlier periods. No cognate terms have as yet been found.

fpriefien, vb., 'to sprout, shoot forth,' from the equiv. MidHG. *sprieʒen* (OHG. **sprioʒan*?), str. vb.; corresponding to Du. *spruiten*, AS. *sprútan*, and E. *to sprout*. From this Teut. root *sprŭt*, 'to grow up,' are derived E. *to sprit*, 'to sprout' (AS. *spryttan*), as well as AS. *spreót*, 'pole, shaft,' equiv. to Du. *spriet*, 'javelin, spear, bowsprit,' whence ModHG. **Spriet** in **Bugfpriet**. Comp. further **fpritʒen** and **Sproffe**. No terms undoubtedly cognate are found in the non-Teut. languages.

fpringen, vb., 'to spring, leap, jump,' from the equiv. MidHG. *springen*, OHG. *springan*, str. vb.; corresponding to the equiv. OSax. *springan*, Du. *springen*, AS. *springan*, E. *to spring*, Goth. **spriggan*. From this common Teut. vb., to which ModHG. **Sprung**, m. (MidHG. and OHG. *sprung*), is allied, the cognates of Ital. *springare*, 'to jog, swing one's legs,' are derived. An allied Aryan root *sprgh*, with a nasal exists in Gr. σπέρχεσθαι, 'to hasten,' σπερχνός, 'hasty.'

fpritʒen, vb., earlier **fprütʒen**, 'to spirt, squirt, syringe, spout forth,' from the equiv. MidHG. *sprützen*, whence Ital. *spruzzare* and *sprizzare* were borrowed; allied to Mid HG. *sprützte*, ModHG. **Spritʒe**, f., 'syringe, squirt'; deriv. of the Teut. root *sprŭt*, 'to grow up, shoot forth' (see **fpriefien**). Comp. E. *to sprit*, 'to spirt' and 'to sprout.'

fpröde, adj., 'brittle; shy, coy,' ModHG. only; corresponding to ModFlem. *sprooi*, early ModDu. *spru*, MidE. *sprēpe*, 'infirm, brittle.' The adj., an old formation (like **blöde** and **müde**) from the Teut. root *sprēw*, 'to be scattered as dust' (see **Spreu**), is not recorded, probably only by chance, in the earlier periods of the language.

Sproffe, f., 'shoot, sprout; rung,' from MidHG. *sproʒʒe*, OHG. *sproʒʒo*, m., 'rung.' This meaning is probably derived from an older signification ('twig'); comp. OIc. *sprote*, 'twig, rod, staff,' AS. *sprota*, 'twig.' These terms are connected with the Teut. root *sprŭt* in **fpriefien**, of which **Spreß**, 'sprout,' is a ModHG. derivative; from the latter **Spreßling** is derived.

Sprotte, f., 'sprat,' prop. a LG. word, which corresponds to the equiv. Du. *sprot*, E. *sprat*, and AS. *sprott*. Its earlier history has not been ascertained.

Spruch, m., 'saying, adage, sentence, judgment,' from MidHG. *spruch*, m., 'that which is uttered, word, speech'; a MidHG. derivative of the vb. **fprechen**.

fprühen, vb., 'to emit sparks, sparkle,' first recorded in ModHG., but MidHG. **spruejen*, OHG. **spruowen*, are to be assumed. Its connection with MidHG. *spræwen*, 'to fly as dust,' and ModHG. **Spreu**, leads to the root *sprīw* (*sprōw*), 'to be scattered as dust'; see further **fpröde**.

fpuchen, vb., 'to haunt' (of a ghost), ModHG. only; its early history cannot be discovered; how it is connected with the root *splw* (see **fpeien**) is uncertain.

Spuk, m., 'spectre, ghost,' ModHG. only, prop. a LG. word; it is unknown to UpG. (the strictly HG. form **Spuch** occurs in early ModHG.); comp. LG. and Du. *spook*, from Teut. *spauka-*. Allied to Swed. *spok*, 'scarecrow,' Dan. *spog*, 'joke, fun,' Norweg. *spjok*, 'ghost' (E. *spook* is of Scand. origin). It is uncertain whether the word is related to Lith. *spúgulas*, 'splendour.'

Spule, f., 'spool, bobbin,' from MidHG. *spuole*, m., 'spool, tube, quill,' OHG. *spuola*, f., *spuolo*, m., 'spool'; corresponding to Du. *spoel*, E. *spool*. From the Teut. cognates are derived the Rom. terms, Ital. *spuola*, 'shuttle,' OFr. *épolet*, 'spindle.' Connected with the root *spa*, 'to draw,' adduced under **fpannen** and **fpinnen**?.

fpülen, vb., 'to rinse, wash,' from the equiv. MidHG. *spüelen*, OHG. *spuolen*, wk. vb.; corresponding to the equiv. Du. *spoelen*, AS. *spélan*. Its connection with the preceding word is not clear. The corresponding collective **Spülicht**, n., 'dishwash, swill,' is based on MidHG. *spüelach* (OHG. **spuolahi*).

Spund, m., 'bung, bunghole, channel,' from MidHG. *spunt* (gen. *spuntes*), m., 'bunghole, valve in the tube of a pump.' The persistent *t* of the MidHG. inflected form points of itself to the foreign origin of the term, and still more so the MidHG. variants *punct* and *pfunt*, as well as Mod HG. (dial.) ꝓunt and ꝓunbe (as to the period when the word was borrowed, comp. ꝳein). Du. *spon*, *spun*, 'bung,' and Fr. *bonde*, 'sluice, plug,' *londen*, 'bung,' are corresponding terms, derived from the Mid HG. words, which are based on Lat. *puncta*, 'prick, puncture, opening made in a pipe.' With regard to the *s* of MidHG. *spunt*, comp. Ital. *spuntone*, 'spontoon,' *spuntare*, 'to blunt,' allied to Lat. *punctum*.

Spur, f., 'track, trace, footstep, vestige,' from MidHG. *spur* (*spür*), n. and f., 'footstep,' beside which the equiv. MidHG. and OHG. *spor* occurs; connected with the Teut. and Aryan root *sper* (see ꝭpern), 'to tread.' To this is allied the ModHG. denominative *spüren*, 'to trace, investigate, discover,' from MidHG. *spürn*, OHG. *spuren*, *spurren*, and *spurien*, wk. vb., lit. 'to follow in search of the track of game,' then 'to go in quest of, trace, examine.' This figurative sense recurs in all the Teut. languages (comp. Du. *speuren*, AS. *spyrian*, OIc. *spyrja*), and is probably a relic of the terms used by OTeut. hunters.

Spuſen, vb., 'to speed, make haste,' from the equiv. MidHG. *spuoten* (not recorded), OHG. *spuotōn*; allied to MidHG. and OHG. *spuot*, f., 'success, dispatch,' which is the abstract of MidHG. and OHG. *spuon* (*spuoan*), 'to succeed, be successful' (*sputen* is wanting in Suab. and Bav.). To the same cognates E. *speed*, from AS. *spēd*, 'success' (AS. *spōwan*, 'to make progress'), Du. *spoed*, 'haste,' *spoeden*, 'to hasten.' With the root *spō* (*spē*) contained in these words, Sans. *sphâ*, 'to swell, grow, thrive,' and OSlov. *spěja* (*spěti*), 'to be successful,' are connected; so too perhaps Lat. *spatium*.

Spützen, vb., equiv. to ſpruꜩen.

Staat, m., 'state, country, pomp, show,' ModHG. only, borrowed, like Du. *staat*, and E. *state*, from Lat. *status*, whence also Fr. *état* and Ital. *stato*. The meaning 'display' also belongs to Fr. *état*. ꝭtaat is a totally different word.

Stab, m., 'staff, stick, staff-officers,' from MidHG. and OHG. *stap* (gen. *stabes*), m., 'stick, prop, staff'; a common Teut. word, represented also by Goth. *stafs* (*b*), AS. *stœf*, E. *staff*, Du. *staf* (comp. also ꝓuch, ſtate under ꝓuch). Its relation to the similarly sounding OHG. vb. *staben*, 'to be stiff,' leads to an Aryan root *stap*, 'to be firm,' which is implied by Sans. *sthâpay*, 'to cause to stand, erect,' or to Aryan *stabh* in Lith. *stôbas*, *stôbras*, 'statue,' *stēbas*, 'staff, buttress.'

Stachel, m., 'sting, prickle, goad,' from the equiv. MidHG. (very rarely) *stachel*, OHG. *stahhulla* (*stacchulla*), f.; a rather late derivative of ſtechen.

Stadel, m., 'barn,' from the equiv. Mid HG. *stadel*, OHG. *stadal*, m.; an old derivative of the Aryan root *stā*, 'to stand,' prop. signifying 'standing-place'; comp. Lat. *stabulum*, 'stable,' allied to *stare*, 'to stand,' Sans. *sthâtra*, 'standing-place,' allied to *sthâ*, 'to stand.' Comp. ꝭcheune also.

Staden, m., 'bank, shore,' from the equiv. MidHG. *stade*, OHG. *stado*, m.; corresponding to Goth. *staþ*, AS. *stæþ*, OSax. *stath*, 'bank.' The common Teut. stem *staþo-* (with which ꝭeſtate, ModHG. only, is connected) is formed from the Aryan root *stā* (see ſtehen and ꝭtätte), and signifies 'bank' in the sense of 'terra firma.' ꝭtaten is the genuine HG. word for the prop. MidG. and LG. Uſer.

Stadt, f., 'city, town,' from MidHG. *stat*, f., 'place, situation, spot, locality, town,' OHG. *stat*, f., 'place, spot.' Prop. identical with ꝭtatt and ꝭtätte (the meaning 'town' was first developed in the Mid HG. period; the earlier term was ꝓurg, OHG. and MidHG. *burc*, f.). See ꝭtatt.

Staffel, f., 'rung; step, degree,' from MidHG. *staffel* (*stäffel*, usually *stapfel*), m. and f., 'grade, degree,' OHG. *stđffal* (*stapfal*), m., *staffala*, f., 'foundation, basis, step.' A derivative of the Teut. root *stap*, 'to go' (in ꝭtapfe and ꝭtufe); allied to the LG. cognates of ꝭtapel.

Staffette, f., 'courier, special messenger,' ModHG. only; see ꝭtapfe.

Stahl, m., 'steel,' from the equiv. Mid HG. *stahel*, m. and n. (contracted *stâl*, with the variant *stachel*), OHG. *stahal* (*stâl*, *stahhal*); corresponding to Du. *staal*, AS. *style*, *steli*, n., E. *steel*, and the equiv. OIc. *stâl* (Goth. **stakla-*), n. A pre-Teut. form *stakło-* is implied by the cognate OPruss. *stakla*, 'steel.' Other corresponding terms are wanting in the Aryan languages (so too in the case of ꝭelb and ꝭilber the Teut. terms are related only to the Slav.).

Staken, m., 'stake, pale, boat-hook,'

ModHG. only, prop. a LG. word; comp. Du. *staak*, AS. *staca*, E. *stake*, and the equiv. OSw. *staki*. From these cognates, which, like Stachel, are connected with stechen, the equiv. Rom. class of Ital. *stacca* is derived.

Stall, m., 'stall, stable, sty,' from MidHG. *stal* (*ll*), m. and n., 'standing or dwelling place, spot, stable,' OHG. *stal* (*ll*), m., 'stable, spot'; prop. identical with Stelle. The two senses of the OHG. word are ramifications of a prim. meaning, 'standing-place.' Corresponding to Du. *stal*, 'stable, stall,' AS. *steall*, 'stable, standing-place,' E. *stall*. The cognates (whence also stellen) are connected with the Aryan root *stal*, appearing in Stuhl. From Teut. *stallo-* are derived the Rom. cognates, Ital. *stallo*, 'spot,' Fr. *étal*, 'butcher's bench,' *étau*, 'butcher's stall,' Ital. *stalla*, 'stable,' Ital. *stallone*, Fr. *étalon*, and the equiv. E. *stallion*.

Stamm, m., 'stem, trunk, stock, tribe,' from MidHG. and OHG. *stam* (*mm*), m., 'trunk, pedigree, race, reason, cause'; corresponding to Du. *stam*, AS. *stemn* (*stæfn*), E. *stem* (see Steven), Olc. *stafn*. The implied Teut. *stamno-* (hardly for *stabno-*, allied to Stab), a derivative of the Aryan root *stā̌*, 'to stand,' is equiv. to Ir. *tamon* (for *stamon-*), 'pedigree,' and Gr. στάμνος, 'wine jar,' the meaning of which recalls ModHG. Stänber.

ſtammeln, vb., 'to stammer, stutter,' from the equiv. MidHG. *stammeln*, *stamelen*, OHG. *stammalôn*, *stamalôn*. A derivative of OHG. *stammal*, *stamal*, 'stammering,' on whose earlier variant *stammêr*, *stam-êr* (nom. sing. masc.), is based OHG. *stammên*, *stamên*, 'to stammer.' Comp. the Goth. adj. *stamms*, Olc. *stamr*, 'stammering,' and also stumm. The prop. LG. ſlammern agrees with Du. *stameren*, E. *to stammer* (comp. AS. *stamor*, 'stammering'). For the root *stam*, 'to check' (ſtammeln, 'to falter frequently'), see ungeſtüm and ſtemmen.

ſtammen, vb., 'to originate (from), descend, proceed,' from the equiv. MidHG. *stammen*; allied to Stamm.

ſtampfen, vb., 'to stamp, pound,' from the equiv. MidHG. *stampfen*, OHG. *stampfôn*; a derivative of ModHG. Stampf, MidHG. and OHG. *stampf*, 'punch'; comp. Du. *stampen*, E. *to stamp*, Olc. *stappa* (for *stampa*), 'to stamp, push.' From these cognates Ital. *stampare*, Fr. *étamper*, 'to impress,' Ital. *stampa*, 'stamp, impression,'

and Fr. *estampe*, are borrowed. Akin to Stempel and ſtumpf. The Teut. root *stamp* (*stump*), 'to push,' contained in these words, seems to be connected with Gr. στέμβω, 'I tread' (and Sans. *stamba*, 'post'?). Comp. Stapfe and Stempel.

Stand, m., 'state, position, rank, stand,' from MidHG. *stant* (*d*), m., 'state, condition'; from the root *stand* (see ſtehen).

Standarte, f., 'standard, banner,' from the equiv. MidHG. *stanthart* (*standert*), m. Borrowed in the 13th cent. from OFr. *estendard* (Fr. *étendard*), 'flag,' or preferably from the equiv. Ital. *stendardo*, which is based on Lat. *extendere*. From the same source E. *standard* is derived.

Ständer, m., 'high desk, pole, watercask,' ModHG. only; a LG. word; corresponding to Du. *stander*, 'pillar'; allied to Staub.

ſtändig, adj., 'standing, stationary, constant,' ModHG. only (MidHG. and OHG. *stęndic* in compounds like inſtändig); allied to Staub, 'continuance.' Comp. *bestęndec*, 'continuous,' an adj. occurring even in MidHG.

Stange, f., 'pole, stake, curb-bit,' from the equiv. MidHG. *stange*, OHG. *stanga*, f.; corresponding to Du. and E. *stang*, Olc. *stǫng*, f., 'pole.' From the Teut. cognates is derived the Rom. class of Ital. *stanga*, 'pole.' Teut. *stangô* is usually connected with the Teut. root *sting* (see ſtechen), preserved in E. *to sting*. For a similar development of meaning see Staſen. Deriv. Stengel.

Stapel, m., 'support, stocks (for ships),' ModHG. only, a LG. word, corresponding to HG. Staffel. Comp. Du. *stapel*, 'heap, staple-town,' E. *staple* (hence Fr. *étape*, 'depot, emporium'). "The development of meaning in the cognates ranges through the meanings 'support (AS. *stapol*), foundation (OHG. *staffol*), frame, heap, piled-up goods.'" See the following word.

Stapfe, m., 'footprint, footstep,' from the equiv. MidHG. *stapfe*, OHG. *stapfo* (*staffo*), m.; allied to MidHG. and OHG. *stępfen*, also MidHG. *stapfen*, OHG. *stapfôn*, 'to tread,' which corresponds to the AS. str. vb. *stæppan*. Comp. Du. *stap*, 'step,' *stappen*, 'to step,' and the E. word *step*. The Teut. verbal root *stap*, 'to tread, step, go,' to which Staffel and Stuſt are allied, appears in a nasalised form in the cognate ſtampfen. From Teut. is borrowed Ital. *staffa*, 'stirrup,' whence *staffetta*, 'courier,' is derived. Since the Aryan root *stab* may have had a variant *stap*, it is possible that OSlav. *stopa*, 'track,' is primit. allied to 𝔖𝔱𝔞𝔭𝔣𝔢.

𝔖𝔱𝔞𝔯, m., 'starling,' from the equiv. MidHG. *star*, m., OHG. *stara*, f.; corresponding to AS. *stær*, *stearn*, E. *stare*, OIc. *stare*, *starre*, 'starling'; primit. allied to Lat. *sturnus*. E. *starling* indicates the derivation of ModHG. 𝔖𝔭𝔢𝔯𝔩𝔦𝔫𝔤 (OHG. *sparo*).

—𝔖𝔱𝔞𝔯, m., 'cataract' (of the eye), has been deduced in ModHG. from MidHG. *starblint* (*d*), OHG. *starablint* (comp. Du. *staarblind*), adj., 'blind from a cataract,' which has no connection with the name of the bird, since it more probably belongs to the same root as ModHG. 𝔰𝔱𝔞𝔯𝔯𝔢𝔫 (OHG. *starēn*), 'to look fixedly, stare.' In AS., besides *stærblind*, a curious form, *púrblind* occurs, the first component of which is AS. *púr*, 'bittern'; comp. Gr. γλαύκωμα, from γλαύξ, 'owl.' Hence the instinctive connection between the name of the bird and the disease is quite comprehensible.

𝔰𝔱𝔞𝔯𝔨, adj., 'strong,' from MidHG. *starc* (and *starch*), OHG. *starc* (and *starah*), adj., 'strong, vigorous, big'; corresponding to OSax. *stark*, Du. *sterk*, AS. *stearc*, E. *stark*, OIc. *sterkr*. To the same Teut. root *stark* belong by a different gradation Goth. *gastaúrknan*, 'to become parched, wither away,' OIc. *storkna*, 'to curdle,' OHG. *storchanēn*, 'to become fixed, hard'; hence perhaps 'fixed' is the primit. meaning of the root. Lith. *strégti*, 'to stiffen, become numb,' and ModPers. *suturg* (base **strga*), 'strong,' are primit. allied. Deriv. ModHG. 𝔖𝔱ä𝔯𝔨𝔢, f., 'starch' (note the E. word).

𝔖𝔱ä𝔯𝔨𝔢, f., 'heifer,' ModHG. only, properly a LG. word. Scarcely allied to ModHG. 𝔖𝔱𝔦𝔢𝔯; connected rather, like MidHG. *stēr*, OHG. *stēro*, 'ram,' with Goth. *staira*, 'sterile,' which is primit. allied to Gr. στεῖρος, στέριφος, 'sterile,' Lat. *sterilis*, Sans. *start*, 'sterile.' Connected with the following word.

𝔰𝔱𝔞𝔯𝔯, adj., 'fixed, staring,' ModHG. only; probably a LG. word. Comp. the rare MidHG. *starren*, 'to become fixed,' allied to the Teut. root *ster*, *star*, with which the cognates of 𝔖𝔱𝔞𝔯 and 𝔖𝔱ä𝔯𝔨𝔢 are connected. With these comp. Sans. *sthira*, 'firm, strong,' Gr. στερεός, 'hard.'—ModHG. 𝔰𝔱𝔞𝔯𝔯𝔢𝔫, vb., 'to look fixedly, stare,' from the equiv. MidHG. *starn*, OHG. *starēn*, which is more closely connected with 𝔖𝔱𝔞𝔯 than with 𝔰𝔱𝔞𝔯𝔯.

𝔖𝔱𝔞𝔱𝔱, f., 'place, stead,' from MidHG. and OHG. *stat*, f., 'place, spot'; from the plur. (OHG. *stęti*, MidHG. *stęte*) is derived ModHG. 𝔖𝔱ä𝔱𝔱𝔢, f., 'place, site.' Corresponding to Du. *stede*, *st-é*, 'spot, place, small town.' The ModHG. prep. 𝔰𝔱𝔞𝔱𝔱 (comp. *kraft*) is properly an oblique case of the subst.; in MidHG. (very rarely) *an*... *stęte*, 'in place of,' &c. ModHG. 𝔷𝔲 𝔰𝔱𝔞𝔱𝔱𝔢𝔫 (as in the phrase 𝔷𝔲 𝔰𝔱𝔞𝔱𝔱𝔢𝔫 𝔨𝔬𝔪𝔪𝔢𝔫, 'to serve one's turn, be useful') is not connected with this word 𝔖𝔱𝔞𝔱𝔱, but is based on MidHG. *stat*, OHG. *stata*, f., 'convenient spot or period, occasion, help'; hence even in MidHG. *ze staten*, OHG. *zi statu*, 'at a suitable time, for assistance.' With this is associated ModHG. 𝔤𝔢𝔰𝔱𝔞𝔱𝔱𝔢𝔫, MidHG. *gestaten*, OHG. *gistatōn*, 'to permit,' lit. 'to furnish a good opportunity.' OHG. *stata* is, like *stat* (gen. *stęti*), a verbal abstract of 𝔰𝔱𝔢𝔥𝔢𝔫.

—ModHG. 𝔰𝔱𝔞𝔱𝔱𝔣𝔦𝔫𝔡𝔢𝔫, 'to take place,' from MidHG. *stats finden*, 'to find a good opportunity.'—𝔰𝔱𝔞𝔱𝔱𝔩𝔦𝔠𝔥, adj., 'stately, magnificent, considerable,' a ModHG. derivative of ModHG. *stat*, 'good opportunity.'

𝔖𝔱𝔞𝔲𝔟, n., 'dust, spray,' from the equiv. MidHG. and OHG. *stoup* (gen. *stoubes*), m.; also, by a different formation, ModHG. 𝔊𝔢𝔰𝔱ü𝔭𝔭, MidHG. *stüppe*, OHG. *stuppi*, 'dust,' which, like Goth. *stubjus*, is connected with 𝔰𝔱𝔦𝔢𝔟𝔢𝔫, 'to fly as dust, scatter.'

𝔖𝔱𝔞𝔲𝔠𝔥𝔢, f., 'veil, sleeve, muff, mitten,' from MidHG. *stûche*, OHG. *stûhha*, f., 'the broad pendant sleeve on a woman's dress, kerchief, veil, cloth, apron'; corresponding to AS. *stocu*, 'long sleeve,' OIc. *stúka*. The Rom. cognate, Fr. *étui* (Ital. *astuccio*), 'case,' has been derived from a Teut. **stúkjo*. Teut. *stûkō* (*stûkjo*) is usually connected with a pre-Teut. root *stûg*; OLG. *stûkan*, Du. *stuiken*, 'to pile up, push,' and Lith. *stùgti*, 'to look aloft.'

𝔖𝔱𝔞𝔲𝔡𝔢, f., 'shrub, bush,' from the equiv. MidHG. *stûde*, OHG. *stûda*, f., a specifically HG. word, wanting in the other Teut. dialects. Its genuine Teut. origin is, however, undoubted. It seems, like 𝔰𝔱𝔢𝔥𝔢𝔫, to belong to a primitively cognate Aryan root *stû*, which appears in Gr. στύλος, 'pillar,' and στύω, 'to look fixedly,' and also in 𝔰𝔱ü𝔱𝔷𝔢𝔫.

𝔰𝔱𝔞𝔲𝔢𝔫, vb., 'to dam in, stow away, pack,' from MidHG. and OHG. *stouwen*, 'to put a stop to, arrest, restrain' (properly identical with MidHG. and OHG. *stouwen*, 'to abuse, rate, accuse'?). Allied to ModHG. 𝔰𝔱𝔞𝔲𝔫𝔢𝔫, 'to be amazed' (orig. a Swiss word, adopted as a literary term in the last century), which is wanting in MidHG. and OHG. For the early history of ſtaunen and ſtaunen the older periods give no further clue, yet comp. root *stû*, 'to look fixedly,' under Staube.

Staupe, f., 'rod, scourge,' from Mid HG. (MidG.) *stûpe*, 'post to which a criminal is bound and beaten with rods'; hence ſtäupen, 'to flog, scourge,' which occurs in ModHG. only. Corresponding to OFris. *stûpa*, 'public chastisement with the rod.' Early history obscure.

ſtechen, vb., 'to prick, stab, engrave,' from the equiv. MidHG. *stëchen*, OHG. *stëhhan*, str. vb. From this strong verbal root *stek*, which is preserved in MidEur. Teut. (OSax. *stëkan*, Du. *steken*, OFris. *steka*); comp. ſticken, Stecken, and Stichel. By passing from the *i* class into the *e* class this root (comp. bitten) originated in an older form *stik*, pre-Teut. *stig*, which has a variant *tig*, 'to be sharp,' in the non-Teut. languages. Comp. Sans. *tij*, 'to be sharp, sharpen' (*tigmá*, 'pointed, sharp'), Gr. στίγμα, 'prick, point,' from στίζω, 'to mark with a pointed instrument, prick,' Lat. *instigare*, 'to goad on, incite.' Whether these are connected further with a prehistoric root *stik*, *stink* (see Stange), is uncertain.—Stecken, m., 'stick, staff,' from the equiv. MidHG. *stëcke* (*stëche*), OHG. *stëccho* (*stëhho*), m. Corresponding to AS. *sticca*, E. *stick*; lit. perhaps 'pricker,' like Stange, allied to E. *sting*.—ModHG. ſtechen, wk. vb., 'to stick, fix, put, place, conceal,' from MidHG. and OHG. *stecken*, 'to fasten by sticking, fix firmly,' lit. 'to make something stick'; a recent factitive of ſtechen (properly *stakjan for *staikjan, from the root *stik*). From the intransit. meaning of MidHG. *stecken*, 'to remain fast,' is derived the equiv. ModHG. ſtecken, str. vb., 'to stick, remain fast, be fixed.' The Rom. cognates, Ital. *stecco*, 'thorn,' *stecca*, 'staff,' Fr. *etiquette*, 'ticket' (on goods, &c.), are based on derivatives of the Teut. root *stik*, *stëk*.

Steg, m., 'path, narrow wooden bridge,' from the equiv. MidHG. and OHG. *stëc* (gen. *stëges*), m.; allied to ſteigen; also dialectically Stege, f., equiv. to Stiege, 'stair.' —ModHG. Stegreif, from the equiv. MidHG. *stëgreif*, OHG. *stëgareif*. An OTeut. term, as is shown by the correspondence between HG. and AS. *stigerâp*, E. *stirrup*, OIc. *stigreip*; lit. 'rope, ring for mounting a horse' (the term Steigbügel,

'stirrup,' equiv. to Du. *stijgbeugel*, is unknown to MidHG. and OHG. See, however, Bügel).

ſtehen, vb., 'to stand, remain,' from the equiv. MidHG. and OHG. *stên*, str. vb.; besides the root *stai*, which may be deduced from this verb, MidHG. and OHG. *stân* indicates another root. The form of this root *stai* (*stá*) was extended to *stand* (*staþ*), from which most of the dialects form the pres. stem; comp. Goth. *standan*, AS. *standan*, E. *to stand* (E. *to stay* is derived from Rom.; comp. OFr. *estaier*), OHG. *stantan*, MidHG. (rarely) *standen*. The pres. stem was, in the Teut. group, formed from the root *stand* (*staþ*), while the substant. derivatives were chiefly based on the Aryan root *stâ* (comp. Stadt, Statt, ſtetig). This recurs (as in the case of kommen, gehen, ſitzen) in all the Aryan languages in the same sense. Comp. Sans. *sthâ*, Gr. ἵ τάναι, Lat. *stâre*, OSlov. *stati*, 'to stand.'

ſtehlen, vb., 'to steal,' from the equiv. MidHG. *stëln*, OHG. *stëlan*; a common Teut. str. vb. Comp. Goth. *stilan*, OIc. *stela*, AS. *stëlan*, E. *to steal* (to which *stealth* is allied), Du. *stelen*, OSax. *stëlan*, 'to steal.' The root is confined to Teut., and corresponds only partly to Gr. στερίσκω, 'to rob'; perhaps the Teut. *l* instead of the Gr. *r* is due to hehlen (on account of the frequent combination of hehlen and ſtehlen). A vb. corresponding to the Gr. κλέπτω, 'to steal,' is preserved in Goth. (comp. Goth. *hlifan*, 'to steal').

ſteif, adj., 'stiff, rigid, pedantic, formal,' from MidHG. *stîf*, 'stiff, fixed, upright, brave, stately'; probably a MidG. and LG. word. Comp. Du. *stijf*, AS. *stîf* (E. *stiff*), OIc. *stîfr*, 'fixed, stiff.' The Teut. root *stîf*, in these cognates, occurs in the non-Teut. languages as *stîp*; Lat. *stîpes*, 'stake, stick,' Lith. *stiprùs*, 'strong, firm,' *stîpti*, 'to become stiff.' Comp. also Stift.

Steig, m., 'path, footway,' from the equiv. MidHG. and OHG. *stîc* (gen. *stîges*), m.; allied to ſteigen, 'to mount,' which is based on the equiv. MidHG. *stîgen*, OHG. *stîgan*, str. vb. The vb. is common to Teut. in the same sense; comp. OSax. *stîyan*, Du. *stijyen*, AS. *stîgan* (E. *to sty*), Goth. *steigan*. The Teut. root *stîg* (comp. also Steg, ſteil) corresponds to the widely-diffused Aryan root *stîgh*, 'to step, stride,' which appears in Sans. (rare) *stigh*, 'to step, stride,' Gr. στείχω, 'to go,' Lat. *vestigium*, 'track, trace,' OSlov. *stignąti*, 'to hasten'; hence the meaning of the verbal root has been modified in Teut.—The vb. ſteigern, 'to raise, increase, put up to auction,' allied to MidHG. and OHG. *steigen*, 'to cause something to ascend, to elevate or extol something,' occurs in early ModHG. only; hence the vb. means lit. 'to cause something to mount in price.'

ſteil, adj., 'steep,' from the equiv. late MidHG.*steil*, the variants of which, *steigel*, OHG. *steigal*, prove the origin of ſteil (lit. 'mounting') from the cognates discussed under Steig. Comp. Du. *steil*, AS. *stǣgl*, *s'ēger*, 'steep'; to these are allied OHG. *stēchal*, *stēhhal*, MidHG. *stěckel* (*stěchel*), 'steep,' Bav., Alsat., MidHG., and LG. *stickel*, 'steep' (in the UpG. dialects ſteil seems to be entirely unknown).

Stein, m., 'stone,' from the equiv. Mid HG. and OHG. *stein*, m.; corresponding to Goth. *stains*, OIc. *steinn*, AS. *stán*, E. *stone* (to which E. dial. *steen*, 'stone vessel,' from AS. *stǣne*, 'pitcher' is allied; comp. OHG. *steinna*, 'pitcher'), Du. *steen*, OSax. *stén*. The common Teut. *staino*- is related pre-historically to OSlov. *stěna*, 'wall' (*stěnĭnŭ*, 'rocky, stony'), as well as to Gr. στία, στίον, 'pebble.'—Steinmetze, see under Metze (1).

Sleiß, m., 'rump, buttocks' (with MidG. *ei* instead of *eu*), from the equiv. MidHG. and OHG. *stiuz* (hence also the early Mod HG. variant Steuß), m., corresponding to Du. *stuit*. It is probably based on a Teut. *stüoot*-, which is primit. allied to Lat. *stiva*, 'plough handle.'

Stelle, f., 'place, spot, situation, office,' from MidHG. *stal*, m., 'standing-place' (comp. Stall), or more probably a recent derivative of ſtellen, MidHG. and OHG. *stellen*, 'to put up, erect, fix, establish,' a denominative of Teut. *stallo*-, standing-place,' discussed under Stall. From the Aryan root *stel*, 'to stand' (an extended form of Aryan *stā*, see ſtehen), comp. Stuhl and Stiel, and especially Gr. στέλλω, 'to put, send,' στόλος, 'expedition,' Sans. *sthūna* (for *sthulna*), 'pillar,' *sthal*, 'to stand firm.' To this word ſtillen and Stelle are also allied.

Stelze, f., 'stilt, wooden leg,' from the equiv. MidHG. *stelze*, OHG. *stelza*, f.; corresponding to Du. *stelt*, Dan. *stylte*, Swed. *stylta*, and the equiv. E. *stilt*. Probably a genuine Teut. word, the early history of which is, however, obscure.

ſtemmen, vb., 'to stem, check, oppose,' from MidHG. and OHG. *stemmen* (*stemen*), 'to check, restrain, cause to stand.' For the root *stam*, see under ſtammeln, ſtumm, ungeſtüm.

Stempel, m., 'stamp, die, pestle,' ModHG. only, properly a LG. word, of which the HG. form is *stempfel*; comp. Du. *stempel*, allied to ſtampfen.

Stengel, m., 'stem, stalk,' from the equiv. MidHG. *stengel*, OHG. *stengil*; a diminutive of Stange.

ſteppen, vb. 'to quilt, stitch,' from Mid HG. *steppen*, 'to prick here and there, sew in rows, stitch'; an intensive form from the root of Stift.

ſterben, vb., 'to die,' from the equiv. MidHG. *sterben*, OHG. *sterban*. str. vb., corresponding to OSax. *sterban*, Du. *sterven*, AS. *steorfan*, 'to die,' E. *to starve*. In East Teut. this term is wanting (comp the root discussed under *tet*). OIc., however, preserves a corresponding *starf*. n., 'work, trouble, effort,' to which *starfa*, 'to take pains,' and *stjarfe*, 'tetanus, locked jaw,' are allied. The parallel development of Gr. οἱ καμόντες, 'the dead,' from κάμνω, 'to take pains,' shows that we may assign, on the basis of the Scand. words, the primary meaning 'to torment oneself' to the West Teut. *sterban*. Unfortunately the early history of the Teut. root *sterb* is obscure. For the primit. Aryan root for 'to die' see under Mord.

Sterke, f., 'cow'; see Stärke.

Sterling, m., from MidHG. *sterlinc* (*ą*), m., 'a coin,' whence E. *sterling*. The Mid HG. word *sterlinc* (*stœrlinc*) indicates by its formation, which is similar to that of Pfenning and Schilling, that it is an old word; its early history is, however, obscure.

Stern, m., 'star,' from the equiv. Mid HG *sterne*, OHG. *sterno*, m. (OHG. and Mid HG. variant *stěrn*); comp. Goth. *stairnô*, f., OIc. *stjarna*, f., 'star.' OHG. *ster-no* seems to be linked with OHG. *sun-no*, *má-no*, like Goth. *stairnô*, f., with Goth. *sun-nô*, f.; the earlier MidHG. variant *sterre*, OHG. and OSax. *sterro*, lead to Du. *ster*, *star*, AS. *steorra*, E. *star*. The primary stem *ster* is common in the same sense to the Aryan group (comp. Mond and Sonne); to it correspond Sans. *star*, Zend *stare*, Gr. ἀστήρ, ἄστρον, Lat. *stella* (for *sterula*). Whether this root *ster* belongs to the Aryan root *str*, 'to scatter' (Stern, lit. 'dispenser of light'?), or to the Sans. root *as*, 'to throw' (Stern, lit. 'thrower of rays'?), is altogether

uncertain. To this is allied the ModHG. collective Gestirn, n., 'stars, constellation,' from MidHG. gestirne, OHG. gistirni.—
Stern, m., 'stern,' ModHG, only, comes from the equiv. E. stern (OIc. stjörn), a derivative of the root of steuern.

Sterz, m., 'tail, rump, plough handle,' from the equiv. MidHG. and OHG. sterz, m.; corresponding to Du. staart, AS. steort, E. start. A Teut. root stert, 'to project' or 'to turn' (see stürzen), has been assumed to explain the cognates; others connect it with Gr. στόρθη, 'prong, projecting point.'

stet, adj., 'fixed, stable, constant,' from the equiv. MidHG stæte, OHG. stâti, adj. (see the following word); a verbal adj. from the root sta in stehen (lit. 'that which can stand'). To this is allied stets, adv., 'steadily, constantly, always,' from the equiv. MidHG. stætes, properly a gen. of the adj.

stetig, adj., 'constant, continual,' from MidHG. stætec (g), with the variant stæte (OHG. stâti), adj., 'firm, constant, stable'; properly a verbal adj. of stehen. Comp. the preceding word.

Steuer (1.), f., 'aid, tax, duty, impost,' from MidHG. stiure, OHG. stiura, f., 'duty, tax,' properly 'aid, contribution, support, help.' With these general meanings the following word is connected.

Steuer (2.), n., 'rudder, helm,' from the equiv. late MidHG. (MidG.) stiure, n.; properly a LG. word, originally belonging only to the Teutons on the sea-coast (in OHG. stiura, f., 'rudder, stern'); comp. stuur, 'rudder,' AS. steór, n. (E. stern, see under Stern), OIc. styre, n., 'helm.' To this is allied steuern, 'to steer, pilot,' which originated under the influence of the substantive Steuer, from MidHG. and OHG. stiuren, 'to guide, lead, support'; comp. Du. stieren, sturen, AS. styran, E. to steer, and the equiv. OIc. stýra (Goth. stiurjan), 'to fix firmly, maintain.' These cognates, on account of their undoubted connection with Steuer, f., 'duty' (lit. 'support'?), have been linked with OIc. starr, 'stake,' and the equiv. Gr. σταυρός.

Stich, m., 'prick, thrust,' from MidHG. stich, OHG. stih (hh), m., 'prick, point' (comp. Goth. stiks, 'period of time'), from the root stik (see stechen). To this Stichel, m., 'graving tool, graver,' from MidHG. stichel, OHG. stihhil, m., 'sting,' is allied.—
sticheln, vb., 'to prick, stitch,' is an intensive of stechen by association with Stich.

stichen, vb., 'to stitch, embroider,' from MidHG. sticken, OHG. sticchen (from Teut. *stikjan), wk. vb., 'to pierce, thrust, stitch, embroider.' Originally a variant of stikan, 'to pierce,' from the root stik (see stechen, Stich); comp. E. to stitch, from AS. *sticcan, Du. stikken.—To this ersticken, 'to choke, suffocate,' from the equiv. MidHG. ersticken, OHG. irsticchen, is allied.

stieben, vb., 'to fly as dust, scatter, disperse,' from the equiv. MidHG. stieben, OHG. stiuban, str. vb. Allied to Du. stuiven, and the cognates of Staub; see the latter and stöbern.

Stief- in compounds is preserved throughout the Teut. group only as the first component; comp. MidHG. stief-bruoder, -kind, -muoter, -sun, -swester, -tohter, -vater; OHG. stiuf-bruoder, -chint, &c. (Du. stief-broeder, -kind, &c.). Corresponding to AS. steóp-sunu, -fæder, E. step-father, &c.: OIc. stjúpfaðer. That the word was used by itself at an earlier period is indicated by the derivatives OHG. stiufen, irstiufen, bistiufen, 'to rob one of his relatives (parents or children),' AS. âstýpan, 'to rob.' All further clue to its early history is unfortunately wanting.

Stiefel, m., 'boot,' from the equiv. Mid HG. stivel, stivâl (OHG. stivâl?), m.; the MidHG. variant stivâl points clearly to a loan-word from the equiv. Ital. stivále, m. (for v equiv. to MidHG. v, f, comp. Vers, Käfig), lit. 'a light summer covering made of leather for the feet' (from MidLat. æstivale, 'pertaining to summer'). The word was borrowed in HG. (it does not occur in the other Teut. dialects), probably in the 12th cent.

Stiege (1.), f., 'stair, staircase,' from the equiv. MidHG. stiege, OHG. stiega, f.; the same as Steg; the broken MidHG. ie is similar to MidHG. wiege, 'cradle,' and schief, 'awry' (see schief).

Stiege (2.), f. (dial. Steig), in the sense of 'score,' has been derived from the allied MidHG. stîge, f., 'stall for small cattle' (Swed. stia, 'pigsty'), it being assumed that a stall contained twenty sheep. Yet it is remarkable that the Crim. Goth. stega was used in the 16th cent. in the sense of 'score' (comp. Schock; E. score, lit. 'notch'; Du. snees, 'score,' lit. 'row, series').

Stieglitz, m., 'goldfinch,' from the equiv. MidHG. stigliz, stigelitz (tz), m.; a Slav. loan-word; comp. Czech stehlec (stehlic), 'thistle-finch,' and also Kiebitz.

Stiel, m., 'handle, stalk, pedicle,' from the equiv. MidHG. and OHG. *stil*, m. Phonetically the assumption that the word was borrowed from Lat. *stilus*, 'style' (for writing), is possible. It is more probable, however, that the words are primit. allied, on account of AS. *stela, steola*, 'handle' (E. diminutive *stalk*), and of Gr. στελεόν, στέλεχος, 'handle.' The cognates of Stall, Stelle, and still may also be primit. allied.

Stier, m., 'bull,' from the equiv. Mid HG. *stier*, OHG. *stior*; a common Teut. term; comp. Goth. *stiur*, AS. *steór*, E. *steer*, Du. *stier*. The remarkable variant OIc. *þjórr*, Dan. *tyr*, Swed. *tjur*, points to pre-Teut. *teuro*- and *steuro*-; to this OSlov. *turŭ*, 'bull,' Zend *staora*, 'draught cattle,' and the Sans. adj. *sthûra*, 'great, mighty' (OIc. *stórr*, OHG. *stûri*), are perhaps allied. Gr. ταῦρος (whence Lat. *taurus*) is based, as is indicated by OIr. *tarb*, on a primit. form *tarvos*.

stier, adj., 'staring,' ModHG. only; allied to starr.

Stift (1.), m., 'peg, tack, style, pencil,' from MidHG. *stift* (*stëft*), m., 'sting, thorn, peg,' OHG. *stëft*, m., 'peg.' A specifically HG. word, which is probably derived from the Aryan root *stĭp*, 'to project,' appearing in steif. Lat. *stĭpes*, 'stake, trunk (of a tree),' has also been connected with the same root.

Stift (2.), n., 'charitable foundation, monastery,' from early MidHG. *stift*, m. and n., 'foundation, establishing, building, ecclesiastical foundation,' also 'founding, regulation, arrangement,' to which MidHG. *stiften*, 'to found, build, arrange, regulate, devise, contrive, cause,' is allied. While the subst. is unknown to OHG., the OHG. vb. *stiften* occurs with the same meaning as the MidHG. vb. (comp. Du. *sticht, stichten*). The *ht* of AS. *stihtan*, 'to regulate, incite,' is abnormal; like OIc. *stëtt*, 'stone floor, foundation, it seems to point to a Teut. root *stihw*, 'to build, found.' The meaning of these cognates precludes any connection with Stift (1).

still, adj., 'still, silent, quiet,' from the equiv. MidHG. *stille*, OHG. (OSax.) *stilli*; corresponding to the equiv. Du. *stil*, AS. *stille*, E. *still* (adj. and adv.). A derivative of the Aryan root *stel*, 'to stand' (see Stall, stellen, and Stelle), with which Sans. *sthânu* (for *sthalnu*), 'standing, immovable,' is also allied.—stillen, vb., 'to still, pacify,' from MidHG. and OHG. *stillen*, 'to cause to be still, bring to a standstill' (E. *to still*), is a derivative of still.

Stimme, f., 'voice, sound,' from the equiv. MidHG. *stimme*, OHG. *stimma*, f., of which the older variant, *stimna*, corresponds to OSax. *stëmna* (*stëmma*), AS. *stëmn, stefn* (E. dim. *steven*, 'noise, cry'), Goth. *stibna*, 'voice.' It is uncertain whether *stebnô*- or *stibnô*- is the older form. The connection with Gr. στόμα, 'mouth,' is dubious.

stinken, vb., 'to stink,' from MidHG. *stinken*, OHG. *stinchan*. In OHG. and early MidHG. the verb signifies 'to emit a smell,' and may even mean 'to give forth a fragrant odour'; in MidHG. the modern meaning prevails. In AS. too, *stincan* may mean 'to emit a fragrant odour' or 'to stink'; comp. E. *to stink*. This West Teut. meaning, 'to emit a (pleasant or unpleasant) smell' (and also 'to perceive by smell, to scent'), can scarcely be reconciled with Goth. *stiggan*, 'to push,' and Scand. *stökkva*, 'to leap, squirt, hasten.' It is probably more closely connected with Gr. ταγγός, 'rancid' (comp. Gr. ταῦρος, equiv. to Goth. *stiur*).

Stirn, f., 'forehead, brow,' from the equiv. MidHG. *stirne*, OHG. *stirna* (for *sternja*), f.; a specifically HG. word (yet also in AS. *steornëde*, 'frontosus'?), for which Du. *voorhoofd*, AS. *foranheáfod*, E. *forehead* (OIc. *enne*, Goth. *anþi*, OHG. *endi*, equiv. to Lat. *antiae*), occur. In Bav., Hirn is generally used instead of Stirn. The form *sternjô*- has been connected with Gr. στέρνον, 'breast,' while 'broad' is assumed to be the intermediate idea, which is deduced from the root *ster*, in Lat. *sternere* and Gr. στρώννυμι, 'to spread out'; comp. OSlov. *strana*, 'district.'

stöbern, vb., 'to fly about, drift, drizzle,' ModHG. only, allied to earlier ModHG. Stöber, m., MidHG. *stöuber*, 'hound,' which is derived from MidHG. *stöuben*, 'to scare up, start up, chase away'; the latter is a factitive of stieben. To this is allied Mod HG. Gestöber, n., 'drifting,' formed from MidHG. *stöuben*, 'to raise dust.'

stochen, vb., ModHG. only, equiv. to E. *to stoke*; a derivative of the Aryan root *stug*, 'to push, thrust,' discussed under Stock.

Stock, m., 'stick, staff,' from MidHG. *stoc* (*ck*), OHG. *stoc* (*cch*), m., 'stick, staff, trunk' (of a tree, &c.); corresponding to Du. *stok*, AS. *stocc*, E. *stock*, OIc. *stokkr*.

The primary meaning 'stake, club, stick,' leads to the Sans. root *tuj*, 'to brandish or hurl weapons, set in violent motion' (for Sans. *t*, equiv. to Teut. *st*, comp. 𝔈𝔱𝔦𝔢𝔯). From Teut. are derived the Rom. class, Ital. *stocco*, 'rapier.' Allied also to 𝔈𝔱𝔲̈𝔠𝔨.

𝔖𝔱𝔬𝔣𝔣, m., 'stuff, material, matter,' ModHG. only, borrowed, like Du. *stof*, E. *stuff*, from Rom. Comp. the equiv. Fr. *étoffe*, Ital. *stoffa*, f., the origin of which has not been explained.

𝔖𝔱𝔬𝔣𝔣𝔢𝔩, m., 'foolish fellow,' an abbrev. of 𝔈𝔥𝔯𝔦𝔰𝔱𝔬𝔭𝔥; comp. 𝔐𝔢𝔱𝔷𝔢 and 𝔎𝔲̈𝔭𝔢𝔩.

𝔣𝔩𝔬̈𝔥𝔫𝔢𝔫, vb., 'to groan,' ModHG. only, properly a LG. word. Comp. the equiv. Du. *stenen*, AS. *stunian*, OIc. *stynja*. The verbal root *sten*, 'to groan,' is common to Teut.; comp. Sans. *stan*, 'to rustle, roar,' Gr. στένω, 'to groan, roar,' OSlov. *stenją*, 'to groan.' The root *sten* is a variant of the Aryan root *ten*, discussed under 𝔡𝔬𝔫𝔫𝔢𝔯𝔫.

𝔖𝔱𝔬𝔩𝔩𝔢, f., 𝔖𝔱𝔬𝔩𝔩𝔢𝔫, m., 'prop, post, gallery (of a mine),' from MidHG. *stolle*, OHG. *stollo*, m., 'support, post.' Derived, like 𝔈𝔱𝔞𝔩𝔩, 𝔰𝔱𝔢𝔩𝔩𝔢𝔫, and 𝔰𝔱𝔦𝔩𝔩, from the root *stal*, which appears also in Sans. *sthúnâ*. The latter points, like OHG. *stollo* (from *stolno-), to Aryan *stelnâ*, 'post'; for *ll* from *ln* comp. *voll* and 𝔚𝔢𝔩𝔩𝔢.

𝔣𝔱𝔬𝔩𝔭𝔢𝔯𝔫, vb., 'to stumble, trip,' early ModHG. only, an imitative form like 𝔥𝔢𝔩𝔣𝔢𝔯𝔫.

𝔖𝔱𝔬𝔩𝔷, adj., 'proud, haughty, arrogant,' from MidHG., late OHG. *stolz*, 'foolish, arrogant, stately, splendid, magnificent, high-minded.' The assumption that the word was borrowed from Lat. *stultus*, 'foolish,' whence Ital. *stolto*, 'foolish,' does not meet the case, for OFr. *estout*, 'arrogant, bold,' is borrowed from pre-HG. *stolto-, the meaning of which is scarcely explicable by Lat. *stultus;* only MidHG. *stolz*, 'foolish,' shows the influence of the Lat. and Ital. signification. Teut. *stolto- is considered to be cognate with 𝔈𝔱𝔢𝔩𝔷𝔢. E. *stout* seems to be borrowed from Mid Du. *stout* (for *stolt*), with a different development in meaning. — 𝔖𝔱𝔬𝔩𝔷, m., 'pride,' is a subst. lately formed from the adj.

𝔖𝔱𝔬̈𝔭𝔣𝔢𝔩, 𝔖𝔱𝔬̈𝔭𝔣𝔢𝔩, m., 'stopper, cork,' a ModHG. derivative of 𝔣𝔱𝔬𝔭𝔣𝔢𝔫, vb., 'to stuff, cram, mend,' MidHG. *stopfen*, OHG. *stopfôn, of which a variant *stoppôn*, wk. vb., 'to stuff,' occurs; to the latter, Du. *stoppen*, AS. *forstoppian*, E. *to stop*, correspond.

The assumption that the word was borrowed from MidLat. *stuppare*, 'to stop with tow' (from Lat. *stuppa*, 'tow'; comp. Ital. *stoppare*, Fr. *étouper*), is open to objection. It is more closely related to Mid HG. *stupfen*, *stüpfen*, OHG. *stopfôn*, 'to pierce.' With the implied Aryan root *stup* (*tup*) is connected Sans. *stump* (*tump*), 'to pu-h, thrust' (Gr. τύπτω ?).

𝔖𝔱𝔬𝔭𝔭𝔢𝔩, f., 'stubble,' properly a MidG. and LG. form; in genuine HG. we have UpG. 𝔖𝔱𝔲𝔭𝔣𝔢𝔩, from MidHG. *stupfel*, OHG. *stupfila*, f.; comp. the equiv. Du. *stoppel*, E. *stubble*, and OSwed. *stubb*. Whether the cognates are borrowed from Lat. *stipula* (late Lat. *stupila*, equiv. to Ital. *stoppio*, Fr. *étouble*, 'stubble') is uncertain ; nor has it been decided what connection there is between the Teut. word and its non-Teut. representatives (such as OSlov. *stĭblo*, 'stubble'). On the other hand, the root-syllable of 𝔖𝔱𝔬𝔭𝔭𝔢𝔩 with that of 𝔰𝔱𝔢𝔭𝔣𝔢𝔫 may point to Aryan *stup*, 'to prick, pierce,' or rather it may with OIc. *stúpa*, 'to project' (to which E. *steeple*, from *steep*, is allied), be traced back to primary meaning, 'to stand out rigid, jut, project.' It might also be connected with the nasalised cognates of 𝔖𝔱𝔲𝔪𝔭𝔣, which, with Swiss *stäbes*, E. *stub*, and OIc. *stúfr*, *stúfe*, 'stump,' presume a Teut. root *stŭp*, *stŭb*, 'to hew off.'

𝔣𝔱𝔬𝔭𝔭𝔢𝔫, vb., 'to stop,' ModHG. only ; borrowed, like other nautical terms, from LG. Comp. E. *to stop* and 𝔙𝔢𝔯𝔟.

𝔖𝔱𝔬̈𝔭𝔣𝔢𝔩, m., see 𝔖𝔱𝔬̈𝔭𝔣𝔢𝔩.

𝔖𝔱𝔬̈𝔯, m, 'sturgeon,' from the equiv. MidHG. *störe*, *stüre*, OHG. *sturo*, *sturio*, m.; corresponding to Du. *steur*, AS. *styrja* (*styra*). The Teut. term *sturjo* passed in the form *sturio* (MidLat.) into Rom. ; comp. Ital. *storione*, Fr. *esturgeon*, whence the equiv. E. *sturgeon*. The origin of the Teut. word is obscure.

𝔖𝔱𝔬𝔯𝔠𝔥, m., 'stork,' from the equiv. MidHG. *storch* (variant *store*, whence 𝔈𝔱𝔢𝔯𝔣, common to UpG. and West Thuring.); OHG. *storah* (*hh*), also *store*, m. ; comp. AS. *store*, E. *stork*, and the equiv. OIc. *storkr*. Its prehistoric connection with Gr. τόργος, 'vulture,' is dubious. On the other hand, the Slav. cognates, OSlov. *stĭrkŭ*, Russ. *sterchŭ*, 'stork,' must have been borrowed from OTeut.

𝔣𝔱𝔬̈𝔯𝔢𝔫, vb., 'to stir up, disturb, poke, rake,' from MidHG. *stœren*, OHG. *stôren* (*störren* from *störjan, *staurjan), wk. vb., 'to scatter, destroy, annihilate'; to these are allied North Fris. *stiuren*, and with gradation AS. *styrian*, E. *to stir*, but hardly the cognates of ſtreuen. The early history is obscure.

Storren, m., 'stump of a tree,' from the equiv. MidHG. *storre*, OHG. *storro*, m., which is connected with OHG. *storrên*, MidHG. *storren*, 'to stand out, project' (Goth. *andstaúrran*, 'to grumble, murmur'; root *stur*, see ſtarr. To this is allied ſtörrig, adv., 'stubbornly, obstinately,' ModHG. only; lit. 'clod-like, of the nature of a clod.'

ſtoßen, vb., 'to push, thrust,' from the equiv. MidHG. *stôӡen*, OHG. *stôӡan*, str. vb., corresponding to Goth. *stautan*, OSax. *stôtan*, Du. *stooten*. The common Teut. strong verbal root *staut* corresponds in non-Teut. to an Aryan root *tud*, by gradation *taud*, which appears in Lat. *tundo*, 'to beat, bruise, stun' (Lat. *tudes*, 'hammer'), and the Sans. root *tud*, 'to push, thrust'; for Teut. *st*, equiv. to Aryan *t*, comp. Stier and Sterb. See the following word.

ſtottern, vb., 'to stutter, stammer.' ModHG. only (in Swab. *gaksen*, Austr. *stückezen*), formed from MidG. and LG., in which *stotteren* (so too in Du.) is an intensive of *stoten*, 'to push, thrust' (ſtottern, lit. 'to stumble repeatedly'); corresponding to E. *to stutter*. See the preceding word.

Stoïӡ, m., 'stump of a tree,' ModHG. only; early history obscure.

ſtrach, adj., 'extended, direct, tense,' from MidHG. *strac* (*ck*), 'straight, tight,' to which ModHG. ſtracks, adv., 'straightway, immediately,' from MidHG. *strackes*, is allied; so too ModHG. ſtrecken, 'to stretch, extend.'

Strafe, f., 'punishment, penalty, fine,' from the equiv. MidHG. (rare), *strâfe*, f.; OHG. *strâfa, f., is, like the verb corresponding to ModHG. and MidHG. *strâfen*, 'to punish,' not recorded. The cognates are specifically HG. (whence Du. *straf*), and are wanting in the other Teut. dialects. The late appearance of the word does not prove that it was borrowed. The history of the cognates is obscure.

ſtraff, adj., 'stretched, tense, tight,' from MidHG. (rare) *straf*(*ff*), 'tense, strict'; probably a LG. word corresponding to Du. *straf*. Its early history is, however, obscure. It has been supposed that Ital. *strappare*, 'to tear out,' is borrowed from Teut. by assuming a root *strap*, 'to draw'; hence ſtraff, lit. 'drawn tight'?.

Strahl, m., 'ray, beam,' from MidHG. *strâl*, *strâle*, m. and f., OHG. *strâla*, f., 'arrow, flash of lightning' (OHG. *donerstrâla*, 'flash of lightning'); corresponding to Du. *straal*, AS. *strǽl*, 'arrow.' These West Teut. cognates (whence Ital. *strale*, 'arrow') are closely connected with OSlov. *strěla*, 'arrow' (whence Russ. *strělá*, 'arrow,' hence Strelize, lit. 'marksman, archer'). To these are allied ſtrahlen, 'to beam, radiate' (occurring in ModHG only), and also the following word.

Strähle, f., 'comb,' from the equiv. MidHG. *stræl*, m., to which ModHG. and MidHG. *strælen*, 'to comb,' is allied; the equiv. OHG. vb. *strâlen* (*strâllen, *strâlian) presumes also for OHG. a subst. *strâl*, meaning 'comb.' It is not improbable that the separate teeth of the comb were regarded as arrows, rays.

Strähne, f., 'skein, hank,' from the equiv. MidHG. *strën*, *strēne*, OHG. *strēno*, m., corresponding to MidDu. *strene*, Du. *streen*. Its connection with the preceding word is uncertain.

ſtramm, adj., 'dense, vigorous, huge.' ModHG. only, a LG. word; corresponding to Du. *stram*, North Fris. *striam*, 'bolt upright.'

ſtrampeln, vb., 'to kick, struggle,' ModHG. only, orig. a LG. word; comp. Du. *strompelen*, 'to stumble, stagger.' Its early history is obscure.

Strand, m., 'strand, beach,' from late MidHG. (MidG.) *strant* (*d*), m., adopted as a literary term from LG.; comp. Du. *strand*, AS. *strand*, E. *strand*, OIc. *strǫnd*. These cognates, from which OFr. *étrain* is borrowed, cannot be traced farther back. To this is allied the ModHG. ſtranden, equiv. to Du. *stranden*, E. *to strand*. Comp. Ufer.

Strang, m., 'rope, string, halter, trace,' from MidHG. *stranc*, *strange*, m. and f., OHG. *strang*, m., 'string, rope'; comp. Du. *streng*, AS. *streng*, E. *string*, OIc. *strengr*, 'string, strap.' This Teut. *strangi*- seems to be the adj. ſtreng (lit. 'strong'), used as a subst. Yet Strang, like Gr. στραγγάλη, 'string,' and Lat. *stringere*, 'to draw tight,' might be connected with an Aryan root *strenk* (*streng*), 'to turn.'

Straße, f., 'street, road,' from the equiv. MidHG. *strâӡe*, f., OHG. *strâӡa*, f.; a common West Teut. term; comp. Du. *straat*, AS. *strǽt*, E. *street*, OSwed. *strata*, 'road,' ModSwed. *strât* (OIc. *strǽti* and OSwed. *strǽti* are derived from OE.). The form *strâta*, 'street,' was borrowed in the 1st cent.

(perhaps contemporaneously with Pfund, Sad, Münze, &c.) from MidLat. *stráta* (scil. *via*, lit. 'paved road') before the Lat. *t* was softened to *d* in Rom.; comp. Ital. *strada*, Span. *estrada*, Fr. (dial.) *étrée*, to which OIr. *sráth*, 'street,' is allied.

sträuben, vb., 'to ruffle or bristle up, resist,' from MidHG. *striuben* (for which *striubeln* occurs), OHG. *strūben*, wk. vb., also MidHG. *strūben*, OHG. *strūbēn*, 'to stand motionless, look fixedly, rise aloft, bristle up, resist.' Comp. MidHG. *strūp (b)*, 'bristling up,' *strobeleht*, *strūbeleht*, 'bristly.' To this ſtreifen is allied. In the non-Teut. languages indubitable cognates of the genuine Teut. root *strūb*, 'to be coarse,' are wanting; yet comp. Gr. στρυφνός, 'bitter, firm, stout' ?.

Strauch, m., 'shrub, bush,' from the equiv. MidHG. *strūch*, m. (to which the ModHG. collective Gesträuch is allied); wanting in OHG. Corresponding to Du. *struik*, 'shrub' (also Du. *stronk*, 'shrub,' equiv. to LG. Strunf, with a nasalised root syllable). The stem is not found in other languages; the relation of the cognates of ModHG. ſtraucheln is dubious.

ſtraucheln, vb., 'to stumble,' from the equiv. MidHG. *strūcheln*, an intensive form of OHG. *strūhhēn*, *strūhhōn*, 'to stumble'; it corresponds to the equiv. Du. *struikelen*. To this is allied the root vb. OIc. *strjūka*, 'to stroke, rub'; but ModHG. Strauch is scarcely connected with this Teut. root *strūk*, 'to glide' (at all events straucheln is not 'to entangle oneself in bushes'). It is uncertain whether Gr. στρεύγεσθαι, 'to grow tired,' is a cognate.

Strauß (1.), m., 'quarrel, conflict, fight,' from the equiv. MidHG. *strūʒ*, m.; to this MidHG. *striuʒen*, 'to resist,' AS. *strútian*, 'to quarrel,' is allied.

Strauß (2.), m., 'crest, tuft, nosegay,' from the equiv. late MidHG. **strūʒ*, m., which may be inferred from *gestriuʒe* and *striuʒach*, 'cluster of bushes.'

Strauß (3.), m., 'ostrich,' from the equiv. MidHG. and OHG. *strūʒ*, m.; it seems to be rather a corruption of late Lat. *s'ruthio*, 'ostrich,' on which AS. *strȳta* is based (comp. Ital. *struzzo*, Fr. *autruche*, whence E. *ostrich*), than a permutation of pre-HG. **strūto*-. The word may have been borrowed contemporaneously with Pfau. On the other hand, a direct connection with Gr. στρουθίον, or rather ἡ μεγάλη στρουθός, 'ostrich' (στρουθός, 'sparrow'), is impos-

sible. Moreover, it is remarkable that the Germans say Vogel Strauß, in the same way as the Fr. *autruche* (Span. *av-estruz*) from *avistrutio*, is linked with Lat. *avis*.

streben, vb., 'to strive, struggle, endeavour,' from MidHG. *strēben*, wk. vb., 'to move violently, exert oneself, contend.' The OHG. strong verb corresponding to the non-recorded wk. vb. **strěběn* would be **strīban (*strifan* ?), as is assumed by the Rom. loan-words. Comp. OFr. *estriver*, 'to fight, wrestle,' *estrif*, 'contest,' whence E. *to strive*, *strife*, are borrowed.

strecken, vb., 'to stretch, extend,' from MidHG. *strecken*, OHG. *strecchan*, wk. vb., 'to straighten, make tense, extend, stretch'; corresponds to Du. *strekken*, AS. *streččan*, E. *to stretch*. The corresponding adj. ſtrad (comp. also OHG. *stracchēn*, 'to be extended'), points to a Teut. root *strak* (for *srak*, a variant of *rak* in recken ?), which is perhaps connected with the root of Strang and ſtrenge. It is doubtful whether the HG. cognates are borrowed from Ital. *straccare*, 'to exhaust, fatigue.'

ſtreichen, vb., 'to rub,' from MidHG. *strīchen*, str. vb., 'to smooth, make strokes, draw, rub, besmear,' OHG. *strīhhan*, str. vb., 'to rub.' To this is allied the Mod HG. wk. vb. ſtreichen, from MidHG. *streichen* (OHG. *streihhōn*), wk. vb., 'to graze, touch, stroke,' as well as ModHG. Streich, m., from MidHG. *streich*, m., 'blow, cut, stroke,' and ModHG. Strich, m., from MidHG. and OHG. *strich*, m., 'stroke, line' (comp. Goth. *striks*). The correspondences in the other Teut. dialects are Du. *strijken*, AS. *strīcan*, E. *to strike* (whence *stroke*). With the pre-Teut. root *strīg* are connected Lat. *stringere*, 'to strip off, unsheath, touch, graze slightly,' Lat. *striga*, 'stroke,' OSlov. *strigą* (*strišti*), 'to shear, cut off.'

Streifen, m., 'stripe, streak,' from late MidHG. *streif*, m., 'expedition,' allied to MidHG. *streifen* (*streipfen*), wk. vb., 'to glide, march, roam'; comp. Du. *strippen*, 'to strip off leaves' (*streep*, 'stripe, streak, stroke'). Further cognates are wanting.

ſtreifen, vb., 'to graze slightly, strip off,' from MidHG. *ströufen* (*stroufen*), wk. vb., besides which a rare form, *streifen*, 'to skin, flay, chastise,' occurs. OHG. **stroufen* and Goth. **straupjan* are also indicated by Du. *stroopen*, 'to strip, strip off leaves, make predatory excursions,' AS. *bestrȳpan*, E. *to strip*. ModHG. ſtrūben is also more remotely allied. Prehistoric

z

cognates of the Teut. root *straup* are wanting. For ModHG. *ei*, equiv. to MidHG. *ou*, see **Schleife**.

Streit, m., 'dispute, quarrel, strife,' from the equiv. MidHG. and OHG. *strît*, m.; allied to ModHG. **streiten**, MidHG. *strîten*, OHG. *strîtan*, str. vb., 'to quarrel, fight.' OHG. *einstriti*, 'stubborn,' OSax. *strîd*, 'zeal,' and OIc. *strīðr*, 'stubborn, severe, strong,' show that **Streit** has gone through the same development of meanings as **Krieg** (lit. 'exertion'); OIc. *strīð*, n., 'pain, grief, oppression,' is, however, remarkable (yet comp. the cognates of Mod HG. *tapfer*). Pre-historic cognates of the Teut. root *strid* (for *strī*?, *srī*?) are wanting; yet comp. Sans. *sridh*, 'enemy.'

streng, adj., 'strict, severe, stern,' from MidHG. *strenge*, adj., OHG. *strengi*, 'strong, brave, hard, unfriendly' (to which the adv. MidHG. *strange*, OHG. *strango*, is allied); comp. OSax. *strang*, Du. *streng*, AS. and E. *strong*, and the equiv. OIc. *strangr*. Its connection with **Strang** (*Strenge*, lit. 'tense') has been already suggested, yet comp. also Lett. *stringt*, 'to grow tight, withered.'—**strengen** (in **anstrengen**), from MidHG. and OHG. *strengen*, 'to press, urge,' is a nominal verb.

Streu, f., 'litter, bed of straw,' from the equiv. MidHG. *ströu*, f., allied to **streuen**, from the equiv. MidHG. *ströuwen* (*strouwen*), OHG. *streuwen* (*strouwen*), wk. vb. To this correspond Goth. *straujan*, OSax. *strewian*, Du. *strooijen*, AS. *streowian*, E. *to strew*. The common Teut. *straujan* (to which **Streb** is allied), whence Ital. *sdrajarsi*, 'to stretch away,' is borrowed, is connected in some inexplicable manner with the Aryan root *ster* (*strō*), in Lat. *sternere*, Gr. στορέν-νυμι, στρώννυμι, and the Sans. root *str*, 'to strew.'

Strich, see **streichen**.

Strich, m., 'string, cord,' from the equiv. MidHG. and OHG. *stric (ck)*, m. Its connection with **Strang** or **streichen** is dubious; it is rather related to Sans. *sraj*, 'winding, twisted ornament,' or Sans. *rajju*, 'string' (for Teut. *str* from Aryan *sr*, comp. **Schwester**, **Strom**, and **strecken**).—ModHG. **stricken**, 'to knit,' from MidHG. *stricken*, OHG. *stricchen*, 'to lace, clasp, plait,' is probably a derivative.

Striegel, m., 'currycomb,' from the equiv. MidHG. *strigel*, OHG. *strigil*, m.; to this **striegeln**, 'to comb,' from the equiv. MidHG. *strigelen*, is allied. The word is borrowed from Lat. *strīgilis*, 'scraper (used by bathers), flesh-brush' (Ital. *stregghia*, *streglia*, Fr. *étrille*, 'currycomb'). It is scarcely related directly to **streichen** (Aryan root *strik*, *strig*).

Strieme, m. and f., 'stripe, streak, scar,' from MidHG. *strieme* (*streime*, *strîme*), m., 'stripe'; OHG. *strīmo* (to which *strimil*, MidHG. *strîmel*, is allied), 'stripe,' is an isolated relic of a Teut.-Aryan root *strī*, which is not found elsewhere.

Strippe, f., 'string, strap, band,' a MidG. and LG. form for the genuine MidHG. *strüpfe*. Yet comp. also Swiss *ltruppe*, 'strap.'

Strobel, m., 'pine cone, strobile,' Mod HG. only, allied to MidHG. *strobelen*, OHG. *strobalôn*. See **stráuben**.

Stroh, m., 'straw,' from the equiv. Mid HG. and OHG. *strô* (gen. *strawes*, *strauwes*, *strôwes*), n.; a common Teut. word. Comp. Du. *stroo*, AS. *streaw*, E. *straw*, OIc. *strá* (Goth. *strawa*-), n. Its connection with **streuen** is evident, yet its exact relation is uncertain (**Stroh**, lit. 'hangings, embossed paper'?).

Strom, m., 'stream, torrent, current,' from the equiv. MidHG. *strôm* (*stroum*), OHG. *stroum*; common to Teut. in the form *straumo*-. Comp. OSax. *strôm*, Du. *stroom*, AS. *streám*, E. *stream*, and the equiv. OIc. *straumr*. Teut. *straumo*- for *srou-mo*- is based on the Aryan root *srū* (*srou*), 'to flow,' which appears in Gr. ῥέω (for *σρεFω; ῥύσις, 'flowing,' for *sru-ti-s*), Sans. root *sru*, 'to flow,' OIr. *sruth*, 'river,' and *sruaim* (base *sroumen*), 'stream.' For the evolution of Aryan *sr* to *str* see **Schwester** and **Strich**.

strotzen, vb., 'to be puffed up, teem, boast of,' from the equiv. late MidHG. *strotzen*, wk. vb. The Tent. root *strŭt*, which is not widely diffused, appears in E. *strut* (to which OIc. *þrútenn*, 'swollen,' is allied; comp. OIc. *þjórr*, equiv. to HG. **Stier**). To this ModHG. **Strauß**, 'contest,' with the evolved meaning 'to swell with anger,' and its cognates are allied ?.

Strudel, m., 'eddy, whirlpool, vortex,' from the equiv. late MidHG. *strudel*, m. A graded form from OHG. *strêdan*, str. vb., 'to roar, bubble'; Lat. *strīdere*, 'to whiz,' is not connected with the HG. cognates.

Strumpf, m., 'stocking,' from MidHG. *strumpf*, m., 'stump, trunk (of a tree, of a body).' These meanings of the MidHG. word show that it is equivalent to the following word (*strumpo- for *strunqo-?). The ModHG. sense results from the originally current compound Hofenftrumpf (hence lit. 'the end of the hose, short hose').

Strunk, m., 'trunk, stem, stump,' from the equiv. late MidHG. strunc, m., which, like the preceding word and Strauch, points to a Teut. root strŭk. It corresponds to Du. stronk.

ftruppig, adj., 'rough, bristly, scrubby,' see ſträubeln. Geſtrüpp, 'brambles, bushes,' is a collective term formed from it in ModHG.

Stube, f., 'room, chamber,' from Mid HG. stube, OHG. stuba, f., 'room with means for heating, sitting-room, bathroom'; common to OTeut.; comp. Du. stoof, 'foot-stove, drying-room,' AS. stofa, E. stove, OIc. stofa, 'room, bathroom with a stove.' Although the Romance origin of the cognates is impossible (Ital. stufa, Fr. étuve, 'sweating-room, stove,' are certainly borrowed from Teut.), this does not prove that the words are genuinely Teut. The word stuba was adopted in Finn. as tupa, in Lith. as stubà; comp. OSlov. istŭba, izba, Hung. szoba, Turk. soba, 'room.' The primary meaning of the Teut. word is 'heated room,' as may be inferred from Du. stoven, 'to stew, warm up' (whence Ital. stufare, Fr. etuver, 'to foment').

Stüber, m., Nafenftüber, m., 'fillip,' ModHG. only, allied to LG. stubben, 'to push.' In the sense of 'stiver' (a coin), the word, which first occurs in ModHG., is obscure; it is, however, met with as Du. stuiver and Swed. styfver.

Stück, n., 'piece, article,'from the equiv. MidHG. stücke, OHG. stucchi, n. ; a common Teut. word ; comp. OSax. stukki, Du. stuk, AS. stýćće, OIc. stykke, n., 'piece.' Allied to Stech, and, like the latter word, probably means lit. 'that which is cut off or hewn to pieces.' The secondary meaning 'bark' of OHG. stucchi is indicated by Ital. stucco, 'gypsum, stucco,' whence again ModHG. Stuck, 'stucco,' m., Studatur, f., 'stucco-work.'

Stufe, f., 'step, degree, grade,' from the equiv. MidHG. stuofe, OHG. stuofa, f., both of which are rare (comp. Du. stoep, 'threshold'). A graded form from the root stap, 'to go' (AS. stôpol, 'footprint'), which appears in ModHG. Staffel and E. to step. Comp. also Tritt in the sense of Stufe.

ftufen, ſtoſen, vb., 'to cook slowly,' ModHG. only, from LG. Comp. Du. stoven under Stube.

Stuhl, m., 'chair, seat,' from the equiv. MidHG. and OHG. stuol, m. ; corresponding to OSax. stôl, Du. stoel, AS. stôl, E. stool, OIc. stôll. A common Teut. noun, derived from the Aryan root stā̆, 'to stand' (see ſtehen), or from the Aryan root stal, 'to put, place' (see ſtellen), hence Stuhl, lit. 'stand, frame'?. It corresponds in the non-Teut. languages to Lith. pastólas, 'stand, frame,' OSlov. stolŭ, 'seat, throne,' Gr. στήλη, 'pillar.'

Stulpe, f., 'pot-lid, coat-cuff,' ModHG. only, from LG. Comp. Du. stulp, 'lid of a stewpot,' and stulpen, 'to cover with a lid,' whence ModHG. ſtülpen, 'to put on a lid' (stelpen, 'to check,' to which OIc. stôlpe, 'post,' is allied). Early history obscure.

ftumm, adj., 'dumb, silent,' from the equiv. MidHG. and OHG. (and OSax.) stum (mm); corresponding to Du. stom, 'dumb.' Its connection with the cognates of ſtammeln (root stam) is undoubted. Mid HG. stęmmen, OHG. stęmmen (from stamjan), 'to stop, check' (comp. ſtemmen and ungestüm), shows that ſtammeln and ſtumm ſein mean lit. 'to falter (in speaking).'

Stummel, m., 'stump,' from MidHG. stummel, stumbel, OHG. stumbal, m., 'piece cut off, stump'; properly an adj. used as a subst., from OHG. stumbal, MidHG. stumbel, 'mutilated.' This word is based (like the equiv. OHG. and MidHG. stumpf, adj. and subst. ; see Stumpf) on a pre-Teut. root sthmb, 'to mutilate,' which appears in Lith. stìmbras, 'stump,' stámbras, stembrýs, and stémbras, 'stem, stalk,' stúmbas, 'trunk, stump,' stambús, 'coarse.'—To this verſtümmeln, vb., 'to mutilate,' from the equiv. MidHG. verstümbelen, OHG. stumbilôn, is allied.

Stump, m., 'stump,' a LG. form for HG. Stumpf, MidHG. and OHG. stumpf. Corresponding to Du. stomp, E. stump (also OIc. stúfr, 'stump'?). (ModHG. Stümper, 'bungler, blunderer,' lit. 'mutilated person,' is also properly LG. ; comp. Du. stomper). The adj. ſtumpf, 'lopped, docked, blunt,' comes from the equiv. OHG. and MidHG. stumpf; Du. stomp, 'blunt.' Its connection with Stummel is certain ; besides the Teut. root stumb (Aryan stemp), in ModHG. Stummel, we have to assume an equiv. root stump (Aryan stemb), which appears in Lith. stambras, 'stump.'—

Stümper, m., 'bungler, blunderer,' early ModHG. only, is a derivative of the LG. form Stump.

Stumpf, adj., see the preceding word.

Stunde, f., 'hour, time, league,' from MidHG. *stunde*, OHG. *stunta*, f., 'time, period of time' (the ModHG. signification 'hora' first occurs in late MidHG., the primary meaning was 'undefined period'). Corresponding to OSax. *stunda*, AS. *stund*, E. dial. *stound*, OIc. *stund*, 'space of time'; Du. *stond*, 'moment.' The pre-historic connections of the word (perchance with **Staub**, **gestauben**; hence **Stunde**, 'rest, repose'?) are uncertain.

stupfen, vb., 'to poke, push,' from MidHG. and OHG. *stupfen* (*stüpfen*). See under **stopfen**.

sturen, vb., 'to stare at,' ModHG. only. A graded form, from **starr**.

Sturm, m., 'storm, tumult,' from MidHG. and OHG. *sturm*, m., 'tempest, fight'; comp. Du. *storm*, AS. and E. *storm*, and the equiv. OIc. *stormr*. From the common Teut. *storm* (*sturm*) are derived the Romance cognates, Ital. *stormo*, 'concourse, encounter, quarrel,' which proves the primitive use of the word in the figurative sense of 'fight' (E. *stour* is based on the corresponding OFr. *estour*). The Teut. root *stur* is a relic of the Aryan root *ser* (*sr* from *stur*?), to which Gr. ὁρμή, 'attack, impact,' Sans. root *sr*, 'to stream, hasten,' belong (for *str* from *sr*, see **Schwester** and **Strom**). Others prefer to regard the word as primitively cognate with Lat. *sternere*, 'to throw down.'

stürzen, vb., 'to hurl, overturn, overthrow, sink, plunge,' from MidHG. *stürzen*, OHG. *sturzen* (from **sturzjan*, **sturtjan*), wk. vb., 'to hurl, sink, turn, cover by inverting'; corresponding to Du. *storten*. Allied probably to E. *to start* (*to startle*, from AS. *steartlian*). The early history of the Teut. root *stert* (to which **Sterz** is allied?) cannot be traced farther back.

Stute, f., 'mare,' from MidHG. *stuot*, f., 'breeding stud, mare' (for the evolution of a collective meaning see **Kamerab** and **Frauenzimmer**), OHG. *stuta*, f., 'drove of horses.' Corresponding to AS. *stód*, equiv. to E. *stud*, AS. *stéda* (E. *steed*), 'stallion'; OIc. *stóð*, 'stud, number of horses,' and *stedda* (from **stádda*), f., 'mare'; comp. also MidE. *stott*, 'horse.' ModHG. **Gestüt**, n., 'stud,' is a recent collective form. OSlov. *stado*, Lith. *stodas*, 'drove of horses,' are clearly related to the Teut. cognates, but they may with as good reason be regarded as loan-words; yet comp. Lith. *stóné*, 'stable' (for horses). The whole of the cognates are connected with the Aryan root *stā*, 'to stand' (OHG. *stuota*, lit. 'stock'? 'stable'?).

stutzen, vb., 'to stop short, hesitate, be startled, to cut short,' from late MidHG. *stutzen*, wk. vb., 'to scare away'; allied to MidHG. *stutz*, 'push, impact' (Teut. root *staut*, see **stoßen**); comp. Du. *stuiten*, 'to check, rebound.'—**Stutzer**, m., 'fop, dandy,' ModHG. only, lit. 'one who wears gay clothes.'—**stutzig**, adj., 'curtailed, stubborn, startled,' is also allied.

stützen, vb., 'to prop, support,' from the equiv. MidHG. (*under-*)*stützen*, OHG. (*untar-*)*stuzzen*; allied to MidHG. and Mod HG. *stütze*. OHG. *stuzzen*, from **stutjan*, points to a Teut. root *stut*, besides which OHG. *studen*, OIc. *styðja*, 'to fix firmly, prop,' and AS. *stuðu*, *studu*, 'post' (E. *stud*), presume a Teut. root *stup* (*stud*). The early history of the cognates is obscure.

suchen, vb., 'to seek, search,' from the equiv. MidHG. *suochen* (*süechen*), OHG. *suohhan* (*suohhen*); a common Teut. verb, properly strong. Comp. Goth. *sôkjan*, AS. *sêcan*, E. *to seek* (and *to beseech*), Du. *zoeken*, OSax. *sôkian*, 'to seek.' The strong verbal root *sôk*, from Aryan *sâg*, has primit. cognates in Gr. ἡγέομαι, 'to lead,' and especially in Lat. *sāgire*, 'to trace out,' and OIr. *sáigim*, 'to seek.' To these are allied the cognates of **Sache**.

Sucht, f., 'sickness, disease,' from the equiv. MidHG. and OHG. *suht*, f.; an abstract formation from Goth. *siukan*, str. vb., 'to be ill'; see **siech** (and **schwach**?). Corresponding to Goth. *sauhts*, OIc. *sótt* (E. only *sick*), Du. *zucht* (and *ziekte*). The Germans often instinctively connect **Sucht** with *suchen* (hence **Sucht nach etwas**, 'rage for something').

sucheln, vb., 'to suckle,' ModHG. only, intensive of **saugen**.

Sud, see **Süden**.

sudeln, vb., 'to splash, soil, daub,' from late MidHG. *sudeln*, 'to dirty'; lit. perhaps 'to cook badly' (MidHG. *sudel*, 'keeper of a cookshop'); allied to **sieden**.

Süden, m., 'south'; the strictly HG. form is **Sund**, which survives in the proper names **Sundgau**, **Sundheim**, &c.; comp. OHG. *sundwint*, 'south wind,' *sundarwint* (MidHG. *sundenvint*). Yet the simple form of the word became obsolete at an early period in UpG. (the term used being **Mittag**), the names of the other cardinal points being also unknown. The loss of the n in Süben (MidHG. *sunden*. OHG. *sundan*) points to the adoption of the word from LG. The primit. Teut. stem *sunþ-*, 'south,' is also assumed by OIc. *sunnan*, AS. *sűðan*, 'from the south,' AS. *sűð*, Du. *zuid*, OSax. *sűth*, 'south.' The term *sunþ-*, 'south,' is as specifically Teut. as Norten and Westen. Whether *sunþ-* is derived from *sun-*, in Goth. *sun-nô*, 'sun,' and means lit. 'sun-side,' is not certain (yet note Ossen as 'dawn-side').

Sühne, f., 'atonement, expiation, reconciliation,' from MidHG. (rare) *süene* (mostly *suone*), f., 'atonement, reconciliation, sentence,' OHG. *suona*, f., 'sentence, court, reconciliation.' To this is allied ModHG. sühnen, vb., 'to atone for, expiate, conciliate,' from MidHG. *sűenen*, OHG. *suonen*, 'to conciliate, reconcile, equalise' (OIIG. 'to judge'). OHG. *suona*, 'court,' and OIc. *són*, 'sacrifice,' appear to be connected with a root *sűn*, 'to set up,' from which Lat. *sânus*, 'healthy,' and ModHG. gesund may have been derived. Deriv. versöhnen, 'to reconcile.'

Sulze, Sülze, f., 'pickle, brine, pickled or salted meat,' from MidHG. *sulze, sülze*, OHG. *sulza* (from **sultja*), f., 'salt water, pickled sausage,' comp. OSax. *sultia*, 'salt water,' Du. *zult*, 'pickled meat'; undoubtedly a graded form of Salz. From the Teut. word is derived Ital *solcio*, 'preserve, pickles.'

summen, vb., 'to hum,' from the equiv. late MidHG. *summen*, wk. vb.; an onomatopoetic form.

Sumpf, m., 'swamp, bog, marsh,' from the equiv. MidHG. *sumpf* (wanting in OHG., in which *sumft* is used). Corresponding to Du. *somp*, and with an old gradation E. *swamp* (dial. *sump*). OHG. *giswumft* and Goth. *swumfsl*, 'pond,' are differently derived. Its connection with schwimmen (Sumpf, 'porous soil'?) is very dubious; it is preferable to connect it with OIc. *svǫppr*, 'sponge.' The Teut. root was probably *swemp*; E. dial. *swanky*, 'marshy,' may point to an orig. *sweng*.

Sund, m., 'sound, strait,' early Mod HG. only, a MidG. and LG. word; comp. AS. *sund*, E. *sound*, OIc. *sund*, 'sea, strait.' The connection with Goth. *sundrô*, 'separated' (see sondern), is open to objection on account of the meaning (Sund, lit. 'division between countries and islands'?). It is preferable to link it with AS. and OIc.

sund, n., 'swimming,' which is an abstract of schwimmen (*sunda-* for *swm-tó-*, allied to the root *swem*); by this assumption Sund is regarded as 'the place where one can swim.'

Sünde, f., 'sin, offence,' from the equiv. MidHG. *sünde*, OHG. *suntu, suntea* (base **sundî*), f. Corresponding to OLG. *sundia*, Du. *zonde*; the equiv. AS. *synn* (E. *sin*) is based on the primary form **sunjô* for **sundjô*; OIc. *synð* also points to a Goth. **sunidi*. Pre-Teut. *sontiá-, swenetiá-*, belong to a pre-Teut. root *swen, sun*, which, with a dental suffix, appear also in Gr. ἄτη, 'guilt, damage,' Lat. *sons*, 'guilty,' *sonticus*, 'injurious.'

Sündflut, f., 'the Flood,' is an early ModHG. corruption of the equiv. Mid HG. and OHG. *sin-vluot*, which means lit. 'great universal overflow.' The term *sin-*, which appears only in OTeut. compounds, signifies 'general, constantly, always' (comp. Singrün, 'periwinkle'), in Goth. *sinteins*, 'daily, everlasting,' AS. *symble*, OSax. *simbla*, OHG. *simblum*, 'always.' Comp. Lat. *sem-per*, 'always.'

Suppe, f., 'soup, broth'; late MidHG. *suppe (soppe)*, f., 'broth, sauce, soup'; properly a MG. and LG. word, the *pp* of which would be represented by *pf* in genuine HG. Allied to the root *sűp*, 'to drink'; comp. MidHG. *supfen*, 'to sip, drink' (Du. *soppen*, E. *to sop*), and ModHG. saufen. Comp. Du. *sop* and *soep*. The LG. word passed into Romance; comp. Ital. *zuppa*, 'wine soup,' Span. *sopa*, Fr. *soupe*, whence the equiv. E. *soup* (OFr. *souppe*, 'sop').

surren, wk. vb., 'to hum, buzz,' Mod HG. only, an imitative word.

süß, adj., 'sweet,' from the equiv. Mid HG. *süeze*, adj. (also *suoze, swuoze*, adv.), OHG. *suozi (swuozi)*, adj., a common Teut. term, occurring also in the other Aryan languages. Comp. OSax. *swôti*, Du. *zoet*, AS. *swête*, E. *sweet*, OIc. *sœtr*, Goth. **swôtus* (for which *sûts* is found), 'sweet.' The Teut. *swôti-u*, from Aryan *swâd-tí*, is based on an Aryan root *swâd*; comp. Sans. *svâdú*, 'sweet, delicious,' and the root *srad*, 'to taste nice' (*svâd*, 'to be rejoiced'), Gr. ἡδύς, 'sweet,' and ἥδομαι, 'I rejoice' (ἡδονή, 'pleasure,' ἁνδάνω, 'to please'), Lat. *sudvis* for **sudávis*, 'sweet' (also *suddere*, 'to advise,' lit. 'to make tasty, pleasant'?). In the Teut. group, AS. *swêlan*, Scotch *swats*, 'beer,' may be allied; on the other hand, the primary verb corresponding to

Aryan *swâddú-*, 'sweet,' was lost at an early period in Teut.

Sutter, m., 'sea-adder,' early ModHG. only, from late MidHG. *sutteren*, 'to boil over'; allied, like MidHG. **Subel**, to **fieben**.

T.

Tabak, m., 'tobacco,' ModHG. only; orig. an American word (like **Kartoffel**), now found in all modern languages; comp. Du. *tabak*, E. *tobacco*, Fr. *tabac*, Ital. *tabacco*, Span. *tabaco*; 'properly the roll through which the smoke of the prepared plant was imbibed.'

Tadel, m., 'blame, censure, reproof,' from MidHG. *tadel*, m. and n., 'fault, stain, defect (bodily or mental).' The word is recorded at a remarkably late period—the end of the 12th cent.—but this, of course, does not prove that it was borrowed. The Teut. root *dap* (*dad*?) contained in it has been compared, probably without just grounds, with Gr. τωθάω (root *dhôdh*), 'to deride, mock.'

Tafel, f., 'table, tablet, slab,' from Mid HG. *tavel*, *tavele*, f., 'tablet, picture, table,' OHG. *tavala* (*tabala*, *tubella*), f., 'tablet'; borrowed during the OHG. period from Lat. *tabula*, *tabella*. Even in the pre-HG. period Lat. *tabula* passed into HG. and was normally permutated; comp. OHG. *zabal*, MidHG. *zabel* (see **Schach**). It corresponds to the Romance cognates, Ital. *tavola*, 'table, tablet, board, picture,' Fr. *table* (E. *table*).—**Tafelrunde**, f., 'Round Table,' like the equiv. MidHG. *tavelrande* (especially of King Arthur); an imitation of Fr. *table ronde*.

Tag, m., 'day, daylight,' from the equiv. MidHG. and OHG. *tac* (*g*), m.; common to Teut. in the form *dago-*; comp. Goth. *dags*, OIc. *dagr*, AS. *dæg*, E. *day* (also *to dawn*), Du. and OSax. *dag*. This specifically Teut. word represents the stem, almost obsolete in Teut., of the equiv. Lat. *dies*, Sans. *dina*, OSlov. *dĭnĭ* (Goth. *sin-teins*, 'daily,' see **Sünbflut**). To explain Teut. *dago-* (to which AS. *dôgor*, OIc. *dœgr*, from *dôgoz*, *dôgiz*, are allied), it has been connected with the Sans. root *dah* (for Aryan *dhêgh*, *dhôgh*?), 'to burn'; this appears further in Lith. *dègti*, 'to burn,' *dàgas*, *dagà*, 'harvest' (also in Sans. *âhar*, n., 'day'?). Hence the base *dhógho-s*, common to G. Tag and Lith. *dágas*, means perhaps 'the hot period of the day or year' (comp. **Oftern** as a proof that names for periods of the day and year may be identical). Tag in G. denoted originally only the light period of the day; the day of twenty-four hours was called **Nacht**.—**täglich**, adj. and adv.. 'daily,' from the equiv. MidHG. *tagelich* (*tegelich*), adj., *tagelichen* (*tege-lîches*), adv., OHG. *tagalîh*, adj., *tagalîhhîn*, *tagolîhhes*, adv. The adj. has been formed from the adv., which is again a combination of two words, as in the phrase (*allaro*) *tago gilîh* (*hes*); for *gilîh* in the sense of 'every,' see **männiglich**; *tago gilîhhes* (lit. 'on each of the days') is an adverb genit. like OHG., MidHG., and ModHG. *des tages*. See further **vertheidigen**.

Takel, n., 'tackle,' ModHG. only, adopted, like many nautical terms, from LG.; comp. the equiv. Du. *takel*, E. *tackle*, Dan. *takkel*, Swed. *takel*. The literal meaning of this, which is peculiar to maritime dialects, was 'implements (in general),' which leads to kinship with Goth. *taujan*, 'to make' (comp. *tooijen*, 'to adorn,' E. *tool*).

Talg, m., 'tallow,' ModHG. only, from LG. (*talg*), hence unknown to Swab. and Bav.; allied to Du. *talk*, AS. **tealg*, E. *tallow*, OIc. *tolgr*. Teut. *talgo-* (*tolgo-*) cannot be traced farther back; yet note AS. *talg*, 'colour' (see **Seife**). It is scarcely connected with Goth. *tulgus*, 'firm' (**Talg**, lit. 'that which has become solid'?). The proper HG. (UpG.) word is **Unschlitt**.

Tand, m., 'toy, trifle, bauble,' from MidHG. *tant*, m., 'idle talk, tricks' (to which MidHG. *tanten*, 'to play a practical joke,' is allied).—**Tändelei**, f., 'toying, trifling, dawdling,' ModHG. only, is a derivative of **Tand** (in MidHG. once only *tenterle*). In OHG. only a corresponding *tantarôn*, 'to be mentally perplexed,' is recorded. No further light can be thrown on the HG. stem *tant*.

Tang, m., 'sea-weed,' ModHG. only, formed from the equiv. Scand. *pang* (Dan. *tang*), whence also E. *tang*, *tangle*.

Tann, m., see the following word.

Tanne, f., 'fir tree,' from the equiv. MidHG. *tanne,* f., OHG. *tanna,* signifies 'fir tree, oak,' hence the primary idea of the word is usually 'forest tree' (see Eiche, Buche). This is supported by ModHG. *Tann,* m., from MidHG. *tan (nn),* m. and n., 'forest' (OHG. *tan-esil,* 'wild ass,' which seems to be based on a collective signification of *Tanne.* The early history of the HG. cognates (to which ODu. *dennia,* Du. *den,* 'fir tree,' is allied) is uncertain. Its connection with Gr. θάμνος, 'thicket,' is dubious.

Tante, f., 'aunt,' ModHG. only, formed from Fr. *tante;* for the genuine G. words preserved dialectically see Base and Muhme.

Tanz, m., 'dance, ball,' from the equiv. MidHG. *tanz,* m., to which MidHG. and ModHG. *tanzen* is allied. The word was first adopted in the 11th cent. In OHG. the verbs were *salzôn* (which, like AS. *sealtian,* was borrowed at an early period from Lat. *saltâre*), and the genuine Teut. *tûmôn* and *leikhan* (comp. Reich). The late appearance of MidHG. *tanzen* tends to show that it is a loan-word; it is based on the equiv. Romance cognates, Ital. *danzare* (Fr. *danser,* whence E. *to dance,* and Du. *dansen*). It is true that, considering the late period at which it was borrowed, the HG. *t* compared to Ital. *d* is abnormal. The Romance cognates are themselves of Teut. origin, which has been sought in OHG. *dansôn,* 'to draw' (allied to Goth. *pinsan;* see gebunsen).

tapfer, adj., 'brave, valiant, bold,' from MidHG. *tapfer (dapfer, tapfel),* 'firm, pressed, full, weighty, important' (only in late MidHG. 'brave'), OHG. *tapfar,* 'heavy, weighty, important'; comp. Du. *dapper,* 'brave, much,' E. *dapper.* The connection in meaning with OSlov. *dobll,* 'strong, able,' *debelŭ,* 'stout,' and *dobrŭ,* 'beautiful, good,' is quite clear, but it is difficult to show how it is related to the corresponding OIc. *dapr,* 'sad'; note, however, Mod HG. *breist,* 'bold, audacious,' OHG. *drīsti,* OLG. *thrīsti,* compared with Lat. *trīstis.*

Tappe, f. (in Swab. and Alem. Depen, m.), 'claw, paw,' from the equiv. MidHG. *tāppe (only *tāpe* is recorded), f.; origin and early history obscure. To this is allied Mod HG. **täppisch,** adj., 'awkward, clumsy,' since MidHG. *tappe (tāpe)* occurs also as 'uncouth, loutish person'; hence also ModHG. **tappen,** vb., 'to flounder along, grope one's way,' lit. 'to behave awkwardly.'

Tarnkappe, f., 'magic cap,' see Kappe; the first component is OTeut. *darni,* 'secret,' OHG. *tarni,* AS. *dyrne.* To this MidE. *dāren,* 'to conceal oneself,' is allied.

Tasche, f., 'pocket, pouch, wallet,' from the equiv. MidHG. *tasche (tesche),* OHG. *tasca,* f. An obscure word, the relation of which to the equiv. Romance cognate Ital. *tasca* cannot be defined. The origin of the word and the history of its further diffusion is unknown.

Tasse, f., 'cup,' ModHG. only, from Fr. *tasse* (comp. Ital. *tazza,* from Arab. *tassah,* 'bowl').

tasten, vb., 'to touch, fumble, grope,' from the equiv. MidHG. *tasten,* wk. vb. Borrowed about 1200 A.D. from the Romance cognate Ital. *tastare* (Fr. *tâter*), 'to feel, fumble,' which is based on a Lat. *taxitare (allied to late Lat. *taxare,* 'to touch sharply').

Tatze, f., 'paw, claw,' from MidHG. *tatze,* f., 'hand, paw.' The origin and history of this word, which cannot be traced farther back, are obscure.

Tau (1.), n. (unknown to Swab. and Bav.), 'rope, cable,' ModHG. only; properly a LG. word, based on OIc. *taug,* 'cord, rope' (whence E. *tow,* Du. *touw*). The latter is connected with the Teut. root *tuh (tang),* in ModHG. ziehen. From the LG. word Fr. *touer,* 'to tow a ship,' is derived. For the words borrowed by HG. from LG. see Strand, Boot, &c.

Tau (2.), m., 'dew,' from the equiv. MidHG. and OHG. *tou* (gen. *touwes*), n. (MidG. also, m.); corresponding to the equiv. OSax. *dau,* Du. *dauw,* AS. *deáw,* E. *dew,* OIc. *dǫgg* (Goth. *daggwa is wanting), whence E. (dial.) *dag.* Teut. *dauwo-,* from pre-Teut. *dhāwo-,* is generally connected with the Sans. root *dhāv,* 'to run, flow, stream.'

taub, adj., 'deaf, torpid,' from MidHG. and OHG. *toup* (b), 'deaf, insensible, stupid, foolish, mad'; corresponding to Goth. *daufs* (b), 'callous,' AS. *deáf,* E. *deaf,* and the equiv. Du. *doof.* Since the meanings of the OHG. and MidHG. adj. border on those of OHG. and MidHG. *tump* (see bumm), the two words are certainly connected. The assumed relation (see bumm) to the Aryan root *dhubh,* 'to be blunt, obtuse, deafened,' preserved in Gr. τυφλός, 'blind,' leads further to toben and its co-nates. ModHG. betäuben, 'to deafen, stun,' from MidHG. töuben, MidHG. and OHG. touben, wk. vb., 'to deprive of sensation or strength, to annihilate,' supports the assumed primary meaning.

Taube, f., 'dove, pigeon,' from the equiv. MidHG. tûbe, OHG. tûba, f. ; corresponding to the equiv. Goth. dúbó, AS. dúfe, E. dore, Du. duif. This common Teut. term (for which Goth. ahaks, AS. culufre, 'dove,' are also found) has been connected with a Teut. root dúb, 'to dive,' which appears in AS. dŷfan, E. to dive, Taube being regarded as orig. 'water-dove.' It is more probably related to OIr. dub, 'black,' duibe, 'blackness'; comp. Gr. πέλεια, 'wild pigeon,' from πελιός, 'dark blue.'—**Tauber**, m., 'male pigeon,' for which tûber occurs in MidHG.

tauchen, vb., 'to dip, dive,' from the equiv. MidHG. tûchen, wk. vb., OHG. túhhan, str. vb. ; comp. Du. duiken, 'to dive, duck,' E. to duck (whence also E. duck, AS. dúce); see further buden. Other terms derived from the Teut. root duk, 'to stoop, dive,' are wanting. The connection of the word with taufen is improbable.—**Taucher**, m., 'diver' (bird), from the equiv. MidHG. túhhære, OHG. túhhári, m.

tauen, vb., 'to thaw,' from MidHG. touwen, töuwen, OHG. douwen, dewen (dóan), wk. vb., 'to dissolve' ; comp. Du. dooijen, AS. þáwan, E. to thaw, OIc. þeyja. With ModHG. Tauwind, m., 'thaw wind,' comp. Du. dooij, E. thaw, OIc. þeyr. If the Teut. root þaw, 'to dissolve' (comp. verrauen), exhibited in all these words, has originated in þagu, equiv. to Aryan téq, Gr. τήκω, 'to melt,' τακερός, 'liquid,' may be counted as cognates. Yet the Teut. words, as well as Osset. t'ayın, 'to thaw,' may point to an Aryan root taw.

Taufe, f., 'baptism, christening,' from the equiv. MidHG. toufe, OHG. toufa (toufi), f. ; allied to taufen, vb., 'to baptize, christen,' MidHG. töufen, toufen, OHG. toufen (from *toufjan). The primary meaning of the vb. is preserved by MidHG. toufen, 'to dip under,' which is properly a causative of tief. Goth. daupjan, OLG. dôpian, Du. doopen, exhibit the Christian meaning, which AS. represented by fulwian (fulwiht, 'baptism'); comp. OIc. kristna, 'to baptize.' In its relation to the history of civilisation taufen is as difficult to determine as Heide (which see). It cannot be positively affirmed whether the MidEurop. term daup-

jan "has been restricted in meaning solely because the Goths, who were first to receive Christianity, rendered the Gr. word βαπτίζω by the corresponding daupjan; this word, as the designation of the first sacrament, was then adopted from them (with Heide, Kirche, Pfaffe, and Teufel) by the Western Teutons, and was so firmly rooted among the latter that the AS. missionaries could no longer think of supplanting it by their corresponding verb fulwian." Perhaps, however, the OTeut. daupjan had even in the heathen acquired a ritual sense which fitted it to become the representative of the Christian-Romance baptizare (Ir. baitsim).

taugen, vb., 'to be of use, be good or fit for,' from MidHG. tugen, OHG. tugan (pres. sing. touc), pret. pres., 'to be capable, useful, suitable, to be of use, to suit.' Corresponding to OSax. dugan, 'to be capable, be of use,' Du. deugen, 'to be of use,' AS. dugan, OIc. duga, Goth. dugan, 'to be fit, of use.' The Teut. verbal root dug (daug) might, like Lith. daúg, 'much,' daúksinti, 'to increase,' point to Aryan dhugh (Gr. τύχη, 'fortune,' τυγχάνω, 'I am fortunate'?). To this are allied tüchtig and Tugend.

Taumel, m., 'reeling, staggering, frenzy,' from MidHG. tûmeln (tûmen, tûmelieren), 'to reel, stagger,' OHG. tûmalón (tûmón), 'to turn.' From the OHG. and MidHG. variant with ú is derived tummeln (comp. also Rehrtrommel). The Teut. root dú contained in these words leads to kinship with the Sans. root dhú, 'to storm along, put in violent motion, shake.'

Tausch, m., 'exchange, barter' ; Mod HG. only ; in late MidHG. (15th cent.) we meet for the first time with rostiuschære, 'horse-dealer' (comp. Du. paardentuischer), and vertüschen, 'to exchange.' The word is properly LG. ; comp. Du. tuischen, 'to barter.' How täuschen, 'to deceive,' from late MidHG. tiuschen (tüschen), 'to deceive, make game of some one' (late MidHG. túsch, 'mockery, joke, deception'), is connected with this word is not clear.

tausend, n. and m., 'thousand,' from the equiv. MidHG. tûsend (tûsunt), OHG. túsunt, dúsunt; corresponding to Goth. þúsundi, AS. þúsend, E. thousand, Du. duizend, OSax. thúsind. While the lower numerals up to a hundred are common to all the Aryan languages, the term for a thousand occurs elsewhere only in the Slav. group ; comp. OSlov. tysęšta, Lith. túk-

stantis. The primary meaning and further history of the Slav.-Teut. word *túsnti, túsonti*, can no longer be discovered; perhaps Slav. borrowed this word in prehistoric times from Teut. (in Sans. *sahasra*, Zend *hazaṅhra*, Gr. χίλιοι for *χέσλιοι, equiv. to *ghesłio-*; in Lat. *milia*, equiv. to Gr. μύρια).—**Tausendgüldenkraut**, n., 'centaury,' ModHG. only, an erroneous version of the Lat. *centaurea* (as if it were a compound of *centum* and *aurum*. It is really Gr. κενταύριον).

Teer, m. and n., 'tar,' early ModHG. only, a LG. word (unknown to Swab. and Bav.); comp. Du. *teer*, AS. *teoro* (*tyrwe*), E. *tar*, and the equiv. OIc. *tjara* (to which OIc. *tyrviðr*,'pine-wood,' is allied). The HG. form Zehr is recorded in the ModHG. period in Hess. These cognates meaning 'tar' are old derivatives of a Teut. word *trewo-*, 'tree' (comp. Goth. *triu*, E. *tree*), which is based upon Aryan *derw-, dorw-* (*dru*), 'tree, wood'; comp. Gr. δρῦς, 'oak' (δόρυ, 'spear'), OSlov. *drẽvo*, 'tree, wood,' and the equiv. Sans. *dấru* (*dru*); see also Trog. Teer means lit. 'the thick oil from trees' (especially from resinous pine-trees?); comp. Lith. *darwà*, 'pine-wood,' and Lett. *darwa*, 'tar.'

Teich, m., 'pond, pool,' from MidHG. *tîch*, m., 'fish-pond, pond' (it is uncertain whether OHG. *dîh*, 'eddy, whirlpool,' is the same word. The LG. cognates of Mod HG. Deich seem to be connected; AS. *dîc*, E. *ditch, dike* (OIc. *díke*), border on the meaning of Teich. Teut. *dîko-* (from *dhîghn-*?) may be primit. allied to Gr. τίφος (from *dhîghos*?), n., 'pond, bog.'

teig, adj., 'mellow' (of fruit), from the equiv. MidHG. *teic*; allied to the following word.

Teig, m., 'dough,' from the equiv. Mid HG. and OHG. *teic* (*g*), m.; corresponding to Du. *deeg*, AS. *dáh*, E. *dough*, and the equiv. OIc. *deig*, n.; a derivative of a Teut. root *dîg*, 'to knead,' from which the adj. teig and ModHG. Tiegel, 'stewpan,' are derived. A more general meaning is exhibited by Goth. *deigan*, 'to form from clay,' which is derived from Aryan *dhîgh*, and is connected with Sans. *dih*, 'to bedaub, cement, besmear.' To these are also allied Lat. *figulus*, 'potter,' *fingere*, 'to form,' *figura*, 'shape,' Gr. τεῖχος, τοῖχος (for θεῖχος, θοῖχος), 'wall.'

Teil, m. and n., 'part, share, portion,' from the equiv. MidHG. and OHG. *teil*,

m. and n.; corresponding to Goth. *dails, daila*, f., OSax. *dêl*, m., Du. *deel*, n., AS. *dǽl* (*dál*), and E. *deal* (*dole*). Teut. *dai-li* (*lo*) seems to point to an Aryan root *dhai* (see tilgen), which is proved by OSlov. *dělŭ*, 'part.'—**teilen**, wk. vb., 'to divide, share,' from the equiv. MidHG. and OHG. *teilen* (Goth. *dailjan*), is a denominative, like OSlov. *děliti*, 'to share.'—**teils**, adv., 'partly,' first used as an adv. in ModHG. —The ModHG. suffix -tel in Drittel, Viertel, &c., is based upon MidHG. *teil* (*dritteil, vierteil*, &c.; see also Urtel from Urteil).

Teller, m., 'plate, salver,' from the equiv. MidHG. *teller, teler* (*telir*), m.; the word was borrowed in the 14th cent. from Ital. *tagliere* (Fr. *tailloir*), 'chopping board,' which belongs, like Ital. *tagliare* (Fr. *tailler*), 'to cut to pieces,' to Ital. *taglia*, 'incision'; comp. Fr. *détail*.

Tempel, m., 'temple,' from the equiv. MidHG. *tëmpel*, m. and n., OHG. *tëmpal*, n.; borrowed during the OHG. period (with ecclesiastical words like Kloster, Altar, &c.) from Lat. *templum*. A Teut. word used in pre-Christian times for the same idea was OSax. *alah*, AS. *calh*, Goth. *alhs*.

Tenne, f., 'threshing-floor,' from the equiv. MidHG. *tenne*, n., f., and m., OHG. *tenni*, n. No corresponding word occurs in this sense in the allied Teut. dialects. It has been connected with AS. *denu*, 'valley,' AS. and E. *den*; but Tenne is rather a derivative of Tanne (lit. 'made of fir').

Teppich, m., 'carpet, tablecloth,' from the equiv. MidHG. and OHG. *teppîch, tëbech*, m. and n.; borrowed probably in the 8th cent. from Romance. The variants OHG. and MidHG. *tepplt, teppît*, point immediately to Ital. *tappeto*, Lat. *tapétum*, or rather *tapét-* (Fr. *tapis*). ModHG. Tapet, Tapete, and tapezieren are more recent loanwords; comp. Ital. *tappezzare*, 'to paper' (a room).

Terne, f., 'three winning numbers (in a lottery),' ModHG. only, from the equiv. Ital. *terno*.

teuer, adj., 'dear, costly, precious,' from the equiv. MidHG. *tiure, tiur*, OHG. *tiuri*; corresponding to the equiv. OSax. *diuri*, Du. *duur*, AS. *dýre, deóre*, E. *dear* (to which *darling*, from AS. *deórling*, is allied), OIc. *dýrr*. For the gradation *ū* (ModHG. *tür*, 'esteem'), *iu*, see tauern (2). The early history of this common Teut. adj., which is wanting only in Goth., cannot be ascertained.

Teufel, m., 'devil, demon,' from the equiv. MidHG. *tiuvel* (*tievel*), m., OHG. *tiuval, tioval*, m. (in the plur., neut. also); corresponding to OSax. *diuǔal*, Du. *duivel*, AS. *deófol*, equiv. to E. *devil*. The West Teut. words have apparently genuine Teut. sounds; on account, however, of the equiv. Goth. *diabaúlus*, Gr.-Lat. *diabolus*, it is certain that the word was borrowed. The early existence of the West Teut. word, attested by the permutation of LG. *d* to HG. *t*, can only be explained by the assumption that it was introduced into HG. in the 5th or 6th cent. through a Goth. medium (as also taufen, Pfaffe, Kirche, Heibe, Samstag, and probably Engel), for the connection of the cognates with Gr.-Lat. (Ecclesiast.) *diabolus* cannot be doubted. The genuine HG. term for 'evil spirit' was Goth *unhulþô*, OHG. *unholda*, lit. 'the demons.'

Text, m., 'text,' even in late MidHG. *tëxt*, formed from Lat. *textus*.

Thal, n., 'valley,' from the equiv. Mid HG. and OHG. *tal*, m. and n.; corresponding to Goth., OSax., and Du. *dal*, AS. *dœl*, E. *dale* (to which E. *dell* is allied), OIc. *dalr*, 'valley.' From the same Aryan root *dhô*, 'to lie low,' is derived AS. *dene, denu*, 'valley.' In the non-Teut. group, Gr. θόλος, 'dome-shaped roof, rotunda' (lit. 'deepening, excavation'?), is regarded as cognate; OSlov. *dolŭ*, 'valley,' is certainly allied.—zu **Thal** (of rivers, 'down-stream') from the equiv. MidHG. *ze tal*, 'down' (comp. Goth. *dalaþ*, 'downwards'); in opposition to zu Berg (see Berg) 'upwards.'

Thaler, m., 'dollar' (three shillings), first recorded in the 15th cent.; an abbreviation of Joachimsthaler for 'florin from Joachimsthal' (in Bohemia). From the Ger. word are derived Ital. *tallero*, Du. *daalder*, E. *dollar*.

That, f., 'deed, act, fact,' from the equiv. MidHG. and OHG. *tât*, f.; a verbal noun formed by gradation from thun. Corresponding to Goth. *dêþs*, OIc. *dáð*, AS. *dǽd*, E. *deed*, Du. *daad*, OSax. *dâd*. Teut. *dê-di-*, from *dhê-tt*, formed from the Teut. root *dê*, *dô*, from Aryan *dhê*, *dhô*. The graded form *ê* (*â*) is seen also in the OHG. partic. *gitân*, MidHG. and ModHG. *getân*.—**thätig**, adj., 'active, energetic,' from MidHG. *lœtec*, OHG. *tâtîc*.

Thau, see Tau (2).

thauen, see tauen.

Thee, m., 'tea,' ModHG. only, derived, like Fr. *thé*, Du. *thee*, and E. *tea*, from Chin. *the*.

Theer, see Teer.

Theidung, n., in Narrentheiding, 'empty talk,' from MidHG. *teidinc, tagedinc*, 'discussion, negotiation, talk' (properly 'the judicial proceeding' appointed for a certain day or period). Comp. Ding and verteibigen.

Theil, see Teil.

Theriak, m., 'antidote; treacle'; in MidHG. *driakel, triakel, triaker* (Du. *teriaak, triakel*), from Gr.-MidLat. θηριακόν, 'remedy for the bite of wild animals.'

theuer, see teuer.

Thier, see Tier.

Thon, m., 'clay,' earlier ModHG. **Than**, *Tahen*, from MidHG. *tâhe, dâhe*, OHG. *dâha*, f., 'clay, loam' (also 'earthen vessel'); corresponding to Goth. *þâhô* (from *þanhô*), f., 'clay,' AS. *þô* (older *þôhœ*), f., 'clay,' OIc. *þá*, f., 'clayey soil.' No words occur in the other Aryan languages to elucidate the implied pre-Teut. *tankân*, 'loam.'

Thor (1.), m., 'fool,' from MidHG. *tôre, tôr*, m., 'insane person, fool'; *tôro*, m., has not yet been found in OHG. The *r* of the adj. has originated in *s* (*z*), as is shown by OHG. *tusig*, AS. *dysig*, 'foolish,' E. *dizzy*, and Du. *duizelig*, 'dizzy.' For further Teut. cognates of the Aryan root *dhus* (*dhaus, dhucs*) see under Dusel; it is uncertain whether Lat. *furere*, 'to rage,' is derived from this root *dhus*.—**thöricht**, adj., 'foolish, silly,' from the equiv. Mid HG. *tôrēht, tœreht* (also *tœrisch, tœrsch*).—**Thorheit**, f., 'foolishness,' from MidHG. *tôrheit*.

Thor (2.), n., 'gate, gateway,' from the equiv. MidHG. and OHG. *tor*, n.; corresponding to Goth. *daúr*, OSax. *dor*, n., 'gate, door.' See Thür.

Thran, m., 'train-oil, blubber,' Mod HG. only, a LG. word, corresponding to Du. *traan*, Dan. and Swed. *tran*. The origin and prim. meaning of the word are unknown.

Thräne, f., 'tear' (in Swab. and Bav. Zähre is the popular term), from the equiv. late MidHG. *trēne*, f.; properly the plur. of the MidHG. sing. *trahen* (contracted *trân*), m.; corresponding to OHG. *trahan* (*trân*), m. (OSax. *trahni*, plur.), 'tears'; Teut. base, *trahnu-*. The equiv. MidHG. *traher* recalls MidHG. *zaher* (see Zähre), so that Teut. *tahru* must have had the parallel forms *trahru* and *trahnu*. More definite information concerning the early history of MidHG. *trahen, traher*, cannot be ascertained.

𝕿𝖍𝖗𝖔𝖓, m., 'throne,' from the equiv. MidHG. *trôn*, m., which originated in Fr. *trône*, or, with the lengthening of the vowel in an open syllable, in Lat. (Gr.) *thronus* (comp. Ital. *trono*).

𝖙𝖍𝖚𝖓, vb., 'to do, perform, make,' from the equiv. MidHG. and OHG. *tuon*; corresponding to OSax. *dûan*, Du. *doen*, AS. *dôn*, E. *to do*. Further details concerning this essentially West Teut. str. verbal root *dô, dê* (in Goth. *taujan*, 'to do'), belongs to grammar; yet see also 𝕿𝖍𝖆𝖙 and the suffix *-tum*. The pre-Teut. *dhô, dhê*, has a wide ramification in the other Aryan languages. Comp. the Gr. root θη, θε, in τίθημι, 'to put, do,' Sans. root *dhâ* (*dudhâmi* and *dhâmi*), 'to put, lay, do' (*dhâtṛ*, 'creator'), OSlov. *dêją* (and *dědą*), 'to do, make,' Lat. *facio* (perf. *féci*, equiv. to Gr. ἔθηκα).

𝕿𝖍𝖚𝖓𝖋𝖎𝖘𝖈𝖍, m., 'tunny,' ModHG. only. from the equiv. Lat. *thunnus* (Gr. θύννος), whence Ital. *tonno*, Fr. *thon* (E. *tunny*).

𝕿𝖍𝖚𝖗, f., 'door,' from the equiv. MidHG. *tür*, OHG. *turi*, f. ; properly a plur. form, the idea being often expressed by such a form; in OHG. we find *turi* as plur. with a sing. meaning (the stem was really *dur-*). Corresponding to OSax. *duri* (*dura*), Du. *deur*, AS. *duru* (*dyre*); OIc. *dyrr* is plur. only. The common Aryan stem *dhur* (*dhwer*) recurs in Gr. θύρα, θύρετρον, 'door,' to which θαιρός, 'hinge of a door,' and θυρών, 'vestibule' (comp. Goth. *daurôns*, plur. only, 'door'), are allied; Lat. *fores*, 'door,' OSlov. *dvĭrĭ*, 'door' (*dvorŭ*, 'court'), Lith. *dùrys*, 'door.' To these are allied the equiv. Sans. *dur, dvâr*, which in the oldest period was inflected only in the dual or plur. (the initial aspirate is dropped, because the case suffix begins with an aspirate). The primary meaning of this word, which has invariably the ModHG. signification, cannot be discovered. Allied to 𝕿𝖍𝖔𝖗.

𝕿𝖍𝖚𝖗𝖒, see 𝕿𝖚𝖗𝖒.

𝖙𝖎𝖊𝖋, adj., 'deep, profound, low,' from the equiv. MidHG. *tief*, OHG. *tiof*; corresponding to OSax. *diop*, Du. *diep*, AS. *deóp*, E. *deep* (*depth* and *to dip*), OIc. *djópr*, and Goth. *diups*, 'deep.' The common Teut. adj. *diupa-*, of which ModHG. *taufen* is a factitive, belongs to a Teut. root *dŭp*, the variant of which, *dŭb*, appears in AS. *dýfan*,

E. *to dive* (see 𝕿𝖆𝖚𝖇𝖊), as well as in E. *dub*. Comp. W. *dwfn*, OIr. *fudomain*, Lith. *dubùs*, 'deep, hollow,' OSlov. *duplĭ*, 'hollow' (see 𝕿𝖔𝖇𝖊𝖑), from an Aryan root *dhub, dhup*. For a nasalised Teut. root *dump*, see 𝕿ü𝖒𝖕𝖊𝖑.

𝕿𝖎𝖊𝖌𝖊𝖑, m., 'stewpan, crucible,' from MidHG. *tigel, tëgel*, OHG. *tëgal*, 'crucible'; corresponding to the equiv. OIc. *digull* (Swed. *degel*, Dan. *digel*). The cognates cannot have been derived from Lat. *tegula* (yet comp. 𝖅𝖎𝖊𝖌𝖊𝖑). The word is probably based on the Teut. root *dig*, 'to knead, form,' discussed under 𝕿𝖊𝖎𝖌.

𝕿𝖎𝖊𝖗, n., 'animal, beast, brute,' from MidHG. *tier*, OHG. *tior*, n., 'animal,' especially 'wild beast' (hence ModHG. 𝕿𝖎𝖊𝖗𝖌𝖆𝖗𝖙𝖊𝖓); corresponding to OSax. *dior*, 'wild beast,' Du. *dier*, 'animal,' AS. *deór*, E. *deer* (in MidHG. also, as well as in the language of sportsmen in ModHG., *tier* is often used in the sense of 'roe' and 'hind'), OIc. *dýr*, n., 'animal,' especially 'wild beast,' and also 'roe, stag.' Goth. *dius*, 'wild beast,' shows that the *r* of the words quoted as based upon Aryan *s* (base *dheuso-*?); to this the AS. adj. *deór*, 'bold,' and OHG. *tiorlîh*, 'wild,' are traced; hence Goth. *dius*, 'animal,' is probably an adj. used as a subst. (lit. 'the wild creature'). 𝕿𝖎𝖊𝖗, therefore, was originally quite distinct from 𝖁𝖎𝖊𝖍, 'useful gregarious animal.' Lat. *animal* with *anima* suggests the supposition that the cognates belong to an Aryan root *dhus*, 'to breathe' (comp. OSlov. *duša, duchŭ*, 'spirit, soul').

𝖙𝖎𝖑𝖌𝖊𝖓, vb., 'to extinguish, erase, eradicate,' from MidHG. *tilgen* (*tiligen*), OHG. *tîligon*, and also *tîlôn*, wk. vb., 'to exterminate, extirpate.' Comp. OSax. *far-dîligôn*, Du. *delgen*, AS. *â-dîlgian*, 'to extirpate.' It is remarkable that the word was borrowed from Lat. *dêlére*, considering its wide diffusion in the West Teut. languages (we should also have expected *tialên* in OHG.).

𝕿𝖎𝖓𝖙𝖊, f., 'ink, tint,' from the equiv. MidHG. *tinte, tinkte* (for *nct* and *nt* comp. 𝖇𝖚𝖓𝖙 and 𝕾𝖕𝖚𝖓𝖙), OHG. *tincta*, f. ; the word is evidently borrowed; it is based on the equiv. Lat. *tincta* (lit. 'coloured, variegnted things'), whence Ital. and Span. *tinta*, 'ink.' It is clear, therefore, that the spelling 𝕿𝖎𝖓𝖙𝖊 is historically more correct than 𝕯𝖎𝖓𝖙𝖊; the latter is due to MidG. and LG. In OHG. *atraminza* (from Lat. *atramentum*, comp. OFr. *errement*) was used. The equiv.

E. *ink*, Du. *inkt*, Rhen. *inkes*, are based on the Romance cognates, Fr. *encre*, OFr. *enques*, Ital. *inchiostro* (the ultimate source is Lat.-Gr. ἔγκαυστον).

Tifch, m., 'table,' from the equiv. Mid HG. *tisch*, OHG. *tisc*, m.; corresponding to OSax. *disc*, Du. *disch*. The OHG. word also means 'dish,' the antiquity of which is proved by AS. *disč*, 'dish, bowl,' E. *dish*. The Gr.-Lat. *discus*, on which the cognates are based, has the late signification 'dish' (post-classical; properly 'disk'); yet comp. also Ital. *desco*, 'table,' OFr. *dois*, 'table' (ModFr. *dais*, 'canopy, dais').

Titel, m., 'title, claim,' from MidHG. *titel* (*tittel*), OHG. *titul, tital*, m.; from the equiv. Lat. *titulus*, whence also Fr. *titre*, Ital. *titolo*.

Tobel, m., 'narrow valley,' from Mid HG. *tobel*, OHG. *tobal*, m., 'forest ravine, valley'; a derivative of the Teut. root *dub*, *dup* (see **Tief**), to which Lith. *daubà*, *daub-urà*, 'valley,' OSlov. *duplĭ*, 'hollow,' *dĭbrĭ*, 'valley, ravine,' are primit. cognate (Aryan root *dhup*, *dhub*).

toben, vb., 'to fume, rage, bluster,' from the equiv. MidHG. *toben*, OHG. *tobēn* (*tobôn*), wk. vb.; corresponding to the equiv. AS. *dofian*, 'delirare' (*gedof*, 'fury, rage, madness'). Based on the Teut. root *dub*, 'to be mentally confused, to be deafened,' from which *taub* and *tumm* are also derived. Whether we have to assume on account of OHG. *tûfar*, *tûbar*, 'silly, foolish,' an Aryan root *dhûp*, *dhûq*, is dubious; perhaps Lith. *dùkti*, 'to grow mad,' *dùkis*, 'fury, madness,' are primit. allied to the cognates of *toben*.

Tochter, f., 'daughter,' from the equiv. MidHG. *tohter*, OHG. *tohter*, f.; a common Teut., and also a primit. Aryan term; comp. Goth. *daúhtar*, AS. *dohtor*, E. *daughter*, Du. *dochter*, OSax. *dohtar*, 'daughter.' The primit. Aryan *dhuktêr* (*dhugatêr*), on which the Teut. cognates are based, is indicated also by Lith. *duktě̃*, OSlov. *dŭšti*; comp. further Gr. θυγάτηρ, Sans. *duhitár*, Zend *duγδar*, 'daughter.' The Aryan word is usually considered to be a derivative of the Sans. root *dugh*, 'to milk,' regarding **Tochter** as equiv. to 'milker.' This assumption is, however, quite as dubious as the derivation of **Water, Mutter**, and **Bruder**.

Tod, m., 'death,' from the equiv. Mid HG. *tôt* (*d*), OHG. *tôd*, m.; corresponding to Goth. *dauþus*, OSax. *dôth*, Du. *dood*, AS. *deáþ*, E. *death*. A verbal abstract of the Teut. verbal root *dau*, which has been preserved in OIc. *deyja*, str. vb. (whence the equiv. E. *to die*); comp. OSax. *dôian* (from *daujan*), OHG. and MidHG. *touwen* (MidHG. *töuwen*), wk. vb., 'to die.' Teut. *dau-þu-* has the Lat.-Sans. suffix *tu-* (base *dhâu-tu-s*). The adj. cognate ModHG. *tot*, 'dead,' is based on the *to* partic. of the same root, *dhôu* (partic. *dhautó*). With these are connected in the non-Teut. languages OSlov. *daviti*, 'to strangle,' Lith. *dóvyti*, 'to torment,' which correspond as causatives to Goth. *dôjan* (for **dôwejan*), 'to torment' (lit. 'to put to death'). The orig. form of the root was *dhēu, dhōw*.

todt, see **tot**.

toll, adj., 'mad, frantic, absurd,' from MidHG. and OHG. *tol* (with one *l*), adj., 'foolish, absurd,' to which OHG. *tulisc*, 'foolish,' is allied. Comp. OSax., Du., and AS. *dol*, 'foolish,' E. *dull*. The Teut. root *dul* contained in these words has a variant *dwal*, which has been preserved in Goth. *dwals*, 'foolish,' AS. *gedwëlan*, 'to err,' OHG. *gitwola*, 'infatuation, delusion, heresy,' OSax. *dwalm*, 'infatuation, delusion.' An Aryan root *dhwel*, *dhul*, 'to be infatuated, deluded,' is also attested by Sans. *dhvr̥*, *dhûr* (*dhru*), 'to deceive, cheat, injure.'

Tölpel, m., 'blockhead, booby,' from MidHG. *törpel*, *dörpel*, properly *dörper*, *dörpære*, m., 'peasant, clownish person, blockhead'; really identical with **Dörfer**, 'villager.' MidHG. *dörper* is a MidG. and LG. form (for genuine MidHG. *dorfære*). The LG. form of the MidHG. word is explained by the fact that Flanders, the medium by which French terms relating to the court and chivalry were introduced into Germany, also furnished some words (comp. **Wappen**) to HG.

Ton, m., 'tone, sound,' from MidHG. *tôn*, *dôn*, m., 'sound, tone, voice, song melody'; from Gr.-Lat. *tŏnus* (τόνος), with lengthening of the *ŏ*; comp. **Thron**. Hence ModHG. *tönen*, vb., 'to sound, resound,' from MidHG. *tænen, dænen*.

Tonne, f., 'tun, cask, barrel,' from the equiv. MidHG. *tunne*, OHG. *tunna*, f. A corresponding word with a similar form is preserved by Du. *ton*, AS. *tunne*, E. *tun*; according to these LG. cognates the HG. word ought to have an initial *z*, or rather the cognates an initial *d*. Hence the word must have been borrowed by one or the other, which is all the more probable since it is wanting in Swab. and Bav. The Rom. languages have Fr. *tonne* (*tonneau*), Span. and Portug. *tonel*. Probably Kelt. is the ultimate source of the word; comp. Ir. and Gael. *tunna*, 'tun, cask.' In that case, the word passed into HG. after 700 A.D., when the *t* could not be permutated to *z*. The form of OSwed. *byn*, 'tun, cask,' shows that it was borrowed at a much earlier period.

Topas, m., 'topaz,' from the equiv. MidHG. *topáze* (*topazie*), m.; derived, like most of the terms for precious stones, through a Lat. medium from Gr. Comp. Gr. τόπαζος, τοπάζιον, 'topaz.'

Topf, m., 'pot,' from the equiv. MidHG. *topf* (with the diminutive variant *tüpfen*), n.; this word, which is rare in MidHG., is wanting in OHG. The primit. word is unknown to UpG. (Hafen being used), yet Alem. has preserved *dipfi*, *düpfi*, 'iron pot with three legs,' Hess. *dippen*, 'pot' (Luther Töpfen); in Du. and E. the divergent form *pot* occurs. MidHG. *topf*, 'olla,' is probably more closely related to MidHG. *topf, topfe*, OHG. *topf, tof* (*topfo*), 'top' (toy), so too ModHG. dial. Topf, 'top' (toy); AS. and E. *top* is exceptional. The word is based on the Teut. root *dup*, 'to be deep, hollow' (see tief); Topf, lit. 'that which has been hollowed out.'

Topp, m., 'top' (of a mast), ModHG. only, borrowed, like most nautical terms, from LG. Comp. Du. *top*, E. *top*. For further cognates see under Zopf.

Torf, m., 'turf, peat,' ModHG. only, a LG. loan-word unknown to Bav.; comp. LG. *torf*, Du., AS., and E. *turf*, and the equiv. OIc. *torf*. In OHG. we find a genuine HG. form *zurba*, 'sward,' with a normal permutation, for which Swiss now has *turbe*, with the LG. permutation. The OTeut. word passed (in a LG. form) into Rom.; comp. Ital. *torbo*, Fr. *tourbe*, 'turf.' This form Terf (lit. 'sward'), orig. common to Teut., is based on pre-Teut. *drbh*, and is connected with Sans. *darbhá*, 'tuft of grass.'

Torkel, f., 'wine-press,' from MidHG. *torkel*, OHG. *torkula*, f., 'wine or oil press.' From Lat. *torcula, torculum*.

torkeln, vb., 'to reel, stagger,' from the equiv. MidHG. *torkeln*; intensive of Mid HG. *turc*(*k*), m., 'reeling, downfall.' Early history obscure.

Tornister, m., 'haversack, knapsack,' adopted in the last cent. from Hungar. *turisznya*, 'satchel.'

Tort, m., 'wrong, vexation,' ModHG. only; the LG. form for HG. Trey.

Torte, f., 'tart,' early ModHG. only, from Fr. *tarte*.

tosen, vb., 'to rage, storm,' from the equiv. MidHG. *dōsen*, OHG. *dōsōn*. Based on a Teut. root *þus* (by gradation *þaus*), from which OIc. *þyss, þausn*, 'tumult,' is also derived.

tot, adj., 'dead,' from the equiv. Mid HG. and OHG. *tôt* (OHG. also *tôt*); corresponding to the equiv. Goth. *dauþs*, AS. *deád*, E. *dead*, Du. *dood*, OSax. *dôd*. Teut. *dau-do-* (*dauþo-*), contained in these words, is properly a partic. (comp. falt, laut, traut) of the Teut. strong verbal root *ddu*, 'to die,' mentioned under Tob.—Derivative töten, factitive vb., 'to put to death,' from the equiv. MidHG. *tœten* (*tœden*), OHG. *tôten* (*tôden*). Comp. Goth. *dauþjan*.

traben, vb., 'to trot, jog,' from MidHG. *draben* (*draven*), wk. vb., 'to walk or ride at an even, rapid pace'; corresponding to Du. *draven*.—**Trabant**, m., 'gentleman-at-arms, life-guardsman,' is a derivative of traben, with a Rom. partic. suffix. Comp. Lappalien.

Tracht, f., 'dress, costume, load,' from MidHG. (OHG.) *traht*, f., 'carrying, load'; verbal abstract of tragen.—**trächtig**, adj., 'pregnant,' is connected with the subsidiary meaning of *traht*, 'pregnancy.'

trachten, vb., 'to aim (at), aspire (to),' from MidHG. *trahten*, OHG. *trahtôn*, wk. vb., 'to think, esteem, consider, strive, invent, excogitate'; corresponding to Du. *trachten*, AS. *trahtian*. Based on Lat. *tractare*, 'to treat, reflect on,' whence Ital. *trattare*, Fr. *traiter*, 'to treat.' The genuine Teut. origin of OHG. *trahtôn* is undoubted, hence it has been thought to be primit. allied to Gr. δέρκομαι, Sans. *dṛç*, 'to see.'

träge, adj., 'indolent, lazy,' from Mid HG. *trœge*, adj. (*trágo*, adv.), OHG. *trâgi*, adj. (*trâgo*, adv.), 'slow, loth, wearied, lazy'; corresponding to Du. *traag*, AS. *trâg*, 'reluctant, difficult.' The assumed primit. Teut. **trêgu-z*, 'reluctant, loth,' belongs to an OTeut. root *trêy*, 'to be sad, disheartened,' which appears in Goth. *trigo*, 'sadness,' OIc. *tregr*, 'reluctant, slow' (*trege*, 'pain'), AS. *trèga*, 'pain,' OSax. *trâgi*, 'vexation' (allied to *trègan*, str. vb., 'to be sorry'). OSwed. *trögher* (ModSwed. *trög*), 'lazy,' has a graded form, *ô*, of the root vowel *ê*. Sans. *drâgh*, 'to torment,' has also been supposed to contain the Aryan root *drĕgh*. The following word is not allied.

tragen, vb., 'to bear, carry, support, endure,' from the equiv. MidHG. *tragen*, OHG. *tragan*, str. vb., 'to bear, hold, bring, lead'; corresponding to OSax. *dragan*, Du. *dragen*, Goth. *dragan*, str. vb., 'to bear.' Whether OIc. *draga*, AS. *dragan*, equiv. to E. *to draw*, are entirely different from these cognates is open to doubt. The Teut. root *drag*, 'to bear' (from Aryan *dhragh*), has been compared with OSlov. *drŭžati*, 'to hold.'

trampeln, vb., from the equiv. Mid HG. *trampeln*, wk. vb., 'to trample'; a MidG. and LG. intensive form from Goth. *trimpan*, 'to tread,' to which a genuine HG. form, MidHG. *trumpfen*, 'to run,' is allied; comp. E. *to tramp, trample*. The forms ModHG. *trappen*, 'to tread noisily,' Du. *trappen*, 'to tread,' E. (dial.) *to trape*, without a nasal, also occur. Comp. also Treppe.—**Trampeltier**, n., a corruption of the equiv. Dromedar, 'dromedary.'

Trank, m., 'drink, beverage,' from the equiv. MidHG. *tranc (k)*, m. and n.; an abstract from trinfen.—To this **Tränke**, f., 'watering-place' (for animals), from the equiv. MidHG. *trenke*, OHG. *trencha*, f., is allied.

Trappe, m. and f., 'bustard,' from the equiv. MidHG. *trap, trappe*, m.; comp. the equiv. Du. *trapgans*. The early history of the word is entirely obscure.

Traß, m., ModHG. only. Derived, like the equiv. Du. *tras (tiras, tieras)* and E. *tarrace (tarras)*, from Ital. *terrazzo*.

Tratte, f., 'draft, bill of exchange,' ModHG. only, from Ital. *tratta*.

Traube, f., 'grape, bunch of grapes,' from the equiv. MidHG. *trûbe*, m. and f., OHG. *trûba (drûba)*, f., *trûbo (druppo?)*, m.; corresponding to Du. *druif*. It is uncertain whether we have to assume Goth. **þrûba*, 'grape' (OIc. *þrûga*, 'grape, winepress,' is a derivative of OIc. *þrûga*; see brücfcn).

trauen, vb., 'to trust, confide; marry,' from MidHG. *trûwen*, wk. vb., 'to hope, believe, trust' (also 'to betroth, unite in marriage'), OHG. *trûên (trûwên)*, 'to believe, trust.' Comp. Goth. *trauan*, wk. vb., 'to trust, confide,' OSax. *trûôn*, Du. *vertrouwen*, 'to trust, confide' (but *trouwen*, 'to marry'). A derivative of the Teut. root *trŭ, treu*, 'to have confidence,' mentioned under traut and treu.

Trauer, f., 'mourning, sorrow, grief,' from the equiv. MidHG. *trûre*, f.; a derivative of MidHG. *trûren*, OHG. *trûrên* (equiv. to ModHG. trauern, 'to mourn, grieve'), wk. vb. Allied to ModHG. traurig, 'mournful, sad,' MidHG. *trûrec*, OHG. **trûrac (g)*; to this adj. AS. *dreôrig*, E. *dreary*, is related by gradation (comp. Du. *treurig*, 'sad.' Borrowed from HG.?). On account of OHG. *trûrên*, 'to lower one's eyes,' the cognates are based on the OTeut. root *driu*, 'to fall, sink' (comp. Goth. *driusan*, AS. *dreôsan*, 'to fall').

Traufe, f., 'dripping of water, eaves, gutter,' from the equiv. MidHG. *troufe*, f., MidHG. and OHG. *trouf*, m. A graded form from triefen, 'to drop, trickle'; so too ModHG. träufeln, träufen, 'to drip, trickle,' from MidHG. *tröufen*, MidHG. and OHG. *troufen*, lit, 'to cause to drop.'

Traum, m., 'dream, vision,' from the equiv. MidHG. and OHG. *troum*, m.; corresponding to the equiv. OSax. *drôm*, Du. *droom*, E. *dream* (recorded about 1200 A.D.), OIc. *draumr*. The signification 'dream,' occurring in all these cognates, may be deduced from the lit. meaning, 'phantom, illusion,' so that Teut. *draumo-* (for *draugmo-* or *draugwmô-*?) would be connected with trügen. In any case, OSax. *drôm* (E. *dream*) and OSax. *drâm* (AS. *dreám*), 'shout of joy, noise,' must be regarded as etymologically different words; the latter is connected with Gr. θρῦλος, 'noise.'—Derivative **träumen**, vb., 'to dream,' from MidHG. *tröumen*, MidHG. and OHG. *troumen*.

traun, interj., 'truly! in faith! forsooth!' from the equiv. MidHG. (MidG.) *trûn, trûwen*, for MidHG. *triuwen, entriuwen*, 'in truth,' allied to Treue.

traut, adj., 'beloved, dear,' from the equiv. MidHG. and OHG. *trût;* allied to MidHG. *trût*, m. and n., 'sweetheart, spouse.' Since there is no corresponding word in the Teut. dialects with a Goth. form of the dental, it cannot be decided whether traut must be connected with trauen; in any case, the form and meaning admit of our regarding it as the old lo partic. (comp. laut, falt, zart) of the root *trŭ, treu*, seen in trauen and treu, so that its lit. meaning is 'one in whom confidence or trust is reposed.' The borrowed Romance words beginning with d (comp. Ital. *drudo*, m., 'lover,' *druda*, f., 'mistress,' *drudo*, 'gallant, brave,' Fr. *dru*) presuppose a Goth.

*𝔡𝔯𝔞𝔡𝔞-, which could not be from the same root as Goth. *trauan*, 'to trust.' The connection with Gael. *drúth*, 'wanton, pert,' W. *drud*, 'bold,' is obscure; it may be primit. allied (Aryan root *dhrū̆*).

𝔗𝔯𝔢𝔟𝔢𝔯, plur., 'husks, grains,' from the equiv. MidHG. *treber*, OHG. *trebir*, plur.; the corresponding sing. would be *trab*. Comp. Ic. *draf*, Du. *draf*, 'sediment of a brewing' (to which *drabbe*, 'lees,' is allied), AS. *dræf*, E. *draff*, 'lees, refuse, dregs' (late AS. *drabbe*, 'lees, dregs, dirt,' whence E. *drab*, applied to colour and a woman). If the medial *b* of the Teut. base *draboz*, n., could have originated in a guttural, the word might be compared with OIc. *dregg* (equiv. to E. *dregs*), and hence be probably allied to Lat. *fræces*, 'grounds, dregs of oil'; Aryan root *dhraq̄*ȋ. It seems to be also connected more remotely with 𝔗𝔯𝔢𝔣𝔱𝔢𝔯, 'husks, skins (of grapes).'

𝔱𝔯𝔢𝔠𝔥𝔢𝔫, vb., 'to drag, haul,' from the MidHG. *trēchen*, 'to drag,' or rather from the intensive form *trecken*; allied to Du. and MidLG. *trekken*.

𝔗𝔯𝔢𝔣𝔣, n., 'club' (at cards), properly 𝔗𝔯𝔢𝔣𝔣𝔩𝔢 (18th cent.), from Fr. *trèfle*, 'clover, trefoil' (Lat. *trifolium*).

𝔱𝔯𝔢𝔣𝔣𝔢𝔫, vb., 'to hit, strike; guess'; occur, happen,' from MidHG. *trëffen*, OHG. *trëffan*, str. vb., 'to hit, reach, fight'; comp. AS. *drëpan*, OIc. *drepa*, 'to hit, push, strike.' As to the Teut. root *drep* (pre-Teut. *dhreb*) contained in these cognates, nothing positive can be asserted. Comp. 𝔈𝔦𝔫𝔱𝔯𝔞𝔠𝔥𝔱.

𝔗𝔯𝔢𝔣𝔣𝔢𝔫, n., 'encounter, engagement'; even in MidHG. *trëffen*, n.; an infinitive used as a subst., from MidHG. *trëffen*, 'to fight.' See 𝔱𝔯𝔦𝔣𝔱𝔦𝔤.

𝔱𝔯𝔢𝔦𝔟𝔢𝔫, vb., 'to drive, impel,' from the equiv. MidHG. *trīben*, OHG. *trīban*, str. vb.; corresponding to OSax. *drīban*, 'to drive, drive away, exercise,' Du. *drijven*, 'to drive, carry on (a business), fly, swim,' E. *to drive* (AS. *drīfan*), OIc. *drīfa*, 'to hasten,' Goth. *dreiban*, 'to drive.' The Teut. str. verbal root *drīb* (from Aryan *dhrībh* ȋ, *dhrīp* ȋ), 'to move quickly, drive,' has not yet been found in the other Aryan languages. See 𝔗𝔯𝔦𝔣𝔱.

𝔱𝔯𝔢𝔦𝔡𝔢𝔩𝔫, vb., 'to tow a boat,' ModHG. only; a LG. loan-word; comp. the equiv. Du. *treilen* (AS. *træglian*, E. *to trail*). On account of Fr. *trailler*, 'to pull,' which is probably a corresponding term, 𝔱𝔯𝔢𝔦𝔟𝔢𝔩𝔫 has been supposed to be connected with Lat. *trahere*. There is no need, however, to ascribe the cognates to a non-Teut. origin.

𝔱𝔯𝔢𝔫𝔡𝔢𝔩𝔫, 𝔱𝔯𝔢𝔫𝔱𝔢𝔩𝔫, vb., 'to dawdle, loiter,' lit. 'to turn, move this way and that,' from late MidHG. *trendeln*, 'to turn,' allied to MidHG. *trendel*, 'ball, top,' which, like AS. *trendel*, 'sphere' (E. *trendle*), and Du. *omtrent*, 'towards, on, about' (Dan. and Swed. *trind*, 'round'), are connected with a root *trend*, 'to move in a circle.'

𝔱𝔯𝔢𝔫𝔫𝔢𝔫, vb., 'to separate, sever,' from MidHG. and OHG. *trennen* (older *trannjan*), wk. vb., 'to split, separate, cleave,' lit. 'to partition off'; factitive of MidHG. *trinnen*, 'to run away, separate' (comp. *abtrünnig*). This verbal stem is unknown to the other Teut. languages, and hence its primit. Teut. and pre-Teut. form and meaning cannot be ascertained.

𝔗𝔯𝔢𝔫𝔰𝔢, f., 'snaffle,' ModHG. only, a LG. word; comp. Du. *trens*. The early history of the word is obscure; it is doubtful whether it has been borrowed from Span. *trenza*, 'plait, braid (of hair).'

𝔗𝔯𝔢𝔭𝔭𝔢, f., 'stairs, staircase,' from MidHG. (MidG.) *treppe*, *trappe*, m. and f., 'stairs, step'; corresponding to Du. *trap*. This word (for which 𝔖𝔱𝔦𝔢𝔤𝔢 occurs in UpG.) belongs to the cognates of 𝔱𝔯𝔞𝔭𝔭𝔢𝔫 (see under 𝔱𝔯𝔞𝔪𝔭𝔢𝔩𝔫), which are likewise of MidG. and LG. origin; the HG. form (of the 16th and 17th cents.) is properly 𝔗𝔯𝔢𝔭𝔣𝔢.

𝔗𝔯𝔢𝔰𝔭𝔢, f., 'brome-grass,' a Sax. and Siles. word, from MidHG. (MidG.) *trësp*, 'darnel,' with the genuine HG. variants *trëfs*, *trëfse*, m. Modern Ger. dialects (e.g., Thuringian) have 𝔗𝔯𝔢𝔣𝔣 (Swab. *trefz*), so that an orig. term *trëf* is probable. Allied to Du. *dravik*, MidE. *drauk* (AS. **drafoc*); non-Teut. cognates are wanting.

𝔗𝔯𝔢𝔰𝔰𝔢, f., 'lace, braid (of hair),' ModHG. only, from Fr. *tresse*.

𝔗𝔯𝔢𝔰𝔱𝔢𝔯, plur., 'husks, grape-skins,' from MidHG. *trester*, OHG. *trestir*, plur., 'grains, residue.' The similarity in meaning to 𝔗𝔯𝔢𝔟𝔢𝔯, 'grains,' points to a primit. kinship of OHG. *trebir* and *trestir* (comp. also AS. *dærstan*, 'lees'), so that *trestir* would represent **trefstir* or **trehstir*. Pruss. *dragios*, OSlov. *droždije* and *droštija*, 'lees,' which are primit. allied to these words, are also similarly related.

𝔱𝔯𝔢𝔱𝔢𝔫, vb., 'to tread, proceed, step,' from the equiv. MidHG. *trëten*, OHG. *tretan*; a common Teut. str. vb.; corresponding to OSax. and AS. *trëdan*, E. *to tread*, Du. *trëden*, Goth. *trudan*. Comp.

also Triſt, Trott, and Trotte. In the non-Teut. languages no Aryan root *dre-t* is found, though Gr. δρόμος, 'course,' Sans. root *dram*, 'to run' (AS. *trem*, 'step'), and the root of the cognates of trampeln seem to be orig. connected with it.

treu, adj., 'true, faithful,' from late MidHG. *triuwe*, for which classical Mid HG. has *getriuwe* (hence ModHG. getreu), OHG. *gitriuwi*, 'true, faithful, trusty, loyal.' Properly a derivative of OHG. *triuwa*, MidHG. *triuwe* (ModHG. Treue), f.; getreu, lit. 'possessing loyalty.' In OSax. *triuwi*, Du. *trouw*, AS. *treówe*, *trýwe* (E. *true*, *truth*, *to trow*, and *to trust*), Goth. *triggws*, 'true.' Teut. *treuwo-* (*treuwi-*?), for pre-Teut. *dréwo-*, is related to the assumed (see trauen) Aryan root *drū*, 'to have confidence,' with which Pruss. *druwis*, 'belief,' is connected. OHG. *triuwa*, f., 'fidelity,' corresponds to OSax. *treuwa*, AS. *treów*, 'fidelity,' Goth. *triggwa*, 'agreement, compact'; with the last signification, Ital. *tregua*, Fr. *trève*, 'armistice,' borrowed from Teut., are connected.

Trichter (in UpG. and LG. dialects Trachter), m., 'funnel,' from the equiv. Mid HG. *trihter*, with older variants *trehter*, *drahter*, OHG. *trahtāri*, m.; corresponding to Du. *trechter*, OAS. *tructer* (Swed. *tratt*?). Based on MidLat. *tractārius*, 'funnel,' corrupted from the equiv. Lat. *trājectōrium* (Lat. *trajicere*, *traicere*), 'to pour from one vessel into another.' For the contraction comp. Utrecht, Maſtricht, from Lat. *Ultrajectum*, *Mosae-Trajectum*. The word was borrowed in Ger. coincident with the introduction of Ital. wine-culture (comp. Kelter, Spund, and Wein). As in the case of Kelter, the Romance languages retain few traces of the Lat. word; comp. Rhet. *trachuoir*, Walloon and Vosges *tretœ* (the more widely diffused Rom. word for 'funnel' is Lat. *infundibulum*, equiv. to Fr. *fondéfle*, yet Alban. *taftár*, 'funnel,' is also based on Lat. *tractdrius* for *trajectorium*).

Trieb, m., 'sprout; instinct, impulse,' ModHG. only; allied to treiben. Comp. Triſt.

triefen, vb., 'to drop, drip, trickle,' from MidHG. *triefen*, OHG. *triofan*, str. vb., 'to drop'; corresponding to OSax. *driopan*, Du. *druipen*, AS. *dreópan*, 'to drop.' To this are allied the cognates of Traufe, träufeln, and Tropfen. With the Teut. root *drūp* (from pre-Teut. *dhrūb*), OIr. *drucht* (base *druptu-*), 'dew, dewdrop,' is also probably connected.

triegen, see trügen.

Trift, f., 'right of pasturage, common,' from MidHG. *trift*, f., 'pasture,' lit. 'place to which something is driven'; not recorded in OHG. Trift (as in the case of Acker) is a relic of the speech of primit. nomad life. MidHG. *trift* also signifies (as a derivative of the root of treiben) 'herd, drove, floating (of wood), actions, mode of life'; comp. E. *drift* and *drove*.

triftig, adj., 'drifting; convincing, sound, valid,' from late MidHG. (rare) *triftec* (*g*), 'striking, pertinent, suitable'; a derivative of treffen.

trillern, vb., 'to trill, warble,' ModHG. only, from the equiv. Ital. *trillare*.

trinken, vb., 'to drink,' from the equiv. MidHG. *trinken*, OHG. *trinchan*; a common Teut. str. vb.; comp. Goth. *drigkan*, AS. *drincan*, E. *to drink*, Du. *drinken*, OSax. *drinkan*. From OTeut. are derived the Romance cognates, Ital. *trincare*, Fr. *trinquer*, 'to touch glasses.' The str. verbal root *drink* (Aryan *dhreng*) is not found in non-Teut.; on the other hand, the Aryan root *pō*, 'to drink' (comp. Sans. *pā*, Gr. πω-, Lat. *pō-tus*, &c.), is wanting in Teut. —Comp. Tranf, Trunt.

trippeln, vb., 'to trip, mince,' ModHG. only; corresponding to Du. *dribbelen*. A recent intensive form from treten or traben.

Tripper, m., 'gonorrhea,' a MidG. and LG. word for which older ModHG. Trüpfer, m. (allied to Tropfen), occurs. Comp. E. *dripper*, allied to *drip*.

Tritt, m., 'step, tread,' from MidHG. *trit*, m. Allied to treten.

trocken, adj., 'dry, barren,' from the equiv. MidHG. *trocken*, *trucken* (*truchen*), OHG. *trochan* (*trucchan*); comp. OSax. *drucno*, *drocno*, 'dry.' Corresponding to the equiv. LG. *dreuge*, Du. *droog* (comp. Drege, to which Du. *droogte*, 'dryness,' is allied), AS. *drýge*, E. *dry* (allied to *drought*), which are derived from cognate roots. With the Teut. root *drūk*, *drūy*, *draug*, 'to be dry,' is also connected OIc. *draugr*, 'dry wood.' A pre-Teut. root *dhrūk* (*dhrūy*) has not yet been found in the other Aryan languages.

Troddel, f., 'tassel, bob,' dimin. of Mid HG. *trâde*, OHG. *trâda*, f. (*trâdo*, m.), 'fringe'; MidHG. *trâdel* (dial. for *trâdel*) signifies 'fibre in wood.' Since the other

Teut. dialects have no word corresponding to OHG. *trådo*, 'fringe,' nothing definite can be ascertained concerning its early history.

tröbeln, vb., 'to deal in second-hand goods, dawdle, loiter,' from MidHG. *tretelen*, which, with the nasalised form *trentelu*, is derived from the same root. Comp. MidHG. *tredel-, trendelmarket*, equiv. to ModHG. Trödelmarkt, 'rag-fair.'

Trog, m., 'trough,' from the equiv. Mid HG. and OHG. *troc* (g), m.; comp. Du. *trog*, AS. *trog*, E. *trough*, OIc. *trog*. The assumed Teut. *trogo-*, from which the cognate Ital. *truogo*, 'trough,' is borrowed, is based on pre-Teut. *dru-kó-*, which is rightly connected with the Aryan stem *dru* (*dreu, deru*), 'tree, wood,' discussed under Teer; comp. Sans. *dru, dåru*, 'wood.' Hence Trog is lit. 'wooden article.'

trollen, vb., 'to roll about, loll, trip,' from MidHG. *trollen*, 'to run with short steps'; perhaps allied to MidHG. *trolle*, 'booby, uncouth person' (lit. 'ghost-like monster'). Fr. *tróler*, 'to stroll about,' is a Ger. loan-word.

Trommel, f., 'drum, cylinder, sieve,' from the equiv. late MidHG. *trumel, trummbel*, f., of which the classical MidHG. form is *trumbe* (*trumme, trume*), 'drum, trumpet'; comp. OHG. *trumpa, trumba*, 'trumpet.' The Rom. languages have a corresponding word, Ital. *tromba*, Fr. *trompe*. Since these have no Lat. form, OHG. *trumba* may be regarded as their source. OHG. *trumba* seems to be identical with OIc. *trumba*, 'pipe, stalk, trumpet,' in which case the latter is probably nearer the primary meaning.—ModHG. Trompete, f., 'trumpet' (even in MidHG. *trûmet, trûmbet*), is based on Rom.; comp. Fr. trompette, Ital. *trombetta*.

Tropf, m., 'needy or stupid person,' from the equiv. late MidHG. *tropfe*. It is considered to be a variant of Tropfen (Tropf, lit. 'least thing, nothing, wight' ?).

Tropfen, m., 'drop, tear,' from the equiv. MidHG. *tropfe* (*troffe*), OHG. *tropfo* (*troffo*), m.; corresponding to OSax. *dropo*, Du. *drop*, AS. *dropa*, E. *drop*, and the equiv. OIc. *drope*. A derivative of the Teut. root *drup* (see triefen).

Troſt, m., 'comfort, consolation,' from MidHG. and OHG. *trôst*, m., 'comfort, help, protection, assurance, confidence'; corresponding to OIc. *traust*, m., 'assurance,' Goth. *traust* (gen. *traustis* for *-eis*), 'treaty, alliance.' The word is a derivative of the Teut. root *traus*, a variant of the root *trû* appearing in trauen. Comp. OIc. *traustr*, adj., 'certain, strong, firm,' lit. 'that in which one has confidence.'—**tröſten**, vb., 'to comfort, console,' from the equiv. Mid HG. *trœsten*, OHG. *trôsten* (*traustjan*).

Troſſ, m., 'baggage, baggage-train, cavalcade,' from late MidHG. *trosse*, f., 'luggage,' formed from Fr. *trousse*, 'truss, bundle.'

Trott, m., 'trot,' ModHG. only, from the equiv. Ital. *trotto* (Fr. *trot*). This Rom. word is apparently based on OHG. *trottôn*, 'to tread' (late MidHG. *trotten*, 'to run'), an intensive form of treten. E. *to trot* has been adopted from the borrowed Fr. term *trotter*. Comp. the following word.

Trotte, f., 'wine-press,' from the equiv. MidHG. *trotte* (*trote*), OHG. *trotta* (*trota*), f.; lit. perhaps 'place where the wine is pressed out by treading.' A derivative of the Teut. root *tred* (*trod*), which has been discussed under treten (see also the preceding word). For a term adopted with the Southern culture of the vine, see under Kelter (comp. also Terfel).

Trotz, m., 'boldness, obstinacy, defiance,' from MidHG. (MidG.) *trotz*, of which the more usual forms are MidHG. *tratz, trutz*, m., 'refractoriness'; allied to MidHG. *tratzen, tretzen*, 'to defy,' *tratz*, 'insolent, defiant, obstinate.' The word is unknown to OHG. and the other OTeut. dialects, but there is no reason to suppose that it has been borrowed.—**trotz**, prep., 'in spite of,' is based on the MidHG. interj. *tratz* (*trotz*), 'I defy you.'

trübe, adj., 'turbid, gloomy, dull, dim,' from MidHG. *truebe*, adj. (*truobe*, adv.), OHG. *truobi*, adj., 'obscure, gloomy, dull'; allied to trüben, 'to darken, tarnish, cast a gloom over,' MidHG. *trueben*, OHG. *truoben*, 'to darken, sadden.' Comp. AS. *drôf*, 'dirty, troubled,' Du. *droef*, 'dull, sad,' Goth. *drôbjan*, 'to confuse, lead astray, excite commotion,' AS. *drêfan*, 'to disturb, agitate, trouble.' In the non-Teut. languages there are no certain cognates of the Teut. root *drôb*, 'to confuse.'—**Trübſal**, n., 'affliction, distress,' from MidHG. *trüebesal*, OHG. *truobisal*; an abstract of trüben.

Trubel, m., 'confusion, trouble,' Mod HG. only, from Fr. *trouble*.

Truchſeß, m., 'lord high-steward,' from the equiv. MidHG. *truh-, truht-sœze* (*-sætze*), OHG. *truhsâzзo* (=). The MidLat. rendering, 'dapifer, discophorus,' shows that the word signified 'he who serves the food.' Yet MidHG. and OHG. *truht* is not used in the sense of 'food'; it signifies 'that which can be carried' (a derivative of *tragen*), and might thus mean also 'the food, served up.' On account of MidHG. and OHG. *truht*, 'crowd, troop,' others with greater reason regard MidHG. *truhsæʒe* as 'he who sits with the retainers (or at the head of the table), provides for their maintenance (hence *dapifer*) and assigns to them their places at table.' The word is also found in LG. dialects; comp. LG. Droſtei, 'district of a Droſte' (high bailiff; MidDu. *drossâte*); Du. *drossaard*, 'high bailiff.'

Trüffel, f., 'truffle,' ModHG. only; corresponding to Du. *truffel*, E. *truffle*, Fr. *truffe*, Span. *trufa*. The equiv. Ital. *tartufo* shows that the word is connected with Kartoffel, which see.

Trug, m., 'deception, illusion,' ModHG. only, allied to trügen, older triegen, which is derived from the equiv. MidHG. *triegen*, OHG. *triogan*, str. vb., corresponding to OSax. *bidriogan*, 'to cheat, deceive.' To these are allied Teut. *draumo-*, 'phantom' (see Traum), as well as OIc. *draugr*, 'ghost,' OSax. *gidrog*, MidHG. *getroc* (*g*), 'ghost' (comp. also Zwerg). The Teut. root *drāg* (*dwerg*), 'to deceive,' contained in these words, is based on an Aryan root *dhrūgh* (*dhwergh*), 'to overreach, injure'; comp. Sans. *druh*, 'to injure (by deceit, craftiness, or enchantment),' OPers. *drauga*, 'lie,' Zend *draoga*, 'lying' (*druj*, 'ghost').

Truhe, f., 'trunk, chest,' from MidHG. *truhe* (**trucke* is indicated by ModHG. dial. Trucke), OHG. *truha* (*truccha*), f., 'chest, cupboard.' OIc. *þró* (from *þrúh*), and AS. *þrúh*, 'chest, drawer,' seem to be allied in meaning although the sounds do not entirely correspond. In any case Lat. *truncus*, 'trunk' (of a tree) is not allied. If AS. *þrúh* is not identical with HG. Truhe (MidLat. *trucca*), the latter may be connected with Trog; Truhe (lit. 'wooden vessel') would then be Aryan *drūk-* (*drukn-*).

Trumm, m., 'end, stump, fragment,' which is found besides only in the plur. Trümmer, 'fragments, ruins,' is based on Mid HG. and OHG. *drum*, n., 'end, piece, end-piece, splinter'; comp. OIc. *þrǫmr*, 'brim, edge, verge,' E. (AS.) *thrum*, 'end-piece.' Teut. *þramu-* (*þrumu-*). from Aryan *trmo-*, has rightly been connected with Lat. *terminus*, Gr. τέρμα, 'boundary, conclusion, end.'

Trumpf, m., 'trump,' ModHG. only, from the equiv. Fr. *triomphe* (Ital. *trionfo*), whence also Du. *troef*, E. *trump*; properly identical therefore with Lat. *triumphus*; hence lit. 'triumphant, victorious card.' Comp. Treff.

Trunk, m., 'drink, draught,' from the equiv. MidHG. and OHG. *trunc*, allied to trinfen.

trunken, adj., 'drunken, intoxicated,' from the equiv. MidHG. *trunken*, OHG. *trunchan*. An old partic. without the prefix ge (see feist), and with an active sense too, 'he who has drunk' (comp. Lat. *potus*), then 'he who has drunk immoderately'; similarly Du. *dronken*, E. *drunk*, and Goth. *drugkans*.

Trupp, m., 'troop, band, gang,' ModHG. only, from Ital. *truppa*.

Truthahn, m., 'turkey-cock,' ModHG. only; Trut is probably an imitation of the cry of the bird.

Tuch, n., 'cloth, stuff; kerchief,' from the equiv. MidHG. *tuoch*, OHG. *tuoh* (*hh*), m. and n.; comp. OLG. *dōk*, Du. *doek*, 'cloth.' To these is also allied OIc. *dúkr*, 'cloth,' whence E. *duck* (canvas). On account of the OIc. signification 'table-cloth,' Tuch has been compared with Goth. *gadauka*, 'messmate.' The early history of the West Teut. *dōko-*, 'cloth' (from pre-Teut. *dhāgo-*), is obscure.

tüchtig, adj., 'fit, able, qualified, excellent,' from MidHG. (MidG.) *tühtic* (*g*), 'serviceable, brave, sturdy'; allied to Mid HG. (MidG.) *tuht*, f., 'ability, fitness,' an abstract of ModHG. taugen (comp. also Tugend). Corresponding to Du. *deugdelijk*, AS. *dyhtig*, E. *doughty*.

Tücke, f., 'trick, spite, malice,' from MidHG. *tücke*; properly plur. of older ModHG. Tuck, MidHG. *tuc*(*k*), *duc*(*ck*), m, 'blow, push, rapid movement, sly trick, sleight of hand, craftiness.' The word is wanting in OHG. and the other OTeut. languages, hence its earlier form cannot be discovered.

Tuff, Tufffſtein, m., 'tufa, tuff,' from the equiv. MidHG. and OHG. *tufstein* (*tub-*, *tupf-stein*); formed from Ital. *tufo* (Fr. *tuf*), based on Lat. *tōphus*.

Tugend, f., 'virtue, chastity,' from Mid HG. *tugent, tugende*, f., 'manly excellence, power, good quality, virtue'; OHG. *tugund*, f., as a derivative of *tugan* (see taugen), signifies lit. 'serviceableness, fitness.' Goth. **dugunþus* (derivative *unþu-*, from pre-

Teut. *entu-*) is also indicated by AS. *dugup*.

Tülle, f., 'socket,' MidHG. *tülle*, n., 'ferule for fastening an iron point on a handle' (usually 'partition of boards, palisade'). OHG. has no corresponding form *tulli* (Goth. *dulja-*), which might be connected by gradation with ModHG. Thal (Thülle, lit. 'deepening'). Others consider Fr. *douille* (from Lat. *ductile*, 'channel'), 'socket,' as the ultimate source of MidHG. *tülle*. Fr. *tuyau* (E. *tewel*), Span. *tudel*, 'pipe,' are certainly not allied. The abnormal double sense of MidHG. *tülle* has not, however, been explained.

Tulpe, f., 'tulip,' earlier ModHG. *Tulipan*, from the equiv. Ital. *tulipa*, *tulipano*.

-tum, suffix, from MidHG. and OHG. *-tuom*; an abstract suffix, which has been formed in compounds from an independent word *tuom*, m. and n., 'relation, rank, dignity, condition.' This is an abstract form of ModHG. thun. Comp. the corresponding Eng. suffix *-dom* in *kingdom*. Eng. has preserved the independent word *doom* (AS. *dôm*), to which *to deem* (AS. *dêman*) is allied; comp. Sans. *dhâman*, 'institution, sacred custom.'

Tümpel, m., 'pool, deep part of a lake'; a MidHG. form for MidHG. *tümpfel*, 'deep place in flowing or standing water, pool, puddle,' OHG. *tumfilo*, m., 'whirlpool' (whence the equiv. Ital. *tonfano*). A derivative of the nasalised Teut. root *dup*, 'to be deep' (see taufen, tief), which appears also in E. *dimple*, Du. *dompelen*, 'to dive, plunge,' *dompelaar*, 'diver' (bird). Pre-Teut. *dhumb*, 'to be deep,' is also assumed by Lith. *dumbu*, 'to get hollow.' Comp. also Topf.

tünchen, vb., 'to whitewash, plaster,' from the equiv. MidHG. *tünchen*, OHG. *tunihhôn*, mostly *mit chalche tunihhôn*. The additional expression in OHG. leads to the assumption that *tunihhôn* means lit. 'to clothe,' from OHG. *tunihha*, 'dress' (borrowed, like AS. *tunuce*, from Lat. *tunica*). The Germans still say eine Wand mit Tünche bekleiden, 'to give a coat of limewash to a wall' (comp. E. *to coat* and *coat*). With this agrees Ital. *intonicare*, 'to plaster, rouge' (*intonico*, *intonicato*, 'plaster'). Note that Lat. *tunica*, Ital. *tonica*, also signifies 'covering.' The Lat.-Ital. word was borrowed at the beginning of the OHG. period;

had it been borrowed earlier it would have appeared as *zunihha* in OHG. It cannot have been introduced much later than Fenster and Turm.

tunken, vb., 'to dip, steep, soak,' from MidHG. *tunken*, *dunken*, OHG. *tunchôn*, *dunchôn*, wk. vb., 'to immerse.' The OHG. variant *thunkôn* leads to a Goth. **pugkôn*, which must be allied to Lat. *tingere*, 'to moisten, dip,' and to Gr. τέγγω, 'to soften, moisten.' Hence tunken cannot be connected with tauchen.

Tüpfel, m., 'dot, iota'; diminut. of earlier ModHG. Tupf, m., which is based on MidHG. *topfe*, OHG. *topfo*, 'point.' Goth. **duppa* (**duppila*) is wanting. Probably cognate with tief.

Turm (UpG. and Rhen. Turn), m., 'tower, steeple,' from the equiv. MidHG. *turm*, with the variant *turn* (*torm*, *torn*), m. ; in OHG. only *turra* and *turri*, which correspond to the equiv. Lat. *turris*. The final *m* of the MidHG. word has not yet been explained, nor the *n* of ODu. *turn*, Du. *toren*, UpG. *turn*; AS. *tŷr*, E. *tower*, with the variant AS. *torr*, 'tower,' also present a difficulty. Comp. further Fr. *tour*, Ital. *torre*, from Lat. *turris*.

turnen, vb., 'to practise gymnastics,' ModHG. only ; no corresponding word is found in MidHG., which has only *turnei*, 'tonrnament,' *turnieren*, 'to hold a tournament, tilt,' borrowed from Fr. The Mod HG. word is probably derived from Fr. *tourner*, 'to turn, turn round.'

Turteltaube, f., 'turtle-dove,' from the equiv. MidHG. *turteltûbe* (*türteltube*), OHG. *turtul-*, *turtil-tûba*, f. ; borrowed and corrupted in the OHG. period (in connection with the Biblical texts) from Lat. *turtur*, whence also Du. *tortelduif*, AS. and E. *turtle*. Comp. also Ital. *tortora*, Fr. *tourtre*, *tourtereau*.

Tusch, m., 'flourish of trumpets'; interj., 'hush! tush!' ModHG only ; a recent formation imitating a sound.

Tusche, f., 'Indian-ink,' ModHG. only ; from Fr. *toucher*, 'to paint, delineate, ink.' **tuten**, vb., 'to blow a horn,' ModHG. only ; a recent onomatopoetic word.

Tüttel, m., 'dot,' ModHG. only ; entirely distinct from Tittel. It is identical with MidHG. *tüttel* (*tüteltn*), n., 'nipple, teat' ; dimin. of the equiv. OHG. *tutta*, MidHG. *tutte*.

Twing, m., see zwingen.

U.

übel, adj., 'evil, bad, wrong; sick,' from MidHG. *übel*, OHG. *ubil*, ' bad, wicked '; a common Teut. adj. corresponding to OSax. *ubil*, Du. *euvel*. AS. *yfel*, E. *evil*, Goth. *ubils*, ' bad.' With these are connected OHG. *uppi* (from Teut. *ubjo-*), ' vicious, malignant; villain,' as well as the cognates of ModHG. *üppig*. The word has been supposed to be related to the prepos. *über* (Aryan *upéri*), so that Teut. *ubilo-*, from *upelo-*, meant lit. 'that which oversteps a limit or is contrary to rule.' Nothing positive, however, can be asserted, since the word is specifically Teut.; or is OIr. *uall*, 'pride,' cognate ?.

üben, vb., 'to practise, exercise,' from MidHG. *üeben*, OHG. *uoben* (from *óbjan*), wk. vb., 'to set agoing, execute, venerate,' corresponding to OSax. *óbian*, 'to celebrate,' Du. *oefenen*, 'to exercise, look after,' OIc. *æfa*, 'to practise.' Allied to OHG. *uoba*, 'celebration,' *uobo*, 'tiller of the soil.' The Teut. root *ób*, 'to execute,' contained in these cognates, seems to have been originally used of tilling the ground and of religious acts. To this corresponds, according to the permutation of consonants, the Aryan root *óp*, with which are allied Sans. *ápas*, n., 'work' (espec. religious work), and Lat. *opus*, n., 'work' (connected with *óperari*, espec., 'to sacrifice').

über, prepos. and adv., 'over, above,' from the equiv. MidHG. *über;* OHG. *ubir*, *ubar*, is a prepos. with the adverb. form *ubiri*. Corresponding to OSax. *obar*, Du. and E. *over*, AS. *ofer*, OIc. *yfer*, Goth. *ufar*, 'over.' This common Teut. word is based on an equiv. Aryan *upéri*, which appears in Sans. *upari*, Gr. ὑπέρ (ὑπείρ), Lat. *super*. With these are connected the prepos. *auf*, and *ob* (*ober*). Comp. also *übel*.

Überdruß, see verdrießen.—**überflüssig**, adj., 'superfluous,' from MidHG. *übervlüȝȝec*, 'overflowing, superabundant, remaining.'—**überhaupt**, adv., 'in general, on the whole,' from late MidHG. *über houbet*, 'without counting the pieces, whole, all' (properly only of buying goods; Mid HG. *houbet* is frequently used to designate a number of men or beasts).

überwinden, vb, 'to wind over; overcome, conquer,' from MidHG. *überwinden*, OHG. *ubarwintan*, str. vb., 'to excel, overpower, conquer'; also with an equiv. meaning MidHG. *überwinnen*, OHG. *ubarwinnan*. While the simple OHG. vb. *wintan* means 'to turn, turn round,' OHG. *winnan* (comp. AS. *oferwinnan*) has the signification ' to contend, quarrel' (comp. gewinnen), which appears in the compound. The *t*, which properly belongs only to the present stem in this sense, is the same as in OHG. *stantan*, *swintan* (see stehen, schwinden).

übrig, adj., 'left over, remaining,' from MidHG. *überic* (*g*), 'left over, excessive, exaggerated, superfluous'; a MidHG. derivative of über.

Ufer, n., 'shore, bank (of a river),' a MidG. and LG. word (adopted like Beet, Strand, &c., in the written language), from the equiv. MidHG. *uover*, n. OHG. *uofar* (Goth. *ófr* ?) is wanting; nor is the word known even now to the UpG. dialects. Comp. MidLG. *óver*, Du. *oever*, AS. *ófer* (obsolete in E.; yet *Windsor* is equiv. to AS. *Windles ófer*, 'the bank of the Windel'). West Teut. *ófor* has been considered, probably without reason, a cognate of Sans. *ap*, 'water' (for the evolution of meaning comp. Au), and Lat. *amnis* (for *apnis* ?), 'river.' UpG. (Bav.) *urvar*, 'haven,' landing-place, bank,' of the MidHG. period, points rather to a Goth. *us-far*, 'haven'; Goth.-Teut. *us* appears in some West Teut. dialects as *ó* ⸱OHG. *uo*). Hence Ufer is lit. 'departure, setting out' ?.

Uhr, f., 'clock, watch, hour,' ModHG. only, from LG. *ûr*, 'clock, hour' (even in the MidHG. period LRhen. *ûr* meant 'hour'); corresponding to Du. *uur*, E. *hour*. Based on Lat. *hóra* (comp. Fr. *heure*, Ital. *ora*).

Uhu, m., 'horned owl,' ModHG. only, a recent onomatopoetic word, which was connected with MidHG. *húwe*, OHG. *húwo*, OLG. *húo*, 'owl.'

ulken, vb., 'to lark,' ModHG. only; allied to LRhen. *ulk*, 'bulb' ?. Comp. Du. *ui*, 'onion, joke.'

Ulme, f., 'elm,' from MidHG. (rare) *ulmboum*, for which MidHG. and OHG. *ëlmboum*, m., is most frequently found. While *ulm-* is adopted from Lat. *ulmus*, the equiv. OHG. and MidHG. *ëlm-* is related prehistorically, by gradation, with Lat. *ulmus;* so too OIc. *almr*, E. *elm*. With the pre-

Teut. stem *el, ol*, the cognates of ModHG. Erle (Eller) are also connected.

um, adv. and prep., 'about, around,' from the equiv. MidHG. *umbe* (*ümbe*), OHG. *umbi*, cannot be regarded as directly corresponding to Gr. ἀμφί, Sans. *abhi*, 'about,' for then the OHG. form would be *umb*. OHG. *umbi* is rather a compound of this **umb*, with the prep. *bî*, 'by'; so too OSax. *umbi*, AS. *ymbe* (but *ymb* directly corresponds to Sans. *abhi*).—**umſonſt**, adv., 'in vain, to no purpose,' from the equiv. MidHG. *umbe sus*. See ſonſt.

un-, prefix, 'not,' from the equiv. MidHG. and OHG. *un-*; a negative prefix common to Teut. and Aryan; comp. OSax. *un-*, Du. *on-*, AS. and E. *un-*, OIc. *ó-*. Corresponding to Gr. ἀ-, Lat. *in-*, Sans. and Zend *a-*, *an-*. With this prefix is connected the common Aryan negation *nê*, 'not' (see nicht), as well as the prep. ohne and its cognates.

Unbill, f., 'iniquity, wrong,' MidHG. only; based on the cognates of billig, instead of the correct ModHG. Unbilfe, f., MidHG. *unbilde*, n., 'wrong, impropriety,' which is properly an abstract from MidHG. (rare) *unbil* (usually *unbillich*), adj., 'incongruous, unjust.' On account of the meaning there is probably no direct historic connection with Bilb. Comp. billig, and especially Weichbild.

und, conj., 'and,' from the equiv. MidHG. *unt, unde*, OHG. *unta, unti* (*inti, enti*); corresponding to OSax. *endi*, Du. *en*, AS. and E. *and*, Sans. *átha*, 'also, further, and,' points, like AS and E. *and*, to Aryan *nthá*.

Unflat, m., 'filth, dirt,' from MidHG. *un-rât*, m., n., and f., 'dirtiness, untidiness'; to which is allied **unflätig**, adj., 'filthy, nasty,' from MidHG. *unvlætic*, 'unclean, untidy.' OHG. **flât*, 'beauty,' is met with only in female proper names (*Sigi-, Muot-, Hruot-flât*). The early history of OHG. **flât* (Goth. *flêd*, AS. *flêd* in proper names) is obscure.

ungefähr, see ehngefähr.

ungeheuer, adj., 'monstrous, atrocious,' from MidHG. *ungehiure*, OHG. *ungihiuri*, 'uncanny, frightful'; allied to **Ungeheuer**, n., 'monster,' from MidHG. *ungehiure*, 'savage, dragon, ghostly creature,' OHG. *ungihiurî*, 'monster.' See geheuer.

ungeſchlacht, see geſchlacht.

ungeſtüm, adj., 'blustering, impetuous,' from MidHG. *ungestüeme*, OHG. *un-gistuomi* (*unstuom*), adj., 'stormy, impetuous'; the unnegatived form of the adj. was extremely rare in OHG. and MidHG. Based on a verbal root *stam*, as in MidHG. *stemen* (ModHG. ſtemmen, from **stamjan*), 'to check, restrain,' which appears also in ModHG. flammeln.—**Ungeſtim**, n., 'monster,' early ModHG. only; unknown to the older periods. Early history obscure.

Ungeziefer, n., 'vermin,' from the equiv. late MidHG. *ungezîbere, unzîver*, n.; properly 'unclean beast not suited for sacrifice.' It is based, in fact, on OHG. *zëbar*, 'beast of offering,' which is connected with the equiv. AS. *tîfer*. The terms borrowed in Rom., OFr. *toivre*, 'cattle,' Portug. *zebro*, 'ox, cow,' prove that *zëbar* was applied to large animals, and that the word was widely diffused in OTeut.

Unke, f., 'ringed snake,' ModHG. only; in MidHG. *üche* (OHG. *ûhha*), f., 'toad'; MidHG. and OHG. *unc*, m., 'snake.' Probably the ModHG. word is due to a combination of the older forms.

unlängſt, adv., 'recently, of late,' from MidHG. *unlanges* (*unlange*), 'short time,' with an excrescent *t* as in Obſt, Art.

Unrat, m., 'trash, rubbish, refuse,' from MidHG. and OHG. *unrât*, m., 'helplessness, want, necessity, useless stuff'; allied to Rat.

uns, pron., 'us, to us,' from the equiv. MidHG. and OHG. *uns*; in the same form common to Teut. to supplement the declension of wir. Comp. Du. *ons*, OLG. and AS. *ûs* (E. *us*), Goth. *uns*. This *uns* (from *ns*) is certainly connected with Lat. *nos* (*noster*), Gr. ἡμεῖς (for **ἀσ-μεῖς*), and Sans. *nas*, 'us'; comp. wir.—Allied to **unſer**, poss. pron., 'our,' from MidHG. *unser*, OHG. *unsêr*. The detailed history of the pronom. stem belongs to grammar.

Unſchlitt, Inſchlitt (Inſelt), n., 'suet, tallow,' from MidHG. *unslit* (*unselt*), *inslit* (*inselt*), n., 'tallow,' of which there are abundant variants in MidHG. Comp. OHG. *unslit*, 'fat, tallow' (AS. *unslit*, or rather *unflit*, 'fat, grease, tallow,' is uncertain). MidHG. *unsleht*, 'tallow' (Rhen.-Franc. *inschlicht*), seems to be connected with MidHG. (*in*)*geslehte*, n., 'entrails.' The derivation of the word cannot be more definitely determined, since the older forms are unknown; Hess. and LG. *ungel*, 'tallow,' suggests the supposition that OHG. *unslit* has originated in **ungslit*.

unten, adv., 'below, beneath, underneath,' from the equiv. MidHG. *unden*, OHG. *untanân*. Allied to **unter**, prep. and adv., 'below, under,' from MidHG. and OHG. *unter*, *under*, OHG. *untar* (prep.); but *untari*, adv.; corresponding to Goth. and OSax. *undar*, Du. *onder*, AS. and E. *under*. The Aryan prep. *ṇdhér*, on which these are based, appears also in Lat. *infra* (comp. *inferior*) and Sans. *adhás*, 'beneath' (*adhara*, 'the lower').

Unterſchleif, m., 'embezzlement, smuggling,' ModHG. only, allied to Mid HG. *undersliufære*, 'cheat'; comp. MidHG. *undersliefen*, 'to cheat, deceive,' *underslouf*, 'hiding-place.'

unterthan, adj., 'subject to, dependent,' from the equiv. MidHG *undertân*, OHG. *untartân*. Properly a partic. of MidHG. *undertuon*, OHG. *untartuon*, 'to subjugate, bring into subjection.' See *thun*.

unterwegen, unterwegs, adv., 'on the way,' from MidHG. *under wëgen*, 'on the way, away.'

unwirſch, adj., 'cross, rude, morose,' from MidHG. (rare) *unwirs*, usually *unwirdesch*, 'unworthy, contemptuous, indignant, angry.' Comp. MidHG. *unwërt*, 'despised, unsuited, disagreeable'; allied to **wert**. See also **wirſch**.

Unze, f., 'ounce,' from MidHG. *unze*, OHG. *unza*, f., 'weight,' from Lat. *uncia*.

üppig, adj., 'luxurious, voluptuous, sumptuous,' from MidHG. *üppic* (*g*), OHG. *uppîg*, 'superfluous, useless, invalid, frivolous, arrogant.' For the connection of this specifically HG. word with Goth. *ufjô*, f., 'superfluity,' and OHG. *uppi*, 'malicious,' as well as with the cognates of **übel** and **über**, see **übel**.

Ur, see **Auer**.

ur-, pref., from MidHG. and OHG. *ur-*; an accented prefix of which **er-** (MidHG. *er-*, OHG. *ir-*) is the unaccented form. In OHG., *ur*, 'out of,' is met with as a prep. The prefix signifies 'out of, originally, in the beginning.' Goth. has *us* (*uz*), of which there are no certain cognates in the other Aryan languages.

Urahn, m., 'great-grandfather,' from MidHG. *urane*; see **Ahn**—**uralt**, adj., 'extremely old, primeval,' from the equiv. MidHG. and OHG. *uralt*; allied to **alt**.—

Urbar, n., 'produce, landed property,' from MidHG. *urbor*, *urbar*, f. and n., 'copyhold, rent, income'; lit. perhaps 'tax, produce, rent' (comp. Goth. *gabaúr*, 'tax'). Hence **urbar**, adj., 'arable,' lit. 'bearing interest, productive' (ModHG. only).—

Urfehde, f., 'solemn oath not to take vengeance on an enemy,' from the equiv. MidHG. *urvêhede* (*urvêhe*), f.; see **Fehde**.—

Urheber, m., 'author, originator,' a Mod HG. derivative of MidHG. *urhap* (*b*), m., 'beginning, cause, origin' (allied to **heben**).

Urkunde, f., 'deed, document, charter,' from MidHG. *urkunde* (*urkünde*), v. and f., 'testimony, proof, document,' OHG. *urchundi*, f., 'testimony'; allied to **erkennen** (hence lit. 'recognition').—**Urlaub**, m., 'leave of absence, furlough,' from MidHG. and OHG. *úrloup* (*b*), m. and n., 'permission'; an abstract from **erlauben**, 'to permit,' MidHG. *erlouben*, OHG. *irloubôn*.—

Urſache, f., 'cause,' from MidHG. *ursache*. —**Urſprung**, m., 'source, origin,' from MidHG. *ursprunc*, *ursprinc* (*g*), OHG. *úrspring*, m. and n., 'source'; allied to **ſpringen**, (**erſpringen**).—**Urtel, Urteil**, n., 'judgment, sentence, decision,' from Mid HG. *urteil*, *urteile*, f. and n., 'judicial decision'; allied to **erteilen** (lit. 'that which is imparted'). Comp. Du. *oordeel*, AS. *ordâl*, 'judgment' (whence Fr. *ordalie*, 'judgment of God,' MidLat. *ordalium*).

uzen, vb., 'to jeer at, mock,' ModHG. only; a derivative of the proper name **Ul3**, an abbrev. form of **Ulrich**. Comp. **häuſeln**.

V.

Vater, m., 'father,' from the equiv. MidHG. *vater*, OHG. *fater*; common to Teut. and Aryan in the same sense; comp. Goth. (rare) *fadar* (usually *atta*), OIc. *faðer*, AS. *fæder*, E. *father*, Du. *vader*, *vaar*, OSax. *fadar*. Teut. *fadér*, from Aryan *patér*; comp. Lat. *pater*, Gr. πατήρ, Sans. *pitṛ* (for *patṛ*), 'father.' Aryan *pa-tér* has been derived from the Sans. root *pâ*, 'to guard, protect,' so that **Vater** would mean lit. 'protector.' An English preacher of the 12th cent. connected the word in a similar way with AS. *fêdan*, E. *to feed* (see **füttern**); hence **Vater**, lit. 'nourisher.' Neither interpretation is historically certain, since Aryan *pa-ter* is probably based on an instinctive sound (comp. Gr. dial. πᾶ, 'father,' πάππα); comp. **Mutter, Bruder**, and **Schwe-**

ſter. For a derivative of Water see under Wetter, Wasſ, and Waſe.

Veilchen, n., 'violet' (plant), dimin. of earlier ModHG. Veil, from MidHG. vîel, older viól, m., víole, f. Borrowed in the early MidHG. period from Lat. viola (with v equal to f, as in Vers, Räſig, Brief, and Vogt). Comp. Ital. viola, dimin. violetta, Fr. violette; also to Du. viool, E. violet.

Veitsbohne, f., 'kidney-bean,' Mod HG. only; it is so called because it begins to bloom on St. Vitus's day (June 15).—

Veitstanz, m., 'St. Vitus's dance' (Mod HG. only), MidLat. chorea sancti Viti, thus named because the help of St. Vitus was implored.

ver-, pref.; in its most frequent significations it is derived from MidHG. ver-, OHG. fir- (far-), which are probably a combination of several other unaccented forms. Comp. the unaccented prefixes Goth. fair-, fra-, faúr- (see also freſſen), which appeared in OHG. as fir- (far-). Goth. fair, fra, and faúr appear to correspond respectively to Gr. περί, πρό, and παρά, though their meanings do not coincide. Comp. Sans. pári, 'round about,' párá, 'away,' purá, 'before,' prá, 'before, away.'—Most of the compounds with ver- (E. for-) are based on Goth. fra-, which denoted 'the opposite, deterioration, change.'

verblüffen, vb., 'to disconcert, confuse,' ModHG. only, from Du. verbluffen, 'to stun, dishearten.' Early history obscure. — **verbrämen,** vb., 'to border, fringe,' from late MidHG. brëm, verbrëmen, n., 'border, trimming,' older ModHG. Brame, 'border, skirts of a wood,' E. brim (AS. brimme).

verdammen, vb., 'to condemn, anathematise,' from the equiv. MidHG. verdamnen, OHG. firdamnón; borrowed, like other ecclesias. terms in the OHG. period, from Lat. damnáre (comp. Fr. damner, Ital. damnare), with the prefix ver- to give a bad sense to the word.—**verdauen,** vb., 'to digest,' from the equiv. MidHG. verdöuwen (verdöun), verdouwen, with the simple forms döuwen, douwen, OHG. douwen (dęwen), firdouwen, 'to digest'; comp. Du. verduwen. The assumed Teut. þaujan, 'to digest,' is probably connected with tauen (lit. 'to dissolve').—**verderben,** str. vb., 'to spoil, destroy, corrupt,' from MidHG. verdĕrben, str. vb., 'to come to nought, perish, die,' with which the corresponding causative MidHG. verdęrben, 'to ruin, kill,' was con-

fused in ModHG. OHG. *dĕrban, Goth. *haírban, str. vb., 'to perish, die,' is wanting. The meaning of the MidHG. words points to a connection with ſterben, so that we must assume a double root, Aryan terbh, sterbh (comp. Stier and Dreſſel (2)); in that case neither terb, with its divergent meaning, nor dürfen can be allied.—**Verderben,** n., 'destruction,' from MidHG. verdĕrben, n., properly an infinitive used as a subst.— **verdrießen,** vb., 'to grieve, vex, trouble,' from MidHG. verdriezen, str. vb., 'to excite anger, produce weariness'; also the equiv. MidHG. be-, erdriezen, from OHG. bi-, irdriozan, str. vb. Comp. Goth. usþriutan, 'to molest, revile,' AS. þreátian (E. to threaten), with á-þreótan,' to be disgusted,' Du. droten, 'to threaten,' with verdrieten, 'to vex,' OIc. prjóta, 'to want, fail' (þrot, 'want,' þraut, 'hard task, trouble.' The great development of the str. verbal root, Teut. þrüt, makes it difficult to find undoubted cognates in non-Teut.; OSlov. trudŭ, 'pain, trouble,' truzdą, 'to torment,' Lat. trúdo, 'to crowd, push,' point to an Aryan root trüd.—Mod HG. **Verdruß,** m., 'vexation, annoyance'; in MidHG. usually urdruz, urdrütze, verdriez. — **verdutzt,** adj., 'disconcerted, abashed,' from MidHG. vertutzt, a partic. of MidHG. vertutzen, vertuzzen, 'to be deafened, become silent'; remoter history obscure. See vertuſchen.

vergällen, vb., 'to embitter,' from MidHG. vergellen, wk. vb., 'to make as bitter as gall, embitter'; allied to Galle.— **vergauen,** see Gau.—**vergattern,** vb., 'to enclose with trellis-work, assemble (soldiers) by beat of drum,' from late Mid HG. (LRhen.) vergatern, 'to assemble.' Properly a LG. word; comp. Du. vergaderen, to which the cognates of E. to gather (see Gatte) are connected.—**vergebens,** adv., 'in vain, to no purpose,' from Mid HG. vergëbene (-gëbenes), 'gratis, in vain'; allied to vergëben (OHG. firgëban), 'useless, to no purpose,' lit. 'given away,' a partic. used as an adj.—**vergeſſen,** vb., 'to forget,' from the equiv. MidHG. vergëzzen, OHG. firgëzzan, str. vb.; a West Teut. word; comp. Du. vergeten, AS. forgitan, E. to forget. Also the equiv. OHG. irgëzzan, MidHG. ergëzzen. The compound verb is the relic of a strong verbal root get, 'to reach, attain,' whence E. to get; comp. Goth. bigitan, 'to find,' OIc. 'to reach, attain.' In non-Teut., Lat. prae-hendere, 'to grasp,' Gr. χανδάνω (Aryan root ghed, *ghend*), are connected with the root *get*. Hence vergeſſen means lit. 'to get beyond one's reach, lose possession of.'—**vergeuden**, vb., 'to squander, dissipate,' from MidHG. *giuden* (*übergiuden*), wk. vb., 'to boast, make a parade, squander with ostentation'; unknown to OHG. Goth. *giwipa* might refer to OHG. *gëicôn*, 'to open one's mouth wide' (see *gähnen*).—**Vergnügen**, n., 'pleasure, enjoyment, amusement,' ModHG. only, from late MidHG. *vernüegen* and *genüegen*, 'to content, satisfy.'

verheeren, vb., 'to ravage, devastate,' from the equiv. MidHG. *verhern* (*verhergen*), OHG. *firherjôn*; lit. 'to destroy by war.' See *Heer*.

verlangen, vb., 'to claim, demand,' from MidHG. (rare) *verlangen*, 'to desire ardently,' usually MidHG. *belangen*, 'to desire, long for.' OSax. *langôn*, Du. *verlangen*, AS. *lengian*, E. *to long*, show the correspondence of the Teut. languages. The word is usually regarded as an old derivative of *lang*, but this is opposed by the meaning; it might be rather compared with the cognates of *gelingen*, the primary meaning of which is 'to aim, strive.'—**verletzen**, vb., 'to hurt, injure,' from MidHG. *verletzen*, 'to check, injure, wound'; allied to *letzen*.—**verläumden**, vb., 'to calumniate, slander,' from MidHG. *verliumden*; see *Leumund*.—**verlieren**, vb., 'to lose,' from the equiv. MidHG. *verliesen*, OHG. *virliosan*; a common Teut. str. vb., to which the equiv. Goth. *fraliusan*, AS. *forlêosan*, Du. *verliez∙n* correspond. Gr. λύω, 'to loosen' (ἀλεύω, 'to avoid, keep far away'?), Lat. *solvo* (partic. *so-lu-tus*), 'to loosen' (Sans. *lû*, 'to tear to pieces'), and Goth. *luns*, 'ransom,' which point to an Aryan *lŭ*, are closely connected with the Teut. root *lus*, to which *los* and *lösen* are also related. —**Verlies**, n., 'subterranean cave, dungeon,' ModHG. only, lit. 'place where one is lost' (comp. MidHG. *verliesen*, 'to kill'?).—**verloben**, vb., 'to engage, alliance, betroth,' from the equiv. MidHG. *verloben*; lit. 'to promise,' in which sense MidHG. *geloben* also occurs; see *geloben* and *Lob*.—**Verluſt**, m., 'loss, damage, injury,' from the equiv. MidHG. *verlust*, OHG. *virlust*, f.; a verbal abstract of *verlieren* (comp. Freſſ with *fretten*).

vermählen, vb., 'to marry, unite,' from late MidHG. *vermehelen*, usually *mehelen*, *mahelen*, lit. 'to give in marriage to a man,' also 'to take to wife,' whence generally 'to affiance, betroth.' The word is usually based on OHG. *mahal*, 'hall of justice' (see Maßl and Gemaßl); it is better to proceed from the equiv. MidHG. *gemahelen*, OHG. *ginahalen*, which are derivatives of OHG. *gimahala*, 'spouse.' For other details concerning its early history see Gemaßl.—**vermeſſen**, adj., 'daring, presumptuous,' from MidHG. *vermëʒʒen*, OHG. *firmëʒʒan*, 'daring, bold'; a partic. of MidHG. *vermëʒʒan*, OHG. *firmëʒʒan*, refl. 'to estimate one's strength too high, have an overweening opinion of oneself.'—**Vermögen**, n., 'ability, power, wealth,' from MidHG. *vermügen*, n., 'power, might, capability.' An infinit. used as a subst., MidHG. *vermügen*, *vermugen*, 'to be in a position, have power,' OHG. *furimugan*, allied to *mögen*, Macht. The prep. *vermöge*, 'in virtue of' (ModHG. only), is based on MidHG. *vermüge*, f., 'might, power,' and is developed like *kraft*.

vernichten, vb., 'to annihilate, annul,' from MidHG. *vernihten*, 'to annihilate, think lightly of'; allied to *nicht*.—**Vernunft**, f., 'reason, understanding,' from MidHG. *vernunft*, OHG. *firnunft*, f., 'activity of perception, sensual perception, comprehension, insight, understanding'; abstract of **vernehmen**, 'to hear, perceive, understand,' MidHG. *vernëmen*, OHG. *firnëman*, 'to perceive, hear, experience, grasp, seize, understand.' These figurative meanings are based on some such meaning as in Goth. *frauiman*, 'to take possession of, seize.' For a similar evolution see vergeſſen (with different senses attached to the prefix); begreifen has been similarly developed in its figurative senses.

verſchämpern, vb., 'to spill, waste foolishly,' ModHG. only, properly a LG. word, of onomatopoetic origin.—**verpönen**, vb., 'to forbid (under penalties), proscribe,' ModHG. only, from Lat. *poena* (whence also Pein).

verquicken, vb., 'to amalgamate (with),' ModHG. only, lit. perhaps 'to combine with quicksilver'; allied to Queckſilber (see also erquicken).—**verquiſten**, vb., 'to spend foolishly,' ModHG. only, from Du. *kwisten*, *verkwisten*, 'to squander, lavish'; comp. Goth. *fraqistjan*, 'to destroy, annihilate' (*usqistjan*, 'to kill'). Early history obscure.

verraten, vb., 'to betray, reveal,' from the equiv. MidHG. *verrâten*, OHG. *firrâtan*; lit. 'to lead astray by wrong advice.' —**verrecken**, vb., 'to die' (of cattle), from

MidHG. (rare) *verrecken*, 'to stretch out the limbs rigidly in death'; allied to reden.—**verrucht**, adj., 'infamous, atrocious,' from MidHG. *verruochet*, 'heedless, careless,' allied to MidHG. *verruochen*, 'to pay no heed, forget.' The meaning of the Mod HG. adj., like that of the cognate ruchlos, is under the influence of anrüchig, berüchtigt, Gerücht, ruchbar.—**verrückt**, adj., 'mad, crazy,' ModHG. only; allied to MidHG. *verrücken*, 'to move from the spot, confuse, disconcert.'

Vers, m., 'verse, couplet,' from the equiv. MidHG. and OHG. *vërs, fërs*, m. and n., which was adopted in the OHG. period (as early as the 9th cent.) from Lat. *versus*, perhaps contemporaneously with Schule and Meister. Comp. Räsig, Brief, and Vesper for the representation of Lat. *v* by HG. *f* (comp. AS. *fers*, and Du. *vers*).

verschieden, adj., 'different, distinct, various,' ModHG. only; not from verscheiden, which even in MidHG. (*verscheiden*) signifies specially 'to die,' but from a LG. word; comp. Du. *verscheiden* (for which *underscheiden* is found in MidHG.).—**verschlagen**, adj., 'cunning, crafty, sly,' properly a partic. of MidHG. *verslahen*, which also means 'to cheat.'—**verschmitzt**, adj., see schmitzen.—**verschroben**, adj., 'distorted, perverse, intricate,' lit. 'screwed the wrong way'; an inorganic partic. of schrauben; see Schraube.—**verschwenden**, vb., 'to squander, waste,' from MidHG. *verswenden*, 'to break to pieces, annihilate, consume,' which as a factitive of MidHG. *verswinden*, ModHG. verschwinden, 'to disappear,' signifies lit. 'to cause something to disappear.'

versehren, vb., 'to wound, injure, damage,' from the equiv. MidHG. *sëren*, lit. 'to cause pain'; allied to MidHG. and OHG. *sêr*, 'pain'; see sehr.—**versiegen**, vb., 'to dry up,' ModHG. only; allied to MidHG. *sigen*, OHG. *sigan*, str. vb., 'to fall, sink, flow, trickle' (see seihen, sickern); versiegen, lit. 'to flow out or away.'—**versöhnen** (same as versühnen), vb., 'to reconcile, atone for,' from the equiv. MidHG. *versüenen*; allied to Sühne. The accented vowel is derived either from LG. or probably from OBav. and OSwab., in which, late in the Middle Ages, œ appears before n, instead of üe (grün for grün; tön for tün).

Verstand, m., 'understanding, intelligence, sense,' from MidHG. *verstant* (*d*), which is used only rarely (in the sense of 'explanation, information'); comp. MidHG. *verstantnisse*, 'intelligence, insight, understanding,' to which MidHG. *verstęndic*, 'intelligent,' is allied. In OHG. too *firstantnissi* is most frequently used. To this word is allied ModHG. **verstehen**, vb., 'to understand, comprehend,' from MidHG. *verstân*, OHG. *firstân* (*firstantan*), 'to perceive, see into, notice, understand'; comp. Du. *verstaan*, AS. *forstondan* (in E. *to understand*). How the meaning can be derived from the root of stehen is not clear; it is usually referred to Gr. ἐπίσταμαι, 'to understand,' compared with the root στα, 'to stand.'—**verstümmeln**, vb., 'to mutilate,' from late MidHG. *verstümbelen*; see Stummel.

verteidigen, vb., 'to defend, maintain, justify,' from the equiv. MidHG. *verteidingen, vertagedingen* (usually *tagedingen*), wk. vb., of which the most frequent meaning is 'to plead before a tribunal, settle and adjust by agreement.' Allied to MidHG. *tagedinc, teidinc* (*g*), 'a lawsuit fixed for a certain date, court-day, negotiation, assembly' (with the meaning 'gossip, talk,' comp. Teiding). OHG. *tagading*, 'legal summons, negotiations,' is based on *tag* in the sense of 'fixed period,' and *ding*, 'judicial proceedings.' Comp. Du. *verdedigen*.

vertrackt, adj., 'distorted, twisted, odd, strange,' properly a partic. of vertreden, 'to confuse.'—**vertragen**, vb., 'to carry away, wear out, tolerate,' from MidHG. *vertregen*, str. vb., 'to tolerate, endure, be indulgent'; hence late MidHG. *vertrac*, ModHG. Vertrag, m., 'agreement, treaty.'—**vertuschen**, vb., 'to hush up,' from MidHG. *vertuschen*, 'to cover, conceal, keep secret, reduce to silence' (to which *verbutzt*, lit. 'stunned,' is allied ?); an onomatopoetic term.

verwahrlost, adj., 'neglected, spoilt,' properly a partic. of MidHG. *verwarlôsen*, 'to treat negligently,' based on OHG. *waralôs*, 'careless, negligent' (MidHG. *warlœse*, 'carelessness, negligence'). For the first part of the compound comp. wahrnehmen.—**verwandt**, adj., 'related, allied, cognate,' from the equiv. late MidHG. (rare) *verwant*, which is a partic. of MidHG. *verwenden* (with the rare signification 'to marry'); the usual term in MidHG. was *sippe* (OHG. *sippi*), adj. Comp. also MidHG. and OHG. *mâc*, m., 'relative, kinsman.'—**verwegen**, adj., 'bold, daring, rash,' from MidHG. *verwëgen*, 'quick and decided,' a partic. of *verwëgen*, 'to decide quickly.'

Verweis, m., 'reprimand, censure,' from the equiv. late MidHG. *verwīʒ*, n.; allied to *verweisen*, from MidHG. *verwīʒen*, OHG. *firwīʒan*, str. vb., 'to reprimand, censure.' Comp. Du. *verwijt*, n., 'reprimand,' and *verwijten*, 'to reproach, upbraid,' Goth. *fraweitan*, 'to revenge.' The meaning 'to punish' also belonged to the simple stem, as is shown by OSax. *wīti*, OHG. *wīʒʒi* (*wīzzi*), MidHG. *wīʒe* (*witze*), n., 'punishment, tortures of hell.' The Teut. root *wīt*, 'to punish,' is based on the common Aryan root *wid*, 'to see,' on which are based Lat. *vidēre*, Gr. ἰδεῖν (for further cognates of this root see *wissen*); comp. Goth. *faírweitjan*, 'to look around,' and *witan*, 'to observe.' The development of meaning is usually compared with that of Lat. *animadvertere*, 'to perceive, punish.' Hence **Verweis** is not directly connected with *weisen*; to the latter *verweisen*, 'to misdirect' (obsolete), is allied.—**verwesen**, vb., 'to decay, rot,' from MidHG. *verwësen* (OHG. *firwësan), str. vb., 'to come to nothing, pass away, destroy.' Comp. Goth. *frawisan*, 'to consume, waste, squander' (note *frawaírþan*, 'to be destroyed'). However clearly these seem to point to a connection with **Wesen** (root *wës*, 'to be'), yet OHG. *wësanēn*, 'to get dry, rotten,' OIc. *visenn*, 'faded, decayed,' and AS. *weornian*, 'to destroy,' suggest a Teut. and Aryan root *wīs*, 'to decay,' from which Gr. ἰός, Lat. *virus* (for *visus), Sans. *viša*, 'poison,' are derived.—**Verweser,** m., 'administrator, manager,' cannot of course be derived from the preceding word; it belongs to MidHG. *verwësen*, 'to manage, provide, look after'; Goth. *faúrawisan, 'to manage,' recalls Goth. *faúragaggja, 'steward' (lit. 'predecessor'); thus the prefixes *ver-* of the two MidHG. words *verwësen* are of different origin.

verwichen, partic., 'past, late, former,' from *verweichen*.—**verwirren,** see *wirr.*—**verwittern,** vb., 'to decompose, decay,' ModHG. only. Allied to E. 'to wither,' from MidE. *widren*, 'to wither, vanish'; also primitively to Lith. *výstu* (*výsti*), 'to wither,' *pavaitìnti*, 'to cause to wither.'

verzeihen, vb., 'to pardon, excuse,' from the equiv. MidHG. *verzīhen*, which usually means 'to deny, refuse,' then 'to renounce, abandon.' To this **Verzicht** and *verzichten* are allied.

Vesper, f., 'vespers, evening,' from the equiv. MidHG. *vësper*, OHG. *vëspera*, f., which was adopted contemporaneously with monastic institutions (comp. **Mette** and **Nonc**), from Lat. *vespera* (whence also Ital. *vespro*, Fr. *vêpre*). The primit. kinship of the Lat. with the MidHG. and OHG. word is inconceivable, because the correspondence of Lat. *v* with OHG. *v* (*f*) is found only in OHG. loan-words (see **Veit** and **Käfig**).

Vettel, f., 'slut,' from late MidHG. *vëtel*, f.; formed from the equiv. Lat. *vetula*.

Vetter, m., 'cousin,' from MidHG. *veter*, *vetere*, m., 'father's brother, brother's son,' OHG. *fetiro*, *faterro*, *fatureo*, m., 'uncle'; for the change of meaning comp. **Neffe** and **Oheim.** The earlier meaning is 'father's brother,' as is indicated by the clear connection with **Vater**, by AS. *fœdera*, 'uncle' (with *faðu*, 'aunt'), and also by the non-Teut. correspondences which point to Aryan *paturyo-, patrıcyo-,* 'uncle on the father's side.' Comp. Lat. *patruus*, Gr. πάτρως (from *πάτραος), Sans. *pítrvya*, Zend *tûirya* (from *ptúrya), 'father's brother.' In ModHG. dialects **Vetter** has acquired the signification of **Vfetter**, 'sponsor, godfather' (MidHG. *pfetter*, equiv. to Ital. *patrino*, see **Pate**), perhaps by connecting it with **Gevatter.**

Vieh, n., 'cattle, beast,' from the equiv. MidHG. *vihe*, *vëhe* (with the dial. variant *vich*, ModHG. **Viech**), OHG. *fihu*, *fëhu*, n. The word is common to Teut. and Aryan; comp. Goth. *faíhu*, AS. *feoh*, Du. *vee*, 'cattle.' Corresponding to the equiv. Sans. *paçu*, Lat. *pecu*, *pecus*, which point to Aryan *péku*, 'cattle.' The word was probably applied originally only to domestic cattle (comp. also **Tier**, **Mann**), for Sans. *paçu* has the special sense 'flock,' and Lat. *pecus*, 'small cattle, sheep.' Hence it is easily explicable how the word acquired in several groups the meanings 'goods, possession, money' (concerning the system of barter comp. also **Schaß**); comp. Lat. *pecúlium*, 'property,' *pecúnia*, 'property, money,' Goth. *faíhu*, 'money,' AS. *feoh*, 'cattle, money,' E. *fee.*

viel, adv. and adj., 'much,' from the equiv. MidHG. *vil*, *vile*, OHG. *filu*, subst. and adv.; properly the neut. of a pre-Teut. adj. *ǰelu-*, of which, however, the OTeut. dialects have preserved only scanty relics; comp. Goth. *filu* (and the gen. *filaus*, adv., 'by much'), AS. *feolu* (*feala*), Du. *reel*, OSax. *filu*, 'much.' The Teut. adj.

filu, from ***félu-*, is based on Aryan adj. *pelu* (*polú-*), from which Sans. *purú*, OPers. *paru*, Gr. πολύ-, OIr. *il*, 'much,' are derived ; so too Lat. *pollëre*, 'to be strong.' The root of these cognates is the same as in *voll*, which see. The disappearance of the old adj. *felu-* was due chiefly to the cognates of 𝔪𝔞𝔫𝔠𝔥𝔢𝔯 (Goth. *manags*) ; yet the other Aryan languages use the adj. only sparingly.—𝔙𝔦𝔢𝔩𝔣𝔯𝔞𝔣, m., 'glutton, Ursus gulo,' ModHG. only, a corruption of Scand. *fjallfress*, m., 'mountain bear.'— 𝔳𝔦𝔢𝔩𝔩𝔢𝔦𝔠𝔥𝔱, adv., from MidHG. *vil lîhte*, lit. 'very easy,' then 'probably,' finally 'perhaps.'

𝔳𝔦𝔢𝔯, num., 'four,' from the equiv. Mid HG. *vier*, OHG. *fior;* corresponding to OSax. *fiuwar*, Du. *vier*, AS. *feower*, *feôwer*, E. *four*; the AS. variant *fyðer-* (in compounds) points, like the corresponding Goth. *fidwôr* (*fidur-*), to a primary form *detwor*, *petur*, for *qetwor*, *qetur*. The latter forms show that Teut. *vier* is connected with Lat. *quattuor*, Gr. τέσσαρες (πίσυρες), Sans. *catur*, OSlov. *četyri*, 'four.' The common Aryan *qetur-*, *ktru-*, is also indicated by ModHG. 𝔑𝔞𝔲𝔱𝔢 (from *hrûdó-*, equiv. to *ktrû-tâ*, lit. 'quaternity.'—𝔙𝔦𝔢𝔯𝔱𝔢𝔦𝔩, n., 'quarter' ; for the suffix, see 𝔗𝔢𝔦𝔩.

𝔙𝔦𝔰𝔦𝔢𝔯, n. 'visor,' borrowed in the 15th cent. from the equiv. Ital. *visiera*, Fr. *visière*.

𝔙𝔦𝔷𝔡𝔬𝔪, m., 'viceregent,' from Mid HG. *viztuom*, m., 'governor, administrator' ; formed from *vicedominus*, whence also Fr. *vidame*.

𝔙𝔩𝔦𝔢𝔣, see 𝔉𝔩𝔦𝔢𝔰.

𝔙𝔬𝔤𝔢𝔩, m., 'bird, fowl,' from the equiv. MidHG. *vogel*, OHG. *fogal*, m. ; a common Teut. term ; comp. Goth. *fugls*, AS. *fugol*, E. *fowl*, Du. *vogel*, OSax. *fugal*, m., 'bird.' This specifically Teut. word has no exact correspondence in non-Teut. Teut. *fugla-* is perhaps derived from the Teut. root *flug*, 'to fly,' thus connecting the word with 𝔊𝔢𝔣𝔩𝔲𝔤𝔢𝔩 (for which *gevügele* occurs, however, in MidHG.) as the collective of 𝔙𝔬𝔤𝔢𝔩. Others prefer to connect it with 𝔉𝔲𝔠𝔥𝔰, which is regarded as 'the animal with a tail.' There is no term in Teut. corresponding to Lat. *avis*, Sans. *vi*, 'bird.'

𝔙𝔬𝔤𝔱, m., 'overseer, steward, bailiff,' from MidHG. *vogt*, *voget*, OHG. *fôgat* (*fogât), m. ; from MidLat. *vocâtus*, with the pronunciation of the Lat. *v* like *f*. as in 𝔙𝔢𝔯𝔰, 𝔙𝔢𝔰𝔭𝔢𝔯 (comp. 𝔎𝔞𝔣𝔦𝔤). The Mid Lat. term is for *advocatus* (whence OHG.

pfogát) ; comp. Fr. *avoué*, 'defender of a church or abbey, attorney.' MidLat. *advocatus* signified lit. 'legal assistant,' whence the meanings 'guardian' (MidHG. and ModHG. dial.) and 'patron, protector.' MidHG. *voget* denotes also 'the protector of the Romish Church, King or Emperor of Rome, king and ruler (generally),' and further 'governor, legal official.'

𝔙𝔬𝔩𝔨, n., 'people, nation, soldiery, troops,' from the equiv. MidHG. *volc* (*k*), OHG. *folc*, n. (rarely m.) ; corresponding to OSax. *folk*, Du. *volk*, AS. *folc*, E. *folk;* OIc. *fólk*, 'people, troops, detachment.' The latter seems to be the primary meaning, from which Lith. *pulkas*, 'heap, crowd,' and OSlov. *plŭkŭ*, 'troops,' are borrowed. The connection of the word with Lat. *vulgus* is uncertain, for it is very dubious whether the Lat. word and the Teut. cognates can be based on a primary form, *qelgos*, *qolgos*.

𝔳𝔬𝔩𝔩, adj., 'full, complete, entire,' from the equiv. MidHG. *vol* (*ll*), OHG. *fol* (*ll*) ; a common Teut. adj., corresponding to the equiv. Goth. *fulls*, AS. and E. *full*, Du. *vol*, and OSax. *full*. Allied to *füllen*, which see. The other Aryan languages also preserve a corresponding *plno-* (*ln* becomes Teut. *ll*) ; comp. Sans. *pûrnâ*, Zend *parena*, Lith. *pilnas*, OSlov. *plŭnŭ*, OIr. *lán* (for *plôno-*), Lat. *plênus*, 'full' (*manipulus*, 'handful'). The Lat. adj. is a partic. in *no-*, from the root *plê*, 'to fill' (Lat. *complêre*, *implêre*; Gr. πίμπλημι, from the root πλη), which appears in Sans. as *pur*, *prâ*, 'to fill.' The cognates of *viel* belong to the similar root *pel*.—𝔳𝔬𝔩𝔩𝔨𝔬𝔪𝔪𝔢𝔫, adj., 'perfect, complete,' from Mid HG. *volkumen*, 'accomplished, grown up, complete' ; properly a partic. of MidHG. *volkumen*, 'to reach the end or goal.'

𝔳𝔬𝔫, prep., 'of, from, concerning,' from the equiv. MidHG. *von*, *vone* (dial. *van*), OHG. *fona* (*funa*) ; corresponding to OSax. *fon*, *fan*, *fana*, 'of,' Du. *van*. The pre-Teut. *pana*, on which the word is based, is rightly regarded as an extension of the shortened Aryan form *apo*, which is discussed under *ab*.

𝔳𝔬𝔯, adv. and prep., 'before,' from Mid HG. *vor*, *vore*, OHG. *fora;* corresponding to Goth. *faúr* and *faúra*, 'before,' OSax. *for*, *fora*, Du. *vor*, AS. and E. *for*. In non-Teut. are found the correspondences Sans. *purâ* and *purás*, 'before,' with *pra*, Gr. πάρος with πρό ; ModHG. *für*, as well as Lat. *pro*, are more remotely allied.

vorder, adj., 'front, anterior, foremost,' from MidHG. *vorder,* OHG. *fordar,* adj., 'standing at the head of, former, anterior'; an old comparative with the Aryan suffix *tero-* (Gr. -τερο-; comp. anter from *aupero-*). Goth. **fahrþara-* is wanting; the connection with the root of Goth. *faŭra* (see vor) is apparent; comp. Sans. *pûrva,* 'being before or in front,' with *purás, purá,* 'before.' Fürst, fertern, and fertern (comp. also Altvordern) are also allied.

vorhanden, adv., 'at hand, extant,' from vor Handen, lit. 'before the hands'; comp. abhanden (and behende).

Vormund, m., 'guardian, tutor,' from MidHG. *vormunt (d),* also *vormunde, vormünde,* m., 'intercessor, protector, guardian,' OHG. *foramunto,* m., 'intercessor.' Allied to Mund (2), under which another equiv. word is mentioned (comp. also Beqt).

vorn, adv., 'in front, before,' from the equiv. MidHG. *vorn, vorne (vornen, vornân);* in OHG. the equiv. *forna* is used only in dialects as an adv. of place. A derivative of Teut. *for-,* appearing in vor and für.

vornehm, adj., 'distinguished, aristocratic,' from MidHG. *vürnœme,* 'preferable, distinguished'; comp. angenehm.

W.

Waare, see Waare.

Wabe, f., 'honeycomb,' from the equiv. MidHG. *wabe,* m. and f. *(waben,* m.), OHG. *waba,* f. *(wabo,* m.); lit. perhaps 'texture,' allied to weben. It is scarcely connected with Lat. *favus.* Allied also to Waffel.

wabern, vb., 'to be agitated,' from MidHG. *wabern,* 'to be in motion, move to and fro'; comp. Olc. *rafra,* 'to move to and fro.'—**Waberlohe,** f., 'flickering flame,' formed like the equiv. Olc. *vafrlogi.*

wach, adj., 'awake, on the alert,' a remarkably late word (of the last cent.), which is entirely wanting in the earlier periods and dialects (in MidHG. *wacker,* see wacker); a recent derivative of weden and wachen. The latter is an old form; comp. MidHG. *wachen,* OHG. *wahhên,* 'to wake, be awake,' OSax. *wakôn,* Du. *waken,* AS. *wacian, wecccan,* E. *to wake, watch;* also in Goth. *wakan,* str. vb., 'to be awake, watch.' For the early history of the cognates see the causative weden. The abstract form **Wache,** f., 'guard, watch,' is from MidHG. (very rare) *wache,* for which *wahte,* f. (ModHG. Wacht), is the usual term; to this ModHG. **Wächter,** m., 'watch, guardian,' from MidHG. *wahtære* is allied.

Wachholder, m., 'juniper, gin'; the word has attained its present form by many inorganic changes; it is based on the equiv. OHG. *wëhhaltura* (MidHG. *wëchelturre*) and *wëhhalter* (MidHG. *wëcholter*); in Mid HG. also *wachalter, quëckolter, rëckholter* (still represented by the modern Alem. form Reckholder). Helunter and Maßholder show that the derivative syllable is Mhd

HG. *-ter;* as in the case of Maßholder, the final syllables were changed to Holder, equiv. to Holunter. The signification of the *l* derivative, OHG. **wëhhal,* 'juniper' (also **wëhhan-* in dial. Wachandel), is entirely inexplicable.

Wachs, n., 'wax,' from the equiv. Mid HG. and OHG. *wahs,* n., common to Teut. in the same sense; comp. Olc. *vax.* AS. *weahs,* E. *wax,* LG. and Du. *was.* OSlov. (Russ.) *vosků,* Lith. *vászkas,* 'wax,' perhaps borrowed from OTeut., are closely related to this word.

wachsen, vb., 'to grow, increase, thrive,' from the equiv. MidHG. *wahsen,* OHG. *wahsan,* str. vb.; corresponding to the equiv. Goth. *wahsjan,* OSax. *wahsan,* Du. *wassen,* AS. *weaxan,* E. *to wax.* The Teut. root *wahs* contained in these words, and perhaps cognate with that of weden, appears in non-Teut. as *weks, uks;* comp. Sans. *vakš, ukš,* 'to grow strong or tall,' Zend *uxš,* Gr. ἀέξω (αὐξάνω), 'to strengthen, increase, grow'; comp. Ochse.

Wachtel, f., 'quail,' from the equiv. MidHG. *wahtel,* OHG. *wahtala,* f.; corresponding to AS. *wyhtel* (rare; usually *erschen*). The term looks like a derivative of Wacht (root *wak,* 'to be awake'). It is probable, however, that the word has attained its present form by many changes; comp. Du. *kwakkel, kwartel,* 'quail' (phonetically cognate with MidLat. *quaccila,* Fr. *quaille,* Ital. *quaglia,* 'quail'). The word for 'quail,' common to Sans. and Gr. but unknown to Teut., was *wortok, wortog;* comp. Sans. *vartikâ,* Gr. ὄρτυξ, 'quail.'

Wacke, f., 'wacke, toadstone,' from Mid

HG. *wacke*, m., 'rock-flint, block of stone projecting from the ground,' OHG. **wacko-* (from the base *waggo*), m., 'pebble, flint.' Further cognates are wanting.

wacheln, vb., 'to shake, rock, totter,' from the equiv. late MidHG. *wackeln* (and also *wacken*). An intensive form from MidHG. *wagen*, OHG. *wagón*, 'to move, totter, shake'; comp. Du. *waggelen*, 'to shake,' AS. *wagian*, also E. *to wag* (from AS. *waggian). These cognates are certainly more closely related to ModHG. *wiegen* (Teut. root *weg*, from the Aryan root *wĕgh*) than to the cognates of *wanken*.

wacker, adj., 'valiant, gallant, honest,' from MidHG. *wacker* (*wacher*), OHG. *wacchar* (*wakhar*), adj., 'cheerful, lively, awake'; comp. Du. *wakker*, 'awake, awakened, cheerful, powerful,' AS. *wacor*, 'awake,' OIc. *wakr*, 'stirring, awake.' An old derivative (corresponding to Sans. *vigra*, 'powerful, active') from the Teut. root *wak*, 'to be stirring, brisk' (see *wecken*); comp. also *nach*.

Wade, f., 'calf' (of the leg), from the equiv. MidHG. *wade*, m. (used chiefly in the plur.), OHG. *wado*, m.; comp. the equiv. Du. *wade*. OIc. *rǫ́ðve*, m., 'muscle,' shows that the more general meaning was 'muscle'; OHG. *wado* (accus. *wadun*) is based on Teut. *waþico*, m. There are no cognates in the non-Teut. languages.

Waffe, f., 'weapon,' from the equiv. MidHG. *waffen, wáfen*, OHG. *waffun, wáfan*, n., 'weapon, sword, armour'; corresponding to Goth. *wépna*, n. plur., 'weapons,' AS. *wǽpn*, E. *weapon*, Du. *wapen*. Comp. also **Wappen**. Teut. *wépno-* (*wapono-*) assumes a Teut. *wébono-* (*wobono-*): its connection with the equiv. Gr. ὅπλον (lit. 'utensil') is conceivable by assuming a double root, *wop, wob*. Whether this root is identical with the Sans. root *vap*, 'to scatter, sow,' in which case 'missile' would be the primary meaning of **Waffe**, is uncertain.

Waffel, f., 'waffle, wafer,' ModHG. only, properly a LG. word; comp. Du. *wafel* (hence E. *waffle*). The **Waffel** was so called from its resemblance to the honeycomb, for the Fr. term *gaufre* signifies both 'honeycomb' and 'waffle.' Comp. E. *wafer* and **Wafer**.

Wage, f., 'balance,' from MidHG. *wâge*, OHG. *wâga*, f., 'balance, weighing-machine' (allied to *wiegen*). Corresponding to OSax. *wâga*, Du. *waag*, AS. *wǽg* (whence E. *to weigh*), OIc. *vág*, f., 'balance.' Allied to the Teut. root *weg* in *wiegen*.

Wagen, m., 'vehicle, carriage, waggon,' from the equiv. MidHG. *wagen*, OHG. *wagan*, m.; corresponding to the equiv. Du. *wagen*, AS. *wǽgn*, E. *wain*, OIc. *vagn*, 'waggon.' Based on the Teut. root *wĕg* (see **Weg**); from the corresponding Aryan root *wĕgh, wogh*, 'to drag, drive,' are derived Gr. ἄχος, Lat. *vehiculum*, OIc. *fén*, 'waggon.' The Aryan words **Rad** and **Rate** show that vehicles were used in primitive times; for the Aryan root *wegh*, 'to drag, to move on,' see *wegen*. — **Wagner**, m., 'cartwright' from MidHG. *wagener*, 'cartwright, driver, carrier,' OHG. *wagandri*, 'cartwright'; hence the proper name **Wagner**.

wagen, vb., 'to venture, risk,' from MidHG. *wâgen*, wk. vb., 'to hazard, venture,' lit. 'to put in the scales.' MidHG. *wâge*, f., 'balance,' also means 'uncertain result'; the word is unknown to ModHG. in this sense.

wägen, vb., 'to weigh,' from MidHG. *wëgen*; identical with *wiegen*.

Wahl, f., 'choice, election,' from the equiv. MidHG. *wal*, OHG. *wala*, f.; to this is allied ModHG. *wählen*, 'to choose,' from the equiv. MidHG. *weln, wellen*, OHG. *wellen* (from *waljan), wk. vb. Comp. OIc. *val*, n., 'choice,' with *velja*, 'to select.' Allied to the Aryan root *wel*, 'to wish,' appearing in *wollen*.

Wahlstatt, Walstatt, f., 'field of battle,' from the equiv. MidHG. *walstat*, f.; MidHG. and OHG. *wal*, m., f., and n., has also the same meaning. The corresponding AS. *wǽl* signifies 'those left on the battlefield,' also 'corpse' (to which *wælstów*, 'place of combat,' is allied); comp. OIc. *valr*, 'the corpses on the battlefield,' *valfǫðr* (lit. 'father of the dead'). It is impossible to recognise in this primit. word a derivative of the root of *wählen*, as if it meant 'the chosen favourites of the god of war, who were led away by the Valkyres.' It is rather based on a root *wâl*, 'destruction,' which appears also in OHG. *wuol*, 'defeat,' AS. *wól*, 'plague, pestilence'; allied to *wühlen*?. — **Walküre**, f., 'Valkyre,' formed from OIc. *valkyrja* (AS. *wælcyrie*), f., prop. 'a divine maiden who makes a selection of the slain on the field of battle.' See *ficien*.

Wahn, m., 'illusion, delusion,' from MidHG. and OHG. *wân*, m., 'uncertain, unfounded opinion, supposition, belief, hoping, thoughts.' The word (comp. **Argwohn**) did not originally contain the secondary meaning 'want of foundation,' as is shown by OSax. *wân*, AS. *wén*, Goth. *wéns*, 'expectation, hope.' Hence the derivative **wähnen**, 'to think, believe, suppose,' MidHG. *wænen*, OHG. *wânnen* (from **wânjan*), 'to mean, suppose, hope,' comp. the equiv. Goth. *wênjan*, AS. *wénan*, OSax. *wânian*. The nominal stem *wéni* is not related to any terms in non-Teut. (Aryan root *wê ?*, *ghwê*, *ghê ?*), unless it be connected with the root *wen*, 'to love,' from which OHG. and OSax. *wini*, 'friend,' Sans. *ran*, 'to love,' and Lat. *venerari*, 'to venerate,' are derived.

Wahnsinn, m., 'frenzy, madness, delirium.' It has properly no connection whatever with the preceding word; it first occurs in ModHG., and is an imitation of the earlier **Wahnwitz**, m., 'delirium,' which is based on MidHG. *wânwitzec*, *wânwitze*, OHG. *wânawizzi*, adj., 'unintelligible, void of understanding.' **Wahnwitz** is the sole relic of an old method of forming compounds with *wâna-*, 'wanting,' which is especially preserved in Scand.; comp. also OHG. *wanaheil*, 'sickly,' lit. perhaps 'deficient in health'; thus too OHG. *wanawizzi*, 'deficient in sense.' 'Goth. *wans*, 'deficient, lacking,' OIc. *vanr*, 'lacking,' is an old partic. with the suffix *ana*, from the Aryan root *û*, 'to be empty,' from which *ête* is derived; comp. the Zend root *û*, 'to want,' Sans. *ûna*, 'wanting,' and OHG. *wanôn*, 'to diminish.'

wahr, adj., 'true, real, genuine,' from the equiv. MidHG. and OHG. *wâr* (also MidHG. *wære*, OHG. *wâri*); corresponding to OSax. *wâr*, Du. *waar*, 'true.' A genuine Teut. word, found only in a few languages; Lat. *vêrus*, OIr. *fîr*, 'true' (and also OSlov. *věru*, 'belief') are primitively allied to it; its primit. meaning has not been discovered. In Goth., only **tuzwêrs*, 'doubtful,' appears to be cognate; but Goth. *unwêrs*, 'indignant,' OHG. *miliwâri*, 'mild,' probably belong to another class. The word for 'true' in Goth. is *sunjis*, in AS., *sóþ*, which are related to ModHG. *fein*, Aryan root *es*; 'the true' is thus 'the existent,' which suggests a connection between Lat. *vêrus*, equiv. to Teut. *wêro-*, through the medium of a prehistoric form, **wes-rô-*, with the Aryan root *wes*, 'to be' (see **Wesen**).

wahren, vb., 'to watch over, preserve,' from MidHG. *warn*, wk. vb., 'to notice, be careful, pay attention to'; OHG. only in *biwardn* (the same as MidHG. *bewarn*, ModHG. **bewahren**, 'to keep, preserve'). Comp. the corresponding OSax. *warôn*, 'to pay attention to.' From Ger. is derived Fr. *se garer*, 'to guard against, mind'; but Fr. *garnir* (Ital. *guarnire*), 'to furnish, stock,' is based on the equiv. OHG. *warnôn*, MidHG. *warnen*, which, like **wahren**, is derived from the same root *war*, 'to take care of, look after.' To this is allied OHG. and OSax. *wara*, MidHG. *war*, f., 'attention,' still preserved in **wahrnehmen**, 'to perceive,' from MidHG. *war nëmen*, OHG. and OSax. *wara nêman*, 'to pay attention to, perceive' (in OHG. and MidHG. construed with the genit.), lit. 'to have regard to.' The Teut. root. *w..r*, 'to take heed, notice,' is rightly regarded as primit. cognate with Gr. ὁράω, 'I see' (Aryan root *wor*, to which *warten* is also allied).

währen, vb., 'to last, continue,' from the equiv. MidHG. *wërn*, OHG. *wërên*, wk. vb.; allied to OSax. *warôn*, 'to last.' The *r* of these verbs is based on an old *s*, which leads to a connection with the Aryan root *wes*, 'to be' (comp. **Wesen**). Deriv. **während**, prep. and conj., 'during, pending, whilst,' properly a partic.

Wahrung, f., 'fixed value or standard,' from MidHG. *wërunge*, 'guaranteed alloy.'

wahrnehmen, see **wahren**.

Wahrsager, m., 'soothsayer, prophet,' from the equiv. late MidHG. (rare) *wârsager*, which is properly LG. Comp. OSax. *wârsago*, 'prophet,' and **weisfagen**.

Wahrwolf, see **Werwolf**.

Wahrzeichen, n., 'mark, token, omen, signal,' from MidHG. *warzeichen*, n., 'token, mark,' for which the equiv. MidHG. and OHG. *wortzeichen* (OSax. *wordtêkan*), n., is ordinarily used. The word has been corrupted; its primit. form and meaning are obscure. Comp. also the cognate, OIc. *jartein*, 'token of recognition.'

Waid, m., 'woad, blue dye,' from the equiv. MidHG. and OHG. *weit*, m.; corresponding to the equiv. Du. *weede*, AS. *wâd*, E. *woad*, Goth. **waida-* (for which *wizdila*, 'woad,' is found), whence MidLat. *guasdium*, Fr. *guède*). From Teut. is derived the equiv. Rom. cognate, Ital. *guado*. Lat. *vitrum*, 'woad,' is historically related to the Teut. cognates, which may be based on pre-Teut. *waitô*.

Waidmann, see **Weite** (2).

Waife, f. (m.), 'orphan,' from MidHG. *weise*, OHG. *weiso* (*weisso*?), n., 'parentless child,' also 'fatherless or motherless child' (the masc. seems to be used in MidHG. for the fem. also) ; corresponding to Du. *wees*, OFris. *wêsa*, 'orphan.' The base (Teut. *waisjôn*?) is probably derived from an Aryan root meaning 'to rob'; comp. Sans. *vidh*, 'to become empty' (see **Witwe**). In Goth. a diminutive of **Witwe** (see **Dirne** and **Eichhorn**), *widuwairna*, m., signifies 'orphan.'

Wald, m., 'wood, forest,' from the equiv. MidHG. *walt* (*d*), OHG. *wald*, n. ; corresponding to OSax. *wald*, Du. *would*, AS. *weald*, E. *wold*, OIc. *vǫllr*, Goth. **walþus*, m., 'wood.' Teut. *walþu-s*, from which OFr. *gaut*, 'brushwood,' is borrowed, points to pre-Teut. *waltus* (*waltwos*?), to which Gr. ἄλσος (for *Fαλτfοs ?), 'grove,' and Sans. *vâṭa* (from *valta), 'garden, district,' are probably related. The connection with *wild* is uncertain.

Walfisch, m., 'whale,' from the equiv. MidHG. *walvisch*, OHG. *walfisc*, m. The first component was orig. sufficient to designate a whale ; comp. ModHG., MidHG., and OHG. *wal*, AS. *hwæl*, OIc. *hvalr*, m., 'whale.' The early history of Teut. *hwala-*, 'whale' (to which MidHG. *walre*, OHG. *welira*, 'whale,' is allied), is obscure.—

Walroß, n., 'walrus,' from the equiv. Dan. *hvalros*, as well as **Narwal** and **Wels**, are from the same root.

walken, vb., 'to full, mill (cloth) ; tread (skins) ; thrash, cudgel,' from MidHG. *walken*, OHG. *walchan*, str. vb., 'to strike, thrash, full, mill (cloth)'; comp. Du. *walken*, 'to press,' AS. *wealcan*, OIc. *valka*, 'to roll, move to and fro.' From Teut. *walkan* are also derived Ital. *gualcare*, 'to calender or press cloth,' *gualchiera*, 'fulling-mill.' The Teut. root *walk*, from Aryan *walg*, seems to coincide with Sans. *valg*, 'to hop or skip along.'—From MidHG. *walker*, *welker*, 'fuller,' is derived the proper name **Welker**.

Walküre, see **Wahlstatt**.

Wall, m., 'rampart, mound, embankment,' from the equiv. MidHG. *wal* (*ll*), m. and n. ; OHG. *wal is by chance not recorded. Comp. OSax. *wal* (*ll*), Du. *val*, 'rampart,' AS. *weall*, E. *wall*. This West Teut. word, which is certainly borrowed from the equiv. Lat. *vallum*, *vallus*, seems to belong to the earliest loan-words from Lat. (comp. **Straße**, **Mauer**) ; primit. kinship with the Lat. word is very improbable.

Wallach, m., 'gelding,' ModHG. only, lit. 'Wallachian' ; "the practice of gelding stallions was introduced into the Middle and West of Europe from Wallachia and Hungary."

wallen (1.), vb., 'to boil, bubble,' from the equiv. MidHG. *wallen*, OHG. *wallan*, str. vb. ; corresponding to OSax. *wallan*, AS. *weallan*, allied to OIc. *vel'a*, 'to boil, bubble.' From the same Aryan root *wel* (*wol*) is derived ModHG. **Welle**, 'wave, billow.'

wallen (2.), vb., 'to wander about, go on a pilgrimage,' from MidHG. *wallen*, OHG. *wallôn*, 'to wander, roam about, go on a pilgrimage'; corresponding to AS. *weallian*, 'to wander.' Allied to MidHG. *wallære*, 'traveller (on foot), pilgrim'; MidHG. *wallevart*, ModHG. **Wallfahrt**, f., 'pilgrimage.' The root *wal* (*wallôn*, from *wal-nô*) is perhaps not different from the root of *wallen* (1). Comp. E. *to walk* (Teut. base *wallagôn*) with AS. *weallian*.

Walnuß, f., 'walnut,' ModHG. only, from the equiv. Du. *walnoot;* comp. AS. *wealhhnutu*, E. *walnut*, OIc. *valhnot;* it signifies 'French or Italian nut.' The first component is *walh-*, a term orig. applied by the Teutons to the Kelts (at first to the Volcae), but later to the Romance tribes of France and Italy. See **welsch**.

Walroß, see **Walfisch**.—**Walstatt**, see **Wahlstatt**.

walten, vb., 'to dispose, manage, govern,' from the equiv. MidHG. *walten*, OHG. *waltan*, str. vb. ; corresponding to OSax. and Goth. *waldan*, OIc. *valda*, AS. *wealdan*, *gewyldan*, E. *to wield*. Teut. *waldan* (from pre-Teut. *waltá-*) has a *t* which properly belonged to the present stem, but was afterwards attached to the verbal stem ; comp. the OIc. pret. *ollr*, from a Teut. base *wol-þó-m, 'I governed.' The root *wal* is also indicated by Lat. *valere*, 'to be strong,' as well as OIr. *flaith*, 'dominion.' The allied Slav. words seem to have been borrowed at an early period from Teut. ; comp. OSlov. *vlada* (*vlasti*) and Lith. *raldýti*, 'to govern,' *valdóvas*, 'ruler,' *pavildĕti*, 'to possess,' *veldĕti*, 'to acquire.'

Walze, f., 'cylinder, roller,' from the equiv. late MidHG. *walze*, f. Allied to **walzen**, 'to roll,' MidHG. *walzen*, str. vb., 'to roll, turn, revolve,' OHG. *walzan*, 'to turn,' also OIc. *velta*, 'to roll, revolve.'—**wälzen**, vb., 'to roll, trundle,' from MidHG. *welzen*, OHG. *welzen*, *walzen* (from *walzjan), wk. vb., 'to roll, turn, trundle'; factitive of walzen, which was orig. only intransit. The Teut. root walt, from Aryan wald, has no cognates in non-Teut.

Wamme, Wampe, f., 'paunch, belly (of a skin), flank, dewlap,' from MidHG. wamme, older wambs (wampe), f., 'belly, paunch, lap,' OHG. wamba, wampa (wamba, wumba), f. Corresponding to Du. wam, 'belly (of a fish),' AS. and E. womb, Olc. vǫmb, Goth. wamba, f., 'belly, body.' There are no non-Teut. cognates of the common Teut. wambô-, 'belly, entrails.'—

Wams, m., 'doublet, jerkin, waistcoat,' from MidHG. wambeis, wambes, n., 'doublet, garment worn under the coat of mail'; a Romance loan-word; comp. OFr. gambais. MidLat. wambasium is itself a derivative of OHG. and Goth. wamba, 'body.'

Wand, f., 'wall, partition,' from MidHG. want(d), OHG. want, f., 'wall, side'; comp. OSax. and Du. wand. This word is wanting in the other dialects (comp. Goth. waddjus, E. wall). To connect it with the phonetically related winten gives no sense; Wand, lit. 'turning'?.

Wandel, m., 'walking, change, behaviour,' from MidHG. wandel, OHG. wantal, m., 'retrogression, vicissitude, stain, fault; trade and commerce, communication, intercourse.' Allied to OHG. wantalôn, MidHG. wandelen, 'to change, transform, associate' (wandeln, 'to walk,' so too MidHG. wandeln; see the next word). The cognates are based on the root of winten.

wandern, vb., 'to travel, wander, migrate,' from MidHG. wandern, 'to go, walk, travel.' Derived, like the equiv. wandeln (MidHG. wandeln), from winten.

Wange, f., 'cheek,' from the equiv. MidHG. wange, OHG. wanga, n.; Goth. *waggô, n., 'cheek,' may be inferred from waggareis, 'pillow.' Comp. OSax. wanga, Du. wang, AS. wǫnge (E. wangtooth, 'jawtooth'); the borrowed Ital. word guancia, 'cheek,' presupposes a term *wankja. The early history of the word is uncertain. AS. wǫng, Olc. vangr, Goth. waggs, 'field, plain,' are usually regarded as the nearest cognates, Wange being explained as 'surface of the face.' Most of the names for parts of the body have, however, no such origin.

Wank, m., in the phrase ohne Wank, 'without hesitation,' MidHG. âne wanc, OHG. âno wanc; MidHG. wanc, m., 'want of stability, fickleness.' Allied to wanken, vb., 'to totter, vacillate, hesitate,' from MidHG. wanken, OHG. wanchôn, 'to totter, waver'; comp. Olc. vakka (for *wankân), 'to totter.' Connected with OHG. wanchal, MidHG. wankel, 'wavering, fickle' (hence Wankelmut, m., 'vacillation,' MidHG. wankelmuot); allied to winten.

wann, adv. and conj., 'when,' from MidHG. and OHG. wanne; an old adverb, derivative of the pronominal stem hwa- in wer.

Wanne, f., 'winnowing fan,' from the equiv. MidHG. wanne, OHG. wanna, f. As in the case of Wall, it is quite possible that the word was borrowed from Lat. (vannus, 'winnowing fan'). There exists, however, a genuine Teut. stem from which Wanne can be derived. Goth. winþjan, and the equiv. E. winnow (from AS. windwian) point to a Teut. root winþ, 'to winnow' (Lat. ventilare), and hence OHG. wanna might stand for *wanþna. In that case the primit. kinship with Lat. vannus (from which E. fan is borrowed) would be conceivable.

Wanst, m., 'paunch, belly,' from the equiv. MidHG. wanst (wenst), OHG. wanast (wenist), m. A specifically HG. word, which, however, like most of the names for parts of the body (comp. Fuß, Herz, and Niere), is genuine Aryan. It is probably connected with Lat. venter, 'belly,' but more nearly with Sans. vastî, 'bladder,' and vanisthu, 'entrails.'

Wanze, f., 'bug,' from the equiv. MidHG. wanze, f. The word first appeared in the 13th cent.; in MidHG. and OHG. the term wantlûs, 'house-bug,' is used in the same sense; probably Wanze is an abbreviation of the latter (comp. Spatz with Sperling). For the meaning comp. Czech stěnice, 'bug,' from stěna, 'wall.'

Wappen, n., '(coat of) arms, escutcheon,' from the equiv. MidHG. wâpen, with the variant wâfen, n. The former is the LG. form, which established itself through the chivalry of the Lower Rhine; comp. Telpel.

Ware, f., 'goods, merchandise,' from the equiv. late MidHG. war, f..; a LG. word, corresponding to the equiv. Du. waar, AS. waru, E. ware, Olc. vara, f. Goth. *warô (but not *wazô) must be assumed; if the latter meant lit. 'valuable article,' wert Teut. wer-þo-) might be regarded as cognate.

warm, adj., 'warm,' from the equiv.

MidHG. and OHG. *warm;* corresponding to OSax., Du. and E. *warm,* Goth. **warms* (comp. *warmjan,* 'to warm'). A common Teut. adj. based on the Aryan root *war,* 'to be hot.' Comp. OSlov. *varŭ,* 'heat,' with *vrěti,* 'to boil, be hot,' *vrŭlŭ,* 'passionate'; Lith. *virti,* 'to boil.' The Teut. cognates have, with less reason, been compared with Sans. *gharmá,* 'heat of fire, glare of the sun,' and Gr. θερμός, Lat. *formus,* 'warm.'

warnen, vb., 'to warn, admonish,' from MidHG. *warnen,* 'to watch over, protect,' OHG. *warnen (wernen),* 'to deny, refuse, decline.' Corresponding to OSax. *wernian,* 'to decline, withhold.' AS. *wyrnan,* E. *warn,* OIc. *varna,* 'to refuse.' On account of the meaning the connection with OHG. *warnôn* (see **wahren**) is dubious; undoubted cognates have not yet been found.

Wart, m., 'warder,' from MidHG. and OHG. *wart,* 'warder, keeper,' which appears only as the second component of compounds. —**Warte,** f., 'watch-tower, belfry,' from MidHG. *warte,* OHG. *warta,* f., 'reconnoitring, ambush.'—**warten,** vb., 'to wait, await, stay,' from MidHG. *warten,* OHG. *wartên,* 'to spy, lurk, expect.' Comp. OSax. *wardôn,* 'to be on one's guard, look after,' AS. *weardian,* 'to guard, keep,' E. *to ward,* OIc. *varða,* 'to watch over, protect' (also Goth. *-wards,* 'keeper,' in compounds). From OTeut. are borrowed Ital. *guardare* and Fr. *garder,* 'to guard.' Hence the primary meaning of the cognates is 'to look after or take charge of some one,' and so they are undoubtedly connected with the root of **wahren.**

-wärts, suffix in compounds, *e.g.,* aufwärts, from MidHG. and OHG. *-wertes (ûfwërtes,* 'upwards'); properly an adverb. genit. of MidHG. and OHG. *-wërt* (MidHG. and OHG. *ûfwërt,* adv., 'upwards'). The latter word is used as an adj. in OHG., but is now represented by **wärtig** (MidHG. and OHG. *-wërtic);* comp. OHG. *inwërt,* adj., 'internal,' Goth. *andwairþs,* adj., 'present.' The word is never used independently; since it forms local adjs. in the sense of 'existing,' some are inclined to connect it with **werden,** 'to arise.'

warum, adv., 'why, for what reason,' from MidHG. and late OHG. *warumbe* (in earlier OHG. *hwanta*). The first part of the word seems to be the adv. *wara,* 'whither,' which is derived from *hwa-* (see **wer**).

Warwolf, see **Werwolf.**

Warze, f., 'wart, teat,' from the equiv. MidHG. *warze,* OHG. *warza,* f.; corresponding to Goth. **wartô,* OIc. *varta,* AS. *wearte,* E. *wart,* and the equiv. Du. *wrat.* The early history of Teut. *wartô-* (from Aryan *wardô-*) is uncertain; some connect it with the Aryan root *wṛd,* 'to grow,' from which **Wurzel** is derived, and regard **Warze** as 'excrescence' (comp. OSlov. *vrědŭ,* 'eruption'). Others prefer to compare it with AS. *wearre,* 'weal,' Lat. *verrūca,* 'wart,' the *rr* in which may have arisen by the loss of an intermediate dental.

was, neu. of **wer,** 'what'; comp. MidHG. and OHG. *waȝ* (from *hwaȝ*); comp. E. *what.* Corresponding to Lat. *quod,* Sans. *kad.*

waschen, vb., 'to wash,' from the equiv. MidHG. *waschen (weschen),* OHG. *wascan,* str. vb.; comp. Du. *wasschen,* AS. *wascan,* E. *to wash,* OIc. *vaska* (Goth. **waskan*), 'to wash.' The *sk* of the old forms was orig. only a part of the present stem, but was afterwards joined to the base; it may have been preceded by a dental. Teut. **watska-* is probably based on the Teut. nominal stem *wat,* 'water' (see **Wasser**); comp. OIr. *usce,* 'water.' Ir. *faiscim,* W. *gwasgu,* 'I press,' may, however, with equal reason, be connected with **waschen.**

Wase, f., see **Base.**

Wasen, m., 'sod, turf, grass,' from MidHG. *wase,* OHG. *waso,* m., 'sward, damp soil or mound'; also OHG. *wasal,* n., 'damp mound.' The word is identical with **Rasen,** just as **sprechen** with E. *to speak;* comp. AS. *wëccëan, wrëccëan,* 'to awake,' and AS. *wrixl* with **Wechsel.** Hence there existed Aryan roots with and without *r;* we must therefore regard *wraso, waso,* as the Teut. base; for the area of diffusion see **Rasen.** From OHG. is derived Fr. *gazon,* 'sward.'

Wasser, n., 'water,' from the equiv. MidHG. *waȝȝer,* OHG. *waȝȝar;* comp. OSax. *watar,* Du. *water,* AS. *wæter,* E. *water;* beside these West Teut forms in *r (watar-o-)* are found the forms in *n,* Goth. *watô,* OIc. *vatn,* n., 'water.' The root *wat* is related by gradation to *ut* in **Otter,** and to *wët* in AS. *wët,* E. *wet,* North Fris. *wiat,* 'damp, wet.' The other Aryan languages have also corresponding graded forms with the same signification; Aryan *ud* in Gr. ὕδωρ (Lat. *unda ?*), OSlov. *voda,* Saus. *udán,* 'water, billow,' *udrín,* 'abounding in water,' and also the root *ud*, 'to moisten' (with which the cognates of ModHG. wasch̀en are connected?). Hence the Aryan root is *ŭd*, *wĕd*, *wŏd*. The Aryan word corresponding to Lat. *aqua* assumed in Teut. (Goth. *ahwa*) the meaning 'river.' See Au.

Wat, f., 'dress, garment,' an archaic word, from the equiv. MidHG. and OHG. *wât*, f., which, with its OTeut. cognates, is referred to the Zend root *waδ*, ' to dress.'

Wate, f., 'scoop-net, seine,' from the equiv. MidHG. *wate*, f.; allied to OIc. *vaðr*, 'fishing-line.' Perhaps it is based on the root of OHG. *giwëtan*, MidHG. *wëtan*, 'to combine, tie together.'

waten, vb., 'to wade,' from MidHG. *waten*, OHG. *watan*, str. vb., 'to wade, go, stride'; a common Teut. word; comp. Du. *waden*, AS. *wadan*, E. *to wade*, OIc. *vaða*, 'to wade, press forwards' (especially in water). The borrowed Ital. term *guadare* has the same meaning, 'to walk through water'; on the OIc. noun *vað*, 'ford,' and the equiv. Du. *wadde*, are based Ital. *guado*, Fr. *gué*, 'ford, shallow part of a river'; comp. Weeb. The Teut. root *wad*, 'to stride, wade,' is identical with the primit. cognate Lat. *vădere*, 'to wade, ford,' to which Lat. *vădum*, 'ford,' is allied. The Aryan root *wādh* has not been preserved in other languages.

Watte, f., 'wadding, fleece,' ModHG. only, from Du. *watte*; allied to the equiv. E. *wad*, Fr. *ouate*, Ital. *ovate*. The origin of the cognates is not to be sought for in Teut., since the Teut. words have appeared only in modern times, and no other undoubted cognates are to be found in the group. The word was also borrowed in Romance.

Wau, m., 'dyer's weed, weld,' ModHG. only, from Du. *wouw* (also in earlier Mod HG. Waute); comp. E. *weld*. From Teut. (Goth. *walda*-) are derived Fr. *gaude* and Span. *gualda*. In non-Teut. there are no cognates that might explain the early history of the word.

weben, vb., 'to weave, entwine, fabricate,' from MidHG. *wëben*, OHG. *wëban*, str. vb., 'to weave, work, plait, spin'; comp. Du. *weven*, AS. *wifan*, E. *to weave*, and the equiv. OIc. *refa*. A widely developed Teut. and Aryan root (*web* from Aryan *webh*), which testifies to the great antiquity of weaving among the Indo-Europeans. Comp. the Sans. root *vabh*, 'to weave,' in *ûrṇavâbhi*, 'spider,' lit.

' woollen-weaver' (also *ubh*, ' to bind '), Gr. ὑφαίνω, ' to weave,' ὕφος, ' web.' Comp. Wabe, Wirtel, and Wespe.

Wechsel, m., 'change. vicissitude,' from MidHG. *wëhsel*, OHG. *wëhsal*, m., 'change, barter, exchange, trade'; corresponding to OSax. *wëhsal*, 'trade, money,' Du. *wissel*. A specifically Ger. derivative with the suffix *-sla*, from the same root as Lat. *vĭces*, 'variation, alternation.' The Aryan root *wĭk* (Lat. *vĭc*-) appears to have had a variant *wĭg*, which occurs in Weche and weichen. For AS. *wrixl* see Mafen.

Weck, m., 'wedge-shaped fine bread,' from MidHG. *wëcke*, OHG. *wëcki* (from *weggi*), m., 'wedge, wedge-shaped bread,' corresponding to Du. *weg*, 'fine white bread,' AS. *wëcg*, E. *wedge*, and the equiv. OIc. *veggr*. Teut. *waggo*-, from pre-Teut. *waghyo*-, is usually regarded as primit. cognate with Lith. *vagis*, 'wedge, plug.' For the terms applied to pastry comp. Kipfel and Krapfe.

wecken, vb., 'to wake, awake,' from the equiv. MidHG. *wëcken*, OHG. *wëcchen* (from **wakjan*), str. vb.; corresponding to Goth. *wakjan* (*uswakjan*), OIc. *vekja*, AS. *wëččean*, Du. *wekken*, OSax. *wëkkian*, 'to awake.' The common Teut. *wakjan* has the form and meaning of an old causative, but presupposes a Teut. **wëkan*, which does not occur (the apparently primary Goth. *wakan*, str. vb., was orig. weak). Sans. too has only the causative *vâjáy*, 'to stir, incite,' of the corresponding root; this meaning throws light on the Teut. cognates; Lat. *vigil*, 'awake,' and *vegére*, 'to be lively, excite,' are also probably allied. The lately formed adj. Mod HG. wach shows that from the primit. causative *wogéy* (Teut. *wakj*-) numerous cognates might be gradually developed.

Wedel, m., 'fan, sprinkling brush, tail, tuft, brush (of foxes),' from the equiv. Mid HG. *wëdel* (*wadel*), OHG. *wëdil* (*wadal*), m. and n.; also dial. Wabel. The specifically HG. word is a derivative of the root *wê* (see wehen), with the suffix -*þlo*; Webel, lit. 'implement for blowing.'

weder, particle, in conjunction with noch, from MidHG. *newëder*, OHG. *niwëdar*; this is properly a neut. of *wëdar*, 'each of two,' *niwëdar . . . noh*, ' neither of the two . . . nor.' Comp. the corresponding development of entweber, and also E. *either* (lit. ' each of two').

Weed, f., 'horse-ford,' ModHG. only,

from the equivalent Du. *wed;* allied to *waten.*

Weg, m., 'way, road,' from the equiv. MidHG. and OHG. *wēc* (gen. *wēges*), m. ; corresponding to OSax., Du., and AS. *weg*, E. *way*, and the equiv. Goth. *wigs*. A common Teut. derivative of the Teut. root *weg*, 'to march, drive, ride'; Lat. *via*, 'way,' is connected with the corresponding Lat. *vehere;* comp. **Wagen** and **wegen**. Allied to **weg**, adv., 'away, gone,' from MidHG. *enwēc* for *in wēc*, lit. 'on the way'; corresponding to Du. *weg*, AS. *onwēg*, E. *away*.—**Wegbreite**, 'plantain,' from the equiv. MidHG. *wēgebreite*, OHG. *wēgabreita;* comp. Du. *wegbree*, AS. *wēgbrǣde*, E. *weybread;* an OTeut. term.—**wegen**, prep., 'on account of, with regard to,' from the equiv. MidHG. *von...wëgen* (with intervening genit.); see **laut** and **kraft**.—**Wegerich**, m., 'plantain,' from the equiv. MidHG. *wēgerich*, OHG. *wēgarīh*, m.; lit. 'sovereign of the road,' formed from Teut. *rīk*, 'king' (see **Reich**).

wegen, vb., in **bewegen**, 'to move,' from MidHG. *wēgen*, OHG. *wēgan*, str. vb., 'to move,' with which the corresponding causative, OHG. *wegen, wecken* (from *wagjan*), 'to cause to move,' was confused; corresponding to Goth. *gawigan*, 'to move.' The primary meaning of the widely diffused Aryan root *wegh*, preserved in **Wagen** and **Weg**, was 'to move on, march, drive, ride,' from which the signification 'to carry, move,' was afterwards developed in Teut. Comp. Sans. root *vah* 'to proceed, drive, ride,' and the equiv. Lat. *vehere*, OSlov. *vesti*.

weh, interj., 'woe! alas!' from the equiv. MidHG. and OHG. *wē;* corresponding to Goth. *wai*, AS. *wá*, E. *woe*. From the Teut. interj. *wai* is derived the equiv. Ital. and Span. *guai* (Fr. *ouais*). As in the case of Lat. *vae* (Gr. *oî*), **weh** is to be regarded as an instinctive sound. The subst. **Weh**, n., 'plaint, misery, woe,' seems to be based on the interj.; comp. OSax., OHG., and MidHG. *wē* (gen. *wēwes*), and OHG. *wēwo*, m., *wēwa*, f., 'woe, pain, sorrow,' and the borrowed Ital. *guajo*, 'sorrow.' See **weinen** and **wenig**.

wehen, vb., 'to blow,' from the equiv. MidHG. *wæjen (wæn)*, OHG. *wâjan (wâen)*, wk. vb.; corresponding to Du. *waaijen*, AS. *wáwan*, Goth. *waian*, 'to blow.' The originally strong (as in Goth. and AS.) verbal root *we*, 'to blow,' is found in other Aryan languages; comp. Gr. ἄημι, 'to blow' (root Fη), OSlov. *vějati*, 'to blow,' Sans. root *vá*, 'to blow.' Allied to **Wind**.

Wehr, f.. 'defence, resistance, protection,' from MidHG. *wer*, OHG. *wert*, f., 'defence, fortification'; allied like Mod HG. **Wehr**, n., 'dam, weir,' late MidHG *wer*, n., 'weir,' to **wehren**, 'to protect, defend; hinder, prevent, oppose, forbid.' This verb is from MidHG. *wern, wergen*, OHG. *werian, weren*, wk. vb., 'to hinder, protect, defend'; comp. Goth. *warjan*, 'to forbid, hinder,' OSax. *werian*, 'to hinder.' On account of the meaning, its connection with **wahren** (root *wor*, 'to look on,' in Gr. ὁράω) is not so apparent as its primit. kinship with the Sans. root *vṛ*, 'to check, restrain, hinder.'

Weib, n., 'woman, wife,' from the equiv. MidHG. and OHG. *wîp (b)*, n.; corresponding to OSax. *wîf*, Du. *wijf*, AS. *wíf*, E. *wife*. It is wanting in Goth., certainly not by accident (the word used is *qinô, qêns*). The term *wibo-* is specifically Teut., while Goth. *qinô* is prehistorically connected with Gr. γυνή, Sans. *gnâ*, 'woman.' Its kinship with Gr. οἴφω is dubious; it is more probably related to Sans. *vip*, 'inspirited, inwardly excited' (of priests), to which OHG. *weibôn*, 'to stagger, be unstable,' is allied. Hence the Teutons must have coined the term **Weib** (*wîbo-* from *wipô-*), because in woman they venerated *sanctum aliquid et providum*. In that case the remarkable gender might perhaps be explained as 'inspiration, something inspired.'

Weibel, m., 'sergeant, apparitor,' from the equiv. MidHG. *weibel*, OHG. *weibil*, m.; allied to MidHG. *weiben*, 'to move to and fro.' The variant **Webel** (in **Feldwebel**) is derived from LG. or East MidG.

weich, adj., 'soft, tender, impressible,' from the equiv. MidHG. *weich*, OHG. *weih (hh)*; corresponding to OSax. *wêk*, Du. *week*, AS. *wác*, OIc. *veikr, veykr* (whence E. *weak*), 'soft, tender.' A derivative of the root of **weichen** (hence **weich**, lit. 'yielding, giving way').

Weichbild, n., 'outskirts of a town, precincts,' from MidHG. *wîchbilde*, n., 'outskirts of a town, jurisdiction over a town and its precincts.' The origin of this compound, first occurring in the 13th cent., is disputed. The assumption that it signifies lit. 'image of a saint' (comp. **weihen** for MidHG. *wîch*, 'holy'), does not suffice to explain the actual meaning. The suggested lit. meaning, 'local image,' is equally unsatisfactory, although MidHG. *wich-* in Mid HG. *wichgrâve*, 'municipal judge,' and *wichvride*, 'municipal peace,' certainly appears in the compound; comp. OSax. *wîc*, 'town, place,' Du. *wijk*, 'quarter of a town,' OHG. *wîh* (*hh*), 'town, city.' The signification of the second component cannot be explained from ModHG. Bild (MidHG. *bilede*). There existed beside OHG. and MidHG. *bil-lîch*, 'suitable, right,' an OHG. **bilida*, 'law, jurisdiction,' which appears only in Mid HG. *unbilde* (see Unbill); hence MidHG. *wichbilde* meant first of all 'municipal jurisdiction,' and then 'municipal territory' (comp. Sprengel).

Weichen, plur., 'groin'; the term was first recorded in the 14th cent., denoting the tender parts of the body between the ribs and loins.

weichen, vb., 'to yield, give away, waver,' from the equiv. MidHG. *wîchen*, OHG. *wîhhan*, str. vb.; corresponding to the equiv. OIc. *ýkva*, *vîkja*, OSax. *wîkan*, Du. *wijken*. The Teut. root *wîq*, 'to yield,' lit. 'to make room for some one, give way,' appears also in Wechsel and weich. Its earlier form *wîg* (in Sans. *vij*, 'to yield, flee') is a variant of *wîk*, which is indicated by Lat. *vices*, 'change,' and espec. by Gr. εἴκω, 'to yield.' Comp. also Weche.

Weichsel, f., 'agriot cherry,' from the equiv. MidHG. *wîhsel*, OHG. *wîhsila*, f. The Teut. character of the word is undoubted; in spite of its absence in the other dialects, it is probably derived from the OTeut. period (hence Ital. *visciola?*). It is connected with OSlov. *višnja*, Lith. *ryszna*, 'agriot cherry.' The name of the river *Vistula*, 'Weichsel' (Lat. *Vistula*, AS. *Wistle*), has nothing to do with the word, nor with Weichselzopf, m., 'elflock, plica Polonica.' The latter is said to have come from Poland, where matted hair is often produced by some disease; comp. Pol. *wieszczyce*, 'elflock.'

Weid, see Wait.

Weide (1.), f., 'willow,' from the equiv MidHG. *wîde*, OHG. *wîda*, f.; comp. OIc. *víðer*, AS. *wîðig*, E. *withy* (isolated MidG. and LG. dialects seem to lengthen the old *î* in the accented syllable). Prehistoric *wît-*, 'willow,' is indicated also by the equiv. Gr. ἰτέα and Lit. *žilvytis*, 'grey willow.' An Aryan root *wî*, 'pliant, capable of being twisted,' has been assumed, and the word compared also with Lat. *vîtis*, 'vine, tendril,' OSlov. *viti* (Lith. *výti*), 'to turn, plait.'

Weide (2.), f., 'pasture, pasture-land,' from MidHG. *weide*, OHG. *weida*, f., 'fodder, food, place for grazing, the search for food and fodder (chase, fishing).' Allied to OIc. *veiðr*, 'chase, fishing,' AS. *wáð*, 'chase,' and also to ModHG. weiden, 'to graze, pasture,' MidHG. *weiden*, OHG. *weidôn*, 'to forage'; MidHG. *wiedeman*, 'hunter,' ModHG. Waidmann (comp. the proper name Weidmann with Jäger, and also Weidner, from MidHG. *weidenære*, 'hunter, sportsman'). If the cognates be traced back to a root *wai*, 'to forage,' Lat. *vê-nâri*, 'to chase, hunt,' may be connected with it; comp. also the Sans. root *vî*, 'to fly at, attack something, take food.' Comp. further Eingeweide, to which ModHG. ausweiden is allied.

Weiderich, f., 'willow herb,' ModHG. only; so called from its willow-like leaves; the term is formed like Wegerich and Hetterich.

weidlich, adj., 'brave, stout, vigorous,' from MidHG. *weidelîch*, *weidenlîch*, 'lively, pert, distinguished, grand'; lit. 'befitting the chase,' from Weide (2); see the latter also for Weidmann.

weifen, vb., 'to wind, reel,' from Mid HG. *weifen*, wk. vb., 'to swing, wind on a reel,' a factitive of MidHG. *wîfen*, str. vb., 'to swing, wind.' It is based on a Teut. root *wîp*, 'to turn,' which appears also in Goth. *weipan*, 'to wreathe' (*waips*, 'wreath'); with this root Lat. *vibrare*, 'to brandish, vibrate,' is primit. cognate. Allied to Wipfel and Wimpel.

Weigand, m., 'warrior, hero,' from the equiv. MidHG. and OHG. *wîgant*, m.; not an inherited term, but borrowed in the last century from MidHG. literature. It is a West Teut. form for 'warrior'; comp. AS. *wîgend*, OSax. *wîgand*; properly a pres. partic. of the nearly obsolete (in West Teut.) root *wîg*, 'to fight' (comp. Goth. *weihan* and **wigan*, str. vb., 'to fight'). This is identical with the Aryan root *wîk*, 'to be strong, bold,' which appears in Lat. *vincere*, 'to conquer,' OIr. *fichim*, 'to fight,' as well as in OSlov. *vêkŭ*, 'strength' (equiv. to OIc. *veig*, 'strength'); comp. Lith. *wikrus*, 'brisk.' Allied to weigern and Gemeih.

weigern, vb., 'to refuse, deny,' from MidHG. *weigern*, OHG. *weigarôn*, 'to oppose, refuse'; allied to OHG. *weigar*, 'foolhardy,' lit. perhaps 'obstinate, resisting.'

This is connected with the Teut. root *wîg*, 'to fight,' mentioned under the preceding word.

Weihe, f. (Weih, m.), 'kite,' from the equiv. MidHG. *wîe*, OHG. *wîe* (*wîjo*), m.; a specifically HG. word (comp. Du. *wouw*?). Connected with the root *wî*, 'to chase,' mentioned under Weibe (2)?. In that case Weih would mean lit. 'hunter, sportsman.'

weihen, vb., 'to consecrate, dedicate,' from MidHG. and OHG. *wîhen* (from *wîhjan*), wk. vb., 'to sanctify'; a derivative of the OTeut. adj. *wîho-*, 'sacred, holy'; comp. MidHG. *wîch* (nom. *wîher*), OHG. and OSax. *wîh*, Goth. *weihs*. The adj. has also been preserved in Weihnachten, from MidHG. *wîhen-nahten*, which is properly a fusion of MidHG. *ze wîhen nahten* (comp. Mitternacht). Nacht (which see) has preserved in this compound of the heathen period the meaning 'day' (the old Teutons celebrated their winter feast from December 26 to January 6); among the Anglo-Saxons Beda transmitted the term *môdra niht*, 'the mothers' nights.' For the adoption of the old word in the service of Christianity, comp. Ostern (also taufen?). Moreover, E. *Yule* preserves another OTeut. designation of the same festival; comp. AS. *giuli* (*gȝle*), Goth. *jiuleis* (OIc. *ýler*), 'January,' OIc. *jól*, AS. *geól*, 'Christmas.'

—Weihrauch, m., 'incense,' from MidHG. *wîchrouch* (*wîhrouch*), OHG. *wîhrouh*, m., lit. 'holy perfume.' Weihbild has no connection with these words.

Weiher, m., 'fish-pond,' from the equiv. MidHG. *wîwer, wîwære*, OHG. *wîwâri, wîâri*, m. (OHG. also 'stable'); corresponding to OLG. *wîweri*. Borrowed in the pre-OHG., probably in the Roman period, from Lat. *vivârium*, 'park, preserve, fish-pond'; corresponding to Fr. *vivier* (Du. *vijver*), Ital. *vivajo*, 'fish-pond.' Comp. also Weiler.

weil, conj., 'because,' from late MidHG. (rare) *wîle*; in classical MidHG. *die wîle*, conj., 'so long as, during, while, since, because' (hence ModHG. dieweil); OHG. *dia wîla unz*, 'so long as'; properly accus. of Weile.—**weiland,** adv., 'formerly, of yore,' from the equiv. MidHG. *wîlent, wîlen;* the *t* form is a recent extension of the earlier word (Du. *wijlen*). Based on OHG. *hwîlôm*, 'at times,' dat. plur. of **Weile,** f., 'while, space of time, leisure.' The latter is based on MidHG. *wîle*, OHG. *wîla* (*hwîl*), f., 'time, period of time, hour'; corresponding to OSax. *hwîl, hwîla*, 'time,' Du. *wijl*, E. *while*, Goth. *hweila*, 'time.' The verb weilen, 'to stay, tarry, sojourn,' from MidHG. and OHG. *wîlên*, 'to stop, stay, sojourn,' in connection with OIc. *hvíla*, 'bed,' *hvíld*, 'rest,' suggests that Weile meant lit. 'resting time.' It has been compared with the Lat. root *qui* (*quiê*), 'to rest' in *quietus, tranquillus*, as well as with OSlov. *počiti*, 'to rest'; Gr. καιρός, 'point of time,' is perhaps cognate.

Weiler, m., 'village, hamlet,' from MidHG. *wîler*, m., 'small farm, hamlet.' OHG. *wîlâri* occurs only as the second component in compound names of places (*e.g., Brûwîlâri*, equiv. to Brauweiler). MidLat. *villâre*, 'farm' (Fr. *villier*), was adopted in local names, just like Lat. *villa* (OHG. *-wîla, e.g.*, in *Rotwîla*, equiv. to Rotweil); comp. Fr. *ville*, 'town.' The word seems to have been borrowed contemporaneously with Weiher.

Wein, m., 'wine,' from the equiv. MidHG. and OHG. *wîn*, m.; corresponding to OSax. *wîn*, m. and n., Du. *wijn*, m., AS. *wîn*, E. *wine*, and the equiv. Goth. *wein*, n. There is no phonological evidence to show that the word was borrowed. The assumption that it was adopted from Lat. *vînum* (equiv. to Goth. *wein*, n.), or rather from Low Lat. *vînus*, m. (equiv. to OHG. *wîn*, m.), is probable from the accounts of ancient writers. The period of adoption was perhaps the first cent. B.C., hence the early diffusion among the OTeut. dialects. An earlier connection of the Teut. with the Lat. word is improbable (Lat. *v* equiv. to Teut. *w* in old loanwords; comp. Pfau, Weiher, Weiler, with Vers and Brief). With regard to the Southern culture of the vine, comp. the following words borrowed from Lat.—Kelter (also Presse), Kelch, Lauer, Spund, Most, Torkel, Trichter, and Winzer. Note, too, Swiss *wîmmen*, OHG. *windemôn* (older *wintimmôn*), equiv. to Lat. *vindêmiare;* Swiss Wümmet, from OHG. *windemôd*, *wintimmôd*, equiv. to Lat. *vindêmiae* (whence also the equiv. OIr. *fînime*, 'vintage,' also *fín*, 'wine').

weinen, vb., 'to weep, cry,' from the equiv. MidHG. *weinen*, OHG. *weinôn;* comp. Du. *weenen*, AS. *wânian*, OIc. *veina*, 'to weep.' Probably a derivative of the Teut. interj. *wai* (see weh); hence weinen, lit. 'to lament' (the origin of the word would be similar to that of ächzen). It is also possible that Goth. *qainôn*, 'to weep,' is based in the other dialects on *wai*, 'woe.'

weis, adj., in einem, etwas weis machen, 'to make one believe, hoax a person,' from OHG., late MidHG. *einen wîs machen,* 'to inform a person, instruct him' (in ModHG. in an ironical sense). Comp. MidHG. and OHG. *wîs tuon,* 'to inform, instruct.' Allied to **weise,** adj., 'wise, prudent, cunning,' from MidHG. and OHG. *wîs* (also MidHG. *wîse,* OHG. *wîsi*), adj., 'intelligible, experienced, acquainted with, learned, wise.' A common Teut. adj.; comp. Goth. *weis,* 'knowing,' OSax. and AS. *wîs,* 'wise, knowing,' E. *wise,* Du. *wijs.* The primary form of the word was a verbal adj. from *wissen* (*wîso-* for *witto-*). Allied to the following word.

Weise, f., 'manner, mode, way,' from MidHG. *wîse,* OHG. *wîsa,* f., 'method'; corresponding to the equiv. AS. *wîse,* E. *wise,* Du. *wijze,* OSax. *wîsa.* From this West Teut. word (in OIc. *vîsa*) the equiv. Rom. cognates, Ital. *guisa,* Fr. *guise,* are derived. Teut. *wîsô-n-* seems, like *weise,* to be derived from the Teut. root *wît,* 'to know'; hence Weise, lit. 'knowledge'?. See Art.—The suffix -weise (*e.g.,* in teilweise) has been developed in ModHG. in connection with MidHG. phrases, such as in *rēgenes wîs,* 'like rain.'

Weisel, m., 'queen bee,' from the equiv. MidHG. *wîsel,* m., lit. 'leader, guide.' Allied to **weisen,** vb., 'to show, direct, point,' from MidHG. *wîsen* wk. (str.) vb., OHG. *wîsen* (from *wîsjan*), wk. vb., 'to show, direct, instruct'; a derivative of weise (hence lit. 'to make wise').

weissagen, vb., 'to foretell, prophesy, predict,' from the equiv. MidHG. *wissagen,* OHG. *wîssagôn,* wk. vb.; it is not organically connected with sagen. Based on OHG. *wîȝȝago* (*wîȝago*), 'prophet,' a derivative of the Teut. root *wît,* 'to know' (comp. AS. *wîtga,* 'prophet'). This form was corrupted to *wîssagôn* in the OHG. period by connecting it with *wîs,* 'wise,' and *sago,* 'speaker,' or rather with OHG. *forasago* (OLG. *wâr-sago*), 'prophet.' OHG. *wîȝȝago* is properly a subst. formed from the Teut. adj. **wîtag,* 'knowing, intelligible, wise' AS. (*wîtig*).

Weistum, n., 'legal precedent, record,' from late MidHG. (rare) *wîstuom,* m. and n., 'sentence, instruction (to the jury),' lit. 'wisdom'; allied to weise (comp. E. *wisdom*).

weiß, adj., 'white, blank,' from the equiv. MidHG. and OHG. *wîȝ* (from *hwîȝ*), adj.; corresponding to Goth. *hweits,* OIc.

hvîtr, AS. and OSax. *hwît,* Du. *wit,* E. *white.* This common Teut. term (*hwîtto-*) is based on an Aryan root *kwîd, kwît,* from which are derived Sans. *çvit,* 'to be white, to shine' (so too *çvêtá, çvitrá, çvitna,* 'white'), Zend *spaeta,* 'white,' OSlov. *světŭ,* 'light,' and Lith. *szvaitýti,* 'to make bright.' Goth. *hwaiteis* (ModHG. Weizen, 'wheat'), is related by gradation.

weit, adj., 'wide, broad, ample,' from the equiv. MidHG. and OHG. *wît*; corresponding to OSax. and AS. *wîd,* E. *wide,* Du. *wijd,* OIc. *vîðr,* 'roomy, extended, spacious.' Allied to Sans *vîtá,* 'straight'?. From its form Teut. *vî-do-* seems to be a partic. derivative of a root *wî.*

Weizen, m., 'wheat,' from MidHG. *weitze,* OHG. *weizzi,* m. The dial. (unknown only in Bav.?) variant Weißen (Swiss, UpSwab., Wetterau, UpHess., Hennegau, and Thuringian) is based on MidHG. *weiȝe,* OHG. *weiȝi* (*tz* and *sz* interchanged in this word on account of the older inflectional interchange of *tj* and *ti*; comp. reiȝen and heiȝen); hence Weißbrod as well as Weiȝen?. Corresponding to the equiv. Goth. *hwaiteis* (dat. *hwaitja*), OIc. *hveite,* AS. *hwǽte,* E. *wheat,* Du. *weit,* OSax. *hwêti.* Lith. *kvėtýjs,* 'grains of wheat,' is borrowed from Teut. Weizen is rightly regarded, on account of the white flour, as a derivative of weiß (comp. Sans. *çvitnyá çvêtá,* 'white').

welch, pron., 'which, what,' from MidHG. *wëlch, wïlich,* interr. pron., OHG. *wë-, wie-lîh* (*hh* and *h*), interr. pron., 'who, which'; corresponding to Goth. *hwîleiks* (*hwéleiks*), OSax. *hwilik,* Du. *welk,* AS. *hwylč,* E. *which.* A common Teut. derivative, from the pronominal stem *hwe-* (see wer) and the suffix *lîko-,* 'constituted' (see gleich and solch); hence welch, lit. 'as constituted.'

Welf, m., 'whelp, cub,' from the equiv. MidHG. and OHG. *wëlf* (earlier *hwëlf,* m. and n.); corresponding to OIc. *hvelpr,* AS. *hwëlp* (E. *whelp*). This Teut. word *hwelpo-,* which was used at an early period, espec. of 'cubs,' has no cognates in the non-Teut. languages. Welf is not allied.

welk, adj., 'withered, faded,' from MidHG. and OHG. *wëlc* (*wëlch*), 'moist, mild, lukewarm, faded'; peculiar to HG.; connected with MidE. *welken,* E. *to welk,* and Welke. The primary meaning of the Teut. root *welk,* from Aryan *welg,* is 'to be moist,' as is indicated also by OSlov. *vlaga,* 'moistness,' *vlŭgŭkŭ,* 'moist,' Lith. *vilgyti,* 'to moisten,' Lett. *wélgans, wálgans*, 'moist,' unless these are more closely allied to AS. *wlacu, wlæc*, 'moist.' From a form **walki*, connected with OHG. *wĕlk*, Fr. *gauche*, 'left,' is usually derived.

𝔚𝔢𝔩𝔩𝔢, f., 'wave, billow, swell,' from the equiv. MidHG. *wĕlle*, OHG. *wĕlla*, f. ; a word peculiar to HG., but found, however, in the OTeut. vocabulary. It is primit. allied to the equiv. OSlov. *vlŭna*, Lith. *wilnis*, and is based like these on an Aryan root *wel*, 'to turn, roll,' which appears in OHG. *wĕllan* and *wallen*. Comp. Lat. *volvere*, Gr. εἰλύειν, 'to roll,' as well as Sans. *úrmi*, equiv. to OHG. *walm*, AS. *wylm*, 'billow.'

𝔚𝔢𝔩𝔰, m., 'shad' (fish), from the equiv. late MidHG. *wels*. Its connection with 𝔚𝔞𝔩𝔣𝔦𝔰𝔠𝔥 (stem *hwalo-*) is not impossible, if MidHG. *wels* is based on OHG. **wĕlis* (from **hwalis-*) ; comp. OHG. *wĕlira*, 'whale.'

𝔴𝔢𝔩𝔣𝔠𝔥, adj., 'foreign, outlandish (espec. Italian or French),' from MidHG. *wĕlsch* (*wĕlhisch, walhisch*), 'Romance, French, Italian,' OHG. *walhisc*, 'Romance' ; a derivative of MidHG. *Walch*, OHG. *Walh*, 'one of the Latin race.' The corresponding AS. *Wealh* was applied to the 'Kelt,' and this is the lit. meaning of the word (comp. the Keltic tribal name *Volcae*, on which Teut. *Walho-* is based ; it was applied to the Latin race when they occupied Gaul, which had been formerly inhabited by the Kelts. Comp. further 𝔚𝔞𝔩𝔫𝔲𝔰 and the E. local names *Wales* (AS. *Wălas*) and *Cornwall*.

𝔚𝔢𝔩𝔱, f., 'world, society,' from the equiv. MidHG. *wĕlt*, usually *wĕrlt, wĕrelt*, OHG. *wĕralt* (*worolt*), f. ; the MidHG. and OHG. word has also the earlier signification 'age, saeculum.' Comp. OSax. *wĕrold*, 'earthly life, age' ; Du. *wereld*, AS. *weorold, worold*, E. *world*, have the ModHG. meaning. The double sense 'world' and 'age' can hardly be explained from one primary form ; the latter meaning is linked with OIc. *ǫld*, AS. *yld*, 'age' ; the former seems to be based on a collective sense, 'humanity,' which follows from OLG. *ĕldi*, AS. *ylde*, OIc. *elder*, 'men.' The first part of the compound (Goth. *wair-aldus*) is Teut. *wĕr*, 'man, person' (see 𝔚𝔢𝔯𝔴𝔬𝔩𝔣). 𝔚𝔢𝔩𝔱, like 𝔥𝔦𝔪𝔪𝔢𝔩 and 𝔥𝔬𝔩𝔩𝔢, is peculiar to Teut.

𝔚𝔢𝔫𝔡𝔢, f., 'turn, turning-point, change,' from MidHG. *wĕnde*, OHG. *wĕntĭ*, f., 'boundary, turning back, turn.'—𝔚𝔢𝔫𝔡𝔢𝔩𝔱𝔯𝔢𝔭𝔭𝔢,

f., 'winding stairs,' based on the equiv. late MidHG. *wĕndelstein*.—𝔴𝔢𝔫𝔡𝔢𝔫, vb., 'to turn, change,' from MidHG. *wĕnden*, OHG. *wĕnten* (from **wantjan*), wk. vb., 'to overturn, cause to retrograde, hinder.' Comp. OSax. *wĕndian*, Goth. *wandjan*, AS. *wĕndan*, 'to turn,' E. *to wend*, Du. *wenden*, 'to change' ; a factitive of *winten*. Hence *auswendig*, 'by heart,' MidHG. *ûzwĕndic*, 'externally, abroad' (*etwas auswendig können* is a ModHG. phrase, and is here used in the sense of 'externally,' *i.e.*, 'without looking into a book') ; *inwendig*, 'internally,' from MidHG. *innewendec*.— *gewandt*, adj., 'skilled, adroit, dexterous,' from MidHG. *gewant*, lit. 'directed to the circumstances, appropriate to the circumstances,' *i.e.*, 'constituted somehow or other.'

wenig, adj., 'little, few,' from MidHG. *wēnec, weinec (g)*, OHG. *wēnag weinag*, adj. As a derivative of the Teut. root *wai* (see *weh* and *weinen*), the adj. signified primarily in OHG. and MidHG. 'deplorable, lamentable, unfortunate' (so too Goth. *wainags*) ; from 'unfortunate,' the MidHG. 'weak, small, trifling, little' is derived.

wenn, conj., 'if, when,' from MidHG. *wenne, wanne ;* identical with *wann*. Comp. the following word.

wer, pron., 'who,' from MidHG. and OHG. *wĕr* (earlier *hwĕr*), interr. pron. ; the nom. sing. preserves the *r* as a representative of old *s ;* comp. Goth. *hwas*, 'who,' also AS. *hwá*, E. *who*. The Teut. stem of the interr. pron. was *hwa-, hwe-.* from Aryan *ko, ke*, which is found in non-Teut. in Lat. *quo-d*, Gr. πότερος, (κότερος), Lith. and Sans. *kas*, 'who.' Hence *wann, weder, welch, wenn, wie*, and *wo*. Further details belong to grammar.

werben, vb., 'to sue (for), solicit,' from MidHG. *wĕrben (wĕrren)*, OHG. *wĕrban, wĕrvan* (earlier *hwĕrfan*), str. vb., 'to turn, walk to and fro, strive hard, make an effort, be active, be doing something, accomplish something.' For the evolution of meaning of ModHG. *werben*, comp. Lat. *ambire*. The lit. sense of the Teut. root *hwĕrf* is 'to move to and fro,' as is shown by 𝔚𝔦𝔯𝔟𝔢𝔩. Comp. OSax. *hwĕrban*, 'to walk to and fro,' Du. *werven*, 'to woo,' Goth. *hwaírban* (and *hwarbón*), 'to wander.' A corresponding Aryan root *qerp (kerp)* is not found in non-Teut. Comp. 𝔚𝔢𝔯𝔣𝔱 (2).

𝔚𝔢𝔯𝔡, equiv. to 𝔚𝔦𝔯𝔱.

werden, vb., 'to become, grow, get,'

from the equiv. MidHG. wĕrden, OHG. wĕrdan; a common Teut. vb.; comp. Goth. waírþan, AS. weorþan (obsolete in E.), Du. worden, 'to become.' The Teut. strong verbal root werþ has no corresponding and equiv. Aryan wert, yet it is undoubtedly connected with Lat. verto, 'to turn,' OSlov. vrŭtěti, vratiti, 'to turn,' Sans. vṛt, 'to turn, roll'; 'to turn' developed in Teut. into 'to become, arise' (comp. Sans. sam vṛt, 'to arise'). The earlier meaning 'to turn' is rightly supposed to exist in the suffix ≈wärts (which see), as well as in MidHG. virtel, 'spindle ring,' equiv. to OSlov. vrĕteno, 'distaff.'

Werder, m., 'small island in a river,' from MidHG. wert (d), m., 'island, peninsula,' OHG. werid, warid, f., 'island.' Corresponding to AS. waroð, 'bank, shore,' with AS. war, OIc. ver, n., 'sea' (for the meaning comp. Au). Its primit. kinship with Sans. vár, 'water,' is not certain.

werfen, vb., 'to cast, throw,' from the equiv. MidHG. wĕrfen, OHG. wĕrfan (wĕrpfan); a common Teut. str. vb.; comp. Goth. waírpan, OIc. verpa, AS. weorpan, E. to warp, Du. werpen, OSax. wĕrpan, 'to throw.' From Teut. are borrowed OFr. querpir, Fr. déguerpir, 'to leave in the lurch.' The Teut. root werp contained in these words is based upon werq, from pre-Teut. werg (comp. Wolf with Gr. λύκος, fünf with quinque, and vier with quattuor); the primit. allied Sans. vṛj, 'to throw down,' and OSlov. vrŭgą (vrěšti), 'to throw,' have a guttural sound. Allied to the following word and to Würfel.

Werft (1.), m., 'woof,' from MidHG. and OHG. warf, n. (comp. ModHG. Hüfte from MidHG. huf), 'warp, yarn, or thread for the warp.' Corresponding to the equiv. AS. wearp, E. warp, OIc. varp, which are usually derived from the vb. werfen. Lith. verpti, 'to spin,' is perhaps derived from the Ger. word.

Werft (2.), f. and n., 'wharf,' ModHG. only; borrowed from LG., like many nautical expressions; comp. Du. werf (scheepstimmerwerf), E. wharf, and the equiv. Swed. varf. The word cannot, on account of the consonants, be connected with werfen. The cognates signify lit. 'work-place,' and are related to the verbal root of werben (which see).

Werg, n., 'tow, oakum,' from the equiv. MidHG. wĕrch, wĕrc (for the double form comp. Storch), OHG. wĕrah (hh), and wĕrc, n.; also OHG. dwirihhi, dwurihhi, n., 'tow, stuppa.' The OHG. and MidHG. forms of Werg are identical with those of Werf, hence the former is usually derived from the latter; this, however, does not explain the development of meaning. OHG. dwurihhi, 'tow,' may be connected with Werf and wirfen, since it means 'the refuse produced by work.' Perhaps the simple word was developed from the compound.

Wergeld, n., from the equiv. MidHG. wĕrgĕld, 'fine for slaughter,' lit. 'man's, person's money.' For the first component comp. Werwolf, Welt.

Werk, n., 'work, deed, production,' from the equiv. MidHG. wĕrc (wĕrch), OHG. wĕrc, wĕrah (hh), n.; for the double forms comp. the cognate Berg. Based on a common Teut. werko-, 'work,' which is attested by OIc. verk, AS. weorc, E. work, Du. and OSax. wĕrk. For further details concerning the root, to which Gr. ἔργον is allied, see wirken.

Wermut, m., 'wormwood, bitterness,' from the equiv. MidHG. wĕrmuot, wĕrmüete, f. and n., OHG. wĕrmuota (wormuota), f. There is no clear etymological connection with Wurm, to which this uncompounded word (comp. E. wormwood, from AS. wĕrmód, wormód). Its relation to warm too is not certain.

Wert (1.), m., equiv. to Werder, 'river island.'

Wert (2.), m., 'worth, value, price,' from the equiv. MidHG. wĕrt (d), OHG. wĕrd, n., 'price, costly articles, splendour'; comp. OSax. wĕrð, 'hero, reward,' Goth. waírþs, 'worth, price'; an adj. used as a subst. Based on the adj. wert, 'worth, dear,' from MidHG. wĕrt (d), OHG. wĕrd, 'costing a certain price, saleable at,' then absolutely 'of high worth, splendid, distinguished.' Corresponding to Goth. waírþs, 'worthy, fit,' AS. weorþ, and E. worth. On account of its meaning its connection with werden is improbable. Lith. wertas and OSlov. vrĕdŭ, with which it is sometimes compared, are probably Teut. loan-words. It may be related to the Aryan root wor, 'to regard, contemplate' (see wahren), of which wert might be a particip. derivative in the sense of 'esteemed'; see also Ware.

Werwolf, m., 'werewolf,' from the equiv. MidHG. wĕrwolf (not recorded in OHG.). It is undoubtedly based on an OTeut. word; comp. AS. wĕrewulf, E. were-

wolf. From the AS. word is derived Mid Lat. *guerulfus,* OFr. *garou,* whence by tautology ModFr. *loup-garou,* 'werewolf.' The presupposed OTeut. *werowulfo-* means lit. 'man-wolf,' *i.e.*, a man who roams about in the form of a wolf (Gr. λυκάνθρωπος). The first component is OHG., OSax., and AS. *wër* (Goth. *wair*), m., 'man,' primit. cognate with Lat. *vir,* Sans. *víras,* 'man.'

Wefen, n., 'being, creature, nature, disposition, manners,' from MidHG. *wësen,* n., 'sojourn, domestic affairs, manner of living, quality, situation.' An infinit. used as a subst.; MidHG. *wësen,* OHG. *wësan* (to which the ModHG. pret. forms of the vb. *fein* are allied), str. vb.; corresponding to Goth. *wisan,* 'to be, tarry, stay' (AS. *wësan;* E. *was,* belong to the sphere of grammar). The verbal root *wes,* 'to be, abide,' to which *wähten* is allied, is found in non-Teut., in the Sans. root *vas,* 'to stay, tarry, pass the night.'—Allied to **wefentlich,** adj., 'essential,' from the equiv. MidHG. *wësentlich* (*wësenlich*); the *t* is excrescent.

Wefpe, f., 'wasp,' from the equiv. Mid HG. *vespe,* earlier *wefse,* f. (m.), OHG. *wefsa* (earlier *wafsa*), f.; a genuine Teut. word; comp. AS. *wæfs, wæps,* m., E. *wasp.* Hence we must probably assume a Teut. *wafs-,* beside which Teut. *wabis-, wabit-,* is presupposed by Bav. *webes,* East Thuringian *wëpschen, wëwetzchen* (in West Thur. *wispel*). Aryan *wops-* (*wobhes-*), which points to the verbal root *weben* (see **Wiebel**), is almost as widely diffused in the Aryan languages as **Horniffe;** OBret. *guohi,* 'wasps' (from *wops-*), Lith. *vapsà,* 'gadfly,' OSlov. *vosa,* 'wasp,' and probably also by gradation Lat. *vespa.* In the MidHG. period a form *vespe* was borrowed from Lat. *vespa ;* on the other hand, Fr. *guêpe* is probably due on account of its initial sound to Ger. influence.

Wefte, f., 'vest, waistcoat,' adopted as a current term in the last cent. Since the word is unknown to the older dialects, it must have been borrowed from Fr. *veste* (Lat. *vestis*); had it, however, appeared earlier in the OTeut. dialects, it would have been primit. allied to Lat. *vestis.* The modern dial. form, MidHG. *wester,* 'christening gown' (found espec. in compounds), is based on the same Aryan root as Lat. *vestis.* With the Aryan root *wes,* 'to clothe' (equiv. to Sans. *vas,* Gr. ἕννυμι for *Fεσ-νυμι, Lat. *ves-tis*), are also connected Goth. *wasjan,* 'to dress,' OHG. and AS. *wërian,* E. *to wear.*

Wefen, m., 'west,' from the equiv. Mid HG. *wësten,* OHG. *wëstan,* n.; also ModHG. **West,** which is found in OHG. and Mid HG. only as the first part of compounds (*e.g.,* OHG. *Wëstfálo,* MidHG. *Wëstvále,* 'Westphalian'). Comp. Du. *west* (in compounds), E. *west* (whence Fr. *ouest*), OIc. *vestr,* n. The explanation of the cognates is difficult, espec. on account of the old term *Visegothae,* 'Visigoths, West Goths,' transmitted by Lat. One is inclined to connect the word with Lat. *ves-per,* Gr. ἑσπέρα, 'evening,' and to regard it as the 'evening quarter'; comp. the corresponding explanations of **Süd** and **Oft** (see also **Abend**).

wett, adj., 'equal, even,' from late MidHG. *wette,* adj., 'paid off.' A recent derivative of the noun **Wette,** f., 'bet, wager,' MidHG. *wette, wete, wet (tt),* n. and f., OHG. *wetti, weti,* n., 'mortgage contract, legal obligation, pledge, stake (in a bet), compensation, fine' (the last three meanings first occur in MidHG.). Comp. AS. *wedd,* OIc. *veð,* Goth. *wadi,* n., 'pledge, earnest.' From OTeut. *wadjo-,* the Romance cognates, Ital. *gaggio* and Fr. *gage,* 'pledge,' are borrowed. The following are also primit. allied to Teut. **Wette;** Lat. *văs* (*vadis*), 'surety,' *vădimonium,* 'bail, security,' Lith. *vadùti,* 'to redeem a pledge,' and perhaps also Gr. ἄεθλος (root Feθ), 'prize (of contest),' which point to an Aryan root *wedh.*

Wetter, n., 'weather, storm, tempest,' from the equiv. MidHG. *wëter,* OHG. *wëtar,* n.; corresponding to OSax. *wëdar,* 'weather, tempest, storm,' Du. *weder, weêr,* AS. *wëder,* E. *weather,* and the equiv. OIc. *veðr* (Goth. **widra-* is wanting). If Teut. *wedro-* is based on pre-Teut. *wedhro-,* OSlov. *vedro,* n., 'fair weather' (*vedrŭ,* 'bright, clear'), is related to it. It is possible, though less probable, that *wetró-* is the Aryan base, with which also OSlov. *vĕtrŭ,* 'air, wind' (from the root *wĕ,* 'to blow'), coincides.—

Wetterleuchten, n., 'sheet lightning,' corrupted from late MidHG. (so even now in ModHG. dials.) *wëterleich* (comp. Norw. *vederleik*), 'lightning'; comp. MidHG. *leichen,* 'to dance, skip' (see **Leich**).

wetzen, vb., 'to whet, sharpen,' from MidHG. *wetzen,* OHG. *wezzen* (from **hwazzjan*), wk. vb., 'to sharpen'; comp. Du. *wetten,* AS. *hwettan,* E. *to whet,* OIc. *hvetja,* 'to sharpen.' A common Teut. wk. vb., properly strong. The Teut. strong verbal root *hwat,* from Aryan *kwod* (by gradation *hwât*), seems to be equiv. to the Sans. root *cud*, 'to whet, sharpen, set on fire, incite' (comp. AS. *hwettan*, OIc. *hvetja*, 'to excite, incite,' prop. 'to sharpen'). The older Teut. periods preserve the adjs. *hwassa-* (Goth. *hwass*, OHG. and MidHG. *was*) and *hwato-* (AS. *hwœt*, OHG. *waʒ*), 'sharp,' from the root *hwat*.

wichſen, vb., 'to black, polish (boots), wax (thread),' from late MidHG. *wihsen*, OHG. *wahsen*, *giwehsen*, wk. vb., 'to wax'; a derivative of 𝔚𝔞𝔠𝔥𝔢.

Wicht, m., 'wight, creature, rāgamuffin,' from MidHG. *wiht*, m. and n., 'creature, being, thing' (used espec. of hobgoblins, dwarfs, &c.), OHG. *wiht*, m. and n., 'thing, being, person'; comp. also the meanings of 𝔅𝔢ſ𝔢𝔴𝔦𝔠𝔥𝔱. Corresponding to OSax. *wiht*, 'thing' (plur. 'demons'), Du. *wicht*, 'little child,' AS. *wiht*, 'being, thing, demon,' E. *wight*. Goth distinguishes between *waihts*, f., 'thing,' and *ni-waiht*, n., 'nothing' (on which Ger. nicht and nichts are based). The meaning 'personal or living being' is probably derived from the primary sense 'thing,' for the early history of which the cognate languages give no clue except through OSlov. *veŝtĭ*, 'thing,' which, like Teut. *wihti-*, is based upon Aryan *wekti-*. The cognates can scarcely be explained by wiegen and wägen. MidHG. *wihtelîn*, *wihtelmennelîn* are still used dial. for 'hobgoblins, dwarfs.'

wichtig, adj., 'weighty, important,' Mod HG. only; a recent variant of gewichtig, lit. 'having weight.' See 𝔊𝔢𝔴𝔦𝔠𝔥𝔱.

Wicke (1.), f., 'vetch, tare,' from the equiv. MidHG. *wicke*, OHG. *wiccha*, f.; corresponding to Du. *wikke*. Borrowed from Lat. *vicia*, 'vetch,' whence the equiv. Ital. *veccia*, Fr. *vesce* (E. *vetch*). The period at which it was borrowed (contemporaneous with 𝔖𝔭𝔢𝔩𝔱?) is fixed by the representation of Lat. *v* by *w* (comp. 𝔓𝔣𝔞𝔲, 𝔓𝔣𝔲𝔥𝔩 with 𝔅𝔢𝔤𝔱 and 𝔅𝔢𝔦𝔩𝔠𝔥𝔢𝔫), as well as the retention of the Lat. *c* as *k* (comp. 𝔎𝔯𝔢𝔲).

Wicke (2.), f. 'wick,' see 𝔚𝔦𝔢𝔠𝔥𝔱.

Wickel, m. and n., 'roll, curl-paper, distaff-ful (of flax),' from MidHG. *wickel*, *wickelîn*, OHG. *wicchilî*, *wicchilîn*, n., 'roll, a quantity of flax or wool to spin off'; cognate with 𝔚𝔦𝔠𝔨, 'wick.' Further cognates are wanting to explain the early history of the word. Allied to **wickeln**, vb. 'to roll, wind, swathe,' from late MidHG. *wickeln*, lit. 'to make into the form of a roll'; also ModHG. 𝔚𝔦𝔠𝔨𝔢𝔩, f., 'swaddling clothes.'

Widder, m., 'ram,' from MidHG. *wider*, OHG. *widar*, m.; corresponding to Goth. *wiþrus*, m. (ram? lamb?), AS. *weðer*, E. *wether*, Du. *weder*, 'ram, wether.' Teut. *weþru-*, from pre-Teut. *wetru-*, is primit. allied to Lat. *vitulus*, 'calf,' Sans. *vatsá*, 'calf, young animal,' which are derived from Aryan *wet-*, 'year'; comp. Lat. *vetus*, 'aged,' Gr. ἔτος, Sans. *vatsara*, 'year.' Hence 𝔚𝔦𝔡𝔡𝔢𝔯 means lit. 'young animal, yearling.'

wider, prep. and adv., 'against,' from MidHG. *wider*, OHG. *widar*, 'against, towards, back, once more'; corresponding to Goth. *wiþra*, prep., 'against, before,' OSax. *wiðar* (and *wið*), prep., 'against,' Du. *weder*, *weer*, AS. *wiðer* (and *wið*), 'against' (hence E. *with*). Teut. *wiþrô*, 'against,' and the equiv. *wiþe* are based on the Aryan prep. *wi*, 'against,' which is preserved in Sans. *ví*, 'asunder, apart' (to which *vitarám*, 'further,' is allied). Comp. hinter.—Allied to **widern**, **anwidern**, vb., 'to loathe, be offensive,' lit. 'to be opposed,' from MidHG. *widern*, 'to be opposite.'— **Widerpart**, m., 'opponent, opposition,' from MidHG. *widerparte*, f. and m., 'opposing party, enmity, enemy, opponent,' allied to MidHG. *part*, 'part,' which is based on Lat. *pars* (Fr. *part*).—**Widerſacher**, m., 'adversary,' from MidHG. *widersache*, OHG. *widarsahho*, m., 'opponent in a lawsuit, accused, opponent (generally)'; allied to 𝔖𝔞𝔠𝔥𝔢, which orig. meant 'legal dispute.'— **widerſpenſtig**, adj., 'refractory, perverse, obstinate,' from the equiv. MidHG. (rare) *widerspenstec*, usually *widerspæne*, *widerspænec*; allied to MidHG. *widerspân*, also *spân*, *span* (nn), 'dispute, quarrel.'— **Widerthon**, m., 'spleenwort,' from the equiv. MidHG. *widertân* (*-tât*, *-tôt*); an obscure word; it has probably been corrupted.—**widerwärtig**, adj., 'adverse, repugnant, repulsive,' from MidHG. *widerwertic*, *-wartic* (*widerwert*, *-wart*), adj., 'striving against, refractory, hostile,' OHG. *widarwart*, *wartic* (*g*), 'opposed.' Comp. wärts—**widrig**, adj., 'contrary, adverse, repugnant,' ModHG. only.

widmen, vb., 'to dedicate, devote, consecrate,' from MidHG. *widemen*, OHG. *widimen*, 'to furnish with a dowry, endow'; allied to OHG. *widamo*, 'wedding present' (see 𝔚𝔦𝔱𝔱𝔲𝔪).

wie, adv., 'how, in what way,' from the equiv. MidHG. *wie*, OHG. *wio*, which is derived from *hwêu* for *hwêwu*, *hwaiwô*; the last form is indicated only by Goth.

hwaiwa, 'how.' Based on the Teut. pronom. stem *hwa*-, Aryan *qe, qo*. The formation of pre-Teut. *koiwŏ* is identical with that of Sans. *ĕvā́*, 'in this manner,' from the pronom. stem *a*, 'this.' Another form is preserved in E. *how*, from the equiv. AS. *hú* (equiv. to OSax. and Teut. *hwó*).

Wiebel, m., 'beetle,' from MidHG. *wibel*, OHG. *wibil*, m.; corresponding to OSax. *wibil*, AS. *wifel*, E. *weevil*. The literal meaning of this word as a derivative of weben (see also Wefpe) is probably 'weaver' (because it surrounds itself with a web on changing into a chrysalis state). Comp. Lith. *vabalas*, 'beetle.'

Wieche, m., 'wick,' from MidHG. *wieche*, m. and f., 'twisted yarn as wick or lint,' OHG. *wiohha* (*wioh*?), 'wick'; also Mid HG. and ModHG. (dial.) *wicke*, with the same signification. The latter is connected with Wickel, from which MidHG. *wieche* was orig. at all events quite distinct; comp. Du. *wiek*, 'lamp wick,' AS. *weoca* (but also *wecca*, equiv. to E. *wick*). There are apparently no other cognates, unless we include Weden.

Wiedehopf, m., 'hoopoe' (bird), from the equiv. MidHG. *witehopfe*, m., OHG. *wituhopfo* (-*hoffo*), m., lit. 'forest hopper.' OHG. *witu*, 'timber,' equiv. to AS. *wudu*, E. *wood* (comp. Kramtsvogel), is primit. allied to OIr. *fid*, 'tree' (or Gr. φιτρός, 'block of wood, log'). Comp. hüpfen.

wieder, adv., identical with wider.

Wiege, f., 'cradle,' from the equiv. Mid HG. *wige, wiege*, OHG. *wiga* (*wiega*?), and, with a different gradation, *waga*, f.; corresponding to Du. *wieg*, OIc. *vagga*, 'cradle' (in AS. *cradol*, E. *cradle*). It is evidently connected with the root weg in bewegen, wadeln; yet some difficulties still remain; the relation of OHG. and MidHG. *ie, i, a*, is not quite clear (see schief and Stiege).

wiegen, vb., 'to weigh, rock,' from the equiv. MidHG. *wëgen*, OHG. *wëgan*, str. vb.; identical with wegen, vb., which see.

wiehern, vb., 'to neigh, shout noisily,' an intensive form of the equiv. MidHG. *wihen* (*wihenen, wihelen*), OHG. *wihón* for *wljón, *hwljón;* formed from the same root as MidHG. *weijen*, OHG. *weiðn* (*hweiðn*), 'to neigh' (E. dial. *to wicker*). With the onomatopoetic root *hwî* are connected, though with a different evolution of meaning, AS. *hwínan*, E. *to whine*, OIc. *hvína*, 'to rustle, drink (of beasts).'

Wiemen, m., 'pole for hanging meat to be smoked above the hearth,' ModHG. only, from LG.; comp. Du. *wieme*, 'smoking-place.'

Wiefe, f., 'meadow, pasture-land,' from the equiv. MidHG. *wise*, OHG. *wisa*, f. From the same root are derived with a different gradation OIc. *veisa*, 'pool, pond with standing water,' AS. *wôs*, 'moisture,' E. (dial.) *woosy*, 'moist.' LG. *wische*, 'meadow,' is based on LG. *wiska*.

Wiefel, m. and n., 'weasel.' from the equiv. MidHG. *wisel, wisele*, OHG. *wisala*, f.; corresponding to Du. *wezel, wezeltje*, AS. *wësle* (*weosule*), E. *weasel*, Dan. *väsel*. It is frequently regarded as a derivative of Wiefe, linking it with the place where the animal is usually found; others, on account of the keen scent of the animal, connect its name with Lat. *virus*, 'poison' (root *wîs*, see verwejen). Both derivations are very uncertain.

wild, adj., 'wild, savage, fierce,' from the equiv. MidHG. *wilde*, OHG. *wildi*, adj., corresponding to Goth. *wilþeis*, AS. *wilde*, E. *wild*, Du. *wild*, OSax. *wildi*; the corresponding OIc. *villr* usually signifies 'going astray, confused.' Fr. *sauvage* (from Lat. *silvaticus*), as a derivative of Lat. *silva*, has led to the assumption that the Teut. cognates are derived from Wald. This view is not probable, since wild seems to be used only of living beings (lit. 'senseless, irrational'?); comp. the Scand. signification. Moreover, the subst. Wild, n. ('wild animals, game, deer'), which cannot be derived from the adj., has a more original form; comp. MidHG. *wilt* (*d*), OHG. and AS. *wild*, n. (AS. also *wildor*, and later *wildeór*), 'wild animals,' from Teut. *wilþiz*, n. (hence pre-Teut. *weltos*-, n., 'wild animals,' but *weltjo*-, 'wild, savage'). Hence the connection with Wald is improbable, though a more certain origin has not yet been found.

Wildbret, n., 'game, venison,' from MidHG. *wiltbrât, -brœte*, n., 'roasted (or boiled) game, game for roasting, venison'; see Braten.—**Wildfang**, m., 'deer-stalking,' from MidHG. *wiltvanc* (*g*), m., 'game preserving, preserves'; late MidHG. in the sense of 'strange person' (one entrapped, as it were, like game).

Wildschur, n., 'wolfskin, fur pelisse,' ModHG. only, from the equiv. Pol. *vilczur*.

Wille, m., 'will, volition, design, wish,' from the equiv. MidHG. *wille*, OHG. *willo*, m.; corresponding to Goth. *wilja*, OSax.

willio, Du. *wil*, AS. *willa*, E. *will;* an abstract from wollen, which see. Allied to willig, adj., 'willing, voluntary, ready,' from MidHG. *willec*, OHG. *willig*.—Willfahren, vb., 'to accede to, grant, humour,' from late MidHG. *willevarn*.—Willkommen, adj., 'welcome, acceptable'; subst. 'welcome, reception'; from MidHG. *willekumen.* Corresponding to Du. *welkom*, AS. *wilcumen*, E. *welcome*, whence OFr. *wilecome* (a form of greeting) was borrowed. —Willkür, f., 'option, discretion, caprice,' from MidHG. *willekür*, f., 'free choice, free will'; see liesen and Kur.

wimmeln, vb., 'to swarm, teem with,' from late MidHG. (MidG.) *wimmen*, 'to be astir, swarm.' From the same root *wem* (*wam*) are derived the equiv. OHG. *wimidôn* and *wimizzen* (*wamezzen*). OHG. *wiuman*, 'to swarm with,' seems to be a reduplicated present of the same root *wen* (*we-wm-*).

wimmern, vb., 'to whimper,' from MidHG. *wimmer*, n., 'whining,' beside which occurs an equiv. MidHG. *gewammer*, with a different stage of gradation; recent imitative forms.

Wimpel, m. and f., 'pennon, flag, streamer,' from MidHG. *wimpel*, f. and m., 'banner, flag, naval ensign, kerchief,' OHG. *wimpal*, 'frontlet, veil.' Allied to Fr. *guimpe* (OFr. *guimple*), 'wimple, stomacher,' Du. *wimpel*, AS. *winpel, wimpel*, E. *wimple*. The exact relation of these apparently compound words to one another is obscure, since the LG. dialects have *mp* coinciding with HG. (we should have expected *mf* in HG.). Since it is not yet known in which group it was borrowed, nothing definite can be said concerning its early history. The evolution in meaning is similar to that of Fahne.

Wimper, f., 'eyelash,' from the equiv. MidHG. *wintbrâ, wintbrâwe*, OHG. *wintbrâwa*, f.; lit. 'the winding eyebrow.'

Wind, m., 'wind,' from the equiv. Mid HG. *wint* (d), OHG. *wint*, m.; corresponding to Goth. *winds*, AS. and E. *wind* (to which *window* from OIc. *vindauga*, lit. 'wind eye,' is allied), Du. and OSax. *wind*, 'wind.' The common Teut. *windo-*, from Aryan *wĕntó-*, is identical in form with the equiv. Lat. *ventus*, and Sans. *vāta*, m., 'wind' (comp. also Gr. ἀήτης?); they are derivatives of the present partic. *wĕ-nt-* of the root *wĕ*, 'to blow' (see wehen); for the form of the word comp. Zahn. While this word extends beyond Teut. the terms for the chief directions of the wind are peculiar to that group (see Nord, Ost, &c.).

Winde, f., 'windlass, winch,' from the equiv. MidHG. *winde*, OHG. *winta*, f.— Windel, f., 'swaddling clothes, napkin,' from the equiv. MidHG. *windel*, OHG. *wintila*, f.; lit. 'means for winding about.' —winden, vb., 'to wind, reel, twine,' from MidHG. *winden*, OHG. *wintan*, str. vb., 'to wind, turn, wrap'; comp. OSax. *windan*, 'to turn' (*biwindan*, 'to wrap up'), Du. *winden*, AS. *windan*, E. *to wind*, Goth. *windan*. For the causative of this Teut. strong verbal root *wind*, 'to turn, wrap,' see wenden; other derivatives are wandern, wandeln. There are no certain cognates in non-Teut. Ital. *ghindare*, Fr. *guinder*, 'to hoist,' are borrowed from Teut.

Windhund, m., Windspiel, n., 'greyhound, harrier,' from the equiv. MidHG. *wintbracke, wintspil;* these compounds are tautological forms for MidHG. and OHG. *wint*, 'greyhound.' It is probably not connected with Wind, though the two words are instinctively associated. On account of the limited area of its diffusion, the prehistoric form cannot be discovered. Its kinship with Hund (Teut. *hundo-*, from *hwundo-*) is perhaps possible (Wind-, from *hwindo-?*); in that case the assonance with Wind must have caused the differentiation.

Windsbraut, f., 'hurricane, tornado,' from the equiv. MidHG. *windes brût*, OHG. *wintes brût*, f.; a remarkable formation, which is usually referred to mythological ideas. Yet OHG. and MidHG. *brût* in this compound might be cognate with Mid HG. *brûs*, ModHG. Braus, if this were connected with pre-Teut. *bhrŭt-to-*.

Wingert, m., 'vineyard,' from MidHG. *wingarte*, OHG. *wingarto*, m.; comp. also E. *vineyard;* lit. 'wine-garden.' For the shortening of MidHG. and OHG. *i*, comp. Winzer.

Winh, m., 'sign, wink, nod, hint,' from the equiv. MidHG. *winc* (k), OHG. *winch*, m.; allied to winken, vb., 'to wink, beckon, nod,' MidHG. *winken*, str. vb., OHG. *winchan*, wk. vb., 'to move sidewards, totter, nod, wink'; corresponding to AS. *wincian*, E. *to wink*. If 'to totter along, move with a sideward motion,' is the primary meaning of the Teut. root *wink*, the Aryan root may be the same as that of weichen (*wĭg, wĭk*). Related to the following word.

𝔚𝔦𝔫𝔨𝔢𝔩, m., 'angle, corner, nook,' from the equiv. MidHG. *winkel*, OHG. *winchil*, m.; corresponding to Du. *winkel*, AS. *wincel*, 'angle,' to which Goth. *waíhsta*, m., 'angle, corner,' formed from a nasalised root, is allied. The primary meaning of the word is probably 'bend.' See 𝔚𝔦𝔫𝔣.

𝔴𝔦𝔫𝔨𝔢𝔫, see 𝔚𝔦𝔫𝔨.

𝔴𝔦𝔫𝔰𝔢𝔩𝔫, v., 'to whine, whimper,' from the equiv. MidHG. *winseln*, an intensive of MidHG. *winsen*, OHG. *winsôn*, *winisôn*, wk. vb., 'to lament.' Probably derived, like *wimmern* (𝔴𝔦𝔢𝔥𝔢𝔯𝔫), from the Teut. root *hwī*. Its connection with *weinen* is less probable.

𝔚𝔦𝔫𝔱𝔢𝔯, m., 'winter,' from the equiv. MidHG. *winter*, OHG. *wintar*, m.; a common Teut. term, wanting in the other Aryan languages. Comp. Goth. *wintrus*, AS. and E. *winter*, OSax. *wintar*. The allied languages used a stem *ghĭm* (*ghiem*); comp. Lat. *hiems*, Gr. χειμών, OSlov. and Zend *zima*, Sans. *hêmanta* (also in the Lex Salica *ingimus*, 'anniculus'). These Aryan cognates, which may also signify 'snow' and 'storm' (comp. Gr. χεῖμα, 'storm'), cannot, for phonological reasons, be allied to the Teut. group. They suggest, however, a connection between 𝔚𝔦𝔫𝔱𝔢𝔯 and 𝔚𝔦𝔫𝔡; yet the Teut. bases *wintru-* and *windo-* do not agree phonologically. Perhaps those are right who regard 𝔚𝔦𝔫𝔱𝔢𝔯 as the 'white period,' referring it to OGall. *vindo-*, 'white' (as in *Vindo-bona*, *Vindo-magus*, *Vindonissa*); comp. OIr. *find*, 'white.' In the OTeut. languages 𝔚𝔦𝔫𝔱𝔢𝔯 also signifies 'year,' which is still retained in the Mod HG. dial. 𝔈𝔦𝔫𝔴𝔦𝔫𝔱𝔢𝔯, 'yearling kid, steer' (AS. *ánetre*, 'of one year').

𝔚𝔦𝔫𝔷𝔢𝔯, m., 'vintager, vine-dresser,' from the equiv. MidHG. *winzürl*, *winzürle*, OHG. *winzuril* (*winzurnil*), m. It can hardly have been borrowed from Lat. *vīnitor*, which must have produced the OHG. form *wīnizâri (MidHG. *wīnzære*, *wīnzer*). OHG. *winzuril* is more probably, however, a compound slightly influenced by the Lat. term; its second component is derived from OHG. *zëran*, 'to tear or pluck off.' Comp. 𝔚𝔢𝔦𝔫, and for the accented vowel 𝔚𝔦𝔫𝔤𝔢𝔯𝔱.

𝔴𝔦𝔫𝔷𝔦𝔤, adj., 'tiny, diminutive, petty,' from the equiv. late MidHG. *winzic* (*g*). A recent diminutive derivative of *wenig* (comp. *einzig* from *einig*, *ein*); yet note Swab. and Alem. *wunzig*.

𝔚𝔦𝔭𝔣𝔢𝔩, m., 'top (of a tree), summit,' from MidHG. *wipfel* (*wiffel*), OHG. *wipfil* (*wiffil*), m., 'top of a tree'; lit. perhaps 'that which rocks, swing,' for the word is based on the Teut. root *wip*, 'to tremble, move, rock' (see 𝔚𝔦𝔭𝔭𝔢).

𝔚𝔦𝔭𝔭𝔢, f., 'critical point, see-saw, seat (of a swing), crane,' ModHG. only, borrowed from LG.; comp. Du. *wippen*, 'to let fly, jerk, rock.' The genuine HG. form is OHG. and MidHG. *wipf*, 'swing, quick movement'; in MidHG. also *wifen*, str. vb., 'to swing' (see 𝔴𝔢𝔦𝔣𝔢𝔫). The Teut. root *wĭp*, 'to move with a rocking motion,' contained in these cognates (and in 𝔚𝔦𝔭𝔣𝔢𝔩), is based on pre-Teut. *wĭb*, whence also Lat. *vibrare*, 'to vibrate'; allied to the earlier Aryan variant *wĭp*, in Sans. *vip*, 'to tremble,' OHG. *weibôn*, 'to totter.'

𝔴𝔦𝔯, pron., 'we,' from the equiv. Mid HG. and OHG. *wir*; corresponding to Goth. *weis*, OSax. *wī*, Du. *wij*, AS. *wé*, E. *we*. The common Teut. *wīz*, with a secondary nomin. suffix *s*, is based on Aryan *wei*, whence Sans. *vayám*, 'we.' The declension of 𝔴𝔦𝔯, which is supplemented by *uns*, belongs to grammar.

𝔚𝔦𝔯𝔟𝔢𝔩, m., 'whirl, vortex, whirlpool, bustle, crown (of the head),' from MidHG. *wirbel*, m., 'vortex, crown (of the head), whirl,' OHG. *wirbil*, *wirfil*, m., 'whirlwind'; comp. OIc. *hvirfell*, 'vortex,' E. *whirl*. Derivatives of the Teut. root *hwerb* (*hwerf*), 'to turn' (see 𝔴𝔢𝔯𝔟𝔢𝔫). With regard to 𝔎𝔬𝔭𝔣𝔴𝔦𝔯𝔟𝔢𝔩 note the evolution of meaning in 𝔖𝔠𝔥𝔢𝔦𝔱𝔢𝔩.

𝔴𝔦𝔯𝔨𝔢𝔫, vb., 'to work, effect, produce,' from the equiv. MidHG. *wirken* (*würken*), OHG. *wirken* (*wurchen*). This verb, properly strong, is common to Teut. in the forms *wirkjan*, *wurkjan*; comp. Goth. *waúrkjan*, AS. *wyrčean*, also OSax. *wirkian*, Du. *werken*. The Teut. verbal root *werk*, *work*, to which ModHG. 𝔚𝔢𝔯𝔨 belongs, is based on an old Aryan root *werg* (*worg*), which occurs in several dialects. With Gr. ἔργον, 'work,' are connected ῥέζω (for *Ϝρεγιω), 'to do, perform,' ὄργανον, 'instrument,' ὄργιον, 'sacred rite'; so too the Zend root *vrz*, *verez*, 'to work, toil.' The meanings, 'to prepare by sewing, embroidering, weaving,' incipient in MidHG., have been preserved in ModHG. There is also in Ger. a compound derivative OHG. *scuoh-wourhto*, MidHG. *schuochwürte*, 'shoemaker,' whence ModHG. proper names such as 𝔖𝔠𝔥𝔲𝔟𝔢𝔯𝔱, 𝔖𝔠𝔥𝔲𝔠𝔥𝔞𝔯𝔡𝔱.

𝔴𝔦𝔯𝔯, adj., 'confused, entangled,' a Mod HG. derivative of *wirren*, 'to twist, entangle, confuse' (mostly now *verwirren*).

This properly str. vb. (as the old ModHG. partic. verworren shows) is based on Mid HG. wërren (verwërren), OHG. wërran (firwërran), str. vbs., 'to entangle, confuse.' On the corresponding subst. OHG. wërra, 'confusion, dispute,' are based Ital. guerra, Fr. guerre, 'war.' It is uncertain whether OHG. and OSax. wërran, str. vb., 'to bring into confusion,' is based on an earlier *wersan, and whether Wurſt is connected with it. A pre-Teut. root wers appears in OSlov. vrěšti, 'to thresh,' and probably also in Lat. verro, 'to sweep.' E. worse (Goth. waírsiza; see the following word) is usually referred to the Teut. root wers, 'to confuse.'

wirſch, adj., 'cross, angry,' ModHG. only, an imitation of MidHG. unwirsch (from unwirdesch, unwürdesch). The signification cannot be explained from the Mid HG. compar. wirs (equiv. to E. worse, Goth. waírsis).

Wirſching, Wirſing, m., 'borecole,' first recorded in ModHG.; the word seems, however, to have been borrowed at an earlier period from Upper Italy, as is also indicated by the Fr. term, chou de Milan ou de Savoie. It is based on Lombard. versa (comp. Ital. verzotto), 'cabbage, borecole,' which is usually referred to Lat. viridia, 'vegetables.' Ficht and Ruppes were borrowed at a much earlier period.

Wirt, m., 'host, landlord,' from Mid HG. and OHG. wirt. m., 'husband, head of the house, sovereign of a country, host, guest, landlord (of an inn, &c.)'; comp. OSax. wërd, 'husband, master of the house,' Du. waard, Goth. waírdus, 'host.' No connection with Lat. vir, 'man' (for Teut. wër, see Werwolf, Welt, and Wergeld), is possible, and it can hardly be related to warten.

Wirtel, m., 'spindle ring,' from the equiv. MidHG. wirtel, m., which is derived from the Aryan root wert, 'to turn' (see werben).

Wiſch, m., 'rag, clout. wisp,' from the equiv. MidHG. wisch, OHG. wisc, m., to which MidHG. and ModHG. wischen, OHG. wisken, is allied. Comp. OIc. visk, 'bundle,' and also E. wisp with a labial instead of a guttural. The base wisku, wisq, wisp, may be connected with Lat. virga (from wizgā ?).

Wiſpel, m., 'twenty-four bushels,' Mod HG. only, a LG. word. The base wichschepel, recorded in the 12th cent., points to a connection with LG. schepel, 'bushel.'

wiſpeln, vb., 'to whisper,' from the equiv. MidHG. wispeln, OHG. wispalôn,

hwispalôn. Also in ModHG. only, wiſpern (properly perhaps a LG. word), corresponding to AS. hwisprian, E. to whisper. These intensive forms seem to be based on an onomat. root hwīs (hais), to which also heiſer is usually referred.

wiſſen, vb., 'to know, beware of,' from the equiv. MidHG. wiȝȝen, OHG. wiȝȝan; a common Teut., and more remotely a primit. Aryan pret. present. Comp. Goth. wait, 'I know,' AS. wât, E. wot, OSax. wêt, OHG. and MidHG. weiȝ. Based on pre-Teut. woid, wid, in Sans. vêda, 'I know,' Gr. οἶδα, OSlov. vědĕti, 'to know.' This primit. unreduplicated perfect is based on a root wid, which in the Aryan languages means lit. 'to find,' then 'to see, recognise'; comp. Sans. vid, 'to find,' Gr. ἰδεῖν, Lat. videre, 'to see,' Goth. witan, 'to observe.' In Ger. comp. gewiß, verweiſen, weiſſagen, Witȝ.

willern, vb., 'to scent, spy out,' from MidHG. witeren, 'to scent something'; comp. the equiv. OIc. viðra; connected with Wind. "E. to wind, and Fr. vent, 'scent,' show that it was possible for the sportsman's phrase to attain this meaning (which is lit. 'to track by the aid of scent')."

Wittib (with a normal b), Witwe, f., 'widow.' from the equiv. MidHG. witewe, witwe, OHG. wituwa (witawa), f.; common to Teut. and Aryan. Comp. Goth. widuwô, OSax. widowa, Du. weduwe, AS. wuduwe, widewe, E. widow. Corresponding to Ir. fedb, Lat. vidua, San. vidhává, OSlov. vĭdova. The primit. Aryan form widhéwá (widhowá), f., 'widow,' implied in these words seems to be an old formation from an Aryan root widh, Sans. root vidh, 'to become empty, be faulty'; comp. Gr. ἠίθεος, 'single, unmarried.' The designations for Witwer, 'widower,' are recent derivatives of the feminine form (comp. Schwieger); comp. OHG. wituwo, MidHG. witware, from which a new fem. could be ultimately formed (MidHG. witwerinne); comp. Mod HG. Witmann (hence Witfrau). ModHG. Waiſe, 'orphan,' is perhaps connected with the same Aryan root widh.

Willum, n., 'widow's jointure,' the proper term is probably Widelum, n. The first component is MidHG. widen, wideme, m. and f., 'bridal gift, present from the bridegroom to the bride,' then also 'endowment of a church,' OHG. widamo, 'wedding gift of the bridegroom to the bride.' The corresponding AS. weotuma, 'money paid for the bride,' leads to kinship with Gr.

vĕdna, vĕdnov, 'bridal presents made by the bridegroom,' to which perhaps OSlov. *vedą* (*vestí*) and the equiv. OIr. *fedaim*, 'to marry,' are allied. There is, in any case, no connection between 𝔐ittum and the preceding word; comp. also witmen.

𝔚itwe, see 𝔐ittib.

𝔚iṫz, m., 'wit, sense, understanding, repartee,' from MidHG. *witze*, OHG. *wizzi*, f., 'knowing, understanding, prudence, wisdom'; an abstract of wiffen (corresponding to AS. and E. *wit*). Allied to wiṫzig, adj., 'witty, clever, brilliant,' from MidHG. *witzec* (*g*), OHG. *wizzīg*, 'intelligent, prudent.'

wo, adv., 'where,' from MidHG. and OHG. *wā* for older *wār*, 'where'; comp. OSax. *hwār*, Du. *waar*, AS. *hwǣr*, E. *where*, and the equiv. Goth. *hwar*. A local adv. from the old interr. pron. *hwa-*, from Aryan *ko-*; comp. Sans. *kárhi*, 'when.' See wer and warum.

𝔚oche, f., 'week,' from the equiv. MidHG. *woche*, OHG. *wohha*, usually with an earlier vowel *wēhha*, f., a common Teut. term based on a primary form, *wikōn-*. Comp. Goth. *wikô*, OSax. *wika*, Du. *week*, AS. *wucu*, *wicu*, E. *week*, and the equiv. OIc. *vika*, f. The assumption that Lat. *vices*, 'change,' was adopted by the Teutons in the sense of 'week' is untenable, for were the notion 'week' borrowed from the Romans, it would have assumed a form corresponding to Ital. *settimana*, Fr. *semaine* (OIr. *sechtman*), 'week.' The Teut. origin of the word is supported by the fact that it is borrowed by Finn. (as *wiika*), as well as by *wice*, f., 'alternate service,' the AS. variant of *wicu*, which makes it probable that 𝔚oche meant 'change' (comp. 𝔚echfel). The assumption of a loan-word is, however, most strongly opposed by the genuine Teut. names of the days of the week, which prove the existence of a developed chronology in the pre-historic period.

𝔚ocken, m., 'distaff,' ModHG. only, from LG.; probably cognate with 𝔚ieche.

𝔚oge, f. (with MidG. *ô* for *â*, as in Obem, Schlot, Ret, &c.), 'wave, billow,' from MidHG. *wāc* (*g*), OHG. *wâg*, n., 'water in commotion, flood, billow, stream, river, sea'; comp. OSax. *wâg*, AS. *wǣg*, Goth. *wêgs*, 'billow, flood.' From OHG. is derived Fr. *vague*. Teut. *wēgo-*, *wēgi-*, from pre-Teut. *wēgho-*, *wēghi-*, is connected with the Aryan root *wĕgh*, 'to move'; hence 𝔚oge, lit. 'motion, that which is moved.'

wohl, adv., 'well, probably,' from the equiv. MidHG. *wol*, OHG. *wola* (earlier *wëla*), adv. from gut; corresponding to OSax. *wĕl*, Du. *wel*, AS. *wĕl*, E. *well*, Goth. *waila*. The primary meaning of this common Teut. adv. is 'as one could wish,' because it is derived from the root of wollen. Aryan *welo-*, 'wish, desire,' is also indicated by Sans. *vára*, m. and n., 'wish, desire,' to which *víram ā* (or *práti víram*), 'as one could wish, as one likes,' is allied. wohlfeil, adj., 'cheap,' from MidHG. *wol veile*, *wolveil*, 'easily purchasable'; comp. feil.—wohlgeboren, adj., 'Mr.,' from MidHG. *wolgeborn* (also *hôchgeborn*), 'distinguished.'—𝔚ohlthat, f., 'benefit, kindness, good deed,' from the equiv. MidHG. *woltât*, OHG. *wolutât*.

wohnen, vb., 'to dwell,' from the equiv. MidHG. *wonen*, OHG. *wonēn*, wk. vb.; corresponding to OSax. *wunōn*, Du. *wonen*, AS. *wunian*, 'to dwell, be, remain.' Beside these West Teut. cognates there are those of gewohnt; the Aryan root *wen*, on which they are based, probably meant 'to please,' which is suggested by Goth. *wunan*, OIc. *una*, 'to rejoice'; the 'wonted thing' is 'that with which one is pleased'; wohnen, lit. 'to find pleasure anywhere.' From the same Aryan root *wen* are derived OSax. and OHG. *wini* (MidHG. *wine*), 'friend,' Lat. *Venus*, 'goddess of love,' the Sans. root *van*, 'to be fond of, love,' Sans. *vánas*, 'delight.' Comp. also 𝔚onne and 𝔚unfch.

wölben, vb., 'to vault, arch,' from MidHG. and OHG. *welben* (from *walbian, *hwalbjan*), wk. vb., 'to assume a curved shape, vault.' Comp. OSax. *bihwelbian*, 'to arch over, cover,' Du. *welven*, OIc. *hvelfa*, 'to arch'; allied to AS. *hwealf*, 'arched,' and Goth. *hwilftri*, 'coffin' (lit. 'arch'). The Teut. verbal root *hwelb*, *hwelf*, from Aryan *qelp* (*qelq*?) is related to Gr. κόλπος, 'bosom' (lit. 'arch'); so too Sans. *kūrcá*, Lat. *culcita*, 'pillow'?.

𝔚olf, m., 'wolf,' from the equiv. MidHG. and OHG. *wolf*, m.; common to Teut. and also to Aryan; comp. Goth. *wulfs*, OSax. *wulf*, Du. *wolf*, AS. *wulf*, E. *wolf*. Teut. *wulfo-*, from *wulpo-*, is based on Aryan *welgo-*, *wlko-*; comp. Sans. *vṛ́ka*, OSlov. *vlǎkǎ*. Lith. *vilkas*, Gr. λύκος, Lat. *lupus*, 'wolf.' On account of this apparent similarity between 𝔚olf and the equiv. words of the other Aryan languages, Lat. *vulpes*, 'fox,' cannot be allied. The Aryan term *wlko-*

has been rightly compared with the Aryan root *welk*, 'to march,' preserved in Gr. ἕλκω, OSlov. *vlěkǫ*, so that 𝔐𝔬𝔩𝔣 meant perhaps 'robber.' The word was often used in Teut. to form names of persons; comp. 𝔐𝔬𝔩𝔣𝔯𝔞𝔪, under 𝔑𝔞𝔟𝔢; 𝔑𝔲𝔡𝔬𝔩𝔣, from *Ruodolf* (lit. 'famous wolf,' see 𝔑𝔲𝔥𝔪), 𝔄𝔡𝔬𝔩𝔣, from *Adalolf* (lit. 'noble wolf,' see 𝔄𝔡𝔢𝔩).

𝔐𝔬𝔩𝔨𝔢, f., 'cloud,' from the equiv. MidHG. *wolken*, OHG. *wolchan*, m.; also in MidHG. (Alem., MidG.) *wolke*, OHG. *wolcha*, f., 'cloud.' Corresponding to OSax. *wolcan*, n., Du. *wolk*, AS. *wolcen*, 'cloud' (to which E. *welkin* is allied). Under 𝔴𝔢𝔩𝔨 a pre-Teut. root *welg*, 'moist,' is assumed, with which the term *wolkôn* (*wolken*-), n., 'cloud' (lit. 'the moist thing'), peculiar to West Teut., is connected.

𝔐𝔬𝔩𝔩𝔢, f., 'wool, down,' from the equiv. MidHG. *wolle*, OHG. *wolla*, f.; corresponding to Goth. *wulla*, AS. *wull*, E. *wool*, Du. *wol*. Teut. *wullô*-, from pre-Teut. *wlnâ* (for *ll* from *ln* see 𝔐𝔢𝔩𝔩𝔢 and 𝔳𝔬𝔩𝔩), correspond in the Aryan languages to Sans. *ûrṇâ*, OSlov. *vlŭna*, Lith. *vílna*, 'wool'; in Lat. *villus*, *vellus*. Sans. *ûrṇâ* is connected with a root *vṛ*, 'to cover, wrap' (pres. *ṛṇômi*); hence 𝔐𝔢𝔩𝔩𝔢 (Aryan *wlnâ*) meant lit. 'that which covers.' Gr. εἶρος, ἔριον, 'wool,' cannot be related to the common Aryan cognates (root *wel*).

𝔴𝔬𝔩𝔩𝔢𝔫, vb., 'to wish, be willing, have a mind to, intend,' from the equiv. MidHG. *wollen* (*wellen*), OHG. *wellan* (*wellan*); an anomalous vb.; the further details belong to grammar. Comp. OSax. *wellian*, *willian*, Du. *willen*, AS. *willan*, E. *to will*, Goth. *wiljan*. The connection between the Teut. root *wel*, 'to wish,' with which 𝔐𝔞𝔥𝔩 and 𝔴𝔢𝔥𝔩 are also connected, and the equiv. Lat. *velle* is apparent; comp. also Sans. *vṛ* (*var*), 'to choose, prefer,' OSlov. *voliti*, 'to be willing.' Gr. βούλομαι, 'to be willing,' is, on the other hand, not allied; it is more probably related to Gr. ἐθέλω, θέλω, 'to wish,' which, like Sans. *hary*, 'to desire,' points to an Aryan *ghel* (*ghwel*), which would produce in Teut. likewise a root *wěl*, 'to be willing.'

𝔐𝔬𝔩𝔩𝔲𝔰𝔱, f., 'delight, voluptuousness,' from MidHG. *wol-lust*, m. and f., 'gratification, joy, pleasure, enjoyment, merry life, voluptuousness.'

𝔐𝔬𝔫𝔫𝔢, f., 'rapture, ecstasy, bliss,' from MidHG. *wunne* (*wünne*), OHG. *wunna* (*wunni*), f., 'joy, pleasure, the most beautiful and best'; corresponding to OSax. *wunnia*, 'joy,' AS. *wynn*. Goth. *wunni (gen. *wunnjôs) was probably a verbal abstract of Goth. *wunan*, 'to rejoice,' the root of which (Aryan *wen*, 'to be pleased') appears in 𝔴𝔢𝔥𝔫𝔢𝔫. OHG. *wunnea* (MidHG. *wünne*), 'pasture-land,' has been considered as identical with 𝔐𝔬𝔫𝔫𝔢; yet that word, like Goth. *winja*, 'pasture, fodder,' has its own early history. It has been preserved in 𝔐𝔢𝔫𝔫𝔢𝔪𝔬𝔫𝔞𝔱, 'month of May,' MidHG. *wunnemânôt* (*winnemânôt*), OHG. *wunni-*, *winni-*, *mânôd*, lit. 'pasture month.'

𝔴𝔬𝔯𝔣𝔢𝔩𝔫, vb., 'to fan, winnow,' ModHG. only; intensive of 𝔴𝔢𝔯𝔣𝔢𝔫.

𝔴𝔬𝔯𝔤𝔢𝔫, see 𝔴𝔲̈𝔯𝔤𝔢𝔫.

𝔐𝔬𝔯𝔱, n., 'word, term, expression,' from the equiv. MidHG. and OHG. *wort*, n.; corresponding to Goth. *waúrd*, OSax., AS., and E. *word*, Du. *woord*. The common Teut. *wordo*, 'word,' based on Aryan *wṛdho*-, is equiv. to Lat. *verbum* (Lat. *b* for Aryan *dh*, as in 𝔅𝔞𝔯𝔱, *rot*), Pruss. *wirds*, 'word,' and Lith. *vardas*, 'name.' 𝔐𝔢𝔯𝔱 has with less reason been regarded as an old particle. *wṛ-tó*- (for the suffix comp. *fatt* and *traut*), and derived from the root *wer* (*wrē*), appearing in Gr. ῥήτωρ, 'orator,' ῥήτρα, 'saying,' ἐρέω, 'to ask,' and with which OIr. *breth*, 'sentence,' based on Aryan *wṛto*-, is connected.

𝔐𝔯𝔞𝔠𝔨, n., 'wreck, refuse,' ModHG. only, from LG.; comp. Du. *wrak*, E. *wreck*. Based on Du. *wrak*, 'useless, damaged,' and *wraken*, 'to cast out.'

𝔐𝔲𝔠𝔥𝔢𝔯, m., 'usury, interest,' from MidHG. *wuocher*, OHG. *wuohhar*, m. and n., 'produce, fruit, gain, profit'; corresponding to Goth. *wôkrs*, 'usury.' The OHG. and MidHG. sense 'descendants' points to a Teut. root *wak*, 'to arise, bear,' which is identical with the Aryan root *wŏg*, 'to be astir, successful, energetic' (see 𝔴𝔢𝔠𝔨𝔢𝔫); comp. Sans. *vâja*, m., 'power, strength, nourishment, prosperity,' and AS. *onwæcnan*, 'to be born.' In meaning the Aryan root *aug*, 'to increase,' cognate with Aryan *wog*, is more closely connected; comp. Lat. *augere*, Goth. *aukan* (Lith. *augti*, 'to grow').

𝔐𝔲𝔠𝔥𝔰, m., 'growth, development'; ModHG. only, a graded form, from 𝔴𝔞𝔠𝔥𝔰𝔢𝔫.

𝔐𝔲𝔠𝔥𝔱, f., 'weight, burden,' ModHG. only, from LG. *wucht*, a variant of 𝔊𝔢𝔴𝔦𝔠𝔥𝔱.

𝔴𝔲̈𝔥𝔩𝔢𝔫, vb., 'to root, grub up, burrow, rummage, stir up,' from the equiv. MidHG. *wüelen*, OHG. *wuolen* (from *wôljan);

corresponding to Du. *woelen*. With this weak verbal root *wôl* is connected the Teut. cognate *walo-* (see 𝔚𝔞𝔥𝔩𝔰𝔱𝔞𝔱𝔱), to which OHG. and MidHG. *wuol* and AS. *wôl*, 'defeat, ruin,' are allied.

𝔚𝔲𝔩𝔰𝔱, f., 'swelling, roll, pad,' from the equiv. MidHG. (very rare) *wulst*, OHG. (rare) *wulsta*, f. (also signifying the 'turned up lip'). A derivative of OHG. *wëllan*, MidHG. *wëllen*, str. vb., 'to make round, roll,' to which 𝔚𝔢𝔩𝔩𝔢 is allied.

𝔴𝔲𝔫𝔡, adj., 'galled, chafed, wounded,' from the equiv. MidHG. *wunt* (*d*), OHG. *wunt*; corresponding to OSax. and AS. *wund*, Du. *gewond*, and Goth. *wunds*; properly an old partic. with the Aryan suffix *to-*. There is also an old abstract of the same root with the Aryan suffix *-tâ* (see 𝔖𝔠𝔥𝔞𝔫𝔡𝔢?), ModHG. 𝔚𝔲𝔫𝔡𝔢, 'wound,' from MidHG. *wunde*, OHG. *wunta*, f., to which OSax. *wunda*, Du. *winde*, AS. *wund*, E. *wound*, correspond. The root on which the word is based would assume the form *wen* in Teut.; comp. Goth. *win-nan*, 'to suffer, feel pain,' to which Gr. ὠτειλή (from *ὀ-Fα-τειλή), 'wound,' is usually referred.

𝔚𝔲𝔫𝔡𝔢𝔯, n., 'wonder, marvel, miracle,' from MidHG. *wunter*, OHG. *wuntar*, n., 'astonishment, object of astonishment, wonder, marvel' (the signification 'astonishment' is preserved in the expression 𝔚𝔲𝔫𝔡𝔢𝔯 𝔫𝔢𝔥𝔪𝔢𝔫, 'to be surprised,' which existed in MidHG.). Comp. OSax. *wundar*, E. and Du. *wonder*. Teut. *wundro-* seems, like Gr. ἀθρέω (for *Fαθρέω?), 'to gaze at, observe, consider,' to point to an Aryan root *wendh*, 'to gaze at, stare at.'

𝔚𝔲𝔫𝔰𝔠𝔥, m., 'wish, desire,' from Mid HG. *wunsch*, OHG. *wunsc*, m., 'wish, desire' (MidHG. also 'capacity for doing something extraordinary'); comp. Du. *wensch*, OIc. *ósk* (for Goth. **wunska*), 'wish.' Hence the derivative 𝔴ü𝔫𝔰𝔠𝔥𝔢𝔫, 'to wish, desire, long for,' MidHG. *wünschen*, OHG. *wunsken*, 'to wish'; comp. Du. *wenschen*, AS. *wŷscéan*, E. *to wish*. Sans. *vâñchâ* (for **vânskâ*), 'wish' (with the root *vâñch*, 'to wish '), is regarded as equiv. to Teut. *wunskô*, 'wish.' The *skâ* derivative is based on the root *wen*, 'to be pleased,' which appears in 𝔴𝔢𝔥𝔫𝔢𝔫.

𝔚ü𝔯𝔡𝔢, f., 'dignity,' from MidHG. *wirde*, f., 'dignity, honour, respect,' OHG. *wirdi*, f.; an abstract from 𝔚𝔢𝔯𝔱.—𝔴ü𝔯𝔡𝔦𝔤, adj., 'worthy, estimable,' from the equiv. MidHG. *wirdec*, OHG. *wirdîg*.

𝔚𝔲𝔯𝔣, m., 'throw, cast, projection,' from the equiv. MidHG. and OHG. *wurf*; allied to 𝔴𝔢𝔯𝔣𝔢𝔫.—With this 𝔚ü𝔯𝔣𝔢𝔩, m., 'die, cube,' from MidHG. *würfel*, OHG. *wurfil*, m., is connected; comp. the equiv. OIc. *verpell*.

𝔴ü𝔯𝔤𝔢𝔫, vb., 'to choke, strangle, throttle,' from the equiv. MidHG. *würgen* (MidG. *worgen*), wk. vb., OHG. *wurgen* (from **wurgjan*). Beside this wk. vb. there existed a strong verbal root, Teut. *werg* (deduced from the equiv. MidHG. *erwërgen*), from Aryan *wergh*, from which Lith. *verszti* (*verżu*), 'to lace together, press firmly,' and OSlov. *vrŭzą*, 'to chain, bind,' are derived. The word has also been compared with the Aryan root *wrengh* (see 𝔯𝔦𝔫𝔤𝔢𝔫).

𝔚𝔲𝔯𝔪, m., 'worm, grub,' from Mid HG. and OHG. *wurm*, 'worm, insect, serpent, dragon'; comp. Goth. *waúrms*, 'serpent,' OSax. *wurm*, 'serpent,' Du. and E. *worm*. The meaning of the common Teut. word varies between 'worm' and 'serpent' (comp. 𝔏𝔦𝔫𝔡𝔴𝔲𝔯𝔪). The former occurs in the primit. allied Lat. *vermis*, 'worm,' with which Gr. ῥόμος (ῥόμοξ for *Fρομο-), 'wood-worm,' is related by gradation. Sans. *krmi*, 'worm,' Lith. *kirmelẽ* and OIr. *cruim* (OSlov. *črŭvĭ*), 'worm,' are not connected with this word; nor is Gr. ἕλμις, 'maw-worm,' related to it.—𝔴𝔲𝔯𝔪𝔢𝔫, vb., 'to become worm-eaten, pry, poke into,' ModHG. only; comp. Du. *wurmen*, 'to torment oneself, languish, work hard'; probably allied to 𝔚𝔲𝔯𝔪.

𝔚𝔲𝔯𝔰𝔱, f., 'sausage, pudding, roll, pad,' from the equiv. MidHG. and OHG. *wurst* (MidG. and Du. *worst*), f. This specifically G. word is rightly regarded as a derivative of the Aryan root *wert*, 'to turn, wind' (see 𝔴𝔢𝔯𝔟𝔢𝔫 and 𝔚𝔦𝔯𝔱𝔢𝔩); hence 𝔚𝔲𝔯𝔰𝔱 (base *wŗtti*, *wrtsti*), lit. 'turning.'

𝔚𝔲𝔯𝔷, f., 'root, herb,' from MidHG. and OHG. *wurz*, f., 'herb, plant' (MidHG. also 'root'); comp. OSax. *wurt*, 'herb, flower,' AS. *wyrt*, E. *wort*, Goth. *waúrts*, 'root.' An Aryan root *wṛd*, *wṛdd*, is indicated by Gr. ῥάδαμνος, 'teudril, shoot' (Gr. ῥίζα from *Fριδjα), and Lat. *râdix* (Gr. ῥάδιξ), with which again OIc. *rót* (whence the equiv. E. *root*) for **wrôt-* is closely connected; comp. also 𝔑ü𝔰𝔰𝔢𝔩. An allied Teut. root *wrt* (from Aryan *wrd*) appears in Goth. **aurti-*, 'herb,' and OHG. *orzôn*, 'to plant.'—To this is allied 𝔚ü𝔯𝔷𝔢, f., 'spice, seasoning, wort (brewing),' from MidHG. *würze*, f., 'spice plant'; corresponding to E. *wort* and OSax. *wurtia*, 'spice.'—𝔴ü𝔯𝔷𝔢𝔫, vb., 'to spice, season,' from the equiv. MidHG. *würzen*, OHG. *wurzen*.

2 C

Wurzel, f., 'root,' from the equiv. Mid HG. *wurzel*, OHG. *wurzala*, f. ; corresponding to Du. *wortel*. The final *l* is not, as in Gichel, a diminut. suffix ; OHG. *wurzala* is rather, according to the evidence of the equiv. AS. *wyrtwalu*, a compound, properly *wurz-walu*. In OHG. the medial *w* was lost, as in Bürger (OHG. *burgâri*), equiv. to AS. *burgware* (comp. further OHG. *eihhorn* with *dcweorn*). Thus too Merchel, OHG. *morhala*, represents *morh-walu*, ModHG. Geisel, OHG. *geisala*, represents *geis-walu*. The second component is Goth. *walus*, 'staff,' AS. *walu*, 'weal, knot'; hence AS. *wyrtwalu* and OHG. *wurzala* meant lit. 'herb stick' (from Wurz).

Wust, m., 'chaos, trash, filth,' from Mid HG. (rare) *wuost*, m., 'devastation, chaos, refuse.'—**wüst**, adj., 'desert, waste, confused, disorderly,' from MidHG. *wüeste*, OHG. *wuosti*, 'desolate, uncultivated, empty'; corresponding to OSax. *wôsti*, Du. *woest*, AS. *wêste*, 'waste.'—**Wüste**, f., 'desert, wilderness,' from the equiv. MidHG. *wüeste*, OHG. *wuostî* (*wuostinna*), f. ; comp. OSax.

wôstinnia, AS. *wêsten*, 'wilderness.' To these West Teut. cognates, which point to a pre-Teut. adj. *wâstu*, OIr. *fás*, and Lat. *vâstus*, 'waste,' are primit. allied. The West Teut. adj. cannot be borrowed from Lat. (only MidHG. *waste*, 'desert,' is probably thus obtained).

Wut, f., 'rage, fury, madness,' from the equiv. MidHG. and OHG. *wuot*, f. ; in OHG. also *wuot*, AS. *wôd*, E. *wood*, adj., 'furious, mad,' Goth. *wôds*, 'possessed, lunatic.' There exist, besides these cognates, AS. *wôð*, 'voice, song,' OIc. *ôðr*, 'poetry, song.' The connection between the meanings is found in the primit. allied Lat. *vâtes*, 'inspired singer' (OIr. *fáith*, 'poet') ; comp. the Sans. root *vat*, 'to animate spiritually.' From the same is prob. derived the name of the OTeut. god *Wôdan* (AS. *Wôden*, **Wêden*, OSax. *Wôdan*, OIc. *Oðenn*, OHG. *Wuotan*), whose name is preserved in Du. *Woensdag*, E. *Wednesday*. The orig. mythological idea of das wütende Heer, 'the spectral host,' is based on Mid HG. (and OHG.) *Wuotanes her*, 'Odin's host.'

Z.

Zacken, m., 'point, peak, prong, tooth (of a comb),' from the equiv. MidHG. (MidG.) *zacke*, m. and f. ; properly a MidG. and LG. word. Comp. Du. *tak*, m., 'twig, branch, point,' North Fris. *tâk*, 'point,' to which OIc. *tág*, m., 'willow twig,' E. *tack*, are also probably allied. The latter are perhaps primit. cognate with Sans. *daçâ*, 'fringe,' or with Gr. δοκός, 'beam' (Teut. *takko-*, Aryan *dokno-*?). It is uncertain whether Zinke is allied.

zag, adj., 'faint-hearted, shy, irresolute,' from MidHG. *zage*, OHG. *zago*, *zag*, adj., 'faint-hearted, cowardly.' A derivative of ModHG. **zagen**, 'to lack courage, hesitate' (comp. wach and wachen), MidHG. *zagen*, OHG. *zagên*. It is not probable that the word was borrowed, in spite of the few cognates of the Teut. stem *tag*. This is probably derived from a Goth. **at-agan* (1st sing. **ataga*, equiv. to Ir. *ad-agur*, 'to be afraid') by apocope of the initial vowel ; *at* is probably a pref. Goth. *agan*, 'I am afraid,' is based on the widely diffused OTeut. root *ag* (Aryan *agh*), 'to be afraid,' with which Gr. ἄχος, 'pain, distress,' is also connected.

zäh, adj., 'tough, viscous, obstinate,' from the equiv. MidHG. *zæhe*, OHG. *zâhi*, adj. ; corresponding to Du. *taai*, AS. *tôh*, E. *tough* ; Goth. **tâhu* (from **tanhu-*) has to be assumed. With the Teut. root *tanh*, 'to hold firmly together,' are also connected AS. *getęnge*, 'close to, oppressing,' and OSax. *bitęngi*, 'pressing.' Zange appears on account of its meaning to belong to a different root.

Zahl, f., 'number, figure, cipher,' from MidHG. *zal*, f., 'number, crowd, troop, narrative, speech,' OHG. *zala*, f., 'number'; corresponding to Du. *taal*, 'speech,' AS. *talu*, E. *tale*. Allied to **zählen**, vb., 'to count out, pay,' from MidHG. *zaln*, OHG. *zalôn*, 'to count, reckon, compute' (OSax. *talôn*), and **zahlen**, vb., 'to number, count,' from MidHG. *zęln*, OHG. *zęllen* (from **zaljan*), wk. vb., 'to count, reckon, enumerate, narrate, inform, say.' Comp. Du. *tellen*, 'to count, reckon, have regard to,' AS. *tęllan*, E. *to tell*. From the originally strong verbal root *tal*, Goth. *talzjan*, 'to instruct,' is also derived. In non-Teut. there is no certain trace of a root *dal*, 'to enumerate.' See Zoll.

ʒaḥm, adj., 'tame, tractable, docile,' from the equiv. MidHG. and OHG. *zam*; corresponding to Du. *tam*, AS. *tǫm*, E. *tame*, and OIc. *tamr*, 'tame, domesticated.' Allied to ʒäḥmen, vb., 'to tame, domesticate, break in, check,' from MidHG. *zęmen* (*zęmmen*), OHG. *zęmmen* (from *zamjan*), wk. vb., 'to tame'; corresponding to Goth. *gatamjan*, OIc. *temja*, Du. *temmen*, 'to tame.' The connection between the Teut. cognates and Lat. *domare*, Gr. δαμᾶν, Sans. *damáy* (*damany*), 'to subdue, compel,' is undoubted. The relation of these cognates based on *dom*, 'to subdue,' to a similar root appearing in ModHG. ʒiemen (Teut. root *tem*, 'to be suitable, be fitted') is obscure. OHG. *zęmmen*, 'to tame,' looks as if it were a causative of OHG. *zēman*, 'to be adapted, suit excellently.' In that case it is remarkable that the primary verb has been preserved in Teut. only; but was it perhaps deduced from the causative? (see weden).

ʒaḥn, m., 'tooth,' from the equiv. MidHG. *zan*, *zant (d)*, OHG. *zan*, *zand*, m.; common to Teut. and also to Aryan. Comp. OSax. and Du. *tand*, AS. *tóþ* (from *tanþ*), E. *tooth*, Goth. *tunþus*. Teut. *tanþ-*, *tunþ-* (from Aryan *dont-*, *dn̥t-*), is primit. allied to Lat. *dens* (stem *dent-*), Gr. ὀδούς (stem ὀδοντ-), Sans. *dat* (nom. sing. *dan*), *danta*, Lith. *dantìs*, OIr. *dét*, 'tooth.' The Aryan primit. stem *dont-* (*dn̥t-*) is in form the pres. partic. of the root *ed*, 'to eat,' with apocope of the initial vowel (see eſſen); hence ʒaḥn is lit. 'the eating organ' (for the Teut. suffix of the pres. partic. *-and-*, *-und-*, see Feind, Freund, and Heiland). To this word ʒinne is allied.

Bäḥre, f., 'tear,' properly neut. plur. of MidHG. *zaher* (**zacher*), OHG. *zahar* (*zahhar*), m.; the form with *ch* in MidHG. is inferred from the derivative *zęchern*, *zachern*, 'to weep' (OHG. *hhr* from *hr*). Comp. AS. *teár* (from **teahor*, with the variant *tæhher*), E. *tear*, OIc. *tár* (for **tahr-*), Goth. *tagr*, n., 'tear.' A primit. Teut. word in the form *dakru*, which is presupposed by Gr. δάκρυ, Lat. *lacruma* (for earlier *dacruma*), OIr. *dacr* (*dér*), 'tear.' The equiv. Sans. *áçru*, if it stands for *dáçru*, is abnormal.

ʒange, f., 'tongs, pincers,' from the equiv. MidHG. *zange*, OHG. *zanga*, f.; corresponding to Du. *tang*, AS. *tǫnge*, E. *tongs*, and the equiv. OIc. *tǫng*. The common Teut. *tangô-* assumes a pre-Teut. *danká-*, which is usually connected with the Sans. root *danç* (*daç*), 'to bite' (comp. Gr. δάκνω); hence ʒange, lit. 'biter.' Comp. OHG. *zangar*, MidHG. *zanger*, 'biting, sharp, lively,' whence Ital. *tanghero*, 'unpolished, coarse.'

ʒanken, vb., 'to quarrel,' from late MidHG. *zanken*, *zęnken*, 'to dispute'; a remarkably late word, not recorded in the earlier Teut. periods. Perhaps MidHG. *zanke* (a variant of ʒinke), 'prong, point,' is the base of ʒanken, which must then have meant 'to be pointed.'

ʒapfe, m., 'peg, plug, tap, bung,' from MidHG. *zapfe*, m., 'tap, espec. in a beer or wine cask' (also *zipfen*, 'to pour out from a tap'), OHG. *zapfo*, 'peg, plug.' Corresponding to North Fris. *táp*. Du. *tap*, AS. *tæppa*, E. *tap*, and the equiv. OIc. *tappe*. From the Teut. cognates are borrowed the equiv. Fr. *tape* and Ital. *zaffo* (Spund, on the other hand, was borrowed from Romance). Teut. *tappon-* cannot be traced back to the other primit. allied languages; only ʒipfel seems to be related to these cognates.

ʒappeln, vb., 'to move convulsively, sprawl, flounder,' from the equiv. MidHG. *zappeln*, a variant of *zabeln*, OHG. *zabalón* (*zappalón*?), 'to sprawl.' A specifically HG., probably of recent onomatopoetic origin.

ʒarge, f., 'border, edge, setting, groove,' from the equiv. MidHG. *zarge*, OHG. *zarga*, f. Corresponding with a change of meaning to AS. and OIc. *targa*, 'shield' (lit. 'shield border'), whence Fr. *targe*, Ital. *targa*, 'shield' (whence MidHG. and Mod HG. *tartsche*, E. *target*, are borrowed). The remoter history of the cognates is obscure.

ʒart, adj., 'tender, soft, fragile, nice,' from MidHG. and OHG. *zart*, adj., 'dear, beloved, precious, confidential, fine, beautiful'; unknown to the other OTeut. dialects. Like the properly equiv. traut, ʒart appears to be a partic. with the suffix *to-*. Teut. *tar-do*, from Aryan *dr̥-tó-* (comp. ſatt, tot), is most closely related to the Zend partic. *dereta*, 'honoured'; comp. Sans. *d-dr̥*, 'to direct one's attention to something.' The Teut. word cannot have been borrowed from Lat. *carus*, 'dear.'

ʒaſer, f., 'fibre, filament,' ModHG. only, unknown to the earlier periods (older Mod HG. *zasel*, Swed. *zasem*). Origin obscure.

ʒauber, m., 'charm, enchantment, magic,' from MidHG. *zouber* (*zouver*), OHG.

zoubar (*zoufar*), m., 'magic, charm, spell'; comp. Du. *tooveren*, 'to enchant,' OIc. *taufr*, n., 'magic.' For the meaning, the corresponding AS. *teáfor*, 'vermilion,' is important; hence Зauber is perhaps lit. 'illusion by means of colour'; others suppose that the runes were marked with vermilion, so that Зauber would mean lit. 'secret or magic writing.' No cognates of the specifically Teut. *taufro-*, *taubro-* (Aryau root *dăp*, not *dăbh*), have been found.

Зaubern, vb., 'to hesitate, delay, procrastinate,' allied to MidHG. (MidG.) *zûwen* (**zûwern*), wk. vb., 'to draw,' which seems like зеgern, to be connected with зiehen.

Зaum, m., 'bridle, rein,' from the equiv. MidHG. and OHG. *zoum*, m.; corresponding to OSax. *tóm*, Du. *toom*, OIc. *taumr*, 'bridle, rein.' The meaning makes it probable that the word is derived from the Teut. root *tug*, *tuh*, 'to draw' (*taumo-* for **taugmo-*, Aryan *doukmo-*; comp. Зraum); hence Зaum is lit. 'drawing strap.'

Зaun, m., 'hedge, fence,' from the equiv. MidHG. *tûn*, m.; comp. OSax. *tûn*, Du. *tuin*, 'hedge, garden,' AS. *tûn*, 'enclosure, place,' E. *town* (also dial. to *tine*, 'to hedge in,' from the equiv. AS. *týnan*), OIc. *tûn*, 'enclosure, farm.' Teut. *tû-no-* (*tû-nu-* ?) is connected pre-historically with -*dûnan* in OKelt. names of places (such as *Augustodûnum*, *Lugdûnum*); comp. OIr. *dûn*, 'citadel, town.'—Зaunkönig, m., 'wren,' in MidHG. merely *küniclîn*, OHG. *chuninglî*, n., 'little king.'

зaufen, vb., 'to tease (wool, &c.), tug, pull about,' from MidHG. and OHG. *erzûsen*, OHG. *zirzûsôn*, wk. vb.; comp. Mid HG. *zûsach*, 'brambles.' Apart from HG. the Teut. root *tûs* (Aryan *dûs*), 'to tear to pieces,' does not occur; the comparison with Lat. *dûmus* (from **dûsmus* ?), 'bramble,' is uncertain.

Зeche, f., 'rotation (of duties), succession, hotel bill, share in a reckoning (at an inn), drinking party (each paying a share), corporation, guild, club,' from the equiv. MidHG. *zěche*, f. (which also means arrangement, association); also in MidHG. *zěchen* (OHG. **zëhhôn*), wk. vb., 'to arrange, prepare, bring about,' also (late), 'to run up a score at an inn.' In OHG. only the word *gizěhôn*, 'to arrange, regulate,' from this stem is found; comp. the allied AS. *teohhian* and *teógan* (from **těhhôn*, *tëhwôn*, *tëhôn*), 'to arrange, determine, regulate,' and *teoh* (*hh*), 'company, troop.' A Teut. root *tĕhw*, *tĕgw* (*tĕw*), is indicated by Goth. *gatĕwjan*, 'to ordain,' *tĕwa*, 'order,' *tĕwi*, 'troop of fifty men.' These imply a pre-Teut. root *dĕq*, 'to arrange, regulate' (to which Gr. δεῖπνον, 'meal,' for *deqnjom*?, is allied). The numerous senses in MidHG. may be easily deduced from the primary meaning.

Зecke, f., 'tick,' from the equiv. Mid HG. *zěcke*, m. and f.; corresponding to Du. *teekt*, AS. **tica* (*ticia* is misspelt for *tiica*), E. *tike, tick*. From the old West Teut. *tĕko*, *tikko*, are derived the equiv. Ital. *zecca*, Fr. *tique*. Aryan *digh-* is indicated by Armen. *tiz*, 'tick,' which is probably primit. allied to the Teut. cognates.

Зeder, f., 'cedar,' from MidHG. *zěder* (*cěder*), m.; from Gr.-Lat. *cedrus* (OHG. *cëdarboum*).

Зeh, m. and f., 'toe,' from the equiv. MidHG. *zěhe*, OHG. *zěha*, f.; corresponding to Du. *teen*, AS. *táhœ*, *tá*, E. *toe*, and the equiv. OIc. *tá*. Beside the base *taihôn*, *taihwôn* (Bav. *zěchen* and Swab. *zaichen*), assumed by these forms, MidHG. and LG. dialects prove the existence of a variant *taiwôn* (from *taigwôn*, *taihwôn*); Swiss and MidRhen. *zěb*, *zěbe*, Franc. and Henneberg. *zěwe*, Thuring. *zĕwe*. Pre-Teut. *daiqá-n*, 'toe,' is usually connected with Gr. δάκτυλος (Lat. *digitus*?), 'finger,' which, on account of the sounds, is, however, improbable, especially as the Teut. word is always used in the sense of 'toe.'

зehn, num., 'ten,' from the equiv. Mid HG. *zěhen*, (*zěn*), OHG. *zěhan*; corresponding to OSax. *tëhan*, Du. *tien*, AS. *týn*, E. *ten*, Goth. *taíhun*; common to Aryan in the form *dekn*; comp. Sans. *dáçan*, Gr. δέκα, Lat. *decem*, and OSlov. *desętĭ*.—зehnte, adj., 'tenth,' from Mid HG. *zěhende* (*zěnde*), OHG. *zëhando*; as subst. 'a tenth, tithe.' —Зehntel, see Зeil. Comp. also :зig.

зehren, vb., 'to eat and drink, live, waste,' from MidHG. *zern*, (*verzern*), 'to consume, use up'; OHG. *firzëran*, str. vb., means only 'to dissolve, destroy, tear' (comp. Винзer). Corresponding to Goth. *gatairan*, 'to destroy, annihilate,' AS. *tëran*, E. *to tear*; allied to Du. *teren*, 'to consume,' OSax. *farterian*, 'to annihilate,' and also to ModHG. зerren and зergen. The Teut. str. verbal root *ter*, 'to tear,' corresponds to Gr. δέρω, 'to flay,' OSlov. *derą*, 'to tear,' and the Sans. root *dar*, 'to burst, fly in pieces or asunder.'

Зeichen, n., 'sign, mark, token, signal,

symptom, indication,' from the equiv. Mid HG. *zeichen*, OHG. *zeihhan*, n.; corresponding to OSax. *têkan*, Du. *teeken*, AS. *tácn*, E. *token*, and the equiv. Goth. *taikns*. A derivative of the Aryan root *dĭg*, *dĭk*, which appears also in ʒeiɥen and ʒeigen; this root with *k* is contained further in AS. *tǽċean*, E. *to teach* (comp. the *g* of Lat. *dignus*, *prodigium*, and of Gr. δεῖγμα).— Der. ʒeiɥnen, vb., 'to mark, draw, delineate,' from MidHG. *zeichenen*, OHG. *zeihhanen*; lit. 'to furnish with marks.'

Zeidler, m., 'keeper of bees,' from the equiv. MidHG. *zidelœre*, OHG. *zîdaldri*, m.; a derivative of OHG. *zidal*-, MidHG. *zidel*-, espec. in the compound *zidalweida*, MidHG. *zidelweide*, 'forest in which bees are kept.' This *zidal* (pre-HG. **tiplo*- probably appears also in LG. *tielbŭr*, 'honey-bear') does not occur in any other OTeut. dialect, but it is not necessary on that account to assume a foreign origin for the word. The word is supposed to have come from Slav. territory, where the keeping of bees is widely spread, being based on OSlov. *bĭčela*, 'keeper of bees' (comp. Lebfuɥen); but this derivation is not quite probable. Its connection with Seibelbaſt (MidHG. *zidel*-, *sidelbast*) and Zeiland is equally uncertain.

zeigen, 'to show, point out, demonstrate,' from MidHG. *zeigen*, OHG. *zeigôn*, str. vb., 'to show, indicate'; a specifically HG. derivative of the Teut. str. verbal root *tĭh*, ModHG. ʒeihen. The latter comes from MidHG. *zîhen*, str. vb., 'to accuse of, depose concerning,' OHG. *zîhan*, 'to accuse'; also ModHG. verʒeihen, 'to pardon,' MidHG. *verzîhen*, OHG. *firzîhan*, 'to deny, refuse pardon.' Based on the Aryan str. verbal root *dik* (for *dig* see Zeichen); comp. Sans. *diç*, 'to exhibit, produce, direct to,' Gr. δείκνυμι, 'to show,' Lat. *dico*, 'to say.' The primary meaning of the root is preserved by Zeichen and ʒeigen, as well as by Goth. *gateihan*, 'to announce, narrate, proclaim, say'; comp. the compounds OSax. *aftîhan*, AS. *oftêon*, 'to deny.' In HG. the word seems to have acquired a legal sense (comp. Lat. *causidicus judex*); comp. Inʒiɥt.

Zeiland, m., 'spurge laurel,' from the equiv. MidHG. *zîlant*; scarcely allied to MidHG. *zîl*, 'briar'; more probably connected with Seibelbaſt. Comp. Zeibler.

Zeile, f., 'line, row, rank,' from the equiv. MidHG. *zîle*, OHG. *zîla*, f. (late MidHG. also 'lane'). A specifically HG. derivative of the Teut. root *tĭ*, from which Ziel and Zeit are also derived.

Zeiſig, m., 'siskin,' from the equiv. Mid HG. *zîsec*, usually *zîse*, f. Borrowed, like Stieglitz and Kiebitz, from Slav. (Pol. *czyż*, Bohem. *čížek*), whence also LG. *ziseke*, *sieske*, Du. *sijsje*. E. *siskin*, Dan. *sisgen*, Swed. *siska*.

Zeit, f., 'time, epoch, period, tense,' from the equiv. MidHG. and OHG. *zît*, f. and n. (OHG. *zîd*, n.); corresponding to OSax. *tîd*, Du. *tijd*, AS. *tîd*, E. *tide* (comp. Du. *tij*, which is also used of the flow of the sea). The root of Teut. *tî-di-*, 'time,' is *tî-*, as is proved by the equiv. OIc. *tîme*, AS. *tîma*, E. *time* (comp. Goth. *hweila* under Weile). A corresponding Aryan root *dî* is presupposed by Sans. *a-diti*, 'unlimited in time and space, unending, endless' (the name of the goddess Aditi). Other Teut. derivatives of the same root are Zeile and Ziel, which also point to the 'limitless in time or space.'—Zeitloſe, f., 'meadow saffron,' from MidHG. *zîtlôse*, OHG. *ziti/ôsa*; the name of the plant is due to the fact that it does not bloom at the ordinary period of flowering plants.—Zeitung, f., 'newspaper, gazette,' from late MidHG. *zîtunge*, 'information, news'; comp. Du. *tijding*, E. *tidings*, OIc. *tîðende*, 'tidings.' The evolution of the meaning from the stem of Zeit is not quite clear; comp., however, E. *to betide*.

Zelle, f., 'cell,' from the equiv. MidHG. *zëlle*; formed from Lat. *cella* (comp. Keller).

Zelt, n., 'tent, pavilion, awning,' from the equiv. MidHG. *zëlt* (more frequently *gezëlt*), OHG. *zëlt* (usually *gizëlt*), n. A common Teut. word; comp. AS. *gëteld*, 'tent, pavilion, cover' (hence E. *tilt*), OIc. *tjald*, 'curtain, tent.' From OTeut., Fr. *taudis*, 'hut' (Span. and Port. *toldo*, 'tent'?), is derived; OFr. *taudir*, 'to cover,' points to the AS. str. vb. *betëldan*, 'to cover, cover over' (E. and Du. *tent* is based upon Fr. *tente*; comp. Ital. *tenda*, from Lat. *tendere*). Hence the evolution of meaning of Zelt may be easily understood from a Teut. root *teld*, 'to spread out covers.' The following word is allied.

Zelte, m., 'cake, tablet, lozenge,' from the equiv. MidHG. *zëlte*, OHG. *zëlto*, m. Perhaps derived from the Teut. root *teld*, 'to spread out' (see the preceding word). Comp. Flaben for the meaning.

Zelter, m., 'palfrey, ambling pace,' from

the equiv. MidHG. *zëlter*, OHG. *zëlidri*, m. Lit. 'a horse that goes at a gentle pace'; allied to Bav. and MidHG. *zëlt*, m., 'amble, gentle pace,' Du. *telganger*, 'ambler.' To this AS. *tealtrian*, 'to totter,' is probably allied.

𝕭𝖊𝖓𝖙- in 𝕭𝖊𝖓𝖎𝖌𝖊𝖗𝖎𝖈𝖍𝖙, n., 'criminal court or jurisdiction'; -𝖌𝖗𝖆𝖋, m., 'judge of a criminal court,' from MidHG. *zënte*, f., 'district, consisting properly of 100 communities'; comp. Ital. *cinta*, MidLat. *centa*, 'district.'

𝕭𝖊𝖓𝖙𝖓𝖊𝖗, m., 'hundredweight,' from the equiv. MidHG. *zëntenære*, m. Formed from MidLat. *centenarius* (Da. *centenaar*); in Fr., however, *quintal*, Ital. *quintale* (and *cantáro*?).

𝕭𝖊𝖕𝖙𝖊𝖗, m. and n., 'sceptre,' from Mid HG. *zëpter*, m. and n., which is again derived from Gr.-Lat. *sceptrum*.

𝖟𝖊𝖗-, prefix from MidHG. *zer-* (MidG. *zur-* and *zu-*), OHG. *zir-*, *zar-*, *zur-*; a common West Teut. verbal prefix, meaning 'asunder'; comp. OSax. *ti*, AS. *tô*. In Goth. only *twis-* occurs as a verbal prefix in *twisstandan*, 'to separate'; the nominal Goth. prefix *tuz-* (OHG. *zûr-*, OIc. *tor-*) corresponds to Gr. δυσ-, Sans. *dus*, 'bad, difficult.'

𝖟𝖊𝖗𝖌𝖊𝖓, vb., 'to torment, tease, vex'; ModHG. only. It may be identical with MidHG. *zern* (and *zergen*), OHG. *zerian* (see 𝖟𝖊𝖍𝖗𝖊𝖓); yet Du. *tergen*, AS. *tergan*, 'to tug, tease, worry' (E. *to tarry*), point to a Goth. *targian, which with Russ. *dergati*, 'to tear, tug,' indicate an Aryan root *drgh* (comp. 𝖙𝖗𝖆𝖌𝖊).

𝖟𝖊𝖗𝖗𝖊𝖓, vb., 'to tug, tease, worry,' from MidHG. and OHG. *zerren*, wk. vb., 'to tear, cleave'; from the same root as 𝖟𝖊𝖍𝖗𝖊𝖓.

𝖟𝖊𝖗𝖗𝖚𝖙𝖙𝖊𝖓, see 𝖗ü𝖙𝖙𝖊𝖑𝖓, 𝖗𝖚𝖙𝖘𝖈𝖍𝖊𝖓.

𝖟𝖊𝖗𝖘𝖈𝖍𝖊𝖑𝖑𝖊𝖓, vb., 'to shatter, shiver,' from MidHG. *zerschëllen*, str. vb., 'to fly to pieces,' lit. 'to burst with a loud noise.'

𝖟𝖊𝖗𝖘𝖙𝖗𝖊𝖚𝖙, adj., 'scattered, dispersed'; first formed in the last cent. from Fr. *distrait*.

𝖟𝖊𝖗𝖙𝖗ü𝖒𝖒𝖊𝖗𝖓, vb., 'to destroy, shatter, lay in ruins,' formed from ModHG. 𝕿𝖗ü𝖒𝖒𝖊𝖗, 'fragments, ruins'; in MidHG. *zerdrumen*, 'to hew to pieces,' from MidHG. *drum*, 'piece, splinter.'

𝖟𝖊𝖙𝖊𝖗, interj. (espec. in 𝖅𝖊𝖙𝖊𝖗𝖌𝖊𝖘𝖈𝖍𝖗𝖊𝖎, 'cry of murder, loud outcry,' from MidHG. *zëtergeschreie*), from the equiv. MidHG. *zëter* (*zëtter*), 'cry for help, of lamentation, or of astonishment'; not recorded elsewhere.

𝕭𝖊𝖙𝖙𝖊𝖑, m., from the equiv. late MidHG. *zëttel*, m., 'design or warp of a fabric'; allied to MidHG. and OHG. *zetten*, 'to scatter, spread out,' whence ModHG. *verzetteln*, 'to disperse, spill.' The early history of the root *tad*, seldom occurring in OTeut., is obscure.—𝕭𝖊𝖙𝖙𝖊𝖑, m., 'note, ticket, playbill, placard,' from MidHG. *zedele* (*zetele*, *zettele*), 'sheet of paper,' is different from the preceding word. It is formed from Ital. *cedola* (Fr. *cédule*), 'ticket,' MidLat. *scedula* (Gr. σχίδη), 'scrap of paper.'

𝕭𝖊𝖚𝖌, n., 'stuff, substance, material, fabric, apparatus, utensils,' from MidHG. *ziuc* (*g*), m. and n., 'tool, implements, equipment, weapons, baggage, stuff, testimony, proof, witness'; OHG. *giziug*, m. and n., 'equipment, implements' (hence ModHG. 𝖅𝖊𝖚𝖌𝖍𝖆𝖚𝖘, 'arsenal'). Allied to ModHG. 𝕭𝖊𝖚𝖌𝖊, m., 'witness,' from the equiv. late MidHG. (rare) *ziuge*. Also 𝖟𝖊𝖚𝖌𝖊𝖓, vb., 'to produce, beget, bear witness, testify,' from MidHG. *ziugen*, 'to beget, prepare, procure, acquire, bear witness, prove,' OHG. *giziugón*, 'to attest, show.' All the cognates are derived from the Teut. root *tuh* (see 𝖟𝖎𝖊𝖍𝖊𝖓), which in a few derivatives appears in the sense of 'to produce, beget'; comp. AS. *teám*, 'descendants' (to which E. *to teem* is allied), Du. *toom*, 'brood.' From the same root the meaning 'to attest, show,' (OHG. *giziugón*), lit. 'to be put on judicial record,' must be derived.

𝕭𝖎𝖈𝖐𝖊, f., 'kid,' from MidHG. *zickelin*, OHG. *zicchî*, *zickîn* (for the suffix *-ln*, see 𝕾𝖈𝖍𝖜𝖊𝖎𝖓), n.; corresponding to AS. *ticcen*. A diminutive of Teut. *tigó-*, 'she-goat.' Comp. 𝕭𝖎𝖊𝖌𝖊.

𝕭𝖎𝖈𝖐𝖟𝖆𝖈𝖐, m. and n., 'zigzag,' ModHG. only; a recent form from 𝖅𝖆𝖈𝖐𝖊.

𝕭𝖎𝖊𝖈𝖍𝖊, f., 'cover of a feather-bed, tick,' from MidHG. *zieche*, OHG. *ziahha*, f., 'coverlet, pillow-case'; corresponding to Du. *tijk*, E. *tick*. Lat.-Gr. *theca*, whence also Fr. *taie*, 'pillow-case,' as well as OIr. *tlach*, 'tick,' was adopted in HG. contemporaneously with 𝕽𝖎𝖋𝖊𝖓 and 𝕻𝖋ü𝖍𝖑, hence *theca* was permutated to *ziahha*.

𝕭𝖎𝖊𝖌𝖊, f., 'she-goat,' from the equiv. Mid HG. *zige*, OHG. *ziga*, f.; a Franc. word, which in the MidHG. period passed also into LG. In UpG., 𝕲𝖊𝖎𝖘, with which 𝕭𝖎𝖊𝖌𝖊 is probably connected etymologically; for Goth. *gait-*, 'goat,' may have had a graded variant **gitó-*, by metathesis **tigó-*. The latter form must also have been current in pre-historic times, as is proved by the AS. diminut. *tiċċen*, equiv. to OHG. *ziccht* (see Zicke), and the form *kittīn*, obtained by metathesis, equiv. to OHG. *chizzī*. In East MidG. Hitte and Hippe are used for Ziege; in Alem. and Bav. and in Thuring. Ziege is the current term.

Ziegel, m., 'brick, tile,' from the equiv. MidHG. *ziegel*, OHG. *ziagal*, m. The word was borrowed in the pre-HG. period, perhaps contemporaneously with Mauer, Pfosten, Spiegel, and Speicher, from Lat. *tēgula*, whence also the Romance cognates, Ital. *tegghia*, *tegola*, Fr. *tuile*; from the same source are derived Du. *tegehel*, *tegel*, AS. *tigel*, E. *tile*. Ziegel is not a cognate, but a genuine Teut. word, although Lat. *tegula* and its Romance forms may be used in the sense of Ziegel.

ziehen, vb., 'to draw, pull, march,' from the equiv. MidHG. *ziehen*, OHG. *ziohan*; a common Teut. str. vb.; comp. Goth. *tiuhan*, OSax. *tiohan*, AS. *teon*. The Teut. verbal root *tuh* (*tug*) corresponds to an Aryan root *duk*, which has been preserved in Lat. *dūco*, 'to lead.' From the same root the cognates of Zaum, Zeug, Zecht (Herzog), and the (properly) LG. Tau, n., are derived.

Ziel, n., 'limit, aim, goal,' from the equiv. MidHG. and OHG. *zil*, n. Allied to Goth. *tils*, *gatils*, 'suitable, fit,' and *gatilōn*, 'to aim at, attain,' OHG. *zilōn*, 'to make haste,' AS. *tilian*, 'to be zealous, till' (E. *to till*), Du. *telen*, 'to produce, create,' OSax. *tilian*, 'to attain.' To the Goth. adj. *tila-*, 'suitable,' the Scand. prep. *til* (whence E. *till*) belongs. Hence the primary meaning of the cognates is 'that which is fixed, definite,' so that it is possible to connect them with the Teut. root *tī* in Zeile and Zeit.

ziemen, vb., 'to beseem, become, suit,' from MidHG. *zëmen*, OHG. *zëman*, 'to beseem, suit, be adapted, gratify'; corresponding to Goth. *gatiman*, OSax. *tēman*, Du. *betamen*, str. vb., 'to be proper, suit.' It has been suggested under zahm that OHG. *zëman*, 'to suit,' is a deduction from the causative zähmen (see zahm and Zunft). Allied to ziemlich, adj., 'suitable, moderate, tolerable,' from MidHG. *zimelich*, 'proper, adapted.'

Ziemer, m., 'buttock, hind-quarter' (of animals), 'haunch (of venison),' from the equiv. MidHG. *zimere*, f. Bav. dialectic forms such as Zem (Zen) and Zemsen indicate the Teut. origin of the word; Teut. base *tëmoz-*, *timiz-*.

Zier, f., 'ornament, decoration,' from MidHG. *ziere*, OHG. *ziarī*, f., 'beauty, magnificence, ornament'; an abstract of the MidHG. adj. *ziere*, OHG. *ziari*, *zēri*, 'precious, splendid, beautiful.' Corresponding to OIc. *tīrr*, OSax. and AS. *tīr*, m., 'fame, honour' (E. *tire*). The relation of the words is difficult to explain, because the stem vowels (OHG. *ia* not equiv. to AS. *ī*) do not correspond. No connection with Lat. *decus*, 'honour' (*decōrus*, 'becoming'), is possible.—**Zierat** (Zierrat is a corruption), m., 'adornment, decoration,' from MidHG. *zierōt*, an abstract of Mid HG. *ziere* (comp. Armut and Kleinod).—**Zierde,** f., 'ornament, decoration,' from MidHG. *zierde*, OHG. *ziarida*, f., with the meanings of OHG. *ziarī*, f. (see Zier).

Ziesel, m., 'shrew-mouse,' from the equiv. MidHG. *zisel* (and *zisemūs*), m.; a corruption of the equiv. Lat. *cisimus*.

Ziestag, see Dienstag.

Ziffer, f., 'figure, numeral, cipher,' from late MidHG. (rare), *zifer*, *ziffer*, f.; corresponding to Du. *cijfer*, E. *cipher*, Fr. *chiffre*, 'cipher, secret characters,' Ital. *cifra*, 'secret characters.' Originally 'cipher, nought'; adopted in the European languages from Arab. *çafar*, 'nought,' along with the Arabic notation.

-zig, suffix for forming the tens, from MidHG. *-zic* (*g*), OHG. *-zug*; comp. zwanzig. In dreißig, from MidHG. *drī-zec*, OHG. *drī-zug*, there appears a different permutation of the *t* of Goth. *tigus*, 'ten'; comp. AS. *-tig*, E. *-ty*. Goth. *tigu-* (from pre-Teut. *dekú-*) is a variant of *taíhan*, 'ten.' See zehn.

Zimmer, n., 'room, chamber,' from Mid HG. *zimber*, OHG. *zimbar*, n., 'timber, wooden building, dwelling, room'; corresponding to OSax. *timbar*, Du. *timmer*, 'room,' AS. *timber*, E. *timber*, OIc. *timbr*. To these are allied Goth. *timrjan*, 'to build up,' OHG. and MidHG. *zimberen*, Mod HG. zimmern, 'to build.' The primary meaning of the subst. was certainly 'wood for building'; it is primit. allied to Lat. *domus*, Gr. δόμος, Sans. *dama*, OSlov. *domŭ*, 'house' (lit. 'building of wood'); and also to the root vb. Gr. δέμω, 'to build' (δέμας, 'bodily frame').

Zimmet, m., 'cinnamon,' from the equiv. MidHG. *zinemīn*, *zinmēnt*, OHG. *sinamin*, m.; from MidLat. *cinamonium*

(Gr. κύναμον). For the Romance term see Ṛanel.

Zimperlich, adj., 'prim, prudish, affected,' a MidG. form for the genuine UpG. zimpferlich; comp. MidDu. zimperlije, usually simpellje, equiv. to Dan., Norw., and Swed. dial. simper, semper, 'fastidious,' E. to simper.

Zindel, m., 'light taffeta,' from the equiv. MidHG. zindâl, zündâl; from MidLat. cendalum (Gr. σίνδων, 'fine linen,' lit. 'Indian stuff'), whence Ital. zendado, and zendale.

Zingel, m., 'stone wall, palisade,' from MidHG. zingel, m., 'rampart,' whence ModHG. umzingeln, 'to encircle, surround' (MidHG. zingeln, 'to make an entrenchment'), formed like Lat. cingulus, cingere.

Zink, n. and m., 'zinc,' ModHG. only; certainly connected with Zinn. It has been thought that Zinn, 'tin,' when borrowed by Slav. was extended by a Slav. suffix k, with which as zink it passed again into Ger. (whence Fr. zinc). Other etymologists assume a connection with the following word, because tin when melting forms spikes (Zinken).

Zinken, m., 'spike, prong,' from the equiv. MidHG. zinke, OHG. zinko, m. How the equiv. MidHG. zint, OIc. tindr, and ModHG. Zacke are connected with this word is not clear. Late MidHG. zinke (and zint), as a designation of a wind instrument (cornet), has been preserved in ModHG.

Zinn, n., 'tin,' from the equiv. MidHG. and OHG. zin, n.; corresponding to Du., AS., E., and OIc. tin; a common Teut. term which has no cognates in the allied languages (Ir. tinne seems to be borrowed). Lat. stannum is the source of Fr. étain, Ital. stagno, but not of the Teut. words.

Zinne, f., 'pinnacle, battlement,' from MidHG. zinne, OHG. zinna, f., 'upper part of a wall with openings or embrasures.' On account of the meaning it is probably not connected with Zahn; MidHG. zint (see Zinke), 'point, peak' (OHG. zinna, from *tinjôn for *tindjôn?), is more nearly allied. See Zahn.

Zinnober, m., 'cinnabar,' from the equiv. MidHG. zinober, m.; formed from Lat.-Gr. κιννάβαρι, whence also Fr. cinabre.

Zins, m., 'tribute, rent, (plur.) interest,' from MidHG. and OHG. zins, m., 'duty, tribute.' Borrowed during the OHG. period (comp. Kreuz) from Lat. census (Ital. censo), 'census, tax.' The HG. word passed in the form tins into OSax.; in Du., cijns.

Zipfel, m., 'tip, point, peak, lappet,' from MidHG. zipfel (zipf), m., 'pointed end, peak'; allied to E. and Du. tip. Zapfen is the only primit. cognate word in Teut. (Zopf has no connection with Zipfel).

Zipperlein, n., 'gout,' from late MidHG. (rare) zipperlîn, 'gout in the feet'; allied to MidHG. zippeltrit, 'tripping step.' Zippeln is an onomat. imitation of zappeln.

Zirbel, f., in Zirbeldrüse, f., 'pineal gland,' from MidHG. zirbel-, in zirbelwint, 'whirlwind'; allied to MidHG. zirben, 'to move in a circle, whirl,' OHG. zerben, AS. tearflian, 'to turn.' The Teut. root tarb, 'to whirl,' cannot be traced farther back.

Zirkel, m., 'circle, circuit, company, society,' from MidHG. zirkel, OHG. zirkil, m., 'circle,' which is again derived from Lat. circulus (Ital. circolo, Fr. cercle), 'circle,' MidHG. and OHG. zirc, 'circle,' from Lat. circus (Ital. circo).

zirpen, vb., 'to chirp,' ModHG. only; a recent onomatop. form. So too zischeln, vb., 'to whisper,' and zischen, vb., 'to hiss, whiz'; ModHG. only; in MidHG., zispezen, n., 'hissing.'

Zistag, see Dienstag.

Zither, Cither, f., 'guitar, zither'; formed like the equiv. OHG. cithara, zitera, f., from the equiv. Lat. cithara. MidHG. has only zitôle, f., 'zither,' from OFr. citole, which, like Ital. cétera, comes from Lat. cithara. Ital. and Span. guitarra, whence Fr. guitare, ModHG. Gnitarre, 'guitar,' is, on the other hand, derived from Gr. κιθάρα.

Zitrone, Citrone, f., 'citron,' ModHG. only, from Fr. citron, which is borrowed from Lat.-Gr. κίτρον. The origin of the latter word (the East?) is unknown.

Zitter, Zieter, f., 'thill, shaft,' from the equiv. MidHG. zieter, OHG. ziotar, zieter, m. and n. The latter can hardly represent *ziohtar (allied to ziehen) on account of AS. teóder, E. tether, OIc. tjóðr, 'rope.' The unintelligible ModHG. word was popularly, but wrongly, connected with zittern (dial. Zetter, Zitterstange).

Zitteroch, m., 'herpetic eruption,' from the equiv. MidHG. zitteroch, OHG. zittaroh (hh), m. (ttr remains unpermutated as in zittern); corresponding to AS. téter, E. tetter, to tetter. Allied in the non-Teut. languages to Sans. dadru, dadruka, 'cutaneous eruption,' Lith. dedervine, 'tether, scab,' and Lat. derbiosus (from derdviosus?). AS. téter is based like Sans. dadru on an Aryan *de-dru-*, a reduplicated form (like 𝔅𝔦𝔟𝔢𝔯); OHG. *zittaroh* is borrowed from it.

𝔷𝔦𝔩𝔱𝔢𝔯𝔫, vb., 'to tremble, shake, quiver,' from the equiv. MidHG. *zitern, zittern*, OHG. *zittarôn*, wk. vb.; corresponding to OIc. *titra*, 'to twinkle, wink, tremble' (old *tr* remains unpermutated in HG.; comp. 𝔟𝔦𝔱𝔱𝔢𝔯, 𝔖𝔭𝔩𝔦𝔱𝔱𝔢𝔯, and 𝔱𝔯𝔢𝔲). 𝔅𝔦𝔱𝔱𝔢𝔯𝔫 is one of the few Teut. vbs. which have a reduplicated present (see 𝔟𝔢𝔟𝔢𝔫). From the implied primit. Teut. **ti-tró-mi* the transition to the weak *ó* conjugation is easily understood, just as the change of Teut. **rí-rai-mi*, 'I tremble' (comp. Goth. *reiran*, 'to shake,' from an Aryan root *rai-*), to the similarly sounding weak *ai* conjugation. In the non-Teut. languages no cognates of 𝔷𝔦𝔱𝔱𝔢𝔯𝔫 have been found (Aryan root *drā'ĭ*). The G. word was adopted by Dan.; comp. Dan. *zittre*, 'to shake.'

𝔅𝔦𝔱𝔴𝔢𝔯, m., 'zedoary,' from the equiv. MidHG. *zitwar, zitwan*, OHG. *citawar, zitwar*, m.; from MidLat. *zeduarium*, the source of which is Arab. *zedwâr*. The zedoary was introduced into European medical science by the Arabs (comp. also Ital. *zettovario*, Fr. *zédoaire*, E. *zedoary*).

𝔅𝔦𝔱𝔷, 𝔅𝔦𝔱𝔰, m., 'chintz,' from the equiv. Du. *sits, chits*, E. *chintz*. The ultimate source of the word is Bengalî *chits*, 'variegated cotton.'

𝔅𝔦𝔱𝔷𝔢, f., 'nipple, teat,' from the equiv. late MidHG. (rare) *zitze*, f.; comp. the corresponding LG. *titte*, f., Du. *tet*, f., AS. *tit*, m. (plur. *tittas*), E. *teat*, Swiss *tisse*, 'teat.' The usual word for 'teat' in OHG. is *tutta, tuta*, f., *tutto, tuto*, m.; MidHG. *tutte, tute*, f., *tütal*, n.; comp. 𝔗ü𝔱𝔱𝔢𝔩. In Romance occur the cognate words—Ital. *tetta, zizza, zezzola*, 'teat,' Fr. *tette*, f., *teton, tetin*, m., 'nipple,' Span. *teta*, as well as Ital. *tettare*, Span. *tetar*, Fr. *teter*, 'to suck'; the double forms with *t* and *z* imply that these words were borrowed from Teut.

𝔅𝔬𝔟𝔢𝔩, m., 'sable (*Mustella zibellina*), sable-fur,' from the equiv. MidHG. *zobel*, m.; borrowed from Russ. *sobol* (comp. Dan. *zobel*). From the same source are derived MidLat. *sabellum* (OFr. *sable*, E. *sable*) and *sabellinus*, whence Ital. *zibellino*, Span. *zebellina*, Fr. *zibeline*.

𝔅𝔬𝔟𝔢𝔯, see 𝔍𝔲𝔟𝔢𝔯.

𝔅𝔬𝔣𝔢, f., 'maid, waiting-woman,' ModHG. only, formed from MidHG. *zâfen* (*zôfen*), 'to draw, arrange suitably, nurse, adorn'; *zâfe*, f., 'ornament'; hence 𝔅𝔬𝔣𝔢, lit. 'adorning maid.'

𝔷ö𝔤𝔢𝔯𝔫, vb., 'to linger, loiter, defer,' ModHG. only, a derivative of MidHG. *zogen*, OHG. *zogôn*, 'to tug, draw, go, defer, retard.' An intensive form of 𝔷𝔦𝔢𝔥𝔢𝔫; comp. OIc. *toga*, E. *to tug*. For the development of meaning comp. further ModHG. dial. 𝔧ä𝔤𝔢𝔯𝔫, 'to wander aimlessly.'

𝔅ö𝔤𝔩𝔦𝔫𝔤, m., 'pupil,' ModHG. only; formed with the suffix *-ling* from MidHG. **zoge*, 'guide, leader,' in *magezoge*, 'tutor,' OHG. *magazogo*, 'paedagogus' (see 𝔥𝔢𝔯𝔷𝔬𝔤); allied to 𝔷𝔦𝔢𝔥𝔢𝔫.

𝔅𝔬𝔩𝔩 (1.), m., 'inch,' from the equiv. MidHG. *zol*, m. and f., which is probably identical with MidHG. *zol*, m., 'cylindrical piece, log'; comp. MidHG. *tzolle*, 'icicle.'

𝔅𝔬𝔩𝔩 (2.), m., 'duty, toll, dues,' from MidHG. and OHG. *zol*, m., 'custom-house, toll, duty'; corresponding to the equiv. OSax. and AS. *tol*, E. *toll*, Du. *tol*, OIc. *tollr*. Usually regarded as borrowed from MidLat. *telonium*, Gr. τελώνιον, 'custom-house, toll.' The Ger. words are, however, in spite of the lack of a Goth. **tulls* (for which *móta* occurs; comp. 𝔐𝔞𝔲𝔱), so old, and correspond so closely, that they must be regarded as of genuine Teut. origin. 𝔅𝔬𝔩𝔩 is connected with the root *tal* (appearing in 𝔷ä𝔥𝔩𝔢𝔫 and 𝔅𝔞𝔥𝔩), of which it is an old partic. in *no-* (*ll* from *ln*), and hence it signified originally 'that which is counted.'—Derivative 𝔅ö𝔩𝔩𝔫𝔢𝔯, m., 'collector,' receiver of customs,' from MidHG. *zolnære, zolner*, OHG. *zollanâri, zolneri*, m. Corresponding to AS. *tolnére, tollére*, E. *toller*, Du. *tollenaar*, OFris. *tolner*, Dan. *tolder*; comp. OSax. *tolna*, 'toll.'

𝔅𝔬𝔫𝔢, f., 'zone,' ModHG. only, from the equiv. Lat.-Gr. ζώνη.

𝔅𝔬𝔭𝔣, m. '(long) plait of hair, pigtail, cue, tuft,' from MidHG. and OHG. *zopf*, m., 'end, peak, cue.' Corresponding to LG. *topp*, Du. *top*, 'end, peak,' AS. and E. *top* (MidE. variant *tuft*), OIc. *toppr*, 'tuft of hair,' OFris. *top*, 'tuft,' Swed. *topp*, Dan. *top*, 'point, end, cue.' A common Teut. word, by chance not recorded in Goth. The lit. meaning seems to be 'projecting end'; hence 𝔅𝔬𝔭𝔣 orig. 'points of the hair when tied together' (comp. 𝔍𝔞𝔭𝔣𝔢𝔫 and 𝔗𝔬𝔭𝔭). The value attached even in the Middle Ages to long plaits of hair as an element of female beauty is attested especially by the fact that the Swab. and Aleman. women when taking an oath held their plaits in their hands. Among the Teutons, to cut a person's hair was to brand him with infamy. From Teut. are derived the Romance cognates, OFr. *top*, 'tuft of hair,' Span. *tope*, 'end,' Ital. *toppo*, ModFr. *toupet*, 'tuft, lock of hair.' No cognate terms are found in the non-Teut. languages.

Zores, Zorus, m.,'confusion,' ModHG. only, from Jewish *zores*, 'oppression.'

Zorn, m., 'anger, wrath, passion,' from MidHG. *zorn*, m., OHG. *zorn*, n., 'violent indignation, fury, insult, dispute'; corresponding to OSax. *torn*, n., 'indignation,' AS. *torn*, n., 'anger, insult,' Du. *toorn*, m., 'anger' (*torn*, 'push, fight'); in Goth. by chance not recorded. It is an old partic. in *no*- from the root *tar*, 'to tear' (Goth. *ga-tairan*, OHG. *zĕran*, 'to tear to pieces, destroy'); hence Zorn meant lit. 'rending of the mind'?. Yet note Lith. *durnas*, 'mad, angry, insufferable,' and *durnúti*, 'to rage.'

Zote, f., 'obscenity,' ModHG. only; of obscure origin, but certainly a loan-word. It is most probably connected with Fr. *sotie*, *sottie*, 'obscene farce' (in the carnival plays obscenity is the main element), Fr. *sottise*, 'abusive language, indecency,' from Fr. *sot*, 'blockhead,' Span. and Port. *zote*, 'booby.' With these are connected Ital. *zotico*, 'coarse, uncouth' (comp. Ital. *zotichezza*, 'coarseness,' *zoticacco*, 'uncouth, clownish'; they are not derived from Lat. *exoticus* (Lat. *x* is never equiv. to Rom. *z*). Comp. further AS. and E. *sot*, Du. *sot*, and Ir. *suthan*, 'blockhead,' *sotaire*, 'fop.'

Zotte (1.), **Zottel**, f., 'lock, tuft, tangle,' from MidHG. *zote*, *zotte*, m. and f., 'tuft of hair,' OHG. *zotta*, *zata*, *zota*, f., *zotto*, m., 'mane, comb (of birds), tuft.' MidHG. *zotte* is normally permutated from *toddón*-; comp. OIc. *todde*, m., 'tuft, bit, tod (weight for wool),' E. *tod*, Du. *todde*, 'rags, tatters'; also Dan. *tot*, 'tuft of hair, tangle,' Du. *toot*, 'hair-net'?. Nothing more definite can be ascertained concerning the early history of the word. From Ger. are derived the Ital. words *zazza*, *zázzera*, 'long hair,' and *tattera*, 'rubbish, trash' (perhaps also Ital. *zatter*, *zattera*, Span. *zata*, *zatara*, 'raft.'

Zotte (2.), f., dial., 'spout of a vessel,' equiv. to Du. *tuit*, 'pipe' (see Düte).

zotteln, vb., 'to move clumsily, shuffle along,' from MidHG. *zoten*, 'to walk slowly, saunter'; comp. E. *tottle*, *toddle*, *totter*; allied to Zotte (1.).

zu, prep., 'to, in addition to, at, in order to'; adv., 'to, towards,' from the equiv. MidHG. *zuo* (MidG. *zū*), OHG. *zuo*, *zua*, *zō*; comp. the corresponding OSax. *tō*, Du. *toe*, OFris. *tō*, AS. *tō*, E. *to*; wanting in OIc. and Goth. (for which Scand. *til* and Goth. *du* occur). It corresponds in non-Teut. to Lith. *da*-, OIr. *do*, as well as to Zend *-da*, Gr. -δε, and Lat. *-do*, which are used enclitically.

Zuber, Zober, m., 'tub,' from MidHG. *zuber*, *zober*, OHG. *zubar*, n., 'vessel'; probably allied primit. to MidE. *tubbe*, E. *tub*, Du. *tobbe*, LG. *tubbe* and *tōver*. In OHG. also *zwibar*, which compared with OHG. *einbar* (see Eimer) is regarded as a 'vessel with two handles,' and is connected in form with Gr. δίφρος (from *dwi*, 'two,' and root φερ).

Zubuße, f., 'additional contribution,' from late MidHG. *zuobuoze*, f., *zuobuoʒ*, m., 'supplement'; comp. Buße.

Zucht, f., 'breeding, rearing, breed, brood, education, discipline,' from Mid HG. and OHG. *zuht*, f., 'marching, expedition; education, discipline; culture, propriety; that which is trained, cultivated; posterity.' A verbal abstract of ziehen (comp. Flucht from fliehen); corresponding to LG. and Du. *tucht*, AS. *tyht*, Dan. *tugt*, Goth. *tauhts (in *ustauhts*, 'completion').— Derivatives—**züchten**, vb., 'to breed, cultivate, bring up, discipline,' from MidHG. *zühten*, OHG. *zuhten*, *zuhtôn*, 'to train up.' —**züchtig**, adj., 'modest, bashful, discreet,' from MidHG. *zühtec*, OHG. *zuhtig*, 'well bred, polite ; punitive ; pregnant.'—**züchtigen**, vb., 'to chastise, correct, punish,' from MidHG. *zühtegen*, 'to punish.'

Zuck, m., 'twitch, start, shrug,' from MidHG. *zuc* (gen. *zuckes*), m., 'quick marching, jerk.' Allied to zucken, zücken, vb., 'to move convulsively, start, jerk, tug,' from MidHG. *zucken*, *zücken*, OHG. *zucchen*, *zukken*, 'to march quickly, snatch away, jerk, tug'; intensive form of ziehen. Hence the ModHG. compounds entzücken, verzücken (MidHG. *enzücken*, *verzücken*), signified orig. 'to snatch away, transport in spirit.' From the base *tukkôn* is derived Fr. *toucher*, Ital. *toccare*.

Zucker, m., 'sugar,' from the corresponding MidHG. *zucker*, *zuker*, m. (OHG. *zucura*, once only); comp. the corresponding Du. *suiker*, MidE. *sucre*, E. *sugar*, Ic. *sykr*, Dan. *sukker*, Swed. *socker*. The word was borrowed from MidLat. *zucara*, which is derived in the first instance from Arab. *sokkar*, *assokhar*; from the same source the Rom. class Fr. *sucre* and Ital. *zucchero* are obtained. Span. *azúcar* was directly adopted from the Arabs, who cultivated the sugar-cane in Spain. Comp. further Lat. *saccharum*, Gr. σάκχαρ, σάκχαρον, Pers. *schakar*, Sans. *çarkarā*, 'granulated sugar,' Prakrit *sakkara*. The primit. source of the word is probably India.—3ucferfanb, m., 'sugar-candy,' ModHG. only, from Fr. *sucre candi*, Ital. *zucchero candito*, 'crystallised sugar, sugar-candy,' which is derived from Arab. *qand;* the ultimate source of the word is Indian *khand*, 'piece.'

zuerſt, adv., 'at first, firstly, in the first place,' from the equiv. MidHG. *ze ĕrest*, *zĕrest*, OHG. *zi ĕrist*, *zĕrist*, 'at first, for the first time'; comp. erſt.

3ufall, m., 'chance, incident, occurrence, accident,' from late MidHG. *zuoval*, m., 'accident, what happens to a person, receipts'; allied to fallen.

zufrieden, adv. and adj., 'contented, satisfied,' ModHG. only; originally only an adv. formed by the combination of the prep. zu and the dat. of the subst. Friede. Hence the orig. meaning of zufrieden is 'in peace, quietly, protection.' In MidHG. *mit vride* (comp. abhanden, behende) was the equiv. expression.

Zug, m., 'pull, march, expedition,' from MidHG. *zuc* (gen. *zuges*), OHG. *zug*, m., a verbal abstract of ziehen (comp. Flug from fliegen). Corresponding to the equiv. Du. *teug*, AS. *tyge*, E. tug, and Dan. *tog*.

Zugang, m., 'admittance, access,' from the equiv. MidHG. and OHG. *zuoganc*, m. (see Gang).

3ügel, m., 'rein, bridle, check,' from MidHG. *ziigel*, *zugel*, m., 'strap, band, rein,' OHG. *zugil*, *zuhil* (*zuol*), m., 'band, cord, rein'; a derivative of ziehen. Corresponding to OIc. *tygell*, m., 'strap, cord, rein,' AS. *tygel*, Du. *teugel*, Dan. *tøile*. See also 3aum.

zugleich, adv., 'at the same time, together,' ModHG. only, implying MidHG. *ze geliche*, 'in the same manner' (see gleich).

zuhand, adv., 'at once, immediately,' from the equiv. MidHG. *zehant*, lit. 'at hand.' In Ger. many adverbial expressions are formed from the word Hand,—abhanden, vorhanden, allerhand; comp. zufrieden.

zuleszt, adv., 'finally, ultimately,' from MidHG. *ze lezzist*, *ze leste*, OHG. *zi lezzist;* comp. leszt.

Zülle, f., 'lighter, boat,' from the equiv. MidHG. *züle*, *zulle;* early history obscure. The G. word is related only to the Slav. class, Russ. *čelnŭ*, Pol. *czołn*, Czech *člun;* on which side the word was borrowed cannot be ascertained.

3ulp, m., 'sucking mark (on the skin), spot made by sucking,' ModHG. only; allied to zullen, 'to suck'; origin obscure. Probably related to Du. *tul*, 'bottle, tippler,' *tullen*, 'to tipple.'

zumal, adv., 'especially, particularly,' from MidHG. and OHG. *ze māle*, 'at the point of time, forthwith, immediately'; comp. Mal.

zünden, vb., 'to take fire, set on fire, kindle,' from MidHG. *zünden*, 'to set on fire,' OHG. *zunten* (from *zuntjan*), wk. vb., 'to kindle'; also in MidHG. *zunden*, 'to burn, give light,' OHG. *zundēn*, 'to be aflame, glow.' Comp. Goth. *tundnan*, 'to be kindled,' *tandjan*, wk. vb., 'to set on fire,' AS. *tyndan*, MidE. *tenden*, E. (dial.) *teend*, *tind*, 'to kindle,' OIc. *tendra*, Swed. *tända*, Dan. *tænde*. MidHG. *zinden*, str. vb., 'to burn, glow,' implies a Goth. str. vb. **tindan;* to this is allied OHG. *zinsilo*, m., *zinsilôd*, 'fomes,' *zinsera*, f. 'censer' (not from Lat. *incensorium*), and *zinsilōn*, 'machinari.' With Goth. *tandjan*, 'to set on fire,' are connected OHG. *zantaro*, MidHG. *zander*, 'glowing coal,' OIc. *tandre*, 'fire.' The Teut. root *tand* (Aryan *dnt*?, *dndh*?), 'to burn,' has no undoubted cognates in the non-Teut. languages.—Derivative Zunder, Bündel, m., 'tinder, touchwood, fuse,' from the equiv. MidHG. *zunder*, m. and n., OHG. *zuntara*, *zuntra*, f. Comp. LG. *tunder*, Du. *tonder*, AS. *tynder*, E. *tinder*, OIc. *tundr*, Swed. *tunder*, Dan. *tønder*. Forms with *l* also occur; comp. OHG. *zuntil*, MidHG. *zundel*, *zündel*, m., 'lighter, tinder' (ModHG. proper name Zündel), Du. *tondel*. From Teut. is borrowed OFr. *tondre*, 'tinder.'

Zunft, f., 'guild, corporation, club, sect,' from MidHG. *zunft*, *zumft*, OHG. *zumft*, f., 'propriety, rule, law; society governed by certain rules, union, association, guild'; allied to ziemen. OHG. *zumft* is derived from *zĕman*, 'to be proper,' by means of the *-ti* (Goth. *-þi*), which forms verbal abstracts; for the intrusion of an *f* in the combination *mt*, comp. Kunft, Nunft, and Ramft. Hence the orig. meaning of Zunft is 'suitability, propriety, that which is becoming or according to law.' For the development of meaning comp. Gilde, derived from LG.

3unge, f., 'tongue, language,' from MidHG. *zunge*, f., 'tongue, tongue-shaped piece, language,' OHG. *zunga*, f., 'tongue, domain of a language.' Comp. OSax. *tunga*, LG. *tunge*, Du. *tonge*, OFris. *tunge*, AS. *tunge*, E. *tongue*, Olc. and Swed. *tunga*, Dan. *tunje*, Goth. *tuggô*. In non-Teut. occurs the cognate Lat. *lingua*, which is usually supposed to come from *dingua* (like *lacrima* for *dacrima*, see Zähre). Teut. *tungôn*, with Zunge, is scarcely allied to the Sans. root *danç*, 'to bite, be pointed' (Zunge should be lit. 'that which licks'); the relation to Sans. *juhû*, *jihvâ*, 'tongue,' is uncertain.

zunichte, adv., 'ruined, undone,' in the phrases zunichte, werben, 'to be ruined,' zunichte machen, 'to ruin, destroy,' from Mid HG. *ze nihte*, 'to nothing'; see nicht.

Zünsler, m., 'pilser,' ModHG. only; probably allied to OHG. *zinsilo*, 'tinder' (comp. MidHG. *zinden*, 'to burn'), mentioned under zünden.

zupfen, vb., 'to pull, pluck,' ModHG. only, earlier ModHG. zopfen; denominative from Zopf; hence zupfen means lit. 'to drag by the hair'?.

zurecht, adv., 'in order, aright,' from MidHG. *ze rëhte*, OHG. *zi rëhte*, 'aright'; comp. LG. *te rechte* (see Recht).

zürnen, vb., 'to be angry,' from Mid HG. *zürnen*, OHG. *zurnen*; denominative from Zorn.

zurück, adv., 'back, backwards,' from MidHG. *zerücks* (MidG. *zurücke*), OHG. *zi rucke*, 'backwards, behind one's back'; comp. LG. *terügge*. Allied to Rücken; comp. E. *back*.

zusammen, adv., 'together,' from Mid HG. *zesamene, zesamt*, OHG. *zisamane*, 'together, jointly'; comp. sammeln, samt.

zusseln, vb., 'to pluck'; probably a derivative of zausen, MidHG. *zûsen*.

Zuversicht, f., 'confidence, reliance, conviction,' from MidHG. *zuoversiht* (MidG. *zûvorsiht*), OHG. *zuofirsiht*, f., 'foreseeing, glance into the future, expectation, hope.' Allied, like Sicht, to sehen.

zuvor, adv., 'before, beforehand, formerly,' from late MidHG. *zuovor, zuovorn* (MidG. *zûvor*), 'formerly, beforehand.' Allied, like bevor, to ver.

zuwege, adv. in zuwege bringen, 'to bring out, accomplish,' from MidHG. *ze wëge*, OHG. *zi wëge*, 'on the (right) way.' Comp. wegen, adv., and Weg.

zuweilen, adv., 'at times, sometimes,' ModHG. only; in MidHG. *under wîlen* or *wîlen, wîlent*, 'once, formerly.' Similarly, ModHG. bisweilen, allweil, weiland; comp. weil.

zuwider, adj. (orig. adv.), 'importunate,' ModHG. only; implying MidHG. *ze wider*, formed in a similar way to ModHG. zugegen (MidHG. *zegegene*), lit. 'against'; see wider.

zwacken, vb., 'to pinch, tease, cheat,' from MidHG. *zwacken*, 'to pluck, tug'; a graded form of zwicken.

zwagen, vb., 'to wash,' see Zwehle.

Zwang, m., 'compulsion, force, restraint,' from MidHG. *twanc, zwanc (g)*, m., 'compulsion, distress, oppression' (comp. MidHG. *des lîbes twanc*, 'tenesmus, constipation'), OHG. *dwang (gidwang)*, m., 'distress, contraction, compulsion'; abstract of zwingen. Allied to **zwängen**, vb., 'to squeeze, constrain, force,' denomin. of Zwang, MidHG. *twengen*, 'to use violence to, squeeze in, oppress,' OHG. *dwengen*, 'to use violence to' (OHG. and MidHG. *zwangen, zwengen*, 'to pinch'; comp. MidHG. *zwange*, 'tongs'); see also zwingen. A Teut. root *pwenh* (Aryan *twenk*) is implied by OHG. *dûhen*, Du. *duwen*, AS. *þyan*, 'to press, oppress' (from **punhjan*).

zwanzig, num., 'twenty,' from the equiv. MidHG. *zweinzec, zwênzic*, OHG. *zweinzug*; a common West Teut. numeral. Comp. OSax. *twêntig*, LG. and Du. *twintig*, OFris. *twintich*, AS. *twêntig* (from *twâgentig*?), E. *twenty* (see *zig). The *n* of the first component seems to be a mark of the nom. plur. masc., as in OHG. *zwên-e*, AS. *twêgen*; see zwei.

zwar, adv., 'indeed, truly, of course,' from MidHG. *zwâre, ze wâre*, 'in truth,' OHG. *zi wâre* (MidHG. *wâr*, n., 'truth,' an adj. used as a subst.). Connected, like fürwahr (MidHG. *vür war*, 'truly), with wahr.

Zweck, m., 'nail, plug; aim, object, design, goal,' from MidHG. *zwëc (-ckes)*, m., 'nail, plug in the centre of the target; aim, object, design'; comp. zwacken, zwicken, and Zwick. How the ModHG. word (orig. 'nail') acquired its most prevalent meaning 'design' is explained by the MidHG. term, of which the central idea is 'the object aimed at in the target'; other cognates of the MidHG. word are wanting.

zween, num., see zwei.

Zwehle, f., 'towel,' from MidHG. *twehele, twehel, dwehele, dwêle*, f. (also *quehele*, Thuring. Quähle), 'drying cloth, towel,' OHG. *dwahila, dwëhila, dwahilla*.

f., 'towel, napkin, small napkin.' The implied Goth. *þwahljô (old AS. *þwehlœ*) is a derivative of *þwahl*, 'bath, washing,' and hence signified 'that which belongs to bathing.' The cognates are connected with ModHG. (dial.) ʒwagen, 'to wash,' from the equiv. MidHG. *twahen, dwahen,* OHG. *dwahan*; an old common Teut. word for 'to wash.' Comp. Goth. *þwahan*, OSax. *thwahan*, AS. *þweán*, OIc. *þvá*, Dan. *toe, tvætte,* Swed. *tvo, tvätta*, 'to wash.' With these are connected Goth. *þwahl*, 'bath,' AS. *þweál*, 'washing,' OHG. *dwahal*, 'bath,' OIc. *þvál*, 'soap,' MidHG. *twuhel*, 'bathing tub.' In the allied Aryan languages only Pruss. *twaxtan*, 'bathing apron,' is cognate; Gr. τέγγω, Lat. *tingo*, 'to moisten,' are not connected with it. From OTeut. is derived the Rom. class, Ital. *tovaglia*, Fr. *touaille*, equiv. to E. *towel*.

ʒwei, num., 'two,' from the equiv. Mid HG. *zwêne*, m., *zwô*, f., *zwei*, n.; OHG. *zwêne*, m., *zwo*, f., *zwei*, n.; common to Teut. and Aryan. Comp. OSax. *twêne*, m., *twô, twá,* f., *twei,* n.; Goth. *twai*, m., *twôs*, f., *twa*, n.; AS. *twégen*, m., *twâ*, f., *tú*, n.; E. *two,* Du. *twé*, OFris. *twêne*, m., *twâ*, f., *twâ*, n.; OIc. *tveir*, m., *tvær*, f., *tvau*, n.; Swed. *tvâ*, Dan. *to, tvende*, m., *to*, f., *to*, n. Comp. further ʒwanʒig and ʒwölf. Corresponding in the non-Teut. languages to Sans. *dva*, Zend *dva*, Gr. δύο, Lat. *duo*, OIr. *dá*, Lith. *dù*, Russ. *dva*. In earlier ModHG. the forms for the different genders were kept separate (ʒween, m., ʒwo, f., ʒwei, n.), until in the 17th cent. the neuter form became the prevalent one. For further cognates see ʒweifel and ʒwist.—ʒweierlei, adv. and adj., 'of two kinds, twofold,' from MidHG. *zweier leige*, 'of a double sort'; comp. *lei*.

ʒweifalter, m., 'butterfly,' from the equiv. MidHG. *zwivalter*, m., corrupted from MidHG. *vîvalter*, OHG. *fîfaltra*, 'butterfly.' See Falter and Schmetterling.

ʒweifel, m., 'doubt, uncertainty,' from MidHG. *zwivel*, m., 'uncertainty, distrust, fickleness, perfidy, despair,' OHG. *zwîfal*, m., 'uncertainty, apprehension, despair.' Comp. Goth. *tweifls*, m., 'doubt,' OSax. *twîfal*, Du. *twijfel*. The following forms also occur, OHG. *zwîfo, zwêho*, m., 'doubt' (equiv. to OSax. *twêho*, AS. *tweó*, 'doubt'), and OIc. *tŷja* (base *twîhjôn*), 'doubt.' All are based on a pre-Teut. *dweiq (dwîp)*, 'to doubt.'—Allied to ʒweifeln, vb., 'to doubt, suspect,' from MidHG. *zwîvelen*, OHG. *zwîfalôn*, 'to waver, doubt'; comp. OSax. *twiflôn*, 'to waver,' Dan. *tvivle*, Du. *twijfelen*, 'to doubt.' These cognates are unquestionably connected with ʒwei (comp. Gr. δοιή, 'doubt,' Sans. *dvayá*, 'falseness'); the formation of the noun is, however, not clear (see ʒweig and ʒwies).

ʒweig, m., 'branch, bough, twig,' from the equiv. MidHG. *zwîc (-ges)*, n. and m., OHG. *zwîg*, m.; corresponding to AS. *twîg*, E. *twig,* Du. *twijg*; also in MidHG. and OHG. *zwî* (gen. *zwîes*), n. The *g* is probably evolved from *j*, and *zwî*, gen. *zwîges*, may be traced back to a nom. *zwîg*. The AS. form *twîg* is implied by the acc. plur. *twîgu (twîggu)*. Yet the primary forms cannot be ascertained with certainty, hence it is not quite clear how ʒweig is connected with the numeral ʒwei (ʒweig, lit. 'a division into two parts'?).

ʒweite, ordin. of ʒwei, 'second,' a Mod HG. form. The form in MidHG. is *ander*, OHG. *andar*, 'the other'; see anber.

ʒwerch, 'athwart, across,' in compounds such as ʒwerchfell, 'diaphragm,' ʒwerchpfeife, 'fife,' ʒwerchsack, 'knapsack, wallet,' from MidHG. *twërch, dwërch* (also *quërch*), adj., 'oblique, reversed, athwart,' OHG. *dwërah, twërh*, 'oblique, athwart.' Corresponding to AS. *þweorh*, 'perverse,' Goth. *þwaírhs*, 'angry' (*þwaírhei*, f., 'anger, dispute'), Du. *dwars*, Dan. *tværs, tvært*, 'athwart.' With these is also connected ModHG. überʒwerch, adj. and adv., 'across, athwart, crosswise' (MidHG. *über twërch, uber zwërch*). The same Aryan root *tverk* appears also perhaps in AS. *þurh*, 'through' (see burch). Beside *twërh*, the MidHG. and OHG. variant *twër*, 'oblique, athwart,' occurs (in MidHG. also *quër*; see quer), OIc. *þverr*, 'athwart, impeding.' Teut. *þwerhwo*- points to an Aryan root *twerk*, with which Lat. *torqueo* is connected.

ʒwerg, m., 'dwarf, pigmy,' from the equiv. MidHG. *twërc(g), getwërc* (also *querch, zwërch*), OHG. *twërg*, m.; a common Teut. word. Comp. Du. *dwerg*, AS. *dweorh*, E. *dwarf*, OIc. *dvergr*, m., Swed. and Dan. *dverg*. The Teut. base is *dwergo*-, which is perhaps also connected with the Teut. root *drug*, 'to deceive'; hence ʒwerg means lit. 'phantom, illusion'?.

ʒwetsche, Quetsche, f., 'damson'; ModHG. only; a difficult word to explain. Bav. *zwëssen, zwëspen,* Swiss *zwetske,* Austr. *zwespen,* Thur. and East MidG. *quatige*, seem to be related like quer and ʒwerch, quängeln and ʒwingen, so that we must perhaps assume an initial *tw*. Since damsons were orig. obtained from Damascus (the Crusaders are said to have introduced them into Europe; comp. E. *damask plum, damascene, damson*, Ital. *amascino*, Portug. *ameixa*), it seems probable that the Teut. cognates (Bav. *zwèschen*) are derived from MidLat. *damascena* or Gr. δαμάσκηνον through the intermediate forms *dmaskîn, dwaskîn*, which appear in Transylvanian *maschen, mäschen*. Yet the phonological relations of the numerous dialectic forms are so indistinct that a final solution of all the difficulties has not yet been found. From HG. are derived Du. *kwets*, Dan. *svedske*, Boh. *švetska*.

Зwіф, m., 'peg, sprig; pinch, nip, twinge,' from MidHG. *zwic*, a variant of *zwēc* (see Зwесf), 'nail, nip, pinch.' From G. is derived the equiv. Dan. *svik*.—Зwіскеl, m., 'wedge,' from the equiv. MidHG. *zwickel*, m.; a derivative of the preceding word.

зwіскеп, vb., 'to pinch, twitch, peg,' from MidHG. *zwicken*, 'to fasten with nails, squeeze in, pinch, tug,' OHG. *zwicchēn*; comp. LG. *twikken*, AS. *twiččian*, MidE. *twicchen*, E. *to twitch* (see зwаскеп, Зwесf).

зwіе=, in compounds 'two,' from Mid HG. and OHG. *zwi*-, LG. *twi*-, Du. *twee*-, OIc. *tvī*-, AS. *twi*-, Goth. *tvi-. It is the form of the numeral зwеі as the first element of a compound; comp. in the non-Teut. languages δι- (from δϜι-), Lat. *bi*-, Sans. *dvi*-, used in a similar way.

Зwіебаф, m., 'biscuit,' ModHG. only; probably a rendering of Fr. *biscuit* (Ital. *biscotto*); comp. Dan. *tvebak*, Du. *tweebak* (also *beschuit*).

Зwіebel, f. (Swiss *zibele*, Bav. *zwifel*, Thuring. *zippel*), 'onion, bulb,' from the equiv. MidHG. *zwibolle, zibolle* (with the variants *zwippel, zwifel, zibel, zebulle*), m. OHG. *zwibollo, zwivolle*, m. A corruption of Lat. *caepulla*, 'onion,' whence also the Rom. words, Ital. *cipolla*, Fr. *ciboule*; Dan. *swible* has been adopted from Ger. The genuine G. word for Зwіebel is Bolle (properly 'bulb, ball'), on which MidHG. *zwibolle* was based. The E. word *bulb* is derived from the Lat. *bulbus* (Gr. βολβός), 'bulb, onion.'

зwіеfaф, adj., 'twofold, double,' from the equiv. MidHG. *zwifach*; for the meaning of the second component see Fаф.—зwіеfältig, adj., 'twofold,' from the equiv. MidHG. *zwivaltic* (also in MidHG. and OHG. *zwivalt*); comp. falt.—Зwіelіфt, n., 'twilight,' ModHG. only, formed from LG. *twelecht*; the MidHG. expression is *zwischenlieht*; comp. E. *twilight*.

зwіer, adv., 'twice,' earlier ModHG., from the equiv. MidHG. *zwir*, OHG. *zwirôr, zwiro*; comp. OIc. *tysvar, tvis-var* (-*var* corresponding to Sans. *vára*, 'time'). OHG. *drirôr*, 'thrice,' is similarly formed.

Зwіеfеl, f., 'fork,' from MidHG. *zwisele*, OHG. *zwisila*, f., 'fork, forked branch'; a derivative, like Зwеig and Зwеіfеl, from the stem *twi*- (see зwіе=).

Зwіеfpalt, m., 'division, discord, schism,' ModHG. only, from зwіе= and Spalt; in MidHG. the form is *zwispeltunge*, f., 'division, discord.'—зwіеfpältig, adj., 'discordant, disunited,' from the equiv. MidHG. *zwispeltic, zwispaltic*, OHG. *zwispaltig*; allied to fpalten.—Зwіеfpraфе, f., 'dialogue, colloquy,' ModHG. only; in OHG. *zwisprëhho*, m., with a different sense, 'bifarius,' and in AS. *twispráce*, adj., 'double-tongued, deceitful.'—Зwіеtraфt, f., 'dissension, discord,' from MidHG. *zwitraht*, f., 'disunion'; зwіеträфtig, adj., 'discordant, at variance,' from Mid HG. *zweitrehtic*, 'disunited, discordant'; as a MidG. word it is allied to treffen (comp. Eintracht).

Зwіllіф, Зwіlф, m., 'twilled cloth, tick,' from the equiv. MidHG. *zwilich, zwilch*, OHG. *zwilih* (hh), m.; properly an adj. used as a subst., from *zwilich*, 'twofold, consisting of two threads' (to this MidHG. *zwilchen*, 'to weave with two threads,' is allied). Formed on the model of Lat. *bilix*, 'consisting of two threads'; comp. Drillich.

Зwіllіng, m., 'twin,' from the equiv. MidHG. *zwinelinc, zwillinc* (g), m. (also *zwiselinc* and *zwilich-kint*), and *zwinelîn*, n., OHG. *zwiniling*, m. A derivative of the OHG. adj., *zwinal*, 'geminus, gemellus,' and also, like *zwinal*, from *zwi*-, 'twofold'; comp. the equiv. E. *twin*, Du. *tweeling*, Dan. *tvilling*.

зwіngen, vb., 'to force, compel, vanquish,' from MidHG. *twingen, dwingen*, 'to press, cramp, force, compel, dominate,' OHG. *dwingan, thwingan*, 'to crowd, suppress, conquer,' corresponding to OSax. *thwingan*, OIc. *þvinga*, Dan. *tvinge*, Du. *twingen*, OFris. *dwinga, twinga*, MidE. *twingen*, 'to force' (E. *twinge*), see also Зwаng.—Derivatives Зwіng, Зwіnk, m., 'fortress,' from MidHG. *twinc*, m., 'that which constrains, confines; jurisdiction.'—

Зwinge, f., 'vice, clamp, holdfast,' lit. that which encloses or presses together; corresponding to the equiv. Dan. *tvinge.*—
Зwinger, m., 'fortified castle, prison, narrow space, wild beast's cage, arena,' from MidHG. *twingære*, m., 'oppressor, space between the walls and ditch of a citadel, promurale, fortress.' Comp. Dan. *twinger*, 'prison, wild beast's cage' (Du. *dwinger*, 'despot, tyrant').

зwinſten, зwinkern, vb., 'to wink, twinkle,' from MidHG. *zwinken, zwingen*, 'to blink, twinkle'; also in MidHG. *zwinzen* (from *zwingezen*) and *zwinzern*. Corresponding to AS. *twinclian*, E. *to twinkle.*

зwirbeln, vb., 'to twirl,' from MidHG. *zwirbeln, zwirben*, 'to move in a circle, whirl' (*zwirbel*, m., 'in circular motion, *zwirbelwint*, 'whirlwind'). Allied to OHG. *zęrben* (*zarbjan*), 'to turn round,' AS. *tearſlian*, 'to roll'?. Undoubted cognates in the non-Teut. languages are wanting.

Зwirn, m., 'thread, twine, twisted yarn,' from MidHG. *zwirn*, m., 'double thread'; like AS. *twīn*, E. *twine*, Du. *twijn* (Dan. *tvinde*, 'twine wheel'), it points to a base *twizna-*. A Teut. root *twis* appears also by a different derivation in E. *twist.*—
зwirnen, vb., 'to twist, twine, throw (silk),' a denominative, from MidHG. *zwirnen*, OHG. *zwirnēn, -nōn*, 'to twist a double thread, twine'; comp. Du. *tweernen*, E. *to twine*, and the equiv. Dan. *tvinde.*

зwiſchen, adv. and afterwards prep., 'between, among,' from the equiv. MidHG. *zwischen, zwüschen*, adv. and prep. Orig. a shortened form of the adverb. expressions MidHG. *inzwischen, under zwischen*, OHG. *in zwiskēn, untar zwiskēn*, 'between each pair.' Allied to MidHG. *zwisc, zwisch*, adj., OHG. *zwisk, zwiski*, adj., 'twofold, two and two'; comp. OSax. *twisk*, Du. *tusschen*, E. *betwixt.*—Derivatives ModHG. baзwiſchen, inзwiſchen.

Зwiſt, m., 'dissension, quarrel; twist,' from the equiv. MidHG. *zwist*, m.; properly a LG. word which has passed into HG. Comp. LG. and Du. *twist*, 'quarrel,' also Du. and E. *twist*, Dan. *twist*, 'twisted stuff,' MidE. *twist*, 'branch' (*twisten*, 'to plait'), OIc. *tvistr*, 'sad, disunited,' Ic. *tvistra*, 'to dissever.' The Aryan root *dwis*, on which these words are based, appears in Sans. as *dviṣ*, 'to hate,' with a signification that resembles ModHG. Зwiſt; it may have been 'to be at variance, disunited.' Perhaps Lat. *bellum, duellum*, 'war,' from the base *dwerlo-*, equiv. to *dwislo-?*, is also connected with this word.

зwilſchern, vb., 'to twitter, chirp, warble,' from the equiv. MidHG. *zwitzern*, OHG. *zwizzirōn*; comp. MidE. *twiteren*, E. *twitter* (Dan. *qviddre*). An onomatopoetic form.

Зwitter (earlier ModHG. Зwieborn), m., 'mongrel, hermaphrodite, hybrid,' from MidHG. *zwitar, zwētorn, zwidorn*, m., 'hermaphrodite, bastard, half-caste,' OHG. *zwitarn, zwitaran*, m., 'nothus, hybris.' A derivative of *zwi-*, 'duplex' (see зwei); comp. ModHG. dial. Зwiſter, 'hermaphrodite.' Different forms occur in OIc. (*tvítóla*) and Dan. (*tvetulle*, 'hermaphrodite').

зwölf, num., 'twelve,' from the equiv. MidHG. *zwęlf, zwęlif*, OHG. *zwelif*. A common Teut. num.; corresponding to OSax. *twelif*, Du. *twaalf*, AS. *twęlf*, E. *twelve*, Goth. *twalif*, OIc. *tolf*, Dan. *tolv*, Swed. *tolf*. It is a compound of Teut. *twa-* (HG. зwei), with the component *-lif*, which appears also in eɪf (Goth. *ain-lif*). In the allied Aryan languages a corresponding form occurs only in Lith. *twylika*, 'twelve,' *vēnolika*, 'eleven'). For the signification of the second component, Teut. *-lif*, Lith. *-lika*, see elf.

ADDITIONS AND CORRECTIONS
By PROFESSOR KLUGE.

Besen, Lat. *ferula*, 'ferula,' is perhaps connected with this word; base *bhes*.

Egge, is derived rather, like Roggen, from UpG. (Swiss *egge*, pronounced *ecke*), but the pronunciation of the *gg* was softened in LG., probably on account of the spelling (see Epheu); yet *egge* is also Livonian. In MidG. and LG. the harrow is called *écke* (in MidG. also *éke*). The term for 'wheat' (Weizen) seems also to be influenced by UpG.

frohn, OHG. *fró* and Goth. *frauja*, 'lord,' are cognate with Sans. *pûrva*, *pûrvya*, and OSlov. *prŭvŭ*, 'first' (OHG. *fró*, from *frawan*, equiv. to *prwo-*, Goth. *frauja*, from *frawjan*, equiv. to *prwyo*; Sans. *pûrvya*, as an attribute of the gods, corresponds to OIc. *Freyr* (comp. Gott).

Geschwister, read OHG. *giswëster*.

Knabe may with OIr. *gnia*, 'servant,' point to a common base, *gnopot*, *gnepot*.

leer, if derived from Teut. *léya*, may be connected with OIr. *lia*, 'hunger.'

Mist, read AS. *mist* (equiv. to LG. *mist*).

INDEX

TO THE WORDS QUOTED FROM GREEK, LATIN, ITALIAN, FRENCH, AND ENGLISH, SHOWING THE GERMAN WORD UNDER WHICH THEY WILL BE FOUND.

GREEK.

(Old, Middle, and Modern Greek.)

ἀ-, un-
ἆτος, fatt
ἀβρότονον, Aberraute
ἀγαθός, gut
ἄγγελος, Engel
ἀγγούριον, Gurke
ἄγκιστρον, Angel
ἁγνός,
ἁγνός, } keusch
ἀγρός, Acker
ἄγχω, eng
ἄγω, Acker, Achse
ἀδελφός, Kalb
ἄδην, satt
ἆεθλος, weit
ἀεί, sve alei
ἀέξω, wachsen
ἀζηχής, Jagd
ἄημι, wehen
ἀήτης, Wind
ἀθρέω, Wunder
αἰεί, je, Ehe
αἶθος, Esse
αἴθω, eitel
αἷμα, Seim
αἰόλος, See
αἰών, Ehe, ewig, je
ἄκαινα, } Ähre
ἄκανος,
ἄκαστος, } Ahorn
ἀκαταλίς,
ἀκή, Art
ἀκίς, Eck
ἄκμων, Hammer
ἀκούω, hören
ἄκρος, Ähre
ἀκτέα, } Attich
ἀ τῇ,
ἄκων, Ähre

ἀλάβαστρον, Alabaster
ἀλείφω, Salbe
ἀλεύω, verlieren
ἀλκυών, Schwalbe
ἄλλος, elend
ἀλμενιχιακά, Almanach
ἄλοχος, liegen
ἅλς, Salz
ἄλσος, Wald
ἄμαθος, Sand
ἀμάρα, Meer
ἀμδρακον, Majoran
ἀμάω, mähen, Mahd
ἄμβροτος, Mord
ἀμέλγω, melken
ἄμεναι, satt
ἄμη, Ohm
ἄμητος, Mahd, mähen
ἀμητός, Mahd
ἀμυγδάλη, Mandel (2)
ἄμυλον, Amelmehl
ἀμφί, bei, um
ἀμφιλύκη, Licht
'Αυγίμαρος, Meer
ἀμφορά, Eimer
ἄμφω, beide
ἀνά, an
ἀναχωρητής, Einsiedler
ἁνδάνω, süß
ἀνδράποδον, Rebse
ἄνεμος, ahnden
ἀνεψιός, Neffe
ἄνευ, ohne
ἀνθηδών, } Drohne
ἀνθρήνη,
ἄνισον, Anis
ἀντί, ant-
ἄνυδρος, Otter
ἀξίνη, Axt

ἄξων, Achse
ἄπελος, Fell
ἀπηνής, gönnen
ἀπό, ab
ἀποθήκη, Bottich
ἀπολαύω, Lohn
ἀργός, flink
ἄργυρος, Silber
ἀρήν, Ramme
ἄρκτος, Bär (2)
ἁρμός, Arm
ἀρόω, Acker, Art
ἄρπη, scharf
ἀρχι-, Erz-
ἀρχιατρός, Arzt
ἀσκηθής, Schade
ἀστήρ, ἄστρον, Stern
ἀτμός, Atem
ἄτρακτος, Drechsel
αὖ γε, auch
αὐξάνω, wachsen
ἀχάτης, Achat
ἄχνη, Ähne
ἀψίς, Abseite
ἄχος, Eidechse zag
ἄχυρον, Ähne

βαίνω, kommen, Rang, led
βαλλίζω, Ball (2)
βάλλω, Armbrust
βάλσαμον, Balsam
βάναυσος, Böhmhase
βάπτω, Bad
βδέω, Fift
βεῦδος, Rote
βήρυλλος, Beryll, Brille
βιβλία, Bibel
βίος, led, kommen
βίοτος, βιόω, led

βλέπω, } pflegen
βλέφαρον,
βλήρ, Löder
βλίτον, Melde
βολβός, Bolle (1) Zwiebel
βόμβυξ, Bombafin, Bombaft
Βόσπορος, Furt
βούβαλος, Büffel
βούκδιον, Pokal
βουκόλος, halten
βούλομαι, wollen
βοῦς, Kuh
βούτυρον, Butter
ῥρέμω, brummen
βρέχω, Regen
βρόγχος, Kragen
βροτός, Mord
βρόχθος, Kragen
βρόχος, Kring
βρύον, Kraut
βρύτον, brauen
βρύω, Kraut
βύας, } Kauz
βύζα,
βύρσα, Börse, Kürschner
βύσσορ, Kranz
βωλίτης, Pilz

γάγγραινα, Ranker (2)
γαῖσον, γαῖσος, Ger
γάλα, Milch
γαλάγγα, Galgant
γαμφαί, } Ramm,
γαμφηλαί, } Kiefer (1)
γαῦλος, γαυλός, Kiel (2)
γε, auch, da
γενειάς, } Kinn
γένειον,

INDEX.

γένος, Rind, Knecht, Knabe, Heil
γένυς, Kinn
γέρανος, Kranich, Krahn
γεύω, kiesen, kauen
γηράσκω, Kranich
γίγνομαι, Rind, Knabe
γιγνώσκω, können
γλαύκωμα, } Star
γλαύξ,
γλήνη, } klein
γλῆνος,
γλιά, } Klei
γλίνη,
γλοιός, Klei, klein, Leim
γλυκύρριζα, Lakritze
γλύπτης,
γλύφανος, } klieben
γλύφω,
γλωῦω, Kinde
γνύξ,
γνυπετεῖν, } Knie
γνῶσις, } können
γνωτός,
γόγγρος, Kanker (2)
γόμφος, Kamm, Kegel (1), Knebel
γόνυ, Knie
γράφω, kerben, Grab
γράω, Kralle
γρύζω, grunzen
γρύλλος, Grille
γρυμέα, Krume
γρυπός, Kropf, krumm, Krüppel
γούτη, Kraut
γρύψ, Greif
γυνή, Rind, Knecht, kommen, Braut, Weib
γυρόω, Geier
γύψος, Gips

δάκνω, Zange, Kleister, rinnen
δάκρυ, Zähre
δάκτυλος, Dattel, Zeh
δαμάω, zahm
δαμάσκηνον, Zwetsche
δαυλός, dürr
δε, zu
δεῖγμα, Zeichen
δείκνυμι, zeigen
δεῖπνον, Zeche
δέκα, zehn
δέλεαρ, } Äber
δέλετρον,
δέλφαξ, } Kalb
δελφύς,
δέμας, } Zimmer
δέμω,
δεξιός, jaht

δέρκομαι, trachten, Drache
δέρω, jehren
δι-, zwie-
διάβολος, Teufel
δίπαλτος, -falt
διπλάσιος, -falt, falten
δίπταμνος, Diptam
δίσκος, Tisch
δίφρος, Zuber
διώκω, Jagd
δοιή, Zweifel
δοκός, Zacken
δολιχός, lang
δολφός, Kalb
δόμος, Gaden, Zimmer
δόρυ, Zeer
δοχή, Daube
δράκων, Drache
δρόμος, treten
δρῦς, Eiche, Teer
δύο, zwei
δυσ-, zer-

ἐ, sich
ἕαρ, Lenz
ἔβενος, Ebenbaum
ἐγγύς, nah
ἔγχελυς, Aal
ἐγχεσίμωοος, Märchen
ἐγώ, ich
ἐδανόν, essen
ἔδνον, Wittum
ἕδομαι, essen
ἕδρα, Sessel
ἕεδνα, Wittum
ἕζομαι, sitzen, Sessel
ἐθέλω, wollen
ἐθνικῶς, Deutsch
ἔθος, Sitte
εἴκω, weichen
εἰλύω, Welle
εἰμί (ἐστί), sein
εἶμι, gehen, eilen, Gasse
εἴργω, rächen
εἶρος, Wolle
ἑκατόν, hundert
ἔκλειγμα, } Latwerge
ἔκλεικτόν,
ἐκυρά, -ός, Schwäher
ἐλάτη, Linde
ἔλαφος, Hirsch
ἐλαφρός, gelingen, leicht, lungern
ἐλαχύς, leicht
ἐλεημοσύνη, Almosen
ἐλεύθερος, lieberlich
ἐλέφας, Elfenbein, Kamel
ἐλίκη, Salweide
ἕλκω, Wolf
ἕλμις, Wurm

ἕλπος, } Salbe
ἔλφος,
ἐμπίς, Imme
ἔμπλαστρον, Pflaster
ἐμφυτεύω, } impfen
ἐμφύω,
ἐν, ἐνί, in
ἐνέπω, sagen
ἐννέα, neun
ἔννυμι, Weste
ἔξ, sechs
ἐξάμιτον, Sami
ἑός, sich
ἐπίπλοος, Fell
ἐπίσκοπος, Bischof
ἐπίσταμαι, Berstand
ἔρομαι, heu, sehen
ἔπος, erwähnen
ἑπτά, sieben
ἔραζε, Erde, Ähren
ἔργον, Werk, wirken
ἐρέβινθος, Erbse
ἐρέτης, Ruder
ἐρετμός, Ruder, Eiche
ἐρεύγω, räuspern
ἔρευθος, } rot
ἐρεύθω,
ἐρευνάω, raunen
ἐρέω, Wort
ἔριθος, reiten
ἔριον, Wolle
ἐρυγή, räuspern
ἐρυθρός, Lende, rot
ἐρυσίπελας, Fell, rot
ἐρωή, Ruhe
ἑσπέρα, Westen
ἕσπερος, Abend
ἔσσετε, sagen
ἔτος, Widder
ἔτυμος, Sitte
Εὐμενίδες, Drude
ἐχῖνος, Igel
ἔχω (ἔσχον), Sieg

ζέσμα, } gären
ζεστός,
ζεύγνυμι, Joch
Ζεύς, Dienstag
ζέω, gären
ζητέω, jäten
ζίγγιβερις, Ingwer
ζυγόν, gären, Joch
ζώνη, Zone

ἡγέομαι, suchen
ἤδομαι, } süß
ἡδονή,
ἡδύς,
ἤϊθεος, Wittib
ἥλιος, Sonne
ἡμεῖς, uns
ἦπαρ, Leber

ἤρι, erst
ἦτορ, Ader, Atem
ἦτρον, Ader
ἠώς, Osten

θαιρός, Thür
θάλλω, } Dolde
θάλος,
θάμνος, Tanne
θαρρέω, } dreist
θάρσος,
θέλω, wollen
θερμός, Bärme, warm
θήκη, Zieche
θηριακόν, Theriak
θίς, Düne
θόλος, Dolde, Thal
θρῆνος, dröhnen
θρόνος, Thron
θρύλος, Traum
θρώναξ, Drohne
θυγάτηρ, Tochter
θύννος, Thunsisch
θύρα, Thür
θύραζε, Düne
θύρετρον, Thür
θύρσος, Dorsche
θυρών, Thür

ἰβίσκος, Eibisch
ἰγνύα, Knie
ἰδεῖν, wissen, Berweis
ἰδίω, schwitzen
ἰδρύω, sitzen
ἰδρώς, schwitzen
ἱέναι, eilen
ἰκμάς, Seihe
ἱμάς, Seile, Seil
ἱμονιά, Seil
Ἴνες, Sehne
ἰός, Gist, verwesen
ἰπνός, Ofen
ἵππος, Heu, Roß (1)
ἵστημι, stehen
ἰτέα, Weide

καγχάζω,
καγχαλάω, } kichern
καγχλάζω,
καδμεία, Galmei
καθαρός, Reyer
καιρός, weil
κακκάω, } kacken
κακός,
κάλαμος, Halm
καλέω, helen, laden (2)
κάλλος, καλός, heil
καλύβη, hehlen
κάλυξ, Kelch
καλύπτω, hehlen
καυδρα, Kammer
κάμαρος, Hummer

INDEX. 419

κάμηλος, Kamel
κάμινος, Himmel
κάμμαρος, Hummer
κάμνω (καμόντες), sterben
κάναστρον, Knaster
κάνθαρος, Kanne
κάνθος, Kante
κάνναβις, Hanf
κάπρος, Haber, Habergeiß, Bock
κάπων, Kapaun
κάρα, Hirn
κάραβος, Krabbe, Krebs
κάρδαμον, Harz
καρδία, Herz
κάρηνον, Hirn
καρκαίρω, Furcht
κάρνον, Horn
κάρον, Karbe
καρπός, Herbst
κάρτα, hart
κάρταλλος, } Kratze (1)
κάρταλος, } Hürde
καρτερός, hart (1)
κασσύω, Säule (2)
κασταναία, } Kastanie
Κάστανα, }
κανλόν, Gauler
καφουρά, Kampfer
καχάζω, lichern
κάχληξ, Hagel
κάχουν, Haber
κέγκει, Hunger
κέδρος, Zeder
κεῖμαι, Nest
κείρω, scheren
κεμάς, Hinde
κενταύριον, tausend
κέντρων, Haber (2)
κεραός, Hirsch
κέρας, Horn, Hirsch, Rind
κερασέα, -ία, } Kirsch
κεράσιον, }
κέρμα, Schersen
κέρνον, Hirn
κεύθω, Hort, Hütte
κεφαλή, Giebel, Kopf, Schädel
κῆρος, Hof, Hufe
κῆρ, Herz
κιθάρα, Zither
κιννάβαρι, Zinnober
κίναμον, Zimmet
κίσσα, Häher
κιστη, Kiste
κίτρον, Bitrone
κιχώριον, Kicher
κλαγγή, Klang, klingen
κλάδος, Holz
κλέος, Leumund, laut
κλέπτω, stehlen, Getichter

κλίμαξ, lehnen (1), Leiter
κλίνη, lehne (1), lehnen (1)
κλίνω, lehnen (1)
κλισία, lehnen (1), Leiter
κλίτος, κλίτος, lehnen (1)
κλιτύς, lehnen (1)
κλοιός, Hals
κλύδων, } lauter
κλύζω, }
κλυτός, } laut
κλύω, }
κνίδη, Nessel
κόβαλος, Kobold
κοῖ, hören
κοέω, schauen
κοίτη, Nest
κόλπος, Wolf, wölben
κόλφος, Golf
κόμη, Haar (2)
κονίλη, Quendel
κόνις, Honig
κονίς, κονίδες, Niß
κοπίς, Hippe (1)
κόπτω, hauen
κορακίνος, Karansche
κόραξ, Rabe
κόρυζα, Rotz
κόρυς, }
κορύσσω, } rüsten
κορώνη, Nabe
κότερος, wer
κοτέω, Hader (1)
κότος, Hader (1), naß, Haß
Κότυς, Haber (1)
κραδαίνω, rasseln
κραιπνός, laufen
κρανίον, Hirn
κρατερός, } hart
κρατύς, }
κρέας, roh
κρεμάννυμι, Rahmen
κριθή, Gerste
κρίνω, rein
κριός, Rind
κρόκη, Rogen
κρυμός, Reif (2)
κρυπτάδιος, einzig
κρύπτη, Kluft, Gruft
κύβος, Hüfte
κυδώνεα, Quitte
κύκλος, Rad
κυμάτιον, Sims
κύμβος, Hunpe
Κύπρος, Kupfer
κυριακόν, Almosen, Samstag, Kirche
κύριε ἐλεῖσον, Leib
κύρτη, -ία, -ος, Hürde
κύσθος, Hort
κύτος, Haut
κυφός, Höcker
κύων, Hund

κώμη, Heim
κύρτη, heben, Hippe (1)

λᾶας, Lei
λάγδην, lecken (2)
λάγνος, -ινος, Legel
λακίζω, Schlag (2)
λαλέω, lallen
λαμπάς, Lampe (1)
λάξ, lecken (2)
λαμπρά, Leber
λέγω, lesen
λεῖος, leise, Schleim
λείπω, leihen, bleiben, Leib
λείχω, lecken (1)
λέκτρον, liegen
λέπος, Laub
λευκός, Licht
λέχος, } liegen
λέχω, }
λιαρός, leise
-λικος, -lich
λιλαίομαι, Lust
λιμήν, Leim
λιναία, -ία, Leine
λίνον, Leinen
λίπα, klein, Leber
λιπαρέω, bleiben, leben, Leib, klein
λιπαρής, leben
λιπαρός, bleiben, klein, Leber, leben
λίπος, bleiben, klein
λίτα, Leinen
λιχνεύω, } lecker (1)
λίχνος, }
λοβός, Lappen
λοίπος, leihen
λούω, laben
λοχέω, λόχος, liegen
λυγγάνομαι, }
λυγόθην, } schluffen
λυγίζω, Loge
λύγξ, Luchs, schlingen
λύγος, Loge, Lauch
λυγόω, Loge
λύζω, schlingen
λυκάνθρωπος, Werwolf
λυκόπερδον, Bofist
λύκος, Wolf, elf, Schaum, werfen
λύρα, Leier
λύω, verlieren

μάγγανον, Mange
μαῖα, Muhme, Mutter
μαίομαι, Mut
μακεδνός, } mager
μακρός, }
μάκων, Mohn

μανδύας, Mantel
μανιάκης, } Mähne
μάννος, μάνος, }
μαραίνω, mürbe
μάρτυρ, -ύριον, Marter
μάτηρ, Mutter
μέ, mein
μέγας, groß
μέδιμνος, }
μέδομαι, } messen
μέδων, }
μέθη, } Met
μέθυ, μεθύω, }
μείω, μείων, minder
μέλδω, schmelzen
μέλι, Mehlsu, Honig
μένος, mahnen, Minne
μεσόδμη, Gaden
μέσος, mitte
μέσπιλον, Mispel
μετά, mit
μέτρον, Mal, Mond
μήδομαι, messen
μηκάομαι, niedern
μήκων, Mohn
μῆλα, schmal
μῆλον, Apfel
μήν, Mond
μήτηρ, Mutter
μήτρα, Mieder
μητρυῖα, Muhme
μίγνυμι, mischen
μικρός, Schmach
μίλτος, Mehlsu
μιμνήσκω, mahnen, Minne
μίνθα, Minze
μινύρθα, } minder
μινύω, }
μίσγω, mischen
μισθός, Miete
μίτος, Samt
μοιχός, Hure
μοναστήριον, Münster
μοναχός, Mönch
μόνος, Mähne
μύαξ, Moos
μυδών, Moder
μυῖα, Moos, Mücke
μυκάομαι, mucken, mucen
μύλη, ίται, }
μύλλω, } mahlen
μύλος, }
μύρια, tausend
μύρον, } Schmeer
μύρω, }
μῦς, Maus (1), (2)
μυών, Maus (2)
μῶλος, μῶλυς, mühen
-μωρος, Märchen

νάρδος, Narde

INDEX.

ναῦς, Kiel (2) Nachen, Naue
νέμομαι, νέμος, νέμω, } nehmen
νέομαι, genesen
νέος, neu
νέπoδες, Neffe
νέρτερος, Nord
νεφέλη, Nebel
νέφος, Nebel
νεφρός, Niere
νέω, nähen
νη- (νηκερδής), nein
νῆμα, nähen
νήπτης, nüchtern
νῆτρον, nähen
νηῦς, Naue
νηφάλιος, νήφω, } nüchtern
νίπτω, Niz
νίφα, νίφει, Schnee
νόμος, nehmen
νόννα, Nonne
νόστος, genesen
νοτερός, νοτέω, naß
νύ, nun
νύμφη, Braut
νῦν, nun
νύξ, Nacht
νυός, Schnur (2)

ξυρός, ξύω, } sauer

ὄγκινος, ὄγκος, } Angel
ὀδούς, Zahn
ὄζος, Aft
οἴ, weh
οἶδα, wissen
οἰδάω, οἴδμα, οἶδος, } Eiter
οἴνη, οἶνός, } ein
δῖς, Aue, Schaf
οἴφω, Weib
ὀκτώ, acht
ὀλίγος, schlecht
ὀλκάς, Holk
ὅλος, selig, all
ὅλπη, Salbe
ὀμιχέω, Hure, Mift
ὀμίχλη, ὁμίχλη, Mift
ὁμός, gleich
ὀμφαλός, Quebel, Nabe, Nabel
ὀμφή, fingen
ὀνίνημι, gönnen
ὀνίσκος, Affel
ὄνομα, Name
ὄνος, Affel
ὄνυξ, Nagel

ὀξύη, Esche
ὅπλον, Waffe
ὀπός, Saft
ὀρδώ, wahren, Wehr
ὄργανον, ὄργιον, } wirken
ὀρέγω, Rechen, recen
ὀρμή, Sturm
ὄρνις, Aar
ὄροβος, Erbse
ὄρρος, Arsch
ὄρυξ, Habicht, Waajtel
ὀρυγμός, röcheln
ὄρυζα, Reis (1), Roggen
ὄρυζον, Reis (1)
ὀρφανός, Erbe
ὅς, sich
ὅσδος, Aft
ὅσσα, erwähnen
ὄσσε, Auge
ὀστέον, Bein
ὄστρεον, Auster
οὖθαρ, Euter
οὖλε, οὖλος, selig
οὐρανός, Himmel
οὖς, Ohr, Öhr
ὀφθαλμός, Auge
ὀφρύς, Braue
ὄψ, erwähnen
ὄχος, Wagen

πᾶ, Vater
πάγη, Fach
παιδεύω, Pedant
παλάμη, fühlen
πάπας, παπᾶς, Pfaffe
πάππα, Vater
πάππας, Papst
πάπυρος, Papier
παρά, ver-, Pferd
παράδεισος, Paradies
πάρδαλις, Parder
παροικία, Pfarre
πάρος, vor
πατέομαι, Futter
πατήρ, lueten, Vater
πάτος, Pfad
πάτρως, Vetter
παχύς, Bug
παχύς, Backbunge
πέδη, Feffel (1)
πέδιλον, πέζος, } Fuß
πεῖθω, bitten
πεῖρα, Gefahr
πεῖσμα, binden
πέλεια, πελιός, } Taube
πέλλα, πέλμα, } Fell
πέμπε, fünf

πέμπτος, fünf, Donner, Pfingtag, Samstag
πενθερός, binden
πέντε, fünf
πεντεκοστή, Pfingften
πέπλος, Fell
πέτων, Pfebe
πέρα, πέραν, fein
πέρδω, farzen
περί-, ver-
πέρκη, Forelle
περκνός, Forelle, Sprenkel (2)
πέρυσι, πέριτι, firn
πέταλος, πετάννυμι, } faden
πέτομαι, Feder
πετροσέλινον, Peterfilie
πεύκη, Fichte
πέφτη, Pfingtag
πηγή, Bad
πηδόν, Pilet
πηλίκος, -lich
πηνίον, πῆνος, } Fahne
πῆχυς, Bug
πίδαξ, πιδύω, } feift
πῖλος, Filz
πίμπλημι, voll
πίνω (πέπωκα), trinken
πιππίζω, piepen
πίσυρες, vier
πίων, Eped, Bier
πλάθανον, Fladen
πλακοῦς, πλάξ, } flach
-πλάσιος, -falt, falten
πλατεῖα, Plaß
πλατύς, Fladen, platt
πλέκω, flechten
πλέω, fließen
πλήγνυμι, Flegel
πλήσσω, fluchen
πλίνθος, Flinte
πλοκή, πλόκος, flechten
πλύνω, Flut
πλωτός, πλώω
πόα, ποίη, } Feu
ποικίλος, Specht
ποίνη, Fchine
πολιός, fahl
πόλις, Felfen
Πολυκράτης, Mangold
πολύς, viel
πολύτλας, dulden
πολύτρητος, drechen
πομπή, Bombaft, Pomp
πορεύω, πορθμεύς, πορθμός, } fahren

πόρις, Farre
πόρκος, Fertel
πόρος, fahren, Furt
πόρτις, Farre
πόσις, Draut
πότερος, wer
πότνια, Braut
πούς, Fuß
πρεσβύτερος, Priefter
πρήθω, braten
πρό, ver-, vor
πρόμος, Fürft
προσηνής, gönnen
πρωΐ, -ία, -ίος, früh
πτέρις, Farn
πτέρνα, Ferse
πτερόν, Feder, Farn
πτέρυξ, Floffe
πτίλον, Feder
πτύω, speien
πυγμαχος, πυγμή, Fauft
πυθμήν, Boden
πύθω, faul
πύϊρ, Feuer
πυνθάνομαι, bieten
πύξ, Fauft
πυξίς, Büchse
πύξος, Büchse, Buch3
πύον, faul
πύος, Bieft
πῦρ, Feuer
πύργος, Burg
πύρεθρον, Bertram
πυρσός, Feuer
πωλέομαι, feil
πῶλος, Fohlen, foltern
πώς, Fuß

ῥάδαμνος, ῥάδιξ, } Durz
ῥαιβός, Reif (1)
ῥαμφή, ῥάμφος, rümpfen
ῥάπις, ῥαφάνη, ῥάφανος, ῥάφυς, } Rübe
ῥάχις, Rücken
ῥέζω, wirken
ῥέμβομαι, rümpfen
ῥέμβω, renken
ῥέω, Strom
ῥήτρα, ῥήτωρ, } Wort
ῥίζα, Durz, Rift
ῥόμβος, renken
ῥόμος, ῥόμος, Durm
ῥῦμα, Riemen
ῥύσις, Strom

σάββατον, Samstag
σάγμα, Saum (2)

INDEX.

σάκκος, Sack
σάκχαρ, -ον, Zucker
σάνταλον, Sandel
σάρδιον, Sarder
σαρκοφάγος, Sarg
σεισοπυγίς, Bachstelze
σήμερον, heute
σηρικός, Seide
σιγάω, σιγή, beschwichtigen, schweigen
σίναπι, Senf
σίνδων, Zindel
σίνομαι, schwinden
σκάζω, hinken
σκαπάνη, schaben
σκάπτον, Schaft (1)
σκάπτω, schaben
σκάφιον, Scheffel
σκαφίς, σκάφος, Schiff
σκέπτω, spähen
σκῆπτρον, Zepter, Schaft (1)
σκήπων, Schaft (1)
σκιά, Schemen, Schein
σκίμπτω, schief
σκίουρος, Eichhorn
σκίπων, Scheibe
σκίρον, schirmen, Schein
σκοῖπος, Scheibe
σκολιός, scheel
σκότος, Schatten
σκύλον, Schoner, Haut
σκῦτος, Haut
σκώπτω, Schimpf
σκώρ, Hure
σμερδαλέος, } Schmerz
σμερδνός,
σμίλη, } Schmied
σμινύη,
σμύχω, Schmauch
σόβη, Schweif
σομφός, Schwamm
σπάθη, Spaten, Span
σπαίρω, Sport
σπαρνός, sparen
σπάω, Gespenst
σπείρω, sparen
σπερχνός, } springen
σπέρχομαι,
στάμνος, Stamm
σταυρός, Steuer (2)
στέγη, Dach
στέγω, Dach, decken
στεῖρος, Stärke
στείχω, } Steig
στελεόν,
στέλεχος, Eitel
στέλλω, Stelle
στέμβω, stampfen
στένω, stöhnen
στερεός, starr
στερίσκω, stehlen

στέριφος, Stärke
στέρνον, Stirn
στήλη, Stuhl
στία, Stein
στίγμα, } stechen
στίζω,
στίον, Stein
στόλος, Stelle
στόμα, Stimme [νυμι
στορέννυμι, see στρώννυμι
στόρθη, Sterz
στραγγάλη, Strang
στρεύγομαι, straucheln
στρουθίον, } Strauß (3)
στροῖθος,
στρυφνός, sträuben
στρώννυμι, Streu, Stirn
στύλος, στύω, Staude
σύ, du
συλλαβή, Silbe
συντρησαι, drehen
σῦς, Sau
σύφαρ, sauber
σφάλλω, fallen, falsch
σχέδη, Zettel
σχέδος, Schatz
σχίζα, Scheit, scheiden
σχίζω, scheiden
σχινδαλμός, Schindel

ταγγός, stinken
ταινία, dehnen
τακερός, tauen
ταναός, dünn
τάνυμαι, dünn, dehnen
ταρσιά, ταρσός, Darre
τάσις, dehnen
ταῦρος, Stier, Kiel (2), stinken
τε, noch (1), (2)
τέγγω, tunken, Zwehle
τέγος, Dach
τείνω, dehnen
τεῖχος, Teig
τέκνον, Degen(1),gedeihen
τέκτων, Dachs
τέλθος, gelten
τελώνιον, Zoll
τενθρηδών, } Drohne
τενθρήνη,
τένων, dehnen, Dohne
τέρετρον, } drehen
τερέω,
τέρμα, Trumm
-τερος, hinter, vorher
τερσαίνω, } Darre
τέρσομαι,
τέσσαρες, vier, Jahr
τετραίνω, drehen
τήκω, tauen
τηλίκος, -λίξ
τίθημι (ἔθηκα), thun

τίκτω, Degen (1)
τίνω, Fehme
τίφος, Teich
τλήμων, τλῆναι, dulden
τό, der
τοῖχος, Teig
τοκεύς, τόκος, Degen (1)
τολμάω, dulden
τόνος, Donner, Ton
τόξον, Dachs
τοπάζιον, } Topas
τόπαζος,
τόργος, Storch
τόρνος, drehen
τορύνη, Quirl
-τος, laut
-τρα, Blatter
τράμις, Darm
τραυλός, bürr
τρεῖς, drei
τρέπομαι, drechseln
τρῆμα, drehen, Darm
τρῆσις, Draht
-τρια, Leiter
τριήρης, Ruder
τρυγών, Drossel (1)
τρύξ, Dreck
τύ, du
τυγχάνω, taugen
τύλη, τύλος, Daumen
τύπτω, stopfen
τύρβη, Dorf
τυφλός, dumm, taub
τύχη, taugen
τωθάω, Tadel

ὕδρα, Otter
ὕδωρ, Wasser, Otter
υἱός, υἱύς, Sohn
ὑλιά, Sohle (2)
ὑπείρ, ὑπέρ, über
ὕπνος, Schlaf (2) Schwefel
ὗς, Sau
ὕσσωπος, Jsop
ὑφαίνω, } weben
ὕφος,

φαγεῖν, Buche, Bauch
φαγός, Buche
φαίρω, bohnen
φακός, Bohne
φάλαγξ, Balken, Bohle
φαρόω, bohren
φασιανός, Fasan
φάσκω, Bann
φαῦλος, böse, faul
φέβομαι, beben
φέρω, Bahre, bohren
φεύγω, biegen
φηγός, Buche
φημί, Bann

φθείρ, φθείρω, Laus
φιτρός, Wiedehopf
φλεβοτόμον, Fliete
φλέγω, blecken, bleichen, Blitz
φλόξ, blecken. Blitz
φράτηρ, Bruder
φρέαρ, Brunn
φρίσσω, Brei
φρύγω, brauen
φρύνη, φρῦνος, braun
φυλή, bauen
φύλλον, Blatt
φύλον, bauen
φῦμα, bauen, Baum
φύσις, bauen
φύσκα, Bauch
φύω, bauen, sein (2)
φώγω, backen

χαῖος, Ger
χαιρέφυλλον, Kerbel
χαίρω, gern
χαμαίδρυον, Gamander
χαμαίμηλον, Kamille
χανδάνω, vergessen, ganz
χανδός, ganz
χάος, } Gaumen
χαῦνος,
χείδ, gähnen
χεῖμα, χειμών, Winter
χελιδόνιον, Schellkraut
χέω, gießen
χήν, Gans
χθές, gestern
χίλιοι, tausend
χιτών, Gaden, Kittel
χλαρός, gelb
χλιαίνω, } glimmen
χλιαρός,
χλόη, χλωρός, gelb
χολέρα, Koller (2)
χολή, χόλος, Galle (1)
χορδή, Korbe
χόρτος, Garten, Gras
χρεμέθω, grein
χρόμαδος, gram
χρυσός, Gold
χῦμα, gießen
χυμός, Alchimie

ψίττακος, Sittich
ψύλλα, Floh

ὠλένη, Elle
ὠόν, Ei
ὦπα, Auge
ὥρα, ὧρος, Jahr
ὠτειλή, wund
ὤχρα, Ocker

LATIN.

Comprising Old, Low, and Middle Latin.

abbas, Abt, Essig, Kette (2)
abbatia, Abtei
Abellanum, Apfel
abrotonum, Abercaute, Ebriz
absida, Abseite
abyssus, Robisbrag
accipio, } Habicht
accipiter, }
acer, Ahorn
acetum, Essig
achates, Achat
acies, Ed, Ecke, Ähre, Art
acre (vinum), Essig
acte, Attich, Lattich
aculeus, Ähre
acus, Ähre
ad, bis
adamas, Demant
adspectus, spähen
advenire, } Abenteuer
adventura, }
advocatus, Vogt
aequus, eben, Ehe
aes, Erz, Eisen
aesculus, Eiche
aestivale, Stiefel
aestumare, Ehre
aeternus, Ehe
aevum, Ehe, ewig, Seele
ager, Acker
agere, Acker, Achse
agnus castus, teusch
agrimonia, Odermennig
ala, Achsel, Deichsel
alabastrum, Alabaster
alba, Albe (1)
albula, Albe (2)
albus, Alber
alces, Elentier
alere, alt
Alisatia, } eleut
alius, }
allodium, Allod
almutia, -um, Mütze
alnus, Erle
Alpes, Alpe
altare, Altar
alter, ander
alumen, Alaun
ama, Ohm
amandola, Mandel (2)
amaracus, Majoran
amare, gönnen
amarellus, Ammer

amarus, Ampfer
ambactus, Amt
ambi-, bei
ambire, werben
ambo, beide
amittere, meiden
amnis, Ufer
ampulla, Ampel
amputare, impfen
amylum, Amelmehl
an-, an
anachoreta, Einsiedel
anas, Ente
anas crecca, } Kriekente
anas quer-quedula, }
anceria, } Anker (2)
ancheria, }
aucilla, Eule
ancora, Anker (1)
angelus, Engel
angere, eng
anguilla, Aal
angulus, Angel
angustine, Angst, eng
angustus, eng
anhelare, Essig
anima, Tier, ahnden
animadvertere, Berweis
animal, Tier
animus, ahnden
anisum, Anis
annona, Ernde
ansa, Öse
anser, Gans
ante, ant-
antiae, Stirn
anus, Mann, Hebamme, Ahn
aper, Eber
apium, Eppich
apostolus, Bischof
apotheca, Bottich
apricus, aber (2)
Aprilis, April
aqua, saff, Au, Wasser
Aquae, Bad
aqueductus, Abzucht, Andauche
aquilegia, Aglei
arare, Art, Acker
arbalista, Armbrust
arbor, Alber, Espe
arca, Arche
archangelus, } Erz-
archi-,

archiater, } Arzt
Archigenes, }
arcora, Erker
arcubalista, Armbrust
arcus, Pfeil, Erker, Armbrust
area, Ar, Ähren
argentum, Silber
argentum vivum, Quecksilber
aries, Krahn
aristolochia, Osterluzei
armenius, Hermelin
arinus, Arm
armutia, Mütze
ars, Art
artista, Arzt
arvum, Ähren, Erde
as, Aß
ascalonium, Aschlauch, Schalotte
ascia, Art
asellus, Esel, Assel
asinus, Esel, Igel
asparagus, Spargel
assis, Aß
astracus, astricus, Estrich
atramentum, Tinte
-atus, Einöde
audire, hören
augere, auch, Wucher
augia, Au
Augustodunum, Düne, Zaun
Augustoritum, Furt
augustus, August, auch
auris, Ohr
aurora, Osten
auscultare, hören, Ohr
avena, Hafer
avis, Vogel, Ei, Strauß (3)
avunculus, Enkel (2) Oheim
avus, Oheim
axilla, Achsel
axis, Achse

babuinus, Pavian
baburrus, Bube
bacar, Becher
bacca, Beere, Becken
baccalaureus, Hagestolz
baccinum, Becken
bacilletum, } Pickelhaube
bacinetum, }
baco, Bache

bajulus, ballia, } Böller
ballivus, }
balneum, Bad
balsamum, Balsam
balteus, Belt
bandum, Banner
barba, Bart, Barte (1), (2), Bade (2), Barte, Barbier, Leube
barbarius, Barbier
barbarus, brav
barbellus, Barbe
barbus, Barbe
baron, Barbe
barcanus, Barchent
barica, Barke
baro, Baron
barracanus, Berlan
Batavia, Au
Baunonia, Bohne
bedellus, Büttel, Pedell
bellum, Swist
benna, Benne
bersare, birschen
beryllus, Beryll, Brille
beta, Beete
betonica, -ula, Batheugel
bi-, zwie-
biber, Biber
bibere, Bier
biblia, Bibel
Bibracte, Biber
bicarium, Becher
bidellus, Pedell
bilix, Zwillich
billa, Bill
birretta, } Barett
birrum, -us, }
bisamum, Bisam
biscopus, Bischof
bitumen, Kitt
blaterare, plaudern
blundus, blond
boja, Boje
boletus, Pilz
bombyx, Bombasin, Bombast
bos, Kuh
braca, Bruch (3)
bracellum, } Bretzel
brachiolum, }
brachium, Bretzel, Brasse
breve, brevis, Brief
Brigantes, -ia, } Berg
Brigiani, }

INDEX.   423

bubalus, Büffel
bucca, Backe (2)
buccina, Posaune
buccula, Buckel (1)
bucina, Posaune
bulbus, Bolle (1), Zwiebel
bulga, Balg, Bulge
bulla, Bill, Bulle (3)
Burgundiones, Berg
burgus, Burg
buscus, Busch
bussa, Büse
butina, Bütte
butyrum, Butter
buxus, Buchs

caccare, laden
cadena, Kette (2)
cadmia, Galmei
caecus, blind
caedere, scheiden
caepulla, Zwiebel
caerefolium, Kerbel
Caesar, Kaiser
caesaries, Haar (2)
cafura, Kampfer
calamancus, Kalmank?
calaminaris, Galmei
calamus, Halm, Schalmei
calare, holen
calcare, Mahr, Kelter
calcatorium, } Kelter
calcatura,
caldumen, } Kaldaunen
caldus,
calendarium, Kalender
calidus, Kaldaunen
calix, Lärche, Kelch
calvus, kahl
calx, Kalk
camamilla, Kamille
camelus, Kamel
caminata, Kamin, Remenate
caminus, Kamin
camisia, Hemd, Kamisol
camphora, Kampfer
campus, Kamp, Kampf, Hof
cancelli, -us, Kanzel
cancer, Kanker (1), (2)
canere, Hahn, Schwan
caniculus, Kaninchen
canis, Hund
canistrum, Knaster
canna, Kanel, Kanne
cannabis, Hanf
cannetta, Kanne
cantharus, Kanne
capa, Kapelle (1)
capella, Kapelle (1), (2)
capellanus, Kaplan

caper, Haberzeiß, Bock, Haber
capere, heben, haben, Habicht, haschen
capillare, kahl
capillus, Haupt
cupito, Knappe
capitulum, Kapitel
capo, Kapaun
cappa, Kappe
captivus, Haft (2)
captus, Haft (2), -haft
capucinus, } Kapuze
capucium,
capulum, Kabel
capus, Habicht
caput, Haupt, Kappes, Laub
carabus, Groppe, Krabbe
carbunculus, Karfunkel
carcer, Kerker
cardus, carduus, Karde
carere, Haar (2)
careum, Karbe
carpere, Herbst, Karpfen
carra, Karren
carruca, Karch
carrus, Karch, Karre
cartusia, Karthause
carus, Hure, zart
caseus, -ius, Käse
cassis, hüten
castanea, Kastanie
castigare, kasteien
castus, keusch
catapulta, Bolz
catena, Kette (2)
catillus, Kessel
catinus, Kessel, Igel
cattus, Katze
Caturiges, Haber (1)
caulis, Kohl
caupo, kaufen
causa, causari, kosen
cavea, Käfig, Kane
cavere, schauen
cavia, Käfig
cedrus, Zeder
celare, hehlen
cella, Zelle
cellarium, Kall, Keller
cellarius, } Kellner
cellenarius,
celsus, Halde
cenialum, Zindel
census, Zins
centa, Zent-
centaurea, tausend
centenarius, Zentner
cento, Haber (2)
centum, hundert
cera, Kerze

ceraseus, Kirsche
cerasum, Kirsche, Pflaume
cerata, Kerze
cerebrum, Hirn
cernere, Räder
cervus, Hirsch
chamandreus, Gamander
chelidonia, Schellkraut
cholera, Koller (2)
chorda, Korde
chorea S. Viti, Beitstanz
cicer, -a, Kicher
cichoria, Kicher
ciconia, Häher
cicoria, Kicher
cinamomium, Zimmet
cingere, } Zingel
cingulus,
cinnabaris, Zinnober
circulus, Zirkel
circus, Bezirk, Zirkel
cirrus, Hirse
cis, heute
cisimus, Ziesel
cista, Arche, Kiste
cithara, Zither
citra, heute
citrus, Zitrone
civis, Heirat
clangor, Klang, klingen
clarus, klar
claudere, Klause, schließen
claudus, lahm
clausa, } Klause
clausarius,
claustrum, Kloster
clausula, Klausel
clausum, Klause
clericus, Pfaffe
clinare, } lehnen (1)
clinus,
clivus,
clocca, Glocke
closum, Klause
cluere, laut
clusa,
clusinaria, } Klause
clusus,
coebloar, Löffel
cofen, Kopf
cognomentum, Leumund
cohors, Garten
coleus, Hode
coliandrum, Koriander
colis, Kohl
collarium, Koller (1)
collis, Halde, Holm
collum, collus, Hals

coma, Haar (2)
combrus, Kummer
comes stabuli, Marschall
commendator, Komtur
communis, ein, Meineid, gemein
companio, Kumpan
compater, Gevatter
compes, Fessel (1)
complere, voll
con-, ge-, Ganerbe
conila, Quendel
conivere, neigen
conscientia, Gewissen
consolida, Günsel
conspicere, spähen [(1)
constare, Kost, (1), kosten
contra, Gegend
contrafactus, hunterbunt
conucula, Kunkel
convenire, bequem
copa, Kufe (2)
copula, Koppel
coquere, kochen, Kuchen
coquina, Küche
coquus, Kuchen, Koch
cor, Herz
coracinus, Karausche
corallium, -ius, Koralle
corbis, Korb, Reff (1)
coriandrum, Koriander
cornix, Rabe
cornolium, Kornelle
cornu, Horn
cornus, Kornelle
corona, Krone
coronare, krönen
corpus, Körper
cortex, Kork
corulus, Hasel
corvus, Rabe
costa, Kost (1), Küste
costare, kosten (1)
costurarius, Küster
costus, Kost (1)
cotagium, Kot (1)
cotonea, Quitte
cotta, Kotze, Kutte
cottanum, Quitte
cottus, Kutte
coxa, coxim, Hechse
crabro, Horniffe
cras, gestern
crates, Korn, Hürde
crecca, Krickente
crecopulus, Rohrdommel
cremare, Herd
creta, Kreide, Seide

cretcus, Räter
cretobulus, Rohrdommel
cribrum, rein, Reiter
crimen, Leumund
crispus, kahl
croca,
croccia,
croces, -us, } Krücke
crucca,
crucea, -ns,
crudus, roh, Räube
cruentus, Räute
cruor, Räube, roh
crusina,-inna, } Kürschner
crusna,
crusta, Kruste
crux, Bims, Kelch, Kreuz, Küster
crystallus, Krystall
cucina, Küche
cuculus, Kuckuck, Gauch
cucurbita, Kartoffel, Kürbis
cucurum, Köcher
culcita, Kissen, wölben
culleus, Kelle
culmen, Halm, Holm
culmus, Halm
cum, ge-
cumbia, Kumpf
cuminum, Kümmel
cunctari, hangen
cuniculus, Kaninchen
-cunque, irgend
cupa, Kopf, Kuppe, Karelle (2), Kiepe, Kübel, Kufe (2) [Kübel
cupella, Kapelle (2),
cupellus, Kübel
cuper, Kupfer
cupere, hoffen
cupla, Koppel
cuppa, Kopf
cuprum, Kupfer
currere, Roß (1)
curtus, kurz, Schurz, mager
curvus, Kürbe
cussinus, Kissen
custor, Küster
custos, Küster, Haus
cutis, Haut
cyprium, Kupfer

dactylus, Attich, Dattel
dama, Dambock
damascena, Zwetsche
damnare, verdammen
decanus, Dechant
decem, zehn
decorus, Zier

decuria, Decher
decus, Zier
defrutum, brauen
delere, tilgen
delirare, Irre, Gleise, lehren
dens, Zahn
densus, dürr
derbiosus, Zitteroch
deus, Gott
dexter, recht
diabolus, Teufel
dicere, zeigen
dictare, dichten
dies, Morgen (2), Tag
dies Lunae, Montag
digitus, Zeh
dignus, Zeichen
discus, Tisch
diurnalis, Morgen (2)
-do, zu
doceo, doctus, gelehrt
domare, zahm
domina, Dambrett, Frau
Dominica in Albis, Pfingsten
dominus, Frau
domus, Dom, Zimmer
draco, Drache, Eule
ducatus, Dukaten
ducere, ziehen
ductile, Tülle
dumus, zausen
duo, Daus, zwei
duodecim, Dutzend
durare, dauern (1)

ebenus, Ebenbaum
ebur, Elfenbein
edere, essen
ego, ich
electuarium, Latwerge
eleemosyne, Almosen
emere, nehmen
emplastrum, Pflaster
eucaustum, Tinte
endivia, Endivie
episcopus, Bottich (Bischof)
equuleus, foltern
equus, foltern, Heu, Roß (1)
errare, irren
eruca, Raute
erugere, räuspern
ervum, Erbse
esse (est), sein
esus, essen
et, oder
examitum, Samt
excellere, Halm, Hals
exclusa, Schleuse

excurare, scheuern
exoticus, Zote
expendere, Speise, Spende
extendere, Standarte

faba, Bohne
fabula, Fabel
facere, heben, thun
facula, Fackel
fagus, Buche
falco, Falke
faldistolium, } falten
faldistorium,
fallere, fallen, falsch, fehlen
falsus, falsch
falx, Falte
far, Barn
fari, Bann
fasianus, Fasan
fastidium, garstig
fastigium, Borste
fatum, Fee
faux, Schlauch
favonius, Föhn
favus, Wabe
fax, Fackel
febris, Essig, Fieber, Bieber
fel, Galle (1)
felix, Bilsenkraut
fenestra, Fenster
feniclum,
-culum, } Fenchel
fenuclum,
feria, Feier
feriae, Feier, Beete
feriari, Feier
ferire, Bär (1)
fermentum, Bärme
ferre, Bahre, gebären, bohren
fertilis, gebären
festum, Fest
fiber, Biber
ficus, Feige, Feigwarze
fidere, bitten
fieri, sein
figulus, } Teig
figura,
filix, Bilsenkraut
filtrum, Filz
fimbria, Franse
findere, reißen, Beil
fingere, Teig
finire, sein
fistula, Fistel
fixus, fix
flado, Fladen
flagellum, Flegel
flagrare, blecken, flackern

flamma, flammen
flare, blähen
flasca, -o, Flasche
flavus, blau
flere, bellen
flexus, Flechse
fligere, bläuen
floccus, Flocke
florere, Blume, Blust
florinus, Florin
flos, Blume, Florin
floscellu-, Flößel
forare,
focarius, } Fächer
foculare,
focus, Fächer, backen
fodere, Bett
foeniculum, Fenchel
folium, Blatt
follis, Balg
forare, bohren
fores, Thür
foresta, } Forst
foris,
forma, Form
formica, Ameise
formula, Formel
formus, Bärme, warm
fotrale, Futteral
fraces, Treber
fragrare, Bracke
framea, Franse
frangere, brechen
frater, Bruder
fremere, Breme, brummen, gram
frendere, Graud, Gerste
frigere, brauen
frigère, fricren
frons, Braue
fructus, Frucht
fruges, } brauchen
frui,
fugere, biegen
fuisse, bauen
fulgur, Blitz
fulica, Belche (2)
fulmen, Blitz
fundere, gießen
fundus, Boden
fungi, Bauch
fur, Frettchen
furca, Furke
furere, Thor (1)
furetum, -us, } Frettchen
furo,
furvus, Bär (2)
fusilis, Fusel
fustis, Bausch
futurus, bauen

gabalus, Gabel

INDEX.

ga=sum, Ger, Kaiser
galanga, Galgant
galatina, Gallerte
galeta, Gelte
galla, Gallapfel, Galle (2)
gamandraea, Gamander
ganta, Gans
gelare, Gallerte, kalt
gelidus, } kalt
gelu,
gena, Kinn
genista, Ginst
gens, Kind
gentilis, Geschlecht
genu, Knie
genuini (dentes), Kinn
genus, } Kind, Knabe,
gignere, } Knecht, Heil
glaber, glatt
gladius, Floß
glesum, Auer, Glas, Bernstein
glis, Klette
globus, Kolben, Knäuel
glocire, Glucke, Klucke
glomus, Knäuel
glubere, klieben
gluere, } Knäuel
gluma,
glus, } Klei
gluten,
(g)noscere, können
gradus, Grab
Graccus, Kaiser
granien, Gras
grandis, groß
granum, Korn, Gran
graphium, Griffel
griphus, Greif
griseus, Greis
grossus, Groschen
grunnire, grunzen
grupta, Gruft
grus, Kranich, Krahn
gula, Kehle
guasdium, Waid
gubernare, schalten
guerulfus, Werwolf
gurges, Kolf
gurgulio, Gurgel
gustare, kiesen, kosten (2)
gustus, kiesen
gypsum, Gips
gyrare, Geier

habere, haben, -haft, heben, hinken
haedus, Geiß
halec, Häring
hamus, Hamen
hariolus, } Garn
haruspex,

hasta, Gerte
hederacea, Hederich
helvus, gelb
heraldus, Herold
Hercynia, Berg
heri, gestern
hiare, gähnen
hic, nun
hiems, Winter
hilla, } Garn
hira,
hiscere, gähnen
Hispanum (viride), Grünspan
hoc enim est corpus meum, Hokuspokus
hodie, heute
holcaa, Holl
homicida, Papst
homo, Brant, man
hora, Uhr
hordeum, } Gerste
horrere,
horridus, garstig
hortus, Garten
hospes, Gast
hospitale, Spital
hostia, } Gast
hostis,
humlo,
humulus, } Hopfen
hupa,
hysopum, Isop

ibiscum, Eibisch
id, er
imperator, Kaiser
implore, roll
imputare, impfen
in, in
in-, un-
incensorium, zünden
inclutus, laut
incubo, Hause
incus, Amboß
inferior, } unten
infra,
infundibulum, Trichter
ingimus, Winter
insece, } sagen
insectiones,
insistere, inständig
instigare, stechen
insula, Insel
intibus, Endivie
intrare, entern
invenire, finden
ire, Gasse, gehen, eisen
is, er
ivus, Eite

Januarius, Jänner

jecur, Leber
joculari, Gaukler
jocus, Juts
jubilare, jubeln
jugerum, Jauchert
jugum, } Joch
jungere,
juniperus, Einbeere
Jupiter, Dienstag
jus, Käse, Jauche
juvencus,
juvenis, } Jung
juventa,

labare, } schlaff
labi,
labina, Lawine
labium, Lippe
labor, Arbeit
Laburdanus, Labberdan
lac, Milch
lacerare, Schlag (2)
lacruma, Zähre, Zunge
lactuarium, Latwerge
lactuca, Attich, Laitich
lacus, Lache, Meer
lagena, -oena, } Legel
lagona,
laicus, Laie
laisius, Leiste (2)
lallare, lallen
lambere, Lippe, Löffel
lampetra, } Lamprete
lampreda,
lancea, Lanze
lapatica,
lapatium, } Lattich
laptica,
laqueus, Latz
larix, Lärche
larva, Larve
lassus, laß, lassen
laterna, Laterne
latinus, lateinisch
lattica, -uca, Lattich
laubia, Laube
laurus, Lorbeer
lautus, lauter
lavare, laben, Lauge
lavendula, Lavendel
lectus, liegen
lesa, Lehne (2)
legere, lesen, Rechen
lenis, lind
lens, Linse
lentus, lind, Linde
leo, Löwe
levis, leicht, leise, Lunge, Schleim
libens, lieb
liber, lebig
libido, lieb, Lob

libum, Lebkuchen
licium, Drillich, Lilie, Litze
ligusticum, Liebstöckel
lilium, Lilie, Rose
lima, } Schleim
limare,
limus, Schleim, Lehm, Leim
linen, Lilie, Linie, Leinen
linere, Kleister, Leim
lingere, lecken 1
lingua, lecken, Zunge
linquere, leihen, bleiben, Leib
linum, Leinen, Leine
liquiritia, Lakritze
lira, lehren, irre, Gleise
lolium, Lolch
longus, lang
lora, Lauer
lubere, } Lieb, Lob
lubido,
lubricus, Schleife, Schlupf
lucere, Licht, Lohe (1)
lucerna, Kall, Licht
lucidus, Licht
lucrum, Lohn
Lugdunum, Düne, Zaun
lumbus, Lende
lumen, Licht
luna, Laune, Licht, cf. Montag
lupus, Wolf, Schaum
lutum, Letten
lux, Licht, Lohe (1)
lycoperdon, Bofist
lycopodium, Bärlapp
lyra, Leier

macarellus, Makrele
macellarius, } Metzger
macellum,
macer, mager
macula, Makel
magister, Meister
magistratus, Einöbe
major, Majoran, Meier
major domus, Meier
majoracus, } Majoran
majorana,
Majus, Mai
maledicere, maledeien
malum, Apfel
malus, Mast (1), Nest
malva, Malve
mancipium, Kebse
mancus, mangeln
mandala, Mandel (1)
mane, Morgen (1)

manipulus, voll
Manuus, Mann
mansio, } Meß-
mansionarius, } ner
mantellum, Mantel
manus, Mund (2)
maquerellus, Matrele
maraginum, Moraſt
marca, Mark (2)
mare, Moſt (1), Marſch, Meer
marga, margila, Mergel
margo, Mark (1)
mariscalcus, Marſchall
mariscus, Marſch
marmor, Marmel
marscalhus, Marſchall
martes, Marder
Martius, März
mertus, Marder
martyr, } Marter
martyrium, }
maserini (scyphi), Maſer
massa, Moſſe, Meſſing
mater, Mutter
matratium, Matratze
matrina, Pate
matrix, Mieder
matta, Matte (2)
mattina, Mette
mattus, matt
matutinus, Mette
Maurus, Mohr
medicus, Arzt
medius, Beſanmaſt, Mitte
mejare, Miſt
mel, Mehltau, Honig
meminisse, } mahnen,
mens, } Minne
mensa, Speiſe
mensis, Mond
menta, mentha, Minze
mentiri, Meineid
mentum, Mund (1)
mercatus, Markt
mergere, Mark (3)
merula, Amſel, Schmerl
mespila, Miſpel
metere, Matte (1)
metiri, Mal (1) meſſen
meus, mihi, mein
milia, Meile, tauſend
mingere, Miſt
minimus, minder
minium, Mennig
minor, } minder
minuere, }
miscere, miſchen
miser, } barm-
miseri, } herzig

misericordia, } barm-
-cors, } herzig
inodius meſſen, Mieze (2)
modus, Maß, meſſen
molere, mahlen, mahnen
moenia, Mund (2)
mola, Mühle
moles, mühen
molina, Mühle
molinarius, Müller
moliri, mühen
mollis, mild
monachus, Mönch
monasterium, Münſter
monere, mahnen, Minne
moneta, Münze (1)
monile, Mähne
monstrare, Muſter
mopsus, Mops
mordere, Schmerz
mordrum, }
mori, } Mord
mors, }
mortuus, }
mortarium, Mörſer, Mörtel
morum, morus, Pflaume, Maulbeere
Mosaetra-} Trichter
jectum, }
muffula, Muff (1)
mulctra, Mulke
mulgere, melken
mulus, Maul (2)
munire, Mund (2)
murmurare, murmeln
murus, Mauer
mus, Maus (1)
musmon-
tanus, } Murmeltier
musmontis, }
musculus, Maus (2) Muſchel, Muskel
muscus, Moos, Mohr
mustum, Moſt, Mieſtert
muta, Mauſe, Maut
mutare, Mauſe, Mutter
mutilus, Hammel

nanciaci, genug
nardus, Narbe
nare, Natter
nares, Naſe
nario, Narr
nassa, Netz
nasus, Naſe
natare, } Natter
natrix, }
natus, alt
navis, Kiel (2) Nachen, Naue
ne, noch (2) nn-, nein

ne-, nein
nebula, Nebel
nectere, Neſtel
nefas, nein
nefrones, Niere
nemus, nehmen
nepos, Neffe, Nichte
neptis, Nichte
neque, noch (2)
nere, nähen
nervus, Nerv
nicere, } neigen
nictare, }
nidus, Neſt, Neſtel
ninguere, Schnee
niti, Neid
nitidus, nett
nix, Schnee
nocturnus, nüchtern
nodus, Neſtel
nomen, Namen
nona, None
nonna, Nonne
nos, uns
noscere, können
noster, uns
nota, Note
notio, } können
notus, }
novem, neun
novicius, Novize
novus, neu
nox, Nacht
nudus, nackt
nunc, nun
nurus, Schnur (2)
nux, Nuß (1)

oblata, Oblate
oblongus, oblang
obscurus, Scheuer
occa, Egge
occulere, hehlen
ochra, Oker
octo, acht
oculus, Auge
offendimentum, binden
offerre, opfern
oleum, Öl
oliva, Olive
onocrotalus, Rohrdommel
operari, } üben
opus, }
orbus, Erbe
ordalium, Urtel
ordinare, } Orden
ordo, }
organa, -um, Orgel
oryza, -on, Reis (1)
os, Bein
ostrea, ostreum, Auſter

ovis, Aue, Schaf
ovum, Ei

pactum, -us, Pacht
paganus, Heide
palafredus, } Pferd
palafrenus, }
palantia, -um, } Pfalz
palatinus, }
palatium, Palaſt, Pfalz
palenca, -um, } Pfalz
palitium, }
palleo, pallidus, fahl
palma, fühlen, Palme
palus, Pfahl, Pfuhl
panceres, Panzer
pangere, fangen
pannus, Fahne, Pfand
panther, -a, Panther
papa, Papſt, Pfaffe
papaver, Mohn
papio, Pavian
pappa, } Pappe
pappare, }
papula, Pappel (1)
papulus, Pappel (2)
papyrum, Papier
par, Paar
paradisus, Paradies
paraveredus, Pferd
parcus, Pferch
pardalis, } Bardel
pardus, }
parifredus, Pferd
parochia, }
parochus, } Pfarre
paroecia, }
parra, }
parricus, Pferch
pars, wider
passer, Spatz
pastata, Paſtete
pater, taeten, Bater, Pate
patere, Foder
patina, Pfanne
patrinus, Pate
patruus, Detter
pausa, Panſe
pavo, Pfau
pax, fangen
pecu, } Bieh
peculium, }
pecunia, Bieh, Schatz
pecus, Bieh
pedellus, Pedell
pedere, Fiſt
pedica, Feſſel (1)
pelicanus, Pelikan
pellicia, Pelz
pellis, Fell, belzen
pena, Fein

INDEX.

penicillus, Pinsel
penna, Feder, Finne (1)
pennale, Pennal
pentecoste, Pfingsten
pepo, Pfebe
perca, Barsch
peregrinus, Pilger
perferre, dulden
periculum, Gefahr
peritus, fahren
perna, } Ferse
pernix,
persicum, Pfirsich
perula, Perle
pes, Fuß
pesna, Finne (1)
pestilentia, Pest
pestis, Pest
petrosilium, Petersilie
Petrus, Beete
phlebotomum, Flinte
pictor, Felle
pictus, } Specht
picus,
pila, pilare, } Pfeiler
pilarius,
pileus, Filz
pilula, Pille
pilum, Pfeil
pilus, Filz
pimpinella, Bibernelle,
   Bimpernelle
pingere, Feile, Finger,
   Specht
pinna, Finne (1) Flosse,
   Pinn
pinsellus, Pinsel
pipa, Pfeife
pipare, Pfeife, piepen
piper, Pfeffer
pipinella, Bibernelle
pipita, Pips
pirum, Birne, Pflaume
piscis, Fisch, Finne (1),
   Mast (1)
pisum, Erbse
pituita, Pips
pix, Pech
placenta, flach
plaga, flach, } Plage,
   Placken
plauca, Planke
plangere, Flegel, fluchen
planta, Pflanze
planus, flach, Flur
plastrum, Pflaster
platea, Platz (1)
platessa, Plattelse
Plautus, Fladen
plectere, flechten
plegium, pflegen
plenus, Korn, voll

plicare, flechten
plorare, flennen
Plotus, Fladen
pluere, fließen
pluma, Flaum, fliegen
poena, Pein, verpönen
poeta, Papst
poledrus, foltern
pollere, viel
pomarancia, Pomeranze
pompa, Pomp
pomum, Pflaume
pondo, } Pfund
pondus,
ponticus(mus), bunt
populus, Pappel (2)
porca, Furche, Gleise
porculetum, Furche
porcus, Ferkel, Barch
porrigere, recken
porta, Lurz, Pforte
porticus, Pforte
portulaca, Burzel
portus, Furt, Port
poscere, forschen
posita, -us, Post
postellus, Pfosten
postis, Pfosten
potio, Gift
potus, trinken, trunken
praeambulum, Priamel
praebenda, Pfründe
praedicare, opfern, pre-
   digen
praehendere, vergessen,
   Preis
praepositus, Propst
precari, } fragen
preces,
presbyter, Priester
pressa, Kelter, Presse
pretiare, preisen
pretium, Preis
princeps, Prinz
prior,
priscus, } frisch
prius,
pro, vor
probare, prüfen
procax, } fragen
procus,
prodigium, Zeichen
propago, propfen
propheta, Papst
proponere, Propfen
propositus, Propst
provenda, Pfründe
pruina, frieren
prunum, Pflaume
prurire, frieren
psittacus, Sittich
pugil, Faust

pugio, Faust
pugna,
pugnare, } Faust, fechten
pugnus,
pulejum, Polei
pulex, Floh
pulletrus, foltern
pullus, Fohlen
pulpito, } Pult
pulpitum,
pulsare, } Puls
pulsus,
pulver, Pulver
pulvinar, } Pfühl
pulvinus,
pumex, Bims
puncta, Spund
punctio, Bunzen
punctum, Spund
punctus, } bunt
puntus,
pupa, Puppe
purgatorium, Fegefeuer
purus, pur
pus, faul
putare, puter, } impfen
putere,
puteus, Pfütze, Brunn
pyrethron, Bertram

quaccila, Wachtel
quadrum, -us, Quader
quantum, Gant
quartana, Kartanne
quarto, Ort (3)
quattuor, werfen, Fohre,
   vier
que, noch (1), (2)
quercus, Föhre
querquedula, Krieknete
querquerus, Furcht
quietare, quitt
quietus, weil
quinque, fünf, werfen
quintinus, Quentchen
quintus, fünf
quod, wer, was

rabarbarum, Rhabarber
racemus, Rosine
radius, Roß (2), Rute
radix, Rettich, Würz
radix barbara, } Rha-
radix pontica, } barber
raja, Roche (1)
rancidus, ranzig
rapa, Rapunzel, Rübe
rapicium, Raps
rapidus, Ratte
raponticum, Rhabarber
raptus, Ratte
rapum, Rübe

rapuncium, } Rapun-
rapunculus, } zel
rarus, rar
ratio, Rede
ratis, Ruder
raudus, groß
rebus, Rebus
rectus, recht
reda, reiten
regere, recht
regius, reich
regula, Regel
relinquere, } leihen
reliquia,
reminisci, mahnen,
   Minne
remus, Ruder
renta, Rente
reri, Rat
res, Rebus
respondere, schwören
reubarbarum, } Rha-
reuponticum, } barber
rex, Reich
Rhaetia, Rießling
rhopalici (versus),
   Knittelvers
rhythmus, Reim
rigare, Regen
ristua, Ries
risus, Reis (1)
-ritum, Furt
robigo, Rost (2)
roccus, Rock
rodere, Rüssel
rosa, Rose
rosina, Rosine
rosmarinus, Rosmarin
rota, Rad, gerade (2)
rotula, -us, Rolle
rotundus, rund
ruber, Leude, Reiter, rot
rubere, rot
rubeta, Kalkranze
rubidus, rot
rubigo, Rost (2)
rubrica, rot, Rubrik
ructare, räuspern
rudis, } groß
rudus,
rufus, rot
ruga, Runzel
rugire, röcheln
ruminare, räuspern
rumpere, Raub
rupicapra, Gemse
rupta, Rotte
ruptarius, Reuter
rus, Raum
ruscus, Rausch (1), Rohr
russus, Rauschgelb
ruta, Raute (1)

rutarius, Renter
rutilus, rot
rutta, Rotte

sabbati dies, Samstag
sabellinus, }
sabellum, } Zobel
sabinus, Sebenbaum
sabulum, Sand
saccellum, Seckel
saccharum, Zucker
saccus, Sack
sacramentum, Sackerlot
sacrista, Sigrist
saeculum, Seele
saevus, See
sagire, suchen
sagma, }
sagmarius, } Saum (2)
sagulum, Segel
sal, Salz
salamandra, Salamander
salix, Salweide
sallere, Salz
salmo, Salm
saltare, Tanz
salvator, Salbader
salvegia, }
salvia, } Salbei
sambuca, Pauke
samitum, Samt
sanus, Sühne, gesund
sapa, }
sapere, } Saft
sapo, Seife
sapor, Saft
sarda, Sardelle, Sarber
sat, satis, }
satur, } satt
satureja, Saturei
Saturni dies, Samstag
sauma, Saum (2)
saxum, Messer
scabellum, Schemel
scabere, schaben
scabinus, Schöffe
scalmeia, Schalmei
scamellum, Schemel
scancio, Schenk
Scandinavia, Au
scandula, Schindel
scapellus, Scheffel
scaphium, }
scaphum, } Scheffel
scapus, Schaft (1)
scarlatum, Scharlach
scarleia, Scharlei
scedula, Zettel
sculus, Schulb
sceptrum, Zepter
schedium, Skizze

scindere, schelten
scindula, Schindel
scirpus, Schilf
sciurus, Eichhorn
sclareia, Scharlei
Sclavus, Sklave
sclusa, Schleuse
scola, Dom, Rose, Schule
scorbutus, Scharbock
scribere, schreiben
scrinium, Schrein
scriptum, Schrift
scrupulus, Srumpel
scrutari, Schrot
scurrare, scheuern
scutella, }
scutula, } Schüssel
scutum, Scheuer, Haut
se, sich
sebum, Seife
secare, Säge, Sense, sehen
secula, Sichel
securis, Säge, Sense
securus, turz, sicher
sedere, Sessel, sitzen
sedile, Saitel
Segestes,
Segimundus, } Sieg
Segiomerus,
segrista(nus), Sigrist
sella, Sessel, sitzen
semen, säen, Same
semiplotia, Flader
semper, Singrün, Sinde
senatus, Einöde
senex, Seneschall
senior, Seneschall, Herr
sensus, }
sentire, } Sinn
sepelire, besehlen
septem, sieben
sequi, Heu, folgen, sehen
sericus, Seibe
serere, säen
seta, Seibe
sex, sechs
sextarius, Sechter
sibi, sich
sidere, sitzen
sigillum, Siegel
signare, }
signum, } Segen
silva, }
silvaticus, } wild
sima, Sims
simila, Semmel
similis, }
simulare, } Gleichner
sinapi, Senf
siniscalcus, Seneschall
situla, Seidel

Slavus, Sklave
smaragdus, Smaragd
sobrius, sauber
socculus, Sockel
soccus, Socke
socer, }
socrus, } Schwäher
sol, Sonne
solarium, Söller
solea, Sohle (1), (2),
solidus, Sold [Schwelle
sollus, selig
solum, Saal
solvere, verlieren
somnus, Schlaf (2)
Schwefel
sonare, Schwan
sons, }
sonticus, } Sünde
sordes, schwarz
soror, Schwester
sparus, Speer
spatium, Spuren
speculum, spähen, Spiegel
spegulum, Spiegel
spensa, Speise
spernere, Kleister, rinnen, Sporn
spesa, Speise
spicarium, Speicher
spina, Spilling
spondere, schwören
spuere, speien (Spott)
spuma, Schaum
sputum, Spott
squiriolus, Eichhorn
stabulum, Marschall, Stabel
stannum, Zinn
stare, Stabel, stehen
status, Staat
stella, Stern
sterilis, Stärke
sternere, Streu, Stirn, Sturm
stilus, Stiel
stipes, steif, Stift (1)
stipula, Stoppel
stiva, Sleiß
strata, Straße
stridere, Strudel
striga, streichen
strigilis, Striegel
stringere, Strang, streichen
struthio, Strauß (3)
stultus, stolz
stupila, Stoppel
stuppa, }
stuppare, } Stöpsel
sturio, Stör

sturnus, Star
suadere, süß, schwätzen
suasuin, schwarz
suavis, süß
subula, Säule (2)
sudare, schwitzen
sudor, Schweiß
suere, Säule (2)
sugere, saugen
sulcus, Pflug
sulphur, Schwefel
super, über
superstitio, Aberglaube
surdus, schwarz
sus, Sau
sutor, Schuster, Säule (2)
suus, Schwester, sich
syllaba, Silbe
synodus, sempersrei

tabella, Tafel
tabula, Tafel, Schach
tacere, Mohn
tapetum, Teppich
taurus, Stier
taxare, tasten
taxus, Dachs
tegere, Dach, behnen, Gewand, becken
tegula, Ziegel, Ziegel
tellus, Diele
telonium, Zoll (2)
temo, Deichsel
templum, Tempel
tempora, Schlaf (1)
tempus, Ding
temulentus, bämisch
tendere, behnen, Zelt
tenebrae, dämmern, düster
tenero, behnen
tenuis, bünn
tenus, behnen, Dohne
terebra, bresten
terminus, Trumm
tertius, britte
testa, Kopf
textus, Teri
theca, Bieche
theodiscus, bentsch
theriacum, Theriat
thronus, Thren
thunnus, Thunfisch
thyrsus, Dorsche
tincta, Tinte
tingere, tunken, Zwehle
titulus, Titel
toga, Dach, Gewand
tolerare, }
tollere, } bulden
tonare, Donner
tongere, bünten

INDEX.

tongitio, blinken
tonitru, Donner
tonus, Ton
topazius, -us, Topas
tophus, Tuff
torcula, Torkel
torcular, brechseln
torculum, Torkel
torquere, brechseln, Zwerch-
torrere, dörren, Darre, garstig
torridus, } Darre
torris,
tractare, trachten
tractarius, } Trichter
tractorium,
trahere, treibeln
trajectorium, } Trichter
trajicere,
trames, Darm
tranquillus, weil
trans, durch
tres, drei
tribus, Dorf
trifolium, Treff
trilix, Drillich
tripudium, Fuß
tristis, dreist, tapfer
triumphus, Trumpf
trua, Quirl
trucca, Truhe
trudere, verdrießen
truncus, Truhe
tu, du
tugurium, Dach
tumere, Daumen
tundere, stoßen
tunica, tünchen
turba, Dorf
turdela, Drossel (1)

turdus, Drossel (1)
turris, Turm
turtur, Turteltaube
tuticus, deutsch

uber, Euter
ulmus, Ulme
ulna, Elle
Ultrajectum, Trichter
umbilicus, } Nabe,
umbo, } Nabel
uncia, Unze
uncus, Angel
unda, Wasser
unguere, Anke
unguis, Nagel
unus, ein, gemein
urceus, Krug (1)
urgere, rächen
ursus, Bär (2)
urus, Auer
uva, Eken

vacca, Ochse
vadere, waten
vadimonium, wett
vadum, waten
vae, weh
valere, walten
valeriana, Baldrian
vallum, } Wall
vallus, }
vannus, Wanne
vas, weit
vasculum, Flasche
vastus, Wust
vates, Wut
vehere, reiten, Weg, wegen
vehiculum, Wagen
velle, wollen

vellus, Wolle, Fließ
venari, Weide (2)
venerari, Bahn
venire, kommen
venter, Wanst
ventilare, Wanne
ventus, Wind
Venus, wohnen
ver, Lenz
verbum, Wort
veredus, Pferd
vernis, Wurm
verrere, wirr
verres, Barch
verruca, Warze
versus, Vers
vertere, werden
verus, wahr
vesica, Wanst
vespa, Wespe
vesper, Westen, Abend
vespera, Vesper
vester, euch
vestigium, Steig
vestis, Weste
vetula, Vettel
vetus, Widder
via, Weg
vibrare, weisen, Wippe
vicedominus, Bizdom
vices, Wechsel, weichen, Woche
vicia, Wicke
videre, wissen, Verweis
vidua, Wittib
vigere, vigil, wecken
villa, villare, Weiler
villus, Wolle
vincere, Weigand
vindemia, Franse, Wein
vindemiare, Wein

vindobona, }
vindomagus, } Winter
-nissa,
vinitor, Winzer
vinum, } Essig, Wein
vinns, }
viola, -etta, Veilchen
vir, Werwolf, Wirt
virga, Wisch
viride Hispanum, Grünspan
viridia, Wirsching
virus, verwesen, Wiesel Gift
viscus, Mistel
Visegothae, Westen
Vistula, Deichsel
vitis, Weide (1)
vitrum, Firnis, Waid
vitulus, Widder
Vitus, Veitstanz
vivarium, Weiher
vivere, led
viverra, Eiche
rivus, led, kommen
vocare, erwähnen
vocatus, Vogt
Volcae, welsch, Falke
volvere, Welle
vorago, } Schlauch
vorare, }
vos, euch
vox, erwähnen
vulgus, Volk
vulpus, Fuchs, Wolf

wambasium, Wams

zeduarium, Zitwer
zona, Zone
zucara, Zucker

ITALIAN.

abate, Abt
aceto, Essig
agosto, August
albaro, Alber
albergo, Herberge
alchimia, Alchmie
alenare, Essig
allarme, Alarm, Lärm
alna, Elle
amascino, Zwetsche
ambasciata, Amt
ancora, Anker (1)
aprile, April
araldo, Herold
arancia, Pomeranze

arciere, Hatschier
argento vivo, Quecksilber
aringo, Ring
arlucchino, Harlekin
arnese, Harnisch
arraffare, } raffen
arrappare, }
arrostir, Rost (1)
asello, Assel, Esel
asino, Esel
aspo, Haspe
astraen (Sicil.) } Estrich
astregh (Mil.) }
astuccio. Etauche

avorio, Elfenbein

babbeo, } Bube
babbole, }
babbuino, Pavian
bacinetto, Pickelhaube
bacino, Becken
baja, Bai (2)
baldacchino, Baldachin
baldo, bald
balestra, Armbrust
balsamo, Balsam
banca, Bank
banco, Bank, Bankett
banda, Bande

bara, barella, Bahre
baracane, Berlan
barbio, Barbe
barca, Barke
basso, Baß
basta, Bast
bastione, } Bastei
bastire, }
basto, Bast, Bastard
beccare, } Bicke
becco, }
benda, } binden
bendare, }
bovero, Biber
bezzo, Batzen

INDEX.

bianco, blank
biavo, blau
bica, Beige
bicchiere, Becher
bidello, Pedell
bieta, Beete
biondo, blond
biscotto, Zwieback
boccale, Pokal
bordo, Borte
borgo, Burg
borragine, Boretsch
borsa, Börse
bosco, Busch
bosso, Buchs
bossolo, Büchse
bottega, Bottich
bozzetto, } Posse
bozzo,
bracciatello, Bretzel
bracco, Bracke
brache, Bruch (3)
brando, Brand
brodo, Brot
bruno, braun
brusco, barsch
bucare, bauchen
buccina, Posaune
buffettare, } rüffen
buffo,
burro, Butter

cacio, Käse
cadenza, Schanze
cadôm (Bologn.), Kalkbaunen
cafura, Kampfer
camamilla, Kamille
camello, Kamel
camera, Kammer
camerata, Kamerad
camicia, Hemd
camminata, Kemenate
camozza, Gemse
campana, Glocke
canella, Kanel
canfora, Kampfer
cantaro, Zentner
canto, Kante
capuccio, } Kappes,
Kapuze
carato, Karat
cardo, Karte
carpione, Karpfen
carvi, Karbe
castagna, Kastanie
cavezzone, Kappzaum
cavoli rape, Kohlrabi
cavolo, Kohl
cece, Kicher
cedola, Zettel
censo, Zins

cerveta, Kriekente
cerfoglio, Kerbel
cesoje, Schere (1)
cetera, Zither
chioccia, } Glucke
chiocciare,
chiostro, Kloster
chiusa, Klause
chollera, Koller (2)
cifra, Ziffer
cinta, Zent
ciovetta, Schuhu
cipolla, Zwiebel
circo, } Zirkel
circolo,
ciriegia, Kirsche
citra, Zither
cizza, Zitze
codatremola, Wachstelze
coltra, Koller 2
composto, Kumpest
compra, } Grempelmarkt
comprare,
coniglio, Kaninchen
conocchia, Kunkel
contrada, Gegend
coppa, Kopf
coracino, Karausche
corniolo, Kornelle
costo, Kost (1)
cotogna, Knitte
cotta, Kot (1), Rohr, Kutte
cerescione, Kresse
creta, Kreide, Seide
croccia, } Krücke
crocco,
crompare, Grempelmarkt
cucina, Küche
cucuzza, Kürbis
cuffin, Kopf
cuocere, kochen
cnoco, Koch
cupola, Kuppel
cuscino, Kissen
cutretta, Wachstelze

damasto, Damast
dannare, verdammen
danzare, Tanz
dar presa, Preis
dattilo, Dattel
decano, Dechant
desco, Tisch
diamante, Demant
digrignare, greinen
donna, Frau
dozzina, Dutzend
droga, Droge
druda, drudo, traut

elmo, Helm (1)

empiastro, Pflaster
ermellino, Hermelin

fagiano, Fasan
falbala, Falbel
falbo, fahl
falcone, Falke
saldistorio, falten
fallire, fehlen
falso, falsch
fata, Fee
favonio, Föhn
feltro, Filz
festa, Fest
fiadone, Fladen
fianco, Flanke, Gelenk
fiasco, Flasche
fico, Feigwarze
fiera, Feier
figa, feige
fino, fein
finocchio, Fenchel
finta, Finte
fiore, Florin
flauto, Flöte
forbici, Schere (1)
formaggio, Käse
franco, frank
frangia, Franse
frasche, Fratze
fresco, frisch
fuga, Fuge
furetto, Frettchen

gabbia,
gabbinolo, } Käfig
gaggia,
gaggio, wett
galanga, Galgant
galea, } Gelle
galeotta,
galla, Galle (2)
gatto, Katze
Gazari, Ketzer
gazza, Elster
gherone, Gehren
ghindare, Winde
giaco, Jack
giga, Geige
girfalco, Geier
giubba, Joppe
giubilare, jubeln
ginoco, Juks
giuppa, Joppe
golfo, Golf
gonfalone, Fahne
gramo, gram
grappa, Krapfen (2)
grattare, tratzen
greppia, Krippe
greto, Grieß

grillo, } Greif
griffone,
grigio, greis
grillo, Grille
grimaldello, Dietrich
griso, greis
grosso, Groschen
grotta, Gruft
gruzzo, Grütze
guadare, waten
guado, Waid, waten
guai, } weh
guajo,
gualcare, walken
gualchiera, walken
guancia, Wange
guardare, Wart
guarentire, } gewähren
guarento,
guarnire, wahren
guerra, wirr
guisa, Weise
guitarra, Zither

incanto, Gant
inchiostro, Tinte
ingombro, Kummer
insalata, Salat
intonicare,
intonicato, } tünchen
intonico,
isola, Insel
isopo, Ysop
izza, Hitze

lacca, Lache
laccio, Latz
laido, Leid
lancia, Lanze
landa, Land
lasco, Äsche (2) lasch
lasso, laß
lasto, Last
lastrico, Estrich
latta, Latte
lattovaro, Latwerge
lauro, Lorbeer
lavagna, Lei
lavendola, Lavendel
leccare, lecken (1)
lega, Meile
lesina, Ahle
lesto, List
levistico, Liebstöckel
limosina, Almosen
lira, Leier
lista, Leiste (1), Liste
liuto, Laute
loggia, Laube
loja, Lauer
lotto, Los
luchina, Lug

INDEX.

luna, Laune
luna di miele, Flitter
lunedì, Montag

madreperla, Perlmutter
maestro, Meister
Maggio, Mai
magon, ⎫
magone, ⎭ Magen
magro, mager
magun, Magen
majo, Male
majorana, Majoran
maledire, maledeien
malva, Malve
mandola, Mandel (2)
mangano, Mange
mantello, Mantel
marca, Mark (1)
marese, Marſch, Moraſt
marga, Mergel
mariscalco, Marſchall
marmotta, Murmeltier
martirio, Marter
martora, Marder
maschera, Maske
mattino, Mette
matto, matt
medico, Arzt
mercato, Markt
mescere, miſchen
messa, Meſſe
mezzana, Beſanmaſt
miele (luna di m.), Flitter
miglia, ⎫
miglio, ⎭ Meile
milza, Milz
monaco, Mönch
moro, Mohr
mostarda, Moſtert
mosto, Moſt
mostra, Muſter
muffo, Muff (2)
mulinaro, Müller
mulino, Mühle

nabisso, Nobiskrug
nappo, Napf
nastro, Neſtel
nespola, Miſpel
niffo, Schnabel
nona, None
nonna, ⎫
nonno, ⎭ Nonne
norte, Nord

ocra, Oker
oleandro, Oleander
ora, Uhr
orda, Horde
organo, Orgel

ostrica, Auſter
ovate, Watte

pacco, Pack (1)
pagano, Heide (2)
palafreno, Pferd
palco, Balken
palizzata, Palliſade
panca, Bank
pancia, ⎫
panciera, ⎭ Panzer
pantofola, Pantoffel
papa, Papſt
pappa, Pappe
pappagallo, Papagei
parco, Pferch
parrochia, ⎫
parroco, ⎭ Pfarre
partita, Partei
passare, paſchen
pasta, Paſtete
patata, Kartoffel
patrino, Pate, Vetter
pausa, Pauſe
pavone, Pfau
pece, Pech
pedante, Pedant
pellegrino, Pilger
pelliccia, Pelz
peluzzo, Plüſch
pena, Pein
pentecoste, Pfingſten
pepe, Pfeffer
pera, Birne
perla, Perle
pesca, Pfirſich
piaga, Plage
pianca, Planke
pianta, Pflanze
piastrello, Pflaſter
piatto, platt
piazza, Platz (1)
picca, Pic
piè d'oca, Gänſerich
piliere, Pfeiler
pillola, Pille
piluccare, pflücken
pincione, Fink
pioppo, Pappel (2)
pipillare, piepen
pipita, Pips
pisciare, piſſen
piva, Pfeife
poleggio, Polei
polso, Puls
polvere, Pulver
pomice, Bims
pomo, Pomeranze
porcellana, Porzellan
porto, Port
posta, ⎫
posto, ⎭ Poſt

potare, impfen
potassa, Pott
pozza, ⎫
pozzo, ⎭ Pfütze
prebenda, Pfründe
predicare, predigen
prence, Prinz
presa, Preis
prete, Prieſter
prevosto, Propſt
prezzare, preiſen
prezzo, Preis
propaggine, pfropfen
prova, Probe
provare, prüfen
provenda, Pfründe
prugna, Pflaume
pulpito, Pult
punto, bunt
punzona, Bunzen

quadrello, ⎫
quadro, ⎭ Quader
quaglia, Wachtel
quartana, Kartaune
quarto, Quart
quarzo, Quarz
quintale, Zentner

rabarbaro, Rhabarber
racimolo, Roſine
rada, Rhede
raja, Roche (1)
ramponzolo, Rapunzel
raucare, ⎫
ranco, ⎭ renken
rangifero, Rennier
raspo, Rapp
ratto, Ratte
razza, Raſſe
recare, reden
rendita, Rente
ricco, reich
riga, ⎫
rigoletto, ⎭ Riege
rima, Reim
risina, Ries
riso, Reis (1)
roba, Raub
rocca, Rocken
rodomontata, Rodomonte, ⎫ Rodomontade
rosa, Roſe
rosso, Rauſchgelb
rotolo, Rolle
ruba, ⎫
rubare, ⎭ Raub
ruca, ⎫
ruchetta, ⎭ Raute
rullare, ⎫
rullo, ⎭ Rolle

ruta, Raute

sabbato, Samstag
sacco, Sack
sagire, ſetzen
sagrestano, Sigriſt
sala, Saal
salata, Salat
salma, Saum (2)
sandalo, Sandel
sapone, Seife
sardella, ⎫
sardina, ⎭ Sardelle
satureja, Saturei
scabino, Schöffe
scacchi (a), ſchachig
scacco, Schach
scaffale, Scheffel
scaglia, Schale
scalco, Schalk
scandola, Schindel
scaraffare, ſchröpfen
scarmuccia, Scharmützel
scarlatto, Scharlach
scarpa, ſcharf
scartata, Schartete
scatola, Schachtel
scellino, Schilling
schermire, ⎫
schermo, ⎭ ſchirmen
scherzare, Scherz
schiaffo, Schlappe (2)
schiarea, Scharlei
schiavo, Sklave
schiena, Schienbein
schiera, Schar (2)
schifo, Schiff
schineco, Schinken
schiniere, Schienbein
schippire, ſchleifen
schiuma, Schaum
schivare, Scheu
schizzo, Skizze
sciabla, Sabel
sciamito, Samt
sciarpa, Schärpe
scito, ſchelten
scodella, Schüſſel
scorbuto, Scharbock
scoss (Lomb.), Schoß (3)
scutolare, Schutt
scotta, Schote (2)
scotto, Schoß (2)
scrigno, Schrein
sdrajarsi, ſtreun
secchin, Seibel
secco, vino, Sekt
seda (Nor. It.), Seibe
segno, Segen
segolo, Sichel
semola, Semmel

2 E

432 INDICE

nena, Senestaum
senno, Sinnen
sostiere, Sechzer
seta, Seide
settimana, Woche
sgabello, Schemel
sghembo, schlimm
sgneppa, Schnepfe
sgraffiare, schraffieren
sguancio, Schwank
sgnrare, scheuern
sicuro, sicher
signora,, -e, Herr
siniscalco, Seneschall
slitta, Schlitten
smacco, Schmach
smalto, Schmalte, schmelzen
smalzo, Schmalz
smeriglio, Schmergel
smeriglione, }Schmerl
smerlo, }
snello, schnell
socco, Socke
soglia, Sohle (1), (2)
solajo, }Söller
solare, }
soldato, }Sold
soldo, }
solzia, Sulze
sorta, Sorte
spada, Spaten
spanna, Spanne
sparagio, Spargel
sparaviere, Sperber
spasso, Spaß
spato, Spat
spaziare, spazieren
specchio, Spiegel
speglio, Spiegel
spelda, }Spelt
spelta, }
spendere, Speise, Spende
spesa, Speise
spezieria, Spezerei
spiare, spähen
spito, Spieß (2)

spillo, Spilling
spione, Spähen
sportula, Sportelin
springare, springen
sprizzare, spritzen
sprone, Sporn
spruzzare, spritzen
spuntare, }Spund
spuntone, }
spuola, Spule
squadrone, Schwadron
squassacoda, Wachstelze
squilla, Schelle
squillare, Schall
stacca, Stalen
staffa, Stapfe
staffetta, Stapfe
stagno, Zinn
stalla, }
stallo, }Stall
stallone, }
stampa, }stampfen
stampare, }
stanga, Stange
stato, Staat
stecca, }stecken
stecco, }
stendardo, Standarte
stinco, Schinken
stivale, Stiefel
stocco, Stock
stoffa, Stoff
stolto, stolz
stoppare, Stöpfel
stoppio, Stoppel
storione, Stör
stormo, Sturm
straccare, strecken
strada, Straße
strale, Strahl
strappare, straff
stregghia, }Striegel
streglia, }
strozza, }Drossel (2)
strozzare, }
struzzo, Strauß
stucco, Stück
stufa, Stube

stufare, Stube
suolo, Sohle (2)

tabacco, Tabak
taccola, Dohle
taccuino (Milan.), Almanach
taglia, }
tagliare, }Teller
tagliere, }
talero, Thaler
tanghero, Zange
tappeto, }Teppich
tappezzare, }
targa, Zarge
tartufo, Kartoffel, Trüffel
tartufolo, Kartoffel
tasca, Tasche
tasso, Dachs
tastare, tasten
tattera, Zotte (1)
tavola, Tafel
tazza, Tasse
tegghia, }Ziegel
tegola, }
tenda, Zelt
terno, Terne
terrazzo, Traß
tetta, }Zitze
tettare, }
tinta, Tinte
titolo, Titel
tonfano, Tümpel
tonica, tünchen
tonno, Thunfisch
toppo, Zopf
torba, Torf
torre, Turm
torso, Dorsche
tortora, Turteltaube
tovaglia, Zwehle
tratta, Tratte
trattare, trachten
tregua, tren
trescare, dreschen
trillare, trillern
trincare, trinken

trionfo, Trumpf
tromba, }Trommel
trombetta, }
trono, Thron
trotto, Trott
truogo, Trog
truppa, Trupp
tufo, Tuff
tulipa, }Tulpe
tulipano, }

uracano, Orkan
urto, hurtig

veccia, Wicke (1)
vernice, Firnis
versa (Lomb.), }Wirverzotta, }sching
vescovo, Bischof
vespro, Vesper
viola, Fiedel
violetta, Veilchen
visciola, Weichsel
visiera, Visier
vivajo, Weiher

zaffo, Zapfe
zafferano, Safran
zatta, }
zattera, }Zotte (1)
zazza, }
zazzera, }
zecca, Zecke
zendado, }Zindel
zendale, }
zenzero, }Ingwer
zenzovero, }
zettovario, Zitwer
zezzolo, Zitze
zibellino, Zobel
zitta, Zitze
zoticacco, }
zotichezza, }Zote
zotico, }
zucchero, Zucker
zucchero candito, Zuckerland
zuppa, Suppe

FRENCH.

h mont, Düne
abbé, Abt
able, Albe (2)
agace, Elster
aire, Ähren
alarme, Alarm, Lärm
alchimie, Alchimie

alcôve, Alkoven
alêne, Ahle
alize, Erle
almanach, Almanach
alun, Alaun
amande, Mandel (2)
ambassade, Amt

anche, Enkel (1)
ancolie, Aglei
ancre, Anker (1)
âne, Esel
anis, Anis
août, August
arbalète, Armbrust

archer, Hatschier
are, Ar
arlequin, Harlekin
Arras, Rasch
artiste, Arzt
as, As
asperge, Spargel

INDEX.

aire, Estrich
auberge, Herberge
aumône, Almosen
aumuce, \
aumusse, } Mütze
aune, Elle
aurone, Aberraute
autruche, Strauß (3)
aventure, Abenteuer
avoué, Vogt
avril, April

babiller, papp In
bâbord, Backbord
babouin, Pavian
bac, bad
bachelier, Hagestolz
baie, Bai (1), (2)
bailif, \
bailli, } Ballei
bal, Ball (3)
balle, \
ballon, } Ball (2), Ballen
ban, Bann
banc, Bank, Bankett
bande, Bande, Band
bannière, Banner,
  Panier
banque, Bank
banquet, Bankett
bar, Vahre
barbeau, Barbe
barbier, Barbier
baron, Baron
baroque, Brockperle
barque, Barke
barre, Barre
barrette, Barett
bassin, Becken
baste, Bastard
bastion, Bastei
bât, \
bâtard, } Bastard
bâtir, Bastei
Baudouin, bald
baume, Balsam
bazar, Bazar
beaupré, Bug
bec, Bick
bec-d'oie, Gänserich
bêche, Bide
bedeau, Büttel, Pedell
belette, Bilch
bélier, \
bélibre, } Bellhammel
Belin, /
benne, Benne
berline, Berline
beton, Blest
bette, Beete
beurre, Butter
bible, Bibel

biche, Petze
bidre, Bahre, Bier
bièvre, Biber
bigot, bigott
billet, Bill
biscuit, Zwieback
bise, Biese
blanc, blank
bleu, blau
bloc, Bloc
blond, blond
bloquer, Block
boc, Bock
bocal, Pokal
boie, Boi
bois, Busch
bolet, Pilz
bombasin, Bombasin
bomerie, Boden
bonde, \
bondon, } Spund
bord, Borte
bordel, Bordell
border, bordieren
bosse, Bosse
bosseler, bosseln (2)
bossette, Büchse
botte, Bütte
bouc, Bock
boucle, Buckel (1)
boude, Boje
boulevard, Bollwerk
bouracan, Berkan
bourg, Burg
bourrache, Boretsch
bourse, Börse
bousiller, pfuschen
bouteille, Butte (2)
boutique, Bottich
brachet, Brack
braies, Bruch (3)
brailler prahlen
brandon, Brand
braque, Brack
bras, Brasse
brasser, Brasse
brave, brav
brèche, Bresche
brême, Brassen
breuil, Brühl
brise, Brise
broche, \
brochet, } Hecht
brn, Kraut
brun, braun
brusque, barsch
buer, bauchen
bufle, Büffel
buis, Buchs
bulle, Bulle (3)
bulo (Vosges), Pilz
bure, Bühre

busard, Bußaar
buste, Büste
butin, Beute (2)

cabane, \
cabinet, } Kabuse
câble, Kabel (1)
cabus, Kappes
cage, Käfig
calamine, Galmei
cajute, Kajüte
calandre, Kalender
calfater, kalfatern
calice, Kelch
calmande, Kalmank
calme, Kalm
camarade, Kamerad
cambuse, Kabuse
camisole, Kamisol
camphre, Kampfer
canelle, Kanel
canette, Kanne
cannelle, Kanel
canot, Kahn
cant, Kante
cape, Kappe
capot, kaput
capuce, Kapuze
carassin, Karausche
carat, Karat
carpe, Karpfen
carraque, Krade
carreau, Quader
carriole, Karre
carte, Karte
carvi, Karbe
cauchemar, Mahr
causer, losen
cavecon, Kappzaum
cédule, Zettel
céleri, Sellerie
cercelle, Kriekente
cercle, Zirkel
cercueil, Sarg
cerfeuil, Kerbel
cerise, Kirsche
chacal, Schakal
chafaut, Schafott
chaîne, Kette (2)
chalemie, Schalmei
chaloupe, Schaluppe
chalumeau, Schalmei
chambre, Kammer
chameau, Kamel
chamoisé, Gemse
chamoiser, Sämischleder
champion, Kampf
chance, Schanze (1)
chancre, Kanker (2)
  Schanker
chapo, \
chapeau, } Kappe

chapelle, Kapelle (2)
chaperon, Kappe
char, Karre
chardon, Karde
charrue, Karch
Chartreuse, Karthause
chat, Katze
châtaigne, Kastanie
châtier, kasteien
chaudin (S.W. Fr.),
  Kaldaunen
chauve, kahl
chélidoine, Schellkraut
cheminée, Kamin, Kemenate
chemise, Hemd
chiche, Kicher
chiffre, Ziffer
Chivert, Hemd
choc, Schaukel
chose, Losen
chou, Kohl
choucroute, Kraut
chouette, Schuhu
chou-rabe, Kohlrabi
ciboule, Zwiebel
cinabre, Zinnober
cingler, Segel
ciseaux, Schere (1)
citron, Zitrone
clair, klar
cloche, Glocke
clocheman, \ Bellhammel
clocman, / mel
cloître, Kloster
coche, Kutsche
coffre, Koffer
coiffe, Kopf
coing, Quitte
colère, Koller (2)
collier, Koller (1)
connétable, Marschall
connin, Kaninchen
contrée, Gegend
coq, Küchlein
coquelourde, Küchenschelle
corde, \
cordelle, } Kerbe
corinthe, Korinthe
cornouille, Kornelle
côte, Küste
cotillon, Kot (1)
coton, Kattun
cotte, Kot (1), Kotze,
  Kutte
coucou, Kuckuck
coupelle, Kapelle (2)
couple, \
coupole, } Kuppel
courbe, Kurbe
cousin, Kissen

coût, Kost (1)
coûter, kosten (1)
coutre, Küster
crabe, Krabbe
craie, Kreide
crampon, Krampe
crèche, Krippe
crèque, Krieche
cresson, Kresse (1)
crevette, Krebs
croc, Krücke
crosse, Krücke
croupe, Kruppe,
croûte, Kruste
cruche, Krug (1)
cuire, kochen
cuisine, Küche
cuivre, Kupfer
cymaise, Sims

dague, Degen (2)
daim,   } Damhock
dain,
dais, Tisch
damas, Damast
dame, Dambrett, Frau
damner, verdammen
danser, Tanz
datte, Dattel
déchirer, Scharteisen
décombres, Kummer
déguerpir, werfen
demain, Morgen (1)
dérober, Raub
détail, Teller
deux, Daus
diamant, Demant
distrait, zerstreut
dogue, Dogge
double, doppelt
doublet, doppeln
douille, Tülle
douve, Daube
douzaine, Dutzend
doyen, Dechant
dragon, Drache
drogue, Droge
drôle, drollig
dru, traut
dune, Düne
durer, dauern (1)

ébaucher, pauschen
èbe, Ebbe
éblouir, blöde
écaille, } Schale
écale,
écarlate, Scharlach
échafaut, Schafott
échalotte, Schalotte
échandole, Schindel
échanson, Schenk

écharpe, Schärpe
échec, Schach, schedig
échevin, Schöffe
échine, Schienbein
échoppe, Schuppen
écluse, Schleuse
écot, Schoß (1), (2)
écrevisse, Krebs
écrin, Schrein
écuelle, Schüssel
écume, Schaum
écurer, scheuern
écureuil, Eichhorn
élan, Elentier
électuaire, Latwerge
élingue, Schlinge
élinque, schlenkern
émail, schmelzen
émerillon, Schmerl
empan, Spanne
empereur, Kaiser
emplâtre, Pflaster
encan, Gant
encombrer, Kummer
encre, Tinte
enseigne, Segen
enter, impfen
épeautre, Spelt
épée, Spaten
épeiche, Specht
épeler, Beispiel
éperon, Sporn
épervier, Sperber
épier, } spähen
épion,
éplucher, pflücken
épois, Spieß (2)
épreuve, prüfen, Probe
équiper, Schiff
escabeau, } Schemel
escabelle,
escadron, Schwadron
escalin, Schilling
escarboucle, Karfunkel
escarmouche, Scharmützel
escarpe, } scharf
oscarper,
esclave, Sklave
espion, spähen, Spion
esquif, Schiff
est, Osten
estampe, stampfen
estourgeon, Stör
étain, Zinn
étal, } Stall
étalon,
étamper, stampfen
étape, Stapel
état, Staat
étau, Stall
étendard, Standarte

étiquette, stecken
étoffe, Stoff
étouble, Stoppel
étoupper, Stöpsel
étrain, Stroh
étrée, Straße
étrille, Striegel
étui, Stauche
étuve, } Stube
étuver,
évêque, Bischof

fable, Fabel
faillir, fehlen
faisan, Fasan
fait, seit
falaise, Felsen
falbala, Falbel
fanon, Fahne
faucon, Falle
fauteuil, falten
fauve, fahl
faux, falsch
fée, Fee
feinte, Finte
fenouil, Fenchel
fête, Fest, feit
fétiche, Fetisch
feurre, Futter
feutre, Filz
figue, Feige
fin, fein
flacon, Flasche
flamberge, Flamberg
flamme, Flicie
flan, Flaben
flanc, Flanke
fléau, Flegel
flèche, Flitzbogen
flin, Flinte
flotte, Flotte
flou, flau, lau
flûte, Flöte
foire, Feier, Messe
fondôsse, Trichter
forêt, Forst
foudre, Fuder
fourreau, Futter
frac, Frack
frais, frisch
framboise, Brombeere
franc, frank
frange, Franse
frasques, Fraze
fret, Fracht
frise, Fries
friser, frisieren
froc, Frack
fromage, Käse
furet, Frettchen

gage, weil

gai, jäh
galanga, Galgant
galiasse, } Selte
galion,
galop, Galopp
gant, Gant
garant, } gewähren
garantir,
garder, Wart
garer, } wahren
garnir,
gaspiller, kostspielig
gauche, weil
gaude, Wau
gaufre, Waffel
gazon, Wasen
gelée, Gallerte
genêt, Ginst
gentil, Geschlecht
geôle, Käfig
gerbe, Garbe (1)
gerfaut, Geier
gibel, Giebel (2)
gigue, Geige
gingembre, Ingwer
giron, Gehren
glacier, Gletscher
glousser, Glucke
glouteron, Klette
golfe, Golf
gonfalon, Fahne
gourde, Kürbis
grain, Gran
grappin, Krapfen (2)
gratter, kratzen
gré, Grab
grêle, } Grieß
grès,
griffe, greifen
griffon, Greif
grippe, Grippe
gripper, greifen
gris, greis
gros, Groschen
grosse, Gros
grotte, Gruft
groupe, Kropf
gruau, Grütze
gué, waten
guède, Wald
guêpe, Wespe
guerre, wirr
guimpe, Wimpel
guinder, Winde
guise, Weise
guitare, Zither
gypse, Gips

hache, Hippe (1)
haillon, Hader (2)
haire, Haar (2)
halener, Essig

INDEX.

halle, Halle
hallebarde, Hellebarde
hanap, Napf
hanter, hantieren
happe, Hippe (1)
harangue, Ring
hardi, hart
hareng, Häring
harlequin, Harlekin
harpe, Harfe
hase, Hase
hâte, Hast
haubert, Hals
heaume, Helm (1)
héraut, Herold
hermine, Hermelin
hêtre, Heister
heure, Uhr
heurt, hurtig
hisser, hissen
hochequeue, Bachstelze
homme, man
honnir, } Höhnen
honte, }
horde, Horde
houblon, Hopfen
houx, Hulst
huile, Öl
huître, Auster
hutte, Hütte

if, Eibe
île, Insel
ivoire, Elfenbein

jale, Gelte
jaque, Jacke
jardin, Garten
jupe, } Joppe
jupon, }

Labourd, Labberdan
lacet, Latz
lâche, lasch
laid, Leid
laie, Lehne (2)
lame, Lahn
lampe, Lampe
lamproie, Lamprete
lande, Land
lanterne, Laterne
lapin, Lampe
las, Laß
laste, Last
latte, Latte
laurier, Lorbeer
lécher, lecken (1)
lendemain, Morgen (2)
lest, Ballast, Last
leste, List
leurre, Luder

levain, }
lever,   } Hefe
levûre, }
lice, Litze
lieue, Meile
lion, Löwe
lippe, Lippe
liste, Leiste (1), Liste
livèche, Liebstöckel
livrer, liefern
loge, Laube
lorgner, }
lorgnon, } -lauern
lorgnette, }
lot, } Los
loterie, }
loup-garou, Werwolf
louvoyer, lavieren
lundi, Montag
lune, Laune
lune de miel, Flitter
luquer (Norm.), lügen
luth, Laute
lyre, Leier

maçon, Metze (1)
madré, Maser
mai, Mai, Maie
maigre, mager
maire, Meier
mais, Mais
maison, Metzger
maître, Meister
malt, Malz
manière, Manier
manteau, Mantel
maquereau, mäkeln, Makele
marais, Marsch, Morast
marche, Mark (1)
marché, Markt
maréchal, Marschall
marjolaine, Majoran
marmotte, Murmeltier
marne, Mergel
marque, Marke
mars, März
martre, Marder
martyre, Marter
masque, Maske
mat, matt
matelas, Matratze
matelot, Matrose
matin (matines), Mette
maudire, maledeien
mauve, Malve
médecin, Arzt
mêler, mischen
mère-perle, Perlmutter
mésange, Meise
messe, Messe
meunier, Müller

meurtre, Mord
meute, Meute (1), (2)
miel, Flitter
mille, Meile
mine, Miene
mizaine, Besanmast
moine, Mönch
momerie, Mumme (2)
mont (à), Düne
montre, Muster
more, Mohr
mort, Mord
mortier, Mörter, Mörtel
mousette, Muff (2)
moufle, Muff (1)
moulin, Mühle
mousse, Moos
mout, Most
moutarde, Mostert
moutier, Münster
mouton, Hammel, Bellhammel
mue, } Mause
muer, }

naïf, naiv
nèfle, Mispel
net, nett
neveu, Neffe
nippe, Nipfsache
noue, None
nonnain, } Nonne
nonne, }
nord, Nord
note, Note
nouilles, Nudel

ocre, Ocker
oeuf, Ei
offrir, opfern
oléandre, Oleander
on, man
oncle, Onkel
opé, impfen
orange, Pomeranze
ordalie, Urtel
orgue, Orgel
ouais, weh
ouate, Watte
oublie, Oblate
ouest, Westen
ouragan, Orkan
ouvrage à bosse, Posse

païen, Heide (2)
paire, Paar
pal, Pfahl
palais, Palast
palefroi, Pferd
pallisade, Pallisade
pamphlet, Pamphlet
panse, Panzer

pantoufle, Pantoffel
paon, Pfau
pape, Papst
papier, Papier
paquet, Pack (1)
parc, Pack, Pferch
paroisse, Pfarre
parrain, Pate
part, wider
partie, Partei
passe-dix, Pasch
passe-poil, Paspel
passer, passieren, rassen (1), (2), paschen
pâte, }
pâté, } -Pastete
pâtée, }
patte, Pfote
pause, Pause
peaux chamoisées, Sämischleder
pêche, Pfirsich
pédant, Pedant
pèlerin, Pilger
pelisse, Pelz
pelletier, belzen
peluche, Plüsch
pentecôte, Pfingsten
pépie, Pips
pépier, piepen
perle, Perle
peuple, Pöbel
peuplier, Pappel (2)
pile, } Pfeiler
pilier, }
pilote, Pilot
pilule, Pille
pimprenelle, Bibernelle, Pimpernelle
pinceau, Pinsel
pinçon, Fink
pipe, Pfeife
pique, Pik, Schürre
piquenique, Picknick
pisser, pissen
placard, Placken
place, Platz (1)
plaie, Plage
plan, Plan
planche, Planke
planchette, Blankscheit
plante, Pflanze
plaque, Placken
plat, platt, Platte
plâtre, Pflaster
poinçon, Bunzen
pois, Erbsen
poison, Gift
poivre, Pfeffer
poix, Pech
pomme de terr., Kartoffel

pompe, Pomp, Bombast
poncer, rauschen
port, Port
poste, Post
pot, } Pott
potasse,
poteau, Pfosten
poudre, Puder, Pulver
pouliot, Polei
pouls, Puls
poupée, } Puppe
poupon,
prébende, Pfründe
prêcher, predigen
presse, Presse
prêtre, Priester
prévôt, Profst
prince, Prinz, König
prise, Preis, Prise
priser, preisen
prix, Preis
prouver, prüfen
provende, Pfründe
provin, pfropfen
prueve (E.Fr.), prüfen
prune, Pflaume
puits, Pfütze
pupitre, Pult

quaille, Wachtel
quart, Quart
quartz, Quarz
quenouille, Kunkel
quintal, Zentner
quitte, quitter, quitt

race, Rasse
rade, Rhede
radis, Rettich
raffer, raffen
raffiner, feim
raie, Roche (1), Roß (2)
raisin, Rosine
râle, Ralle
rame, Ries
rampe, Rampe
rance, ranzig
rang, Rang, Ring
rangier, Renntier
râpe, Rapp, Rappe (3),
  Raspe, Rappier
râpes, Rappe (2)
rapier, Rappier

rapontique, Rhabarber
rare, rar
rat, Ratte
rébus, Rebus
remarquer, Marke
renne, Renntier
rente, Rente
reste, Rest
rêver, rappeln
rhubarbe, Rhabarber
rhum, Rum
riche, reich
rime, Reim
riper, reiben
riz, Reis (1)
robe, Raub
roc, Roche (2)
rochet, Rock
rodomontade, Rodo-
  montade
rôle, Rolle
rond, rund
roquette, Rauke
rose, Rose
roseau, Rohr
rosse, Roß (1)
rôtir, Rost (1)
rouler, Rolle
rubrique, Rubrik
rue, Raute (1)
rum, Rum

sabre, Säbel
sac, Sack
sacré, sackerlot
sacristain, Sigrist
safran, Safran
sage-femme, Hebamme
saisir, setzen
salle, Saal
samedi, Samstag
sandal, Sandel
sarcelle, Kriekente
sarriette, Saturei
sauge, Salbei
saule, Salweide
sauvage, wild
savon, Seife
scorbut, Scharbock
seigneur, Herr
semaine, Woche
semaque, Schmacke
semoule, Semmel
senau, Schnaue

séné, Senesbaum
sénéchall, Seneschall
servant, Scharwenzeln
setier, Sechter
seuil, Sohle (2)
simple, Simpel
smalt, Schmalte
soc, Sod
socle, Sockel
soie, Seide
soldat, } Sold
solde,
sole, Sohle (1), (2)
somme, Saum (2)
sot,
sotie, sottie, } Jete
sottise,
sou, Sold
souffler, } puffen
soufflet,
soupe, Suppe
spath, Spat
sucre, Zucker, Zuckerland
sur, sauer
sûr, sicher

tabac, Tabak
table, Tafel
taie, Zieche
taillor, } Teller
tailloir,
taisson, Dachs
tante, Tante
tape, Zapfe
tapis, Terrich
targe, Zarge
tarir, Darre
tarte, Torte
tasse, Tasse
tâter, tasten
taudis, } Zelt
tente,
tête, Kopf
teter,
tetin, } Zitze
teton,
tette,
thé, Thee
thon, Thunfisch
tique, Zecke
titre, Titel
tonne, } Tonne
tonneau,
tort, Tort

touaille, Zwehle
toucher, Tusche
touer, Tau (1)
toupet, Zopf
tour, Turm
tourbe, Torf
tourner, turnen
tourtereau, } Turtel-
tourtre,   taube
trailler, treideln
traiter, trachten
trâle, Drossel (1)
trèfle, Treff
tresse, Tresse
trève, treu
trinquer, trinken
triomphe, Trumpf
trôler, trollen
trompe, } Trommel
trompette,
trône, Thron
trot, } Trott
trotter,
trouble, Trubel
trousse, Troß
truffe, Trüffel
tuf, Tuff
tuile, Ziegel
tuyau, Tülle

vague, Woge
vaisseau, Schiff
valise, Felleisen
vendange, Franse
vent, wittern
vêpre, Vesper
vernis, Firnis
vesce, Wicke
veste, Weste
vidame, Bizdom
vif, Quecksilber
ville, } Weiler
villier,
vinaigre, Essig
viole, Fiedel
violette, Veilchen
virelai, Firlefanz
visière, Visier
vivier, Weiher

zédoaire, Zitwer
zibeline, Zobel
zinc, Zink

INDEX.

ENGLISH
(Including Scotch).

a, ein
abbot, Abt
Aberdeen, Labberdan
above, oben
ache, Etel
acorn, Eder
acre, Acker
adder, Näter, Otter, Natter
after, Alter
aftermath, Mahd
again, gegen, entgegen
aghast, Geist
ails, Ähre
alb, Albe (1)
alcove, Alkoven
alder, Erle
alison, Ahle
all, all
almond, Maubel (2)
alms, Almosen
alone, allein
also, also
alum, Alaun
amelcorn, Amelmehl
among, mengen
an, ein
anchor, Anker (1), (2)
and, und
angel, Engel
angle, Angel
anis, Anis
ankle, Enkel (1)
answer, Antwort, schwören
ant, Ameise
anvil, salzen, Amboß
ape, Affe
apple, Appledore, } Apfel
arbalist, Armbrust
arch-, Erz-
ark, Arche
arm, Arm
army, Heer
arras, Rasch
arse, Arsch
as, als, also
ash, Esche
ashes, Asche (1)
ask, Eidechse, heischen
asker, Eidechse
asp, Espe
ass, Esel
asunder, sonder
atter, Eiter
auger, Näber
aware, gewahr

away, Weg
awfshots, Alp
awm, Ohm
awns, Ähne
ax(e), Axt
axle,
axle-tree, } Achse
aye, je

babble, pappeln
baboon, Pavian
baby, Bube
bac, Back
bachelor, Hagestolz
back, Back, Backbord, zurück
bacon, Bache
bailiff, Ballei
bait, beizen
baize, Bol
bake, backen
baker, Beck
bald, baar
baldrick, Belt
bale, Ballen
balk, Balken
ball, Ball (2)
ballast, Ballast
balm, Balsam
ban, Bann
band, Band
bang,
bangle, } Bengel
barb,
barbel, } Barbe
barbs, Borte (2)
bare, baar
barge, Barke
bark, Borke
barley, Barn, Gerste
barm, Bärme, barmherzig
barn, Barn
barracan, Berkan
barrow, Barch, Bahre
barse,
bass, } Barsch
bast, Bast
bat, Fledermaus
batch, backen
bath, Bath,
bathe, } Bad
bay, Bai (1), (2), beugen
baysalt, Boisalz
be, sein 2
be-, bei
beacon, Bake
beadle, Büttel

beaker, Becher
beam, Baum
bean, Bohne
bear, Bär (2), gebären, Bahre
beard, Bart
beastings, Biest
beat, Amboß, Beutel (1)
beaver, Biber
beck, Bach
beckon, Bake
become, bequem
bed, Bett, Beet
bee, Biene
beebread, Brot
beech, Buche
beer, Bier
beet, Beete
beetle, Beutel (1)
beff, baf
before, bevor
beg, bitten
begin, beginnen
behind, hinten
behoof, Behuf
belief, Glaube
bell, bellen, Bellhammel
bellows, Balg
bell-wether, Bellhammel
belly, Balg
belt, Belt
bench, Bank
bend, Band, binden
beneath, nieden
bent,
bentgrass, } Binse
Bentley, Binse
berry, Beere
beseech, suchen
besom, Besen
best, besser
betide, Zeitung
better, besser
betwixt, zwischen
bible, Bibel
bickiron, Bicke
bid, bieten, bitten
bide, bitten
bier, Bahre
biestings, Biest
bight, Bucht
bile, Beule
bilge, Bulge
bill, Bill, Bille
bin, Benne, Bühne
bind, binden
bing, Beige

birch, Birke
bird, Brut
bire, Bauer (1)
birth, Geburt
bishop, Bischof
bit, beißen
bitch, Petze
bite, beißen, Bissen
bitter, bitter
blab, plappern
black, Blackfisch
bladder, Blatter
blade, Blatt
blank, blank
blare, plärren
blast, blasen
blaze, blaß
bleak, bleich
bleat, blöken
bleed, Blut
blind, blind, blenden
blink, blinken
block, Block
blood, Blut
bloom,
blooth, } Blume
blossom,
blow, blähen, blühen, bläuen
blue, blau
blunder, klind
boar, Bär (3)
board, Bord, Bort
boat, Boot
bode, bieten
body, Bauch, Bottich, Rumpf
boil, Beule
bold, bald
bole, Bohle
bolster, Polster
bolt, Bolz
bombasine, Bombasin
bombast Bombast
bond, binden
bone, Bein
bone-ash, Asche (1)
book, Buch
boom, Baum
boon, bohnen
boose, Bause
boot,
boosy, } Beute (2), Buße
booth, Bude
booty, Bente (2)
borage, Boretsch
bordel, Bordell
bore, bohren

INDEX.

borough, Burg
borrow, borgen
bosh, Posse
bosom, Busen
bote, Buße
both, beide
bottom, }
bottomry, } Boden
bough, Bug
bought, Bucht
bouk, bauchen
bourn, Brunn
bouse, bausen
bow, biegen, Bogen
bower, Bauer (1)
bowl, Bolle (2), Bowle
bowsprit, Bugspriet
box, boren, Buchs, Büchse
boy, Bube
boyhood, -heit
brace, Brasse
brach, Bracke
brack, Brack, Brackwasser
brackish, Brackwasser
brain, Bräzen, Hirn
bramble, Brombeere
brand, Braud
brasse, Brassen
brawl, prahlen, brüllen
bread, Brot
break, brechen
bream, Brassen
breast, Brust
breath, Brodem
breech, }
breeches, } Bruch (3)
breed, Brut
breeze, Breme, Brise
brew, brauen
bridal,
bride, } Braut
bridegroom,
bridge, Brücke
bright, -bert
brim, verbrämen
brimstone, Brummen
bring, bringen
brink, Brink
brisket, Brößchen, Brausche
bristle, Borste
broad, breit
brood, Brut
brook, brauchen, Bruch (2)
broom, Brombeere, Ginst
broth, Brot
brothel, Bordell
brother, Bruder
brow, Braue
brown, braun

bruise, Braus, Brojam, larg
brush, Bürste
buck, Bock, bauchen, Bauch
buckmast, }
buckwheat, } Buche
buff, Büffel
buffet, puffen
build, Bude, Bild
bulb, Belle (1), Zwiebel
bulge, Bulge
bull, Bulle (1), (3)
bullfist, Bofist
bullock, Bulle (1)
bulwark, Bollwerk
bundle, Bündel
buoy, Boje
burden, Bürde
burial, bergen
burn, brennen
burr, Borste
burrow, Burg
burst, bersten
burthen, Bürde
bury, Berg, bergen, Burg
bush, Busch
buss, Bisse
but, Butte
butt, Bütte
butter, Butter
butterfly, Schmetterling
buxom, biegen
by, be-, bei

cabbage, Kappes
cabin, Kabuse
cable, Kabel (1)
caboose, Kabuse
caddow, Dohle
cage, Käfig
cake, Kuchen
calamanco, Kalmant
calf, Kalb
callow, kahl
calm, Kalm
can, Kanne, können
canker, Kanker (2)
cant, Kante, Gant
cap, Kappe
capon, Kapaun
car, Karre
caraway, Karbe
carbuncle, Karfunkel
care, Karfreitag, larg
carl, Kerl
carp, Karpfen
cart, Kratze (1)
carve, kerben
cat, }
caterwaul, } Kate

cellar, Keller
chafer, Käfer
chaff, Kaser, Spreu
chain, Kette (2)
chalk, Kalk
chamber, Kammer
champion, Kampf
chancel, Kanzel
chap, Kappe
chapman, kaufen
chary, karg
chastise, Lasteien
cheap, kaufen
checky, schekig
cheese, Käse
chervil, Kerbel
chest, Kiste
chestnut, Kastanie
chew, kauen
chiches, Kicher
chickpeas, Kicher
chicken, Küchlein
chill, kalt, kühl
chilver, Kalb
chimney, Kamin, Kemenate
chin, }
chinbone, } Kinn
chincough, keuchen
chints, }
chintz-cotton, } Zitz
choose, kiesen
chough, Dohle
Christmas, Messe
church, Kirche
churl, Kerl
churn, kernen
cipher, Ziffer
clamp, Klammer, Klampe
clang, }
clank, } Klang, klingen
clap, Klaff, klabastern
clash, klatsch
clay, Klei
clean, klein
clear, klar
cleat, Kloß
cleave, kleben, klieben
cleft, Kluft
clew, Knäuel
cliff, Klippe
clift, Kluft
climb, klimmen
cling, Klüngel
clink, klingen
clip, Klafter
cloam, Klei
clock, Glocke
clot, Kloß
clotbur, Klette
cloth, Kleid
clove, Knoblauch

clover, Klee
club, Kolben
club-foot, Klumpe
cluck, Glucke, Klucke
clump, Klumpe
coach, Kutsche
coal, Kohle
coast, Küste
coat, Kot (1), Kotze, kützchen
cock, Hahn, Henne, Küchlein
cold, kalt
cole, Kohl
colemouse, Kohle, Kohlmeise
comb, Kamm
comber, Kummer
come, kommen
comrade, Kamerad
cony, Kaninchen
cook, Koch
cool, kühl
coom, Kahm
coomb, Kumpf
coop, Kufe (2)
cooper, Küfer
cop, Kopf
cope, Kappe
copper, Kupfer
corb, Korb
cord, Korde
coriander, Koriander
cork, Kork
corn, Korn
cornelian-tree, Kornelle
Cornwall, welsch
cost, kosten (1)
cot, }
cottage, } Kot (1)
cotton, Kattun
couchgrass, Quecke
cough, keuchen
couple, Koppel
couth, Kund
cove, Koben
cow, Kuh
cower, kauern
crab, Krabbe
crack, krachen
cradle, Krätze (1), Wiege
craft, }
crafty, } Kraft
crag, Kragen
cramp, }
cramp-irons, } Krampe, Krampf
cranberry, Krammetsvogel
crane, Krammetsvogel, Kranich
craneberry, Krammetsvogel

INDEX.

crank, } krank, Kring
crankle,
craple, Krapfen (2)
cratch, Krippe
crate, Krätze
crave, Kraft
craw, Kragen
creak, krieksen
creep, kriechen
cress, Kresse (1)
crib, Krippe
crimple, Krampf, krumm
crinkle, krank, Kring
cripple, Krüppel
crisp, kahl
crop, Kropf
cross, Kreuz
crouch, kriechen
croup, Kruppe
crow, Krähe, krähen
crown, Krone
crucian, Karausche
crum, Krume
crumb, Krume
crump, } krumm
crumple,
crust, Kruste
crutch, Krücke
cuckoo, Kuckuck
cud, Köder
cudgel, Kugel
cup, Kopf
cushion, Kissen

daft, heftig
dag, Tau (2)
dale, Thal
dally, bahlen
dam, Damm
damascene, Zwetsche
damask, Zwetsche, Damast
damp, Dampf
dance, Tanz
dank, dumpf
dapper, tapfer
darling, teuer
date, Dattel
daughter, Tochter
daw, Dohle
dawn, Tag
day, Tag
dead, tot
deaf, taub
deal, Teil
dean, Dechant
dear, teuer
death, Tod.
deed, That
deem, -tum
deep, tief
deer, Tier

dell, Thal
den, Tenne
depth, tief
deuce, Daus
devil, Teufel
dew, Tau (2)
die, Tod
dike, Deich, Teich
dill, Dill
dimple, Tümpel
ding, bengeln
dip, tief
dish, Tisch
ditch, Teich
dive, tief, Taube
dizzy, Dusel, Thor (1)
do, thun
dock, Dock
dodder, Dotter (2)
doe, Damboch
dog, Dogge, Hund
doit, Deut
dole, Teil
dollar, Thaler
-dom, } -tum
doom,
dot, Dotter (1)
dough, Teig
doughty, tüchtig
dovecot, Kot (1)
dove, Taube
dowel, Döbel
down, Daune, Düne
dozen, Dutzend
drab, } Treber
draff,
dragon, Drache
drake, Ente
drake-fly, Drache
draw, tragen
dregs, Drusen, Treber
dream, Traum [Trauer
dreary, bauern (2),
drift, Trift
drink, trinken
drip, } Tripper
dripper,
drive, treiben
droll, } drollig
drollish,
drone, Drohne
drop, Tropfen
drought, trocken
drove, Trift
drunk, trunken
dry, trocken
dub, tief
duck, Ente, Tuch, tauchen
dull, toll
dumb, dumm
dun, dunkel
dung, Dung

dure, dauern (1)
dust, Dunst, Dust
Dutch, deutsch
dwarf, Zwerg

e-, ge-
Eames, Oheim
ear, Ähre, Lefze, Ohr, Öhr
earn, Ernte
earnest, Ernst
earth, Erde
east, Osten
Easter, Ostern
eat, essen
ebb, Ebbe
edge, Eck
Edward, Allod, Kobold
eel, Aal
egg, Ei
eider, } Eider
eiderdown,
eiderduck,
eight, acht
eils, Ähre
either, jeder, weder
eke, auch
elbow, Elle
elder, Holunder
electuary, Latwerge
eleven, elf
elf, Elf
elk, Elentier
ell, Elle
elm, Ulme
else, elend
emboss, bossein (2)
eme, Oheim
emmet, Ameise
emplaster, Pflaster
empty, einsig
end, Ende
endure, dauern (1)
enough, genug, ge-
ere, eher
eve, Abend
even, eben
evening, Abend, Morgen (1)
ever, immer
evil, übel
ewe, Aue, Schaf
eye, Auge
eyeball, Apfel
eyelid, Lid

fadge, fügen
fail, fehlen
fair, fegen
fairy, Fee
falcon, Falke
fall, fallen

fallow, fahl, Felge
false, falsch
falsehood, -heit
fan, Wanne
fane, Fahne
fang, fangen
far, fern
fare, fahren
farrow, Ferkel
fart, farzen
farthing, Pfennig, Schilling
fast, fasten, fest
fat, feist
father, Mutter, Vater
fathom, Faden
fay, Fee, fügen
fear, Gefahr, Furcht
feast, Fest
feather, Feder
fee, Vieh, Schatz
feed, Futter, Vater
feel, fühlen
fell, Fell
felly, Felge
felt, Filz
fennel, Fenchel
fern, Farn
ferret, Frettchen
ferry, Fähre
fetlock, Fuß
fetters, Fessel (1)
fever, Fieber
fey (Scot.), feige
fiddle, Fiedel
field, Feld
fiend, Feind
fifth, fünf
fight, fechten
fig-tree, Feige
file, Feile
fill, füllen
film, Fell
fin, Finne (1)
finch, Fink
find, finden
fine, fein
finger, Finger
fir, Föhre
fire, Feuer
fireboot, } Lufte
fire-bote,
firelock, Flinte
first, Fürst
fish, Fisch
fist, Faust
five, fünf
flag, Flagge
flail, Flegel
flask, Flasche
flat, flach
flat-footed, glatt

flatter, flattern
flawn, Fladen
flax, Flachs
flea, Floh
fleam, Fliete
fledge, flügge
flee, fliehen
fleece, Flies
fleet, fließen, Flotte, Floß
flesh, Fleisch
flew, flau
flick, Fleisch
flicker, flackern
flight, Flucht
flint, Flinte, Linse
flitch, Fled, Fleisch
flite, Fleiß
flitter, flattern
flittermouse, Fledermaus, Flitter
float, Floß
flock, Flocke
flood, Flut
flook,
flook-footed, } flach
floor, Flur
flounder, Flunder
flow, Flut
fluke, flach
flute, Flöte
flutter, flattern
fly, Fliege, fliegen
foal, Fohlen
foam, Feim, Schaum
fodder, Futer, Futter
foe, Fehde
fold, falten
-fold, -falt
folk, Volk
follow, folgen
food, Futter
foot, Fuß
for-, vor
for-, ver-
forbid, bieten
ford, Furt
forehead, Stirn
forget, vergessen
fork, Furke, Gabel
forth, fort
fortnight, Nacht
foster,
fosterbrother, } Futter
fother, Futer
foul, faul
four, vier
fowl, Vogel
fox, Fuchs
fraught, Fracht
freak, frech, Sprenkel (2)
freckle, Sprenkel (2)

froe, frei
freeze, frieren
freight, Fracht
fresh, frisch
fret, fressen
Friday, Freitag
friend, Freund
frieze, Fries
fright,
frighten, } Furcht
frisk, frisch
friz,
frizzle, } Fries
frock, Frosch, Frack
frog, Frosch
frolic, frohloden
from, fremd
frosk, Frosch
frost, Frost
full, voll
funk, Funke
furbelow, Falbel
furlong, Furche
furrow, Furche
further, fürder

gaggle, gackern
gait, Gasse
galangal, Galgant
gall, Galle (2)
gall-oak, Gallapfel
gallows, Galgen
gallow-tree, Gallapfel
gander, Gans
gang,
gangway, } Gang
gangweek,
gannet, Gans
gaol, Käfig
gape, gaffen
garden, Garten
garlic, Lauch
gate, Gasse, Gaden, Gatter
gather, Gatte, gut, vergattern
geld, gelt (2)
get, vergessen
gherkin, Gurke
ghost, Geist
gilt, gelt (2)
ginger, Ingwer
gird,
girdle, } Gurt
give, geben
glad, froh, glatt, schmeicheln
glass, Glas
gleam, glimmen
gleed, glühen
glide, gleiten
glimmer, glimmen

glitter, gleißen, glitern
gloat, glotzen
gloom, glühen
gloss, glosten
glow, glühen
gnaw, nagen
go, gehen
goad, Ger, Gerte
goat, Geiß
god, Gott
godfather, Gete
gold, Gold
good, gut
goose, Gans
gore, Gehren
gospel, Beispiel
gourd, Kürbis
gowk, Gauch
grab, grapsen, krabbeln
grabble, Garbe (1), krabbeln
grapple, krabbeln
grasp, grapsen
grass, Gras
grasshopper, Heuschrecke
grave, graben
gray, grau
great, groß
greaves, Griebe
green, grün
greet, Gruß
grev, gran
griffin, Greif
grim, grimm
grin, greinen
grind, Grand
gripe, greifen
grist, Gerste
grit, Grütze
groan, greinen
groat, Groschen, Grütze
groom, Braut
groove, Grube
ground, Grund
grove, Grube
grow, grün
grub, Grube
grunt, grunzen
guest, Gast
guild, Gilde
gulf, Golf
gums, Gaumen

haberdine, Labberdan
hack, haden
hackle, Hechel
hag, hager, Hexe
haggard, hager
hail,
hailstone, } Hagel
hair, Haar (2)
hale, holen

half, halb (1)
hall, Halle
halm, Halm
halse, Hals
halter, Halfter
hamble, Hammel
hammer, Hammer
hand, Hand (1)
handicraft,
handiwork, } ge-
handle, hanteln
hang, hangen
harbour, Herberge, Heer
hard, hart
hards, Haar (1), Hede
hardy, bart
hare,
hare-lip, } Hase
hark, horchen
harm, Harm
harness, Harnisch
harns, Hirn
harp, Harfe
harrow, Heer, Harke
harry, Heer
harsh, barsch
hart, Hirsch
harvest, Herbst
hasp, Haspe
haste, Hast
hat, Hut (1), hüten
hatch, Hede (2)
hatchel, Hechel
hate, Haß
have, haben
haven, Hafen (2)
haver, Hafer
haw, Hag
hawk, Habicht
hawthorn, Hagedorn
hay, Heu
hay-boot, Hede (1)
hazel, Hasel
he, heute
head, Haupt, Kopf
-head, -heit
heal, hehlen, heilen
health, heilen
heap, Haufe
hear, hören
hearken, horchen
heart, Herz
hearth, Herd
heat, heizen
heath, Heide (1)
heathen, Heide (2)
heave, heben
heaven, Himmel
hedge, Hede (1), (2)
hedgehog, Igel
heed, hüten
heel, Hade, Ferse

INDEX. 441

heifer, Farre, Klee
hell, Hölle [ter
helm, Helm (1), (2), Hals-
help, helfen
helve, Halfter
hemlock, Schierling
hemp, Hanf
hen, Henne
hence, hinnen
herd, Herde
here, hier
heriot, Heer
herring, Häring
hew, hauen
hide, Haut, Hufe, Haus, Hütte
high, hoch
hill, Halde, Halle, Holm
him, heute
hind, Hinde, Heirat
hindberries, Himbeere
hinder, hindern
hip, Hüfte, hüpfen
hirse, Hirse
hive, Heirat
hoar, hehr
hoard, Hort
hoarse, heiser
hoary, hehr
hogshead, Oxhoft
hoist, hissen
hold, halten
hole, hohl
hollow, hohl
holly, Hulst
holm, Holm
holster, Holster
holy, heilig
home, Heim
honey, Honig
honeycomb, Raum
honeymoon, Flitter
hood, Hut (1)
-hood, -heit
hoof, Huf
hook, Hake, Hechel
hop, Hopfen, hüpfen
hope, hoffen
horde, Horde (1)
horn, Horn
hornet, Horniss
horse, Ross (1)
horse-radish, Meer-
rettig
hose, Hose
hot, heiss
hotbed, Beet
hound, Hund
hour, Uhr
house, Haus
housebote, Busse
how, wie

-how, hoch
huckster, Hoke (2)
hulk, Holk
hulver, Hulst
humble-bee, Hummel
hundred, hundert
hunger, Hunger
hunt, Hand (1), Hinde
hurdle, Hürde
hurricane, Orkan
hurst, Horst
husband, }
hussy, } Haus
hustings, }
hut, Hütte

I, ich
ice, Eis
idle, eitel
if, ob (2)
ilt, gelt (2)
imp, impfen
in, in
ink, Tinte
irk, } Ekel
irksome, }
iron, Eisen
island, Au, Eiland
itch, jucken
ivory, Elfenbein
ivy, Epheu

jacket, Jacke
jail, Käfig
jig, Geige
joke, Juks

kabljau, Kabliau
keam, } Rahm
keans, }
keech, Kuchen
keel, Kil (2)
keen, kühn, schnell
kernel, Kern, Korn
kettle, Kessel
key, Keil
kid, Kitze (1)
kidney, Niere
kiln, Kohle
king, König
kingdom, -tum
kipe, Kiepe
kirtle, Kittel
kiss, küssen
kitchen, Küche
kitling, } Kitze (2)
kitten, }
kittle, kitzeln
knack, tnacken
knapsack, knappen
knar, Knorre
knave, Knabe

knead, kneten
knee, } Knie
kneel, }
knell, Knall
knick, kniden
knight, Knecht
knit, Knoten
knitch, Knode
knob, Knopf
knock, Knochen, tnacken
knoll, Knollen
knop, Knopf
knot, Knoten
know, können, Name
knuckle, Knöchel

lace, Latz
ladder, Leiter
lade, laden (1)
lady, Laib
lair, Lage
lake, Lache
lamb, Lamm
lame, lahm
lammas, Laib, Messe
lamprey, Lamprete
land, Land
lantern, Laterne
lap, Lappen
larch, } Lärche
lark, }
larum, Lärm
last, leisten, Last, letzt, Leiste (2), Leisten
late, letzt
lath, Latte
lathe, Lade
lather, Seife
latin, lateinisch
lattermath, Mahd
laugh, } lachen
laughter, }
laverock, Lerche
lax, Lachs
lay, legen
lead, Blei, Lot, leiten
leaf, Laub
leak, lechzen
leap, laufen
learn, lernen
lean, los
lease, lesen
leather, Leder
leave, bleiben
lee, See
leech, Arzt
leek, Lauch
leer, leer
left, link
lend, lehnen (2), leihen
lent, Lenz
-less, los

let, lassen, letzen
letter, Buch
lewd, Laie
lick, lecken (1)
lid, Lid
lie, liegen, Lug, Lauge
lief, lieb
life, Leib
lift, lichten, Luft
light, leicht, Licht, licht, Lunge
lights, leicht, Lunge
like, gleich
lily, Lilie
limb, Glied
lime, Leim
limetree, Linde
linchpin, Länse
lind, }
linden, linden- } Linde
.tree, }
line, Leine
lion, Löwe
lip, Lippe
lisp, lispeln
list, Lauschen, Leiste (1), List, Lust
listen, lauschen
lithe, lind
live, leben
liver, Leber
loadsman, leiten, Lotse
loadstar, } leiten
loadstone, }
loaf, Laib
loam, Lehm
loan, lehnen, leihen
loath, } Leid
loathe, }
lobster, Hummer
lock, Loch, Locke, Block
long, lang, verlangen
look 1, lugen
look 2 (Nor. E.), Locke
loose, los
lord, Laib, Brot
lore, Lehre
lot, Los
loud, laut
louse, Laus
love, lieb, Lob
low, Lehre
lower, horchen, lauern
luck, Glück
lunacy, }
lunatic, } Laune
lune, }
lungs, Lunge
lunt, Lunte
lurk, horchen, lauern
lust, Lust
-ly, -lich

INDEX

lye, Lauge
lyre, Leier

Macaulay, Magd
mackerel, Makrele, mäkeln
mad, }
maggot, } Made
maid, }
maiden, } Magd
maidenhead, }
maidenhood, } -heit
maize, Mais
make, machen
mallow, Malve
malt, Malz
man, Mann
mane, Mähne
mangle, Mange, mangeln
mantle, Mantel
many, manch
maple, }
mapletree, } Maßholder
march, Mark (1)
March, März
mare, Mähre
marjoram, Majoran
mark, }
market, } Marke
marrow, Harke, Mark (3)
marsh, Marsch
marten, Marder
Mary, Rosmarin
mash, Meisch
masker, Maske
maslin, Messing
mass, Messe
mast, Mast (1), (2)
master, Meister
mat, Matte (2)
match, machen
mate, matt
math, Mahd
mattock, Meißel, Metze (1)
mattress, Matratze
maund, Mandel (1)
maw, Magen
mawk, Made
may, mögen
mead, Matte (1), Met
meadow, Matte (1)
meager, mager
meal, Mahl (2), Mehl
mean, gemein, meinen
measles, Maser
meat, Messer
meed, Miete
meek, meuchel-
mere, Meer
merl, Amsel

merlin, Schmerl
mermaid, }
merman, } Meer
mesh, Masche
mew, Möwe
middle, mitte, mittel, Mittel
midge, Mücke
midland, }
midlent, }
midnight, } -mitte
midriff, }
midst, }
midwife, Hebamme, mit
midwinter, mitte
might, Macht
milch, melk
mild, milde
mildew, Mehltau
mile, Meile
milk, Milch, melken
mill, Mühle
milt, Milz
mind, Minne
mingle, mengen
minster, Münster
mint, Minze, Münze (1)
mire, Ameise, Moos
miss, missen
mist, Mist, Mistel, Nebel
mister, Meister
mistle, Mistel
mitch, meuchel-
mix, mischen
mixen, Mist
mizzen, Besanmast
moan, meinen
mole, Mal (1)
Monday, Montag
money, Geld
monk, Mönch
month, Monat
mood, Mut
moon, Mond
moor, Moor
mop, Mops
morass, Morast
more, Möhre, mehr, Abend
morning, Morgen (1)
mortar, Mörser, Mörtel
moss, Moos
most, meist
moth, Motte
mother, Moder, Mutter, Perl-mutter
mould, Maulwurf, Malm
moult, Mause
mouse, Maus (1)
mouth, Mund (1)
mow, mähen
mud, Moder

muff, Muff (1)
mule, Maul (2)
mulberry, Maulbeere
mum, Mumme (1)
mumble, }
mumm, } Mumme (2)
murder, Mord
must, Most, müssen
mustard, Mostert
muster, Muster

nail, Nagel
naked, nackt
name, Name, nennen
nape, Nacken
narrow, Narbe
narwal, Narwal
nave, Nabe
navel, Nabel
near, nah
neb=nib
neck, Hals, Nacken, Säge
need, Not
needle, Nadel
neighbour, Nachbar, Bauer (1)
nephew, Neffe
nesh, naschen
nest, Nest
nestle, nisteln
net, Netz
nether, nieder
nettle, Nessel
never, nimmer
new, neu
next, nah
nib, Schnabel
nick, Nick, Nix
nigh, nah
night, Nacht
nightingale, Nachtigall
nightmare, Mahr
nine, neun
nip, kneipen
nipple, nippen
nit, Niß
no, nein
noon, Neue
north, Nord
nose, Lab, Nase
nostrils, Nüster
not, nicht
nought, nicht
now, nun
nun, Nonne
nut, Nuß (1)

oak, Eiche
oak-gall, Gallapfel
oar, Ruder
oath, Eid
oats, Hafer

of, ab
offer, opfern
oft, often, oft
oil, Öl
old, alt
on, an
once, einst
one, ein
open, offen
or, oder
orchard, Garn
ore, Erz
organ, Orgel
ostrich, Strauß (3)
other, ander
otter, Otter
ought, eigen
ousel, Amsel
out, aus
oven, Ofen
over, ober (2), über
owe, eigen
owl, Eule
own, eigen
ox, Ochse
Oxford, Furt
oyster, Auster

pack, Pack (1)
paddock, Schildkrot
pail, Pegel
pain, Pein
pair, Paar
pale, Pfahl
palfrey, Pferd
pamphlet, Pamphlet
pan, Pfanne
pap, Pappe
paper, Papier
parish, Pfarre
park, Pferch
paste, }
pasty, } Pastete
patch, Flacken
path, Pfad
pause, Pause
paw, Pfote
pea, Erbse
peach, Pfirsich
peacock, Pfau
pear, Birne
pearl, Perle, Perlmutter
pease, Erbse
peel, Pelle
peep, piepen
peewit, Kibitz
pelt, Pelz
penny, Pfennig
people, Pöbel
pepper, Pfeffer
pick, Pökel, picken
pickle, Pökel

INDEX. 443

pickle-herring, Pickelhäring
picnic, Picnick
pigeon-cove, Koben
pike, Hecht, picken
pile, Pfeil, Pfeiler
pilgrim, Pilger
pillar, Pfeiler
pillow, Pfühl
pin, Pinn
pinch, Fink
pine, Pein
pink, Fink
pip, Pips
pipe, Pfeife
piss, pissen
pit, Pfütze
pitch, Pech
place, Platz (1)
plague, Plage
plaice, Platteise
plank, Planke
plant, Pflanze
plaster, Pflaster
platch, Pladen
plate, Platte
plat-footed, platt
play,
pledge, } pflegen
plight, Pflicht
plough,
ploughshare, } Pflug
pluck, pflücken
plug, Pflock
plum, Pflaume
plump, plump
pock,
pocket, } Pocke
poke, Pocke, pochen
pole, Pfahl
pool, Pfuhl
pope, Papst
popinjay, Papagei
poplar, Pappel (2)
poppy, Mohn
porch, Pforte
pose, pusten
post, Pfosten
pot, Pott, Topf
potash, Asche (1), Pott
potato, Kartoffel
pound, Pfund
pout, Pute
praise, preisen
prame, Prahm
preach, predigen
preen, Pfriem (1)
price, Preis
prick,
prickle, } prickeln
priest, Priester
prince, König, Prinz

prize, Preis
prong, Pranger
proof, prüfen
prop, Pfropfen
provost, Propst
puff, puffen
pulpit, Pult
pulse, Puls
pump, Pumpe
punch,
puncheon, } Bunzen
puncher,
puppet, Puppe

quack, Quacksalber, quaken
quart, Quart
quartz, Quarz
queen, Kind, König
quick, keck
quicksilver, Quecksilber
quill, Kiel (1)
quince, Quitte
quit, quitt
quitch-grass, Quecke
quite, quitt
quiver, Köcher

race, rasen, Rasse
rach, Brache
rack, Rachen, recken
radish, Rettich
raff, raffen
rail, Ralle, Riegel
rain,
rainbow, } Regen
raise, Reise
raisin, Rosine
rake, Rechen
ram, Ramme
rampion, Rapunzel
rand, Rand
rank, Rang
rant, ranzen
rap, raffen, rappeln
rape, Rapp
rapier, Rappier
rare, rar
rasp,
rasper, } Raspel
rat, Ratte
rattle, rasseln
rave, rappeln
raven, Rabe
raw, roh
ray, Reihen (1), Roche (1)
ray-grass, Raigras
reach, reichen
read, Rat, lesen
ready, bereit
ream, Rahm, Ries
reap, relf

rear, Reise
rearmouse, rühren
reave, Raub
rebus, Rebus
reck, geruhen
reckless, ruchlos
reckon, rechnen
red, retten, rot
reed, Riet
reef, Reff (2), Riff
reek, Rauch
reindeer, Renntier
rest, Rast
ret, röften (2)
rhyne, Rein
rib, Rippe
rice, Reis (1)
rich, reich
riddle, Rätsel, Reiter
ride, reiten
ridge, Rücken
rifle, Riese
right, recht
righteous, gerecht
rim, Rinde
rime, Reif (2)
rinple, rümpfen
rind, Rinde
rindle, Rinne
ring, Rädelsführer, Ring, ringen
ringleader, Rädelsführer
rip, Reff (1)
ripe, reif
ripple, reffen
rise, Reise
rivel, Riese
roach, Roche (1)
road, reiten, Rhede
roan, Rogen
roar, röhren
roast, Rost (1)
roch, Roche (1)
rochet, Rock
rock, Roche (2), Rocken, Ruck
rocket, Rauke
rod, Rute
roe, Rogen, Reh
roll, Rolle
rood, Rute
room, Raum
roost (Scot.), Rost (2)
root, Rüssel, Wurz
rope, Reif (1)
rose, Rose
rosmary, Rosmarin
rot, rösten
rough, rauh
roun, raunen
round, raunen, rund

rouse, Rausch (2)
rout, Rotte
row, Reihe, Ruder
rubric, Rubrik
rud, rot
rudder, Ruder
ruddle,
ruddock, } rot
rue, Raute (1), Reue
rule, Regel
rum, Rum
rumble, rumpeln
rummer, Römer
rump, Rumpf
rumple, rümpfen
run, rinnen
rung, Runge
rush, Rausch (1), rauschen
rushes (bed of), Beet
rust, Rost (1)
ruth, Reue
rye, Roggen
ryegrass, Raigras

sable, Zobel
sabre, Säbel
sack, Sack, Sekt
sad, satt
saddle, Sattel
saffran, Safran
sage, Salbei
sail, Segel
sake, Sache
sallow, Salweide
salt, Salz
salve, Salbe
same, gleich
samel,
sand, } Sand
sap, Saft
satchel, Seckel
Saturday, Samstag
savin, Sebenbaum
saw, Sage, Säge
say, sagen
scale, Schale
scarlet, Scharlach
school, Schule
schooner, Schoner
scissors, Schere (1)
score, Stiege (2)
scot, Schoß (2)
scour, scheuern
scrape, schrappen, scharf
screw, Schraube
scrimp, schrumpfen
scrub, schrubben
scum, Schaum
scurf, Schorf
scurvy, Scharbock
scuttle, Schüssel
sea, See

INDEX.

seal, Robbe
seam, Saum (1), (2)
see, sehen, Sicht
seed, Saat
seek, suchen
seethe, sieden
seldom, selten
sell, Salbuch
send, senden
senna, Sennebaum
sennight, Nacht
set, setzen
settle, Sessel
seven, sieben
sew, Säule (2)
sexton, Sigrist
shab, shabby, } schäbig
shade, shadow, Schatten
shaft, Schaft (1)
shale, Schale
shall, sollen
shallop, Schaluppe
shallow, schal
shame, Scham
shammy, Sämischleder
shank, Schenkel
shape, schaffen
shard = sherd
sharp, scharf
shave, Schabe (2), schaben
sheaf, Schaub
shear, scheren
shears, Schere (1)
sheath, Scheide
sheave, Scheibe
shed, scheiden, Scheitel
sheen, schön
sheep, Schaf
sheep-cote, Kot (1)
sheer, schier (1)
sheet, Schoß (3)
sheets Schote (2)
shell, Schale, Schellfisch
shellac, Schellack
shepherd, Hirt
sherd, Scharte
sheriff, Graf
shide, Scheit
shield, Schild (1)
shift, Schiefer
shilling, Schilling
shim, shimmer, } Schimmer
shin, Schienbein
shine, Schein
shingle, Schindel
ship, Schiff
shippen, Schuppen
shire, schier (1)

shirt, Schurz
shit, scheißen
shive, Scheibe, Schiefer
shiver, Schiefer
shoal, Scholle (1)
shock, Hode (1)
shoe, Schuh
shoot, schießen
shop, Schuppen
shore, Schornstein
short, kurz, Schurz
shoulder, Schulter
shove, schieben
shovel, Schaufel
show, schauen
shower, Schauer (2)
shred, Schrot
shrift, schreiben
shrill, schrill
shrimp, schrumpfen
shrine, Schrein
shrink, schrumpfen
shrive, schreiben
shroud, Schrot
shudder, schaudern
shy, Scheu
sick, siech, Sucht
sickle, Sichel
side, Seite
sieve, Sieb
sift, sichten
sight, Sicht
silk, Seide
sill, Schwelle
silly, selten
silver, Silber
simper, zimperlich
sin, Sünde
since, seit
sinew, Sehne
sing, singen
singe, sengen
sink, sinken
sinter, Sinter
sip, saufen
siskin, Zeisig
sister, Schwester
sit, sitzen
sithe, Säge, Sense
six, sechs
skew, schief
skin, schinden
skirmish, Scharmützel
skute, Schüte
slag, Schlacke
slap, Schlappe (2)
slaughter, Schlacht
slave, Sklave
slay, Schlag (2)
sled, Schlitten
sledge, Schlegel, Schlitten

sleek, schleichen
sleep, Schlaf (2)
sleet, Schloße
slide, Schlitten
slight, schlecht
slim, schlimm
slime, Schleim
sling, Schlinge, schlendern
slip, slippers, } schleifen
slit, schleißen, Schlitz
sloat (N. Eng.), schließen, Schloß
sloe, Schlehe
sloom, schlummern
sloop, Schaluppe
slot (N. Eng.), schließen, Schloß
slough, Schlauch
sluice, Schleuse
slumber, schlummern
sly, schlau
smack, schmecken, Schmack
small, schmal
smart, Schmerz
smear, Schmeer
smelt, schmelzen
smicker, Schminke
smile, schmeicheln
smite, schmeißen
smith, smithy, } Schmied
smock, Schmuck
smoke, Schmauch
smother, schmoren
smug, Schmuck
smuggle, schmuggeln
smut, Schmutz
snail, Schnecke
snake, Schnake
snap, schnappen
snarl, schnarchen
sneeze, niesen
snell, schnell
sniff, schnüffeln
snip, Schnippchen
snipe, snite, } Schnepfe
snivel, beschnäuseln, schnüffeln
snore, snort, } schnarchen
snot, schneuzen
snout, Schnauze
snow, Schnee, Schnaue
snuff, schnüffeln, beschnäuseln, Schnuppe
snuffle, beschnäuseln
snurls, schnarchen
so, so
soap, Seife

sob, seufzen
sock, Socke
soft, sanft
soldier, Sold
sole, Sohle (1)
sollar, Söller
son, Sohn
son-in-law, Eidam
soon, be
sook, Ruß
sop, Suppe
sore, sehr
sorrow, Sorge
sot, Sote
soul, Seele
sound, gesund
soup, Suppe
sour, sauer
souter (N. Eng., Scot.), Schuster
sow, Sau, säen
spade, Spaten
span, Spanne
spangle, Spange
spar, Sparren
spare, sparen
sparrow, Sperling
speak, Sprache, Wasen
spear, Speer
speck, Specht
speech, Sprache
speed, sputen
speight, Specht
spell, Beispiel
spelt, Spelt
spend, Spende
spew, speien
spike, Speiche
spin, spinnen
spit, spenzen, Spieß (2)
splint, splinter, split, } spleißen
spoke, Speiche
spook, Spuk
spool, Spule
spoon, Span, Löffel
sprat, Sprotte
spread, spreiten
spring, springen
springe, Sprenkel (1)
sprit, sprießen, spritzen
sprout, sprießen
spur, spurn, } Sporn
spy, spähen
squirrel, Eichhorn
staff, Knittelvers, Stab
stake, Staken
stalk, Stiel
stall, stallion, } Stall

INDEX. 445

stammer, stammeln
stamp, stampfen
stand, stehen
standard, Standarte
stang, Stange
staple, Stapel
star, Stern
starch, Stärk
stare, Star
stark, stark
starling, Sperling, Star
start, sterz, stürzen
startle, stürzen
starve, sterben
state, Staat
stay, stehen
steal, } stehlen
stealth,
steed, Stute
steel, Stahl
steen, Stein
steep,   } Stoppel
steeple,
steer, Steuer (2), Stier
stem, Stamm
step, Stapfe, Stufe
stepfather, Stiefvater
sterling, Sterling
stern, Stern, Steuer (2)
steven, Stimme
stick, Stecken
stiff, steif
still, still
stilt, Stelze
sting, Stange, Stechen
stink, stinken
stir, stören
stirrup, Stegreif
stitch, sticken
stock, Stock
stoke, stochen
stone, Stein
stool, Stuhl
stop, Stöpsel, stopfen
stork, Storch
storm, Sturm
stound, Stunde
stour, Sturm
stout, stolz
stove, Stube
strand, Strand
straw, Stroh
stream, Strom
street, Straße
stretch, strecken
strew, streun
stride, schreiten
strife, streben
strike, streichen
string, Strang
strip, streifen
strive, streben

stroke, streichen
strong, streng
strut, strotzen
stub,   } Stoppel
stubble,
stud, Stute
stuff, Stoff
stump, Stumpf
sturgeon, Stör
stut, stutter, stottern
sty, Steig
such, solch
suck, saugen
sugar, Zucker
summer, Sommer
sump, Sumpf
sun, Sonne
Sunday, Sonne
sup, saufen
swallow, Schwalbe, schwelgen
swamp, Sumpf
swan, Schwan
swanky, Sumpf
sward, Schwarte
swarm, Schwarm
swart, schwarz
swats (Scot.), süß
swear, schwören
sweat, Schweiß
sweep, schweifen
sweet, süß
swell, schwellen
swift, schweifen
swim, schwimmen
swine, Schwein
swing, } schwingen
swink,
swoop, schweifen
sword, Schwert

table, Tafel
tack, Zacken
tackle, Tafel
tail, Schwanz, Mähe
tale, Zahl
talk, horchen
tallow, Talg
tame, zahm
tang,   } Tang
tangle,
tap, Zapfe
tar, Teer
target, Zarge
tarrace, } Traß
tarras,
tarry, zergen
tea, Thee
teach, zeichen
tear, Zähre, zehren
teat, Zitze
teem, Zeug

teend, zünden
tell, horchen, Zahl
ten, zehn
tenden, zünden
tent, Zelt
tether, Zitter
tetter, Zitteroch
tewel, Tülle
thane, Degen (1)
thank, Dank
that, daß
thatch, Dach
thaw, tauen
the, desto
theft, Dieb
then, dann
thence, dannen
there, da
therf, derb
thick, dick
thief, Dieb
thill, Deichsel
thimble, Daumen, Ermel
thin, dünn
thine, dein
thing, Ding
think, denken, dünken
third, dritte
thirst, Durst
this, dieser
thistle, Distel
thorn, Dorn
thorough, durch
thorp, Dorf
thou, du
though, doch
thousand, tausend
thrash, dreschen
thread, Draht
threat, verdrießen
threaten, drohen
three, drei
thresh,   } dreschen
threshold,
thrill, drillen
throat, Drossel (2)
throng, Drang, dringen
throp, Dorf
throstle, Drossel (1)
throttle, Drossel (2)
through, durch
throw, drehen
thrum, Trumm
thrush, Drossel (1)
thumb, Daumen, Ermel
thunder, } Donner
Thursday,
thy, dein
tick, Zecke, Zieche
tickle, tigeln
tide, Zeit
tiding, Zeitung

tight, dicht
tike, Zecke
tile, Ziegel
till, Ziel
tilt, Zelt
timber, Zimmer
time, Zeit
tin, Zinn
tind, zünden
tinder, Zunder
tine, Zain
tip, Zipfel
tire, Zier
titmouse, Meise
to, zu
toad, Kröte
tobacco, Tabak
tod, Zotte (1)
toddle, zotteln
toe, Zeh
together, Gatte, gut
token, Zeichen
toll, Zoll
toller, Zöllner
to-morrow, Morgen (1)
tongs, Zange
tongue, Zunge
tool, Zatel
tooth, Zahn
top, Topf, Toyp, Zopf
torsk, Dorsch
totter,   } zotteln
tottle,
tough, zäh
tow, Tau (1)
towel, Zwehle
tower, Turm
town, Zaun
trail, treibeln
tramp,   } trampeln
trample,
trape, trampeln
tread, treten
tree, Baum, Teer
trendle, trendeln
trot, Trott
trough, Trog
trow,   } treu
true,
truffle, Trüffel
trump, Trumpf
trust, truth, treu
tub, Zuber
Tuesday, Dienstag
tug, zögern, Zug
tun, Tonne
tunder, Zunder
tunny, Thunfisch
Turkey-pout, Pute
turtle, Turteltaube
tusk, Dorsch
twelve, zwölf

INDEX.

twenty, zwanzig
twig, Zweig
twilight, Zwielicht
twin, Zwilling
twist, Zwirn, Zwist
twine, Zwirn
twinge, zwingen
twinkle, zwinken
twitch, zwicken
twitter, zwitschern
two, zwei
twofold, -falt
-ty, -zig

udder, Euter
un-, un-
uncouth, kund
under, unten
understand, Verstand
up, auf
us, uns

valerian, Baldrian
vane, Fahne
varnish, Firnis
vat, Faß
vessel, Schiff
vetch, Wicke (1)
vinegar, Essig
violet, Veilchen
vixen, Fuchs

wad, Watte
wade, waten
wafer, } Waffel
waffle,
wag, wackeln
wagtail, Bachstelze
wain, Wagen
wake, wachen
Wales, welsch
walk, horchen, wallen (2)
wall, Wall, Wand
wallop, Galopp
walnut, Walnuß
wangtooth, Wange
ward, Wart
ware, Ware

warm, warm
warn, warnen
warp, werfen, Werft (1)
warrant, gewähren
wart, Warze
was, Wesen
wash, waschen
wasp, Wespe
watch, wach
water, Wasser
wax, Wachs, wachsen
way, } Weg
waybread,
we, wir
weak, weich
weapon, Waffe
wear, Weste
weasel, Wiesel
weather, Wetter, Wetter
weave, weben
wedge, Weck
Wednesday, Wut
week, Woche
weevil, Wiebel
weigh, Wage
weight, Gewicht
welcome, Wille
weld, Wau
welk, welk
welkin, Wolke
well, wohl
wend, wenden
werewolf, Werwolf
west, Westen
wet, Wasser
wether, Widder
wharf, Werft (2)
what, was
wheat, Weizen
wheel, Rad
wheeze, Husten
whelp, Welf
where, wo
whet, wetzen
which, welch
while, weil
whine, wiehern
whirl, Wirbel
whisper, wispeln

whistle, Heiser
white, weiß
Whitsunday, Pfingsten
who, wer
whole, heil
whoost, Husten
whore, Hure
wick, Wieche
wicker, wiehern
wide, weit
widow, Witwe
wield, walten
wife, Weib
wight, Wicht
wild, wild
will, wollen, Wille
wimple, Wimpel
win, gewinnen
wind, Wind, Winde, wittern
window, Fenster, Wind
Windsor, Ufer
wine, Wein
wink, Wink
winnow, Wanne
winter, Winter
wisdom, Weistum
wise, weis, Weise
wish, Wunsch
wisp, Wisch
wit, Witz
with, wider
wither, verwittern
withy, Weide (1)
woad, Waid
woe, weh
wold, Wald
wolf, Wolf
womb, Wamme
wonder, Wunder
wood, Krammetsvogel, Wut, Wiedehopf
wool, Wolle
woosy, Wiese
word, Wort
work, Werk
world, Welt
worm, Wurm
wormwood, Wermut
worse, wirr, wisch

wort, Wurz, Würze
worth, Wert (2)
wot, wissen
wound, wund
wrangle, ringen
wreak, rächen
wreck, Wrack
wrench, Rank, reuten
wretch, Recke
wring, ringen
wrinkle, Runzel
wrist, Rist
write, kerben, schreiten, reißen
writhe, Riß
wrong, ringen

yacht, Jacht
yard, Garten
yare, gar
yarn, Garn
yarrow, Garbe (2)
yea, ja
yean, Schaf
year, Jahr
yeast, gären, Gischt
yellow, gelb, Dotter (1)
yellow-hammer, Ammer
yes, ja
yest, Gischt
yesterday, gestern
yew, Eibe
yield, gelten
yoke, Joch
yolk, Dotter (1)
yon, } jener
yonder,
York, Eber
you, euch
young, jung
youngling, Jüngling
younker, Junker
your, euer
youth, Bursche, Junge, Jugend
yule, weihen

zedoary, Zitwer

www.ingramcontent.com/pod-product-compliance
Lightning Source LLC
Chambersburg PA
CBHW022114300426
44117CB00007B/710